Presented by office
on 28 February 1983.

WISDEN
Anthology 1940-1963

WISDEN

Anthology 1940-1963

EDITED BY BENNY GREEN

Queen Anne Press
Macdonald & Co · London & Sydney

First published in Great Britain in 1982 by
Queen Anne Press, a division of
Macdonald & Co (Publishers) Ltd
London & Sydney
Maxwell House
Worship Street, London EC2A 2EN
ISBN 0 356 08547 3

Typeset by Spottiswoode Ballantyne Ltd.,
Colchester and London.
Printed and bound in Great Britain
by Hazell Watson and Viney, London and Aylesbury

FOREWORD

As a friend of mine – not wont to be demonstrative – assured me the other day that he had no pleasanter evenings in the whole year than when the appearance of *Wisden* enabled him to fight the battles of the cricket season over again, I am fortified in the belief that the Almanack fulfils its mission and preserves in a readable and attractive form a record of all that is essential in connection with our glorious game. Lest there should seem to be any suspicion of vanity or egotism in my saying this, I may point to the ever-increasing favour with which *Wisden* is received, and to a constantly-growing circulation.

Sydney H. Pardon 1893

To Leo

CONTENTS

i

Introduction

The codification of cricket history is by no means a precise science. The researcher has to follow what patterns he is able to discern, which is why although all three volumes of this anthology to have appeared so far are more or less alike, none is identical in structure to either of the others. In the first volume, I treated the years between 1864 and 1900 as though they had been one eternal season; once I decided on that plan, the contents fell neatly into place, for all that was left to do was to arrange the material of thirty seven seasons in the way that the Pardons would have arranged them had the thirty seven seasons been one. But with Volume Two there was a difficulty, a new factor, the Great War. Only a lunatic would attempt to treat the life of pre- and post-war England as though nothing had happened. So I divided the volume into two main sections, with the Almanacks covering the war years as a bloodstained causeway leading from one to the other.

In the present volume the challenge is subtly different again. Another war, this time not sundering two disparate periods, but beginning the proceedings. This means that the present volume of the anthology begins with a curious twilit prelude covering the seasons from 1940 to 1945. But what then? A long main section bringing together what are often laughingly referred to as the peacetime years of our age, just as in Volume One I brought together the peacetime years of our grandfathers? That would have been a foolish tactic. From 1864 to 1900 there is a discernible continuity, not just in the history of cricket, but in the history of Britain generally. That is not to say that there were no changes, rather that change took place at a rate compatible with the human capacity for absorbing it without too much discomfort. But a great breach opened up in English cricket in the early 1960s. The game, faced with a choice between radical amendment and financial ruin, chose the amendment. The result was survival, but survival at a cost so great as to transform the technique, morality and social significance of cricket not just in Britain but all over the world. It seemed therefore politic to regard the postwar years as falling into two distinct parts, and to keep those periods to their own volumes.

This resolution of my task brought yet another problem: where to locate the schism. Was the point of no return the introduction of one-day, limited-overs, prize-money cricket? Was it the point when, with the apotheosis of Basil D'Oliveira, cricket and politics became so inextricably enmeshed that nobody has ever been able to separate them since? Was it perhaps the moment when the battle for Australian television rights suddenly plunged the game into the arms of Mr Kerry Packer, into the Law Courts, into fancy dress? Or was it that tragic moment when South Africa was acknowledged to be beyond the pale? One day the historian of the game will see all these moments as watersheds in the story of first-class cricket, moments which changed the face of the game, for better or for worse, irrevocably. For however unhappy the cricket lover might be at the fortunes of his game over the last generation, at least it has been a life packed with incident. An anthology which embraces all from D'Oliveira to Benson and Hedges, from Packer to Robin Jackman, would be a thriller if nothing else.

In the end I decided it would be wiser to reserve the melodrama for the fourth and final volume of the anthology, and to acknowledge that the English domestic game was pushed irreversibly towards the age of financial expediency with the emergence of one-day limited-overs cricket. That innovation was more than what it seemed at the time. It was final acceptance of the fact that when the patrician disappeared from our national life, so did patronage. No longer could a languishing county look to the local landowning Croesus for subsidy. Croesus had been taxed out of existence, and the first-class clubs would have to live from now on by the proceeds from the turnstiles. But who could afford to attend a three-day match and witness its last ball as well as its first? None but the drones, among whose company the present writer has always been proud to number himself. But cricket had either to die the slow death of deserted Tuesday morning grounds, or grasp the nettle of commercialism by offering a briefer and slightly coarsened version of the real thing.

The general feeling was that there was no alternative, and no doubt the view is justified. But as the period under review in this volume drew to its close, I conceived a fantastic scenario which might just conceivably have worked. By the mid-1960s the first-class counties were losing annually between them around £200,000 – or roughly half the annual subsidy awarded to the Covent Garden Opera House. On the grounds that English Cricket is as much an art, as much a tourist attraction, as much a part of the national heritage, as Opera, could not some politicising cricket lover have procured for Cricket what the nation gives to Wagner and Puccini? Nobody ever tried it, and so the first-class game as it had always been since the 1890s, lumbered slowly towards its closure, allowing the compiler of this series of volumes to end the third act on a statistical landmark, the season of 1962, recorded in the 100th edition of the most extraordinary yearbook in the world.

1940-1945

At the Hove ground on Friday, 1 September, 1939, the home side, having collapsed on a rain-damaged pitch, went down by nine wickets to Yorkshire, thanks mainly to the brilliant bowling of Hedley Verity. On the same day, up at Leicester, the players waited for the rain to stop and give the home side a chance to knock off the runs required for victory against Derbyshire. But they waited in vain; all that day the rain came down, washing away not just an inconsequential county match but a whole era, leaving the overnight batsmen Lester and Armstrong with their innings in a state of suspension destined never to be resolved. The only other match in the county programme that day was taking place in Manchester between Surrey and Lancashire; both sides turned up at Old Trafford that morning only to be told that the game had been abandoned owing to something called "The Crisis", which was evidently more acute in Manchester than it was either at Leicester or Hove. On that same morning of Friday, 1 September, thousands of schoolboys, including the present writer, who might in the normal course of events have been going off to watch their county sides in action, were on the move in a rather different style, with labels in their buttonholes, entraining for a destination officially defined as "Somewhere in England". Another war to end wars was about to begin, and of the cricketers who performed those last sad rites that day, none seems more tragic in retrospect than Hedley Verity, whose seven for 9 in six overs at Hove was to be the last recorded first-class performance of his life.

The contrast between official reactions towards cricket in the first and second wars is striking. In August 1914, with the publication of Dr Grace's clarion call in *The Sportsman*, any indulgence in games-playing was acknowledged as an unpatriotic act. Messing about with bats and balls, thundered the voice of patriotic England, was an unpardonable frivolity at a moment when the fate of the nation hung in the balance, with the result that for four years first-class cricket vanished from the face of England and the slender wartime editions of *Wisden* contained little else but the death notices of young men who had not so very long ago been playing for their schools. As a facet of social history, this banishing of cricket – and many other popular spectator sports – from British life is one example among many of the extraordinary hysterical idiocy of the time. When Dr Grace announced that the act of playing cricket was no longer compatible with the demands of citizenship, he was expressing the sentiments of the Victorian home front rather than the Georgian empiricism of the soldiers, who continued to play what games they could when and wherever they could. At Vermelles on 24 June, 1915, Robert Graves records:

> This afternoon we had a cricket match, officers versus sergeants, in an enclosure between some houses out of observation from the enermy. Our front line is perhaps three-quarters of a mile away. I made top score, 24; the bat was a bit of a rafter, the ball a piece of rag tied round with string; and the wicket a parrot cage with the clean, dry corpse of a parrot inside. It has evidently died of starvation when the French evacuated the town. Machine-gun fire broke up the match.

One cannot help wondering whether Dr Grace would have regarded that ghostly, ghastly cricket match as evidence of lack of patriotism among those who participated, but at any event, it was not an issue destined to be raised in the new war, which was notable for the complete reversal of the attitudes of the fathers. Quite rightly, the British saw that cricket, so far from being an indiscreet distraction from more pressing affairs, was a priceless weapon in the war to keep the national spirit buoyant. It is a nebulous question as to how far cricket contributed to the morale of those who played and watched it, but there can be no question that, fund-raising prodigies apart, cricket took its place alongside the theatre, the cinema and the concert hall as living proof that the locals were muddling along in as close an approximation as was humanly possible to ordinary life.

Although there was no question of a county championship or international contests, there were ways in which first-class players could continue to display their skills before the public. On a local level, county secretaries did what they could, and as London was inevitably the vast pot into which servicemen were constantly being flung, it followed that those matches most closely resembling the real thing would be those staged at Lord's. Spectators soon became accustomed to watching the fortunes of two cricketing gallimaufries called London Counties and the British Empire Eleven, each composed largely of county players; these two clubs toured around, helping to keep the first-class flag flying and raising funds for charity, besides playing frequently at headquarters. Then there were the various service elevens, both Home and Commonwealth, and civilian organisations like the Police, the Fire Service and Civil Defence, all of whom were capable now and then of fielding strongish sides. Every man who played in those and other sides during the war, and every spectator who attended their efforts, was reassured by the knowledge that cricket, so far from being the illicit delight of 1914, was now not only respectable but actually patriotic. In the 1944 edition of the Almanack, the editor was proud to place on record the desire of the Adjutant-General of the Forces and of Mr Ernest Bevin, Minister of Labour, that the first-class game be encouraged in every way.

It has not altogether escaped the notice of the cricket historian that what these wartime matches may have lacked in status or immediacy, they more than made up in their wonderful, extraordinary, unpredictably comic eccentricity. The annals of the game, already rich in empirical philosophers, impromptu comedians and freakish enterprises, were now enriched beyond the dreams of the wildest lunatic. The student has only to examine the events at one ground in one month to appreciate this. At Lord's on 10 August, 1940, London Counties played the British Empire XI, the match being utterly memorable for the unexpected comeback of Frank Woolley, who not only scored 38 but also had the pleasure of dismissing Denis Compton. Five days later, a Public Schools XI found itself opposed by another veteran who had come out of retirement to chance his arm; the man following the comeback trail was Patsy Hendren, by which time patrons of the cricket were beginning to become acquainted with one of the first principles of wartime spectating, which was that you never knew who you might see in action. On the 22nd of that month it also became plain that nor could you ever predict which player would be representing which club, for on that day the West Indies side opposing Sir Pelham Warner's XI included the most improbable wicketkeeper ever to represent them. On the 31st the MCC President, Sir Stanley Christopherson, accompanied by Sir Stanley Jackson, Lord Lucan and Mr H. D. G. Leveson-Gower, who had been spending the night commanding the local Home Guard, turned up to watch a game between the Buccaneers and the British Empire XI; alas, with the Buccaneers going for victory, the match was called off owing to The Battle of Britain. On the 7th the war reduced the match between a Middlesex XI and a Lord's XI to hopeless chaos, when an air raid warning obliged the cricketers to take cover and not resume until the All-Clear had sounded.

That 1940 season was, of course the one most prone to disruption by enemy action, but at other grounds in other seasons there occurred events, or a concatenation of events, which had never been dreamed of by John Wisden or the Pardon brothers. In a Whitsuntide match between Nottinghamshire and Derbyshire, one of the umpires also took part as a Derbyshire player. At Lord's in July 1944 the programme included a timely reminder that the first recorded international match in cricket history had been contested by Canada and the United States; a Lord's XI was down to play against Americans, whose players, however, had subsequent engagements, leaving Canada to take the brunt of the local opposition. At Gloucester in the previous summer, R. E. S. Wyatt, captaining the RAF against the home side, allowed the opposition to field an extra man, while a thirteenth player was also allowed to bowl for Gloucestershire, dressed, it appeared, in a football shirt borrowed from Sam Barkas the old Manchester City international full-back. But there is nothing to compare with the Carrollian events surrounding the match in August 1943 at Lord's billed as "Middlesex and Essex v Kent and Surrey". With the match due to start at the usual time, torrential rain was teeming down, and, with prospects of play exceedingly thin, permission was granted for the Compton brothers to depart to play for Arsenal in the opening game of the football season against Charlton Athletic at the Valley. By half past two, with the sun shining and the Comptons gone beyond recall, the covers were taken off and play found to be possible. The Middlesex-Essex side soon discovered that it was further weakened owing to the bizarre accident sustained by the Essex opener Avery, who in his excitement at the prospect of playing in the match, tripped over his bag while leaving home and was unable to take any further part in the proceedings. Nor was the opposition entirely trouble-free, because Arthur Fagg, who should have been opening for them, spent the day in the less salubrious pursuit of following the mysterious spoor of his cricket bag as it wandered unattended down the labyrinth of the railways. One straw in the wind that day was a not-out half century by a Sergeant T. G. Evans. In this regard of future stars, the match between New South Wales and Queensland in December 1939, and the Middlesex-Essex v Kent-Surrey fixture at Lord's in the summer of 1942 are of special interest.

There was only one aspect of first-class cricket which proceeded uninterrupted by the war, and that was that irresistible stimulus to the annalists of *Wisden*, Death. The losses of young men like Verity, Kenneth Farnes, Maurice Turnbull, Robert Nelson and others, to say nothing of the living death endured by E. W. Swanton as a prisoner-of-war, are a reminder to the reader that although altogether less tragic a chronical than its Great War counterparts, *Wisden* in the Second World War was the purveyor of much grief and suffering. But those old players and patrons who died in their beds during the period took their places in what have been recognized for many years now as among the richest, most readable, most amusing, most pathetic footnotes to the Dictionary of National Biography. During the war years some great figures died, including A. J. Webbe, Bobby Peel, Tom Garrett, Cecil Parkin, Fred Tate, Richard Tyldesley, J. T. Hearne, A. C. MacLaren and C. T. B. Turner. But it is not always the greatest players who achieve the most memorable obituaries, as regular readers of *Wisden* will know, and the period of the war was no less rich than any other in its eccentrics and comedians.

There is Arthur Churchill Bartholomew, who formed a cricket side and called it The Guinea Pigs "because it has no tail". And George Pickering Harrison, a Yorkshire professional who, on being invited to play in his first game at Lord's, asked the MCC secretary to meet him at Kings Cross because he did not know the way, never having been to London before. There is C. F. Tufnell, an otherwise undistinguished Kent player who was buried in 1940, fifty six years after his death had been announced in Simla. There is the apparently bellicose F. C. Cole, who served under McClellan and Sheridan in the American Civil War, involved himself in several other military events, and finally found a peaceful haven with the Sheffield Gas Company. Clinging to the hem of literary history is George Henry Remnant, whose path once crossed that of Charles Dickens in most bizarre circumstances. And Sir Jeremiah Colman, although evidently no cricketer at all, deserves a mention, not only for his support of Surrey, but also because of the fondness with which he would quote his father, the "Mustard Millionaire", who had insisted that the family fortunes came "not from the mustard people ate, but from what they left on their plates", which paradox looks well in an Almanack dedicated to the art. As for Lord Gainford, who found that his prowess as a Rugby player enabled him to affect the course of Anglo-Irish parliamentary history, perhaps it may be said that *Wisden* has done him more justice than Hansard ever did. There is Cecil Parkin, Neville Cardus's Card, who once claimed to have dismissed Herbie Collins in an Old Trafford Test match as an indirect result of a spectator's failure to grasp the subtler nuances of English literary history. A finer witticism is attributed to the Umpire William Reeves, who made a permanent contribution to cricketing repartee. Nor must we forget J. E. K. Studd, who expressed as well as any Englishman ever has the idea of Cricket the Great Game as a paraphrase of Christianity.

There is, however, one death in this section which appeals more than any other as the epitome of sporting endings. In a match at Lord's on 23 July, 1942, whose official designation, "Surrey Home Guard v Sussex Home Guard", may well tempt posterity to some risible comments, the veteran double international Andrew Ducat went in for Surrey third wicket down. Quickly moving on to 29 not out, with his side's score at 132, he played a ball out to mid-on. The ball was returned to the bowler, who was just about to send down the next delivery when Ducat fell dead at the crease. Both in its abruptness and in its circumstances in the context of a match at Lord's, poor Ducat's death was unique. Great cricketers have died in a bizarre variety of ways, from wounds in the firing line to being hit on the head by a crane while unloading bananas, from suicide to the hangman's noose, from falling on hard times to falling out of windows. The most benign deaths are usually considered to be those of extremely ancient heroes who pass away so gently that they seem not to have been dismissed so much as having retired to give someone else a knock. But in its own pathetic way, Ducat's death had something perfectly appropriate about it. An outstanding games player who appears to have been born for football and cricket, he is one of the very few sporting figures in English history of whom it could be said that the next ball was literally his dying thought.

Benny Green

CRICKET IN ENGLAND

NOTTINGHAMSHIRE IN 1940

In an effort to provide as much cricket as possible Nottinghamshire played six matches, three with Royal Air Force teams and one each with Derbyshire, Leicestershire, and the Notts and Derby Border League. Not only did these games show that leading county players now in the Services retained their skill, but they brought to light some promising talent. Particularly noteworthy was the work as opening batsman of R. T. Simpson, a young policeman, of whom competent judges formed a high opinion. Among members of the county side who joined the forces were: J. Hardstaff, C. B. Harris, H. Butler, all sergeants, and J. Knowles (Army), and F. G. Woodhead and E. A. Meads (Royal Air Force). W. Voce undertook munitions work. The 1940 accounts showed a surplus of £43, but repairs and painting have not been done at Trent Bridge since the war began, and there is a bank overdraft of £525.

NOTTINGHAMSHIRE v DERBYSHIRE

Played at Nottingham, May 11, 13, 1940

Drawn. Tradition was upheld by playing a Whitsuntide match at Trent Bridge, but Derbyshire, instead of Surrey, were the visitors. Copson failed to arrive, but George Lee, one of the umpires, batted when Derbyshire faced arrears of 95. The completion of the side proved unnecessary, as Alderman withstood the Nottinghamshire attack for two hours and three-quarters, scoring more than half the runs from the bat, so enabling Derbyshire in turn to declare and avoid defeat. Leslie Townsend, by sound defence and clean hitting, took the chief part in a recovery on the first day. Payton and Worthington put on 66 of the 85 scored while four wickets fell, and then Townend mastered the bowling. Hounsfield showed freedom in a stand for 67, but the most attractive batting of the match came from the home county. Keeton and Gunn in sixty-five minutes scored 107 together, and on Monday Heane completed a brilliant century after less than two hours at the wicket. As usual, Heane played the left-hander's strong off-side game, brilliant cuts and off-drives earning most of his twelve 4s; also powerful in pulling, he hit one 6. Gunn, who hit ten 4s, fell to a wonderful left-handed catch in the gulley early on Monday; he also proved effective with the ball.

Derbyshire

A. E. Alderman c Meads b Voce	5	– not out ... 100
A. Townsend b Hall	0	– b Gunn ... 34
Rev. W. E. G. Payton c and b Gunn	25	– c Meads b Gunn ... 0
T. S. Worthington c Woodhead b Cox	44	– b Gunn ... 41
A. F. Skinner st Meads b Cox	4	– not out ... 6
L. Townsend c Voce b Woodhead	69	– b Cox ... 2
A. Rhodes c Meads b Gunn	10	– b Woodhead ... 10
T. D. Hounsfield c Woodhead b Cox	44	
C. Gladwin c Meads b Voce	13	
H. Pope not out	15	
G. Lee (did not bat)		– c Marshall b Gunn ... 1
B 7, l-b 2, w 1	10	B 6, l-b 1 ... 7
	239	(6 wkts dec.) 201

Nottinghamshire

W. W. Keeton b Pope	66	– b Rhodes	0
J. Knowles b Rhodes	5	– not out	29
G. V. Gunn c Gladwin b Worthington	77	– not out	35
R. Giles lbw b Pope	0		
G. F. H. Heane c Pope b L. Townsend	101		
H. R. Cox b Worthington	1		
B. A. Marshall c Gladwin b Rhodes	19		
J. B. Hall not out	34		
W. Voce c Hounsfield b Pope	0		
F. G. Woodhead c Hounsfield b L. Townsend	24		
B 4, l-b 3	7	L-b 1	1
	(9 wkts dec.) 334		**(1 wkt) 65**

E. A. Meads did not bat.

Nottinghamshire Bowling

	Overs	Mdns	Runs	Wkts	Overs	Mdns	Runs	Wkts
Voce	13	3	46	2	7	1	35	—
Hall	12	1	57	1	5	—	24	—
Woodhead	7.3	—	39	1	8	—	26	1
Cox	12	2	39	3	14.5	3	47	1
Gunn	11	1	48	2	10	—	44	4
Marshall					3	1	18	—

Derbyshire Bowling

	Overs	Mdns	Runs	Wkts	Overs	Mdns	Runs	Wkts
Rhodes	14	—	77	2	4	—	20	1
Gladwin	12	—	46	—	4	—	17	—
Pope	12	—	91	3	2	—	8	—
Worthington	12	—	48	2	4	—	15	—
L. Townsend	10.6	—	65	2				
Skinner					1	—	4	—

Umpires: J. Hardstaff, Senr., and G. Lee.

BRITISH EMPIRE XI v LONDON COUNTIES XI

Played at Lord's, July 13, 1940

London Counties won by 104 runs. Consistently good batting and bowling earned a handsome victory over a side whose run-getting powers failed unexpectedly when a close fight seemed in prospect. Parslow drove admirably until missing a ball on the leg stump, and, after he was second out, the remaining eight Empire wickets fell for 67 more runs. Durston, bowling off-breaks, did specially good service in getting Denis Compton caught at mid-on and bowling Conradi in quick succession. Bridger showed sound defence and skill in scoring strokes while the second wicket added 63 and he maintained his mastery of the bowling to the end. Fagg began the day with a steady display while the total reached 104; Hulme and Wellard, by free cricket, added 93, the Middlesex man hitting nine 4s during an hour and three-quarters of faultless batting against a well-varied attack. About 8,000 people watched the game; 6,425 paid at the gates, and a collection by Red Cross nurses realised £120 8s. 3d.

London Counties XI

L. C. Eastman (*Essex*) c Clarke b Judge ... 27	F. S. Lee (*Somerset*) c Judge b Smith 16
A. Fagg (*Kent*) c Emtage b Compton...... 40	J. Smith (*Middlesex*) c Davies b Clarke 13
L. J. Todd (*Kent*) c Parslow b Webster..... 7	W. F. Price (*Middlesex*) c Emtage b Clarke . 1
J. O'Connor (*Essex*) c Conradi b Compton . 19	
J. Hulme (*Middlesex*) not out............ 78	B 7, l-b 4, n-b 2 13
A. W. Wellard (*Somerset*) c Bebbington	
b Davies. 45	(8 wkts dec.) 259

A. Watt (*Kent*) and J. Durston (*Middlesex*) did not bat.

British Empire XI

L. F. Parslow (*Chingford*) b Watt........ 54	Gnr W. M. F. Bebbington (*Darjeeling*)
R. Smith (*Essex*) b Smith 14	c Hulme b Durston. 15
J. R. Bridger (*Cambridge Univ.*) not out.... 48	A/c P. F. Judge (*Glamorgan*) b Wellard ... 0
Sgt D. Compton (*Middlesex*) c Eastman	C. B. Clarke (*West Indies*) lbw b Durston .. 5
b Durston. 1	J. Webster (*Cambridge Univ.*) b Wellard ... 1
E. R. Conradi (*Cambridge Univ.*) b Durston 0	B 1, l-b 3 4
J. G. W. Davies (*Kent*) b Todd........... 7	
J. B. Emtage (*Barbados*) b Todd 6	155

Empire XI Bowling

	Overs	Mdns	Runs	Wkts
Smith	10	—	83	1
Judge	15	1	59	1
Clarke...........	7.2	—	35	2
Webster	8	1	30	1
Compton	5	—	29	2
Davies...........	3	1	10	1

Counties Bowling

	Overs	Mdns	Runs	Wkts
Smith	8	1	20	1
Wellard..........	8.2	1	27	2
Watt	4	—	30	1
Durston	13	1	51	4
Todd............	8	—	23	2

Umpires: F. Chester and W. Reeves.

BRITISH EMPIRE XI v LONDON COUNTIES XI

Played at Lord's, August 10, 1940

British Empire XI won by 53 runs. Over 13,000 people saw the British Empire inflict the first defeat of the London Counties. An opening stand of 113 by Parslow and Nelson gave the Empire side a solid foundation, and Parslow went on to hit his first century at Lord's. After some free hitting by Bridger, Davies and Compton punished the bowling severely, adding 97 before Woolley, whose appearance proved tremendously popular, gained his second wicket. Bartlett declared, and the Counties were left nearly three hours to bat. Fagg and Sandham began with a partnership of 67, but both were bowled by Allen. Then came some delightful strokes by Woolley and O'Connor, who put on 62, but when Compton took a return catch from Woolley he altered the whole position by claiming six successive wickets. Seven men were out for 180, but Watt, who hit Compton for two 6s, and Brooks threatened to save the game. Having completed his 50 the Surrey man was splendidly caught off the next ball, the match being finished with five minutes to spare. As many as 10,326 people paid at the gates, the receipts being £258, and a collection for the Red Cross and Cricketers' Friendly Society yielded £145.

British Empire XI

L. F. Parslow (*Chingford*) b Wellard 101
R. P. Nelson (*Northamptonshire*) c Brooks
    b Woolley. 44
J. R. Bridger (*Cambridge Univ.*) b Durston . 40
Sgt D. Compton (*Middlesex*) c Eastman
    b Woolley. 60

H. T. Bartlett (*Sussex*) not out 7
Pte J. G. W. Davies (*Kent*) not out 51
    B 1, l-b 4 5

               (4 wkts dec.) 308

R. Smith (*Essex*), C. B. Clarke (*West Indies*), W. M. F. Bebbington (*Darjeeling*), L. Allen (*Middlesex*) and A/c P. F. Judge (*Glamorgan*) did not bat.

London Counties XI

A. Fagg (*Kent*) b Allen 44
A. Sandham (*Surrey*) b Allen 20
J. O'Connor (*Essex*) c Bartlett b Compton. . 32
F. E. Woolley (*Kent*) c and b Compton 38
J. Hulme (*Middlesex*) lbw b Compton 13
L. C. Eastman (*Essex*) lbw b Compton 0
A. W. Wellard (*Somerset*) c and b Compton 2

A. Watt (*Kent*) c Smith b Compton 31
E. W. Brooks (*Surrey*) c Davies b Judge . . . 50
J. Smith (*Middlesex*) b Clarke 6
J. Durston (*Middlesex*) not out. 5
    B 8, l-b 5, n-b 1 14
                    255

Counties Bowling

	Overs	Mdns	Runs	Wkts
Smith	12	1	65	—
Wellard.	18	1	76	1
Watt	9	2	51	—
Eastman	10	2	40	—
Durston	11	—	48	1
Woolley	5	1	23	2

Empire XI Bowling

	Overs	Mdns	Runs	Wkts
Smith	2	—	16	—
Judge	6.3	1	26	1
Allen.	13	—	78	2
Clarke.	9	2	26	1
Compton	10	—	81	6
Davies.	4	—	14	—

Umpires: F. Chester and W. Reeves.

BUCCANEERS v BRITISH EMPIRE XI

Played at Lord's, August 31, 1940

Drawn. "The Battle of Britain" interfered with the match, causing late arrivals, which necessitated an altered batting order and bringing about an early cessation when the Buccaneers seemed within sight of victory. F. R. Brown accepted the unaccustomed honour of opening batsman so successfully that he hit two 6s and eight 4s in scoring 77 out of 114 in sixty-five minutes. He drove superbly. De Soysa, one of six left-handed batsmen on view, was a sound partner for the powerful hitter; Unwin showed good form, and Conradi, though not sure of all his strokes, played the second highest innings of the day. Clarke, if severely punished at times, bowled cleverly, but was surpassed by Brown, who took all the six Empire wickets that fell. Pitching well up, with his customary varied spin. Brown lured unwary batsmen to attempt big hits that often brought disaster. His success began when Herbert held a grand left-hand catch at short leg behind the wicket. Nelson was strong as well as discreet in his hitting, but like his partner, Parslow, he fell to a good catch. When Bartlett was bowled by a ball which turned a lot, Davies and M. D. Lyon gave evidence that they retained their skill. Bebbington was a capable wicketkeeper. Mr Stanley Christopherson, MCC president, Sir Stanley Jackson, Lord Lucan and Mr H. D. G. Leveson-Gower, after a night in command of the local Home Guard, were among the company of about 3,000 who supported the Red Cross Fund to which the gate receipts were devoted.

Buccaneers

Lt F. R. Brown c Parslow b Davies	77	
G. R. de Soysa b Clarke	36	
Lt E. J. Unwin lbw b Clarke	40	
L. B. Fishlock b Clarke	18	
C. K. Herbert b Clarke	5	
J. M. Leiper c Smith b Clarke	21	
Sig. E. R. Conradi c Bartlett b Clarke	56	

O/Cdt H. D. King c Bebbington b Davies .. 1
A. J. Gillespie not out 12
G. W. Moore b Davies 0

N-b 2...................... 2
___
(9 wkts dec.) 268

A/c P. F. Judge did not bat.

British Empire XI

L. F. Parslow c Herbert b Brown 16
2nd Lt R. P. Nelson c Fishlock b Brown.... 45
W. G. Spencer c and b Brown............ 1
W. M. F. Bebbington lbw b Brown 8
H. T. Bartlett b Brown 29
Pte J. G. W. Davies lbw b Brown 16

Capt. M. D. Lyon not out 14
C. B. Clarke not out 3

B 5, l-b 2, n-b 2............... 9
___
(6 wkts) 141

R. Smith, N. L. Hills and L. Allen did not bat.

Empire XI Bowling

	Overs	Mdns	Runs	Wkts
Smith	3	—	16	—
Allen	4	—	42	—
Lyon	2	—	17	—
Clarke	19	2	97	6
Davies	16.6	1	85	3
Spencer	2	—	9	—

Buccaneers Bowling

	Overs	Mdns	Runs	Wkts
Leiper	8	—	35	—
Judge	7	1	38	—
Brown	9	—	59	6

Umpires: D. Jenkins and H. L. Goodered.

DULWICH COLLEGE v KING'S COLLEGE SCHOOL, WIMBLEDON

Played at Dulwich, June 11, 1941

Dulwich won by 161 runs. This match fully illustrated the immense value to Dulwich of T. E. Bailey and H. P. H. Kiddle. Both batted finely, and Kiddle, with his fast bowling, completely demoralised the King's College batsmen. He took eight wickets for three runs, including the "hat-trick", a feat that constituted a record in public school cricket.

Dulwich College

A. F. Harlow b Chase	17	D. W. Walton c Chase b Palmer		3
R. G. Hulbert lbw b Penfold	12	A. R. Langston not out		0
A. W. H. Mallett b Penfold	17			
T. E. Bailey not out	84	Extras		4
H. M. Buckland b Cotton	2			
H. P. H. Kiddle b Penfold	32		(6 wkts dec.)	171

H. A. Beardwell, H. R. Woolmer and O. F. Jackson did not bat.

King's College School, Wimbledon

P. R. Chase b Kiddle	3	A. F. Welsted b Kiddle	0
D. H. L. Wadsworth lbw b Kiddle	0	P. B. Chapman c Mallett b Bailey	0
J. C. Penfold run out	0	E. G. Ostime c Langston b Kiddle	0
J. M. L. Cook c and b Kiddle	0	L. T. Cotton not out	0
W. B. Palmer b Kiddle	3	Extras	4
P. H. Nunnerley c Woolmer b Kiddle	0		
I. H. Christie b Kiddle	0		10

METROPOLITAN POLICE v BRITISH EMPIRE XI

Played at Imber Court, August, 2, 3, 1941

British Empire won by 153 runs. As in the first meeting between these two sides the previous year, Clarke, the West Indies player, was the outstanding performer. On this occasion, he achieved the notable feat of taking all ten wickets in one innings, including the "hat-trick". Altogether he dismissed fifteen men in the game for 58 runs. On the opening day, when the Police won the toss and sent in the visitors, a third-wicket stand of 74 between Bennett and Bebbington enabled the Empire to put together a useful total. The best display came from Avery, who brought off some admirable strokes in his sound 54. The Police soon found Clarke too much for them and they lost eight men for 90 runs before stumps were drawn. The next day Oliver tossed up his leg-breaks so successfully that he did the "hat-trick" by sending back Carter, Forde and Hills with successive deliveries. His match record was ten wickets for 93. The Police wanted 226 to win, but they broke down completely before Clarke. At one period Clarke dismissed three men in six balls and next came his "hat-trick". At the finish the Police presented him with the ball.

British Empire XI

H. P. Crabtree lbw b Taylor	1	– c Crowhurst b Taylor	59
A. C. L. Bennett b Ould	34	– not out	10
C. V. G. Haines lbw b Wood	4	– b Oliver	11
W. M. F. Bebbington lbw b Oliver	44	– c Ould b Wood	30
A. V. Avery c Taylor b Crowhurst	54	– b Taylor	3
N. E. Carter b Oliver	7	– b Oliver	2
H. M. Forde b Oliver	2	– b Oliver	0
N. L. Hills c Fullwood b Taylor	1	– st Fullwood b Oliver	0
C. B. Clarke lbw b Oliver	1	– b Oliver	18
R. Saphin c Oliver b Wood	19	– st Fullwood b Oliver	4
D. L. Donnelly not out	1		
B 1, l-b 3	4	B 9, l-b 2	11
	172	(9 wkts dec.)	184

Metropolitan Police

D. Wilson b Clarke	9	– b Clarke	7
A. Reynolds b Forde	11	– c Bebbington b Clarke	18
J. Wills c Donnelly b Crabtree	2	– b Clarke	9
K. Crowhurst c Donnelly b Clarke	24	– c Bennett b Clarke	0
F. Meeres c Haines b Forde	22	– b Clarke	4
J. Cosham b Clarke	0	– st Carter b Clarke	14
F. Wood st Carter b Clarke	4	– b Clarke	0
G. Ould b Crabtree	0	– b Clarke	0
T. Oliver c Haines b Clarke	6	– not out	0
H. Taylor c Carter b Forde	7	– c and b Clarke	8
W. C. Fullwood not out	3	– c Bennett b Clarke	0
B 3, l-b 4	7	B 8, l-b 2, w 2	12
	95		**72**

Metropolitan Police Bowling

	Overs	Mdns	Runs	Wkts	Overs	Mdns	Runs	Wkts
Taylor	13	3	44	2	11	—	31	2
Wood	12.3	3	38	2	10	—	38	1
Oliver	13	2	58	4	9.4	1	35	6
Ould	4	—	18	1	3	—	17	—
Crowhurst	2	—	10	1	3	—	16	—

British Empire XI Bowling

	Overs	Mdns	Runs	Wkts	Overs	Mdns	Runs	Wkts
Clarke	15	4	29	5	9.3	1	29	10
Forde	8	1	21	3	5	—	13	—
Crabtree	4	—	23	2	4	1	8	—
Avery	2	—	7	—				
Bebbington	1	—	8	—	1	—	10	—

SURREY HOME GUARD v SUSSEX HOME GUARD

Played at Lord's, July 23, 1942

Abandoned. This match was given up in tragic circumstances after Andrew Ducat, the Surrey and England cricketer and international footballer, collapsed and died at the wicket. The Surrey side having been sent in to bat, Ducat began his innings before lunch and was 17 at the interval. On resuming he scored steadily, carrying his score to 29. Then he hit a ball from Eaton to mid-on. The ball was returned to the bowler, who was about to send down the next delivery when Ducat fell forward and apparently died immediately though he was moved to the pavilion and quickly taken by ambulance to a nearby hospital. The score of the match as officially recorded by MCC was:

Surrey Home Guard

Pte H. Moss b Eaton	32	Lt R. H. Attwell not out	1
Pte H. E. Wood b Bartlett	8		
Pte P. Cowan c and b Eaton	26	B 4, l-b 2	6
Lt D. A. M. Rome lbw b Eaton	30		
Pte A. Ducat not out	29	**(4 wkts) 132**	

Pte J. C. Johnston, Pte R. A. Levermore, Pte R. A. Eede, Pte A. Jeffery and Lt Col T. C. D. Hassall did not bat.

Sussex Home Guard

Pte H. S. Mather, Pte J. V. Eaton, Pte V. C. Humphrey, Pte C. Steele, Lt N. C. Fuente, Pte T. Bartlett, Pte D. V. Smith, Lt A. C. Somerset, Lt Col W. E. Grace, Pte H. R. Sexton, Major E. H. Firth.

Sussex Home Guard Bowling

	Overs	Mdns	Runs	Wkts
Eaton	18.2	7	34	3
Smith	12	2	35	—
Bartlett	8	—	47	1
Fuente	5	1	10	—

Umpires: T. W. Natcham and Pte J. Moyer.

MIDDLESEX AND ESSEX v KENT AND SURREY

Played at Lord's, August 3, 4, 1942

Drawn. A splendid match, worthy of the players engaged, produced much fine cricket, sensational incidents, and a finish that compensated for the inconclusive result which came after a glorious effort to snatch victory. Trevor Bailey, the Dulwich College captain, put enthusiasm into a Bank Holiday crowd of 22,000 people – 16,693 paid for admission – by dismissing three batsmen in his first over. G. O. Allen gave way at 33 to Bailey, whose second ball beat Bennett; Ames hit 3 to the on, but the seventh delivery got Bridger leg-before and the next sent Todd's middle stump flying. Nichols, bowling Fishlock, claimed the first wicket, and by similarly dismissing Parker he made the score five wickets for 37 before Ames prevented Bailey doing the hat-trick. Carefully nursed by G. O. Allen, Bailey resumed after lunch and bowled Bedser, while Nichols accounted for more seasoned batsmen. By adding 70 in fifty minutes Holmes and Ames checked the collapse, and Evans, with a six to the on from Nichols and six 4s, hit up 55 at one a minute while 77 runs were scored and two wickets fell. He and Gover, batting in admirable style, added 65 in thirty-five minutes. Evans drove splendidly and fell to a catch at mid-on, which Haig with his high reach only just grasped.

A stand of 82 by Brown and Edrich gave Middlesex and Essex the upper hand, but Pierpoint bowling fairly fast, straight and a good length, dismissed them and Denis Compton during a spell of eight overs which cost 37 runs. Nichols and Allen increased their side's advantage on Tuesday morning. The arrears of 88 were cleared off before Bennett was second out, but not until E. R. T. Holmes advanced himself in the batting order did Kent and Surrey pull the game round. Going in third wicket down, Holmes justified his policy of taking first innings by giving a superb forcing display at the critical period. The game proceeded without a tea interval, but Holmes received only moderate support until Todd, relying on defence, stayed while 85 runs came in fifty-five minutes. Having scored 114 out of 189 in an hour and three-quarters Holmes declared at five minutes past five. Besides driving two consecutive balls from Peter Smith high up into the pavilion, he found the boundary nine times, mainly by drives. Middlesex and Essex were left with a hundred minutes in which to get the 190 runs required for victory.

Accurate bowling and sure fielding kept the runs to 87 when Brown was dismissed, but in Denis Compton Edrich found a partner equal to himself at the forcing game. The two England batsmen brought off every possible run, their judgement and speed between the wickets supplementing audacious stroke play. Holmes changed his pace bowlers so that none of them tired, but only an amazing catch separated the dashing batsmen. Edrich drove a half volley back knee high with tremendous force and Bedser, knocking the ball up with his left hand, caught it with his right. This third wicket put on 68 in thirty-five minutes. Leslie Compton showed the nerve required for the exciting situation, but with only five minutes left 26 runs were needed. Denis Compton hit three boundaries among other strokes, but, jumping in to drive the sixth ball of the last over, he failed in the desperate attempt and was stumped. So the match ended amidst tremendous cheering from eight thousand people, with Middlesex and Essex four runs short of victory. Besides the grand finish he gave to the match, Denis Compton distinguished himself by catching Evans brilliantly at long-on. The match produced £417 for King George's Fund for Sailors (War Fund).

Kent and Surrey

L. B. Fishlock (*Surrey*) b Nichols	18	– c L. Compton b Bailey	15
J. R. Bridger (*Surrey*) lbw b Bailey	9	– c Edrich b Sims	41
A. C. L. Bennett (*Surrey*) b Bailey	3	– c Smith b Allen	27
Flt Lt L. E. G. Ames (*Kent*) c L. Compton b Allen	34	– c Brown b Bailey	22
Sgt L. J. Todd (*Kent*) b Bailey	0	– c Sims b Smith	17
Sgt J. F. Parker (*Surrey*) b Nichols	0	– not out	12
Major E. R. T. Holmes (*Surrey*) lbw b Nichols	39	– not out	114
Sgt T. G. Evans (*Kent*) c Haig b Nichols	55	– c D. Compton b Smith	17
Sgt A. V. Bedser (*Surrey*) b Bailey	2		
CSMI A. R. Gover (*Surrey*) not out	20		
Sgt F. G. Pierpoint (*Surrey*) b Allen	1		
B 4, l-b 3, w 4, n-b 1	12	L-b 5, w 1, n-b 6	12
	193	**(6 wkts dec.)**	**277**

Middlesex and Essex

A. V. Avery (*Essex*) b Bedser	27	– lbw b Todd	15
Cpl S. M. Brown (*Middlesex*) c Evans b Pierpoint	58	– lbw b Pierpoint	34
Sq Ldr W. J. Edrich (*Middlesex*) c Parker b Pierpoint.	46	– c and b Bedser	73
Sgt Instr D. Compton (*Middlesex*) lbw b Pierpoint	10	– st Evans b Bedser	57
PC L. H. Compton (*Middlesex*) b Gover	33	– not out	4
Sgt Instr M. S. Nichols (*Essex*) b Bedser	51		
T. E. Bailey (*Essex*) b Parker	0		
Major G. O. Allen (*Middlesex*) c Ames b Pierpoint	29		
Lt P. Smith (*Essex*) c Todd b Bedser	11		
Capt. N. Haig (*Middlesex*) b Bedser	0		
J. Sims (*Middlesex*) not out	1		
B 7, l-b 2, n-b 6	15	B 1, n-b 2	3
	281	**(4 wkts)**	**186**

Middlesex and Essex Bowling

	Overs	Mdns	Runs	Wkts	Overs	Mdns	Runs	Wkts
Nichols	14	3	47	4	8	1	25	—
Allen	9.1	1	32	2	6	—	28	1
Bailey	7	1	36	4	8	—	42	2
Edrich	3	—	26	—	6	—	24	—
Smith	6	—	40	—	8	—	62	2
Sims					12	1	58	1
Haig					5	—	26	—

Kent and Surrey Bowling

	Overs	Mdns	Runs	Wkts	Overs	Mdns	Runs	Wkts
Gover	12	1	45	1	7	—	54	—
Todd	9	—	48	—	4	—	23	1
Bedser	19.7	—	72	4	6.6	—	44	2
Parker	8	—	31	1	2	—	22	—
Bridger	3	—	28	—				
Pierpoint	10	1	42	4	4	—	40	1

Umpires: G. Beet and A. Fowler.

GLOUCESTERSHIRE SERVICES v DOMINIONS

Played at Clifton College, Bristol, May 29, 1943

Gloucestershire Services won by 107 runs. Nutter, of Lancashire, was their best batsman. He began quiety, but finished by punishing the bowling whole-heartedly. Outtram, medium-fast, bowled well. The Dominions team, although including several capable batsmen, fared poorly against a strong attack and only Dempster showed to advantage. Laidlaw took three of the last four wickets for four runs. The scorers did not keep the bowling analysis.

Gloucestershire Services

Sgt D. Brookes c Stanford b Outtram...... 29	W. E. Cranfield b Lawrence............. 2
Surgn Lt J. A. Nunn b Williams.......... 35	W. H. Lewis not out................... 1
Cpl R. Howorth c Broad b Williams....... 2	Lt Laidlaw b Outtram.................. 3
L/A/C A. E. Nutter c Stanford b Outtram . 77	
Lt F. M. Sibbles b Carmody............. 11	B 15, l-b 8.................. 23
W. Neale c Stanford b Carmody.......... 18	
F/O T. W. Goddard c Hodges b Outtram .. 1	(9 wkts dec.) 202

Sgt G. Lambert did not bat.

Dominions XI

Lt C. S. Dempster lbw b Laidlaw......... 37	P/O W. K. Hodges b Laidlaw............ 5
P/O D. K. Carmody c Nutter b Sibbles 5	P/O E. Lawrence c Cranfield b Goddard ... 1
Flt Lt R. G. Emery b Lambert........... 0	F/O G. Falkinder not out............... 2
F/O E. G. Broad b Lambert............. 9	Major W. S. Outtram b Laidlaw.......... 7
Sgt E. A. Williams run out............. 11	B 13, l-b 2, n-b 2............. 17
L/A/C K. C. James c Nunn b Nutter...... 1	
Sgt R. M. Stanford c Lambert b Nutter 0	95

GLOUCESTERSHIRE v RAF

Played at Gloucester, July 24, 1943

Drawn. The county side were indebted to their guests for a good score. Brookes (Northamptonshire) and Barling (Surrey) both RAF men, began with 146 in two hours, and Barling went on to make a splendid hundred, including many well-timed strokes, in two and three-quarter hours. Brookes, like Barling, hit seven 4s. With Wilson batting briskly, Goddard declared and set his opponents to make 265 in two and a half hours. The fast bowling of Hawker proved disconcerting, and although Nutter hit nine 4s the RAF could not score quickly enough. Mills, the old Gloucestershire spin bowler, reappeared at the age of 60 after a lapse of fourteen years, but bowled only two overs. Sgt V. D. Guthrie of the Australian Air Force, who bowled for Gloucestershire but was not included in their batting order, wore an England football shirt borrowed from S. Barkas, the former England international, an instructor at his station. As the Gloucestershire organisers asked thirteen men to attend, Wyatt agree to let them play twelve, but declined to augment his own eleven.

Gloucestershire

Sgt D. Brooks b Warburton............. 69	Flt Lt P. L. Hahn lbw b Bedser.......... 6
P/O T. H. Barling c and b Beveridge......103	F/O A. H. Deavin b Jackson............ 4
T. D. Hounsfield b Jackson.............. 0	T. W. Goddard c Berry b Bedser......... 8
Flt Sgt G. S. Mobey b Warburton......... 3	B 8, l-b 6................... 14
P/O A. Wilson not out................. 52	
F/O E. J. Drake st James b Beveridge 5	(8 wkts dec.) 264

Cpl D. J. Guy, L Cpl F. Hawker and P. T. Mills did not bat.

RAF

F/O R. J. Gregory b Hawker 19	L/A/C A. E. Nutter b Goddard 57
Sgt L. G. Berry lbw b Drake............. 34	A/C2 L. Warburton not out 32
Sgt L. J. Todd b Hawker................ 7	B 1, l-b 3 4
F/O R. E. S. Wyatt lbw b Drake.......... 24	
Wing Cdr R. G. Musson b Hawker 20	(6 wkts) 197

F/O J. Beveridge, L/A/C K. James, Flt Sgt A. V. Bedser and Sgt P. F. Jackson did not bat.

RAF Bowling

	Overs	Mdns	Runs	Wkts
Todd.............	10	1	42	—
Bedser............	21.6	1	86	2
Warburton	12	—	44	2
Jackson...........	15	2	57	2
Beveridge	4	—	21	2

Gloucestershire Bowling

	Overs	Mdns	Runs	Wkts
Hawker...........	14	—	79	3
Guthrie...........	4	—	16	—
Drake............	8	1	42	2
Wilson	4	—	10	—
Goddard..........	9.3	—	31	1
Mills	2	—	15	—

Sgt V. D. Guthrie (RAAF) bowled, but was not included in the batting order.

ENGLAND v THE DOMINIONS

Played at Lord's, August 2, 3, 1943

England won by eight runs. A match remarkable for many changes of fortune and sensational incidents ended at quarter to seven in a narrow victory for England, thanks to Robertson taking the last two wickets in the only over he bowled. Robins won the toss, and England in uneven batting displays did well enough to warrant the closure of each innings. Denis Compton and Ames checked a poor start by adding 56 and, with Holmes in good form, 71 more runs came quickly, while Bailey, exercising discreet defence, helped the Kent batsmen add 112. Compton played a dashing game, but the honours belonged to Ames, who hit splendidly all round the wicket; his chief strokes during two hours forty minutes were two 6s and eleven 4s.

After scoring 93 for two wickets, The Dominions collapsed so badly before Denis Compton at the practice ground end that eight men fell for 22 runs before stumps were drawn, and when Robins in the morning decided that England, although 209 ahead, should bat again, they lost four men for 6 runs – altogether twelve consecutive wickets for 28 under conditions apparently quite favourable to batsmen. Not until Robins joined Holmes did England recover, and they played such fine cricket that 106 runs came in 55 minutes. Robins, quite in his old dashing style, made the bowling the length he desired by jumping in or stepping back, and audacity brought him a 6 and ten 4s.

The Dominions did not shirk the big task of getting 360 in roughly four hours and a half. Dempster played grandly. Workman proved such a useful opening batsman that he saw the total reach 80, and Carmody, going in second wicket down, gave such assistance that 104 were added. Third out, Dempster scored his 113 out of 187 in an hour and fifty minutes, hitting ten 4s by beautiful strokes. After tea Constantine played in his own aggressive style, but from a hard drive Leslie Compton caught him with the left hand at full stretch while leaning on the pavilion rails with feet on the ground. This perfectly fair catch caused much criticism as the ball might have been over the boundary, but Constantine knew the rules and said "That is cricket". With seven out for 218, The Dominions looked well beaten, but Sismey and Clarke put on 108 and the final sensation, with two very good catches, finished the match amidst much excitement. The wicket-keeping by Sismey and Evans was always high-class. On Monday the teams were presented to the Duke of Gloucester before lunch. The exact numbers paying for admission were 23,993 on Monday and 14,217 on Tuesday. The proceeds went to the Red Cross Fund.

England

H. Gimblett (Somerset) c Sismey b Roper	10	– b Roper. 0
Capt J. D. Robertson (*Middlesex*) b Constantine.	33	– c Sismey b Roper 1
L Cpl L. Compton (*Middlesex*) b Martindale.	1	– b Martindale. 1
Sgt Instr D. Compton (*Middlesex*) run out.	58	– c Miller b Martindale 17
Sq Ldr L. E. G. Ames (*Kent*) c and b Clarke	133	– c Sismey b Martindale 13
Major E. R. T. Holmes (*Surrey*) c and b Clarke	39	– not out 45
Flt Lt R. W. V. Robins (*Middlesex*) b Martindale	2	– not out 69
2nd Lt T. E. Bailey (*Royal Marines*) not out	30	
L Cpl A. W. H. Mallett (*Royal Marines*) lbw b Clarke	2	
Sgt T. G. Evans (*Kent*) b Clarke.	5	– b Roper. 0
B 5, l-b 5, n-b 1	11	B 3, l-b 1 4

(9 wkts dec.) 324   (6 wkts dec.) 150

Flt Sgt A. V. Bedser (*Surrey*) did not bat.

The Dominions

F/O D. K. Carmody (*Australia*) c Evans b Mallet	43	– c Ames b D. Compton 49
Lt C. S. Dempster (*New Zealand*) c Ames b Bedser	18	– b Mallett 113
Sgt K. Miller (*Australia*) c L. Compton b D. Compton.	32	– c Evans b Bedser 2
Sgt J. Workman (*Australia*) c Mallett b Bedser	8	– b D. Compton. 16
L. N. Constantine (*West Indies*) c Mallett b D. Compton.	2	– c L. Compton b Bedser. 21
O/Cdt D. P. Morkel (*S. Africa*) lbw b D. Compton	2	– c and b Bedser 0
E. A. Martindale (*West Indies*) b D. Compton.	4	– c D. Compton b Bedser 0
F/O S. Sismey (*Australia*) lbw b Bedser	0	– c Bedser b Robertson 70
P/O A. D. McDonald (*Australia*) lbw b D. Compton	0	– not out 9
C. B. Clarke (*West Indies*) c and b D. Compton	0	– b D. Compton. 52
F/O A. W. Roper (*Australia*) not out.	0	– c Bailey b Robertson 2
B 3, l-b 1, n-b 2	6	B 11, w 1, n-b 5. 17

115   351

The Dominions Bowling

	Overs	Mdns	Runs	Wkts	Overs	Mdns	Runs	Wkts
Roper	9	—	51	1	7	1	36	3
Martindale	10	—	50	2	9	1	28	3
Clarke.	19.7	1	89	4	3	—	29	—
Constantine	10	—	61	1	4	—	32	—
Miller	4	1	25	—	4	1	21	—
Morkel	1	—	6	—				
McDonald	8	1	31	—				

England Bowling

	Overs	Mdns	Runs	Wkts	Overs	Mdns	Runs	Wkts
Bedser............	10.6	1	33	3	25	1	108	4
Bailey............	4	—	15	—	6	1	31	—
Mallett...........	8	1	26	1	9	4	28	1
Robins...........	3	—	20	—	12	—	75	—
D. Compton.......	8	2	15	6	20	3	60	3
L. Compton.......					3	—	12	—
Holmes...........					1	—	14	—
Robertson........					1	—	6	2

LESLIE COMPTON'S CATCH

The two-day match between England and The Dominions at Lord's provided an example of the risk run by applying the declaration after taking first innings. R. W. V. Robins won the toss, declared with nine men out, and secured a lead of 209; yet he preferred to bat again, and his second declaration, after a collapse of batsmen who were forcing the pace, produced a grand finish: Robertson dismissed two men in the only over he bowled and England won by eight runs at a quarter to seven. The effort to get 360 in four hours and a half only just failed, and the result might and probably would have been different but for the left-handed catch by Leslie Compton leaning on the pavilion rails which dismissed Constantine. That grand catch aroused much discussion, but it was perfectly fair because Compton was standing within the boundary when he held the ball.

Notes by the Editor, 1944

MIDDLESEX AND ESSEX v KENT AND SURREY

Played at Lord's, August 28, 1943

Kent and Surrey won by nine wickets. Steady rain lasting many hours suggested a wet day, but after an early lunch the downfall ceased and the precaution of covering the pitch entirely enabled a start at half-past two. Meanwhile, when everyone present regarded cricket as impossible, the Arsenal club obtained permission for the brothers Compton to play at Charlton in the opening match of the football season. An injury to A. V. Avery of Essex, who tripped over his bag when leaving home for Lord's, further weakened what could be called the home team, and Arthur Fagg spent the day looking for his bag mislaid on the railway. This mishap merely necessitated a substitute fielding, but G. O. Allen, on winning the toss, found his side so seriously reduced in batting strength that, against an attack which always looked menacing, except in one over by A. V. Bedser, they collapsed badly. In a hundred minutes they fell for 75 runs, the best stand by Nichols and Allen realising 20. Todd started the trouble with a splendid ball, but best of the five bowlers, all in fine form, was Wright, who kept a perfect length with his leg breaks and returned a remarkable analysis. The loss of Fishlock to a juggled slip catch preceded a forcing partnership by E. A. Bedser, who shaped very well, and Ames, the runs being hit off when the innings had lasted seventy minutes; altogether they added 106 in an hour and a quarter. T. G. Evans again gave evidence of his batting ability following admirable work behind the stumps, where the beaten side were further handicapped, R. H. Twining, one of the substitutes, at the age of 53 naturally lacking the skill of Leslie Compton. After the winning hit the game was treated lightly. Considering the weather the attendance was good, 3,456 paying at the gates. The proceeds went to King George's Fund for Sailors.

Middlesex and Essex

Capt. J. D. Robertson c Mallett b A. V. Bedser. 7	2nd Lt T. E. Bailey c Evans b Wright 7
Cpl S. M. Brown b Todd 0	R. H. Twining c Parker b Wright 0
H. P. Crabtree b A. V Bedser 2	Sgt J. Sims not out 11
Sgt Instr M. S. Nichols c Evans b Todd 11	Capt. I. A. R. Peebles c Parker b A. V. Bedser. 0
Major G. O. Allen b Wright 19	L-b 4 4
Sq Ldr R. W. V. Robins c Todd b Parker... 11	___
G. E. V. Crutchley b Mallet 3	75

Kent and Surrey

L. B. Fishlock c Nichols b Allen 3	Sgt L. J. Todd not out.................. 33
Flt Sgt E. A. Bedser c Sims b Peebles 54	B 10, l-b 1, w 3, n-b 1 15
Sq Ldr L. E. G. Ames c Allen b Robins 47	___
Sgt T. G. Evans not out................. 56	(3 wkts) 208

Major E. R. T. Holmes, Sgt J. F. Parker, L Cpl A. W. H. Mallet, Flt Sgt A. V. Bedser, Lt D. V. P. Wright and A. E. Fagg did not bat.

Kent and Surrey Bowling

	Overs	Mdns	Runs	Wkts
Todd.............	7	—	17	2
A. V. Bedser	4.2	—	21	3
Parker............	3	—	13	1
Wright	5	3	8	3
Mallet............	4	—	12	1

Middlesex and Essex Bowling

	Overs	Mdns	Runs	Wkts
Allen.............	5	—	14	1
Nichols	5	1	12	—
Bailey	5	—	34	—
Sims	7	1	46	—
Peebles	6	—	54	1
Robins	3	—	33	1

WEST OF ENGLAND v LORD'S XI

Played at Lord's, July 8, 1944

Lord's XI won by five wickets. For their first appearance at Lord's West of England were originally matched against A.A. Command, but, owing to the gunners being engaged with the flying-bombs, the opposition was changed to a Lord's XI. The brothers Lyon were the rival captains, and on being sent in to bat the West found some moisture in the pitch, a condition which Todd turned to such account that four wickets fell for 32. Meanwhile Sinfield made no mistake and Berry and Nutter helped in stands of 60 and 70. Altogether Sinfield resisted the bowling for three hours. The best batting of the match came from Townsend, who in just over two hours hit 91 out of 196; but he gave three chances behind the wicket.

West of England

J. C. W. MacBryan b Todd	1	P. L. Hahn c Townsend b Todd	12
R. A. Sinfield st Fullwood b Skene	90	R. J. O. Meyer lbw b Lyon	0
F. R. Santall c Thompson b Waddy	17	H. Yarnold not out	0
H. J. Williams b Todd	3	T. Goddard lbw b Skene	0
B. H. Lyon b Todd	2	B 2, l-b 5	7
L. G. Berry b Skene	37		
A. E. Nutter lbw b Todd	34		203

Lord's XI

D. C. H. Townsend b Meyer	91	R. W. Skene c Williams b Goddard	9
L. J. Todd lbw b Meyer	20	M. D. Lyon not out	13
A. G. Doggart b Goddard	0	B 4, l-b 5, w 1, n-b 2	12
J. T. Morgan c MacBryan b Goddard	30		
A. H. Wolstenholme not out	29	(5 wkts)	204

A. S. G. Thompson, B. B. Waddy, W. C. Fullwood and H. Taylor did not bat.

Lord's XI Bowling

	Overs	Mdns	Runs	Wkts
Taylor	12	1	38	—
Todd	20	5	46	5
Waddy	8	—	33	1
Skene	11.3	3	19	3
Lyon	9	4	16	1
Wolstenholme	8	1	32	—
Morgan	3	—	12	—

West of England Bowling

	Overs	Mdns	Runs	Wkts
Nutter	11	1	23	—
Meyer	18	1	72	2
Goddard	21.1	2	74	3
Sinfield	5	—	12	—
Santall	4	2	7	—
Lyon	1	—	4	—

A LORD'S XI v CANADA

Played at Lord's, July 20, 1944

A Lord's XI won by 213 runs. Americans were to have appeared at Lord's on this date, but their team, chosen entirely from bomber crews, were too busily engaged in the initial stages of the liberation of Europe campaign. Consequently Canada found themselves against stronger opposition. They began well enough, the first ball of the day disposing of Dempster, but afterwards their bowling was mastered. Todd, the Kent left-hander, hit his 151 in two and a half hours, MacBryan and Twining helping him in stands of 111 and 145. The West Indies fast bowler, Padmore, who served in the Canadian Army, bowled almost throughout the innings. Steady slow bowling upset Canada. Northwood and Simpson put on 86 for the second partnership, but the last eight wickets went down for 22 runs. It was interesting to see the flag of Canada over the Lord's pavilion.

A Lord's XI

C. S. Dempster c Stacey b Padmore	0	E. M. Wellings not out	27
J. C. W. MacBryan c Moffatt b Padmore	57	Capt. B. B. Waddy not out	0
Sgt L. J. Todd c Court b Bartlett	151	B 6, l-b 2. n-b 1	9
R. H. Twining b Padmore	77		
A. P. F. Chapman b Padmore	8	(5 wkts dec.)	329

Lt Col G. H. M. Cartwright, Flt Lt D. Stewart, R. C. A. FitzGerald and Sgt J. Townson did not bat.

Canada

Cpl J. Court b Todd	2	Sgt Major C. Stacey lbw b Cartwright	0
Capt. J. Northwood c Wellings b Cartwright	35	Major E. S. Williams not out	6
Capt. S. Simpson lbw b Stewart	60	SQMS G. McIlvenny b Waddy	1
Cpl H. Padmore lbw b Cartwright	3	Cpl J. Bartlett c Townson b Waddy	0
Capt. R. Moffatt b Cartwright	0		
Flt Lt E. Spriggs b Cartwright	3	B 4, l-b 2	6
CSM E. Matsuyama c Todd b Cartwright	0		116

Canada Bowling

	Overs	Mdns	Runs	Wkts
Padmore	21	1	112	4
Moffatt	6	—	39	—
Court	15	1	71	—
Simpson	6	—	46	—
Bartlett	8	1	52	1

A Lord's XI Bowling

	Overs	Mdns	Runs	Wkts
Todd	7	—	15	1
FitzGerald	5	—	12	—
Wellings	5	2	21	—
Waddy	4	2	14	2
Stewart	7	1	22	1
Cartwright	7	1	26	6

ENGLAND v AUSTRALIA

Played at Lord's, August 7, 1944

England won by 33 runs. All those who saw this Bank Holiday game went away filled with admiration of Hammond. The England captain gave one of his best exhibitions in a crisis. At one time seven wickets were down for 118, but Hammond, who went in at 51, stayed till the total reached 210. The Australians bowled and fielded splendidly, but, despite packing the off-side, they could not completely check Hammond. He continually moved out to the pitch of the ball and hammered the field with powerful drives and skilfully placed hits on either side of cover. The slow left-arm bowler, Ellis, gave him most trouble and nearly bowled him when 20, while the stroke off Calvert, which completed his 50, should have been snapped up by Sismey, the wicket-keeper. These were small blemishes in a notable innings that occupied two and a quarter hours and included twelve 4s. The two war-time discoveries from Dulwich College, Bailey and Mallett, gave Hammond excellent support, Bailey staying while the eighth wicket put on 78 in an hour.

Australia were left three and a quarter hours in which to hit off the runs and, thanks to Miller, they looked like accomplishing the task. At 13 brilliant fielding by Washbrook accounted for Workman, but Miller, after being nearly bowled by Bailey, emulated Hammond for hard driving. He made 85 out of 119 in one hundred minutes, getting twelve 4s. The turning point came with the total 142 for four wickets, when Hammond brought on Wright for a second spell, and the Kent man kept his end going until the finish. He got Williams taken at the wicket by Evans, and after Mallett bowled Stanford at 160, Wright destroyed any hopes of an Australian success by sending back Cristofani, McDonald and Roper in the course of five deliveries. Half an hour remained when the last man, Ellis, joined Henderson, and not until five minutes from time did Wright win the match by dismissing Henderson leg before. It was a grand day's cricket, full of surprises, with each side enjoying changes of fortune. Sixteen thousand people were present.

England

Flt Sgt C. Washbrook c Roper b Cristofani	20	Lt A. W. H. Mallett b Roper	16
F/O R. T. Simpson st Sismey b Ellis	16	Lt T. E. Bailey lbw b Roper	13
Lt J. D. Robertson st Sismey b Cristofani	15	Sgt T. G. Evans not out	10
Flt Lt W. R. Hammond c Roper b Ellis	105	Lt D. V. P. Wright c Williams b Ellis	4
Sq Ldr W. J. Edrich c Workman b Cristofani	14	B 4, l-b 2	6
Capt. D. C. H. Townsend b Ellis	6		
Sgt L. J. Todd b Roper	1		**226**

Australia

Flt Lt S. G. Sismey b Bailey	10	F/O D. R. Cristofani b Wright	0
Flt Sgt J. Workman run out	8	Flt Lt A. D. McDonald c Bailey b Wright	0
P/O K. R. Miller c and b Todd	85	Flt Lt A. W. Roper b Wright	2
Flt Sgt C. P. Calvert c Hammond b Wright	10	F/O R. E. Ellis not out	5
F/O R. Stanford b Mallett	36	B 2, l-b 1, n-b 1	4
F/O E. A. Williams c Evans b Wright	2		
Flt Lt J. R. Henderson lbw b Wright	31		**193**

Australia Bowling

	Overs	Mdns	Runs	Wkts
Roper	13	3	37	3
Calvert	16	2	38	—
Cristofani	22	4	63	3
Ellis	24.5	3	82	4

England Bowling

	Overs	Mdns	Runs	Wkts
Bailey	13	3	46	1
Todd	12	2	35	1
Wright	18.2	3	62	6
Edrich	2	—	8	—
Mallett	16	5	38	1

MATCHES AT LORD'S IN 1944

Until the flying-bombs arrived in London in the middle of June there was every indication that the 1944 cricket season at Lord's would break all war-time records in the matter of crowds and gate receipts. As it was, the raising of the flat-rate admission charge of sixpence to one shilling resulted in more money than ever being given to charity. The sum, £4,117, was allocated as follows: Duke of Gloucester's Red Cross and St John Fund £2,568, Army Cricket Association £352, Colonial Comforts Fund £313, RAAF Welfare Fund £242, King George's Fund for Sailors £220, and RAF War Emergency Committee £167. Altogether the total paid to charities during the war reached £11,557. Despite various difficulties 167,429 people paid for admission, against 232,390 in 1943. Bad weather accounted partly for this reduction and the flying-bomb menace caused some fixtures to be cancelled – including three big school matches, Clifton v Tonbridge, Rugby v Marlborough, and Cheltenham v Haileybury. These were re-arranged and the descriptions and scores will be found in the Public Schools section. Altogether 41 matches took place at Lord's during the summer, and, again, the cricket at headquarters gave enjoyment to everyone concerned.

ENGLAND v AUSTRALIA

(First Victory Match)

Played at Lord's, May 19, 21, 22, 1945

Australia won by six wickets. In a dynamic finish, true to the exhortation expressed in the post-war cricket plans, Pepper made the winning hit off the fourth ball of the last possible over just at seven o'clock. To the majority of the 18,000 people who saw the cricket this really fine climax gave intense pleasure and the Australian batsmen reached the pavilion amidst enthusiastic applause. The England team deserved equal praise for the splendid sportsmanship in doing their part in the speediest manner, changing positions quickly and starting each over without a suggestion of delay when the waste of seconds might have meant a drab draw.

While giving Australia hearty congratulations for their triumph, it must be indicated clearly that the prevailing conditions favoured them. After heavy rain overnight England batted on a green pitch with the outfield slow. The immediate loss of Hutton from a poor stroke gave Robertson the opportunity to prove his worth, and for 85 minutes he mastered the well-varied attack. He and Washbrook added 53, Hammond showed his form until after lunch a fast ball took his off stump, Ames and Edrich put on 75, but Stephenson alone of the remainder caused trouble, the last three wickets falling at 267.

Australia made 82 for two wickets before the close, and on Whit-Monday, when some 30,000 watched the game, they found the pitch – completely covered during the week-end and so protected from much rain – after being mown in the morning according to custom, quite favourable to scoring. Also better reward came for scoring strokes. Hassett increased his 27 by 50 before hitting over a yorker. Batting in quiet, resolute fashion, with hooks and cuts his most effective strokes, Hassett maintained his reputation. An interruption by rain did not help the fielding side and the bowling was mastered, Miller and Stanford making 99 runs together while Pepper gave an idea of his power in a stand for 73.

Miller accounted largely for Australia gaining the upper hand, his elegant, emphatic style fully meriting the hundred he earned before his first lifted stroke gave Ames a catch at deep mid-off. Batting three and a half hours, Miller hit only six 4s, but he was always getting runs with the soundness characteristic of most Australians. Williams and Price forced the pace with such effect that 88 runs cam in fifty minutes for the ninth partnership, Williams, last out to a catch at the wicket, hit eleven 4s in his 53. A repatriated prisoner of war, Williams hit hard in front of the wicket and cut cleanly.

Rain fell as play ceased shortly before half-past six, and in the morning England, 188 behind, batted on turf drying in sunshine. Pepper used his height and strong finger spin and, with the ball keeping low, he dismissed Hutton at 52 and Washbrook at 75, but Robertson, in another admirable display, stayed two hours forty minutes, hitting two 6s to the on and five 4s before Sismey, standing back, caught him off the first delivery by Cheetham, coming on with the new ball. Edrich and Robins further improved matters for England in a stand for 68, but, through haste for runs when victory was out of the question, both left at 286, and the remaining three wickets went for eight runs.

Wanting 107 runs with seventy minutes at their disposal, Australia soon lost Whitington and Miller – dismissed when starting for an impossible second run. Then Pepper joined Hassett and Hammond spread his field out so as to prevent fours, but singles came very frequently and often the boundary could not be saved. Fielding at deep mid-off, Hammond, running across behind the bowler, caught Hassett cleverly, and

Cheetham lost his wicket when Pepper refused a sharp run. Then Price came in with twelve minutes left and 31 runs wanted. Hammond did not use the opportunity afforded by these wickets falling to change his bowling. He kept the onus of attack with his two fast bowlers, who stuck heroically to their work, but the effect of such unusual toil was shown when Stephenson, whose first match this was since 1941, got both hands to a high catch at short slip but could not hold the ball.

So Pepper escaped after a cut for four, and in the next over there came four singles and a six from a mighty on-drive into one of the grand-stand boxes. With the clock almost at seven. Price scored one from the second ball by Gover; Pepper followed with a couple of two's to leg, and the terrific strain was over: Australia victorious over a side lacking a left-handed batsman or bowler and generally unfortunate in all the circumstances of the match, hastily extended to three days as a cricket celebration of "V" Day. About 17,000 people saw the finish, while altogether 67,660 paid the shilling admission during the three days, the proceeds of £1,935 3s. 6d. going to Red Cross and Australian charities. Entertainment tax absorbed £957 10s. 10d.

England

L. Hutton c Sismey b Williams	1	– b Pepper	21
Flt Sgt C. Washbrook st Sismey b Ellis	28	– lbw b Pepper	32
Capt. J. D. Robertson lbw b Ellis	53	– c Sismey b Cheetham	84
W. R. Hammond b Williams	29	– lbw b Ellis	33
Sq Ldr L. E. G. Ames c Price b Cheetham	57	– b Ellis	7
Sq Ldr W. J. Edrich b Miller	45	– c Workman b Price	50
Sq Ldr R. W. V. Robins b Cheetham	5	– c Hassett b Pepper	33
Lt Col J. W. A. Stephenson c Sismey b Price	31	– b Price	1
Lt Col S. C. Griffith c Sismey b Cheetham	9	– not out	4
Lt D. V. P. Wright b Price	0	– run out	1
A. R. Gover not out	0	– st Sismey b Pepper	1
B 1, l-b 6, w 1, n-b 1	9	B 18, l-b 8, n-b 1	27

1/1 2/54 3/97 4/130 5/205   267   1/52 2/75 3/149 4/175 5/218   294
6/213 7/233 8/267 9/267   6/286 7/286 8/289 9/292

Australia

Flt Sgt J. A. Workman b Gover	1		
Capt. R. S. Whitington c Griffith b Wright	36	– lbw b Stephenson	0
W/O A. L. Hassett b Stephenson	77	– c Hammond b Gover	37
Sq Ldr S. G. Sismey c Wright b Edrich	37		
P/O K. R. Miller c Ames b Stephenson	105	– run out	1
F/O R. M. Stanford st Griffith b Stephenson	49		
Sgt C. G. Pepper c Griffith b Stephenson	40	– not out	54
Capt. A. G. Cheetham c Hammond b Wright	0	– run out	0
W/O R. G. Williams c Griffith b Wright	53		
Sgt C. F. Price c Robertson b Stephenson	35	– not out	10
F/O R. S. Ellis not out	1		
B 9, l-b 10, n-b 2	21	B 4, l-b 1	5

1/11 2/52 3/136 4/171 5/270   455   1/9 2/11 3/63 4/76   (4 wkts) 107
6/357 7/358 8/366 9/454

Australia Bowling

	Overs	Mdns	Runs	Wkts	Overs	Mdns	Runs	Wkts
Cheetham	13.1	1	49	3	17	2	44	1
Williams	19	2	56	2	21	7	47	—
Pepper	19	2	59	—	32.4	7	80	4
Ellis	31	8	59	2	17	3	33	2
Miller	9	2	11	1	9	1	23	—
Price	9	1	24	2	19	3	40	2

England Bowling

	Overs	Mdns	Runs	Wkts	Overs	Mdns	Runs	Wkts
Gover	25	3	90	1	11.4	1	51	1
Stephenson	36	4	116	5	11	—	51	1
Edrich	17	2	61	1				
Wright	37.3	9	122	3				
Robins	10	—	45	—				

Umpires: G. Beet and A. Fowler.

ENGLAND v AUSTRALIA
(Second Victory Match)
Played at Sheffield, June 23, 25, 26, 1945

England won by 41 runs. The finest match of the season, played on a natural wicket at the bomb-scarred Bramall Lane ground, was memorable for a wonderful hundred by Hammond on the opening day when the pitch was at its worst, and the successful bowling of Pope and Pollard, each making his first appearance for England. Hassett put in England on a drying wicket and events moved quickly. In the sixth over Sismey was struck on the chin by a rising ball from Cheetham which touched Hutton's pads and the wound required three stitches. Carmody deputised behind the wicket and performed splendidly. Though Washbrook cut and drove to fine purpose, five England wickets were down for 141, and the two slow bowlers, Pepper and Ellis, were really menacing when Pope joined Hammond. For a time Hammond, who needed all his resource to keep up even his own end, shielded Pope, and there was a rare battle of wits between Hammond and Pepper. Playing back almost the whole while, Hammond delayed his stroke until the last split second and managed to steer the turning ball off his wicket. He never neglected a scoring opportunity and hit two 6s and eight 4s. The stand yielded 107 in ninety minutes, runs coming freely in the latter stages when both men used their height to get to the tossed-up slows.

In the last half-hour on Saturday, Australia made 23 without loss, but on the Monday bowlers met with such success that Hutton with 46 was top scorer while twenty wickets fell for 314 runs. In the heavy northern atmosphere Pope bowled perfectly to his aggressive leg trap, Pollard (three catches), Robertson (one run out) and Wright (one great catch). Pope dismissed the Australian opening pair for 36, but the most damaging blow was a beautiful ball by Pollard which took Hassett's middle stump. Miller offered resistance until he attempted a foolish single when trying to pierce and drive back the closely set leg side. Carmody produced some nice strokes, but Hammond made two sharp chances at slip look ridiculously easy and the remaining Australians were unequal to the occasion, the last five wickets falling for 27.

So England gained a handsome lead of 139, which Hutton and Washbrook augmented with a stand of 56. During their association Miller sent down one remarkable over. Bowling short at a great speed, he rapped Hutton on the left forearm and struck Washbrook on the foot. Washbrook had scarcely recovered from this shock than a short bumper hit him on top of the head, and it was small wonder that he presented Sismey — behind the stumps again — with a catch.

At the tea interval the score was 76 for two, and in less than an hour it changed to 122 for seven before stout and well-judged hitting by Griffith and Pollard produced 55, only one run less than the best of the day by the England first pair.

The Bramall Lane pitch has a reputation for its staying powers, and when first thing on Tuesday Australia began their task of trying to get 330 in the last innings the conditions for batting were possibly better than at any time in the match. It was a cold morning, and this probably accounted for Hammond dropping Whitington, who was 7 and the score 19. Neither Whitington nor Workman looked comfortable, but both faced the bowling determinedly, even if streaky strokes off Pope and Pollard flew past the slips. The Australian pair made a splendid bid for victory and their stand of 108 was the highest of the match. In all, Workman defied the bowling for three and three-quarter hours. There remained Hassett and Miller, but both were bowled by almost unplayable balls, and Sismey suffered a similar fate. In avenging their defeat at Lord's, England played grand cricket, and the Australians also excelled in bowling and fielding. About 50,000 people were present during the three days, the recepts being £7,311.

England

L. Hutton c Cheetham b Williams	11	– b Ellis	46
C. Washbrook c Carmody b Pepper	63	– c Sismey b Miller	24
J. D. Robertson c Whitington b Ellis	26	– lbw b Miller	1
W. R. Hammond c Hassett b Cheetham	100	– b Ellis	38
E. R. T. Holmes b Ellis	6	– c Sismey b Pepper	2
W. J. Edrich lbw b Pepper	1	– c Hassett b Pepper	1
G. H. Pope c Ellis b Cheetham	35	– c Pepper b Ellis	2
S. C. Griffith c Hassett b Cheetham	2	– st Sismey b Price	35
R. Pollard b Pepper	11	– c Whitington b Price	25
W. B. Roberts b Williams	4	– c Carmody b Price	6
D. V. P. Wright not out	7	– not out	1
B 3, l-b 10, n-b 5, w 2	20	B 1, l-b 4, n-b 4	9

1/28 2/81 3/129 4/136 5/141   286   1/56 2/62 3/97 4/104 5/120   190
6/248 7/262 8/264 9/272   6/122 7/122 8/177 9/184

Australia

R. S. Whitington c Wright b Pope	17	– lbw b Wright	61
J. A. Workman c Pollard b Pope	6	– c Hammond b Pollard	63
A. L. Hassett b Pollard	5	– b Pope	32
K. R. Miller run out	17	– b Pollard	8
D. K. Carmody c Hammond b Wright	42	– run out	14
C. G. Pepper c Hammond b Wright	21	– c Pollard b Pope	27
A. G. Cheetham b Pope	10	– c Hammond b Pollard	18
S. G. Sismey c Pollard b Pope	0	– b Pollard	17
C. F. T. Price c Pollard b Pope	0	– b Pope	11
R. G. Williams not out	5	– lbw b Pollard	2
R. S. Ellis run out	1	– not out	9
B 5, l-b 12, n-b 6	23	B 17, l-b 6, n-b 3	26

1/33 2/36 3/44 4/80 5/122   147   1/108 2/121 3/171 4/189 5/221   288
6/131 7/132 8/132 9/145   6/231 7/244 8/260 9/280

Australia Bowling

	Overs	Mdns	Runs	Wkts	Overs	Mdns	Runs	Wkts
Williams	16	4	31	2	9	2	23	—
Cheetham	15	3	47	3	7	1	19	—
Ellis	33	9	66	2	25	5	47	3
Miller	13	3	19	—	13	2	28	2
Pepper	30.5	6	86	3	15	3	46	2
Price	3	—	17	—	4.4	—	18	3

England Bowling

	Overs	Mdns	Runs	Wkts	Overs	Mdns	Runs	Wkts
Pope	21.5	4	58	5	28.4	9	69	3
Pollard	17	5	42	1	33	6	76	5
Wright	9	3	14	2	22	6	50	1
Edrich.	5	—	10	—	4	1	13	—
Roberts.					13	4	40	—
Hutton					2	—	14	—

Umpires: G. P. Heaton and H. Thomas (Bradford League).

ENGLAND v AUSTRALIA

(Third Victory Match)

Played at Lord's, July 14, 16, 17, 1945

Australia won by four wickets. For this game England tried the experiment of playing three of the best schoolboy cricketers of 1944 – Dewes, White and Carr – but they scored only 47 runs, and Carr, the bowler, sent down only nine overs. In any event a heavy responsibility would have fallen on the other members of the side, and to aggravate matters Hammond, stricken down with lumbago, retired from the match after the first day, and Washbrook so severely bruised his right thumb that he was of little use on the last day. Yet England would have done better but for missed catches; Hassett in the first Australian innings was twice dropped, and at a vital stage in the final innings Miller, when 38 and the total 167, ought to have been taken at deep leg by Dewes.

After an eclipse of the sun earlier in the week, storms of wind and rain made cricket conditions problematical on Saturday, but, following a sharp shower that delayed the start until ten minutes past twelve, rain held off during the playing hours and the pitch was for the most part of neutral character – rather slow, seldom helping the ball unless delivered very short, but sometimes responding to spin. Batting until twenty minutes past six, England scored enough runs to ensure an interesting struggle. Hutton showed to much advantage – altogether he made 173 out of his side's 418.

He took two hours twenty minutes in scoring his first 52 out of 97, bowlers looking more difficult during this time than at any other period in the match, but he doubled his runs while the total rose by 72 in an hour. A single from the first ball after tea gave him the hoped-for century, but Miller in his next over upset the Yorkshireman's leg stump with a very fast ball.

Losing Washbrook at 11, Hutton received most help from Dewes, the Cambridge left-hander, in a stand for 65. Confidently facing a severe trial of nerve, Dewes, in rather crouched style, played sound cricket for an hour and a half, although twice struck on the thigh by Miller, who eventually sent the off-stump flying with an extra fast ball to which Dewes played back. Hammond stayed while 31 were added, and that was the last seen of the England captain in the match.

By good defence White countered the menace of "silly" point and mid-on – both stood very close – for three-quarters of an hour, but Carr, the third 18-year-old tyro, soon fell to a fine ball that shook off the leg bail. Then came the best stand of the innings and the most attractive batting, Edrich and Griffith putting on 66 in seventy minutes by good resolute cricket.

Not covered completely during the week-end, as was the case in the Whitsun match, the pitch recovered from heavy rains on Saturday night, and seemed in good order on Monday morning when Hammond reported unfit and Griffith took over the England captaincy. Besides leading the side soundly, he kept wicket admirably, but in gaining a lead of 60 England owed most of the sound bowling to Pollard, Wright and Roberts. Hassett saw half his team leave for 72, and then Carmody helped him put on 55, the best stand of the innings thanks to missed catches. In the absence of Washbrook, Dewes opened the England second innings with Hutton, and Miller soon sent his leg stump flying. Then Edrich excelled with hook and drive, and the second stand produced 105, the day ending with the total 118 for three wickets.

When Hutton (49) and Pollard (7) resumed, Hassett placed his field to cut down Hutton's scoring strokes and closed in for the other batsmen. This policy of attacking the weaker members paid; in seventy minutes the six outstanding wickets went down for 46. In his first match of the series Cristofani was certainly a success. He varied his pace and flight and turned his leg-break or googly sufficiently to beat the bat. Miller also did valuable work with the ball, though when fielding to his own bowling he strained a back muscle, which often worried him when bowling for the rest of the tour.

During a spell of extraordinary weather the sun shone consistently for the first time in four days while Australia obtained the necessary runs by five minutes to six. Off the second ball, without a run scored, Australia lost Whitington, but Workman and Sismey turned the scale with a second partnership of 82. Afterwards Miller, taking few risks, hit 71 of the last 121 in just under two hours. Pollard always toiled hard, but he badly missed the support of Pope. About 84,000 people were present during the match.

England

L. Hutton b Miller	104	– c Sismey b Cristofani	69
C. Washbrook c Sismey b Williams	8	– not out	13
J. G. Dewes b Miller	27	– b Miller	0
W. R. Hammond st Sismey b Pepper	13	– absent ill	0
Hon. L. R. White st Sismey b Cristofani	11	– lbw b Cristofani	4
W. J. Edrich lbw b Cristofani	38	– b Miller	58
D. B. Carr b Miller	4	– c Pepper b Cristofani	1
S. C. Griffith c Pepper b Cristofani	36	– c Pepper b Cristofani	0
R. Pollard not out	1	– b Miller	9
W. Roberts b Cristofani	1	– b Ellis	0
D. V. P. Wright lbw b Ellis	5	– c Hassett b Cristofani	6
B 2, l-b 1, n-b 3	6	L-b 3, n-b 1	4

1/11 2/76 3/107 4/162 5/169   254   1/1 2/106 3/107 4/122 5/127   164
6/175 7/241 8/248 9/249   6/129 7/150 8/151

Australia

R. S. Whitington b Pollard	19	– c Griffith b Pollard	0
J. A. Workman c Edrich b Wright	7	– b Wright	30
A. G. Cheetham b Roberts	5	– not out	9
A. L. Hassett lbw b Pollard	68	– c Edrich b Wright	24
K. R. Miller b Pollard	7	– not out	71
C. G. Pepper lbw b Pollard	0	– lbw b Edrich	18
D. K. Carmody c White b Pollard	32	– c Edrich b Roberts	1
D. R. Cristofani b Roberts	32		
S. G. Sismey c Griffiths b Pollard	9	– lbw b Pollard	51
R. G. Williams b Wright	4		
R. S. Ellis not out	0		
L-b 4, n-b 7	11	B 1, l-b 15, n-b 5	21

1/29 2/29 3/50 4/71 5/72   194   1/0 2/82 3/104 4/151   (6 wkts) 225
6/127 7/149 8/183 9/194   5/186 6/193

Australian Bowling

	Overs	Mdns	Runs	Wkts	Overs	Mdns	Runs	Wkts
Williams	19	6	45	1	3	—	10	—
Cheetham	19	4	47	—	4	—	7	—
Pepper	19	2	44	1	10	3	22	—
Ellis.............	19.1	6	25	1	14	1	29	1
Miller	18	3	44	3	16	2	42	3
Cristofani	13	1	43	4	29.3	8	49	5
Whitington					1	—	1	—

England Bowling

	Overs	Mdns	Runs	Wkts	Overs	Mdns	Runs	Wkts
Edrich...........	7	—	25	—	12	1	37	1
Pollard	23	4	75	6	21	4	71	2
Wright	24.1	3	49	2	25	4	59	2
Roberts..........	14	5	24	2	13	4	24	1
Carr	3	1	10	—	6	2	13	—

Umpires: G. Beet and A. Fowler.

ENGLAND v AUSTRALIA

(Fourth Victory Match)

Played at Lord's, August 6, 7, 8, 1945

Drawn. After their defeat in the third match, England relied entirely on experienced players, bringing in Fishlock for the first time during the series; but though the side from first ball to last made every effort to force a win, Australia concentrated mainly on avoiding defeat and achieved that objective, so they ensured themselves against losing the rubber. The match began on Bank Holiday, when 34,000 people, probably a record for the ground, saw grand bowling for England by Pope, Pollard and Wright and a stubborn display of batting by Australia. The whole course of the match can be said to have centred on Sismey, who, going in when Workman left at 15, spent one hundred minutes over his first 15 runs and altogether defied the England attack for four hours. It was certainly a great effort for his side and no doubed paved the way for a century by Miller in taking off some of the edge from the bowling.

Towards the end of the innings Sismey was struck on the thumb, and on Tuesday, when England replied with 249 for the loss of three men, Workman, acting as wicket-keeper, conceded 51 "extras". On the third morning Hammond made a sensible move in allowing Carmody to keep wicket. Though against tradition, this action had a precedent in 1905 when, at The Oval, Joe Darling, on Lilley being injured, consented to A. O. Jones, the twelfth man, deputising.

Repeating his Whitsun hundred on the same ground, Miller used three bats. He joined Sismey at 108 for three wickets, and in two hours they put on 121 before Sismey was struck on the thumb. He retired, and, out soon after resuming, he could not keep wicket. Miller experienced some uncomfortable overs from Pope and Pollard, but his straight driving was always sure, and sixth to leave at 301 he made his 118 in three hours twenty minutes, hitting ten 4s.

Mr Clement Atlee, the Prime Minister, was present on the second day when Miller completed his effort, England being kept in the field until lunch-time. Whereas Australia occupied seven hours over their 388, England passed them in an hour and a quarter less time for the loss of four men – Hutton, Fishlock, Robertson and Hammond. Immediately Hutton and Fishlock opened the character of the cricket changed. Hutton off-drove superbly, and the success of Fishlock only emphasised how handicapped were England in the preceding games without a class left-handed batsman. In his stay of two hours thirty-five minutes Fishlock proved very strong when forcing to leg, and he also drove and cut well. There were twelve 4s in his 69 out of 173, including 38 extras.

If uncertain on Tuesday evening, Hammond produced his best form on Wednesday morning, when he and Washbrook by adding 157 took part in the best stand in all the five matches. Delightful strokes through the covers and straight drives were the feature of Hammond's 83, which included eleven 4s, and only a wonderful catch at backward point by Workman, released from the onerous duty of wicket-keeper, closed the England captain's innings. Workman dived to the right and held the ball inches from the turf.

Washbrook went on to hit a brilliant century – his first for England – and apart from a difficult chance to slip off Ellis when 43, he did not make a mistake until after he passed three figures. His finest strokes were his crisp square cut and delightful off drive. He seldom missed an opportunity to hook and one of these at the expense of Cristofani earned 6, while he also hit eight 4s, his innings lasting four hours. Edrich, who assisted Washbrook in a stand of 105, too, batted splendidly. England stood little chance of forcing a win, but Hammond declared, and Australia lost four men in clearing off their deficit of 80 runs.

Australia did not reach England's standard of high-class fielding, but their bowling was more varied. Williams and Ellis were extremely accurate over long periods and Miller commanded respect by virtue of his pace, though he was sometimes erratic. Both Pepper and Cristofani came in for a deal of punishment. The perfect pitch gave little encouragement to bowlers and during the three days only 21 wickets fell. Altogether 93,000 people were present.

Australia

R. S. Whitington c Hutton b Pope	46	– lbw b Pope	7
J. A. Workman lbw b Pollard	6	– c Fishlock b Pope	9
S. G. Sismey c Fishlock b Pollard	59		
A. L. Hassett c Wright b Pope	20	– b Pollard	7
K. R. Miller b Pope	118	– not out	35
R. M. Stanford b Pope	2	– not out	33
C. G. Pepper c and b Roberts	57		
J. Pettiford c Wright b Pollard	32	– b Wright	39
D. R. Cristofani c Edrich b Pollard	14		
R. G. Williams c Fishlock b Roberts	1		
R. S. Ellis not out	0		
B 16, l-b 8, n-b 9	33	B 5, n-b 5	10

1/15 2/70 3/108 4/262 5/265   388   1/12 2/30 3/54 4/80   (4 wkts) 140
6/301 7/359 8/374 9/380

England

L. B. Fishlock b Pettiford	69	S. C. Griffith c Stanford b Pettiford	7
L. Hutton lbw b Williams	35	R. Pollard not out	2
J. D. Robertson c Miller b Pettiford	25		
W. R. Hammond c Workman b Ellis	83	B 27, l-b 12, w 14, n-b 4	57
C. Washbrook c sub b Williams	112		
W. J. Edrich not out	73	1/73 2/136 3/173 (7 wkts dec.) 468	
G. H. Pope c Hassett b Williams	5	4/330 5/435 6/443 7/464	

D. V. P. Wright and W. B. Roberts did not bat.

England Bowling

	Overs	Mdns	Runs	Wkts	Overs	Mdns	Runs	Wkts
Pope............	43	11	83	4	12	3	42	2
Pollard..........	37.3	7	145	4	13	2	58	1
Wright..........	28	5	75	—	7	1	23	1
Edrich...........	6	—	13	—				
Roberts..........	16	4	39	2	6	2	7	—

Australian Bowling

	Overs	Mdns	Runs	Wkts
Miller...........	23	5	49	—
Williams..........	39	9	109	3
Pepper..........	18	3	63	—
Cristofani........	12	3	41	—
Pettiford.........	18	2	62	3
Ellis..............	36	9	80	1
Whitington........	1	—	7	—

Umpires: G. Beet and A. Fowler.

ENGLAND v AUSTRALIA

(Fifth Victory Match)

Played at Old Trafford, August 20, 21, 22, 1945

England won by six wickets. For the first time since 1905 the Mother Country triumphed over Australia at Manchester, and so made the sides all square with two victories apiece in the Victory series. Throughout the three days the cricket reached a high standard, due to the natural wicket which encouraged the bowlers and at times gave them much assistance. It was really a wonderful match, memorable for the excellent all-round performance of the 24-year-old Australian, Cristofani, who, after bowling superbly in England's first innings – taking five wickets for 55 runs – came to the rescue of Australia by hitting 110 not out. For England, Phillipson made a notable début, dismissing nine men in the match with his fast-medium outswingers, and Griffith distinguished himself behind the stumps by making seven catches, six in the second innings – nearly all masterly efforts. At the beginning of the match Hammond brought off two wonderful slip catches.

After six years of transport restrictions the sight of dozens of special omnibuses labelled "Cricket Ground" was something remarkable with VJ Day less than a week behind. The first day went through without interruption, and with fifteen wickets falling for 335 runs

England established a mastery, finishing only 11 behind Australia with half their wickets in hand, including those of Edrich, Washbrook and Pope.

England took the risk of making their left-arm slow bowler, W. B. Roberts, twelfth man, but events proved that Hammond, relying mainly on pace, correctly summed up the possibilities of the pitch. Knowing that only victory would enable them to draw the rubber, the England team rose to the occasion. Before lunch when half the Australian team fell for 104, Hammond kept his three bowlers, Pollard, Pope and Phillipson, fresh by using them in short relays, but afterwards he relied on the Lancashire pair, who operated till the innings ended. Phillipson, the fastest of the three, was the best because he persistently aimed at the wicket; Pollard was always troublesome, but Pope, who made the ball swing considerably, too often pitched short and off the wicket.

Miller stood out as the one Australian batsmen equal to the occasion, but considering his ability he went in rather late in the innings and had to be satisfied in taking out his bat for 77, the result of a stay of two and a quarter hours. The heavy unrolled outfield reduced the value of many strokes, and there were periods in the match when runs came very slowly, but so keen was the play no one minded.

The impregnable defence of Hutton was extremely valuable to England. Fishlock was not at his best, and at 33 he mistimed a slow yorker, while Robertson gave square-leg an easy catch before Hammond put the England batting on a different plane. At once he took the initiative by three times driving Williams straight for four runs apiece, and in seventy minutes he hit 57 out of 97 with Hutton, who altogether stayed two and a half hours.

Rain halved the second day's cricket, but thousands of northerners showed their keenness for cricket by turning up first thing in the morning in the drenching rain. The weather turned fine at twelve o'clock, and England resumed their innings in brilliant sunshine at 2.15. At first the drying pitch played slowly, but the two right-arm slow bowlers, Cristofani and Pepper, never looked easy. During this period England owed much to Washbrook, who used the pull with rare judgement, and Edrich, Phillipson and Wright all did valuable work in this dour contest in which every run was vital.

Hassett surprised many people by not having the wicket rolled between the innings. In any case the heavy roller was not available, as it was requisitioned during the war and used to lay out airfields in the Middle East. The position was tense and evenly balanced, for a prolonged stand at this stage could have produced an Australian win on such a sporting pitch. Phillipson placed only cover-point, silly mid-off and silly mid-on in front of the bat, while Pope put four men in his leg-trap. Hammond being at slip and Edrich in the gully. The first Australian setback was at 13, Pettiford being easily taken at silly mid-off, and four runs later Sismey, discarding the monumental patience he showed at Lord's, attempted to hook the wrong ball and was leg-before. Only 27 runs came in the first hour, six fewer than England on Monday, and before the heavy clouds caused stumps to be drawn twenty minutes early Whitington was the first of Griffith's six victims. The England wicket-keeper flung himself like a goalkeeper and held the ball left-handed while suspended in mid-air. Whitington withstood the bowling for eighty-five minutes, a praiseworthy effort for usually a fluent player.

Australia resumed on Wednesday with their score 37 for three wickets, and everything seemed to depend on their two best batsmen, Miller and Hassett, but inside half an hour both were well caught by Griffith for the addition of only 9 runs. The Lancashire pair, Phillipson and Pollard, often made the ball lift unpleasantly from a good length, the pitch being hard underneath while the damp surface was drying in brilliant sunshine. Promoted in the batting order, Cristofani came in at 69, and although he from the start attacked the bowling cheekily, things continued to go so badly for his side that by a quarter-past one eight wickets were down for 105 and the match looked as good as over; but there ensued a glorious partnership of 95 between Cristofani and Williams. While Williams defended valiantly for ninety-five minutes, Cristofani, using the square cut, hook and off-drive, raced to his century after lunch. He hooked Pope for a spectacular six — a carry of 90 yards — on to the pavilion terraces, and when a powerful pull off Wright gave him 101 out of 126 the whole crowd held up the game while they stood and cheered.

As soon as the total reached 200 Hammond claimed the new ball, and Phillipson with his first delivery got Williams out to another fine catch by the wicket-keeper. Ellis soon gave short-leg a catch and Cristofani took out his bat. Beside the 6, he hit thirteen 4s in his 110 out of 141 in two hours twenty-three minutes.

England wanted 141 in two hours twenty minutes – a light task in ordinary conditions, but there was a possibility that the Australian bowling would prove troublesome. A shock occurred with only 5 runs on the board, Williams bowling Fishlock, but Hutton and Robertson, both full of good strokes, added 69, and later Hammond and Edrich took control, putting on 54 before the substitute, E. A. Williams, caught Hammond beautifully near the sight screen. Eventually Edrich, England's best batsman in the final hour, made the winning hit with three-quarters of an hour to spare. During the three days the attendance reached 72,463 and the receipts £11,627. As at Sheffield, this match outside London was staged by the Inter-Services Sports Committee, and German prisoners were paid three farthings an hour for painting the buildings (outside) and putting certain parts of the bomb-scarred ground in a safe condition.

Australia

R. S. Whitington c Hammond b Pollard	19	– c Griffith b Phillipson ... 10
J. Pettiford b Pollard	28	– c Robertson b Phillipson ... 8
D. K. Carmody c Hammond b Pollard	7	– c Griffith b Pollard ... 3
S. G. Sismey b Phillipson	5	– lbw b Phillipson ... 4
A. L. Hassett c Pollard b Pope	6	– c Griffith b Pollard ... 1
K. R. Miller not out	7	– c Griffith b Phillipson ... 4
C. G. Pepper run out	9	– b Wright ... 23
R. M. Stanford run out	1	– c Griffith b Wright ... 23
D. R. Cristofani c Edrich b Pollard	8	– not out ... 110
R. G. Williams c Griffith b Phillipson	5	– c Griffith b Phillipson ... 12
R. S. Ellis c Pollard b Phillipson	0	– c Pollard b Phillipson ... 3
L-b 2, n-b 6	8	B 1, l-b 5, n-b 3 ... 9

1/41 2/59 3/64 4/66 5/102   173   1/13 2/17 3/37 4/41 5/46   210
6/117 7/125 8/138 9/155   6/69 7/87 8/105 9/200

England

L. Hutton c Sismey b Williams	64	– lbw b Pepper ... 29
L. B. Fishlock lbw b Miller	9	– b Williams ... 4
J. D. Robertson c Williams b Pepper	13	– lbw b Pepper ... 37
W. R. Hammond c Pettiford b Cristofani	57	– c sub b Ellis ... 16
W. J. Edrich c and b Pepper	23	– not out ... 42
R. Pollard lbw b Cristofani	0	
C. Washbrook c Carmody b Cristofani	38	– not out ... 11
G. H. Pope c Pepper b Cristofani	1	
W. E. Phillipson not out	18	
S. C. Griffith c Ellis b Cristofani	0	
D. V. P. Wright st Sismey b Pettiford	9	
B 3, l-b 6, w 1, n-b 1	11	B 2 ... 2

1/14 2/46 3/143 4/159 5/162   243   1/5 2/69 3/70 4/124   (4 wkts) 141
6/198 7/201 8/218 9/221

England Bowling

	Overs	Mdns	Runs	Wkts	Overs	Mdns	Runs	Wkts
Phillipson	27	4	72	3	29	12	58	6
Pope	10	3	15	1	19	6	49	—
Pollard	22	3	78	4	23	11	46	2
Wright					13	3	44	2
Edrich					3	1	4	—

Australian Bowling

	Overs	Mdns	Runs	Wkts	Overs	Mdns	Runs	Wkts
Miller	9	—	20	1	11	1	41	—
Williams	18	7	40	1	8	—	41	1
Pepper	24	3	74	2	12	5	18	2
Ellis..............	7	—	21	—	7	2	13	1
Pettiford	6.2	—	22	1				
Cristofani	22	3	55	5	7	—	25	—
Hassett					0.1	—	1	—

Umpires: F. Chester and H. Elliot (Lancashire).

ENGLAND v DOMINIONS

Played at Lord's, August 25, 27, 28, 1945

Dominions won by 45 runs with eight minutes to spare. One of the finest games ever seen produced 1,241 runs, including sixteen 6s, a century in each England innings by Hammond, and grand hundreds for the Dominions by Donnelly, the New Zealand left-hander, and Miller, of Australia. In addition, the result was a triumph for Constantine, who, in the absence of Hassett through illness, was chosen captain by the Dominions players just before the match began. Both sides experienced various changes of fortune and the issue remained in doubt till the end. Although Craig, a left-hander from South Australia, forced the pace from the beginning, the Dominions lost half their side for 109. Then Pepper and Donnelly added 120. Always master of the bowling, Donnelly hit two 6s and eighteen 4s, being last out. With Gimblett suffering from cramp, Hammond changed his order, and before the first day ended England lost Fishlock, Robertson and Phillipson for 28.

By twenty minutes to one on Monday six England wickets were down for 96, but Hammond and Edrich lifted their side out of trouble with a stand of 177, of which Edrich's share was 65. Against keen bowling Hammond never made a mistake. Three drives off Cristofani went into the pavilion for 6, and he also hit ten 4s, getting his 121 in two hours forty minutes. Edrich, missed in the slips off Williams when 17, scored freely to the on. After Hammond left the innings was soon over, the last three wickets falling at the same total. As Gimblett and Phillipson were unfit, England fielded two substitutes when the Dominions batted again. Fell and Craig opened with a stand of 49, and the second day closed with Donnelly and Miller together and the total 145 for three wickets.

The final stage will be remembered chiefly for the glorious driving of Miller. He outshone everyone by his dazzling hitting. In ninety minutes he raised his overnight 61 to 185, and in three-quarters of an hour of superb cricket he and Constantine put on 117. Though travelling at such a pace, Miller played faultlessly. One of his seven 6s set the whole crowd talking. It was a terrific on-drive off Hollies, and the ball lodged in the small roof of the broadcasting box above the England players' dressing-room. Besides his 6s Miller hit thirteen 4s, his 185 taking him only two and three-quarter hours. This was a wonderful finish to his season at Lord's, where in four first-class matches he scored 568 runs in eight innings, twice not out, with three centuries and an average of 94.68.

England wanted 357 in four and a half hours, and thanks to Hammond, they made a worthy challenge. Always seeking runs, the England captain was twice missed in the deep before completing 50, but, though tiring, he carried on freely getting 102 out of 152 in two hours. His main strokes were one 6 and ten 4s. By hitting two separate hundreds in a match for the seventh time, Hammond set up an individual record. After he left there followed some daring batting by Davies and Griffith, who added 83 in fifty-eight minutes, but England for victory needed to get 74 in three-quarters of an hour when Phillipson joined Davies. Brilliant fielding by Constantine accounted for Phillipson, and next Pepper bowled Davies. Only fifteen minutes remained when the last man, Hollies, joined Wright. In tense excitement Ellis and Pepper each delivered a maiden with the fielders crowded round the batsmen. Constantine then brought back Cristofani, who bowled Wright, and the Dominions gained a grand victory. While some batsmen dominated the cricket, mention must be made of the splendid bowling, particularly that of Wright, who took five wickets in each Dominions innings. Hollies stood up gallantly to heavy punishment and Pepper kept going for long spells in the final innings without losing his length.

The Dominions

D. R. Fell c Griffith b Wright	12	– b Davies		28
H. S. Craig c Davies b Phillipson	56	– c Hammond b Davies		32
J. Pettiford b Davies	1	– b Wright		6
K. R. Miller lbw b Hollies	26	– c Langridge b Wright		185
M. P. Donnelly c and b Hollies	133	– b Wright		29
L. N. Constantine c Hollies b Wright	5	– c Fishlock b Hollies		40
C. G. Pepper c Hammond b Wright	51	– c Robertson b Hollies		1
D. R. Cristofani lbw b Edrich	6	– b Wright		5
R. G. Williams lbw b Wright	11	– c Hammond b Wright		0
R. S. Ellis b Wright	0	– st Griffith b Hollies		0
C. D. Bremner not out	1	– not out		0
L-b 3, w 2	5	B 1, l-b 8, n-b 1		10

307   336

England

L. B. Fishlock c Pettiford b Ellis	12	– run out		7
J. D. Robertson lbw b Constantine	4	– c Fell b Pettiford		5
James Langridge lbw b Cristofani	28	– b Pepper		15
W. E. Phillipson b Pepper	0	– run out		14
S. C. Griffith c Bremner b Williams	15	– c Pepper b Pettiford		36
W. R. Hammond st Bremner b Pepper	121	– st Bremner b Cristofani		102
H. Gimblett c Pettiford b Cristofani	11	– b Pepper		30
W. J. Edrich c Pepper b Cristofani	78	– c Pepper b Ellis		31
J. G. W. Davies lbw b Pepper	1	– b Pepper		56
D. V. P. Wright lbw b Pepper	0	– b Cristofani		0
E. Hollies not out	0	– not out		0
B 7, l-b 6, w 2, n-b 2	17	B 6, l-b 5, n-b 4		15

287   311

England Bowling

	Overs	Mdns	Runs	Wkts	Overs	Mdns	Runs	Wkts
Phillipson	16	2	40	1	2	1	1	—
Edrich	9	1	19	1	3	—	13	—
Wright	30	2	90	5	30.1	6	105	5
Davies	22	9	43	1	13	3	35	2
Hollies	20.2	3	86	2	29	8	115	3
Langridge	6	1	24	—	8	—	57	—

The Dominions Bowling

	Overs	Mdns	Runs	Wkts	Overs	Mdns	Runs	Wkts
Miller	1	—	2	—	5	—	28	—
Williams	22	4	49	1	2	—	11	—
Constantine	15	2	53	1	6	—	27	—
Pepper	18	3	57	4	33	13	67	3
Ellis	4	3	4	1	20	4	54	1
Cristofani	23.3	4	82	3	21.3	1	64	2
Pettiford	5	—	23	—	14	3	45	2

NOTES BY THE EDITOR, 1946

Empire Teams Take the Field

After five seasons of what may be called impromptu cricket the sudden end of the European war came just in time to permit a partial resumption of the first-class game last summer. To celebrate victory, three days were allotted to the Whitsuntide match with the Australian Services at Lord's; then the MCC and the Combined Services Committee further extended this start into five Victory matches of three days each between England and Australia. The remarkable success that attended this spontaneous gesture of renewing the happy accord associated with contests of this nature emphatically proved the enormous value of keeping the game going during the uphill years of strife. The RAAF players of 1944, augmented by the AIF, soon ripened into a capable all-round side that underwent little alteration in this rubber series of 1945. England, on the other hand, seemed to experience difficulty in finding the best of the available players. This was more noticeable at Lord's than at either Sheffield or Manchester. Some of the chosen men, coming almost straight from battlefields to the headquarters of cricket, must have regarded the first encounter primarily as a reunion with many old friends, so that a thoroughly serious view of the game, such as the Australians clearly held, was too much to expect. In the first match the onus of attack for the final stage was borne by two fast bowlers of mature age, A. R. Gover and Colonel J. W. A. Stephenson, both tired from their exertions on the previous day; and C. G. Pepper made the winning hit just at seven o'clock in the last over of this very much enjoyed contest. For the third match – the second at Lord's – the choice of three youngsters without any experience of representative cricket afforded the strongest contrast; and again England lost. The work of George Pope, Pollard and Phillipson – kept out by injury until the final match at Old Trafford, which England won comfortably – showed that good bowlers of pace were available. This result, which divided the honours, came as a happy conclusion, and everyone could feel contented, especially as the last expressed wish of Mr John Curtin, Prime Minister of Australia, for an immediate resumption of Test cricket, became practically an accomplished fact during the summer, even before his death in July.

Directly after the end of the season Dr H. V. Evatt, Australian Minister for External Affairs, appealed to the MCC to send a side to Australia as soon as possible, with the natural outcome of the acceptance of a definite invitation from the Australian Cricket Board of Control for England to visit Australia in the 1946-47 season. On the same occasion Dr Evatt stressed that the tour of the Australian Services team which sailed in October last to India was official. So, with the Dominions, West Indies and New Zealand putting teams in the field, the whole British Commonwealth of Nations became identified actively with cricket almost before the joyous shouts for peace, raised on the collapse of Japan, ceased to echo. And now a very powerful side from India, under the leadership of the Nawab of Pataudi, further accentuates the happy relations which cricket brings to all competing countries.

Big Hitting

Of the eleven matches, each of three days, played last summer which the MCC ranked as first-class, that between England and Dominions at Lord's rivalled as an attraction those in which Australia took part, and we saw in M. P. Donnelly, the left-handed New Zealander, who toured England in 1937, a batsman ready to join company with the best exponents of the game now that he will have regular first-class experience while at Oxford University. His fine stroke play, notably to the off, provided some of the best cricket seen last season, and for arousing spectators to enthusiasm was exceeded only by gigantic hitting in which C. G. Pepper and Keith Miller emulated the giants of the past – not in the rate of scoring but in the carry of their big drives. In that same Dominions match at Lord's, Miller on-drove a ball to the roof of the broadcasting box over the England dressing-room at a height said to exceed that of the record hit by Albert Trott which cleared the pavilion. That was one of seven 6s by Miller in a score of 185. Pepper hit six 6s while making 168 in two hours and a half at Scarborough against H. D. G. Leveson Gower's eleven. He revelled in straight drives, one of which off Hollies cleared the four-storied houses and landed the ball in Trafalgar Square. In this he rivalled the historic efforts of C. I. Thornton in 1886, when A. G. Steel was the bowler and Thornton's 107 included eight 6s. While these tremendous drives remain chronicled because earning six runs, one may doubt if the length of carry and height of any of them equalled that by G. J. Bonnor in the first England and Australia match at the Oval in 1880. Always associated with the superb catch which G. F. Grace made, this hit was described to me quite recently by Mr S. F. Charlton, an Old Cranleighan, who saw all the match. He wrote that Shaw, the bowler from the Vauxhall end, signalled with a gesture of his hand for G. F. Grace to look out, and the next ball with this guile in it brought about the catch near the sight screen – most certainly an amazing piece of cricket. The youngest of the three Graces playing for England just waited while the batsmen twice ran up and down the pitch before the ball fell into his safe hands. Hitherto my efforts to discover in what position G. F. Grace was fielding always failed.

Laws of the Game

Until the MCC publish the Laws of Cricket as re-drafted, mainly under the direction of Colonel Rait Kerr, the provisional decision for a declaration on the first day of the match when 300 runs have been scored, and the optional use of a new ball after 55 overs, must help towards definite decisions, and will be acceptable in all grades of cricket. The necessity for a closer observance of the laws became apparent when G. O. Allen, playing for South of England against the Australians at Lord's on June 30, was given out by umpire Fowler "handled the ball" on an appeal by A. W. Roper, the bowler. No matter what Roper thought or intended, he may be congratulated on bringing about the dismissal of a former England captain for an obvious infringement of Law 29 at the headquarters of cricket. "The rigour of the game" cannot be too strongly impressed on all young players; and I may feel some personal satisfaction in having described in my notes last year what I saw at Weston-Super-Mare, where a batsman picked up the ball, tossed it to the bowler, and took his guard as if this was a regular procedure – a sad reflection on strict match play. Close followers of the game will remember previous cases of "handled the ball", some of which may be mentioned. A. D. Nourse, the South African left-hander, paid the penalty at Hove in 1907, when he stopped the ball that might have rolled on to the stumps. Then in February 1930, at Auckland F. J. Benson, of the MCC Australian touring team, was given out when he "stooped as if to pick up the ball", – a still stronger warning for a batsman always to leave the ball to the fieldsman.

An equal or even greater offence by a batsman is kicking at a ball wide of the stumps. Very rightly "leg-byes may not be scored" in this way, but surely to kick at the ball is "obstructing the field"; and merely pushing out the pad comes under the same category when no attempt is made to use the bat for a stroke. The wicket-keeper is prevented from taking the ball and so is obstructed. I will cite Keith Miller, the Australian, as being guilty of this ugly gesture – a strange weakness for so fine a batsman – and he was admonished for it by the umpire at Lord's.

So long ago as 1888, at the general meeting of the Marylebone Club at Lord's, it was recommended by the committee "that the practice of deliberately defending the wicket with the person instead of the bat is contrary to the spirit of the game and inconsistent with strict fairness, and the MCC will discountenance and prevent this practice by every means in their power." Yet batsmen have been guilty of doing this on several occasions to my own knowledge, and once Frank Chester sent back a batsmen who ran after kicking the ball through the slips.

Troublesome Last Over

More finishes on time caused "the last over" to remain a "bone of contention", and I was taken to task by R. E. S. Wyatt for my remarks about play ceasing at Coventry in 1944 when a wicket fell to the second ball of the over with ten runs wanted for victory by the side having four more men to bat. Mr Wyatt thought that I condemned him for allowing the umpire to pull up stumps instead of letting another batsman come in. He explained that neither he nor the captain had power to over-rule the umpire. My intention was far from criticising Wyatt, the captain, or the umpire, but to call attention to difficulties bound to arise in such circumstances, and to strengthen my plea for a clear ruling that the last over should be finished in order that either the fielding or batting side could have the opportunity to snatch a victory and so bring about a definite result – always desirable in every contest. The difficulties of deciding the precise time for calling "last over" and allowing another batsman to hasten to the wicket are obvious. Umpires' watches or outside clocks may differ from those inside the pavilion, and if that "last over" were played out there would not be any hopeless discussions or heart-burnings. Another point: Who decides that it is to be the last over? Notes on Law 13 state that "an over should always be begun if 'time' has not been reached". This applies to lunch and tea intervals and the close of play each day without any specific reference to the last over of the match – and that is what matters most.

Entertainment Tax

While we have Australia emphasising the value of cricket in cementing the brotherhood of all countries in the British Empire and the imperative desire to maintain the happy gestures always apparent when England and Australia take the field in the keenest of Test matches, the Government cannot see that entertainment tax charged on gate receipts, not on profits, of a match is a heavy drag on county cricket, besides handicapping the organisations responsible for the international fixtures which mean so much for the general welfare of Great Britain and our various Commonwealth visitors – Australia, South Africa, New Zealand, West Indies and India. This continuous drain on revenue becomes all the more serious now when all the counties face the heavy cost of renovating their grounds, re-building blitzed pavilions and stands, with improved accommodation necessary to meet the requirements of the large crowds which are certain to assemble. True, the Chancellor of the Exchequer has reduced the tax on some outdoor sports, a concession partly turned by cricket clubs to the benefit of the paying public. We may hope that more may be done in this direction, so helping the clubs which further cricket as a game for recreative amusement and not for financial gain.

CRICKET IN AUSTRALIA

SOUTH AUSTRALIA v NEW SOUTH WALES
Played at Adelaide, December 15, 16, 18, 1939

South Australia won by seven wickets. The superb batting of Bradman, who scored 341 without being dismissed, overshadowed everything else in a remarkable match. In his first innings of 251, scored at one run a minute, he included every possible stroke, and bowlers with the exception of O'Reilly, were helpless. Bradman, who hit thirty-eight 4s and two 6s, often scored three times as fast as his partners, of whom Waite gave valuable support in a stand of 147. When South Australia wanted 155 for victory, Bradman dominated the cricket to such a degree that he almost reached three figures before the winning hit was made. Solomon proved the outstanding New South Wales batsman. He displayed sound defence and strong attacking strokes which reached the boundary eighteen times in his 131. With McCabe, Chipperfield and Pepper, he also batted well in the second innings.

New South Wales

S. J. McCabe lbw b Grimmett	40	– lbw b Grimmett	47
J. H. Fingleton c Bradman b Grimmett	29	– b Klose	2
S. G. Barnes b Waite	2	– c Walker b Ward	33
C. M. Solomon c Tregoning b Klose	131	– c Tregoning b Grimmett	46
A. G. Chipperfield b Cotton	32	– lbw b Grimmett	57
A. G. Cheetham c Bradman b Tregoning	32	– b Grimmett	2
C. Pepper lbw b Klose	22	– c Grimmett b Klose	47
A. Roper c Ridings b Grimmett	15	– c and b Ward	0
W. J. O'Reilly c Walker b Klose	16	– c Tregoning b Grimmett	5
S. Sismey not out	5	– c Tregoning b Grimmett	3
J. Walsh b Klose	1	– not out	0
B 2, l-b 8, w 1	11	B 1, l-b 5	6
	336		**248**

South Australia

R. S. Whitington c Sismey b Roper	6		
K. L. Ridings c Sismey b Walsh	29	– b Cheetham	20
D. G. Bradman not out	251	– not out	90
R. A. Hamence lbw b Pepper	41	– lbw b Pepper	12
M. G. Waite b Cheetham	46	– not out	28
T. Klose c and b O'Reilly	4	– b Roper	2
J. E. Tregoning b O'Reilly	0		
C. W. Walker b O'Reilly	1		
F. A. Ward b O'Reilly	4		
C. V. Grimmett b O'Reilly	17		
H. J. Cotton absent hurt	0		
B 21, l-b 4, n-b 6	31	B 1, l-b 3	4
	430		**(3 wkts) 156**

South Australia Bowling

	Overs	Mdns	Runs	Wkts	Overs	Mdns	Runs	Wkts
Cotton	12	—	51	1				
Waite	19	—	98	1	12	1	22	—
Grimmett	20	—	102	3	20.5	—	122	6
Ward	5	—	42	—	15	4	61	2
Tregoning	3	—	9	1				
Klose	5.4	1	23	4	7	1	37	2

New South Wales Bowling

	Overs	Mdns	Runs	Wkts	Overs	Mdns	Runs	Wkts
Roper	14	—	83	1	3	—	26	1
Cheetham	15	1	80	1	7	—	33	1
O'Reilly	22.1	4	108	5	10	—	29	—
Pepper	9	—	56	1	8	—	31	1
Walsh	12	—	72	1	2.2	—	33	—

Umpires: J. D. Scott and A. G. Jenkins.
H. C. Newman last two days (Jenkins ill).

SOUTH AUSTRALIA v QUEENSLAND

Played at Adelaide, December 22, 23, 25, 26, 1939

South Australia won by an innings and 222 runs. The power of their batsmen and the cunning bowling of Grimmett and Ward gave them overwhelming success. K. L. Ridings, Bradman, Badcock and Waite all reached three figures in helping to set up a record score for the Adelaide Oval. Ridings, a strong driver, shared with his captain in a second-wicket stand of 196. The fourth partnership yielded 136, and the next, between Badcock and Waite, realised 281. Using a wide range of strokes in stylish fashion, Badcock completed a brilliant double hundred in four hours before being bowled. The fifth century stand of the innings came from Whitington and P. L. Ridings, who added 108. Tallon and Rogers were the only batsmen to offer protracted resistance in Queensland's first innings. A better show was forthcoming in the follow-on when Queensland faced huge arrears of 599, but a gallant 156 by Brown proved unavailing as a safety effort.

South Australia

K. L. Ridings lbw b Baker.................151	R. S. Whitington c Rogers b Christ........ 67	
T. Klose c Ellis b Cook.................. 13	P. L. Ridings not out................... 44	
D. G. Bradman c Hansen b Ellis..........138		
R. A. Hamence lbw b Cook.............. 6	B 10, l-b 17, n-b 2............. 29	
C. L. Badcock b Dixon.................236		
M. G. Waite c and b Dixon..............137	(7 wkts dec.) 821	

C. V. Grimmett, F. A. Ward and C. W. Walker did not bat.

Queensland

W. A. Brown b Grimmett	20	– st Walker b Ward 156
G. G. Cook st Walker b Ward	27	– c Waite b Grimmett 15
T. Allen c Klose b Ward	35	– c Waite b Ward 22
R. Rogers c Waite b Grimmett	49	– c Klose b Grimmett 50
G. Baker c Walker b Klose	0	– lbw b Grimmett 52
D. Tallon c Badcock b Ward	70	– c Waite b Ward 14
D. Hansen b Grimmett	2	– c Walker b Grimmett 15
D. Watt c Waite b Grimmett	6	– lbw b Grimmett 8
C. Christ c Walker b Ward	1	– b Ward 12
P. L. Dixon not out	3	– c Walker b Grimmett 17
J. Ellis c Badcock b Ward	5	– not out 1
L-b 3, n-b 1	4	B 8, l-b 3, w 1, n-b 3 15
	222	**377**

Queensland Bowling

	Overs	Mdns	Runs	Wkts
Ellis	14	—	95	1
Cook	22	1	129	2
Dixon	24	—	142	2
Christ	27.1	3	144	1
Baker	22	—	127	1
Watt	14	1	135	—
Rogers	4	1	20	—

South Australia Bowling

	Overs	Mdns	Runs	Wkts	Overs	Mdns	Runs	Wkts
P. L. Ridings	5	—	29	—	11	1	48	—
Waite	9	2	40	—	13	2	21	—
Grimmett	19	2	71	4	33.4	5	124	6
Ward	16.7	2	62	5	30	3	165	4
Klose	5	1	16	1	3	—	4	—

Umpires: J. D. Scott and H. C. Newman.

NEW SOUTH WALES v QUEENSLAND

Played at Sydney, December 29, 30, 1939

New South Wales won by an innings and 130 runs. Devastating bowling by O'Reilly, who took 14 wickets for little more than three runs apiece, bewildered Queensland and brought the match to an end in two days. Making the fullest use of a stiff breeze, O'Reilly was practically unplayable with his variety of spin, change of pace and tantalizing length. On the first day he sent back eight men for 23 runs. Brown alone proving capable of getting more than twenty. Barnes, with a well-hit hundred, Mudge and Lush batted splendidly for New South Wales, and Queensland went in a second time needing 274 to avert defeat in an innings. The task was far beyond them. O'Reilly again found little opposition and, taking six wickets for 22 runs, finished the game in summary fashion with a match record of fourteen for 45 runs.

Queensland

W. A. Brown c Chipperfield b Lush	24	– c Mudge b O'Reilly.............	14
G. G. Cook lbw b O'Reilly....................	15	– c Sismey b Pepper..............	3
T. Allen b O'Reilly	2	– lbw b Pepper..................	17
R. Rogers c Sismey b O'Reilly	18	– b Cheetham	18
G. Baker run out...........................	10	– c Mudge b O'Reilly.............	51
D. Tallon b O'Reilly	16	– c Solomon b O'Reilly	0
D. Watt b O'Reilly	0	– b O'Reilly	6
W. Tallon b O'Reilly........................	3	– c Lush b O'Reilly	0
C. Christ not out...........................	5	– b Walsh	9
P. L. Dixon b O'Reilly.......................	2	– c Mudge b O'Reilly.............	7
J. Ellis b O'Reilly...........................	2	– not out	4
B 7, n-b 1.......................	8	B 9, l-b 4, n-b 2..........	15
	105		**144**

New South Wales

H. Mudge lbw b Baker	79	J. G. Lush b Ellis.....................	54
S. J. McCabe c Brown b Ellis	13	W. J. O'Reilly c and b Christ	26
C. M. Solomon b Dixon	24	S. Sismey c and b W. Tallon	5
S. G. Barnes c Ellis b Baker 119		J. Walsh not out	10
A. G. Chipperfield b Cook	10	B 4, l-b 5, n-b 1	10
A. G. Cheetham st D. Tallon b Christ	21		
C. Pepper st D. Tallon b Cook	8		**379**

New South Wales Bowling

	Overs	Mdns	Runs	Wkts	Overs	Mdns	Runs	Wkts
Lush	6	—	27	1	3	—	18	—
Cheetham........	4	1	10	—	5	—	18	1
Pepper	13	2	37	—	14	2	45	2
O'Reilly	11.1	3	23	8	15.2	7	22	6
Walsh					5	—	26	1

Queensland Bowling

	Overs	Mdns	Runs	Wkts
Ellis..............	16.3	—	60	2
Cook.............	12	—	67	2
Baker	11	—	65	2
Dixon	7	2	26	1
W. Tallon	11	—	71	1
Christ	12	—	53	2
Watt	4	—	27	—

Umpires: G. Borwick and R. McGrath.

VICTORIA v SOUTH AUSTRALIA

Played at Melbourne, December 29, 30, 1939, January 1, 2, 1940

Drawn. Insufficient time prevented South Australia hitting off the runs needed for victory. Another great innings by Bradman eclipsed everything else in the match. Ridings and Klose took the edge off the bowling in an opening stand of 108, and then their captain scored as he pleased. He used all the strokes in a masterly display which brought him 267 runs, including twenty-seven 4s before Fleetwood-Smith, who received heavy punishment, took his wicket. Victoria's batsmen showed to advantage in their first innings, despite the good pace bowling of Burton, who was making his Shield début. Miller and Beames hit splendid centuries. Hassett, who narrowly missed a hundred, also showed sparkling form in the second innings, and South Australia were set 179 to get. They were 118 behind with nine wickets left when the game ended.

South Australia

K. L. Ridings c Johnson b Ring	56	– not out	29
T. Klose b Scott	54	– lbw b Ring	15
D. G. Bradman c Johnson b Fleetwood-Smith	267		
C. L. Badcock lbw b Ring	58		
R. A. Hamence lbw b Fleetwood-Smith	20	– not out	11
R. S. Whitington c Ring b Scott	41		
C. W. Walker lbw b Scott	1		
M. G. Waite c Hassett b Ring	64		
F. A. Ward c and b Ring	26		
C. V. Grimmett c Sievers b Ring	6		
G. Burton not out	1		
B 6, l-b 9, w 1	16	B 3, l-b 1, n-b 1	5
	610	**(1 wkt)**	**60**

Victoria

I. S. Lee b Klose	36	– c Grimmett b Ward	39
G. E. Tamblyn c Walker b Ward	38	– absent hurt	0
A. L. Hassett st Walker b Grimmett	92	– c and b Ward	66
K. R. Miller c Bradman b Burton	108	– c Bradman b Klose	1
I. W. Johnson lbw b Waite	14	– lbw b Klose	23
P. J. Beames c and b Burton	104	– b Burton	32
B. A. Barnett b Burton	7	– lbw b Klose	46
M. W. Sievers lbw b Burton	16	– c Badcock b Grimmett	36
D. T. Ring st Walker b Grimmett	32	– not out	41
R. B. Scott c Waite b Burton	7	– b Grimmett	17
L. O'B. Fleetwood-Smith not out	11	– st Walker b Ward	4
B 5, l-b 5	10	B 5, l-b 3	8
	475		**313**

Victoria Bowling

	Overs	Mdns	Runs	Wkts	Overs	Mdns	Runs	Wkts
Scott	25	—	135	3	3	—	9	—
Sievers	29	1	120	—	3	—	12	—
Ring	25.4	1	123	5	4	1	13	1
Fleetwood-Smith	27	—	156	2				
Johnson	13	—	60	—	5	2	14	—
Hassett					1	—	7	—

South Australia Bowling

	Overs	Mdns	Runs	Wkts	Overs	Mdns	Runs	Wkts
Burton	20.2	—	99	5	11	1	44	1
Waite	21	3	90	1	10	1	38	—
Grimmett	33	2	136	2	21	2	78	2
Klose	21	3	42	1	17	4	43	3
Ward	19	—	98	1	14.4	2	102	3

Umpires: W. J. Craddock and A. N. Barlow.

NEW SOUTH WALES v COMBINED QUEENSLAND AND VICTORIA

Played at Brisbane, November 22, 23, 25, 26, 1940

New South Wales won by one wicket. R. Saggers, the New South Wales wicket-keeper, equalled a world record by catching seven men in the second innings of the combined side. Tallon, the Queensland wicket-keeper, incidentally one of the players who shares the record of dismissing seven men in an innings, showed to fine advantage as a batsman, his grand second innings almost enabling his side to snatch success when heavy defeat seemed certain. With hard hitting in the first innings, Tallon gave of hint of what was to come. In the second he reached three figures in ninety minutes before lunch, and took less than two hours over 152, which included a 6 and twenty 4s. Hassett assisted him in a stand of 162. Barnes, with a masterly century, was largely responsible for the big first innings total reached by New South Wales. He failed when facing the task of getting 190 to win, but McCabe helped New South Wales to an exciting victory.

Combined Team

W. A. Brown c Chegwyn b Trumper	13	– c Jackson b O'Reilly	43
G. G. Cook b Jackson	5	– c Saggers b Gulliver	22
R. Rogers c and b O'Reilly	29	– c Saggers b Gulliver	34
D. Tallon c Chegwyn b O'Reilly	55	– c Trumper b Cohen	152
A. L. Hassett c McCool b Trumper	14	– c Saggers b McCool	96
K. R. Miller c Saggers b McCool	8	– c Saggers b Jackson	24
G. Baker c Gulliver b Trumper	22	– c Saggers b Gulliver	12
M. W. Sievers not out	23	– c Saggers b Gulliver	25
M. Raymer c Saggers b McCool	15	– b Jackson	1
D. T. Ring st Saggers b McCool	5	– c Saggers b Gulliver	0
J. Ellis c Chegwyn b O'Reilly	1	– not out	1
Extras	12	Extras	6
	202		**416**

New South Wales

M. B. Cohen c Tallon b Ellis	0	– b Baker	34
K. Carmody b Sievers	7	– run out	36
S. G. Barnes c Tallon b Ring	144	– lbw b Baker	3
S. J. McCabe c Cook b Ring	43	– c Cook b Ring	53
J. Chegwyn c Tallon b Sievers	37	– c and b Raymer	21
R. Saggers c Hassett b Raymer	58	– c Tallon b Baker	5
V. Jackson c Rogers b Ring	7	– lbw b Raymer	2
K. Gulliver not out	66	– c Brown b Ring	0
C. McCool c Miller b Raymer	52	– not out	27
V. Trumper c Baker b Raymer	4	– run out	0
W. J. O'Reilly b Cook	4	– not out	4
Extras	7	Extras	7
	429		**(9 wkts) 192**

New South Wales Bowling

	Overs	Mdns	Runs	Wkts	Overs	Mdns	Runs	Wkts
Trumper	9	—	37	3	10	2	46	—
Jackson	6	—	18	1	17.5	2	69	2
O'Reilly	10.4	—	46	3	17	1	85	1
Gulliver	7	—	44	—	16	—	80	5
Barnes	1	—	6	—				
McCool	9	—	39	3	11	—	91	1
Cohen					9	2	39	1

Combined Team Bowling

	Overs	Mdns	Runs	Wkts	Overs	Mdns	Runs	Wkts
Ellis............	20	5	76	1	10	3	26	—
Sievers	17	1	68	2	5	1	20	—
Ring	20	—	143	3	9.4	2	50	2
Cook.............	12.3	3	29	1	7	1	17	—
Raymer..........	17	—	85	3	9	—	55	2
Baker	3	—	21	—	9	1	17	3

VICTORIA v SOUTH AUSTRALIA

Played at Melbourne, December 13, 14, 16, 17, 1940

Drawn. Badcock and Hamence created Australian cricket history when each made two
centuries in a match. Thoroughly on top of the bowling, both used drives, cuts, hooks,
pulls and glances with equal facility. Hamence scored 233 for once out; Badcock's
aggregate was 222. Victoria, for whom Lee, Miller and Hassett batted soundly, found
Grimmett still a force and his skill brought him seven first innings wickets at moderate
cost. Victoria, 126 behind on the first innings, were left to get 372, and when the game
ended they still required 210 with only three wickets standing.

South Australia

K. Ridings c Baker b Ring	69	– lbw b Johnson	22
T. Klose c Ring b Dudley	2		
C. L. Badcock c Ring b Sievers	120	– c Tamblyn b Sievers	102
C. W. Walker c Johnson b Sievers	10		
M. G. Waite b Dempster	15		
R. A. Hamence c Dudley b Sievers	130	– not out	103
B. H. Leak b Dudley	79		
C. V. Grimmett st Baker b Johnson	14		
P. Ridings lbw b Johnson	42		
F. A. Ward c Dempster b Johnson	7	– b Ring	10
H. J. Cotton not out	7		
Extras	20	Extras	8
	515	**(3 wkts dec.)**	**245**

Victoria

I. S. Lee b Cotton	93	– b Ward	41
G. Tamblyn b Grimmett	32	– c and b Ward	29
R. Dempster lbw b Grimmett	10	– lbw b Waite	2
K. R. Miller b Grimmett	63	– b Waite	16
A. L. Hassett c Waite b Grimmett	67	– not out	36
P. Beames st Walker b Grimmett	42	– c Cotton b Grimmett	1
I. W. Johnson c Klose b Grimmett	0	– c P. Ridings b Ward	9
M. W. Sievers lbw b Waite	41	– b Ward	1
E. A. Baker lbw b Grimmett	15	– not out	12
D. Ring not out	12		
W. Dudley c Cotton b Waite	4		
Extras	10	Extras	14
	389	**(7 wkts)**	**161**

Victoria Bowling

	Overs	Mdns	Runs	Wkts	Overs	Mdns	Runs	Wkts
Dudley	24	—	71	2	10	—	45	—
Sievers	30	3	100	3	9.5	—	49	1
Johnson	26	10	117	3	12	—	50	1
Ring	27	1	139	1	14	4	56	1
Dempster	15	1	65	1	4	—	16	—
Miller	1	—	3	0				
Hassett					3	—	21	—

South Australia Bowling

	Overs	Mdns	Runs	Wkts	Overs	Mdns	Runs	Wkts
Cotton	11	2	47	1	4	—	8	—
Waite	19.1	—	55	2	11	3	14	2
P. Ridings	7	—	23	—	4	1	11	—
Grimmett	38	6	114	7	17	1	36	1
Klose	14	3	46	—				
Ward	13	—	94	—	15	2	53	4
Hamence					4	—	25	—

NEW SOUTH WALES v QUEENSLAND

Played at Sydney, December 26, 27, 28, 29, 30, 1940

New South Wales won by 404 runs. The match brought distinction to A. Morris, the New South Wales opening batsmen, who created a record by making two separate hundreds on his first appearance. His batting greatly impressed, and he employed a wide range of strokes, particularly in the second innings. His match aggregate was 259. On the opening day Morris helped Barnes to put on 261 for the second wicket, and in the second innings he joined with Cohen in a three-figure first-wicket stand. Rogers showed good form in Queensland's first innings, but only Brown did much against the spin bowling of Pepper and O'Reilly when the visitors were set to get 552 to win.

New South Wales

M. B. Cohen c Christ b Ellis .... 5 – b Cox 118
A. Morris b McCarthy ....148 – b Watt 111
S. G. Barnes c McCarthy b Cook ....133 – c Tallon b Cook 5
S. J. McCabe c Rogers b Watt 75
C. McCool lbw b Christ .... 45 – lbw b Ellis.................... 0
R. Saggers b Christ.......................... 1 – c Tallon b Cox 33
V. Jackson c McCarthy b Ellis .... 47 – not out 47
C. Pepper c Brown b Watt .... 7 – c Tallon b Watt.............. 6
W. J. O'Reilly b Cook....................... 30 – c Baker b Watt 13
V. Trumper not out......................... 5 – c Ellis b Watt 11
R. B. Scott run out .... 4 – c Brown b Cox 2
    Extras 16   Extras................. 23

                516   (9 wkts dec.) 369

Queensland

W. A. Brown c Pepper b Trumper	7	– c Scott b Pepper	57
G. G. Cook b Scott	4	– run out	25
R. Rogers c Pepper b Jackson	114	– b Pepper	26
D. Tallon lbw b O'Reilly	34	– c and b Pepper	0
G. Baker b Jackson	48	– c Barnes b Pepper	3
D. Watt b Pepper	13	– c Trumper b Pepper	0
M. Raymer not out	41	– b Pepper	10
J. McCarthy run out	18	– lbw b O'Reilly	4
D. Cox b McCool	16	– b O'Reilly	14
J. Ellis st Saggers b McCool	0	– not out	1
C. Christ b Jackson	18	– st Saggers b O'Reilly	0
Extras	21	Extras	7
	334		**147**

Queensland Bowling

	Overs	Mdns	Runs	Wkts	Overs	Mdns	Runs	Wkts
Ellis	17	1	82	2	12	1	54	1
Cook	13.7	—	67	2	12	—	66	1
Cox	10	1	73	—	11.5	—	63	3
Christ	17	—	78	2	5	—	23	—
Raymer	5	—	46	—	4	—	23	—
Watt	11	—	110	2	10	—	90	4
McCarthy	9	1	44	1	5	1	27	—

New South Wales Bowling

	Overs	Mdns	Runs	Wkts	Overs	Mdns	Runs	Wkts
Scott	8	—	36	1	4	—	12	—
Trumper	7	—	34	1	3	—	13	—
Jackson	9.6	1	30	3	7	2	15	—
Pepper	16	2	82	1	13	2	57	6
O'Reilly	7	1	34	1	13.6	1	43	3
McCool	12	—	96	2				
Cohen	3	2	1	—				

W. R. HAMMOND IN FIRST-CLASS CRICKET
1920-1939

WALTER REGINALD HAMMOND

By R. C. ROBERTSON-GLASGOW

(Statistics by E. L. Roberts)

Some judge batsmen by the number of their runs, others by the manner of their making. By either criterion W. R. Hammond, England's captain, must rank among the great. For seven seasons consecutively up to the end of 1939 he headed the English first-class averages. His batting average, since he began to play for Gloucestershire in 1920, stands in all first-class cricket at 55.72, nearly 4 units higher than his nearest rival, Sutcliffe. He has made 155 centuries. But, far more than this, he has adorned cricket and entertained the public with a style of batting in which splendour of manner, grace of execution, and muscular power of stroke have been combined to a degree rarely equalled in the history of the game. "Let's go and see Hammond", we used to say. It was worth a journey even to see him walk out to bat; for the true stamp of greatness was printed on him.

His bowling, though never great, was good enough to be used successfully for England. He has taken good wickets in Test matches, including that of W. M. Woodfull, in the days when the batting of Woodfull was a headline. At about medium pace, Hammond had a late swerve from leg with the new ball, and at any time could tax a batsman with an awkward break-back. He had great pace from the pitch, and an action for a boy to imitate, with easy rhythm and the left shoulder pointing at the batsman just before delivery.

As a fielder he will be remembered as one of the greatest of slips, intelligent, so quick in anticipation and movement that no catch seemed difficult. In earlier times he would field anywhere, and he threw like an Australian.

Born at Dover on June 19, 1903, Hammond toured early, playing young cricket in China and Malta. Returning to England he went to Cirencester Grammar School, where he distinguished himself by playing an innings of 365 not out in a house match. In 1920 he played for Gloucestershire as an amateur, but his qualification was questioned by the Kent authorities. He turned professional, and 1923 was his first season of regular appearance. I remember him then as a batsman of freedom and power, but still unsound in judgment and defence.

Unlike Hutton, of Yorkshire, and D. Compton, of Middlesex, he did not jump into full panoply. He batted like a very promising undergraduate, took risks and enjoyed them. But from the start he fielded like an archangel. Little, if anything, was yet seen of his bowling. In his first match, against Surrey at Bristol, he scored 110 and 92. His aggregate for the county was 1,313: average 28.54. At The Oval he made 46 and 19 for the Players against the Gentlemen. Consistency was yet to come. In 1924 his performance in figures showed little change, but he played one remarkable innings, 174 not out on a difficult pitch against Middlesex at Bristol. Gloucestershire had been out for 31, Middlesex for 74, when this happened. It was followed by some great bowling by Charles Parker − he did the "hat-trick" in each innings − and Gloucestershire won by 61 runs.

Next summer, his defence much strengthened, he was fit to play for England. He scored 1,818 runs in all matches, including an innings of 250 not out against Lancashire at Old Trafford, when he and Dipper put on 330 for the third wicket. In the autumn he sailed with the Hon. F. S. G. Calthorpe's team to the West Indies. In the first unofficial Test, at Barbados, he played an innings of 238 not out and made five catches. His average in representative matches was 87. Here, then, was England's number three for the coming Australian Tests in England. But he fell ill, and in 1926 played no cricket at all.

In 1927 he returned, climbed the heights, and has remained there ever since. Refreshed, stronger than ever, he showed a masterful brilliance against every variety of bowling. He made 135 against Yorkshire at Gloucester, then 108 and 128 in the next match, against

Surrey at The Oval; took breath at Dewsbury with 11 and 17, then roused Old Trafford with 99 and 187. In this last century, he hit four 6s and twenty-four 4s, and annihilated the redoubtable fast bowler, E. A. McDonald, whose two wickets cost him 165 runs. Back at Bristol, he scored 83 and 7 against Middlesex. There were two days of May left, and Hammond needed 164 for his 1,000 runs; so, at Southampton, he made 192, and joined that old king of Gloucestershire and English cricket, who had done the same feat in 1895 in his forty-seventh year.

In the autumn of 1927 he sailed to South Africa with Captain R. T. Stanyforth's MCC team. In the Tests he scored 390 runs, highest innings 90, average 40. His bowling, so far more admired by the connoisseur than remarked by the critics, yielded 15 wickets at 26 each. He was now, beyond question, an all-rounder.

He had reached the meridian of his powers. He was twenty-five years old, an athlete from top to toe, of an agile and flexible strength more often seen in Dominion than English cricketers, brimming with health and natural confidence. Each to his own view; but in the years since the last war, for skill fortified by endurance, for harmony and control of attack and defence. I have not known his like. Bradman may have been more starkly efficient, Frank Woolley have shown more charm, Hobbs a more exquisite technique; but to me, whether trying to bowl him out or to field those terrific strokes, Hammond remains the greatest of them all. Without need of reflection or memory, I can still feel and hear those off-drives.

The best know failure, and it came to Hammond in the Australian Tests here in 1930, when he scored only 306 runs and only one century; a performance that would have set up some cricketers for life, but, in Hammond, caused a welter of theory and vapouring. Grimmett, whom he had dominated in Australia, worried him in England. The little man bowled grandly, it is true, attacking Hammond's leg stump. But it was not only Grimmett who troubled him. Some virtue had temporarily ebbed from him. He lost confidence, and tended to play off his back foot balls that he was accustomed to bang against the rails behind cover-point. It was the husk, not the body, that was batting. I doubt, too, if he was in full health. Yet even his ghost scored in that season 2,032 runs with an average of 53. A second journey to South Africa, under A. P. F. Chapman, did much to restore him. He scored 517 in nine Test innings, average 65, and his 136 not out was the only century for England in the series.

To return to 1928. In all first-class matches he scored 2,825 runs, average 66, including nine centuries. In bowling, he took 84 wickets at 23 each. His fielding, especially at short slip to the leg-spinners of Charles Parker, was superb. The Cheltenham Festival that year was nearly all Hammond. Against Surrey he made 139 and 143, caught four men in the first innings and six in the second. In the next match, against Worcestershire, he scored 80, took 9 for 23 in the first innings and 6 for 105 in the second. Against the West Indies, in three Tests, he scored only 111 runs, average 37.

But he was soon to rob the critics of their adjectives. Sailing to Australia with the England team under A. P. F. Chapman in one of the strongest batting sides that any country had produced, he took control of the Australian bowlers. In the second Test he played an innings of 251, in the third 200. In the fourth, still untamable, he made 119 not out and 177, and his Test average ended at 113.12 for just over 900 runs. This triumph was won not by vigilance and attrition, but by exuberant and offensive batting. They could not hold that driving. In the English season of 1929 he finished second to J. B. Hobbs, scoring 2,456 runs, with ten centuries, at an average of 65. Against the South Africans, who were led by H. G. Deane, he cooled down to two centuries, both not out.

Two lean years followed. First, the seasons against the Australians, mentioned before; then 1931, when his average sank to 42. Probably he was stale. Even so, he played an innings of 100 not out against New Zealand at The Oval, and in all made six centuries. In 1932 he fared better, scoring 2,528 runs at an average of 56 and he more often showed that brilliancy in attack which had marked him out as a batsman apart; but, as a whole, it was evident that some of the superb contempt had left his style, which became more thoughtful; he was batting from knowledge rather than instinct. Perhaps too much was expected of him. Critics tended to exaggerate his failures and neglect his successes. He was now, so to speak, the Prime Minister, a target for any passing fool. To recover completely, he needed a month of golf at the seaside or a cricket tour round the clubs and villages. Instead, he went out to the grimmest series of Tests ever played between two countries – to Australia under D. R. Jardine.

Dismal quarrels, public and personal, arguments and recriminations produced an atmosphere wholly at variance with his free and genial temperament. Small wonder that "he did not repeat his record-breaking achievements of the previous tour". Great wonder that, in a style of cricket shot through with commerce and acrimony, Hammond, mixing iron with gold, scored 440 runs during the Tests, as did Herbert Sutcliffe, and alone of the side made two centuries in the series. His parting present to Sydney, scene of his greatest triumphs, was a cracking drive for six, which ended the fifth Test and heralded an exhibition in New Zealand which none but he could have given. In three innings he scored 59, 227 and 336 not out. The last two were in the Tests, giving him an aggregate that was also an average, 563. In his 336 not out, at Auckland, he batted for 318 minutes, hitting thirty-four 4s and ten 6s (three off consecutive balls). A New Zealand Test cricketer, who has played against the best in Australia and England, has told me that, even allowing for the comparative mediocrity of the bowling, it was quite the most wonderful display, in power and variety, that he has ever seen. So back to England.

In summer 1933 he took part in the three Tests against the West Indies, but did nothing of note, scoring only 74 runs for an average of 25. For Gloucestershire his form was brilliant. He scored 239 against Glamorgan, 126 not out against Lancashire; then, against Worcestershire, at Worcester, for the fourth time in his career, scored a century in each innings. In this match, C. C. Dacre brought off the same feat. After a double century (206) at Leicester, he played one of his greatest innings against Middlesex at Lord's, 178, which so nearly won the match against all expectation. Centuries against Nottinghamshire and Surrey followed, both at Bristol, and then, in the return match against Lancashire, at Old Trafford, he made 120. Still the spate swelled on: 231 against Derby at Cheltenham: then, to balance failure in the Tests, 264 against West Indies at Bristol. Lastly, two centuries in the Folkstone Festival, 184 for South of England v MCC, 133 for England Eleven v West Indies. At Folkestone, I remember, he took a fancy for square-cutting balls of good length off the off stump, and third man's boots nearly caught fire. So he ended that season with 3,323 runs at an average of 68.

As in 1930, so in 1934 Hammond failed in the Tests against Australia in England. It would be idle to attribute this failure to a back injury owing to which he played hardly any cricket till the middle of June. Nor was it any one Australian bowler, as has often been suggested, who overcame him. Hammond has always been a batsman of moods, and in this series his failure was as much temperamental as technical. Half England had gone crazy about the Tests. Thousands of sandwiches were cut, hundreds of articles were written. And somehow, as he moved in the middle of the turmoil, I found Hammond faintly but undeniably bored. Naughty, perhaps, but to me, I must confess, enjoyably comical. Everything was ready for the coronation, but the king refused to get out of bed! Further, it was his benefit year.

And richly did he give of his art to Gloucestershire. In thirteen matches he averaged 126. He made 302 not out against Glamorgan, 290 against Kent, 265 not out against Worcestershire. He was as sure a draw as ever on the county grounds, and his benefit totalled £2,650, a magnificent and unparalled sum for a west country cricketer, but no more than was due to one who, wisely directed and handled by that remarkable leader, B. H. Lyon, had raised Gloucestershire to an eminence it had not imagined since the golden days of the Graces.

There is little rest in modern cricket, and in the winter of 1934 Hammond was off to the West Indies under the captaincy of R. E. S. Wyatt. He did nothing great in the Tests, though in all matches he had an average of 56, with a highest score of 281 not out. 1935 was another ordinary year for him. He looked stale, which was not surprising. Indeed, English cricket seemed aweary of its life and to go through its motions because it must. A young and virile South African team, under H. F. Wade, won the Test rubber. It was the end of a rather melancholy chapter. Hutton had only just begun in Yorkshire, D. Compton was still in the "nursery", young Joseph Hardstaff appeared in but one Test, at Leeds. Middle-age prevailed.

In April 1936, having had his tonsils removed, he began slowly, but soon warmed to it. An All-India team visited us. Hammond played in the second and third Tests; in the second he played an innings of 167, reaching 100 in 100 minutes, mainly by off-driving of his own inimitable sort; in the third he made 217, and his Test average finished at 194. But his most remarkable innings was one of 317 for Gloucestershire against Nottinghamshire in Goddard's benefit match. It contained but one false stroke, and the third hundred was made in 70 minutes. In this month of August Hammond scored 1,281 runs, so exceeding the 1,278 of Dr W. G. Grace, made in the year 1876.

In the winter of 1936 he visited Australia for the third time, G. O. Allen captaining. He began with 141 against Western Australia, 107 against a reinforced Western Australian team, 104 and 136 against South Australia; and he had not yet reached his favourite Sydney. There, in the second Test, he played an innings of 231 not out. It was seriously and, for Hammond, slowly built up; but it suited the occasion. In Australia's second innings he took 3 for 29 in 127 balls, and England won by an innings. Thereafter he was less successful against an attack mainly directed, in the case of O'Reilly, at his leg stump. His next highest score was 56, and his Test average 58. England won the second Test, Australia the next three and so the rubber.

In the three Tests of 1937 against New Zealand he averaged 51, scoring 140 at Lord's. In all matches his aggregate was 3,252 with 13 centuries and average 65. During the following winter it was announced the he had turned amateur. For the Tests against Australia here in 1938 he was appointed England's captain. He had long been king among our cricketers. As a strategist he would not rank among our great leaders; but he was safe, observant and experienced. His colossal achievements commanded the respect as his sociable nature invited the confidence of every sort of cricketer.

His responsibility, so far from weighing him down, seemed quietly to elate him, and his genius reached its height in an innings of 240 in the second Test at Lord's. When he walked down the pavilion steps. England had lost two wickets for only 20 runs to the fast bowling of McCormick. From the start Hammond was "simply and severely great", master of each bowler and every stroke. He and Paynter put on 222 for the fourth wicket, a new record. On the next day, before a record crowd, Hammond and Ames added 186 for the sixth wicket. At length, after he had batted for just over six hours, Hammond, soon after receiving a painful blow on the elbow, was bowled by McCormick on the leg stump. His 240 was the highest score for England up till then in any home Test. But that sort of thing hardly mattered in comparison to the quality of the innings. He gave only one chance, if I may so describe a drive that split the fielder's finger.

At Leeds, he played a fine first innings of 76 out of a total of 223, but failed to score in the second, Australia winning a grand match by five wickets. At The Oval, in the deciding Test, he led England to overwhelming victory. This was Hutton's match, for he scored his famous 364 in 13 hours and 20 minutes. Hammond played very quietly for 59. For Gloucestershire he scored 2,180 runs at an average of 83.84.

In the winter of 1938 he led the MCC team in South Africa. This is no place for a history of those strange and often tedious Tests on chemically over-perfect pitches. The last match, in spite of lasting for ten days, was never finished. Hammond scored 609 runs in the Tests, including three centuries, for an average of 87.

Back in England for the season of 1939, which seems so far away, he showed no decline in his colossal skill. For a cricketer so widely travelled, so drenched in runs, he retained his keeness to a remarkable degree; but it was observable that his method was changing. He now played more strokes of his back foot − the first hint, perhaps, of a need to conserve energy. Be that as it may, he scored seven centuries, one of them against the West Indies in the Test at The Oval, totalled 2,479 runs for the season, and with 63.56 yet again headed the averages.

Figures must largely fill a sketch of so great a batsman, but I should like future generations of cricketers, if they turn over Hammond's pages on some peaceful evening, to think of him as something far more than a wonderful maker of runs, many more of which, we hope, are yet to flow from his bat. For, as an all-rounder, he is the greatest cricketer of this generation, not merely in centuries, in the taking of wickets, and in the making of catches, but in his attitude to the game which he, while drawing from it his fame, has enriched with a grace, a simplicity and a nobility that may never be seen again.

CAREER AT A GLANCE

In England

Year	Complete Innings	Runs	100s	Average	Wickets	Runs	Average	Catches
1920	3	27	—	9.00	—	—	—	—
1921	3	2	—	0.66	—	76	—	—
1922	9	88	—	9.77	—	8	—	2
1923	51	1,421	1	27.86	18	742	41.22	19
1924	41	1,239	2	30.21	29	775	26.72	30
1925	53	1,818	3	34.23	68	2,003	29.45	62
1926				(Did not play owing to illness)				
1927	43	2,969	12	69.04	20	884	44.20	41
1928	43	2,825	9	65.69	84	1,914	23.10	78
1929	38	2,456	10	64.63	28	978	34.92	36
1930	38	2,032	5	53.47	30	928	30.93	31
1931	42	1,781	6	42.40	47	1,457	31.00	43
1932	45	2,528	8	56.17	53	1,483	27.98	45
1933	49	3,323	13	67.81	38	1,375	36.18	54
1934	31	2,366	8	76.32	21	1,059	50.42	22
1935	53	2,616	7	49.35	60	1,636	27.26	52
1936	37	2,107	5	56.94	41	1,046	25.53	13
1937	50	3,252	13	65.04	48	1,094	22.79	37
1938	40	3,011	15	75.27	14	847	60.50	33
1939	39	2,479	7	63.56	3	39	13.00	34

In Australia and New Zealand

Year	Complete Innings	Runs	100s	Average	Wickets	Runs	Average	Catches
1928-29	17	1,553	7	91.35	11	661	60.09	10
1932-33	18	1,511	5	83.94	20	597	27.35	15
1936-37	21	1,242	5	59.14	27	577	21.37	10

In South Africa

Year	Complete Innings	Runs	100s	Average	Wickets	Runs	Average	Catches
1927-28	19	908	2	47.78	27	644	23.85	13
1930-31	17	1,045	3	61.47	15	494	32.93	18
1938-39	17	1,025	4	60.29	7	270	38.57	15

In West Indies

Year	Complete Innings	Runs	100s	Average	Wickets	Runs	Average	Catches
1925-26	15	732	2	48.80	20	573	28.65	15
1934-35	14	789	3	56.36	2	161	80.50	14
Total	846	47,145	155	55.72	731	22,348	30.57	742

Note – W. R. Hammond played 98 not out innings.

SUMMARY

	Complete Innings	Runs	Highest Innings	100s	Average	Wickets	Runs	Average
Test matches	112	6,883	336*	22	61.45	83	3,127	37.67
Gentlemen v Players	26	979	138	3	37.65	34	752	22.41
County matches	539	29,930	317	100	55.52	474	13,804	29.12
Other matches	169	9,353	281	30	55.34	140	4,665	33.32
Total	846	47,145	336*	155	55.72	731	22,348	30.57
In England	708	38,340	317	124	54.15	602	18,371	30.51
Abroad	138	8,805	336*	31	63.80	129	3,977	30.82
Total	846	47,145	336*	155	55.72	731	22,348	30.57

* *Signifies not out.*

In the last thirteen English seasons W. R. Hammond was top of the English batting averages in seven consecutive seasons (1933-1939), and in only two of the thirteen seasons averaged fewer than 50 runs per innings – 42.40 in 1931 and 49.35 in 1935.

In addition to his 155 hundreds, Hammond scored over 50 on 158 occasions. He has been dismissed without scoring 47 times.

His all-round figures in 1928 provided one of the most remarkable records in cricket history – 2,825 runs, 84 wickets and 78 catches.

Hammond's batting averages in his three Australian tours should be noted: 91.35 in 1928-29, 83.94 in 1932-33, and 53.25 in 1936-37. In these three tours he scored 4,342 runs and averaged 73.59 runs per innings.

For his sixteen full English seasons Hammond has an average aggregate of 2,389 runs. For the last thirteen seasons (1927-1939) his average aggregate is 2,596 runs.

HAMMOND IN COUNTY CRICKET

Year	Complete Innings	Runs	100s	Average	Wickets	Runs	Average
1920	3	27	—	9.00	—	—	—
1922	9	88	—	9.77	—	8	—
1923	46	1,313	1	28.54	18	712	39.55
1924	37	1,085	2	29.32	25	662	26.48
1925	49	1,571	2	32.06	61	1,695	27.78
1927	35	2,522	10	72.05	16	712	44.50
1928	30	2,471	9	82.46	63	1,393	22.11
1929	26	1,730	7	66.53	17	597	35.11
1930	23	1,168	3	50.78	22	490	22.27
1931	30	1,389	5	46.30	39	1,115	28.58
1932	33	2,039	6	61.78	46	1,294	28.13
1933	40	2,578	10	64.45	38	1,293	34.02
1934	16	2,020	8	126.25	12	518	43.16
1935	39	1,803	5	48.72	37	1,222	33.02
1936	30	1,432	3	47.73	33	768	23.27
1937	36	2,393	10	66.47	33	646	19.57
1938	26	2,180	13	83.84	11	640	58.18
1939	31	2,121	6	68.41	3	39	13.00
Total	539	29,930	100	55.52	474	13,804	29.12

In thirteen successive seasons (1927-1939) Hammond has been top of the Gloucestershire batting averages. In his other three full seasons he was second in 1925 and third in 1923 and 1924. During these sixteen seasons he averaged 1,863 runs and 29 wickets in Championship matches.

An interesting comparison may be drawn between the records of W. G. Grace and W. R. Hammond in county matches:

	Runs	100s	Average	Wickets	Average
W. R. Grace	21,738	47	40.78	1,265	18.29
W. R. Hammond	29,930	100	55.52	474	29.12

INNINGS BY INNINGS IN TEST CRICKET

Opponents	No. of Tests	Innings	Not Outs	Runs	100s	Average
Australia	29	50	3	2,684	9	57.10
South Africa	24	42	7	2,188	6	62.51
West Indies	13	20	2	639	1	35.50
New Zealand	8	10	2	936	4	117.00
India	3	5	1	436	2	109.00
Total	77	127	15	6,883	22	61.45

Note – Hammond took 83 wickets at an average of 37.67 and held 101 catches in Test cricket.

Year	Opponents	Innings	Runs	Average
1927-28	South Africa	51, 43, 14, 90, 1*, 28, 25, 66, 3	321	40.12
1928	West Indies	45, 63, 3	111	37.00
1928-29	Australia	44, 28, 251, 200, 32, 119*, 177, 38, 16	905	113.12
1929	South Africa	18, 138*, 8, 5, 65, 0, 17, 101*	352	58.65
1930	Australia	8, 4, 38, 32, 113, 35, 3, 13, 60	306	34.00
1930-31	South Africa	49, 63, 57, 65, 136*, 75, 15, 29, 28	517	64.62
1931	New Zealand	7, 46, 100*, 16	169	56.33
1932	India	35, 12	47	23.50
1932-33	Australia	112, 8, 23, 2, 85, 20, 14, 101, 75*	440	55.00
1932-33	New Zealand	227, 336*	563	563.00
1933	West Indies	29, 34, 11	74	24.66
1934	Australia	25, 16, 2, 4, 37, 20, 15, 43	162	20.25
1934-35	West Indies	43, 29*, 1, 9, 47, 1, 11, 34	175	25.00
1935	South Africa	28, 27, 27, 63, 87*, 29, 63*, 65	389	64.83
1936	India	167, 217, 5*	389	194.50
1936-37	Australia	0, 25, 231*, 32, 51, 20, 39, 14, 56	468	58.50
1937	New Zealand	140, 33, 0, 31	204	51.00
1938	Australia	26, 240, 2, 76, 0, 59	403	67.16
1938-39	South Africa	24, 58, 181, 120, 1, 61*, 24, 140	609	87.00
1939	West Indies	14, 30*, 22, 32, 43, 138	279	55.80

* *Signifies not out.*

HUNDREDS IN TEST CRICKET (22)

Lord's	Leeds	Birmingham	Manchester
140 (1937)	113 (1930)	138* (1929)	167 (1936)
240 (1938)			

The Oval	Adelaide	Melbourne	Sydney
101* (1929)	119* (1929)	200 (1929)	251 (1929)
100* (1931)	177 (1929)		112 (1932)
217 (1936)			101* (1933)
138 (1939)			231* (1936)

Durban	Cape Town	Christchurch	Auckland
136* (1931)	181 (1939)	227 (1933)	336* (1933)
120 (1939)			
140 (1939)			

In each of his first two Test matches – v South Africa in 1927-28 – W. R. Hammond scored 50 runs and took 5 wickets.

Against Australia in 1928-29 he scored 779 runs in five consecutive Test innings – 251, 200, 32, 119 not out, and 177.

In 1930-31, v South Africa, he had five consecutive innings each over fifty – 63, 57, 65, 136 not out and 75. Immediately preceding these innings he had scored 49 (v South Africa) and 60 (v Australia).

Hammond is the only cricket who has scored over 700 runs in four consecutive Test innings: 101 and 75 not out (v Australia), 227 and 336 not out (v New Zealand) – all in 1933.

He is the only England captain who has scored a double hundred in a Test match – 240 v Australia at Lord's in 1938.

In Test cricket Hammond's record is unparalleled. No other cricketer has played over 125 innings, scored over 6,000 runs (including 22 hundreds), taken over 80 wickets, and made over 100 catches.

TWO HUNDREDS IN ONE MATCH

108 and 128   Gloucestershire v Surrey at The Oval, 1927
139 and 143   Gloucestershire v Surrey at Cheltenham, 1928
119 and 177   England v Australia at Adelaide, 1929
122 and 111* Gloucestershire v Worcestershire at Worcester, 1933
104 and 136   MCC v South Australia at Adelaide, 1936
110 and 123   Gloucestershire v Derbyshire at Burton-on-Trent, 1938

FIFTY AND HUNDRED IN ONE MATCH

110 and 92   Gloucestershire v Surrey at Bristol, 1923
 99 and 187   Gloucestershire v Lancashire at Manchester, 1927
123 and 55   Gloucestershire v Kent at Dover, 1927
197 and 58   Gloucestershire v Somerset at Taunton, 1927
 50 and 134   Gloucestershire v Middlesex at Lord's, 1929
147 and 71* Gloucestershire v Yorkshire at Bradford, 1932
 70 and 133   Gloucestershire v Middlesex at Lord's, 1932
101 and 75* England v Australia at Sydney, 1933
160* and 57   Gloucestershire v Somerset at Bristol, 1936
108 and 62   Gloucestershire v Surrey at Cheltenham, 1936
 86 and 100* South v North at Lord's, 1937
121 and 63* Gloucestershire v Glamorgan at Newport, 1937
121 and 56   Gloucestershire v Glamorgan at Bristol, 1937
110 and 55   Gloucestershire v Somerset at Bristol, 1937
121 and 75   Gloucestershire v Lancashire at Manchester, 1937
 86 and 101* Gloucestershire v Somerset at Bristol, 1938

TWO FIFTIES IN ONE MATCH

58 and 82   Gloucestershire v Somerset at Taunton, 1925
56 and 52   MCC v Trinidad at Port-of-Spain, 1926
76 and 63   Gloucestershire v Lancashire at Bristol, 1927
55 and 68   Gloucestershire v Kent at Folkestone, 1928
66 and 61   Gloucestershire v Sussex at Bristol, 1928
64 and 65   Gloucestershire v Hampshire at Southampton, 1928
57 and 65   England v South Africa at Cape Town, 1931
53 and 92* Gloucestershire v Northamptonshire at Northampton, 1932
59 and 95   Gloucestershire v Sussex at Horsham, 1932
59 and 64   MCC v Victoria at Melbourne, 1933
55 and 51   Gloucestershire v Worcestershire at Worcester, 1933
63 and 87* England v South Africa at Leeds, 1935
66 and 71   Gloucestershire v Oxford University at Oxford, 1935
50 and 63   An England XI v New Zealanders at Folkestone, 1937
71 and 56   Gloucestershire v Hampshire at Southampton, 1937
66 and 64   Sir P. F. Warner's XI v England Past and Present at Folkestone, 1938
60 and 71   Gloucestershire v Middlesex at Lord's, 1939

* *Signifies not out.*

TEN WICKETS IN A MATCH

15 for 128 Gloucestershire v Worcestershire at Cheltenham, 1928
10 for 134 Gloucestershire v Sussex at Brighton, 1928
12 for 74   Gloucestershire v Glamorgan at Clifton, 1930

HUNDREDS (155)

FOR GLOUCESTERSHIRE (106)

v Surrey (11): 205*, 199, 143, 139, 135, 128, 120, 113, 110, 108, 108
v Glamorgan (10): 302*, 302, 239, 218*, 177, 156, 140, 121, 121, 119
v Lancashire (9): 271, 264, 250*, 187, 164, 155, 126*, 121, 120
v Nottinghamshire (9): 317, 217, 153, 140, 119, 118*, 116, 111, 103
v Middlesex (8): 178, 174*, 166, 134, 124, 116, 113, 104*
v Somerset (8): 197, 160, 140, 120, 116, 110, 101*, 100
v Derbyshire (6): 237, 231, 134, 134, 123, 110
v Essex (6): 244, 207, 164*, 154, 127, 105*
v Kent (6): 290, 163, 153*, 136, 123, 121
v Worcestershire (6): 265*, 178, 160, 122, 111*, 100
v Leicestershire (4): 252, 217, 206, 114
v Sussex (4): 168*, 160, 137, 116
v Yorkshire (4): 162*, 147, 135, 124
v Hampshire (3): 192, 112, 112
v Northamptonshire (3): 193, 131, 102
v Warwickshire (3): 238*, 192*, 142
v Cambridge University (2): 113*, 110
v Oxford University (1): 211*
v West Indies (1): 264
v South Africans (1): 123
v New Zealanders (1): 108

  * *Signifies not out.*

OTHER MATCHES (49)

England v Australia (9): 251, 240, 231*, 200, 177, 119*, 113, 112, 101
England v South Africa (6): 181, 140, 138*, 136, 120, 101*
England v New Zealand (4): 336*, 227, 140, 100*
England v India (2): 217, 167
England v West Indies (1): 138
MCC v South Australia (3): 145, 136, 104
MCC v Victoria (2): 203, 114
MCC v New South Wales (1): 225
MCC v Western Australia (1): 141
MCC v Western Australia Combined XI (1): 107
MCC v Border (1): 166
MCC v Transvaal (1): 132
MCC v Natal (1): 122
MCC v Cape Province (1): 126
MCC v Western Province (1): 100
MCC v British Guiana (2): 111, 106*
MCC v West Indies XI (1): 238*
MCC v Barbados (1): 281
MCC v Trinidad (1): 116
Players v Gentlemen (3): 138, 110, 106
South v North (2): 130, 100*
England v The Rest (1): 107
England XI v West Indies (1): 133
South of England v MCC (1): 184
L. H. Tennyson's XI v A E. R. Gilligan's XI (1): 120

  * *Signifies not out.*

DOUBLE HUNDREDS

336* England v New Zealand at Auckland, 1933
317 Gloucestershire v Nottinghamshire at Gloucester, 1936
302* Gloucestershire v Glamorgan at Bristol, 1934
302 Gloucestershire v Glamorgan at Newport, 1939
290 Gloucestershire v Kent at Tunbridge Wells, 1934
281 MCC v Barbados at Barbados, 1935
271 Gloucestershire v Lancashire at Bristol, 1938
265* Gloucestershire v Worcestershire at Dudley, 1934
264 Gloucestershire v West Indies at Bristol, 1933
264 Gloucestershire v Lancashire at Liverpool, 1932
252 Gloucestershire v Leicestershire at Leicester, 1935
251 England v Australia at Sydney, 1929
250* Gloucestershire v Lancashire at Manchester, 1925
244 Gloucestershire v Essex at Chelmsford, 1928
240 England v Australia at Lord's, 1938
239 Gloucestershire v Glamorgan at Gloucester, 1933
238* MCC v West Indies XI at Barbados, 1926
238* Gloucestershire v Warwickshire at Birmingham, 1929
237 Gloucestershire v Derbyshire at Bristol, 1938
231* England v Australia at Sydney, 1936
231 Gloucestershire v Derbyshire at Cheltenham, 1933
227 England v New Zealand at Christchurch, 1933
225 MCC v New South Wales at Sydney, 1929
218* Gloucestershire v Glamorgan at Bristol, 1928
217 England v India at The Oval, 1936
217 Gloucestershire v Leicestershire at Gloucester, 1937
217 Gloucestershire v Nottinghamshire at Bristol, 1934
211* Gloucestershire v Oxford University at Oxford, 1930
207 Gloucestershire v Essex at Westcliff-on-Sea, 1939
206 Gloucestershire v Leicestershire at Leicester, 1933
205* Gloucestershire v Surrey at The Oval, 1928
203 MCC v Victoria at Melbourne, 1933
200 England v Australia at Melbourne, 1929

WHERE THE HUNDREDS WERE MADE

ENGLAND

Bristol	29	Clifton	2	Horsham	1
Gloucester	12	Leicester	2	Hull	1
Cheltenham	10	Newport (Mon.)	2	Leeds	1
Lord's	10	Westcliffe-on-Sea	2	Leyton	1
The Oval	9	Bradford	1	Liverpool	1
Manchester	6	Brentwood	1	Maidstone	1
Folkestone	5	Brighton	1	Oxford	1
Nottingham	3	Cardiff	1	Peterborough	1
Taunton	3	Chelmsford	1	Portsmouth	1
Worcester	3	Derby	1	Southampton	1
Birmingham	2	Dover	1	Swansea	1
Burton-on-Trent	2	Dudley	1	Tunbridge Wells	1
Canterbury	2				

ABROAD

Australia: Adelaide 5, Sydney 5, Melbourne 3, Perth 2.
South Africa: Durban 4, Cape Town 2, East London 2, Johannesburg 1.
West Indies: Barbados 2, Georgetown 2, Port-of-Spain 1.
New Zealand: Auckland 1, Christchurch 1.

Note – Hammond made his hundreds on fifty different grounds, thirty-seven in England and thirteen abroad.

ONE THOUSAND RUNS IN MAY

May 7-31, 1927

For Gloucestershire	Innings	
	1st	2nd
v Yorkshire at Gloucester	27	135
v Surrey at The Oval	108	128
v Yorkshire at Dewsbury	17	11
v Lancashire at Manchester	99	187
v Leicestershire at Leicester	4	30
v Middlesex at Bristol	83	7
v Hampshire at Southampton	192	14

Note – During the month of May, Hammond played fourteen innings, scoring a total of 1,042 runs at an average of 74.42.

In 1927 Hammond scored over 1,800 runs in May and June, and owing to bad weather he had only one innings in the last two county matches in June.

NOTES

Playing for Gloucestershire against Surrey and Worcestershire at Cheltenham in 1928, Hammond obtained the following figures in the two matches:

	Batting	Bowling	Fielding
v Surrey	139	1 wicket for 71	10 catches
	143		
v Worcestershire	80	9 wickets for 23	1 catch
		6 wickets for 105	
Total	362	16 wickets for 199	11 catches

Probably a record week's all-roundness.

On three occasions Hammond has scored double hundreds in two consecutive innings: for England v Australia in 1929, for England v New Zealand in 1933, and for Gloucestershire v West Indies and Derbyshire in 1933.

In two successive seasons (1927 and 1928) he scored two separate hundreds in Gloucestershire–Surrey matches. Also in consecutive seasons (1923 and 1924) he obtained "spectacles" v Worcestershire.

In 1933 W. R. Hammond scored 3,323 runs (average 67.81) in the season – the fourth highest aggregate in a season.

He shares with K. S. Ranjitsinhji and H. Sutcliffe the distinction of scoring two aggregates of 3,000 runs in consecutive seasons (1937 and 1938).

W. R. Hammond is the only English batsman who has scored four innings over 300 runs.

On six occasions he has scored two separate hundreds in a match, a record shared by J. B. Hobbs.

In three seasons – 1927, 1933, 1936 – he has scored 1,000 runs in a month.

In sixteen consecutive years (1923-1939) – excluding 1926, when owing to illness he did not play – Hammond made 740 catches, an average of 46 per year. In purely English cricket he averaged 39 per year during the period.

At Bristol in 1934 and at Newport in 1939 Hammond scored 302 v Glamorgan, being not out at Bristol.

In 1936-37 Hammond scored four hundreds in consecutive innings in Australia. He scored three hundreds in successive innings four times – in 1927, 1928-29 (Australia), 1937, 1938.

In Gloucestershire matches in 1938 he scored seven hundreds in eight successive innings.

RECORDS

W. R. Hammond broke and set up many records, the following being a selection of the more important ones:

IN TEST CRICKET

1. He has scored most runs (6,883) and most hundreds (22).
2. Most runs in a series of Test matches by an English batsman (905 v Australia in 1928-29).
3. He has made (*a*) most appearances (77) in Test matches, (*b*) most catches (101), and (*c*) played most innings (127).
4. Twice he has scored two double hundreds in consecutive Test innings – 251 and 200 v Australia in 1928-29, 227 and 336 not out v New Zealand in 1932-33.
5. He is the only cricketer who has scored 700 runs in four consecutive innings in Test matches – 101 and 75 not out v Australia at Sydney, 227 and 336 not out v New Zealand at Christchurch and Auckland, all in 1933.
6. (*a*) Highest third-wicket partnership in Test cricket – 264 v West Indies at The Oval in 1939 (with L. Hutton). (*b*) Highest fifth-wicket partnership – 242 v New Zealand at Christchurch in 1933 (with L. E. G. Ames).

IN FIRST-CLASS CRICKET

1. Most catches in a season (78 in 1928) and most in a match (10 v Surrey at Cheltenham in 1928).
2. The quickest century of centuries on record – Hammond scored his first hundred in 1923 and his hundredth in 1935.
3. Record aggregate for English batsmen in tours abroad – 1,553 runs (average 91.35) in Australia in 1928-29.
4. Record aggregate for one month in English cricket – 1,281 (average 98.53) in August, 1936.
5. Thirteen hundreds in a season in Gloucestershire matches in 1938.
6. W. R. Hammond's average all-round record, statistically, is only exceeded by that of W. G. Grace, but it must be remembered that whereas the Doctor's covered over thirty full seasons, Hammond's has been compiled in sixteen, although this includes several winters abroad. Here are the latter's yearly figures: 2,939 runs, 45 wickets, 46 catches.

HERBERT SUTCLIFFE IN FIRST-CLASS CRICKET

Herbert Sutcliffe was born on November 25, 1894. In 1914 he played for Yorkshire 2nd eleven, scoring 249 runs and averaging 35.57 runs per innings. After serving in France as a commissioned officer, Sutcliffe was demobilised early in 1919, and immediately set to work to win a place in the Yorkshire team.

In a match played at Leeds in May, between Yorkshire and Sixteen Colts, Sutcliffe opened the innings for the Colts, and retired after scoring 51 runs. He was included in Yorkshire's first match (v MCC at Lord's), scored 38 out of 120, and has been an essential part of the Yorkshire team ever since.

Sutcliffe remains one of the most reliable of all English batsmen, his record in Test cricket being unique. He has an ideal temperament for "big cricket", and that probably is the reason why his figures in Test cricket are even better than his record in county matches, great as that is.

CAREER AT A GLANCE

In England

Year	Innings	Not Out	Runs	100s	Average	Other Innings over Fifty	Ducks	Catches
1919	45	4	1,839	5	44.85	7	1	22
1920	45	3	1,393	4	33.16	7	2	14
1921	43	2	1,235	—	30.12	8	3	15
1922	48	5	2,020	4	45.95	12	1	16
1923	60	6	2,220	3	41.11	15	1	24
1924	52	8	2,142	6	48.68	9	5	19
1925	51	8	2,308	7	53.67	7	4	31
1926	47	9	2,528	8	66.52	12	—	31
1927	49	6	2,414	6	56.13	11	1	25
1928	44	5	3,002	13	76.97	13	1	13
1929	46	4	2,189	9	52.11	8	1	15
1930	44	8	2,312	6	64.22	13	2	19
1931	42	11	3,006	13	96.96	9	—	19
1932	52	7	3,336	14	74.13	8	3	24
1933	52	5	2,211	7	47.04	6	2	33
1934	44	3	2,023	4	49.34	12	2	18
1935	54	3	2,494	8	48.90	12	—	16
1936	53	7	1,532	3	33.30	6	4	20
1937	54	5	2,162	4	44.12	11	1	22
1938	50	7	1,790	5	41.62	8	2	11
1939	29	3	1,416	6	54.46	1	1	7

In Australia and New Zealand

Year	Innings	Not Out	Runs	100s	Average	Other Innings over Fifty	Ducks	Catches
1923-25	18	—	1,250	5	69.44	4	1	5
1928-29	16	—	852	2	53.25	5	—	3
1932-33	21	1	1,342	5	64.04	6	1	4

In South Africa

Year	Innings	Not Out	Runs	100s	Average	Other Innings over Fifty	Ducks	Catches
1927-28	23	3	1,030	2	51.50	9	1	3

In Jamaica

Year	Innings	Not Out	Runs	100s	Average	Other Innings over Fifty	Ducks	Catches
1935-36	4	—	81	—	20.25	—	—	2
Total	1,086	123	50,127	149	52.05	219	40	431

SUMMARY

	Innings	Not Outs	Runs	100s	Average
Test matches	84	9	4,555	16	60.73
Gentlemen v Players	28	5	1,113	2	48.39
County matches	721	74	32,814	100	50.71
Other matches	253	35	11,645	31	53.41
Total	1,086	123	50,127	149	52.05
In England	1,004	119	45,572	135	51.49
Abroad	82	4	4,555	14	57.69
Total	1,086	123	50,127	149	52.05

INNINGS BY INNINGS IN TEST CRICKET

Year	Opponents	Innings	Runs	Average
1924	South Africa	64, 122, 83, 29*, 5	303	75.75
1924-24	Australia	59, 115, 176, 127, 33*, 59, 143, 22, 0	734	81.55
1926	Australia	13*, 82, 26, 94, 20, 76, 161	472	78.66
1927-28	South Africa	102, 41*, 29, 99, 25, 8, 37, 3, 51, 23	418	46.44
1928	West Indies	48, 54, 63	165	55.00
1928-29	Australia	38, 32, 11, 58, 135, 64, 17	355	50.70
1929	South Africa	26, 114, 100, 10, 37, 4, 9, 104, 109*	513	64.12
1930	Australia	29, 58*, 32, 28*, 74, 161, 54	436	87.20
1931	New Zealand	117, 109*	226	226.00
1932	India	3, 19	22	11.00
1932-33	Australia	194, 1*, 52, 33, 9, 7, 86, 2, 56	440	55.00
1933	New Zealand	0, 24	24	12.00
1933	West Indies	21, 20	41	20.50
1934	Australia	62, 24, 20, 63, 69*, 38, 28	304	50.66
1935	South Africa	61, 3, 38	102	34.00

* *Signifies not out.*

Opponents	No. of Tests	Innings	Not Outs	Runs	Average
Australia	27	46	5	2,741	66.85
South Africa	17	27	3	1,336	55.66
West Indies	5	5	—	206	41.20
New Zealand	4	4	1	250	83.33
India	1	2	—	22	11.00
Total	54	84	9	4,555	60.73

Note – Sutcliffe held 23 catches in Test cricket.

HUNDREDS IN TEST CRICKET (16)

Lord's	The Oval	Manchester	Birmingham
122 (1924)	161 (1926)	109* (1931)	114 (1929)
100 (1929)	109* (1929)		
	104 (1929)		
	161 (1930)		
	117 (1931)		

Sydney	Melbourne	Johannesburg
115 (1924)	176 (1925)	102 (1927)
194 (1932)	127 (1925)	
	143 (1925)	
	135 (1929)	

* Signifies not out.

HUNDREDS (149)

FOR YORKSHIRE (112)

v Leicestershire (10): 234*, 212, 200, 189, 187, 174, 129, 119, 109, 105
v Essex (9): 313, 255, 194, 166, 150*, 133*, 129, 125, 108*
v Lancashire (9): 195, 165, 140, 135, 135, 132, 126, 122, 106
v Surrey (9): 232, 203, 176, 138, 131*, 129, 123, 114, 101*
v Warwickshire (8): 205, 205, 153*, 142, 130, 129, 109, 102
v Middlesex (7): 235, 202, 177, 175, 120*, 104, 103
v Hampshire (6): 131, 116, 112, 107, 104*, 100
v Nottinghamshire (6): 169, 135, 111, 110*, 107, 100
v Glamorgan (5): 147*, 135*, 132*, 121, 121
v Northamptonshire (5): 150, 145, 113, 107*, 104
v Sussex (5): 270, 228, 173, 160, 122*
v Gloucestershire (4): 134, 132, 118, 110
v Somerset (4): 213, 183, 139, 136
v Worcestershire (4): 200*, 187, 138, 112
v Derbyshire (3): 182, 138, 111
v Kent (3): 230, 174, 110
v MCC (7): 171, 109*, 108, 107, 107, 102*, 101
v Cambridge University (4): 173*, 152, 108, 105
v Rest of England (2): 124, 114*
v South Africans (1): 113
v Oxford University (1): 125*

OTHER MATCHES (37)

England v Australia (8): 194, 176, 161, 161, 143, 135, 127, 115
England v South Africa (6): 122, 114, 109*, 104, 102, 100
England v New Zealand (2): 117, 109*
MCC v Tasmania (2): 188, 101
MCC v South Australia (2): 154, 122
MCC v Combined XI (1): 169
MCC v New South Wales (1): 182
MCC v Griqualand West (1): 100
Players v Gentlemen (2): 120, 107
North v South (2): 131, 110
England v The Rest (2): 227, 101

Rest of England v Lancashire (2): 139, 136
H. D. G. Leveson-Gower's XI v New Zealanders (1): 126
H. D. G. Leveson-Gower's XI v All India (2): 106, 102
MCC Australian Team v H. D. G. Leveson-Gower's XI (1): 119*
C. I. Thornton's XI v MCC South African Team (1): 114
Rest of England v Lord Cowdray's XI (1): 119

    * *Signifies not out.*

DOUBLE HUNDREDS (17)

313   Yorkshire v Essex at Leyton, 1932
270   Yorkshire v Sussex at Leeds, 1932
255   Yorkshire v Essex at Southend, 1924
235   Yorkshire v Middlesex at Lord's, 1925
234* Yorkshire v Leicestershire at Hull, 1939
232   Yorkshire v Surrey at The Oval, 1922
230   Yorkshire v Kent at Folkestone, 1930
228   Yorkshire v Sussex at Eastbourne, 1928
227   England v The Rest at Bristol, 1927
213   Yorkshire v Somerset at Dewsbury, 1924
212   Yorkshire v Leicestershire at Leicester, 1935
206   Yorkshire v Warwickshire at Dewsbury, 1925
205   Yorkshire v Warwickshire at Birmingham, 1933
203   Yorkshire v Surrey at The Oval, 1934
202   Yorkshire v Middlesex at Scarborough, 1936
200* Yorkshire v Worcestershire at Sheffield, 1935
200   Yorkshire v Leicestershire at Leicester, 1926

    * *Signifies not out.*

WHERE THE HUNDREDS WERE MADE

IN ENGLAND

The Oval	14	Cambridge	4	Bristol	1
Scarborough	14	Nottingham	4	Derby	1
Sheffield	12	Leyton	3	Dover	1
Bradford	11	Northampton	3	Eastbourne	1
Lord's	9	Bournemouth	2	Folkestone	1
Leeds	8	Brighton	2	Hastings	1
Birmingham	7	Gloucester	2	Kettering	1
Hull	7	Huddersfield	2	Neath	1
Dewsbury	5	Portsmouth	2	Oxford	1
Leicester	5	Southend	2	Peterborough	1
Manchester	5	Worcester	2		

ABROAD

Australia (10): Melbourne 4, Sydney 3, Adelaide 2, Perth 1.
South Africa (2): Johannesburg 1, Kimberley 1.
Tasmania (2): Hobart 1, Launceston 1.

    Sutcliffe has scored hundreds on forty different grounds – thirty-two in England and eight abroad. He has been most successful on two widely different grounds – The Oval (large) and Scarborough (small).

TWO HUNDREDS IN ONE MATCH

176 and 127   England v Australia at Melbourne, 1925
107 and 109* Yorkshire v MCC at Scarborough, 1926
111 and 100* Yorkshire v Nottinghamshire at Nottingham, 1928
104 and 109* England v South Africa at The Oval, 1929

FIFTY AND HUNDRED IN ONE MATCH

103 and 78   Yorkshire v Middlesex at Lord's, 1919
124 and 50* Yorkshire v Rest of England at The Oval, 1925
 59 and 115   England v Australia at Sydney, 1924
 76 and 161   England v Australia at The Oval, 1926
 71 and 131   Yorkshire v Surrey at The Oval, 1926
107 and 50* Players v Gentlemen at Lord's, 1926
 95 and 135   Yorkshire v Lancashire at Leeds, 1927
 58 and 135   England v Australia at Melbourne, 1929
161 and 54   England v Australia at The Oval, 1930
 76 and 150   Yorkshire v Essex at Dewsbury, 1930
173 and 59   Yorkshire v Sussex at Brighton, 1930
 83 and 132   Yorkshire v Gloucestershire at Bradford, 1932
 96 and 110* North v South at Manchester, 1932
138 and 56   Yorkshire v Surrey at Bradford, 1937

TWO FIFTIES IN ONE MATCH

62 and 59   Yorkshire v Surrey at The Oval, 1920
60 and 91   Yorkshire v Hampshire at Sheffield, 1921
65 and 73*   Yorkshire v Lancashire at Sheffield, 1922
61 and 62   Yorkshire v MCC at Scarborough, 1923
94 and 55*   Yorkshire v Sussex at Brighton, 1926
57 and 81   Yorkshire v Hampshire at Sheffield, 1927
59 and 57   MCC v Transvaal at Johannesburg, 1927
91 and 52   England v The Rest at Lord's, 1929
76 and 70   MCC v South Australia at Adelaide, 1928
75 and 72*   Yorkshire v Leicestershire at Sheffield, 1931
58 and 78*   Yorkshire v Gloucestershire at Bristol, 1931
63 and 69*   England v Australia at Manchester, 1934
60 and 63   Yorkshire v Oxford University at Oxford, 1934

   * *Signifies not out.*

555 FOR ONE WICKET!

On June 15 and 16, 1932, cricket history was made at Leyton when Yorkshire met Essex. Winning the toss, the Yorkshiremen took first innings, and Holmes and Sutcliffe began a partnership which lasted for seven and a half hours. During this time the famous Yorkshire pair scored 555 runs, thus beating by one run the record for any wicket set up in 1898 by two other Yorkshiremen, J. T. Brown and J. Tunnicliffe.

The latter made their runs in 305 minutes compared with 450 minutes required by Holmes and Sutcliffe, but it must be remembered that Chesterfield – the ground where Brown and Tunnicliffe made history – is a small one compared with Leyton. Moreover, in 1898 the Derbyshire attack was much weaker than the Essex bowling in 1932.

Sutcliffe's share of the new record was 313, made without a chance, and – as in 1898 – the partnership only ended when one of the batsmen made a present of his wicket to the opposition. In 1898 Brown threw away his wicket; in 1932 Sutcliffe followed his example.

It may be noted that in this game both Holmes and Sutcliffe were on the field when every ball was bowled.

NOTES

In eight consecutive English seasons (1925-1932) and four overseas tours Sutcliffe never failed to average over 50 runs per innings. During this period his average ranged from 51.50 in South Africa in 1927-28 to 96.96 in England in 1931.

On sixteen occasions Sutcliffe shared partnerships for the first wicket exceeding 250 runs – eleven times with P. Holmes, three times with Hobbs, and twice with Hutton.

Holmes and Sutcliffe scored 100 or more runs for the first wicket 74 times. In all first-class cricket Sutcliffe helped to score 100 for the first wicket on 145 occasions.

On eleven occasions Hobbs and Sutcliffe scored 100 or more runs for England's first wicket in Test matches.

During one period of 24 months – May 1931 to May 1933 – Sutcliffe scored 7,687 runs, including 32 hundreds and 22 other innings over fifty. His average for this period was 79.24.

In Yorkshire matches Sutcliffe is credited with many remarkable performances and records, of which the following may be noted:

1. His aggregate – 38,554 runs – is greater than that of any other Yorkshire batsman, D. Denton with 33,068 runs being the nearest.
2. He has averaged 8 runs per innings more than any Yorkshireman who has scored 20,000 runs.
3. On two occasions in 1924 Sutcliffe was on the field throughout a match – v Cambridge University at Cambridge and v Essex at Southend.
4. Sutcliffe has shared 38 partnerships exceeding 200 runs in Yorkshire matches – nineteen with P. Holmes, five with M. Leyland, three each with L. Hutton and E. Oldroyd, two with W. Barber, D. Denton and A. Mitchell, and one each with R. Kilner and A. Wood.
5. For Yorkshire Sutcliffe has carried his bat through the innings six times – v Essex (1920), v Hampshire (1932), v Rest of England (1933), v Worcestershire (1934), v Glamorgan (1936), and v Oxford University (1939).
6. Holmes and Sutcliffe scored a hundred or more in each innings of a match twice – 105 and 265 (unfinished) v Surrey at The Oval (1926), and 184 and 210 (unfinished) v Nottinghamshire at Nottingham in 1928.
7. In six seasons – 1925, 1928, 1931, 1932, 1935 and 1937 – Sutcliffe scored over 2,000 runs in Yorkshire matches.
8. On 98 occasions Sutcliffe has shared a first-wicket partnership of 100 runs or more for Yorkshire – sixty-nine times with P. Holmes, fifteen with L. Hutton, six with A. Mitchell, four with M. Leyland, twice with W. Barber, and once each with P. A. Gibb and E. Robinson.
9. In his first season (1919) Sutcliffe headed the Yorkshire batting averages.

SUTCLIFFE'S RECORDS

1. Sutcliffe is the only cricketer who has:–

    (*a*) Scored 50 or more runs in each innings of a Test match seven times.
    (*b*) Scored over 2,000 runs in a season in fourteen consecutive seasons (1922-1935).
    (*c*) Scored four hundreds in consecutive innings, and in the same season three other hundreds in successive innings (1931).
    (*d*) Scored two separate hundreds in a Test match twice (1925 and 1929), and also four hundreds in a Test series twice (1924-25 and 1929).
    (*e*) Averaged over 90 runs per innings for an aggregate of 3,000 runs – in 1931 (a wet season) he scored 3,006 runs, average 96.96.
    (*f*) Averaged 2,387 runs per year while scoring over 50,000 runs.

2. Sutcliffe is the oldest cricketer to (*a*) carry his bat through the innings while scoring the first hundred of the season (125 not out v Oxford University in 1939), and (*b*) score four hundreds in consecutive innings (1939). He was 44.

3. Sutcliffe is the only English cricketer who has:–

    (*a*) Scored three hundreds in consecutive innings in two Test matches.
    (*b*) Averaged 50 or more runs per innings in each of six consecutive series of England–Australia matches.
    (*c*) Scored 1,000 runs in his first ten Test matches (he did not bat in one),
    (*d*) Scored three hundreds in successive Test matches.

4. With P. Holmes he shares the record partnership for the first, or any, wicket in first-class cricket – 555 v Essex at Leyton in 1932.

5. In Australia in 1924-25 J. B. Hobbs and Sutcliffe scored over 100 runs for England's first wicket in three consecutive innings. On the third occasion they batted a whole day without being parted, scoring 283 runs.

6. Sutcliffe was the first batsman to obtain three aggregates of 3,000 runs in a season, two being in consecutive seasons.

7. In each of his first three innings in Test cricket Sutcliffe scored over 50 – 64, 122, 83 v South Africa in 1924. (P. A. Gibb equalled this record v South Africa in 1938-39, but scored fewer runs.)

8. Sutcliffe is the only cricketer who played regularly in each of the twenty-one inter-war seasons. He scored over 1,000 runs in each.

9. In Test matches v Australia Sutcliffe has averaged 66.85 runs per innings – 16.59 runs per innings more than his average for Yorkshire.

DEATHS IN THE WAR

FARNES, PILOT OFFICER KENNETH, RAF, the Cambridge, Essex and England fast bowler, was killed during the night of October 20, 1941, when the plane in which he was pilot crashed. His death at the age of 30 came as a great shock to countless friends and the whole world of cricket. After training in Canada he desired to become a night-flying pilot, and within four weeks of his return to England he met his disastrous end.

Discovered when 19 years of age by Mr Percy Perrin in an Essex Club and Ground match against Gidea Park in 1930, Kenneth Farnes took five Kent wickets for 36 runs in his second county match and was welcome in the Essex team whenever available. After three years in the Cambridge eleven, he went as a master to Worksop College, and consequently his appearances in first-class cricket were limited. His university experiences brought continuous improvement. In 1933 his work for Cambridge showed 41 wickets at 17.39 runs apiece, and he was by far the most effective amateur bowler in the country with a record of 113 wickets at 18.38 each. In a drawn match with Oxford seven wickets fell to him at a cost of 71 runs. His best performance that season – 11 wickets for 114 runs, 7 for 21 in the second innings – enabled Essex to beat Surrey by 345 runs at Southend, their first success against these opponents since 1914. In ten matches for the county, Farnes claimed 67 wickets at an average cost of 16.07, and this form brought him the honour of representing England in the first Test against Australia in 1934. Despite his fine performance – ten wickets for 179 runs – England lost by 238 runs. Strangely enough, when England won by an innings and 38 runs at Lord's. Farnes did not meet with any reward, Verity taking the honours. Farnes was not called upon again in that series, but in 1938 he took most wickets in Tests against Australia – 17 at 34.17 each.

In 1934 he was largely responsible for the first victory of Essex over Yorkshire since 1911 by taking 11 wickets for 131, Southend again proving a favourable ground for him. Thanks to Farnes dismissing seven men for 59 in the final stage, Essex brought about a great triumph by an innings and 46 runs. After a tour in West Indies knee trouble prevented Farnes from playing in 1935, but next season, for the Gentlemen at Lord's, he created a sensation by bowling Gimblett, Hammond and Hardstaff in quick succession, a stump being sent flying in each case. With four men out for 33, the Players were in danger of defeat, but, after the complete loss of Wednesday owing to rain, there was not time to reach a finish in two days. This fine work influenced the choice of Farnes to tour Australia with the team captained by G. O. Allen in the winter of 1936. Never did he bowl better than in the last Test, when he took six wickets for 96 runs in a total of 604; Australia won by an innings and 200 – a result that decided the rubber.

Farnes bowled well in Test trials at Lord's. In 1938 he gave special proof of being in great form by dismissing eight Players for 43 runs in the first innings and three in the second for 60, so doing a lot towards the Gentlemen winning by 133 runs – their second victory in this encounter since the last war. In the following winter he went with the England touring team to South Africa, where he was second in Test bowling to Verity. His 16 wickets cost 32.43 each, while in the whole tour 44 wickets fell to him at 27.43 apiece. He did the best bowling of the third Test, the only one brought to a definite finish, which gave W. R. Hammond's side the rubber. With four wickets for 29, Farnes was mainly instrumental in making South Africa follow on, and he dismissed three men for 80 in their second innings of 353, which left England still 13 runs to the good after a declaration with only four men out. Paynter, 243 – a South African record – and Hammond, 120, were the great batsmen on that occasion; their stand realised 242.

Farnes made his first appearance of the season in 1939 for the Gentlemen, and showed his fondness for Lord's by disposing of the last three Players in the course of six balls. This final effort by Farnes at headquarters recalls how well he bowled in university matches;

but in 1932 he disfigured an analysis of five wickets for 98 runs by being "called" 21 times. The discipline then brought to bear was effective in correcting a faulty approach to the crease. Nearly six feet five inches tall, Farnes, taking a comparatively short and easy run, brought the ball down from a great height with the inevitable effect of sharp lift, which made him extremely difficult to time when retaining a good length. Altogether in first-class cricket Farnes took 720 wickets at an average of 20.55 each.

A very good field near the wicket, Farnes reached many catches that would have been impossible for a man of medium height. He had no pretensions as a batsman, but in 1936, at Taunton, hit up 97 not out in two hours, Wade helping to add 149 for the last wicket; dismissing six men in the match. Farnes was largely responsible for Essex winning by an innings and 66 runs. He laughed at just failing to get a century – the ambition of every batsman.

Farnes wrote a very interesting book – *Tours and Tests*, published in 1940; among his hobbies were painting and music.

GANDAR-DOWER, MR KENNETH CECIL, was lost at sea through Japanese action in February 1944 at the age of 36. He played for Harrow against Winchester in 1927, but not in the Eton match. At Cambridge he did well in the Freshmen's Match and was a Crusader, but his time was mainly given up to tennis, at which he captained the University team. One of the most versatile players of games of any period, he was amateur squash champion in 1938, won amateur championships at fives, and played lawn tennis for Great Britain. In all, he represented Cambridge at six forms of sport: tennis, lawn tennis, Rugby fives, Eton fives, squash rackets and billiards. In fact, time hardly sufficed for their rival calls. He probably created a record when he played simultaneously in the Freshmen's Match and Freshmen's Tournament, with the connivance of the tennis but not the cricket authorities; he disappeared to play off a round during the early part of his sides's innings, with relays of cyclist friends to keep him informed as to the fall of wickets! He few a private aeroplane to India. In spite of other demands he continued to find time for cricket, making some ten appearances for the Frogs each season almost to the outbreak of war, and got many runs and wickets.

Famous as a big game shot, and extensive traveller, he introduced a team of cheetahs from Kenya jungle to London and on greyhound tracks they set up speed records. A writer of articles and books, he acted as war correspondent in various theatres of operations up to the time of his death.

NELSON, MR ROBERT PRYNNE, became a Second Lieutenant in the Royal Marines and was killed in October, 1940. His death at the age of 28 brought grief to his many cricket associates. A free left-handed batsman with good style, he made many runs when at St. George's School, Harpenden, where he became a master. He got his Cambridge Blue in 1936, and, scoring 91 at Lord's, gave a delightful display. Controlling his lively strokes by clever placing, he cut and drove to the off in beautiful style. He was unfortunate, when so near a century, to fall to a remarkable catch at short leg. Walford knocked up the ball over his shoulder and, turning round, held the catch an inch from the ground as he fell full length. His stand of 113 with N. W. D. Yardley contributed largely to the Cambridge total of 432 and the eventual victory by eight wickets. He got only a single while the 17 runs wanted were knocked off, but his highest score of the season was the best in the match. After a few appearances for Middlesex, Nelson joined Northampton-shire, and captained the eleven with such good effect in the last two seasons of first-class cricket that in 1939 a decisive win at Cambridge was followed by victory in a county match after a prolonged spell of misfortune extending over three years. The success over Leicestershire enabled Northamptonshire to rise from the bottom of the Championship, a position which they had occupied in five consecutive seasons.

Besides exercising the heartening influence of a buoyant personality, Nelson stood out as one of the chief batsmen for the county, scoring 1,031 runs, average 27.13 in 1938, and 1,078, average 32.66, next season. He showed skill in managing his attack and knew when to use his own slow left-hand bowling. His possibilities as an all-rounder were seen at The Saffrons in 1937, when for MCC he scored 183 not out and dismissed six Eastbourne batsmen for 13 runs.

He appeared for the British Empire XI several times, heading the averages with 49.83, and played also for Club Cricket Conference at Lord's last summer.

D. L. Donnelly, who organised the British Empire eleven, received this tribute to Nelson from W. C. Brown, the Northamptonshire captain from 1933 to 1935, and present honorary secretary of the county club:

"Robert Nelson's death is a tragedy. Having known him, you will appreciate what his loss means to this county. His own prowess allied to his patience with, and encouragement to, those under him worked wonders. At the end of 1937 the Northamptonshire side was a disorganized rabble. In two seasons he quietly and imperceptibly moulded them into a team which it was impossible to recognize as the same lot who had done duty before he took over the captaincy. His promise to carry on for at least one season after the war had been the mainspring of the Committee's exertions to keep the club together since county cricket lapsed. His loss has left a great gap".

Donnelly himself wrote: "Robert Nelson was a source of inspiration to us this summer. In our efforts to raise funds for the Red Cross and in our desire to provide attractive, keen cricket on the field he was always eager to help. From his quiet, unassuming manner it was impossible to gather that he was a personality in the cricket world. We who played with him admired him immensely".

From the time of his first match for St. George's School, Harpenden, at the age of 12, R. P. Nelson kept a record of his performances without a break. He played for his school for seven years, from 1925 to 1931 inclusive, and his figures, comprising his complete cricket career, were:

Batting	Innings	Not Outs	Runs	Highest Innings	Average
All games	795	118	26,008	183*	38.41
First-class matches	136	12	3,394	123*	27.37

Bowling	Overs	Maidens	Runs	Wickets	Average
All games	6,479	1,580	17,958	1,423	12.61
First-class matches	794	208	2,202	62	35.51

MAURICE TURNBULL

(Born March 16, 1906. Killed in action August 5, 1944)

By J. C. Clay

Major Maurice Joseph Turnbull, Welsh Guards, was killed in action near Montchamp in Normandy on August 5, 1944. He was 38. During an attack his company got cut off, and while making a reconnaissance he was shot through the head by a sniper and killed instantaneously.

"Maurice was such a grand person. So often have I seen him go into action and never have I seen him rattled. He was always the same: quiet, confident, thinking always of his men and disregarding all danger to himself. A really great person". This extract from a letter written from France is a straightforward appreciation of him as a soldier; there are other and sometimes more fulsome tributes paid to him. But I choose this one because it also exactly describes his leadership of Glamorgan in the days of peace, and shows that in his greatest Test of all he did not alter his style but played his own game to the end.

His Achievements

Maurice Turnbull played cricket for England and Rugby football and hockey for Wales; he also held the South Wales Squash Rackets Championship. He captained Cambridge at cricket, was a member of the Test Match Selection Committee, and Captain and Secretary of the Glamorgan Club since 1930. He was top scorer in his first innings for Glamorgan (40 v Lancashire in 1924) and was again top scorer in his last innings (156 v Leicestershire, 1939). In between those dates he made, in first-class cricket, nearly 18,000 runs, averaging 30 per innings, 29 centuries, and held over 300 catches.

These are the bare statistics; as he was only 33 when the war broke out, they are formidable achievements fully entitling him to the position he held in the public estimation – a very prominent games-player. But to those of us who knew him well mere facts and figures do him scant justice. A great player he may have been, but an astute brain made him an even greater captain – the best of his generation who never captained England – and there is little doubt that he would have become one of the game's foremost administrators. And finally, what a grand fellow.

He Started Young

I first met Maurice in July 1924, when as a boy of 17, fresh from many triumphs at Downside, he came down to play against Lancashire at Swansea. In the nets at Cardiff the day before he batted so badly that he wondered if he ought not to stand down. Luckily he played, and by making 40 in the first innings and 16 in the second he contributed very largely to a Glamorgan victory – a sensation in those days. The wicket was never easy (153 was the highest total of the four innings), but he faced that celebrated trio of bowlers, McDonald, Parkin and R. Tyldesley, all at their best, with the assurance of one accustomed to meet them regularly and with success. It was not a case of novice's luck, but of sound and mature judgment worthy of one double his age. Which encourages me to believe that, when a year or so later he sent for the majestic wine waiter of a London hotel and administered a rebuke on the quality of the claret, he was probably quite right!

Maurice, in fact, was something of an infant prodigy, but, unlike so many of them, he did not fade out after a year or two of glorious life: he became a celebrity in 1924 and remained one to the finish. 1925 found him still at Downside, and that it was almost unfair to ask schoolboys to bowl to him is shown by his figures – 1,400 runs, average 95. In 1926 he went up to Cambridge, got his Blue, and also his first century for Glamorgan. In 1927 he was unable to play owing to injury, and he hardly recovered his best form in 1928. But in 1929 he captained Cambridge and scored a thousand runs for them with an average of 50. And here the carefree days of youth ended, for in 1930 he took over the captaincy of Glamorgan.

What He Did For Glamorgan

Glamorgan became a first-class county in 1921, but, except for one good season and one or two sensational victories, failed to live up to that high-sounding title. The side sadly lacked a regular captain, and by the close of the 1929 season, during which it had no less than seven leaders, it resembled a bedraggled flock without a shepherd. Moreover, no public likes seeing its side beaten too frequently: the English are annoyed while the Welsh are hurt, but both show their displeasure in the same way – they stay away. It is not surprising, therefore, to fine that Glamorgan, with little tradition and a very small membership, were in dire financial trouble.

At this unpropitious moment Maurice took charge, comforted perhaps by the knowledge that any change he could bring about was almost bound to be for the better. And change there was, not only in the playing results but in the whole atmosphere: and this better spirit enabled the club to overcome the financial disaster which was shortly to face it.

Noteworthy success did not come all at once, but by linking Monmouthshire with Glamorgan, running a Minor Counties side, and going all out to encourage local talent, he not only found players but widened the interest; and earned his reward in 1937 when Glamorgan won 13 matches in all and finished seventh in the County Championship.

With all due respect, the general public is not frightfully interested in the doings of boards of control, committees and secretaries; it is far more concerned with what happens on the field of play between 11.30 and 6.30. But Maurice's administrative achievements were so great that they must be referred to here.

Briefly, then, Glamorgan at the end of 1932 were in debt to the tune of about £5,000, and as something drastic had to be done, and quickly, an appeal was launched. Now Glamorgan knew all about appeals to the sporting public – it had lived on them since 1921 – but nothing like this one organised by Maurice ever happened before. Whereas a faithful few contributed time and again, on this occasion nobody was left out: every town and every village was encouraged to run a dance or similar function, and to each of these Turnbull made a point of going. If the figures were known, the number of miles he danced for Glamorgan might be favourably compared with the number of runs scored by some of the side! Anyhow, this big effort realised £3,500 and, maybe, gave him valuable ideas, for whenever subsequently funds run low he found means to supplement them.

He was indeed a most efficient Secretary: always on the job, and his suggestions were based on practical knowledge and experience. He went all out, successfully, for an increased membership and paid great attention to the comfort of the spectators. In short, by 1939 he converted a shambling, shamefaced, bankrupt into a worthy and respected member of society with a bank balance of £1,000.

Batting: A Gay Adventure

For a batsman who appeared in nine Tests and held for many years what amounted to a standing invitation for the Gentlemen v Players, an average of 30 is moderate enough: honest toilers with no great gifts have attained better figures. The reason is that Maurice never made runs unnecessarily; he seldom indulged in those large, average-raising, but meaningless, innings which with everything in the batsman's favour might have been played by almost anybody who could bat at all. An innings by him invariably had some definite effect on the game, and he was at his best when others were failing or when runs were required at a pace to beat the clock. He always looked a class batsman and was always attacking the bowler.

In his early days an on-side player, he soon developed all the recognised strokes and a few of his very own, which, though they did not appeal to the purist, were extremely good value for the ordinary spectator and poison to the bowler. Contrary to some belief, bowlers do not enjoy being hit any more than a fox enjoys being hunted; but if they must receive punishment, let it be correctly administered and according to the book. I only bowled against him once: it was most disquieting!

From all of which it can be gathered that an innings by him was a delight to watch; it contained that element of impudence and unorthodoxy which added spice to the rather stolid pudding of accepted county batmanship.

It is difficult to state with certainty which were his best seasons or his best innings, but his appearances in Tests were between 1930-1936, when he played against South Africa, five times, and New Zealand, once, abroad; and against New Zealand, West Indies and India in England. His most noteworthy innings, looked at in retrospect, was perhaps his double century (one of three he made altogether) against Larwood and Voce at Cardiff in the last match of 1932 season. Three months later this celebrated pair, bowling in exactly the same way, were causing a rumpus in Australia. In the same year, on a crumbling Swansea wicket, against Parker and Goddard, and incidentally the clock, he played a magnificent match-winning innings of 119 which enabled Glamorgan to win with ten minutes to spare.

Was There A Better Captain?

I say "No"; but with the reservation that it is only human to get to appreciate highly that which you see often and at its best. Which may account, incidentally, for any element of truth in the cheap gibe that a cricketer must play for a "fashionable" county or do well at Lord's to gain official recognition. But he certainly was very good and must have been near to being selected to lead England: he did actually captain one of the sides in a Test trial match.

Above all things Maurice was a "quiet" captain: there was no fuss, no gesticulating, no shouting on the field. He never got rattled or irritable and always contrived to make the bowlers feel that, although the score board said otherwise, they were really doing pretty well. A grand "boss" to work for: I always bowled much better for him than I ever did for myself or anybody else. As with his batting, he never played for safety, but so sound was his judgement that decisions which appeared almost foolhardy at the time turned out to have been extremely well-calculated risks.

Needless to say, the professionals thought the world of him; and well they might, for nobody kept their interests more at heart or gave them sounder advice. The result was that he always got the best out of what was really a moderate side and did not have to contend seriously with those petty grievances and squabbles which may arise. For cricketers, like other public entertainers, can grow temperamental. Those who are not playing well, or are "out of luck" as it is politely called, become moody or depressed; others, while welcoming favourable notices, are deeply wounded by any hint of adverse criticism.

The example he set in the field, of course, accounted largely for his beneficial influence. He could field anywhere, but short-leg was his real position: the risks he ran and the catches he caught there had to be seen to be believed. Sometimes he literally picked the ball off the defensively held bat and at others he would hang on to red-hot drives although standing but a few yards away from the batsman. Such efforts inspired the bowler and convinced the luckless batsman that there was indeed no justice in the world.

"Quiet, confident, thinking always of his men" – yes, it is a good description.

He Will be Missed

Maurice was so closely identified with sport that his name will always be associated with it. Yet he had views and interests which covered a far wider field. He was very well read, he appreciated good music, and could talk knowledgeably on a variety of subjects, and always with a subtle sense of humour in which he abounded. With M. J. C. Allom he wrote *The Book of the Two Maurices* and *The Two Maurices Again*, giving accounts of their tours in New Zealand and South Africa. These books contain some descriptive writing which is remarkable when compared to the utilitarian accounts of cricket tours to which we are accustomed.

He will be sadly missed – by sport generally, by cricket in particular; but most of all by his friends. As one of them – and, when you have knocked about England together as much as he and I did, you get to know each other pretty well – I say farewell to a fine player, a great sportsman and a grand fellow.

The news of his death came through while Glamorgan were fulfilling one of their war-time fixtures at Cardiff Arms Park, the scene of his first century and many subsequent triumphs. And, as the crowd stood in respectful silence, perhaps the more imaginative or sentimental among them may have pictured for a fleeting instant the well-known figure out there on the field, and derived some small measure of comfort. For Glamorgan were carrying on: and he would have wished that.

HEDLEY VERITY

(Born May 18, 1905; died of wounds received in action, July 31, 1943)

By R. C. Robertson-Glasgow

Hedley Verity, Captain, The Green Howards, died of wounds a prisoner of war in Italy on July 31, 1943, some two months after his thirty-eighth birthday. He had been reported wounded and missing, and the news of his death came on September 1, exactly four years after he had played his last match for Yorkshire and, at Hove, taken seven Sussex wickets for nine runs in one innings, which finished county cricket before the war.

He received his wounds in the Eighth Army's first attack on the German positions at Catania, in Sicily. Eye-witnesses, who were a few yards from Verity when he was hit, have told the story. The objective was a ridge with strong points and pillboxes. Behind a creeping barrage Verity led his company forward 700 yards. When the barrage ceased, they went on another 300 yards and neared the ridge, in darkness. As the men advanced, through corn two feet high, tracer-bullets swept into them. Then they wriggled through the corn, Verity encouraging them with "Keep going, keep going". The moon was at their back, and the enemy used mortar-fire, Very lights and fire-bombs, setting the corn alight. The strongest point appeared to be a farm-house, to the left of the ridge; so Verity sent one platoon round to take the farmhouse, while the other gave covering fire. The enemy fire increased, and, as they crept forward, Verity was hit in the chest. "Keep going", he said, "and get them out of that farmhouse". When it was decided to withdraw, they last saw Verity lying on the ground, in front of the burning corn, his head supported by his batman, Pte Thomas Reynoldson, of Bridlington. So, in the last grim game, Verity showed, as he was so sure to do, that rare courage which both calculates and inspires.

His Bowling Art

Judged by any standard, Verity was a great bowler. Merely to watch him was to know that. The balance of the run up, the high ease of the left-handed action, the scrupulous length, the pensive variety, all proclaimed the master. He combined nature with art to a degree not equalled by any other English bowler of our time. He received a handsome legacy of skill and, by an application that verged on scientific research, turned it into a fortune. There have been bowlers who reached greatness without knowing, or, perhaps, caring to know just how or why; but Verity could analyse his own intentions without losing the joy of surprise and describe their effect without losing the company of a listener. He was the ever-learning professor, justly proud yet utterly humble.

In the matter of plain arithmetic, so often torn from its context to the confusion of judgement, Verity, by taking 1,956 wickets at 14.87 runs each in ten years of first-class cricket, showed by far the best average during this century. In the recorded history of cricket the only bowlers of this class with lower averages are: Alfred Shaw, 2,072 wickets at 11.97 each; Tom Emmett, 1,595 wickets at 13.43 each; George Lohmann, 1,841 wickets at 13.73 each; James Southerton, 1,744 wickets at 14.30 each. It might be argued that during the period 1854 to 1898, covered by the careers of these cricketers, pitches tended to give more help to the bowler than they did during Verity's time. Verity, I know, for one, would not have pressed such a claim in his own favour. He never dwelt on decimals; and, while he enjoyed personal triumph as much as the next man, that which absorbed his deepest interest was the proper issue of a Test match with Australia or of an up-and-down bout with Lancashire; and if, in his country's or county's struggle towards victory, he brought off some recondite plot for the confounding of Bradman or McCabe or Ernest Tyldesley or Edward Paynter, well, then he was happy beyond computing.

Notable Feats

Yet his bowling achievements, pressed into but overflowing the ten years of his career, were so rich and various that they here demand some concentrated notice:

He played in 40 Test matches, taking 144 wickets at 24.37 runs each. He took 100 wickets in Test cricket in a shorter period than any other English bowler.

He is the only cricketer who has taken 14 wickets in a day in a Test match, this feat being performed against Australia at Lord's in the second Test, 1934. During this match, he took 15 wickets for 104 runs, thus sharing with Wilfred Rhodes, his Yorkshire predecessor, the honour of taking most wickets in an England v Australia match.

Twice he took all ten wickets in an innings; in 1931, against Warwickshire at Headingley, Leeds, for 36 runs in 18.4 (6-ball) overs, six maidens; in 1932, on the same ground, against Nottinghamshire, for 10 runs in 19.4 (6-ball) overs, 16 maidens – a world record in first-class cricket for the fewest number of runs conceded by a bowler taking all ten wickets in an innings, and it included the hat-trick.

Again Essex at Leyton, in 1933, he took 17 wickets in one day, a record shared only by C. Blythe and T. W. Goddard.

In each of his nine full English seasons he took at least 150 wickets, and he averaged 185 wickets a season; thrice consecutively (1935-36-37) he took over 200 wickets. His average ranged from 12.42 to 17.63. He headed the first-class English bowling averages in his first season (1930) and in his last (1939), and never came out lower than fifth.

How He Began

Verity was born at Headingley, but passed his twenty-fifth birthday before he played for Yorkshire, in 1930, the year that W. Rhodes retired. Some of his earlier seasons were spent in playing as an amateur for Rawdon in the Yorkshire Council; for Accrington in the Lancashire League; and for Middleton in the Central League. He was then, as always afterwards when allowed, an all-rounder. As a batsman, his height, reach, concentration and knowledge of what to avoid raised him distinctly from the ruck of mediocrity; but, whereas his bowling included grace, his batting had only style. The former was nature embellished by art; the latter was art improved by imitation.

As a bowler, Hedley Verity stands, and will stand, with his illustrious predecessors in the Yorkshire attack: Edmund Peate (1879-1887), Robert Peel (1882-1899), Wilfred Rhodes (1898-1930) – the dates indicate the time of their respective playing careers – but Verity was not a slow left-hander in the accepted sense, and he used to reject comparison with Rhodes so far as method was concerned, saying: "both of us are left-handed and like taking wickets; let's leave it at that."

Verity's mean pace was what is called slow-medium; on fast pitches, often about medium; and he would send down an inswinging yorker of an abrupt virulence not unworthy of George Hirst.

Naturally, on wet or crumbled or sticky pitches, he reduced pace and tossed the leg-spinner higher, but even here his variety of pace and of angle of delivery was remarkable. He was a born schemer; tireless, but never wild, in experiment; as sensitive in observation as a good host, or as an instrumentalist who spots a rival on the beat; the scholar who does not only dream, the inventor who can make it work.

Comparison of Giants

Just how good a bowler was he? In relation to rivals in his own craft but of an earlier day, such a question is useless except to amuse an idle hour or to excite an idle quarrel. We can only say that, in his own short time, he was the best of his kind. In England, day in day out, he may never have quite touched the greatness of Robert Peel, Colin Blythe or Wilfred Rhodes. In Australia, neither in 1932-3 or 1936-7, did he perplex their batsmen quite as J. C. White perplexed them in 1928-29, but, as a workman-artist, he will take some beating. H. B. Cameron, that fine wicket-keeper-batsmen of South Africa, playing against Yorkshire in 1935, hit him for three fours and three sixes in one over; but very rarely did a batsman survive a liberty taken with Verity. He had, besides, a wonderful skill in restoring the "rabbits", early and with little inconvenience, to the hutch.

If a touchstone of Verity's greatness be needed, there is D. G. Bradman, the most inexorable scorer of runs that cricket has yet seen, whose Test match average against England stands at 91.42 in 46 innings. I think it was Verity who kept that average under 150. He was one of only three or four bowlers who came to the battle with Bradman on not unequal terms (*haud impar congressus!*); and Bradman was reported as saying: "I think I know all about Clarrie (Grimmett), but with Hedley I am never sure. You see, there's no breaking-point with him".

Beating the Best

Verity timed his blows. In the fifth Test match, at Sydney, early in 1933, Australia, 19 runs behind on the first innings, lost Victor Richardson for 0. Woodfull and Bradman added 115; Larwood, injured, had left the field – and that particular Larwood never came back – then Verity deceived Bradman in flight, bowled him for 71 and went on to take five for 33 in 19 overs and win the match. In the earlier Tests, amid the fast bowling and the clamour, not much had been heard of Verity, except as a rescuing batsman. But, when the last pinch came, there he was to relieve the weary line; very Yorkshire.

Verity never allowed the opinion that Bradman was less than a master on damaged pitches, refusing to stress the evidence of his own triumph at Lord's in 1934 (Bradman c and b Verity 36; c Ames b Verity 13) and referring to Bradman's two innings of 59 and 43 in 1938 against Yorkshire at Sheffield, "It was a pig of a pitch", he said, "and he played me in the middle of the bat right through." Maybe Verity's opinion of Bradman was heightened by a natural generosity in its giver, but on this matter I think that Verity had reason to know best.

As an all-round fielder, Verity was no more than sound, but to his own bowling, or at backward point, he sometimes touched brilliance; and there sticks in the memory the catch that he made at Lord's in 1938, when McCabe cut one from Farnes crack from the bat's middle.

Opened England Batting

As a batsman for Yorkshire, Verity was mostly kept close to the extras. His build and reach suggested power and freedom, but it remained a suggestion; and he was analogous to those burly golfers who prod the tee-shot down the middle to a prim 180 yards. A casual observer might have mistaken Verity for Sutcliffe a little out of form, for he seemed to have caught something of that master's style and gesture, and, like Sutcliffe, he could be clean bowled in a manner that somehow exonerated the batsman from all guilt. He never quite brought off "the double", though in 1936 he took 216 wickets and scored 855 runs. But he had the sovereign gift of batting to an occasion. In the 1936-37 visit to Australia, G. O. Allen could find no opening pair to stay together, so he sent in Verity with C. J. Barnett in the fourth Test, at Adelaide, and they put up partnerships of 53 and 45. Not much, perhaps; but the best till then. In all Test matches, his batting average was close on 21; nearly 3 units higher than his average in all first-class cricket.

Verity had the look and carriage of a man likely to do supremely well something that would need time and trouble. His dignity was not assumed; it was the natural reflection of mind and body harmonised and controlled. He was solid, conscientious, disciplined; and something far more. In all that he did, till his most gallant end, he showed the vital fire, and warmed others in its flame. To the spectator in the field he may have seemed, perhaps, a little stiff and aloof; but among a known company he revealed geniality, wit, and an unaffected kindness that will not be forgotten.

There was no "breaking-point" with Verity; and his last reported words: "Keep going", were but a text on his short and splendid life.

HEDLEY VERITY WITH THE BALL

ALL FIRST-CLASS MATCHES

Year	Runs	Wickets	Average
1930	795	64	12.42
1931	2,542	188	13.52
1932	2,250	162	13.88
1932-33 (Australia)	698	44	15.86
1932-33 (New Zealand)	64	1	64.00
1933	2,553	190	13.43
1933-34 (India)	1,180	78	15.12
1934	2,645	150	17.63
1935	3,032	211	14.36
1936 (Jamaica)	360	16	22.50
1936	2,847	216	13.18
1936-37 (Australia)	1,043	38	27.44
1937	3,168	202	15.68
1938	2,476	158	15.67
1938-39 (South Africa)	937	47	19.93
1939	2,509	191	13.13
Total	29,099	1,956	14.87

COUNTY CHAMPIONSHIP MATCHES

Year	Runs	Wickets	Average
1930	595	52	11.44
1931	1,703	138	12.34
1932	1,856	135	13.74
1933	1,826	153	11.93
1934	1,210	79	15.31
1935	2,196	161	13.63
1936	1,942	153	12.69
1937	2,270	157	14.45
1938	1,523	111	13.72
1939	2,095	165	12.69
Total	17,216	1,304	13.20

BOWLING SUMMARY

In England	Runs	Wickets	Average
Yorkshire (County Championship)	17,216	1,304	13.20
Yorkshire (Other matches)	4,150	254	16.33
Tests (v Australia)	930	38	24.47
Tests (v South Africa)	250	12	20.83
Tests (v West Indies)	207	9	23.00
Tests (v New Zealand)	166	6	27.66
Tests (v India)	228	15	15.20
Gentlemen v Players	515	27	19.07
Other first-class matches	1,155	67	17.23

In Australia

Tests	726	21	34.57
Other first-class matches	1,015	61	16.80

In South Africa

Tests	552	19	29.05
Other first-class matches	385	28	13.75

In New Zealand

Tests	64	1	64.00

In India

Tests	387	23	16.82
Other first-class matches	793	55	14.41

In Jamaica

First-class matches	360	16	22.50
Total	29,099	1,956	14.87

10 WICKETS IN AN INNINGS

10 for 36 Yorkshire v Warwickshire at Leeds, 1931
10 for 10 Yorkshire v Nottinghamshire at Leeds, 1932

9 WICKETS IN AN INNINGS

9 for 60 Yorkshire v Glamorgan at Swansea, 1930
9 for 44 Yorkshire v Essex at Leyton, 1933
9 for 59 Yorkshire v Kent at Dover, 1933
9 for 12 Yorkshire v Kent at Sheffield, 1936
9 for 48 Yorkshire v Essex at Westcliff, 1936
9 for 43 Yorkshire v Warwickshire at Leeds, 1937
9 for 62 Yorkshire v MCC at Lord's, 1939

8 WICKETS IN AN INNINGS

8 for 33 Yorkshire v Glamorgan at Swansea, 1931
8 for 39 Yorkshire v Northamptonshire at Northampton, 1932
8 for 47 Yorkshire v Essex at Leyton, 1933
8 for 43 England v Australia at Lord's, 1934
8 for 28 Yorkshire v Leicestershire at Leeds, 1935
8 for 56 Yorkshire v Oxford University at Oxford, 1936
8 for 40 Yorkshire v Worcestershire at Stourbridge, 1936
8 for 42 Yorkshire v Nottinghamshire at Bradford, 1936
8 for 80 Yorkshire v Sussex at Eastbourne, 1937
8 for 43 Yorkshire v Middlesex at The Oval, 1937
8 for 38 Yorkshire v Leicestershire at Hull, 1939

17 WICKETS IN A MATCH

17 for 91 Yorkshire v Essex at Leyton, 1933

15 WICKETS IN A MATCH

15 for 104 England v Australia at Lord's, 1934
15 for 38   Yorkshire v Warwickshire at Bradford, 1936
15 for 129 Yorkshire v Oxford University at Oxford, 1936
15 for 100 Yorkshire v Essex at Westcliff, 1936

14 WICKETS IN A MATCH

14 for 54   Yorkshire v Glamorgan at Swansea, 1930
14 for 83   Yorkshire v West Indies at Harrogate, 1933
14 for 78   Yorkshire v Hampshire at Hull, 1935
14 for 132 Yorkshire v Sussex at Eastbourne, 1937
14 for 92   Yorkshire v Warwickshire at Leeds, 1937
14 for 68   Yorkshire v Glamorgan at Bradford, 1939

13 WICKETS IN A MATCH

13 for 83   Yorkshire v Hampshire at Bournemouth, 1930
13 for 97   Yorkshire v Warwickshire at Leeds, 1931
13 for 145 Yorkshire v Sussex at Hove, 1931
13 for 102 Yorkshire v Northamptonshire at Leeds, 1933
13 for 97   Yorkshire v Leicestershire at Leeds, 1935
13 for 107 Yorkshire v Hampshire at Portsmouth, 1935
13 for 88   Yorkshire v Worcestershire at Stourbridge, 1936

12 WICKETS IN A MATCH

12 for 117 Yorkshire v Glamorgan at Swansea, 1930
12 for 74   Yorkshire v Nottinghamshire at Leeds, 1932
12 for 53   Yorkshire v Derbyshire at Hull, 1933
12 for 137 Yorkshire v Kent at Dover, 1933
12 for 96   Yorkshire v MCC at Lord's, 1935
12 for 114 Yorkshire v Leicestershire at Hull, 1939
12 for 85   Yorkshire v MCC at Lord's, 1939

11 WICKETS IN A MATCH

11 for 69   Yorkshire v Derbyshire at Leeds, 1932
11 for 74   Yorkshire v Essex at Dewsbury, 1933
11 for 92   Yorkshire v Middlesex at Lord's, 1933
11 for 153 England v India at Madras, 1933-34
11 for 73   Yorkshire v Middlesex at Leeds, 1935
11 for 111 Yorkshire v Glamorgan at Swansea, 1936
11 for 90   Yorkshire v Nottinghamshire at Bradford, 1936
11 for 181 Yorkshire v MCC at Scarborough, 1937
11 for 88   Yorkshire v Cambridge University at Cambridge, 1938
11 for 66   MCC v Griqualand West at Kimberley, 1938-39

HEDLEY VERITY WITH THE BAT

ALL FIRST-CLASS MATCHES

	Innings	Not Outs	Runs	Highest Innings	Average
1930	14	3	164	32	14.90
1931	25	6	234	28	12.31
1932	33	7	494	46	19.00
1932-33 (Australia)	17	3	300	54*	21.42
1932-33 (New Zealand)			(did not bat)		
1933	42	6	620	78*	17.22
1933-34 (India)	18	4	384	91*	27.42
1934	41	11	520	60*	17.33
1935	45	8	429	35	11.59
1936 (Jamaica)	4	—	195	101	48.75
1936	41	14	855	96*	31.66
1936-37 (Australia)	22	2	180	31	9.00
1937	37	14	335	76	14.56
1938	34	11	385	45*	16.73
1938-39 (South Africa)	12	2	245	39	24.50
1939	30	15	263	54	17.53
Complete batting figures	415	106	5,603	101	18.13

COUNTY CHAMPIONSHIP MATCHES

	Innings	Not Outs	Runs	Highest Innings	Average
1930	11	2	133	32	14.77
1931	18	3	183	28	12.20
1932	25	4	384	36*	18.28
1933	36	3	572	78*	17.33
1934	22	4	309	38	17.16
1935	28	3	256	35	10.24
1936	29	9	535	89	26.75
1937	24	9	229	76	15.26
1938	20	5	176	41	11.73
1939	27	13	248	54	17.71
Total	240	55	3,025	89	16.35

Note – In all Yorkshire matches Verity scored 3,883 runs at an average of 17.89.

OUTSTANDING ACHIEVEMENTS

1. During his career (1930-39) Hedley Verity took 1,956 wickets at a cost of 14.87 runs apiece; scored 5,603 runs, average 18.13; and made 238 catches.

2. Verity played in 40 Test matches, taking 144 wickets for 24.37 runs each, and scoring 669 runs at an average of 20.90.

3. Verity took 100 wickets in Test circket in a shorter period than any other English bowler.

4. He is the only cricketer who has taken 14 wickets in a day in a Test match, this feat being accomplished against Australia at Lord's in 1934. During this match he took 15

wickets for 104 runs, thus sharing with Wilfred Rhodes, his Yorkshire predecessor, the honour of taking most wickets in an England v Australia match.

5. Twice Verity took all ten wickets in an innings. His ten wickets for 10 runs for Yorkshire against Nottinghamshire at Leeds in 1932 is a world record for the fewest number of runs conceded by a bowler taking ten wickets, and it included the hat-trick. Full analysis was 19.4–16–10–10. In his last three overs he took seven wickets for 3 runs. The next best average recorded for ten wickets is ten for 18 runs by G. Geary for Leicestershire against Glamorgan at Pontypridd in 1929. In seven other innings Verity took nine wickets.

6. Against Essex at Leyton in 1933, seventeen wickets fell to him in one day – a record shared with Colin Blythe and Tom Goddard.

7. Verity started County Championship cricket at Hull on May 31, 1930, against Leicestershire, taking in the match eight wickets, four for 15 runs in the second innings; and finished at Hove on September 1, 1939, the last day of county cricket before war began, with this remarkable analysis: 6–1–9–7. His first-class début for Yorkshire was in a friendly against Sussex on May 21, 1930.

8. In each of his nine full English seasons he took at least 150 wickets, and his average was 185 wickets per season; three times consecutively he took over 200 wickets in a season (1935-36-37).

9. In each of his ten seasons of first-class cricket Verity's average ranged from 12.42 to 17.63, in 1930 and 1934 respectively. He headed the English bowling averages in his first season, a feat which he accomplished again in 1939, and he never came out lower than fifth, twice being second, five times third, and once fifth. In his nine full English seasons his wickets ranged from 150 to 216.

10. In 1936, Verity took his 100th wicket in first-class cricket as early as June 19 – a record for a Yorkshireman, though J. T. Hearne (Middlesex) in 1896 took his 100th wicket on June 12. In 1931, C. W. L. Parker (Gloucestershire) equalled this, and next day, A. P. Freeman (Kent) completed 100 wickets.

11. Verity bowled 766 balls in two innings at Durban in the final Test match against South Africa in March, 1939 – a record number of balls by one bowler in a match. This match was the longest ever played – drawn after ten days.

12. Verity scored only one century in first-class cricket – for Yorkshire against Jamaica at Sabina Park, Jamaica, in 1936.

13. At Adelaide, in January 1937, he opened the batting with C. J. Barnett, and scored 19 out of 53 for the first wicket, the best start to an innings for England in the first four Tests of that rubber.

14. Verity's best all-round season was in 1936, when he took his greatest number of wickets, 216; and made his highest aggregate of runs, 855.

15. During Verity's ten years Yorkshire won the County Championship seven times; in six of these seasons Brian Sellers led the team.

The Best Bowler this Century

According to the list in 1940 *Wisden* of bowlers who have taken 1,500 wickets, Hedley Verity, with 1,956 wickets in ten years at 14.87 each, showed by far the best average during this century, and in the history of cricket the only bowlers of this class showing lower averages are:

Alfred Shaw, 2,072 wickets at 11.97 in 34 years.
Tom Emmett, 1,595 wickets at 13.43 in 23 years.
George Lohmann, 1,841 wickets at 13.73 in 15 years.
James Southerton, 1,744 wickets at 14.30 in 22 years.

As the careers of these four famous professionals extended from the year 1854, when Shaw began, to 1898, when Lohmann finished, their remarkable records were achieved during an era when bowlers received far more help from the pitches than was the case during the period in which Verity earned such great reward for his skill.

Four Great Yorkshiremen

Of slow left-handers comparable with Verity as England players, his three predecessors of similar type in the Yorkshire eleven stand out:

Edmund Peate (1879 to 1887), 1,063 wickets at 13.86.
Robert Peel (1882 to 1899), 1,754 wickets at 16.21.
Wilfred Rhodes (1898 to 1930), 4,188 wickets at 16.71.
Hedley Verity (1930 to 1939), 1,956 wickets at 14.87.

These four Yorkshiremen excelled through a period of sixty-one years.

Other Notable Exponents

Other slow left-handers of this category in chronological order have been:

John Briggs, Lancashire (1879 to 1900), 2,200 wickets at 16.10.
Colin Blythe, Kent, killed in the last war on November 8, 1917, aged 38 (1899 to 1914), 2,506 wickets at 16.81.
C. W. L. Parker, Gloucestershire (1903 to 1935), 3,278 wickets at 19.48.
Frank E. Woolley, Kent (1906 to 1938), 2,068 wickets at 19.86.
J. C. White, Somerset (1909 to 1937), 2,358 wickets at 18.56.

AN AUSTRALIAN APPRECIATION

By Don Bradman

(Sent by Airgraph from Adelaide, November 23)

The present war has already taken heavy toll of gallant men who, after faithfully serving their countries on the cricket field in peace-time, have laid down their lives for a greater cause. Of those who have fallen, Hedley Verity was perhaps the most illustrious and from the Dominion of Australia I feel it my sad duty to join with cricketers of the Motherland in expressing sorrow that we shall not again see him on our playing fields.

It could truthfully be claimed that Hedley Verity was one of the greatest if not THE greatest left-hand bowler of all time. Most certainly he could lay just claim to that honour during the 1918-1939 period. No doubt his Yorkshire environment was of great assistance for left-hand bowling seems to be in the blood of Yorkshiremen. It is one of their traditions and inalienable rights to possess the secrets of the art.

Although not a young man from a cricketing standpoint when the call came, Verity was little if any beyond the zenith of his powers. He was always such a keen student of the game, and his bowling was of such a type, that brains and experience played perhaps a greater part in his successes than natural genius.

Although opposed to him in many Tests, I could never claim to have completely fathomed his strategy, for it was never static nor mechanical.

Naturally he achieved his most notable successes when wickets were damp. Nobody privileged to witness that famous Test at Lord's in 1934 (least of all the Australian batsmen) will forget a performance to which even the statistics could not do justice. But it would be ungenerous to suggest that he needed assistance from the wicket, as his successful Australian tours will confirm. The ordinary left-hander who lacks the vicious unorthodox finger-spin of the Fleetwood-Smith variety, needs uncommon ability to achieve even moderate success in Australia, yet Verity was the foundation stone of England's bowling in both countries during his era.

Apart from his special department of the game, Verity could also claim to be a remarkably efficient fieldsman close to the wicket where safe hands and courage are greater attributes than agility. Add this to the fact that once he opened a Test match innings for England, not without success, and we have a fairly general picture of a really fine player.

Those of us who played against this swarthy, capless champion (I never remember having seen him wear a cap) probably appreciated his indomitable fighting spirit even more than his own colleagues. We knew, when war came, that he would plainly see his duty in the same way as he regarded it his duty to win cricket matches for Yorkshire no less than England.

During our association together I cannot recall having heard Verity utter a word of complaint or criticism. If reports of his final sacrifice be correct, and I believe they are, he maintained this example right to the end.

His life, his skill, his service all merited the highest honour, and with great sorrow I unhesitatingly pay humble tribute to his memory.

YORKSHIRE CAPTAIN'S TRIBUTE

By Major A. B. Sellers

My association with Hedley began during my first game for Yorkshire second eleven at Middlesbrough in June 1930. Being new to that type of cricket, I kept a careful eye on what was going on and the fellows with whom I was playing. Our "skipper", Brigadier R. C. Chichester-Constable, DSO, duly introduced me to all the team, and my first impressions of Hedley were that he was a very quiet type of man who did not say very much but had a great sense of humour.

At that time he played for the first eleven when Rhodes was not available, and at the end of the season he topped the English bowling averages. There was nothing in his conversation to lead anyone into thinking that he had ever played for the first team. However, as the game progressed I kept my eye on him and found him to be quite casual about everything he did. There was no fuss; he just got on with the game. An occasional appeal to the umpire; if it was refused he made no signs whatsoever as to what he thought about it.

I came away from that game thinking that there was a man who would not be driven by anyone into doing anything that he did not want to do, and how true that turned out to be. When I became "skipper" of the first eleven I found that Hedley would work hard all day and every day in his own little way, no fuss or hurry or rush. If you studied his bowling action closely, that gave you an insight to his character – steady, even, coupled with determination.

I look back upon my cricketing days with Hedley and find that he never really changed from the Hedley I first met at Middlesbrough on that June day. His advice was sound and good. He was prepared to sit and talk with anyone on most subjects, and of course, like most of us, would talk cricket all day and all night. His bowling always improved, and, as we all know, he played for England so often that he became an automatic choice like Hobbs and Sutcliffe in their day.

His character and disposition never changed amidst all his many triumphs; he just remained Hedley Verity. On many occasions, in order to win a match, I turned to him and said, "Well Hedley, everything depends on you". That was sufficient; although he might be very tired indeed, his determination to help the side win was something to wonder at. If I had given him a direct order, a lot of that determination would not have come to the fore. It was not his nature to be ordered about, although he never gave any outward sign of resentment. His answer was to keep going along in his own sweet way. He knew what he could do and what he could not do.

Hedley lost his life playing a game of war, and I can guarantee that as he lay wounded on the battlefield in Sicily the grim determination to go forward prevailed more than ever before. His death draws a line under his name and the finish to a remakable cricket career. England and Yorkshire lose a great player and I a great friend. I feel honoured to have met and played with him.

OTHER WARTIME DEATHS

BARTHOLOMEW, MR ARTHUR CHURCHILL, of Oxford, the oldest cricket Blue, passed away on March 29, 1940 some five weeks after completing his 94th year. Born on February 21, 1846, at Lympstone, Devon, he was more than a year senior to the Rev. E. E. Harrison Ward, the oldest Cambridge Blue, who died on Easter Monday, five days earlier. The passing of Mr Bartholomew, Oxford, and Mr Ward within this brief space of time left Mr F. A. MacKinnon, Chief of the Scottish Clan, the senior living Blue of either University. He and Mr Ward both played for Cambridge in the "Cobden" match to which further reference will be found in the biography of Mr Harrison Ward.

It is of interest to add here that Mr MacKinnon, now aged 92, who went to Australia in 1878 with the team captained by Lord Harris, is the oldest living cricketer who has represented England. H. C. Maul, another member of that touring side, died early in the year; Mr A. J. Webbe, Middlesex president for so many years, who reached the age of 86 in January, five weeks before his death, played in the only "test" of that tour.

A. C. Bartholomew went to Marlborough and appeared at Lord's against Rugby in 1865, when he was described as "a good bat with patient defence". Going to Trinity College, Oxford, he headed the University averages in 1867, but did not play against Cambridge until the following season, when, in a match of small totals, he scored 7 and 11 not out. He was regarded as one of the best cover points of the day and a contemporary described "his quick returns straight to the wicket, after running hard to the ball, as a pleasure to see".

For some years failing eyesight prevented him reading, but Mr. Bartholomew retained such a keen interest in the game that as recently as the summer of 1939 he listened eagerly while his daughter read the scores and descriptions of matches. He greatly prized the disc from a blotter presented to him when a master at Durham School. It is inscribed "To A. C. B., Durham School, for his score of 166 against Northumberland at Newcastle-upon-Tyne, June 3, 1871." At one time he played for his native county, Devon, and he organised a cricket week at Reading, where he owned a private school, and coached E. H. Bray, L. P. Collins and J. F. Ireland before they gained their Blues. He founded a cricket eleven and called them "Guinea-pigs" – because, he said, "they had no tail". One of his scholars was Major-General Sir Walter Kirke, Inspector-General of the Home Forces. His son, Major-General A. W. Bartholomew, was appointed Lieutenant of the Tower of London in March 1939.

CAHN, SIR JULIEN, Bart., who died on September 26, 1944, at his home, Stanford Hall, Loughborough, Leicestershire, aged 62, was a great supporter of cricket. The eleven which he captained played good matches each season at his West Bridgford ground, and he took teams on many tours, including Jamaica, 1929, Argentine, 1930, Denmark and Jutland, 1932, Canada, USA and Bermuda, 1933, Ceylon and Singapore, 1937 and New Zealand, 1939. Twice he was President of the Nottinghamshire club and defrayed the cost of building new stands at Trent Bridge; he also provided a covered practice shed so that the county players could keep in training throughout the winter. He represented Leicestershire for some years on the Advisory County Cricket Committee and attended the meetings at Lord's dealing with the post-war plans. Keenly interested in hunting, he was at different times Master of the Burton Woodland, Pytchley and Fernie Hunts. Sir Julien inherited a fortune from his father and, apart from business interests, devoted his life to sport and philanthropy.

MR COLE, FREDERICK LIVESAY, an occasional wicket-keeper for Gloucestershire from 1879, when he first appeared at Lord's, died at Sheffield on July 1, 1941. While he would be a useful cricketer to pass muster with W. G. Grace as captain, a more interesting point than his prowess behind the stumps concerns his age. In *Scores and Biographies* the date of his birth is given as October 4, 1856. This tallied with *Wisden* until 1934, when the year was altered to 1842 – a possible misprint due to re-setting "Births and Deaths". Yorkshire papers described how "he joined the Federal Army when 19 and served four years under Generals McClellan and Phil Sheridan"; also that during the Franco-Prussian war he was in the siege of Paris and that he was with Sir Archibald Forbes, the war correspondent, in the Russo-Turkish war before being invalided home in 1876. Inquiries at the Bristol Grammar School, where he was said to have been educated, failed to trace him, neither can any mention of his name between 1837 and 1887 be found in the Registers of the Yeovil district, though his birthplace was recorded as Ilminster, together with the date, at the time of his first match at Lord's.

In response to a question in the *Bristol Evening Post*, Mr Harry Wookey wrote that he played "with Fred Cole for Schoolmasters against Bath Association in 1880, when I was only 17 years of age. Fred Cole was born on October 4, 1856". Another Bristol cricketer confirmed that opinion. Yet it was asserted in the Yorkshire papers that "he had three centenarian brothers all living" and that he was 90 when he retired from the Sheffield Gas Company, though no one knew his exact age and thought he was 60: "George", one of the "centenarian" brothers, could not be traced in Bristol.

Fred Cole made plenty of runs in club cricket, and H. E. Roslyn, of the Gloucestershire County Committee, recalls that "Fred Cole scored the first hundred ever made on our county ground and I kept wicket while he did so" – that was the year before the formal opening in 1889.

COLMAN, SIR JEREMIAH, JP, died on January 15, 1942, aged 82, at his home, Gatton Park, Reigate, Surrey. A year before he underwent a severe operation from which he never fully recovered, but until a few hours before his passing he attended to business and signed cheques. That was characteristic of the close interest and unflagging zeal which he applied to cricket. The game was in his blood, for his father was one of eleven brothers who played as a team in Norfolk about a century ago. He used to say that he had no chance of cricket at school, but at St John's College, Cambridge, he learned to bowl with such good results that he became captain of the College XI in 1882.

He never played first-class cricket, but occupied his leisure watching all the best matches, particularly those between England and Australia and the Universities. A member of the Surrey Club from an early age, he became President in 1916, retained the office for seven years, and remained an enthusiastic Vice-President until his end. Famous in commerce as the "Mustard Millionaire", he related that his father, one of the founders of the firm – J. and J. Colman – once said that "the family fortunes were made, not from the mustard people ate, but from what they left on their plates." He had a splendid collection of cricket pictures and was one of the best-known growers of orchids in the world.

GAINFORD, LORD, who died at Headlam Hall, near Darlington, on February 15, 1943, aged 83, captained Durham County Club from 1886 to 1891, and continued playing cricket until he was 74, when, as he wrote to Mr Bulmer, secretary of Durham County C.C., "Inability to take a quick run forced me to give up the game". His last innings was 9 not out. Joseph Albert Pease, known as "Jack", joined the county club on its formation in 1882 and was the oldest member. He played for the county until 1892, having a batting average of nearly 19, and he kept wicket. In 1878 he went to Cambridge, captained Trinity College cricket eleven, played in the polo team, was master of the drag hounds, and sometimes played Rugby for the University without getting his Blue. One of the proudest moments of his life, he used to relate, was when "I took a catch in the outfield off W. G. Grace, who shook me by the hand". That was in a match for MCC, of which he was a member for many years.

During thirty-four years in the House of Commons he became Postmaster-General, President of the Board of Education, Chancellor of the Duchy of Lancaster, and Chief

Liberal Whip. He was raised to the Peerage in 1916 and took an active part in House of Lords debates. Shortly before his death he recalled an occasion in the Commons some fifty years ago when a fray arose over the Home Rule for Ireland Bill, and he used the Rugby tackle to keep Dr Tanner out of the "maul" until John Burns separated the combatants.

HARRISON, GEORGE PICKERING, a typical Yorkshireman of the old school, died, aged 78, at Scarborough, his home, in September, 1940. He came to the front when first given a trial in 1883, and his career ended almost as suddenly in 1892 from the effects of injury. A right-handed fast bowler, he appeared for Colts of the North at Lord's and clean bowled nine Colts of the South – five of them in six balls – at the low cost of 14 runs. Chosen for the Yorkshire XI without delay, he excelled in his first county match at Dewsbury against Kent; he bowled unchanged through both innings with Ted Peate, the slow left-hander. Harrison came out with eleven wickets for 76 runs as his share in disposing of the visitors for totals of 65 and 79, so surpassing the work of his England colleague. The distinction of being chosen for Players against Gentlemen at Lord's followed, and in the whole season he took 100 wickets at an average cost of 13 runs, his Yorkshire record being 88 at less than 12 runs each.

After such an exceptional start, Harrison suffered an injury when throwing in from the deep field. This accident occurred when he was acting as substitute, and it necessitated the abandonment of fast bowling. Reducing his speed, he met with some success, but could not retain his place in the County eleven.

In Yorkshire Council cricket for Bowling Old Lane he took 878 wickets, and in three seasons for Idle 215 fell to him, the average cost for all this effective work being about 9 runs a wicket. He enjoyed a day of great success for the North and East Ridings of Yorkshire touring in the South, taking 15 Chiswick Park wickets for 38 runs.

Known familiarly as "Shoey", an abbreviation of his trade as shoemaker, Harrison often umpired in first-class cricket, and at every Scarborough Festival in recent years his favourite corner in the pavilion was alive with humour and reminiscences. Of many tales told of him, one mentioned in *The Cricketer* goes back to his first match at Lord's. When accepting the invitation to play for the Colts he asked Mr Henry Perkins, the MCC secretary, to meet him at King's Cross as he had never been to London.

ANDREW DUCAT

By Hubert Preston

The sudden death at Lord's, on July 23, 1942, of Andrew Ducat, Surrey batsman of high talent and effective execution, England international Association footballer, captain of a cup-winning Aston Villa team, and in recent years cricket coach at Eton, came as a shock to countless friends and admirers. A man of delightful disposition, quiet and unassuming, he endeared himself to all who met him and as a reporter of games, after giving up activity in the field, he revealed his character in unbiased, accurate descriptions of matches and criticisms of the high-class players who were his successors. The last time I saw Ducat he sat a few feet from me in the Press box at Lord's. He passed a pleasant remark as he joined his fellow writers and we watched the cricket, intent on the players in the field. Next thing I heard of him, a few days afterwards, was his final and fatal appearance at the crease, where we had seen other cricketers play the game with all the energy of keen sportsmen such as always identified his own efforts.

That Ducat should collapse and die, bat in hand, was the last thing anyone would have expected of such a well-set-up, vigorous, healthy-looking and careful-living man. Evidence of those in the field proved clearly that he expired directly after playing a stroke and as he prepared to receive another ball, for he was dead when carried to the pavilion. The medical report gave the cause of death – failure of a heart that showed signs of definite weakness.

The loss of Ducat in this way may be attributed to the war, but for which there would not have been the Home Guard for him to join. His Surrey Unit were playing their Sussex brothers-in-arms, and Ducat was not out at lunch-time. On resuming, he raised his score from 12 to 29 before the catastrophe occurred.

Class Company

Born on February 16, 1886, at Brixton, in South London. Ducat died at the age of 56, cut off when apparently in the full glow of health. In his youth and subsequently he lived at Southend, and there he played cricket well enough to induce him to become a member of The Oval staff in 1906. Good batting for the Surrey second eleven soon took him to the first-class rank in which he stood out conspicuously from 1909 to 1931. In his first full season he gave proof of his ability by scoring a century at The Oval against Somerset and averaging 27 for an aggregate of 1,080. From that form he never looked back. At a time when Surrey possessed a wealth of attractive fast run-getting batsmen anyone might have failed to shine in the splendour revealed by Tom Hayward, Jack Hobbs, Ernest Hayes, Alan Marshal the Australian giant, and J. N. Crawford; but Ducat bore comparison with all this array of talent. In 1910, a summer of indifferent weather, he played the highest innings for Surrey – 153 against Yorkshire at The Oval. He got the runs, in his best display so far, in less than three hours, his driving, pulling, leg-hitting and cutting being brilliant. In seventy-five minutes he and Hobbs put on 121, and Hitch helped in such a hurricane of hitting that 127 runs came in an hour. That performance, typical of Ducat at his best, was the forerunner of many grand displays. Naturally, and by preference, a forcing batsman, he used his height, five feet ten inches, in perfect forward strokes which brought the drive into action with a minimum of effort, such was the accuracy in timing of his pendulum swing of the bat propelled by strong arms and shoulders.

Highest Innings

Altogether he put together 52 three-figure innings, all for Surrey, the highest being 306 not out against Oxford University at The Oval in 1919. This really sumptuous display, at the expense of a by no means poor bowling side, was not the only proof that he had not suffered from lack of first-class cricket during the four years of war. In fact, that season he scored 1,695 runs, entirely for Surrey, and his 52.96 placed him sixth in the batting averages for the whole country. Before this happy resumption of cricket, accidents caused serious checks in Ducat's career. An injured knee kept him out of several matches in 1912, and when football began that winter a broken leg incapacitated him completely. It seemed that he might be a permanent cripple, but a silver plate in the shin bone enabled him to recover so thoroughly that the loss of 1913, so far from prejudicing his prospects, preceded a prosperous season, for in 1914 he hit four centuries in championship matches and with 42 came out second to Hobbs – in superb form – in the Surrey averages. Again misfortune overtook him when in net practice prior to the start of the 1924 season a ball from Hitch fractured a bone in his arm, and "Mac", as he was called by all his friends, could not play during that summer.

Meanwhile the highest honour of the game rewarded Ducat. For the good reason of his skill and resolution in playing fast bowling and his unfailing courage he was picked for the Leeds Test match against Australia in 1921, when J. M. Gregory and E. A. McDonald struck terror into the hearts of many batsmen. Speed and sure hands in deep fielding also influenced his selection. Honoured with the distinguished place of number four, Ducat still found himself dogged by ill-luck, for, in playing McDonald, the shoulder of his bat was broken and the ball went to the slips, where Gregory held the catch, while the splinter of wood fell on the stumps, shaking off a bail. So Ducat was doubly out. Carter, the Australian wicket-keeper, handed to Ducat the piece of wood – a souvenir which could not compensate the batsman for such an unfortunate dismissal; and he stumped Ducat in the second innings! That was in keeping with the lamentable way in which everything went against England in that series of Tests against W. W. Armstrong's team, the first three wickets falling very cheaply in each of three consecutive defeats which cost England the rubber.

A Great Sequence

When incapacitated in 1924, Ducat became manager of the Fulham football club, and while holding that appointment he was not always available for Surrey, but he invariably resumed full of runs. Sometimes Hobbs was kept idle by strains, and during one such period in 1928 Ducat scored 119 at Old Trafford, 179 not out against Warwickshire at The Oval, 101 not out and 42 at Horsham against Sussex, and 208 off the Essex bowlers in consecutive matches – 649 runs for twice out. His chief partners were Sandham, 282 retired ill, who helped to add 299 in three hours and a half against Lancashire, and Shepherd, 145 not out, who hit so finely at Leyton that 317 runs came for the third wicket in two hours and three-quarters. All this happened in seventeen days; and with a fifth century, 121 against Somerset, Ducat, although not playing in every engagement, made 994 runs in less than six weeks.

Until the end of the 1930 season, in which he scored 1,593 runs, average 45.51, in Championship matches, and 2,067, average 49.21, in all engagements, with 218 against Nottinghamshire at The Oval, the best of five three-figure innings, Ducat maintained his full value as batsman and fieldsman in the Surrey team; but he fell off next year and, his agreement with Surrey having expired, he was called upon to retire. So he said farewell to first-class cricket, at the age of 44, carrying with him the good will of colleagues and the satisfaction of having gained the highest honours at both cricket and Association football. Altogether in first-class cricket he scored 23,373 runs at an average of 38.31.

At Eton

No wonder that when a vacancy occurred at Eton for a coach that choice should fall upon a professional who himself might have been modelled on the style associated with R. A. H. Mitchell, the Lytteltons, the Studds, and carried on through succeeding generations on Agar's Plough – the forward stroke with the bat kept straight by the left elbow pointing to mid-off. Certainly the controlled off-drive, the square and late cut could be shown by this capable coach for young talent to copy, and the quiet, explanatory manner of Ducat during five years earned popularity which will make his place on the Eton cricket staff difficult to fill. In the Public School section, Mr C. H. Taylor, master of cricket at Eton, Oxford Blue from 1923 to 1926, who played for Leicestershire, pays a tribute to Andrew Ducat.

Just as at cricket so at football Ducat prospered during a long career which reached its climax in the years immediately following the protracted war break. When with Woolwich Arsenal in the old days at Plumstead he played right-half for England in all three internationals in the spring of 1910, and ten years later, when he was with Aston Villa, I saw him in two of the most remarkable matches ever played. On the day Wales visited Highbury in March 1920, pools of water stood on the sodden mud to which the turf was reduced, and the Welshmen literally splashed their way to victory by the odd goal in three. With Arthur Grimsdell on the left and Barson in the centre, Ducat completed a grand half-back line. A month later, on a sea of mud at Hillsborough, Sheffield, England, when apparently losing, fought back so valiantly that they beat Scotland by the odd goal in nine. Games of that kind live in the memory even if, by force of circumstance, they do not provide a display of perfect football. Ducat played his last international in 1921 against Ireland, England winning by two clear goals at Sunderland, and that summer came his England honour at cricket. Yet, of all his distinctions. Ducat must have prized most that April afternoon in 1920 at Stamford Bridge, when, as captain of Aston Villa, he received the Football Association Cup as reward for a hard-fought victory by the only goal scored over Huddersfield Town. In this way Aston Villa won the Cup for the sixth time, a record which Blackburn Rovers equalled in 1926.

So far as I have seen, no one has mentioned any parallel case to the suddenness of the Ducat tragedy, with death of a first-class cricketer occurring on the field of play, but in 1870, at Lord's, John Platts, the Derbyshire fast bowler, playing for MCC against Nottinghamshire, bowled a ball which caused the death of George Summers. The batsman received so severe a blow on the head that he died from the effects of the accident a few days afterwards. Pitches at Lord's at that time were notoriously bad, and, as the outcome of this accident, far more attention was paid to the care of the turf. Over the grave of George Summers at Nottingham the MCC erected a memorial tablet "testifying their sense of his qualities as a cricketer and regret at the untimely accident on Lord's ground".

HEARNE, JOHN THOMAS, one of the finest bowlers the game has ever known, who played for Middlesex and England, died on April 17, 1944, after a long illness at Chalfont St. Giles in Buckinghamshire, the place of his birth on May 3, 1867. From 1891 to 1914 he held a prominent place among the very best bowlers, and finished his career with a record of 3,060 wickets, an aggregate surpassed only by W. Rhodes, 4,188, A. P. Freeman, 3,775, and C. W. L. Parker, 3,274.

Right-hand medium-pace, he took a fairly long run up to the wicket, and it would be difficult to recall a bowler with a more beautiful delivery, made as his left hand pointed down the pitch. Standing nearly five feet eleven inches, he brought the ball over with a perfectly straight arm, and such was his command of length that a batsmen might wait many overs for a ball from which he was certain to score. Even on the best of wickets he got on quite an appreciable off-break and, varying his pace cleverly, he used at times to send down a fast ball which swung with his arm. On a bowler's wicket he could dismiss the strongest sides, and on one of the crumbling pitches which occasionally bothered batsmen forty years ago he was simply unplayable. The leading bowler, not only for Middlesex but for the MCC in the days when the club programme included quite a number of first-class matches, he was called upon for an amount of work which would have tired out most men in a very few years, but his splendid methods served him so well that a career in first-class cricket, which opened in 1888, did not close until the 1914 war, and in 1923 at Edinburgh he took six wickets for 64 for Middlesex against Scotland.

Jack Hearne came of famous cricket stock. A newphew of old Tom Hearne and of George Hearne, both of whom played for Buckinghamshire and Middlesex, before the latter went to Catford Bridge, he was a cousin of G. G. Hearne, Frank Hearne and Alex Hearne, all distinguished professionals for Kent. His brother, Walter Hearne, also a good Kent bowler, broke down through knee trouble when he looked to have many years of success before him and then became scorer, as did Alec Hearne when his cousin died.

J.T. used to relate how chance helped him into first-class cricket. "I was born and bred in Buckinghamshire, which, in my young days, did not have a county club or I might have got no further than that", but A. J. Webbe, having watched him on the Evelyn School ground, where Hearne coached, asked him to play in a Middlesex Colts match, and then against the Australians in 1888. He took two cheap wickets, but a further invitation for the next match against Surrey could not be accepted, one of the masters advising him that he was not qualified. By living with his brother in London this difficulty was overcome, but he still worked at Evelyn School during the summer, and in June 1890 he received a telegram asking him to play for Middlesex that very day.

"I turned over my pitch-mowing job to someone else, dashed to the station, and from a newspaper found that Middlesex were playing Nottinghamshire. When I arrived at Lord's just before lunch-time I saw 99 for no wicket on the score-board. Not until reaching the dressing-room did I learn that my side were batting. If Nottinghamshire had been at the wickets I should not have played in that match. I remember Mr Webbe leaning out of the pavilion window as I passed down the little alley to the player's room and saying, 'It is quite all right but I nearly left you out.'

"When Nottinghamshire batted near the end of the day I bowled J. A. Dixon with a real beauty, and as we left the field the great Arthur Shrewsbury said to me, 'Well bowled, young 'un. If you bowl like that you will get someone else out tomorrow' – and I did – six for 62. That is how I began my connection with Middlesex and, barring a couple of matches missed through a strained arm, I went on playing for the county without a break until I retired from county cricket in 1914."

Next season at Lord's he took 14 Yorkshire wickets for less than five runs apiece, and in 14 matches the capture of 118 wickets for ten runs each put him top of the first-class averages. From that proof of ability he went steadily ahead, and in 1893 the fine reward of 212 wickets fell to him, while his aggregate rose to 257 wickets at 14.72 each in 1896: only Tom Richardson with 246 at 16.79 each fared nearly as well. In fact, that was Hearne's greatest year. He appeared for the Players against the Gentlemen at The Oval and Lord's, but those matches were comparatively of small importance in view of his doings against the Australians. With 56 wickets at 13.17 runs apiece he far surpassed the work of any other bowler during the summer against the touring team, though his rivals for fame included Robert Peel, George Lohmann, John Briggs, Tom Richardson and A. D. Pougher. He finished at Hastings for South of England by taking six Australian wickets for eight runs in 17 overs, 13 of them maidens. He also made 29 not out, the next highest score of his side to 53 by W. G. Grace. In the three Test matches that season he took 15 wickets at 14.1 each, dividing the honours with Tom Richardson, whose 24 wickets cost 18.7 each. At Lord's his bowling was not required until the second innings, when he sent down 36 overs for 76 runs and five wickets; but at The Oval, where Australia scored only 119 and 44, he took six wickets for 41 and four for 19 – ten in all for six runs apiece, so having a large share in winning the rubber match by 66 runs.

An even more memorable game that season was at Lord's in June when MCC avenged the disaster of 1878 by dismissing the Australians for 18, one less than the club fell for eighteen years previously. On that occasion Spofforth and Boyle brought undying fame to our visitors – in fact, made a name for Australian cricket in England. The revenge performance earned most renown for A. D. Pougher, who, going on to bowl with three wickets down for 18, disposed of five batsmen without a run being scored off him and the innings ended without addition. Yet Hearne took a greater part than did the Leicestershire bowler in gaining a single innings victory for MCC. In the first innings he sent down eleven overs for four runs and four wickets, and in the second, when the Australians put together a total of 183, he took at a cost of 73 runs, all nine wickets that fell – the visitors batted one man short, Giffen being ill.

In the winter of 1897 he went to Australia with A. E. Stoddart, and his nine wickets for 141 in the first Test at Sydney helped materially in England's only win in the rubber of five matches, which all told yielded him no more than twenty victims. He took part in three Test matches in 1899 – the first experience of a rubber of five in England – and at Leeds set up a record that still stands by doing the only hat-trick against Australia in a Test match in England. His victims were those formidable opponents Clem Hill, Sidney Gregory and M. A. Noble. He did three other hat-tricks; and another big achievement when meeting Australians occurred nine years earlier for Middlesex at Lord's, where he bowled W. L. Murdoch, the Australian captain and great batsman, for nought in each innings.

Besides coaching during several winters in India for the Maharaja of Patiala, Jack Hearne went to South Africa in 1891-92 and, with the two left-handers, J. J. Ferris and "Nutty" Martin, as colleagues, he claimed 163 wickets for less than seven runs each. South African batting was very weak at that time, and Ferris, the Australian, then qualified for Gloucestershire, with 235 wickets at 5.91 each, eclipsed Hearne's performance.

In fifteen different seasons Jack Hearne took over a hundred wickets; three times more than 200. From 1891 to 1904 the only exception was 1901, when the number fell to 99, partly, no doubt, because that was his best batting year with 522 runs, average 20.88. In addition to his exceptional effectiveness with the ball. Hearne score 7,137 runs, average 11.04, and held 382 catches, mostly close to the wicket, where he was a dependable and often a brilliant fieldman. Statistics vary as to J. T. Hearne's total wickets, but the runs scored and catches held are from Sir Home Gordon's *Form at a Glance*.

From 1891 to 1924 Hearne was engaged at Lord's, and the MCC voted him, in lieu of a benefit, the sum of £500. Middlesex gave him the match with Somerset in 1900 as a benefit, and in 1920 he was elected a member of the Committee of the Middlesex County Club, an honour for a professional previously awarded only to William Gunn by Nottinghamshire in 1906. When acting as coach during many seasons at Oxford, Jack Hearne endeared himself to the University undergraduates in the same way that all who met him were impressed by the modest kindliness that marked his whole life.

To be on friendly terms with "J.T." for fifty years, as I was, meant an education in cricket and good fellowship.   H.P.

KITCAT, MR SIDNEY AUSTYN PAUL, an accomplished batsman for Marlborough in 1885 and 1886, and for Gloucestershire when able to appear in country cricket until 1904, died at Esher, aged 73, on June 17, 1942. In 1896, at Bristol, he scored 77 not out, helping W. G. Grace, who made 301, put on 193 for the ninth wicket against Sussex. Another good display was in 1897, when his 93 not out off the Middlesex bowling was largely responsible for his inclusion in the Gentlemen's XI against Players at The Oval. Business prevented him from playing much first-class cricket, but he was very prominent in the Esher eleven for many seasons, and when over 70 years of age he captained the veterans against the colts in their annual match. He went to Portugal in 1895 and 1898 with teams captained by Mr T. Westray.

When captain of Marlborough in 1886, his second season in the eleven, and Rugby won by 37 runs, Kitcat was the victim of an irregularity which certainly influenced the result. At that time Law 14 read:

> "The bowler may not change ends more than twice in the same innings, nor bowl more than two overs in succession."

The Rugby bowlers and the umpires were responsible for the error. C. W. Bengough, the Rugby captain, went on to bowl twice at each end, and in his first over when bowling a second time from the pavilion end, Kitcat, when well set, was caught at cover-point for 27. The umpires after discussion gave Kitcat out, and Mr Perkins, the MCC secretary, supported the verdict; but Bengough, after completing the over, was not allowed to bowl another ball in the innings. Much argument and correspondence ensued, and largely because of this incident the law was amended in 1889, allowing a bowler "to change ends as often as he pleases provided that he does not bowl two consecutive overs in one innings".

Kitcat played Rugby football for the College and Marlborough Nomads; also hockey for Marlborough, Moseley, Middlesex, Surrey, the South, and England.

MacLAREN, MR ARCHIBALD CAMPBELL, very prominent in cricket during a long career lasting altogether from 1887 to 1923, died on November 17, 1944; when nearly 73 years of age. An immaculate batsman possessing the grand manner, he would have gained still higher renown on the playing field but for periods of poor health and the calls of business. Expert knowledge, obtained by careful study of every intricacy of the game, besides experience in leading his school, his county, the Gentlemen and England, might have made him supreme as captain, but he lacked the buoyant optimistic temperament so necessary for complete success in cricket and was easily upset by disagreement with selectors in being given players whom he did not consider suitable to the occasion.

To satisfy his own exacting ideas of perfect play and leadership, as described in his book *Cricket Old and New*, he required the position of dictator in order to pick his own eleven and control them with expectation of ready response to his every word or gesture. Unfortunately for MacLaren, such idealistic conditions were never forthcoming on the big occasion, but the responsibility for this rested partly with him more than once, when he was one of the selectors. Facts bear this out, as will be seen; but in batting he accomplished much, and will remain a magnificent figure in the eyes of all who saw him making runs.

He will always be remembered for his 424 for Lancashire against Somerset at Taunton in 1895, a first-class score that stood unbeaten for nearly thirty years and has been exceeded only by Don Bradman, who now holds the record with 452 not out, and W. H. Ponsford in Australia. For choice as a Test captain he remains unrivalled, having in the course of eleven years led England in 22 matches, and his 35 appearances against Australia have been surpassed only by Hobbs and Rhodes during far longer periods. Often unfortunate when commander in these big events, he never led England to victory in a rubber, but showed his exceptional knowledge of the game when, having asserted that he could pick a side capable of beating the all-conquering Australian team of 1921, he fulfulled his prophecy by selecting and captaining eleven amateurs, who, at Eastbourne at the end of August, gained a victory by 28 runs after being 130 behind on the first innings. In that climax to his career in England he retained his superb figure, though white hair suggested more age than the approach of his fiftieth birthday. He finished his intimate association with first-class cricket by acting as manager to S. B. Joel's team that toured South Africa in 1924-25.

Son of Mr James MacLaren, for many years Hon. Treasurer of Lancashire CC, Archie MacLaren was born on December 1, 1871, at Manchester, and began his important cricket life auspiciously when only fifteen years of age by scoring 55 and 67 for Harrow against Eton in 1887. He finished four years in the eleven as captain, and with 76 in a total of 133 off the Eton bowlers at Lord's showed such form that a month later he appeared in country cricket, and in his first match for Lancashire played a fine innings of 108 against Sussex at Hove.

His obvious powers took some time to ripen, but within a few years he reached the front rank of batsmen. Possessed of great resource, he could, according to circumstances, play a cautious or a brilliant game that made him splendid to watch from the ringside. Standing erect with bat raised well behind him, he was ready to receive any kind of delivery and would force the ball away with every sort of powerful stroke.

Captain of Lancashire from 1894 to 1896, and again from 1899 to 1907, he reasserted himself in 1921 as described, and in the winter of 1922-23, at the age of 51, when leading an MCC side in New Zealand, he scored 200 not out at Wellington in a representative match. Besides his record 424, he three times exceeded two hundred for his county, 226 at Canterbury against Kent in 1896, next year 244 in the same fixture, and 204 at Liverpool against Gloucestershire in 1903. From 1893 to 1909 he frequently appeared for Gentlemen against Players, making 728 runs in these games with an average of 45; in 1903, when he and C. B. Fry added 309 in three hours for the third wicket without being separated, he scored 168.

Eight times in England and once in Australia he obtained over 1,000 runs in a season, his largest aggregate being 1,886 (average 42) in the summer of 1903. He enjoyed pronounced success on the Sydney ground, where in the winter of 1897-98 against New South Wales he scored 142 and 100 in one match, 109 and 50 not out a month later against Australia, 61 and 140 in another match with New South Wales, and 65 in the last Test. He also got 124 against Australia at Adelaide and 181 at Brisbane, altogether six centuries on that tour, in which he made 1,037 runs, average 54.57, in first-class matches. No wonder that MacLaren is still talked of in Australia, and especially at Sydney, for his wonderful batting as an object lesson for everyone.

In Test matches between England and Australia he made 1,931 runs, four times reaching three figures and averaging nearly 34. Twice in the "nineties" he toured Australia with teams led by A. E. Stoddart, and in the winter of 1901-2 he himself took out a side; but in Test matches this team, like the second captained by Stoddart, suffered four defeats and gained only one victory. In three home seasons – 1899, 1902 and 1909 – England, captained by him, won only two of fourteen engagements and lost each rubber. MacLaren visited America with K. S. Ranjitsinhji's team in 1899, and the Argentine in 1911-12 with the MCC side led by Lord Hawke, and he also played in India.

He astonished everyone by taking S. F. Barnes, of small experience in first-class cricket, on the 1901-2 tour in Australia. Yet he could not keep that wonderful bowler in the Lancashire county eleven, and in 1909 he failed to persuade his county colleague, Walter

Brearley, then the best of our fast bowlers, to accept a last-moment invitation to play for England at Lord's.

Opinions differ as to the ability of MacLaren as a captain. Everyone agrees that he held strong views and was loath to depart from them even if his leadership actually suffered. In fact, it appeared more than once that he pursued ways that showed up some curious decision of selection committees in carrying out their duties.

Undoubtedly he found occasional brilliant inspirations, born of his exceptional knowledge of cricket, but he committed some blunders difficult to understand in a man of his experience. A notable illustration of his erratice disposition occurred at The Oval in the Test match of 1909. To begin with, having the final word in the composition of the eleven, he decided, despite fine weather and a hard wicket, that England should take the field without a good fast bowler, John Sharp, of Lancashire, being preferred to Buckingham, of Essex. Then, with the score 9 and one man out, he took Sidney Barnes off in favour of Sharp, mainly a batsman, and kept D. W. Carr, a googly bowler, aged 37, on at one end for an hour and a half, an action for which it would have been difficult to excuse anybody. That was the match in which Warren Bardsley made 136 and 130.

Another lapse from wisdom was at Old Trafford in 1902, when he sent to deep square leg Fred Tate, always a short slip: and that historic dropped catch brought about England's defeat in a match upon which the rubber depended – only victory in that engagement could have prevented the honours going to Australia. Yet such was his knowledge of the game that at Leeds in 1904 he gave Yorkshire first innings, and Lancashire, by avoiding defeat in George Hirst's benefit match, went through the season unbeaten and were champions for the only time under MacLaren's captaincy.

An incident in which MacLaren took strong action was of a kind without precedent or repetition, so far as known, and it aroused severe criticism. In July 1907 at Lord's on the second day the paying public were admitted although saturated turf showed no sign of drying and any cricket was extremely unlikely. Yet the stumps were set, and when pulled up at quarter to five some of the crowd, after demonstrating in front of the pavilion, walked across the pitch. After prolonged discussion between the captains – Gregor MacGregor led Middlesex – and umpires, this statement was handed to the Press by A. C. MacLaren himself: "Owing to the pitch having been deliberately torn up by the public, I, as captain of the Lancashire Eleven, cannot see any way to continue the game, the groundsman bearing me out that the wickets could not be again put right. – A. C. MacLaren." As described in the 1908 *Wisden*, the match was accordingly abandoned. Rolled next morning for the regulation ten minutes, the pitch showed little trace of the damage.

Naturally such a cricketer received many tributes to his ability. In January 1896 the Lancashire club elected him a life member and presented him with a gold watch and chain in recognition of his record score and three successive hundreds hit in the course of eight days at the end of August that same season – 152 at Old Trafford against Nottinghamshire, 108 at Lord's against Middlesex, and 135 at Leicester. Ten years later Lancashire made him a special presentation. In September 1921 he accepted an appointment to coach young players of the county, but an injured knee compelled his resignation early in the 1923 season.   H.P.

PARKIN, HENRY CECIL, who died on June 15, 1943, in a Manchester hospital, earned the description of cricket's chief comedian. Of medium height and rather slim, eccentric in character and in action, he brought every known device besides his own special jugglery into his right-arm bowling. For variation of pace and spin he ranked with the cleverest of attackers, his high-pitched very slow ball being specially deceptive. He chiefly used the off-break, but overdid experiments, so that the most experienced captain found it difficult to place a field able to check run-getting when punishing batsmen faced Parkin. Yet a well-known amateur said in The Oval pavilion that he would like Parkin on his side because he took wickets quickly and left his batsmen plenty of time in which to get runs.

League cricket occupied much of Parkin's time before he started for Lancashire by taking 14 Leicestershire wickets at Liverpool in 1914, and after the last war his Saturdays were engaged similarly; but in 1919 at Old Trafford he helped materially in the defeat of Yorkshire by taking 14 wickets at exactly 10 runs apiece, the margin, curiously enough, being 140 runs – precisely the number hit off Parkin in 60 overs. Chosen for The Players at The Oval and Lord's, he did nothing exceptional, but next season at The Oval he dismissed nine Gentlemen, six clean bowled, in the first innings for 85 runs, a performance which influenced his choice for the team which visited Australia that winter. Except at Adelaide, where five wickets fell to him for 60 runs in the first innings, Parkin, like other England bowlers during that ill-fated tour, suffered severely in the Tests: but he took most wickets, and 73 at 21 runs apiece during the whole campaign. Next summer he again proved the most effective bowler when appearing in four of the five Tests, but England were still far below their best, and altogether Parkin was on the losing side eight times without knowing the satisfaction of victory when playing for his country against Australia.

Of the drawn match at Old Trafford, where he took five wickets for 38 runs, he told a story well suited to his own character. "H. L. Collins, the Australian, batted seven hours for 40 runs. A spectator shouted to our skipper, Lord Tennyson, 'Eh, Tennyson, read him one of your poems!' – and with the very next ball I got Collins lbw." When England batted a second time, 187 runs ahead, Parkin went in first, and so could claim the proud privilege of being one of the few men who have opened both the bowling and batting for England.

He was in the eleven which beat South Africa by an innings and 18 runs at Edgbaston in 1924. Arthur Gilligan, six wickets for 7 runs, and Maurice Tate, four for 12, dismissed the visitors for 30 – the lowest Test match total – and again shared the honours when South Africa following-on, scored 390.

Parkin was at his best about that time, being the most effective Lancashire bowler both in 1923 and the following season, with records of 209 wickets at 16.94 runs apiece, and 200 at the low cost of 13.67 each. His deadliness declined in 1925, when his analysis showed 121 wickets at 20.79 each. E. A. MacDonald and Richard Tyldesley were then his superiors in the powerful Lancashire attack. His benefit match with Middlesex that season realised £1,880. In 1926 he played in eleven county matches, taking 36 wickets at 15.13 apiece, and so shared in Lancashire gaining the championship of the first time since 1904; but his finish in important cricket in his 40th year was regrettable – due to a breach with the Lancashire authorities. Altogether in first-class cricket Parkin was credited with 1,060 wickets at an average cost of 17.49.

As a batsman he was useful at times and showed good style, but his average of 11.47 denotes uncertainty to a high degree. Parkin told his early cricket life in a very vivacious book and, in conformity with his cricket gestures, was a conjurer of no mean ability. Born on February 18, 1886, he was 57.

PEEL, ROBERT, who died at Morley on August 12, 1941, aged 84, was one of the finest all-round cricketers of any time. Primarily he was a bowler, the second in the remarkable succession of slow left-handers – Edmund Peate, Peel, Wilfred Rhodes and Hedley Verity – who rendered such brilliant service to Yorkshire over a period of sixty years. Born at Churwell, near Leeds, on February 12, 1857, "Bobby" Peel first played for his county in 1882, when Yorkshire were singularly rich in bowling talent, so that he had to wait several years before attaining real distinction. Still, being a capital fieldsman, especially at cover-point, and a punishing left-handed batsman, he kept his place in the team, and when Peate's connection with the county ceased in unhappy circumstances Peel came to the fore. For nine seasons, with his fine length, easy action and splendid command of spin, this sturdily built left-hander regularly took over 100 wickets for Yorkshire, his county total amounting to 1,550 at an average cost of 15 runs each. He was often a match-winner. In 1887 he took five Kent wickets for 14 runs in an innings and, with 43 runs in a low-scoring match, helped largely in a victory by four wickets. In the same season eleven Leicestershire wickets fell to him for 51 runs at Dewsbury, five in the first innings for four runs. A year later he took eight Nottinghamshire wickets in an innings for 12 runs, while 1892 five wickets for 7 runs in an innings and eight for 33 in the match against Derbyshire at Leeds was a startling performance. He did even better in 1895 against Somerset, 15 wickets falling to him in 36 overs for 50 runs, nine for 22 in one innings causing a sensation. At Halifax in 1897, a month before his county career ended, Peel dismissed eight Kent men in an innings for 53 runs, his match average showing eleven for 85; this performance gave Yorkshire an innings victory with 103 runs to spare in two days. Peel's full return in bowling in first-class cricket was 1,754 wickets at 16.21 runs apiece.

He did some remarkable things in Test matches with Australia, against whom he played for England twenty times. At Sydney in 1894, Australia, set to get 177, hit off 113 of the runs for the loss of two wickets before stumps were drawn on the fifth day. The result then appeared a foregone conclusion, but strong sunshine followed heavy rain during the night. Peel slept through the storm. Astounded when he saw the drying pitch, he said to the English captain, "Mr Stoddart, gie me t' ball", and with "Johnny" Briggs, the Lancashire left-hander, also at his best, the remaining eight batsmen were disposed of for 53 runs. So England gained an extraordinary win by 10 runs after facing a total of 586, then a record for these Tests, the previous best being Australia's 551 at The Oval in 1884. Peel's analysis in the fourth innings was six for 67. Peel also enjoyed a large share in winning the rubber match of that tour. He took seven wickets, scored 73 in a stand for 152 with A. C. MacLaren, and, following a grand partnership for 210 by Albert Ward, of Lancashire, and J. T. Brown, of Yorkshire, the two best scorers in England's first innings hit off the runs, the victorious total being 298 for four wickets. In 1896 at The Oval, with conditions very difficult for batsmen, he and J. T. Hearne got rid of Australia for 44. Peel's share in the victory by 66 runs was eight wickets for 53 runs, and his last innings analysis six wickets in 12 overs for 23 runs – some revenge for getting "a pair". Hearne's figures showed ten wickets for 60. That was the last match in which W. G. Grace led England to success over Australia.

Besides his great achievements as a bowler, Peel scored over 11,000 runs for Yorkshire, hitting ten centuries. His highest innings was 226 not out against Leicestershire in 1892, and four years later he obtained 210 not out in a Yorkshire score of 887 against Warwickshire at Edgbaston, a total which remains a county match record. Peel and Lord Hawke, who added 292 for the eighth wicket, F. S. Jackson and E. Wainwright all reached three figures in that innings – then a record, four centuries in an innings. In 1889, the year in which the over was increased from four balls to five, Peel put together 158 in the Yorkshire second innings at Lord's, but yet was on the losing side, a brilliant 100 not out in eighty minutes by T. C. O'Brien taking Middlesex to victory by four wickets with ten minutes to spare. Yielding 1,295 runs for thirty-six wickets, the game produced a record aggregate for a match in England at the time.

Peel went four times to Australia, in 1884-5, 1887-8, 1891-2 and 1894-5, and in Test matches with Australia he took 102 wickets for less than 17 runs each. He also figured in Players teams against the Gentlemen from 1887 to 1897, taking in those games 48 wickets at a cost of 16 runs apiece.

He scored 1,206 runs and took 128 wickets in all matches in 1896, the year before his remarkable career came to an end. Sent off the field by Lord Hawke during a game at Bramall Lane and suspended for the remainder of the 1897 season, he was not seen again in the Yorkshire team. He did, however, appear for an England XI against Joe Darling's Australian side at Truro two years later, taking five wickets. His benefit match at Bradford in 1894 realised £2,000.

REMNANT, GEORGE HENRY, who died in February, 1941, aged 92, was the oldest living Kent professional cricketer and a friend of Charles Dickens. Born at Rochester on November 20, 1848, he made the first of 42 appearances for his county at the age of 20. His best score for Kent was 62 against Hampshire at Canterbury in 1877, but in minor cricket he hit 238 and 211 not out for Chilham Castle. He was a magnificent fieldman. As a young man, Remnant played in the village team at Gad's Hill, Higham. He used to relate how, when playing in the meadow adjoining the house where Charles Dickens lived, he drove a ball in the back of a trap in which sat the novelist's children and their governess. The pony bolted; Remnant dropped his bat, dashed in pursuit, and checked the runaway before any harm could be done.

REEVES, WILLIAM, a very useful bat and bowler for Essex and in recent years one of the best of the first-class umpires, died after an operation on March 24, 1944, aged 67. Born at Cambridge, he joined the ground staff at Leyton, where his life centred, for he married into the family of E. C. Freeman, head groundman. A free, hard-hitting batsman and right-arm bowler of medium pace, Reeves fielded keenly and altogether accomplished much useful work for Essex from 1897 to 1921. Altogether he scored 6,603 runs, averaged 16.63, took 595 wickets at an average cost of 27.93, and held 116 catches. His best bowling season was 1904, when 106 wickets fell to him at 26 runs apiece. Next year, when he did his best batting with 1,174 runs, average 29.35, he scored 135 against Lancashire in two hours and 101 against Surrey – both at Leyton. In 1906 his only other century for Essex, 104 against Sussex, was a dashing performance, he and C. P. Buckenham (68) making 163 for the eighth wicket in seventy minutes. Another, noteworthy effort came in 1919 when he and G. M. Louden, the fast bowler put on 122 for the last Essex wicket against Surrey. All these efforts were at Leyton, where also he twice severely punished the powerful Yorkshire attack, and with 71 out of 90 in fifty minutes in 1904, with Charles McGahey as partner, helped in a total of 521. The champions had to follow-on and only just escaped defeat with three wickets in hand, Ernest Smith, who stayed an hour without getting a run, being not out with Lord Hawke. Some of his best bowling performances also were achieved at Leyton, then regarded as a batsman's paradise. In the course of 11 balls he took the last five Derbyshire wickets without conceding a run in 1901. Six years later he and Walter Mead bowled unchanged through both innings of Nottinghamshire, who won a low-scoring game by only seven runs and went on to carry off the Championship without suffering defeat.

A member of the Lord's ground staff for many years, he played in some good matches for MCC, and at Lord's in 1920 he dismissed five Nottinghamshire batsmen for 13 runs. Recently Bill Reeves took part in the special Easter coaching class for schoolboys at Lord's, but the present generation knew him best as an admirable umpire who stood in many Test matches. In this capacity he often gave evidence of his caustic humour. Once when a batsman protested that he was not out, Reeves retorted, "Weren't you? Wait till you see the papers in the morning". To a bowler notorious for appealing, he remarked, "There's only one man who appeals more than you do." "Oh, who's that?" asked the bowler, "Dr Barnardo", replied Reeves.

SPROT, MR EDWARD MARK, an all-round sportsman of much ability, died on October 8, 1945, at his home at Farnham, Surrey, aged 75. Born in Scotland and educated at Harrow he made a name in Army cricket before playing first for Hampshire in 1898 and in company with many noted soldiers (among them Captain E. G. Wynyard, Major R. M. Poore, Colonel J. G. Grieg – giving their rank at that time), he helped to raise Hampshire to such a good standard that during his captaincy they reached fifth place in the county championship. He held the reins from 1903 until 1914, and under his lead Hampshire invariably played attractive cricket with enterprise and enthusiasm. Himself a fine free hitter with zest for the forcing game, Captain Sprot, for a man of medium physique put plenty of power into his strokes, made in free style that meant quick run-getting when he was at the crease.

In first-class cricket he scored 12,251 runs, including 13 hundreds, averaging 28.55 an innings, and with slowish bowling took 54 wickets, besides holding 208 catches. Clearly a valuable man for any county, and as captain in 1918 at Southampton he aroused admiration and astonishment by declaring the innings closed when Hampshire, with a wicket to fall, were 24 behind their visitors, Northamptonshire, at lunch time on the third day, after rain had hindered the progress of the match. By this action he saved the interval between the innings and he soon put on Philip Mead, little known as a bowler. Six wickets for 18 runs fell to Mead's left-hand slows. Hampshire wanted no more than 86 runs for victory and when A. C. Johnston was out at three, Sprot hit up 62 in less than an hour, two 6s and eight 4s being characteristic of his determined aggression. Alec Bowell was the watchful partner in gaining a victory which *Wisden* described as "without parallel, which makes a unique incident in the history of the game". Sprott saw the possibility of victory by dismissing the opposition on a drying pitch and went for runs with the success described – a splendid example of "dynamic" cricket which Sir Stanley Jackson's Committee has asked for in first-class cricket of the future.

When serving with the Shropshire Light Infantry in 1899 Sprot, with Colonel J. Spens, won The Army Rackets Challenge Cup. An admirable golf player, a sure shot and clever fisherman, Sprot found billiards the most fascinating indoor recreation, and on a strange table in Cairo he won a 200 up game from the opening left by his opponent on starting the play.

STUDD, MR GEORGE BROWN, died on February 13, 1945, aged 85. The second eldest of three famous cricketing brothers, Sir J. E. Kynaston Studd and C. T. Studd being the others, all of whom played for both Eton and Cambridge, and established a record by captaining the University in consecutive years. Born at Netheravon House, near Amesbury, Wiltshire, on October 20, 1859, G. B. Studd got his Colours for Eton in 1877 when he scored 32 and 23 against Harrow and 54 against Winchester. He fared less well in the following year, but going up to Cambridge he got his Blue as a Freshman and appeared in the University match four times. Against Oxford in 1880 he made 38 and 40, and two years later, when captain of the Light Blues, he played a great innings of 120, which was the seventh three-figure score, and, at the time, the second highest in University matches. True to Eton form he showed special skill and power in driving, notably to the off, and in the field saved many runs by sure picking up, but did not always hold a catch. He enjoyed his best season for Cambridge in 1881, in which year and the following summer all three brothers were in the University Eleven. In 1882 he made 819 runs in first-class matches – a big achievement in those days – and put together for the Cambridge Long Vacation Club 289 in a grand display of forcing cricket. In the autumn G. B. and C. T. Studd went with the team taken out to Australia by the Hon. Ivo Bligh (afterwards Earl of Darnley) which brought back "The Ashes" by defeating W. L. Murdoch's team in two out of three matches, but G. B. failed to produce his best form. He assisted Middlesex occasionally from 1879 to 1886.

During his last two years at Cambridge he represented the University against Oxford in the tennis matches – both singles and doubles. He was called to the Bar, but owing to a severe illness was compelled to winter abroad and did not practise. Like his brother C. T., G. B. Studd became a missionary, first in India and China, but from 1891 onwards at Los Angeles, California.

Altogether six brothers Studd played in the Eton XI; those besides the three seniors who captained Cambridge – J. E. K., G. B. and C. T. – were A. H., H. W. and R. A. The youngest of the six, R. A., got his Blue in 1895. An elder half-brother E. J. C., who played in the Cheltenham XI in 1866, died in 1909. C. T. Studd died in 1931, J. E. K. Studd on January 14, 1944. G. B. was the last survivor of the 1879 University match.

As written in last years's *Wisden* of Sir J. E. K. Studd, the three brothers helped Cambridge to beat by six wicket the Australian team which won "The Ashes" match by seven runs. The opening stand of 106 by G. B. (48) with J. E. K. (68), largely accounted for the splendid victory by Cambridge, but C. T. Studd, scoring 118 and 17 not out, after taking eight wickets, contributed still more to the triumph. G. B. played for Past and Present of Cambridge, who that season beat the Australians by 20 runs at Portsmouth, and altogether in 10 innings against that 1882 team he averaged 25.20.

TATE, FREDERICK WILLIAM, died at Burgess Hill, Sussex, on February 24, 1943, aged 75. He first played for Sussex in 1888, and not until 1905 did his career end. Subsequently he went to Derby as coach to the County Club and in 1921 to Trent College as professional coach. Two of his three sons played county cricket, Maurice, so well known with Sussex and England, and C. L. Tate, who played for Derbyshire and Warwickshire.

A slow to medium-paced right-hand bowler, with easy action and good command of length, Fred Tate took over 100 wickets in five different seasons. His great year came when he was 35, 180 wickets falling to him for less than 16 runs apiece in 1902. His full record in first-class cricket shows 1,324 wickets at an average cost of 21 runs apiece. He accomplished many good performances. When Hampshire were a second-class county he took nine wickets for 24 runs, and at Leicester in 1902 he again got nine wickets in an innings at a cost of 73 runs. Perhaps his best achievement was that year at Lord's when against Middlesex he dismissed fifteen men for 68 runs in a day. Other exceptional feats were five wickets for one run against Kent at Tonbridge in 1888 and seven for 17 against Gloucestershire at Bristol in 1891; and in 1901 he did the hat-trick against Surrey at The Oval. This was his benefit year and the match against Yorkshire at Hove brought him £1,051.

In his best season, 1902, Tate played against The Gentlemen at Lord's and for England in the fourth Test against Australia at Old Trafford – one of the most dramatic struggles in the history of cricket, Australia winning by three runs after astonishing changes of fortune and incidents that I still can see clearly. Rain-drenched ground influenced the last-minute preference of Tate over George Hirst, and to the last choice fell the lot of being the central figure in a fielding error and in the final scene. Quite recently Len Braund, whom I met by chance, told me that when Joe Darling, the Australian captain, a left-handed batsman, and S. E. Gregory changed ends during an over he wanted Lionel Palairet, fielding at square-leg, as customary when Braund bowled for Somerset, to cross the ground. A. C. MacLaren, the England captain, sent Tate to the position, although he invariably fielded slip or near the wicket for Sussex – never in the deep. At once Darling lifted a catch and Tate dropped it – an absolute disaster for England, 48 more runs coming before the fourth wicket fell at 64. Unquestionably this, the only stand of the innings, determined the issue of the tensely close struggle. In this second innings of Australia Tate bowled five overs and took two wickets for seven runs. Next day, on a very treacherous pitch, England, striving to hit off 124 runs before a threatening storm burst, lost their ninth wicket with eight wanted for victory. Rain then interrupted the game for three-quarters of an hour before Tate joined Rhodes and edged the next ball to the leg boundary; but the fourth ball he received from Saunders bowled him, and so finished the memorable match with a victory that gave Australia the rubber, no matter what might happen in the last encounter at The Oval. A few minutes later torrents of rain fell and washed us all back to Manchester.   H.P.

TURNER, MR CHARLES THOMAS BIASS, a bowler ranking with the best ever produced by Australia, and by many who played against him considered without superior, died on New Year's Day 1944 in Sydney, aged 81. Records that stand to his name tell of his work with the ball, but it is remarkable that in the first set of photographs that appeared in *Wisden* he is holding a bat and wearing pads in company with his colleague J. J. Ferris, grasping a ball in his left hand. Chosen with G. A. Lohmann, of Surrey, Robert Peel, of Yorkshire, John Briggs, of Lancashire, and S. M. J. Woods, of Cambridge University and Somerset – himself an Australian – the two members of the team captained by P. S. McDonnell fully deserved the honour, for they practically dominated every match in which they played on this their first visit to England. In a season when bowlers accomplished wonderful things, almost beyond belief in these days, Turner took 314 wickets at 11.12 runs apiece and Ferris 224 at 14.10 each – G. H. S. Trott coming next with 48 at 23.41. In nine matches against specially chosen sides, three representing England, 70 wickets fell to Turner and 41 to Ferris, seven others claiming only 23 between them. The habit prevailed at that time of relying upon two or three bowlers on a side for the chief work of the season and McDonnell carried this custom to the extreme limit, but of the other specialists picked by C. F. Pardon, Lohmann for Surrey was almost as supreme with 253 wickets at 10.69, Beaumont, with 59, giving most help in carrying off the championship in this year of bowler's triumphs mainly on rain-affected pitches.

To have seen these masters of the art at The Oval is a pleasant recollection, and not one of them creates a happier memory than Turner in his rather long rhythmic run and beautiful right-arm action without any effort to make the most of his medium height – five feet nine inches. He delivered the ball almost facing square down the pitch, and, added to his off-break with slightly varied pace about fast-medium, was ability to turn the ball from leg, send down a fast yorker, and, above all, to get quick lift from the turf. As sufficient evidence of Turner's skill, Sir Stanley Jackson said in last year's *Wisden*, "I always regarded Charles Turner as the best medium-paced bowler I ever played against" – and he could gather an opinion as he scored 91 at Lord's and 103 at The Oval in the Tests in 1893, when Turner, on his third and last visit to England, fell from his greatest achievement to 149 wickets at 14 each, after 215 at 12 in 1890.

Turner earned fame in the 1886-87 season against Arthur Shrewsbury's team. After taking 13 wickets for 54 runs for New South Wales, he in his first Test match dismissed six batsmen for 15 runs, England being all out for 45, which remains the lowest total by England against Australia. He excelled again for New South Wales with 14 wickets for 59, clean bowling Shrewsbury for nought in each innings. In the following season, when Shrewsbury again captained a side in Australia, Turner for New South Wales took 10 wickets for 45 and 16 for 79. G. F. Vernon led another team in Australia at that time, and against the Combined England sides Turner claimed 12 wickets for 87, but, thanks to Peel and Lohmann, the visitors beat Australia by 126 runs. Altogether in 1887-88 Turner took 106 wickets at 13.59 apiece and his record of being the only bowler to take a hundred wickets in first-class cricket in a season in Australia still stands.

So expectations were rife and at once we knew in England that no one had overrated "The Terror". Turner and Ferris routed side after side, actually disposing of England at Lord's for 53 and 62 and steering Australia to victory by 61 runs. Ten wickets for 63 was Turner's share at the expense of very powerful batting, as shown in the other two Tests played on hard turf and both won by England with an innings to spare. Turner also gave early proof of his batting ability, for in the third victory of the tour, each gained in two days, he played a dashing innings of 103 at The Oval, and then, taking nine wickets for 101 runs, was chiefly instrumental in beating Surrey, the champion county of the year, by an innings and 154 runs. Checks were bound to occur when so many strong teams were opposed, but at Lord's Turner returned an average of eleven Middlesex wickets for 59 runs in a low-scoring match, and whenever helped by the state of the turf he did wonders. Twelve wickets for 64 runs at Old Trafford against North of England: 11 for 76 at Liverpool; 11 for 64 at Leicester, where the county won a sensational match by 20 runs – thanks to Pougher, 10 for 91, and Arnall-Thompson, nine for 65; then 13 for 46 at Derby and 13 for 48 at Stoke against an England XI in the course of five days. In the first innings of the Stoke match Turner bowled seven men and got two leg-before, the other being run out. So he paved the way for that big performance in the first meeting with England at Lord's. Ten wickets for 46 against Yorkshire and ten for 59 against Kent also may be cited, and still more extraordinary was his greatest return, 17 wickets for 50 runs against an England XI, at Hastings in August. In the two innings Turner hit the stumps 14 times, got two men lbw, and one stumped – further wonderful proof of how he did beat the bat. When Turner, owing to indisposition, was compelled to rest, Gloucestershire beat the Australians by 257 runs, and altogether nine of the last eleven matches were lost without marring the wonderful work of Turner and Ferris.

Such performances tell of the conditions that so often helped these two consistent bowlers, who repeated their excellence in 1890, if inevitably not quite so deadly. Exact figures show best how they share the attack and the honours in these two tours, their wickets being equal on the second visit when W. L. Murdoch last led an Australian team.

	Matches	Overs	Maidens	Runs	Wickets	Average
1888						
Turner	39	2,589.4	1,222	3,492	314	11.12
Ferris	40	2,222.2	998	3,101	220	14.10
1890						
Turner	35	1,651.1	724	2,725	215	12.60
Ferris	35	1,685.4	688	2,838	215	13.20

Four balls to the over was the rule in 1888, five in 1890.

In 1893 Turner again headed the Australian bowling figures with 160 wickets at 13.76 each; Hugh Trumble, 123 at 16.39, and George Giffen, 148 at 17.89, afforded more help than when Ferris, who at this time was playing for Gloucestershire, fairly shared the honours.

By comparison, the figures of W. J. O'Reilly, the best Australian bowler in the 1938 tour, are interesting: 709.4 overs, 215 maidens, 1,726 runs, 104 wickets, 16.59 average. Six balls an over certainly; and he complained of over-work.

Altogether in 17 Test matches – all against England – Turner took 101 wickets at 16.53 runs apiece in the course of ten years. This average just beats Robert Peel's 102 wickets at 16.81 and far surpasses the next best Australian record, 141 at 20.88 by Hugh Trumble in 32 Tests.

In all first-class matches Turner in credited with 1,061 wickets at 13 runs each, as mentioned in *Scores and Biographies*.

After some years in the Australian Joint Stock Bank, Turner was associated with other business, and when he left Sydney for Queensland in 1897 his first-class cricket career ended. H.P.

TUFNELL, MR CARLETON FOWELL, died on May 26, 1940, aged 84. He left Eton when sixteen without a chance of getting into the Eleven, but played for Cooper's Hill from 1876 to 1878, being captain in the last two seasons. A useful batsman and medium-paced bowler, he played in a few matches for Kent in 1878 and 1879 before going to India. In May 1884 a report reached England of his death at Simla.

TYLDESLEY, RICHARD KNOWLES, youngest and only survivor of four brothers, all of whom were on the Old Trafford ground staff and played for Lancashire, died at his home, Little Hulton near Bolton, on September 17, 1943, aged 45. His father, J. D. Tyldesley, a Westhoughton club professional, taught his sons cricket, and "Dick" reached a high standard. Constant practice at the nets in boyhood brought perfection in length, and with experience he mastered spin, varied pace and other artifices which brought him a trial for Lancashire in 1919 when county matches after the war were restricted to two days. His skill as a slow bowler increased like his bulk, and he gradually gained renown as a slow bowler of the heaviest build in county cricket, looking older than his years but carrying his weight with remarkable ease while toiling for long spells without tiring. Above medium height, he flighted the ball naturally and used the top spinner in a way often earning the umpire's agreement with the leg-before appeal. His leg-break, expected by batsmen rather than operative, turned little if at all under normal conditions but, given a responsive pitch, Dick Tyldesley could be devastating, though length, adjusted to a batsman's ability, was his most effective means of attack.

Regularly from 1922 his victims numbered at least 100 a season, and he showed little if any deterioration in 1931 when the Lancashire committee could not concede to his request for an engagement for a definite period at a fixed salary of £400 a year, no matter whether he could play or not; and his association with the county ceased.

In 1923 he took 106 wickets in Championship matches at 15 runs apiece. Nest season, when the South Africans toured England. Tyldesley appeared to considerable advantage in four of the five Test matches, but his most brilliant achievement was six wickets for 18 runs at Leeds, where, thanks to him and Parkin, Yorkshire were dismissed for 33 and beaten by 24 runs.

This form gained Tyldesley a place in the side which visited Australia in the following winter under A. E. R. Gilligan, but he met with little success on the "shirt-front" wickets, and played against Australia only in the Test match at Melbourne, being dismissed for one and nought, and sending down 37 overs for 136 runs without getting a wicket.

In 1930 Dick Tyldesley played for England against Australia at Nottingham, where England triumphed, and at Leeds in a drawn match, dismissing seven batsmen at an average of 33 runs in the two encounters, but he was not called upon again. He headed his county's bowling with 121 wickets at 14.73 each, and Lancashire were champion county for the fourth time in five seasons, the first of the successes coming in 1926 after an interval of twenty-two years when A. C. MacLaren captained the side. He was again the most effective bowler for Lancashire in 1931 with a record of 116 wickets at a fraction under 16 runs each, but his county dropped to sixth place; and that ended his country career. During several seasons he enjoyed considerable success with the bat, and in 1922 he hit up 105 against Nottinghamshire at Old Trafford.

Parkin and Dick Tyldesley did some remarkable performances besides the triumph at Leeds. In 1924 they shared the wickets in both innings at Old Trafford for Lancashire against the South Africans, Tyldesley's figures being seven for 28 and five for 50; they were unchanged against Warwickshire, ten wickets falling to Tyldesley for 103 runs. In that season he dismissed five Leicestershire batsmen, three clean bowled and the other two leg-before-wicket, in five maiden overs – all he bowled in the innings. Another fine performance was seven Northamptonshire wickets for six runs at Aigburth. Against the same county at Kettering in 1926 he dismissed eight men for 15 runs. Also a unique performance stands to his credit at Derby in 1929, when he dismissed two men with the last two balls of one innings and two more with the first two deliveries he sent down in the second innings.

Altogether in first-class cricket he took 1,513 wickets at 17.15 runs apiece, scored 6,424 runs, average 15.04, and held 328 catches – mostly at short-leg. For Lancashire his record showed 1,447 wickets, a number exceeded only by John Briggs and Arthur Mold. After giving up county cricket, Tyldesley helped Nantwich to win the North Staffordshire and District League championship twice, and he did good service for Accrington, who he joined in 1934.

In 1930 his benefit match, when Surrey visited Old Trafford, realised £2,027, although it clashed with England versus Australia at Trent Bridge where Tyldesley was engaged. At different periods Dick Tyldesley shared in the Lancashire bowling honours with Cecil Parkin and E. A. McDonald, the Australian – and now all three are dead: McDonald passed on in 1937, Parkin three months before Richard Tyldesley.

So much doubt has prevailed as to the relationship of the six Tyldesleys who played for Lancashire that it is opportune to emphasize that the brothers John Thomas, who died in 1930, and Ernest, both famous batsmen and England Test players, belonged to a Worsley family and were not related to the four Westhoughton professionals; these were:

William K. Tyldesley, a batsman. Killed in 1918 during the last war while a Lieutenant in the North Lancashire Regiment. Obituary 1919 *Wisden*.

James Darbyshire Tyldesley, a fast bowler and good batsman; played first for Lancashire in 1910, died in 1923. Obituary 1924 *Wisden*.

Harry Tyldesley, died in 1935. Played first for the county in 1914, at Derby on July 11, when two pairs of Tyldesley brothers figured in the Lancashire eleven; that season the Lancashire averages included five Tyldesleys. Harry toured with A. C. MacLaren's team in the winter of 1922 and headed the bowling averages both in Australia and New Zealand. Obituary 1936 *Wisden*.

Richard Tyldesley, the youngest, the subject of this obituary.

WARD, REV. EDWARD EWER HARRISON, of Cambridge, prominent in the "Cobden" match of 1870, died on March 25, 1940, at his home at Gorleston, Norfolk, aged 92. His death five days before that of A. C. Bartholomew, of Oxford, left F. A. MacKinnon, Chief of the Scottish Clan of Morayshre, the oldest living Cambridge Blue. Mr MacKinnon, who also played in the 1870 match, now holds seniority among University as well as International cricketers. He went to Australia in 1878 with the team captained by Lord Harris, and took part in the only representative match of the tour, which Dave Gregory's eleven won by ten wickets. H. C. Maul, who died on October 10, aged 90, was another member of that side, but did not play in the game which long afterwards was classed as a "Test". Mr A. J. Webbe, "number three" for England in that match, was 86 in January this year; he passed away in February.

Born on July 16, 1847, at Timworth Hall, Suffolk, in the family of Harrison, "E.E." adopted the surname Ward after leaving Bury St Edmund's School, where Mr J. H. Marshall, a Cambridge Blue of 1859, taught him spin and length.

So well did young Harrison master control of his left-hand medium-paced bowling that, despite somewhat moderate physique and indifferent health, he accomplished long spells of successful bowling in University and county cricket. Making the ball go with his arm, he often pitched well to the off and hit the leg stump, delivery from little higher than the shoulder helping this natural flight − so awkward for right-handed batsmen − quite different to imparted swerve with high delivery.

When talking of his University experiences, Mr Ward used to say: "I was never robust, and knew my own strength and weakness, and always wanted to be my own captain. During Oxford's second innings in the 'Cobden' match there was a stand after I had taken the second and third wickets, and I asked to be given a rest. My captain agreed, and when I was put on again I soon took four more wickets".

In an interview at Mulbarton Rectory with an *Eastern Daily Press* representative some twenty years ago, Mr Ward fully described Cobden's feat, about which many varying descriptions have appeared. This may be accepted as authentic.

"From the first ball a run was made by Hill, and the match stood two to tie, three to win, and three wickets to go down. One hundred pounds to one on Oxford was offered and taken. The second ball Butler hit to cover point, a hard catch which Bourne managed to hold. Two more wickets were left − Stewart's and Belcher's. Cobden's third ball bowled Belcher off his pads. Stewart, the last man, was deadly pale and nervous when he walked past me, padded and gloved. A dead silence came over the players and spectators. Cobden crammed his cap on his head, rushed up to the bowling crease, and bowled what I have always thought was a plain long hop. Anyhow, the bails flew, and amid a scene of the wildest excitement Cambridge won by two runs!"

The Hon. Robert Lyttelton, in the Badminton Library account of the match, did justice to Ward's share in the victory. He wrote: "The unique performance of Cobden has unduly cast into the shade Mr Ward's performance in the second innings. It was a good wicket and Oxford had certainly on the whole a good batting eleven. Yet Mr Ward bowled 32 overs for 29 runs and got six wickets and of these five were certainly the best batsmen in the side. He clean bowled Messrs Fortescue, Pauncefote, and Tylecote, and got out in other ways Messrs Ottoway, Townshend, and Francis. It is hardly too much to say that in this innings Mr Ward got the six best wickets and Mr Cobden the four worst. In the whole match Mr Ward got nine wickets for 62 runs, and this again, let it be said, on an excellent ground."

Ward was doubtful about playing in the 1871 match, which, curiously enough, made further University cricket history. S. E. Butler took all ten wickets in the Cambridge first innings, another record. The Dark Blues won by eight wickets. Owing to illness Ward wanted to stand down, but his captain, "Bill" Yardley, of high renown, would not hear of this. That Ward's knowledge of himself was sound came true, for, though bowling 36 overs (four ball each) at a cost of only 38 runs, he did not get a wicket.

When playing for Suffolk, Ward met with much success. At Bury he once scored 46 out of 60 for the last wicket after dismissing six men cheaply, and in 1872 he took 13 MCC wickets for 46 runs. He became Secretary of the Suffolk County Club on its revival in 1876, and, as a prominent member of the side, excelled against Norfolk that year, taking 11 wickets at Bury, and in 1877 returning this extradinary analysis:

	O.	M.	R.	W.
First innings	21	18	7	5
Second innings	13	8	7	3

Thirteen I Zingari wickets once fell to him for 47.

Mr Ward gave 59 years of service to the Church of England, holding appointments in Suffolk, Northumberland, Yorkshire, Derbyshire and Norfolk, his last living being at Mulbarton, where he ministered for 24 years before resigning in 1931.

WEBBE, MR ALEXANDER JOSIAH, of high renown in Harrow, Oxford University and Middlesex cricket, died on February 19, 1941, at his home, Fulvens Farm, Abinger Hammer, Surrey, aged 86. Born on January 16, 1855, he had not been seen on a cricket field in active pursuit of the game in an important fixture for over forty years, but during all that time he still exercised much influence at Lord's as President of Middlesex and member of the Marylebone Club Committee, to which he was first elected in 1886.

Like the Walkers before him, he first made his name in Harrow cricket, and was a member of the Eleven from 1872 to 1874, finishing as captain of the School Eleven when, in the big match at Lord's, notwithstanding his personal contributions of 77 and 80, Eton were victorious by five wickets. Going up to Trinity College, Oxford, Webbe got his Blue as a freshman, and on his first appearance against Cambridge he made 55, the highest score in the match, and 21, so helping materially in a narrow victory by six runs. As evidence of his popularity and excellence as a cricketer, he was twice captain of Oxford, and, when first the leader, his side won handsomely by ten wickets, he and his brother, H. R. Webbe, hitting off 47 runs needed for victory. It is of special interest to recall that he and W. S. Patterson, the Cambridge captain, both played that year for Gentlemen against Players at Lord's, in what was described as "the glorious match", which the Gentlemen won by one wicket when everybody present anticipated a triumph for the Players. W. S. Patterson and A. J. Webbe were the last survivors of the twenty-two engaged in that game and, after Patterson passed away in October 1939, A. J. Webbe remained as the oldest living University captain.

Another very interesting episode during his early period at Oxford was that in 1875 he played for the Gentlemen at Lord's and, going in first, helped W. G. Grace make 203 in the opening stand, his share being 65; "the champion" scored 152. Writing in his book, W. G. Grace said of that occasion. "In a sticky-wicket season, batting suffered, but one player, Mr A. J. Webbe, came to the front with a rush; when we put on 203 runs his defence and patience were perfect." Those attributes expressed by the greatest of batsmen fairly described some of Webbe's characteristics at the wicket.

Webbe also started playing for Middlesex during his first year at Oxford when twenty years of age, and his success in the strongest company still serves as an example of how the best schoolboy cricketers in those days quickly reached the front rank. In every particular a great batsman, he possessed skill in defence, with untiring patience and remarkable power in stroke play. True to type, like many Harrow batsmen of the period, he stood at the wicket with legs wide apart, a position well suited to playing back in defence or cutting – something like the posture adopted and made memorable in later years by Gilbert Jessop, "the Croucher". Webbe cut splendidly, both square and late, used the "Harrow drive", now known as the hit through "the covers", and placed the ball to the on or hit to leg with perfectly timed strokes. In fact, an admirable exponent of the batsman's art. Of middle height and good build, his early stamina had proof in an innings of 299 not out for Trinity College against Exeter; also in 1875 he made his first hundred in important cricket, 120 for the University against Gentlemen of England.

Ripening to maturity, Webbe got more runs as pitches became less favourable to bowlers, and in 1887 he enjoyed his best season, scoring 1,244 runs, with an average of

47, his highest innings being 243 not out against Yorkshire at Huddersfield; 192 not out at Canterbury off the Kent bowlers was another highly meritorious display. When set he exemplified what Robertson-Glasgow now calls a "Difficult Target". Altogether in first-class cricket A. J. Webb scored 11,761 runs, with an average of 23.75, as given in Sir Home Gordon's *Form at a Glance*.

Lord Harris accepting an invitation from the Melbourne Club for a team of Amateurs to visit Australia in the autumn of 1878, A. J. Webbe was one of the chosen. The impossibility of finding amateur bowlers able to go necessitated the inclusion of Tom Emmett and George Ulyett of Yorkshire. By no means representative of England, the side lost the one match against Australia. The death of A. J. Webbe leaves as the only survivor of that touring team F. A. MacKinnon, head of the clan MacKinnon, who has maintained his interest in Kent, his cricketing county, by going to the Canterbury Festival regularly up to 1939.

Free to give practically all his time to cricket, A. J. Webbe kept up his close connection with the game, as known to the public, for nearly seventy years – from his presence in the Harrow eleven to his resignation of the Middlesex Club presidency in 1937; and even to the last, as a trustee of MCC, he held an honoured place in cricket.

Besides his first-class activities, A. J. Webbe, on leaving school, went on the annual tours of Harrow Wanderers, under the lead of I. D. Walker, and he took teams to Oxford and Cambridge each season. After captaining Oxford Harlequins for several years, he was elected president of the club. For such sides he used to bowl medium pace, but really his skill was confined to batsmanship and fielding. Good everywhere, he excelled in the deep, and some magnificent catches stand to his credit.

At other games A. J. Webbe ranked high. He represented Oxford twice at racquets in the doubles, and in 1888 he won the tennis silver racquet at Lord's. Added to his fondness for games and skill in their practice, he served on hospital committees and in many ways helped to relieve the troubles and sufferings of people less fortunate than himself.

MISCELLANY

THE TOM BROWN CENTENARY

RUGBY MEMORIES REVIVED

To mark the centenary of the first visit of an MCC team to Rugby School in 1841, a game immortalised in *Tom Brown's School Days*, the Club sent a powerful side to oppose the School on the Close at Rugby on June 17, 1941. Thomas Hughes, the author, captained the original School team in his last match there.

The 1841 precedent was followed, when the School won the toss and, "with the usual liberality of young hands", sent MCC, by no means either "hard-bitten" or "whiskered", in to bat on a pitch of differing paces. MCC captained, as 100 years ago when Mr Benjamin Aislabie led the side, by their secretary, Lieut-Col R. S. Rait Kerr, himself an old Rugbeian, began badly but recovered. R. I. Scorer batted steadily, and after lunch Major E. R. T. Holmes, the old Surrey captain, "giving no rest and no catches to anyone", scored freely. Of the remainder of the batsmen, nobody accomplished much. While the exact derivation of the term "small cobs" remains a mystery, nothing in the nature of such implied leniency was shown to Lieut-Col Rait Kerr, the leg-break bowling of E. M. I. Robertson and the left-hand deliveries of A. V. Guthrie remaining steady and the fielding of the keenest description till the declaration – long after "half-past twelve o'clock". One or two of the catches might well have merited the 1841 captain's remark of "Pretty cricket!"

Two Rugby wickets fell before tea, and afterwards a "hat-trick" by big Jim Smith, of Middlesex and England, in his second over and the accurate attack maintained by R. E. S. Wyatt, the former England captain, proved too much for School batting admittedly none too strong. The School followed on, and thus those spectators who had doubtless hoped for a repetition of the spectacle of the Marylebone eleven "working like horses" to save the match were disappointed.

So "the Lord's men were declared the winners", this time by 118 runs, but in cheaply disposing of such formidable opponents, Rugby must have felt well satisfied with themselves.

As was the case a century before, luncheon was taken in Old Big School, but it is open to doubt whether any warning was issued as to "keeping spiritous liquors out of the close". Links with Tom Brown's team were provided by the attendance of Mr R. B. V. Currie, a nephew of "– Currie, Esq, major" and "– Currie, Esq, minor", and Mr Philip A. Landon, a great-grandson of Mr Aislabie, first holder of the office of secretary of MCC. Sir Pelham Warner, another famous Old Boy and war-time deputy MCC secretary, was also present.

MCC

R. H. Twining c Wadham b Boddington ...	0	J. Smith c Melly b Robertson 2
R. I. Scorer b Robertson	38	R. A. Boddington c Boyes b Guthrie....... 15
R. E. S. Wyatt c Melly b Guthrie	19	Lt-Col R. S. Rait Kerr not out 2
H. C. Munro c Guthrie b Hussey	14	
Major E. R. T. Holmes b Robertson.......	36	Extras 8
L. G. H. Hingley c Boyes b Boddington	0	———
Major G. O. Allen st Macaulay b Guthrie ..	15	(9 wkts dec.) 149

Lt Col G. H. M. Cartwright did not bat.

Rugby School

J. I. Johnson Gilbert b Wyatt	6	– lbw b Scorer	5
J. A. Boyes b Wyatt	6	– b Munro	10
H. I. Melly b Smith	3	– b Allen	0
J. C. Wardill lbw b Wyatt	4	– not out	12
R. W. Wadham lbw b Smith	0	– not out	3
D. H. G. Lyon b Smith	0		
M. A. Boddington b Wyatt	5		
J. D. Macaulay b Smith	3		
M. J. Hussey b Smith	0		
E. M. I. Robertson c Boddington b Smith	2		
A. V. Guthrie not out	0		
Extras	2	Extras	4
	31		**(3 wkts) 34**

Rugby School Bowling

	Overs	Mdns	Runs	Wkts
Boddington	18	3	41	2
Wadham	8	1	24	—
Robertson	13	2	30	3
Guthrie	11	2	28	3
Hussey	8	1	18	1

MCC Bowling

	Overs	Mdns	Runs	Wkts
Wyatt	11	5	14	4
Smith	8	3	8	6
Allen	3	—	7	—

The score of the orginal match, contained in *Scores and Biographies*, is as follows:

At Rugby, June 17, 1841

Marylebone

T. Chamberlayne, Esq. b Wrottesley	11	– st Hughes b Thompson	9
T. M. Wythe, Esq. c Currie major b Thompson	11	– b Wrottesley	1
L. Huddlestone, Esq. b Wrottesley	6	– b Thompson	3
Lord C. Russell c Currie minor b Wrottesley	3	– run out	3
B. Thackeray, Esq. c Orlebar b Wrottesley	30	– b Wrottesley	58
I. J. Pigou, Esq. b Wrottesley	10	– b Wrottesley	21
G. A. P. Bentinck, Esq. c Blunt b Currie major	27	– lbw b Wrottesley	0
R. Wellesley, Esq. not out	28	– b Hughes	0
H. Rodwell, Esq. b Currie major	0	– c Currie major b Hughes	2
B. Aislabie, Esq. c Currie major b Wrottesley	1	– b Hughes	0
W. P. Bolland, Esq. hit wkt b Currie major	2	– not out	1
B 7	7	B 1	1
	136		**99**

Rugby

T. Hughes, Esq. c Pigou b Wellesley	29	– c Bentinck b Wellesley	0
Thompson, Esq. b Thackeray	7	– b Thackeray	24
A. Orlebar, Esq. b Thackeray	12	– not out	1
Walford, Esq. c Chamberlayne b Wellesley	11	– b Thackeray	0
Hon. A. Wrottesley b Thackeray	0	– c Bentinck b Thackeray	7
Beard, Esq. run out	3	– c Wythe b Wellesley	1
H. W. Lindow, Esq. b Thackeray	0	– run out	14
Blunt, Esq. c Wellesley b Thackeray	5	– b Wellesley	10
Currie, Esq. minor c Huddlestone b Thackeray	12	– not out	4
Currie, Esq. major not out	9	– b Thackeray	13
Thornhill, Esq. run out	1	– not out	1
B 18, w 12, n-b 1	31	B 24, w 3	27
	120		**102**

Unfinished, Rugby having one wicket to go down.

This match is celebrated in *Tom Brown's School Days*.

The Tom Brown hero of the fight against Slogger Williams was the Rev. Augustus Orlebar and his defeated adversary became the Rev. Bulkeley Owen Jones. Each of the clergymen held a living for half a century, and sixty years after their fight they met at Rugby at the unveiling of the memorial to Judge Thomas Hughes, the cricket captain and the Tom Brown of the cricket match as described in his book. As a happy sequel to their school experience the two clergymen discovered each other's identity by accident: their reminiscences were not disclosed.

NOTES BY THE EDITOR, 1943

PROFESSIONALS AND AMATEURS

This is a question that calls for plain speaking and honest thinking. Its treatment demands realism, which you will rarely find either on a soap-box in Hyde Park or in a deep armchair of the Carlton Club.

I think that any man who has had the happiness of playing, even occasionally, in what is called first-class cricket will extend that somewhat arid adjective far beyond the confines of batting, bowling, and fielding. For in no other cricket, however rich in the strife, humour and benevolence of Nature, will you find such good company among players of all ages and all walks of life, or make and, if you will, keep such effortless and enduring friendships. But I also think that the hour is ripe, indeed over-ripe, for the sweeping away of anachronisms and the exploding of humbug.

Under the word "professional" in the *Concise Oxford Dictionary* you will find the words "playing for money"; under "amateur" you will find "one who is fond of" and "one who cultivates a thing as a pastime". You will also find, but not in the dictionary, that, as regards modern cricket, these respective definitions are to a remarkable degree interchangeable; for, all professionals whom I have known are fond of cricket and regard it as a pastime as well as a living, and many amateurs, besides being fond of cricket, play it for the equivalent of money, namely for the publicity which attracts clients to themselves or to the business for which they may be working. The only difference here is that the professional's pay is direct, and the amateur's indirect. To both, cricket is in fact, whatever it may be in law, their source, partly or entirely, of livelihood. To distinguish between these two sorts of cricketer, on any commercial consideration, is surely humbug.

In the season of 1939 there still existed in county cricket a few, a very few, amateurs who earned no money, directly or indirectly, from the playing of their game. They received only their travelling and hotel expenses, and, in some cases, not even these. Long may cricket encourage and be encouraged by such men. Their unbiased leadership and natural generosity have served cricket honourably and long, and they have given to the game, from half-legendary times, many illustrious players, many great captains, many prudent legislators. But they are survivors of an almost lost society, of an age that is nearly gone.

For these reasons, with whatever feelings of regret or pleasure they may be regarded, and for many other reasons, some too obvious, others too intimate to be mentioned, I would welcome the total deletion of all distinction between professionals and amateurs in first-class cricket. To me at least such questions as the position of a cricketer's initials and the precise gate from which he is to enter the field have long seemed vastly absurd. Once on the field, a bowler is as good as a batsman, and a wicket-keeper probably better than either. But, how much county cricketers of the future are going to be paid, and whence the money is to come, are questions that I do not mean to discuss – yet.

NOTES BY THE EDITOR, 1944

CRICKET'S PLACE IN WAR-TIME

To borrow a phrase used by the Prime Minister in his speech at the Guildhall on Lord Mayor's Day, we have passed "the fourth milestone" in war-time cricket; and have not lost sight of the first-class game, to which we all hope to return before much more effort is expended in keeping the flag flying. This symbol of activity on the playing fields, as hoisted above the pavilion every match day at Lord's, is suggested for each club – a small matter but helpful in showing the zeal of all concerned in providing an antidote to war-gloom. Far more than in the similar period of four summers over which the last war extended, cricket has proceeded alike for the recreation of all men in the various services both as players and spectators, while the general public in their thousands flocked regularly to the grounds where any men of known fame were expected. These opportunities accorded with the desire of the Adjutant General of the Forces. Mr Stanley Christopherson, President of the Marylebone Club, emphasised this before the 1940 season, and there has not been any relaxation of this stimulus, Mr Ernest Bevin, Minister of Labour, last summer asking that cricket should be encouraged in every way.

Indeed, the efforts of MCC, the organisers of London Counties and British Empire teams, found splendid support with corresponding energy forthcoming in every part of the country. Civil authorities and town councils welcomed cricket as an aid to their "Holidays at Home" efforts, and the public of all types, many new to the game, found it entertaining – a real recreation worth studying in its intricacies.

Such modern war-time evidence of the great hold cricket has attained and the insistence of its lovers to indulge in their favourite pastime takes us back 150 years. We read in *The Cricket Field*, by the Rev. James Pyecroft: "Let us trace these Hambledonians in all their contests from the 1786 to the 1800, the eventful period of the French Revolution and Nelson's victories, and see how the bank stopping payment, the mutiny of the Fleet, and the threatened invasion, put together, did not prevent balls from flying over the tented field in a far more innocent and rational way on this than on the other side of the water".

That period reminds us of the foundation of MCC and, if debarred from the sight of the "tented fields", typical of Canterbury Week and other festivals, we have revelled in many hits for six, some out of the ground at Lord's, where the Tavern was often bombarded, and once a full glass perished from the blow of a robust batsman's pull. The lost drink was not of the kind described by Nyren as on tap at Hambledon: "Barleycorn Ale – genuine Boniface! vended at twopence per pint".

Perpetual Memorials

For closer links with the distant past I would mention first the purchase by East Molesey Club of their part of old Moulsey Hurst, the historic sports ground commemorated in an oil painting by Richard Wilson, RA, of a match played there in 1780. The picture belongs to MCC. The first record of a match at Moulsey Hurst dates back to 1732, and twelve years later Surrey met there a team got together by Frederick Prince of Wales. This summer the King, through his secretary, expressed to the East Molesey Club the hope that their match with Buccaneers, played in aid of the fund to purchase the freehold of the ground as a perpetual memorial to Captain F. E. Smith, other members and visiting players killed in the war, would be in every way successful; so the close touch of our Royal Family with cricket repeated itself in the personal interest taken by our King in a match on the same ground. And His Majesty is Patron of both MCC and Surrey.

For over sixty years the East Molesey Club have used the five acres now acquired permanently, and the Robins family, of whom R. W. V., of Cambridge University, Middlesex and England, is best known, maintain their intimate and active connection with the doings of the club. Mr. E. W. Kent, who stroked the Oxford boat to victory over Cambridge in 1891, was one of the Trustees who agreed to sell the land to the club at a reasonable sum for use as a cricket ground for all time. This will be gratifying to lovers of the game, as declared in this cable from General Freyberg, V.C., Officer Commanding New Zealand Forces, Middle East: "All comrades of F. E. Smith will approve Molesey Cricket Club's fitting memorial to brilliant all-rounder who fell in gallant action at Alamein". Frederick Edward Smith was the club's best all-rounder. Captain of Waitaki, in New Zealand, he came to England in 1936, and for East Molesey scored 1,000 runs and took 100 wickets in two consecutive seasons. He hit centuries, did the hat-trick, and took all ten wickets in an innings.

Lascelles Hall

Coincidences occur with the march of time, and the Lascelles Hall Club, which celebrated their centenary in 1925, with the help of cricket lovers, especially Yorkshiremen, also have saved their ground from the hands of builders. I recall walking to Lascelles Hall when on duty for a Yorkshire match at Huddersfield. Every Yorkshireman knows Lascelles Hall as the home of the Thewlis family, who put an eleven on the field and won a match in 1866, the year when the ground, as it is now, was opened. Ephraim Lockwood, of high fame, came from this rural spot. He toured America in 1879 with Richard Daft's team, and when at Niagara, looking at the falls, Lockwood exclaimed, "Well, if this is Niagara, I think now't of it; I'd rather be at Lascelles Hall".

Cricket always will be enriched by the retention for futurity of these two old grounds as examples showing the growth of the game both among players and those who support it. So when the question of war memorials is under discussion, nothing could prove more appropriate than the acquisition of the local cricket ground as a perpetual reminder of what this greatest of games has done for the youth and manhood of Great Britain and her offspring in all parts of the world. Already Club Cricket Conference are concerned at the danger of many club enclosures being used as a help towards solving the housing problem; consequently an immediate move would seem advisable to secure such well-kept places as health resorts for the players and people of all ages, besides those already zealous in watching over the future of cricket.

CRICKET UNDER THE JAPS

By Major E. W. Swanton, RA

It is strange, perhaps, but true, how many of us agreed on this: That we were never so thankful for having been cricketers as we were when we were guests of the Japanese. These were periods when we could play "cricket" if our antics do not desecrate the word. There were occasions when we could lecture, and be lectured to, about it. It was a subject that filled countless hours in pitch-dark huts between sundown and the moment that continued to be euphemistically known as lights-out. And it inspired many a daydream, contrived often in the most gruesome setting, whereby one combated the present by living either in the future or the past.

In the days that followed shortly on the fall of Singapore, before work for prisoners had become widely organized, there was a certain amount of play on the padangs of Changi camp that really deserved the name of cricket. It is true that one never seemed able to hit the ball very far, a fact probably attributable about equally to the sudden change to a particularly sparse diet of rice, and the conscientious labours of generations of corporals in charge of sports gear, for whom a daily oiling of the bats had clearly been a solemn, unvarying rite. These Changi bats must have reached saturation point in the early thirties, and I never found one that came up lighter than W. H. Ponsford's three pounder. However, the pitches were true – matting over concrete – and there were even such refinements as pads and gloves. After most of us had been moved to Singapore City on the first stage of the journey up to Thailand, Lieut.-Colonel A. A. Johnson, of the Suffolk Regiment, promoted some excellent matches with the Australians, whose captain was none other than B. A. Barnett; I cannot write of these from first-hand knowledge, but this was, so to speak, Cricket de Luxe, and our jungle cricket bore little outward relation to it.

The first of the camps on the Thai-Burma railway in which we played cricket was Wampo. Christmas Day, 1942, was our first holiday, I think, since our arrival in October, and it was perhaps the fact of our so occupying the afternoon that caused our guards to receive subsequent requests to play cricket with suspicion, as having some religious significance and being therefore good for morale. (It was always the policy to keep prisoners' morale at the lowest level compatible with their being considered able to undertake whatever work was on hand. It was no doubt on this principle that, later on, the Allied chaplains were solemnly and sternly forbidden to pray for victory!)

This particular game was notable, I remember, for what is probably the fastest hundred of all time. It was scored in about five overs by a very promising young Eurasian cricketer called Thoy, who, with graceful ease, kept hitting the tennis ball clear over the huts! Nothing, of course, could have been more popular than the victory of the Other Ranks over the Officers, but the broad lesson of the match was that the merit of any contest depends on the preservation of the balance between attack and defence. (One could not help wondering, earlier in the war, when bombs were raining down on The Oval, whether the Surrey committee were taking the hint.) For jungle cricket our bat, surreptitiously made by the carpenter, was obviously too big.

Our cricket for the next twelve months was confined to theory and reminiscence, but lower down the line, at the base camps of Tarsao and Chungkai, various forms of play were improvised, while still later, at Nakom Patom, the hospital camp, the technique was exploited in front of large and happy crowds of men anxious to forget the tiresomeness of dysentery, beri-beri, and malaria.

Cricket at Nakom Patom reached its climax on New Year's Day, 1945, when a fresh, and certainly hitherto unrecorded, page was written in the saga of England v Australia. The scene is not easy to put before you, but I must try. The playing area is small, perhaps sixty yards by thirty, and the batsman's crease is right up against the spectators, with the pitch longways on. There are no runs behind the wicket, where many men squat in the shade of tall trees. The sides are flanked by long huts, with parallel ditches – one into the ditch, two over the hut. In fact all runs by boundaries, 1, 2, 4 or 6. An additional hazard is washing hung on bamboo "lines". Over the bowler's head are more trees, squaring the thing off, and in the distance a thick, high, mud wall – the camp bund – on which stands a bored and sulky Korean sentry. (Over the bund no runs and out, for balls are precious.) In effect, the spectators are the boundaries, many hundreds of them taking every inch of room. The dress is fairly uniform, wooden clogs, and a scanty triangular piece of loin-cloth known (why?) as a "Jap-Happy". Only the swells wear patched and tattered shorts. The mount at long-on is an Australian preserve, their "Hill". The sun beats down, as tropical suns do, on the flat beaten earth which is the wicket. At the bowler's end is a single bamboo stump, at the other five – yes, five – high ones. There is the hum of anticipation that you get on the first morning at Old Trafford or Trent Bridge, though there are no score cards, and no "Three penn'orth of comfort" to be bought from our old friend "Cushions".

The story of the match is very much the story of that fantastic occasion at The Oval in August 1938. Flt-Lieut John Cocks, well known to the cricketers of Ashtead, is our Hutton; Lieut Norman Smith, from Halifax, an even squarer, even squatter Leyland. With the regulation bat – it is two and a half inches wide and a foot shorter than normal – they play beautifully down the line of the ball, forcing the length ball past cover, squeezing the leg one square off their toes. There seems little room on the field with the eight Australian fielders poised there, but a tennis ball goes quickly off wood, the gaps are found, and there are delays while it is rescued from the swill basket, or fished out from under the hut. As the runs mount up the barracking gains in volume, and in wit at the expense of the fielders. When at last the English captain declares, the score is acknowledged to be a Thailand record.

With the Australian innings comes sensation. Captain "Fizzer" Pearson, of Sedbergh and Lincolnshire, the English fast bowler, is wearing BOOTS! No other cricketer has anything on his feet at all, the hot earth, the occasional flint being accepted as part of the game. The moral effect of these boots is tremendous. Captain Pearson bowls with shattering speed and ferocity, and as each fresh lamb arrives for the slaughter the stumps seem more vast, the bat even punier. One last defiant cheer from "the Hill" when their captain, Lieut-Colonel E. E. Dunlop, comes in, another and bigger one from the English when his stumps go flying.

While these exciting things proceed one of the fielders anxiously asks himself whether they will brew trouble. "Should fast bowlers wear boots? Pearson's ruse condemned – where did he get those boots? . . . boots bought from camp funds: Official denial . . . Board of Control's strong note . . ." headlines seem to grow in size. Then he remembers gratefully that here is no press box full of sick columnists and Test captains, no microphones for the players to run to – in fact, no papers and no broadcasting. The field clears at last. As he hurries off to roll-call he thinks of a New Year's Day six years before when the bund was Table Mountain, the field was the green of Newlands, and he decides that even the South Africans who jostled their way cheerfully back into Cape Town that evening had not enjoyed their outing more than the spectators of this grotesque "Cricket Match".

There was much more "cricket" at Nakom Patom of similar sort, and not a few who came to jeer stayed on to cheer. One was reminded how hitting a moving ball demands the observance of certain principles, whatever the circumstances, while, as for bowling, I defy anyone who does not obey the cardinal rules to pitch six running to a length with a tennis ball.

Talks on cricket were given at many camps, and there were cricket "Quizzes" too, wherein a few so-called experts were showered with questions from all sides. These occasions were never lacking in humour, and there were generally enough Australians among the audience to give, as one might say, a bite to the thing. Sometimes the game was presented from a particular angle. Thus Len Muncer, of Middlesex, a sergeant in the Sherwood Foresters, described the life of a cricket professional, while Lieut-Colonel D. V. Hill, of Worcestershire, showed the game from the point of view of a county captain. Admittedly in a prison camp there was not much in the way of alternative diversion. None the less the interest was wide enough and genuine enough to emphasize what a tremendously strong hold cricket has in England; a hold that among Australians is even stronger.

A few days after the Japanese surrender our camp at Kanburi began to assemble frequently for news bulletins. Emissaries, we heard, were flying hither and thither, instructions and encouragement were being relayed from Governments to POW's; the air was heavy with the most momentous happenings. Moreover, many of those present had had no news of the outside world for months, or longer; yet, no item commanded so much attention as the Test match at Manchester.

I had, by then, already taken my first walk for three and a half years as a free man. We found ourselves in a Thai village on the edge of the jungle. In the little café our hosts politely turned on the English programme. Yes, we were at Old Trafford, and a gentleman called Cristofani was getting a hundred. . . .

1946-1963

At first everything seemed to be much as it had always been. There were the Test matches, and a tour of Australia in prospect. Hammond, featured in "Picture Post" as England's natural leader, took a double century off the Nottinghamshire bowling, and Hardstaff another off the Indians. Yorkshire won the County Championship again. Death had left less gaping wounds in the ranks than in the first war, and match cards bore a comforting resemblance to those of the old days. Certainly there seemed to be as many whimsical, unpredictable and freakish events taking place as ever, most of them at The Oval, where the Indian tourists slipped into cricket history not once but twice. In the match against Surrey, their numbers ten and eleven, Banerjee and Sarwate went on batting for ever; in the Test, Merchant was run out when Denis Compton, drawing on the techniques which had made him a double international, dashed in from a close fielding position and left-footed the ball into the stumps, an exhilarating and faintly comic happening which the Almanack inexplicably described as "a sad finish". And in May a match between Surrey and Old England saw the return to the cricket field of Sutcliffe, Sandham, Woolley, Fender, Tate and M. J. C. Allom, the only man in the history of the world to perform the hat trick for England and also participate as a saxophonist on a jazz record. Indeed, the occasion was so joyous that even Douglas Jardine agreed to emerge from his tent long enough to score a cultured fifty. In a county match at Lord's, Denis Compton apparently opened the batting, and in the game between Derbyshire and Yorkshire, the pitch was found to be too long. Everything, it seemed, was much the same. Nothing had changed.

The illusion was sustained in the following season, when the flourishing popularity of the county game was balm for the raddled nerves of club secretaries. There were two main reasons for this renaissance, the vintage summer weather coming in the wake of an arctic winter, and the deeds of Denis Compton, whose *annus mirabilis* it turned out to be. Ancient records tumbled. Scoreboards rattled along in a breathless attempt to keep up. Day after day, week after week, the headlines intoned the same litany: Edrich and Compton, Compton and Edrich. Another huge stand, another quick hundred. Before the end, Compton had transcended mere cricketing fame. Like Hobbs in 1926 and Hutton in 1938 he took the giant stride from the back page to the front, hitting blinding centuries all over England while his effigy looked down from the hoardings in handsome brylcreemed splendour. It is often forgotten that most of Compton's runs came in a torrent towards the end of the summer, making his achievements more remarkable than ever. When it comes to a rush of blood to the head, the figure usually invoked is that of Major Robert Poore of Hampshire, whose eight-week spell in 1899 attained mythic status; it is revealing to compare his burst with Compton's between July 12 and September 17, 1947:

Poore   21   4   1551   304   91.2
Compton   25   6   2074   246   109.1

And if Poore in his great summer also found the time to play on the winning side in the final of the Army Polo Championships and win the mounted event for the best Man-at-Arms in the Army, then Compton must be credited with the winning of a First Division Championship medal with Arsenal in the winter that followed.

Moreover, in addition to eighteen centuries and nearly 4000 runs, he also took 73 wickets, with the singlehanded route of Surrey at The Oval as his finest hour.

But 1947 proved to be an Indian summer in quite a different way from the previous season. Never again were championship attendances to be so high, and there now began the steady decline, imperceptible at first, into crisis. Those who believe in portents may have found one in the legend of Compton's Knee, the cricketing counterpart of Achilles' Heel. The first postwar Australian side arrived, scored 700 in a day at Southend, and won a Test by scoring over 400 in the fourth innings. Glamorgan won their first championship. Compton scored the fastest triple century in history. In a match between Kent and Middlesex at Canterbury, the generations reached out and touched when Ames and Evans shared wicketkeeping duties. There was the Curious Incident of the Bowler's Bat, which mysteriously went clean through the Long Room window at Lord's one afternoon when the Derbyshire bowler Gladwin was returning to the pavilion after being run out. The seasons slipped by. Ramadhin and Valentine, May and Cowdrey, the former making an appearance in the Almanack under his nautical definition, ''Writer May''. In a match between Lancashire and Nottinghamshire, R. T. Simpson ensures the speed of foot of his fielding side in order not to rob the enemy of victory. Hutton becomes England's first professional captain; it is Coronation Year, and, as the title of Jack Fingleton's book suggests, the Ashes crown that year. There is the blistering pace of Tyson, and Jack Hobbs becomes Sir Jack. Lancashire win a match without losing a wicket, and Keith Miller turns out for Nottinghamshire. The age of Worrell, Weekes and Walcott merges into the age of Sobers. The West Indies under Worrell share a tied Test with Benaud's Australians, and the editor of the Almanack spots a promising youngster called Milburn, whom he describes with more tact than accuracy as ''a well-built lad''.

Then there are the throwers. Every generation has them, and this one boasts Griffin and Meckiff and Lock among others. Griffin in particular wins a place in the record books by taking a hat trick in a Test match and becoming, in the same match, the first bowler to be called for throwing in a Test in England. A university cricketer called J. M. Brearley is selected for his wicketkeeping, and one day in 1956 Laker breaks every Test bowling record in the books. At Bristol in 1961, Gloucestershire settle on the batting order against Yorkshire in the oddest of ways. One day at Southend the pitch is under four feet of sea water, and in a match at Sydney between New South Wales and Victoria there is staged the unsolved mystery of The Immovable Bail, the beneficiaries of this freakish event being Burke, Donaldson and Saggers. Then there are the visiting luminaries, Montgomery at Horsham, Attlee at The Oval, Eisenhower at Karachi. Lord Alexander offers to cancel an England tour and Sir Harold Wilson finds the Russian secret police to be poor close fielders. All of these incidents, however, pale before the happy fate of the Somerset side in 1946, who, on one occasion, found themselves to be strengthened by the presence in the side at Melton Mowbray against Leicestershire of no less renowned a captain than Caesar himself. Naturally Caesar appeared as an Amateur, a fact to remind the reader that it was in the period emcompassed by this volume that English cricket underwent one of the profoundest changes in its long history with the dropping of the distinction between the Gentlemen and the Players.

Last of all, and perhaps richest of all, there are the assorted departures, comprising as always a representative cross-section of British life. There were among this number the hardened professionals who tempered their affection for the game with good-natured cynicism expressing itself in asides like that of Harris of

Nottinghamshire on arrival at the wicket: "Good morning, fellow workers", or that of Skelding of Leicestershire on leaving it: "And that concludes the entertainment for today, gentlemen". Laughter from a vanished age, but a laughter not entirely without point, for both Harris and Skelding were expressing the contradiction of their situation, which was to play a pastime for a living. One who might have understood their worldliness was Alfred Isaac Russell who one day made a quick appeal to a slow umpire and was duly rebuffed.

Even more touching are those accidental curiosities whose origins are so ancient and so obscure as to be lost forever. The connoisseur of such affairs, ruminating on the odd academic fortunes of John Villiers Young, cannot help wondering if there was not some absurdly bizarre story behind his indecision regarding Oxbridge and Camford. And what of Tom Knight Hargreaves, an otherwise forgotten county reliable who could reasonably have claimed, and perhaps did, the honour of hitting a cricket ball further than any other man, and whose feat of striking a delivery in a Yorkshire Council match into Scunthorpe makes nonsense, of the pretensions of the Rev. W. Fellows, Albert Trott and company. To Father William Ignatius Rice falls distinction of a different kind, for although dedicating his life to teaching and theology, he fell into a habit of a less monastic cut by opening the batting occasionally for Warwickshire and becoming the only monk whose behaviour was monitored in the Almanack. But then the off-season antics of the cricketers may often render them more famous than the game itself, especially C. A. "Round-the-Corner" Smith, who, having captained England at cricket and played for the Carthusians at football, used this experience to considerable advantage by masquerading as Rudolph Rassendyll and Professor Henry Higgins before going on to become a celluloid companion to Tarzan of the Apes and a chortling chaperone for Shirly Temple. The facts suggest that Round-the-Corner never allowed these experiences to erase recollections of a happy sporting past. He eventually formed the Hollywood cricket club, administered it with the iron fist inside the iron glove, and remains one of the very few cricketers in history to have a ground named after him.

Rising to higher peaks of eccentricity, we find ourselves confronted by lives so singular and actions so *outré* as to defy belief. Tom Wass's expression of conjugal devotion was whimsical but not excessively so, and the orphaning of Colonel Turner seems doubly sad when we realise how little it deterred him from carrying on with the game. It is when we glimpse the figure of the Reverend George William Gillingham that we are struck dumb with admiration. It falls to a great many reverend gentlemen to cast their bread upon the waters, but to very few of them to cast themselves after it. This was what happened to George William Gillingham, whose devotion to duty concerning the county account books reduces Lord Byron's feat of swimming the Hellespont to the proportions of a paddle at the shallow end. And how can anyone make a coherent comment on the enigma of The Shifting Sands of Jeacocke's House, which might well be sub-titled in true Gilbertian style, "An Englishman's Home Are his Castles". Mention must also be made of the Incident of Newton's Snake, incorporating as it does one of the most interesting reasons for field-placing. As for Lieutenant-Colonel Frank Harris, his act at the age of 70 of embarking on a thirteen hour walk because his father told him to makes a later age wonder if he was not THE Frank Harris.

The palm, however, should go to Edward Humphrey Dalrymple Sewell, a man so eccentric that he would include menus in his books on cricket, and whose life embraced so multifarious a range of activities that the Almanack's obituarist is clearly unable to decide whether Sewell was an amateur who sometimes took money or a professional who occasionally refused it. The priceless euphemism, ''A curiously varied life'' means that Sewell managed to reconcile cheerfully enough his status as Indian civil servant, Essex professional, Surrey Coach, Buckinghamshire secretary and an author so wilful that in one of his published works he reproduced a photograph of himself wearing a mask so inscrutable that it was probably somebody else entirely. By the end of the period covered by this volume his type was indubitably in danger of extinction, a fact so sad that only a doctrinaire imbecile could fail to be depressed by it. It is perhaps just as well that Sewell finally took his leave only four days after the conclusion of Denis Compton's record-breaking season, no doubt happy in the illusion that nothing much had changed after all.

Benny Green

AUSTRALIANS IN ENGLAND

AUSTRALIA AND ENGLAND [1948]

SIDELIGHTS ON THE TESTS

By V. G. J. Jenkins

It is a truism that you cannot have the best of anything in this life without having the worst of it as well. This applies to the history of England-Australia Test cricket as surely as it does to the freedom of the Press, Elizabethan drama, Aunt Agatha's cooking, or any other institution subject to the whims and caprices of human nature.

For some reason, wherever there have been Tests there has also been Trouble.

Larwood and "bodyline" we all know, except those fortunates still in their 'teens. More recently the umpiring controversies of the 1946-47 tour "down under" are too fresh in the memory to need recalling. But these are only the more recent instalments in a serial that has gone on since the earliest days. As far back as 1879 there occurred in Sydney an incident which, if it were repeated today, would call for the combined efforts of UNO to restore order. Lord Harris's XI, beaten in the first Test match, were due to play a return, but it never took place owing to the high feeling caused by some remarkable scenes when the Tourists met New South Wales.

Umpires, even in those days, and an English one in particular, named Coulthard, caused the trouble. So enraged were the crowd by one of his decisions that they invaded the pitch. Those players best tactically situated were able to grab hold of the stumps to defend themselves. Others had to use their fists. Lord Harris was struck by a man with a stick, but A. N. Hornby intervened and carried off the culprit struggling to the pavilion. One can only imagine what repercussions this would have today.

Much the same happened to Sir Pelham Warner's team on the same ground in 1903-4, but this time physical intervention by the onlookers was limited to long-range bombardment with bottles and other missiles. Once again the reason for the outburst had a familiar ring – "Rain stopped play – crowd not agreeing".

Money, too, has always been a bone of contention. Five of the first nine teams to visit Australia, from 1862 and 1886, were all-professional ones under professional captains; this might surprise many moderns who constantly clamour for this as though it were something new.

Not unnaturally, with cricket not thoroughly established then as now, the financial side was a matter of some hazard. Therefore it came as a shock to Arthur Shrewsbury's team of 1884-85 when they found after their arrival in Australia that their opponents, supposedly amateurs, also wanted a half share of the gate receipts. This was against W. L. Murdoch's team, recently back from a successful tour of England. They were at last grudgingly offered 30 per cent of the takings for the first Test at Adelaide. This they refused to accept, but after further wrangling finally agreed to take a flat guarantee of £450 from the South Australian Cricket Association.

In the next Test at Melbourne, Murdoch's men withdrew absolutely, and though they came back to the fold by ones and twos for future matches the whole series became a farce. At Adelaide, Murdoch refused to accept James Lillywhite as an umpire, and two local men were brought in with dire results.

Another extraordinary interlude occurred in 1887-88, when two English teams went off to tour Australia concurrently. One under the Hon. M. B. Hawke, who returned to England because of the death of his father; the other C. Aubrey Smith, now better known in the role of a Bengal Lancer, with variations. They combined for the one Test, W. W. Read being captain.

Not unnaturally both teams suffered a severe financial loss, but provided an all-time deterrent to similar experiments in the future.

In those days Australian teams came to England on a "share all profits" basis, except for a few junior members, who had to be satisfied with a half-share as compared with their seniors. Victor Trumper was one such, but was so successful on his first tour that he was promoted to "full-sharing" status at the end of it.

Managers have always been fair game when other means of causing trouble have exhausted themselves. In 1912 six leading Australian players, Trumper, Clem Hill, Warwick Armstrong, Carter, Ransford and Cotter refused to come to England for the Triangular Tournament unless they were allowed to select their own manager.

To the credit of the Australian Board of Control, they stood firm in the matter and sent the team without the six players concerned, even though it caused a tremendous hullabaloo at the time.

For providing the real touch sinister, however, there has never been anything to beat dark hints about betting. We had a faint echo of it at Sydney in 1946-47. Yet it was in 1888 that some errant spirit, possibly no more than a misguided reveller, broke in to the Adelaide Oval overnight to water the pitch and hack lumps out of the turf, and George Giffen was impelled to write: "Whatever his object could have been is a mystery. If he had backed the Englishmen he did not need to damp the pitch, for they had us under the whip already, whilst if he was a South Australian backer he was not likely to improve our chance by watering the wicket." Presumably this accounts for the armed policemen who now stand guard over the wickets at night in Brisbane and elsewhere.

Not that bets have always been made *sub rosa*. George Bonnor once won a wager of £100 from a fellow-passenger on the ship to England that he would throw a cricket ball 115 yards on his first throw on landing. He did so – 119 yards 5 inches – on the parade ground of Raglan Barracks. At once he offered to make it £200 or nothing on the next throw being 125 yards, but the loser was taking no more chances.

Catering deficiencies, very often with good reason, have frequently stirred the public to wrath. Yet it was an alleged excess of catering zeal that caused one of the noisiest scenes ever witnessed at Kennington Oval.

When the Australians, in 1884, needed only 11 runs to win with nine wickets to fall against the Players, lunch was taken for the sole reason, the crowd thought, of "avoiding the caterer's loss". Whether rain might or might not have intervened appears not to have concerned them, and it took the united efforts of players and committeemen to restore order.

So it has gone on. Trouble in major or minor degree all along the line. But what of it? These have been but transient murmurings, squawks from the groundlings long since forgotten.

But Trumper is not forgotten. Nor Grace, Lohmann, Jackson, "Ranji", MacLaren, Fry, Noble, Murdoch, Spofforth, Clem Hill, Joe Darling, Warren Bardsley, and a host of others whose names trip off the tongue more easily than any list of Cabinet Ministers.

Arguments on the respective merits of Hobbs and Bradman, Hammond and Macartney, S. F. Barnes and O'Reilly will continue long after the storms about umpires' decisions have faded as surely as the minor squabbles of Gengis Khan's courtiers.

"Never the best without the worst." But it is only the best that survives. For what we have received . . .

ESSEX v AUSTRALIANS

Played at Southend, May 15, 17, 1948

Australians won by an innings and 451 runs. In light-hearted vein, they made history by putting together the highest total scored in a day of six hours in first-class cricket. Bradman led the run-getting revel on the Saturday. Complete master of the Essex bowlers on a fast pitch, he scored 187 in two hours five minutes, and by a wide variety of orthodox and unorthodox strokes hit thirty-two 4s and a 5. Brown's 153 occupied three hours and contained seventeen 4s. Loxton (fourteen 4s and a 6) and Saggers (nine 4s) also scored centuries. The biggest partnerships were 219 in ninety minutes between Brown and Bradman for the second wicket, 166 in sixty-five minutes by Loxton and Saggers for the sixth, and 145 in ninety-five minutes between Barnes and Brown for the first. Bailey dismissed Brown and Miller with successive balls, but generally the bowlers failed to stem the scoring. Because of injury Bailey did not bat in either innings. Essex, dismissed twice on Monday, first failed against the pace of Miller and the cleverly varied left-arm deliveries of Toshack; then in the follow-on – apart from Pearce and P. Smith, who made a stand of 133 – they broke down in face of Johnson's off-spinners. The attendance and receipts – 32,000 and £3,482 – were ground records.

Australians

S. G. Barnes hit wkt b R. Smith	79	
W. A. Brown c Horsfall b Bailey	153	
D. G. Bradman b P. Smith	187	
K. R. Miller b Bailey	0	
R. A. Hamence c P. Smith b R. Smith	46	
S. J. Loxton c Rist b Vigar	120	
R. A. Saggers not out	104	
I. W. Johnson st Rist b P. Smith	9	
D. Ring c Vigar b P. Smith	1	
W. A. Johnston b Vigar	9	
E. R. H. Toshack c Vigar b P. Smith	4	
B 7, n-b 2	9	
	721	

Essex

T. C. Dodds c Ring b Miller	0 – b Toshack	16
S. J. Cray b Miller	5 – b Johnson	15
A. V. Avery b Johnston	10 – c Brown b Johnson	3
F. H. Vigar c Saggers b Miller	0 – c Johnson b Toshack	0
R. Horsfall b Toshack	11 – b Johnson	8
T. N. Pearce c Miller b Toshack	8 – c and b Johnson	71
R. Smith c Barnes b Toshack	25 – c Ring b Johnson	0
T. P. B. Smith b Toshack	3 – lbw b Barnes	54
F. Rist c Barnes b Toshack	8 – b Johnson	1
E. Price not out	4 – not out	4
T. E. Bailey absent hurt	– absent hurt	
B 2, l-b 6, n-b 1	9 B 6, l-b 3, n-b 6	15
	83	**187**

Essex Bowling

	Overs	Mdns	Runs	Wkts
Bailey	21	1	128	2
R. Smith	37	2	169	2
P. Smith	38	—	193	4
Price	20	—	156	—
Vigar	13	1	66	2

Australian Bowling

	Overs	Mdns	Runs	Wkts	Overs	Mdns	Runs	Wkts
Miller	8	3	14	3	2	1	4	—
Johnston	7	1	10	1	10	4	26	—
Toshack	10.5	—	31	5	17	2	50	2
Ring	11	4	19	—	7	3	16	—
Loxton					12	3	28	—
Johnson					21	6	37	6
Barnes					9.4	5	11	1

Umpires: W. H. Ashdown and D. Hendren.

ENGLAND v AUSTRALIA
First Test Match

Played at Nottingham, June 10, 11, 12, 14, 15, 1948

Australia won by eight wickets. Bravely as England fought back, the result became nearly a foregone conclusion by the end of the first day after their disastrous batting against a fast attack of exceptionally high standard. Until the last moment considerable doubt existed about the composition of the England side. As Wright was doubtful through lumbago the Selectors sent for Pope (Derbyshire) on the eve of the match, but neither played, Wright being omitted through unfitness. Simpson (Nottinghamshire) was twelfth man. Although only twenty minutes' play was possible before lunch on Thursday, Miller struck a vital blow by clean bowling Hutton with an extra-fast ball and, on a pitch affected sufficiently by a heavy downpour during the interval to make the ball skid through, England lost eight wickets before tea for 74. True, the light never became good and the bowling reached a high level, but England played poorly and there could be no criticism of Yardley's decision to bat first. Washbrook hooked a short-rising ball to long-leg where Brown took a good running catch, Compton trying a leg sweep, missed a straight ball and Edrich was late with his stroke. Johnston, in the fifth over of his first Test against England, achieved the splendid feat of dismissing Edrich and Hardstaff, out second ball, and he continued to bowl left-arm medium-fast deliveries of sustained hostility – accurate in length, varied in pace and swing.

When Laker and Bedser came together, Australia were so much on top that there seemed every likelihood that England would be out for less than the lowest score made before in a Test at Nottingham – 112 by England in 1921 – but the two Surrey all-rounders batted so confidently that they more than doubled the total by adding 89 runs in seventy-three minutes. Laker hooked firmly and made many fine off-drives during a stay of ninety minutes, and Bedser mixed good defence with clean driving. A dazzling slip catch by Miller set the keynote on Australia's excellent fielding, but Australia suffered a handicap when Lindwall pulled a groin muscle midway through the innings and could not bowl again in the match. Johnston's full analysis was 25-11-36-5. Less than quarter of an hour remained for Australia to bat and neither Barnes nor Morris took a risk. Barnes made an unsuccessful appeal against the light after the first delivery of the innings – a wide by Edrich.

Although a good spell by Laker gave England great encouragement at one period on the second day Australia recovered and pressed home their advantage, but on a perfect pitch and in ideal weather conditions England deserved equal praise for limiting the batsmen to 276 runs in six hours. For the most part Yardley set a defensive field and, though lacking penetration, his bowlers performed their allotted tasks in concentrating on and just outside the leg stump. At one period Laker's off-breaks put the Australians into a position where they struggled for runs. Laker broke the opening stand of 73 and when he dismissed Barnes and Miller at 121 his analysis read: 12.4-5-22-3. Laker owed a great deal to Evans for disposing of Barnes who cut a ball hard on to the wicket-keeper's thigh whence it bounced into the air; Evans whirled round and diving full length held the ball with one hand inches from the ground. Miller played for an off-break, but the ball went with Laker's arm and resulted in an easy catch at slip. Then Yardley caused surprise by taking off Laker in order to use the new ball against Brown, normally an opening batsman accustomed to swing. The change in bowling provided Bradman with an opportunity to hit his first 4 after eighty-three minutes, but again he relapsed into long periods of defence and, as Brown followed suit, scoring became very slow with Australia fighting to restore their early superiority. They passed England's total without further loss, but at 184 Yardley went on for the first time in the innings and once again he showed his usefulness as a change bowler in Tests by getting Brown leg-before with his fourth delivery. England met with no other success on Friday; an unbroken stand of 108 between Bradman and Hassett left Australia 128 ahead. Seldom had Bradman been so subdued in a big innings as he was over the 28th Test century of his career. He did not welcome Yardley's tactics in asking his bowlers to work to a packed leg-side field, and he spent over three hours and a half in reaching his 100, the last 29 runs taking seventy minutes.

When play began on the Saturday Bradman needed only two runs to become the first player to complete 1,000 for the season. These he obtained, but in the third over Hutton at short fine-leg held the first of his series of catches given by Bradman off Bedser's late in-swinger. Bradman's unusually subdued innings lasted four hours and three-quarters. For the most part he allowed himself no liberty. On Bradman's departure Hassett became the big problem. Johnson fell to Laker's fifth ball and Young took a brilliant return catch from Tallon during a remarkable spell of bowling, before Hassett found an able partner in the hard-driving Lindwall, who did not require a runner in spite of his groin trouble. In one period of over an hour Young sent down eleven overs without conceding a run and his figures for a complete spell of two hours and a half were: 26-16-14-1. In the innings Young gave away only 79 runs in 60 overs. The eighth-wicket stand added 107 before Bedser knocked Hassett's off-stump, so taking his 50th wicket in Test cricket. Four runs later Evans caught Lindwall smartly on the leg side. Though Hassett pursued his policy of defence for five hours and fifty minutes he hit hard whenever the opportunity arose and his strokes included a 6 and twenty 4s. A last-wicket partnership of 33 emphasised England's difficulties which were increased immediately they began the second innings, 344 behind. Once more Australia gained the incentive of a fine start, when in Miller's second over Washbrook attempted to hook a bumper and edged a catch to the wicket-keeper. Misjudgement in cutting a ball outside the off stump cost Edrich his wicket at 39, but Hutton showed sparkling form and Compton overcame an anxious start against Johnson. In a delightful display of stroke-making Hutton reached 50 with two successive 4s off Miller in an over which produced 14 runs. At this period Miller bowled medium-paced off-breaks, but he turned again to fast deliveries and incurred the noisy displeasure of sections of the crowd when he bowled five bumpers to Hutton in his last eight balls, one of which struck the batsman high on the left arm. By the most attractive batting so far in the match Hutton and Compton scored 82 together in the last seventy minutes.

Before play began on Monday the Nottinghamshire Secretary, Mr H. A. Brown, broadcast an appeal to the crowd to leave the conduct of the game to the umpires and he deplored the barracking of Miller on Saturday. The not-out batsmen continued their good work, but the light became even worse than in the first innings. After an unsuccessul appeal play was held up when the ground caught the edge of a thunderstorm. Almost immediately on the resumption Miller produced a fast break-back which beat Hutton completely in the still gathering gloom. Bad light interrupted the game soon afterwards and though the stoppage was brief conditions became so bad again that the players retired a second time. On this occasion Compton wanted only three runs for his century. After fifty-five minutes the umpires thought the light good enough to continue, but it was still bad. Indeed, rarely can a Test Match have been played under such appalling conditions as on this day. Great credit was due to Compton and Hardstaff, even in the absence of Lindwall, for their resolution. Although Hardstaff went at 243 and Barnett did not settle down Compton batted in masterly fashion when continuing his third century in successive Tests at Trent Bridge, and Yardley gave sound aid till Johnston took a return catch smartly. England faced an almost hopeless task at the beginning of the last day when they stood only one run ahead with four wickets left, but hope remained as long as Compton was undefeated. He found another fine partner in Evans and in spite of two short breaks for rain they held out till ten minutes before lunch when Miller released a lightning bumper at Compton. The ball reared shoulder-high, Compton shaped to hook then changed his mind and tried to get his head out of the way. As he ducked Compton lost his balance on the muddy turf and tumbled into his wicket.

This tragic end to one of the best innings of Compton's career and his highest in Test cricket against Australia sealed England's fate. No praise could be too high for the manner in which Compton carried the side's responsibilities and defied a first-class attack in such trying circumstances. He held out for six hours fifty minutes and hit nineteen 4s.

Evans completed a gallant 50, which included eight boundary strokes, but the end of the innings soon came and Australia wanted only 98 to win. Miller, who accounted for England's two best batsmen, Hutton and Compton, in each innings, and Johnston shared chief bowling honours. Australia fielded grandly, in contrast to England, and no one was better than the twelfth man, Harvey, substituting for Lindwall, whose absence threw much extra work on the other bowlers.

Bedser added interest to the last stages by bowling Morris at 38 and dismissing Bradman for his first "duck" in a Test in England, caught in exactly the same manner as in the first innings; but Barnes and Hassett quickly hit off the runs, Barnes showing tremendous power in square-cutting. The match ended humorously. After making a boundary stroke Barnes thought the game was over when the scores were level, and he snatched a stump before racing towards the pavilion. Barnes was halfway up the pavilion steps when the shouts of the crowd made him realise the error and he returned to the crease. When Hassett did make the winning hit another scramble for souvenirs took place; and in this Barnes was unlucky.   R.J.H.

England

L. Hutton b Miller	3	– b Miller	74
C. Washbrook c Brown b Lindwall	6	– c Tallon b Miller	1
W. J. Edrich b Johnston	18	– c Tallon b Johnson	13
D. C. S. Compton b Miller	19	– hit wkt b Miller	184
J. Hardstaff c Miller b Johnston	0	– c Hassett b Toshack	43
C. J. Barnett b Johnston	8	– c Miller b Johnston	6
N. W. D. Yardley lbw b Toshack	3	– c and b Johnston	22
T. G. Evans c Morris b Johnston	12	– c Tallon b Johnston	50
J. C. Laker c Tallon b Miller	63	– b Miller	4
A. V. Bedser c Brown b Johnston	22	– not out	3
J. A. Young not out	1	– b Johnston	9
B 5, l-b 5	10	B 12, l-b 17, n-b 3	32

1/9 2/15 3/46 4/46 5/48   165   1/5 2/39 3/150 4/243 5/264   441
6/60 7/74 8/74 9/163   6/321 7/405 8/413 9/423

Australia

S. G. Barnes c Evans b Laker	62	– not out	64
A. R. Morris b Laker	31	– b Bedser	9
D. G. Bradman c Hutton b Bedser	138	– c Hutton b Bedser	0
K. R. Miller c Edrich b Laker	0		
W. A. Brown lbw b Yardley	17		
A. L. Hassett b Bedser	137	– not out	21
I. W. Johnson b Laker	21		
D. Tallon c and b Young	10		
R. R. Lindwall c Evans b Yardley	42		
W. A. Johnston not out	17		
E. R. H. Toshack lbw b Bedser	19		
B 9, l-b 4, w 1, n-b 1	15	L-b 2, w 1, n-b 1	4

1/73 2/121 3/121 4/185 5/305   509   1/38 2/48   (2 wkts) 98
6/338 7/365 8/472 9/476

Australia Bowling

	Overs	Mdns	Runs	Wkts	Overs	Mdns	Runs	Wkts
Lindwall	13	5	30	1				
Miller	19	8	38	3	44	10	125	4
Johnston	25	11	36	5	59	12	147	4
Toshack	14	8	28	1	33	14	60	1
Johnson	5	1	19	—	42	15	66	1
Morris	3	1	4	—				
Barnes					5	2	11	—

England Bowling

	Overs	Mdns	Runs	Wkts	Overs	Mdns	Runs	Wkts
Edrich............	18	1	72	—	4	—	20	—
Bedser............	44.2	12	113	3	14.3	4	46	2
Barnett	17	5	36	—				
Young	60	28	79	1	10	3	28	—
Laker	55	14	138	4				
Compton	5	—	24	—				
Yardley...........	17	6	32	2				

Umpires: F. Chester and E. Cooke.

ENGLAND v AUSTRALIA
Third Test Match

Played at Manchester, July 8, 9, 10, 12, 13, 1948

Drawn. Fate dealt its sharpest blow of the series to England by the breaking of the weather over the week-end at a time when defeat for Australia appeared more than a possibility. By the end of the third day England had recovered so well from another disastrous start that they stood 316 runs on with only three wickets down in the second innings, but visions of Australia struggling to avoid being beaten were dispelled by rain which made further play impossible till after lunch on the last day. Another interruption then meant that Australia needed to bat only two hours and a half, and on a pitch reduced to sluggishness by nearly two days of heavy rain they found little difficulty in saving the game. So the sequence of unfinished England-Australia Tests at Manchester since 1905 remained unbroken.

The England Selectors aroused intense pre-match discussion by their omission of Hutton. Wright, Coxon and Laker also stood down, their places being taken by Emmett, Young, Pollard and Crapp, with Wardle (Yorkshire) twelfth man. Emmett's mettle was soon tested, for Bradman, playing in his 50th Test, again lost the toss and England took first innings on a pitch lively for the first few overs. Probably upset by narrowly escaping a run-out off the first ball of the match, the new opening combination did not look comfortable and Johnston began an early collapse by yorking Washbrook. The second English misfortune came when Emmett pushed out his bat with one hand after losing sight of a short-pitched ball which lifted. Barnes, at short-leg, took an easy catch. With Edrich seemingly afraid to play his strokes in a determined effort to redeem previous low scores and Compton not settled down, Lindwall began a number of bouncers one of which led to an accident to Compton. After being struck on the arm he took a big hit at a "no-ball" bumper, but the ball flew off the edge of his bat on to his forehead. Compton staggered around and was led off the field with a cut head. Stitches were inserted and though he wanted to go back at the fall of the next wicket he was ordered to rest. The situation called for the relentless defence which Edrich and Crapp adopted. At one period they scored only one run in twenty-five minutes and by lunch the total stood at 57, the result of two hours of laboured batting. Mixed with similar caution, Crapp afterwards began to reveal his scoring strokes and drove Johnson for a 6 and three 4s before Lindwall and Johnston returned with the new ball. Then in brief time Crapp was leg-before, Dollery hit over a yorker and Edrich touched a rising flier. Edrich deserved more credit for staying three hours five minutes while Compton was able to rest than criticism for scoring only 32 runs in that period. After a short knock at the nets, Compton resumed with five men out for 119. At once he introduced an air of confidence into the batting and, after losing Yardley, he found a fine partner in Evans whose bold hitting helped to bring 75 runs in seventy minutes. At the close England were 231 for seven, Lindwall and Johnston having shared the bowling honours.

Though the new ball was in use at the start of the second day Australia could not retain their grip, for Compton received splendid support from Bedser, who in two hours and a half shared in a stand of 121, only three short of England's eighth-wicket record against Australia. Bedser used his height and feet well in dealing with the pace attack and looked capable of going on for a long time; unfortunately he was run out through an error of judgment by Compton. Soon after Bedser's dismissal occurred a second distressing accident. Barnes, fielding in his usual position about five yards from the bat at short-leg, received a fierce blow under the ribs from a full-blooded pull by Pollard. After being carried off by four policemen Barnes was removed on a stretcher to hospital where examination showed that no bones were broken. Compton, who remained undefeated at the end of the innings, might have been caught at the wicket four times – three chances were very difficult – but he gave a grand display of skill and courage. For five hours twenty minutes he carried his side's responsibilities and nothing earned more admiration than the manner in which he withstood some lightning overs of extreme hostility by Lindwall. Compton hit sixteen 4s.

Pollard unwittingly struck a big blow for England when he hit Barnes, because Australia, having dropped Brown after the Second Test, possessed only one recognised opening batsman. The necessary re-arrangement no doubt played its part in Australia's only batting failure of the Tests, but Bedser and Pollard deserved full credit for their share in gaining England a lead of 142. A fine catch by Evans sent back Johnson, the emergency partner to Morris, and soon Bradman was leg-before to persistent Pollard. This was a great start for England on a slow, easy pitch and when Hassett misjudged Young's flight three men were out for 82. During these set-backs Morris, the left-hander, batted cautiously with distinction, but he and Miller left early on the third morning when Pollard and Bedser each took a wicket with the new ball. So began a day when again everything went in England's favour. At the fall of Miller's wicket Barnes, who had practised in the nets where he collapsed after a few minutes, surprisingly went out to bat, but he was obviously in great pain and, after staying half an hour for a single, he sank to the ground and had to be assisted off. He was taken to hospital again and kept for ten days under observation. Loxton, Tallon and Lindwall drove hard in helping to avoid the possibility of a follow-on, however unlikely its enforcement, but Bedser and Pollard maintained their grip and altogether on Monday the last six wickets fell for 95.

Australia naturally flung everything into attack in the effort to recover lost ground. A dazzling right-hand catch by Tallon dismissed Emmett off the first ball he received from Lindwall, but Washbrook and Edrich stood firm in a period of tenseness in which Miller, called upon for the first time since the Nottingham Test, and Lindwall bowled at great speed. The absence of Barnes from short-leg removed one nagging worry from the minds of Washbrook and Edrich who, helped by unusually poor Australian fielding, strengthened England's position in a second-wicket stand of 124 which vindicated their retention in the side. Washbrook was twice dropped at long-leg and once at slip, but Edrich did not offer a chance. Immediately after reaching 50 with a six Edrich was run out, a fast throw from cover by Morris knocking two stumps out of the ground. Edrich played one of his best and most confident innings, and was not affected by a succession of bumpers from Miller which annoyed sections of the crowd. Compton did not score, but Crapp gave solid support to Washbrook through a new-ball period and the partnership was unbroken at the declaration. Washbrook batted three hours twenty-five minutes and hit eleven 4s; he got within 15 of what would have been his first Test century against Australia in England.

Then the weather intervened. No play took place on Monday and cricket was not resumed till after lunch on Tuesday. Yardley declared first thing in the morning but more showers lessened the hope of victory. Although Young caused brief excitement when he got rid of Johnson with his second ball, the pitch was too lifeless to give bowlers help and Morris and Bradman contented themselves with dead-bat tactics, each remaining at one end. In one spell of a hundred minutes they did not change ends. Morris completed his fourth consecutive Test half-century and, like Bradman, showed adaptability to the conditions. The aggregate attendance of 133,740 was higher than that at Lord's a fortnight earlier. R.J.H.

England

C. Washbrook b Johnston	11	– not out	85
G. M. Emmett c Barnes b Lindwall	10	– c Tallon b Lindwall	0
W. J. Edrich c Tallon b Lindwall	32	– run out	53
D. C. S. Compton not out	145	– c Miller b Toshack	0
J. F. Crapp lbw b Lindwall	37	– not out	19
H. E. Dollery b Johnston	1		
N. W. D. Yardley c Johnson b Toshack	22		
T. G. Evans c Johnston b Lindwall	34		
A. V. Bedser run out	37		
R. Pollard b Toshack	3		
J. A. Young c Bradman b Johnston	4		
B 7, l-b 17, n-b 3	27	B 9, l-b 7, w 1	17

1/22 2/28 3/96 4/97 5/119   363   1/1 2/125 3/129   (3 wkts dec.) 174
6/141 7/216 8/337 9/352

Australia

A. R. Morris c Compton b Bedser	51	– not out	54
I. W. Johnson c Evans b Bedser	1	– c Crapp b Young	6
D. G. Bradman lbw b Pollard	7	– not out	30
A. L. Hassett c Washbrook b Young	38		
K. R. Miller lbw b Pollard	31		
S. G. Barnes retired hurt	1		
S. J. Loxton b Pollard	36		
D. Tallon c Evans b Edrich	18		
R. R. Lindwall c Washbrook b Bedser	23		
W. A. Johnston c Crapp b Bedser	3		
E. R. H. Toshack not out	0		
B 5, l-b 4, n-b 3	12	N-b 2	2

1/3 2/13 3/82 4/135 5/139   221   1/10   (1 wkt) 92
6/172 7/208 8/219 9/221

Australia Bowling

	Overs	Mdns	Runs	Wkts	Overs	Mdns	Runs	Wkts
Lindwall	40	8	99	4	14	4	37	1
Johnston	45.5	13	67	3	14	3	34	—
Loxton	7	—	18	—	8	1	29	—
Toshack	41	20	75	2	12	5	26	1
Johnson	38	16	77	—	7	3	16	—
Miller					14	7	15	—

England Bowling

	Overs	Mdns	Runs	Wkts	Overs	Mdns	Runs	Wkts
Bedser.	36	12	81	4	19	12	27	—
Pollard	32	9	53	3	10	8	6	—
Edrich.	7	3	27	1	2	—	8	—
Yardley.	4	—	12	—				
Young.	14	5	36	1	21	12	31	1
Compton					9	3	18	—

Umpires: D. Davies and F. Chester.

ENGLAND v AUSTRALIA
Fourth Test Match

Played at Leeds, July 22, 23, 24, 26, 27, 1948

Australia won by seven wickets. By the astonishing feat of scoring 404 for three wickets on the fifth day of the match when the pitch took spin, Australia won the rubber. Until that fatal last stage England were on top, but a succession of blunders prevented them gaining full reward for good work on the first four days.

The biggest mistake occurred before the game started, for the selectors decided to leave out Young, the slow left-arm bowler who had been invited to Leeds as one of the original party. Consequently England took the field with an unbalanced attack. Having only one slow bowler available, Yardley did not know what to do for the best on the last day, and he was forced to make Compton the spearhead and to employ Hutton, who to that point had bowled no more than 22 overs in the season. Even then England should have won. Evans, behind the wicket, fell a long way below his best form, and three catches were dropped in the field.

Australia put together the biggest fourth innings total in a Test match between the two countries in England; also the aggregate of 1,723 runs was the highest for any match in England.

Handicapped through injuries to Barnes and Tallon, the Australians were forced to make two changes, Harvey and Saggers appearing for the first time against England. The English selectors brought in Hutton, Cranston and Laker for Young, Dollery and Emmett; after being omitted from the original twelve, Emmett was unexpectedly called from Torquay, where he was playing for Gloucestershire in a friendly match, and made twelfth man. The explanation for this surprising move was never officially given, but it was understood that the selectors were worried in case anything unexpected should happen to one of their batsmen.

When Yardley won the toss for the third time in four matches, England gained first use of a perfect pitch. Without Barnes, Bradman did not place a fieldsman close in at forward short leg and the batsmen welcomed their freedom. After their disappointing starts together in the earlier games, Hutton and Washbrook gave England a great send-off with an opening stand of 168, their best partnership in any Test match. Hutton completely justified his recall to the side and Washbrook successfully eliminated the dangerous high hook stroke which often caused his downfall in earlier Tests. He completed an almost faultless hundred out of 189 and fell in the last over of the day after batting five hours twenty minutes. His second stand with Edrich produced 100.

Bedser, sent in to play the last four balls overnight, proved such an efficient stop-gap that the third successive century partnership resulted. For the second day running the Australians met with no success before lunch, and the third wicket realised 155 before Bedser, who made his highest score in any Test, gave a return catch. Edrich left three runs later after batting five hours ten minutes. This quick fall of wickets revitalised the Australians and the England batting broke down badly. From a total of 423 for two, England were all out 496.

Hassett and Morris opened the Australian innings, but did not shape confidently. Morris left at 13, and next morning Pollard, in his first over, sent back Hassett and Bradman in three balls, making Australia 68 for three. Then nineteen-year-old Neil Harvey joined Miller, and, delivering a terrific onslaught on the England attack, they rescued Australia from their precarious position. In just over an hour and a half they put on 121 by glorious stroke-play. Loxton carried on the big hitting and, with Harvey, added 105 in ninety-five minutes. Harvey hit seventeen 4s while making 112 − his second successive Test century. Loxton's terrific driving brought five 6s and nine 4s. Yet despite this punishment England held the upper hand, for with eight wickets down Australia were 141 behind. Then occurred a similar experience to that at Lord's, where Australia's tail-end batsmen could not be dislodged. Johnston and an injured Toshack, who batted with the aid of a runner, in turn helped Lindwall with such success that the last two wickets added 103 and England's lead was restricted to 38.

Hutton and Washbrook opened with a century stand for the second time in the match and created a new world record for Test cricket in accomplishing the feat twice. Both left at 129, but England consolidated their position by rapid scoring. Edrich and Compton put on 103 at more than one a minute and, although a slight collapse followed, Evans, with help from Bedser and Laker, punished the bowling. At the close of the fourth day England led by 400 with two wickets left.

To most people Yardley's decision to continue batting for five minutes next day came as a surprise and the reason for it aroused plenty of comment. The main idea was to break up the pitch by the use of the heavy roller. Three runs were added in two overs, and then Yardley declared, leaving Australia to score 404 in 345 minutes. The pitch took spin and the ball lifted and turned sharply. Unfortunately, Laker was erratic in length. Compton, bowling his left-hand off-breaks and googlies, baffled the batsmen several times, but without luck. Evans should have stumped Morris when 32, and Compton only gained reward when he held a return catch from Hassett at 57, but he ought to have dismissed Bradman, Crapp dropping a catch at first slip. In half an hour before lunch Morris and Bradman put on 64, and after the interval, against a succession of full tosses and long hops, runs continued to flow. When 59 Bradman had another escape off Compton, and Yardley, in despair, called for the new ball even though the pitch favoured spin. Evans should have stumped Bradman when 108, and Laker at square leg dropped Morris when 126. Not until 301 had been put on did England break the stand, and by that time the match was as good as won. Morris batted four hours fifty minutes for 182. Miller did not last long, but Harvey made the winning stroke within fifteen minutes of time. No fewer than 66 fours were hit in the innings, 33 by Morris and 29 by Bradman.

The attendance figures of 158,000 created a record for any match in England. Receipts amounted to £34,000. **L.S.**

England

L. Hutton b Lindwall	81	– c Bradman b Johnson	57
C. Washbrook c Lindwall b Johnston	143	– c Harvey b Johnston	65
W. J. Edrich c Morris b Johnson	111	– lbw b Lindwall	54
A. V. Bedser c and b Johnson	79	– c Hassett b Miller	17
D. C. S. Compton c Saggers b Lindwall	23	– c Miller b Johnston	66
J. F. Crapp b Toshack	5	– b Lindwall	18
N. W. D. Yardley b Miller	25	– c Harvey b Johnston	7
K. Cranston b Loxton	10	– c Saggers b Johnston	0
T. G. Evans c Hassett b Loxton	3	– not out	47
J. C. Laker c Saggers b Loxton	4	– not out	15
R. Pollard not out	0		
B 2, l-b 8, w 1, n-b 1	12	B 4, l-b 12, n-b 3	10

1/168 2/268 3/423 4/426 5/447   496   1/129 2/129 3/232   (8 wkts dec.) 365
6/473 7/486 8/490 9/496   4/260 5/277 6/278 7/293 8/330

Australia

A. R. Morris c Cranston b Bedser	6	– c Pollard b Yardley	182
A. L. Hassett c Crapp b Pollard	13	– c and b Compton	17
D. G. Bradman b Pollard	33	– not out	173
K. R. Miller c Edrich b Yardley	58	– lbw b Cranston	12
R. N. Harvey b Laker	112	– not out	4
S. J. Loxton b Yardley	93		
I. W. Johnson c Cranston b Laker	10		
R. R. Lindwall c Crapp b Bedser	77		
R. A. Saggers st Evans b Laker	5		
W. A. Johnston c Edrich b Bedser	13		
E. R. H. Toshack not out	12		
B 9, l-b 14, n-b 3	26	B 6, l-b 9, n-b 1	16

1/13 2/65 3/68 4/189 5/294   458   1/57 2/358 3/396   (3 wkts) 404
6/329 7/344 8/355 9/403

Australia Bowling

	Overs	Mdns	Runs	Wkts	Overs	Mdns	Runs	Wkts
Lindwall	38	10	79	2	26	6	84	2
Miller	17.1	2	43	1	21	5	53	1
Johnston	38	13	86	1	29	5	95	4
Toshack	35	6	112	1				
Loxton	26	4	55	3	10	2	29	—
Johnson	33	9	89	2	21	2	85	1
Morris	5	—	20					

England Bowling

	Overs	Mdns	Runs	Wkts	Overs	Mdns	Runs	Wkts
Bedser	31.2	4	92	3	21	2	56	—
Pollard	38	6	100	2	22	6	55	—
Cranston	14	1	51	—	7.1	—	28	1
Edrich	3	—	19	—				
Laker	30	8	113	3	32	11	93	—
Yardley	17	6	38	2	13	1	44	1
Compton	3	—	15	—	15	3	82	1
Hutton					4	1	30	—

Umpires: F. Chester and H. G. Baldwin.

ENGLAND v AUSTRALIA
Fifth Test Match

Played at Kennington Oval, August 14, 16, 17, 18, 1948

Australia won by an innings and 149 runs, so completing their triumph in the rubber with four victories and one draw.

England having been placed in a humiliating position already, the selectors tried further experiments which aroused strong condemnation. Washbrook, suffering from a damaged thumb, was replaced by Dewes, and Watkins, an unknown quantity in representative cricket, not then prominent for Glamorgan, completed the side, with Simpson twelfth man. These changes proved unfortunate, and Australia met with little hindrance on the road to their most emphatic victory in this series of Tests.

Extraordinary cricket marked the opening day. So saturated was the ground by copious rain during the week that the groundsmen could not get the pitch into a reasonable state for a punctual start. The captains agreed that play should begin at 12 o'clock, and Yardley, having won the toss, chose to bat – an inevitable decision with the conditions uncertain and the possibility of more rain. As it happened, apart from local showers early on Sunday morning, the weather proved fine until England fared badly for the second time. All things considered, the Australians found everything favourable for them, as was the case at Lord's. This does not explain the lamentable collapse of England for the lowest score by either side in a Test at The Oval, apart from the 44 for which Australia fell in 1896, the last occasion on which W. G. Grace led England to victory. This followed their dismissal at Lord's in the first of three Tests, for 53, the bowlers being J. T. Hearne and R. Peel.

The sodden state of the pitch, with sawdust covering large patches of turf nearby, made one doubt its fitness for cricket. Bowlers and batsmen found much sawdust necessary for a foothold. This supposed handicap did not seem to trouble the Australians, and reasons for the downfall of England in two hours and a half for such a meagre score were the splendid attack maintained by Lindwall, Miller and Johnston in humid atmosphere against batsmen whose first error proved fatal. Hutton, the one exception to complete failure, batted in his customary stylish, masterful manner throughout the innings, being last out from a leg glance which Tallon held with the left hand close to the ground as he fell – a great finish to Australia's splendid performance.

Lindwall, with his varied pace and occasional very fast ball, excelled. Always bowling at the stumps, he made the ball rise at different heights. Four times he clean bowled a hesitant opponent. Except that Watkins received a blow on the shoulder that destroyed his supposed value as a bowler, the batsmen escaped injury during a most pitiful display. After lunch Lindwall bowled 8.1 overs, four maidens, and took five wickets at a cost of 8 runs!

Everything became different when Australia batted. Barnes and Morris, with controlled assurance and perfect stroke play, made 117, and shortly before six o'clock Bradman walked to the wicket amidst continued applause from the standing crowd. Yardley shook hands with Bradman and called on the England team for three cheers, in which the crowd joined. Evidently deeply touched by the enthusiastic reception, Bradman survived one ball, but, playing forward to the next, was clean bowled by a sharply turning break-back – possibly a googly. As if to avenge the fall of these two wickets in an over, Morris twice hooked Hollies to the boundary and the score rose to 153, while on Monday it reached 226 before Hassett left – 109 for the third wicket. That those runs occupied two hours and a quarter testified to good bowling and fielding by a side in a forlorn position, and the next best partnership was the sixth, which added 39.

Morris missed the special distinction of making 200 through his own ill-judged call for a sharp run, Simpson, fielding substitute for Watkins, with a good return from third man causing his dismissal for 196. Scoring these runs out of 359 in six hours forty minutes, Morris hit sixteen 4s. His strokes past cover-point were typical of the highest class left-handed batsmen. His drives and hooks beat the speediest fieldsmen, and he showed marked skill in turning the ball to leg. He was eighth out, and Tallon got most of the 30 runs added before Bedser at last earned reward for steady bowling by taking the tenth wicket.

Facing arrears of 337, England lost Dewes with 20 scored, but Hutton and Edrich raised the total to 54 before bad light stopped play. The conditions remained anything but good on Tuesday, when the early fall of Edrich to a fine ball from Lindwall preceded the only stand of consequence, Compton and Hutton putting on 61 in an hour and fifty minutes before Lindwall, with his left hand at second slip, held a hard cut from Compton. Hutton maintained his sound form until a bumper from Miller struck Crapp on the head, soon after which the Yorkshireman gave Tallon a catch. Batting four hours and a quarter for 64 out of 153, Hutton was always restrained but admirable in defence.

After he left three wickets fell in deepening gloom for 25 runs. Evans, from the way he shaped without attempting a stroke, obviously could not see the ball which bowled him. Lindwall, with the pavilion behind him, sending down something like a yorker at express speed. The umpires immediately responded to the appeal against the light, and rain at four o'clock delayed the finish until Wednesday morning, when the remaining three wickets realised only ten runs in a sad spectacle for England. The usual scramble for the stumps and bails as Morris held a lofted catch from Hollies marked the close; but much happened subsequently. Mr H. D. G. Leveson Gower on the players balcony called for three cheers for Bradman and the victorious Australians. Responses over the microphone came in due course, the crowd of about 5,000 enthusiasts coming up to the pavilion to hear and see all that happened as a curtain to this series of Test matches in which Australia completely outplayed and conquered England.   H.P.

England

L. Hutton c Tallon b Lindwall	30	– c Tallon b Miller	64
J. G. Dewes b Miller	1	– b Lindwall	10
W. J. Edrich c Hassett b Johnston	3	– b Lindwall	28
D. C. S. Compton c Morris b Lindwall	4	– c Lindwall b Johnston	39
J. F. Crapp c Tallon b Miller	0	– b Miller	9
N. W. D. Yardley b Lindwall	7	– c Miller b Johnston	9
A. Watkins lbw b Johnston	0	– c Hassett b Ring	2
T. G. Evans b Lindwall	1	– b Lindwall	8
A. V. Bedser b Lindwall	0	– b Johnston	0
J. A. Young b Lindwall	0	– not out	3
W. E. Hollies not out	0	– c Morris b Johnston	0
B 6	6	B 9, l-b 4, n-b 3	16

1/2 2/10 3/17 4/23 5/35   52   1/20 2/64 3/125 4/153 5/164   188
6/42 7/45 8/45 9/47   6/167 7/178 8/181 9/188

Australia

S. G. Barnes c Evans b Hollies	61	D. Tallon c Crapp b Hollies	31
A. R. Morris run out	196	D. Ring c Crapp b Bedser	9
D. G. Bradman b Hollies	0	W. A. Johnston not out	0
A. J. Hassett lbw b Young	37		
K. R. Miller st Evans b Hollies	5	B 4, l-b 2, n-b 3	9
R. N. Harvey c Young b Hollies	17		
S. J. Loxton c Evans b Edrich	15	1/117 2/117 3/226 4/243 5/265	389
R. R. Lindwall c Edrich b Young	9	6/304 7/332 8/359 9/389	

Australia Bowling

	Overs	Mdns	Runs	Wkts	Overs	Mdns	Runs	Wkts
Lindwall	16.1	5	20	6	25	3	50	3
Miller	8	5	5	2	15	6	22	2
Johnston.	16	4	20	2	27.3	12	40	4
Loxton	2	1	1	—	10	2	16	—
Ring					28	13	44	1

England Bowling

	Overs	Mdns	Runs	Wkts
Bedser.	31.2	9	61	1
Watkins	4	1	19	—
Young.	51	16	118	2
Hollies	56	14	131	5
Compton	2	—	6	—
Edrich.	9	—	38	1
Yardley.	5	1	7	—

Umpires: D. Davies and H. G. Baldwin.

GENTLEMEN v AUSTRALIANS

Played at Lord's, August 25, 26, 27, 1948

Australians won by an innings and 81 runs. Bradman celebrated his farewell appearance at Lord's with his ninth century of the tour in the course of which he became the first overseas cricketer to score 2,000 runs during each of four visits to England. Once again the Australians' big total robbed the match of much competitive interest. Brown, who hit his eighth century in his most attractive innings of the season, showed even more freedom than Bradman, with whom he shared a second-wicket stand of 181. With leg-glances and on-drives he repeatedly found gaps in the field, and he hit a 5 and fifteen 4s. Bradman (nineteens 4s) threw away his wicket after reaching 150, but Hassett and Miller took part in the third century stand in succession, the Australians finishing the first day with 478 for three. After hooking the second and third deliveries next morning for four and six, Miller gave deep square-leg a catch off the fourth, but Hassett continued effortlessly and reached 200 in the last over before lunch when Bradman declared. Hassett's first century at Leed's included eighteen boundaries. A sound stand of 55 by Edrich and Simpson promised well for the Gentlemen, but thereafter the varied attack generally held command. The Gentlemen's follow-on was notable for a free display by Edrich and skilful leg-break bowling by Ring. Simpson helped in an opening partnership of 60 and Palmer shared a second-wicket stand of 113 with Edrich, who made 128 out of 217 in three and a quarter hours. Edrich, who hit twenty-two 4s, went from 72 to 100 in boundary strokes alone.

Australians

S. G. Barnes c Wooler b Bailey. 19	S. J. Loxton c Griffith b Bailey 17
W. A. Brown c Bailey b Wooller. 120	R. A. Hamence not out. 24
D. G. Bradman c Donnelly b Brown. 150	B 6, l-b 4, w 1 11
A. L. Hassett not out. 200	___
K. R. Miller c Simpson b Wooller. 69	(5 wkts dec.) 610

I. W. Johnson, R. R. Lindwall, R. A. Saggers and D. Ring did not bat.

Gentlemen

R. T. Simpson c Brown b Johnson	60	– c Bradman b Ring	27
W. J. Edrich b Ring	27	– c Saggers b Ring	128
C. H. Palmer c and b Johnson	3	– b Miller	29
M. P. Donnelly lbw b Johnson	15	– c Barnes b Miller	8
N. W. D. Yardley b Miller	25	– b Ring	18
F. G. Mann lbw b Lindwall	7	– c and b Ring	0
R. W. V. Robins b Johnson	30	– b Johnson	19
W. Wooller c Johnson b Hamence	11	– c Loxton b Ring	5
T. E. Bailey c Hamence b Ring	20	– not out	14
F. R. Brown c Hamence b Ring	18	– c Brown b Johnson	17
S. C. Griffith not out	13	– b Johnson	0
B 8, l-b 8	16	B 11, l-b 7, w 1	19

245   284

Gentlemen Bowling

	Overs	Mdns	Runs	Wkts
Bailey	27	4	112	2
Wooller	24	1	131	2
Palmer	21	3	58	—
Edrich	16	3	49	—
Yardley	24	5	88	—
Brown	27	—	121	1
Robins	4	—	22	—
Donnelly	6	—	18	—

Australian Bowling

	Overs	Mdns	Runs	Wkts	Overs	Mdns	Runs	Wkts
Miller	7	3	18	1	19	6	58	2
Lindwall	13	3	39	1				
Johnson	23	7	60	4	28.5	9	69	3
Hamence	8	2	23	1	3	1	18	—
Ring	25.3	7	74	3	32	8	70	5
Barnes	3	2	4	—	5	—	24	—
Loxton	8	2	11	—	13	7	26	—

Umpires: P. T. Mills and J. Smart.

SIR DONALD BRADMAN [1949]

By R. C. Robertson-Glasgow

Don Bradman will bat no more against England, and two contrary feelings dispute within us: relief, that our bowlers will no longer be oppressed by this phenomenon; regret, that a miracle has been removed from among us. So must ancient Italy have felt when she heard of the death of Hannibal.

For sheer fame, Dr W. G. Grace and Don Bradman stand apart from all other cricketers – apart, indeed, from all other games-players. The villagers used to crowd to their doors when "W.G." and his beard drove through their little main street. Bradman, on his visits to England, could never live the life of a private citizen. He couldn't stroll from his hotel to post a letter or buy a collar-stud. The mob wouldn't let him. There had to be a car waiting with engine running, and he would plunge into it, like a cork from a bottle. When cricket was on, Bradman had no private life. He paid for his greatness, and the payment left some mark. The informal occasion, the casual conversation, the chance and happy acquaintance, these were very rarely for him, and his life was that of something between an Emperor and an Ambassador. Yet, for all that, there remained something of that boy who, thirty years before, had knocked a ball or ball-like object about in the backyard of a small house in New South Wales. He never lost a certain primitive and elemental "cheekiness", and mingled, as it were, with his exact and scientific calculations, there was the immortal impudence of the *gamin*.

But, above all, Bradman was a business-cricketer. About his batting there was to be no style for style's sake. If there was to be any charm, that was for the spectator to find or miss. It was not Bradman's concern. His aim was the making of runs, and he made them in staggering and ceaseless profusion. He seemed to have eliminated error, to have perfected the mechanism of stroke. Others before him had come near to doing this; but Bradman did it without abating the temperature of his attack. No other batsman, surely, has ever been able to score so fast while at the same time avoiding risk. He was, as near as a man batting may be, the flawless engine. There were critics who found surfeit in watching him. Man, by his nature, cannot bear perfection in his fellow. The very fact that something is being done which had been believed to be impossible goads and irritates. It is but a short step from annoyance to envy, and Bradman has never been free from envy's attacks. So, when, first in 1930, he reeled off the centuries, single, double and treble, there were not wanting those who compared him unfavourably with other great ones – Trumper, Ranjitsinhji, Hobbs, Macartney. And Bradman's answer was more runs. Others, perhaps, *could* have made them, but they didn't. No one before had ever been quite so fit, quite so ruthless.

It was a coolly considered policy. Cricket was not to be his hobby, his off-hours delight. It was to be his life and his living. A few hundreds here and there for Australia and State – what use in that? Others had done it, would do it again. He did not mean to be just one of the stars, but the sun itself. Never was such ambition achieved and sustained. Never was the limelight directed so unwaveringly on one man in one game. To set such a standard was unique. To keep it was a miracle.

But the sun itself has degrees of splendour; and, whatever the numbers may say, Bradman was never again quite so incredible as in England in the summer of 1930. Like all great artists, he knew how to begin. So he made 236 at Worcester and 185 not out at Leicester. Then, with a mere trifle of 78 against Yorkshire he relented into rest. At Nottingham, in the first Test, he was set fair to win the match for Australia when R. W. V. Robins bowled him with a googly. It is a freak of chance that in both his first and last Test matches in England he should have fatally mistaken a googly for a leg-break. It is also reassurring to mere mortality. In that first Test he scored 131. This was a *hors d'œuvre* of the feast to follow. At Lord's, in the second Test, he made 254, and the innings only ended with one of those catches that set A. P. F. Chapman apart from the other England fieldsmen. Then, at Leeds, he scored 334.

George Duckworth, who was keeping wicket for England, rates this innings as the greatest he ever saw. Archie Jackson, that glorious and ill-fated batsman, had opened the Australian innings with W. M. Woodfull. Off the fifth ball of the second over from Maurice Tate, Jackson was caught at short-leg. Bradman joined his captain. The first ball that he received from Tate whizzed just over his off-stump, and Duckworth, believing that Bradman must be bowled, let it go for byes. Then the show began. Bradman never hit in the air. Boundaries sprang from his bat with murderous precision and calculated profusion. Larwood, Tate and Geary – no mean trio – were helpless. A new machine was at work. A new standard of ambition had been set. At Manchester, Ian Peebles induced Bradman into error to the leg-break. But Bradman returned to himself with 232 at the Oval in the fifth Test. In the five Tests he had scored 974 runs at an average of 139. Statistics cannot record the number of runs he carried with him to each innings. But, in a country of great fieldsmen, he stood out pre-eminent. His gathering and throwing approached perfection. Only in catching, probably owing to the smallness of his hands, he was no better than the next man.

Then, after he had taken his pleasure of the South African bowling in Australia, came the first eclipse. A new style of attack, popularly known as "Body-Line", with the great fast bowler Larwood as its spearhead, was launched on the Australians in Australia by D. R. Jardine. This is no place for discussing the ethics of the matter. Technically, Bradman found no satisfactory answer. He met it, certainly, with a virtuosity of footwork possible to him alone. But his average in eight Test innings sank to a mere trifle of 57, including a score of 103 not out.

When Bradman next came to England, in 1934, there was no Larwood against him, and no Voce. He resumed his mastery. In the Leeds Test he scored 304; at The Oval 244. But, whereas in 1930 he had annihilated doubt, there were now certain qualifications. He was found to be incomplete against that great left-hand bowler, Hedley Verity, on a sticky wicket. At Lord's, in the second Test, he lost his head, if one may use such a phrase of such a master of calculation and coolness. Perhaps it was attributable to his uncertain health. But too much emphasis has been laid on this failure. Verity himself did not agree with the popular generalisation that Bradman "couldn't play on the bad ones". And he knew. But it should be said that, with the exception of Larwood in Australia during the 1932-33 tour, Verity was the one bowler who battled with Bradman on something like level terms, even on the truest of pitches. Besides this failure at Lord's in 1934, another man, one of his own team, contributed to some dimming of the Bradman glory. That was W. H. Ponsford, of Victoria. He was playing in his last Test series against England. Most of his records, once seemingly unassailable, had been stolen by Bradman; but now Ponsford, one of the greatest players of spin bowling that ever batted, ran level with his rival, and actually beat him in the matter of Test average by a decimal point.

Already Bradman had proved his power to live on a pinnacle of success. Now, against G. O. Allen's team in Australia, 1936-37, he was to show that he could return from failure. He started downright badly, and the vultures that await the fall of the great hovered expectantly. But he disappointed them, and, by the end of the tour, he was once more the authentic Bradman. In 1938, his third visit to England, he came as captain. Henceforward, in Tests, except for one innings of 234 at Sydney, he was to deal in single centuries only. It was a concession to old man Time.

Where does Bradman stand as a captain? Such a question opens the way to opinions which, even when gathered from those who played with him from day to day, cannot be reduced to any certain conclusion. On the field he was superb. He had seen and weighed it all. Shrewd and tough, he was not likely to waste anything in dreams or mercy. No one ever saw Bradman not attending. Cricket, to one who made and kept his way from hard beginnings, was a business, not a pastime.

He made mistakes. He took only three regular bowlers on to the field for the last Test at The Oval in 1938. For him, as for Australia, the match was a disaster. Bradman, when bowling, fell and injured his leg. England scored 903 for seven wickets; Hutton 364. Both these totals are Test records. Bradman was unable to bat, and Australia lost by the record margin of an innings and 579. How different from the scene of ten years later, when Lindwall went through the England batting like a steam drill. But, in all, Bradman was the supreme tactician.

On the personal side, his success was more doubtful. Great captaincy begins off the field. True leadership springs from affection even more than from respect. Bradman certainly earned the respect. But, by his very nature, he was bound to have admirers rather than friends. Stripped to the truth, he was a solitary man with a solitary aim. It was what the man did rather than what he was that invited obedience. There are humorously affectionate stories about most great cricketers; intimate, if somewhat apocryphal tales about them; of what Dr Grace said when Ernest Jones bowled a ball through his beard; of Patsy Hendren's reply to a criticism from the Sydney "Hill"; of what Johnny Douglas uttered when second slip floored a catch. But there are no funny stories about the Don. No one ever laughed about Bradman. He was no laughing matter.

During the War, disturbing rumours reached England about his health; and, whatever truth there may have been in them, certainly the England team under W. R. Hammond found Bradman uncommonly near to being a sick man. But, happily, he recovered. So did his batting. Not without luck, surely earned, he first groped, then rushed, his way back to normal. Enough of the old skill returned from him to score 187 at Brisbane and 234 at Sydney.

There followed his last visit as a Test cricketer to England. As a batsman he no longer flamed high above his fellows. He was now no more than a very fine player, and it was arguable that both S. G. Barnes and A. R. Morris were stronger factors in the quelling of bowlers. But Bradman's fame, if possible, increased. Next to Mr Winston Churchill, he was the most celebrated man in England during the summer of 1948. His appearances throughout the country were like one continuous farewell matinée. At last his batting showed human fallibility. Often, especially at the start of the innings, he played where the ball wasn't, and spectators rubbed their eyes. But such a treasury of skill could spare some gold and still be rich. He scored 138 against England at Nottingham, and, when it much mattered, 173 not out at Leeds.

Most important of all, he steered Australia through some troubled waters and never grounded on the rocks. Returning home, he received the first Knighthood ever given to a playing cricketer.

Bradman's place as a batsman is among the few who have been blessed with genius. He was the most wonderful run-scorer that the game has yet known, and no batsman in our own time has so highly excited expectation and so rarely disappointed it.

HONOURS FOR BRADMAN

During the match with Gentlemen of England at Lord's, Don Bradman was presented with a special birthday cake and a copy of Sir Pelham Warner's *Lord's 1787-1945* inscribed, "Presented to Don Bradman on his 40th birthday by the President, committee and members of the Marylebone Cricket Club in memory of the great pleasure he has given at Lord's since 1930 to countless lovers of cricket."

Bradman said: "To bid farewell to cricket on this great ground is for me a very sad occasion. I hope, however, to come to England again, though not as a player, and watch many Tests."

At Scarborough Don Bradman received the honorary life membership of the Yorkshire County Club. He was presented by Mr T. L. Taylor, President of the club, with a 1948 Yorkshire handbook and a silver salver inscribed with his scores made in the four Test matches in which he played at Headingley. Apart from Yorkshire players, Bradman was the first recipient of this distinction.

As the outcome of a testimonial match at Melbourne in December, Sir Donald Bradman received in January a cheque for £9,342 18s. 8d.

ENGLAND v AUSTRALIA

First Test Match

Played at Nottingham, June 11, 12, 13, 15, 16, 1953

Drawn. So stirring was the cricket of the first three days that the anti-climax brought about by prolonged bad weather aroused bitter disappointment. Chiefly through the magnificent bowling of A. V. Bedser, England finished on Saturday needing 187 to win with nine second innings wickets left. The position promised a tremendous struggle, but heavy rain washed out any hopes of play on Monday and a resumption was impossible until half-past four on the last day. In the two hours remaining England did not attempt a task which would have been charged with risk and, with the conditions of no use to bowlers, the cricket contained little other than academic interest.

The consequences of the weather break must have been particularly galling to Bedser. He was England's hero, with a match analysis of fourteen wickets for 99 runs. Only the Yorkshiremen, Wilfred Rhodes and Hedley Verity, who took fifteen wickets apiece, had dismissed more batsmen in any of the previous 159 Tests between England and Australia. Bedser deserved to join them, but, as it was, he made the match memorable for himself by passing the English Test record of 189 wickets held by S. F. Barnes, who, at 80 years of age, saw his own figures overtaken. Barnes was among the first to congratulate the new record-holder.

The omission of Statham from the original twelve meant that England went into the field with only four front-line bowlers, but Bedser put Australia on the defensive by uprooting Hole's middle stump with the first ball of his second over. Hassett and Morris countered with extreme care, only 11 runs coming in the first half-hour and 34 in the hour. Rain stopped the game a quarter of an hour before lunch, by which time the score had rise to 54. Afterwards the bowlers were handicapped by a wet ball, but Bedser was always menacing, and, when he took the new ball, he promptly broke the century stand and followed by trapping Harvey into giving a leg-side catch. When bad light brought the day's play, restricted to four and a half hours, to a close, Bedser's figures told of his toil. They were 25-12-26-3. Hassett was Australia's most accomplished batsman.

Australia, 157 for three, resumed confidently against bowlers using a towel and sawdust on a ball saturated by grass still wet from rain in the night and intermittent light drizzles during play. Although the soggy ball would not swing in the damp, heavy atmosphere, the possibilities of a new ball doing so, should the rain abate and the grass dry, were unmistakable. No doubt this influenced Hutton to give Bedser only a short spell before lunch. Bailey, who conceded only 17 runs in ten overs, kept the batsmen tied down, but, on first going on, Wardle was erratic. Hassett gratefully punished two short balls and so completed his ninth century in Test cricket. Still, a few minutes before the interval Wardle broke the big stand, Bailey at mid-wicket taking a fine catch from Miller over his shoulder as he ran backwards. At lunch Australia were 243 for four.

The game moved so swiftly afterwards that by the end of the day most of the spectators felt exhausted through the sustained excitement. By this time the outfield had dried but the atmosphere remained favourable to swing bowling, and, with the new ball, Bedser and Bailey swept away the rest of the Australian batting in three-quarters of an hour, the six wickets crashing for six runs. From Bailey's first delivery with the new ball Evans began the debacle by a superb left-hand catch off Benaud's leg-glance, hit from the middle of the bat.

Evans made several feet before hurling himself sideways and grasping the ball full stretch as he thudded to the ground. Next Bedser, fresh and alive to his chance, brought Hassett's innings to a close with a ball which pitched on the leg stump and hit the top of the off. For six hours and a half Hassett devoted himself to his defensive role with that sure application and calm so typical of him. He was never anything but graceful. Tallon could offer no answer to a similar ball from Bedser; the Evans-Bailey combination quickly disposed of Lindwall, and Bedser wrecked the wickets of Davidson and Hill. His three spells with a new ball in Australia's innings of seven hours twenty minutes gave him figures of one for seven, two for five, and four, all clean bowled, for two.

The Australian collapse, however, was but a prelude to a series of England failures caused by Lindwall's skill in exploiting the conditions, with late swing at slightly varying shades of fast bowling. In Lindwall's fourth over Kenyon edged an in-swinger to short fine-leg, where he was well caught. Another in-swinger dismissed Simpson second ball, and a lovely swooping catch in the gulley sent back Compton, who drove square and low.

These three wickets fell to Lindwall in eight balls at the same total, 17. Hutton and Graveney checked the collapse, but, in worsening light, England's batting slumped again. Benaud made excellent catches from Graveney, at short-leg, and Hutton, from a forcing stroke to gulley, and soon after an unsuccessful appeal against the light May edged Hill to the wicket-keeper. Immediately afterwards the umpires decided the gloom was too much. England finished this eventful day with six men out for 92 and requiring eight runs to avoid the danger of following-on. Between lunch and the close twelve wickets fell for 98. The honours went to Lindwall and Bedser, and to the fieldsmen on both sides. Everything to hand was snapped up.

Conditions for the third day were almost identical with those on the second. Before lunch bowlers had to use a wet ball, but afterwards the grass had dried and the new ball moved considerably in thick atmosphere. Once more the cricket moved at breathtaking pace, fifteen wickets going down in the day for 217 runs. First, England saved the follow-on easily. Australia's lead was restricted to 105. Bailey performed the first of his many defensive acts in the series by staying an hour and forty minutes for ten runs. Wardle, hitting cheerfully, was second highest scorer in the innings. Australia opened their innings just before the first interval and afterwards Morris began a fierce assault. Bedser, however, soon penetrated Hole's defence, and when a good-length ball stood up and struck Hassett on the glove before lobbing to short-leg, two wickets were down for 44.

Australia never recovered from this, and the manner of their batting indicated that they distrusted the pitch. Yet Hassett received one of the few balls which behaved awkwardly from the turf and, for all the considerable ability of Bedser, several batsmen were out attempting strokes bordering on the reckless. Bedser, who took the first five wickets for 22 runs, was again in his most dynamic form and, and when Bedser took a rest, Tattersall maintained England's grip. Morris, who batted freely for 60 out of 81 in an hour and three-quarters, was his first victim, bowled round his legs. More spectacular catches, this time by Graveney and Simpson, accounted for Davidson and Tallon, and, with Tattersall's help in the field, Bedser swiftly closed the innings. Once again Bedser was a model of accuracy and his controlled swing took effect so late that not one of the batsmen shaped well against him. Morris, the most successful run-getter, received comparatively few balls from him.

After a break of ten minutes for bad light England began their task of making 229 to win. Against a close encircling field, Hutton and Kenyon played safely through the new-ball attack, and Kenyon looked to be going well until he lifted a full toss to mid-on. Simpson might have been caught at slip second ball, but, that apart, the batting was more than adequate. Bad light again brought play to an early closure and left the match in the intriguing situation the development of which was ruined by the heavy rain over the week-end. Attendance 86,000; receipts £29,261.   T.J.H.

Australia

G. B. Hole b Bedser	0	– b Bedser	5
A. R. Morris lbw b Bedser	67	– b Tattersall	60
A. L. Hassett b Bedser	115	– c Hutton b Bedser	5
R. N. Harvey c Compton b Bedser	0	– c Graveney b Bedser	2
K. R. Miller c Bailey b Wardle	55	– c Kenyon b Bedser	5
R. Benaud c Evans b Bailey	3	– b Bedser	0
A. K. Davidson b Bedser	4	– c Graveney b Tattersall	6
D. Tallon b Bedser	0	– c Simpson b Tattersall	15
R. R. Lindwall c Evans b Bailey	0	– c Tattersall b Bedser	12
J. C. Hill b Bedser	0	– c Tattersall b Bedser	4
W. A. Johnston not out	0	– not out	4
B 2, l-b 2, n-b 1	5	L-b 5	5

1/2 2/124 3/128 4/237 5/244   249   1/28 2/44 3/50 4/64 5/68   123
6/244 7/246 8/247 9/248   6/81 7/92 8/106 9/115

England

L. Hutton c Benaud b Davidson	43	– not out	60
D. J. Kenyon c Hill b Lindwall	8	– c Hassett b Hill	16
R. T. Simpson lbw b Lindwall	0	– not out	28
D. C. S. Compton c Morris b Lindwall	0		
T. W. Graveney c Benaud b Hill	22		
P. B. H. May c Tallon b Hill	9		
T. E. Bailey lbw b Hill	13		
T. G. Evans c Tallon b Davidson	8		
J. H. Wardle not out	29		
A. V. Bedser lbw b Lindwall	2		
R. Tattersall b Lindwall	2		
B 5, l-b 3	8	B 8, l-b 4, w 2, n-b 2	16

1/17 2/17 3/17 4/76 5/82   144   1/26   (1 wkt) 120
6/92 7/107 8/121 9/136

England Bowling

	Overs	Mdns	Runs	Wkts	Overs	Mdns	Runs	Wkts
Bedser	38.3	16	55	7	17.2	7	44	7
Bailey	44	14	75	2	5	1	28	—
Wardle	35	16	55	1	12	3	24	—
Tattersall	23	5	59	—	5	—	22	3

Australia Bowling

	Overs	Mdns	Runs	Wkts	Overs	Mdns	Runs	Wkts
Lindwall	20.4	2	57	5	16	4	37	—
Johnston	18	7	22	—	18	9	14	—
Hill	19	8	35	3	12	3	26	1
Davidson	15	7	22	2	5	1	7	—
Benaud					5	—	15	—
Morris					2	—	5	—

Umpires: D. Davies and Harold Elliott (Lancashire).

ESSEX v AUSTRALIANS

Played at Southend, August 12, 13, 1953

Australians won by an innings and 212 runs. The pitch, which had been submerged by four feet of sea-water during the February floods, favoured run-getting while the Australians batted, but it crumbled on the second day and Essex were powerless against the spin bowling first of Ring and then of Johnston. Essex made a good start when getting down two wickets for 50, but Hole, after some early escapes, drove well and he and the enterprising de Courcy put on 150 in two hours. Hole hit eight 4s during a stay of two and a half hours. de Courcy found more help from Craig and 88 came for the fourth wicket. Then de Courcy inflicted dire punishment upon the leg-break bowling of Greensmith and, with drives for 6, 6, 6, 4 and 6 from successive deliveries, took 28 runs in an over. Altogether de Courcy hit 164 out of 278 in two hours twenty-five minutes, with four 6s and eighteen 4s as his chief hits. Benaud, badly missed when six by Watkins at mid-on, shared with Davidson in a partnership of 85, and the total reached 477 for seven wickets by the close. Morris declared next morning and Essex soon found themselves struggling. In the first innings the highest stand was 34 between Avery and Horsfall. In the follow-on 348 behind, Greensmith, batting just over an hour, alone offered much resistance and the match ended before half-past five. Johnston's six wickets for 39 represented his best analysis of the tour.

Australians

A. R. Morris c Vigar b Preston	33	
G. B. Hole c Gibb b Watkins	89	
R. N. Harvey lbw b Smith	3	
J. H. de Courcy lbw b Bailey	164	
I. D. Craig lbw b Bailey	22	
A. K. Davidson lbw b Greensmith	58	
R. G. Benaud c Preston b Watkins	67	
R. G. Archer not out	28	
D. Ring not out	1	
B 5, l-b 7	12	

1/45 2/50 3/200   (7 wkts dec.) 477
4/288 5/328 6/413 7/476

G. R. Langley and W. A. Johnston did not bat.

Essex

T. C. Dodds c Johnston b Archer	3	– b Benaud	17
A. V. Avery c and b Ring	19	– c Langley b Johnston	17
P. A. Gibb c and b Johnston	4	– b Benaud	3
R. Horsfall b Ring	26	– c Hole b Johnston	0
D. J. Insole lbw b Benaud	6	– c and b Johnston	22
T. E. Bailey st Langley b Ring	11	– b Johnston	9
W. T. Greensmith run out	16	– lbw b Johnston	31
F. H. Vigar b Ring	2	– b Ring	2
D. Watkins run out	0	– b Johnston	10
R. Smith b Ring	24	– c Benaud b Ring	3
K. C. Preston not out	8	– not out	13
B 8, l-b 2	10	B 8, l-b 1	9

1/3 2/14 3/48 4/55 5/71   129   1/27 2/31 3/36 4/37 5/57   136
6/71 7/82 8/86 9/115   6/76 7/93 8/113 9/118

Essex Bowling

	Overs	Mdns	Runs	Wkts
Bailey	18	1	71	2
Preston	21	1	88	1
Smith	20	2	123	1
Insole	1	—	5	—
Watkins	15	3	49	2
Greensmith	27	2	129	1

Australian Bowling

	Overs	Mdns	Runs	Wkts	Overs	Mdns	Runs	Wkts
Johnston	9	3	16	1	21.5	5	39	6
Archer	5	—	11	1	2	—	80	—
Ring	17	5	47	5	9	—	28	2
Benaud	13	1	45	1	14	2	33	2
Davidson					4	1	19	—

Umpires: A. E. Boulton-Carter and A. Skelding.

ENGLAND v AUSTRALIA

Fifth Test Match

Played at The Oval, August 15, 17, 18, 19, 1953

England won by eight wickets and so won the Ashes for the first time since 1932-33. It was a most welcome victory in Coronation year and a triumph for Len Hutton, the first modern professional to be entrusted with the captaincy of England. Moreover, he led his team to success on the ground on which he made the world record Test score of 364 in 1938 – the last previous occasion England beat Australia in this country. This was the first time England had won the rubber at home since A. P. F. Chapman's team finished 289 runs ahead on the fourth day on this very ground in 1926.

There was something unique in the victory of Hutton's men as far as England and Australia were concerned. Hutton was the only captain who had lost the toss in all five Tests and yet won the series. In 1905, when Sir Stanley Jackson won the toss in the five Tests, England were victorious in the only two matches that were decided. In 1909, when M. A. Noble equalled Jackson's feat, Australia carried home the Ashes by two matches to one. John Goddard, of the West Indies, was similarly successful in India in 1948-49, and the only parallel to the failure of Hassett's team occurred in South Africa in 1928-29. Then H. G. Deane successfully spun the coin five times, but England won by two clear victories.

The absence of a genuine spin bowler proved a severe handicap to Australia. The issue was virtually decided on the third afternoon when Australia, 31 behind on the first innings, lost half their side to Laker and Lock for 61.

Compared with the fourth Test, England brought in May and Trueman for Watson and Simpson, and made Wardle twelfth man. For the first time in the series England possessed a properly balanced attack. The introduction of Trueman, who faced Australia for the first time, proved a wise decision. As Johnston had recovered from his knee injury, Australia preferred him to Benaud.

As in 1926, stories of long all-night queues frightened away many would-be spectators on the first day when the ground was comfortable with 26,300 people present. The news that Hassett had again won the toss was received gloomily by most England supporters, but by mid-afternoon, when seven Australian wickets were down for 160, pessimism changed to optimism.

At first the cricket took the expected course. With six days at their disposal, there was no need for Australia to hurry, but like true cricketers they never ignored the loose ball. For example, the second ball of the day, a full toss from Bedser, was hit truly by Hassett to the long-leg boundary.

Trueman was given a great welcome. He set a normal field for an easy-paced pitch: two slips, a gully and two short legs. He began with a lively over. The fifth ball Morris tried to sweep, and as it landed in Evans's gloves Trueman appealed for a catch. The last ball nearly earned a wicket, Compton at short fine leg just failing to reach a very hard chance.

Clearly neither bowler intended to allow Australia any complacency. It was all-out attack with both sides striving for the mastery. Trueman, taking one of the longest runs known in cricket, covered a distance of at least 25 yards in fifteen long strides and required forty-five minutes to complete his first spell of five overs which cost 12 runs.

Then came Bailey, but the initiative appeared to be with Australia. Towards the end of an hour Bedser broke the opening stand in his eighth over when his swerve deceived Morris, who, offering no stroke, turned his back and was leg-before. The Surrey giant had now dismissed Morris five times in nine Tests innings in this series and altogether eighteen times in twenty Tests. This success gave England timely encouragement, and within ten minutes Bailey claimed the dangerous Miller, who, padding up, was also lbw. Hutton used Trueman in short spells, and at lunch the total was 98 for two wickets — Hassett 51, Harvey 29.

Light rain during the interval seemed to enliven the pitch, and suddenly Bedser and Trueman drilled a big hole in the Australia batting. A fine stand of 66 between Hassett and Harvey was terminated when Hassett, playing forward, gave a catch to Evans. In the following over Harvey mistimed a hook and Hutton, running with his back to the pitch from short square leg, brought off a grand catch.

Another shower held up the game for ten minutes, and then de Courcy, having already flashed at Trueman, repeated his error and Evans held another catch — wide of the off stump. That made half the side out in only two and a half hours for 118, but while Archer defended Hole played a splendid innings. Hole declined to be subdued, and though he narrowly escaped when Lock dived in Bedser's leg-trap, he pulled and drove until Trueman beat him by pace and Evans seized his third catch. Without addition, Archer, having stayed nearly an hour, lifted the first ball on Bedser's return to the attack back to the bowler. This turned out to be Bedser's final wicket in the series, but it was an historic one. It gave him his 39th of the 1953 Tests and so he beat M. W. Tate's 38 of 1924-25, the previous best in England-Australia matches.

Now came Lindwall, and with only three wickets to fall he launched a hot attack, ably assisted by the left-handed Davidson. For a hour and fifty minutes Lindwall indulged in a magnificent display of clean hitting. His off and cover drives were of the highest class. The new ball at 210 did not halt him and he hit eight sparkling boundaries before he was last out to the fourth catch of the innings by Evans. By adding 157 the last five wickets more than doubled the score, and in the circumstances no one could deny that Australia had made an excellent recovery.

Although there had been some fine catching, England's fielding again left room for much criticism, for Davidson, Lindwall and Johnston were missed by Edrich, Graveney and Bedser respectively. Still, England had every reason to be satisfied in dismissing Australia for 275. Trueman fully justified his selection. Always hostile, he made good use of the occasional bouncer and he looked the part.

Before bad light stopped the struggle at 6.17 p.m. there was time for Lindwall and Miller each to send down one over, and England might well have lost Hutton in Lindwall's tearaway effort. The fourth and fifth balls were bouncers. The fifth flew off the handle of Hutton's bat and five slips surged forward for the catch which unexpectedly never arrived. The ball dropped short because it lost its pace in transit through striking Hutton's cap, which it removed. The cap just missed the stumps or Hutton might have been out hit wicket.

If Saturday belonged to England, Monday went to Australia, for the close of play found England 235 for seven – 40 behind with only three wickets left. The gates were closed long before play was resumed at 11.30 a.m. and thousands failed to gain admission. Upon England's batting this day everyone felt that the destination of the Ashes depended, but after a promising beginning the initiative passed to Australia.

The conditions were not in their favour, but they bowled and fielded as if their very lives were at stake. They dropped only one catch compared with five by England on Saturday and they tied England down to a scoring rate of less than 40 runs an hour. For a time England prospered. An early setback occurred when Edrich, having batted splendidly, left at 37, but there followed a grand partnership of 100 between Hutton and May, who were together two hours twenty minutes. When that was broken England went through a very bad time, chiefly because of the uncertainty of Compton.

Previously Hutton had been master of the situation, but when joined by Compton he added only six in the next half hour before being bowled by a well-pitched-up ball from Johnston which moved from leg and hit the middle stump. Third out at 154, Hutton made his 82 in three hours forty minutes and hit eight 4s. The departure of Hutton was a serious setback for England. The new ball was due, but Johnston was so dominant with cleverly flighted left-arm slows that Hassett was able to save Lindwall and Miller for an all-out assault after tea.

When the interval arrived with the total 165 for three, Compton had spent an hour over 16 and Graveney half an hour for two. On a day made for batting, the bowling figures read: Johnston 10-5-14-2; Hole 7-4-8-0. Lindwall and Miller were only warming up after tea with the old ball when Compton's disappointing exhibition ended in a spectacular flying catch by Langley well wide of the leg stump.

Not until the 78th over did Australia take the new ball, and it brought immediate success. The second ball was enough for Graveney, who fell to a brilliant first slip catch, Miller holding a catch at ankle height. That meant half the England wickets down for 170. Miller had five slips, but Evans did not allow anything to worry him. Soon he was hitting cleanly, and in an over which cost Lindwall 10 were two smashing hooks. England had stopped the slump, but the position was still precarious, particularly when Davidson at square leg cut off a vicious stroke by Evans from Johnston. Evans slipped on being sent back and Langley swept a lightning return into the stumps.

Meanwhile Bailey had begun with 15 in thirty-five minutes, but on being joined by

Laker he changed his methods and brilliant strokes to the off gave him 11 in an over from Johnston. Laker soon went, but Lock closed an end for the last forty minutes of a dramatic day, England finishing at 235 for seven wickets – Bailey 35, Lock 4.

The way England pulled the game round on the third day was scarcely believable. Light rain at 6 a.m. and the heavy roller left the pitch easy paced. Again Bailey foiled the Australian bowlers, but they gained an early success. The first ball of Lindwall's second over lifted and Lock was caught off his glove in the leg trap. More dazzling fielding, notably by de Courcy, saved many runs, but not even the odd bouncer troubled Bailey, and he and Trueman put on 25, so that only 13 runs separated the totals when the last man, Bedser, walked to the crease.

England took twenty minutes to get those runs. Every ball seemed vital until Bedser lifted one from Johnston over mid-off and the batsmen ran four. Miller misjudged its pace and delayed chasing it. Now Australia became concerned mainly in preventing scoring strokes and Hassett widened the field, but Bailey, to whom Miller bowled round the wicket, drove and hooked beautifully until, going forward to Archer, he was bowled on the stroke of lunch time by a fine ball which hit the top of the stumps. Hitting seven 4s and never offering a chance, Bailey withstood the bowling for three and three-quarter hours, his final stand with Bedser yielding 44. Johnston bowled his left-arm slows with rare skill and Lindwall and Miller never spared themselves.

To Hutton must be given the credit for bringing about Australia's subsequent collapse. He realised by the way Morris slammed Bedser past cover and Trueman to leg that the batsmen would thrive on pace bowling on this somewhat lifeless pitch for which Hassett had ordered the heavy roller. Hutton allowed Trueman only two overs and Bedser three before at 19 he introduced the Surrey spinners, Laker (right-arm off-breaks) and Lock (left-arm slow). That was the move that brought home the Ashes. The Australian batsmen had not settled down before they were confronted by spin, and their vulnerability to the turning ball as well as their fear of it led to their undoing. Suddenly a day which began so gloomily for England swung completely Hutton's way.

Laker started the Australian procession. Bowling round the wicket, he twice beat Hassett, and then with the last ball of his first over he got the Australian captain leg-before as he retreated into his wicket. One hour later half the Australia team were back in the pavilion for 61.

In one astonishing spell of fourteen minutes four wickets fell while only two runs were scored. Lock went over the wicket to the left-handed batsmen, but Hole threatened danger with free hitting at the expense of Laker. Again Hutton countered. He placed a deep extra cover as well as a long-on, and Laker with his very next ball got Hole lbw.

Lock never erred in length or direction from the pavilion end, and as Harvey shaped to drive he knocked back his off stump. In the next over Trueman at short square leg hugged a sharp catch from Miller, and then Morris, playing back and trying to force Lock away, was leg-before. So on this gloriously sunny afternoon Australia found themselves confronted with impending defeat. With half their wickets down they were no more than 30 runs ahead.

Hassett saw that the only possible escape was a repetition of Lindwall's method. Young Archer began the offensive by helping himself to 11 in an over from Laker, but at 85 de Courcy was brilliantly run out by Bailey who at mid-wicket swooped on a stroke by Archer. de Courcy tried to get back but Lock broke the wicket at his leisure.

When Archer on-drove Lock magnificently for 6, Hutton placed May on the pavilion rails and Trueman at deep extra cover, but Archer and Davidson still hit at will. A boundary to long leg and then a hook for 6 gave Davidson 10 in two balls from Laker, so that at tea Australia were 131 for six – Archer 44, Davidson 21.

The break gave England a chance to review the position. Clearly they needed to plan to avoid more heavy punishment. Next Laker exploited leg-theory with only three off fielders and Lock off-theory with only three leg fielders. This sensible arrangement plus two steady spells by Bedser resulted in the four remaining wickets being taken for 31 more runs. Archer, who besides his 6 hit seven 4s, batted an hour for his thrilling 49. Lindwall hooked

Lock for 6, received a life at slip from the same bowler, and then, essaying another six, was caught on the pavilion fence by Compton.

England, having dismissed Australia in two hours forty-five minutes for 162, needed 132 to win with ample time at their disposal. They owed much to Lock. The pitch gave him little help, yet such was his finger spin allied to skilful flighting and change of pace that he took five wickets for 45. Laker, too, played a valuable part. He did not approach Lock in accuracy, but he accounted for the dangerous right-handed hitters, Hassett, Miller, Hole and Lindwall. Lock removed three left-handers, Morris, Harvey and Davidson, as well as Archer and Langley.

Fifty minutes remained on Tuesday when Hutton and Edrich began England's final task. Both produced some excellent strokes, but at 24 Hutton brought about his own dismissal. He hit Miller firmly to square leg and took the obvious single, but when de Courcy fumbled he tried to steal a second run and failed to get home. Hutton looked terribly disappointed as he walked slowly back to the pavilion. May stayed with Edrich for the last quarter of an hour and England finished at 38 for one wicket.

They now needed 94, and only rain and a sticky pitch were likely to deprive them of the victory so near their grasp. How those Australians fought to hold the Ashes! Johnston bowled tantalising slows from the Vauxhall end without relief and little help from the slightly worn pitch from 11.30 a.m. till 2.45 p.m., when, with only nine more runs wanted, Hassett ended the struggle by going on with Morris. Lindwall bowled for seventy-five minutes in his first spell, returned for the last ten minutes before lunch, and continued for another half hour. Here is their analysis for the fourth day: Johnston 23-12-36-0; Lindwall 19-5-38-0.

At first Edrich and May made very slow progress: 14 in the first half hour and 24 in the hour. Harvey, Davidson and Lindwall excelled in the field. The attack was always directed at the stumps. Only rarely did Lindwall risk a bumper; runs were too precious to be given away. Slowly the score crept to 88, and then Miller, having dispensed with his slips – five men were on the leg side for his off-spin – got May caught at short fine leg. The stand produced 64 in one hour fifty minutes.

Earlier Edrich magnificently hooked two successive bumpers from Lindwall. Now he was joined by his Middlesex colleague, Compton, and they took England to victory. Compton made the winning hit at seven minutes to three when he swept Morris to the boundary.

At once the crowd swarmed across the ground while Edrich, who batted three and a half hours and hit six 4s, fought his way to the pavilion with Compton and the Australian team. In a memorable scene both captains addressed the crowd, stressing the excellent spirit in which all the matches had been contested both on and off the field.

The attendance for the Test reached 115,000 and the receipts amounted to £37,000.   N.P.

Australia

A. L. Hassett c Evans b Bedser	53	– lbw b Laker	10
A. R. Morris lbw b Bedser	16	– lbw b Lock	26
K. R. Miller lbw b Bailey	1	– c Trueman b Laker	0
R. N. Harvey c Hutton b Trueman	36	– b Lock	1
G. B. Hole c Evans b Trueman	37	– lbw b Laker	17
J. H. de Courcy c Evans b Trueman	5	– run out	4
R. G. Archer c and b Bedser	10	– c Edrich b Lock	49
A. K. Davidson c Edrich b Laker	22	– b Lock	21
R. R. Lindwall c Evans b Trueman	62	– c Compton b Laker	12
G. R. Langley c Edrich b Lock	18	– c Trueman b Lock	2
W. A. Johnston not out	9	– not out	6
B 4, n-b 2	6	B 11, l-b 3	14

1/38 2/41 3/107 4/107 5/118   275   1/23 2/59 3/60 4/61 5/61   162
6/160 7/160 8/207 9/245   6/85 7/135 8/140 9/144

England

L. Hutton b Johnston	82	– run out	17
W. J. Edrich lbw b Lindwall	21	– not out	55
P. B. H. May c Archer b Johnston	39	– c Davidson b Miller	37
D. C. S. Compton c Langley b Lindwall	16	– not out	22
T. W. Graveney c Miller b Lindwall	4		
T. E. Bailey b Archer	64		
T. G. Evans run out	28		
J. C. Laker c Langley b Miller	1		
G. A. R. Lock c Davidson b Lindwall	4		
F. S. Trueman b Johnston	10		
A. V. Bedser not out	22		
B 9, l-b 5, w 1	15	L-b 1	1

1/37 2/137 3/154 4/167 5/170   306   1/24 2/88   (2 wkts) 132
6/210 7/225 8/237 9/262

England Bowling

	Overs	Mdns	Runs	Wkts	Overs	Mdns	Runs	Wkts
Bedser	29	3	88	3	11	2	24	—
Trueman	24.3	3	86	4	2	1	4	—
Bailey	14	3	42	1				
Lock	9	2	19	1	21	9	45	5
Laker	5	—	34	1	16.5	2	75	4

Australia Bowling

	Overs	Mdns	Runs	Wkts	Overs	Mdns	Runs	Wkts
Lindwall	32	7	70	4	21	5	46	—
Miller	34	12	65	1	11	3	24	1
Johnston	45	16	94	3	29	14	52	—
Davidson	10	1	26	—				
Archer	10.3	2	25	1	1	1	—	—
Hole	11	6	11	—				
Hassett					1	—	4	—
Morris					0.5	—	5	—

Umpires: F. S. Lee and D. Davies.

COMBINED SERVICES v AUSTRALIANS

Played at Kingston, September 5, 7, 1953

Australians won by an innings and 261 runs. They overwhelmed the Services in a one-sided match. On an easy pitch the Australians lost three wickets for 89 runs, but the next wicket added 377 in 205 minutes, Miller and de Courcy each making the highest score of his career. Miller's 262 not out was also the biggest innings of the tour. He hit thirty-six 4s, mainly flowing drives, and de Courcy's 204 included five 6s and twenty-seven 4s. Craig also found scoring easy against a tired attack and played his best innings of the tour. Trueman was heavily punished and only the off-breaks of Wells caused the slightest concern. Services batted briskly, but were no match for the Australians, and were dismissed twice on the second day. Horton, the 19-year-old Worcestershire all-rounder, batted well in the first innings and was asked to open the innings when Services followed-on 431 behind. This time he failed and was actually out twice in three balls. Ingleby-Mackenzie and Fenner put on 74 in thirty-seven minutes in the second innings. Ring, because of a back strain, did not play after lunch.

Australians

C. C. McDonald b Spencer	16	I. D. Craig not out	71
A. R. Morris b Spencer	0		
K. R. Miller not out	262	B 7, l-b 6, n-b 1	14
R. N. Harvey b Shirreff	25		
J. H. de Courcy c Spencer b Shirreff	204	1/2 2/29 3/89 4/466 (4 wkts dec.)	592

R. Benaud, R. R. Lindwall, D. Ring, D. Tallon and J. C. Hill did not bat.

Combined Services

Major A. H. Parnaby c Tallon b Ring	29	– lbw b Hill	7
Mdn A. C. Walton b Miller	0	– b Benaud	2
Instr-Lt G. G. Tordoff b Miller	14	– b Miller	15
Lt-Cmdr M. L. Y. Ainsworth c Craig b Ring	20	– b Hill	2
Sq Ldr A. C. Shirreff c Lindwall b Ring	15	– c and b Benaud	27
Mdn A. C. D. Ingleby-Mackenzie lbw b Benaud	22	– b Hill	66
A/c M. J. Horton c sub b Benaud	45	– b Lindwall	0
F/O M. D. Fenner b Lindwall	1	– b Hill	28
Pte T. Spencer b Lindwall	4	– b Hill	4
A/c F. S. Trueman b Miller	6	– not out	6
Pte B. D. Wells not out	0	– b Hill	0
B 4, l-b 1	5	B 10, l-b 3	13

1/8 2/26 3/54 4/74 5/89	161	1/1 2/24 3/24 4/43 5/63	170
6/140 7/141 8/147 9/157		6/77 7/151 8/155 9/170	

Combined Services Bowling

	Overs	Mdns	Runs	Wkts
Trueman	14	2	95	—
Spencer	19	—	106	2
Shirreff	33	1	147	2
Wells	17	4	79	—
Horton	17	3	53	—
Tordoff	15	2	68	—
Ainsworth	3	—	20	—
Parnaby	1	—	10	—

Australian Bowling

	Overs	Mdns	Runs	Wkts	Overs	Mdns	Runs	Wkts
Lindwall	16	1	44	2	5	1	15	1
Miller	8	4	17	3	12	2	41	1
Hill	5	—	11	—	21.4	9	34	6
Ring	11	—	40	3				
Benaud	12	1	44	2	17	3	67	2

Umpires: F. S. Lee and G. S. Mobey.

T. N. PEARCE'S XI v AUSTRALIANS

Played at Scarborough, September 9, 10, 11, 1953

Australians won by two wickets after three days of wonderful cricket by two teams each of which included ten men who had taken part in the Tests. Set to make 320 in three hours forty minutes, the Australians got home when Hill pulled Bedser high over the boundary for 6 off the fifth ball of the final over on the stroke of time. It is impossible to pay tribute to everyone for such a grand display. Altogether the match produced thirty-four 6s and, crowning all, was the feat of Benaud in the fourth innings when he put his side on the path to victory by making 153 out of 209 in one hour fifty minutes. He hit eleven 6s and nine

4s. Benaud went to 99 by hooking Bedser for 6. A single gave him his first hundred in England, and then he launched a terrific attack. Scoring 25 in one over from Tattersall, he pull-drove the first four balls each for 6 and then in the following over was caught in the deep. Morris helped Benaud to score 163 in ninety minutes in the Australians' best opening stand of the tour, but after Benaud left the struggle for supremacy was renewed, for both Bedser and Wardle bowled extremely well. The match was watched by 55,000 people.

T. N. Pearce's XI

L. Hutton c Langley b Hill	49	– st Langley b Hassett	102
R. T. Simpson c Craig b Johnston	86	– c Craig b Johnston	12
T. W. Graveney run out	24	– c Hassett b Hill	66
P. B. H. May lbw b Hill	29	– c Hassett b Hill	43
W. J. Edrich b Johnston	5	– c Langley b Davidson	33
N. W. D. Yardley b Hill	6	– c Benaud b Davidson	19
T. E. Bailey lbw b Benaud	35	– not out	24
T. G. Evans c Hassett b Hill	10	– st Langley b Hill	1
A. V. Bedser c Craig b Benaud	40		
J. H. Wardle not out	17	– st Langley b Davidson	10
R. Tattersall lbw b Benaud	4		
B 13, l-b 2	15	B 4, l-b 2	6

1/71 2/145 3/182 4/188 5/206   320   1/24 2/167 3/213   (8 wkts dec.) 316
6/219 7/243 8/290 9/307   4/258 5/262 6/292 7/293 8/316

Australians

R. Benaud c and b Bedser	29	– c May b Bedser	135
A. R. Morris b Tattersall	20	– b Tattersall	70
G. B. Hole run out	52	– c and b Bedser	26
I. D. Craig lbw b Wardle	9	– c Tattersall b Bedser	2
A. L. Hassett c Yardley b Bailey	74	– c Evans b Bedser	25
R. N. Harvey b Tattersall	41	– lbw b Wardle	3
J. H. de Courcy lbw b Tattersall	0	– b Wardle	8
A. K. Davidson c Wardle b Bedser	39	– not out	27
G. R. Langley b Bedser	25	– c Wardle b Bedser	9
J. C. Hill c Edrich b Bedser	18	– not out	9
W. A. Johnston not out	0		
B 9, l-b 1	10	B 4, l-b 6, n-b 1	11

1/36 2/69 3/117 4/123 5/190   317   1/163 2/209 3/218 4/237 (8 wkts) 325
6/190 7/274 8/276 9/317   5/246 6/278 7/287 8/309

Australian Bowling

	Overs	Mdns	Runs	Wkts	Overs	Mdns	Runs	Wkts
Johnston	26	4	93	2	14	1	71	1
Davidson	11	3	27	—	22.3	5	72	3
Benaud	17.2	1	98	3	8	—	41	—
Hill	24	6	65	4	15	2	94	3
Hassett	3	—	17	—	5	—	18	1
Morris	1	—	5	—				
Hole					2	—	14	—

T. N. Pearce's XI Bowling

	Overs	Mdns	Runs	Wkts	Overs	Mdns	Runs	Wkts
Bedser	22.5	6	66	4	26.5	3	86	5
Bailey	15	2	74	1	7	1	23	—
Tattersall	24	4	70	3	13	1	98	1
Wardle	22	3	97	1	23	2	107	2

Umpires: H. G. Baldwin and H. Elliott (Lancashire).

AUSTRALIANS IN ENGLAND, 1953

After having held the Ashes for 19 years, the longest period on record, Australia surrendered them at Kennington Oval where after four drawn Tests England won the fifth and last in convincing fashion by eight wickets. If the winning of Test Matches were the only thing that mattered, then the team which Lindsay Hassett brought to Great Britain in 1953 did not carry out its mission. That was very far from the truth.

Rarely has any series of matches produced such interesting and exciting cricket. Day after day and sometimes hour after hour the pendulum swung first towards Australia and then towards England. Time and again it seemed that one of the teams had established absolute mastery only for it to be taken away. No other series of Tests captured such public attention. What with day-by-day front page newspaper articles and radio and television broadcasts there were times when industry almost stood still while the man in the street followed the tense battle between bat and ball.

Above everything else was the true spirit of cricket which existed between the England and Australian players both on and off the field. A cricket tour can provide plenty of strain with its constant travel, change of hotels and strenuous matches, but wherever they went Lindsay Hassett's men were agreeable companions and foes. For the most part their cricket was breezy and attractive and if in the occasional match, such as against Middlesex at Lord's and Warwickshire at Edgbaston, they did not show the enterprise the onlookers expected, these were isolated instances among a host of praiseworthy performances.

The Australians' ambition was to enjoy their cricket. In this respect they provided a lesson for many English county cricketers. Naturally the Tests were their main consideration but as soon as the tension was over they gave some magnificent displays of hitting, culminating in that thrilling victory in their last important match at Scarborough, where Benaud hit eleven 6s in his wonderful 135.

In assessing the merits of this team it must be remembered they followed possibly the finest Australian combination to visit this country — Bradman's team of 1948. Yet the overall records were not very different. Bradman's men played 34 matches, won 25 and drew nine. Hassett's men played 35, won 16, drew 16 and lost one, the final Test. The fall in the number of victories could be partly attributed to the wet weather. As many as nine of the 16 wins — all in first-class matches — were accomplished in two days and eleven victories came with an innings to spare. On the other hand the 1948 side won half their 34 matches without batting a second time. Moreover they made 350 runs or more in 24 innings against only 10 innings by the 1953 side.

These facts show clearly that the main difference between the teams was in batting. Since 1926 until last season all Australian sides in England had enjoyed the services of Bradman, who in that period broke almost every individual batting record. Hutton has said he considered Bradman was worth three men to any team. By making his colossal scores at a colossal pace Bradman lightened the responsibility as well as the task of his colleagues. The gap his retirement left in Australian cricket can be seen in the batting figures. For the first time in 50 years not a single Australian batsman could show an average of 40 in the Tests.

Yet in all matches 30 centuries were shared by 10 of the 17 players, and although only six scored 1,000 runs the potential talent was there. Where did Australia come to grief in the Tests? Certainly not in the matter of the toss which Hassett won in all five matches. One would have thought that by gaining choice of innings each time they would have produced some big totals, yet only three times in the Tests did they muster 300, with 368 in the second innings at Lord's the best.

Many of these Australian Sheffield Shield players seemed to be confronted with the same problem that affects so many capable English county batsmen. They were found wanting when lifted into a higher sphere and opposed to Test Match bowlers. With the exception of Hassett and Morris there was a noticeable lack of concentration. They were at a loss in dealing with the turning ball due probably to their own pitches in Australia being protected from rain. Their sorry exhibitions in the Manchester and Oval Tests were notable examples and their decision not to attempt to hit off 166 in 170 minutes at Edgbaston on a pitch taking spin was because they feared a collapse against Hollies, the Warwickshire slow bowler.

Lack of capable opening batsmen contributed to these deficiencies. Only rarely was the side given a sound start. Morris and McDonald were the only two recognised openers in the party and the latter never really settled down to English conditions. Consequently, Hassett experimented with Hole before going in first himself with Morris in the last four Tests.

Hassett, like his rival captain, Hutton, stood out in a lean summer for batsmen. Hassett alone hit two centuries in the Tests. A man for the big occasion, he suited his game to the task in hand and when free to enjoy himself in the less important engagements he gave some delightful displays. Morris never touched his form of 1948, when in the Tests he scored 696 runs, averaging 87, but at times he was a tenacious opponent. Again he found Bedser his main problem and he fell to him five times in the ten Test innings. Much was expected from Harvey who gave some scintillating exhibitions up and down the country, scoring 2,040 runs; yet he could show no more than 346 for his efforts in the Tests. His solitary century came after Evans dropped him at Manchester.

With their seniors failing it was not surprising that the strangers to England, Hole, de Courcy, Davidson and Benaud, fell easy prey when Bedser and his fellow bowlers were in the full flush of success, but enough was seen of these youngsters to make one realise that the experience they gained on this tour may well help them to become better players as they mature. Indeed, I shall be surprised if a lot more is not heard of the three-all-rounders, Davidson, Archer and Benaud.

Turning to the bowling there was an appreciable weakness due to the absence of top-class spin to support the thrust of Lindwall, Miller and Johnston. I should imagine that in such a wet summer Hassett must have regretted the decision to leave behind Ian Johnson, the off-break bowler. None of the three leg spinners, Ring, Hill and Benaud, was seen to advantage in the Tests. It was ironical that while the question of spin remained a permanent problem, two former Australian Test players, Tribe and Dooland, were thriving in English county cricket and a third, McCool, was hidden in the Lancashire League.

Johnston, the only bowler to take 100 wickets in 1948, played in five fewer matches and his victims dropped to 75, there being only seven in the Tests compared with 27 five years before. Johnston's finest effort was in the fifth Test, when he turned to slow spinners. A defiant number eleven batsman, he headed the batting averages by virtue of the fact that he was dismissed only once during the tour. His best innings was 28 not out. A leg injury in a practice match before the tour commenced in earnest gave Johnston much trouble and may have caused Hassett to recast his plans. Although Johnston was able to play in three Tests, he never appeared to be thoroughly sound and his effectiveness was further reduced by the necessity of altering the position of his right foot at the point of delivery. Had Johnston produced his 1948 form, Miller could have been used more sparingly as a bowler.

As it was, Miller, who began the tour in dazzling form with the bat, was forced to expend his energy on bowling, to the detriment of his run-getting powers which would have been invaluable. Still, Miller was one of the personalities of the season. His aggregate of 1,433 (average 51.17) was second only to Harvey's. In this first innings at Worcester, Miller made 220 not out – the highest of his career – and in his final innings against Combined Services at Kingston he surpassed this with 262 not out. It was significant that his only Test hundred was made when Australia put together their highest total.

One man England feared more than any other was Lindwall. Truly one of the world's finest fast bowlers of all time, he may have shed some of his fire. Yet he remained at the peak of his form, taking 26 wickets at 18.84 runs apiece in the Tests compared with 27 for 19.62 in 1948. Whenever Lindwall took the new ball there was a possibility of a collapse, and when the shine had gone England breathed again. Allied to his rhythmic run were speed and control. A highly intelligent bowler, Lindwall never wasted his physical resources. He used his utmost pace only occasionally when its suited his side best. He swung the ball late either way, and given any help from the pitch he caused it to lift from a good length. Both he and Miller exploited the short pitched bumper, never persistently, but within the agreement made between MCC and the Australian Board of Control when the team arrived. In the Lord's and Oval Tests Lindwall also revealed his ability as a batsman of quality.

Two promising young pace bowlers were seen in Archer, who always aimed at the stumps, and the left-handed Davidson. Hill, the surprise choice of the tour, came as a stock bowler. Mostly he delivered top spinners at medium pace with an occasional leg break. Every follower of cricket in England awaited eagerly the arrival at the crease of Craig, who at the age of 17 was the youngest Australian cricketer to be sent overseas, but seldom did he show his home form and he and McDonald were the only two not to appear in a Test.

No combination of 17 cricketers have given a better show in the field. It was a sheer joy to see Harvey at cover, Davidson, Benaud, Hole, Archer, de Courcy, as well as Hassett, Lindwall and Miller close to the wicket, and Morris and Craig in the deep. In marked contrast to England, scarcely a catch was allowed to escape. Finally, praise to Langley for his capable wicket-keeping. He never attempted to challenge Evans in showmanship, but he was always reliable, taking his chances without fuss. Tallon had days of brilliance. He kept well in the first Test, but fell away, and Langley played in the remaining four.

Australia received some measure of compensation for losing the Ashes by taking home a record profit of over £100,000. Their share from the five Tests alone amounted to £55,000. More money was taken in the second Test than in any previous cricket match in the world. The total receipts of £57,000 surpassed the previous highest of £44,063 at Melbourne during the MCC tour of 1946-47.   N.P.

TWO ERAS OF AUSTRALIAN PACE

GREGORY – McDONALD TO LINDWALL – MILLER

By I. A. R. Peebles

This summer we welcome the Australians again to our shores. Already they have been here twenty-one times since their first visit in 1878. They come as challengers, for England hold the Ashes which were regained at Kennington Oval in 1953. We, in England, regard the Australians as our most formidable opponents and another exciting series of Tests can be expected. Usually the Australians ride rough-shod over the County clubs. Not since 1912 has a County eleven lowered their colours. During that tour the Australians were without some of their leading players and they suffered eight defeats including five by the Counties: Nottinghamshire, Surrey, Lancashire (twice), and Hampshire. The nearest any County has come to mastering them since then was in 1930 when Gloucestershire tied at Bristol. (*Editor.*)

Barring mishaps, it does seem certain that once again England will see the old firm of Lindwall and Miller in action. In the past there have been premature reports of their impending retirement, and even at the moment of writing when Sheffield Shield cricket in Australia is well under way and the selectors are doubtless studying the individual form of the players with anxious eyes, both have been troubled by injury. Whatever the future may bring, a comparison between Lindwall and Miller and their only rivals as a pair in the present century of Australian cricket, Gregory and McDonald, is fascinating as it is inevitable.

In making any such comparison it is necessary to recognise that fashions and techniques in cricket, as in other matters, have changed with the passing of the generation which separates two distinct eras. It is a wide subject and, as space will allow only the study of certain aspects, these few reflections are perforce confined to the bowlers' point of view, and again largely to that of the pace bowler.

This will be the third Australian team to visit England since the war, and it will embark on the sixth series since that major interruption. In the number of matches and in actual years this period is almost the exact counterpart of that between the end of the first war and the eve of the 1930 tour. There is also a close parallel in the trend of events. In both cases England were outplayed in the reopening tour and the return visit, achieved a solitary victory in the third series and won the fourth in each case by a final deciding match at The Oval. The succeeding series, those of 1928-29 and 1954-55, saw England once more in the ascendancy by a good margin. The similarity in result during these decades was reflected by a close resemblance in the actual play. A period of Australian supremacy, achieved by a combination of powerful batting, devastating fast bowling and much superior fielding, was followed by a gradual English resurgence led by an outstanding fast-medium bowler. Finally, there comes a complete reversal of the balance, largely brought about by a counterblast of fast bowling. Certainly there were many other factors which contributed to the ebb and flow of the tide, some alike and some totally dissimilar, but few cricket cycles can have been so alike in broad outline.

Bradman Intervenes

They were divided by the era of Bradman who made his first appearance in the 1928-29 series and led the triumphant teams of 1946-47 and 1948. Despite the overlap, the division may be regarded as fairly clear, for on the one hand, despite early success, he was still something of an unknown quantity and, on the other, although still a tremendous force, he was scarcely the man who changed the character of international cricket in the 'thirties. In comparing the two eras, it is possible to identify several elements which affected tactics and techniques; but to say for how many of these Bradman was directly or indirectly accountable or to estimate his total influence on the game as a whole is very difficult. What is plain is that the game as played in the post second war years differed considerably in form from that of 1921.

To start with cold, impersonal figures – if indeed cricket figures can ever be cold or impersonal – surely the most pertinent item amongst Mr Roy Webber's exhaustive figures dealing with these years is the fact that in the 1920-21 and 1921 series England, a well-beaten side, scored forty-nine and fifty runs per hundred balls bowled. Australia were naturally rather more expeditious scoring fifty-three and fifty-six. In the first two post second war series the rates dropped to thirty-seven and thirty-eight for England and fifty and forty-six for Australia. Thereafter the Australian rate dropped farther back. The trend in the intervening years had been a steady decline in the pace of scoring despite a large proportion of runs supplied by Bradman at an exceptionally high personal rate. Even if the 1920-21 and 1921 seasons were abnormal, it hardly calls for the mass of additional evidence available to demonstrate that the play of thirty-five years ago was of a considerably freer character. Whether it was as efficient is another matter.

What is the main reason for this change or deceleration? The broad answer must surely be the transference of the bowlers' focus from the region of the off-stump to that of the leg and the consequent throttling of off-side play but, equally importantly, the denial of the safe deflecting stroke to leg. The causes of this transference are several and complex, and the credit or responsibility must be shared between groundsman, bowler and batsman in what proportion we may later determine. Somewhat unfashionably I am inclined to exculpate the legislators.

In 1921 the spearhead of the Australian attack, the speed of Gregory and McDonald, was directed at the stumps and supported by three slips. The good length ball aimed at the stumps pitched regularly to the off and it was desirable that any error should be further in that direction. If the error was to drop the ball outside the leg-stump the batsman could play boldly in the knowledge that he had free passage to a distant fine-leg who could, at most, rob him of three runs.

When Lindwall and Miller bowled the slips had increased in number and some of them had now migrated to the hitherto uninhabited regions on the leg-side. For England, Bedser, with his sharp in-swerver, had perfected the same technique and the impact on batsmanship must have been as profound as the introduction of the googly. What had been a safe and attractive scoring shot had now elements of suicide, for if the ball "moved" a little to the on a mis-hit was almost certain to result in a catch. Indeed, a correctly executed stroke was often fatal, owing to the difficulty of placing and keeping the ball down in this sector. The dangers of this situation were clear when Bradman, who seldom repeated a serious mistake, fell three times in succession to the backward short-leg position during the 1948 series.

The development of this form of attack is, as I have said, attributable to several causes. Most are agreed that the glory of cricket exists on the off-side, the highest art of the bowler to make the ball go away, and the beauty of batsmanship the variety of stroke between third-man and mid-off. But with the undoubted improvement in defensive back-play and the increase of dead, over-prepared pitches the bowler was given little incentive to attack, especially on the off-side.

While the old lbw rule prevailed it was extremely hard to dislodge a batsman who made good use of his pads, for under its terms the ball had to pitch on and hit. Geometrically it is almost impossible for the faster bowler to drop the ball on a good length and comply with these requirements, unless he turns the ball from the leg – a tall order in the circumstances where it is most required. (In passing, it seems strange that those who advocate the reintroduction of the old law, having robbed the bowler of what little opportunity the present rule affords him in that quarter, expect thereby a return to off-side play.)

When the bowler was shorn of practically all means of positive action on the off-side it was not unnatural that he should seek some line of defence, or at least economy, and the on-side offered decided advantages in time of stress. It was seen as an area of attack in the 1932-33 series, a state of affairs largely precipitated by the tremendous off-side attacks of

Bradman on the paceless pitches of 1930. At the same time O'Reilly dimmed much of Hammond's brilliance by concentrating on his relatively weaker on-side play. From then on much thought was given to the placing and feeding of the close leg-side field.

In the present age the "in-coming" form of attack, so to speak, has been brought to a very fine art and one speculates on the reactions of the great stroke players of the past suddenly confronted with Bedser at his best. On the other side one wonders what additional problems Barnes and Tate might have raised by systematic use of the close leg field.

It is important to distinguish between the legitimate leg stump attack and "leg-theory" applied in a purely negative sense to discourage scoring. That any bowler should be permitted to pack the leg-side field and bowl outside the batsman's legs is deplorable and to be discouraged at all costs. Appeals to the spirit of the game are, to my mind, of dubious value, for the very good reason that the "spirit" is inclined to vary greatly with circumstances and in interpretation. A clear-cut law operates with certainty in all conditions, but the difficulty in this case is, admittedly, to frame such a law without adding further complication to an already intricate code.

My own suggestion to meet this situation has just that disadvantage but seems to have a basis of justice. If, which is perhaps improbable, this form of bowling should ever become widespread, would it not be possible to say that, when five or more fielders were posted to the on, any ball pitching outside the leg stump should be a no-ball? This may be cumbersome but it would exercise restraint where it is needed without interfering with the honest citizen.

The real answer to all cricket problems is, of course, to give the bowler fair incentive and opportunity to attack at all times. In doing so he will get wickets but will be more prone to make mistakes from which the striker can derive benefit and, indeed, in the absence of any guaranteed security, will be anxious to do so. This is hardly the place in which to reopen the discussion as to the best ways and means of achieving this healthy state of affairs, but, as I have implied, a return to the old lbw law is surely not one of them.

The point of these rather rambling reflections is really to say that could the modern spectator be wafted back thirty-five years he would not only see a faster scoring match but one of largely different character. It might or might not be that he would find them more interesting that the battles of attrition to which he has grown accustomed. It might be more accurate to say "had grown accustomed", for it must be borne in mind that the recent series in Australia was the most exciting cricket, whatever is standard. But it was also exceptional.

Much of the action and excitement was due to the fact that the pitches gave considerable, and not always fair, help to the prevailing type of bowling. Their inconsistency occasionally gave the proceedings an air of hit or miss which went beyond the bounds of "glorious uncertainty" and must always detract from an equally balanced and scientific contest. To one who has played on it, the thought constantly recurs that the matting wicket of the old Wanderers ground at Johannesburg, with all its disadvantages, was the one surface which gave both departments full scope for their talents and was at all times a true reflection of merit.

The highlights of each era, Gregory and McDonald attacking Hobbs and Woolley or Lindwall and Miller in action against Compton and Hutton obviously transcended the differences in character to which I have referred and even the one-sided nature of the matches. The chief point in common amongst the batsmen is that they formed a first line of defence with little reserve behind them. The bowlers have much similarity in circumstance and in performance. They reigned supreme at a time when there was a world shortage of fast bowling and batsmen were ill-equipped to meet it.

Which was the finer pair and which the greatest individual must ever be open to argument and is much a matter of opinion. Certainly in span and in the matter of statistics the moderns have a much more impressive record. Gregory and McDonald appeared together in but eleven Test matches, eight against England and three against South Africa. The latter then left the international field at the height of his powers but his senior partner played for another seven years, a total of 24 matches. There is no doubt, however, that his powers declined greatly after the dissolution of the partnership.

Comparison of Figures

Up to the present Lindwall and Miller have appeared together on 46 occasions and have played 49 and 47 Test matches respectively. In his Test career Gregory took 75 wickets at 35.30 runs apiece and McDonald 43 at 35.60 each. So far Lindwall has taken 192 wickets for 21.88 apiece and Miller 147 at 22.99 runs each.

There can be little doubt that McDonald was the most graceful of the quartette and possibly the most perfect cricket machine of all time. In the opinion of many well-qualified judges he could produce a faster ball than anyone within living memory. In his county days he seldom exerted himself to the full; only recently I was given an enthralling eye-witness account of one of his latter bursts of speed, occasioned by the appearance of an amateur who had treated him roughly in a previous match. This apparently irritated him out of his customary impassive calm and the results were spectacular. My informant, who has played most of the fast bowlers of the last thirty years, says it was the fastest bowling he has ever seen and only approached by Lindwall's stupendous three-over burst at Manchester in 1948. It was interesting to hear that the only perceptible increase in effort was that he accelerated in the last five yards of the impeccable run up to a swift gallop. His point established he reverted to the normal cruising speed which carried him through many strenuous seasons.

Gregory was to my mind the most inspiring. One might apply to him the words of a motoring critic who said of a famous make of sports car that others might have gone faster but none had achieved the glorious frenzy of its progress. Estimates as to his maximum speed vary, but it must have been extremely swift especially in the opening overs, and his height and very high arm added greatly to the general hostility of the performance. It might also be said of both Gregory and Miller that, in contrast to the polished craftsmanship of their partners, they were both children of nature.

Lindwall Comes First

A large mass of opinion places Lindwall first of all fast bowlers, a judgement based on pace, variation, control and consummate technique of seam and swerve. In addition he is a wonderfully shrewd and discerning tactician. I have already dwelt on the modern emphasis on the leg stump and the close surrounding field. Lindwall has retained the classical off-side attack but has added to it the cramping assault on the region of the batsman's pads. The so-called "Carmody field", which consists of a cover-point and a short-leg to the fore and the rest of the field spread on either side of the wicket-keeper like the horns of a Zulu Impi, would doubtless appear monstrous and absurd to an eye reopened after thirty years. In the hands of the master it is in fact a formidable instrument. When it is new, the bowler pitches the ball well up, almost to half-volley length, and invites the batsman to drive him into the untenanted foreground. But swinging bat and very late swinging ball are ill met and the mis-hit from either edge means almost certain disaster with the Australian in-field to hand.

Batsmen have told me that Lindwall's low arm gives the ball an awkward angle of flight in addition to the complication of his late and unpredicted dip in either direction. When, as in the last series, the ball came at varying heights from the pitch the skill demanded of the modern opener is such that it is not surprising that few regularly succeed in such circumstances. It may be observed that doped, paceless wickets kill these dangers just as effectively as they obliterate any other point of interest.

Of Miller it might be said that he is the most mercurial but, in the mood, as deadly as any. His careless, almost casual air bears no relation to the power and fire of his action which seems to develop its maximum effort and weight as the arm comes to the downward sector of its swing so that the ball hits the pitch with a resounding thump. Although it may be with less design than in the case of Lindwall, he makes the ball move sharply in either direction.

Miller The Menace

After the splendid performances of our own fast bowlers in Australia in 1954-55 it may seem almost ungrateful to say so but, with Lindwall in at least a temporary decline, Miller was the most menacing bowler of the series with the new ball. He may have lost something of his stamina but his opening assaults at Brisbane, Melbourne and Adelaide were positively hair-raising as seen through the eyes of a visiting supporter. Three balls at the start of the crucial second innings at Adelaide all but wrecked English hopes and remain vividly in the imagination. First there was a ferocious "in-dipper", which appeared to affect Edrich's nervous system as violently as it did his middle and leg stumps. This was followed at uncomfortably short intervals by two very fast balls to Hutton and Cowdrey which left the pitch like leg-breaks and resulted in bullet-like catches, both beautifully picked up in the slips. The challenge was met by magnificent batting by May and Compton, but until the first welcome signs of fatigue appeared the final target of 94 runs seemed immeasurably distant.

Miller has the additional virtue of being a most entertaining bowler, and his impish delight in loosing off googlies and round armers without previous notice must be highly disconcerting, if it does not seem to meet with any great material success.

The Combined Effort

But when all is said and done, which of these great pairs will be given premier place in Australian cricket history in the years to come is a very open question. Gregory and McDonald have one very special niche in all cricket history. At least so far as international cricket is concerned they were the pioneers of all-fast opening attack. Since then it has been regarded as the most effective use that can be made of the new ball, and it can well be argued that two fast bowlers, provided they are of quality, have had more influence on the result of a given series than any other factor, with the possible exception of the phenomenal Bradman. In support of this view I would cite Larwood and Voce; Martindale and Constantine in their own country, Lindwall and Miller and finally Statham and Tyson. There have been many fine individual performers during the same time, but it seems that the combined effort is necessary to derive the fullest service from the individual.

SURREY v AUSTRALIANS

Played at The Oval, May 6, 17, 18, 1956

Surrey won by ten wickets, so becoming the first county for forty-four years to triumph over an Australian team. There could be no doubt about their superiority in a sensational match, and Johnson, in presenting his cap to the Surrey captain, Surridge, admitted it freely.

To Laker belonged the great distinction of taking all ten wickets. Not since 1878, when E. Barratt, another Surrey man, did so for the Players, also at The Oval, had a bowler taken all ten wickets against an Australian side, and Laker was given the ball and a cheque for £50 by the Surrey Committee. He and, in the second innings, the left-handed Lock, fully exposed the weakness of the Australian batsmen against the turning ball.

Winning the toss appeared to have given the Australians a considerable advantage, and Burke and McDonald emphasised this view while scoring 62 in ninety-five minutes. McDonald, though enjoying two "lives", brought off many good strokes during a stay of three hours thirty-five minutes and he fell only 11 runs short of his second century in successive innings. When he was taken at the wicket the total stood at 151 for four wickets, but Laker brought about such a series of disasters that five more batsmen were dismissed while the total rose by 48. Of these runs 12, including a drive for 6, were hit by Davidson in one over from Laker and 16 came in three strokes by Crawford at the expense of the same bowler. Fortunately for the Australians, Miller, getting as much of the bowling as possible, scored briskly after a careful start, and he and Wilson put on 42 for the last wicket. Even so Laker, maintaining a splendid length in a spell of four hours and a quarter broken only by the lunch and tea intervals, exploited off spin on the dry pitch so skilfully that he came out with this analysis:

Overs	Maidens	Runs	Wickets
46	18	88	10

In the hope that he might achieve similar success, Johnson kept himself on for most of the Surrey first innings, but though he flighted the ball well, his off-breaks caused nothing like the same trouble. Apart from three overs by the fast bowlers, the Australian attack remained in the hands of spin bowlers throughout, a policy which not only failed to bring the desired results, but came in for much criticism.

Still, Surrey did not for a long time find run-getting an easy matter, though Fletcher (six 4s) drove hard during an opening stand with Clark which realised 53. Waiting for the ball to punish and then putting plenty of power into strokes all round, Clark stayed till another 59 were added and then became the second victim of Maddocks at the wicket. Giving no chance during two hours and ten minutes, he hit eight 4s.

Constable, cautious at first, gradually developed more freedom, but wickets fell steadily and six were down for 221. Then Laker attacked the bowling. He helped himself to 16, including a drive for 6 and two 4s, in an over from Johnson, and altogether hit 43 out of 57 added by the seventh partnership in thirty-nine minutes, taking Surrey ahead.

Constable's long stay ended with a return catch when he had batted for four hours thirty-five minutes. Without making a serious mistake, he hit seven 4s, chiefly by on-side strokes, in a most valuable innings. Surridge and Loader put on 34 for the last wicket, and so Surrey gained a lead of 88.

Three overs by the opening Surrey bowlers at the end of the second day did not yield a run, and next morning Surridge reverted to an all-spin attack. For a time matters went well enough with the Australians and an opening stand of 56 in ninety-five minutes by Burke and McDonald seemed to have made them reasonably safe from defeat.

Then the course of the game changed completely, for Lock, able by now to make the ball turn quickly and occasionally get up awkwardly from a dusty pitch, caused such a breakdown that in a further ninety-five minutes the innings was all over for another 51 runs. Lock, who took the first six wickets at a cost of 40 runs, finished with an analysis of seven for 49 – a marked contrast to his 0 for 100 in the first innings! Actually he achieved all his success from the Pavilion end – that from which Laker bowled in the first innings – in a spell of 23.1 overs, 6 maidens, for 36 runs. He owed something to smart fielding, the catch by which May at slip disposed of Davidson being first-rate.

Surrey required only 20 runs to win, but Lindwall and Crawford bowled so fast and accurately that they took fifty-five minutes to accomplish the task.

Australians

J. W. Burke lbw b Laker	28	– c and b Lock	20
C. C. McDonald c Swetman b Laker	89	– c Laker b Lock	45
K. Kackay c Surridge b Laker	4	– lbw b Laker	4
R. N. Harvey c Constable b Laker	13	– c May b Lock	10
K. R. Miller not out	57	– c Swetman b Lock	2
L. Maddocks b Laker	12	– c Laker b Lock	0
R. R. Lindwall b Laker	0	– c Constable b Lock	4
I. W. Johnson c Swetman b Laker	0	– run out	5
A. K. Davidson c May b Laker	21	– c May b Laker	7
P. Crawford b Laker	16	– not out	5
J. Wilson c Swetman b Laker	4	– st Swetman b Lock	1
B 4, l-b 8, n-b 3	15	L-b 4	4

1/62 2/93 3/124 4/151 5/173   259   1/56 2/73 3/83 4/85 5/85   107
6/173 7/175 8/199 9/217   6/89 7/92 8/101 9/104

Surrey

D. G. W. Fletcher c Maddocks b Johnson	29 – not out	9
T. H. Clark c Maddocks b Burke	58 – not out	8
B. Constable c and b Johnson	109
P. B. H. May st Maddocks b Johnson	27
K. Barrington c Miller b Johnson	4
R. Swetman st Maddocks b Davidson	0
D. F. Cox b Davidson	13
J. C. Laker c McDonald b Johnson	43
W. S. Surridge c Harvey b Johnson	38
G. A. R. Lock b Davidson	0
P. J. Loader not out	12
B 10, l-b 3, w 1	14 B 1, l-b 1, n-b 1 3

1/53 2/112 3/147 4/192 5/195   347   (No wkt) 20
6/221 7/278 8/302 9/313

Surrey Bowling

	Overs	Mdns	Runs	Wkts	Overs	Mdns	Runs	Wkts
Loader	15	4	30	—	2	2	—	—
Surridge	8	2	8	—	1	1	—	—
Laker	46	18	88	10	25	10	42	2
Lock	33	12	100	—	31.1	9	49	7
Cox	5	—	18	—				
Clark					8	4	12	—

Australians Bowling

	Overs	Mdns	Runs	Wkts	Overs	Mdns	Runs	Wkts
Lindwall	2	1	10	—	8	4	8	—
Crawford	1	—	4	—	7	3	9	—
Johnson	60.3	12	168	6				
Davidson	44	14	101	3				
Wilson	19	9	34	—				
Burke	7	2	16	1				

Umpires: K. McCanlis and L. H. Gray.

ENGLAND v AUSTRALIA
Fourth Test Match

Played at Manchester, July 26, 27, 28, 30, 31, 1956

England won by an innings and 170 runs, with just over an hour to spare and so retained the "Ashes". This memorable game will always be known as "Laker's Match" because of the remarkable performance by the Surrey off-break bowler in taking nine wickets for 37 runs in the first innings and ten wickets for 53 in the second. Laker broke all the more important bowling records in the history of cricket. His achievements were:

1. Nineteen wickets in a match, the most in any first-class game. The previous best was 17, achieved twenty times. The most in a Test Match was 17 for 159 by S. F. Barnes for England against South Africa at Johannesburg in 1913-14.
2. Ten wickets in an innings for the first time in Test cricket. The previous best for England against Australia was eight for 35 by G. Lohmann of Surrey in 1886-87. The best for England in any Test innings nine for 28 by G. Lohmann against South Africa in 1895-96.
3. Ten wickets in an innings twice in one season for the first time. Laker previously took ten for 88 for Surrey, also against the Australians at The Oval in May.
4. Thirty-nine wickets in four Test Matches, equalling the record of A. V. Bedser as the highest number in an England-Australia series, with one match to play.
5. Fifty-one wickets in five matches against the Australians to date in the season.

Apart from Laker's personal records, other noteworthy points about the match were:

1. It was the first definite result in a Test Match between England and Australia at Manchester since 1905.
2. For the first time since 1905 England won two matches in a home series against Australia.
3. For the first time since five Test Matches were played in a series regularly from 1897-98 England held the "Ashes" for three series.

Those are bare facts, interesting in themselves, but they fail to capture the drama of one of the most exciting and controversial matches for a long time. The excitement came towards the last day, first when England were trying hard to make up for the time lost by rain to gain the victory which would settle the destination of the "Ashes", and later as Laker drew nearer and nearer his ten wickets in the innings. The controversy arose over the preparation of the pitch and for days cricketers, officials, critics and the general public could talk of little else.

The England selectors sprang a surprise when they named Rev. D. S. Sheppard among the twelve from whom the team would be chosen. Sheppard, who had given up regular cricket to take up Holy Orders had played only four innings for Sussex during the season, when selected. One of these was 97 against the Australians at Hove. His previous Test appearance was two years earlier when he captained England against Pakistan. Like nearly every move the Selection Committee made during the season, this one proved fully justified.

Graveney, originally in the twelve, dropped out because of a bruised hand and Oakman, who played at Leeds, was added to the party. The selectors continued their policy of relying on a four-man attack and Trueman was omitted. This meant two changes from the side which won at Leeds, Sheppard and Statham replacing Insole and Trueman. The Australians, with their injured men fit, were able to choose from all seventeen members of their party for the first time since the first Test. They omitted Burge and gave Craig his first chance in a Test against England. Langley, the wicket-keeper, was intended to play, but an unusual mishap kept him out. During the night he slept on his hand and damaged it.

May won the toss for the third time in the series and he gave England a big advantage. The pitch was completely useless to fast and fast-medium bowlers and Richardson and

Cowdrey, as at Nottingham, gave delightful displays. They took command from the first over and in three hours ten minutes scored 174 for the opening stand. This was England's best start against Australia since 1938 when L. Hutton and C. J. Barnett began with 219 at Trent Bridge. Both batsmen went all out for their strokes and their perfect understanding in running enabled them to offset the value of Australia's defensive field.

Cowdrey, strong in driving, was first to leave, but Richardson did not survive much longer, batting three hours forty minutes for 104, his first Test century. Most of eleven 4s, the same number as Cowdrey, came from well-timed leg-side strokes, but he also brought off some good cover drives, notably two in an over from Lindwall which were models of execution.

Sheppard and May continued the mastery of the Australian attack, but towards tea time, puffs of dust became noticeable when the ball landed and it seemed that the pitch was breaking up unusually early. Johnson and Benaud, the Australian spin bowlers, were unable to exploit the conditions and England finished the first day with a total of 307 for three. Towards the close May was caught off a quickly spun and lifting leg-break after helping Sheppard add 93. A curiosity was that the first five England batsmen were all amateurs, something that had last happened against Australia in 1899 when C. B. Fry, A. C. MacLaren, K. S. Ranjitsinhji, C. L. Townsend and F. S. Jackson were the men concerned.

Mutterings about the pitch could be heard that evening, but they rose to full fury next day. The Australians still could not get the ball to bite as much as they ought to have done and England went gaily on, adding 152 in two hours eleven minutes before being all out for the highest total against Australia since 1948. Sheppard, 59 overnight, completed a chanceless century and batted five minutes under five hours for 113 which included one 6 and fifteen 4s. He drove delightfully and gave not the slightest suggestion of lack of match practice.

Evans, revelling in the situation, hit lustily and scored 47 out of 62 in twenty-nine minutes. England made their 459 runs in 491 minutes, an unusually rapid rate for Test cricket in recent years.

Australia began their reply just after half-past two and before play ended on the second day they had lost eleven wickets. McDonald and Burke began steadily with a stand of 48, but they had to fight hard against the spin of Laker and Lock, who were brought on early. Laker did not start his devastating work until switched to the Stretford end, from where he took each of his nineteen wickets. McDonald and Harvey fell at the same total and after tea, taken at 62 for two, the last eight wickets went in thirty-five minutes for 22 runs. Lock took his only wicket with the first ball after the interval and Laker did the rest, his after tea spell being seven wickets for eight runs in 22 balls. While admitting that Laker spun his off-breaks appreciably, the Australian batsmen gave a sorry display and appeared to give up too easily.

Following on 375 behind, Australia were unfortunate to lose McDonald, who retired with a knee injury after scoring 11. Harvey replaced him and was out first ball, hitting a full toss into the hands of short mid-on. Harvey failed to score in either innings. Australia finished the day with one wicket down for 51 and the controversial storm broke that night.

Accusations were made that the pitch had been prepared specially for England's spin bowlers and these were denied by the Lancashire authorities. The Australians were said to be extremely bitter over the condition of the pitch, but their captain, Johnson, declined to comment on the subject. The arguments continued over the week-end and not until Laker's wonderful bowling on the last day overshadowed everything did they abate.

The weather changed completely on Saturday, when rain allowed only three-quarters of an hour's cricket between ten minutes past two and five minutes to three. In that brief period Australia added six runs and lost the wicket of Burke. Sunday was an atrocious day and Monday was almost as bad. In two spells of forty-five minutes and fifteen minutes Australia took their score to 84 without further loss. Conditions were terrible for cricket, a fierce wind making batting and bowling extremely difficult. Lignum bails were used and were most successful, not once being blown off.

England looked like being robbed of victory by the weather but it improved considerably on the last day and play began only ten minutes late. The soaking the pitch received left it slow and easy-paced and by fighting, determined cricket, McDonald and Craig remained together until lunch time when the score was 112 for two with four hours left.

Shortly before the interval the sun appeared and almost immediately the ball began to spin quickly. Afterwards Laker began another devastating spell, sending back Craig, Mackay, Miller and Archer in nine overs for three runs. Craig, who helped McDonald add 59, gave a fine, courageous display for four hours twenty minutes; the other three failed to score, Mackay, like his fellow left-hander, Harvey, for the second time in the match. Benaud stayed with McDonald for an hour and a quarter to tea when, with a hour and fifty-five minutes left, England needed to capture four wickets.

Occasionally Laker changed ends, but only when he returned to the Stretford end did he continue his success. After tea the ball spun quicker than at any time in the match and Australia's last hope vanished when McDonald fell to the second ball. His 89, made in five hours thirty-seven minutes, showed that the bowling could be played by determined concentration and he deserved the highest praise for his great effort.

The tension mounted as Laker captured his eighth and ninth wickets. There was never a question of giving Laker his tenth wicket for England's only thought was victory. Lock repeatedly beat the bat, but it was not his match and at twenty-seven minutes past five a great cheer went up as Laker successfully appealed to the umpire, Lee, for lbw against Maddocks. The match was over and Laker had taken all ten wickets.

He earned his triumph by remarkable control of length and spin and it is doubtful whether he bowled more than six bad length balls throughout the match. As Johnson said afterwards: "When the controversy and side issues of the match are forgotten, Laker's wonderful bowling will remain."

That night the rain returned and the following day not a ball could be bowled in any of the first-class matches, so it can be seen how close was England's time margin, and how the greatest bowling feat of all time nearly did not happen.   L.S.

England

P. E. Richardson c Maddocks b Benaud....104	J. C. Laker run out 3
M. C. Cowdrey c Maddocks b Lindwall.... 80	G. A. R. Lock nout out................. 25
Rev. D. S. Sheppard b Archer 113	J. B. Statham c Maddocks b Lindwall...... 0
P. B. H. May c Archer b Benaud 43	
T. E. Bailey b Johnson 20	B 2, l-b 5, w 1 8
C. Washbrook lbw b Johnson............ 6	
A. S. M. Oakman c Archer b Johnson 10	1/174 2/195 3/288 4/321 5/327 459
T. G. Evans st Maddocks b Johnson....... 47	6/339 7/401 8/417 9/458

Australia

C. C. McDonald c Lock b Laker 32	– c Oakman b Laker 89
J. W. Burke c Cowdrey b Lock.................. 22	– c Lock b Laker 33
R. N. Harvey b Laker........................ 0	– c Cowdrey b Laker............ 0
I. D. Craig lbw b Laker....................... 8	– lbw b Laker................. 38
K. R. Miller c Oakman b Laker 6	– b Laker................. 0
K. Mackay c Oakman b Laker 0	– c Oakman b Laker 0
R. G. Archer st Evans b Laker 6	– c Oakman b Laker 0
R. Benaud c Statham b Laker................... 0	– b Laker................. 18
R. R. Lindwall not out........................ 6	– c Lock b Laker 8
L. Maddocks b Laker 4	– lbw b Laker................. 2
I. W. Johnson b Laker........................ 0	– not out 1
	B 12, l-b 4.............. 16

1/48 2/48 3/62 4/62 5/62	84	1/28 2/55 3/114 4/124 5/130 205
6/73 7/73 8/78 9/84		6/130 7/181 8/198 9/203

Australia Bowling

	Overs	Mdns	Runs	Wkts
Lindwall	21.3	6	63	2
Miller	21	6	41	—
Archer	22	6	73	1
Johnson	47	10	151	4
Benaud	47	17	123	2

England Bowling

	Overs	Mdns	Runs	Wkts	Overs	Mdns	Runs	Wkts
Statham	6	3	6	—	16	9	15	—
Bailey	4	3	4	—	20	8	31	—
Laker	16.4	4	37	9	51.2	23	53	10
Lock	14	3	37	1	55	30	69	—
Oakman					8	3	21	—

Umpires: F. S. Lee and E. Davies.

LAKER'S WONDERFUL YEAR

By Neville Cardus

Against the Australians in 1956, J. C. Laker bowled himself to a prominence which might seem legendary if there were no statistics to prove that his skill did indeed perform results and deeds hitherto not considered within the range of any cricketer, living or dead.

No writer of boys' fiction would so strain romantic credulity as to make his hero, playing for England against Australia, capture nine first innings wickets; then help himself to all ten in the second innings. Altogether, 19 for 90 in a Test match. If any author expected us to believe that his hero was not only capable in one chapter of a marvel as fantastic as all this, but also in another chapter, and our earlier chapter, bowled a whole Australian XI out, 10 for 88, the most gullible of his readers would, not without reason, throw the book away and wonder what the said author was taking him for.

Yet as far back as 1950 Laker was hinting that he possessed gifts which on occasion were at any moment likely to be visited by plenary inspiration and accomplish things not only unexpected but wondrous. At Bradford, five miles from his birthplace, Laker, playing for England v The Rest, took 8 wickets for 2 runs in 14 overs – a feat which probably the great S. F. Barnes himself never imagined within mortal bowler's scope – or even desirable. Against Nottinghamshire at The Oval in 1955, Laker took 6 wickets for 5.

Between 1947 and 1953 he did the "hat trick" four times.

Obviously the gods endowed him in his cradle with that indefinable power which from time to time generates talent to abnormal and irresistible achievement. And he has done his conjurations – they have been nothing less – by one of the oldest tricks of the bowlers' trade. Not by the new-fangled "swing" and not by "googlies" or Machiavellian deceit by flight through the air, has Laker hypnotised batsmen into helpless immobility, but by off-breaks of the finger-spin type which would have been recognised by, and approved by, cricketers who played in Laker's own county of Yorkshire more than half a century ago. He really follows the great succession of Yorkshire off-spinners – from Ted Wainwright, Schofield Haigh, not forgetting F. S. Jackson, to George Macaulay, reaching to Illingworth of the present day.

Laker's actual finger spin probably has seldom been surpassed on a "sticky" or dusty wicket, in point of velocity and viciousness after pitching. I can think only of Ted Wainwright, Cecil Parkin and Tom Goddard who shared Laker's ability to "fizz" the ball right-handed from the off-side. There was more temper in Macaulay's attack than there is in Laker's, more vehemence of character. But for sheer technical potentiality, often for sheer actual spitefulness, Laker's off-spin must be regarded as entirely out of the ordinary, and very much his own.

Any great performer needs to be born at the right time. If Laker had begun to play for Surrey in the 1930s, when wickets at The Oval and on most large grounds were doped and rolled to insensibility, he might have made one or two appearances for Surrey, then vanished from the scene. Or maybe he would have remained in Yorkshire where pitches were never absolutely divorced from nature and original sin.

Laker was clever, too, to begin playing cricket and bowling off-spin after the alteration to the lbw rule dangerously penalised batsmen who had brought to a fine art the use of the pads to brilliant off-breaks pitching off the stumps and coming back like a knife – as Cecil Parkin's frequently did. Laker has been quick to adapt his arts to the deplorably unresourceful footwork of most batsmen of the present period; moreover he has, with the opportune judgment of those born to exceptional prowess, taken advantage of the modern development of the leg-trap.

On a good wicket, his attack naturally loses sting. His tempting slowish flight enables – or should enable – batsmen to get to the pitch of his bowling. He thrives on success in perhaps larger measure than most bowlers. He likes, more even than most bowlers, to take a quick wicket. There is sometimes an air of indolence in his movements, as he runs his loose lumbering run, swinging his arm slowly, but with the flick of venom at the last split second. At the end of his imperturbable walk back to his bowling mark he stares at the pavilion as though looking for somebody, but looking in a disinterested way. He is entirely what he is by technique – good professional technique, spin, length and the curve in the air natural to off-spin. He does not, as Macaulay and Parkin did, assert his arts plus passion of character and open relentless lust for spoils and the blood of all batsmen.

He is the Yorkshireman, at bottom, true enough; but Southern air has softened a little the native and rude antagonism. Even when he is "on the kill" on a wicket of glue there is nothing demonstrably spiteful in his demeanour; he can even run through an Australian XI in a Test match, as at Manchester in his "wonderful year", and seem unconcerned.

His bowling is as unassuming as the man himself and on the face of it as modest. That's where the fun comes in; for it is fun indeed to see the leisurely way Laker "sends" his victims one after another, as though by some influence which has not only put the batsmen under a spell, but himself at the same time. Somebody has written that all genius goes to work partly in a somnambulistic way. Jim Laker is certainly more than a talented spinner.

NOTES BY THE EDITOR, 1961
Avoiding a Catastrophe

At one time it seemed that the Australian tour of England might be marred by another altercation. Indeed, Sir Donald Bradman on his return to Australia from the Imperial Cricket Conference, said that, if allowed to get out of hand, the throwing controversy could lead to the greatest catastrophe in cricket history. "It is the most complex question I have known in cricket, because it is not a matter of fact, but of opinion and interpretation", he said. "It is so involved that two men of equal goodwill and sincerity could take opposite views. It is quite impossible to go on playing with different definitions of throwing. This was the great hurdle of the Conference and it unanimously and amicably agreed on a uniform definition. It was a major achievement, but it still has to run the gauntlet of time. We must find some answer which places due regard on the integrity, good faith and judgement of all countries, their umpires, players and administrators. I have good reason to think that certain proposals under examination might lead us into calmer waters. I plead that a calm, patient attitude be exercised while we pursue and resolve the problem."

Throw Defined in 1899

The Imperial Cricket Conference's definition of a throw is not exactly new. On going through various books and brochures which I acquired on the death of my father last August, I came across the following in a booklet compiled for The Australian Visit to England in 1899 written by James Phillips, the Australian umpire who used to spend his summers alternately in England and Australia. Moreover by his vigilance and the action he took he did much to stamp out throwing at the turn of the century:

Phillips wrote:

"I am one of those who hold the opinion that **to bowl a fair ball it is immaterial whether the arm be straight or at an angle so long as there is no perceptible movement in the elbow-joint at the precise moment the ball leaves the hand of the bowler.**

"Just as one bowler, in his desire to make his delivery more difficult, gets as near the return crease as possible, and occasionally inadvertently oversteps the mark, thereby bowling a 'no-ball', so another bowler will, in attempting an increase of pace, use his elbow, especially if he be a bowler whose arm is not quite straight. In each of these instances it does not seem just to suppose that either bowler is wilfully unfair.

"In my capacity as an umpire I have found that there is great difficulty in detecting the elbow movement at the bowling end, whereas when standing at the batting end, near short-leg, this difficulty is overcome, and every movement of the bowler's arm is noticeable."

In those days only the umpire at the bowler's end could call "no-ball". Phillips went on to plead that either umpire should be allowed to call and the Law was changed that year to that effect.

Sixty years later we get the Imperial Cricket Conference version: **A ball shall be deemed to have been thrown if, in the opinion of either umpire, the bowling arm having been bent at the elbow, whether the wrist is backward of the elbow or not, is suddenly straightened immediately prior to the instant of delivery.**

The Truce

While the Imperial Conference was deliberating on the issue of throwing, it was seriously suggested in outside quarters in England and Australia that for the good of cricket it might be expedient to postpone the Australian tour of 1961. The Australian public apparently were convinced the open condemnation of Griffin as a thrower had been done as a preliminary skirmish and that the real target was the Australian fast attack.

Another suggestion advocated a moratorium on throwing for the whole of the 1961 season. Later came the final agreement between MCC and the Australian Board to call a truce for the first seven weeks of the season before the first Test. The cynics said the truce was nothing more than a "Charter for Chuckers". H. L. Hendry, the former Australian Test cricketer, stated that it is well known that some Australian bowlers chucked and that to argue otherwise was sheer hypocrisy. He advised that the Australian Board instruct the Selectors not to pick anyone whose bowling action was suspicious and to see that no bowler was called in England as it was essential that the tour proceeded without incident.

Sensible Compromise

Looking at the problem from all angles, the truce would appear to be a sensible compromise. All who desire to see cricket played in the true spirit should thank those who have striven behind the scenes to restore harmony to the game, particularly Mr Harry Altham, the MCC President, whose firm and courteous chairmanship won high praise from the delegates who attended the Conference.

Already there are indications that all should be well in England this summer. Three of the four Australian bowlers, G. Rorke, J. W. Burke and K. Slater, whose suspicious actions caused so much criticism during the MCC tour of 1958-59, seem to have disappeared from the Test Match scene and I. Meckiff, the central figure of the argument, could not, after smoothing his action, produce the same venom against West Indies. His two wickets in two Tests against West Indies cost 117 runs apiece and his loss of penetrative power caused the selectors to leave him out of the team they selected to visit England this summer.

What is to happen to English bowlers who have been called for throwing during the past two seasons? I recollect Lock, Rhodes, White, Pearson, Aldridge and Bryant. None has been condemned universally by the umpires. There has been the odd case and some of these men, if not all, have taken pains to correct their faults. Are Lock and Rhodes, both Test men, to be barred by England for ever? There was the isolated instance of White, the very promising Hampshire bowler, being called when he had a good chance of going to New Zealand with MCC. His action had never been questioned until umpire P. A. Gibb no-balled him and I am not aware of any opposing batsmen who considered his bowling unfair. Obviously, MCC, having taken such tough action in their war against throwers, cannot invite such men for representative matches – especially overseas – until their names have been cleared. Surely any bowler called by an umpire for throwing should have his action investigated, so that he can be either advised of his fault or have his name cleared. The umpire may be right, but because a bowler has been under suspicion once, that should not rule him out of big cricket for all time, especially if he is satisfying umpires day after day in the County Championship.

CAMBRIDGE UNIVERSITY v AUSTRALIANS

Played at Cambridge, May 17, 18, 19, 1961

Australians won by nine wickets with forty minutes to spare. Some remarkable batting took place on a perfect pitch against ordinary bowling by both sides. The first four Australian batsmen each scored centuries, the team averaging 88 an hour for five hours before Benaud declared. This was the first time any Australian touring side had accomplished such a feat, but India did it against Sussex at Hove in 1946. McDonald had the distinction of reaching three figures before lunch in one hour fifty-seven minutes. As Gaunt strained his left side and Benaud, though he sent down six overs late in the match, could not play a vital part in the attack, much work fell on Misson, Mackay and Quick. Even Harvey had to be pressed into service. Nevertheless, the first seven Cambridge wickets fell for only 113. At this stage Brearley, a 19-year-old Freshman, chosen as wicket-keeper, took control. Showing the utmost confidence and a wide variety of strokes he made 73 (eleven 4s) in two hours. As Alwyn had broken a toe, Brearley went in first when Cambridge followed on 219 behind and he was 69 at the close. Next day Brearley again hit freely until he tried to cut a high toss and was caught by the wicket-keeper for 89 (fifteen 4s). Altogether Brearley made 162 runs and defied the Australians for five hours and twenty minutes – a wonderful achievement for a young man with only three weeks' experience of first-class cricket.

Australians

W. M. Lawry b Jefferson	100	– not out	24
C. C. McDonald b Brodrick	100	– c sub b Jefferson	1
B. C. Booth c Minney b Brodrick	113		
K. Mackay not out	106		
R. N. Harvey not out	28		
P. J. Burge (did not bat)		– not out	40
B 1, l-b 1	2	L-b 2	2

1/177 2/207 3/405   (3 wkts dec.) 449   1/9   (1 wkt) 67

*R. Benaud, †B. N. Jarman, I. W. Quick, F. M. Misson and R. A. Gaunt did not bat.

Cambridge University

N. Alwyn c Lawry b Gaunt	18	– c Harvey b Misson	0
E. J. Craig b Quick	20	– c Lawry b Misson	1
A. R. Lewis c and b Quick	5	– b Mackay	35
M. J. L. Willard b Quick	25	– c Benaud b Quick	14
P. D. Brodrick c Jarman b Mackay	11	– not out	22
N. S. K. Reddy c Burge b Quick	22	– b Quick	43
*D. Kirby b Mackay	2	– lbw b Mackay	27
†J. M. Brearley lbw b Mackay	73	– c Jarman b Quick	89
J. H. Minney c Benaud b Misson	32	– st Jarman b Benaud	38
R. I. Jefferson b Mackay	14	– b Mackay	12
S. Douglas-Pennant not out	1	– lbw b Misson	0
B 2, l-b 4, n-b 1	7	B 2, l-b 2	4

1/33 2/42 3/47 4/68 5/105   230   1/3 2/73 3/103 4/167 5/197   285
6/107 7/113 8/180 9/216   6/213 7/232 8/284 9/285

Cambridge University Bowling

	Overs	Mdns	Runs	Wkts	Overs	Mdns	Runs	Wkts
Jefferson	21	2	91	1	9	—	28	1
Douglas-Pennant	17	2	67	—	7	1	15	—
Willard	4	1	29	—				
Brodrick	38	7	118	2	6	3	7	—
Kirby	36	4	142	—				
Reddy					4.1	—	15	—

Australians Bowling

	Overs	Mdns	Runs	Wkts	Overs	Mdns	Runs	Wkts
Gaunt	5	1	18	1				
Misson	22	7	40	1	25	4	65	3
Quick	41	18	107	4	26	8	60	3
Mackay	18.1	3	43	4	33	8	71	3
Harvey	7	2	8	—	27	10	61	—
Booth	4	1	7	—	1	—	4	—
McDonald					1	—	8	—
Benaud					6	3	12	1

Umpires: D. Davies and A. E. Rhodes.

ENGLAND v AUSTRALIA

First Test Match

Played at Edgbaston, June 8, 9, 10, 12, 13, 1961

Drawn. Australia held the initiative for most of the match, but both sides proved weak in bowling and on the last day England, having faced a first innings deficit of 321 runs, effected a recovery similar to the one they achieved on the same ground in 1957 when West Indies put them out on the opening day for 186.

Personal honours went to Subba Row who saved England by making 59 and 112 on his début against Australia and to Dexter whose 180 on the last day was a superb innings of stylish, forceful strokes. For Australia, Harvey hit his fifth Test hundred against England and his twentieth in Test cricket; O'Neill, if at times uncertain, revealed his class while making 82 and Mackay excelled as an all-rounder. After taking three wickets in four balls he helped Australia to reach 516 by getting 64 in his own characteristic way.

This was the first time since 1909 that England had met Australia at Edgbaston and the Warwickshire officials and their supporters' association deserved the highest praise for the excellent conditions provided for the players, spectators and commentators. Unfortunately, the weather was disappointing. Biting winds and frequent showers of heavy rain spoiled the first and fourth days; cricket proceeded in a light drizzle throughout Saturday and only on Friday and Tuesday did batsmen really enjoy themselves in sunshine. Time lost amounted to seven hours forty minutes during the five days; otherwise a definite result might have been possible.

England, still without P. B. H. May, originally chose twelve men, including B. R. Knight, the young Essex all-rounder. When Dexter became doubtful the selectors called up J. H. Edrich, the Surrey left-hander, but in the end they stuck mainly to the players who had appeared the previous season against South Africa, the only newcomer being Murray, the Middlesex wicket-keeper.

Australia had their worries. Benaud, the captain, was a doubtful starter because of a damaged tendon in his right shoulder and O'Neill, like Dexter, was bothered with an injured knee. Yet, apart from Benaud, the "invalids" acquitted themselves splendidly. Benaud batted well but when he was wanted most as a bowler on the last day, the pain was so severe he sent down only nine overs. If Benaud had been properly fit it might have been a very different story. Australia also had one man new to Test cricket in Lawry.

England having won the toss ten times in their two previous Test series against West Indies (May 3, Cowdrey 2), and South Africa (Cowdrey 5), were successful for the eleventh consecutive time when Benaud called wrongly after Cowdrey spun the coin. It was a green pitch and Richie did not seem to be worried.

The game had been in progress only fifteen minutes when the first interruption occurred in the fifth over with England 10 for no wicket. It proved to be a day of shocks for between the showers eight wickets fell for 180 runs. Subba Row defied Australia for two hours, fifty minutes. At the height of the struggle Mackay, whose main virtues as a bowler were steadiness in length and direction, dismissed Barrington, Smith and Subba Row in the course of four deliveries split between overs.

Between half-past four and half-past six, Mackay bowled without relief sending down 19 overs, eight maidens for three wickets at a cost of 32 runs. Next day, Cowdrey did not have the pitch rolled, and Mackay and Benaud needed only twenty minutes to capture the two remaining wickets. While the rain-affected pitch encouraged the Australian bowlers, much of the England batting was careless.

Australia having dismissed England for 195 in 85 overs proceeded to take the lead in only 59 overs thanks mainly to a fine third wicket stand of 146 between Harvey and O'Neill. Cowdrey varied his bowling but throughout the long innings which lasted eight hours and thirty-five minutes and extended till half-past five on Saturday Statham alone did justice to his reputation. Trueman lacked fire and consequently much of his work was done against the wind. His solitary wicket came in his thirty-second over after he had conceded 106 runs. The two off-spinners, Illingworth and Allen, failed because of imperfect direction and failure to maintain a tightly placed field.

Lawry and McDonald gave Australia a steady start and nearly an hour had passed before Illingworth held McDonald low in the gully. After lunch, taken at 85 for one wicket, Lawry was second to leave, caught by Murray at the second attempt very wide of the off-stump. Then came the big stand by Harvey and O'Neill which established Australia's supremacy.

A short ball from Trueman struck O'Neill in the ribs before he had scored and during his first hour at the crease Australia's young star dealt carefully with some accurate bowling by Statham and Illingworth. Some of the fielding was slow and untidy, but Dexter and Barrington did dazzling work in the covers. When Dexter put in a spell of five overs he gained more lift than either Trueman or Statham. O'Neill really got going with a glorious cover-drive off the back foot and he proceeded to produce a wide range of excellent strokes. For a time he outshone Harvey and raced to his 50 in eighty-nine minutes.

England took the second new ball at 213 without unduly troubling the batsman until at 242 O'Neill chopped the ball into his stumps when he intended to late-cut. O'Neill took less than two hours making 82 out of a stand of 146 and he hit eleven 4s. Harvey's only mistake occurred when at 97 he lay back to punish a short length ball from Statham and was dropped by Trueman at cover. In the end Harvey was leg-before playing back rather casually. He batted splendidly for three and a half hours and hit fifteen 4s. Burge played well for over an hour and at the close, with Simpson and Davidson in command, Australia were 359 for five wickets.

On a miserable cold and wet third day a record crowd for Edgbaston of 25,000 saw the Australian batsmen again subdue England. The pitch remained easy-paced, but stoppages caused two and a half hours' cricket to be lost. Simpson, Mackay and Benaud scored freely and Australia's total of 516 was their highest in England since their 701 at The Oval in 1934. Murray, the England wicket-keeper, was put out of action temporarily with a gash on the side of the left eyebrow when a ball from Illingworth lifted from the rough in the bowlers' run-up.

England faced fifty minutes' batting before the close, but Davidson and Misson had each sent down one over when bad light and more rain ended play for the day with the score five for no wicket. The weather interfered again on Monday, limiting cricket to two hours and twenty minutes. Persistent rain set in at half-past two when England were 106 for one wicket. Only five minutes remained before lunch when Misson sent a loose ball down the leg-side and a poor stroke by Pullar provided a catch for Grout.

Subba Row repeated his fighting display of the first day, but just before the rain came Dexter (nought and four) twice edged Davidson to second slip where Mackay lost sight of the ball against the dark background of the terraced stand. The umpires waited one and three-quarter hours and then decided the ground was so saturated no more cricket would be possible before the last day.

The sun shone on Tuesday, but the Australian bowlers never received the help they had reason to expect from the turf which played easily all day. England cleared their deficit of 321 for the loss of only three men and stood 80 ahead with six wickets left when the struggle was given up.

Dexter gave a glorious exhibition. He excelled with the drive, hitting thirty-one 4s in his 180, made in five and three-quarter hours. Australia did not see the back of him until England's total stood at 400 and only eight more minutes were left for play. Subba Row and Dexter added 42 in the first half hour and the left-hander, making his 112 out of 202, stayed just over four hours, hitting fourteen 4s. His stand with Dexter yielded 109 in under two hours. Cowdrey surrendered the initiative to the opposition before playing on for the second time in the match.

Then Dexter found another valuable partner in Barrington who in a stand of 161 played most unselfishly for three hours and ten minutes, being content to let Dexter push the score along. When all danger had passed Dexter hit with complete abandon and was yards down the pitch when Grout stumped him. So England maintained their record of never having lost a Test at Edgbaston.

The total attendance during the five days including members was 83,000 compared with 91,000 who saw the West Indies in 1957. The receipts, £38,000, were a record for a Test at Edgbaston.   N.P.

England

G. Pullar b Davidson	17	– c Grout b Misson	28
R. Subba Row c Simpson b Mackay	59	– b Misson	112
E. R. Dexter c Davidson b Mackay	10	– st Grout b Simpson	180
*M. C. Cowdrey b Misson	13	– b Mackay	14
K. F. Barrington c Misson b Mackay	21	– not out	48
M. J. K. Smith c Lawry b Mackay	0	– not out	1
R. Illingworth c Grout b Benaud	15		
†J. T. Murray c Davidson b Benaud	16		
D. A. Allen run out	11		
F. S. Trueman c Burge b Benaud	20		
J. B. Statham not out	7		
B 3, 1-b 3	6	L-b 18	18

1/36 2/53 3/88 4/121 5/121   195   1/93 2/202 3/239   (4 wkts) 401
6/122 7/153 8/156 9/181   4/400

Australia

W. M. Lawry c Murray b Illingworth	57	K. D. Mackay c Barrington b Statham	64
C. C. McDonald c Illingworth b Statham	22	*R. Benaud not out	36
R. N. Harvey lbw b Allen	114	†A. W. T. Grout c Dexter b Trueman	5
N. C. O'Neill b Statham	82	B 8, 1-b 4, n-b 1	13
P. J. Burge lbw b Allen	25		
R. B. Simpson c and b Trueman	76	1/47 2/106 3/252 4/299 (9 wkts dec.) 516	
A. K. Davidson c and b Illingworth	22	5/322 6/381 7/469 8/510 9/516	

F. M. Misson did not bat.

Australia Bowling

	Overs	Mdns	Runs	Wkts	Overs	Mdns	Runs	Wkts
Davidson	26	6	70	1	31	10	60	—
Misson	15	6	47	1	28	6	82	2
Mackay	29	10	57	4	41	3	87	1
Benaud	14.3	8	15	3	20	4	67	—
Simpson					34	12	87	1

England Bowling

	Overs	Mdns	Runs	Wkts
Trueman	36.5	1	136	2
Statham	43	6	147	3
Illingworth	44	12	110	2
Allen	24	4	88	2
Dexter	5	1	22	—

Umpires: F. S. Lee and J. S. Buller.

KENT v AUSTRALIANS

Played at Canterbury, June 17, 19, 20, 1961

Drawn. Cowdrey dominated the match, scoring a century in each innings – the first player to do so against the Australians in England. Kent came within seven runs of beating the Australians for the first time since 1899, but even if the county had been successful their victory would not have detracted from the England captain's magnificent batting. The touring team had shown during the first day that the pitch would give no help to the bowlers and hundreds by Lawry and O'Neill enabled Harvey to declare at 428 for six. The Kent batsmen found runs as easy to score on the Monday. Cowdrey reached his century in just under three hours and then hit 49 in the next fifty-two minutes before falling to a catch at fine-leg. He closed the innings 88 behind and after some more attractive batting from the Australians, Harvey left Kent to score 291 in three hours ten minutes to win. The county lost three wickets for 71 and Cowdrey came in with 222 needed in two hours. While he was at the crease anything seemed possible. Harvey manipulated his field well, but Cowdrey always found the gaps with an unending flow of beautifully timed strokes. His century took only ninety-three minutes and in all he spent an hour and forty-nine minutes over 121, which included a 6 and nineteen 4s. Leary helped his captain add 164 at nearly two a minute, but Kent still needed 13 for victory when the last over began. Jones scored five off four balls, but Misson ended their hopes by bouncing the fifth ball over the batsman's head. Davidson, the Australians' premier fast bowler, did not bowl during the last day after a bad attack of asthma.

Australians

R. B. Simpson b Sayer	65	– st Ufton b Jones	41
W. M. Lawry c Richardson b Jones	100	– c Ufton b Brown	17
*R. N. Harvey c Wilson b Halfyard	40	– c Dixon b Jones	66
N. C. O'Neill not out	104	– c Brown b Jones	24
B. C. Booth c Sayer b Halfyard	29	– not out	33
A. K. Davidson b Jones	35	– c and b Jones	3
†A. W. T. Grout b Jones	34	– not out	7
G. D. McKenzie not out	14		
L-b 6, n-b 1	7	L-b 6, w 4, n-b 1	11

1/131 2/177 3/217   (6 wkts dec.) 428   1/41 2/95 3/142   (5 wkts dec.) 202
4/285 5/353 6/405   4/167 5/193

F. M. Misson, I. W. Quick and L. F. Kline did not bat.

Kent

P. E. Richardson c Davidson b Misson	20	– c Harvey b Misson	29
A. H. Phebey c Simpson b Misson	59	– c Quick b Simpson	33
R. C. Wilson lbw b Quick	28	– c Simpson b Quick	5
*M. C. Cowdrey c Booth b Misson	149	– c Booth b McKenzie	121
S. E. Leary c Harvey b Quick	51	– run out	60
P. H. Jones not out	29	– not out	22
A. L. Dixon c Harvey b Quick	1	– c Harvey b Misson	2
†D. G. Ufton not out	0	– not out	0
L-b 3	3	B 5, l-b 6, n-b 1	12

1/29 2/75 3/148 4/300   (6 wkts dec.) 340   1/42 2/69 3/71   (6 wkts) 284
5/317 6/318   4/235 5/264 6/279

D. J. Halfyard, A. Brown and D. M. Sayer did not bat.

Kent Bowling

	Overs	Mdns	Runs	Wkts	Overs	Mdns	Runs	Wkts
Halfyard	20	2	69	2	9	1	32	—
Brown	17	1	82	—	7	—	29	1
Sayer	17	3	66	1	5	—	28	—
Jones	42	14	96	3	15	3	41	4
Dixon	28	4	108	—	12	1	61	—

Australian Bowling

	Overs	Mdns	Runs	Wkts	Overs	Mdns	Runs	Wkts
Davidson	16	4	65	—				
Misson	22	4	61	3	16	1	80	2
McKenzie.........	25	6	64	—	18	—	69	1
Quick	17	4	80	3	11	—	53	1
Kline.............	8	2	33	—	3	—	20	—
Simpson	13	4	34	—	10	—	50	1

Umpires: John Langridge and L. H. Gray.

ENGLAND v AUSTRALIA
Third Test Match
Played at Leeds, July 6, 7, 8, 1961

England won by eight wickets with two days to spare. This will be remembered as "Trueman's Match". Two devastating spells by him caused Australia to collapse. The first occurred immediately after tea on the first day when Australia had reached 183 for two wickets. Then in the course of six overs he dismissed five men for 16 runs. His figures were even more remarkable when he came on at 3.40 p.m. on Saturday with Australia 98 for two. At once he conceded a single to O'Neill before he again claimed five wickets, this time in 24 deliveries, for 0. Trueman finished the match with eleven wickets for 88 runs, easily his best in Test cricket.

The game will also be remembered for the controversy over the state of the pitch. In the previous Test the Lord's ridge loaded the dice in favour of the bowlers. This time the batsmen were at the mercy of the bowlers on a whitish-green piebald surface. It had been chemically treated only a few weeks before the contest and never played true although it did not carry the same physical danger to the batsmen as the one at Lord's. The main trouble was that no one could judge how the ball would behave. Sometimes it came through fast and low; at other times it would check in the broken soft places and stand up so that the batsmen had almost completed their strokes before establishing contact. It favoured all types of bowlers and Trueman came out triumphant.

Consequently, England inflicted the first defeat of the tour on the Australians and made the series all square with two Tests to play by taking revenge for their defeat at Lord's.

Compared with Lord's both sides were under "new management". Peter May took over the England captaincy from Colin Cowdrey – leader and winner of the toss in nine consecutive matches – and Richie Benaud considered himself fit enough to return to the Australian side so that Neil Harvey was relieved of the captaincy after one successful campaign.

Whereas at Lord's it seemed that the loss of Benaud would be a calamity for Australia – and everyone was proved wrong – England entered this match without Statham suffering from a strain. That appeared to be a crippling blow, but not for the first time the selectors sought a player of experience to face Australia and in Leslie Jackson, the 40-year-old Derbyshire opening bowler, they found the man they wanted.

England left out D. B. Close from their final twelve and Benaud was presumed to have gained Australia a big advantage when he won the toss, thus breaking England's sequence of twelve successful tosses. Jackson soon proved he was worthy of his place. He bowled throughout the first hour from the pavilion end during which Lawry and McDonald scored 33 from twenty overs. Jackson also put in another spell of an hour after lunch, but meanwhile England had broken the opening stand ten minutes before the lunch interval when Lawry was leg before to Lock, having offered no proper stroke. He seemed to lose sight of the ball. At the interval Australia had every reason to be satisfied with their score of 77 for one wicket.

McDonald had been at the crease for three hours when Lock bowled for the first time at the Kirkstall Lane end and produced a leg-break which left him stranded down the pitch. Meanwhile, Harvey had become firmly settled. Quick on his feet he drove cleanly and anything short was pulled vigorously. O'Neill helped him to put on 50 in less than an hour so that by tea Australia reached 183 for two off 87 overs; Harvey 66, O'Neill 27.

Then came the transformation. Jackson promptly took the new ball at the pavilion end and Harvey square-cut his first delivery for 4. O'Neill faced Trueman and from the Yorkshireman's first ball he was splendidly caught low in the gully by Cowdrey, the stand having yielded 74 in seventy minutes.

Nine minutes later, Harvey also left, beautifully caught off Trueman by Lock at backward short-leg. Apart from Davidson no other Australian offered much resistance. Jackson snapped up Burge and Mackay and in successive overs Trueman, bowling with his long run and at his fastest through the air, removed Simpson, Benaud (first ball) and Grout before Allen relieved the tiring Jackson and finished the innings by taking McKenzie's off-stump.

Undoubtedly it was this inspired spell by Trueman on the first day which really decided the match. In ninety minutes after tea England captured the remaining eight Australian wickets for the addition of only 54 runs to the interval score.

Friday belonged to the England batsmen. Overnight Pullar and Subba Row had made nine together and they took their stand to 54 in eighty-five minutes before Davidson, coming on for the second time at the pavilion end with a shortened run, dismissed the Northamptonshire captain, leg before. There followed the biggest stand of this low-scoring match. Cowdrey was at his best for the only time in this series and he and Pullar added 86 in five minutes under two hours before Pullar played a slow highly flighted ball from Benaud via his pad on to his stumps. It was the first ball sent down by Benaud in his second spell. Pullar batted three hours and twenty minutes – care being essential on such a difficult pitch.

Whereas most of the Australian batsmen had been at fault in their timing by playing too soon, the England players, until Dexter arrived, effectively used the dead bat. Most of them avoided the drive which was fatal, but May signalled his arrival with a beauty off McKenzie past extra cover. At one period when Davidson and Benaud shared the attack Cowdrey and May did not score for twenty minutes. Still England were 176 for two at tea; Cowdrey 68, May 16.

Australia did not take the new ball until the 94th over and then Davidson promptly induced a return catch from May who had spent eighty-nine minutes over 26 – clear evidence of the troubles which beset the batsmen. Dexter had an uncomfortable time against Davidson and Benaud, but he struggled along for nearly an hour before he lost Cowdrey who had proved safe for four and a quarter hours. His was the innings of a master. Cowdrey hit eleven 4s and was trying to sweep a loose ball when it rose and touched his glove. Thereupon Dexter and Barrington carried through the remaining half hour, Barrington giving England the lead by hitting Benaud to the fine leg boundary.

England resumed on Saturday morning four runs ahead with six wickets standing. They had fought with great tenacity but Dexter, Barrington and Murray rather overdid their caution on this third day. The first half hour yielded only a single against Davidson (leg-cutters) and Benaud. The two ace Australian bowlers sent down eleven successive maiden overs, but for all his patience Dexter was bowled leg-stump, having occupied over two hours for 28.

Trueman tried to take the offensive but after one powerful drive, Burge held him in the same over on the boundary. Australia were on top, but Lock launched a severe attack on Benaud while Murray offered the dead bat to Davidson. In seventeen glorious minutes Lock smote Benaud seven times to the boundary, scoring 30 off the Australian captain in three overs. The ball went in all diretions but only one four over slip was the outcome of a false stroke. It was impossible to set a field to quieten him.

McKenzie returned and trapped Lock leg-before with his second ball; Murray played on when retreating and after Jackson had twice straight-driven McKenzie fiercely to the boundary, McKenzie ran him out from cover in the next over.

Australia had exceeded expectations in taking the last six England wickets in eighty-five minutes for the addition of only 61 to the overnight total. Davidson's analysis during this period was 14-11-9-3 and he finished with five for 63 – similar figures to his performance in the first innings at Lord's where he took five for 42.

England appeared to have missed their chance; their lead was no more than 62 and they had to face the fourth innings. Jackson, at once, brought fresh hope for his fifth ball flattened McDonald's leg stump.

Harvey again played superbly. Like Cowdrey, he showed his class by keeping his head down and never committing himself too soon to a stroke. May varied his bowling, trying to find the right combination, but had the mortification of dropping Harvey in the gully off Trueman when the left-hander was 10.

Allen's first ball of the innings at 49 proved a winner. It whipped across for Lawry to edge into Murray's gloves, but Australia progressed satisfactorily when O'Neill joined Harvey. The arrears were cleared without further loss and then at 98 Trueman returned. He began with his full run and his third ball found Harvey playing too soon. Dexter had to wait for the ball to fall into his hands at cover. That was the beginning of the procession already described.

The secret of Trueman's success in this spell was that after Harvey left, May advised him to bowl off-cutters off his shorter run to a tight leg-trap. By this method Trueman compelled the batsmen to play at every ball. He bowled Benaud for a pair and in thirty-five minutes to tea the score changed to 109 for eight wickets.

Afterwards, Jackson held a return catch from Grout and Cowdrey gained Trueman his sixth wicket by diving to his left and holding Davidson at second slip – another brilliant catch. Trueman's exact analysis from the moment he went on at 98 read 7.5-4-5-6.

Already sixteen wickets had fallen in four and a quarter hours during this amazing day's cricket when just after five o'clock Pullar and Subba Row began the final task of knocking off the 59 runs England needed for victory.

After Australia's downfall, England took no liberties. Davidson upset Subba Row's leg stump at 14, but Pullar and Cowdrey shaped confidently. With forty minutes left before the close England were within 20 of their objective when Cowdrey drove Benaud straight for the only 6 of the match.

Cowdrey left with only 14 needed and May, whose inspiring captaincy had done so much, was at the crease when at 6.17 p.m. Pullar off-drove Benaud for the winning hit.

During the three days nearly 75,000 people were present and the receipts came to £27,723.　　　　　　　　　　　　　　　　　　　　　　　　　　N.P.

Australia

W. M. Lawry lbw b Lock	28	– c Murray b Allen	28
C. C. McDonald st Murray b Lock	54	– b Jackson	1
R. N. Harvey c Lock b Trueman	73	– c Dexter b Trueman	53
N. C. O'Neill c Cowdrey b Trueman	27	– c Cowdrey b Trueman	19
P. J. Burge c Cowdrey b Jackson	5	– lbw b Allen	0
K. D. Mackay lbw b Jackson	6	– c Murray b Trueman	0
R. B. Simpson lbw b Trueman	2	– b Trueman	3
A. K. Davidson not out	22	– c Cowdrey b Trueman	7
*R. Benaud b Trueman	0	– b Trueman	0
†A. W. T. Grout c Murray b Trueman	3	– c and b Jackson	7
G. D. McKenzie b Allen	8	– not out	0
B 7, l-b 2	9	L-b 2	2

1/65 2/113 3/187 4/192 5/196　　　　　　237　　1/4 2/49 3/99 4/102 5/102　　　　120
6/203 7/203 8/204 9/208　　　　　　　　　　　　6/105 7/109 8/109 9/120

England

G. Pullar b Benaud .... 53 — not out 26
R. Subba Row lbw b Davidson .... 35 — b Davidson 6
M. C. Cowdrey c Grout b McKenzie .... 93 — c Grout b Benaud 22
*P. B. H. May c and b Davidson .... 26 — not out 8
E. R. Dexter b Davidson 28
K. F. Barrington c Simpson b Davidson 6
†J. T. Murray b McKenzie 6
F. S. Trueman c Burge b Davidson 4
G. A. R. Lock lbw b McKenzie 30
D. A. Allen not out 5
H. L. Jackson run out 8
     L-b 5 5

1/59 2/145 3/190 4/223 5/239   299   1/14 2/45   (2 wkts) 62
6/248 7/252 8/286 9/291

England Bowling

	Overs	Mdns	Runs	Wkts	Overs	Mdns	Runs	Wkts
Trueman	22	5	58	5	15.5	5	30	6
Jackson	31	11	57	2	13	5	26	2
Allen	28	12	45	1	14	6	30	2
Lock	29	5	68	2	10	1	32	—

Australia Bowling

	Overs	Mdns	Runs	Wkts	Overs	Mdns	Runs	Wkts
Davidson	47	23	63	5	11	6	17	1
McKenzie	27	4	64	3	5	—	15	—
Mackay	22	4	34	—	1	—	8	—
Benaud	39	15	86	1	6	1	22	1
Simpson	14	5	47	—				

Umpires: J. S. Buller and John Langridge.

NORTHAMPTONSHIRE v AUSTRALIANS

Played at Northampton, July 19, 20, 21, 1961

Drawn. Northamptonshire, needing one run off the last ball of the match to beat the Australians, failed to get it in one of the most exciting finishes seen on the ground for many years. When Davidson, the Australian left-arm fast bowler, took the ball for the last over, Northamptonshire wanted four to win with six wickets left. Crump scored a single off the second ball. Lightfoot pushed the third down the wicket and started for a run, but Davidson, running forward, overtook Crump and broke the wicket ahead of him. The new batsman, Scott, hit Davidson for two next ball, which put the scores level. He swung and missed at the next and, when he also failed to connect against the last, tried for a bye. The ball went behind to Simpson, deputising as wicket-keeper for the injured Grout, and with Lightfoot at the other end remaining in his crease until it was too late, Simpson ran forward and broke the wicket before Scott could regain his ground.

The honours of the match went to Northamptonshire. They had been left to get 198 in two hours twenty-five minutes as the result of some inspired fielding and bowling against the Australians who batted in their second innings without McDonald, injured wrist, and Grout, stomach upset. The Australians had made a good start to the game thanks to a hard-hit century by O'Neill in two hours after Larter had Lawry caught at slip off his second ball. In reply Northamptonshire were given a fine start by Norman and Reynolds who shared the best opening partnership of the season for the county to that point. Lightfoot also scored freely and seemed assured of a century but Subba Row declared 24 behind.

Australians

W. M. Lawry c Subba Row b Larter	0	– c Andrew b Larter	100
R. B. Simpson c and b Lightfoot	30	– lbw b Larter	22
N. C. O'Neill b Dilley	142	– c Allen b Lightfoot	2
B. C. Booth run out	16	– c Lightfoot b Crump	16
C. C. McDonald retired hurt	38	– absent hurt	0
A. K. Davidson c Lightfoot b Dilley	3	– c and b Scott	8
*R. Benaud run out	27	– c Norman b Scott	15
†A. W. T. Grout c and b Scott	49	– absent ill	0
G. D. McKenzie c Watts b Scott	6	– c Larter b Allen	4
L. F. Kline b Larter	0	– c Andrew b Scott	0
R. A. Gaunt not out	0	– not out	1
L-b 1, w 1	2	L-b 4, w 1	5

1/0 2/81 3/145 4/221 5/231   313   1/36 2/64 3/73 4/97 5/123   173
6/298 7/312 8/313 9/313   6/152 7/152 8/173

Northamptonshire

M. Norman b Benaud	66	– c sub b Davidson	84
B. L. Reynolds c Kline b Davidson	60	– b Davidson	2
P. J. Watts c Benaud b McKenzie	37	– b Davidson	13
*R. Subba Row b McKenzie	5	– c Booth b Benaud	33
A. Lightfoot not out	80	– not out	57
B. Crump b Gaunt	2	– run out	3
M. E. Scott lbw b Kline	12	– run out	2
†K. V. Andrew not out	12		
B 7, l-b 2, w 2, n-b 4	15	B 2, w 1	3

1/128 1/136 3/143   (6 wkts dec.) 289   1/3 2/33 3/88 4/183   (6 wkts) 197
4/211 5/218 6/263   5/195 6/197

M. H. J. Allen, M. R. Dilley and J. D. F. Larter did not bat.

Northamptonshire Bowling

	Overs	Mdns	Runs	Wkts	Overs	Mdns	Runs	Wkts
Larter	13.5	2	56	2	12.3	3	34	2
Dilley	17	2	64	2	11	3	33	—
Lightfoot	26	6	70	1	9	1	21	1
Allen	13	5	34	—	14	7	23	1
Crump	21	7	42	—	16	10	18	1
Scott	11	1	45	2	17	6	39	3

Australian Bowling

	Overs	Mdns	Runs	Wkts	Overs	Mdns	Runs	Wkts
Davidson	20	8	26	1	14	1	42	3
Gaunt	17	2	48	1	6	—	24	—
Benaud	24	11	33	1	11	—	70	1
Kline	25	7	63	1				
McKenzie	20	7	49	2	13	—	58	—
O'Neill	5	1	24	—				
Simpson	8	—	31	—				

Umpires: D. J. Wood and W. H. Copson.

ENGLAND v AUSTRALIA

First Test Match

Played at Old Trafford, July 27, 28, 29, 31, August 1, 1961

Australia won by 54 runs and made certain of retaining The Ashes. They deserved great credit for fighting back three times when in difficulties, but England, on top for a large part of the match, disappointed, particularly on the last day. Dropped catches proved costly to England and had an important bearing on the result. The game was intensely keen throughout and was the best of the series.

England were without Cowdrey, suffering from a throat infection, and the selectors decided to play three fast bowlers and omit Lock. Close and Flavell were included and Statham returned, Jackson losing his place. Flavell gained his first Test honour at the age of 32. Booth, another newcomer, replaced the injured McDonald for Australia.

Benaud won the toss for Australia, who batted on a "green" pitch which helped the faster bowlers appreciably on the first day. Simpson fell in Statham's first over and, switching ends, the Lancashire fast bowler also dismissed Harvey at 51. O'Neill, never happy, was struck frequently on the thigh and body when facing Flavell and the game had to be held up occasionally while he recovered. Once he vomited when at the bowler's end, but he continued. O'Neill was out when he fell into his wicket in trying a hook. The ball hit him on the wrist and broke a blood vessel in his left forearm, but it was not serious and he continued for the rest of the match. Flavell took his first Test wicket when he bowled Burge shortly after lunch and Australia, despite the sound batting of Lawry, were 106 for four. A little later rain ended play for the day, three and a half hours being lost.

Next morning the remaining six wickets fell in an hour and a half for 66, Statham and Dexter each claiming three. Lawry's splendid 74 took three hours. Statham thoroughly deserved his five wickets for 53, frequently beating the batsmen with his swing and movement off the ground.

England lost Subba Row and Dexter cheaply, but gained the upper hand with a third-wicket stand of 111 between Pullar and May. By the close of the second day England, with seven wickets left, were only three runs behind, but they ran into trouble first thing on Saturday, losing May and Close at the same total with 25 added. May missed a century by five runs, being caught at first slip when Grout dived and scooped the ball up for Simpson. May batted just over three and three-quarter hours and hit fourteen 4s.

Barrington and Murray carefully put England back on top by adding 60 and another good stand came for the seventh wicket, Barrington and Allen adding 86. Then Simpson quickly ended the innings, but England led by 177.

Lawry and Simpson knocked off 63 of the arrears before the end of play, but England should have ended the stand at 38, Subba Row, at second slip, missing Lawry (25) off Trueman. This proved an expensive mistake for Lawry went on to his second century of the series. The opening stand reached 113. Another fielding lapse occurred when Harvey was dropped in the slips by Close when two and he was missed again in the slips, this time by Barrington off Flavell when 26.

Australia cleared their deficit for the loss of two wickets, but a fine catch by Trueman at backward short leg ended Lawry's stay of four and a half hours. Firm drives and, as usual powerful hooks and leg-side deflections, brought Lawry most of his thirteen 4s. Although O'Neill, again received a painful blow on the thigh, he fought hard, but England steadily captured wickets. On the last morning Australia lost three men while adding three runs and the total went from 331 for six to 334 for nine. Allen took all three without cost in 15 balls.

At that point Australia were only 157 on and England looked to have the game comfortably won, but there developed a splendid last-wicket stand between Davidson and

McKenzie. Davidson took 20 in an over off Allen and removed his menace on a pitch taking a fair amount of spin. The other bowlers could make no impression and 98 were added before the innings closed. It was Australia's highest last-wicket Test stand in England. This not only made England's task harder in terms of runs, but it took valuable time away from them. They were set to get 256 in three hours, fifty minutes.

Pullar and Subba Row began with a brisk partnership of 40. Then came a glorious display of controlled hitting by Dexter which put England right up with the clock. Driving with tremendous power and cutting and hooking splendidly, Dexter took only eighty-four minutes to score 76, which included one 6 and fourteen 4s. The second stand with Subba Row produced 110 in that time.

Suddenly the position changed completely. Benaud, bowling round the wicket and pitching into the rough of Trueman's footholds, brought such a collapse that in twenty minutes to tea England virtually lost the game. After getting Dexter caught at the wicket, Benaud bowled May round his legs, had Close, following one drive for 6, caught at backward square leg and bowled the solid Subba Row.

England resumed after tea needing 93 in eight-five minutes with only Barrington of their leading batsmen left. When Murray and Barrington fell for the addition of eight all thoughts of an England victory had gone and it became only a question of whether Australia could finish the match in time. They did so with twenty minutes to spare and thus Australia gained their first Test win at Old Trafford since 1902. Benaud claimed six for 70, his best performance against England. Owing to his shoulder trouble he attempted little spin, being content to let the ball do its work on dropping into the rough.

Good crowds were present on the first four days; the gates being closed on Monday with 34,000 inside. The total attendance was 133,739.   L.S.

Australia

W. M. Lawry lbw b Statham	74	– c Trueman b Allen	102
R. B. Simpson c Murray b Statham	4	– c Murray b Flavell	51
R. N. Harvey c Subba Row b Statham	19	– c Murray b Dexter	35
N. C. O'Neill hit wkt b Trueman	11	– c Murray b Statham	67
P. J. Burge b Flavell	15	– c Murray b Dexter	23
B. C. Booth c Close b Statham	46	– lbw b Dexter	9
K. D. Mackay c Murray b Statham	11	– c Close b Allen	18
A. K. Davidson c Barrington b Dexter	0	– not out	77
*R. Benaud b Dexter	2	– lbw b Allen	1
†A. W. T. Grout c Murray b Dexter	2	– c Statham b Allen	0
G. D. McKenzie not out	1	– b Flavell	32
B 4, l-b 1	5	B 6, l-b 9, w 2	17

1/8 2/51 3/89 4/106 5/150   190   1/113 2/175 3/210 4/274 5/290   432
6/174 7/185 8/185 9/189   6/296 7/332 8/334 9/334

England

G. Pullar b Davidson	63	– c O'Neill b Davidson	26
R. Subba Row c Simpson b Davidson	2	– b Benaud	49
E. R. Dexter c Davidson b McKenzie	16	– c Grout b Benaud	76
*P. B. H. May c Simpson b Davidson	95	– b Benaud	0
D. B. Close lbw b McKenzie	33	– c O'Neill b Benaud	8
K. F. Barrington c O'Neill b Simpson	78	– lbw b Mackay	5
†J. T. Murray c Grout b Mackay	24	– c Simpson b Benaud	4
D. A. Allen c Booth b Simpson	42	– c Simpson b Benaud	10
F. S. Trueman c Harvey b Simpson	3	– c Benaud b Simpson	8
J. B. Statham c Mackay b Simpson	4	– b Davidson	8
J. A. Flavell not out	0	– not out	0
B 2, l-b 4, w 1	7	B 5, w 2	7

1/3 2/43 3/154 4/212 5/212   367   1/40 2/150 3/150 4/158 5/163   201
6/272 7/358 8/362 9/367   6/171 7/171 8/189 9/193

England Bowling

	Overs	Mdns	Runs	Wkts	Overs	Mdns	Runs	Wkts
Trueman.........	14	1	55	1	32	6	92	—
Statham	21	3	53	5	44	9	106	1
Flavell...........	22	8	61	1	29.4	4	65	2
Dexter...........	6.4	2	16	3	20	4	61	3
Allen...........					38	25	58	4
Close...........					8	1	33	—

Australia Bowling

	Overs	Mdns	Runs	Wkts	Overs	Mdns	Runs	Wkts
Davidson	39	11	70	3	14.4	1	50	2
McKenzie........	38	11	106	2	4	1	20	—
Mackay	40	9	81	1	13	7	33	1
Benaud..........	35	15	80	—	32	11	70	6
Simpson	11.4	4	23	4	8	4	21	1

Umpires: John Langridge and W. E. Phillipson.

T. N. PEARCE'S XI v AUSTRALIANS

Played at Scarborough, September 6, 7, 8, 1961

Australians won by three wickets with ten minutes to spare. This match yielded 1,499 runs, the second largest aggregate for a three-day fixture. It was played in a light-hearted manner with no ducks because each batsman was given an easy ball to get off the mark and no lbw decisions because there was no appeal when the ball hit the pads. The batsmen were encouraged to hit as both captains set their normal fields. That the majority of the spectators enjoyed the gay exhibition of free hitting was emphasised by the presence of 15,000 people on each of the three days. In two hours before lunch on the first day Edrich hit 110 out of the total of 202 for four wickets. Dexter and Peter May were also seen at their best and Trueman, with two 6s and twelve 4s reached his highest score in first-class cricket in forty-six minutes. On Thursday as many as twenty-one 6s were hit while five hours' cricket yielded 579 runs. Eleven 6s were shared by the Australians: Jarman six, Burge two and one each by Booth, Mackay and Kline. Then G. J. Smith hit three 6s and Dexter, who completed his hundred in sixty-four minutes, hit seven 6s and eleven 4s. Finally, the Australians finished their first-class programme by knocking off 357 in three and a half hours after a generous declaration by May. Simpson scored his excellent 121 in two hours.

T. N. Pearce's XI

G. J. Smith c Jarman b McKenzie...............	8	– st Jarman b Mackay...............	100
J. H. Edrich st Jarman b Kline..................	110	– c Benaud b Simpson.............	20
E. R. Dexter c Simpson b Mackay..............	57	– b Mackay......................	110
M. J. K. Smith c McKenzie b Quick.............	2	– c Booth b Mackay..............	30
*P. B. H. May b Mackay	100	– c and b Kline	41
†J. M. Parks c and b Benaud	2	– c Booth b Mackay..............	60
T. E. Bailey c O'Neill b Benaud...............	4	– not out	7
D. A. Allen b Mackay........................	3		
F. S. Trueman not out.......................	80		
M. H. J. Allen not out	1		
B 1, l-b 7	8	B 4, l-b 1...............	5

1/13 2/99 3/105 4/202   (8 wkts dec.) 375   1/40 2/118 3/235   (6 wkts dec.) 373
5/209 6/235 7/262 8/359   4/295 5/347 6/373

J. D. F. Larter did not bat.

Australians

*R. Benaud c Parks b Trueman	1	– c Parks b Dexter 41
R. B. Simpson b Trueman	28	– b M. Allen 121
N. C. O'Neill c Dexter b D. Allen	63	– b Dexter 34
P. J. Burge c D. Allen b M. Allen	71	– b Trueman 49
B. C. Booth c D. Allen b Trueman	77	– b Trueman 38
K. D. Mackay c Edrich b D. Allen	33	– c D. Allen b M. Allen 14
†B. N. Jarman not out	80	– c Edrich b D. Allen 32
G. D. McKenzie b Trueman	1	– not out 16
I. W. Quick b Bailey	17	– not out 5
L. F. Kline c M. Allen b Bailey	16	
R. A. Gaunt b M. Allen	2	
B 3	3	L-b 8, w 1 9

1/3 2/68 3/143 4/165 5/238   392   1/100 2/177   (7 wkts) 359
6/312 7/314 8/360 9/378   3/213 4/283 5/292 6/318 7/348

Australian Bowling

	Overs	Mdns	Runs	Wkts	Overs	Mdns	Runs	Wkts
Gaunt	6	—	23	—	8	2	12	—
McKenzie	5	3	7	1	9	2	35	—
Mackay	24	1	136	3	29	4	110	4
Quick	8	—	44	1				
Kline	13	3	60	1	11	1	48	1
Benaud	13	1	59	2				
Simpson	4	—	38	—	15	—	139	1
O'Neill					7	1	24	—

T. N. Pearce's XI Bowling

	Overs	Mdns	Runs	Wkts	Overs	Mdns	Runs	Wkts
Trueman	13	—	59	4	16	1	75	2
Larter	8	—	35	—	7	—	40	—
Bailey	12	2	50	2	4	—	32	—
M. Allen	17	3	102	2	16	2	80	2
D. Allen	15	2	118	2	12.1	—	53	1
Dexter	6	1	25	—	15	1	70	2

Umpires: J. S. Buller and D. Davies.

SOUTH AFRICANS IN ENGLAND

ENGLAND v SOUTH AFRICA
Second Test Match

Played at Lord's, June 21, 23, 24, 25, 1947

England won by ten wickets. From first to last this was a delightful match. South Africa put up a brave fight and were by no means as inferior as the result would suggest. Their bowlers again provided an object lesson in length, direction and bowling to a field, and, in spite of a trying ordeal, their fielding remained at a superlatively high standard of efficiency and keenness. Moreover, Melville, Mitchell and Nourse once more proved their worth as batsmen of contrasting characters. Yet these factors were outweighed by the advantage England gained in winning the toss, the greatness of Edrich and Compton, who established a new world record in Test Matches with a third-wicket stand of 370, the shock bowling and slip catching of Edrich, and the consistently fine work of Wright on his first appearance of the season against the touring side.

Through their excellent performance in the First Test, the South Africans attracted big crowds to Lord's, and the gates were closed half an hour before the start on the first day, when the attendance was officially given as 30,600. The thousands of people turned away missed extremely interesting cricket. Except for an occasional ball which lifted in the early stages, conditions favoured batsmen, and England received a sound start from Hutton and Washbrook, who achieved their first objective of staying together for the ninety minutes before lunch. Yet Hutton never found his true form. He batted an hour and fifty minutes for 18 out of 75 before playing outside an off-break. Hutton made only fourteen scoring strokes – twelve singles, a 4 and a 2 – from the 121 balls delivered to him. By comparison, Washbrook found gaps in the field with grand off and cover-drives, but he profited little from his favourite square-cut, for Melville cleverly blocked the stroke with two fieldsman at third man, one deep and square, the other short and slightly backward. Washbrook looked set for a big score until, with the new ball just in use and the total 96, he flashed at a rising ball outside the off stump. A conjuring catch at second slip, where Tuckett held the ball at the third attempt, ended this attractive display. In view of the obviously long tail, no little responsibility rested on Edrich and Compton, and an enthralling struggle developed between them and a determined attack, splendidly supported in the field, before the two Middlesex batsmen assumed mastery. Then followed a sparkling exhibition of fluent stroke-play, and South Africa conceded 370 runs before the partnership ended. Compton used everything in his complete repertoire, including the brilliant leg-sweep off a slow bowler, and Edrich specially excelled in on-side play. He hooked Rowan for one glorious

6 and frequently brought off a powerful lofted pulled-drive. In three hours ten minutes to the close the stand produced 216 runs, Edrich reaching his first Test century in England and Compton his second in successive Test innings against South Africa. Taking into account the slow start and the twenty-five minutes lost through rain, England's average scoring rate was satisfactory. The day was marred by an unfortunate accident to Melville. Shortly before the close a throw-in from the deep struck him over the right eye. Melville sank to the ground, but, after attention, was able to resume, though during the week-end his eye turned black and became almost completely closed.

Compton and Edrich thrilled another 30,000 crowd on the second day. Both were supremely confident, and by swift and sure running took full value for every stroke. No relief, in fact, came to South Africa until twenty minutes after lunch, when Edrich at last relaxed his concentration and was bowled. He gave a difficult stumping chance when 47, but that was his only blemish. He hit a 6 and twenty-six 4s in 189 out of 391, in five minutes under six hours. The partnership beat by 51 the 319 made by Melville and Nourse in the Nottingham Test and fell only 12 short of the highest for England by any wicket – 382 by Hutton and Leyland against Australia at The Oval in 1938. Compton, dismissed at 515, obtained twenty boundaries in his 208 out of 419 in five hours fifty minutes. His first Test double century brought his total to 436 in three Test innings against South Africa. Barnett led the way in care-free hitting by the following batsmen, so that England after lunch obtained 111 in sixty-five minutes for six wickets before Yardley declared. Tuckett maintained pace and hostility to the end. In his last spell he dismissed five men for 20 in seven overs, and at all times looked a better fast bowler than anyone England possessed.

At first everything went well for South Africa in their reply. Mitchell and Melville made runs surprisingly fast and easily against a constantly changed attack, and not until Compton joined in was the stand broken at 95, when Mitchell fell to a swift stumping by Evans. With only nine added, Viljoen played on to Wright's faster ball, but Nourse stayed with Melville to the end of the day. Third ball on Tuesday morning provided Melville with the opportunity of obtaining the four runs which completed his fourth successive Test century against England, the only comparable feat to which in Test cricket is that of J. H. Fingleton (Australia), who in 1936 made three against South Africa and one against England. Melville and Nourse saw their side safely through the first vital hour, and their third-wicket stand added 118 before Melville played a tired-looking stroke at a long hop and gave backward short-leg an easy catch. Melville offered a return chance to Wright when 40 and an awkward one at the wicket when 93, but he played another great innings for his side. His easy, elegant strokes charmed the purist – and brought him thirteen 4s. Eight runs later Nourse hit too soon when trying to hook. A fifth-wicket stand of 60 by Dawson and Harris gave South Africa fresh hope, but their separation at 290 was the beginning of the end. In one particularly successful spell of 22 balls Wright bowled Rowan, Tuckett and Mann with fizzing leg-breaks. His figures did him less than justice, for Melville alone played him with complete confidence. South Africa followed-on 227 behind, and, with 15 scored, play was held up for twenty minutes while the cricketers were presented to the King and Queen and the Princesses, Elizabeth and Margaret. Upon the resumption Edrich bowled at a tremendous pace. His second ball flattened Melville's middle stump, and two overs later he sent Viljoen's middle stump flying. These dramatic events caused Mitchell to concentrate almost solely on defence, and he and the more aggressive Nourse remained together during the last one hundred minutes, adding 92 runs.

So South Africa, with eight wickets to fall, began the last day needing 107 to make England bat again, a position similar to England's at Nottingham. Obviously such a recovery could not again be expected, but South Africa received a nasty shock when, with the first ball of the day, Edrich shattered Nourse's wicket. From that point the main question became the margin of England's victory, though Mitchell and Dawson added 72 for the fourth partnership and Rowan made some good hits. Mitchell defended dourly for four hours fifteen minutes before an acrobatic slip catch brought his dismissal. Edrich flung himself full length sideways and grasped with one hand a ball going away from him. His catch off Dawson was nearly as good, and Yardley also distinguished himself with two fine efforts. Again Wright was England's best bowler. True, seven of his ten wickets in the match were those of batsmen in the lower part of the order, but his improved length, direction, sharp spin and lift made him always dangerous. Edrich and Compton gave good bowling support; Bedser would have taken several wickets with normal fortune, for at least four chances off him went to ground, but Pope's inclusion was not a success. In England's brief second innings Hutton appeared more like his former self.   R.J.H.

England

L. Hutton b Rowan	18	– not out	13
C. Washbrook c Tuckett b Dawson	65	– not out	13
W. J. Edrich b Mann	189		
D. C. S. Compton c Rowan b Tuckett	208		
C. J. Barnett b Tuckett	33		
N. W. D. Yardley c Rowan b Tuckett	5		
T. G. Evans b Tuckett	16		
G. H. Pope not out	8		
A. V. Bedser b Tuckett	0		
B 2, l-b 10	12		

1/75 2/96 3/466 4/515   (8 wkts dec.) 554   (No wkt) 26
5/526 6/541 7/554 8/554

D. V. P. Wright and W. E. Hollies did not bat.

South Africa

A. Melville c Bedser b Hollies	117	– b Edrich	8
B. Mitchell st Evans b Compton	46	– c Edrich b Wright	80
K. G. Viljoen b Wright	1	– b Edrich	6
A. D. Nourse lbw b Wright	61	– b Edrich	58
O. C Dawson c Barnett b Hollies	36	– c Edrich b Compton	33
T. A. Harris st Evans b Compton	30	– c Yardley b Compton	3
A. M. B. Rowan b Wright	8	– not out	38
L. Tuckett b Wright	5	– b Wright	9
N. B. F. Mann b Wright	4	– b Wright	5
J. D. Lindsay not out	7	– c Yardley b Wright	5
V. I. Smith c Edrich b Pope	11	– c Edrich b Wright	0
L-b 1	1	B 3, l-b 4	7

1/95 2/104 3/222 4/230 5/290   327   1/16 2/28 3/120 4/192 5/192   252
6/300 7/302 8/308 9/309   6/201 7/224 8/236 9/252

South Africa Bowling

	Overs	Mdns	Runs	Wkts	Overs	Mdns	Runs	Wkts
Tuckett	47	7	115	5	3	—	4	—
Dawson	33	11	81	1	6	2	6	—
Mann	53	16	99	1	3.1	1	16	—
Rowan	65	11	174	1				
Smith	17	2	73	—				

England Bowling

	Overs	Mdns	Runs	Wkts	Overs	Mdns	Runs	Wkts
Edrich	9	1	22	—	13	5	31	3
Bedser	26	1	76	—	14	6	20	—
Pope	39.2	5	49	1	17	7	36	—
Wright	29	10	95	5	32.2	6	80	5
Hollies	28	10	52	2	20	7	32	—
Compton	21	11	32	2	31	10	46	2

Umpires: H. G. Baldwin and D. Davies.

SOUTH OF ENGLAND v SOUTH AFRICANS

Played at Hastings, September 3, 4, 5, 1947

South Africans won by nine wickets. The splendid victory achieved by their superior cricket over a powerful side was, from a public viewpoint, rather overshadowed by the achievement of Denis Compton, who created cricket history in beating the 1925 record of J. B. Hobbs of 16 centuries in a season. Compton's seventeenth hundred of the summer, sixth against South Africans and twelfth in 25 innings, naturally aroused unusual excitement. The South Africans made him fight keenly for every run, and when he reached three figures the game was held up for five minutes while crowd and players showed their appreciation. His county colleagues, Robins and Edrich went on to the field to join in congratulations. Compton dashed down the pitch to the first ball after the resumption and was stumped. He made 101 out of 151 in 108 minutes, hit thirteen 4s and offered nothing like a chance. By making 30 in the second innings he brought his season's aggregate against South Africa in first-class matches to 1,187. Compton's superb display followed bright batting by the South Africans. An attractive century by Mitchell ensured them of a big score, and Dawson and Fullerton provided Festival entertainment with a fifth-wicket stand of 110 in fifty-five minutes. On the last over of the first day Dawson reached 100 for the first time on the tour, and next morning added 54 in forty-five minutes. He hit a 6 and twenty-two 4s. So as not to waste time for an interval between innings on the third morning, Robins declared at the overnight score, though South stood 169 behind with a wicket to fall. Melville countered by enforcing the follow-on, and, in spite of a second good innings by Edrich, Rowan and Mann ensured a win for the South Africans. Between them Rowan and Mann claimed all nineteen South wickets.

South Africans

B. Mitchell c Valentine b Goddard	145		
A. Melville c Griffith b Perks	14		
K. G. Viljoen lbw b Compton	50		
A. D. Nourse c Edrich b Bailey	27		
O. C. Dawson not out	166	– not out	0
G. M. Fullerton b Wright	46	– not out	22
N. B. F. Mann b Goddard	20		
A. M. B. Rowan run out	1		
J. B. Plimsoll b Perks	14		
J. D. Lindsay not out	6	– b Goddard	5
B 12, l-b 1, w 2, n-b 6	21	L-b 4	4
	(8 wkts dec.) 510		**(1 wkt) 31**

V. I. Smith did not bat.

South of England

J. D. Robertson c Melville b Rowan	55	– b Mann	12
W. J. Edrich lbw b Rowan	64	– lbw b Rowan	54
D. C. S. Compton st Lindsay b Mann	101	– b Rowan	30
B. H. Valentine b Rowan	9	– st Lindsay b Mann	33
T. E. Bailey b Rowan	18	– b Rowan	6
H. T. Bartlett c Viljoen b Mann	46	– c Lindsay b Mann	19
R. W. V. Robins c Nourse b Rowan	33	– c Lindsay b Mann	14
S. C. Griffith c Lindsay b Mann	1	– b Rowan	11
R. T. D. Perks c and b Mann	0	– c Dawson b Rowan	4
D. V. P. Wright not out	1	– lbw b Mann	1
T. W. Goddard not out	1	– not out	0
B 9, l-b 2, n-b 1	12	B 6, l-b 8, n-b 1	15
	(9 wkts dec.) 341		**199**

South of England Bowling

	Overs	Mdns	Runs	Wkts	Overs	Mdns	Runs	Wkts
Perks............	20	8	51	2				
Bailey...........	20	1	84	1				
Compton	22	—	97	1				
Goddard.........	35	7	136	2	3	—	13	1
Wright	22	2	90	1	2.5	—	14	—
Robins	6	—	31	—				

South Africans Bowling

	Overs	Mdns	Runs	Wkts	Overs	Mdns	Runs	Wkts
Plimsoll..........	20	4	57	—	6	—	15	—
Dawson	10	—	40	—	9	2	15	—
Mann	35	6	97	4	28	11	71	5
Rowan	28	4	108	5	24.2	3	83	5
Smith	3	—	27	—				

Umpires: F. Chester and A. Skelding.

DERBYSHIRE v SOUTH AFRICANS

Played at Derby, July 16, 17, 18, 1947

South Africans won by three wickets. Rain seriously curtailed the first two days, and when the last day's play began South Africans, with one first innings wicket in hand, were 52 behind. Yet, in heavy atmosphere and on a damp pitch, the game was finished in three hours and a half on Friday. One ball from Copson ended the South Africans' innings. Then Derbyshire collapsed in extraordinary fashion. Dawson and Plimsoll dismissed the first three batsmen for 12, and leg-break bowler Smith accomplished a feat unique in English first-class cricket by taking six wickets for one run. Smith finished the innings with a hat-trick – Revill, Marsh and Copson the victims – and the last seven wickets fell while the score rose from 30 to 32. Turning the ball sharply at good length, Smith returned match figures of thirteen wickets for 66. Only after a stern struggle did the South Africans gain victory. Five men were dismissed for 39, but Fullerton hit out boldly.

Derbyshire

C. S. Elliott c Fullerton b Smith	56	– st Fullerton b Smith	18
A. F. Townsend c Mitchell b Dawson	3	– b Dawson	0
J. D. Eggar c Mitchell b Smith	19	– c Melville b Plimsoll	0
G. H. Pope b Dawson	5	– c Melville b Plimsoll	4
A. E. Alderman st Fullerton b Smith	13	– lbw b Plimsoll	6
A. Revill c Melville b Smith	60	– c Fullerton b Smith	1
R. M. Watson not out	25	– lbw b Smith	1
A. E. Rhodes c Mitchell b Smith	0	– st Fullerton b Smith	0
L. B. Blaxland c Plimsoll b Smith	18	– not out	0
E. Marsh b Rowan	10	– b Smith	0
W. H. Copson c and b Smith	0	– c Melville b Smith	0
B 10, l-b 3, w 1, n-b 1	15	B 1, l-b 1	2
	224		**32**

South Africans

B. Mitchell c Blaxland b Pope	23	– b Copson	16
A. Melville c Alderman b Pope	7	– c Marsh b Pope	2
A. M. B. Rowan c Marsh b Pope	5	– c Copson b Pope	3
A. D. Nourse b Copson	2	– b Pope	13
O. C. Dawson c Pope b Rhodes	30	– b Rhodes	14
D. W. Begbie c Watson b Marsh	22	– c Rhodes b Pope	11
G. M. Fullerton b Copson	28	– not out	23
N. B. F. Mann c and b Copson	45	– b Pope	0
J. B. Plimsoll c Revill b Copson	6	– not out	1
L. Tuckett c Elliott b Pope	3		
V. I. Smith not out	0		
N-b 1	1	N-b 2	2
	172		**(7 wkts) 85**

South Africans Bowling

	Overs	Mdns	Runs	Wkts	Overs	Mdns	Runs	Wkts
Plimsoll	16	1	33	—	13	3	13	3
Dawson	22	8	33	2	9	3	16	1
Rowan	25	11	48	1				
Tuckett	9	1	19	—				
Smith	27.2	8	65	7	4.5	3	1	6
Mann	9	5	11	—				

Derbyshire Bowling

	Overs	Mdns	Runs	Wkts	Overs	Mdns	Runs	Wkts
Copson	17.1	6	38	3	14	6	38	1
Pope	24	6	60	5	16.2	5	36	5
Rhodes	14	1	41	1	3	—	9	1
Marsh	7	1	32	1				

Umpires: F. Chester and B. Flint.

ENGLAND v SOUTH AFRICA

First Test Match

Played at Nottingham, June 7, 8, 9, 11,12, 1951

South Africa won by 71 runs. A most remarkable match ended with South Africa gaining their first Test victory for sixteen years and their second in England. Between those two successes they had failed to lower the colours of England and Australia in a total of 28 Tests. Undoubtedly the hero was Nourse, the South African captain. He carried his side with a lion-hearted not out 208. Mere figures cannot convey the magnitude of Nourse's performance. His innings occupied nine and a quarter hours, and during the whole of that time he batted under a great handicap. The left thumb which he had broken at Bristol three weeks previously gave him severe pain, particularly when he tried to impart any power into his strokes, and the longer he stayed the more it swelled. Nourse declined to have an injection to relieve the pain because he feared that it might numb his hand and affect his grip.

When his long innings was over, he followed medical advice and took no further part in the match, so that South Africa were reduced to ten men in the second innings. The captaincy devolved on Eric Rowan, who enjoyed the honour of leading the team to victory in the field. Nourse's 208 was the highest individual score for South Africa in the 75 matches between the two countries – seven weeks later Eric Rowan beat it with 236 in the Leeds Test.

Other splendid features of this match were centuries by Compton and Simpson – the first by a Nottinghamshire player at Trent Bridge – some grand bowling by Mann, Athol Rowan and Bedser, and magnificent close-in fielding by both sides throughout the five days.

After Nourse won the toss, South Africa occupied the crease for almost the whole of the first two days. They adopted the modern Test technique of refusing to take the slightest risk. The pitch was of the placid kind which gives not the slightest encouragement to the bowler and only three wickets fell during the first day while 239 runs were scored at an average of 40 an hour. Their batting had been so uncertain in the preliminary matches that Nourse's negative policy was reasonable. With Eric Rowan going early, South Africa were compelled to rely almost entirely on Nourse, but before he arrived two youngsters, Waite and McGlew, withstood the England bowling for one and three-quarter hours, adding 76.

Another long period elapsed before Tattersall, at square leg, picked up a hit by Nourse and ran out Waite, who batted four and three-quarter hours. Then Cheetham, by staying two hours, gave his captain valuable support. He fell on the second morning when, for the first time, Bedser acquired some lift and Cheetham gave an easy catch to forward short leg.

England waited three more hours for their next success, and in that time Nourse and Fullerton added 121 in South Africa's best stand. Nourse never relaxed his concentration, but after Bedser and Bailey took the fourth new ball at 400, the other batsmen were less cautious and following tea, taken at 410 for five wickets, the resistance was broken. Nourse was ninth to leave when Brown threw down the wicket at the bowler's end. Crisp square cuts and perfect drives past cover brought Nourse most of his twenty-five 4s.

Almost as soon as he reached the pavilion Nourse declared, leaving England to bat for five minutes on Friday evening, and in that brief spell South Africa dealt England a heavy blow by getting Ikin smartly caught at short fine-leg, where McCarthy dived for the ball. So Chubb took a wicket with his second ball in Test cricket.

The cricket on Saturday went in three phases. Before lunch came a dazzling display by Simpson, who, with Hutton, put on 124, including seventeen 4s. There followed some grand off-break bowling by Athol Rowan, who began with a spell of ninety minutes before lunch and reached his peak afterwards when the scoring dropped to 37 in an hour. Simpson experienced a perilous time against Athol Rowan and also Chubb, but he stayed four and a half hours, hitting twenty-one 4s.

The third phase on Saturday belonged mainly to South Africa and succeeded a break of eighty minutes at tea-time for rain. To the surprise of many people Eric Rowan did not call immediately on his pace bowlers, McCarthy and Chubb. Half an hour elapsed, but as soon as McCarthy appeared he ended Simpson's innings. Half an hour remained for play that day, and Watson, in his first Test match, showed he possessed the right temperament by remaining with Compton, who when 45 and the total 250 was missed at the wicket off Chubb.

Throughout the match Brown adopted an enterprising policy, and particularly was this noticeable on Monday after the ground had been drenched by a thunderstorm the previous day. The heavy roller glistened with moisture, but Compton and Watson overcame the conditions and batted through the two hours before lunch, adding 93. Subsequently England risked losing wickets in going for runs. The big stand, which produced 141 in three hours, finished soon after Compton completed his hundred, Watson being beaten by sheer pace. Compton earned the distinction of hitting a century on each of his four Test appearances at Trent Bridge: 1938, 102 v Australia; 1947, 163 v South Africa; 1948, 184 v Australia; 1951, 112 v South Africa.

McCarthy paid little heed to length or direction, and, in trying to sweep a bumper off his eyebrows, Compton was caught by the wicket-keeper on the leg-side. Compton occupied five hours twenty minutes over his 112 and hit eleven 4s.

As the pitch was difficult, Brown declared with England 64 behind. Eight men were stationed close to the batsman when Bedser began the assault. It was at this stage that South Africa needed Nourse's steadying influence, for in two hours, England transformed the match by dismissing five men for 99.

So the last day began with South Africa, on the face of it, possessing not the slightest chance of victory, and when, thanks to Bedser, those four remaining Springbok wickets went down in forty minutes for only 26, it looked a simple matter for England. Bedser bowled superbly in taking six wickets for 37.

England, wanting 186 in the comfortable time of five hours ten minutes, were soon made to realise that the South Africans had not given up hope of success. From the start Eric Rowan set an attacking field and Hutton and Ikin faced a salvo of bumpers from McCarthy. One of these may have accounted for Hutton's early dismissal, for soon after the Yorkshireman received a blow above the heart he gave an easy return to Athol Rowan.

England really lost the match in those sixty-five minutes before lunch, for during that period the only notable strokes were two off-drives for three by Ikin. No more than 25 runs were scored and the initiative had been snatched by South Africa. After lunch the rain-affected pitch was fully exploited by Mann and Athol Rowan, both of whom turned the ball appreciably. Compton could not rise to the occasion as he would have done in his youth and, except when Wardle indulged in some desperate hitting, the England innings was little better than a procession. The match ended at eight minutes past four when McLean, youngest member of the South African team and acting substitute, held a skier in the deep from Wardle. He threw the ball as high again in the air while his jubilant colleagues danced and leapt for joy. On the balcony Nourse paid a special tribute to Eric Rowan for his part in the victory.

The popularity of the five-day Test was reflected in the attendance. Over 100,000 people were present, of whom 92,921 paid. Receipts were £11,361.   N.P.

South Africa

E. A. B. Rowan c Evans b Brown	17	– c Ikin b Bedser ... 11
J. H. B. Waite run out	76	– c Ikin b Tattersall ... 5
D. J. McGlew b Brown	40	– st Evans b Bedser ... 5
A. D. Nourse run out	208	– absent hurt ... 0
J. E. Cheetham c Ikin b Bedser	31	– b Bedser ... 28
G. M. Fullerton c Compton b Tattersall	54	– c Brown b Tattersall ... 13
C. B. van Ryneveld lbw b Bedser	32	– c Hutton b Bedser ... 22
A. M. B. Rowan b Bedser	2	– c Evans b Bedser ... 5
N. B. F. Mann c Tattersall b Wardle	1	– b Tattersall ... 2
G. W. A. Chubb not out	0	– not out ... 11
C. N. McCarthy not out	1	– b Bedser ... 5
B 3, l-b 17, n-b 1	21	B 4, l-b 9, n-b 1 ... 14

1/31 2/107 3/189   (9 wkts dec.) 483   1/12 2/20 3/24 4/52 5/87   121
4/273 5/394 6/465 7/467   6/98 7/103 8/106 9/121
8/476 9/482

England

L. Hutton c Waite b A. Rowan	63	– c and b A. Rowan ... 11
J. T. Ikin c McCarthy b Chubb	1	– b Mann ... 33
R. T. Simpson c Waite b McCarthy	137	– c and b A. Rowan ... 7
D. C. S. Compton c Waite b McCarthy	112	– lbw b A. Rowan ... 5
W. Watson lbw b McCarthy	57	– lbw b Mann ... 5
F. R. Brown c Fullerton b Chubb	29	– c McCarthy b A. Rowan ... 7
T. G. Evans c sub b Chubb	5	– c van Ryneveld b Mann ... 0
J. H. Wardle c Fullerton b Chubb	5	– c sub b A. Rowan ... 30
T. E. Bailey c Fullerton b McCarthy	3	– c Waite b Mann ... 11
A. V. Bedser not out	0	– b McCarthy ... 0
R. Tattersall (did not bat)	–	not out ... 0
B 4, l-b 3	7	L-b 5 ... 5

1/4 2/148 3/234 4/375   (9 wkts dec.) 419   1/23 2/41 3/57 4/63 5/67   114
5/382 6/395 7/410 8/419 9/419   6/80 7/83 8/84 9/110

England Bowling

	Overs	Mdns	Runs	Wkts	Overs	Mdns	Runs	Wkts
Bedser............	63	18	122	3	22.4	8	37	6
Bailey............	45	13	102	—	2	—	10	—
Brown............	34	11	74	2				
Tattersall	47	20	80	1	23	6	56	3
Wardle...........	49	21	77	1	4	3	4	—
Compton	2	—	7	—				

South Africa Bowling

	Overs	Mdns	Runs	Wkts	Overs	Mdns	Runs	Wkts
McCarthy.........	48	10	104	4	8	1	8	1
Chubb............	46.2	12	146	4	6	2	9	—
A. Rowan.........	46	10	101	1	27.2	4	68	5
Mann	20	5	51	—	24	16	24	4
van Ryneveld	3	—	10	—				

Umpires: F. Chester and H. G. Baldwin.

MCC v SOUTH AFRICANS

Played at Lord's, May 21, 23, 24, 1960

Drawn. An even match ended with the South Africans having to fight hard to save the game. The match was notable for the no-balling of Griffin for throwing on Saturday. Lee called him first in his fifth over and when Griffin returned for a second spell Langridge called him twice from square-leg. Once Griffin was called simultaneously for throwing and dragging. No further action was taken against him during the match, but afterwards a special meeting was held to discuss the point, the umpires saying that his basic action was all right. According to the South African Cricket Annual, Griffin had been called twice before, in February and March 1959 while playing for Natal against Transvaal and also against a Combined Border and Eastern Province XI. Put in to bat on a soft pitch, MCC struggled following an opening stand of 60, but a good innings by Walker rescued them. Waite batted soundly for the South Africans, who were troubled by spin, and bowlers continued to hold the upper hand when MCC went in again 59 ahead. When Cowdrey declared, the South Africans needed 197 to win in two hours fifty minutes. They were always behind the clock. Cowdrey claimed the additional half-hour when the sixth wicket fell, but the South Africans held out.

MCC

*M. C. Cowdrey c Tayfield b Goddard............	37	– c Goddard b Tayfield	38
J. H. Edrich b Griffin.........................	36	– c Goddard b Pothecary	13
E. R. Dexter b Griffin	9	– c Waite b Pothecary.............	2
M. J. K. Smith c Waite b Pothecary	6	– b Fellows-Smith	6
D. E. V. Padgett c Griffin b Goddard.............	20	– c O'Linn b Goddard	6
R. W. Barber lbw b Pothecary	7	– c Waite b Goddard..............	8
†J. M. Parks c Wesley b Griffin	12	– c and b Tayfield	17
P. M. Walker b Fellows-Smith	57	– st Waite b Tayfield	13
R. Illingworth b Fellows-Smith.................	13	– not out	6
P. J. Loader b Goddard........................	3	– c Carlstein b Tayfield	13
K. Higgs not out	1	– not out	7
L-b 5, n-b 2	7	B 5,1-b 2, n-b 1.........	8

1/60 2/72 3/87 4/95 5/120   208   1/24 2/42 3/59 4/77   (9 wkts dec.) 137
6/126 7/147 8/191 9/204   5/77 6/95 7/105 8/105 9/123

South Africans

*D. J. McGlew b Loader	9	– c and b Illingworth	5
T. L. Goddard c and b Illingworth	18	– c Walker b Barber	56
†J. H. B. Waite b Walker	50		
R. A. McLean b Walker	2	– c Higgs b Barber	22
S. O'Linn b Barber	19	– not out	6
C. Wesley b Illingworth	1	– b Illingworth	0
P. R. Carlstein c Parks b Illingworth	1	– c Illingworth b Barber	22
J. P. Fellows-Smith st Parks b Walker	9	– b Higgs	6
H. J. Tayfield c Higgs b Loader	13	– not out	0
G. Griffin b Higgs	19	– b Higgs	3
J. E. Pothecary not out	0		
B 6, 1-b 2	8	B 5, 1-b 1	6

1/18 2/33 3/38 4/75 5/82   149   1/24 2/42 3/77 4/82   (7 wkts) 126
6/84 7/114 8/127 9/149   5/108 6/115 7/125

South Africans Bowling

	Overs	Mdns	Runs	Wkts	Overs	Mdns	Runs	Wkts
Griffin	24	10	47	3	8	1	22	—
Pothecary	16	4	50	2	9	3	29	2
Goddard	29.3	10	64	3	11	5	17	2
Tayfield	14	6	33	—	18	9	33	4
Fellows-Smith	8	3	7	2	8	1	28	1

MCC Bowling

	Overs	Mdns	Runs	Wkts	Overs	Mdns	Runs	Wkts
Loader	11	—	34	2	7	2	18	—
Higgs	4.2	3	1	1	15	4	31	2
Walker	27	16	36	3	5	3	5	—
Illingworth	28	11	46	3	16	5	33	2
Barber	19	11	24	1	15	5	33	3

Umpires: F. S. Lee and John Langridge.

NOTTINGHAMSHIRE v SOUTH AFRICANS

Played at Nottingham, May 28, 30, 31, 1960

Drawn. Frequent no-balling of Griffin, the South African opening bowler, eight times in all for throwing and seven times for dragging, was a feature of this match. Griffin was penalised by both umpires, but mainly by Bartley. Eleven of the calls against him, five of them for throwing, came on the first day, and during the match the South African manager announced that the bowler would be sent to Gover, former Surrey and England fast bowler, for special coaching. In Nottinghamshire's second innings, on the third day, Griffin was used only in short spells, but was no-balled on four further occasions, thrice for throwing. Splendid weather and an excellent batting pitch favoured the match and Nottinghamshire made good use of the conditions on the opening day. Apart from Griffin, the attack lacked penetration, and only when the county batsmen tried to force the pace late in the day did wickets fall rapidly. Then the persistent Goddard achieved a string of successes. The South Africans found the batting conditions much to their liking. McGlew and Goddard began with a partnership of 116, broken when McGlew went off for attention to a slight back strain, and resumed at the fall of the second wicket. Carlstein displayed a wide range of powerful strokes, and with useful contributions from Pithey and O'Linn the touring team established a lead of 153, despite consistently good pace-bowling from Cotton, who took three of the last four wickets in four balls. In their second innings Nottinghamshire batted soundly and experienced no difficulty in forcing a draw.

Nottinghamshire

N. Hill c Tayfield b Griffin	51	– c Goddard b Tayfield	48
H. M. Winfield c Waite b Griffin	58	– b Goddard	0
M. Hill b McKinnon	25	– c Fellows-Smith b Tayfield	45
*R. T. Simpson c Pithey b Goddard	63	– c Waite b Goddard	27
C. J. Poole b Griffin	22		
J. D. Springall c McGlew b Goddard	34	– not out	42
C. Forbes c O'Linn b Goddard	7		
†G. Millman b Goddard	1	– not out	27
J. Cotton c Waite b Goddard	6		
I. Davison c O'Linn b Tayfield	2		
B. D. Wells not out	0		
B 1, l-b 2, n-b 8	11	B 1, n-b 3	4

1/99 2/114 3/152 4/204 5/252   280   1/2 2/92 3/115   (4 wkts) 193
6/269 7/272 8/273 9/278   4/125

South Africans

*D. J. McGlew c Winfield b Davison	68	H. J. Tayfield b Cotton	0
T. L. Goddard lbw b Cotton	68	G. Griffin c Poole b Forbes	0
A. J. Pithey hit wkt b Cotton	59	A. H. McKinnon not out	2
†J. H. B. Waite c and b Forbes	34		
R. A. McLean c M. Hill b Wells	24	W 2, n-b 2	4
P. R. Carlstein lbw b Wells	80		
S. O'Linn c Millman b Cotton	72	1/125 2/198 3/233 4/235	433
J. P. Fellows-Smith c Poole b Cotton	22	5/267 6/373 7/430 8/431 9/431	

South Africans Bowling

	Overs	Mdns	Runs	Wkts	Overs	Mdns	Runs	Wkts
Griffin	22	5	60	3	7	4	11	—
Goddard	33	12	71	5	20	9	37	2
Fellows-Smith	9	1	37	—				
Tayfield	29.5	8	62	1	32	12	59	2
McKinnon	14	1	39	1	14	3	54	—
McGlew					7	1	28	—

Nottinghamshire Bowling

	Overs	Mdns	Runs	Wkts
Cotton	31	7	69	5
Davison	25	—	96	1
Forbes	33.3	8	95	2
Wells	54	22	132	2
Springall	8	1	37	—

Umpires: T. J. Bartley and W. H. Copson.

HAMPSHIRE v SOUTH AFRICANS

Played at Southampton, June 18, 20, 21, 1960

South Africans won by nine wickets, McLean finishing the match by hooking the first two balls of the last over of extra time to the boundary. After losing two wickets for 19, the South Africans thrashed the Hampshire attack on a fast, true pitch. Wesley (fourteen 4s) and McGlew pulled the side round with a third-wicket partnership of 112. The other batsmen played aggressively, particularly Carlstein and Griffin. Carlstein, who scored most of his runs in front of the wicket, hit 151 (one 6, twenty-nine 4s). Griffin gave the South African tail considerable sting and his principal hits were three 6s and three 4s. White never gave up and despite poor fielding took five wickets for 134. Hampshire put up a miserable performance and apart from Baldry offered little resistance. Extremely strong on the off, he hit two 6s and ten 4s in his entertaining innings. They did much better when they followed-on. Gray and Marshall gave them a good start and Horton and Barnard played attractively to add 139 in two hours. Horton, strong all round the wicket, batted two and a half hours and when he was sixth out, Hampshire needed two runs to avoid an innings defeat. Once again, the tail folded up against Tayfield, who had a match analysis of eleven for 144. Griffin, the South African fast bowler, was no-balled for throwing six times in the match, twice in the first innings and four times in the second. It was the first occasion that he had been called for throwing since attending a London cricket school in an attempt to correct his action.

South Africans

*D. J. McGlew c Harrison b Shackleton	62		
A. J. Pithey b White	5		
†C. A. R. Duckworth run out	0	– st Harrison b Shackleton	11
C. Wesley run out	84		
R. A. McLean b White	31	– not out	21
P. R. Carlstein lbw b White	151	– not out	3
J. P. Fellows-Smith c Ingelby-Mackenzie b Heath	57		
H. J. Tayfield b White	37		
G. Griffin not out	65		
J. E. Pothecary lbw b Heath	1		
A. H. McKinnon c Harrison b White	5		
B 2, l-b 4, w 3	9	L-b 2	2

1/18 2/19 3/131 4/164 5/190   507   1/25   (1 wkt)   37
6/336 7/412 8/481 9/484

Hampshire

J. R. Gray c Carlstein b Griffin	0	– c and b Tayfield	51
R. E. Marshall c Griffin b Pothecary	14	– c sub b Fellows-Smith	43
H. Horton c Duckworth b Fellows-Smith	8	– c and b McGlew	117
D. O. Baldry c Carlstein b Tayfield	70	– b Tayfield	9
H. M. Barnard b Griffin	29	– c McGlew b Tayfield	77
*A. C. D. Ingelby-Mackenzie b Tayfield	0	– b Tayfield	1
P. J. Sainsbury b Tayfield	21	– c Duckworth b Griffin	20
†L. Harrison c sub b Tayfield	22	– b Tayfield	1
D. Shackleton c Duckworth b Pothecary	11	– c Pothecary b Tayfield	1
D. W. White lbw b Tayfield	1	– b Griffin	10
M. Heath not out	10	– not out	3
B 3, l-b 4, w 1, n-b 1	9	B 5, l-b 1, w 2, n-b 5	13

1/2 2/16 3/55 4/110 5/110   195   1/89 2/127 3/146 4/285 5/289   346
6/134 7/150 8/171 9/172   6/310 7/326 8/329 9/337

Hampshire Bowling

	Overs	Mdns	Runs	Wkts	Overs	Mdns	Runs	Wkts
Shackleton	36	7	142	1	5	2	12	1
White	32	5	134	5	4.2	—	23	—
Heath	28	3	104	2				
Gray	8	3	18	—				
Sainsbury	21	7	60	—				
Baldry	4	—	40	—				

South Africans Bowling

	Overs	Mdns	Runs	Wkts	Overs	Mdns	Runs	Wkts
Griffin.	14	6	25	2	21.3	8	63	2
Pothecary	23	4	58	2	13	4	37	—
Fellows-Smith.	11	4	29	1	14	3	54	1
Tayfield.	23.2	8	66	5	48	21	78	6
McGlew	2	—	8	—	13	2	40	1
Carlstein					14	—	61	—

Umpires: J. H. Parks and Harry Elliott.

ENGLAND v SOUTH AFRICA
Second Test Match

Played at Lord's, June 23, 24, 25, 27, 1960

England won by an innings and 73 runs with over a day to spare and placed themselves two up in the series. The game was made memorable by the several incidents which occurred while Griffin was bowling. He became the first South African to achieve a hat-trick in a Test match and the first man for any country to accomplish that feat in a Test at Lord's. He also gained a less enviable record, for he became the first player to be no-balled for throwing in a Test Match in England. There had been two previous instances abroad, E. Jones of Australia against England at Melbourne in 1897-98 and G. A. R. Lock of England against West Indies at Kingston, Jamaica, in 1953-54.

Griffin was called eleven times during the course of the England innings, all by F. Lee at square-leg. Then, when the match ended at 2.25 p.m. on the fourth day, an exhibition game took place and Griffin's only over consisted of eleven balls. S. Buller no-balled him for throwing four times out of five. On the advice of his captain, McGlew, who had spoken to Buller, Griffin changed to underarm bowling, but was promptly no-balled again by Lee for forgetting to notify the batsman of his change of action. Griffin's last three balls were bowled underarm.

These events tended to overshadow the match itself, which provided England with an easy victory against a disappointing South African side. England made two changes, Barrington coming in for the injured Pullar and a third fast bowler, Moss, replacing Barber. The South Africans preferred Wesley to Pithey.

To avoid the possibility of the supposed ridge near a length at one end interfering with the game, the pitch was moved a yard nearer the pavilion. Rain caused the start to be delayed by three-quarters of an hour. England won the toss for the seventh successive time and batted under conditions which gave slight help to the fast bowlers. Cowdrey soon fell to a catch at second slip, but despite a number of interruptions through bad light and rain, Subba Row and Dexter put England on top. Dexter produced many fine drives and scored 56 out of the second wicket stand of 96 in just over two hours. All told, three and a quarter hours were lost on the first day which ended with England 114 for two.

Next morning Subba Row batted well on a far from easy pitch. Barrington helped him add 62 and Subba Row and Smith took the total to 220 before Subba Row was out. He hit only five 4s during a stay of five hours, but he fought extremely well and placed his strokes cleverly. When their fifth wicket fell at 227 England were not too well placed, but a partnership of 120 in two hours, twenty minutes between Smith and Walker changed the situation.

Smith, after batting just over four hours, missed his century by one run and became the first victim in Griffin's hat-trick to the last ball of an over. Against Goddard, Walker pulled two 6s over long leg, but was bowled by the first ball of Griffin's next over. Then Trueman tried a mighty hit and over went his middle stump.

England were 362 for eight at the close and Cowdrey declared first thing on Saturday when a crowd of just over 27,000 saw South Africa collapse before magnificent fast bowling by Statham. The innings lasted three hours, five minutes and Statham bowled almost throughout. He kept a perfect length and moved the ball either way off the ground to the discomfiture of all the batsmen. He was well supported by Moss. Cowdrey held two great catches at second slip and Parks took three comfortable ones behind the wicket.

Following on 210 behind, South Africa lost McGlew, again to Statham, before a thunderstorm ended play for the day an hour and a half early with the score 34 for one. After week-end rest Statham came back refreshed and South Africa were 72 for six before Wesley, in his first Test, and Fellows-Smith added 54. The end came a quarter of an hour after lunch with Statham hitting the middle stump twice. When bowling Griffin he broke the top of the middle stump. Taking eleven wickets for 97 Statham achieved the best Test match figures of his career and became the first English fast bowler to take eleven wickets in one game since the war.

The crowds, even with the weather doubtful at times, were good, a total of just over 80,000 being present on the four days. The Queen and the Duke of Edinburgh arrived during the exhibition match and just after Griffin had been no-balled by Buller. They saw Trueman hit a mighty six on the top of the pavilion.   L.S.

England

*M. C. Cowdrey c McLean b Griffin	4	R. Illingworth not out		0
R. Subba Row lbw b Adcock	90	F. S. Trueman b Griffin		0
E. R. Dexter c McLean b Adcock	56	J. B. Statham not out		2
K. F. Barrington lbw b Goddard	24	B 6, l-b 14, w 1, n-b 11		32
M. J. K. Smith c Waite b Griffin	99			—
†J. M. Parks c Fellows-Smith b Adcock	3	1/7 2/103 3/165 4/220	(8 wkts dec.)	362
P. M. Walker b Griffin	52	5/227 6/347 7/360 8/360		

A. E. Moss did not bat.

South Africa

*D. J. McGlew lbw b Statham	15	– b Statham	17
T. L. Goddard b Statham	19	– c Parks b Statham	24
S. O'Linn c Walker b Moss	18	– lbw b Trueman	8
R. A. McLean c Cowdrey b Statham	15	– c Parks b Trueman	13
†J. H. B. Waite c Parks b Statham	3	– lbw b Statham	0
P. R. Carlstein c Cowdrey b Moss	12	– c Parks b Moss	6
C. Wesley c Parks b Statham	11	– b Dexter	35
J. P. Fellows-Smith c Parks b Moss	29	– not out	27
H. J. Tayfield c Smith b Moss	12	– b Dexter	4
G. Griffin b Statham	5	– b Statham	0
N. A. T. Adcock not out	8	– b Statham	2
L-b 4, n-b 1	5	N-b 1	1

1/33 2/48 3/56 4/69 5/78   152   1/26 2/49 3/49 4/50 5/63   137
6/88 7/112 8/132 9/138   6/72 7/126 8/132 9/133

South Africa Bowling

	Overs	Mdns	Runs	Wkts
Adcock	36	11	70	3
Griffin	30	7	87	4
Goddard	31	6	96	1
Tayfield	26	9	64	—
Fellows-Smith	5	—	13	—

England Bowling

	Overs	Mdns	Runs	Wkts	Overs	Mdns	Runs	Wkts
Statham	20	5	63	6	21	6	34	5
Trueman..........	13	2	49	—	17	5	44	2
Moss.............	10.3	—	35	4	14	1	41	1
Illingworth					1	1	—	—
Dexter...........					4	—	17	2

Umpires: F. S. Lee and J. S. Buller.

ENGLAND v SOUTH AFRICA

Third Test Match

Played at Trent Bridge, July 7, 8, 9, 11, 1960

England won by eight wickets with a day to spare and, with three successive victories, settled the rubber. Again there was no disputing England's superiority in fast bowling and close fielding. On the other hand, South Africa again found the dice loaded against them. McGlew lost the toss for the third consecutive time; Waite dislocated the little finger of his left hand when keeping wicket early in the afternoon of the first day so that he batted at number eight instead of three and, after the touring team followed-on 199 behind and were battling bravely, McGlew was run out in unfortunate circumstances which caused a heated controversy.

The Nottinghamshire County Club deserved to be complimented on solving the problem of their hitherto docile pitch. More use of the heavy roller and less watering produced a dry, hard surface so that the ball came through at a good pace and the bowlers acquired reasonable lift from a decent length. As at Lord's, England left out R. W. Barber from the chosen twelve; South Africa introduced Pothecary to Test cricket in place of Griffin.

South Africa did extremely well on the first day for, although Cowdrey at last regained form for his country, they put down half the wickets for 154 before a stand of 75 by Barrington and Illingworth held them up. At the close seven wickets had fallen for 242. England, 82 for one at lunch, could claim to have begun satisfactorily, but Adcock bowled Dexter first ball after the interval. While Pothecary was steady and commanded respect, Adcock, Goddard and Tayfield proved a resolute trio and despite Cowdrey staying two hours and fifty minutes for 67 (eight 4s), England never mastered the attack.

A fine return by McLean from the deep ran out Parks and then came the partnership between Barrington and Illingworth. At length Tayfield held a hard return and disposed of Illingworth. With five minutes left, Goddard surprised Barrington with a ball which lifted and O'Linn, the efficient deputy wicket-keeper, seized the catch. Barrington (seven 4s) gave an almost faultless display lasting three hours and fifty minutes.

More fine bowling by Goddard marked the beginning of the second day. A dull morning gave way to a clear sky, but the cricket scarcely matched the brilliant sunshine. Apart from a few gay strokes by Trueman, the England tail were in stubborn mood. Walker took ninety-five minutes to make 30 and England occupied seventy-five minutes adding only 45. Goddard achieved a fine performance in taking five wickets for the third time in a Test innings in England.

Whereas the England innings occupied seven hours, South Africa were dismissed in two hours fifty minutes for 88, their lowest total in England for 36 years – 30 at Edgbaston in 1924. It was also the lowest total of a completed innings in any Test at Trent Bridge. The batsmen were powerless against an attack consisting solely of fast bowlers. Statham and Trueman were in deadly form. The collapse began when McGlew, fending a rising ball from his head, was caught by Parks off his glove from the last delivery of the first over. The early loss of their captain on top of the injury to Waite proved a demoralising blow to South Africa. O'Linn was brilliantly caught at short square leg and then Goddard and McLean unwisely attempted a sharp single to Dexter at cover and Goddard paid the penalty.

When Statham, bowling for the first time at Trueman's end, promptly sent back McLean and Wesley with successive balls, half the side were out for 33 and South Africa's fate was sealed. Fellows-Smith alone gave any trouble and the batsmen remained helpless when they followed on at 4.45 p.m. This time Fellows-Smith went in at number three, but in forty minutes Goddard, Fellows-Smith and McLean were put out for 34 before bad light followed by rain ended cricket sixty-five minutes early.

McGlew, O'Linn and Waite won the admiration of the crowd of 11,000 on Saturday for the tenacious way they faced the bowling and took the Test into the fourth day after it had looked to be almost over on Friday evening. This was a noble fight in the best traditions of cricket and emphasised once more that a game is never lost until it is won.

For the first time on the tour McGlew gave of his best. He looked a class batsman again and was receiving all the help he needed when, with the stand having put on 91 in two hours, the South African captain was run out. The left-handed O'Linn played a ball from Moss to extra cover and went for a reasonably quick single. Moss dashed across the pitch to chase it and McGlew ran into his back. He stumbled and darted for the crease, but Statham had picked up and with unerring aim hit the stumps.

Cowdrey and the other England players near the broken wicket promptly appealed and Elliott, the square-leg umpire, signalled out. Elliott's decision was correct because Moss had not deliberately baulked McGlew. McGlew never hesitates when given out, but as he hastened towards the pavilion the crowd voiced their disapproval of the circumstances of his dismissal. Three times Cowdrey called to him to come back, and when he did the England captain asked the umpires if it was possible to change the verdict, but they were adamant.

There was an incident at Christchurch in March 1951 believed to be unique in Test cricket. Washbrook was given out leg-before but Hadlee, the New Zealand captain, stopped Washbrook on his way out and told the umpire that he felt certain that Washbrook had hit the ball on to his pad. Washbrook was allowed to continue his innings and Wisden *reported that the ethics of his action caused considerable discussion.*

O'Linn did not allow the departure of his captain to affect him, but soon after lunch Statham again took two wickets with successive balls, Carlstein being caught at second slip and Wesley brilliantly snapped up by Parks diving low with the left hand. Wesley had the misfortune to be out first ball in both innings – a "king pair".

This meant six wickets down for 122, but O'Linn found another worthy helper in Waite and even Trueman and Statham with the new ball did not deter them. They put on 109 in two and a half hours before Moss, England's best bowler that day, had Waite leg-before, the ball keeping low. O'Linn continued to battle away in his own peculiar style. Perseverance and concentration were his main assets, but he hooked, cut and drove past cover with flashing strokes until, looking for the shot that would have given him a well-deserved hundred, he was splendidly caught high with the right hand by Cowdrey at second slip. Excepting the first half-hour, O'Linn batted through an innings of six hours and his sure judgment in choosing the ball to punish earned him fifteen 4s.

England wanted only 49 to win and Cowdrey and Subba Row made 25 in the last half-hour on Saturday. Then the weather intervened and nothing could be done before 3 p.m. on Monday. Heavy clouds still threatened to stop the game and when the scores were level both Cowdrey and Dexter fell. South Africa sent down 19 more deliveries before Barrington made the winning hit, a chance to Goddard in the slips. So ended yet another controversial Test. N.P.

England

R. Subba Row b Tayfield	30	– not out	16
*M. C. Cowdrey c Fellows-Smith b Goddard	67	– lbw b Goddard	27
E. R. Dexter b Adcock	3	– c Adcock b Goddard	0
K. F. Barrington c O'Linn b Goddard	80	– not out	1
M. J. K. Smith lbw b Goddard	0		
†J. M. Parks run out	16		
R. Illingworth c and b Tayfield	37		
P. M. Walker c O'Linn b Tayfield	30		
F. S. Trueman b Goddard	15		
J. B. Statham b Goddard	2		
A. E. Moss not out	3		
B 2, l-b 2	4	B 4, l-b 1	5

1/57 2/82 3/129 4/129 5/154   287   1/48 2/48   (2 wkts) 49
6/229 7/241 8/261 9/267

South Africa

*D. J. McGlew c Parks b Trueman	0	– run out	45
T. L. Goddard run out	16	– b Trueman	0
S. O'Linn c Walker b Trueman	1	– c Cowdrey b Moss	98
R. A. McLean b Statham	11	– c Parks b Trueman	0
P. R. Carlstein c Walker b Statham	2	– c Cowdrey b Statham	19
C. Wesley c Subba Row b Statham	0	– c Parks b Statham	0
J. P. Fellows-Smith not out	31	– c Illingworth b Trueman	15
†J. H. B. Waite c Trueman b Moss	1	– lbw b Moss	60
H. J. Tayfield b Trueman	11	– c Parks b Moss	6
J. E. Pothecary b Trueman	7	– c Parks b Trueman	3
N. A. T. Adcock b Trueman	0	– not out	1
B 4, l-b 4	8		

1/0 2/12 3/13 4/33 5/33   88   1/1 2/23 3/23 4/91 5/122   247
6/44 7/49 8/68 9/82   6/122 7/231 8/242 9/245

South Africa Bowling

	Overs	Mdns	Runs	Wkts	Overs	Mdns	Runs	Wkts
Adcock	30	2	86	1	7.4	2	16	—
Pothecary	20	5	42	—	2	—	15	—
Fellows-Smith	5	—	17	—				
Goddard	42	17	80	5	5	1	13	2
Tayfield	28.3	11	58	3				

England Bowling

	Overs	Mdns	Runs	Wkts	Overs	Mdns	Runs	Wkts
Trueman	14.3	6	27	5	22	3	77	4
Statham	14	5	27	3	26	3	71	2
Moss	10	3	26	1	15.4	3	36	3
Illingworth					19	9	33	—
Barrington					3	1	5	—
Dexter					6	2	12	—
Walker					3	—	13	—

Umpires: F. S. Lee and C. S. Elliott.

WEST INDIANS IN ENGLAND

SURREY v WEST INDIES

Played at The Oval, May 13, 15, 16, 1950

Drawn. On their first appearance in London the West Indies outplayed Surrey but were not dominating enough in the field on the third day when they allowed the county to escape defeat. Brilliant sunshine inspired the men from the Caribbean on the opening day, when their batting was really dazzling, but a bitterly cold wind chilled everyone on Monday and Tuesday, so that Surrey could be excused to some extent for not showing their true form with the bat. Rae, the left-hander, saw the total reach 188, but he never approached the standard set by Walcott and Weekes, whose stand of 247 was a record for the fourth wicket for the West Indies in this country. Both excelled with magnificent drives off the back foot. Walcott hit fifteen 4s and Weekes, who stayed almost six hours, hit twenty-six 4s. For the most part the Surrey bowling and fielding were splendid, although Walcott when 68 was dropped at slip. Parker alone gave the tourists much trouble in the Surrey first innings. His off-drives were specially fine. Surrey wanted 388 to avert an innings defeat, and thanks to Fishlock, who made the first century against Goddard's men, and a defiant display by Barton, who stayed four hours, they left the visitors the hopeless task of scoring 48 in the last ten minutes. A collection for Fishlock on Saturday realised £215.

West Indies

A. F. Rae c and b Laker	96	– not out	4
R. Marshall c Barton b A. Bedser	4		
F. M. Worrell c Surridge b Laker	17		
E. Weekes b A. Bedser	232		
C. L. Walcott lbw b A. Bedser	128		
R. J. Christiani not out	32	– c Kirby b A. Bedser	9
B 13, l-b 7, n-b 8	28	N-b 1	1
	(5 wkts dec.) 537		**(1 wkt) 14**

G. E. Gomez, J. D. Goddard, C. B. Williams, H. H. Johnson and A. L. Valentine did not bat.

Surrey

L. B. Fishlock c and b Gomez	10	– c Christiani b Johnson	110
E. A. Bedser c Valentine b Williams	37	– lbw b Johnson	8
J. F. Parker not out	94	– b Worrell	19
B. Constable c Christiani b Worrell	0	– c Rae b Gomez	15
M. R. Barton b Worrell	1	– lbw b Worrell	99
G. J. Whittaker lbw b Worrell	0	– c Christiani b Johnson	14
J. C. Laker c Goddard b Valentine	18	– lbw b Gomez	23
A. V. Bedser c Christiani b Valentine	0	– c sub b Gomez	4
W. S. Surridge b Williams	11	– c Weekes b Gomez	27
G. N. G. Kirby b Gomez	16	– c Gomez b Valentine	32
J. W. McMahon c Christiani b Johnson	0	– not out	23
B 4, l-b 2	6	B 13, l-b 3, n-b 1	17
	193		**391**

Surrey Bowling

	Overs	Mdns	Runs	Wkts	Overs	Mdns	Runs	Wkts
A. Bedser	31.1	5	75	3	1.1	—	6	1
Surridge	21	2	106	—	1	—	7	—
Parker.	17	2	52	—				
Laker	36	11	83	2				
McMahon.	29	2	111	—				
E. Bedser	14	1	82	—				

West Indies Bowling

	Overs	Mdns	Runs	Wkts	Overs	Mdns	Runs	Wkts
Johnson	14.3	2	43	1	27	8	79	3
Gomez	13	3	31	2	40	8	110	4
Williams	19	3	67	2	10	2	42	—
Worrell	13	6	13	3	23	7	50	2
Valentine.	11	2	26	2	30.2	10	83	1
Goddard	2	1	7	—				
Walcott.					8	5	10	—

Umpires: E. Robinson and F. S. Lee.

CAMBRIDGE UNIVERSITY v WEST INDIES

Played at Cambridge, May 17, 18, 19, 1950

Drawn. Batsmen held the mastery throughout on a pitch almost farcically unfavourable to bowlers. The match produced 1,324 runs while seven wickets fell, and a series of new records were set up. Dewes and Sheppard, in scoring 343 in four hours and forty minutes for the first Cambridge wicket, shared in the highest opening stand for Cambridge and the best anywhere in the world against a West Indies team. Neither batsman gave a chance and each hit hard all round. Dewes obtained nineteen 4s, and Sheppard, who batted six hours and a quarter for his highest score in first-class cricket, hit twenty-one 4s. Doggart helped Sheppard add 144 in ninety minutes, and Cambridge declared on the second day at the second highest total made against a West Indies team. Stollmeyer and Christiani, each missed early in his innings began for the visitors with a stand of 178 in two hours and fifty minutes. Christiani, first to leave, drove, cut and hit to leg freely after a quiet start, but Stollmeyer was very restrained, and in his stay of nearly three hours and a half he hit only three 4s. There followed an entertaining stand between Weekes and Worrell. Both drove and hit to leg powerfully and, despite specially fine ground fielding by the University, put on 350 in three hours and three-quarters, a record for any West Indies wicket in England. Weekes took out his bat for 304, which – the biggest score by a West Indies player in this country and the highest at Fenner's – occupied him five hours and twenty-five minutes and included forty 4s. Worrell, batting four hours and a half, hit twenty-seven 4s. The West Indies total exceeded all previous scores by a team from the Caribbean in England.

Cambridge University

J. G. Dewes c Weekes b Goddard. 183	M. H. Stevenson not out	53
D. S. Sheppard c Trestrail b Williams. 227		
G. H. G. Doggart c and b Williams 71	B 3, l-b 3	6
P. B. H. May not out. 44		
A. G. J. Rimell c Christiani b Goddard. 10	(4 wkts dec.) 594

T. U. Wells, O. J. Wait, J. J. Warr, P. A. Kelland and H. W. Denman did not bat.

West Indies

R. J. Christiani lbw b Warr.............111	K. B. Trestrail not out.................. 56
J. B. Stollmeyer c Doggart b Kelland 83	B 3, 1-b 8, w 2, n-b 3 16
F. M. Worrell b Wait 160	
E. D. Weekes not out 304	(3 wkts) 730

J. D. Goddard, C. B. Williams, P. E. Jones, H. H. Johnson, S. Ramadhin and A. L. Valentine did not bat.

West Indies Bowling

	Overs	Mdns	Runs	Wkts
Johnson	15	1	55	—
Jones.............	17	4	77	—
Valentine.........	32	3	97	—
Ramadhin........	20	2	86	—
Williams	12	—	62	2
Worrell...........	12	—	45	—
Goddard..........	32	2	128	2
Stollmeyer........	5	1	38	—

Cambridge University Bowling

	Overs	Mdns	Runs	Wkts
Warr.............	35	3	121	1
Wait	28	3	127	1
Kelland...........	33	—	105	1
Doggart	25	2	123	—
Rimell............	36	1	128	—
Stevenson	12	1	69	—
Wells.............	3	—	28	—
May	2	—	13	—

LANCASHIRE v WEST INDIES

Played at Manchester, June 3, 5, 6, 1950

West Indies won by an innings and 220 runs. This was the first time a team from the Caribbean had defeated Lancashire and, coming just before the First Test, due to be played on an adjacent pitch, they derived much encouragement. By steady consistent batting, the West Indies built a substantial total on the opening day when in nearly six and a half hours they scored 344 runs for the loss of only four men. As usual, Rae waited for the occasional loose ball and then he drove or pulled powerfully. He offered three chances while making his first ten runs and gave another when 77. Slow at first, Stollmeyer produced many stylish forcing strokes while the opening stand yielded 204. Altogether Rae stayed four hours twenty minutes, his chief strokes bringing him one 6 and fourteen 4s. Weekes pulled vigorously, and on the second day Walcott excelled in driving. Lancashire failed ingloriously with the bat. They never recovered after Ikin from the first ball of the innings called Place for an impossible single. Goddard walked from square leg and removed the bails. The pitch became dusty and very worn at one end, conditions which Valentine exploited to the full with his left-arm slows. On the second day, when thirteen Lancashire wickets fell, Valentine took ten for 43 runs, and he finished the match with thirteen at a cost of only 67 runs. Four of the last seven wickets went to Goddard.

West Indies

A. F. Rae st Barlow b Tattersall	114	G. E. Gomez not out	41
J. B. Stollmeyer c and b Hilton	83	J. D. Goddard hit wkt b Tattersall	9
R. Marshall c Barlow b Grieves	44	C. B. Williams not out	8
E. Weekes b Grieves	59	B 19, l-b 5, n-b 1	25
C. L. Walcott c Grieves b Hilton	63		
R. J. Christiani c Barlow b Pollard	8	(7 wkts)	454

L. R. Pierre and A. L. Valentine did not bat.

Lancashire

W. Place run out	0	– b Valentine	14
J. T. Ikin c Goddard b Valentine	19	– c Weekes b Williams	29
G. A. Edrich c Marshall b Valentine	20	– c Marshall b Valentine	11
K. Grieves b Valentine	5	– c Marshall b Valentine	22
A. Wharton b Valentine	8	– c Walcott b Goddard	12
N. D. Howard b Valentine	2	– c Gomez b Goddard	3
J. G. Lomax c Christiani b Valentine	7	– c Gomez b Goddard	6
R. Tattersall not out	18	– c Stollmeyer b Goddard	0
M. J. Hilton c Stollmeyer b Valentine	2	– c Rae b Valentine	8
R. Pollard c Marshall b Valentine	10	– not out	6
A. Barlow c Stollmeyer b Williams	1	– c Marshall b Valentine	9
B 7, l-b 4	11	B 4, l-b 3, n-b 4	11
	103		131

Lancashire Bowling

	Overs	Mdns	Runs	Wkts
Pollard	26	6	59	1
Lomax	23	6	47	—
Wharton	10	1	34	—
Grieves	29	3	97	2
Hilton	32	10	65	2
Tattersall	40	13	80	2
Ikin	16	2	47	—

West Indies Bowling

	Overs	Mdns	Runs	Wkts	Overs	Mdns	Runs	Wkts
Pierre	6	2	11	—	4	—	6	—
Gomez	4	1	8	—	10	4	15	—
Valentine	22	9	26	8	20.2	10	41	5
Williams	20.3	4	47	1	7	—	25	1
Marshall					4	2	9	—
Goddard					13	8	24	4

Umpires: H. Elliott and E. Robinson.

ENGLAND v WEST INDIES

First Test Match

Played at Manchester June 8, 9, 10, 12, 1950

England won by 202 runs. When the individual performances of the Manchester Test are forgotten it will be remembered chiefly because of the arguments aroused by the remarkable nature of the pitch. In their earnest desire to adjust the balance between batsmen and bowlers the Lancashire Ground Committee issued an edict to their groundsman before the 1950 season that less use should be made of water and the heavy roller in the preparation of a pitch. Throughout the summer cricket at Old Trafford went in favour of spin bowlers, and the Test provided no exception, a week of hot, dry weather before the game hastening the crumbling effect. Aware of the likely conditions, Yardley, after a long inspection, omitted A. V. Bedser in order to rely principally on a slow attack, and Goddard adopted similar strategy by including only Johnson of his three pace bowlers.

England looked to have gained a considerable advantage by batting first, but the pitch before lunch was a shade more difficult than at any time in the match. At this stage the straight good-length ball turned just enough to compel a stroke and often touched the edge of the bat, whereas afterwards it turned so much that not infrequently it missed bat and wicket. Moreover, the batsmen had to watch carefully for the ball which lifted sharply.

All went well for England until at 22 Hutton received such a painful blow on the hand from Johnson that he was forced to retire. This was the first of a series of disasters. Valentine, going on one run later, found the turf so responsive to his quick left-arm spin that in seventeen overs before lunch he took five successive wickets for 34 runs. All the batsmen were uncomfortable against the ball which turned from the bat, and good catching by Gomez and Goddard helped Valentine to his deserved reward.

Half the England side were out for 88, but Evans and Bailey wrested the initiative from the bowlers in a splendid stand of 161, a new record sixth-wicket partnership in England v West Indies Tests. In contrast to Bailey, who concentrated mainly on defence, Evans neglected no opportunity to hit hard. In his maiden Test century and his first in a first-class match in England, Evans scored all but 57 added for the wicket, and his powerful strokes included seventeen boundaries. He batted two hours twenty minutes.

Hutton resumed after the dismissal of Evans and, although in such discomfort that he constantly took his damaged hand from the bat as he played his stroke, he again showed his masterly defensive skill until beaten by a fine ball. When Valentine followed by bowling Laker, he had disposed of eight batsmen consecutively. His prospects of creating history by taking all ten wickets in his first Test disappeared when Ramadhin at last gained compensation for highly skilled slow bowling in which he beat the bat many times without hitting the wicket.

England were indebted to Bailey, who presented a straight bat in defence for over three and a half hours and occasionally opened his shoulders for the sweep or cut, but West Indies deserved sympathy over the loss of Johnson, who pulled a side muscle in his first spell and bowled only two overs in his second before being compelled to retire. He did not field after tea and was unable to bowl again in the match.

Their hero was 20-year-old Valentine, whose feat of taking eight wickets was without parallel for a bowler on Test début. Earlier in the week on the same ground Valentine dismissed eight Lancashire batsmen in an innings. Valentine bowled an accurate length on and around the off stump and turned the ball quickly enough to compel hurried strokes.

The England batting had been patchy, but that of the West Indies was worse. Weekes and Stollmeyer alone appeared capable of dealing with Berry (left-arm slow) and Hollies (leg-breaks). Going on at 51, Berry bowled unchanged to the end of the innings. His spin was not so vicious as that of Valentine, but his variations of pace and flight showed him to be an intelligent bowler with distinct possibilities of greatness.

With a lead of 97, England began their second innings well placed, but Hutton was not fit enough to open, Simpson failed without a run scored, and Doggart and Dollery fell to Valentine by the time the total reached 43. Then Yardley and Edrich pulled the side together, and England finished the second day 205 ahead with six wickets intact. An unusual feature of the innings was that Walcott, the burly West Indies wicket-keeper, started their attack in place of the injured Johnson, and Christiani kept wicket.

Next day Edrich and Bailey batted on against the craft of Valentine and Ramadhin until Ramadhin found the edge of Edrich's bat and Weekes at slip snapped up a difficult catch. Edrich played gallantly for three hours ten minutes and hit ten 4s. More defiance of the bowlers came from Bailey and Hutton, who went in at 151, at the fall of the sixth wicket.

Hutton, with his finger heavily bandaged and in obvious pain, stayed two hours and helped to add 115. He was called upon to face a spell of short rising balls from Goddard, but usually avoided trouble by ducking and to other deliveries demonstrated his skill in playing the dead-bat stroke. For two hours five minutes Bailey again mixed rigid defence with prompt acceptance of any opportunity to hit a bad ball.

On a pitch so much in favour of spin bowlers, West Indies held little hopes of scoring the 386 required to win. As it was, only a superb display by Stollmeyer, the tall, elegant opening batsman, enabled them to obtain nearly half that total. His quick footwork and classical stroke-play stamped him as a batsman of distinct merit. Only an hour's play was needed on the fourth day. In this time the last six wickets went down for 61 runs. Some excitement was provided by Johnson, who punished Laker for 20, including a 6 and three 4s, in two overs, but Hollies and Berry maintained their mastery, Berry bringing his analysis to nine for 116. Even allowing for his fortune in bowling on a pitch so suitable to him, this was a most satisfactory first appearance in Test cricket. The attendance figures reached 48,451, with receipts £13,204.   R.J.H.

England

L. Hutton b Valentine	39	– c and b Worrell 45
R. T. Simpson c Goddard b Valentine	27	– c Weekes b Gomez 0
W. J. Edrich c Gomez b Valentine	7	– c Weekes b Ramadhin 71
G. H. G. Doggart c Rae b Valentine	29	– c Goddard b Valentine 22
H. E. Dollery c Gomez b Valentine	8	– c Gomez b Valentine 0
N. W. D. Yardley c Gomez b Valentine	0	– lbw b Gomez 25
T. E. Bailey not out	82	– run out 33
T. G. Evans c and b Valentine	104	– c Worrell b Ramadhin 15
J. C. Laker b Valentine	4	– c Stollmeyer b Valentine 40
W. E. Hollies c Weekes b Ramadhin	0	– c Walcott b Worrell 3
R. Berry b Ramadhin	0	– not out 4
B 8, l-b 3, n-b 1	12	B 17, l-b 12, n-b 1 30

1/51 2/74 3/79 4/83 5/88   312   1/0 2/31 3/43 4/106 5/131   288
6/249 7/293 8/301 9/308   6/151 7/200 8/266 9/284

West Indies

A. F. Rae c Doggart b Berry	14	– c Doggart b Hollies 10
J. B. Stollmeyer lbw b Hollies	43	– c sub b Laker 78
F. M. Worrell st Evans b Berry	15	– st Evans b Hollies 28
E. Weekes c sub b Bailey	52	– lbw b Hollies................... 1
C. L. Walcott c Evans b Berry	13	– b Berry 9
R. J. Christiani lbw b Berry	17	– c Yardley b Hollies 6
G. E. Gomez c Berry b Hollies	35	– st Evans b Berry................ 8
J. D. Goddard run out	7	– not out 16
H. H. Johnson c Dollery b Hollies	8	– b Berry 22
S. Ramadhin not out	4	– b Berry 0
A. L. Valentine c and b Berry	0	– c Bailey b Hollies 0
L-b 6, n-b 1	7	B 4, w 1................. 5

1/52 2/74 3/74 4/94 5/146   215   1/32 2/68 3/80 4/113 5/126   183
6/178 7/201 8/211 9/211   6/141 7/146 8/178 9/178

West Indies Bowling

	Overs	Mdns	Runs	Wkts	Overs	Mdns	Runs	Wkts
Johnson	10	3	18	—				
Gomez	10	1	29	—	25	12	47	2
Valentine	50	14	104	8	56	22	100	3
Ramadhin	39.3	12	90	2	42	17	77	2
Goddard	15	1	46	—	9	3	12	—
Worrell	4	1	13	—	5.5	1	10	2
Walcott					4	1	12	—

England Bowling

	Overs	Mdns	Runs	Wkts	Overs	Mdns	Runs	Wkts
Bailey	10	2	28	1	3	1	9	—
Edrich	2	1	4	—	3	1	10	—
Hollies	33	13	70	3	35.2	11	63	5
Laker	17	5	43	—	14	4	43	1
Berry	31.5	13	63	5	26	12	53	4

Umpires: F. Chester and D. Davies.

ENGLAND v WEST INDIES
Second Test Match

Played at Lord's, June 24, 26, 27, 28, 29, 1950

West Indies won by 326 runs. They fully merited their first Test victory in England, which, to their undisguised delight, was gained at the headquarters of cricket. In batting, bowling and fielding they were clearly the superior side, with Ramadhin this time the more successful of the two 20-year-old spin bowlers who during the 1950 summer wrought such destruction among English batsmen. In the match Ramadhin took eleven and Valentine seven wickets.

England, already without Compton, suffered further setbacks before the game began by the withdrawal through injury of Simpson and Bailey. In view of heavy rain on Friday, the selectors gambled on the pitch being helpful to spin by choosing Wardle, left-arm slow, to replace Bailey, but instead the turf played easily from the start, and Yardley found himself with three slow bowlers who turned the ball from leg; he would have wished to bowl all of them from the same end. The teams were presented to the King just before the start when 30,500 were inside the ground, the gates having been closed.

Although Wardle took a wicket with his first ball in Test cricket in England by getting rid of Stollmeyer at 37, West Indies were so much on top that shortly after four o'clock the total stood at 233 for two. Brilliant stroke-play came from Worrell, who drove delightfully and made some astonishing late cuts, and Weekes, whose 63 in ninety minutes contained ten 4s, but Rae, in much less spectacular manner, performed even more important work for West Indies.

A fine ball by Bedser which swung away and broke back after pitching shattered the wicket of Weekes at 233, and from that point England fought back splendidly. Clever slow bowling by Jenkins, in particular, raised England hopes after tea. In a twenty-minute spell of seven overs he sent back Walcott, Rae and Gomez. Rae, who was badly missed in the gully off Bedser when 79, made no other mistake during a patient innings lasting four hours forty minutes, in which he scored 106 out of 273. At times he appeared content to continue a passive defensive policy, but occasionally he would abandon these tactics, as when in one over he hit Jenkins for three of his fifteen 4s. Largely through the inspiration of Yardley, England atoned for earlier catching errors by first-class ground fielding, and in view of the nature of the pitch they could feel satisfied with their performance of taking seven wickets for 320 runs on the opening day. Bedser was the most consistent and reliable bowler, but luck went against him, especially when he saw two catches missed off him during a fine spell of 22 overs for 17 runs with the new ball.

No more than ten minutes were required to finish the innings on Monday, but England's reply was disappointing in the extreme. Neither Hutton nor Washbrook was in his best form, but both played well enough to take the score to 62 before Hutton dashed down the pitch and was stumped yards out. This began a rout which was checked only by spirited hitting by Wardle, who punched six 4s and took part with Berry in the second highest stand of the innings, 29 for the last wicket.

No blame could be attached to the pitch. It gave slow bowlers a little help, but only to those who used real finger spin as did Ramadhin and Valentine. Ramadhin bowled with the guile of a veteran. He pitched a tantalising length, bowled straight at the wicket and spun enough to beat the bat. No English batsman showed evidence of having mastered the problems of deciding which way Ramadhin would spin and he was too quick through the air for any but the most nimble-footed to go down to meet him on the half-volley with any consistency. Valentine lent able support, but the English batsmen might, with profit, have tackled him more boldly. England's score was their lowest for a completed innings in a home Test against West Indies.

Thanks to a remarkably sustained spell of bowling by Jenkins, England prevented West Indies in their second innings from placing themselves in an impregnable position until the association of Walcott and Gomez. Previously Weekes, Worrell and Stollmeyer gave another exhibition of masterly stroke-play, but with only a twenty-minute rest Jenkins kept one end going from the start until tea, and deserved the reward of the four wickets which fell to him.

Unfortunately for England a second series of fielding blunders played into the hands of West Indies at a time when a slight prospect of victory seemed to exist. The most expensive of these occurred when Walcott had scored nine. He was missed at slip off Edrich, who bowled with plenty of life in using the new ball. Before England met with another success Walcott and Gomez put on 211, beating the record for the sixth wicket in England v West Indies Tests established a few weeks earlier at Manchester by Evans and T. E. Bailey. Walcott and Gomez also set up a record Test stand for any West Indies wicket in England. When Goddard declared, setting England 601 to get to win with nearly two days to play, Walcott, the six-foot-two wicket-keeper-batsman, was only one short of the highest score by a West Indies player in Test cricket in England, 169 not out by G. Headley in 1933. As usual, Walcott scored the majority of his runs by drives, even against the good-length or shorter ball, and leg sweeps. He hit twenty-four 4s. Gomez did not put such force into his strokes, but he provided an admirable and valuable foil.

Two batsmen distinguished themselves in England's second innings. For five hours and a half Washbrook withstood the attack, and his only mistake occurred when, at 93, he gave a hard chance to mid-on. Otherwise he batted excellently; although for the most part refusing to take a risk he hit one 6 and fourteen 4s.

The only other success was Parkhouse, who signalised his first Test with a very good innings, in which he showed encouraging confidence and a variety of strokes until he hit a full toss straight to silly mid-off in the last over of the fourth day when wanting only two runs for 50. This mistake came at a time when thoughts were raised that Washbrook might be capable of saving the match if someone could stay with him. Hutton again was dismissed curiously. He made no stroke at a ball which came with Valentine's arm and hit the middle stump.

England started the last day with six wickets left and 383 runs required to win, but when Ramadhin yorked Washbrook, who did not add to his score, the end was in sight and nothing happened to check the inevitable defeat. Ramadhin and Valentine were again the chief executioners. During the five days the full attendance was 112,000.   R.J.H.

West Indies

A. F. Rae c and b Jenkins	106	– b Jenkins ... 24
J. B. Stollmeyer lbw b Wardle	20	– b Jenkins ... 30
F. M. Worrell b Bedser	52	– c Doggart b Jenkins ... 45
E. Weekes b Bedser	63	– run out ... 63
C. L. Walcott st Evans b Jenkins	14	– not out ... 168
G. E. Gomez st Evans b Jenkins	1	– c Edrich b Bedser ... 70
R. J. Christiani b Bedser	33	– not out ... 5
J. D. Goddard b Wardle	14	– c Evans b Jenkins ... 11
P. E. Jones c Evans b Jenkins	0	
S. Ramadhin not out	1	
A. L. Valentine c Hutton b Jenkins	5	
B 10, l-b 5, w 1, n-b 1	17	L-b 8, n-b 1 ... 9

1/37 2/128 3/233 4/262 5/273   326   1/48 2/75 3/108   (6 wkts dec.) 425
6/274 7/320 8/320 9/320   4/146 5/199 6/410

England

L. Hutton st Walcott b Valentine	35	– b Valentine ... 10
C. Washbrook st Walcott b Ramadhin	36	– b Ramadhin ... 114
W. J. Edrich c Walcott b Ramadhin	8	– c Jones b Ramadhin ... 8
G. H. G. Doggart lbw b Ramadhin	0	– b Ramadhin ... 25
W. G. A. Parkhouse b Valentine	0	– c Goddard b Valentine ... 48
N. W. D. Yardley b Valentine	16	– c Weekes b Valentine ... 19
T. G. Evans b Ramadhin	8	– c Rae b Ramadhin ... 2
R. O. Jenkins c Walcott b Valentine	4	– b Ramadhin ... 4
J. H. Wardle not out	33	– lbw b Worrell ... 21
A. V. Bedser b Ramadhin	5	– b Ramadhin ... 0
R. Berry c Goddard b Jones	2	– not out ... 0
B 2, l-b 1, w 1	4	B 16, l-b 7 ... 23

1/62 2/74 3/74 4/75 5/86   151   1/28 2/57 3/140 4/218 5/228   274
6/102 7/110 8/113 9/122   6/238 7/245 8/258 9/258

England Bowling

	Overs	Mdns	Runs	Wkts	Overs	Mdns	Runs	Wkts
Bedser	40	14	60	3	44	16	80	1
Edrich	16	4	30	—	13	2	37	
Jenkins	35.2	6	116	5	59	13	174	4
Wardle	17	6	46	2	30	10	58	—
Berry	19	7	45	—	32	15	67	
Yardley	4	1	12	—				

West Indies Bowling

	Overs	Mdns	Runs	Wkts	Overs	Mdns	Runs	Wkts
Jones	8.4	2	13	1	7	1	22	—
Worrell	10	4	20	—	22.3	9	39	1
Valentine	45	28	48	4	71	47	79	3
Ramadhin	43	27	66	5	72	43	86	6
Gomez					13	1	25	—
Goddard					6	6	—	—

Umpires: D. Davies and F. S. Lee.

LEICESTERSHIRE v WEST INDIES

Played at Leicester, July 12, 13, 14, 1950

West Indies won by an innings and 249 runs. In a remarkable opening day on an easy pitch West Indies scored 651 for two wickets, and thereby approached the Australians' feat against Essex at Southend, where 721 runs were made in six hours in 1949, the highest total in one day in first-class cricket. Again Worrell (225) and Weekes (190) shared a colossal stand which produced 309 in the last 145 minutes. Next morning, in twenty-five minutes before Goddard declared, the partnership was raised to 340, only ten short of the stand by the same pair earlier in the tour at Cambridge. Each of these brilliant batsmen hit one 6 and twenty-six 4s. At the beginning of his innings Weekes hit the fastest century of the whole season in sixty-five minutes. Marshall made his 188 (thirty-one 4s) in three and a half hours; his straight drives were superb and his stand with Worrell produced 247 in just over two hours. Leicestershire were handicapped through Jackson, their off-break bowler, straining his back. At the age of 44, Berry, who first played for the county in 1924, hit his 41st hundred. Slow at first, Berry scored freely after reaching 50 in three hours, and Tomkin shaped splendidly, but on the third day sixteen Leicestershire wickets went down for 126, Ramadhin taking eight for 43.

West Indies

A. F. Rae b Jackson	26	
R. Marshall c and b Sperry	188	
F. M. Worrell not out	241	
E. Weekes not out	200	
B 18, l-b 6, w 1, n-b 2	27	
	(2 wkts dec.) 682	

C. L. Walcott, R. J. Christiani, G. E. Gomez, J. D. Goddard, P. E. Jones, S. Ramadhin and A. L. Valentine did not bat.

Leicestershire

L. G. Berry c and b Valentine	121	– c Walcott b Jones	5
G. S. Watson c Goddard b Jones	10	– c Walcott b Valentine	6
M. Tompkin c Rae b Marshall	74	– c Marshall b Ramadhin	11
C. H. Palmer b Ramadhin	9	– b Ramadhin	20
V. E. Jackson b Valentine	56	– c Jones b Ramadhin	1
G. Lester b Ramadhin	27	– b Ramadhin	6
K. D. Smith not out	14	– lbw b Ramadhin	2
J. W. R. Smith c Walcott b Valentine	1	– b Ramadhin	0
J. E. Walsh c Marshall b Valentine	0	– not out	24
C. Wooler b Ramadhin	0	– st Christiani b Valentine	4
J. Sperry b Ramadhin	16	– c Ramadhin b Valentine	1
B 16, l-b 8	24	L-b 1	1
	352		**81**

Leicestershire Bowling

	Overs	Mdns	Runs	Wkts
Sperry	34	—	171	1
Wooler	28	6	103	—
Walsh	21	1	133	—
Jackson	9	3	24	1
Palmer	16	1	79	—
Lester	20	—	122	—
K. Smith	3	—	23	—

West Indies Bowling

	Overs	Mdns	Runs	Wkts	Overs	Mdns	Runs	Wkts
Jones............	21	3	55	1	7	2	13	1
Gomez..........	12	7	21	—	2	2	—	—
Ramadhin........	40.3	14	90	4	15	7	27	6
Valentine.........	57	27	101	4	19.4	8	40	3
Worrell..........	10	2	25	—				
Marshall.........	12	4	36	1				

Umpires: F. Chester and A. Skelding.

ENGLAND v WEST INDIES
Third Test Match
Played at Nottingham, July 20, 21, 22, 24, 25, 1950

West Indies won by ten wickets. A gallant attempt by England to fight themselves out of an almost hopeless position failed, and good bowling on the first day, supported by a wonderful innings by Worrell, gave West Indies an easy victory.

More bad luck dogged England in the matter of team selection. On the eve of the match Hutton was found to be suffering from a recurrence of lumbago and Gimblett was troubled by a boil on his neck. The selectors, at 10 p.m. on Wednesday, made a hurried telephone call for Dewes of Middlesex to join the team. From the side beaten at Lord's, England were without Hutton, Edrich, Doggart and Wardle. They brought in Simpson (recovered from injury), Dewes, Insole, Shackleton and Hollies. West Indies preferred Johnson to Jones reverting to the eleven defeated at Old Trafford.

Yardley had many doubts when he won the toss, for the pitch was a little green, and if it were to help bowlers at all in the match it was likely to do so only during the first hour or so. He decided that the risk of putting West Indies in was too great and England batted. The result was disastrous and in the first hour England virtually lost the match. In that period four wickets fell for 25 runs, and although the other batsmen tried hard and brought a partial recovery the side were all out for 223 and the pitch by that time had become perfect.

Insole although far from comfortable against spin, helped Yardley add 50. The Essex player was virtually bowled off his pads, but Chester signalled him out lbw before the ball hit the stumps. Yardley played his best innings of the series, and Shackleton, in his first Test, drove powerfully, scoring 42 out of 69 in seventy minutes. In the last sixty-five minutes on Thursday West Indies scored 77 for the loss of Stollmeyer.

Next day the English bowling was trounced, particularly during a fourth-wicket stand between Worrell and Weekes. Christiani, the overnight stopgap, left at 95, but Rae and Worrell put West Indies ahead during a partnership of 143. Rae, as usual, concentrated on defence, and took four hours ten minutes to score 68 out of 238. Worrell, on the other hand, batted in scintillating style, and the bowlers and fieldsmen were unable to check a wonderful array of fluent strokes. Weekes, usually a quicker scorer, was overshadowed until Worrell tired near the end of the day. At the close West Indies were 479 for three, with Worrell 239 and Weekes 108. They had put on 241, and so easily did he play the bowling that there were many people who considered that Worrell stood a good chance of beating Hutton's record Test score of 364.

In less than half an hour on Saturday Worrell was out. He batted five hours thirty-five minutes and hit two 6s and thirty-five 4s while scoring 261 out of 426. Weekes did not stay much longer; his 129 (seventeen 4s) was scored in three hours forty minutes.

Deadly bowling by Bedser that morning caused the fall of the seven remaining wickets in eighty minutes for 79 runs, and just on one o'clock Washbrook and Simpson opened the second innings with England 335 behind. Showers caused frequent stoppages, but the two batsmen were in no way disturbed, and when rain finally ended play for the day the score stood at 87 without loss.

They were not separated until a quarter past three on Monday, by which time 212 runs were on the board – the highest opening stand by either side in this series of Test matches. Washbrook, first to go, batted five hours twenty minutes for 102, revealing, like Simpson, tremendous concentration. Simpson lasted only a quarter of an hour longer, being run out when going for a sharp single.

Even then England were far from finished, for Dewes and Parkhouse, without looking as safe as the first pair, batted well, and at one period the score stood at 326 for two with England only nine runs behind. A shocking last half-hour turned the course of the game, England losing Parkhouse, Yardley and Insole. Thus in a few minutes the great start had been wasted.

England began the last day 15 ahead with five wickets left, and, despite a merry 63 out of 84 by Evans, wickets fell steadily, and West Indies were set to get 102 to win. In bowling 92 overs in the innings, Valentine delivered more balls than any other Test bowler during one innings. Stollmeyer and Rae made light of the task and hit off the runs in an hour and forty minutes, the match being over at ten minutes to four.

During their first innings of 558 West Indies established several records, the most important of which were:

(a) Their highest total in any Test Match against England.
(b) The highest total by either side in England.
(c) Worrell's 261 was the highest Test score ever made at Trent Bridge.
(d) Worrell made the highest score by a batsman for either country in a Test match in England.
(e) The fourth-wicket partnership between Worrell and Weekes of 283 was the highest stand for any wicket for either side in this Test series in England.
(f) The partnership was the highest Test stand for West Indies in any part of the world.
(g) The stand was the highest fourth-wicket partnership for West Indies in any match in England.   L.S.

England

R. T. Simpson c Walcott b Johnson	4	– run out 94
C. Washbrook c Stollmeyer b Worrell	3	– c Worrell b Valentine ...102
W. G. A. Parkhouse c Weekes b Johnson	13	– lbw b Goddard 69
J. G. Dewes c Gomez b Worrell	0	– lbw b Valentine 67
N. W. D. Yardley c Goddard b Valentine	41	– b Ramadhin 7
D. J. Insole lbw b Ramadhin	21	– st Walcott b Ramadhin 0
T. G. Evans b Ramadhin	32	– c Stollmeyer b Ramadhin 63
D. Shackleton b Worrell	42	– c Weekes b Valentine 1
R. O. Jenkins b Johnson	39	– not out 6
A. V. Bedser c Stollmeyer b Valentine	13	– b Ramadhin 2
W. E. Hollies not out	2	– lbw b Ramadhin 0
L-b 12, n-b 1	13	B 11, l-b 10, w 2, n-b 2 25

1/6 2/18 3/23 4/25 5/75	223	1/212 2/220 3/326 4/346	436
6/105 7/147 8/174 9/191		5/350 6/408 7/410 8/434 9/436	

West Indies

A. F. Rae st Evans b Yardley .... 68 – not out 46
J. B. Stollmeyer c and b Jenkins .... 46 – not out 52
R. J. Christiani lbw b Shackleton 10
F. M. Worrell c Yardley b Bedser .... .261
E. Weekes c and b Hollies..................... .129
C. L. Walcott b Bedser 8
G. E. Gomez not out.......................... 19
J. D. Goddard c Yardley b Bedser 0
H. H. Johnson c Insole b Bedser 0
S. Ramadhin b Bedser........................ 2
A. L. Valentine b Hollies...................... 1
          B 2, l-b 10, n-b 2 14   N-b 5 5

1/77 2/95 3/238 4/521 5/535   558   (No wkt) 103
6/537 7/538 8/539 9/551

West Indies Bowling

	Overs	Mdns	Runs	Wkts	Overs	Mdns	Runs	Wkts
Johnson	25.4	5	59	3	30	5	65	—
Worrell	17	4	40	3	19	8	30	—
Gomez	3	1	9	—	11	3	23	—
Goddard..........	6	3	10	—	12	6	18	1
Ramadhin.........	29	12	49	2	81.2	25	135	5
Valentine.........	18	6	43	2	92	49	140	3

England Bowling

	Overs	Mdns	Runs	Wkts	Overs	Mdns	Runs	Wkts
Bedser............	48	9	127	5	11	1	35	—
Shackleton	43	7	128	1	6	2	7	—
Yardley...........	27	3	82	1				
Jenkins	13	—	73	1	11	1	46	—
Hollies	43.4	8	134	2	7	6	1	—
Simpson					1.3	—	9	—

Umpires: F. Chester and H. Elliott.

NOTES BY THE EDITOR, 1951

UMPIRING VAGARIES

From Frank Chester standing in the Test Match at Trent Bridge to an official acting in a club game in Australia is a far cry, but each gave a decision beyond the knowledge of regular players and followers of cricket down the ages. Chester called "out" to an appeal for leg-before against D. J. Insole and insisted that his ruling should go on the score sheet although the ball went off the batsman's pads on to the stumps; surely this meant bowled. How Chester contrived to signal "out" before the ball reached the stumps is difficult to realise, but, however that may be, his refusal to withdraw his verdict in favour of the more definite and satisfactory form of dismissal cannot be understood. Both for bowler and batsman "bowled" looks far better than "lbw" in the score, and the obstinacy of such an expert as Frank Chester, regarded as the most sagacious, quickest and reliable umpire for many years, in declining to alter his attitude is more than surprising. Can it be that having given his decision he regarded the ball as "dead" before it reached the stumps?

Umpires in Australia often come under criticism. An incident in a district game at Melbourne last October shows that clear understanding of the laws is just as necessary as practical knowledge of the game. In the case under notice Neil Harvey, the left hander, had scored 17 when a fast bowler hit the middle stump. Both bails flew into the air, but dropped into the grooves on the stumps. Harvey was on the way back to the pavilion when the umpire recalled him, saying that he was not out, his reason being that the bails must fall to the ground. Nothing in the laws makes this essential to dismissal. The bails might lodge in the wicket-keeper's pads or be caught by fieldsmen. If these suggestions seem to be stretching the point, they are mentioned to emphasise Law 31, which reads: "The wicket shall be held to be 'down' if either ball or striker's bat or person completely removes either bail from the top of the stumps", etc.

Note to this law: "A wicket is not 'down' merely on account of disturbance of a bail, but it is 'down' if a bail in falling from the wicket lodges between two of the stumps". Surely this applied to the case in question when the "bails" flew into the air".

WARWICKSHIRE v WEST INDIES

Played at Birmingham, August 9, 10, 11, 1950

Warwickshire won by three wickets. The only county side to beat West Indies in 1950, they owed their success mainly to the splendid fast-medium bowling of Grove, who at the age of 38 achieved his best performance in first-class cricket by taking eight wickets for 38. On a greenish pitch Grove moved the ball either way and he claimed the first five wickets that fell for 97. Marshall batted stubbornly for two hours and Williams and Jones hit boldly, but Warwickshire fielded splendidly, Spooner, Dollery and Hollies all making fine catches. Taylor, the New Zealander, shaped well in each county innings, but the real mastery was established by Wolton and Spooner, whose stand realised 123. Wolton drove strongly, being specially severe on Valentine. Hollies caused West Indies most trouble in their second innings. Although Warwickshire wanted only 95 they experienced great difficulty in hitting off the runs on a sporting pitch. In thirty-five minutes before lunch, Gardner and Thompson could score only eight, but their opening stand produced 34. Dollery fell to a magnificent right-hand catch, but Taylor remained firm, and amidst scenes of tremendous enthusiasm Pritchard made the winning hit. Fifty thousand people saw the match. This was the first victory by any county side over a touring team since Worcestershire beat the South Africans in the opening match in 1947.

West Indies

J. B. Stollmeyer c Spooner b Grove	17	– lbw b Grove	29
A. F. Rae c Spooner b Grove	1	– c Kardar b Pritchard	28
F. M. Worrell b Grove	29	– c Dollery b Pritchard	46
R. Marshall c and b Grove	33	– c Pritchard b Hollies	9
C. L. Walcott c Dollery b Grove	14	– lbw b Hollies	41
K. B. Trestrail b Grove	0	– b Hollies	28
R. J. Christiani c Hollies b Pritchard	4	– st Spooner b Hollies	18
C. B. Williams c Taylor b Kardar	21	– lbw b Hollies	0
P. E. Jones lbw b Grove	20	– not out	0
A. L. Valentine b Grove	5	– lbw b Pritchard	1
L. H. Pierre not out	0	– b Hollies	0
B 9, l-b 2, n-b 1	12	B 15, l-b 5, n-b 2	22
	156		222

Warwickshire

F. C. Gardner c Worrell b Pierre	8	– hit wkt b Valentine	13
J. R. Thompson c Stollmeyer b Jones	26	– c Worrell b Jones	16
Donald Taylor c Rae b Worrell	24	– not out	36
J. S. Ord c Trestrail b Jones	7	– lbw b Pierre	1
H. E. Dollery lbw b Valentine	3	– c Jones b Valentine	0
A. V. Wolton b Pierre	89	– b Pierre	5
R. T. Spooner not out	66	– c Walcott b Valentine	3
A. H. Kardar b Jones	5	– b Valentine	8
T. L. Pritchard c Christiani b Valentine	15	– not out	4
C. W. Grove b Valentine	11		
W. E. Hollies c Marshall b Valentine	6		
B 9, l-b 14, n-b 1	24	B 8, l-b 1, w 1	10
	284	**(7 wkts)**	**96**

Warwickshire Bowling

	Overs	Mdns	Runs	Wkts	Overs	Mdns	Runs	Wkts
Pritchard	23	6	55	1	19	5	57	3
Grove	26.4	8	38	8	35	6	69	1
Hollies	14	3	39	—	29.3	12	57	6
Kardar	10	3	12	1	3	—	14	—
Donald Taylor					1	—	3	—

West Indies Bowling

	Overs	Mdns	Runs	Wkts	Overs	Mdns	Runs	Wkts
Pierre	15	—	57	2	5	1	17	2
Worrell	23	6	51	1				
Jones	31	10	66	3	21.4	4	33	1
Valentine	23	5	57	4	26	13	36	4
Williams	4	—	29	—				

Umpires: H. W. Parks and A. Skelding.

ENGLAND v WEST INDIES

Fourth Test Match

Played at The Oval, August 12, 14, 15, 16, 1950

West Indies won by an innings and 56 runs. Even a wonderful display by Hutton could not save England, and West Indies won the rubber by three matches to one, confirming their all-round superiority in emphatic style. For the first time in the series Denis Compton was available, but chances of England fielding a full-strength team were upset when Evans broke a thumb, Washbrook was injured in a county match, and Parkhouse developed a bad cold. Once again the selectors had to call on late substitutes. Sheppard was brought in after the team had been announced, and the day before the match Coxon, the Yorkshire bowler, was asked to attend. Some confusion arose, for Lowson, the Yorkshire batsman, was first chosen, but when the selectors heard that there was doubt about Bailey they changed their minds and selected a bowler. In fact, England fielded almost a completely new team. Brown took over the captaincy from Yardley, and Hutton, Sheppard, Compton, Bailey, McIntyre, Hilton and Wright replaced Washbrook, Parkhouse, Insole, Shackleton, Evans, Jenkins and Hollies. That left only Simpson, Dewes and Bedser of the beaten Nottingham eleven. Coxon was twelfth man.

Goddard won the toss, making matters even in that respect, and, as events turned out, this became vitally important. It was soon obvious that the new England attack would fare no better than its predecessors, despite the fact that Wright bowled superbly. Rae and Stollmeyer scored slowly, and their opening stand produced 72 in one and three-quarter hours. Worrell was nearly dismissed before scoring, but Simpson's throw from mid-wicket to McIntyre went too high and the chance was lost. This proved very costly, for the second wicket put on 172. Rae remained as solid as ever and took five hours to score 109.

Worrell did not show anything like the same skill as at Nottingham in the previous Test, and, indeed, batted like a man out of form. The batsmen were handicapped because the ball came slowly off the pitch and for most of the time played it far higher up the bat than usual. When Rae left at half-past five, England faced the prospect of the last hour bowling to Worrell and Weekes, but Weekes, too, did not show his best form, and he hit a long-hop into the hands of mid-off, giving Wright his only success off one of the extremely rare bad balls he sent down that day.

On Monday, Worrell took three-quarters of an hour over six runs, but his slowness was explained when he retired through an attack of giddiness due to stomach trouble. Walcott and Christiani did not last long, but England were checked by Gomez and Goddard, who put on 109, and their partnership, lasting two hours, gave Worrell time to recover. The sight of Worrell resuming his innings at 446 for six must have been a heart-breaking moment for the England team, but he added only 22 runs. Worrell batted five hours five minutes for 138 and hit seventeen 4s.

Hutton and Simpson making little effort to score during the last seventy minutes obtained 29 runs, but Simpson, when four, might have been caught off Jones at first slip. Next day the grim fight for runs continued, and when Simpson left after two hours twenty minutes only 73 runs were on the board. Sheppard did not inspire confidence during a short stay, and at 120 for two Compton joined Hutton.

Compton took some time to fathom the wiles of Ramadhin and Valentine, but Hutton never looked in trouble and he completed his first 100 of the tests in four and a quarter hours. Then he opened out and brought off many scorching cover drives. Compton showed increasing confidence and all looked to be going well when tragedy occurred. Their stand of 109 ended when Compton was run out. Hutton turned a ball to leg and Compton ran. Hutton started, but checked himself and refused the call. Compton, instead of turning back, ran on and was out by half the length of the pitch.

Rain held up play for an hour and Dewes left soon afterwards, but Hutton remained all day and was 160 not out at the close. Heavy overnight and morning rain followed by warm sunshine made the pitch treacherous on Wednesday and the early play was packed with drama. Everything hinged on whether England's last six wickets could score 72 more runs to make West Indies bat on the difficult surface. England failed by ten.

Hutton again rose magnificently to the occasion, but he lost partners rapidly against balls which lifted and turned nastily after the first few overs. Wright, the last man, joined Hutton with 28 still wanted to save the follow-on. Hutton took most of the bowling and excitement became intense as the runs slowly came, but at length Wright was lbw and England were made to bat again 159 behind. Hutton carried his bat for 202 and did not give a single chance during his stay of seven hours fifty minutes. He hit twenty-two 4s in the highest innings ever played against West Indies in England. It beat his own 196 made at Lord's in 1939. Nobody who saw his effort of concentration and perfect stroke play will forget the great attempt he made to save his country.

Hutton immediately went in again and, not unnaturally, this time he failed. The England innings was almost a procession. At tea-time the score stood at 70 for four, and the match was over three-quarters of an hour later. Sheppard made a brave show lasting two hours, but nobody else reached 20. The sixth, seventh and eighth wickets all fell at 83, the left-arm spinners of Valentine being almost unplayable. Because of a strained groin Worrell did not bowl or field on the last day, but he was not really wanted because Goddard filled the breach admirably with his sharp off-breaks delivered at medium pace. The West Indies fielded splendidly, notably Weekes at slip and short-leg. In the match Weekes held five catches and Trestrail, who acted as deputy for Worrell, made two catches.   L.S.

West Indies

A. F. Rae b Bedser 109
J. B. Stollmeyer lbw b Bailey 36
F. M. Worrell lbw b Wright 138
E. Weekes c Hutton b Wright 30
C. L. Walcott b Wright 17
G. E. Gomez c McIntyre b Brown 74
R. J. Christiani c McIntyre b Bedser 11
J. D. Goddard not out 58

P. E. Jones b Wright 1
S. Ramadhin c McIntyre b Wright 3
A. L. Valentine b Bailey 9
    B 5, l-b 11, n-b 1 17
                                     503

1/72 2/244 3/295 4/318 5/337
6/446 7/480 8/483 9/490

England

L. Hutton not out ....202 – c Christiani b Goddard 2
R. T. Simpson c Jones b Valentine .... 30 – b Ramadhin 16
D. S. Sheppard b Ramadhin .... 11 – c Weekes b Valentine 29
D. C. S. Compton run out .... 44 – c Weekes b Valentine 11
J. G. Dewes c Worrell b Valentine .... 17 – c Christiani b Valentine 3
T. E. Bailey c Weekes b Goddard .... 18 – lbw b Ramadhin 12
F. R. Brown c Weekes b Valentine .... 0 – c Stollmeyer b Valentine 15
A. J. McIntyre c and b Valentine .... 4 – c sub b Ramadhin 0
A. V. Bedser lbw b Goddard .... 0 – c Weekes b Valentine 0
M. J. Hilton b Goddard .... 3 – c sub b Valentine 0
D. V. P. Wright lbw b Goddard .... 4 – not out 6
    B 5, l-b 6 11   B 6, l-b 3 9

1/73 2/120 3/229 4/259 5/310   344   1/2 2/39 3/50 4/56 5/79   103
6/315 7/321 8/322 9/326   6/83 7/83 8/83 9/85

England Bowling

	Overs	Mdns	Runs	Wkts
Bailey	34.2	9	84	2
Bedser	38	9	75	2
Brown	21	4	74	1
Wright	53	16	141	5
Hilton	41	12	91	—
Compton	7	2	21	—

West Indies Bowling

	Overs	Mdns	Runs	Wkts	Overs	Mdns	Runs	Wkts
Jones	23	4	70	—				
Worrell	20	9	30	—				
Ramadhin	45	23	63	1	26	11	38	3
Valentine	64	21	121	4	26.3	10	39	6
Gomez	10	3	24	—	8	4	6	—
Goddard	17.4	6	25	4	9	4	11	1

Umpires: W. H. Ashdown and F. S. Lee.

GLOUCESTERSHIRE v WEST INDIES

Played at Cheltenham, August 19, 21, 1950

West Indies won by an innings and 105 runs. This match provided yet another triumph for young Ramadhin. In his best bowling performance of the tour he took eight wickets for 15 runs in the Gloucestershire first innings and finished with the remarkable match analysis of thirteen wickets for only 51 runs. Heavy rain delayed the start until 2.45 p.m., and then Stollmeyer put in the county. Johnson and Gomez claimed the first two wickets before Ramadhin, going on at 31 proceeded to bring the innings to a close. In one spell of eleven balls he took four wickets without conceding a run, and would up with four wickets in ten balls for four runs. He did not bowl a loose ball, and by cleverly disguised finger spin he turned his deliveries sharply either way. West Indies lost their opening pair for 39 before Weekes and Walcott took charge. Not out 64 on Saturday, Walcott by powerful back play hit magnificently to leg besides excelling with the off-drive. His defence proved very sound and, batting three and a half hours, he hit eighteen 4s. Mortimore, 17 years old, deputised for Goddard and, bowling off-breaks, showed considerable promise, but the best bowling for Gloucestershire was done by Cook, left-arm slow. Ramadhin threatened to run through the county a second time until Valentine intervened and ended the one-sided encounter by taking the last four wickets for seven runs.

Gloucestershire

G. M. Emmett b Ramadhin	26	– c Stollmeyer b Johnson	9
Sir D. Bailey c Christiani b Johnson	1	– st Christiani b Ramadhin	6
B. O. Allen c and b Gomez	2	– c Weekes b Ramadhin	5
T. W. Graveney b Ramadhin	19	– c Stollmeyer b Ramadhin	23
D. M. Young lbw b Ramadhin	0	– c Williams b Valentine	30
A. E. Wilson b Ramadhin	0	– b Ramadhin	0
C. A. Milton c Weekes b Ramadhin	0	– st Christiani b Ramadhin	2
G. E. Lambert c Weekes b Ramadhin	13	– c Christiani b Valentine	1
J. K. Graveney c Trestrail b Ramadhin	0	– b Valentine	9
C. Cook lbw b Ramadhin	0	– c Gomez b Valentine	1
J. Mortimore not out	4	– not out	5
B 4	4	L-b 6	6
	69		**97**

West Indies

R. E. Marshall c Lambert b Cook	19	C. B. Williams c Allen b Mortimore	0
J. B. Stollmeyer lbw b Lambert	0	H. H. Johnston st Wilson b Cook	2
C. L. Walcott b Mortimore	126	S. Ramadhin c sub b Cook	0
E. Weekes c Bailey b Cook	57	A. L. Valentine not out	9
K. B. Trestrail c Wilson b Lambert	0	B 9, l-b 1, n-b 1	8
R. J. Christiani b Mortimore	23		
G. E. Gomez c Milton b Cook	27		**271**

West Indies Bowling

	Overs	Mdns	Runs	Wkts	Overs	Mdns	Runs	Wkts
Johnson	9	4	10	1	9	3	11	1
Gomez	9	5	16	1	4	1	5	—
Valentine	7	2	24	—	17.2	6	31	4
Ramadhin	6.4	2	15	8	19	6	36	5
Weekes					2	—	8	—

Gloucestershire Bowling

	Overs	Mdns	Runs	Wkts
Lambert	20	4	72	2
J. Graveney	19	4	69	—
Cook	24.4	8	60	5
Mortimore	18	3	62	3

Umpires: C. H. Welch and T. Spence.

ESSEX v WEST INDIES

Played at Southend, August 23, 24, 25, 1950

West Indies won by seven wickets. Led on the first innings, West Indies fought back well and gained victory with five minutes to spare. Essex began splendidly with an opening partnership of 126 between Dodds and Avery, who mixed restraint and aggressiveness judiciously against a varied attack and well-placed field. Dodds drove and pulled strongly and showed admirable concentration in defence. Making his first century of the season, he batted four hours and hit ten 4s. Ramadhin and Gomez, who bowled his off-breaks with skill, completely perplexed most of the batsmen, and the last five wickets fell for 39 runs. The West Indies first innings followed a similar pattern, for Christiani and Stollmeyer began with a partnership of 104, but the last six wickets added only 28 runs. Bailey, bowling with the aid of a strong wind, took five wickets for 13 runs after lunch on the second day, but heavy rain caused a long delay late in the afternoon, and Gomez and Ramadhin made good use of the drying pitch on the final day. West Indies were left two hours ten minutes to score 186, and they succeeded largely because of a stand of 97 in fifty-five minutes between Weekes and Christiani. During the match Ray Smith of Essex completed the "double" of 1,000 runs and 100 wickets, a feat he alone accomplished during the season.

Essex

T. C. Dodds b Ramadhin	106	– run out 25
A. V. Avery c Jones b Stollmeyer	52	– c Stollmeyer b Ramadhin 18
D. J. Insole b Ramadhin	0	– lbw b Gomez 18
R. Horsfall b Ramadhin	15	– b Gomez 17
E. A. Stanley b Gomez	3	– st Walcott b Ramadhin 25
T. E. Bailey lbw b Gomez	3	– lbw b Gomez 5
F. H. Vigar b Ramadhin	1	– lbw b Ramadhin 11
R. Smith c Rae b Gomez	6	– b Gomez 1
T. P. B. Smith run out	19	– c Weekes b Gomez 18
T. H. Wade c Stollmeyer b Gomez	3	– c Gomez b Ramadhin 19
K. C. Preston not out	1	– not out 5
B 14, l-b 6	20	B 5, l-b 2 7
	229	**169**

West Indies

R. J. Christiani c P. Smith b Preston	60	– not out	53
J. B. Stollmeyer hit wkt b P. Smith	43	– b Preston	16
K. B. Trestrail b R. Smith	8		
G. E. Gomez lbw b Bailey	46		
E. Weekes c Vigar b Preston	23	– not out	84
C. L. Walcott c Wade b Bailey	5	– c Wade b Preston	0
A. F. Rae c Preston b R. Smith	0	– c Bailey b R. Smith	30
C. B. Williams c P. Smith b Bailey	5		
P. E. Jones lbw b Bailey	2		
S. Ramadhin not out	4		
L. R. Pierre c Wade b Bailey	0		
B 11, l-b 6	17	B 1, l-b 2	3
	213		**(3 wkts) 186**

West Indies Bowling

	Overs	Mdns	Runs	Wkts	Overs	Mdns	Runs	Wkts
Pierre	7	—	17	—	3	—	14	—
Jones	10	1	38	—	7	3	9	—
Gomez	21	7	34	4	39	14	79	5
Williams	29	12	52	—	4	—	11	—
Ramadhin	37	16	53	4	25.5	9	49	4
Stollmeyer	3	—	15	1				

Essex Bowling

	Overs	Mdns	Runs	Wkts	Overs	Mdns	Runs	Wkts
Bailey	16.4	3	44	5	12	—	71	—
Preston	16	2	59	2	7	1	27	2
R. Smith	24	7	44	2	16.2	1	85	1
P. Smith	22	2	49	1				

Umpires: A. Skelding and E. Robinson.

MIDDLESEX v WEST INDIES

Played at Lord's, August 26, 28, 29, 1950

Chief honours went to Christiani, who enjoyed a distinction which hitherto belonged alone to George Headley by scoring two centuries in a match in England. Despite fine batting for two hours by Stollmeyer (ten 4s) and a stand of 85 between him and Weekes (eight 4s), West Indies began the last day 74 behind the Middlesex first innings total with eight men out. Then Christiani, cleverly contriving to get most of the bowling, shared with Johnson a stand of 96, a record for a West Indies ninth wicket in England. Valentine helped to put on 40, and Christiani took out his bat after two hours and a half batting marred only by a chance when 39. Specially good in drives and leg-side strokes, Christiani hit one 6 and twenty-one 4s – five of them in an over from Sims. When, thanks to a partnership of 103 by Dewes and Edrich, the county set the West Indies 178 to win in ninety-three minutes, Christiani, going in first, again played with enterprise, and he completed three figures a second time by hitting 13 in the last over of the game. His chief figures were fourteen 4s, and in the two innings he obtained 231 runs without being dismissed. Robertson (twelve 4s), driving and hitting to leg well, and Sharp, each of whom stayed four hours, were chiefly responsible for the Middlesex first innings total.

Middlesex

J. G. Dewes b Valentine	21	– lbw b Weekes		86
J. D. Robertson c Walcott b Johnson	105	– c and b Valentine		27
W. J. Edrich lbw b Johnson	8	– c and b Worrell		36
D. C. S. Compton b Goddard	38	– c Rae b Weekes		24
H. P. Sharp c Gomez b Valentine	72			
S. M. Brown st Walcott b Valentine	36	– not out		13
J. M. Sims b Johnson	1	– not out		20
J. J. Warr c Rae b Valentine	6			
M. L. Laws st Walcott b Valentine	1			
J. A. Young c Gomez b Goddard	14			
A. E. Moss not out	0			
B 6, l-b 2, n-b 1	9	L-b 2, w 1		3
	311		**(4 wkts dec.)**	**209**

West Indies

A. F. Rae c Laws b Moss	3			
J. B. Stollmeyer lbw b Sims	81			
R. Marshall b Sims	9	– lbw b Warr		9
F. M. Worrell b Warr	1	– not out		7
E. Weekes c Compton b Young	52	– st Laws b Young		7
C. L. Walcott c Laws b Young	7	– b Young		24
R. J. Christiani not out	131	– not out		100
G. E. Gomez c Laws b Young	7			
J. D. Goddard c Edrich b Compton	6			
H. H. Johnson c Warr b Sims	25			
A. L. Valentine lbw b Compton	2			
B 12, l-b 7	19	B 1		1
	343		**(3 wkts)**	**148**

West Indies Bowling

	Overs	Mdns	Runs	Wkts	Overs	Mdns	Runs	Wkts
Johnson	43	10	85	3	4	—	11	—
Gomez	19	5	45	—	17	4	36	—
Valentine	52.1	23	72	5	8	4	20	1
Marshall	20	7	51	—	9	1	41	—
Goddard	19	5	49	2				
Worrell					19	5	73	1
Weekes					4	—	25	2

Middlesex Bowling

	Overs	Mdns	Runs	Wkts	Overs	Mdns	Runs	Wkts
Warr	19	3	57	1	11	—	32	1
Moss	12	1	54	1	2	—	23	—
Sims	23	5	96	3				
Young	36	11	79	3	15	4	54	2
Compton	9	3	19	2	6	—	38	—
Edrich	3	—	19	—				

Umpires: D. Davies and C. H. Welch.

HOW WEST INDIES CRICKET GREW UP

By Learie N. Constantine

The West Indies have been close to England for a long time by virtue of the relationship and status of Colonies. Even at cricket England has stood in the unassailable position of parent and tutor; the fact that the parent can now be beaten at her own game has never altered the relationship. But West Indies cricket has grown up and in the summer of 1950 reached a peak that it has since striven to maintain, but without success.

We like to think in my family that when cricket was born in the West Indies a Constantine was there as chief midwife. Test match status was not granted to the West Indies until after 1928, but I was included in a West Indies side that toured England in 1923 and my father did the same on two previous occasions many years before that. Trinidad was discovered by Columbus in 1492 and by the MCC in 1895; when I discovered England in 1923 there had already been quite a lot of cricket between the two countries.

In my boyhood there was an enthusiasm for cricket in Trinidad such as I have seldom seen equalled anywhere else in the world. My father set the family to work to make a private pitch from rolled clay covered with matting; it was the fashion everywhere and tremendous cricket battles were fought out between neighbouring families. My mother could keep wicket almost as well as a Test 'keeper; my sister had as much aptitude for batting as I had; one of my uncles was an international player and another was just as skilled. When we small boys were not playing in bigger games, we incessantly opposed each other, using oranges for balls and coconut branches for bats.

Such intense interest bred great young cricketers. I shall always remember watching two famous Trinidad clubs play a match during my boyhood. One of them, Stingo, boasted no less than seven bowlers in the International class. Stingo won the toss, and put in their rivals for the fun of skittling them out. But this time their opponents had prepared a surprise. The name of this rival club was Victoria, for which my father played, so you can guess where my sympathies lay. I could hardly bear to breathe as the Victoria opening pair took their places at the wicket. One was the "secret weapon", a slim and immature-looking boy called Wilton St Hill – alas! now no more. He was smoking as he walked out; he took his stance, still smoking, glanced idly round the field, then threw away his cigarette. George John – also now gone to the "great divide" – one of the most formidable fast bowlers who ever handled a ball, thundered up at the other end and sent down a red lightning flash – atomic if you wish – but the slender boy flicked his wrists and the ball flew to the boundary faster than sound. The next went the same way. The boy batted from his wrists; he never seemed to use any force. I don't believe he had the strength even if he so desired. His was just perfect timing. Wilton St Hill became famous later, but I never saw him or anyone else play a more heart-lifting innings than he did that day.

I began in club cricket in Trinidad when such men as St Hill, George Challoner, Pascal, Cumberbatch, Bertie Harragin, John Small, Dewhurst, Tarilton, Austin, C. R. Browne and my father were the great players of the day. Then came my selection for the 1923 voyage to England.

In the first games in England most of us youngsters found that we could not tell one white player from another. It was bewildering and annoying, especially when, as it seemed to us, people like Jack Hobbs, Andy Sandham, Ernest Tyldesley and Harry Makepeace, having been dismissed and sent back to the pavilion, immediately came walking out to bat again! It was many years after that I learnt that some English players shared the same thoughts and anguish about us.

The last match of that tour was the most exciting of all. At Scarborough, against what was really an All-England XI, we were twice put out for low scores on a nasty wicket and in the final knock our opponents needed only 31 runs to win. Hobbs, Stevens, Tyldesley, Rhodes, Chapman and Mann were sent back by John and Francis for 19 runs, and for a moment it looked as if we had a chance. Then some unfavourable lbw decisions robbed us of our hopes. Sir H. D. G. Leveson Gower stated later that it was mainly because of that terrific game that the West Indies won Test Match status for the next tour in 1928.

I was selected for that tour, also. We did not win a Test, but I shall always remember a match at Lord's against Middlesex. I had torn a muscle just previously and was ordered not to play. But we needed financial help and as our team-manager considered me a "drawing-card", he asked me if I could possibly manage to turn out. The doctor was very worried and said that if I played I must on no account do any bowling.

Middlesex, batting first, declared at 352 for six. We began with 79 for five; then I got 86 in fifty-five minutes and we managed a total of 230. After that, I *had* to bowl! I took six wickets for 11 in one spell and when we walked in after the innings closed, the members in the pavilion rose for me. Again our first five wickets went down for a poor score, but my star was in the skies; I made a century in an hour and we won by three wickets. As we walked in, the members rose for me a second time, as they did for Keith Miller last summer.

I was with the first West Indies side to tour Australia. That was in 1930-31 and I shall never forget it. Being a "drawing-card" is an exacting business. For example, during this tour of 15 games I played in 14 and rested once. In one big match I took six for 45 and made 59 in thirty-five minutes including four 6s; and in another a century in fifty minutes. I also had the pleasure of clean-bowling Sir Don Bradman and Stan McCabe on the same day. But far more important to me and to us all was the terrific thrill of beating Australia in the final Test. That, too, made history for my country.

In the autumn of 1934 came on of the happiest events of my life – an invitation to visit India and play in the Gold Cup Tournament. I stayed in a Maharajah's palace for a few days amidst such beauty and luxury as had seemed formerly to belong only to dreams – gold coaches, gold chairs, diamonds, turquoises, sapphires, ivories and silks. I found Indian cricketers equal to the best in the world in technique and invariably sporting and cheerful, however the game went. I was amazed and impressed at the fine condition of many of the Indian cricket grounds, and even more by the magnificent enthusiasm of both players and non-players for their country's fortunes.

I went back to the West Indies for the 1934 Tests against England. Wyatt, the English skipper, said publicly that his side was the strongest ever sent to visit us. It included Hammond, Hendren, Ames, Iddon, Holmes, Leyland, Farnes and others as good: I doubt whether any team as powerful has visited the West Indies since. I did not reach home in time to play in the first Test, which England won, but in the second, bowling the last over of the match, I took the final English wicket with my fifth ball with sixteen seconds to go! For the second time in history, West Indies had beaten England in a Test Match – and my hand had discharged the fatal missile.

The next Test was drawn and the fourth and final one provided another terrific thrill – more than one, in fact. First, Wyatt, the England captain, was knocked out and had to leave the match in the hands of a deputy. Then Grant, our skipper, sprained an ankle at a critical point of the game, and so the Test deputy-captaincy fell on me. But again our fortunes were in the ascendant and once more a ball from me took the last wicket; this time we had won a rubber against England and for the first time.

I was back again in Test cricket in 1939 just before World War II began. In fact, as an "old man" (as cricketers go) I made 79 in fifty-five minutes and took five for 75 beneath the silvery barrage-balloons that were already floating over The Oval ground. Then our team had to cut short its tour and get home as best it could the long way round via Glasgow and Montreal, with the U-boats already hunting the seas for victims.

Big cricket for me ended with the sunny pre-war era when nobody had heard of atom bombs and when cricket could compete for the headlines. But West Indian cricket has gone from strength to strength. Such names as Worrell, Weekes, Ramadhin, Valentine, Walcott, Rae, Stollmeyer and Gomez and many more have rung around the world. Records have been gleefully made in the sunshine on many a green field; Test matches have been doggedly fought; Commonwealth countries have played each other and also challenged on equal terms the might of England and, I think it just to say, covered themselves with honour.

Even as an old man in his fifties I, myself, can go and cheer at such games – and I can add a little more to my store of cricket knowledge. It all comes in useful, especially at such times as three years ago when I went out to Ceylon on a coaching and cricket-lecturing tour. There are some grand young players coming on in Ceylon; they are well worth watching. Some are now engaged in English League cricket, enlarging and cementing the philosophy of Commonwealth solidarity.

Of English cricket I would say that on its showing against Australia and South Africa the standard is improving rapidly. Never let anyone tell you that the heroes of yesterday's English cricket will never be equalled. I know so many of them so well and they are the first to laugh at such a statement and to say that cricket, like other forms of sport, should and will steadily *improve*. We old fellows who set up records made them for youngsters to break, just as we broke our predecessors' records whenever we could.

The West Indies tour of England in 1950 stands out as the finest in our history. Whether we shall be able to repeat the performances and win the rubber again, I have grave doubts. Ramadhin and Valentine, I suspect will be there. The terrible trio – Worrell, Weekes and Walcott – will also be there. Goddard has accepted the captaincy and will lead the side. His task will not be as simple as in 1950 when English cricket was struggling to shake off the effects of the years the war had eaten. Nevertheless, the material at his disposal will be good and if England maintains its progress under May, a terrific series of Tests should ensue, with the odds in favour of England.

MILESTONES IN WEST INDIES CRICKET

1842   Trinidad C.C. already "of very long standing".
1863   Kingston C.C. formed in Jamaica.
1864-5   Barbados and British Guiana met in first representative match.
1887-8   Philadelphians (USA) first overseas team to tour West Indies.
1891   First Triangular Tournament between Barbados, Trinidad and Demerara.
1894-5   First visit of an English team (captain R. S. Lucas).
1900   First West Indies team toured England.
1901-2   First matches of an English touring team (captain R. A. Bennett) against the combined West Indies.
1906   Second West Indies tour of England. S. G. Smith achieved "the double".
1910-11   First MCC team (captain A. F. Somerset) visited West Indies.
1923   Third West Indies team visited England.
1925-6   Second MCC team toured West Indies.
1927-8   G. A. Headley made his début, scoring 409 runs in five innings, with 211 (made out of 348) his highest, against Lord Tennyson's touring team.
1928   Fourth West Indies team toured England, playing Test matches for first time. England won all three.
1929-30   MCC visited West Indies, playing four Test matches in which G. A. Headley hit 176; 114 and 112 in the third; and 223. In winning at Georgetown, West Indies gained their first Test victory. A. Sandham, with 325 in the last, scored the first treble-century in Test cricket.
1930-1   West Indies toured Australia for first time.
1933   Fifth West Indies team to England.
1934-5   MCC toured West Indies. For the first time in history, West Indies won Test rubber.
1939   Sixth West Indies team to England.
1947-8   MCC visited West Indies and did not win any of their first-class engagements.

1950   Seventh West Indies team to England (captain J. D. Goddard). West Indies
          gained first Test victory in England and won rubber.
1951-2   Second West Indies team to Australia.
1952-3   First Indian team to West Indies.
1953-4   MCC team toured West Indies, drawing rubber. With 681 for eight wickets at
          Port of Spain, West Indies hit their highest Test total. A. L. Valentine (24)
          became youngest player to complete 100 Test match wickets.
1954-5   First Australian team visited West Indies; were first visiting side to win Test
          rubber in Caribbean.

ENGLAND v WEST INDIES
First Test Match

Played at Birmingham, May 30, 31, June 1, 3, 4, 1957

Drawn. The return of Test cricket to Edgbaston after an interval of 28 years produced one
of the most remarkable matches of all time. Blessed with fine weather throughout,
although the last day turned cold, the contest was notable for some excellent personal
performances and a wonderful recovery by England who seemed on the brink of defeat
when they began their second innings 288 behind. In the end, West Indies had their backs
to the wall and had to fight strenuously to ward off disaster.

Among the records set, the following were most notable:

(1) May and Cowdrey put on 411 together, a Test record for the fourth wicket: the
highest stand ever made for England and the third highest for any side in the history of
Test cricket. It fell 40 short of the highest – 451 by Bradman and Ponsford for the
Australian second wicket against England at The Oval in 1934. Roy and Mankad made
an opening stand of 413 for India against New Zealand at Madras in 1955-56.

(2) May's 285 not out was the best score by an England captain, surpassing
Hammond's 240 against Australia at Lord's in 1938. England's best against West Indies is
325 by Sandham at Kingston in 1930.

(3) May's 285 not out was his highest in first-class cricket and the highest individual
score in all post-war Test cricket, beating Compton's 278 v Pakistan at Nottingham in
1954.

(4) Cowdrey's 154 was his highest score in Test cricket and his first Test century in
England.

(5) Ramadhin, in his marathon performance, bowled 774 balls, the most delivered by a
bowler in a Test, beating Verity's 766 against South Africa at Durban in 1939. He also
bowled most balls (588) in any single first-class innings, including Tests, beating his
colleague Valentine who sent down 552 balls in the second innings against England at
Nottingham in 1950. The highest number of balls ever bowled by one man in a first-class
match was 917 by C. S. Nayudu for Holkar v Bombay in 1944-45.

(6) O. G. Smith gained the distinction of hitting a century on his first appearance
against England, a feat he had previously accomplished on his first appearance against
Australia at Kingston, Jamaica, in 1954-55. Denis Compton hit hundreds on début
against Australia, South Africa and West Indies.

England were fortunate when May won the toss for the twelfth time in sixteen matches. From the original thirteen players selected, they left out Graveney and Wardle and West Indies omitted Valentine.

Seldom can England have given such a disappointing exhibition on a perfect pitch. In four hours the whole side were dismissed for 186 and Ramadhin, with seven wickets for 49, had achieved his best performance in Test cricket.

Ramadhin kept his opponents guessing by his peculiar flick of the right wrist. None could tell his intention, whether he was attempting off spin or leg spin. As usual, he kept his shirt sleeves buttoned at the wrists and it was difficult to see how the ball left his right hand. He acquired very little spin and the majority of his wickets were taken with straight balls.

Gilchrist, a wiry, long-armed fast bowler, provided a contrast to Ramadhin. After lunch he bowled without relief for an hour and fifty minutes, maintaining a fiery pace for seventeen overs.

West Indies lost Pairaudeau to a yorker in Trueman's second over, but Rohan Kanhai and Walcott took command and saw the total to 83 for one wicket by the close of the first day. Early the next day, Walcott, stealing a single, pulled a leg muscle so severely that he collapsed and fainted. Soon he was compelled to have Pairaudeau as a runner and later in the innings Pairaudeau also acted as runner for Worrell. Further ill-luck overtook West Indies at another stage when Gilchrist went lame so that neither he nor Worrell could take part in the attack.

The second day produced an unfinished stand of 119 by O. G. Smith and Worrell. When Statham removed Kanhai with the first ball of the day, and later Walcott went for 90 and Sobers for 53, England were holding their own.

A wonderful slip catch by Bailey, who flung himself to his left and held with both hands a vicious cut, dismissed Sobers. Walcott showed much patience in an innings of four hours twenty minutes, but his punishing powers were revealed in the shape of eleven 4s. By mid-afternoon half the West Indies wickets had gone for 197. They were no more than 11 ahead and Trueman and Statham had the new ball. Here began the long stand by Smith and Worrell. Often each was beaten by the two pace bowlers, but they survived, taking the score to 316 for five wickets.

A record attendance for Edgbaston of 32,000 people saw the cricket on Saturday and still West Indies held the mastery. Indeed, the England bowlers toiled from 3.20 p.m. on Friday until 1.30 p.m. on Saturday before they managed to break the Smith–Worrell partnership of 190 made in five hours.

Pairaudeau occupied an abnormal amount of time in the middle for a man who scored only a single. He spent three and a quarter hours as runner for Walcott and then five hours for Worrell.

Even after Statham bowled Worrell with the last ball before lunch England had to wait another eighty-five minutes for their success. Altogether Smith stayed six hours and fifty-two minutes for his 161, being eighth out at 469. He hit one 6 and eighteen 4s and scored quite quickly after completing his hundred.

When England batted a second time, West Indies had Hall and Asgarali as substitutes for Walcott and Worrell; later Alexander appeared for Gilchrist, who began the bowling with Atkinson. Ninety minutes elapsed before Ramadhin caused more consternation by deceiving Richardson and then bowling Insole in the next over.

Fortunately for England, Close, despite a blow on the left hand, defended resolutely and he and May raised the score to 102 for two wickets at the close of the third day.

Monday was memorable for the feat of May in batting all day and, excepting the first twenty minutes, Cowdrey was with him the whole time. It was a tremendous struggle. Both found the answer to Ramadhin by playing forward to him. His analysis for the day read: 48 overs, 20 maidens, 74 runs, 0 wickets. At the close England were 378 for three wickets; May 193, Cowdrey 78. While May took four hours ten minutes to reach three figures, Cowdrey, avoiding all risks, completed 50 out of 160 in three hours forty minutes.

As the wonderful partnership ripened on the last day many new cricket records were established. With the position still critical, defence remained the prime objective. Just after one o'clock Cowdrey completed his century in seven and three-quarter hours and thereupon he changed his tactics, driving and cutting powerfully so that his third fifty came in fifty-five minutes.

At length, Asgarali caught Cowdrey at long on. The stand had lasted eight hours twenty minutes, Cowdrey having hit sixteen 4s and 63 singles. In the next half-hour May and Evans put on 59 more runs before May declared. Beginning his match-saving effort at 5.40 p.m. on Saturday, May batted till 3.20 p.m. on Tuesday, and helped to change the total from 65 for two wickets to 583 for four. No man could have done more for England than the captain, whose record innings of 285 not out lasted five minutes short of ten hours. May hit two 6s, twenty-five 4s and 111 singles. The perfect stylist and excelling with the cover drive, he made very few false strokes for such a long stay.

Both Ramadhin and Atkinson bowled tirelessly. West Indies used only two balls throughout the innings, the first being changed after 96 overs so that 162 overs were bowled with the second.

After their gruelling time in the field, West Indies, set to make 296 in two hours twenty minutes, lost Kanhai and Pairaudeau to Trueman for only nine runs. Then with the fielders clustered round the batsmen, Laker and Lock ran riot, seven wickets going for 68 runs, but Goddard, the captain, defended solidly for forty minutes, constantly putting his pads to the ball, and Atkinson was there for the final seven minutes.

No doubt May could have declared when Cowdrey left, but having seen his side out of trouble he was not prepared to give West Indies the slightest chance of success. Attendance 64,968; receipts £29,496. N.P.

England

P. E. Richardson c Walcott b Ramadhin	47	– c sub b Ramadhin	34
D. B. Close c Rohan Kanhai b Gilchrist	15	– c Weekes b Gilchrist	42
D. J. Insole b Ramadhin	20	– b Ramadhin	0
P. B. H. May c Weekes b Ramadhin	30	– not out	285
M. C. Cowdrey c Gilchrist b Ramadhin	4	– c sub b Smith	154
T. E. Bailey b Ramadhin	1		
G. A. R. Lock b Ramadhin	0		
T. G. Evans b Gilchrist	14	– not out	29
J. C. Laker b Ramadhin	7		
F. S. Trueman not out	29		
J. B. Statham b Atkinson	13		
B 3, l-b 3	6	B 23, l-b 16	39

1/32 2/61 3/104 4/115 5/116   186   1/63 2/65   (4 wkts dec.) 583
6/118 7/121 8/130 9/150   3/113 4/524

West Indies

Rohan Kanhai lbw b Statham	42	– c Close b Trueman	1
B. H. Pairaudeau b Trueman	1	– b Trueman	7
C. L. Walcott c Evans b Laker	90	– c Lock b Laker	1
E. D. Weekes b Trueman	9	– c Trueman b Lock	33
G. Sobers c Bailey b Statham	53	– c Cowdrey b Lock	14
O. G. Smith lbw b Laker	161	– lbw b Laker	5
F. M. Worrell b Statham	81	– c May b Lock	0
J. D. Goddard c Lock b Laker	24	– not out	0
D. Atkinson c Statham b Laker	1	– not out	4
S. Ramadhin not out	5		
R. Gilchrist run out	0		
B 1, l-b 6	7	B 7	7

1/4 2/83 3/120 4/183 5/197   474   1/1 2/9 3/25   (7 wkts) 72
6/387 7/466 8/469 9/474   4/27 5/43 6/66 7/68

West Indies Bowling

	Overs	Mdns	Runs	Wkts	Overs	Mdns	Runs	Wkts
Worrell	9	1	27	—				
Gilchrist	27	4	74	2	26	2	67	1
Ramadhin	31	16	49	7	98	35	179	2
Atkinson	12.4	3	30	1	72	29	137	—
Sobers					30	4	77	—
Smith					26	4	72	1
Goddard					6	2	12	—

England Bowling

	Overs	Mdns	Runs	Wkts	Overs	Mdns	Runs	Wkts
Statham	39	4	114	3	2	—	6	—
Trueman	30	4	99	2	5	3	7	2
Bailey	34	11	80	—				
Laker	54	17	119	4	24	20	13	2
Lock	34.4	15	55	—	27	19	31	3
Close					2	1	8	—

Umpires: E. Davies and C. S. Elliott.

ENGLAND v WEST INDIES
Third Test Match

Played at Nottingham, July 4, 5, 6, 8, 9, 1957

Drawn. This match will be remembered mainly for the feats of Graveney, Worrell and O. G. Smith. The Gloucestershire batsman, after so many disappointing Test displays, made 258, his highest score in first-class cricket, and Worrell and Smith clearly saved West Indies by brilliant and determined centuries. There were two other hundreds – by Peter Richardson and May – and Goddard played a match-saving defensive innings for West Indies on the last day.

For most of the five days bowlers experienced a lean time in a heat-wave. Only nine wickets fell on the first three days while 914 runs were scored. Thunderstorms on Saturday evening and on Sunday drenched the ground, but the pitch was firm when West Indies resumed their first innings promptly on time on Monday. They broke down before Trueman, but following on 247 behind, kept England in the field until after tea on Tuesday. England wanted 121 in the final hour, a task that proved impossible.

Two factors told against England. They dropped Lock from their original twelve which left them with only four front-line bowlers who were reduced to three when Bailey ricked his back. Secondly, having shown the highest standard of ground fielding, England later missed at least five possible chances when West Indies were struggling to avoid defeat.

As usual when batsmen shine at Trent Bridge the pitch came in for a deal of mixed criticism. It was a beauty and remained in perfect order to the end. No doubt, it benefited from the week-end rain which it readily absorbed. With West Indies collapsing, it was rolled twice before lunch on Monday so that not even in the later stages did it become dusty or responsive to spin.

England were fortunate to win the toss in such excellent conditions, but they suffered an early reverse when D. V. Smith nibbled at a short ball in Worrell's third over. Then came Graveney at 11.45 p.m. on Friday and he was not dismissed until 2.20 p.m. on Saturday, during which time he not only hit his first Test century in twenty-two appearances in England but went on to score 258.

Except when he opened his score in lofting Worrell close to backward short leg,

Graveney rarely looked in trouble. He drove with tremendous power, making the fullest use of his height. Fourth out at 510, he batted for seven hours fifty-five minutes and altogether hit thirty 4s.

Richardson, who excelled with the cut and pull, made his 126 (ten 4s) in four hours forty minutes, his stand of 266 with Graveney being the highest for England's second wicket against West Indies. The bowling was thoroughly mastered when May joined Graveney and the crowd greatly enjoyed seeing these two artists together.

The end of the first day found England 360 for two wickets; Graveney 188, May 40. The two batsmen continued in the same vein until O. G. Smith, in only his sixth over of the innings, dismissed May leg-before at 487. The England captain scored his faultless 104 (fourteen 4s) in just over three hours.

Whereas Ramadhin and Valentine were innocuous, Smith also disposed of Graveney so that in eleven overs he claimed two wickets for only 14 when over 500 runs were on the board. It was at this stage that Derek Richardson began his first innings as an England player. Staying seventy minutes, he left no doubt as to his promise. Later, when Cowdrey and Evans were punishing the tired bowlers, Ramadhin limped off the field with a strained leg muscle.

West Indies had toiled manfully for ten hours when May declared at the tea interval. They wanted 470 to avoid a follow-on and introduced a new pair of opening batsmen in Worrell and the tall left-handed Sobers. Both rose to the occasion and at the close of the second day West Indies were 59 for no wicket.

Worrell went on to bat all through Saturday, waging a remorseless battle with his colleagues against some splendid bowling and excellent fielding. Laker, in particular, served England admirably. Laker broke the opening stand at 87, after Sobers had defended carefully for two and three-quarter hours, and just before lunch he held a high return from Walcott with the left hand, but another three hours passed before England gained their next success, during which time Kanhai helped Worrell to put on 129.

For the first five hours on Saturday West Indies averaged no more than 30 runs an hour compared with England's steady 60 earlier in the match, but in the last hour Weekes took command with Worrell and they added 66, so that West Indies finished the third day 295 for three wickets; Worrell 145, Weekes 33.

The game underwent a big transformation on Monday. West Indies broke down so badly that they lost twelve wickets in less than six hours. Anxiety over the week-end rain rather than the wiles of Trueman, Statham and Laker − well as these three bowled − caused their downfall. The collapse began when Weekes, trying to hook the third ball of the day, was a shade too soon and it went off the back of a glove on to his wicket. Worrell proceeded to demonstrate that the bowling could be dealt with efficiently, but the loss of Weekes seemed to demoralise the other players and England captured the last seven first innings wickets for the addition of only 77 to Saturday's total. Trueman never made the ball lift or fly in a manner to cause alarm, but he did the main damage in the first hour when in seven overs he took five wickets for 11 runs − a very fine piece of sustained hostile bowling.

Ramadhin, who had Valentine as runner, stayed forty-five minutes while the last wicket put on 55. So Worrell carried his bat through an innings lasting just over nine and a half hours for 191 including twenty-six 4s. He was a tired man, but again opened with Sobers only to fall at the end of another hour to a very fine ball that moved in late. Worrell was on the field continuously from 11.30 a.m. on Thursday until 3.00 p.m. on Monday − altogether twenty and a half hours, probably the longest time any cricketer has endured.

When the first five West Indies second innings wickets fell for only 89, England seemed to be galloping to victory, but O. G. Smith, aided in turn by Atkinson and Goddard, applied the brake. Smith played a great innings for his side. Occasionally he indulged in carefree strokes, but for the most part he disciplined himself to the urgency of the occasion. He might well have gone during the last hour on Monday for when only 44 he was dropped on the square-leg boundary off Laker by Pressdee of Glamorgan who was acting substitute for Bailey.

But for that mistake England ought to have won with plenty of time to spare, but West Indies were still in a precarious position at the end of the fourth day when their score stood at 175 for five wickets; Smith 67, Atkinson 36.

With victory almost in sight, England saw their advantage gradually slip away as West Indies fought magnificently for a draw. Above everything else stood out the wonderful innings by O. G. Smith. He surpassed his 161 of the Edgbaston Test and, staying seven hours, was eighth out at 352 having hit three 6s and ten 4s. Just after midday, when Trueman and Statham took the new ball, Atkinson's superb effort of two and a half hours ended in a catch to Evans.

Nearly five and a half hours remained for play, and West Indies had only four wickets left when Goddard, their captain, arrived. He survived an early chance, when only six, off Statham to Evans, and later, when 47, was dropped twice in the same over off Laker by Trueman and Bailey. Unperturbed by these incidents, the left-handed Goddard batted heroically for three hours forty minutes while he and Smith added 154, a record for the West Indies' seventh wicket against England.

Even after Goddard left, England needed another half-hour to finish the innings, for Ramadhin was missed by Graveney at slip. With Bailey taking little part in the attack an abnormal amount of work fell on Trueman, Statham and Laker. All responded nobly.

With only 16 overs bowled in the final hour, England needed to average over seven runs an over and at no time did they look like accomplishing the task. They still wanted 57 when the umpires called time. Attendance 61,167, receipts £30,239.   N.P.

England

P. E. Richardson c Walcott b Atkinson	126	– c Kanhai b Gilchrist	11
D. V. Smith c Kanhai b Worrell	1	– not out	16
T. W. Graveney b Smith	258	– not out	28
P. B. H. May lbw b Smith	104		
M. C. Cowdrey run out	55		
D. W. Richardson b Sobers	33		
T. G. Evans not out	26		
T. E. Bailey not out	3		
B 1, l-b 10, w 1, n-b 1	13	B 7, l-b 2	9

1/14 2/280 3/487   (6 wkts dec.) 619   1/13   (1 wkt) 64
4/510 5/573 6/609

J. C. Laker, F. S. Trueman and J. B. Statham did not bat.

West Indies

F. M. Worrell not out	191	– b Statham	16
G. Sobers b Laker	47	– lbw b Trueman	9
C. L. Walcott c and b Laker	17	– c Evans b Laker	7
Rohan Kanhai c Evans b Bailey	42	– c Evans b Trueman	28
E. D. Weekes b Trueman	33	– b Statham	3
O. G. Smith c Evans b Trueman	2	– b Trueman	168
D. Atkinson c Evans b Trueman	4	– c Evans b Statham	46
J. D. Goddard c May b Trueman	0	– c Evans b Statham	61
R. Gilchrist c D. Richardson b Laker	1	– b Statham	0
A. L. Valentine b Trueman	1	– not out	2
S. Ramadhin b Statham	19	– b Trueman	15
B 5, l-b 10	15	B 2, l-b 10	12

1/87 2/120 3/229 4/295 5/297   372   1/22 2/30 3/39 4/56 5/89   367
6/305 7/305 8/314 9/317   6/194 7/348 8/352 9/365

West Indies Bowling

	Overs	Mdns	Runs	Wkts	Overs	Mdns	Runs	Wkts
Worrell	21	4	79	1	7	1	27	—
Gilchrist	29	3	118	—	7	—	21	1
Atkinson	40	7	99	1	1	—	1	—
Ramadhin	38	5	95	—				
Valentine	23	4	68	—				
Sobers	21	6	60	1				
Goddard	15	5	26	—	1	—	2	—
Smith	25	5	61	2				
Walcott					1	—	4	—

England Bowling

	Overs	Mdns	Runs	Wkts	Overs	Mdns	Runs	Wkts
Statham	28.4	9	78	1	41.2	12	118	5
Trueman	20	8	63	5	35	5	80	4
Laker	62	27	101	3	43	14	98	1
Bailey	28	9	77	1	12	3	22	—
Smith	12	1	38	—	12	5	23	—
Graveney					5	2	14	—

Umpires: F. S. Lee and J. S. Buller.

HAMPSHIRE v WEST INDIES

Played at Southampton, July 13, 15, 16, 1957.

Drawn. The three Hampshire seam bowlers, Shackleton, Heath and Gray, surprised West Indies on the first day when they dismissed them for 110 on a pitch which encouraged swing. With Gray also shaping splendidly with the bat, Hampshire enjoyed a lead of 17 with half their wickets in hand at the close on Saturday. Subsequently West Indies made a fine recovery. With Dewdney performing the hat-trick, Hampshire could add only 32 more runs and then Pairaudeau proceeded to make 163, the highest score of his career. Showing excellent style, he hit two 6s and twenty-nine 4s in a dazzling display which occupied him four hours and ten minutes. With Weekes and Walcott taking part in three-figures stands with Pairaudeau and Worrell completing a charming fifty, West Indies were able to set Hampshire to score 339 in five hours. Unfortunately, only seven more overs proved possible before rain brought a grand match to a premature conclusion.

West Indies

N. Asgarali run out	34	– lbw b Shackleton	5
A. Ganteaume lbw b Heath	0	– b Shackleton	4
B. H. Pairaudeau b Heath	3	– b Shackleton	163
E. D. Weekes b Gray	12	– lbw b Shackleton	62
C. L. Walcott st Harrison b Gray	4	– b Shackleton	34
G. Sobers not out	37	– c Eagar b Burden	11
O. G. Smith lbw b Shackleton	9	– lbw b Shackleton	1
F. M. Worrell lbw b Heath	8	– not out	56
F. C. M. Alexander b Shackleton	1	– b Shackleton	22
W. Hall b Heath	0	– b Heath	20
T. Dewdney c Eagar b Shackleton	1	– b Heath	0
L-b 1	1	B 4, l-b 4, n-b 1	9

1/11 2/23 3/42 4/52 5/54   110   1/4 2/31 3/163 4/265 5/282   387
6/64 7/81 8/86 9/91   6/288 7/288 8/352 9/387

Hampshire

R. E. Marshall b Worrell	11	– not out		18
J. R. Gray c Sobers b Dewdney	83	– not out		23
H. Horton b Dewdney	8			
E. D. R. Eagar b Sobers	14			
H. M. Barnard lbw b Sobers	0			
A. C. D. Ingleby-Mackenzie c Alexander b Hall	16			
P. J. Sainsbury not out	13			
L. Harrison b Sobers	5			
D. Shackleton c Alexander b Dewdney	0			
M. Heath b Dewdney	0			
M. D. Burden c Alexander b Dewdney	0			
B 3, l-b 2, n-b 4	9	N-b 2		2

1/32 2/55 3/82 4/82 5/113   159   (No wkt) 43
6/149 7/154 8/159 9/159

Hampshire Bowling

	Overs	Mdns	Runs	Wkts	Overs	Mdns	Runs	Wkts
Shackleton	18.5	10	31	3	37	11	103	7
Heath	21	4	58	4	30.4	9	114	2
Gray	13	6	20	2	9	1	46	—
Sainsbury					13	4	29	—
Burden					20	4	86	1

West Indies Bowling

	Overs	Mdns	Runs	Wkts	Overs	Mdns	Runs	Wkts
Hall	10	2	31	1	3	—	9	—
Worrell	16	2	41	1				
Dewdney	19.3	2	38	5	4	—	32	—
Sobers	18	9	40	3				

Umpires: A. E. Pothecary and L. H. Gray.

ENGLAND v WEST INDIES
Fourth Test Match

Played at Leeds, July 25, 26, 27, 1957

England won by an innings and five runs, the match being all over by a quarter to three on Saturday afternoon. This hollow victory gave England the rubber and brought personal distinction to Loader who, in taking nine wickets for 86 runs, performed the hat-trick when the West Indies, last four first innings wickets were taken in four balls. Trueman bowled O. G. Smith with the last ball of an over and then Loader removed Goddard, Ramadhin and Gilchrist.

It was only the second hat-trick accomplished by an Englishman in a home Test, the first being by J. T. Hearne against Australia and also at Leeds in 1899. At Manchester, in 1912, T. J. Matthews did the hat-trick twice on the same afternoon for Australia against South Africa in the first match of the Triangular tournament.

Loader, who had not played in the first three Tests, received his chance because Statham was injured and could not be considered for selection. When Bailey dropped out with a split hand, D. W. Richardson was added to the party and he duly became twelfth man. West Indies intended to include Dewdney but an abscess in the mouth put him in hospital and so Pairaudeau completed the eleven which included Alexander for the first time. Atkinson also was unfit.

A heavy overcast sky and stiff cross breeze made the conditions ideal for seam bowling on a well-marled pitch but few people could have anticipated such a poor batting performance by West Indies after Goddard had won the toss. Forty minutes passed while Worrell and the left-handed Sobers played cautiously against the accurate attack of Trueman and Loader who had eight fielders behind the striker.

May was just preparing for his first bowling change when Sobers turned Loader sharply and Lock, diving to his right, brought off an amazing catch at leg-slip. England appeared to have missed a great chance of dismissing Worrell cheaply when Richardson, by a brilliant pick-up at cover, cut off a sizzling drive which left Worrell stranded in mid-pitch, but in his excitement Richardson sent his return high above Evans's head.

Smith, the Sussex left-arm bowler, put in a very steady spell from the pavilion end and when Loader returned at the opposite end his late swing accounted for both Worrell and Weekes in the same over, the latter also being deceived by a subtle decrease of pace.

With three men out for 42, West Indies were in a bad position, but Rohan Kanhai and Walcott made a stubborn stand, raising the total to 112 for three at tea. Kanhai was treated to a very heavy dose of short-pitched balls by Trueman, but despite a painful blow on the back of the left hand which required strapping the young batsman faced up bravely to the rough treatment.

Laker broke the stand soon after the interval when for the third successive time in the series he deceived Walcott, Cowdrey holding a sharp slip catch. More resistance came from Kanhai and O. G. Smith in an appalling light and it was no surprise when, immediately Smith appealed to them, the umpires stopped the proceedings for nearly half an hour.

Again Laker effected a separation by getting Kanhai, who had defied England for nearly four hours, leg-before. Loader and Trueman took the new ball and in less than three overs the remaining five wickets fell. Trueman hit Pairaudeau's off-stump and bowled Smith round his legs via the pads in one over before Loader completed the rout with his hat-trick.

Worrell struck back for West Indies with a fine ball that swung across the left-handed D. V. Smith and took his off-stump so that England finished the day 11 for one. On Friday, Worrell bowled superbly and achieved his best performance with the ball by finishing with seven wickets for 70 runs. Valentine, Atkinson, Gomez and Ramadhin were the only other West Indies bowlers who had taken as many as seven wickets in a Test innings

A grey morning and occasional light showers made the conditions unpleasant for both sides. West Indies faced the handicap of bowling with a wet ball, which the umpires dried, but the turf recovered so well that no sawdust was required. Richardson left to the third ball of the morning, caught by the new Test wicket-keeper, and Graveney, after a few challenging strokes, was indisputably bowled by Gilchrist, who sent his middle stump flying. At this stage West Indies stood all square for England's first three wickets – like theirs – had gone for 42, but determined batting by May, Cowdrey and Sheppard turned the scales.

Sobers put in a very good spell of left-arm slow bowling, maintianing the attack from the Kirkstall end from 12.35 p.m. until 3.45 p.m., when the new ball was taken. During this period Sobers' analysis read 28-8-65-1, his solitary prize being May's wicket. May's quest for runs led to his undoing. He was using the cut and drive freely to pierce Sobers' packed off-side field when, essaying a cut, he gave Alexander his second catch of the day, May hit nine 4s.

The May-Cowdrey stand yielded 94 and Cowdrey and Sheppard followed with one of 91. Whereas Cowdrey never became fluent and hit only four 4s, Sheppard introduced a touch of sparkle to the cricket. Occasionally his timing lacked precision but he treated everyone to a fine variety of strokes. Beginning with four boundaries Sheppard swept to his 50 in ninety-five minutes and when seventh out at 264 he had made his 68 (ten 4s) in two hours twenty-five minutes compared with three hours forty minutes taken by Cowdrey over the same score and two hours thirty-five by May for 69.

West Indies were at the cross-roads when Worrell took the second new ball at 3.45 p.m. with England 179 for four wickets. From that point he bowled without relief to the end of the innings on the stroke of 6.30 p.m., his only respite coming from a ten minutes' break for rain and when another shower caused the tea interval to extend to half an hour. During that period Worrell's figures were 22.2-7-42-5. Actually the last five wickets fell for 52 runs, but England gained a valuable lead of 137 runs.

The introduction of Alexander as wicket-keeper brought a noticeable improvement in the West Indies fielding although their returns still fell a long way below the England standard. Rarely, indeed, have England proved so efficient in this vital part of the game and in this match particularly their splendid work went a long way towards keeping their opponents in subjection.

In fact the dramatic breakdown in the second innings came after another wonderful effort by Lock and again at the expense of Sobers. As patient methods failed them in their first innings West Indies seldom wasted a scoring opportunity when they batted a second time. During the innings they despatched the ball to the boundary nineteen times but the final result was the same. Sobers hooked and drove with such skill that he scored 20 from the first four overs. He saw Cowdrey dispose of Worrell with an excellent right-handed slip catch and then he himself was run out by Lock who, fielding between deep point and cover, swooped down on a peerless off-drive and, turning swiftly, landed the ball at the top of the stumps with Sobers helpless in the middle of the pitch.

After that incident, Walcott alone offered real resistance and by lunch time seven wickets were down for 108. Another half-hour sufficed to finish the match and give England their first rubber against West Indies since 1939.

Evans distinguished himself by not conceding a bye and in catching O. G. Smith he raised his number of dismissals in eighty Tests to 200, a figure far in excess of his nearest rival, the Australian, W. A. Oldfield, who claimed 130 victims in fifty-four Tests.

Although only 66,629 people were present during the three days, the receipts amounted to £27,100, including £20,600 taken in advance bookings, some for the fourth and fifth days. Attendance, 54,903; receipts, £28,164.   N. P.

West Indies

F. M. Worrell b Loader	29	– c Cowdrey b Trueman	7
G. Sobers c Lock b Loader	4	– run out	29
Rohan Kanhai lbw b Laker	47	– lbw b Loader	0
E. D. Weekes b Loader	0	– c Cowdrey b Trueman	14
C. L. Walcott c Cowdrey b Laker	38	– c Sheppard b Loader	35
O. G. Smith b Trueman	15	– c Evans b Smith	8
B. H. Pairaudeau b Trueman	6	– c Trueman b Loader	6
J. D. Goddard b Loader	1	– c Loader b Lock	4
F. C. M. Alexander not out	0	– b Laker	11
S. Ramadhin c Trueman b Loader	0	– run out	6
R. Gilchrist b Loader	0	– not out	6
L-b 2	2	L-b 5, n-b 1	6

1/16 2/42 3/42 4/112 5/125   142   1/40 2/40 3/49 4/56 5/71   132
6/139 7/142 8/142 9/142   6/92 7/103 8/112 9/122

England

P. E. Richardson c Alexander b Worrell	10	J. C. Laker c Alexander b Worrell 1
D. V. Smith b Worrell	0	F. S. Trueman not out.................. 2
T. W. Graveney b Gilchrist	22	P. J. Loader c Pairaudeau b Worrell....... 1
P. B. H. May c Alexander b Sobers	69	
M. C. Cowdrey c Weekes b Worrell	68	B 2, l-b 5, w 1 8
Rev. D. S. Sheppard c Walcott b Worrell	68	
T. G. Evans b Worrell	10	1/1 2/12 3/42 4/136 5/227 279
G. A. R. Lock b Gilchrist	20	6/239 7/264 8/272 9/278

England Bowling

	Overs	Mdns	Runs	Wkts	Overs	Mdns	Runs	Wkts
Trueman..........	17	4	33	2	11	—	42	2
Loader	20.3	9	36	6	14	2	50	3
Smith	17	6	24	—	4	1	12	1
Laker	17	4	24	2	6.2	1	16	1
Lock.............	14	6	23	—	1	—	6	1

West Indies Bowling

	Overs	Mdns	Runs	Wkts
Worrell	38.2	9	70	7
Gilchrist	27	3	71	2
Sobers............	33	8	79	1
Ramadhin.........	19	5	34	—
Smith	8	1	17	—

Umpires: D. Davies and J. S. Buller.

NEW ZEALANDERS IN ENGLAND

CAMBRIDGE UNIVERSITY v NEW ZEALANDERS

Played at Cambridge, May 18, 19, 20, 1949

New Zealand won by an innings and 50 runs. They never lost the firm grip obtained before lunch on the first day when seven Cambridge wickets fell for 45. By taking the first three wickets for five runs after changing ends, Hayes broke the back of the University batting. A stand of 61 between Popplewell and Stevenson alone prevented a complete rout. In turn the fast bowling of Warr gave the New Zealanders early shocks. His pace accounted for three wickets falling for 19. Any visions of a serious collapse were dispelled by a fourth-wicket stand of 324 between Reid and Wallace, who both narrowly missed a double hundred. In his fourth century of the tour Wallace (sixteen 4s) again batted splendidly. Reid went steadily till he reached 100. Then he hit with power all round, his strokes including twenty-three 4s. Cambridge showed more confidence in the second innings, when Morris, Doggart and Insole did best. Rabone bowled leg-breaks and googlies and he took five wickets for five runs each.

Cambridge University

J. G. Dewes b Hayes	8	– b Hayes	32
R. J. Morris lbw b Cresswell	19	– c Reid b Rabone	56
G. H. G. Doggart lbw b Hayes	2	– lbw b Cresswell	62
W. N. Coles b Hayes	0	– c Burtt b Cresswell	12
A. G. J. Rimell c Sutcliffe b Cresswell	7	– c Donnelly b Hayes	3
D. J. Insole st Reid b Burke	1	– not out	79
R. B. Hawkey c Reid b Cresswell	2	– b Rabone	13
M. H. Stevenson c Burke b Burtt	34	– lbw b Rabone	0
O. B. Popplewell st Reid b Burke	19	– b Rabone	3
B. J. K. Pryer b Burtt	1	– b Rabone	0
J. J. Warr not out	0	– b Rabone	0
B 7, l-b 7	14	B 3, l-b 5, w 8	16
	107		**284**

New Zealanders

B. Sutcliffe c Morris b Warr	2	M. P. Donnelly c Popplewell b Doggart 27
W. A. Hadlee c Popplewell b Warr	4	G. O. Rabone not out 1
J. R. Reid not out	188	B 8, l-b 2, w 2, n-b 1 13
F. B. Smith c Insole b Warr	9	
W. M. Wallace c Popplewell b Warr	197	(5 wkts dec.) 441

T. B. Burtt, C. C. Burke, J. A. Hayes and G. F. Cresswell did not bat.

New Zealanders Bowling

	Overs	Mdns	Runs	Wkts	Overs	Mdns	Runs	Wkts
Hayes	17	5	26	3	27	5	77	2
Cresswell	21	11	26	3	17	4	42	2
Burtt	14	11	5	2	24	9	50	—
Rabone	3	—	4	—	11	6	25	5
Burke	11.1	2	32	2	31	10	56	1
Sutcliffe					9	3	18	—

Cambridge University Bowling

	Overs	Mdns	Runs	Wkts
Warr.............	35	7	81	4
Hawkey	18	4	44	—
Insole	2	—	16	—
Pryer.............	17	2	69	—
Stevenson........	22	3	95	—
Doggart	15	3	62	1
Rimell............	17	4	37	—
Morris...........	8	1	24	—

Umpires: F. S. Lee and H. Palmer.

OXFORD UNIVERSITY v NEW ZEALANDERS

Played at Oxford, May 25, 26, 27, 1949

Oxford University won by 83 runs. The New Zealanders suffered their only defeat of the tour through their inability to master the lively, quick bowling of Wrigley and Whitcombe on a pitch drying out after a flooding. Oxford deserved success if only for the many brilliant catches they held. Without Cowie, the New Zealanders, especially on the first day, were unable to take full advantage of conditions strange to many of them. Hofmeyr, who resisted their attack for five hours, carried his bat for 95, and even the fall of the last five wickets for 33 — three in one over to Rabone — did not disturb his placid play. The New Zealanders lost three men for 67 before the close. The second day produced remarkable cricket. Twenty-two wickets fell for 160. With the pitch at its worst and the ball often flying both the New Zealanders and Oxford batsmen were in severe trouble. The plucky innings of Wallace, who was struck twice on the right thumb, and the hard hitting of Winn were fine efforts at critical times. Burtt, in his element, took six Oxford wickets for 18, and Rabone at slip held five catches. When the New Zealanders lost half their second innings wickets for 45 the issue seemed settled, and on the last morning the University, thanks to more splendid pace bowling, won the match before lunch. Kardar in the gully helped with two grand catches off fierce slashes. Wallace and Donnelly made a gallant but vain effort in an eighth wicket stand of 49.

Oxford University

M. B. Hofmeyr not out 95	– c Rabone b Hayes	0
B. Boobbyer b Cave 5	– c Hadlee b Burtt................	8
C. E. Winn c Scott b Rabone 58	– b Burtt	37
C. B. Van Ryneveld b Hayes.................. 16	– c Mooney b Cave	1
D. B. Carr b Cave........................... 34	– c Rabone b Burtt	0
A. H. Kardar b Smith 8	– c Reid b Burtt.................	7
P. A. Whitcome b Rabone 6	– c Rabone b Burtt	4
J. Wiley b Rabone........................... 6	– c Rabone b Hayes	0
J. A. G. C. Law b Rabone..................... 0	– c Rabone b Cave	0
G. H. Chesterton c Reid b Rabone 0	– not out	10
M. H. Wrigley b Hayes....................... 4	– c Hadlee b Burtt	0
B 11, l-b 2, n-b 2 15	B 1, l-b 4................	5

247   72

New Zealanders

V. J. Scott c Van Ryneveld b Chesterton	23	– c Wiley b Whitcombe	4
W. A. Hadlee b Wrigley	1	– b Whitcombe	21
J. R. Reid lbw b Whitcombe	6	– c Kardar b Wrigley	4
W. M. Wallace b Whitcombe	43	– c Whitcombe b Wrigley	37
F. B. Smith c Boobbyer b Wrigley	20	– c Kardar b Whitcombe	4
M. P. Donnelly c Carr b Wrigley	0	– b Kardar	32
G. O. Rabone c Law b Whitcombe	1	– c Van Ryneveld b Chesterton	10
F. L. H. Mooney c Whitcombe b Wrigley	4	– b Kardar	1
T. B. Burtt c Hofmeyr b Whitcombe	3	– c Kardar b Whitcombe	0
J. A. Hayes c Winn b Wrigley	0	– not out	0
H. B. Cave not out	3	– lbw b Wrigley	9
B 4, l-b 2	6	L-b 4	4
	110		**126**

New Zealanders Bowling

	Overs	Mdns	Runs	Wkts	Overs	Mdns	Runs	Wkts
Hayes	19.5	6	44	2	14	6	28	2
Cave	20	5	40	2	18	10	21	2
Reid	6	2	7	—				
Burtt	24	5	65	—	16	9	18	6
Rabone	23	7	60	5				
Donnelly	2	—	10	—				
Smith	2	—	6	1				

Oxford University Bowling

	Overs	Mdns	Runs	Wkts	Overs	Mdns	Runs	Wkts
Whitcombe	22.2	8	45	4	24.3	7	65	4
Wrigley	17	3	28	5	13	5	23	3
Chesterton	7	2	19	1	5	3	15	1
Kardar	4	1	12	—	7	2	19	2

Umpires: F. Chester and J. J. Hills.

HAMPSHIRE v NEW ZEALANDERS

Played at Southampton, June 15, 16, 17, 1949

New Zealanders won by seven wickets. A fluctuating, enjoyable game ended with the New Zealanders, left only thirty-five minutes to get 109 to win, snatching a memorable victory with five minutes to spare. The first Test bowlers being rested, Hayes, Cresswell and Burke did splendidly in dismissing Hampshire cheaply on a hard pitch. Cresswell, who took four wickets for seven runs each, bowled eight successive maiden overs. Scott and Sutcliffe made 142 for the first New Zealand wicket, Scott and Hadlee 100 for the second, and

Reid and Donnelly 105 for the fourth in just under an hour. Hampshire again started badly, losing two men for 24, but Eagar and McCorkell led a splendid recovery and Arnold contributed a sound century. The game appeared heading for a certain draw, but the two left-handers, Sutcliffe and Donnelly, scored 50 in ten minutes, and the runs were hit off amid rising excitement. Sutcliffe's 46 in thirteen minutes included three 6s and four 4s.

Hampshire

N. McCorkell lbw b Cresswell	11	– c Reid b Burtt	67
N. H. Rogers st Reid b Cresswell	1	– b Hayes	4
D. R. Guard c Rabone b Hayes	6	– b Hayes	12
J. Bailey c Rabone b Cresswell	4	– c Rabone b Burtt	13
E. D. R. Eagar b Burtt	16	– b Burke	82
J. Arnold c Hayes b Cresswell	16	– c Cresswell b Burtt	110
D. Shackleton b Burke	16	– b Burtt	21
C. Walker b Hayes	20	– b Burtt	16
C. Hill c Reid b Burke	0	– not out	49
V. J. Ransom c Sutcliffe b Burke	19	– c Rabone b Burke	9
C. J. Knott not out	9	– c Cresswell b Burtt	0
B 2, l-b 1, n-b 8	11	B 15, l-b 10, w 1	26
	129		**409**

New Zealanders

V. J. Scott c Walker b Bailey	129		
B. Sutcliffe b Knott	71	– c Eagar b Ransom	46
W. A. Hadlee c Rogers b Knott	33	– not out	9
J. R. Reid b Knott	50	– b Shackleton	9
M. P. Donnelly not out	100	– not out	39
F. B. Smith st McCorkell b Eagar	23	– b Shackleton	0
G. O. Rabone not out	15		
B 4, l-b 5	9	L-b 5, w 1	6
	(5 wkts dec.) 430		**(3 wkts) 109**

T. B. Burtt, C. C. Burke, J. A. Hayes and G. F. Cresswell did not bat.

New Zealanders Bowling

	Overs	Mdns	Runs	Wkts	Overs	Mdns	Runs	Wkts
Hayes	17.5	3	45	2	33	5	108	2
Cresswell	26	14	28	4	16	4	42	—
Burke	13	3	40	3	29	9	65	2
Rabone	1	1	—	—	27	9	65	—
Burtt	11	7	5	1	42.2	19	76	6
Hadlee					2	—	12	—
Smith					1	1	—	—
Sutcliffe					3	—	15	—

Hampshire Bowling

	Overs	Mdns	Runs	Wkts	Overs	Mdns	Runs	Wkts
Ransom	23	3	51	—	6	—	47	1
Shackleton	18	2	58	—	5.5	—	56	2
Knott	34	3	109	3				
Bailey	33	9	88	1				
Hill	17	4	66	—				
Walker	11	1	42	—				
Eagar	1	—	7	1				

Umpires: H. Baldwin and D. Hendren.

SURREY v NEW ZEALANDERS

Played at The Oval, June 18, 20, 21, 1949

Drawn. Remarkable for many new records, the match emphasised the lack of first-rate bowlers. The ball was apt to rise at varying heights from hard turf, but several batsmen excelled. Sutcliffe, revealed his home form after unfortunate experiences. Lucky in being missed when 17 by Parker at slip off Alec Bedser, he batted over five hours without another mistake, and hit one 5 and twenty-one 4s. His stroke play all round the wicket was admirable. Scott helped in the best start of the tour, 229 runs coming in three hours and a half; short in uplift, he hit only five 4s. Laker beat Sutcliffe with what was a leg-break to the left-handed batsman when the third wicket was worth 98 runs. A collapse ensued, but on Monday morning the New Zealanders raised the total to the best of the tour, and then Surrey surpassed all scores for the season and Parker made his personal highest and the best of the season. Going in with three men out for 77, he batted six and a half hours without any noticeable mistake and hit twenty-five 4s while scoring 255 out of 568. Whittaker, with a straight drive which went through the open window in the secretary's office in the pavilion and thirteen 4s, got his 91 in as many minutes out of 140 after being joined by Parker, who took part in three other three-figure stands – 100 in seventy-two minutes with Barton, 126 in ninety minutes with Eric Bedser, and 116 with Alec Bedser. Slight lumbago prevented Alec bowling when the tourists batted 180 behind, but Eric, keeping a good length with spin, broke the opening partnership at 95 and claimed a third victim in Rabone, whose all-round performance – two innings of over 50 and four wickets – deserved high praise. In the three days 1,237 runs were scored for twenty-two wickets.

New Zealanders

B. Sutcliffe b Laker	187	– c and b E. A. Bedser	48
V. J. Scott c Barton b A. V. Bedser	96		
W. A. Hadlee c Barton b A. V. Bedser	7	– lbw b E. A. Bedser	7
W. M. Wallace c A. V. Bedser b E. A. Bedser	47		
M. P. Donnelly lbw b Laker	15	– not out	2
F. B. Smith c McIntyre b Laker	19	– not out	11
J. R. Reid b Laker	8		
G. O. Rabone c McIntyre b A. V. Bedser	51	– c and b E. A. Bedser	52
T. B. Burtt b Laker	1		
J. A. Hayes c and b Laker	2		
H. B. Cave not out	13		
B 7, l-b 5, n-b 7	19	B 6, n-b 1	7
	465	**(3 wkts)**	**127**

Surrey

L. B. Fishlock c and b Rabone	41	E. A. Bedser c Smith b Cave	65
D. G. W. Fletcher b Cave	4	J. C. Laker c Burtt b Cave	14
H. S. Squires c Sutcliffe b Cave	28	A. V. Bedser not out	45
G. J. Whittaker lbw b Rabone	91		
J. F. Parker c Sutcliffe b Rabone	255	B 21, l-b 10, n-b 1	32
M. R. Barton c and b Donnelly	38		
A. J. McIntyre c Hadlee b Rabone	32	**(9 wkts dec.)**	**645**

J. W. McMahon did not bat.

Surrey Bowling

	Overs	Mdns	Runs	Wkts	Overs	Mdns	Runs	Wkts
A. V. Bedser	38.5	10	94	3				
Parker.	18	1	73	—	3	2	1	—
Laker	45	11	112	6	12	4	27	—
McMahon.	11	—	45	—	15	4	52	—
E. A. Bedser	18	2	76	1	10	4	21	3
Squires	10	—	46	—	6	2	11	—
Fishlock					3	1	8	—

New Zealanders Bowling

	Overs	Mdns	Runs	Wkts
Hayes	39	5	151	—
Cave.	40	9	126	4
Burtt	37	11	103	—
Rabone.	28.2	3	138	4
Sutcliffe.	3	2	10	—
Smith	5	—	31	—
Donnelly.	4	—	30	1
Hadlee	1	—	10	—
Scott	3	—	14	—

Umpires: F. S. Lee and S. J. Staples.

ENGLAND v NEW ZEALAND

Second Test Match

Played at Lord's, June 25, 27, 28, 1949

Drawn. On a pitch which seemed to improve the longer the match progressed, there appeared little hope of a definite result, but the game was made memorable by an incorrect declaration on the part of F. G. Mann, the England captain, and a brilliant innings of 206 by M. P. Donnelly, the New Zealand left-hander. Shortly after six o'clock on Saturday, with England's total 313 for nine wickets, Mann closed the innings and New Zealand in fifteen minutes scored 20 without loss. At the time he did not realise his mistake, but on Sunday he issued the following statement:

"When I declared the England innings closed on Saturday evening I thought that the experimental rule which allows a declaration to be made on the first day of a three-day match applied to the present series of Test Matches. I regret very much that I was wrong in this respect, but I am very glad indeed that we did not in fact gain any advantage from the declaration." An official announcement from Lord's stated that as no protest was made at the time the match would carry on as if no breach of regulations occurred.

Because of an injured leg, Washbrook stood down from the England side, his place being taken by Robertson. Wharton, also hurt, withdrew after being selected, and Watkins deputised. A further change was Gladwin for Bedser. New Zealand fielded an unchanged eleven.

So lively was the pitch for the first three hours that it began to look as if Mann was not so fortunate in again winning the toss as was at first considered. The New Zealanders bowled and fielded magnificently, and England lost their first five wickets for 112 runs. Cowie, during a long spell, maintained a perfect length at a fast pace and several times he made the ball lift nastily.

Eventually the pitch eased and Cowie tired in the oppressive heat. The change in England's fortunes came when Bailey joined Compton. Fortunate to receive two loose balls down the leg side which he turned for four apiece immediately he went in, Bailey showed complete confidence and for a long time he overshadowed Compton. Bailey continued to punish anything loose, mainly by going down on one knee and sweeping the ball hard to the square-leg boundary. Ten 4s came in his first 50 made in sixty-seven minutes. With his side in danger. Compton concentrated on wearing down the attack, and not until England were out of trouble did he take the slightest risk. Then he brought into play his wide range of strokes and scored much faster than his partner. Bailey was unlucky to miss his first Test hundred, for which only seven wanted he cut a ball on to the wicket-keeper's foot, whence it rebounded into the hands of second slip. His splendid innings lasted two and a half hours and contained sixteen 4s.

The stand of 189 was a record for the sixth wicket in Test Matches between the two countries. Compton, who left six runs earlier than Bailey, stayed three and three-quarter hours for 116, which included eleven 4s. After the big stand had been broken, three further wickets fell for 12 runs, and Mann, not wishing to waste any more time, decided on his declaration. His attempt to secure a wicket before the close failed, Sutcliffe and Scott were not content merely to play out time, but scored readily off loose bowling.

On Monday, Sutcliffe and Scott carried their partnership to 89, Sutcliffe showing delightful form for an hour and a half. With this stand broken, the England bowlers met with reasonable success for a time, and at lunch, with the New Zealand total 160 for four, the game stood in an even position. Then Donnelly took complete control of the attack and, with most of the other batsmen giving him good support, the game swung round in New Zealand's favour. England claimed only one wicket between lunch and tea, that of Smith. Donnelly was quite content to wait for the loose ball and batted much more cautiously than usual. He took three and a half hours to complete his first hundred, but on Tuesday he changed his style completely and in under an hour and a half he obtained 80 out of 112. Altogether he batted five minutes short of six hours, and his 206, made out of 347, contained twenty-six 4s. His innings was the highest for New Zealand in any Test Match. Powerful pulls and neat late cuts brought him a large number of his runs and he made no mistake until, after passing 200, he hit out at every ball. Rabone, during a seventh wicket stand of 78, and Burtt, who helped to add 85 for the eighth partnership, gave Donnelly most help. New Zealand's total of 484 was the highest by either country in England.

Facing arrears of 171, England soon averted any danger of defeat, Hutton and Robertson scoring 143 together in the best first-wicket stand for their country against New Zealand. England went ahead for the loss of Hutton, and with the game safe the remaining play was of little account. Edrich helped Robertson put on 73. Compton and Robertson were out to successive balls, and Watkins just failed in an attempt to complete 50 before the close. Robertson batted three and three-quarter hours and hit one 6 and eleven 4s.

L. S.

England

J. D. Robertson c Mooney b Cowie	26	– c Cave b Rabone 121
L. Hutton b Burtt	23	– c Cave b Rabone 66
W. J. Edrich c Donnelly b Cowie	9	– c Hadlee b Burtt............. 31
D. C. S. Compton c Sutcliffe b Burtt	116	– b Burtt 6
A. Watkins c Wallace b Burtt	6	– not out 49
F. G. Mann b Cave	18	– c Donnelly b Rabone 7
T. E. Bailey c Sutcliffe b Rabone	93	– not out 6
T. G. Evans b Burtt	5	
C. Gladwin run out	5	
J. A. Young not out	1	
B 9, l-b 2	11	B 9, l-b 1 10

1/48 2/59 3/72 4/83 5/112   (9 wkts dec.) 313   1/143 2/216 3/226   (5 wkts) 306
6/301 7/307 8/307 9/313   4/226 5/252

W. E. Hollies did not bat.

New Zealand

B. Sutcliffe c Compton b Gladwin. 57	T. B. Burtt c Edrich b Hollies 23
V. J. Scott c Edrich b Compton 42	H. B. Cave c and b Young 6
W. A. Hadlee c Robertson b Hollies. 43	J. Cowie not out 1
W. M. Wallace c Evans b Hollies 2	
M. P. Donnelly c Hutton b Young 206	B 16, l-b 3, w 3, n-b 1 23
F. B. Smith b Hollies. 23	
G. O. Rabone b Hollies 25	1/89 2/124 3/137 4/160 5/197 484
F. L. H. Mooney c Watkins b Young 33	6/273 7/351 8/436 9/464

New Zealand Bowling

	Overs	Mdns	Runs	Wkts	Overs	Mdns	Runs	Wkts
Cowie	26.1	5	64	2	14	3	39	—
Cave.	27	2	79	1	7	1	23	—
Rabone.	14	5	56	1	28	6	116	3
Burtt.	35	7	102	4	37	12	58	2
Sutcliffe.	1	—	1	—	16	1	55	—
Wallace.					1	—	5	—

England Bowling

	Overs	Mdns	Runs	Wkts
Bailey	33	3	136	—
Gladwin	28	5	67	1
Edrich.	4	—	16	—
Hollies	58	18	133	5
Compton	7	—	33	1
Young.	26.4	4	65	3
Watkins	3	1	11	—

Umpires: W. H. Ashdown and F. Chester.

COMBINED SERVICES v NEW ZEALANDERS

Played at Gillingham, June 29, 30, 1949

New Zealanders won by an innings and 50 runs. Cowie did not attempt to produce his quickest pace, but he dismissed the first three Services batsmen for only eight runs and the side never recovered. Sutcliffe was the dominating personality in an opening New Zealand stand of 247. He gave a glorious display, but Scott seldom relaxed from vigilant defence during a stay of five and a half hours. The Services redeemed themselves in the second innings. Manners, top scorer in each innings, hooked and drove finely while making 123 out of 160, and in a whirlwind eighth-wicket stand Deighton and Wilson added 111 in fifty-three minutes. The New Zealanders fielded brilliantly and thoroughly enjoyed the brief interval from Test and county cricket.

Combined Services

Sq Ldr W. E. G. Payton (RAF) b Cowie	8	– c Sutcliffe b Cresswell.	7
Major A. H. Parnaby (Army) c Scott b Cowie	0	– c Cowie b Burke	10
Lt M. L. Y. Ainsworth (RN) b Cowie.	0	– c Wallace b Cowie	17
Writer P. B. H. May (RN) c Mooney b Hayes	15	– lbw b Sutcliffe.	32
Lt Cdr J. E. Manners (RN) c Wallace b Burke	36	– b Cresswell	123
Wing Cdr W. R. Ford (RAF) b Cresswell	0	– st Mooney b Sutcliffe	0
Flt Lt A. C. Shirreff (RAF) c Scott b Cresswell	0	– lbw b Cresswell.	14
Capt. J. H. G. Deighton (Army) b Hayes	0	– c Smith b Burke	59
Sq Ldr R. G. Wilson (RAF) not out	5	– c Wallace b Burke.	68
Capt. D. W. M. Gay (Army) c Sutcliffe b Burke	0	– not out	0
A/c P. I. Bedford (RAF) c Smith b Burke	7	– st Mooney b Sutcliffe	15
N-b 1.	1	B 1, l-b 1.	2
	72		**347**

New Zealanders

B. Sutcliffe c Deighton b Shirreff. 144	F. L. H. Mooney b Shirreff	5
V. J. Scott lbw b Deighton 203	C. C. Burke not out.	44
J. R. Reid c sub b Deighton. 10		
W. M. Wallace c sub b Deighton 4	B 20, l-b 1	21
M. P. Donnelly c and b Deighton 19		
F. B. Smith c Parnaby b Bedford 19	(7 wkts dec.) **469**

J. Cowie, J. A. Hayes and G. F. Cresswell did not bat.

New Zealanders Bowling

	Overs	Mdns	Runs	Wkts	Overs	Mdns	Runs	Wkts
Cowie.	8	3	22	3	15	4	52	1
Cresswell	12	3	22	2	20	7	34	3
Hayes	8	1	21	2	12	2	48	—
Burke	3.5	1	6	3	28	4	109	3
Reid					6	1	22	—
Sutcliffe.					15.4	3	80	3

Combined Services Bowling

	Overs	Mdns	Runs	Wkts
Deighton.	30.1	2	119	4
Shirreff	33	3	131	2
Gay.	31	4	94	—
Bedford.	10	—	46	1
Wilson	12	—	58	—

Umpires: F. Chester and W. H. Ashdown.

ESSEX v NEW ZEALANDERS

Played at Southend, August 10, 11, 12, 1949

Drawn. Sutcliffe, in a fine left-hand display, proved the central figure. His 243 was the highest score made by a New Zealander touring this country; his 100 not out in the second innings made him the first New Zealander to complete 2,000 runs during a tour of England, and the first to register two separate centuries in a match for his country abroad.

He was favoured by much good fortune on the opening day, being missed no fewer than four times during a stay of five hours forty minutes, in which he hit twenty-nine 4s. His second innings was faultless and, lasting only two hours contained eleven 4s. He drove, hooked and hit to leg with splendid skill. Hadlee in each innings was his best partner, helping to add 97 in the first innings and 109 in the second. Thanks to Dodds, who hit eleven boundaries, Vigar, rather less free, and Eve, the Essex score stood at 262 for four at the tea interval on the second day, but the last six wickets fell for 42. Essex, left to get 335 to win, began so slowly that all chance of success soon disappeared, but Eve drove with power for eighty minutes.

New Zealanders

B. Sutcliffe c Pearce b Vigar	243	– not out	100
V. J. Scott b P. Smith	29	– c Wade b Pullinger	25
J. R. Reid b R. Smith	4	– lbw b R. Smith	7
W. A. Hadlee b P. Smith	55	– b R. Smith	57
M. P. Donnelly c Vigar b R. Smith	20	– lbw b Vigar	1
F. B. Smith c Vigar b R. Smith	0	– c Wade b Pullinger	7
F. L. H. Mooney c Wade b R. Smith	4	– c Vigar b Pullinger	4
T. B. Burtt b P. Smith	18	– c and b Vigar	7
C. C. Burke not out	27	– lbw b Vigar	5
H. B. Cave c P. Smith b Vigar	2		
G. F. Cresswell c Wade b P. Smith	1		
B 8, l-b 7, w 2	17	B 1, l-b 4	5
	420	**(8 wkts dec.)**	**218**

Essex

T. C. Dodds lbw b Burtt	82	– c Sutcliffe b Cave	7
S. J. Cray c Donnelly b Burtt	29	– c Sutcliffe b Burtt	60
F. H. Vigar c Sutcliffe b Cave	89	– st Reid b Burke	46
S. C. Eve c Scott b Cresswell	40	– b Cave	69
D. J. Insole c Mooney b Cave	23	– not out	25
R. Horsfall c and b Cresswell	9		
T. N. Pearce run out	6		
R. Smith b Cresswell	12		
T. P. B. Smith b Cave	0		
T. H. Wade not out	2		
G. R. Pullinger b Cave	0		
B 9, l-b 1, n-b 2	12	B 4, l-b 5	9
	304	**(4 wkts)**	**216**

Essex Bowling

	Overs	Mdns	Runs	Wkts	Overs	Mdns	Runs	Wkts
R. Smith	36	9	93	4	24	1	68	2
Pullinger	30	3	113	—	19	3	58	3
P. Smith	43.4	4	148	4	8	—	46	—
Vigar	12	—	49	2	7	—	41	3

New Zealanders Bowling

	Overs	Mdns	Runs	Wkts	Overs	Mdns	Runs	Wkts
Cave	24.5	2	82	4	15	1	39	2
Cresswell	29	7	63	3	16	3	32	—
Burtt	23	6	65	2	16	5	47	1
Burke	14	—	52	—	11	1	66	1
Sutcliffe	6	—	30	—	3	—	23	—

Umpires: F. Chester and S. J. Staples.

MIDDLESEX v NEW ZEALANDERS

Played at Lord's, August 27, 29, 30, 1949

New Zealanders won by nine wickets. The last match of the season at Lord's brought further honours to the New Zealanders, whose only previous victory there was in 1931 when they beat MCC by an innings and 22 runs. Middlesex, who had just assured themselves of finishing at least level at the head of the Championship, were well beaten. Opening the bowling for the first time in the tour, Reid dismissed Brown and Edrich quickly, and, with Robertson falling to Cowie, the first three wickets went for 11. The total was only 21 when Dewes was dropped before scoring by the wicket-keeper off Cowie. For a long time Dewes was uncertain, particularly against Cowie, who bowled splendidly throughout, but he played a valuable part in helping Denis Compton to effect a complete recovery. They stayed together three hours twenty minutes and put on 210. Compton (nineteen 4s) gave a faultless display. Twice when Warr and Edrich used the new ball the New Zealanders ran into trouble, but the total reached 241 with only half the side dismissed. Middlesex appeared to lose their determination and batted badly against more good bowling by Cowie and Burtt, so that the New Zealanders were left needing 157 in two and three-quarter hours. Through the brilliance of Sutcliffe they hit off the runs with seventy minutes to spare. Sutcliffe drove and pulled as he pleased, hitting one 6 and seventeen 4s. He finished the match by sweeping Mann three times to the leg boundary. He was dropped off his final stroke, but that was the only mistake in a dazzling exhibition.

Middlesex

J. D. Robertson c Mooney b Cowie	6	– b Cowie	4
S. M. Brown b Reid	0	– b Burtt	16
W. J. Edrich b Reid	2	– b Cowie	1
D. C. S. Compton c Burtt b Cowie	148	– b Burtt	10
J. G. Dewes c Reid b Cowie	92	– b Burke	60
H. Sharp c Donnelly b Cowie	8	– run out	10
F. G. Mann b Cowie	4	– b Reid	0
L. Compton c Mooney b Burtt	1	– c Donnelly b Burtt	41
J. Sims b Reid	37	– c Mooney b Burtt	13
J. A. Young b Burtt	4	– b Cowie	4
J. J. Warr not out	5	– not out	2
B 4, l-b 3, w 1	8	L-b 8	8
	315		**169**

New Zealanders

B. Sutcliffe lbw b D. Compton	59	– not out	110
V. J. Scott c L. Compton b Edrich	5	– b Sims	23
J. R. Reid b Sims	18		
W. M. Wallace c Brown b Young	58		
M. P. Donnelly lbw b Edrich	72		
G. O. Rabone lbw b Sims	3	– not out	18
W. A. Hadlee b Edrich	50		
F. L. H. Mooney lbw b Warr	1		
T. B. Burtt c and b D. Compton	19		
C. C. Burke not out	21		
J. Cowie c Mann b D. Compton	3		
B 10, l-b 9	19	B 4, l-b 2	6
	328		**(1 wkt) 157**

New Zealanders Bowling

	Overs	Mdns	Runs	Wkts	Overs	Mdns	Runs	Wkts
Cowie	36	8	87	5	21	3	68	3
Reid	10.4	3	38	3	13	2	24	1
Rabone	8	1	47	—	3	—	8	—
Burtt	14	4	44	2	18.3	2	50	4
Burke	27	5	80	—	6	2	11	1
Sutcliffe	3	1	11	—				

Middlesex Bowling

	Overs	Mdns	Runs	Wkts	Overs	Mdns	Runs	Wkts
Edrich	16	1	60	3	5	—	17	—
Warr	18	2	50	1	3	—	18	—
Sims	22	3	86	2	9	2	32	1
Young	24	8	47	1	10	1	47	—
D. Compton	14.3	—	66	3				
Sharp					4	—	25	—
Mann					0.5	—	12	—

Umpires: A. Skelding and J. J. Hills.

SUSSEX v NEW ZEALANDERS

Played at Hove, June 14, 16, 17, 1958

Drawn. This was a most enjoyable match, both sides playing attractive cricket and going all out for a result. Either side could have won in the final few minutes. Smith repeated his performance of the previous year against West Indies in saving Sussex in the first innings. He batted four and three-quarter hours for 142 and strong drives, hooks and pulls brought him one 6 and nineteen 4s. Petrie dismissed him with a brilliant leg-side catch at the wicket and held four other catches in the innings (eight in the match). Next day Reid hit a century in eighty-six minutes and spent only two hours for 118. Mighty drives brought most of his four 6s and sixteen 4s. He hit one ball out of the ground. Sutcliffe, reappearing after breaking a wrist, helped him add 172 for the fifth wicket. He claimed three of the nine 6s hit in the innings. Facing arrears of 111, Sussex looked doomed when their ninth wicket fell at 194, but Sheppard and Marlar put on 49 in forty minutes. Sheppard went from 56 to 102 in that period. The New Zealanders made a bold effort to get 143 in eighty-five minutes, but were almost defeated. Their eighth wicket fell with eight minutes left and they finished 29 short of their objective.

Sussex

L. J. Lenham b Sparling	31	– c Petrie b Sparling	21
D. V. Smith c Petrie b Hayes	142	– c Petrie b Hayes	0
A. S. M. Oakman c Petrie b Blair	7	– c and b Sparling	25
J. M. Parks c Petrie b Blair	16	– c Cave b Reid	44
Rev. D. S. Sheppard c and b Reid	10	– c and b Blair	102
K. G. Suttle b Sparling	5	– b Sparling	6
R. V. Bell c Petrie b Hayes	13	– c Petrie b Hayes	9
N. I. Thomson c Petrie b Hayes	10	– c Hayes b Reid	18
A. E. James not out	9	– run out	1
R. G. Marlar c Harford b Blair	17	– not out	9
R. T. Webb (did not bat)	–	c D'Arcy b Hayes	10
B 4, l-b 5, n-b 5	14	B 2, l-b 3, n-b 3	8

1/88 2/109 3/129 4/158 (9 wkts dec.) 274   1/0 2/17 3/54 4/63 5/115   253
5/174 6/234 7/235 8/247 9/274   6/130 7/153 8/187 9/194

New Zealanders

L. S. M. Miller c Oakman b Bell	45	– c James b Oakman	47
J. W. D'Arcy st Webb b James	0	– b Marlar	1
W. R. Playle b Marlar	38	– c Marlar b Thomson	17
N. S. Harford c Lenham b Bell	16	– c Sheppard b Marlar	9
B. Sutcliffe c Webb b Marlar	99		
J. R. Reid b Oakman	118	– c Thomson b James	1
J. T. Sparling c Sheppard b Oakman	3	– run out	10
H. B. Cave c Suttle b Marlar	26	– b Thomson	0
R. W. Blair c and b Marlar	0	– st Webb b James	6
J. A. Hayes b Oakman	15	– not out	3
E. C. Petrie not out	9	– not out	6
B 10, l-b 5, n-b 1	16	B 8, l-b 6	14

1/7 2/81 3/93 4/112 5/284   385   1/10 2/45 3/76   (8 wkts) 114
6/320 7/346 8/346 9/369   4/94 5/102 6/103 7/103 8/108

New Zealanders Bowling

	Overs	Mdns	Runs	Wkts	Overs	Mdns	Runs	Wkts
Hayes	20	4	63	3	20	5	53	3
Blair	20	3	54	3	14	4	39	1
Cave	31	11	45	—	17	6	34	—
Sparling	21	2	64	2	25	5	71	3
Reid	11	2	34	1	12	4	28	2
Sutcliffe					3	—	20	—

Sussex Bowling

	Overs	Mdns	Runs	Wkts	Overs	Mdns	Runs	Wkts
Thomson	21	2	71	—	8	—	22	2
James	16	4	50	1	3	—	13	2
Smith	6	—	23	—				
Bell	28	5	94	2				
Marlar	24.5	7	78	4	10	—	48	2
Oakman	19	6	46	3	6	1	17	1
Parks	2	—	7	—				

Umpires: A. E. D. Smith and T. W. Spencer.

ENGLAND v NEW ZEALAND
Second Test Match

Played at Lord's, June 19, 20, 21, 1958

England won by an innings and 148 runs with more than two days to spare, the match being completed by half-past three on Saturday. New Zealand had the ill luck to be trapped twice on a wet pitch after England, with May, winning the toss, had batted on a true surface, and they were dismissed for 47, the lowest total in the long history of Tests at Lord's and the fourth lowest in England. In 1924, South Africa were put out at Edgbaston for 30, and further back Australia could muster only 36 at Edgbaston in 1902 and 44 at The Oval in 1896. Again the Surrey spinners, Lock, nine wickets for 29, and Laker, five for 37, proved almost unplayable. It was Lock's first Test at Lord's.

While England relied on the eleven who won at Edgbaston, New Zealand welcomed the return of Sutcliffe, who played with his right forearm encased in a felt cover and they also brought in Blair, leaving out Meale and Cave.

The match began in sad circumstances with the announcement that news had just been received of the death of Douglas Jardine in a Swiss nursing home. Jardine captained

England at Lord's in 1931 when New Zealand played their first Test match. The MCC and New Zealand flags were lowered to half mast.

The honours of the first day went to New Zealand. They restricted England to less than 40 runs an hour, taking seven wickets for 237 runs. While full credit must be given to Hayes, MacGibbon, Blair and Reid for their steadiness on an easy-paced pitch, some of the England batsmen showed little imagination in dealing with bowling generally short in length.

With Richardson and Smith concentrating solely on defence the first hour produced only 27 runs and fifty minutes later the total stood at 54 when Petrie caught Richardson on the leg side. In two hours before lunch Smith made only 17. One could sympathise with him in his anxiety to do himself justice, but he looked a vastly different cricketer from the one who had set up a University record by hitting three hundreds for Oxford against Cambridge on this same ground in successive matches.

Smith was missed off Blair by MacGibbon at second slip off the third ball after the interval, and when third to leave he had occupied three hours fifty minutes over 47. Both Graveney and May fell trying to change the tempo of England's scoring and Cowdrey arrived in time to face Hayes and MacGibbon with the new ball. Bailey gave Cowdrey valuable help in a stand of 60. It was sheer joy to see Cowdrey pierce the field with dazzling cover drives and powerful on-side strokes, but runs never came easily against keen opponents.

Petrie caught four of the first six batsmen behind the stumps and Hayes (short-leg) and Playle and D'Arcy (covers) were often prominent. Hayes made a grand catch at short-leg in disposing of Evans and at the end of the day he was still fresh enough to put in a final burst of bowling, taking Cowdrey's off-stump with a yorker. Cowdrey made 65 in two hours ten minutes, hitting nine 4s.

So much rain fell in London after the close of play that next day the match could not be resumed until 3.20 p.m. and then wickets went down in a heap, thirteen in all in the space of two hours twenty minutes.

In such circumstances the England tail had little to fear. Lock played really well, demonstrating the value of the straight bat, but Trueman, Laker and Loader were willing to hit at anything and in half an hour 32 runs were added before the innings ended.

Trueman started the New Zealand debacle by removing Miller in the first over. Then for half an hour D'Arcy and Playle managed to subdue Trueman and Loader, but May gave them only four overs before he turned to Laker and Lock with the total at 12. The change was electrifying. The pitch could not be described as sticky, but it was treacherous enough for Laker to make the occasional ball stand up as well as turn from the off.

Most of the New Zealanders contributed to their own downfall by picking the wrong ball to punish. Playle, the first of Laker's victims, slammed a catch to mid-off; Harford fell in almost the same way, but D'Arcy stood his ground for fifty minutes. Then as soon as he faced Laker he was taken in the leg trap. Sutcliffe showed that the conditions were not so difficult as his predecessors had imagined, but any hopes New Zealand entertained of avoiding a complete collapse went when Reid, having hit Lock for a tremendous 6 in front of the tavern, gave Loader a skier at mid-on.

So Lock broke Laker's sequence, and the left-arm bowler, whipping the ball across from leg to the right-handers, quickly accounted for MacGibbon and Alabaster, but he found a worthy foe in Petrie while Sutcliffe concentrated on taking Laker. In this way both men avoided off spin, but May countered by bringing in Bailey for an over so that the two Surrey bowlers could change ends.

Lock, from his new station, immediately pierced Sutcliffe's defence with his quicker ball and Petrie, who kept up his end for forty minutes without scoring, was cheered all the way back to the pavilion on being caught in Laker's leg trap. Hayes gave Lock his fifth wicket with a slip catch and so New Zealand, following on 222 behind, had to face the music for another ten minutes.

New Zealand's fate had been virtually settled on Friday and more rain left the pitch and outfield in a sodden state. The players needed plenty of sawdust to maintain their footholds when the match was resumed in sunshine after a delay of half an hour.

This time all five England bowlers met with some degree of success. D'Arcy alone offered real resistance. Sixth out, he kept up his end for just over two hours, and while mainly on the defensive he did not hesitate to punish the ball he fancied. Three of his four boundaries came at the expense of Trueman.

Sutcliffe fell to a fine ball from Bailey that took his off-stump and nine men were out for 56 when Hayes spoiled Laker's figures by sweeping him twice for 6, but Lock soon tempted him into giving a return catch. It was one of the shortest Tests for many years, being completed in eleven and a half hours. In 1946, when Australia dismissed New Zealand at Wellington for 42 and 54 and won by an innings and 103 runs, the issue was decided around lunch time on the second day.

With 25,000 people present, the captains arranged an exhibition match of 20 overs each which, played in a light-hearted way, caused plenty of fun, Richardson kept wicket for England while Evans bowled.   N.P.

England

P. E. Richardson c Petrie b Hayes	36	F. S. Trueman b Hayes	8
M. J. K. Smith c Petrie b Hayes	47	J. C. Laker c Blair b MacGibbon	1
T. W. Graveney c Petrie b Alabaster	37	P. J. Loader c Playle b MacGibbon	4
P. B. H. May c Alabaster b MacGibbon	19		
M. C. Cowdrey b Hayes	65	L-b 1	1
T. E. Bailey c Petrie b Reid	17		
T. G. Evans c Hayes b MacGibbon	11	1/54 2/113 3/139 4/141 5/201	269
G. A. R. Lock not out	23	6/222 7/237 8/259 9/260	

New Zealand

L. S. M. Miller lbw b Trueman	4	– c Trueman b Loader	0
J. W. D'Arcy c Trueman b Laker	14	– c Bailey b Trueman	33
W. R. Playle c Graveney b Laker	1	– b Loader	3
N. S. Harford c and b Laker	0	– c May b Lock	3
J. R. Reid c Loader b Lock	6	– c Cowdrey b Trueman	5
B. Sutcliffe b Lock	18	– b Bailey	0
A. R. MacGibbon c May b Lock	2	– c May b Lock	7
J. C. Alabaster c and b Lock	0	– b Laker	5
E. C. Petrie c Trueman b Laker	0	– not out	4
R. W. Blair not out	0	– b Lock	0
J. A. Hayes c Cowdrey b Lock	1	– c and b Lock	14
L-b 1	1		

1/4 2/12 3/12 4/19 5/25 6/31   47   1/11 2/21 3/34 4/41 5/44   74
7/34 8/46 9/46   6/44 7/56 8/56 9/56

New Zealand Bowling

	Overs	Mdns	Runs	Wkts
Hayes	22	5	36	4
MacGibbon	36.4	11	86	4
Blair	25	6	57	—
Reid	24	12	41	1
Alabaster	16	6	48	1

England Bowling

	Overs	Mdns	Runs	Wkts	Overs	Mdns	Runs	Wkts
Trueman	4	1	6	1	11	6	24	2
Loader	4	2	6	—	9	6	7	2
Laker	12	6	13	4	13	8	24	1
Lock	11.3	7	17	5	12.3	8	12	4
Bailey	1	—	4	—	5	1	7	1

Umpires: C. S. Elliott and D. Davies.

INDIANS IN ENGLAND

SURREY v INDIA

Played at Kennington Oval, May 11, 13, 14, 1946

India won by nine wickets. A record-breaking last-wicket stand between Sarwate and Banerjee featured India's first victory of the tour. Although Merchant and Gul Mahomed put on 111 the third wicket, nine men were out for 205 when the last pair came together. They were not separated for three hours ten minutes, their partnership of 249 being the highest ever recorded for the last wicket in England. Never before in history had Nos. 10 and 11 in the batting order each scored a century in the same innings. Both Sarwate and Banerjee gave masterly displays and neither at any time appeared in difficulties. Fishlock drove well for Surrey, who collapsed badly before the Indian spin bowlers. Nayudu, dismissing Fishlock, Bennett and A. V. Bedser, performed the hat-trick. Following on 319 behind Surrey made a better fight. Fishlock, again in good form, and Gregory opened with a stand of 144, but next day the slow bowlers were again on top. Sarwate followed his fine batting by clever variation of spin, and India were left to get only 20 runs for victory. Gregory batted just short of three hours. Surrey were handicapped by an injury to Gover, who could not bowl again in the match after straining a tendon in his heel before lunch on the first day.

India

V. M. Merchant b Squires	53	– not out	15
V. S. Hazare lbw b A. V. Bedser	0		
R. S. Modi b A. V. Bedser	0	– not out	4
Gul Mahomed b A. V. Bedser	89		
R. B. Nimbalkar c Mobey b Parker	18		
Mushtaq Ali lbw b Parker	6		
S. W. Sohoni lbw b Watts	6		
V. Mankad c Mobey b A. V. Bedser	16		
C. S. Nayudu c Bennett b A. V. Bedser	9		
C. T. Sarwate not out	124	– c Watts b A. V. Bedser	1
S. Banerjee b Parker	121		
B 7, l-b 4, n-b 1	12		
	454	**(1 wkt)**	**20**

Surrey

R. J. Gregory lbw b Sohoni	16	– lbw b Mankad	100
L. B. Fishlock hit wkt b Nayudu	62	– c Merchant b Hazare	83
H. S. Squires c Nimbalkar b Hazare	4	– st Nimbalkar b Nayudu	21
T. H. Barling b Hazare	8	– b Mankad	16
J. F. Parker c Merchant b Banerjee	20	– b Sarwate	20
E. A. Bedser lbw b Mankad	6	– lbw b Sarwate	21
E. A. Watts b Mankad	2	– st Nimbalkar b Sarwate	2
N. H. Bennett c Mushtaq Ali b Nayudu	0	– c Mankad b Sarwate	24
A. V. Bedser b Nayudu	0	– not out	31
A. R. Gover lbw b Banerjee	7	– lbw b Sarwate	0
G. S. Mobey not out	6	– lbw b Mankad	5
B 1, l-b 1, n-b 2	4	B 5, l-b 9, w 1	15
	135		**338**

Surrey Bowling

	Overs	Mdns	Runs	Wkts	Overs	Mdns	Runs	Wkts
Gover............	7	2	18	—				
A. V. Bedser.......	47	8	135	5	3	—	14	1
Watts............	38	7	122	1	2.5	—	6	—
Parker............	27.2	7	64	3				
Squires..........	12	1	36	1				
E. A. Bedser.......	8	—	25	—				
Gregory..........	5	1	23	—				
Fishlock..........	3	—	19	—				

India Bowling

	Overs	Mdns	Runs	Wkts	Overs	Mdns	Runs	Wkts
Hazare...........	16	9	20	2	16	5	36	1
Sohoni..........	9	1	31	1	6	—	15	—
Banerjee..........	9	—	42	2	11	1	45	—
Nayudu...........	12	3	30	3	25	4	93	1
Mankad..........	5	1	8	2	25	7	80	3
Sarwate..........					16	5	54	5

ENGLAND v INDIA

First Test Match

Played at Lord's, June 22, 24, 25, 1946

England won by ten wickets. The seventh consecutive single brought the match to an emphatic success for England just at half-past one on the third day. This concluding fight for runs typified the cricket from first to last and, though defeated so severely, India deserved high credit for the way they put the utmost keenness and effort into all their doings. Beyond question batting first proved anything but an advantage, for after much rain the ground remained heavy throughout the opening day, and, while the pitch never seemed difficult, it gave bowlers just enough help to make run-getting a struggle throughout Saturday. To take first innings on winning the toss was the obvious course for Pataudi, but only two stands checked the cheap dismissal of batsmen – 57 for the seventh wicket and 43 for the tenth. Modi, very doubtful in timing the ball until after six men were out for 87, continued cramped, while Hafeez, a left-hander, scored freely with good cuts, drives and leg hits, and only in the final effort to improve matters did one of the soundest batsmen in the side force the pace. Then Modi brought off drives and forcing strokes that gave character to his play and Shinde offered stubborn resistance until completely beaten by Bedser.

This event appropriately finished the innings, for Alec Bedser, one of the Surrey twins, accomplished probably the finest performance ever recorded by a bowler in his first Test match. Using his height, six feet two inches, to the full extent and putting his weight behind every ball, Bedser maintained an admirable length at fast-medium pace, with swerve or spin which often turned the ball appreciably from the sodden turf. For each of the four bowlers considered necessary Hammond placed an attacking field with three short legs and a silly point usually on duty; sometimes even more men stood very close to the bat.

England started just as badly by losing Hutton and Compton – bowled first ball – for 16. Hammond and Washbrook added 45, but both left while the total reached 70, and the success of Amarnath, with his short quick run and downward flip of the ball, required all the skill of Hardstaff and Gibb to prevent further disaster in a prelude to their batting on Monday, when the Nottingham man brought out his highest skill in stroke play while the bespectacled Yorkshireman relied on stubborn defence. Appreciably faster after a finer Sunday, the pitch and outfield meant greatly improved conditions for scoring, and so the total mounted from 135 to 252 in less than two hours before Gibb gave slip a catch. By adding 182, the fifth partnership put England on the highroad to victory, and with continued support, Hardstaff surpassed his previous highest Test Match innings – 169 against Australia.

During five and a quarter hours at the wicket Hardstaff maintained close concentration on every ball. Bareheaded, as usual, he stood erect, holding the bat at full length, defending or forcing the ball away with wristy strokes; amidst the cheers that greeted his 200 he remained unruffled and as watchful as ever until the last wicket fell. He trusted to perfect timing for every kind of scoring stroke with the ball kept down, and one lifted drive from Amarnath to the pavilion rails caused surprise calling for special comment. Smailes put power into a few strokes, and two boundaries past cover-point by Bedser gave a hint of batting ability.

Before India began their second innings the King came from the pavilion with General Adams, President of MCC, and the teams were introduced to His Majesty.

Mankad, after long spells of bowling, batted very well and 67 runs came before Merchant gave Ikin his only wicket of the match, and India entered upon the last day only 66 behind with six wickets in hand, but Bedser and Wright, who beat Pataudi with a specially deadly leg-break, caused a collapse, checked once by Amarnath and Hindlekar in a stand for 59. Amarnath, Mankad and Hazare proved themselves valuable all-round players. Practically all the Indians showed a preference to attack the bowling rather than defend, and their lively zeal certainly pleased the 15,000 people present at the finish. On each of the first two days the gates were closed about noon, when the crowds numbered nearly 30,000.   H. P.

India

V. M. Merchant c Gibb b Bedser	12	– lbw b Ikin	27
V. Mankad b Wright	14	– c Hammond b Smailes	63
L. Amarnath lbw b Bedser	0	– b Smailes	50
V. S. Hazare b Bedser	31	– c Hammond b Bedser	34
R. S. Modi not out	57	– lbw b Smailes	21
Nawab of Pataudi c Ikin b Bedser	9	– b Wright	22
Gul Mahomed b Wright	1	– lbw b Wright	9
Abdul Hafeez b Bowes	43	– b Bedser	0
D. D. Hindlekar lbw b Bedser	3	– c Ikin b Bedser	17
C. S. Nayudu st Gibb b Bedser	4	– b Bedser	13
S. G. Shinde b Bedser	10	– not out	4
B 10, l-b 6	16	B 10, l-b 2, n-b 3	15

1/15 2/15 3/44 4/74 5/86   200   1/67 2/117 3/126 4/129 5/174   275
6/87 7/144 8/147 9/157   6/185 7/190 8/249 9/263

England

L. Hutton c Nayudu b Amarnath	7	– not out	22
C. Washbrook c Mankad b Amarnath	27	– not out	24
D. Compton b Amarnath	0		
W. R. Hammond b Amarnath	33		
J. Hardstaff not out	205		
P. A. Gibb c Hazare b Mankad	60		
J. T. Ikin c Hindlekar b Shinde	16		
T. F. Smailes c Mankad b Amarnath	25		
A. V. Bedser b Hazare	30		
D. V. P. Wright b Mankad	3		
W. F. Bowes lbw b Hazare	2		
B 11, l-b 8, n-b 1	20	L-b 1, w 1	2

1/16 2/16 3/61 4/70 5/252   428   (No wkt) 48
6/284 7/344 8/416 9/421

England Bowling

	Overs	Mdns	Runs	Wkts	Overs	Mdns	Runs	Wkts
Bowes............	25	7	64	1	4	1	9	—
Bedser............	29.1	11	49	7	32.1	3	96	4
Smailes...........	5	1	18	—	15	2	44	3
Wright	17	4	53	2	20	3	68	2
Ikin.............					10	1	43	1

India Bowling

	Overs	Mdns	Runs	Wkts	Overs	Mdns	Runs	Wkts
Hazare	34.4	4	100	2	4	2	7	—
Amarnath.........	37	18	118	5	4	—	15	—
Gul Mahomed	2	—	2	—				
Mankad	48	11	107	2	4.5	1	11	—
Shinde............	23	2	66	1				
Nayudu...........	5	1	15	—	4	—	13	—

Umpires: H. G. Baldwin and J. Smart.

SUSSEX v INDIA

Played at Hove, July 27, 29, 30, 1946

India won by nine wickets. Except on the last day, when George Cox made the highest score of his career, the Indians were always on top. On Saturday they found the hard wicket and fast outfield so much to their liking that they averaged ninety runs an hour while recording their biggest total of the tour. The first four batsmen reached three figures – an extremely rare achievement. Merchant and Mankad led off with a stand of 293. Merchant drove and cut brilliantly in scoring his second double century out of 314 in just over three and a half hours; he hit twenty-three 4s. Pataudi and Amarnath added 219. India declared first thing on Monday; overnight rain made the ground slower but the wicket never became difficult, and much of the Sussex batting proved disappointing, though Stainton defended soundly for over three hours. Following on 280 behind, Sussex lost three men for 17 runs, but Cox and James Langridge, in a fine stand, added 171. When the seventh wicket fell, Sussex needed 26 to avoid an innings defeat. Then Hammond, missed when two, and Cox put on 107 in an hour. Cox, not out 72 overnight, added 100 in an hour and three-quarters before lunch on Tuesday, and altogether batted four hours fifty minutes. Hard, clean driving brought him a six (four overthrows), a five (four overthrows) and twenty 4s. Merchant and Modi hit off the runs by adding 120. Merchant in the match scored 268 for once out.

India

V. M. Merchant c Hammond b Cox 205	– not out	63
V. Mankad c James Langridge b Cox 105	– c Hammond b James Langridge ...	8
Nawab of Pataudi not out......................110		
L. Amarnath c Griffith b J. N. Bartlett...........106		
R. S. Modi (did not bat)	– not out	72
B 4, l-b 2, n-b 1 7	B 5	5

(3 wkts dec.) 533   (1 wkt) 148

V. S. Hazare, Gul Mahomed, S. N. Banerjee, C. S. Nayudu, D. D. Hindlekar and S. G. Shinde did not bat.

Sussex

John Langridge lbw b Banerjee	7	– c Modi b Banerjee	2
H. W. Parks c Pataudi b Amarnath	56	– c Pataudi b Amarnath	4
R. G. Stainton st Hindlekar b Mankad	72	– b Banerjee	6
G. Cox c Hazare b Amarnath	8	– not out	234
James Langridge c Pataudi b Shinde	45	– c Modi b Amarnath	79
C. Oakes lbw b Mankad	4	– st Hindlekar b Mankad	8
H. T. Bartlett c Mankad b Shinde	33	– b Mankad	0
S. C. Griffith c Mankad b Shinde	0	– c Hindlekar b Mankad	8
H. E. Hammond c Banerjee b Mankad	2	– b Mankad	33
J. K. Nye not out	0	– c Hindlekar b Shinde	16
J. N. Bartlett c Hindlekar b Shinde	0	– lbw b Mankad	10
B 15, l-b 5, n-b 6	26	B 17, l-b 6, n-b 3, w 1	27
	253		**427**

Sussex Bowling

	Overs	Mdns	Runs	Wkts	Overs	Mdns	Runs	Wkts
Nye	25	2	122	—	11	—	39	—
Hammond	32	4	109	—	7	—	24	—
Cox	27	4	86	2	2	—	15	—
James Langridge	17	2	76	—	16	6	33	1
J. N. Barltett	11.5	1	55	1	4	1	14	—
Oakes	19	—	78	—	4	—	1	—
H. T. Bartlett					1	—	1	—

India Bowling

	Overs	Mdns	Runs	Wkts	Overs	Mdns	Runs	Wkts
Banerjee	11	2	32	1	10	—	50	2
Amarnath	26	10	39	2	26	8	60	2
Mankad	26	10	44	3	40.4	9	140	5
Nayudu	10	—	33	—	4	—	17	—
Shinde	27	3	60	4	31	3	116	1
Hazare	7	1	19	—	2	—	17	—

ENGLAND v INDIA

Third Test Match

Played at The Oval, August 17, 19, 20, 1946

Drawn. Utterly ruined by the weather, the match was abandoned at lunch time on Tuesday, the result leaving England winners of the rubber by virtue of the victory gained at Lord's. Rain that fell until one o'clock so affected the ground that it was doubtful if play would have been attempted even at five o'clock on Saturday but for the crowds of people who waited around the walls from early in the morning. As it was about ten thousand people saw Merchant and Mushtaq Ali score 79, a stand which lasted twenty minutes longer on Monday morning before Fishlock, with a lightning throw from mid-on, hit the stumps; the partnership realised 94 in 110 minutes. In two and a half hours before lunch that day India lost four wickets altogether and scored 122 runs, a rate of progress indicating length bowling and smart fielding but, as on Saturday, some false strokes went perilously near outstretched hands.

Merchant maintained his mastery without ever becoming menacing as a hard hitter, and then lost his wicket unluckily. He started for a short run, was sent back by Mankad but moved too slowly and Compton, running behind the bowler from mid-on, kicked the ball on to the stumps – an incident reminiscent of that by Joe Hulme, another Arsenal and England forward, who in the same way dismissed Iddon of Lancashire in 1938 when

Middlesex visited Old Trafford. This was a sad finish to a remarkable display of skilled concentration lasting five hours and a quarter. Merchant hit twelve 4's, excelling in late cuts and pulls, while placing on record the highest innings for India in a Test Match against England. He and Mankad were forcing the pace when the disaster happened – they added 46 in half an hour for the seventh wicket, Merchant leaving at 272. Mankad, bowled playing forward, scored 42 out of 87 in an hour, his pulls and drives coming as a refreshing change after much extreme care on a dead pitch which afforded bowlers only the doubtful help of the occasional rising ball.

Hammond frequently changed his attack, allowing no one a long spell. Edrich, always straight with some off-break, proved most effective, but, after the use of the heaviest roller, Pataudi relied mainly on Amarnath and Mankad. Two splendid catches disposed of Washbrook, taken at short leg, and Fishlock, at deep square leg, while Hutton, second out at 55, fell playing back at a perfect length ball that kept low; Mankad's figures then read – 9 overs, 4 maidens, 9 runs, 2 wickets – reward for clever left-hand slow bowling, with mixed break. Compton, often going in to the ball and making some brilliant strokes, played out time with Hammond, and nothing could be done on the last day.

The official return of attendance on Monday was 26,285, of whom 20,253 paid 3s. 6d. at the turnstiles, and 4,080 were holders of tickets bought before the match.

The Prime Minister and Mrs Attlee were present on Saturday and Monday.   H.P.

India

V. M. Merchant run out 128	S. W. Sohoni not out................... 29
Mushtaq Ali run out 59	C. S. Nayudu c Washbrook b Bedser 4
Nawab of Pataudi b Edrich.............. 9	D. D. Hindlekar lbw b Edrich............ 3
L. Amarnath b Edrich.............. 8	B 1, l-b 5, n-b 4 10
V. S. Hazare c Compton b Gover 11	
R. S. Modi b Smith 27	
Abdul Hafeez b Edrich 1	1/94 2/124 3/142 4/162 5/225 331
V. Mankad b Bedser 42	6/226 7/272 8/313 9/325

England

L. Hutton lbw b Mankad 25	W. R. Hammond not out 9
C. Washbrook c Mushtaq Ali b Mankad ... 17	B 11, l-b 1 12
L. B. Fishlock c Merchant b Nayudu 8	
D. Compton not out 24	1/48 2/55 3/66 (3 wkts) 95

W. J. Edrich, James Langridge, T. P. B. Smith, T. G. Evans, A. V. Bedser and A. R. Gover did not bat.

England Bowling

	Overs	Mdns	Runs	Wkts
Gover	21	3	56	1
Bedser............	32	6	60	2
Smith	21	4	58	1
Edrich............	19.2	4	68	4
Langridge	29	9	64	—
Compton	5	—	15	—

India Bowling

	Overs	Mdns	Runs	Wkts
Amarnath.........	15	6	30	—
Sohoni	4	3	2	—
Hazare	2	1	4	—
Mankad	20	7	28	2
Nayudu...........	9	2	19	1

Umpires: J. Smart and F. Chester.

OXFORD UNIVERSITY v INDIA

Played at Oxford, May 21, 22, 23, 1952

India won by nine wickets. A great fourth-wicket stand of 366 by Umrigar and Hazare – the highest for any wicket by India against an English team – played the major part in bringing the tourists their victory at the end of six games. The Indians were badly placed, with three men out for 32, when the pair came together, and they raised the score to 398 in three and three-quarter hours before Hazare declared. Both drove gloriously. Umrigar hit three 6s and thirty-three 4s in his not out 229 made in four and a quarter hours. He joined Hazare and Merchant as the only Indians who have scored a double hundred against English teams. Hazare, who had been out of form, hit twenty-nine 4s. The off-spin bowling of Ghulam Ahmed was another factor in the Indians' success. He took 13 wickets for 150 in the match. Cowdrey played two good innings for Oxford, and the stylish batting of Dowding in the second innings earned him his Blue.

Oxford University

B. Boobbyer b Ghulam Ahmed	37	– b Shinde	28
W. G. E Wiley c Hazare b Ghulam Ahmed	23	– lbw b Shinde	35
P. D. S. Blake b Ghulam Ahmed	5	– b Shinde	0
M. C. Cowdrey b Ghulam Ahmed	92	– b Hazare	54
A. L. Dowding b Hazare	0	– b Ghulam Ahmed	69
J. de Villiers b Divecha	45	– lbw b Ghulam Ahmed	6
P. J Whitcombe lbw b Ghulam Ahmed	4	– lbw b Ghulam Ahmed	22
I. D. F. Coutts b Ghulam Ahmed	1	– c and b Ghulam Ahmed	0
D. C. P. R. Jowett not out	12	– run out	0
W. M. Mitchell c Hazare b Ghulam Ahmed	2	– c and b Ghulam Ahmed	9
A. J. Coxon b Ghulam Ahmed	0	– not out	1
L-b 6	6	B 4, l-b 4	8

1/43 2/56 3/70 4/71 5/181   227   1/53 2/53 3/72 4/117 5/173   232
6/196 7/200 8/221 9/227   6/190 7/192 8/197 9/231

India

P. Roy c Wiley b Coxon	0	– c Boobbyer b Coxon	8
D. K. Gaekwad c Whitcombe b Coxon	4	– not out	16
P. R. Umrigar not out	229	– not out	29
H. R. Adhikari b Coutts	1		
V. S. Hazare not out	161		
B 1, l-b 2	3	L-b 8, n-b 1	9

1/0 2/19 3/32   (3 wkts dec.) 398   1/25   (1 wkt) 62

V. L. Manjrekar, C. D. Gopinath, S. G. Shinde, R. V. Divecha, P. Sen and Ghulam Ahmed did not bat.

India Bowling

	Overs	Mdns	Runs	Wkts	Overs	Mdns	Runs	Wkts
Divecha	17	7	35	1	11	2	33	—
Hazare	27	14	28	1	9	3	16	1
Umrigar	7	—	18	—				
Ghulam Ahmed	41.1	13	84	8	43.4	16	66	5
Shinde	20	6	56	—	47	13	107	3
Roy					4	2	2	—

Oxford University Bowling

	Overs	Mdns	Runs	Wkts	Overs	Mdns	Runs	Wkts
Coxon............	15	3	49	2	5	1	18	1
Coutts...........	24	3	93	1	5	—	22	—
Mitchell..........	17	3	78	—				
Jowett............	23	1	112	—				
de Villiers	2	—	19	—				
Cowdrey..........	6	—	44	—				
Boobbyer					0.5	—	13	—

Umpires: D. Hendren and F. Chester.

ENGLAND v INDIA
First Test Match

Played at Leeds, June 5, 6, 7, 9, 1952

England won by seven wickets. History was made in the match which, if not reaching the high standard expected from Test cricketers, was crammed with exciting incidents, remarkable collapses and gallant recoveries. But, above all, were the events which occurred at the commencement of India's second innings. They went in facing a first innings deficit of 41, and within a few minutes the match seemed almost over. India lost their first four wickets without a run scored and the crowd were stunned into silence as the drama unfolded before them. No Test side had ever before made such a bad start to an innings, although memories went back to the time when Australia lost three men before scoring against England at Brisbane in 1950. India possessed a reasonable chance of victory before this disaster overtook them, and although they tried hard to make up for it the blow was too severe. In the end England won comfortably enough, but the margin does not show how hard they had to fight under conditions which were mostly in favour of their rivals. Success by India might well have given them the confidence they so badly needed and which never came throughout the tour.

For Hutton the match was a personal triumph. Tradition had been broken with his appointment as a professional captain of England and he must have known that the eyes of the world were upon him. He did not falter and his astute leadership earned him many admirers and, perhaps, guided future policy. When Hazare beat Hutton in the toss there seemed little reason, except for past failures, why India should not have produced a good total. The pitch gave no help to bowlers, but India were on the defensive almost from the first ball. Rapid bowling changes unsettled them, and when their first three wickets fell for 42 another of their total collapses seemed imminent. At that stage young Manjrekar joined his captain, Hazare, and by thoroughly good batting they pulled the game round. Hazare chose the occasion to play himself back to form, but it was the performance of Manjrekar which caught the imagination of most people. He showed skill and nerve far in excess of that normally associated with a youth of 20. They carried the total to 264 before Hazare, who batted four hours, twenty minutes, edged a catch to Evans.

That was the wicket England had been waiting for, and they showed their appreciation with another devastating spell which undid nearly all the good work of the fourth pair. In the next over Manjrekar was brilliantly caught at second slip, Watkins diving to his left and holding the ball while rolling over. Manjrekar's 133 occupied four and a half hours and included nineteen 4s. The total was still 264 when yet another wicket fell, Gopinath being yorked, and although Phadkar and Mantri played out the remaining twenty minutes England must have been well satisfied with their day's work.

An overnight downpour changed their ideas, for India's total, moderate as it was under good conditions, became much more formidable on a difficult pitch. And so it turned out. Only thirty-five minutes were needed to capture the four remaining Indian wickets, Laker taking them all in the course of nine balls. Then came England's turn to bat, and it soon became obvious that they were in for a difficult time. Hazare quickly brought on his off-spinner Ghulam Ahmed, and Hutton and Simpson had to call upon all their skill to save themselves. Simpson was lucky on a number of occasions, but Hutton left first, caught in the leg-trap off a ball which turned and lifted. Simpson fell in similar fashion, and May hit over a ball he turned into a yorker and was bowled. When a struggling Compton provided Ramchand with his third catch at short leg, England were in serious trouble, but they, too, found the men for the occasion. Graveney and Watkins, the successes of the tour in India the previous winter, fought back grimly, and their stand of 90 proved the turning point of the match. Watkins fell towards the close, the day ending with England 87 behind and half their wickets left. Ghulam Ahmed must have been a tired man, having bowled 46 overs (17 maidens) for his four for 75.

The cricket, already exciting, became even tenser before the large Saturday crowd. Graveney, whose fine innings of the previous day helped to save his side, did not last much longer, but the audacious batting of Evans placed England on top. Even the accurate Ghulam Ahmed was mastered and not until four were needed for the lead did Evans falter. He made 66 in ninety-seven minutes, and a determined Jenkins helped him add 79 for the seventh wicket. Considering that they would have to bat in the fourth innings on a pitch always likely to be difficult, England's lead of 41 did not appear enough.

Then came that astonishing Indian breakdown that virtually settled the issue. In the course of the first 14 balls Trueman claimed three wickets and Bedser one. Only the dismissal of Gaekwad by Bedser was the result of the ball doing the unexpected. Trueman upset Roy, Manjrekar and Mantri by his fiery pace and hostility. Hazare had changed the batting order, sending in Mantri and Manjrekar early, but it was left to Hazare himself to stop the rot. First he prevented Trueman's hat-trick, Mantri and Manjrekar having fallen to successive balls. Then, after losing Umrigar, fifth out at 26, he found a defiant partner in Phadkar. Yet again the game swung round. Gradually the excitement eased as it was seen that Hazare and Phadkar were in no way unsettled, and at one stage India, despite their disasters, must have started thinking of victory. Ten minutes before the close Hutton brought back Trueman for a final fling and the move worked, Hazare being beaten and bowled by sheer pace. His great effort with Phadkar added 105. It was the best Indian sixth-wicket stand against England.

So India began the fourth and what proved to be the last day 95 ahead with four wickets left, but there was no more fight left in them. Jenkins dismissed Gopinath and Ramchand with successive deliveries, and with another wicket falling at the same total England were set to get only 125 to win. Even then the match was not without surprises, for England made heavy weather of the task, struggling all the way and taking two and a half hours over the runs. Hutton had his middle stump knocked flat, and Simpson, although making 51, should have been out when 16. May soon left, but Compton and Graveney, taking an hour, carefully knocked off the remaining 36 runs. Trueman, in his first Test, emerged as England's most successful bowler with seven wickets for 116 runs, but, lively as he was, weak batting on the part of the Indians helped him. The attendance for the four days was 74,000 and receipts were over £17,000. – L.S.

India

P. Roy st Evans b Jenkins	19	– c Compton b Trueman	0
D. K. Gaekwad b Bedser	9	– c Laker b Bedser	0
P. R. Umrigar c Evans b Trueman	8	– c and b Jenkins	9
V. S. Hazare c Evans b Bedser	89	– b Trueman	56
V. L. Manjrekar c Watkins b Trueman	133	– b Trueman	0
D. G. Phadkar c Watkins b Laker	12	– b Bedser	64
C. D. Gopinath b Trueman	0	– lbw b Jenkins	8
M. K. Mantri not out	13	– b Trueman	0
G. S. Ramchand c Watkins b Laker	0	– st Evans b Jenkins	0
S. G. Shinde c May b Laker	2	– not out	7
Ghulam Ahmed b Laker	0	– st Evans b Jenkins	14
B 1, l-b 7	8	L-b 5, w 1, n-b 1	7

1/18 2/40 3/42 4/264 5/264   293   1/0 2/0 3/0 4/0 5/26   165
6/264 7/291 8/291 9/293   6/131 7/143 8/143 9/143

England

L. Hutton c Ramchand b Ghulam Ahmed	10	– b Phadkar	10
R. T. Simpson c Ramchand b Ghulam Ahmed	23	– c Mantri b Ghulam Ahmed	51
P. B. H. May b Shinde	16	– c Phadkar b Ghulam Ahmed	4
D. C. S. Compton c Ramchand b Ghulam Ahmed	14	– not out	35
T. W. Graveney b Ghulam Ahmed	71	– not out	20
A. J. Watkins lbw b Ghulam Ahmed	48		
T. G. Evans lbw b Hazare	66		
R. O. Jenkins c Mantri b Ramchand	38		
J. C. Laker b Phadkar	15		
A. V. Bedser b Ramchand	7		
F. S. Trueman not out	0		
B 15, l-b 11	26	B 4, l-b 3, n-b 1	8

1/21 2/48 3/62 4/92 5/182   334   1/16 2/42 3/89   (3 wkts) 128
6/211 7/290 8/325 9/329

England Bowling

	Overs	Mdns	Runs	Wkts	Overs	Mdns	Runs	Wkts
Bedser	33	13	38	2	21	9	32	2
Trueman	26	6	89	3	9	1	27	4
Laker	22.3	9	39	4	13	4	17	—
Watkins	11	1	21	—	11	2	32	—
Jenkins	27	6	78	1	13	2	50	4
Compton	7	1	20	—				

India Bowling

	Overs	Mdns	Runs	Wkts	Overs	Mdns	Runs	Wkts
Phadkar	24	7	54	1	11	2	21	1
Ramchand	36.2	11	61	2	17	3	43	—
Ghulam Ahmed	63	24	100	5	22	8	37	2
Hazare	20	7	22	1	3	—	11	—
Shinde	22	5	71	1	2	—	8	—

Umpires: H. Elliott (Lancashire) and H. G. Baldwin.

ENGLAND v INDIA
Third Test Match
Played at Manchester, July 17, 18, 19, 1952

England won by an innings and 207 runs. The fast bowling of Trueman and England's superlative catching and fielding made this a memorable Test. Sensing the opportunity presented him through a pitch greasy on top after rain, Trueman produced so much pace and extracted such life from the turf that he thoroughly demoralised the opposition. Much as he was assisted both by a series of splendid catches close to the wicket and by a surprising amount of irresolute batting, he looked to be England's best fast bowling prospect since the war. His pace and lift were only two of the factors which created this impression. Just as important were his considerable improvement in control compared with his bowling in the first two Tests, his abounding confidence and his ardour.

Conditions typical of Manchester's weather reputation provided the background to the opening day's play. Not only did showers limit the cricket to three hours and fifty minutes, but the atmosphere was always heavy and the light never good. After Hutton won the toss for the first time in the series, he and Sheppard took such care to give England a safe start that only 28 runs came in the first hour and 48 in the second. Their task was not altogether easy, as Phadkar and Divecha moved the ball late in the humid air and occasionally a ball lifted awkwardly.

In the second over after lunch, when the light was at its worst, Sheppard's impressive innings ended. Only one more ball was bowled before the umpires decided to suspend play. Soon after the resumption Hutton (56) passed the Test aggregate of 5,410 of J. B. Hobbs, and he continued his polished display to the end of the day, when he required 15 for his 16th century in Test cricket and the 111th of his career. All day India were handicapped by a wet ball. No doubt this was responsible for the limited use Hazare made of his slow bowlers.

Cold, drab weather and showers persisted also throughout the second day, when play was restricted to three and a quarter hours. Until the advent of Evans, England's innings remained as sombre as the setting. Hutton, taking an hour and a quarter to complete his century, did not reach his form of the first day and for a long time May batted with exceeding caution. When he became more free May excelled with the on-drive, and once he drove Mankad high over mid-on with a stroke perfect in timing and punishing in its power. For half an hour before the close Evans brought gaiety to the cricket and, to the delight of 25,000 people, he continued his assault on the third morning. In two periods amounting to an hour and ten minutes he hit 71 out of 84. In his last over Evans took a 2 and three 4s from successive balls and gave the bowler a return catch from the next.

During the closing stages of England's innings the pitch appeared to be easy, but, with his extra pace, Trueman quickly demonstrated the devil which could be pounded from it. Bowling down wind at extreme speed, making the ball whip from the ground and often rear nastily, Trueman was the chief instrument in India's rout for a score equalling their lowest in Test cricket, that against Australia at Brisbane in 1947-48. A magnificent catch at short-leg by Lock when he touched the ball for the first time in a Test match helped Bedser to Mankad's wicket, and, equally well supported in the field, Trueman took the next six. His field contained three slips, three men in the gulley, two at short-leg and a short mid-off, and every chance, no matter how fast or difficult, was taken with assurance. Trueman's analysis was one of the best in Test history.

Trueman began India's second collapse by dismissing the unfortunate Roy, who failed to score in either innings, and such was the measure of England's ascendancy that Hutton did not need to recall him for a second spell. After a short stand by Adhikari and Hazare, India crumpled so much against Bedser and Lock that the last seven wickets fell for 27. In their two innings India batted only three hours and three-quarters. This provided the only modern instance of a Test team dismissed twice in one day. The victory ensured England of the rubber. – R.J.H.

England

L. Hutton c Sen b Divecha	104	J. C. Laker c Sen b Divecha	0
D. S. Sheppard lbw b Ramchand	34	A. V. Bedser c Phadkar b Ghulam Ahmed	17
J. T. Ikin c Divecha b Ghulam Ahmed	29	G. A. R. Lock not out	1
P. B. H. May c Sen b Mankad	69	B 2, l-b 2	4
T. W. Graveney lbw b Divecha	14		
A. J. Watkins c Phadkar b Mankad	4	1/78 2/133 3/214 4/248 (9 wkts dec.) 347
T. G. Evans c and b Ghulam Ahmed	71	5/252 6/284 7/292 8/336 9/347

F. S. Trueman did not bat.

India

V. Mankad c Lock b Bedser	4	– lbw b Bedser	6
P. Roy c Hutton b Trueman	0	– c Laker b Trueman	0
H. R. Adhikari c Graveney b Trueman	0	– c May b Lock	27
V. S. Hazare b Bedser	16	– c Ikin b Lock	16
P. R. Umrigar b Trueman	4	– c Watkins b Bedser	3
D. G. Phadkar c Sheppard b Trueman	0	– b Bedser	5
V. L. Manjrekar c Ikin b Trueman	22	– c Evans b Bedser	0
R. V. Divecha b Trueman	4	– b Bedser	2
G. S. Ramchand c Graveney b Trueman	2	– c Watkins b Lock	1
P. Sen c Lock b Trueman	4	– not out	13
Ghulam Ahmed not out	1	– c Ikin b Lock	0
L-b 1	1	B 8, n-b 1	9

1/4 2/4 3/5 4/17 5/17   58   1/7 2/7 3/55 4/59 5/66   82
6/45 7/51 8/53 9/53   6/66 7/66 8/67 9/77

India Bowling

	Overs	Mdns	Runs	Wkts
Phadkar	22	10	30	—
Divecha	45	12	102	3
Ramchand	33	7	78	1
Mankad	28	9	67	2
Ghulam Ahmed	9	3	43	3
Hazare	7	3	23	—

England Bowling

	Overs	Mdns	Runs	Wkts	Overs	Mdns	Runs	Wkts
Bedser	11	4	19	2	15	6	27	5
Trueman	8.4	2	31	8	8	5	9	1
Laker	2	—	7	—				
Watkins					4	3	1	—
Lock					9.3	2	36	4

Umpires: D. Davies and F. S. Lee.

SURREY v INDIA

Played at The Oval, July 26, 28, 29, 1952

India won by six wickets and provided the biggest shock of the season for the ultimate County Champions. A hat-trick by Divecha and the no-balling of Lock for alleged throwing made the match memorable. On a lively pitch, Surrey were out just before lunch in two hours. No one faced the quick, swinging deliveries of Divecha confidently. He did the hat-trick when disposing of Whittaker, Laker and Bedser at 59, and deserved his analysis of six wickets for 29 runs. Loader, the young Surrey fast bowler, shone when India batted and except for missed chances he would have had better figures than five for

63. After tea the no-balling of Lock by umpire Price from square-leg caused a sensation. Watching Lock's action very closely, Price "called" the Surrey left-arm spin bowler once in an over, then, a little later, twice in an over. Lock's delivery seemed to be called into question when he bowled his quicker ball.

Surrey, 108 behind on the first innings, turned the fortunes of the game on the second day, thanks largely to May, who captained them for the first time. Excelling with the cover-drive and square-cut, he hit twenty-four 4s in a stay of four and a quarter hours. India wanted 212 to win, and when Gaekwad fell into Bedser's leg trap with only a single on the board their task seemed heavy, but next morning Adhikari, the vice-captain, took his side to victory. He made the winning hit after resisting the county for four hours. Phadkar shared with him in the match-winning unfinished fourth-wicket partnership of 107.

Surrey

D. G. W. Fletcher c Adhikari b Ramchand	7	– b Divecha	22
T. H. Clark c Manjrekar b Ramchand	18	– c Sen b Ramchand	4
B. Constable c Umrigar b Divecha	12	– c Hazare b Divecha	18
P. B. H. May c Ramchand b Divecha	5	– c Sen b Phadkar	143
A. F. Brazier c Adhikari b Ramchand	0	– c Umrigar b Ramchand	42
G. J. Whittaker c Umrigar b Divecha	14	– c Umrigar b Ghulam Ahmed	20
A. J. McIntyre c Ghulam Ahmed b Ramchand	6	– run out	35
J. C. Laker c Phadkar b Divecha	6	– c Ramchand b Ghulam Ahmed	4
A. V. Bedser b Divecha	0	– c Manjrekar b Ghulam Ahmed	1
G. A. R. Lock not out	8	– not out	0
P. J. Loader b Divecha	0	– c Manjrekar b Ghulam Ahmed	0
N-b 1	1	B 14, l-b 6, w 1, n-b 9	30

1/10 2/33 3/43 4/43 5/53 6/59   71   1/10 2/44 3/50 4/217 5/275   319
7/59 8/59 9/65   6/277 7/300 8/308 9/319

India

P. Roy st McIntyre b Bedser	32	– c Lock b Laker	15
D. K. Gaekwad c Lock b Loader	8	– c Laker b Bedser	0
H. R. Adhikari c May b Bedser	5	– not out	98
V. S. Hazare c Laker b Loader	5	– c May b Lock	32
P. R. Umrigar c McIntyre b Loader	6	– lbw b Loader	8
D. G. Phadkar c Constable b Loader	17	– not out	50
V. L. Manjrekar c Lock b Laker	44		
R. V. Divecha c Bedser b Loader	15		
G. S. Ramchand st McIntyre b Laker	37		
P. Sen c Lock b Laker	3		
Ghulam Ahmed not out	0		
B 1, l-b 2, n-b 4	7	B 5, l-b 4, n-b 2	11

1/17 2/37 3/48 4/59 5/60   179   1/1 2/28 3/88 4/107   (4 wkts) 214
6/77 7/118 8/172 9/176

India Bowling

	Overs	Mdns	Runs	Wkts	Overs	Mdns	Runs	Wkts
Phadkar	9	4	18	—	26	11	44	1
Divecha	11	3	29	6	28	7	94	2
Ramchand	13	4	23	4	28	7	85	2
Ghulam Ahmed					22.5	8	50	4
Hazare					7	2	16	—

Surrey Bowling

	Overs	Mdns	Runs	Wkts	Overs	Mdns	Runs	Wkts
Bedser............	24	9	46	2	23	5	49	1
Loader	22	3	63	5	19	4	59	1
Lock.............	12	1	37	—	22	9	32	1
Laker	7.1	1	26	3	20	3	54	1
Clark					2	—	9	—

Umpires: C. H. Welch and W. F. Price.

WORCESTERSHIRE v INDIA

Played at Worcester, April 29, 30, May 1, 1959

Drawn. The first big match of the tour was notable mainly for the action of Buller, the Test umpire and former Worcestershire wicket-keeper, in no-balling Pearson, the county fast bowler, five times on the opening day for throwing. Kenyon, Worcestershire's new captain, persevered with Pearson and he emerged with the best figures on either side in taking five wickets for 63 runs. A cold wind did not help India who lost half their wickets for 82 but Borde, ninth out on the second morning, hit strongly to leg and also drove and cut well while scoring thirteen 4s in his 90. Worcestershire began by losing four men for 46 and then came a grand display of powerful hitting by Dews who with two 6s and fourteen 4s made 122 out of a partnership of 187 with Broadbent in three hours. Broadbent concentrated on defence and though he hit one 6 and eleven 4s he occupied four and three-quarter hours for his not out 102. India, by capturing the last five county wickets on the third morning for the addition of 44, effected a recovery though they faced a deficit of 86. A painstaking effort by Contractor was in marked contrast to the batting of Umrigar who, when his side looked safe, pulled and drove so freely at the expense of the slow bowlers, Horton and Slade, that he hit one 6 and thirteen 4s while getting 87 out of 124 added with Contractor.

India

P. Roy lbw b Pearson	13	– c Slade b Flavell ... 0
N. J. Contractor c Booth b Pearson	17	– c Broadbent b Pearson ... 46
P. R. Umrigar b Flavell	9	– c Aldridge b Slade ... 87
V. L. Manjrekar c Booth b Pearson	29	– not out ... 19
D. K. Gaekwad run out	10	– not out ... 4
A. G. Kripal Singh c Booth b Flavell	0	
C. G. Borde c Slade b Pearson	90	
N. S. Tamhane c Dews b Aldridge	7	
S. P. Gupte c Kenyon b Aldridge	8	
R. Surendranath c Pearson b Slade	14	
R. B. Desai not out	0	
L-b 13, n-b 9	22	L-b 1 ... 1

1/34 2/36 3/56 4/80 5/82   219   1/6 2/130 3/144   (3 wkts) 157
6/115 7/154 8/176 9/219

Worcestershire

D. Kenyon c Tamhane b Desai ... 3	D. B. Pearson c Tamhane b Gupte ... 5
L. Outschoorn c sub b Gupte ... 34	J. A. Flavell b Gupte ... 2
M. J. Horton b Desai ... 0	K. J. Aldridge c Manjrekar b Gupte ... 0
D. W Richardson b Gupte ... 25	
R. G. Broadbent not out ... 102	
G. Dews c sub b Gupte ... 122	B 1, l-b 5, w 1 ... 7
D. N. F. Slade c Tamhane b Desai ... 5	1/7 2/17 3/53 4/66 5/253 305
R. Booth c sub b Desai ... 0	6/270 7/272 8/283 9/295

Worcestershire Bowling

	Overs	Mdns	Runs	Wkts	Overs	Mdns	Runs	Wkts
Flavell	34	10	70	2	15	6	27	1
Aldridge	27	10	59	2	12	5	21	—
Pearson	22	10	40	4	10.1	4	23	1
Slade	25.1	20	14	1	17	5	57	1
Horton	3	—	14	—	9	3	28	—

India Bowling

	Overs	Mdns	Runs	Wkts
Desai	33	6	88	4
Surendranath	26	5	61	—
Gupte	39.5	17	92	6
Borde	9	4	25	—
Umrigar	11	2	32	—

Umpires: J. S. Buller and E. Davies.

MINOR COUNTIES v INDIA

Played at Longton, Stoke-on-Trent, June 10, 11, 12, 1959

Minor Counties won by six wickets. This was a remarkable match. The rival captains, Gaekwad and Ikin, each hit a century, but dwarfing both these fine displays was that by Sharpe, the young Yorkshireman, who, when India declared and set Minor Counties to make 334 in four hours fifty minutes, scored 202, including five 6s, one 5 and twenty-nine 4s in three and a half hours. He offered many chances during his bold assault and received splendid help from Bailey, who provided the backbone to a winning stand of 284. Sharpe left when only six more runs were required and was quickly followed by Bailey and Ikin, but though rain deprived them of twenty minutes the Minor Counties still had thirty-five minutes to spare. Gaekwad was taken ill during the tea interval on the first day, and though he completed his innings he took no further part in the match, the side being led by Roy on the last two days. It was the Minor Counties' first win over a touring team since 1928 when they beat West Indies by 42 runs at Exeter.

India

N. J. Contractor b Young	7	– b Birkenshaw	26
A. L. Apte b Craig	1	– run out	44
P. Roy b Craig	4	– st Simons b Atkinson	22
A. G. Kripal Singh c Ikin b Young	8	– not out	66
J. M. Ghorpade b Laitt	67	– c Sharpe b Atkinson	52
M. L. Jaisimha c Laitt b Birkenshaw	51	– c Birkenshaw b Laitt	12
D. K. Gaekwad c Birkenshaw b Laitt	100		
N. S. Tamhane c Simons b Laitt	22	– run out	29
R. Surendranath c Ikin b Laitt	4		
R. B. Desai c Laitt b Young	15	– b Laitt	13
V. M. Muddiah not out	0		
B 5, l-b 3	8	B 4, l-b 6	10

1/6 2/12 3/12 4/45 5/117   287   1/43 2/65 3/98   (7 wkts dec.) 274
6/181 7/242 8/246 9/287   4/145 5/178 6/254 7/274

Minor Counties

P. J. Sharpe (*Yorkshire*) c Desai b Surendranath . . . . 6 – c Contractor b Muddiah 202
D. H. Cole (*Devon*) c Jaisimha b Muddiah . . . . 36 – c Muddiah b Surendranath 22
F. R. Bailey (*Staffordshire*)
           c Contractor b Surendranath. 5 – c Kripal Singh b Muddiah 79
R. M. James (*Berkshire*) b Jaisimha . . . . 5 – not out 4
J. T. Ikin (*Staffordshire*) b Muddiah . . . . .118 – c Tamhane b Jaisimha 0
C. R. M. Atkinson (*Durham*) b Ghorpade . . . . 23 – not out 1
J. Birkenshaw (*Yorkshire*) c Tamhane b Kripal Singh 18
R. G. Simons (*Hertfordshire*) run out 0
I. T. Craig (*Cambridgeshire*) c and b Kripal Singh . . 1
D. J. Laitt (*Oxfordshire*) not out 7
S. H. Young (*Durham*) c Ghorpade b Kripal SIngh . 0
         B 5, l-b 4 9   B 19, l-b 7 26

1/19 2/41 3/50 4/86 5/135   228   1/44 2/328   (4 wkts) 334
6/192 7/200 8/209 9/225   3/329 4/330

Minor Counties Bowling

	Overs	Mdns	Runs	Wkts	Overs	Mdns	Runs	Wkts
Young	25	1	94	3	15	3	54	—
Craig	17	—	46	2	15	2	39	—
Laitt	15.1	3	58	4	13.3	1	53	2
Cole	4	—	20	—				
Birkenshaw . . . . . . :	10	2	23	1	16	3	67	1
Atkinson	6	—	38	—	7	—	51	2

India Bowling

	Overs	Mdns	Runs	Wkts	Overs	Mdns	Runs	Wkts
Desai	17	4	46	—	15	2	64	—
Surendranath	20	9	42	2	11	—	62	1
Jaisimha	3	1	7	1	10	—	22	1
Muddiah	25	8	56	2	17	2	74	2
Kripal Singh	17	3	54	3	14	1	53	—
Ghorpade	6	—	14	1	4	—	33	—

Umpires: F. H. Moore and H. C. Turner.

MIDDLESEX v INDIA

Played at Lord's, July 18, 20, 21, 1959

India won by four wickets, their second victory against a county side. Dominant feature was the remarkable début by Baig, the Oxford University batsman. During his two hours at the crease he hit nineteen 4s in his magnificent 102 and shared a fourth-wicket partnership of 117 with Umrigar. Another young player, M. J. Smith, playing his first game for Middlesex, bowled sensibly to take four for 84. Despite a determined innings by Hooker, the county never recovered from losing their first two wickets to successive balls from Surendranath before a run had been scored and they followed on 156 behind. They did little better when they batted a second time, being dismissed for 222. Borde captured five wickets with his leg-breaks. India lost six wickets in scoring the 67 runs they needed to win, mainly through impetuosity.

India

P. Roy c Bick b Smith	51		
N. J. Contractor c Smith b Robins	55	– lbw b Bick	14
A. A. Baig st Murray b Smith	102	– c Murray b Smith	29
C. G. Borde run out	11	– b Smith	4
P. R. Umrigar b Smith	51		
R. G. Nadkarni c Gale b Smith	13	– b Bick	0
A. L. Apte not out	39	– b Bick	5
A. G. Kripal Singh lbw b Bick	33	– not out	8
M. L. Jaisimha not out	7	– c Robertson b Bick	1
R. Surendranath (did not bat)	–	– not out	1
B 5, l-b 4, w 2	11	L-b 5	5

1/105 2/112 3/157   (7 wkts dec.) 373   1/11 2/34 3/39   (6 wkts) 67
4/274 5/281 6/294 7/361   4/46 5/57 6/61

N. S. Tamhane did not bat.

Middlesex

R. A. Gale c Kripal Singh b Surendranath	0	– c Borde b Jaisimha	17
W. E. Russell b Nadkarni	33	– c Umrigar b Nadkarni	36
R. A. White c Borde b Surendranath	0	– c Borde b Nadkarni	28
R. W. Hooker b Borde	80	– st Tamhane b Borde	9
E. A. Clark b Umrigar	19	– c Surendranath b Nadkarni	46
J. D. Robertson b Nadkarni	15	– b Borde	19
J. T. Murray c Borde b Umrigar	19	– st Tamhane b Borde	5
D. A. Bick c Tamhane b Umrigar	9	– b Nadkarni	26
M. J. Smith not out	17	– c Tamhane b Borde	0
R. V. C. Robins b Nadkarni	3	– lbw b Borde	6
J. Shepperd b Nadkarni	13	– not out	11
B 8, n-b 1	9	B 9, l-b 8, w 1, n-b 1	19

1/0 2/0 3/75 4/124 5/124   217   1/33 2/79 3/99 4/99 5/163   222
6/169 7/179 8/190 9/199   6/192 7/201 8/201 9/206

Middlesex Bowling

	Overs	Mdns	Runs	Wkts	Overs	Mdns	Runs	Wkts
Shepperd	18	1	54	—	2	—	7	—
Hooker	18	7	56	—				
Clark	20	2	61	—	2	—	4	—
Smith	31	9	84	4	9.5	4	27	2
Robins	9	—	57	1				
Bick	15	5	50	1	10	3	24	4

India Bowling

	Overs	Mdns	Runs	Wkts	Overs	Mdns	Runs	Wkts
Surendranath	9	2	34	2	16	5	35	—
Jaisimha	6	1	15	—	12	1	45	1
Umrigar	27	7	66	3	17	4	39	—
Nadkarni	34	22	34	4	33	17	41	4
Kripal Singh	12	1	34	—	4	1	10	—
Borde	6	—	25	1	16.5	5	33	5

Umpires: W. H. Copson and N. Oldfield.

ENGLAND v INDIA

Fourth Test Match

Played at Manchester, July 23, 24, 25, 27, 28, 1959

England won by 171 runs. This was the most interesting match of the series and the only one that went into the fifth day. England might have finished it earlier, but Cowdrey, with India having six wickets down for 127, announced before play began on the third day that in view of the settled weather and the Manchester holidays next week he would not enforce the follow-on if this situation arose.

An excellent pitch provided ideal conditions for batsmen and Pullar, in only his second Test, gained the distinction of becoming the first Lancastrian to hit a hundred for England at Old Trafford, M. J. K. Smith also established himself by scoring his maiden Test century, but overshadowing everything else was the achievement of Abba Ali Baig, the 20-year-old Oxford Freshman, who, drafted into the Indian side, hit a brilliant hundred on his first appearance in Test cricket.

With the rubber already decided the England selectors brought M. J. K. Smith, Dexter and Illingworth into the team to the exclusion of Cowdrey, Moss and Close, but on Peter May becoming ill – he underwent an operation during the match although he saw the first two days' play – Cowdrey was recalled and he captained England for the first time. India showed three changes, Baig, Joshi and Contractor replacing Manjrekar, Tamhane and Apte.

Some skilful bowling by Desai, Surendranath and Umrigar, who made the ball swing in the sweltering atmosphere, induced false strokes, and before lunch on the opening day England offered five chances, but only one was accepted when Parkhouse mistimed a hook.

Three weeks earlier Pullar had made 75 in his first Test innings at Headingley. Again he showed he possessed the big-match temperament. Safe when facing the new ball, he moved his feet well in going forward to the spinners, and whenever he decided to drive he made his stroke with the full flow of the bat. Cowdrey, too, delighted with his powerful drives, but opposed to much leg-theory bowling England spent two and a half hours reaching 100.

Cowdrey had hit one 6 and ten 4s and the stand had yielded 131 when the captain chopped the ball into the wicket-keeper's gloves. After tea India took the new ball but Pullar, as sure as ever, not only completed his hundred but went on to make 131 (fourteen 4s) before he was taken by the wicket-keeper on the leg-side after batting five and a half hours.

Meanwhile, M. J. K. Smith, batting for England for the first time in his normal position at number four and not as an opener where he was tried against New Zealand the previous year, played extremely well and never offering the semblance of a chance during the last two and a half hours, put on 98 with Pullar and 42 with Barrington, England scoring 304 for three wickets on the first day, Smith finishing with 55 and Barrington 22.

Next morning the sun again shone powerfully and both not-out batsmen played confidently, but Smith, having reached his hundred, was caught off a mighty pull, having hit one 5 and twelve 4s in an innings of three and a half hours. His stand with Barrington realised 109. While Smith made most of his runs on the leg-side, Barrington excelled with the cover drive as well as the pull, but Dexter, opposed to Gupte and Nadkarni, shaped uncertainly against the two spinners. Nevertheless, England were 417 for four at lunch and subsequently wickets were sacrificed in a chase for more runs, the last six adding only 73 after the interval. Barrington, getting his last 34 runs in six overs off the new ball, was leg-before making a violent hook. Besides two 6s he hit eleven 4s, and his 87, his best in Test cricket, came in three hours.

India owed much to Surendranath. It was a great feat to send down forty-eight overs in almost exhausting heat, and he finished with five wickets. Nadkarni bowled accurately and always commanded respect, and if a few fielders spoiled the work of the side, Baig, Contractor and Desai could not be faulted. Joshi, who took three catches, gave his best display behind the stumps.

When India batted the difference between the two attacks was soon evident. Cowdrey set an umbrella field for Trueman and Rhodes, and Roy might have gone in the first over, Dexter failing to accept a sharp chance in the slips. As if was, Rhodes removed both opening batsmen, and before the end of the second day India, with six wickets down for 127, were in a hopeless position.

A sterling display by Borde, a 25-year-old professional with Lancashire League experience, was one of the few good features of the third day's play. He drove and pulled to leg with assurance in scoring 75, his best in Test cricket. There was also much to admire in the leg-spin bowling of Barrington, who, seldom used by May, his England and Surrey captain, was given plenty of scope to reveal his hidden talent by Cowdrey and he responded by taking three wickets for 12 runs each. He kept a perfect length and mixed leg spin with the googly.

When England batted again, 282 ahead, it was not surprising that Desai and Surendranath bowled defensively and listlessly. Parkhouse and Pullar, both anxious to gain places in the MCC team to tour West Indies, declined to take risks and the purposeless cricket was derided by the majority of the crowd of 13,000. Later they enjoyed some fine stroke-play by Dexter and Barrington and England wound up an unsatisfactory day 547 in front.

On Monday India, and in particular Baig, restored dignity to the struggle. A splendid second-wicket stand of 109 – the best of the series for the touring team – between Contractor and Baig enabled India to master the bowling, but when Baig had made 85 he was struck on the right temple by a bouncer from Rhodes and was led off the field in a dazed condition. Happily he soon recovered, and next morning when India resumed at 236 for four and Rhodes and Trueman immediately took the new ball, he continued his innings on the departure of Nadkarni. The first ball Baig received (from Rhodes) was another bouncer, but the batsman did not flinch although the Derbyshire bowler subjected the fragile-looking Indian to a hot assault on the leg side and generally pitched much too short.

Baig hovered at 96 for nearly half an hour when to everyone's relief he swept Rhodes to the boundary. The England team joined in the wholehearted applause and Cowdrey shook hands with Baig as he crossed at the end of the over. A natural player with a splendid eye, Baig generally placed himself behind the ball, moving so quickly into position that he always had plenty of time for his strokes. The drive, cut, hook and pull were finely executed, and with Umrigar going most confidently India were beginning to threaten England.

Baig and Umrigar were pressing for victory. They stole sharp singles and were clearly masters of the situation when Baig pulled Mortimore. He thought the ball had beaten Dexter at mid-on, but Dexter picked up brilliantly and Baig had gone too far for when he turned the ball was in Swetman's hands. Both Baig (twelve 4s) and Umrigar (thirteen 4s) batted for four hours twenty minutes.

Actually Umrigar was 94 when Baig left at 321, and on completing his first and only Test hundred in England he realised the cause was hopeless and was eighth to leave, skying Barrington to extra cover with the field spread deep. Trueman finished the match by holding Surendranath at mid-on and shattering Gupte's wicket. So England won with three and a quarter hours to spare.   N.P.

England

W. G. A. Parkhouse c Roy b Surendranath	17	– c Contractor b Nadkarni	49
G. Pullar c Joshi b Surendranath	131	– c Joshi b Gupte	14
M. C. Cowdrey c Joshi b Nadkarni	67	– c Borde b Gupte	9
M. J. K. Smith c Desai b Borde	100	– c Desai b Gupte	9
K. F. Barrington lbw b Surendranath	87	– lbw b Nadkarni	46
E. R. Dexter c Roy b Surendranath	13	– c Umrigar b Gupte	45
R. Illingworth c Gaekwad b Desai	21	– not out	47
J. B. Mortimore c Contractor b Gupte	29	– c Nadkarni b Borde	7
R. Swetman c Joshi b Gupte	9	– not out	21
F. S. Trueman b Surendranath	0	– c Baig b Borde	8
H. J. Rhodes not out	0		
B 7, l-b 7, w 2	16	B 9, l-b 1	10

1/33 2/164 3/262 4/371 5/417   490   1/44 2/100 3/117   (8 wkts dec.) 265
6/440 7/454 8/490 9/490   4/132 5/136 6/196 7/209 8/219

India

P. Roy c Smith b Rhodes	15	– c Illingworth b Dexter	21
N. J. Contractor c Swetman b Rhodes	23	– c Barrington b Rhodes	56
A. A. Baig c Cowdrey b Illingworth	26	– run out	112
D. K. Gaekwad lbw b Trueman	5	– c Illingworth b Rhodes	0
P. R. Umrigar b Rhodes	2	– c Illingworth b Barrington	118
C. G. Borde c and b Barrington	75	– c Swetman b Mortimore	3
R. G. Nadkarni b Barrington	31	– lbw b Trueman	28
P. G. Joshi run out	5	– b Illingworth	5
R. Surendranath b Illingworth	11	– c Trueman b Barrington	4
S. P. Gupte not out	4	– b Trueman	8
R. B. Desai b Barrington	5	– not out	7
L-b 1, w 4, n-b 1	6	B 8, l-b 5, n-b 1	14

1/23 2/54 3/70 4/72 5/78   208   1/35 2/144 3/146 4/180   376
6/124 7/154 8/199 9/199   5/243 6/321 7/334 8/358 9/361

India Bowling

	Overs	Mdns	Runs	Wkts	Overs	Mdns	Runs	Wkts
Desai	39	7	129	1	8	2	14	—
Surendranath	47.1	17	115	5	8	5	15	—
Umrigar	19	3	47	—	7	3	4	—
Gupte	28	8	98	2	26	6	76	4
Nadkarni	28	14	47	1	30	6	93	2
Borde	13	1	38	1	11	1	53	2

England Bowling

	Overs	Mdns	Runs	Wkts	Overs	Mdns	Runs	Wkts
Trueman	15	4	29	1	23.1	6	75	2
Rhodes	18	3	72	3	28	2	87	2
Dexter	3	—	3	—	12	2	33	1
Illingworth	16	10	16	2	39	13	63	1
Mortimore	13	6	46	—	16	6	29	1
Barrington	14	3	36	3	27	4	75	2

Umpires: C. S. Elliott and J. S. Buller.

PAKISTANIS IN ENGLAND

ENGLAND v PAKISTAN
Second Test Match
Played at Nottingham, July 1, 2, 3, 5, 1954

England won by an innings and 129 runs. Pakistan, still striving to acclimatise themselves to cold, wet weather and to adjust their cricket to soft pitches, offered moderate opposition to a side which, although lacking Hutton, who was unfit, showed superiority in all phases. England achieved their first victory at Trent Bridge since 1930, with over ten hours to spare.

When Pakistan began batting on a true pitch, Hanif and Alim-ud-Din faced the England opening attack confidently enough and, despite the dismissal of Alim-ud-Din, neither team could claim appreciable advantage in the first hour. Then Sheppard, deputy to Hutton as captain and opening batsman, called upon Appleyard for his first bowl in Test cricket. No one could have wished for a better start than made by the 30-year-old Yorkshireman, who resumed big cricket that season after two years' illness.

Hanif was leg-before to Appleyard's second ball; Maqsood snicked a catch to the wicket-keeper in his third over; the first ball of the next hit Waqar's middle stump and the second of his fifth sent the off stump of Imtiaz flying. In this dramatic spell of 26 balls, during which the Pakistan total changed from 37 for one to 55 for five, Appleyard took four wickets for six runs. His mixture of in-swingers, off-spinners and leg-cutters, his variation of pace and flight, bore the stamp of a high-skilled craftsman. That exciting period broke the back of the innings and, although Kardar led a commendable rally, Pakistan were all out before tea. On turf so favourable to batsmen, the need for improvement in forward play was clearly revealed.

By contrast, Simpson at once settled into his most pleasing game, driving and hooking with full power and timing his glances admirably. By the close England stood 36 behind with eight wickets left. The one batting failure was May, who, attempting to force a ball well outside his off-stump, pulled it into his wicket.

The sureness of Simpson and Compton's batting next morning carried ominous signs for Pakistan, whose best bowler, Fazal Mahmood, was handicapped by a pulled leg muscle which forced him to shorten his run. Soon after England went in front, however, Compton (20) gave a sharp chance off Fazal. That turned out to be a most expensive miss. Immediately after reaching a handsome century, Simpson picked the wrong ball to hit, but Pakistan's troubles were only in their infancy. First came a fourth-wicket stand of 154 in eighty-five minutes. Well as Compton batted, Graveney played even better. Some of his punishing drives left the bat with the sound of a pistol shot. So did the stroke from which Maqsood courageously, or in self-preservation, caught him at mid-off. England held a formidable position when Bailey joined Compton. This became further strengthened by a partnership of 192 in an hour and three-quarters. Compton scored all but 27 of the runs, yet he owed much to Bailey, who, recognising his partner's form and mood, did all he could to give him the bowling. Making full use of further escapes when 120 and 171, Compton sent the bowling to all parts of the field with a torrent of strokes, orthodox and improvised, crashing and delicate, against which Kadar could not set a field and the bowlers knew not where to pitch. By methods reminiscent of his former glories, Compton raced through his second hundred in eighty minutes and he made his highest score in his 100 innings for England in four hours fifty minutes before missing a leg-break from Khalid

Hassan who, at 16, was the youngest cricketer to be chosen for a Test Match. In the record Test innings played in Nottingham, Compton hit a 6 and thirty-three 4s. Until Sheppard declared, the rest of the England innings came as anti-climax.

Pakistan faced an hour's batting before the close, as well as arrears of 401, but so spiritedly did Hanif and Alim-ud-Din tackle the situation that they made 43 in the first half hour and stayed together to the end. A day on which 496 runs were scored for four wickets remained a triumph for Compton, but the memory of Hanif's fierce hooks and cuts lingered nearly as much.

Next day Hanif resumed his aggressiveness until, having crisply made all but eleven of his runs in boundaries, he fell to the alertness of Evans behind the wicket. Rain limited play to three-quarters of an hour before lunch and cricket was then held up until after tea. For a short time afterwards the ball lifted nastily. One delivery which kicked from a length brought Statham the wicket of Waqar, but soon the turf eased, so that Pakistan's closing score of 189 for six was again disappointing. The best and most adventurous batting was that of Maqsood, who hit two 6s and eight 4s. Unfortunately for Pakistan he did not show discretion in trying for another six off Appleyard, Statham confidently atoning for a previous fielding mistake. Off the previous ball May had held a mighty hit just over the square-leg boundary. Much rain fell during the week-end, but the game began promptly on Monday, when, notwithstanding solid work by Fazal, Sheppard brought it to a close by catching Aslam a quarter of an hour before lunch.   R.J.H.

Pakistan

Hanif Mohammad lbw b Appleyard	19	– c Evans b Bedser	51
Alim-ud-Din b Statham	4	– b Statham	18
Waqar Hassan b Appleyard	7	– c Evans b Statham	7
Maqsood Ahmed c Evans b Appleyard	6	– c Statham b Appleyard	69
Imtiaz Ahmed b Appleyard	11	– lbw b Wardle	33
A. H. Kadar c Compton b Bedser	28	– c Graveney b Wardle	4
Fazal Mahmood c Sheppard b Bedser	14	– b Statham	36
M. E. Z. Ghazali b Statham	18	– c Statham b Bedser	14
Mohammad Aslam b Wardle	16	– c Sheppard b Appleyard	18
Khalid Hassan c May b Appleyard	10	– not out	7
Khan Mohammad not out	13	– c Compton b Wardle	8
B 9, l-b 1, n-b 1	11	B 4, l-b 3	7

1/26 2/37 3/43 4/50 5/55   157   1/69 2/70 3/95 4/164   272
6/86 7/111 8/121 9/138   5/168 6/189 7/216 8/242 9/254

England

D. S. Sheppard c Imtiaz b Khan	37	T. G. Evans b Khan	4
R. T. Simpson b Khalid Hassan	101	J. H. Wardle not out	14
P. B. H. May b Khan	0	B 2, l-b 1, n-b 1	4
D. C. S. Compton b Khalid Hassan	278		
T. W. Graveney c Maqsood b Kardar	84	1/98 2/102 3/185 (6 wkts dec.) 558	
T. E. Bailey not out	36	4/339 5/531 6/536	

A. V. Bedser, J. B. Statham and R. Appleyard did not bat.

England Bowling

	Overs	Mdns	Runs	Wkts	Overs	Mdns	Runs	Wkts
Bedser	21	8	30	2	30	11	83	2
Statham	18	3	38	2	20	3	66	3
Appleyard	17	5	51	5	30.4	8	72	2
Bailey	3	—	18	—				
Wardle	6	3	9	1	32	17	44	3

Pakistan Bowling

	Overs	Mdns	Runs	Wkts
Fazal Mahmood ...	47	7	148	—
Khan Mohammad ..	40	3	155	3
Kardar	28	4	110	1
Khalid Hassan	21	1	116	2
Maqsood Ahmed ...	3	—	25	—

Umpires: F. Chester and T. Spencer.

SUSSEX v PAKISTAN

Played at Hove, May 23, 24, 25, 1962

Sussex won by seven wickets. It was their first victory over a touring team for ten years and they owed it mainly to Dexter, their captain, who had just been named captain of England for the first Test. On the first day, Dexter proved justified sending in Pakistan to bat. He also helped to bring about a collapse; on the second morning he hit a brilliant century before lunch – his first for Sussex for two seasons. On the third morning he took three wickets in seven balls. Burki, the rival captain, though falling leg-before for nought to Dexter, in the first innings, excelled in driving and cutting while getting his first century of the tour. Sussex were also indebted to Thomson, Buss and Bates who with Dexter comprised a very keen seam attack. Dexter was the man of the match at the very end when he made the winning hit. So Pakistan were beaten for the first time during the tour.

Pakistan

Alim-ud-Din b Bates	17	– c Dexter b Thomson 0
Ijaz Butt c Oakman b Dexter	24	– c Bell b Bates 31
Shahid Mahmood c Dexter b Bates	0	– b Bates 19
Mushtaq Mohammad c Bates b Thomson	44	– lbw b Thomson 3
*Javed Burki lbw b Dexter	0	– not out 110
†Imtiaz Ahmed b Bates	1	– c Parks b Buss 29
Intikhab Alam c Suttle b Thompson	19	– b Dexter 41
Afaq Hussain run out	7	– c Parks b Dexter 0
Mahmood Hussain b Bates	16	– c Bell b Dexter 0
Munir Malik b Buss	10	– c Thomson b Bates 16
Mohammad Farooq not out	0	– c Thomson b Dexter 7
B 1, l-b 5	6	L-b 4 4

1/42 2/44 3/45 4/46 5/47   144   1/0 2/54 3/57 4/65 5/92   260
6/89 7/113 8/130 9/136   6/190 7/198 8/198 9/229

Sussex

A. S. M. Oakman c Burki b Mahmood	28	– lbw b Mahmood.............. 2
R. J. Langridge c Intikhab b Munir	8	– not out 10
K. G. Shuttle c and b Afaq	55	– c Intikhab b Munir 13
†J. M. Parks lbw b Munir.....................	36	– c Alim b Munir 4
*E. R. Dexter lbw b Shahid 117		– not out 27
L. J. Lenham lbw b Mahmood	27	
G. C. Cooper run out	55	
N. I. Thomson not out	0	
A. Buss not out..............................	5	
B 10, l-b 5, n-b 2	17	B 4 4

1/18 2/50 3/134 4/134   (7 wkts dec.) 348   1/5 2/20 3/26   (3 wkts) 60
5/203 6/339 7/340

R. V. Bell and D. L. Bates did not bat.

Sussex Bowling

	Overs	Mdns	Runs	Wkts	Overs	Mdns	Runs	Wkts
Thomson	18	7	46	2	19	8	46	2
Buss	17.3	3	55	1	12	3	39	1
Bates	11	7	13	4	27	6	65	3
Dexter	11	3	24	2	23.1	5	80	4
Bell					5	3	10	—
Cooper					3	—	16	—

Pakistan Bowling

	Overs	Mdns	Runs	Wkts	Overs	Mdns	Runs	Wkts
Mahmood	24	7	76	2	10	4	21	1
Munir	31	7	101	2	9.5	1	35	2
Farooq	12	—	71	—				
Afaq	10	2	42	1				
Intikhab	4	—	23	—				
Shahid	5	1	18	1				

Umpires: F. S. Lee and R. S. Lay.

THE COUNTY MATCHES

MODERN COUNTY CRICKET

MORE ENTERPRISE NEEDED

By Colonel R. S. Rait Kerr

The following article which deals with some of the problems connected with present-day cricket was first given as a speech by Colonel Rait Kerr, Secretary of MCC, at the annual meeting of County Secretaries at Lord's on December 11, 1951.

Many people are highly critical of modern cricket and are asking if all is well with it. Following the First World War cricket boomed only to fall into the doldrums after a few years. This was the reason why, before the Second World War ended, a Select Committee sat to look into the dim future. It might be salutary if we all re-read that report from time to time, and in particular the following section:

We are agreed that no recommendation in regard to many of the proposals standing on the agenda in connection with the conduct and administration of County Cricket can be fully effective unless the game is played in the best possible manner and spirit. In the few years preceding the outbreak of war cricket was increasing in its appeal, and the credit was due to County Committees, Captains and Players.

We consider that a satisfactory standard was attained in 1939, and we do not believe that any radical changes in the conduct of the game are called for.

In 1937 the report of the Findlay Commission stressed the importance of "attacking play" and in our view a wholesome rivalry and determination can be demonstrated to the benefit of the game in ways other than "batting" and "bowling". For example, in the past teams who have paid attention to good fielding and efficient running between the wickets have always been attractive. In particular, we wish to stress the importance of avoiding any delay in changing the field. We do not advocate that County Cricket should develop into displays of unskilled hitting, but rather that the batsman's task is to demonstrate the full artistry of the game by his stroke play, and that the bowler's first duty is to take wickets.

We *RECOMMEND* that Counties before each season should make it clear to their Captains and Players that it remains the policy of their Committee that:

 (i) The team shall aim for victory from the first ball of a match, and maintain an enterprising attitude towards the game until the last over is bowled.

 (ii) The players shall adopt a dynamic attitude towards the game, whether batting, bowling or fielding.

(iii) The intervals and Hours of Play as provided for in the Laws of Cricket or in Match Regulations must be strictly adhered to. In particular, the two minutes allowed for the incoming batsman to take his place is a generous allowance which should rarely be utilised to the full, and never exceeded.

That these recommendations were largely taken to heart would certainly seem to be suggested by the verdict of the Editor of *Wisden* on the 1947 season. It read as follows:

In every way the season of 1947 bears favourable comparison with any year within living memory. Attendances which rose beyond those known in the past, with obvious appreciation by ever-increasing multitudes, clearly demonstrated the great hold the game takes on spectators once they are aware that both sides and every individual mean to expend all their energies striving for a definite result. The fine weather enjoyed, notably in August, might have meant that with batsmen supreme, drawn games would have predominated, but actually about three-quarters of the County Championship matches were won outright.

I can hardly imagine that his view could be so sanguine to-day especially were he to look at the graph shown here. The curve for "finished matches" omits all those in which no decision was reached on the first innings, thus removing one factor which might otherwise have given a distorted picture.

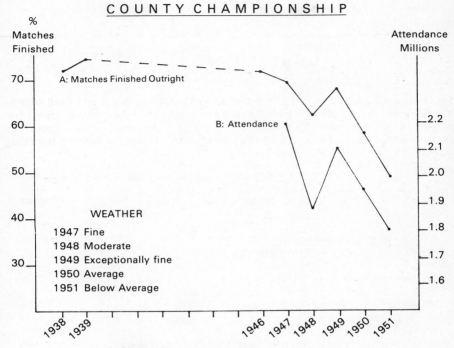

COUNTY CHAMPIONSHIP

N.B. Attendance figures before 1947 not available

We naturally would all expect "attendance" figures to reflect the weather conditions experienced during any season, and it has generally been held that in a wet season the percentage of unfinished matches tends to rise. The graph, of course, has eliminated a major weather factor but I have made an attempt to examine the overall effect of weather in order to ascertain what bearing it has on the incidence of drawn matches.

Before the introduction of the present scoring system in 1938, a correlation between bad weather and a high percentage of drawn matches appears to have existed, and a similar correlation can be seen in the years 1948, 1949 and 1950, but exactly the opposite effect is found in 1938, 1939 and 1947.

I think it is fair to say, therefore, that, after eliminating matches in which no decision was reached on the first innings, the incidence of drawn matches depends by no means entirely on weather.

If you look at the graph the similarity in the trends of the curves is at once apparent and it is really remarkable how the decrease in matches finished appears to be so closely reflected by a decrease in attendance. The fall in gates is due, besides weather, to a combination of causes, for example, personal incomes, other attractions and the way in which the game is played.

It is surely alarming that the average of 25 per cent of drawn matches in 1938, 1939 and 1946 has steadily risen by the end of the 1951 season to about 50 per cent. The percentage of drawn matches in earlier years was one of the problems specially studied by the Findlay Commission in 1937 and the scoring system for the Championship which they recommended and which was introduced in 1938, was specifically designed to reduce the number of drawn matches. It had an immediate effect and it is therefore all the more disturbing to find that the percentage of "finished matches" in 1951 was the lowest since 1930.

All of us – and I do not exclude the MCC – are only too keenly aware of our financial problems and if, as I suggest, this marked increase in drawn matches has a powerful bearing on them, surely the cause for such an increase is well worth seeking.

Ultra perfect pitches are often blamed, but this can hardly be the primary cause for the recent increase in drawn matches as they are certainly no more perfect than in 1938 or 1939 and are probably less so in most cases. Much has been written and spoken about the desirability of faster wickets. The dead pitch invites negative cricket. The faster the pitch the more must something happen, runs or wickets. I was interested the other day to hear a very distinguished cricketer repeat in almost identical words what was said by an equally great cricketer many years ago. He said:

Cricket, to maintain its hold on the national character, must be eager, quick and full of action. To-day it is the reverse. . . . Fifty per cent of the matches are drawn and the game itself, becoming listless and dull, is bound to suffer. When cricket ceases to provide excitement for the spectator and player, when it not once but continually allows whole days to be monopolised by two or three batsmen, the rest loafing in the pavilion, then it will cease to attract and spectators and players alike will go elsewhere.

So wrote A. G. Steel in *Wisden* in 1900.

In recent years we have seen the rate of scoring in Test cricket under easy conditions of pitch as low as 40 runs per hour, and if the rate reaches 50 runs per hour it is considered satisfactory. No doubt the bowling is accurate and the fielding splendidly tight, but can the game in this country really survive the emphasis on security first and last?

Modern cricketers have been known to maintain that it is better to be 70 for nought at lunch on the first day than 120 for three. I would suggest that a match is often made or marred by tea-time on the first day. "Made" if a match-winning rate of scoring has been maintained, or "marred" if the reverse has made it probable that only declarations in the later stages of the game can instil any life into it. Unfortunately, much of the most laborious play is seen on the first day of a match. Saturday is a first day, and Saturday gates are vital to finances.

I know, too, that some players will maintain that modern batting technique has been forced upon them as a result both of the off-side lbw law and of a definite development in the art of field setting. I would ask them to remember that the present lbw law has been in existence for sixteen years and whatever truth there may be in these arguments they cannot entirely explain why, when required, batsmen can score quickly on a Tuesday from the same bowling, supported by the same fielding, as had appeared to make the game so difficult on the previous Saturday.

A friend, whose judgment in cricket matters is always balanced, stressed two points, which appeared to him to be fundamental. First, that the technical developments since the war have all been defensive, especially in bowling tactics and field placing – with a leg-side bias. The game must be brought back on to the off-side if we are to recapture its beauty and appeal. Second, that county cricket is now a "professional" game, but the average professional does not seem to realise that in the long run his livelihood depends on the appeal of the game to the public.

There are no doubt other ills for which cures can be sought, but to me the problem of the drawn match transcends all others. The counties unanimously accepted the Report of the Select Committee in 1944, and as a first step I feel that nothing but good could follow from carrying out the recommendation I have quoted that each season committees should encourage their captains and players in the belief that cricket must be "eager, quick and full of action".

A CALL FOR CULTURE [1952]

SAFETY-FIRST CAN RUIN CRICKET

By Neville Cardus

Cricket, more than any other game, is able at its best to rise above competitive appeal and results; it can show its fine arts entirely for our pleasure – our aesthetic pleasure. In fact as a game, pure and simple, dependent on who loses and who wins, cricket is often a poor substitute for football, tennis, racing or tiddly-winks. I am, of course, discussing first-class matches running to three days and more; the crowd is usually largest on the first day when there's no prospect of a decision. A third afternoon, promising a fight, is played to empty benches and to the apparently homeless ancients of the pavilion.

Obviously a game that absorbs so long a time for a match, so that the end is not clearly seen in the beginning, must, at bottom, depend on a spectacular and human interest; the players must possess something about them that allures us, apart from what the score-board says.

Cricket is in full attractive health when all its departments are being exhibited by exponents with a personal touch; we will gladly forget the clock and the fact that no finish is likely to be approached until tomorrow at the earliest, if all the time there are strokes to look at, good bowling of variety to look at, and good swift fielding in all positions to look at. No game equals cricket for range of technique and duration of scene. It cannot hope in the present age to hold its own with other and faster competitive games unless also the players are constantly interested in themselves.

Of how many cricketers at the moment may we say that they are worth watching for distinguished individual skill? Of how many contemporary batsmen may we say that if they stay at the wicket an hour we are sure to see fine free strokes? I can't think of six. Hutton, the "Master", is not certain in an innings of three hours not to bore us and deny his powers.

Nobody ever saw an innings by Woolley that, given half an hour's duration, was not glorified by at least three glorious hits. The same can be said of Duleepsinhji, Hammond, Barnett, Dacre, Cyril Walters, Bakewell, Bowley of Sussex, Ernest Tyldesley ... but I could fill much valuable space with the list, all names more or less of cricketers in action in the same seasons.

Any organism to be really vital must function in all its parts. "Masterful" batsmanship does not mean the ability, patience and endurance to amass runs. The art of batsmanship comprises strokes to all parts of the field. Everybody has heard of the square-cut. But how many times do we get the opportunity nowadays to applaud the flashing beauty of it?

Years ago J. T. Tyldesley of Lancashire scored 165 against Surrey at Old Trafford, and when he was out there was a streak of white powder in front of the rails of the pavilion (the pavilion at Old Trafford is square to the wicket). Tyldesley's square cuts had knocked the paint off. It is argued that bowlers these times can't pitch to the off? Very well, then; genius is resourceful and discovers other ways and means.

Batsmanship signifies square cuts, drives, straight and to the on and off, on the ground or over the in-fielders' heads, leg glances and leg-hits; hooks and pulls. I do not exaggerate if I say here and now that it is possible to go to a cricket match in our present period and not in a whole day witness half the strokes that are the game's crown jewels; what is more, we won't see many attempts to perform some of them.

So with bowling. The art of bowling comprises pace, spin, medium and slow, left or right hand, variations of flight, and all the rest. English cricket, as I write these lines, lacks a great fast bowler, lacks a great slow left-hand bowler. How, then, is it arguable that the contemporary cricket is "as good as ever" and in a state of health, if in so many of its departments there is no life, no distinguished executant?

You wouldn't say of a man that he was proof that the human physique is as good as ever it was if he happened to be deaf, unable to walk well, but was sound of heart. You wouldn't maintain that an orchestra was as good as it might be if it didn't have any good brass nowadays, and no first flute.

And without strokes in all directions, fielding is bound to lose power to charm the eye for want of opportunity. And good fielding is essential to cricket as a constantly entertaining spectacle, guaranteed to convey pleasure to thousands, runs or no runs.

The tendency to put emphasis on cricket as competition, an affair of match-winning and percentages, is dangerous, and if it is not checked the game may easily, as a three-day matter, become obsolete after another decade. The result is important; we all want to win. But by its constitution, cricket must retain its unique fascination as spectacle, as pageant in summer time, and medium or vehicle for the expression of character in action.

I can't believe there is less innate talent for cricket in English boys and men to-day than in the past. But I do insist that the atmosphere and general governance don't bring the best out of a gifted player. The pressure of the spirit of the age hinders freedom and individuality. Life in this country is rationed. Can we blame Bloggs of Blankshire if in a four-hour innings he lets us know that his strokes are rationed?

The times we live in are against the bold extravagant gesture. Our first-class cricketers seldom are allowed to play for fun. Their "committees" are shortsighted enough to imagine that the crowd will flock for ever to sit in silence while batsmen wait for the shine to wear off and then "dig themselves" in; while bowlers wheel them up mechanically on the short and safe side. The multitude storms your gates in a season when your team is winning the County Championship. But you can't hope to win it every year. . . .

The future of the game in its present first-class shape and procedure is dependent on the revival of personal art and initiative. In 1905 the Australians discovered that Frank Laver had learned to swing the ball dangerously. The English air and the green turf helped his swerve, and for weeks he carried all before him. When he arrived at Old Trafford he clean bowled my hero, R. H. Spooner, for 0. Johnny Tyldesley came in next and he and A. C. MacLaren sternly watched the new ball "demon" and defended with unusual asperity. After a quarter of an hour, though, nothing had been done to clear the atmosphere; the score-board stood menacingly at 7 for 1. Then, while the Australian field changed over, MacLaren and Tyldesley held converse in mid-wicket, and what they said was audible to everyone present, including Laver.

"Johnny", said MacLaren, "I propose to drive this fellow." And Tyldesley replied: "You'll, of course, do as you please, Mr MacLaren; but I'm going to cut him."

You see, they were free enough, and men and cricketers enough, to form an individual plan. Whether it would succeed rested with the hazards of sport. The point is that they did not intend to submit to bondage or negation. The style is the man himself, in cricket or in any other occupation. Too much is said to-day of the material setting and organisation of cricket; of schools and coaching.

But what is to be taught? Technique in the abstract, divorced from spirit, tradition and faith in the impulse (and native skill) of a born player of games? Was Woolley coached or Macartney or Compton or Gimblett or Keith Miller or Victor Trumper or McCabe? Or Grimmett?

More than all material factors, cricket is in dire need of a great personal example. Most young folk are imitative to begin with: they'll push from behind the crease, content to wait for the loose ball, if that's the way their "betters" behave. They'll rub the new ball on their trousers, like so many bereft Alladins' rubbing the lamp, for want of a better trick, for so long as no master of more artistic accomplishments is there to inspire them.

Where there is no vision . . . certain as to-morrow is it that, failing a renaissance of the game as art and spectacle, with character and the personal touch dictating and directing the competitive issues, cricket's days are numbered, or at any rate likely to be chequered.

Already it lives more or less on the profits which come from the Test matches. The first sign of the renaissance will be heralded when once more a Test match does not give us a different kind of cricket from that of a county match, but is an ordinary first-class match in apotheosis.

In the past, great players didn't think that in a Test match they were under an obligation to deny their best gifts and to inhibit themselves for safety's sake. Grace, MacLaren, Ranji, Trumper, Hobbs, Woolley – and on and on to yesterday – found the challenge of a Test match an incentive to their greatest deeds. What has been done in the past by mortal cricketers it is possible to do again, given the love and the desire. At least – as Pooh-Bah would say – a man might try.

NOTES BY THE EDITOR, 1954

A Spur to Enterprise

It will be interesting to see whether the award of trophies and cash prizes has any stimulating effect on the game this summer. A business firm is offering silver mementoes and cheques of one hundred guineas each for the fastest hundred and for certain bowling, fielding and wicket-keeping performances. Such inducements should not be necessary to foster dynamic cricket. As Mr Aird said, the whole matter depends on the attitude of the players. Possibly the added incentive may help them to develop the right frame of mind in all phases of the game. Speed, of course, is not the first essential in cricket, and it is obvious that the fastest hundred may not be the best or the most valuable of the season. The comparatively small crowd who paid for admission on the fifth day of the Lord's Test last June sat enthralled while they watched the dour batting of Watson and Bailey against the might of Australia. There were few runs but every moment and every ball was vital. This pair saved England that day as surely as did T. G. Evans at Adelaide in 1947 when he spent ninety-five minutes with D. Compton before scoring.

THE EARLY COUNTY CHAMPIONS [1959]

By Rowland Bowen

Recent controversy has drawn attention to the doubts which have often been expressed down the years on the accepted list of County Champions in the early days of first-class cricket. At the request of the Editor of *Wisden* I have conducted extensive research into contemporary publications to see what light they cast on the early years. The four principal annuals consulted were *Fred Lillywhite's Guide* for seasons from 1854 up to and including 1865 (referred to as the *Guide*); *John and James Lillywhite's Companion* from season 1865 to 1884 – it incorporated the *Guide* from season 1866 (referred to as the *Companion*); *James Lillywhite's Annual* from season 1871 till its cessation – it incorporated the *Companion* from season 1885 (referred to as the *Annual*); and, of course, *Wisden* from 1864. A very large number of other annuals – usually individual and often unofficial – and county cricket annuals have also been examined, as well as individual county cricket histories and other publications. They are mentioned by name where necessary.

This examination has led to the following conclusions: (1) there has been an uncritical acceptance and repetition of statements concerning earlier periods, or statistics about earlier cricket, which would horrify a professional historian; (2) the concepts of first-class cricket, and of a county cricket championship *as we know them* were things quite alien to the minds of cricket enthusiasts and writers of 80 and more years ago; (3) there is no evidence that the championship started in 1873; (4) there was no agreement amongst various contemporary publications as to how the championship was to be decided in the early years; (5) the hitherto accepted list of champions is certainly wrong for two of the years given, and in four further years there can be legitimate argument.

The proof of the first conclusion will become obvious during the course of this article.

As regards the second conclusion, there was generally no agreement whether Hampshire and Somerset were to be considered among the "celebrated" counties;

averages often included all county matches even against such teams as Buckinghamshire. For example, W. G. Grace's published records for first-class matches include such games as MCC v Hertfordshire. Moreover, there seems to be a distinction between the county champions and the county championship. In other words, the county champions were the best county *against all comers*; the idea of restricting the choice of champions by reference only to games against other counties did not appear to exist, certainly in the minds of the editors of the *Companion* or *Annual* until some time in the late 70s or early 80s.

As regards the third conclusion, the *Companion* said of 1865, "if one county was better than any other, it was Nottinghamshire," and of 1866, "Middlesex occupy premier position," and of 1867, "Middlesex forfeited the premiership to Yorkshire"; no comment in 1868, but in 1869 "Yorkshire and Nottinghamshire were champion counties"; in 1870 "Yorkshire now fairly champion county" – supported by *Wisden* for that season; in 1871 *Companion* and *Wisden* agreed that Nottinghamshire were champions, but conceded that Sussex were the champions of the south; the *Annual* said "Nottinghamshire will not be deprived of the championship"; in 1872 *Companion* and *Annual* agreed Nottinghamshire were champions. The only significant thing about 1873 was that for that season, rules governing qualification for counties were agreed – nothing else was decided – certainly not how the championship should be run. The fact that those rules were found necessary indicated clearly that the best county was already being designated champion county, and that it was not right that a county should be so designated when it engaged players who had appeared for some other county that season. There was no organised championship; in fact there was no championship in the strict sense until 1890, when the counties themselves agreed how the championship should be decided; or even until 1894, when MCC were asked in future to designate the county champions.

As regards the fourth conclusion, it was stated (and has been repeated blindly since 1895 so far as I have been able to gather) that the county with the fewest losses were champions up to and including season 1886. This was not so; had it been the *Annual* would scarcely have said of season 1874 that "the most partial supporter would hardly venture to compare Derbyshire with Gloucestershire" which latter county was stated unequivocally to have been champions. Moreover, *Cricket* for September 21, 1882, used the system not stated to have been adopted until 1887, viz.: one point for a win, half for a draw. Again, between 1873 and 1886 inclusive, the contemporary annuals disagreed with each other on four occasions and they disagreed with the modern list in two further years. Had the champions been designated in the manner stated there could have been no such disagreement. Moreover, in none of those six years was the disagreement affected by the question of whether the two doubtful counties, Hampshire and Somerset, were first-class.

As regards the fifth conclusion, I think it will be conceded that if contemporary publications all agreed that a certain county were champions for a certain year, and if by claiming the championship early histories of that county supported those contemporaries but not the modern list, then the modern list is wrong. Those conditions are fulfilled.

It is worthwhile examining the origins of the present list. It appeared first in Alfred Gibson's *County Cricket Championship* published in 1895 – I have not been able to find an earlier list.

The list from 1873 to 1895 is exactly as now accepted. Gibson appears to have been a statistician who tried to read back into the minds of the writers of twenty years earlier his own ideas; hence the faults in the list. It was copied and brought up to date by the Rev. R. S. Holmes in a publication of the same name up to 1896. *Wisden* was the first annual to show the list, in 1901, but omitted 1873 and 1874. It was then copied into various county yearbooks, notably the one printed by Yorkshire, and into other annuals. It was reprinted by *Wisden* in 1907 and again in 1911, when 1873 and 1874 were added as in Gibson's list.

I now propose to examine the situation before 1873, year by year, and from 1873 in the years in which there is any argument. The contemporary annuals are not as helpful as they might be. *Wisden* did not always designate a champion, and did not publish a table until 1888; it published an order of merit for the two previous seasons, however. Earlier, the order in which the counties appeared in *Wisden* is evidence, for Surrey were always shown first, until 1877, and thereafter Middlesex, and the next county shown is usually found to have been considered champions. The *Companion* never published a table, but usually listed the counties in their order of merit. The order of merit in the *Companion* has to be deduced since Surrey were always conventionally shown first, and Middlesex second, until season 1870. The *Annual* first published a table for 1872 (though it included all games), omitted one for 1874, 1887 and 1888 and had a table in purely alphabetical order for 1877 and 1880; from 1873 to 1885 the order in which the counties appeared in the *Annual* was purely alphabetical. It will be seen that something can be disinterred!

Before 1864, the *Guide* does not claim any county as champions.

1864 Surrey had easily the best record, winning seven games and drawing one. They were conventionally placed first in *Wisden*, *Guide* and *Companion*, but there was still no claim made nor implication that they were champions by whatever names designated. This would imply that the concept of champions – or premiers, call it what you will – only came in during the next two or three years.

1865 The *Companion* said "if one county were better than any other it was Nottinghamshire." No other publication made this statement; nor do the various orders in which the counties are listed assist us. Nottinghamshire's record was, won five, lost two. The *Companion* listed second to Surrey (conventionally first in all three annuals) Middlesex – won three, drawn one, lost one; the *Guide* gave Kent as second – won two, drawn two, lost two. Perhaps Nottinghamshire were best – but *not* on the basis of least lost.

1866 The *Companion* said Middlesex occupied premier position. Their playing record was won seven, drawn one, lost one; and no one else came near them. *Perhaps* it is the statement in the following season that enables us to date the first champion county – though not, perhaps, the county championship – from 1866, for in

1867 The *Companion* said "Middlesex forfeited the premiership to Yorkshire." Of this there can be no possible doubt, for Yorkshire won all their seven games, and no other county had even an unbeaten record.

1868 No one was designated champions. Nottinghamshire were listed second by *Wisden* to the conventionally first Surrey. Nottinghamshire had the best record, won four, lost two, but the counties seem to have been even. Probably Nottinghamshire were champions, but I can find no statement or claim to this effect.

1869 The *Companion* unequivocally said "Yorkshire and Nottinghamshire were champions" – and this was the first use of the term; hereafter it was always used (or implied in years of argument). There can be no doubt then about the propriety of dating back the list of county champions to this season.

1870 The *Companion* said "Yorkshire are now fairly champion county." This was supported by the order of counties in *Wisden*, since Yorkshire appeared second to the conventionally first Surrey, by a statement in *Wisden* for that season and also by the *History of Yorkshire County Cricket*, the earliest claim in any individual county history.

1871 The *Companion* said "Nottinghamshire were champions"; the *Annual* supported this at page 57: "Nottinghamshire will not be easily deprived of the championship." *Wisden* agreed about Nottinghamshire. Both the *Companion* and *Wisden* agreed Sussex were champions of the south. The playing records were Nottinghamshire won four, drawn one, lost one; Sussex won four. The orders in which the counties appeared supported the statement that Nottinghamshire were champions. It seems a little hard on Sussex, but the writers of those days were very chary of awarding the championship to counties which had played only a few matches. Anyway, no contemporary put Sussex first and that seems sufficient.

1872 The *Companion* and *Annual* said Nottinghamshire were first; the orders in *Wisden* and *Annual* supported this, Surrey being conventionally first. Nottinghamshire's record was won two, drawn five; Lancashire, however, won all their four games; yet there was no suggestion at all that they were champions. Once more the contemporary judgment of which was the better team must be accepted; this judgment was not based solely on actual results of games, but made some attempt (one cannot help but feeling as one reads those old comments) to take into account how the games actually went, how strong were the opponents and so on. This was the year of the first table, in the *Annual*; it does not help us much since it listed all games played, not only county games. However, F. S. Ashley-Cooper, in his *Nottinghamshire Cricket and Cricketers*, made the claim for Nottinghamshire being champions in 1871 and 1872.

1873 This, the first year now shown in the list of champions, is also the first year in which the statement in that list gives rise to argument. *Wisden*, commenting on the 1873 season, was quite definite that Nottinghamshire were champions. Ashley-Cooper did not make this claim. The *Companion* was unequivocal that Gloucestershire were champions. The *Annual* said at one point when dealing with Gloucestershire that Gloucestershire were champions, but when dealing with Nottinghamshire said that "Nottinghamshire were co-equal". There was no claim to the sole championship in the *History of Gloucestershire County Cricket Club*. The playing records of the two counties were Gloucestershire won four, drawn two; Nottinghamshire won five, drawn one. On the face of it, the 1874 *Wisden* would appear to have been correct, but there was no unanimity at the time, and in view of all the statements made, it is probably right to accept what the present list (derived from Alfred Gibson) says, bracketing Gloucestershire and Nottinghamshire as co-equal.

1874   Here again there is grave dispute. The present list shows Derbyshire as champions. The *Annual* I have already quoted – it will bear repetition – "the most partial supporter would hardly venture to compare Derbyshire with Gloucestershire." Both *Annual* and *Companion* were in no doubt that Gloucestershire were champions, and *Wisden* listed them second to the conventionally placed Surrey (listing Derbyshire last!). *The History of Gloucestershire County Cricket Club* made the definite claim that Gloucestershire were champions in 1874; *Derbyshire County Cricket*, by Piper, published 1897, made no claim for Derbyshire to have been champions in 1874, though it said they were the only unbeaten county, but it is fair to say that the unofficial *Derbyshire Cricket Guide* for 1896 did make the claim (prompted no doubt by A. Gibson). On the other hand "Feats and Facts of Derbyshire Cricket" in the *Derbyshire Cricket Annual* for 1887 did not mention Derbyshire as champions in 1874 – surely it would have if anyone in or out of the county had made the claim? In the face of contemporary unanimity on the subject, there can be no doubt that the present list is wrong, both in supposing that the champions were designated with reference to fewest matches lost, and in designating Derbyshire as champions. At the time, Gloucestershire were accepted as champions, and claimed to be champions; Derbyshire were not, and did not, and the modern list should therefore be corrected. As a matter of interest, Gloucestershire – playing Yorkshire, Surrey and Sussex – won four, drew one and lost one; Derbyshire – playing only Kent and Lancashire, both very weak teams at that time – won three and drew one.

1875   There was no controversy about this season till recently. There need be none, particularly if it is remembered that "least matches lost" was *not* a rule, but a guide to deciding who were champions. All three annuals were quite positive that Nottinghamshire were champions, and Ashley-Cooper supported this. Sussex made no claim to be champions at the time, nor did they do so until 1958. They did not have an unbeaten record, as they lost to the very weak Hampshire team, in that season reckoned by all three contemporary annuals as among "the" counties, as they were indeed for the next three seasons. The records were Nottinghamshire won six, drawn three, lost one; Sussex won five, drawn one, lost two. Both *Companion* and *Annual* put Yorkshire (won six, drawn one, lost three) second to Nottinghamshire, as does the *History of Yorkshire County Cricket* – this seems a little unfair to Sussex, but it is clear that they were not even equal first. Both Lillywhites, as well as *Wisden*, were Sussex men; it is inconceivable that their annuals would have failed to make a claim for Sussex as champions if there had been any sort of justification for such a claim.

1876 and **1877**   Complete agreement with the present list that Gloucestershire were champions.

1878   The present list shows Middlesex. Volume one of the *History of Middlesex CCC* at page 154 did not claim Middlesex as champions, though they had an unbeaten record; it said that "probably Nottinghamshire, and certainly Yorkshire were stronger." The records were Middlesex won three, drawn three; Nottinghamshire won seven, drawn four, lost three; Yorkshire won seven, drawn two, lost five. Middlesex drew both games with Nottinghamshire, and beat Yorkshire twice. Neither the *History of Yorkshire County Cricket* nor *Nottinghamshire Cricket and Cricketers* made any claim for Yorkshire or Nottinghamshire. The *Companion* twice said that "no one county were champions" and in a third place, that Nottinghamshire held the leading place amongst counties. The *Annual* did not commit itself. *Wisden* did not help, since it now listed Middlesex first instead of Surrey, but it is clear that the convention changed this season, for from now on Middlesex were listed conventionally first with Surrey often second. The contemporary evidence seems plain, and the correct entry in the list should be "undecided".

1879   The present list shows Nottinghamshire and Lancashire bracketed. The *Companion* supported this, more or less, though it rather spoke with two voices. The *Annual* also supported this. *Wisden* listed Nottinghamshire second to the conventionally first Middlesex, with Lancashire eighth. Ashley-Cooper said that Nottinghamshire were agreed to have been the better team, and there were strong implications in *Lancashire County Cricket*, by F. Reynolds (published 1883), that 1881 was the first year in which Lancashire were champions (though this could just be taken as meaning "sole champions"). It should be added that *Lancashire Cricket Records* 1865-1908 gave Lancashire as champions in 1881, 1897 and 1904 and tied in 1889; it made no claim for 1879, nor 1882. The records were Lancashire won five, drawn four, lost one; Nottinghamshire won five, drawn six, lost one. In all the circumstances, it would seem better to accept the present list, since it is to a great extent supported by contemporary annuals – even if not by *Wisden* of that time.

1880 and 1881 Complete agreement with the present list that Nottinghamshire in 1880 and Lancashire in 1881 were champions. A recent publication suggests Gloucestershire might be considered as joint champions in 1880. Contemporaries did not support this view. Gloucestershire won four, drew five and lost one against Nottinghamshire's won six, drawn three, lost one – it is clear why contemporaries admitted no argument about Nottinghamshire's supremacy.

1882 The present list shows Nottinghamshire and Lancashire bracketed. The *Companion* at one point said Lancashire had a short-head over Nottinghamshire, at another point an opposite opinion, and at a third that the two counties divided the honours equally. The *Annual* said "Lancashire and Nottinghamshire were fairly equal"; it published a table showing these two teams first; the table included Hampshire and Somerset which the *Annual* called Minor Counties. This is important as Lancashire beat Somerset twice. *Wisden* said this was Somerset's début amongst the first-class counties; listed Middlesex and Surrey conventionally first and second, Lancashire third and Nottinghamshire fourth; and said: "In all matches Lancashire lost four games and Nottinghamshire two, therefore Nottinghamshire must be considered champions." It will be noticed that *Lancashire Cricket Records*, already quoted, made no claim for Lancashire to have been champions, while Ashley-Cooper said Nottinghamshire were surpassed by no other county (which is one way of admitting that they tied!). *Cricket*, however, in its issue for September 21, 1882, awarded one point for a win and a half for a draw, and put Lancashire first. The records were Lancashire won ten, drawn three, lost one against counties, plus won two v Somerset: Nottinghamshire won eight, drew three, lost one. The matter has been discussed at length (as in the case of season 1879) only because the contemporary *Wisden* gave a different opinion from the present list, and because a Lancashire publication specifically excluded Lancashire from being champions in these two seasons. One finds oneself unable to agree with *Wisden* for 1883 and in view of the two Lillywhite statements, the present list should be accepted as correct.

1883 The present list shows Nottinghamshire as champions. The *Companion* said "Nottinghamshire were fully entitled to the honours of county champions" but conceded that the difference between them and Yorkshire was minute. The *Annual* said Nottinghamshire were champions under the recognised system of awarding the championship. *Cricket* placed Nottinghamshire first, *Wisden* said that Yorkshire were first and had an undeniable claim, and put Yorkshire third and Nottinghamshire fourth to the conventionally first Middlesex and second Surrey. Ashley-Cooper said that Nottinghamshire were first. *The History of Yorkshire County Cricket* at page 60 gave Yorkshire first. The records were Nottinghamshire won four, drawn seven, lost one (they won one and drew the other game with Yorkshire); Yorkshire won nine, drew five, lost two, and drew two with Leicestershire, not reckoned to be first-class by any contemporary. In the circumstances one can agree with *Wisden* for 1884 that Yorkshire had a claim, but accept the other contemporary evidence that the claim was not conceded.

1884-1888 There was complete agreement with the present list in contemporary annuals.

1889 A very minor point. *Wisden* for 1890 bracketed the top three teams in the following order: Nottinghamshire, Lancashire, Surrey. In terms of their records, that was surely correct. Nottinghamshire won nine, drew three, lost two; Lancashire and Surrey won ten, drew one, lost three. From 1887 the custom of awarding one point for a win and a half for a draw had been adopted (as foreseen by *Cricket* five years before), so certainly a triple tie was correct; and equally certain, the *Wisden* order of placing the teams in 1890 was correct. Not until five years later do we find a list which puts them in the order now found, which is neither by merit nor alphabet – Surrey, Lancashire, Nottinghamshire. It is clear that this minor correction should be made in the current list, for the only reason for putting Surrey first among the three is that they were champions in the two previous seasons – even so, Nottinghamshire had a better record than Lancashire.

From 1890 there is no argument about who were first.

We can now sum up with a new list. The only point remaining to be decided is from what date should the list run? It has been clearly shown that one can logically and consistently run the list from 1869, and even from 1865, since that was the first time a county was stated to have been better than any other with gaps in 1868 and 1878. It has been clearly shown that 1873 is not a significant date, except for the one point of qualification. On the other hand, there is a legitimate doubt which counties were first-class, at least until 1886. Cambridge appear from 1863 to 1869. Hampshire were so reckoned in 1863-67 and 1870, but not in 1868 or 1869, nor 1871-73. *Wisden* included them from 1874 to 1878 and against from 1880 to 1885. The *Guide* included them in 1863 and 1864 (in 1854 it said that Hampshire were once, but now no longer). The *Annual* and the *Companion* generally exclude Hampshire except in 1865-67, 1870 and 1874-78). From 1881-85 *Wisden* included Somerset, whereas the others excluded them, save that the *Annual* showed Somerset in its table for 1882. Derbyshire were included from 1871-87 by *Wisden* and *Annual* and by the *Companion* from 1872. Lancashire did not appear until 1867 (though they played Middlesex twice in 1865), and Gloucestershire not until 1870. Surrey, Kent, Sussex, Yorkshire and Nottinghamshire were "Celebrated counties" from early days, while Middlesex, who were "creeping along" in 1857 were accepted as "celebrated" by 1864. The method of reckoning, one point for a win, was introduced in 1887. That would seem, then, to be another suitable date to commence the list. 1890 would be another suitable date; then the counties themselves decided the method of scoring in the championship. The choice is between 1865 and 1869 or between 1887 and 1890. I have selected 1865, merely for the sake of historical completeness.

Period 1865-86. The method of deciding who were county champions was generally by "fewest losses". This led to anomalous results and was tempered in several years by a critical judgment of which was the strongest county. The counties most generally selected by contemporaries as champions were:

1865	Nottinghamshire	1876	Gloucestershire
1866	Middlesex	1877	Gloucestershire
1867	Yorkshire	1878	Undecided
1868	Undecided (probably Nottinghamshire)	1879	Nottinghamshire and Lancashire
1869	Nottinghamshire and Yorkshire	1880	Nottinghamshire
		1881	Lancashire
1870	Yorkshire	1882	Nottinghamshire and Lancashire
1871	Nottinghamshire		
1872	Nottinghamshire	1883	Nottinghamshire
1873	Gloucestershire and Nottinghamshire	1884	Nottinghamshire
		1885	Nottinghamshire
1874	Gloucestershire	1886	Nottinghamshire
1875	Nottinghamshire		

Period 1887-89. One point for a win, half for a draw.

1887	Surrey	1889	Nottinghamshire, Lancashire,
1888	Surrey		Surrey

Period 1890 to date. As shown in *Wisden* in 1901, 1907 and ever since 1911.

May I conclude by saying that the only evidence that is acceptable from an historical point of view is contemporary evidence even if contemporaries seem, from our point of view, to have been wrong – for they were not wrong from their own point of view; a list of county champions can only name those who were at the time accepted as champions. Critics cannot, twenty, forty or eighty years later, air their views with the same authority.

I have only attempted to decide between the contemporary publications for 1873, 1879, 1882 and 1883 because there is sufficient weight of contemporary opinion and evidence to enable one to do so; and to award the honours equally to the two claimants for three of those years; because it is 75 years after the event I have not inclined to alter the result for 1883. I have had no such doubts for 1874 and 1878 were contemporaries were in complete agreement – nor, of course, for the years 1875 and 1880 which have been the subject of recent discussion, but which presented contemporaries with no problems.

Editor's Note: Without in any way disputing the conclusions reached by the author, I do not think we can alter the accepted list as regularly published in Wisden for over forty years, even where there are good grounds for disagreeing with it.

A POSTSCRIPT [1960]

No evidence nor reasonable inference has been produced to controvert the findings on this subject in last year's *Wisden*, but during the year that has passed further points have arisen that need comment.

On the existence of the championship before 1873 *Wisden* for 1888, referring to Surrey's victory the previous season, says that "it was after an interval of 23 years." W. W. Read in his *Annals of Cricket* also claims Surrey as Champions in 1864, and his year-by-year review of the seasons gives, as Champions, almost precisely those in the list in last year's article, even to altering the order in 1889 in favour of Nottinghamshire (this agreed with the general sentiment at the end of the 1889 season also). *Cricket* for April 26, 1883, quoting from the *Sheffield Telegraph*, gives Yorkshire as Champions in 1867 and 1870. R. Daft in *Cricket* for September 21, 1893, quoting from an unidentified newspaper cutting, goes even further back: "on this occasion (1853) they (Nottinghamshire) are fully entitled to the flag and may for the present possess the honour of being the 'Champion County'."

When dealing with season 1875, the recently made claim for (but not by) Lancashire for that season was not met. No contemporary made any suggestion that Lancashire were then Champions, nor does *Lancashire Cricket Records* 1865-1908 nor has Lancashire at any time. The claim may be safely ignored.

Nottinghamshire's record in season 1865 was won 6, lost 1 and not won 5 and lost 2 as stated last year.

Now for the question of the "least matches lost" method. The only authority who has been able to make any reasoned defence to me of that method was compelled to qualify it in order to account for the anomalies that exist between the application of that method and the generally accepted list. It is true that references were made to the least matches lost method as far back as 1884 but *Lillywhite's Annual*, which did this, did not consistently apply it. Last year I quoted *Cricket* in 1882, which did not use that method; in the issue of *Cricket* for September 23, 1886, there is an article from *The World* on "The Year's Cricket" which placed Surrey unquestionably first that season not only "because of the *right and generally recognised rule* that *drawn games count as half wins* which places Surrey fractionally ahead of Nottinghamshire" but also *because Surrey twice beat the Australians* whereas Nottinghamshire could only draw. (There is, by the way, no other claim for Surrey that season.)

W. G. Grace's *Cricket* published in 1891 gives championship tables back to 1870 which used the method then in vogue (1 for a win, minus 1 for a loss). The resulting list of champions gained wide currency during the next dozen or more years, and was quoted, for example, by J. B. Payne in *The Cricket Field* for December 1892 when he gives Yorkshire as Champions in 1874.

This is clear proof that the least matches lost method was far from being generally accepted by contemporary writers, and we see also further evidence that playing quality counted at least as much as methods of scoring points.

There are three interesting points concerning Derbyshire. In 1874 their team of players against Nottinghamshire numbered sixteen. No county generally accepted as "first-class" ever batted odds against another county and, contemporaries being unanimous that they were not Champion County that year, the question arises whether even in the vague terminology of those days they were one of "the counties". It is interesting that W. G. Grace omitted all Derbyshire matches in the championship tables given in his book. Lastly, the fluidity of membership of the championship in those days as considered by the Press is well shown by *Cricket*, regularly including Derbyshire in its weekly tables for 1888 until early August, other contemporaries having dropped Derbyshire before the beginning of that season.

Lastly, but by no means least, a rather qualified *amende honorable* to the Rev. R. S. Holmes. Though it is true that Alfred Gibson's pamphlet preceded Holmes's, the latter's derived directly from a series of articles in *Cricket* commencing in October 1894 which repeated much of what he had said in an earlier article in *Cricket* in January 1893. Holmes's list then given tallies exactly with the generally accepted list save for 1879, when he did not bracket Lancashire with Nottinghamshire but showed Nottinghamshire alone. This in itself contradicts his surmise that "so far as I could learn, the smallest number of matches lost decided the order from 1873 to 1886," which he rightly calls "an absurd test and occasionally most unfair". Holmes can hardly have searched very hard, and one reason why he said this may have been because his editor was the same as the editor of *Lillywhite's Annual*, which seems to have been the first to refer to this method and which, as we have seen, did not apply it consistently. Holmes, however, very clearly had his doubts for in the *History of Yorkshire County Cricket* not only does he give Yorkshire as Champions in 1870 (at p. 48, thus contradicting p. 51, where he says the championship started in 1873!) but also on pp. 57-58 where he says that according to the accepted test Nottinghamshire were Champions in 1883, thus contradicting p. 60 where he says, "True, in that year (1883) Yorkshire was the champion county"! It is abundantly clear that one cannot appeal with any certainty to Holmes, the apparent originator of the present list.

The matter can, I think, be safely left there. The hitherto accepted list is undoubtedly wrong in places, nor can it be made to follow the least matches lost method without severe qualifications to that method; the method itself was not the generally accepted one of determining the champion county – indeed there was no generally accepted method; and the championship – or at least the naming of a champion county (not quite the same thing) – long preceded 1873.

DERBYSHIRE

DERBYSHIRE v YORKSHIRE

Played at Chesterfield, June 29, July 1, 1946

Yorkshire won by four wickets. Any extraordinary incident marked the commencement. Two overs bowled; then the discovery that the pitch was two yards over length necessitated a re-start. Showing much improved form, Derbyshire gained a first innings lead and kept the issue in doubt until near the end. Batting with unwonted restraint, Smith played finely for 51, but Yorkshire lost Hutton and Gibb for 2. Barber, by staying in four hours, prevented a complete breakdown. Then Derbyshire collapsed in their second innings, and splendid slow left-hand bowling by Armstrong could not prevent Yorkshire getting the required runs.

Derbyshire

D. Smith b Bowes	61	– c Gibb b Smailes	13
A. Townsend b Booth	21	– c Gibb b Bowes	8
G. S. Elliott c Hutton b Bowes	4	– b Coxon	8
A. E. Rhodes b Bowes	4	– b Bowes	0
P. Vaulkhard c Watson b Bowes	0	– c Bowes b Coxon	1
C. Gladwin b Smailes	25	– b Bowes	16
G. F. Hodgkinson c Bowes b Coxon	4	– c Booth b Coxon	10
A. Revill c Robinson b Bowes	0	– c Watson b Robinson	10
E. Marsh not out	23	– b Booth	4
T. R. Armstrong b Smailes	8	– not out	1
W. H. Copson b Smailes	0	– c Robinson b Booth	7
B 4, l-b 5	9		
	182		**78**

Yorkshire

L. Hutton b Copson	2	– b Armstrong	36
P. A. Gibb b Rhodes	0	– c Smith b Armstrong	6
W. Barber c Vaulkhard b Armstrong	71	– not out	22
W. Watson c and b Armstrong	23	– b Armstrong	5
H. Beaumont c and b Copson	6	– c Smith b Armstrong	3
A. B. Sellers b Copson	3	– c Vaulkhard b Armstrong	10
T. F. Smailes c Townsend b Gladwin	21	– c Smith b Rhodes	1
A. Coxon lbw b Armstrong	1		
E. P. Robinson b Armstrong	11	– not out	4
W. E. Bowes b Copson	1		
A. Booth not out	4		
B 9, l-b 20, w 1	30	B 1	1
	173	**(6 wkts)**	**88**

Yorkshire Bowling

	Overs	Mdns	Runs	Wkts	Overs	Mdns	Runs	Wkts
Bowes	27	6	66	5	15	4	29	3
Smailes	12.5	1	37	3	7	3	15	1
Coxon	14	2	45	1	7	2	14	3
Hutton	4	—	18	—	1	—	1	—
Booth	10	5	7	1	6.2	2	8	2
Robinson					7	2	11	1

Derbyshire Bowling

	Overs	Mdns	Runs	Wkts	Overs	Mdns	Runs	Wkts
Copson...........	28	8	46	4	9	3	26	—
Rhodes...........	14	3	22	1	9	3	20	1
Gladwin..........	19	4	31	1	3	—	9	—
Armstrong	25.3	9	44	4	12.2	2	32	5

DERBYSHIRE v ESSEX

Played at Chesterfield, August 6, 7, 8, 1947

Essex won by five wickets. A record Essex tenth wicket stand of 218, lasting two hours and a half, by Vigar and Peter Smith, completely altered the course of the game, for when they came together Essex were 24 behind. Smith, who dominated the partnership, offered two difficult chances in a very exceptional display by a last man; he drove and pulled freely, hitting three 6s and twenty-two 4s in his 163, and punished Marsh for 22 in one over. Vigar, by contrast, batted patiently for five hours. Townsend took batting honours while completing his 1,000 runs, but Derbyshire, despite good work by Elliott, lost eight wickets on the second day before clearing off arrears of 194. Then Gladwin, Gothard and Copson scored freely, but Essex easily accomplished a light task.

Derbyshire

A. Townsend b P. Smith	86	– b R. Smith....................	1
C. S. Elliott b R. Smith	2	– run out	68
T. S. Worthington c P. Smith b Bailey	0	– b Bailey......................	9
D. Smith run out............................	10	– b R. Smith....................	35
G. H. Pope c Insole b Bailey.................	5	– c Dodds b Bailey	11
A. E. Alderman b Bailey.....................	20	– c Insole b Bailey	27
E. Marsh c Crabtree b P. Smith	24	– c Horsfall b Bailey	4
A. E. Rhodes c Insole b P. Smith	4	– c Horsfall b R. Smith	0
E. J. Gothard not out	24	– b R. Smith....................	40
C. Gladwin c Insole b Bailey..................	27	– c Wilcox b Bailey	52
W. H. Copson b Bailey.......................	0	– not out	38
B 16, l-b 4, n-b 1	21	B 9, l-b 8, w 1, n-b 1	19
	223		**304**

Essex

T. C. Dodds lbw b Copson	20	– c Townsend b Copson	23
S. J. Cray b Copson	11	– b Pope.......................	9
A. V. Avery c Pope b Copson.................	0	– lbw b Pope	0
H. P. Crabtree lbw b Pope	2	– c Worthington b Gladwin	30
F. H. Vigar not out	114	– not out	40
R. Horsfall b Pope.........................	8	– not out	3
D. R. Wilcox b Gladwin	9		
T. E. Bailey b Worthington..................	19		
D. J. Insole b Copson	48		
R. Smith c Marsh b Pope	21		
T. P. B. Smith b Worthington................	163	– c Worthington b Copson	4
B 1, n-b 1..........................	2	L-b 5...................	5
	417		**(5 wkts) 114**

Essex Bowling

	Overs	Mdns	Runs	Wkts	Overs	Mdns	Runs	Wkts
Bailey	24.2	1	83	5	30.5	6	92	5
R. Smith	18	3	50	1	49	14	122	4
T. P. B. Smith	18	2	59	3	22	6	53	—
Vigar.	2	—	10	—	5	—	18	—

Derbyshire Bowling

	Overs	Mdns	Runs	Wkts	Overs	Mdns	Runs	Wkts
Copson	36	8	117	4	14	3	36	2
Pope	27	8	73	3	15	5	39	2
Gladwin	13	3	54	1	3.1	—	15	1
Worthington	21.5	1	90	2				
Rhodes	18	4	44	—	5	—	19	—
Marsh	11	3	37	—				

Umpires: D. Hendren and N. Harris.

DERBYSHIRE v YORKSHIRE

Played at Chesterfield, June 26, 28, 29, 1948

Drawn. The magnificent all-round cricket of George Pope placed Yorkshire in a seemingly hopeless position by the end of the first day, but then rain washed out the second day and allowed only ninety minutes' play on the Tuesday. Yorkshire were powerless against the aggressive fast-medium bowling of Gladwin and Pope, supported by keen fielding. Although the pitch was never difficult, no Yorkshireman reached double figures in the county's lowest total since 1935. The Derbyshire innings provided a complete contrast, for hard hitting was the feature. Pope hit a six and eleven 4s and Revill ten 4s, but left-arm slow bowler Wardle gained deserved success. Yorkshire lost three second innings wickets for 15 runs before the end of an extraordinary opening day, which was watched by 14,000 people. Yorkshire defended dourly in the brief subsequent play, while Pope brought his match figures to ten wickets for 25 runs – a brilliant performance, apart from his innings of 73.

Yorkshire

H. Halliday c Dawkes b Pope.	5	– b Pope.	0
E. Lester c Elliott b Gladwin	0	– c Dawkes b Pope	3
W. Watson run out	4	– c Revill b Gladwin	0
J. V. Wilson c Elliott b Gladwin	2	– lbw b Jackson	8
K. Smales b Pope	1	– c Dawkes b Pope	6
R. Aspinall c and b Gladwin	5	– c Revill b Pope	0
A. B. Sellers b Pope.	8	– not out	0
J. P. Whitehead b Pope	7		
T. F. Smailes b Pope.	7	– not out	16
J. H. Wardle not out	2		
D. V. Brennan lbw b Pope.	0		
L-b 1, w 1, n-b 1	3	B 1, l-b 1, n-b 2	4
	44		**(6 wkts) 37**

Derbyshire

C. S. Elliott lbw b Whitehead 62	A. E. Rhodes c Wilson b Wardle 1
A. Alderman b Wardle 20	E. J. Gothard lbw b Wardle 7
D. Smith c Smales b Wardle 22	C. Gladwin b Wardle 4
E. Marsh run out..................... 0	L. Jackson not out.................... 0
G. H. Pope c Watson b Wardle.......... 73	B 4, l-b 3, n-b 1 8
A. Revill b Wardle 12	—
G. Dawkes c Sellers b Wardle............ 68	277

Derbyshire Bowling

	Overs	Mdns	Runs	Wkts	Overs	Mdns	Runs	Wkts
Pope	14.1	9	12	6	17	11	13	4
Gladwin	14	3	29	3	10	8	5	1
Rhodes					10	5	12	—
Jackson..........					3	2	3	1

Yorkshire Bowling

	Overs	Mdns	Runs	Wkts
Aspinall	13	1	49	—
Whitehead	15	5	46	1
Wardle	37.4	13	87	8
Smailes	14	4	38	—
Smales	16	6	49	—

Umpires: H. Elliott and B. Flint.

DERBYSHIRE v SOMERSET

Played at Derby, May 14, 16, 1949

Derbyshire won by ten wickets. The splendid form of Rhodes, who took nine wickets for 58 in the match and batted soundly for 54, played a large part in Derbyshire's easy success. The first Somerset collapse was surprising after Hill off-drove confidently in making 60 of the first 93 runs, but Copson and Rhodes puzzled the other batsmen, Rhodes claiming the last four wickets for six runs. Gimblett cut and drove with power in the second Somerset innings, but the tail failed ignominiously, the last six wickets making only 24 runs.

Somerset

H. Gimblett c Revill b Copson 11	– c Dawkes b Jackson............ 51
E. Hill c and b Copson 60	– b Copson 6
H. T. F. Buse c Dawkes b Rhodes 14	– c Jackson b Copson 6
N. S. Mitchell-Innes c Elliott b Gladwin 16	– b Copson 1
M. Coope c Revill b Copson 11	– lbw b Rhodes 5
G. E. S. Woodhouse lbw b Rhodes.............. 13	– c Dawkes b Jackson............ 2
M. F. Tremlett b Copson..................... 0	– c Dawkes b Rhodes 4
J. Lawrence b Rhodes....................... 3	– b Jackson 0
H. W. Stephenson not out.................... 1	– not out 11
A. W. Wellard b Rhodes..................... 2	– c Elliott b Rhodes............. 5
H. Hazell st Dawkes b Rhodes 0	– b Rhodes. 1
L-b 1 1	L-b 1 1
132	93

Derbyshire

C. S. Elliott c Coope b Wellard	17	– not out	21
A. Townsend c Wellard b Buse	29	– not out	11
D. Smith c Mitchell-Innes b Tremlett	1		
A. Revill c Wellard b Buse	0		
A. E. Rhodes c Stephenson b Wellard	54		
D. A. Skinner b Buse	6		
G. Dawkes c Gimblett b Hazell	31		
C. Gladwin c Mitchell-Innes b Wellard	23		
E. Marsh b Lawrence	3		
W. H. Copson st Stephenson b Buse	23		
L. Jackson not out	0		
B 4, l-b 3, n-b 1	8		
	195	**(No wkt)**	**32**

Derbyshire Bowling

	Overs	Mdns	Runs	Wkts	Overs	Mdns	Runs	Wkts
Copson	13	4	24	4	8	2	24	3
Gladwin	11	3	25	1	10	2	47	—
Jackson	20	7	33	—	10	5	12	3
Rhodes	14.1	4	49	5	9.2	4	9	4

Somerset Bowling

	Overs	Mdns	Runs	Wkts	Overs	Mdns	Runs	Wkts
Wellard	21	5	31	3	8	2	12	—
Buse	17.5	2	46	4	6	1	13	—
Tremlett	17	4	48	1				
Hazell	14	5	28	1				
Lawrence	8	—	34	1				
Gimblett					1	—	7	—

Umpires: E. Cooke and K. McCanlis.

HISTORY OF DERBYSHIRE CRICKET [1954]

By W. T. Taylor

(*County Secretary since* 1908)

The history of Derbyshire cricket is that of a gallant struggle against adversity and financial difficulties. In scarcely one year since the club was formed eighty-two years ago has there been a credit balance. In fact, more than once Derbyshire have carried on only through the generosity of the cricketing public of the county, who have risen nobly to the club's many appeals for monetary assistance.

Derbyshire were formed on November 4, 1870, at a meeting called in the Guildhall, Derby, by an exceptionally enthusiastic cricket-lover, Mr Walter Boden. A large and influential gathering passed the resolution: "That a cricket club be formed, representing the whole strength of the county, to be called the Derbyshire County Club."

Upon the election of a committee and officials, the Earl of Chesterfield, patron of all manly sports, accepted the Presidency. The Hon. W. M. Jervis was asked to be the first Honorary Secretary. Unfortunately for Derbyshire, the Earl died in the first year of the club's existence. The Hon. W. M. Jervis succeeded him as President until 1887, when, on the appointment of Mr G. H. Strutt to the Presidency, he resumed his secretarial duties.

FINANCIAL CRISIS

In those days the subscription list was small and the loss of a few hundred pounds on the year's working, a matter of much concern. In 1887 the debt was fully £1,000 and the position critical. With the help of Mr Boden and other friends of the club, the Hon. W. M. Jervis immediately set about removing this burden, and in one year the liabilities were liquidated. This is only one instance of the generosity which has been manifested through the years. Heavy taxation now prevents assistance from those who would wish to give it and the flag is kept flying with the help of receipts from Test Match profits and the organisation of various extraneous forms of raising money.

Although Derbyshire have not the colourful cricket traditions as some counties, the game has always held a warm corner in the hearts of the sports-loving people of the Peak County. Exact details of cricket's origin in Derbyshire are difficult to obtain, but records indicate that games were played in many parts of the county soon after the opening of the nineteenth century. Certainly in 1824 Derby defeated Chesterfield by an innings and 23 runs. One of the leading clubs in Derby at that time was the Derby Old Club and a prominent one in Chesterfield was the North Derbyshire Cricket Club.

Chesterfield continued to be a key point in the early history of Derbyshire. Tom Hunt, one of the most versatile of cricketers, was born there in 1819. He excelled in every phase of the game and, in fact, was so gifted that he became known as the "Star of the North". In 1856 he scored 102 for North v South at Manchester, a tremendous innings in those days.

ALL-ENGLAND BEATEN

Seven years earlier, when twenty of the County beat the famous All-England XI by an innings and seven runs, Hunt had made 61 and John Paxton, a fast bowler from Ilkeston, had taken eleven wickets for 47. Next year, 1850, when the match ended in a draw, the same two players were outstanding. Paxton must have been a bowler of unusual merit. In six matches against the All-England XI he took forty wickets – no mean feat against batsmen acknowledged to be the best in the land.

One of the most important events leading to the formation of the County Club occurred in 1863 when the South Derbyshire Cricket Club, one of the most prominent in the County, who combined with the Derby Town Club in the use of the Holmes ground in Derby, were given notice to leave. At once they acquired a ground from the Derby Recreation Company which held a lease from the corporation. The new ground was prepared for cricket, and to this day it is the leading headquarters of the game in Derbyshire. For many years the Derby County Football Club used the same ground, and not only played there under the auspices of the Cricket Club, but wore their colours of chocolate, amber and pale blue.

About this period a match is reported as having taken place in front of the Grand Stand on the Race Course, within a short distance of the present match centre. It may be interesting to mention at this stage that the Derbyshire Committee now have a scheme in hand for adopting this site for their matches at Derby and of making use of the Grand Stand with its covered accommodation for considerably more spectators.

LANCASHIRE TO THE RESCUE

The main problem arising from the inaugural meeting in 1870 was that of arranging matches against other counties. For the first three seasons Lancashire alone were willing to make fixtures, a fact that should never be forgotten by Derbyshire cricketers. The first of these games, at Manchester in May 1871, ended in victory for Derbyshire by an innings and eleven runs. Lancashire's first innings total of 25 remains their lowest to this day. The Lancashire batsmen were thrown into confusion by the pace of the Derbyshire fast bowler, Dove Gregory, who took six wickets for nine runs. In the ensuing years, however, Lancashire gained ample revenge.

Derbyshire's inability to secure any additional county opponents caused a good deal of despondency among officials and supporters, but the turning point came in 1873 when a match was arranged at Wirksworth between sixteen of the County and the Nottinghamshire eleven. Considering that at the time Nottinghamshire were a cricket power, the result was staggering. Derbyshire won by an innings and eight runs. In their first innings Nottinghamshire scored a beggarly 14 runs; Joe Flint took six wickets for 7 runs and William Mycroft four for 6.

HOSPITALITY

Through the years a tale has been handed down about that batting debacle. The story is that a local Derbyshire celebrity, a keen and generous supporter of the club – and the proprietor of an important wine and spirit business, where he blended an attractive and potent brand of whisky – entertained the visitors lavishly at his establishment on the morning when they were to begin their innings.

Who can say that his fanatical enthusiasm for Derbyshire was responsible for the heaviness of his hand when he poured out refreshment for his guests? Might it not have been just the warmth of his hospitality?

That thrilling victory created intense interest in Derbyshire fortunes during the following season, but no one could have been prepared for the outcome. Derbyshire became Champion County in 1874. Vicissitudes too numerous to record in detail had to be encountered and overcome before that title was theirs again sixty-two years later.

When Derbyshire were first proclaimed Champion County, the smallest number of games lost decided the order of merit. What an inducement to play for draws! Through no fault of their own, however, Derbyshire were able to arrange matches only against Lancashire and Kent, three of which ended in victory and the other in a draw.

In the early days of Derbyshire county cricket the side was graced by many stalwart players, but as a counter came a series of exceptional misfortunes. Dove Gregory, a bowler who enjoyed much success, died in 1873 when only 35; the career of William Mycroft (left-arm fast), whom many considered one of the best bowlers produced by a club renowned for its strength in attack, was interfered with by ill-health, and William Cropper, an all-round cricketer of much merit, met with death on the football field before reaching the zenith of his powers. In addition, Frank Sugg and Frank Shacklock left to assist other counties. Almost inevitably such a sequence of disasters meant a lean period on the field, and in 1888 Derbyshire were relegated to second class.

"WISDEN" DECIDES

I would point out that the classification of rank was not then decided by the authority of MCC. The chief arbiters in this matter were the London sporting press, who might be said to have ruled supreme in everything appertaining to county cricket. Thus it was, that, after much discussion, Derbyshire's relegation was a decision of the press rather than of any cricketing body. Incidentally, Mr Charles F. Pardon, then Editor of *Wisden*, was a leading protagonist in the move. Despite strong Derbyshire protests, the other first-class counties and the cricketing public in general assented to the change.

Derbyshire remained in the wilderness until 1894, when they were again designated first-class. On a motion of the captains of the leading counties, they, together with Essex, Leicestershire and Warwickshire, were given first-class status, but the result of matches did not count in the Championship until 1895, by which time Hampshire had also been admitted. The County Championship was reorganised accordingly.

During Derbyshire's period in exile many fine players wore their colours. Prominent among them was S. H. Evershed, who in later years was knighted for public services to his native town of Burton-on-Trent. He captained the eleven with marked ability for many years. Another was that grand veteran, L. G. Wright, a magnificent batsman and unsurpassed as a fieldsman in the old-fashioned position of square-point. So keen and alert was he in 1952 that at the age of 90 he regularly visited the County Ground to watch the matches and he still played an excellent game of bowls. He died early this year.

Other players of top class were George Davidson, whose 274 against Lancashire at Manchester in 1896 remains a Derbyshire batting record, and who, in 1895, scored 1,296 runs and took 138 wickets, the first professional to accomplish this, and only the second player to do the "double", the first being W. G. Grace; William Chatterton, a batsman of delightful strokes who toured South Africa with an English team in 1891; and William Storer, a skilled wicket-keeper who played in Tests against Australia both at home and abroad. Against Yorkshire in 1896 Storer hit centuries in each innings – a feat performed previously only by W. G. Grace, A. E. Stoddart and George Brann, all amateurs.

Youthful readers may not be aware that the celebrated Australian, F. R. Spofforth, known always as "The Demon Bowler", played some cricket for Derbyshire. Spofforth last toured England with an Australian side in 1886, and afterwards, when he set up home in Derbyshire, the County authorities sought to persuade the County Cricket Council to allow him to play without waiting for the usual two years' residential qualification. This application was, quite rightly, refused. Even so, Yorkshire generously offered to waive the point so that Spofforth could turn out against them. He did so in two matches in the 1889 season and, moreover, showed his appreciation of their action so much that in one game he took fifteen of their wickets for 81 runs. Next season Spofforth shared the captaincy with S. H. Evershed and, as might have been expected, headed the bowling averages with 42 wickets at 11.36 runs each. He made one appearance in 1891. That was his last.

For many years Derbyshire's participation in the County Championship was uneventful, but occasionally they accomplished performances to be remembered. The defeat of Essex by nine wickets at Chesterfield in 1904 provided the most notable of these. When Essex made 597 in their first innings (P. A. Perrin 343 not out) they looked safe enough from defeat, but Derbyshire replied with 548 (C. A. Olliviere 229), dismissed Essex for 97 in the second innings, and won the game with 149 for one (Olliviere 92 not out) in the last innings.

WORLD RECORD STAND

Another memorable match was that against Warwickshire at Blackwell in 1910, when J. Chapman (165) and Arnold Warren (123) put on 283 for Derbyshire's ninth wicket. This still stands as a world record in first-class cricket. Then in my third year as Derbyshire Secretary, I remember the occasion well. At lunch time on the last day Warwickshire looked certain of a comfortable win. Derbyshire, with eight second innings wickets down, were a long way behind Warwickshire's first innings score and, well as Chapman and Warren were batting, few Derbyshire folk could hope that defeat would be avoided.

In view of their strong position, Warwickshire, I knew, were hoping to catch an early afternoon train, and, in conversation during the interval, I remarked to their fast bowler, Frank Field: "You look like catching your train all right, Frank." The reply was, "I'm not so sure about that, Mr Taylor. These chaps are pretty good bats, you know." How right he was. Chapman and Warren made their runs in less than three hours and Warwickshire had to be content with a draw.

Another historic Derbyshire achievement was the defeat of the Australian Imperial Forces XI in 1919 by 36 runs. This was the only victory gained by a county side against the Australians during their tour. Furthermore, it was accomplished without that great-hearted fast bowler, William Bestwick, who, at the age of 43, was making his first appearance for the Players against the Gentlemen at Lord's. James Horsley – he did the hat-trick – and Arthur Morton shared nineteen wickets in the two Australian innings.

Because Bestwick's début for Derbyshire had been as far back as 1898 and he had not played for them since 1909, nearly everyone thought he would be past first-class cricket when he returned to the game in 1919. He surprised them all by his powers. In 1921 Bestwick was fourth in the first-class bowling averages with 147 wickets for less than 17 runs each, including all ten for 40 in an innings against Glamorgan at Cardiff. Not bad for a fast bowler of 45 making a come-back! No county ever had a better servant. The stronger the opposition and the better the pitch the harder he tried. His total of 1,452 wickets is a Derbyshire record. On his only Test appearance, at Leeds against Australia in 1905, Bestwick's contemporary, Arnold Warren, a very fast bowler with a lovely action, took five wickets for 57 runs.

One of the features of Derbyshire's cricket from 1899 to 1914 was the wicket-keeping of Joe Humphries. Surely his stumping of batsmen on the leg side when standing up to the fast bowling of Bestwick and Warren has never been surpassed since the days of Gregor MacGregor of Middlesex fame. He toured Australia with the England side of 1907 and, by scoring 16 at a critical time, assisted materially in the winning of the Second Test by one wicket.

BESTWICKS MEET QUAIFES

Those who enjoyed the spectacle regretted that A. E. Lawton and G. Curgenven, both batsmen of tremendous hitting powers, were able to assist only infrequently. Limited as were his appearances, Curgenven rarely lost time playing himself in. At Gloucester, for instance, in 1922, he scored 65 in the first innings at little more than one a minute and his 68 out of 119 in the second took less than twenty-five minutes. That year two Derbyshire players figured in an occurrence considered unique in county cricket. When W. Bestwick and R. Bestwick shared the bowling against W. G. Quaife and B. W. Quaife of Warwickshire, spectators witnessed father and son bowling against batsmen likewise related. Similarly, no history of Derbyshire cricket would be complete without reference to the all-round work of Sam Cadman and Arthur Morton. Over a long period of years they were almost always the chief run-getters and wicket-takers. Too much credit cannot be accorded to them.

County cricket resumed in 1919 only through a big effort by everyone connected with the game. At first matches were restricted to two days, but the experiment was not repeated. Unsatisfactory as the season may have been, it was auspicious for Derbyshire because that year marked the beginning of G. R. Jackson's long association.

In 1920 came the most disastrous season ever experienced by any side since the County Championship came into existence. Of the 18 matches played, Derbyshire lost 17 outright. The other was abandoned without a ball being bowled. The only pleasurable memories for Derbyshire were the first appearances of Harry Elliott and Harry Storer. Elliott could be regarded as a most unfortunate wicket-keeper in that his career coincided with the peak years of Herbert Strudwick of Surrey. His big-match honours were confined to tours of South Africa (1927) and India (1933) and one home Test, at Manchester against West Indies in 1928. In first-class cricket Elliott stumped or caught 1,206 victims, a number exceeded by only three players. His 1,183 dismissals for Derbyshire are easily a county record. Two special feats by him were in not conceding a bye in 25 completed innings in 1936 and in missing only one match through injury from 1920 to 1927. Harry Elliott's nephew, Charles, began to play for Derbyshire in 1932. Twenty years later, when he headed the batting averages, he was still one of the County's most able batsmen. Harry Storer, a nephew of the old wicket-keeper, William Storer, was a most dependable first-wicket batsman, equally at home on fast or slow pitches. But for the claims of first-class football, at which he was capped by England, probably he would have played for his country at cricket as well.

Worried by the appalling results of 1920, G. M. Buckston returned, at 40 years of age, to lead the side next season with the fixed intention of instilling determination into a dispirited eleven. Buckston had not played county cricket since 1907, but a pronounced revival in Derbyshire fortunes coincided with his appointment. Only those who played under him knew how much the team owed to the "skipper" for his example, cheerfulness and leadership. Having accomplished his mission, Buckston refused to be dissuaded from his intention to retire. Instead, he was elected chairman of the Committee.

G. R. JACKSON ERA

G. R. Jackson took over the captaincy for 1922. Throughout Derbyshire's cricket history no appointment has been followed by such happy results. For nine seasons G. R. Jackson led Derbyshire with masterly judgment. Although a stern disciplinarian, he held the affection and respect of every player. When he retired at the end of the 1930 summer he had laid the foundations of the Championship team six years later. This was *Wisden's* interpretation of G. R. Jackson's effort for Derbyshire cricket: "For his work in leading and inspiring the team, Jackson deserves immense thanks. He took over control when the fortunes of the county were at a very low ebb, steadily raised the standard of the cricket, and now retires with Derbyshire well established amongst the leading teams of the day."

During G. R. Jackson's captaincy many cricketers destined to give magnificent service over a protracted period entered the county ranks. One was Leslie Townsend (1922), a gifted all-rounder who in 1933 scored 2,268 runs and took 100 wickets. In 1924 that fine aggressive cricketer, Stanley Worthington, embarked upon his county career. He was no mean fast-medium bowler, an attractive batsman on hard pitches and a superb close fielder. A particularly joyous match for Worthington was that against Nottinghamshire at Ilkeston in 1938. Not only did he score two separate centuries, but, in the course of his second innings, he heard of the birth of his only child, a son.

DENIS SMITH ARRIVES

In 1927 Derbyshire were further strengthened by the advent of Denis Smith. At one time this left-hand batsman of beautiful stroke-play was described as a second Frank Woolley. He developed to a high state of efficiency but never quite reached the class expected. Even so, his total of 20,516 runs for Derbyshire constitutes a county record. A year after Worthington came Albert Alderman and Tom Mitchell. Alderman was a steady opening batsman and second to none in the outfield. His catch at The Oval in 1936 when he dismissed Barling is still recalled by those privileged to witness it. When Barling swept a ball from Copson to fine leg the stroke looked certain to produce six runs, but Alderman, sprinting hard for 30 yards, held the ball with his right hand close to the palings.

Mitchell's discovery was unusual and intriguing. With time on his hands during the General Strike of 1926, Mitchell, a miner, practised bowling near the pit-head of the Creswell Colliery at which he normally worked. An old cricketer who saw him turning the ball prodigiously from leg at once recommended him to the local cricket club. They invited Mitchell to play for them. Mitchell not only gathered a harvest of wickets immediately in club cricket, but by 1928 had advanced to the county eleven. Against Leicestershire in 1935 he took all ten for 64 in an innings. Much excellent service was to come also from Alf Pope, a fast-medium bowler and useful batsman who began in county cricket in 1930. Four of Jackson's men, Townsend, Worthington, Denis Smith and Mitchell, played for England and all helped Derbyshire to carry off the Championship in 1936. How lucky were Derbyshire to find so many above average cricketers over so short a period!

Derbyshire were fortunate also in persuading A. W. Richardson to become captain in 1931. Richardson continued as leader until the end of that wonderful 1936 season. Without doubt the chief architects in this glorious episode of Derbyshire cricket were the two captains, G. R. Jackson (1922-30) and A. W. Richardson (1931-36), and the coach, Sam Cadman. By their skill and acumen, Jackson and Richardson gradually moulded Derbyshire into a match-winning combination, and, with the flair for discerning the potentialities of young players, Cadman produced from the cricket nursery no fewer than eight of the Championship team. With Middlesex and Yorkshire issuing late, though strong, challenges, interest in the side was aflame in the closing weeks of the 1936 season and, when he heard the news that the result of the Championship had at last been settled, the Derbyshire President, the Duke of Devonshire, hurriedly left his shooting party at Bolton Abbey to journey to Derby and join the public reception given to the players on their return. The Duke, who had accepted the Presidency in 1909, always showed the deepest interest in the club's affairs. He attended home matches regularly and was always ready to come to the rescue when financial problems presented themselves. When he died in 1938 he was succeeded in the Presidency by his son, who in turn was succeeded by his son, the present eleventh Duke of Devonshire.

DEVASTATING COPSON

Two players of outstanding merit, Bill Copson (1932) and George Pope (1933), began with Derbyshire under A. W. Richardson. Apart from being one of the most likeable fellows who stepped on to a cricket field, Copson was a devastating fast-medium bowler whose gift of making the ball appear to leave the turf faster than he bowled it through the air caused the downfall of scores of first-rate batsmen. Copson did not enjoy the best of health. Nevertheless, he played a vital part in much of Derbyshire's glory. He could not have wished for a better start in big cricket. With the first ball he sent down in a county game, at The Oval in 1932, he dismissed no less a player than Andrew Sandham of Surrey. Copson's most noteworthy feat was that against Warwickshire in the first innings at Derby in 1937. His eight wickets for eleven runs there included four with successive balls. Although Copson did the hat-trick three times, that distinction has been surpassed by the present Derbyshire leg-break bowler, Bert Rhodes (five times). Only three men – D. V. P. Wright (seven), T. W. Goddard (six) and C. W. L. Parker (six) – have exceeded this number.

George Pope was an all-rounder of abundant possibilities whose natural talent should have produced better results than it did. Both he and Copson played for England at home and, along with his county colleague, Worthington, Copson went to Australia in 1936-37 as a member of G. O. Allen's team, but did not make a Test appearance there. R. H. R. Buckston, who followed A. W. Richardson in the leadership, gave every possible encouragement to the younger players. Since the war Buckston has rendered equal aid as captain of the second eleven. His understanding of the "outlook" of the young cricketer has been valuable in the extreme.

The resumption of county cricket in 1946 presented more problems, the main one affecting Derbyshire being that of finding a regular captain. With the exception of E. J. Gothard, who carried out the duties in 1947 and 1948, no one was available for more than one year. Although no more than a moderate change bowler, Gothard performed a remarkable hat-trick at Derby against Middlesex in their Championship year of 1947 by dismissing A. Fairbairn, W. J. Edrich and R. W. V. Robins. To his credit also went the bowling of Sir Donald Bradman at Derby in 1948.

Luckily for Derbyshire, a regular captain became available from 1951 onwards when G. L. Willatt took over. Under his leadership in 1952 the side finished fourth, their highest position since 1937. Continuity of captaincy is always beneficial to a team, and all followers of Derbyshire cricket must be glad that Willatt signified his ability to continue in 1953. Whenever Willatt was absent in 1952, the side played under the command of D. B. Carr, who, following his tour with the MCC team in India the previous winter, added a balance to the eleven through his all-round skill. Since the Second World War several noteworthy victories have been recorded by Derbyshire. These included the defeat of Somerset in one day in 1947 – by an innings and 125 runs.

C. GLADWIN AND L. JACKSON

A further highlight of this period has been the fast-medium bowling of Clifford Gladwin, who, except for 1950 when unfitness kept him out of nearly half the matches, has taken over 100 wickets for Derbyshire in each season. As a fact, Derbyshire are said to have an uncanny facility for producing fast-medium bowlers ("Derbyshire bowlers" they are called). Another of this variety is Leslie Jackson, who came into the side in 1947. At times Jackson is good enough to run through a batting side and even on the hardest pitches he will move the new ball either way. The Australian touring team of 1948 were genuine in their declaration that only two bowlers in England moved the ball away from the bat as much as Jackson. He toured India with the Commonwealth team in the winter of 1950, suffered an injury to his elbow which necessitated his returning to undergo an operation, resumed cricket late in the 1951 season, and returned to his best form in 1952, heading the county bowling with a total of 114 wickets.

PICTURESQUE CHESTERFIELD

Although Derby remains the county ground of the club, it is by no means as pleasing to the eye as the beautiful Queen's Park enclosure at Chesterfield, which Derbyshire first used in 1898 for a match against Surrey. Despite the superb lob bowling of D. L. A. Jephson, who shortened the match by taking nine Derbyshire wickets for 55 runs in the two innings, the size of the crowd at that game made the experiment well worth while and further fixtures were arranged there. In fact Chesterfield became a regular venue for several matches a season. Since those days also the Committee have extended their fixtures to other centres in the county and now no less than five grounds are used. Those responsible for the county's policy believe that they owe a duty to their followers which they can best repay by offering them an opportunity of watching first-class cricket within a reasonable distance of their homes.

The first game at Chesterfield did not pass without incident. Derbyshire supporters were most hostile about Jephson's lobs, against which they protested vigorously, saying that this was "unfair bowling". Only a few weeks after that exciting contest Chesterfield was the scene of the establishment of a batting record which stood for thirty-four years. Yorkshire's opening pair, J. T. Brown and J. Tunnicliffe, scored 554 together against Derbyshire in W. Sugg's benefit match before Brown deliberately knocked down his wicket. That partnership was not beaten until two more Yorkshiremen, Percy Holmes and Herbert Sutcliffe, made 555 for the first wicket against Essex at Leyton in 1932.

To record in detail the efforts of all the splendid cricketers who have played for Derbyshire would be quite impossible, but all omissions are regretted. What of the future? Within the next few years some of the present Derbyshire side will finish their careers. Replacements for them have to be found. Many promising young cricketers in the county have been discovered and developed through the medium of the Derbyshire Youth Cricket Advisory Council, who are carrying out the scheme sponsored by the MCC Youth Cricket Association. Properly developed, some of these should mature into top-class players, and I believe that in years ahead Derbyshire will continue to flourish as an attractive county.

From 1889 until the present time only three Secretaries have held office for Derbyshire. Mr. W. B. Delacombe did so until his retirement in 1908. He was followed for a few months by Mr. R. S. T. Cochrane. Mr Taylor, who has been Secretary ever since, is to-day the longest-serving of the county Secretaries. Although he assisted Derbyshire in a few matches from 1905 onwards, he is better known for his administrative efficiency. In the organisation of special efforts which over the years have raised more than £20,000 for the county club his share has been large – and always, unstinted. *Editor.*

DERBYSHIRE v MIDDLESEX

Played at Chesterfield, July 17, 18, 19, 1957

Derbyshire won by an innings and 22 runs, taking 14 points. Middlesex, sent in by Carr, were dismissed in their second innings for the lowest total in first-class cricket for three years, and they looked likely to be out for the lowest score for fifty years when their seventh, eighth and ninth wickets all fell at 13, but Bennett and Moss more than doubled the score. In both innings Gladwin, with accurate fast-medium bowling, was the main source of trouble to Middlesex, and he received good support from Morgan, Smith and Jackson. A damp pitch was helpful throughout to bowlers. Derbyshire, too, found conditions difficult; they owed much to a lively seventh wicket stand of 50 between Dawkes and Morgan for their useful lead of 51.

Middlesex

J. D. Robertson c Dawkes b Gladwin	38	– lbw b Jackson 0
R. A. Gale c Kelly b Smith	8	– c Dawkes b Gladwin........... 4
D. O. Baldry lbw b Morgan	4	– b Gladwin.................... 1
W. J. Edrich c Revill b Gladwin	10	– c Carr b Gladwin.............. 0
G. P. S. Delisle b Morgan	0	– b Jackson 6
F. J. Titmus c Carr b Smith	22	– c Morgan b Gladwin........... 0
J. T. Murray c Dawkes b Gladwin	1	– c and b Gladwin 0
D. Bennett c Dawkes b Gladwin	13	– not out 14
H. W. Tilly c Jackson b Gladwin	0	– lbw b Jackson................ 0
R. J. Hurst c Carr b Gladwin	2	– run out 0
A. E. Moss not out	0	– c Hamer b Morgan............ 2
B 4	4	L-b 2................. 2

1/24 2/34 3/55 4/62 5/86   102   1/0 2/1 3/1 4/1 5/9   29
6/86 7/93 8/93 9/99   6/9 7/13 8/13 9/13

Derbyshire

A. Hamer b Moss 5	E. Smith c Murray b Tilly.............. 0
C. Lee c and b Titmus................. 33	C. Gladwin not out 5
J. M. Kelly b Tilly 23	L. Jackson c Titmus b Hurst 0
A. C. Revill b Hurst 17	
D. B. Carr c Murray b Tilly 4	B 4, l-b 5 9
D. J. Green c Edrich b Hurst 1	
G. O. Dawkes c Gale b Tilly........... 28	1/12 2/53 3/82 4/82 5/87 153
D. C. Morgan c Bennett b Hurst........ 28	6/87 7/137 8/143 9/149

Derbyshire Bowling

	Overs	Mdns	Runs	Wkts	Overs	Mdns	Runs	Wkts
Jackson...........	6	4	4	—	11	6	7	3
Gladwin	25.2	14	23	6	14	8	18	5
Morgan...........	19	5	42	2	4.2	3	2	1
Smith	17	6	29	2	1	1	—	—

Middlesex Bowling

	Overs	Mdns	Runs	Wkts
Moss.............	5	2	12	1
Bennett..........	2	—	4	—
Titmus	10	—	33	1
Hurst	21.1	10	50	4
Tilly	13	4	45	4

Umpires: W. E. Phillipson and A. Skelding.

DERBYSHIRE v HAMPSHIRE

Played at Burton, August 13, 14, 1958

Derbyshire won by 103 runs taking 14 points and administering a most disturbing defeat to Hampshire at a vital stage of the Championship competition. Derbyshire, put in to bat, made eight for one wicket in 20 minutes' play possible before rain ended the first day. Next day thirty-nine wickets fell on drying turf. When Shackleton and Heath, unchanged, dismissed Derbyshire cheaply, Hampshire seemed in a good position, but they found the pace and lift of Jackson and Rhodes even more disconcerting. In seventy minutes Hampshire were out for 23, the lowest post-war score in English first-class cricket and the lowest ever obtained against Derbyshire. For a second time Heath and Shackleton, fast-medium, bowled unchanged and only Morgan of the Derbyshire batsmen offered much resistance. Needing 159 to win, Hampshire again failed against Rhodes and Jackson, being disposed of in an hour and three-quarters.

Derbyshire

C. Lee c Horton b Shackleton	8	– c Horton b Heath 6
F. C. Brailsford c Barnard b Heath	4	– c Horton b Heath 14
D. J. Green c Sainsbury b Heath	6	– c Barnard b Shackleton 4
A. Hamer c Pitman b Heath	5	– c and b Heath 7
D. C. Morgan c Horton b Shackleton	3	– c Marshall b Shackleton 46
D. B. Carr c Burden b Heath	12	– lbw b Heath 19
H. L. Johnson c Harrison b Heath	4	– c and b Shackleton 6
G. O. Dawkes c Burden b Heath	19	– b Heath....................... 0
H. J. Rhodes b Shackleton	0	– c Sainsbury b Heath 2
E. Smith not out	6	– b Heath....................... 0
H. L. Jackson b Shackleton	4	– not out 0
L-b 2, w 1	3	L-b 1, n-b 2 3

1/8 2/13 3/24 4/27 5/27   **74**   1/21 2/25 3/25 4/40 5/94   **107**
6/35 7/52 8/56 9/68   6/100 7/100 8/106 9/107

Hampshire

R. E. Marshall c Dawkes b Rhodes	4	– lbw b Jackson 0
J. R. Gray b Rhodes	0	– c Dawkes b Rhodes 1
H. Horton b Jackson	5	– b Jackson 8
R. W. C. Pitman run out	0	– c Carr b Rhodes 11
H. M. Barnard c Morgan b Rhodes	5	– c Carr b Jackson.............. 16
A. C. D. Ingleby-Mackenzie c Lee b Rhodes	2	– b Rhodes..................... 4
P. J. Sainsbury b Jackson	4	– c Dawkes b Jackson........... 4
L. Harrison not out	2	– c Jackson b Morgan 0
D. Shackleton c Lee b Jackson	0	– c Jackson b Morgan 1
M. Heath b Jackson	0	– b Morgan 4
M. D. Burden b Jackson	0	– not out 0
N-b 1	1	L-b 6.................... 6

1/4 2/5 3/7 4/12 5/17   **23**   1/1 2/1 3/13 4/23 5/32   **55**
6/17 7/23 8/23 9/23   6/46 7/47 8/47 9/55

Hampshire Bowling

	Overs	Mdns	Runs	Wkts	Overs	Mdns	Runs	Wkts
Shackleton	16.4	8	36	4	18.2	4	52	3
Heath	16	5	35	6	18	4	52	7

Derbyshire Bowling

	Overs	Mdns	Runs	Wkts	Overs	Mdns	Runs	Wkts
Jackson..........	8.4	5	10	5	15	8	16	4
Rhodes..........	8	3	12	4	9	1	29	3
Morgan..........					5.3	3	4	3

Umpires: J. S. Buller and H. G. Baldwin.

DERBYSHIRE v ESSEX

Played at Chesterfield, August 12, 13, 14, 1959

Drawn. Rain spoiled the match, allowing little more than an hour's play on the second day. Hamer, well supported by Hall and Lee, gave Derbyshire a sound start and Johnson also batted well, but the pace of Knight brought about a startling collapse, for he took the last four wickets in seven balls. Essex began poorly, but typically dour batting by Bailey, who helped Insole to add 167, swung the game in their favour. Insole batted enterprisingly, but failed narrowly to ensure bonus points for Essex. In the late stages of the innings, with little time left, Preson hit fiercely.

Derbyshire

A. Hamer c Taylor b Bailey	91		
I. W. Hall c Preston b Hurd	38		
C. Lee c Taylor b Hurd.........................	38		
D. B. Carr c Taylor b Hurd.....................	1		
H. L. Johnson lbw b Knight	63		
D. C. Morgan b Greensmith	12	– not out	14
G. O. Dawkes c Savill b Knight	28		
G. W. Richardson b Knight	4		
H. J. Rhodes b Knight.........................	0	– not out	3
E. Smith b Knight	0	– c Preston b Hurd	5
R. Berry not out	2		
B 2, l-b 5	7		

1/86 2/148 3/153 4/196 5/213   284   1/7   (1 wkt) 22
6/260 7/281 8/281 9/281

Essex

L. A. Savill c Dawkes b Richardson	16	B. R. Knight not out	27
J. Milner lbw b Rhodes	2	K. C. Preston c Johnson b Carr	70
B. Taylor c Hall b Rhodes.	7	A. Hurd c and b Lee	4
D. J Insole c Hamer b Berry	155		
T. E. Bailey c Morgan b Rhodes..........	68	B 8, l-b 10, w 1, n-b 1	20
M. Bear c Carr b Richardson	17		
W. T. Greensmith c Dawkes b Richardson..	0	1/3 2/11 3/39 4/206 5/251	403
G. Smith c and b Smith.................	17	6/251 7/300 8/304 9/393	

Essex Bowling

	Overs	Mdns	Runs	Wkts	Overs	Mdns	Runs	Wkts
Bailey	26	3	78	1				
Knight	17.2	3	44	5				
Preston	16	2	42	—				
Greensmith........	15	1	49	1	4	3	7	—
Hurd	25	4	64	3	3	—	15	1

Derbyshire Bowling

	Overs	Mdns	Runs	Wkts
Rhodes	24	6	51	3
Richardson	27	6	62	3
Morgan	26	5	67	—
Smith	21	3	88	1
Berry	22	5	62	1
Carr	7	—	37	1
Hamer	2	1	12	—
Lee	1.5	—	4	1

Umpires: P. A. Gibb and D. Davies.

DERBYSHIRE v WORCESTERSHIRE

Played at Derby, June 18, 20, 21, 1960

Derbyshire won by eight wickets, taking 12 points. Worcestershire made a shaky start on a good batting pitch, but recovered well in a fifth-wicket partnership of 141 between Sedgley and Dews, who hit fourteen 4s. After Lee, Carr and Johnson had all batted well and enabled Derbyshire to declare, Jackson, late on the second day, undermined Worcestershire with a hat-trick, the second of his career. Dews again batted soundly, but a good spell by Morgan prevented a real recovery and Derbyshire made light of the task of scoring 97 to win.

Worcestershire

R. G. A. Headley c Milner b Lee	20	– b Jackson	3
J. B. Sedgley run out	95	– b Jackson	2
A. H. Spencer lbw b Lee	3	– lbw b Jackson	8
D. W. Richardson b Carr	20	– c Dawkes b Jackson	0
R. G. Broadbent lbw b Jackson	4	– b Morgan	22
*G. Dews c Dawkes b Jackson	86	– lbw b Carr	48
†R. Booth c Carr b Richardson	0	– c Dawkes b Morgan	1
D. N. F. Slade not out	34	– b Carr	11
D. B. Pearson c Hall b Richardson	2	– c Berry b Morgan	9
K. J. Aldridge b Carr	19	– c Berry b Morgan	0
J. Flavell c and b Carr	2	– not out	4
B 1, l-b 3, n-b 2	6	B 1	1

1/52 2/59 3/83 4/87 5/228   **291**   1/4 2/5 3/5 4/22 5/59   **109**
6/233 7/233 8/242 9/287   6/63 7/86 8/105 9/105

Derbyshire

C. Lee b Aldridge	76		
I. W. Hall lbw b Flavell	1	– not out	49
*D. B. Carr c Booth b Richardson	67	– c Booth b Aldridge	20
H. L. Johnson c Aldridge b Slade	96	– not out	5
D. Milner c Spencer b Flavell	18		
W. F. Oates st Booth b Slade	19		
D. C. Morgan run out	4		
G. W. Richardson b Flavell	4		
†G. O. Dawkes not out	3	– c Slade b Flavell	22
B 4, l-b 10, n-b 2	16	L-b 1	1

1/7 2/133 3/154 4/200   (8 wkts dec.) **304**   1/35 2/87   (2 wkts) **97**
5/265 6/272 7/287 8/304

H. L. Jackson and R. Berry did not bat.

Derbyshire Bowling

	Overs	Mdns	Runs	Wkts	Overs	Mdns	Runs	Wkts
Jackson..........	23	7	43	2	21	6	33	4
Richardson.......	22	7	50	2	15	3	19	—
Morgan..........	15	5	46	—	12	7	9	4
Lee	17	4	47	2				
Berry............	20	7	51	—	8	5	11	—
Carr	9.2	2	32	3	16.1	5	36	2
Oates	4	—	16	—				

Worcestershire Bowling

	Overs	Mdns	Runs	Wkts	Overs	Mdns	Runs	Wkts
Flavell...........	25	1	74	3	9	1	19	1
Aldridge	26	6	58	1	11	3	25	1
Pearson..........	23	3	72	—	10	2	19	—
Slade............	36.2	12	63	2	10.1	2	23	—
Richardson.......	7	—	21	1				
Spencer..........					2	—	10	—

Umpires: H. G. Baldwin and D. J. Wood.

DERBYSHIRE v OXFORD UNIVERSITY

Played at Buxton, June 24, 26, 27, 1961

Drawn. Rhodes returned to the team after a spell of work in correcting his suspect bowling action and he gained encouraging success by performing the hat-trick. He and Eyre upset the University batting, apart from the hard-hitting Fry, during the first innings. Derbyshire began their reply in enterprising manner, but rain prevented a resumption until after tea on the second day. Then wickets fell quickly and Derbyshire declared 15 runs behind. Again a keen Derbyshire attack troubled the University, despite an elegant innings by the Nawab of Pataudi, who hit thirteen 4s in a stay of ninety-three minutes. Rhodes finished the innings with a hat-trick, the first of his career. Set to make 196, Derbyshire began badly, but Carr batted defiantly against his former University.

Oxford

D. M. Green b Eyre............................	24	– c Hall b Eyre	45
D. R. Worsley c Dawkes b Rhodes...............	0	– c Johnson b Buxton	11
A. A. Baig c Carr b Eyre......................	16	– b Buxton	2
*Nawab of Pataudi c Carr b Rhodes	26	– c Beet b Morgan...............	70
C. A. Fry c and b Carr	61	– b Smith.......................	8
C. D. Drybrough b Eyre.......................	13	– c Beet b Smith................	10
†R. H. C. Waters c Carr b Rhodes..............	22	– not out	23
A. R. Duff run out	4	– b Morgan	0
J. D. Piachaud b Rhodes......................	28	– lbw b Rhodes	1
T. R. Jakobson not out	8	– b Rhodes......................	0
N. P. Thompson c Dawkes b Buxton	2	– b Rhodes......................	0
B 2, l-b 3, n-b 1	6	B 7, l-b 2, n-b 1	10

1/0 2/38 3/41 4/80 5/116   210   1/49 2/55 3/65 4/88 5/111   180
6/155 7/163 8/194 9/206   6/179 7/179 8/180 9/180

Derbyshire

D. C. Morgan b Jakobson	18	– b Jakobson	7
I. W. Hall c Waters b Green	35	– lbw b Jakobson	4
H. L. Johnson c Waters b Thompson	48	– c Duff b Thompson	5
W. F. Oates c Jakobson b Thompson	2	– c Thompson b Piachaud	27
G. A. Beet c Waters b Jakobson	3	– b Jakobson	1
*D. B. Carr c Jakobson b Thompson	1	– not out	45
I. R. Buxton not out	43	– not out	16
†G. O. Dawkes c Pataudi b Thompson	26		
E. Smith c Pataudi b Green	11		
T. J. P. Eyre not out	7		
L-b 1	1	B 4, l-b 2	6

1/28 2/92 3/103 4/107   (8 wkts dec.) 195   1/9 2/14 3/20   (5 wkts) 111
5/107 6/109 7/154 8/188   4/21 5/64

H. J. Rhodes did not bat.

Derbyshire Bowling

	Overs	Mdns	Runs	Wkts	Overs	Mdns	Runs	Wkts
Rhodes	29	11	57	4	16.5	5	37	3
Eyre	21	9	54	3	10	1	33	1
Buxton	15.1	4	34	1	11	5	20	2
Smith	17	5	30	—	10	2	40	2
Morgan	15	9	17	—	8	2	24	2
Carr	8	3	12	1	4	—	16	—

Oxford Bowling

	Overs	Mdns	Runs	Wkts	Overs	Mdns	Runs	Wkts
Jakobson	25	5	91	2	12	3	27	3
Thompson	19	4	72	4	9	2	11	1
Green	8	—	26	2				
Drybrough	3	1	5	—	6	4	7	—
Piachaud					11	4	31	1
Duff					8	1	25	—
Pataudi					1	—	4	—

Umpires: N. Oldfield and R. Aspinall.

ESSEX

ESSEX v GLOUCESTERSHIRE

Played at Brentwood, June 26, 27, 28, 1946

Gloucestershire won by an innings and 23 runs. Fine bowling by Goddard, who took fourteen wickets for 169 runs, enabled Gloucestershire to gain a convincing victory. The off-spin bowler made the ball turn and come off the turf quickly; only Avery seemed master of such craft, and he carried his bat through the first innings after scoring more than half the total. For Gloucestershire, Crapp used the leg hit and drive to advantage in making his first century of the season, his strokes including thirteen 4s. Barnett, Emmett and Cranfield were all in form.

Gloucestershire

C. J. Barnett c and b Taylor	79
B. O. Allen c Dodds b Appleyard	14
W. L. Neale c Wade b P. Smith	39
W. R. Hammond st Wade b Taylor	14
J. F. Crapp c and b R. Smith	102
G. M. Emmett c and b Vigar	66
A. E. Wilson b Vigar	0
L. M. Cranfield not out	49
G. Lambert c Taylor b P. Smith	7
T. W. Goddard c Taylor b P. Smith	19
C. Cook c Pearce b R. Smith	1
B 1, l-b 4, w 1	6
	396

Essex

A. V. Avery not out	83	– b Cranfield 44
F. H. Vigar b Goddard	2	– lbw b Goddard 31
R. M. Taylor c Emmett b Goddard	0	– c Hammond b Goddard 7
T. N. Pearce run out	1	– c Allen b Cook 30
R. F. T. Paterson lbw b Goddard	19	– b Goddard 11
T. C. Dodds c Hammond b Goddard	6	– b Cook 13
T. P. B. Smith b Goddard	12	– c Goddard b Cranfield 43
D. F. Cock c Cook b Goddard	14	– c Cranfield b Goddard 0
R. Smith lbw b Barnett	18	– c Cook b Goddard 0
T. H. Wade c Allen b Goddard	1	– not out 14
F. W. Appleyard c Cook b Goddard	0	– lbw b Goddard 1
B 8, l-b 1	9	B 8, l-b 5, w 1 14
	165	208

Essex Bowling

	Overs	Mdns	Runs	Wkts
R. Smith	28.4	4	95	2
Appleyard	16	7	31	1
P. Smith	52	12	121	3
R. Taylor	24	4	79	2
Paterson	3	—	9	—
Vigar	19	4	55	2

Gloucestershire Bowling

	Overs	Mdns	Runs	Wkts	Overs	Mdns	Runs	Wkts
Lambert	9	—	21	—	3	—	12	—
Barnett	6	3	5	1	12	4	25	—
Goddard..........	40.1	12	88	8	33.2	7	81	6
Cook.............	36	18	42	—	31	13	42	2
Emmett..........					2	—	20	—
Cranfield.........					14	5	14	2

ESSEX v GLAMORGAN

Played at Brentwood, June 16, 17, 18, 1948

Glamorgan won by an innings and 190 runs. Their batsmen excelled – particularly E. Davies and Jones, each of whom hit a double century. Then Muncer, taking full advantage of a rain-affected pitch, won the game with his splendid off-spin bowling. Essex could do little to check the grand stroke-play of Davies and Jones, and their stand for the third wicket yielded 313 in three and a quarter hours. Davies hit two 6s and thirty 4s in an innings of five hours, and Jones three 6s and twenty-two 4s in a stay of four hours. Muncer's accurate bowling, backed by smart catching close to the wicket, upset Essex first time after rain, and when they followed-on, Muncer, once more suited by the conditions, fared even better. He took the first eight wickets, caught the next man, and finished with nine for 62 and fifteen for just under 11 runs each in the match. Glamorgan again held their catches in first-rate style.

Glamorgan

E. Davies c Preston b Dines 215	J. Eaglestone lbw b Pearce 60
P. Clift b Preston..................... 14	J. Pleass not out 2
W. G. A. Parkhouse b Preston 69	B 6, l-b 4 10
W. E. Jones not out...................212	
A. Watkins lbw b Vigar................ 4	(5 wkts dec.) 586

W. Wooller, L. Muncer, H. Davies and N. Hever did not bat.

Essex

T. C. Dodds c Watkins b Wooller................	0 – b Muncer	37
S. J. Cray c Wooller b Muncer	37 – b Muncer	21
A. V. Avery c Watkins b Muncer	8 – b Muncer	41
F. H. Vigar c Watkins b Muncer................	9 – lbw b Muncer	1
R. Horsfall lbw b Watkins.....................	43 – c Watkins b Muncer...........	13
T. N. Pearce b Muncer	64 – c Pleass b Muncer.............	4
R. Smith c Parkhouse b Muncer	16 – lbw b Muncer	2
F. Rist not out..............................	20 – c Wooller b Muncer	6
W. B. Morris c Clift b Jones	20 – c Muncer b Jones	29
W. J. Dines c Clift b Muncer..................	0 – not out	2
K. C. Preston lbw b Jones....................	5 – b Muncer	0
L-b 4, w 1, n-b 1	6	B 12 12
	228	**168**

Essex Bowling

	Overs	Mdns	Runs	Wkts
Preston	20	—	101	2
Smith	40	12	106	—
Vigar.	26	3	123	1
Morris.	21	3	94	—
Dines	15	1	77	1
Avery	8	—	38	—
Pearce.	5	—	37	1

Glamorgan Bowling

	Overs	Mdns	Runs	Wkts	Overs	Mdns	Runs	Wkts
Wooller.	11	4	19	1	10	1	30	—
Hever	8	2	11	—	5	1	17	—
Muncer.	35	8	99	6	29.4	8	62	9
Jones.	11.4	1	64	2	16	4	38	1
E. Davies	4	—	8	—				
Watkins	4	—	21	1	3	2	3	—
Clift					5	3	6	—

Umpires: A. R. Coleman and D. Davies.

ESSEX v DERBYSHIRE

Played at Colchester, July 21, 22, 23, 1948

Essex won by an innings and 44 runs. Derbyshire, championship leaders at the time, were overplayed in a game of fluctuating fortunes. Most of the excitement occurred in the Essex first innings. Dodds and Avery opened with the first century stand – 138 – made against their rivals, then Rhodes, the Derbyshire leg-break bowler, did the hat-trick for the second time in the season. Ray Smith capped the day's spirited play by hitting the fastest century of the summer in sixty-three minutes – the second fifty runs in nineteen minutes. Altogether he batted eighty-one minutes and hit seventeen 4s. Vigar, at the crease four hours, took part with Smith in an eighth-wicket stand of 152. Both Essex Smiths bowled well in making Derbyshire follow-on 242 behind, and Peter again proved disturbing with his leg-breaks when they gave another moderate batting display.

Essex

T. C. Dodds lbw b Jackson 71	T. P. B. Smith lbw b Rhodes 0
A. V. Avery lbw b Jackson 118	R. Smith c Revill b Gladwin 112
T. E. Bailey b Pope 6	T. H. Wade b Gladwin 0
F. H. Vigar lbw b Pope 94	E. Price not out 0
R. Horsfall c Dawkes b Jackson 0	B 6, l-b 11, n-b 1 18
T. N. Pearce c Smith b Rhodes 27	
D. J. Insole b Rhodes 0	446

Derbyshire

C. S. Elliott b R. Smith	45	– run out	13
A. F. Townsend c Price b P. Smith	27	– b R. Smith	13
D. Smith b R. Smith	30	– b Price	43
D. C. Brooke-Taylor lbw b R. Smith	3	– c Avery b P. Smith	21
A. Revill b R. Smith	28	– c Wade b P. Smith	6
G. H. Pope c Wade b P. Smith	5	– c Vigar b P. Smith	23
G. Dawkes not out	30	– b P. Smith	16
A. E. Rhodes c Vigar b P. Smith	0	– c Insole b R. Smith	18
C. Gladwin c Dodds b P. Smith	13	– not out	36
E. J. Gothard st Wade b P. Smith	8	– run out	3
L. Jackson b P. Smith	0	– run out	2
B 13, l-b 2	15	B 1, l-b 3	4
	204		**198**

Derbyshire Bowling

	Overs	Mdns	Runs	Wkts
Jackson	35	7	114	3
Gladwin	37	8	89	2
Pope	21.2	2	72	2
Rhodes	49	7	133	3
Revill	2	—	20	—

Essex Bowling

	Overs	Mdns	Runs	Wkts	Overs	Mdns	Runs	Wkts
Bailey	6	1	18	—	4	—	10	—
R. Smith	38	18	58	4	23.5	4	64	2
T. P. B. Smith	41.4	7	80	6	32	7	94	4
Price	9	1	33	—	2	2	—	1
Vigar					6	1	26	—

Umpires: B. Flint and C. N. Woolley.

ESSEX v DERBYSHIRE

Played at Westcliff, June 29, 30, 1949

Derbyshire won by eight wickets. Splendid in-swing bowling by Gladwin, who took advantage of much hesitant stroke play, caused Essex to be dismissed in ninety minutes on the first morning. With Elliott, Revill and Smith all batting soundly, Derbyshire gained a lead of 185 runs and, when Essex lost three men for 22 in the last half an hour, it seemed likely that Derbyshire would win by an innings. Pearce and Bailey emphasised the earlier batting weaknesses by sharing a fourth-wicket partnership of 166 in 160 minutes. Pearce straight drove a no-ball from Gladwin out of the ground and also reached the boundary eleven times while making his runs out of 229. Morris injured a finger while batting.

Essex

T. C. Dodds lbw b Copson	25	– c Revill b Jackson	9
F. H. Vigar c Dawkes b Gladwin	0	– c Dawkes b Jackson	4
W. B. Morris retired hurt	5	– b Copson	17
S. C. Eve c Dawkes b Gladwin	9	– c Dawkes b Jackson	0
T. E. Bailey b Gladwin	4	– b Copson	71
T. N. Pearce c Marsh b Gladwin	6	– b Jackson	111
R. Smith b Gladwin	8	– c Dawkes b Copson	4
T. P. B. Smith c Marsh b Jackson	0	– c Gladwin b Copson	0
T. H. Wade not out	0	– c Johnson b Copson	31
E. J. Price c Dawkes b Jackson	0	– c Johnson b Jackson	4
G. R. Pullinger b Jackson	0	– not out	0
B 1, l-b 1, w 4	6	B 8, l-b 2, w 1, n-b 2	13
	63		**264**

Derbyshire

C. S. Elliott lbw b P. Smith	45	– not out	38
E. Marsh c sub b Pullinger	5	– lbw b Bailey	1
A. Revill c sub b Price	58	– c Eve b R. Smith	24
D. Smith b Bailey	51	– not out	9
L. Johnson c and b Price	14		
C. Gladwin c Wade b Bailey	5		
D. A. Skinner c Wade b Bailey	0		
A. E. Rhodes b Price	33		
G. Dawkes c Pearce b Price	21		
W. H. Copson b Price	0		
L. Jackson not out	0		
B 9, l-b 7	16	B 8	8
	248	(2 wkts)	**80**

Derbyshire Bowling

	Overs	Mdns	Runs	Wkts	Overs	Mdns	Runs	Wkts
Copson	8	2	19	1	20	8	43	5
Gladwin	11	2	36	5	21	5	63	—
Jackson	3.5	1	2	3	23.1	6	52	5
Rhodes					19	1	81	—
Johnson					5	—	12	—

Essex Bowling

	Overs	Mdns	Runs	Wkts	Overs	Mdns	Runs	Wkts
Bailey	22	3	103	3	6	2	17	1
P. Smith	9	1	32	1	2.4	—	11	—
Pullinger	9	3	20	1	7	—	25	—
Price	17	6	47	5				
R. Smith	8	1	30	—	5	1	19	1

Umpires: H. G. Baldwin and E. Cooke.

ESSEX v SOMERSET

Played at Clacton, August 20, 22, 23, 1949

Somerset won by an innings and 50 runs. They were far too strong all round for an Essex side which disappointed badly on a perfect pitch. Despite a bright opening by Dodds, who scored 56 out of 69 in under an hour, Essex lost eight wickets for 117. They could not master Tremlett, who, in a deadly spell of 15 balls, took four wickets for 1 run. Three times Tremlett knocked the middle stump out of the ground. A last-wicket stand of 99 between Peter Smith and Wade saved Essex from complete disaster. Gimblett and Walford opened with 116 for Somerset; Buse helped Gimblett in a third stand of 124, and Tremlett and Woodhouse put on 103 for the fifth wicket. Gimblett batted four and a half hours and Tremlett hit his first hundred in England. Insole and Eve were unable to bat in the Essex second innings and the side again collapsed.

Essex

T. C. Dodds c Gimblett b Tremlett	56 – b Lawrence	57
S. J. Cray lbw b Buse	5 – c Hazell b Tremlett	25
F. H. Vigar b Tremlett	24 – c Stephenson b Hazell	1
R. Horsfall lbw b Buse	3 – c Stephenson b Tremlett	38
D. J. Insole b Buse	4 – absent ill	0
T. E. Bailey c Stephenson b Tremlett	16 – not out	21
S. C. Eve b Tremlett	0 – absent hurt	0
T. N. Pearce lbw b Lawrence	18 – c Tremlett b Wellard	35
R. Smith b Tremlett	0 – c Stephenson b Tremlett	2
T. P. B. Smith not out	64 – c Wellard b Hazell	7
T. H. Wade c Lawrence b Tremlett	45 – c Buse b Lawrence	1
B 8, w 1	9 B 4, l-b 2, w 1	7
	244	**194**

Somerset

H. Gimblett b Bailey	156	S. S. Rogers c Dodds b Vigar	9
M. M. Walford c Wade b Vigar	40	J. Lawrence c Bailey b Vigar	12
H. E. Watts b Vigar	1	A. W. Wellard b Vigar	9
H. T. F. Buse run out	53	H. L. Hazell not out	0
G. E. S. Woodhouse lbw b Vigar	59	B 9, l-b 17, w 1, n-b 4	31
M. F. Tremlett st Wade b P. Smith	104		
H. W. Stephenson c and b Vigar	14		**488**

Somerset Bowling

	Overs	Mdns	Runs	Wkts	Overs	Mdns	Runs	Wkts
Buse	28	9	44	3	7	—	29	—
Wellard	13	1	62	—	17	2	50	1
Tremlett	25	6	78	6	16	2	58	3
Lawrence	12	1	32	1	6.4	1	16	2
Hazell	6	1	19	—	13	3	34	2

Essex Bowling

	Overs	Mdns	Runs	Wkts
Bailey	36	2	133	1
R. Smith	39	8	118	—
P. Smith	31	3	104	1
Vigar	23.2	—	102	7

Umpires: C. N. Woolley and K. McCanlis.

ESSEX v WORCESTERSHIRE

(Avery's Benefit Match)

Played at Romford, May 27, 29, 30, 1950

Drawn. Worcestershire looked the better-equipped side, but they did not make the most of their chances. Outschoorn tried the patience of the crowd by taking seven hours over 140 in the first innings. Whiting, in contrast, drove attractively for his first century and he hit eighteen 4s. His fourth-wicket stand with Outschoorn realised 198 in just under three and a half hours. Avery appropriately batted confidently for Essex, and Insole, with splendid cover-driving, reached a century before hitting his wicket and breaking a bail in the act, but Worcestershire led by 60 runs. There was no hope of a result when Worcestershire, with three hours remaining, batted again, and Kenyon and Cooper scored 154 together for the first wicket. Dews hit 33 in eleven minutes, but Outschoorn, very slow once more, spent forty-five minutes over 15. Two professionals tossed for innings in this game – Avery, for Essex, and Perks, captain for the first time in the absence of R. E. Bird, for Worcestershire.

Worcestershire

E. Cooper b Preston	17	– b Avery	79
D. J. Kenyon c Wade b Preston	15	– c Wade b R. Smith	84
L. Outschoorn c Preston b Bailey	140	– not out	15
G. Dews c Preston b R. Smith	52	– c Bailey b R. Smith	33
N. H. Whiting st Wade b P. Smith	118	– not out	3
R. O. Jenkins b Bailey	9		
R. Howorth c and b P. Smith	13		
H. Yarnold b Bailey	17		
R. T. D. Perks c Insole b P. Smith	3		
P. F. Jackson b P. Smith	8		
J. Flavell not out	0		
L-b 16, n-b 1	17	B 5, l-b 6	11
	409		**(3 wkts) 225**

Essex

T. C. Dodds b Perks	22	R. Smith b Jenkins	10
A. V. Avery b Howorth	72	T. P. B. Smith lbw b Perks	28
S. J. Cray lbw b Howorth	5	T. H. Wade c Yarnold b Flavell	1
F. H. Vigar b Perks	37	K. C. Preston not out	0
D. J. Insole hit wkt b Jenkins	105	B 6, l-b 5	11
T. E. Bailey b Perks	51		
T. N. Pearce c and b Howorth	8		**350**

Essex Bowling

	Overs	Mdns	Runs	Wkts	Overs	Mdns	Runs	Wkts
Bailey	40	19	59	3	3	1	6	—
Preston	26	6	83	2	7	1	39	—
P. Smith	65.3	14	182	4	5	2	8	—
R. Smith	27	5	68	1	25	3	80	2
Vigar					11	1	43	—
Avery					9	1	38	1

Worcestershire Bowling

	Overs	Mdns	Runs	Wkts
Perks	32.5	5	89	4
Flavell	13	2	34	1
Howorth	45	17	75	3
Jenkins	46	7	125	2
Jackson	8	2	16	—

Umpires: H. W. Parks and J. J. Hills.

ESSEX v WARWICKSHIRE

Played at Ilford, June 3, 5, 6, 1950

Drawn. Gardner distinguished himself by becoming the sixth player to hit two centuries in a match for Warwickshire. He supplied the steadiness while most of his colleagues hit freely. Spooner saw the opening stand realise 88, and by the tea interval on the first day the total reached 284 for five wickets. Afterwards Essex reaped the reward for hard toil in the relentless heat. Insole had the satisfaction of scoring his second successive hundred, and it was during this match that the Essex committee appointed him captain in succession to Pearce. When Warwickshire wanted runs quickly, Ord and Dollery (one 6 and five 4s) hit splendidly. Essex needed 316 in three and a half hours, and when Dodds and Avery began with 50 in half an hour a definite finish seemed probable. Cray helped himself to one 6 and ten 4s, but he concentrated so much on defence that his side fell behind the clock. Kardar, at slip, smartly "stumped" Vigar off Hollies, but as the wicket-keeper did not remove the bails the bowler under Laws 41 and 42 was not credited with the wicket.

Warwickshire

F. C. Gardner c P. Smith b Pullinger	113	– not out	101
R. T. Spooner c Wade b R. Smith	48	– b R. Smith	23
A. Townsend c Insole b R. Smith	34	– c and b Vigar	46
J. S. Ord c Avery b P. Smith	44	– c Cray b P. Smith	55
H. E. Dollery lbw b P. Smith	17	– c Wade b Pullinger	38
A. V. Wolton c Wade b R. Smith	38	– not out	15
A. H. Kardar c Insole b Bailey	4		
R. E. Hitchcock c Pearce b P. Smith	11		
C. W. Grove b R. Smith	0		
T. L. Pritchard not out	13		
W. E. Hollies lbw b R. Smith	4		
B 1, l-b 2, w 3, n-b 3	9	B 5, l-b 4, n-b 2	11
	335	**(4 wkts dec.)**	**289**

Essex

A. V. Avery lbw b Hollies	19	– c Townsend b Pritchard	45
T. C. Dodds c Spooner b Pritchard	8	– b Pritchard	35
S. J. Cray c Townsend b Hollies	39	– not out	75
F. H. Vigar lbw b Hollies	0	– run out	20
D. J. Insole c and b Townsend	106	– not out	3
T. E. Bailey c Townsend b Hollies	6		
T. N. Pearce b Hollies	6		
R. Smith b Townsend	42	– c Wolton b Grove	15
T. P. B. Smith c Dollery b Townsend	63	– c Spooner b Grove	15
T. H. Wade run out	8		
G. R. Pullinger not out	2		
B 1, l-b 9	10	B 1, l-b 2, w 1, n-b 1	5
	309	**(5 wkts)**	**213**

Essex Bowling

	Overs	Mdns	Runs	Wkts	Overs	Mdns	Runs	Wkts
Bailey	23	1	77	1	18	2	60	—
Pullinger	21	2	75	1	8	—	54	1
P. Smith	40	14	97	3	16	3	61	1
R. Smith	31.2	10	77	5	30	8	87	1
Vigar					7	1	16	1

Warwickshire Bowling

	Overs	Mdns	Runs	Wkts	Overs	Mdns	Runs	Wkts
Pritchard.........	30	6	102	1	17	3	59	2
Grove...........	24	3	73	—	11	1	53	2
Hollies	40	16	74	5	25	5	72	—
Kardar	8	1	27	—				
Townsend........	13.2	2	23	3	9	1	24	—

Umpires: A. E. Pothecary and E. Cooke.

ESSEX v NOTTINGHAMSHIRE

Played at Ilford, June 7, 8, 9, 1950

Drawn. Essex gained a first innings lead, but a further result never seemed likely. Hardstaff, the best Nottinghamshire batsman, took the eye. Powerful drives and strong leg-side strokes showed him in good light in the first innings when he hit eighteen 4s, and Winrow helped him add 124 for the fourth wicket. Essex were as well served by Cray, who hit twenty-two 4s, mainly by excellent leg-side strokes, in scoring 163 – his highest innings. Horsfall and Eve each shared with him in a century partnership and Essex declared leading by two runs. Hardstaff again batted stylishly in face of more steady bowling by the cousins Smith, but Essex, left to get 252 in one hundred minutes could do no better than respond with a three-figure opening partnership by Dodds and Avery in just over an hour. Sime, the Nottinghamshire captain, was involved in an unusual incident in his second innings. He was given out to what seemed a catch in the slips and returned to the pavilion, but Insole, the Essex captain, requested him to resume.

Nottinghamshire

C. B. Harris b R. Smith........................	2	– c Dodds b R. Smith	50
H. Winrow c Horsfall b Vigar....................	59	– c and b R. Smith...............	17
C. J. Poole c Wade b R. Smith	4	– c Vigar b Pullinger	11
J. Hardstaff c Avery b R. Smith	145	– c Vigar b P. Smith...........	69
R. Giles b P. Smith	67	– c and b Vigar	6
F. W. Stocks c Vigar b P. Smith	11	– b P. Smith...................	18
P. F. Harvey c Vigar b P. Smith	4	– not out	28
W. A. Sime c and b Vigar	44	– c Horsfall b R. Smith	8
A. Jepson not out	18	– b P. Smith...................	17
E. A. Meads b Vigar	0	– c Avery b P. Smith..............	20
H. J. Butler b R. Smith	7		
B 4, l-b 5, w 2	11	B 4, l-b 5...............	9

372   (9 wkts dec.) 253

Essex

T. C. Dodds c Jepson b Butler	6	– not out	59
A. V. Avery b Jepson	8	– not out	51
S. J. Cray c Harris b Harvey...................	163		
R. Horsfall b Stocks	85		
D. J. Insole c Meads b Stocks..................	5		
S. C. Eve c Hardstaff b Stocks	42		
F. H. Vigar not out	46		
R. Smith c Meads b Harvey	1		
T. P. B. Smith not out	8		
B 6, l-b 1, n-b 3	10	B 8	8

(7 wkts dec.) 374   (No wkt) 118

T. H. Wade and G. R. Pullinger did not bat.

Essex Bowling

	Overs	Mdns	Runs	Wkts	Overs	Mdns	Runs	Wkts
R. Smith	37.1	4	150	4	30	9	64	3
Pullinger	24	4	70	—	7	2	25	1
P. Smith	30	12	70	3	38.1	12	83	4
Vigar	20	3	71	3	16	—	72	1

Nottinghamshire Bowling

	Overs	Mdns	Runs	Wkts	Overs	Mdns	Runs	Wkts
Butler	29	5	80	1	3	—	10	—
Jepson	24	6	64	1	2	—	7	—
Harvey	32	1	99	2	3	—	9	—
Harris	11	2	30	—				
Stocks	29	10	63	3	6	—	15	—
Sime	7	1	28	—	4	—	14	—
Hardstaff					5	1	28	—
Winrow					4	—	27	—

Umpires: A. E. Pothecary and E. Cooke.

ESSEX v LEICESTERSHIRE

Played at Westcliff, July 8, 10, 11, 1950

Drawn. The bare result gives no hint of the excitement which marked the closing phase of this game which either side could have won off the last ball. Leicestershire were set to score 236 in 160 minutes, and Watson, helped by Prentice, proceeded to go for the runs. After an opening stand of 130 in ninety minutes, Watson went on to complete 105 out of 172 in 120 minutes before being one of three batsmen run out through over-anxiety to keep in front of the clock. Wickets continued to fall, and when the last over arrived Leicestershire required nine with the ninth pair, Smith and Corrall (limping from a knee injury) together. Three runs came off the first four balls, and then Corrall was run out. Smith faced the remaining ball. A six would have given his side victory or the fall of his wicket 12 points to Essex, but Skinner's ball sped harmlessly past the off stump. On the opening day Essex lost six men for 91 before Bailey and Ray Smith added 64 by bright stroke play. Leicestershire, too, found runs difficult until Tompkin joined Palmer in a sixth-wicket stand of 95. Ray Smith bowled admirably during a long spell, and when Essex batted again Cray showed good form. Few of the other batsmen played the leg-breaks of Walsh with any assurance.

Essex

A. V. Avery b Wooler	0	– c Smith b Wooler	9
S. J. Cray lbw b Walsh	36	– hit wkt b Walsh	84
F. H. Vigar b Jackson	14	– c Jackson b Walsh	32
T. E. Bailey c Smith b Jackson	68	– lbw b Walsh	0
D. J. Insole b Walsh	4	– c Jackson b Walsh	10
W. B. Morris b Jackson	13	– b Palmer	6
D. C. Levick hit wkt b Jackson	1	– lbw b Walsh	6
R. Smith c Smith b Wooler	27	– not out	41
T. P. B. Smith b Jackson	6	– b Walsh	38
T. H. Wade b Jackson	5	– c sub b Walsh	8
I. J. Skinner not out	0	– not out	1
B 4, l-b 5, w 2, n-b 1	12	B 20, l-b 9, n-b 1	30

186   (9 wkts dec.) 265

Leicestershire

G. S. Watson lbw b R. Smith	16	– run out	105
F. T. Prentice b R. Smith	0	– c Avery b Skinner	44
K. D. Smith c Wade b Skinner	20	– not out	4
C. H. Palmer c Wade b R. Smith	65	– c Avery b P. Smith	1
V. E. Jackson b R. Smith	5	– run out	3
G. Lester b R. Smith	0	– c Wade b P. Smith	10
M. Tompkin st Wade b P. Smith	66	– c Avery b R. Smith	48
J. E. Walsh lbw b P. Smith	7	– c R. Smith b P. Smith	5
C. Wooler b Skinner	12	– run out	0
P. Corrall b Skinner	14	– run out	3
J. Goodwin not out	4	– not out	0
L-b 7	7	B 4, l-b 2, w 1	7

216   (9 wkts) 230

Leicestershire Bowling

	Overs	Mdns	Runs	Wkts	Overs	Mdns	Runs	Wkts
Goodwin	16	5	33	—	14	4	27	—
Wooler	18	6	23	2	18	5	45	1
Palmer	9	2	19	—	11	5	23	1
Jackson	23.5	13	46	6	23	12	37	—
Walsh	17	3	53	2	39	12	92	7
Lester					3	1	11	—

Essex Bowling

	Overs	Mdns	Runs	Wkts	Overs	Mdns	Runs	Wkts
R. Smith	47	16	94	5	13	—	52	1
Skinner	16.3	7	44	3	19	—	67	1
P. Smith	31	13	56	2	16	1	83	3
Vigar	4	—	15	—	4	1	21	—

Umpires: W. H. Ashdown and T. Spencer.

ESSEX v SURREY

Played at Southend, August 8, 9, 10, 1951

Drawn. The performance of May in scoring, for the first time, two separate hundreds in a match overshadowed everything else. In the first innings, May made 167 in four hours and a half, hitting a 6 and twenty-three 4s; in the second, by the continued use of a variety of well-timed strokes, he scored 103 in an hour and fifty-five minutes, with sixteen 4s his chief figures. He gave no chance. Missed when 11, Barton hit thirteen 4s while helping May to add 241 in three hours and a half on the opening day, and Whittaker, profiting from an early escape, registered three 6s and two 4s in a brisk display. Despite stands of 99 by Horsfall (ten 4s) and the dogged Gibb, and 90 by Smith (one 6, eight 4s) and Bailey, Essex fared badly; but Bailey (sixteen 4s) came to the rescue, reaching his first century of the season in just over three hours and a half. Putting on 122 in an unfinished partnership, May and Constable enabled Surrey to declare, but Essex, though losing four wickets for 33, were never in real danger.

Surrey

L. B. Fishlock b Preston	12	– c Vigar b R. Smith	20
M. R. Barton b R. Smith	117	– b Jerman	1
P. B. H. May c Insole b Greensmith	167	– not out	103
B. Constable b R. Smith	12	– not out	51
J. F. Parker st Gibb b R. Smith	8		
G. J. Whittaker not out	51		
A. J. McIntyre b R. Smith	5		
J. C. Laker c and b Vigar	34		
A. V. Bedser c Gibb b Vigar	0		
W. S. Surridge lbw b Vigar	6		
G. A. R. Lock not out	1		
B 6, l-b 10, n-b 3	19	N-b 2	2
	(9 wkts dec.) 432		**(2 wkts dec.) 177**

Essex

T. C. Dodds lbw b Bedser	5	– c Parker b Bedser	20
A. V. Avery b Bedser	17	– b Bedser	5
P. A. Gibb c Whittaker b Lock	33	– c McIntyre b Surridge	0
R. Horsfall c and b Lock	79	– run out	4
D. J. Insole b Bedser	16	– not out	4
T. E. Bailey not out	104		
R. Smith b Laker	57		
F. H. Vigar c McIntyre b Lock	8	– not out	2
W. T. Greensmith c Parker b Laker	5		
K. C. Preston c McIntyre b Laker	2		
L. C. S. Jerman b Bedser	8		
B 15, l-b 4, w 2, n-b 1	22	B 8	8
	356		**(4 wkts) 43**

Essex Bowling

	Overs	Mdns	Runs	Wkts	Overs	Mdns	Runs	Wkts
Preston	19	5	55	1	5	—	23	—
Jerman	24	2	79	—	6	—	39	1
Insole	8	2	29	—				
R. Smith	33	4	107	4	15	1	48	1
Bailey	9	1	30	—				
Greensmith	22	3	80	1	6	1	28	—
Vigar	11	—	33	3	6	2	26	—
Dodds					1	—	5	—
Horsfall					1	—	6	—

Surrey Bowling

	Overs	Mdns	Runs	Wkts	Overs	Mdns	Runs	Wkts
Bedser	28	3	68	4	8	1	14	2
Surridge	25	2	84	—	9	—	19	1
Parker	10	5	23	—				
Laker	39	16	66	3	4	3	2	—
Lock	35	11	93	3	4	4	—	—

Umpires: E. Cooke and K. McCanlis.

ESSEX v NOTTINGHAMSHIRE

Played at Clacton, August 18, 20, 21, 1951

Drawn. Essex did remarkably well to head a total of 576. All through, batsmen were masters and six partnerships of over a hundred were registered. Simpson drove superbly for 212, made out of 370 in five hours forty minutes, and hit a 6 and twenty-nine 4s. Stocks, hitting ten 4s in his first 50, and Clay shared in century stands with Simpson, and Martin and Smales added 112 in seventy minutes. Essex lost Dodds without a run scored, but Avery and Gibb made 148 together and Gibb and Horsfall joined in another three-figure partnership. With the Nottinghamshire attack ineffective apart from Matthews, left-arm fast-medium, Insole, Bailey, R. Smith and Vigar took Essex in front for the loss of six wickets.

Nottinghamshire

W. W. Keeton c Preston b R. Smith	14
R. T. Simpson c Greensmith b P. Smith	212
P. F. Harvey c Gibb b R. Smith	13
J. D. Clay b Greensmith	39
C. J. Poole b Greensmith	6
F. W. Stocks c Preston b R. Smith	100
E. Martin c Dodds b P. Smith	93
K. Smales run out	53
A. J. Underwood c Preston b Bailey	0
E. A. Meads not out	24
B 10, l-b 6, w 2, n-b 4	22
(9 wkts dec.)	576

C. S. Matthews did not bat.

Essex

T. C. Dodds b Matthews	0
A. V. Avery lbw b Matthews	70
P. A. Gibb c Meads b Matthews	118
R. Horsfall c Meads b Matthews	123
D. J. Insole b Simpson	88
T. E. Bailey st Meads b Simpson	48
R. Smith st Meads b Harvey	82
F. H. Vigar not out	30
W. T. Greensmith not out	12
B 8, l-b 11, w 2, n-b 1	22
(7 wkts)	593

T. P. B. Smith and K. C. Preston did not bat.

Essex Bowling

	Overs	Mdns	Runs	Wkts
Preston	21	3	84	—
Bailey	29	4	104	1
R. Smith	42	7	139	3
P. Smith	36	8	121	2
Greensmith	28	6	78	2
Insole	4	—	21	—
Vigar	1	—	7	—

Nottinghamshire Bowling

	Overs	Mdns	Runs	Wkts
Matthews	38	13	71	4
Underwood	32	5	110	—
Stocks	37	10	98	—
Harvey	33	11	120	1
Smales	45	13	105	—
Simpson	32	11	67	2

Umpires: G. S. Mobey and W. F. Price.

ESSEX v NOTTINGHAMSHIRE

Played at Romford, June 10, 11, 12, 1959

Essex won by an innings and 132 runs. Simpson's policy of sending them in to bat thus ended in dismal failure. Nottinghamshire paid a heavy price for missing Insole when 17. So far did he overshadow the unduly cautious Bailey that he obtained 159 of the 196 added for the fourth wicket. Each batted for three and a quarter hours, Insole, by powerful all-round strokes, hitting twenty-four 4s. Careful play by the Nottinghamshire batsmen proved fruitless against the swinging deliveries of Ralph and they followed on 226 behind. Winfield again showed sound defence, but there never existed a chance that Nottinghamshire would save the game. In taking twelve wickets for 104 runs, Ralph gained the best match-analysis of his career.

Essex

G. Smith c Millman b Jepson 22	W. T. Greensmith b Davison 12
G. Barker st Millman b Morgan 31	L. H. R. Ralph b Springall 19
B. Taylor b Morgan 50	K. C. Preston not out 1
D. J. Insole c Martin b Morgan. 180	
T. E. Bailey c Davison b Springall 43	B 2, l-b 6, w 1, n-b 6 15
M. Bear run out. 22	
J. Milner run out 1	1/27 2/90 3/127 4/323 5/349 396
B. R. Knight b Morgan 0	6/350 7/353 8/371 9/390

Nottinghamshire

R. T. Simpson b Ralph 8	– lbw b Ralph	10
N. Hill c Taylor b Ralph 29	– b Preston	9
J. D. Clay b Knight. 40	– c Milner b Preston	2
E. J. Martin b Ralph 0	– b Ralph.	10
C. J. Poole c Milner b Ralph 23	– c Knight b Preston	0
H. M. Winfield c Taylor b Greensmith 38	– b Ralph.	29
J. D. Springall b Knight. . : 1	– c Knight b Greensmith	2
G. Millman lbw b Preston 0	– c Insole b Ralph	19
A. Jepson c Milner b Ralph 19	– b Ralph.	10
M. Morgan c Smith b Ralph 5	– b Ralph.	0
I. Davison not out 0	– not out	0
B 5, w 1, n-b 1 7	W 3	3

1/40 2/41 3/41 4/89 5/114   170   1/14 2/18 3/22 4/23 5/33   94
6/125 7/142 8/150 9/167   6/44 7/74 8/85 9/85

Nottinghamshire Bowling

	Overs	Mdns	Runs	Wkts
Jepson.	23	4	71	1
Davison	25.4	4	72	1
Morgan.	36	4	144	4
Springall	27	3	94	2

Essex Bowling

	Overs	Mdns	Runs	Wkts	Overs	Mdns	Runs	Wkts
Preston	22	6	47	1	20	8	23	3
Ralph	25.1	5	55	6	20.3	6	49	6
Knight	14	3	26	2	5	—	11	—
Bailey	9	4	19	—	2	2	—	—
Greensmith.	7	1	16	1	8	3	8	1

Umpires: C. S. Elliott and L. H. Gray.

ESSEX v LEICESTERSHIRE

Played at Colchester, June 24, 25, 26, 1959

Leicestershire, after being sent in to bat, won by 126 runs. The match provided a triumph for Spencer, the fast-medium bowler, who on a well-grassed pitch took fourteen wickets for 94 besides scoring 63 for once out. He was specially effective when Essex went into get 249 to win, dismissing seven of the last eight batsmen for 13 runs. Watson (ten 4s) batted beautifully in the Leicestershire first innings, but in face of accurate bowling by Bailey eight wickets were down for 138 before Spencer and Smith added 77. Essex never looked like making a fight for first-innings points and Leicestershire started their second innings badly. Then Gardner, with help from the later batsmen, effected a recovery. Bold driving by Taylor (one 6, eight 4s) lessened the severity of the first Essex defeat of the season.

Leicestershire

M. R. Hallam c Insole b Bailey	20	– b Bailey	4
J. van Geloven c Preston b Bailey	2	– c Insole b Knight	8
W. Watson lbw b Bailey	75	– c Bailey b Preston	0
L. R. Gardner c Insole b Bailey	12	– c Taylor b Bailey	51
J. Carter c Ralph b Knight	7	– lbw b Bailey	19
A. C. Revill b Preston	12	– b Knight	19
M. Turner lbw b Preston	4	– b Knight	28
R. Julian c and b Bailey	1	– b Preston	12
R. C. Smith c Taylor b Bailey	31	– not out	12
C. T. Spencer not out	51	– b Preston	12
B. S. Boshier b Preston	1	– b Knight	3
L-b 7, n-b 3	10	L-b 6	6

1/3 2/49 3/69 4/93 5/128   226   1/6 2/7 3/23 4/69 5/88   174
6/132 7/137 8/138 9/215   6/109 7/140 8/148 9/169

Essex

T. C. Dodds c Revill b Spencer	24	– c Julian b Spencer	0
G. Barker c Hallam b Spencer	11	– c Julian b Boshier	4
B. Taylor c Julian b Spencer	3	– c Watson b Boshier	50
D. J. Insole b van Geloven	14	– c Julian b Spencer	26
T. E. Bailey b Spencer	4	– c van Geloven b Spencer	1
M. Bear b Boshier	42	– c Watson b Spencer	2
B. R. Knight c Revill b Spencer	24	– c van Geloven b Spencer	23
W. T. Greensmith c Julian b Spencer	2	– b Spencer	3
L. H. R. Ralph b van Geloven	17	– c Hallam b Spencer	0
Dr C. B. Clarke b Boshier	5	– not out	6
K. C. Preston not out	0	– b Spencer	6
B 5, l-b 1	6	L-b 1	1

1/30 2/35 3/38 4/52 5/57   152   1/4 2/4 3/78 4/79 5/82   122
6/116 7/119 8/147 9/147   6/91 7/107 8/107 9/110

Essex Bowling

	Overs	Mdns	Runs	Wkts	Overs	Mdns	Runs	Wkts
Bailey	24	2	65	6	19	7	43	3
Preston	16.2	2	52	3	19	4	47	3
Ralph	17	2	47	—	8	3	25	—
Knight	11	2	26	1	15	2	53	4
Clarke	6	—	26	—				

Leicestershire Bowling

	Overs	Mdns	Runs	Wkts	Overs	Mdns	Runs	Wkts
Spencer...........	21	4	53	6	25.2	9	41	8
Boshier...........	24.2	6	76	2	25	8	77	2
van Geloven.......	12	5	17	2	2	—	3	—

Umpires: W. H. Copson and D. J. Wood.

ESSEX v KENT

Played at Westcliff, July 15, 16, 17, 1959

Kent won by 17 runs. They were saved from disaster on a green pitch on Wednesday by Pretlove and Evans, who put on 118 for the fifth wicket. Savill drove so strongly that he hit one 5 and nine 4s in scoring 52 of an Essex opening partnership of 70, but Kent led by 31. Against the pace of Knight, who earned a match record of ten wickets for 146, Kent struggled in the second innings, but Pretlove and Leary added 61 and Wilkinson and Halfyard 58. So Essex needed 211 to win. Barker, driving splendidly and without fault for three hours twenty minutes, hit seventeen 4s. Insole and Milner helped him in partnerships of 56 and 52, but despite the absence with knee trouble of Ridgway, the last six wickets fell for 60. In catching Savill, Evans brought his total of wickets to 1,000.

Kent

A. H. Phebey b Knight	19	– lbw b Knight...................	22
R. C. Wilson c Barker b Knight	13	– b Knight	7
S. E. Leary c Barker b Knight...................	2	– c Barker b Knight..............	40
J. F. Pretlove c Knight b Clarke	70	– c Bear b Knight	26
A. L. Dixon b Knight	7	– b Ralph.......................	8
T. G. Evans b Clarke	58	– c Barker b Ralph	8
R. Wilkinson run out..........................	43	– c Taylor b Knight..............	30
D. J. Halfyard lbw b Insole....................	13	– c Barker b Clarke..............	29
F. Ridgway c Insole b Ralph...................	23	– b Clarke	3
A. Brown b Knight	10	– not out	0
J. C. T. Page not out	1	– c Milner b Ralph...............	4
B 1, l-b 7, w 3, n-b 2	13	L-b 1, n-b 1..............	2

1/30 2/38 3/45 4/57 5/175   272   1/24 2/38 3/96 4/105 5/109   179
6/190 7/213 8/260 9/265   6/113 7/118 8/176 9/177

Essex

G. Barker lbw b Ridgway	23	– c Phebey b Halfyard.............	105
L. A. Savill lbw b Halfyard...................	52	– c Evans b Ridgway..............	1
L. H. R. Ralph c Phebey b Halfyard..............	33	– c Evans b Brown................	9
B. Taylor c Pretlove b Wilkinson...............	22	– b Halfyard	7
D. J. Insole c Leary b Wilkinson...............	4	– c Leary b Brown................	29
J. Milner c Evans b Brown	12	– c Wilkinson b Pretlove	25
M. Bear b Brown..............................	39	– c Evans b Brown................	5
B. R. Knight lbw b Ridgway	1	– c Leary b Halfyard.............	2
W. T. Greensmith c Leary b Ridgway	39	– b Halfyard	1
Dr C. B. Clarke b Ridgway....................	0	– lbw b Halfyard.................	0
W. Dow not out	9	– not out	0
B 2, l-b 2, w 1, n-b 2	7	B 4, l-b 4, n-b 1...........	9

1/70 2/83 3/132 4/136 5/138   241   1/14 2/25 3/81 4/133 5/145   193
6/153 7/154 8/214 9/214   6/170 7/183 8/188 9/189

Essex Bowling

	Overs	Mdns	Runs	Wkts	Overs	Mdns	Runs	Wkts
Ralph	26	5	85	1	17	3	65	3
Knight	20.5	4	83	5	18	3	63	5
Dow	13	1	46	—	6	2	17	—
Clarke.	11	1	34	2	6.4	—	32	2
Insole	2	—	11	1				

Kent Bowling

	Overs	Mdns	Runs	Wkts	Overs	Mdns	Runs	Wkts
Ridgway	24	8	41	4	6.2	1	23	1
Halfyard.	33	5	102	2	14	2	54	5
Wilkinson	11	5	31	2	5	1	19	—
Brown.	17	4	60	2	18	5	45	3
Page					13	3	38	—
Pretlove					1	—	5	1

Umpires: J. B. Bowes and H. Yarnold.

ESSEX v WORCESTERSHIRE

Played at Leyton, August 1, 3, 4, 1959

Drawn. Worcestershire, for a long time overplayed, deservedly saved the game. Kenyon put Essex in on a damp green pitch and batting failures followed, but Knight, driving stylishly in making his maiden century, and Bailey pulled the game round. Bailey swung the ball disconcertingly in helping to dispose cheaply of Worcestershire in their first innings, but when they followed on 214 behind Horton, who hit the first double hundred of his career, and Dews turned the fortunes of the match in a fine fifth-wicket stand of 203. Attractive all round the wicket, Horton hit twenty-six 4s in an innings lasting five and three-quarter hours, and Dews, who drove powerfully, sixteen 4s and five 6s. Although Worcestershire were 200 on with ninety minutes left, Kenyon did not declare and the game ended on a farcical note, every Essex man, except the wicket-keeper, sharing the bowling.

Essex

L. A. Savill lbw b Flavell.	5	B. R. Knight c Headley b Flavell 103
G. Barker b Aldridge.	2	W. T. Greensmith not out 3
B. Taylor c Horton b Coldwell	37	
D. J. Insole b Coldwell	9	L-b 11, w 3, n-b 5 19
T. E. Bailey b Coldwell	90	
C. C. P. Williams b Coldwell	0	1/2 2/28 3/49 4/54 (8 wkts dec.) 327
J. Milner c Booth b Coldwell.	59	5/54 6/152 7/323 8/327

L. H. R. Ralph and A. Hurd did not bat.

Worcestershire

M. J. Horton b Bailey	0	– c Barker b Greensmith	212
R. G. A. Headley c Taylor b Ralph	10	– lbw b Bailey	0
D. W. Richardson b Knight	1	– b Knight	4
D. Kenyon c Knight b Bailey	30	– lbw b Bailey	63
R. G. Broadbent c Taylor b Bailey	2	– lbw b Greensmith	7
G. Dews lbw b Bailey	0	– c Hurd b Savill	130
L. Outschoorn lbw b Ralph	14	– c Williams b Barker	29
R. Booth not out	26	– not out	26
J. Flavell c Taylor b Knight	8	– b Greensmith	2
L. J. Coldwell c Taylor b Bailey	17	– st Taylor b Greensmith	6
K. J. Aldridge run out	0	– b Greensmith	5
B 2, l-b 1, n-b 2	5	B 5, l-b 2, n-b 2	9

1/0 2/1 3/38 4/42 5/43 113   1/5 2/10 3/144 4/167 5/370 493
6/45 7/65 8/78 9/108   6/436 7/458 8/463 9/485

Worcestershire Bowling

	Overs	Mdns	Runs	Wkts
Flavell	35	7	107	2
Aldridge	18	3	61	1
Coldwell	36.4	7	116	5
Horton	4	—	18	—
Richardson	2	—	6	—

Essex Bowling

	Overs	Mdns	Runs	Wkts	Overs	Mdns	Runs	Wkts
Bailey	20	8	35	5	22	6	71	2
Knight	13	4	42	2	22	5	71	1
Ralph	21	10	28	2	20	5	65	—
Hurd	2	—	2	—	18	2	74	—
Greensmith	1.3	1	1	—	32.2	1	123	5
Insole					6	1	26	—
Barker					5	2	13	1
Savill					2	—	26	1
Williams					2	1	1	—
Milner					2	—	14	—

Umpires: A. E. Fagg and T. W. Spencer.

ESSEX v GLOUCESTERSHIRE

(K. C. Preston's Benefit)

Played at Leyton, August 5, 6, 7, 1959

Tied. The match had a dramatic finish two minutes from the end of the extra half-hour. Gloucestershire, set to make 212 in two hours fifty minutes, looked doomed to defeat when losing eight men for 131, but Brown, driving and pulling with great force, played a grand innings of 91, including four 6s and ten 4s. When he was ninth out, caught at the wicket off the new ball, Gloucestershire needed three runs to win and six minutes remained. Bailey was called for a wide, and Mayer brought the scores level with a single, but Cook deflected a ball to short-leg and Milner brought off a brilliant left-hand catch. Insole was the man of the match, scoring 267 for once out. Driving and pulling magnificently, he hit twenty-five 4s and two 6s in his 177 not out, made in three and a half hours, and he was almost as dominating in the second innings. Bailey shared with him in a fourth wicket stand of 175. Milton, captaining Gloucestershire in the absence of Graveney and Emmett, narrowly missed his seventh hundred of the season. Savill and Knight, the latter bowling well, were awarded their county caps during the game. Preston, because of an injured arm, could not play, although he fielded as substitute for a short period.

Essex

L. A. Savill c Brown b Allen	25	– b Brown	10
G. Barker c Mortimore b Brown	6		
B. Taylor c Brown b Allen	74	– b Brown	6
D. J. Insole not out	177	– c Cook b Brown	90
T. E. Bailey c Meyer b Bernard	50	– c Milton b Bernard	10
C. C. P. Williams b Brown	3	– c Meyer b Smith	1
J. Milner c Milton b Brown	6	– c Meyer b Brown	11
B. R. Knight not out	17	– c Meyer b Smith	0
L. H. R. Ralph (did not bat)		– b Bernard	13
W. T. Greensmith (did not bat)		– not out	28
L-b 5, n-b 1	6	B 2, l-b 2, n-b 3	7

1/16 2/101 3/114   (6 wkts dec.) 364   1/21 2/22 3/32 4/59   (8 wkts dec.) 176
4/289 5/305 6/325   5/82 6/83 7/109 8/176

A. Hurd did not bat.

Gloucestershire

D. M. Young b Knight	14	– c Ralph b Bailey	0
C. A. Milton c Ralph b Knight	99	– run out	23
R. B. Nicholls c Taylor b Hurd	64	– c Milner b Knight	41
J. B. Mortimore c Taylor b Hurd	30	– c Williams b Ralph	12
D. Carpenter c and b Greensmith	1	– b Greensmith	13
A. S. Brown b Knight	35	– c Taylor b Bailey	91
J. R. Bernard c Insole b Bailey	9	– b Knight	1
D. R. Smith c Williams b Knight	1	– c Taylor b Greensmith	6
D. A. Allen c Bailey b Greensmith	37	– lbw b Knight	5
B. J. Meyer c Taylor b Greensmith	21	– not out	13
C. Cook not out	0	– c Milner b Knight	0
B 3, l-b 12, n-b 3	18	B 4, w 1, n-b 1	6

1/19 2/133 3/199 4/211 5/238   329   1/0 2/61 3/73 4/82 5/104   211
6/263 7/267 8/276 9/326   6/110 7/111 8/131 9/209

Gloucestershire Bowling

	Overs	Mdns	Runs	Wkts	Overs	Mdns	Runs	Wkts
Smith	23	2	86	—	22	8	44	2
Brown	24	4	66	3	18.5	2	60	4
Milton	2	—	13	—				
Cook	20	11	38	—	8	1	22	—
Mortimore	28	7	82	—				
Allen	8	4	6	2	6	—	20	—
Bernard	13	1	67	1	8	1	23	2

Essex Bowling

	Overs	Mdns	Runs	Wkts	Overs	Mdns	Runs	Wkts
Bailey	29	5	74	1	14	1	46	2
Knight	25	4	69	4	17.4	2	64	4
Ralph	23	6	56	—	7	1	30	1
Greensmith	30.2	4	80	3	8	1	65	2
Hurd	18	6	32	2				

Umpires: A. E. Fagg and T. W. Spencer.

ESSEX v OXFORD UNIVERSITY

Played at Brentwood, June 18, 20, 21, 1960

Oxford University won by seven wickets. Set to get 258 at nearly 86 an hour, they succeeded with thirteen minutes to spare. No such result appeared likely when two wickets fell for 28, but Burki (one 6, twelve 4s), hitting his second century of the match, and Green (two 6s and thirteen 4s) drove and pulled so well that they put on 203 in two hours five minutes. Bailey (fifteen 4s), Bear, his partner in a fifth-wicket stand of 170, and Barker took the honours on the opening day. Burki (fourteen 4s), batting nearly five hours, enabled Oxford to restrict their first innings deficit to 71. Savill (two 6s, eleven 4s) shared in a partnership of 80 with Insole which led to a second Essex declaration. Carr and Taylor made their first first-class appearances.

Essex

G. Barker c Pataudi b Drybrough	62	– b Jakobsen	9
G. J. Smith c Dyson b Sayer	9	– c Dyson b Jakobsen	25
L. A. Savill c Smith b Drybrough	35	– c Burki b Green	81
*D. J. Insole lbw b Sayer	12	– lbw b Sayer	35
T. E. Bailey c Burki b Drybrough	118		
M. Bear c Pataudi b Pithey	79	– not out	9
B. R. Knight c Jakobsen b Drybrough	4	– c Jakobsen b Green	18
W. T. Greensmith c Fry b Pithey	15	– run out	1
†J. Taylor b Pithey	4	– not out	2
R. Carr not out	7		
K. C. Preston not out	10		
L-b 1	1	B 2, l-b 3, n-b 1	6

1/29 2/102 3/111 4/119   (9 wkts dec.) 356   1/17 2/51 3/131   (6 wkts dec.) 186
5/289 6/297 7/319 8/335 9/339   4/164 5/168 6/176

Oxford University

D. M. Green c Taylor b Bailey	15	– run out	113
E. M. Dyson lbw b Bailey	1	– c Knight b Bailey	0
D. B. Pithey b Knight	9		
J. Burki not out	144	– not out	109
Nawab of Pataudi c Taylor b Greensmith	37	– not out	15
C. A. Fry b Preston	40	– c Barker b Bailey	15
C. D. Drybrough b Knight	15		
D. M. Sayer b Knight	8		
T. R. Jakobsen c Insole b Knight	5		
*†A. C. Smith run out	0		
J. D. Piachaud lbw b Bailey	7		
L-b 2, n-b 2	4	B 1, l-b 5	6

1/2 2/25 3/25 4/74 5/190   285   1/0 2/28 3/231   (3 wkts) 258
6/246 7/260 8/267 9/267

Oxford University Bowling

	Overs	Mdns	Runs	Wkts	Overs	Mdns	Runs	Wkts
Sayer	18	5	58	2	27.5	9	65	1
Jakobsen	11	2	40	—	19	6	32	2
Burki	3	—	13	—				
Green	20	4	50	—	16	2	54	2
Piachaud	23	6	47	—	3	—	29	—
Drybrough	32	8	107	4				
Pithey	11	1	40	3				

Essex Bowling

	Overs	Mdns	Runs	Wkts	Overs	Mdns	Runs	Wkts
Bailey	25.2	9	44	3	12	1	50	2
Knight	24	6	86	4	16	—	66	—
Preston	21	4	59	1	13	1	56	—
Greensmith	20	2	59	1	4	—	29	—
Carr	12	1	33	—	4	—	29	—
Insole					3	—	22	—

Umpires: W. E. Phillipson and P. A. Gibb.

GLAMORGAN

GLAMORGAN v SOMERSET

Played at Pontypridd, June 15, 17, 18, 1946

Glamorgan won by eight wickets. "Freak" declarations agreed upon by the two captains, J. C. Clay and C. J. P. Barnwell, with the object of bringing interest into a rain-spoiled match – the only one of the season at Pontypridd – produced some remarkable cricket. Play ended on the first day at three o'clock, and could not be resumed until Tuesday. Somerset immediately declared at their Saturday's score, and Glamorgan, as part of the plan, having scored a similar total off loose bowling, also declared. Four and a half hours remained for play when Somerset on the drying pitch collapsed; A. D. G. Matthews, with eight fieldsmen close to the bat, proved unplayable. Somerset were all out in less than two hours, and Glamorgan, despite a stoppage by rain, won the match with time to spare.

Somerset

F. S. Lee c Wooler b Judge	15	– c Wooler b Matthews	29
H. Gimblett not out	26	– c Judge b Matthews	12
J. Lawrence not out	4	– b Matthews	0
*C. J. P. Barnwell (did not bat)		– c Dyson b Matthews	0
J. W. Seamer (did not bat)		– c Wooler b Judge	0
H. T. F. Buse (did not bat)		– c Clay b Matthews	0
W. H. R. Andrews (did not bat)		– b Judge	5
A. W. Wellard (did not bat)		– b Matthews	3
A. T. M. Jones (did not bat)		– c Watkins b Matthews	0
W. T. Luckes (did not bat)		– not out	0
H. L. Hazell (did not bat)		– b Judge	0
B 6	6	B 1, l-b 3	4
	(1 wkt dec.) 51		**53**

Glamorgan

W. E. Jones not out	40	– lbw b Wellard	5
A. Watkins c Seamer b Jones	3		
G. Lavis not out	8		
A. H. Dyson (did not bat)		– b Buse	18
E. Davies (did not bat)		– not out	21
W. Wooler (did not bat)		– not out	0
		B 10	10
	(1 wkt dec.) 51		**(2 wkts) 54**

E. C. Jones, H. Davies, J. C. Clay, A. D. G. Matthews and P. F. Judge did not bat.

Glamorgan Bowling

	Overs	Mdns	Runs	Wkts	Overs	Mdns	Runs	Wkts
Matthews	13.2	8	14	—	17	9	12	7
Judge	10	3	14	1	13.5	1	35	3
Wooller	3	—	17	—				
Clay					3	1	2	—

Somerset Bowling

	Overs	Mdns	Runs	Wkts	Overs	Mdns	Runs	Wkts
Lee	3.4	—	30	—				
Jones.	3	—	21	1				
Wellard.					14	4	22	1
Andrews					8	3	11	—
Buse					6	1	9	1
Hazell					0.2	—	2	—

NOTES BY THE EDITOR, 1947

FREAK DECLARATIONS

The advisability of the captain who wins the toss always taking first innings received more than one contradiction, the most noticeable example of the reverse action proving effective being the occasion when E. D. R. Eager put Yorkshire in at Bournemouth and Hampshire won by ten wickets. That clever and successful venture earned full reward and popular praise, but that same captain and P. E. Murray Willis, of Northamptonshire, mixed matters sadly when, at Portsmouth on June 20, they tried a "freak declaration" scheme with the idea of producing a satisfying struggle but staged a farce. The visitors declared on the second day and Hampshire in the pavilion were prepared to do the same as "arranged", but their action would have come too late in the day for this to be permitted, and Northamptonshire continued their innings from the position of 38 for one wicket. The umpires would have taught a valuable lesson by insisting that that first declaration must stand; and Hampshire, batting against such a total, might well have gained a complete victory on the third day instead of Northamptonshire taking the points for the first-innings lead.

That was not the only case of an attempt to overcome the vicissitudes of the weather by a "freak" declaration; and one created a situation which brought condemnation from Headquarters. Reproof from MCC meant that the extreme care in framing the laws exercised by the special committee, representing all parts of the country, was nullified when captains made "arrangements" in the manner of proceeding with a match interfered with by rain. At Pontypridd, J. C. Clay very rightly wanted to give pleasure on the third day to the crowd seldom able to see county cricket, and he agreed to declare when Glamorgan's total equalled Somerset's 51 for one wicket. After this was done the visitors fell in their second innings for 53; Glamorgan gained an easy victory by eight wickets and so received 12 points. This, of course, was unfair for all the other competitors, and with either side well placed for the championship might have influenced the result of the competition. Surely Somerset, with 51 runs scored, could have striven to force a victory by ordinary means on the Tuesday; and Glamorgan, seeing that Matthews took seven wickets for 12 runs, could very likely have triumphed in a straightforward fight without any subterfuge. Keen matches have been finished in one day, and, with real zest for victory without any waste of time over the declaration business, one could imagine a struggle with real cricket delighting the crowd. It comes to this, "It isn't cricket" will cease to be a rebuke if means are adopted to obtain false results to matches. Another case came to nought. Brian Sellers declared with a score of 171 for three wickets, the idea being that when Lancashire equalled that total they should declare and the remaining time be equally divided in a fight for a result; as it happened, the visitors, batting slowly at Bramall Lane, could not reach the Yorkshire score, and there was a very flat termination to a "no-decision" match.

GLAMORGAN v SUSSEX

Played at Swansea, July 7, 8, 9, 1948

Glamorgan won by six wickets. A solid innings by John Langridge, who completed his century in just under four hours, contrasted strikingly with the indecision shown by most of the other batsmen against Muncer's skilful off-break bowling. That Glamorgan established a lead of 145 was largely due to Parkhouse, whose maiden hundred was made on the ground where he first learned cricket. Eaglestone, less restrained, hit a 6 and fourteen 4s in fifty minutes. Another good opening partnership by John Langridge and Parks gave Sussex a sound start, before Muncer, maintaining an immaculate length on a pitch unresponsive to spin, enabled Glamorgan to regain their grip. Taking fifteen wickets for 201, Muncer became the first to claim 100 wickets for the season. He was brilliantly supported in the field.

Sussex

John Langridge c Clift b Muncer	104	– c Clift b Muncer 30
H. W. Parks c Eaglestone b Wooller	50	– c Clift b Muncer 53
S. C. Griffith b Muncer	5	– lbw b Muncer 1
G. Cox c Wooller b Muncer	11	– lbw b Muncer 27
James Langridge c Clift b Muncer	4	– c Clift b Muncer 35
C. Oakes b Muncer	7	– b Trick 5
H. T. Bartlett not out	38	– c Watkins b Jones.......... 17
A. S. Oakman c Clift b Muncer	0	– not out 0
P. A. Carey run out	9	– run out 57
A. James c Watkins b Muncer	3	– b Muncer 2
D. J. Wood lbw b Muncer	0	– c Watkins b Muncer......... 0
B 17, l-b 10, n-b 3	30	B 5, l-b 5 10
	261	**237**

Glamorgan

E. Davies lbw b Oakes	20	– c John Langridge b Carey 11
P. Clift b Carey	43	– c Wood b Oakes............. 22
W. G. A. Parkhouse b James	117	– run out 26
W. E. Jones lbw b James Langridge	26	– c Wood b Bartlett........... 24
A. Watkins b James	48	– not out 6
J. Eaglestone c Parks b James Langridge	72	– not out 4
J. Pleass not out	38	
W. Wooller b James Langridge	12	
L. B. Muncer b Oakes	11	
H. Davies c Carey b Oakes	12	
S. Trick c and b Oakes	0	
B 6, l-b 1	7	
	406	**(4 wkts) 93**

Glamorgan Bowling

	Overs	Mdns	Runs	Wkts	Overs	Mdns	Runs	Wkts
Wooller	14	2	33	1	14	5	33	—
Watkins	9	2	8	—	14	7	15	—
Trick	45	22	64	—	33	14	73	1
Muncer	46	12	99	8	44.5	16	102	7
Jones	3	—	27	—	6	4	4	1

Sussex Bowling

	Overs	Mdns	Runs	Wkts	Overs	Mdns	Runs	Wkts
Carey	19	2	51	1	4	1	17	1
Wood	15	3	45	—	7	3	14	—
James	17	2	70	2	3	—	8	—
Oakes	21.3	3	87	4	3	—	17	1
Cox	3	—	4	—				
Oakman	13	2	53	—	2	—	13	—
James Langridge	26	2	88	3	4	—	20	—
John Langridge	1	—	1	—				
Bartlett					1	—	4	1

Umpires: D. Hendren and K. McCanlis.

GLAMORGAN v SURREY

Played At Cardiff, August 18, 19, 1948

Glamorgan won by an innings and 24 runs. This victory ranked amongst their best performances and was a personal triumph for Clay, who, returning to the side at the age of 50, captured ten wickets in the match for 66 runs. While the pitch was wet and lifeless Emrys Davies and Dyson scored 91 runs for the first wicket and then, when the Surrey bowlers threatened to gain the initiative Wooller produced his best form of the season, driving and square cutting with great power. Surrey fared disastrously in the last hour of the day, losing nine men for 47. The following morning they followed on 189 runs behind and with Fishlock scoring easily, there was no suggestion of the drama to follow. Then from 61 for one the score went to 62 for five wickets, a position from which Surrey never recovered. Scenes of remarkable enthusiasm marked the end of the match – Glamorgan's last county fixture of the season in Wales – and the players were mobbed by a cheering crowd as they left the field.

Glamorgan

E. Davies c Parker b Laker	47
A. H. Dyson lbw b Laker	51
W. G. A. Parkhouse b Laker	0
W. E. Jones st McIntyre b Laker	1
W. Wooller lbw b Squires	89
J. Eaglestone c Squires b E. A. Bedser	6
J. Pleass lbw b E. A. Bedser	0
B. L. Muncer c Laker b E. A. Bedser	4
H. Davies c E. A. Bedser b Squires	17
N. G. Hever not out	1
J. C. Clay st McIntyre b Laker	4
B 16, l-b 1, w 1, n-b 1	19
	239

Surrey

L. B. Fishlock b Hever	7	– st H. Davies b Muncer ... 38
M. R. Barton b Wooller	2	– b Muncer ... 12
H. S. Squires b Hever	5	– lbw b Clay ... 9
A. J. McIntyre st H. Davies b Clay	17	– c Clay b Jones ... 19
J. F. Parker b Muncer	6	– b Muncer ... 0
E. A. Bedser lbw b Clay	3	– b Clay ... 1
B. Constable c Dyson b Muncer	1	– b Clay ... 30
J. C. Laker lbw b Clay	0	– b Clay ... 11
T. Clark lbw b Clay	0	– c Wooller b Clay ... 0
W. S. Surridge b Clay	9	– not out ... 33
J. W. McMahon not out	0	– c Clay b Jones ... 6
		B 5, l-b 1 ... 6
	50	165

Surrey Bowling

	Overs	Mdns	Runs	Wkts
Surridge	6	1	11	—
Parker...........	9	1	24	—
Laker	44.2	10	86	5
McMahon........	14	8	33	—
Squires	10	5	11	2
E. A. Bedser	30	13	55	3

Glamorgan Bowling

	Overs	Mdns	Runs	Wkts	Overs	Mdns	Runs	Wkts
Wooller..........	6	1	14	1	5	1	11	—
Hever	10	2	14	2	6	1	13	—
Clay	8.2	3	15	5	27	9	51	5
Muncer..........	4	1	7	2	25	5	61	3
Jones............					5	1	23	2

Umpires: T. J. Bartley and B. Flint.

GLAMORGAN IN 1948

On the afternoon of Tuesday, August 24, 1948, Glamorgan set the seal on a wonderful season by winning the County Championship for the first time.

Appropriately, J. C. Clay, a member of the original side which entered the competition in 1921 and whose name has become synonymous with Glamorgan cricket, played a leading part in the victory that day over Hampshire at Bournemouth which ensured for them the honours after an exciting race with Surrey, Yorkshire and Derbyshire. He took nine wickets in the game for 79, and in the preceding fixture against Surrey at Cardiff he claimed a full analysis of ten for 66 – two bowling performances which bear eloquent testimony to the skill and physical fitness of one in his fifty-first year. On this form it was a pity that Clay could not play more often, but he was frequently engaged on his duties as a Test Team selector.

GLAMORGAN v SOMERSET

Played at Neath, June 11, 13, 1949

Glamorgan won by 115 runs. On a very difficult pitch batsmen nearly always groped for the ball and 66 by Muncer for Glamorgan proved the highest score of the match. As an all-rounder, he played the principal part in their victory, his devastating off-spin bowling bringing him twelve wickets for 94 in the game. Somerset's bowlers were not quite so effective, but Wellard, Tremlett, Hazell, and Buse all did useful work. The ball moved at such strange paces and angles that normal strokes were practically useless. Somerset's batsmen frequently hit out in sheer desperation, but Tremlett alone enjoyed much success.

Glamorgan

E. Davies c and b Tremlett	19	– b Tremlett	47
P. Clift c Wellard b Buse	7	– c Stephenson b Buse	0
W. G. A. Parkhouse lbw b Hazell	10	– c Gimblett b Buse	4
W. E. Jones st Stephenson b Tremlett	6	– c Stephenson b Buse	7
W. Wooller lbw b Wellard	23	– lbw b Wellard	5
B. L. Muncer c Buse b Wellard	66	– c Stephenson b Tremlett	24
M. Robinson st Stephenson b Hazell	1	– b Lawrence	14
J. T. Eaglestone st Stephenson b Hazell	23	– b Tremlett	4
H. G. Davies c Gimblett b Wellard	0	– b Tremlett	22
N. G. Hever not out	16	– c Stephenson b Wellard	1
S. A. Trick c Tremlett b Wellard	0	– not out	5
B 8, l-b 8, n-b 1	17	B 10, l-b 5, w 1, n-b 1	17
	188		**150**

Somerset

H. Gimblett c Trick b Wooller	1	– c Parkhouse b Muncer	8
E. Hill c Clift b Hever	0	– run out	13
H. W. Stephenson lbw b Muncer	28	– c and b Muncer	5
G. E. S. Woodhouse b Muncer	9	– c H. Davies b Muncer	1
M. Coope b Trick	18	– c Robinson b Muncer	8
H. T. F. Buse lbw b Jones	0	– c H. Davies b Muncer	7
S. S. Rogers c Clift b Jones	8	– c Clift b Muncer	1
M. F. Tremlett b Trick	29	– st H. Davies b Trick	31
J. Lawrence lbw b Muncer	0	– c Clift b Muncer	19
A. W. Wellard b Muncer	4	– c Clift b Muncer	11
H. L. Hazell not out	7	– not out	3
L-b 5	5	B 6, l-b 1	7
	109		**114**

Somerset Bowling

	Overs	Mdns	Runs	Wkts	Overs	Mdns	Runs	Wkts
Wellard	24.2	5	63	4	22	9	43	2
Buse	9	3	17	1	15	5	28	3
Tremlett	13	4	26	2	12	3	19	4
Hazell	23	8	49	3	12	4	26	—
Lawrence	4	—	16	—	5.2	1	17	1

Glamorgan Bowling

	Overs	Mdns	Runs	Wkts	Overs	Mdns	Runs	Wkts
Wooller	4	1	9	1	3	—	11	—
Hever	5	1	9	1	6	—	14	—
Muncer	14	2	46	4	15	4	48	8
Jones	6	1	16	2	3	—	10	—
Trick	7.5	2	24	2	9.2	2	24	1

Umpires: H. W. Parks and A. E. Pothecary.

GLAMORGAN v KENT

Played at Swansea, June 18, 20, 1949

Glamorgan won by ten wickets. Dampness in the pitch through watering probably assisted bowlers, but feeble methods found reflection in Kent's paltry first innings total of 49. The quick deliveries of Wooller and Watkins soon upset their calculations, and Muncer completed the rout by taking four wickets in eight overs for three runs. In contrast

Glamorgan made a good score in free and easy style. Clift, in particular, gave an impressive display of forcing cricket. He made his century in three hours, and three 6s and fifteen 4s meant 78 in eighteen strokes. Kent did much better when they batted again, but left Glamorgan the simple task of getting 18 to win.

Kent

R. Mayes b Wooller	4	– c Watkins b Jones 37
L. J. Todd b Watkins	2	– b Trick 65
L. E. G. Ames c Parkhouse b Watkins	3	– lbw b Muncer 69
P. Hearn lbw b Muncer	20	– c Wooller b Muncer 0
A. H. Phebey c H. Davies b Watkins	0	– run out 8
T. G. Evans c Robinson b Wooller	17	– b Trick 10
B. Edrich c H. Davies b Muncer	0	– lbw b Muncer 27
D. G. Clark c Parkhouse b Muncer	3	– c H. Davies b Wooller 22
R. R. Dovey lbw b Muncer	0	– st H. Davies b Muncer 28
D. V. P. Wright not out	0	– absent hurt 0
C. Lewis c Clift b Wooller	0	– not out 2
		B 18, l-b 1 19
	49	**287**

Glamorgan

E. Davies b Todd	43	– not out 6
P. Clift lbw b Lewis	104	– not out 13
W. G. A. Parkhouse b Lewis	35	
W. E. Jones c and b Edrich	54	
A. Watkins b Dovey	38	
B. L. Muncer b Dovey	2	
M. Robinson lbw b Edrich	20	
W. Wooller c Phebey b Edrich	0	
J. T. Eaglestone st Evans b Dovey	4	
H. G. Davies c Clark b Dovey	1	
S. A. Trick not out	0	
B 17, n-b 1	18	
	319	**(No wkt) 19**

Glamorgan Bowling

	Overs	Mdns	Runs	Wkts	Overs	Mdns	Runs	Wkts
Wooller	22.3	10	23	3	12	1	44	1
Watkins	14	6	23	3	3	—	13	—
Muncer	8	5	3	4	41.5	11	120	4
Trick					20	7	49	2
Jones					17	4	42	1

Kent Bowling

	Overs	Mdns	Runs	Wkts	Overs	Mdns	Runs	Wkts
Todd	16	5	55	1				
Dovey	43	18	72	4				
Wright	3	1	2	—				
Edrich	37.2	9	94	3				
Lewis	19	3	71	2				
Ames	2	—	7	—				
Evans					2	—	8	—
Hearn					2	—	6	—
Clark					1	—	5	—

Umpires: A. Lockett and W. F. Price.

GLAMORGAN v ESSEX

Played at Ebbw Vale, June 22, 23, 24, 1949

Glamorgan won by nine wickets. An exciting finish was a fitting climax to a keen struggle. After a declaration by Pearce, Glamorgan, set 177 for victory in 105 minutes, gained success with nearly half an hour to spare. They found the man for the occasion in Clift, who completed a remarkable not out century in seventy-nine minutes. He put considerable power behind well-timed forcing forward strokes and his chief hits were two 6s and fourteen 4s. For first innings lead of 21 Glamorgan owed much to Watkins, whose flawless technique earned a brilliant hundred. Robinson gave him best support in a stand of 101 which occupied eighty-five minutes. Avery stood out for Essex with a century in each innings. He mixed sound defence with polished stroke play, and his deflections to leg were models of accurate timing.

Essex

T. C. Dodds b Watkins	22	– c and b Wooller	6
A. V. Avery c Clift b Muncer	117	– c Watkins b Wooller	100
F. H. Vigar lbw b Jones	24	– not out	1
S. C. Eve b Wooller	27	– lbw b Wooller	1
T. E. Bailey b Wooller	11	– c Watkins b Wooller	0
T. N. Pearce c Parkhouse b Jones	25	– b Muncer	55
R. Smith b Wooller	25	– c H. Davies b Wooller	23
A. B. Lavers lbw b Muncer	6	– b Hever	0
T. H. Wade b Watkins	27		
E. J. Price b Wooller	5		
G. R. Pullinger not out	0		
B 4, l-b 8	12	B 2, l-b 9	11
	301	**(7 wkts dec.)**	**197**

Glamorgan

E. Davies c Vigar b Bailey	16	– b R. Smith	51
P. Clift c Wade b Bailey	22	– not out	101
W. G. A. Parkhouse lbw b Pullinger	37	– not out	9
W. E. Jones st Wade b Price	12		
A. Watkins b Price	104		
B. L. Muncer b Pullinger	4		
M. Robinson run out	50		
W. Wooller b Bailey	45		
J. T. Eaglestone b Bailey	10		
H. G. Davies b Price	2		
N. G. Hever not out	9		
B 4, w 2, n-b 5	11	B 13, l-b 3	16
	322	**(1 wkt)**	**177**

Glamorgan Bowling

	Overs	Mdns	Runs	Wkts	Overs	Mdns	Runs	Wkts
Muncer	30	6	56	2	15	7	25	1
Jones	21	7	52	2				
Wooller	33	10	85	4	26	8	57	5
Watkins	19.1	2	44	2	10	2	32	—
Hever	17	2	52	—	19.3	4	72	1

Essex Bowling

	Overs	Mdns	Runs	Wkts	Overs	Mdns	Runs	Wkts
Bailey	28	5	91	4	8	—	57	—
Pullinger	24	6	72	2	7	1	43	—
Smith	13	2	30	—	9.1	—	61	1
Price	38	5	92	3				
Lavers	12	4	26	—				

Umpires: W. F. Price and A. Lockett.

GLAMORGAN v LANCASHIRE

Played at Llanelly, July 13, 14, 15, 1949

Drawn. The fortunes of the game fluctuated to a considerable extent, and Lancashire, with their last pair together in an exciting situation, still wanted four runs for victory when stumps were pulled up. In Glamorgan's first innings Wooller and Parkhouse were seen to most advantage in a third wicket partnership of 105, but Pollard and Greenwood exploited the new ball so effectively that the last five wickets went for 20. Apart from Edrich, who stayed three hours for 62, Lancashire, after rain, were completely baffled by Muncer. His off-spinners turned so quickly that in his last spell he dismissed five batsmen for eight runs. Then Glamorgan were routed by Pollard and Tattersall, and Lancashire, requiring only 133 to win, were once more thwarted by Muncer, whose full match analysis was fourteen wickets for 103.

Glamorgan

E. Davies b Greenwood	9	– b Pollard	23
P. Clift c Pollard b Greenwood	5	– c Berry b Pollard	4
W. G. A. Parkhouse b Greenwood	59	– c Kelly b Pollard	25
W. Wooller b Grieves	71	– c Barlow b Greenwood	17
A. Watkins lbw b Pollard	34	– c Barlow b Tattersall	1
B. L. Muncer c Grieves b Pollard	6	– lbw b Tattersall	4
A. Porter b Greenwood	10	– not out	1
J. Pleass c Edrich b Greenwood	0	– c Ikin b Tattersall	2
J. Eaglestone c Barlow b Pollard	5	– b Tattersall	0
H. G. Davies c Greenwood b Pollard	3	– c Berry b Greenwood	10
N. G. Hever not out	0	– lbw b Tattersall	0
B 10, l-b 3, n-b 2	15	B 5, l-b 2, w 1, n-b 1	9
	217		**96**

Lancashire

J. T. Ikin b Muncer	21	– st H. Davies b Muncer	2
J. Kelly c H. Davies b Muncer	8	– run out	12
G. A. Edrich lbw b Muncer	62	– c Parkhouse b Muncer	14
A. Wharton b Watkins	11	– c Muncer b Watkins	0
K. Grieves b Muncer	24	– c Clift b Muncer	50
N. D. Howard c H. Davies b Wooller	9	– lbw b Muncer	39
P. Greenwood c Clift b Muncer	21	– b Muncer	2
A. Barlow c E. Davies b Muncer	5	– c Watkins b Muncer	0
R. Pollard b Muncer	8	– not out	1
R. Berry c Clift b Muncer	1	– not out	1
R. Tattersall not out	0	– b Wooller	6
B 11	11	L-b 2	2
	181		(9 wkts) **129**

Lancashire Bowling

	Overs	Mdns	Runs	Wkts	Overs	Mdns	Runs	Wkts
Pollard	29.1	12	45	4	13	2	37	3
Greenwood.......	26	6	71	5	14	4	32	2
Grieves	21	3	51	1				
Tattersall	14	6	22	—	13.1	7	18	5
Berry............	6	1	7	—				
Ikin.............	2	—	6	—				

Glamorgan Bowling

	Overs	Mdns	Runs	Wkts	Overs	Mdns	Runs	Wkts
Wooller..........	16	3	31	1	21	7	50	1
Hever	15	3	46	—				
Muncer..........	24.5	11	49	8	25	9	54	6
Watkins	19	4	44	1	9	4	23	1

Umpires: A. E. Pothecary and E. Cooke.

GLAMORGAN v SOMERSET

Played at Cardiff, June 3, 5, 6, 1950

Drawn. Time was called when Somerset's ninth wicket went down, and after an exciting finish Glamorgan were deprived of victory. Parkhouse was again their outstanding batsman. Exploiting all the strokes with ease and assurance, he hit a century in each innings, and virile efforts earned him thirty-three 4s. Muncer made his first century for Glamorgan in three and a half hours, 66 coming in sixteen strokes. When the home county batted a second time, Emrys Davies and Parkhouse shared an opening partnership of 241 in two and a half hours. Rogers and Tremlett were aggressive for Somerset, and Buse and Angell also did well. Ellis Robinson, their off-spin bowler, was the only player to take more than five wickets in the match.

Glamorgan

E. Davies lbw b Buse.........................	18	– b Hazell	98
W. G. A. Parkhouse lbw b Robinson	121	– c Redman b Robinson	148
M. Robinson c Hill b Buse	7	– not out	5
W. E. Jones b Buse	13	– not out	9
J. Pleass b Robinson	9		
B. L. Muncer c Redman b Hazell	114		
B. Hedges c Hazell b Robinson.................	3		
J. McConnon c Redman b Hazell................	1		
H. G. Davies lbw b Robinson	5		
N. G. Hever not out	0		
D. Shepherd b Robinson......................	0		
B 9, l-b 8	17	B 1, l-b 1, n-b 1...........	3
	308		**(2 wkts dec.) 263**

Somerset

F. L. Angell c H. Davies b Shepherd	18	– run out	73
E. Hill c H. Davies b Shepherd	0	– run out	6
M. F. Tremlett c H. Davies b Hever	14	– c Pleass b Hever	80
H. Gimblett c Parkhouse b Hever	4	– c H. Davies b Shepherd	30
H. T. F. Buse lbw b Jones	92	– c H. Davies b E. Davies	0
J. Lawrence b Muncer	38	– c Jones b Muncer	5
S. S. Rogers st H. Davies b Muncer	88	– b E. Davies	0
H. W. Stephenson st H. Davies b Muncer	7	– b Shepherd	12
J. Redman c and b Muncer	8	– not out	13
H. L. Hazell b Jones	0		
E. P. Robinson not out	9	– lbw b E. Davies	10
B 6, l-b 7	13	B 1, l-b 1	2
	291		**(9 wkts) 231**

Somerset Bowling

	Overs	Mdns	Runs	Wkts	Overs	Mdns	Runs	Wkts
Redman	18	3	54	—	8	—	49	—
Buse	28	8	81	3	14	1	61	—
Lawrence	12	3	40	—				
Robinson	34.1	8	70	5	14	1	72	1
Hazell	33	15	46	2	20	2	78	1

Glamorgan Bowling

	Overs	Mdns	Runs	Wkts	Overs	Mdns	Runs	Wkts
Hever	30	12	39	2	16	2	81	1
Shepherd	23	6	44	2	13	3	40	2
Muncer	37	7	99	4	14	1	45	1
Jones	26	6	66	2	7	—	32	—
E. Davies	10	1	30	—	10	3	31	3

Umpires: A. Skelding and T. Spencer.

GLAMORGAN v DERBYSHIRE

Played at Cardiff, June 2, 4, 5, 1951

Glamorgan won by an innings and 120 runs. Before declaring they made their highest score in first-class cricket, beating their 586 for five wickets against Essex in 1948. Davies shared an opening stand of 135 with Clift and Parkhouse helped him add 177 for the second wicket. A variety of well-timed strokes brought Parkhouse sixteen 4s and Davies nineteen. Afterwards the Derbyshire bowling came in for severe treatment, Jones and Watkins adding 113 in sixty-five minutes. Splendid off-spin bowling by McConnon, who did his best work for the county so far, also played a prominent part. His full analysis was fourteen wickets for 153 runs.

Glamorgan

E. Davies c Revill b Morgan	146	B. L. Muncer not out	23
P. B. Clift c Elliott b Jackson	61	J. McConnon lbw b Eato	2
W. G. A. Parkhouse b Rhodes	107	H. G. Davies not out	30
W. E. Jones run out	58		
A. J. Watkins c Morgan b Hamer	72	B 12, l-b 9, n-b 5	26
W. Wooller b Jackson	62		
J. Pleass run out	0	**(8 wkts dec.) 587**	

N. G. Hever did not bat.

Derbyshire

C. S. Elliott c Muncer b McConnon	52	– lbw b Muncer	32
A. Hamer c Wooller b Muncer	44	– c H.Davies b McConnon	35
J. Kelly b McConnon	46	– b Muncer	8
A. C. Revill b McConnon	29	– b McConnon	0
G. L. Willatt c H. Davies b McConnon	2	– not out	89
D. Smith b E. Davies	15	– b McConnon	20
A. E. G. Rhodes b E. Davies	3	– c E. Davies b McConnon	15
G. Dawkes c Hever b McConnon	0	– c Watkins b McConnon	19
D. C. Morgan c Parkhouse b McConnon	0	– c H. Davies b Watkins	12
A. Eato b McConnon	10	– lbw b McConnon	0
L. Jackson not out	1	– c Jones b McConnon	4
B 7, l-b 2	9	B 22	22
	211		**256**

Derbyshire Bowling

	Overs	Mdns	Runs	Wkts
Jackson	31	8	100	2
Morgan	34	5	133	1
Eato	26	4	106	1
Rhodes	36	10	100	1
Hamer	24	5	98	1
Revill	2	—	24	—

Glamorgan Bowling

	Overs	Mdns	Runs	Wkts	Overs	Mdns	Runs	Wkts
Hever	15	5	30	—	9	4	23	—
Wooller	11	1	38	—	2	1	4	—
Watkins	11	2	26	—	11.1	4	24	1
Jones	4	3	4	—				
Muncer	16	6	18	1	34	11	85	2
McConnon	25	6	69	7	44	19	84	7
E. Davies	15	8	17	2	7	2	14	—

Umpires: H. Elliott and J. S. Buller.

GLAMORGAN v KENT

Played at Neath, July 3, 4, 5, 1957

Glamorgan won by 46 runs. When Glamorgan collapsed in two hours to the pace of Halfyard their chances of success seemed slight but they fought back magnificently and turned the tables on Kent. Halfyard, practically unplayable on a drying pitch, took nine wickets for 39 runs, the best performance of his career. Kent, who passed their opponents' score with only three wickets down, led by 146, but Glamorgan faced up to their task dourly. With Parkhouse leading the resistance they batted so surely that Kent were left to get 207 to win – a task beyond them against inspired off-spin bowling by McConnon. Parkhouse showed his class in a faultless display which lasted five hours twenty minutes. He hit one 6 and eighteen 4s.

Glamorgan

W. G. A. Parkhouse c Ufton b Halfyard.	9	– c Wilson b Wright. 133
G. Dauncey c Pretlove b Halfyard	6	– c Ufton b Halfyard 7
B. Hedges c Page b Halfyard	15	– c Page b Wright 37
W. E. Jones c Pettiford b Halfyard	0	– c Fagg b Dixon 41
L. N. Devereux c Wilson b Halfyard.	5	– run out 18
P. Walker lbw b Halfyard	0	– c Wilson b Wright. 0
D. J. Ward c Dixon b Halfyard.	1	– c Wilson b Wright. 15
J. E. McConnon c Page b Halfyard	36	– lbw b Halfyard 43
H. G. Davies c Dixon b Halfyard	0	– c Phebey b Dixon 21
D. J. Shepherd c Wilson b Dixon	12	– c Page b Dixon 3
H. D. Davies not out.	3	– not out 3
B 1, l-b 1	2	B 24, l-b 7 31

1/10 2/23 3/25 4/32 5/32   **89**   1/31 2/110 3/207 4/246 5/250   **352**
6/37 7/48 8/48 9/77   6/266 7/324 8/346 9/346

Kent

A. H. Phebey c Jones b H. D. Davies	1	– lbw b Walker 4
R. C. Wilson c H. G. Davies b H. D. Davies	0	– b H. D. Davies 35
J. F. Pretlove b McConnon	59	– c H. G. Davies b H. D. Davies 27
J. Pettiford c Parkhouse b H. D. Davies	43	– run out 15
S. E. Leary b Shepherd	40	– c Devereux b McConnon 23
A. L. Dixon c H. D. Davies b Walker	6	– c H. G. Davies b H. D. Davies 27
D. G. Ufton b McConnon	15	– c Walker b McConnon 0
A. E. Fagg c Devereux b Shepherd	14	– c Shepherd b McConnon 0
D. J. Halfyard c Parkhouse b McConnon.	5	– c Shepherd b McConnon 14
D. V. P. Wright not out.	28	– not out 7
J. C. T. Page b H. D. Davies.	23	– c Parkhouse b H. D. Davies 2
L-b 1	1	B 1, l-b 4, n-b 1 6

1/1 2/14 3/80 4/115 5/124   **235**   1/10 2/63 3/74 4/88 5/120   **160**
6/147 7/170 8/183 9/187   6/123 7/123 8/144 9/159

Kent Bowling

	Overs	Mdns	Runs	Wkts	Overs	Mdns	Runs	Wkts
Halfyard.	17.2	7	39	9	38	13	89	2
Dixon	12	3	35	1	40.3	13	91	3
Page	5	—	13	—	22	7	57	—
Wright					31	14	70	4
Pretlove					1	1	—	—
Pettiford					4	—	14	—

Glamorgan Bowling

	Overs	Mdns	Runs	Wkts	Overs	Mdns	Runs	Wkts
H. D. Davies.	25.3	4	88	4	23.4	6	66	4
Walker	20	7	34	1	6	2	21	1
Shepherd.	21	2	64	2	6	—	17	—
McConnon	20	5	48	3	12	3	26	4
Devereux					13	4	24	—

Umpires: L. H. Gray and A. R. Coleman.

GLAMORGAN v LANCASHIRE

Played at Cardiff, August 6, 7, 8, 1958

Drawn. Rain, which washed out play on the final day, almost certainly saved Glamorgan
from complete humiliation. After putting in their opponents on a damp pitch they had the

mortification of seeing Lancashire total 351, thanks to splendid displays by Marner and Grieves. Worse followed, for Glamorgan were shot out for 26, the season's lowest total, being one less than Lancashire's 27 against Surrey. The Glamorgan batsmen were nonplussed by the sheer pace and accuracy of Statham, who hit the stumps five times, and by the spin of Tattersall. The only resistance came from the last pair, Wooller and Gatehouse, who defended stubbornly for half an hour.

Lancashire

R. W. Barber b McConnon............. 48	A. Wilson not out...................... 3
A. Wharton c Walker b McConnon....... 47	T. Greenhough c Pressdee b Ward........ 0
G. Pullar b Walker 89	R. Tattersall b Shepherd................ 2
P. Marner c Wooller b Gatehouse........ 83	
K. Grieves c Parkhouse b Ward.......... 37	B 12, l-b 4, w 1 17
N. H. Cooke st Evans b Ward 18	
M. J. Hilton b Shepherd 0	1/79 2/110 3/242 4/302 5/327 351
J. B. Statham c McConnon b Ward 7	6/335 7/339 8/347 9/347

Glamorgan

W. G. A. Parkhouse b Statham..................	1 – not out	0
B. Hedges c Hilton b Tattersall..................	0	
J. Pressdee c Hilton b Statham	2	
P. Walker b Statham.........................	4	
D. L. Evans b Statham	0	
D. J. Ward b Statham........................	4	
A. C. Burnett b Statham......................	0	
J. E. McConnon b Tattersall....................	2	
W. Wooller not out	2 – not out	0
D. J. Shepherd c Statham b Tattersall.............	1	
P. W. Gatehouse c Hilton b Tattersall.............	8	
B 1, l-b 1	2	

1/0 2/3 3/4 4/7 5/10   26   (No wkt) 0
6/10 7/13 8/13 9/15

Glamorgan Bowling

	Overs	Mdns	Runs	Wkts
Gatehouse.........	26	6	58	1
Shepherd..........	21.3	3	64	2
McConnon........	27	11	59	2
Ward	9	1	51	4
Walker	33	10	102	1

Lancashire Bowling

	Overs	Mdns	Runs	Wkts	Overs	Mdns	Runs	Wkts
Statham	16	9	12	6	2	2	—	—
Tattersall	15.4	7	12	4	1	1	—	—

Umpires: R. S. Lay and J. S. Buller.

GLAMORGAN v SUSSEX

Played at Newport, June 3, 4, 5, 1959

Glamorgan won by four wickets. On a pitch responding to spin, bowlers held the upper hand until the final stage. Then a fifth-wicket partnership of 111 between Walker and Watkins tipped the scales in Glamorgan's favour and fittingly Walker remained to make the winning stroke. He hit one 6 and eleven 4s in his stay of three hours ten minutes but only a few people saw him bat for the gates were not open to the public after rain delayed the resumption for seventy minutes and continued to threaten. Glamorgan had been left to get 224, a seemingly difficult task in view of their first-innings failure against Marlar. Shepherd and McConnon did the damage for Glamorgan, only Oakman and Smith facing them with any success.

Sussex

A. S. M. Oakman c Walker b McConnon	55	– c and b McConnon	19
L. J. Lenham lbw b Shepherd	15	– c Walker b Shepherd	3
E. R. Dexter b Shepherd	19	– b Shepherd	22
J. M. Parks c Pressdee b McConnon	16	– c Parkhouse b McConnon	26
K. G. Suttle c Parkhouse b Shepherd	0	– c Parkhouse b Shepherd	15
D. V. Smith c Hedges b McConnon	21	– not out	60
G. C. Cooper not out	32	– c and b Shepherd	14
N. I. Thomson c McConnon b Shepherd	6	– c Evans b Shepherd	2
R. V. Bell c Walker b McConnon	1	– c Clarke b Shepherd	8
D. L. Bates c Parkhouse b McConnon	2	– c Watkins b Walker	8
R. G. Marlar b Shepherd	0	– c Hedges b Walker	3
L-b 2	2	B 4, l-b 2	6

1/54 2/86 3/105 4/107 5/107   169   1/45 2/59 3/79 4/86 5/92   186
6/156 7/160 8/165 9/169   6/120 7/130 8/152 9/172

Glamorgan

W. G. A. Parkhouse c Parks b Marlar	23	– c Parks b Thomson	8
B. Hedges c Oakman b Bell	20	– c Oakman b Bell	21
J. Pressdee run out	16	– b Marlar	21
L. N. Devereux b Marlar	19	– c Smith b Bell	0
A. J. Watkins lbw b Marlar	1	– c Parks b Thomson	48
P. Walker c Smith b Bell	1	– not out	83
D. J. Ward c Oakman b Marlar	15	– c Parks b Thomson	35
J. E. McConnon b Bell	16	– not out	1
D. L. Evans not out	4		
D. J. Shepherd b Marlar	8		
F. Clarke c Cooper b Marlar	1		
B 1, l-b 7	8	B 1, l-b 4, n-b 2	7

1/41 2/49 3/75 4/77 5/84   132   1/11 2/33 3/33   (6 wkts) 224
6/94 7/109 8/119 9/128   4/59 5/170 6/218

Glamorgan Bowling

	Overs	Mdns	Runs	Wkts	Overs	Mdns	Runs	Wkts
Clarke	6	—	28	—	4	1	13	—
Watkins	5	—	13	—				
Shepherd	24.2	7	47	5	37	7	71	6
McConnon	26	6	73	5	28	2	84	2
Ward	2	1	6	—				
Walker					5.1	2	12	2

Sussex Bowling

	Overs	Mdns	Runs	Wkts	Overs	Mdns	Runs	Wkts
Thomson	4	2	6	—	33	7	65	3
Bates	1	—	3	—	14	2	47	—
Marlar	27.4	7	66	6	10	3	30	1
Bell	25	11	49	3	11	—	60	2
Suttle					2	—	8	—
Dexter					2	—	7	—

Umpires: J. F. Crapp and H. G. Baldwin.

GLAMORGAN v WARWICKSHIRE

Played at Neath, July 22, 23, 24, 1959

Glamorgan won by nine wickets. A thunderstorm of almost tropical intensity on the second day transformed the game after large first-innings scores. Warwickshire were tumbled out in just under two hours for 61 runs and Glamorgan raced to victory in forty-seven minutes after a breezy innings by Hedges. Warwickshire collapsed against the off-spin of Shepherd who took five wickets in his last nine overs at a personal cost of three runs. Although the drying pitch gave considerable help it was never as vicious as the batting breakdown might appear to suggest. In the opening play Horner and Stewart hit centuries for Warwickshire sharing a third-wicket partnership of 175. A century by Hedges, who was helped in an opening stand of 152 by Rees on his second appearance for the county enabled Glamorgan to declare as soon as they were ahead.

Warwickshire

F. C. Gardner c Walker b Watkins	6	– b McConnon 24
N. F. Horner lbw b J. B. Evans	126	– c Ward b J. B. Evans 8
T. W. Cartwright b Watkins	2	– c D. L. Evans b J. B. Evans 4
W. J. Stewart c and b Shepherd	155	– c Pressdee b J. B. Evans 4
A. Townsend not out	48	– b Shepherd 2
R. E. Hitchcock (did not bat)		– c Hedges b Shepherd 8
J. D. Bannister (did not bat)		– not out 8
R. T. Spooner (did not bat)		– lbw b Shepherd 3
W. B. Bridge (did not bat)		– c D. L. Evans b Shepherd 0
G. H. Hill (did not bat)		– b Shepherd 0
R. G. Thompson (did not bat)		– run out 0
B 4, l-b 5, w 1	10	

1/37 2/47 3/222   (4 wkts dec.) 347   1/21 2/31 3/35 4/40 5/50   61
4/347   6/53 7/56 8/60 9/60

Glamorgan

B. Hedges c and b Hill	107	– not out 51
A. Rees c Spooner b Bridge	65	– lbw b Thompson................ 0
J. Pressdee c Gardner b Bridge	17	– not out 13
P. M. Walker c Townsend b Thompson	68	
A. J. Watkins c Spooner b Thompson	25	
L. N. Devereux c Spooner b Thompson	24	
J. E. McConnon not out	28	
D. J. Ward c Spooner b Thompson	3	
J. B. Evans not out	4	
B 4, l-b 3	7	

1/152 2/176 3/194   (7 wkts dec.) 348   1/4   (1 wkt) 64
4/231 5/301 6/324 7/344

D. J. Shepherd and D. L. Evans did not bat.

Glamorgan Bowling

	Overs	Mdns	Runs	Wkts	Overs	Mdns	Runs	Wkts
J. B. Evans	26	4	93	1	13	2	35	3
Watkins	27	12	50	2	6	2	10	—
Walker	17	1	55	—				
Shepherd..........	24.5	4	71	1	12	7	9	5
McConnon........	9	—	44	—	5.1	2	7	1
Ward	4	—	8	—				
Rees	5	1	16	—				

Warwickshire Bowling

	Overs	Mdns	Runs	Wkts	Overs	Mdns	Runs	Wkts
Thompson	27.5	6	61	4	3	1	5	1
Bannister	31	8	89	—	1	—	1	—
Cartwright	16	4	57	—				
Townsend.........	10	3	33	—				
Hitchcock.........	14	3	33	—	3	2	2	—
Bridge............	19	7	42	2	5	—	13	—
Hill	14	5	26	1	3	—	32	—
Gardner					1	—	2	—
Horner					1	—	9	—

Umpires: W. E. Phillipson and D. J. Wood.

GLAMORGAN v DERBYSHIRE

Played at Llanelly, May 18, 19, 20, 1960

Glamorgan won by 119 runs. Glamorgan appeared set for a large first-innings score, passing 200 for the loss of three wickets. Then Jackson took the new ball and he captured five wickets in 13 balls with a magnificent spell of fast bowling. Derbyshire experienced a similar collapse, losing five wickets, mainly against the off-spin of McConnon, while only eight runs were added. In their second innings the recognised Glamorgan batsmen never really mastered Jackson and Smith, although their last two wickets added 51. Derbyshire needing 286 to win, were given a good start by Hamer and Hall but subsequently the batting broke down before the spin of McConnon and Shepherd, who were backed up by superb fielding.

Glamorgan

W. G. A. Parkhouse run out	72	– lbw b Rhodes	34
B. Hedges c Berry b Jackson....................	9	– run out	22
J. Pressdee c and b Rhodes	74	– c Dawkes b Jackson	20
P. M. Walker c Hall b Smith	6	– c Dawkes b Jackson	0
A. J. Watkins b Rhodes.......................	55	– c Rhodes b Smith	27
*W. Wooller c Lee b Jackson	10	– lbw b Jackson	15
J. E. McConnon c Dawkes b Jackson...........	0	– c Lee b Smith	0
J. B. Evans b Jackson	1	– b Smith......................	3
†D. L. Evans lbw b Jackson	0	– c Carr b Buxton	18
P. Gatehouse b Jackson	0	– b Buxton.....................	20
D. J. Shepherd not out.......................	0	– not out	12
B 1, l-b 8, n-b 1	10	B 2, l-b 5	7

1/23 2/118 3/138 4/206 5/231   237   1/45 2/69 3/70 4/81 5/115   178
6/231 7/233 8/237 9/237   6/119 7/123 8/127 9/161

Derbyshire

Batsman	1st	2nd
A. Hamer lbw b J. Evans	0 – c Wooller b Shepherd	42
I. W. Hall c D. Evans b McConnon	21 – c Walker b McConnon	65
C. Lee c Shepherd b McConnon	30 – c Walker b Shepherd	4
*D. B. Carr b J. Evans	20 – c Pressdee b McConnon	4
H. L. Johnson c McConnon b J. Evans	13 – c Pressdee b McConnon	27
I. Buxton c Walker b McConnon	1 – lbw b McConnon	3
†G. O. Dawkes c Parkhouse b McConnon	0 – c Pressdee b McConnon	1
E. Smith lbw b Walker	27 – c D. Evans b Shepherd	5
H. J. Rhodes c Walker b McConnon	0 – c Watkins b McConnon	10
R. Berry b Shepherd	15 – b Shepherd	3
H. L. Jackson not out	0 – not out	2
B 2, l-b 1	3	

1/0 2/26 3/61 4/81 5/86 6/86 7/88 8/89 9/126 **130**

1/86 2/110 3/112 4/125 5/130 6/132 7/150 8/160 9/164 **166**

Derbyshire Bowling

	Overs	Mdns	Runs	Wkts	Overs	Mdns	Runs	Wkts
Rhodes	19.1	5	37	2	24	9	48	1
Jackson	20	5	52	6	26	7	44	3
Buxton	12	5	29	—	1.5	—	13	2
Berry	29	13	49	—	4	—	12	—
Smith	20	6	60	1	30	15	54	3

Glamorgan Bowling

	Overs	Mdns	Runs	Wkts	Overs	Mdns	Runs	Wkts
J. Evans	21	6	26	3	10	3	17	—
Gatehouse	8	3	13	—	5	—	25	—
McConnon	26	8	50	5	23.2	8	51	6
Shepherd	12.4	6	33	1	26	9	40	4
Walker	3	—	5	1	13	3	33	—

Umpires: A. Jepson and N. Oldfield.

GLAMORGAN v YORKSHIRE

Played at Swansea, August 17, 18, 19, 1960

Glamorgan won by 87 runs. Glamorgan were never able to master Illingworth, who by skilful variation of flight captured eight wickets for 70. There was some spirited resistance by Ward and J. B. Evans, who hit strongly to add 62 for the eighth wicket in fifty minutes. Stott, who played the dominant part, and Bolus gave Yorkshire a sound start but once

Shepherd broke the opening partnership with his 1,000th wicket for Glamorgan, Yorkshire collapsed against his spin. Illingworth again worried the Glamorgan batsmen and only Parkhouse and A. Jones batted with any confidence. Illingworth's seven wickets for 53 gave him his best-ever match analysis of fifteen wickets for 123. Needing 232 to win, Yorkshire, with the exception of Taylor, failed against the spin of Ward and Shepherd.

Glamorgan

W. G. A. Parkhouse st Binks b Close	9	– run out	49
B. Hedges b Illingworth	35	– c Binks b D. Wilson	25
A. R. Lewis c D. Wilson b Illingworth	45	– c and b Close	14
A. Jones run out	8	– c Close b Illingworth	35
P. M. Walker c Cowan b Illingworth	28	– c Close b Illingworth	19
J. Pressdee c Birkenshaw b Illingworth	11	– c J. Wilson b Illingworth	0
*W. Wooller b Illingworth	0	– c Bolus b Illingworth	7
D. J. Ward c Birkenshaw b Illingworth	32	– c Sharpe b Illingworth	4
J. B. Evans c and b Illingworth	36	– b Illingworth	23
†D. L. Evans not out	2	– not out	13
D. J. Shepherd c D. Wilson b Illingworth	0	– b Illingworth	0
		B 10, l-b 3	13

1/13 2/66 3/95 4/105 5/128   **206**   1/30 2/58 3/133 4/151 5/153   **202**
6/128 7/141 8/203 9/206   6/161 7/165 8/165 9/202

Yorkshire

W. B. Stott c Wooller b Walker	52	– c D. Evans b Shepherd	12
J. B. Bolus b Shepherd	28	– c Walker b Wooller	28
P. J. Sharpe c J. Evans b Shepherd	16	– c Walker b Shepherd	11
D. B. Close c and b Shepherd	3	– c Parkhouse b Ward	3
K. Taylor c Wooller b Walker	0	– lbw b Shepherd	46
R. Illingworth c Lewis b Ward	11	– c and b Ward	4
*J. V. Wilson b Shepherd	13	– st D. Evans b Ward	0
J. Birkenshaw c Wooller b Ward	3	– c Pressdee b Ward	0
D. Wilson b Shepherd	12	– c Walker b Shepherd	8
†J. G. Binks b J. Evans	20	– not out	20
M. J. Cowan not out	1	– c Shepherd b Ward	4
B 9, l-b 9	18	B 5, l-b 3	8

1/80 2/94 3/102 4/102 5/106   **177**   1/17 2/88 3/92 4/94 5/113   **144**
6/130 7/132 8/143 9/157   6/122 7/122 8/122 9/131

Yorkshire Bowling

	Overs	Mdns	Runs	Wkts	Overs	Mdns	Runs	Wkts
Cowan	8	1	21	—	7	—	15	—
Close	7	3	12	1	16	4	33	1
Illingworth	29.3	10	70	8	26.4	13	53	7
Taylor	4	—	16	—				
D. Wilson	20	4	60	—	25	7	74	1
Birkenshaw	5	—	27	—	8	3	14	—

Glamorgan Bowling

	Overs	Mdns	Runs	Wkts	Overs	Mdns	Runs	Wkts
J. Evans	8.4	3	26	1	2	—	13	—
Wooller	3	—	11	—	11	7	12	1
Shepherd	29	10	52	5	26	9	55	4
Walker	18	2	44	2	4	1	13	—
Ward	6	1	26	2	14.2	1	43	5

Umpires: R. S. Lay and D. J. Wood.

GLAMORGAN v NOTTINGHAMSHIRE

Played at Newport, June 7, 8, 1961

Glamorgan won by 155 runs. A remarkable bowling performance by the Glamorgan off-spinner, Shepherd, during which he captured six wickets without conceding a run, gave his team the mastery which they never lost. Batting first, Glamorgan experienced difficulty against the off-spin of Wells after Jones and Hedges had given them a sound start. When Wells left the field with a strained back, Walker and Ward added 138 for the sixth wicket before Wells returned to break the partnership. Walker went on to score 112 not out (one 6, eighteen 4s). Nottinghamshire made a wretched start, losing two wickets before a run had been scored. Then Shepherd, who, in a spell of eleven overs claimed six wickets without having a run scored off him, wrecked the innings. Wheatley soon declared his second innings and set Nottinghamshire to score 332. Shepherd again broke the back of the innings and Glamorgan won easily. Wells, who hit Shepherd for two 6s and four 4s, spoiled his figures but nevertheless Shepherd had a match analysis of ten wickets for 69 runs.

Glamorgan

A. Jones c Davison b Wells	42	– c Millman b Davison 10
B. Hedges c Davison b Wells	58	– c Hill b Cotton 6
A. Rees c Millman b Wells	13	– c Forbes b Davison........... 21
W. Slade lbw b Wells	0	– c Millman b Wells............. 7
J. Pressdee c Wells b Springall	15	– c Forbes b Davison........... 35
P. M. Walker not out	112	– not out 13
D. J. Ward c Rhodes b Wells	65	
J. B. Evans b Wells	0	
†D. L. Evans c Davison b Wells	0	
B 2, l-b 8, w 1	11	B 2, l-b 6, w 1 9

1/69 2/99 3/99 4/126   (8 wkts dec.) 316   1/21 2/21 3/34 4/62   (5 wkts dec.) 101
5/146 6/284 7/312 8/316   5/101

*O. S. Wheatley and D. J. Shepherd did not bat.

Nottinghamshire

N. Hill b J. B. Evans	0	– c Walker b Shepherd 10
W. E. Rhodes b Ward	15	– b Shepherd 21
C. Forbes c Walker b J. B. Evans	0	– c Slade b Shepherd 9
H. M. Winfield c Walker b Shepherd	30	– c D. L. Evans b Wheatley........ 32
*J. D. Clay c Walker b Shepherd	3	– lbw b Wheatley................ 15
C. J. Poole c Walker b Shepherd	0	– c Hedges b Wheatley 6
J. D. Springall c Pressdee b Shepherd	20	– c D. L. Evans b J. B. Evans 23
†G. Millman lbw b Shepherd	7	– c Walker b Wheatley 1
I. Davison c J. B. Evans b Shepherd	0	– not out 19
J. Cotton c Walker b Ward	7	– b Shepherd 0
B. D. Wells not out	0	– b Wheatley 32
B 1, l-b 3	4	B 8 8

1/0 2/0 3/29 4/36 5/44   86   1/19 2/52 3/78 4/88 5/98   176
6/61 7/70 8/76 9/86   6/100 7/125 8/129 9/129

Nottinghamshire Bowling

	Overs	Mdns	Runs	Wkts	Overs	Mdns	Runs	Wkts
Cotton	15	4	61	—	10	3	32	1
Davison	15	6	49	—	10.4	4	21	3
Wells	41	17	66	7	14	4	39	1
Springall	20	6	57	1				
Forbes	17	4	72	—				

Glamorgan Bowling

	Overs	Mdns	Runs	Wkts	Overs	Mdns	Runs	Wkts
J. B. Evans	8	3	25	2	7	2	34	1
Wheatley	3	—	14	—	14.4	4	36	5
Shepherd.........	16	14	5	6	27	10	64	4
Ward	11.2	4	38	2	5	2	14	—
Walker					8	1	20	—

Umpires: J. H. Parks and W. H. Copson.

GLAMORGAN v LEICESTERSHIRE

Played at Margam, July 19, 20, 21, 1961

Glamorgan won by 178 runs. On a pitch that helped seam bowlers throughout, Glamorgan lost their first four wickets for 23 runs, but determined batting by Walker and Ward prevented a complete collapse. Leicestershire fared even worse and only Wharton, who hit boldly to score 52 in an hour and a quarter, offered any resistance. Walker was again in form when Glamorgan batted a second time and he found a good partner in Slade. Together they added 84 for the fifth wicket. Needing 274 to win, Leicestershire were given a sound start by Hallam and Wharton before J. B. Evans, with a spell of 5.3–3–8–6, wound up the innings.

Glamorgan

*W. G. A. Parkhouse c Pratt b Spencer	0	– c and b van Geloven............	24
B. Hedges c Hallam b Boshier..................	0	– c Wharton b Boshier............	10
A. Jones c and b Spencer	7	– c van Geloven b Savage	17
P. M. Walker c Wharton b Boshier...............	56	– c Hallam b Savage	51
J. Pressdee b Spencer	2	– b Savage	1
W. Slade b van Geloven	19	– c Wharton b van Geloven........	50
D. J. Ward lbw b Savage......................	50	– c Pratt b Savage	0
J. B. Evans c Hallam b Spencer	6	– b van Geloven.................	31
†D. L. Evans b van Geloven...................	13	– lbw b van Geloven	0
D. J. Shepherd b Spencer	18	– b van Geloven.................	3
I. J. Jones not out	2	– not out	0
B 7, l-b 1, w 4, n-b 1	13	B 2, l-b 1, w 1	4

1/0 2/0 3/13 4/23 5/63   186   1/16 2/52 3/54 4/57 5/141   191
6/117 7/133 8/160 9/184   6/141 7/170 8/184 9/184

Leicestershire

*M. R. Hallam b I. Jones	1	– lbw b J. Evans.................	35
A. Wharton c J. Evans b Ward.................	52	– lbw b J. Evans.................	21
J. van Geloven b J. Evans	3	– lbw b Ward...................	0
L. R. Gardner c Walker b J. Evans..............	6	– c Slade b Ward................	9
J. Birkenshaw c D. Evans b I. Jones	8	– c D. Evans b J. Evans...........	0
G. Cross run out	0	– lbw b Ward...................	0
R. L. Pratt b Shepherd	10	– c sub b J. Evans	15
†R. Julian c D. Evans b I. Jones	2	– b J. Evans....................	0
C. T. Spencer b I. Jones	6	– not out	13
J. S. Savage not out.........................	3	– c Walker b J. Evans	0
B. S. Boshier c Pressdee b I. Jones	6	– b J. Evans....................	0
B 4, l-b 2, n-b 1	7	L-b 2	2

1/2 2/11 3/15 4/51 5/51   104   1/40 2/63 3/67 4/67 5/67   95
6/79 7/87 8/95 9/95   6/67 7/80 8/83 9/83

Leicestershire Bowling

	Overs	Mdns	Runs	Wkts	Overs	Mdns	Runs	Wkts
Spencer...........	24	9	39	5	7	2	19	—
Boshier...........	22	6	48	2	10	2	23	1
van Geloven	23.2	6	43	2	22.3	5	46	5
Pratt.............	4	1	18	—				
Savage	8	4	25	1	35	13	72	4
Birkenshaw........					9	1	25	—
Wharton..........					2	1	2	—

Glamorgan Bowling

	Overs	Mdns	Runs	Wkts	Overs	Mdns	Runs	Wkts
I. Jones...........	12.1	1	37	5	6	1	20	—
J. B. Evans	5	1	22	2	13.3	5	32	7
Shepherd..........	12	4	26	1	5	1	7	—
Walker	4	1	10	—	1	—	4	—
Ward	1	—	2	1	9	6	22	3
Slade.............					1	—	8	—

Umpires: D. Davies and J. Arnold.

GLOUCESTERSHIRE

GLOUCESTERSHIRE v OXFORD UNIVERSITY

Played at Bristol, June 29, July 1, 2, 1946

Gloucestershire won by an innings and 101 runs. They found little difficulty in facing an attack lacking variety. Wilson reached three figures on his first appearance as opening batsman and hit eleven 4s in helping to add 192 in three hours with Crapp, whose second century in successive innings included fourteen 4s. Donnelly, in the Oxford first innings, overshadowed all his colleagues, who, on a dry pitch, failed against spin bowling. Driving beautifully, he hit two 6s and fifteen 4s in scoring 117 out of 159 in two hours and a half. Sutton shared in the best stand of the innings, 70 for the ninth wicket, of which Donnelly obtained 68. Following on 287 behind, Oxford made a better start, but, despite the absence of Goddard, suffering from bronchitis, lost their last six batsmen on the third morning for 81.

Gloucestershire

B. O. Allen c Rumbold b Maudsley 3	A. G. S. Wilcox c sub b Bloy 57
A. E. Wilson b Macindoe 104	T. W. Goddard b Macindoe 22
V. Hopkins run out 6	C. J. Scott c Rumbold b Sutton.......... 4
J. F. Crapp c Newton-Thompson b Sutton..121	C. Cook not out 17
A. H. Mills c Newton-Thompson b Sutton .. 32	B 16, l-b 7, w 2 25
L. M. Cranfield st Wheatley b Bartlett 24	
G. M. Emmett b Bartlett............... 44	459

Oxford University

J. S. Rumbold b Scott	4	– b Scott	23
G. E. Beck lbw b Goddard	1	– b Crapp	8
R. H. Maudsley c Allen b Cook	12	– b Goddard	42
M. P. Donnelly c Allen b Cook.............	117	– b Scott	6
N. C. F. Bloy b Goddard	2	– b Cook	35
J. O. Newton-Thompson c and b Goddard.........	7	– run out	20
G. A. Wheatley b Cranfield....................	14	– c Scott b Cook	1
D. F. Henley b Cranfield.......................	0	– c Cook b Cranfield..............	16
D. H. Macindoe b Goddard	5	– c Scott b Cranfield	10
M. A. Sutton b Goddard...................	2	– st Wilson b Cook	11
J. N. Bartlett not out	0	– not out	5
B 6, l-b 2	8	B 5, l-b 3, n-b 1..........	9
	172		186

Oxford University Bowling

	Overs	Mdns	Runs	Wkts
Macindoe	38	6	87	2
Maudsley	13	3	28	1
Bartlett	34	7	91	2
Sutton	41	5	132	3
Newton-Thompson .	5	—	21	—
Bloy	18.4	—	75	1

Gloucestershire Bowling

	Overs	Mdns	Runs	Wkts	Overs	Mdns	Runs	Wkts
Scott	5	3	4	1	15	1	66	2
Crapp	1	—	3	—	7	2	26	1
Cook	16	6	41	2	15.2	4	37	3
Goddard	22.1	3	81	5	8	4	13	1
Cranfield	9	2	35	2	13	3	35	2

GLOUCESTERSHIRE v NOTTINGHAMSHIRE

Played at Bristol, July 3, 4, 5, 1946

Drawn. That Gloucestershire, on a pitch so favourable to batsmen that only seventeen wickets fell for an aggregate of 1,278 runs, gained first innings points, chief credit was due to Hammond, who, after bringing off four splendid catches, made 211, including twenty-six 4s, by faultless cricket. He and Emmett added 226 in an unbroken partnership. Barnett, scoring 171 in three hours and a half by powerful all-round strokes, hit two 6s and twenty-three 4s. For Nottinghamshire, Hardstaff in the first innings and Keeton in the second took chief honours. Hardstaff scored his century on his thirty-fifth birthday.

Nottinghamshire

W. W. Keeton lbw b Lambert	24	– not out ... 100
C. B. Harris c Barnett b Lambert	51	– c sub b Cranfield ... 16
T. B. Reddick c Wilson b Lambert	84	– c Neale b Cranfield ... 48
J. Hardstaff c Hammond b Lambert	113	– not out ... 0
G. F. H. Heane c Hammond b Cranfield	22	
H. Winrow b Cook	77	
F. W. Stocks c Hammond b Cook	6	
H. Butler c Hammond b Lambert	13	
A. Jepson not out	44	
F. G. Woodhead b Cranfield	9	
E. A. Meads run out	7	
B 12, l-b 5	17	B 3, l-b 1 ... 4
	467	**(2 wkts) 168**

Gloucestershire

C. J. Barnett c Hardstaff b Heane	171	B. O. Allen lbw b Harris	41
A. E. Wilson c Hardstaff b Heane	65	G. M. Emmett not out	81
W. L. Neale b Woodhead	46	B 13, l-b 8, n-b 2	23
W. R. Hammond not out	211		
J. F. Crapp b Heane	5	**(5 wkts dec.) 643**	

C. Cook, C. J. Scott, L. M. Cranfield and G. Lambert did not bat.

Gloucestershire Bowling

	Overs	Mdns	Runs	Wkts	Overs	Mdns	Runs	Wkts
Lambert	42	8	109	5	6	1	22	—
Scott	38	5	133	—	8	2	28	—
Cook	36.5	17	46	2	9	2	29	—
Cranfield	42	8	151	2	14	1	59	2
Barnett	2	—	1	—				
Neale					2	—	26	—

Nottinghamshire Bowling

	Overs	Mdns	Runs	Wkts
Butler	40	7	130	—
Jepson.	32	2	122	—
Woodhead	30	3	138	1
Harris	31	7	86	1
Heane	35	6	144	3

GLOUCESTERSHIRE v SURREY

Played at Cheltenham, August 14, 15, 16, 1946

Gloucestershire won by 55 runs. The match provided a triumph for Goddard, who defied the handicap of a fractured finger and snatched victory when Surrey appeared to have the game in hand. After a first innings failure when sent in to bat, Gloucestershire recovered splendidly on a pitch that became easy. Barnett hit 101 in two hours and a half, and Allen also scored skilfully. Surrey were left 292 to get with a possible four hours ten minutes remaining. A stand of 97 between Gregory and Barling put them in a strong position, but Goddard bowled with such skill that, after he changed ends, the last eight wickets fell for 79 runs.

Gloucestershire

C. J. Barnett c Watts b Gover	2	– lbw b E. A. Bedser	101
A. E. Wilson lbw b Parker.	23	– b E. A. Bedser.	59
W. L. Neale b Gover	1	– c Mobey b E. A. Bedser	15
J. F. Crapp c Bennett b A. V. Bedser	34	– b A. V. Bedser	18
B. O. Allen c Squires b E. A. Bedser	15	– c Watts b A. V. Bedser	47
G. M. Emmett run out	6	– lbw b A. V. Bedser	0
G. Lambert b A. V. Bedser	0	– b A. V. Bedser	8
L. M. Cranfield c Fishlock b A. V. Bedser	18	– not out	28
C. J. Scott b Parker	18	– not out	0
T. W. Goddard c Watts b Parker	4		
C. Cook not out	2		
B 5, l-b 3, n-b 1	9	B 15, l-b 7, n-b 1	23
	132	**(7 wkts dec.)**	**299**

Surrey

L. B. Fishlock c Barnett b Goddard	38	– b Cook	10
R. J. Gregory lbw b Goddard	5	– c Wilson b Goddard	87
H. S. Squires c Crapp b Cook	22	– c and b Goddard	11
T. H. Barling b Cook	15	– lbw b Goddard	49
J. F. Parker lbw b Goddard	31	– c Crapp b Goddard	36
E. A. Bedser lbw b Goddard	4	– lbw b Goddard	0
E. A. Watts b Cook	0	– b Goddard	3
N. H. Bennett c Scott b Cook	13	– b Goddard	0
A. V. Bedser b Cook	3	– c Barnett b Goddard	25
G. S. Mobey not out	1	– not out	2
A. R. Gover c Lambert b Cook	4	– b Goddard	7
B 3, l-b 1	4	B 3, l-b 3	6
	140		**236**

Surrey Bowling

	Overs	Mdns	Runs	Wkts	Overs	Mdns	Runs	Wkts
Gover	11	3	23	2	16	—	87	—
A. V. Bedser	21	3	49	3	29	4	72	4
Parker.	11.3	4	18	3	3	1	9	—
Watts	4	1	9	—	6	—	13	—
E. A. Bedser	14	6	24	1	29	5	79	3
Squires					5	1	11	—
Gregory					3	1	5	—

Gloucestershire Bowling

	Overs	Mdns	Runs	Wkts	Overs	Mdns	Runs	Wkts
Lambert	4	—	13	—	3	2	20	—
Scott	2	—	9	—	2	—	11	—
Goddard	22	8	45	4	33.3	11	82	9
Cook.	23	6	63	6	31	6	84	1
Cranfield.	2	—	6	—	8	1	23	—
Barnett					4	—	10	—

GLOUCESTERSHIRE v WORCESTERSHIRE

Played at Cheltenham, August 17, 19, 20, 1946

Worcestershire won by ten wickets. In a game which showed few batsmen to advantage, Perks, the Worcestershire fast-medium bowler, took chief honours. In the second Gloucestershire innings, when bowling unchanged on soft turf, he was unfortunate not to become the first Worcestershire player to take all ten wickets in an innings. He dismissed nine men in succession, but when Scott, one of the last pair of batsmen, skied a catch to slip, Singleton allowed the spinning ball to evade his grasp. Worcestershire required only 70 runs to win, and Singleton and Yarnold achieved the task in forty-five minutes.

Gloucestershire

C. J. Barnett lbw b Perks.	32	– c Bird b Perks	4
A. E. Wilson c Singleton b Perks.	1	– lbw b Perks	3
W. L. Neale lbw b Perks	33	– c Buller b Perks	10
J. F. Crapp b Perks	0	– lbw b Perks	25
B. O. Allen b Jackson	4	– c White b Perks	7
G. M. Emmett c Singleton b Jackson	16	– lbw b Perks	2
A. H. Brodhurst b Perks	3	– b Perks	0
L. M. Cranfield b Jackson.	4	– c Buller b Perks.	8
C. J. Scott b Jackson.	27	– c Wyatt b Jackson	11
T. W. Goddard c Buller b Jackson	0	– not out	2
C. Cook not out	6	– c Singleton b Perks	0
B 3, l-b 6, n-b 4	13	N-b 2	2
	139		74

Worcestershire

A. P. Singleton c Crapp b Scott	0	– not out 54
A. F. T. White c and b Barnett	1	
R. Howorth c Allen b Cook	38	
R. E. S. Wyatt lbw b Cook	24	
R. E. Bird lbw b Goddard	3	
D. M. Young lbw b Goddard	7	
H. Yarnold b Cranfield	32	– not out 14
R. Jenkins b Cranfield	10	
R. T. D. Perks c Barnett b Goddard	9	
P. F. Jackson b Cranfield	0	
S. Buller not out	9	
B 2, l-b 9	11	N-b 2 2
	144	**(No wkt) 70**

Worcestershire Bowling

	Overs	Mdns	Runs	Wkts	Overs	Mdns	Runs	Wkts
Perks	22	7	54	5	21	6	42	9
Wyatt	9	3	27	—	7	2	15	—
Jackson	20.1	6	40	5	12.5	6	15	1
Jenkins	2	1	4	—				
Singleton	1	—	1	—				
Howorth					1	1	—	—

Gloucestershire Bowling

	Overs	Mdns	Runs	Wkts	Overs	Mdns	Runs	Wkts
Scott	8	1	25	1	2	—	11	—
Barnett	6	2	5	1	1	1	—	—
Cook	20	4	38	2	4	1	14	—
Goddard	26	11	41	3	7	2	18	—
Cranfield	8.2	2	24	3				
Neale					3	—	18	—
Allen					1	—	7	—

GLOUCESTERSHIRE v DERBYSHIRE

Played at Bristol, June 18, 20, 1949

Gloucestershire won by an innings and one run. The match provided yet another triumph for Goddard, who, on a pitch of easy pace, took fifteen wickets with off-breaks for 107 runs. Apart from Elliott and, in the second innings, Revill, none of the Derbyshire batsmen played him confidently. This pair put on 88 for the second wicket when Derbyshire faced first innings arrears of 143. Then Goddard, in fourteen overs and a ball, dismissed nine men at a cost of 20 runs, bringing the match to a summary conclusion. Twice he took two wickets with following deliveries. Consistent batting against a steady attack, of which Rhodes, with leg-breaks, was the most effective member earned Gloucestershire their first innings advantage. Allen, during two hours and three-quarters, gave the brightest display, and Milton again showed admirable form.

Derbyshire

C. S. Elliott c Wilson b Cook	41	– st Wilson b Goddard	69
A. Townsend b Milton	19	– c Wilson b J. K. Graveney	0
A. Revill lbw b Cook	20	– lbw b Goddard	42
L. Johnson b Goddard	23	– lbw b Goddard	6
A. E. Rhodes c and b Goddard	11	– b Goddard	0
D. A. Skinner b Cook	11	– c Wilson b Goddard	4
E. Marsh lbw b Goddard	8	– c Allen b Goddard	8
C. Gladwin not out	16	– c Allen b Goddard	7
K. A. Shearwood b Goddard	4	– st Wilson b Goddard	2
W. H. Copson b Goddard	4	– b Goddard	0
L. Jackson c Wilson b Goddard	4	– not out	0
B 11, l-b 4, n-b 1	16	B 1, l-b 3	4
	177		**142**

Gloucestershire

A. E. Wilson c Skinner b Rhodes	32	J. K. Graveney st Shearwood b Rhodes	3
G. M. Emmett b Gladwin	29	Sir D. Bailey b Rhodes	4
J. F. Crapp c Elliott b Rhodes	33	T. W. Goddard b Rhodes	4
T. W. Graveney c Elliott b Rhodes	24	C. Cook not out	15
B. O. Allen lbw b Rhodes	93	B 3, l-b 2, w 2, n-b 1	8
G. Lambert lbw b Jackson	25		
C. A. Milton c Revill b Gladwin	50		**320**

Gloucestershire Bowling

	Overs	Mdns	Runs	Wkts	Overs	Mdns	Runs	Wkts
Lambert	10	—	26	—	6	1	12	—
J. K. Graveney	6	—	10	—	4	—	9	1
Milton	8	4	11	1				
Cook	27	8	68	3	28	10	56	—
Goddard	22.4	9	46	6	29.1	9	61	9

Derbyshire Bowling

	Overs	Mdns	Runs	Wkts
Copson	18	3	55	—
Gladwin	26.2	4	70	2
Jackson	15	1	46	1
Johnson	13	4	27	—
Rhodes	36	4	114	7

Umpires: A. E. Pothecary and T. J. Bartley.

GLOUCESTERSHIRE v WARWICKSHIRE

Played at Gloucester, July 20, 21, 22, 1949

Warwickshire won by 112 runs. They were mainly indebted to the batting of Dollery and the slow bowling of Hollies. In both innings Dollery overshadowed everybody. On the opening day he put together his highest score in first-class cricket, off-driving and cutting beautifully for three hours and twenty-five minutes and hitting four 6s and twenty-two 4s without making any serious error. Wolton and Kardar helped him in stands of 135 and 86, and Townsend also batted brightly. In the second innings, when his team-mates failed against Goddard, Dollery, scoring 73 in sixty-five minutes, hit the off-spin bowler for five 6s and also obtained five 4s. The Gloucestershire batsmen, with the exception of Crapp and T. W. Graveney, fared indifferently against Hollies, who took eleven wickets for 180 runs. Crapp hit fourteen 4s in three hours five minutes in the first innings. He and Graveney put on 92, and when Gloucestershire went in needing 270 to win, they scored 84 together. During the match Hollies and Goddard each took his 100th wicket of the season.

Warwickshire

K. A. Taylor b Cook	24	– c Crapp b Goddard	11
F. C. Gardner lbw b Lambert	0	– lbw b Goddard	28
A. Townsend run out	72	– c T. W. Graveney b Cook	7
J. S. Ord b Goddard	12	– lbw b Goddard	0
H. E. Dollery c Crapp b Goddard	200	– c T. W. Graveney b Goddard	73
A. V. Wolton lbw b Lambert	44	– b Goddard	7
A. H. Kardar not out	21	– c Allen b Goddard	9
C. W. Grove c Young b Cook	1	– b Goddard	0
T. L. Pritchard c Allen b Cook	13	– lbw b Goddard	6
R. T. Spooner st Wilson b Cook	1	– not out	11
B 1, l-b 9, n-b 2	12	B 1, l-b 4	5
	(9 wkts dec.) 400		**(9 wkts dec.) 157**

W. E. Hollies did not bat.

Gloucestershire

G. M. Emmett c Spooner b Townsend	37	– c Dollery b Pritchard	0
D. M. Young b Kardar	8	– b Kardar	3
B. O. Allen c Townsend b Hollies	15	– c Gardner b Kardar	6
J. F. Crapp run out	102	– c and b Hollies	50
T. W. Graveney b Grove	45	– c Gardner b Hollies	33
A. E. Wilson b Hollies	32	– c Spooner b Hollies	27
C. A. Milton st Spooner b Hollies	16	– c and b Hollies	27
G. Lambert b Hollies	12	– c Townsend b Hollies	0
J. K. Graveney b Hollies	2	– c Gardner b Hollies	0
T. W. Goddard run out	6	– not out	0
C. Cook not out	0	– b Pritchard	3
B 1, l-b 10, n-b 2	13	B 2, l-b 5, n-b 1	8
	288		**157**

Gloucestershire Bowling

	Overs	Mdns	Runs	Wkts	Overs	Mdns	Runs	Wkts
Lambert	25	6	93	2	6	1	26	—
J. K. Graveney	20	4	76	—	5	1	13	—
Milton	15	7	14	—				
Cook	44.3	14	119	4	15	3	43	1
Goddard	25	3	86	2	14.3	3	70	8

Warwickshire Bowling

	Overs	Mdns	Runs	Wkts	Overs	Mdns	Runs	Wkts
Pritchard	16	1	48	—	9.5	—	19	2
Grove	16	6	25	1	8	3	8	—
Hollies	44.1	16	101	5	32	11	79	6
Kardar	35	9	81	1	18	6	43	2
Townsend	11	3	20	1				

Umpires: A. Lockett and C. N. Woolley.

GLOUCESTERSHIRE v NORTHAMPTONSHIRE

Played at Bristol, August 27, 29, 30, 1949

Drawn. The batting of Brookes, who put together the biggest score of his career and equalled the highest ever made by a Northamptonshire batsman, dwarfed all else in the match. Specially strong in leg-side strokes and drives through the covers, he gave nothing like a chance during an innings of six hours and three-quarters; he hit a 5 and twenty-six 4s. E. Davies helped him add 144 for the second wicket, and Oldfield and Barrick batted skilfully. Gloucestershire were handicapped on the first day because Goddard, suffering from a strain, could not bowl. Despite bright play by Emmett, Gloucestershire lost four wickets for 121, but Crapp and Allen put on 117. Both Crapp, very patient, and Emmett completed 2,000 runs for the season. Leading by 94, Northamptonshire played out time. A century by Oldfield (thirteen 4s) lost merit when the regular bowlers were rested.

Northamptonshire

D. Brookes lbw b Goddard	257	– b Lambert	5
N. Oldfield run out	42	– not out	108
E. Davies run out	49	– lbw b Cook	17
F. Jakeman c Wilson b Scott	37	– b J. K. Graveney	2
D. Barrick b Goddard	50	– not out	27
F. R. Brown st Wilson b Goddard	2		
V. Broderick not out	0	– b Lambert	2
B 13, l-b 7, n-b 3	23	B 1, l-b 1, n-b 1	3

(6 wkts dec.) 460　　　　　　　　　　　　　　　(4 wkts) 164

R. W. Clarke, A. E. Nutter, R. G. Garlick and K. Fiddling did not bat.

Gloucestershire

G. M. Emmett lbw b Clarke	74	J. K. Graveney c Fiddling b Clarke	27
A. E. Wilson b Nutter	5	C. J. Scott run out	17
T. W. Graveney b Clarke	32	T. W. Goddard b Brown	1
J. F. Crapp c Fiddling b Nutter	114	C. Cook not out	2
C. A. Milton b Clarke	0	B 6, l-b 17, n-b 1	24
B. O. Allen b Garlick	70		
G. Lambert b Broderick	0		366

Gloucestershire Bowling

	Overs	Mdns	Runs	Wkts	Overs	Mdns	Runs	Wkts
Lambert	28	1	115	—	16	3	48	2
J. K. Graveney	30	3	95	—	8	—	13	1
Milton	9	1	19	—				
Cook	37	4	110	—	4	—	20	1
Scott	30	3	81	1	5	1	13	—
Goddard	6.1	1	17	3	9	3	18	—
Allen					4	1	27	—
Crapp					5	2	14	—
Emmett					2	—	8	—

Northamptonshire Bowling

	Overs	Mdns	Runs	Wkts
Nutter	30	4	82	2
Clarke	38	7	107	4
Brown	21.4	5	50	1
Garlick	31	8	52	1
Broderick	14	3	46	1
Barrick	1	—	5	—

Umpires: W. H. Ashdown and S. J. Staples.

GLOUCESTERSHIRE v KENT

Played at Bristol, May 13, 15, 16, 1950

Drawn. The bare result conveys none of the excitement which this match produced, especially on the afternoon of the third day. By that time Gloucestershire had been set the task of scoring 201 to win in 125 minutes, and seemed well on the way to accomplishing it when the scoreboard read 155 for four with half an hour remaining. Admirable off-spin bowling by Dovey, however, quickly transformed the situation, and the last over arrived with Gloucestershire still 15 short of their objective. Dovey took the eighth and ninth wickets with his third and fifth deliveries, but, in a tense atmosphere, Goddard survived the final ball. Earlier Ames scored a hundred in each innings for the third time in his career, the first taking two hours ten minutes and the second occupying an hour longer. His display of 112 saved Kent from complete collapse against the sustained pace bowling of Lambert, who took ten wickets in the match. Gloucestershire owed most for their commanding lead to Emmett, who revealed a wide range of strokes and made many runs by skilful placing. Young helped him in a three-figure opening partnership, though the remaining batsmen appeared uncertain against Wright.

Kent

A. E. Fagg lbw b Lambert	3	– b Lambert	0
A. H. Phebey b Lambert	10	– c Cook b Goddard	48
L. E. G. Ames c Wilson b Lambert	112	– b Lambert	119
P. Hearn st Wilson b Cook	22	– b J. Graveney	8
L. J. Todd b Cook	1	– run out	73
T. G. Evans c J. Graveney b Goddard	7	– c Allen b Lambert	66
A. C. Shirreff b Cook	5	– c Wilson b Milton	6
D. G. Clark b Lambert	16	– c Milton b Lambert	32
R. R. Dovey not out	4	– b Lambert	9
D. V. P. Wright c Cook b J. Graveney	1	– not out	11
F. Ridgway b Lambert	4		
B 3, l-b 4, n-b 1	8	B 4, l-b 8, n-b 2	14
	193	**(9 wkts dec.)**	**386**

Gloucestershire

G. M. Emmett c Fagg b Wright	188	– c and b Shirreff	13
D. M. Young c Evans b Shirreff	67	– c Ames b Dovey	75
T. W. Graveney b Shirreff	0	– b Shirreff	23
J. F. Crapp c Fagg b Wright	5	– c Phebey b Shirreff	2
C. A. Milton c Evans b Ridgway	15	– not out	12
B. O. Allen st Evans b Wright	24	– c Ames b Wright	6
A. E. Wilson c Evans b Dovey	2	– lbw b Dovey	4
G. E. Lambert b Wright	11	– b Dovey	3
J. K. Graveney c Shirreff b Wright	40	– b Dovey	38
T. W. Goddard lbw b Wright	13	– not out	0
C. Cook not out	1	– b Dovey	4
B 4, l-b 6, w 3	13	B 1, l-b 10, w 1, n-b 1	13
	379	**(9 wkts)**	**193**

Gloucestershire Bowling

	Overs	Mdns	Runs	Wkts	Overs	Mdns	Runs	Wkts
Lambert	15.5	2	41	5	36	4	131	5
J. Graveney	14	3	39	1	20	4	59	1
Milton	7	2	19	—	13	1	44	1
Cook	23	9	44	3	27	5	76	—
Goddard	23	8	42	1	23	3	62	1

Kent Bowling

	Overs	Mdns	Runs	Wkts	Overs	Mdns	Runs	Wkts
Ridgway	26	5	86	1	11	—	55	—
Shirreff	21	6	66	2	9	1	47	3
Wright	24.5	4	138	6	7	—	46	1
Dovey	26	10	53	1	9	1	32	5
Todd	6	—	23	—				

Umpires: D. Davies and A. E. Pothecary.

GLOUCESTERSHIRE v LANCASHIRE

Played at Gloucester, June 7, 8, 9, 1950

Lancashire won by 82 runs. Bowlers dominated the game to such an extent that seventeen wickets fell on the first day for 240 runs. The Lancashire batsmen found the slow left-arm deliveries of Cook required careful watching on a pitch responsive to spin, and most of them lost their wickets making defensive strokes. Gloucestershire gave an equally indifferent display against Tattersall and Hilton, and, despite bold strokes by Lambert, failed by 33 to reach their opponents' total. When Lancashire batted again, Ikin and Place adopted cautious methods which later events justified. They put on 82 before Cook repeated his successes and earned a match analysis of thirteen for 87. Gloucestershire, left to score 197 on wearing turf, never looked like succeeding after the opening pair were separated. Tattersall and Hilton shared the bowling honours, Tattersall's full figures being twelve for 68.

Lancashire

W. Place c Wilson b Cook	21	– c Wilson b Scott	27
J. T. Ikin b J. Graveney	1	– lbw b Cook	60
G. A. Edrich lbw b Lambert	5	– b Cook	0
K. Grieves c Emmett b Lambert	17	– b Cook	11
A. Wharton c Milton b Lambert	34	– c Emmett b Cook	27
N. D. Howard c Scott b Cook	39	– c Wilson b Cook	1
J. G. Lomax c Scott b Cook	8	– c T. Graveney b Cook	0
R. Tattersall st Wilson b Cook	10	– c Young b Goddard	15
M. J. Hilton c J. Graveney b Cook	24	– st Wilson b Cook	3
R. Pollard not out	1	– not out	9
A. Barlow c Scott b Cook	0	– lbw b Goddard	1
L-b 4	4	L-b 9	9
	164		**163**

Gloucestershire

G. M. Emmett c and b Hilton	8	– c Grieves b Hilton	38
D. M. Young b Tattersall	4	– lbw b Hilton	41
T. W. Graveney c Tattersall b Hilton	23	– b Tattersall	0
J. F. Crapp c and b Tattersall	9	– c Grieves b Tattersall	0
C. A. Milton c Ikin b Tattersall	4	– c Barlow b Hilton	0
A. E. Wilson c Ikin b Hilton	0	– c Barlow b Tattersall	8
J. K. Graveney c Edrich b Hilton	3	– c Place b Hilton	12
G. E. Lambert c Pollard b Tattersall	44	– c Edrich b Tattersall	8
C. J. Scott b Tattersall	2	– b Tattersall	0
T. W. Goddard not out	12	– not out	0
C. Cook c Lomax b Tattersall	6	– c Ikin b Tattersall	0
B 11, l-b 5	16	B 7	7
	131		**114**

Gloucestershire Bowling

	Overs	Mdns	Runs	Wkts	Overs	Mdns	Runs	Wkts
Lambert	22	2	49	3	4	—	9	—
Scott	7	—	18	—	20	3	43	1
J. Graveney	4	2	6	1	4	1	4	—
Milton	8	3	13	—				
Goddard	20	9	42	—	21.2	7	43	2
Cook	15	6	32	6	42	17	55	7

Lancashire Bowling

	Overs	Mdns	Runs	Wkts	Overs	Mdns	Runs	Wkts
Pollard	5	1	12	—	3	—	7	—
Lomax	3	—	4	—	2	—	7	—
Tattersall	28.4	13	39	6	21	8	29	6
Hilton	27	12	51	4	24	8	55	4
Grieves	2	—	9	—	.4	1	9	—

Umpires: T. Spencer and A. Skelding.

TOM GODDARD RETIRES

Thomas William John Goddard

(Gloucestershire and England, 1922-1951)

By David Moore

When, in the spring of 1951, Tom Goddard was struck down by pneumonia and pleurisy it was feared that such a severe illness might hasten the end of a wonderful career which had already extended far beyond the normal span. And so, unhappily, it proved. It was clear when he took his place in the Gloucestershire team at the end of May that he was far from fit, and though he struggled on for several weeks he found himself obliged in mid-July to withdraw from the side and to announce his retirement from first-class cricket. So there passed from the scene the greatest off-break bowler of recent times.

For Thomas William John Goddard, born October 1, 1900, the road to fame was no easy one. When he first played for Gloucestershire he bowled fast-medium, and success was slow to come. Indeed, the result of his first six seasons' work was so undistinguished that after the summer of 1927 he left the county and joined the MCC staff. It seemed then that no more would be heard of him in first-class cricket.

Then one day in 1928 Beverley Lyon saw him practising off-breaks in the nets at Lord's. He was so impressed that he immediately urged the Gloucestershire authorities to re-engage him. And so it came about that in 1929 he rejoined his native county.

The sequel was sensational. In his first season as a spin bowler Goddard actually took more wickets than had come his way in the whole of his earlier career. For years Gloucestershire had been practically a one-man bowling side. Now, at last, Charles Parker had the supporter he needed. The two men, orthodox left-hander and off-spinner, afforded a perfect contrast, and for three seasons they were – not forgetting Larwood and Voce – the most deadly pair of bowlers in the land. Thanks to their efforts Gloucestershire were fourth in the Championship in 1929 and second in 1930 and 1931. During this period they took between them in purely county matches 904 wickets at an average cost of 15.82. Their greatest triumph occurred at Bristol in 1930, when, thanks to their superlative bowling on a worn wicket, the Australians were held to a tie.

For four seasons after 1931 Parker continued to play for Gloucestershire, but he was not the power of former years. Consequently, the role of senior partner devolved on Goddard, and how well he shouldered his new responsibility may be seen in the records.

When Parker retired Goddard found a new partner in Sinfield. The old contrast was lacking, but in two of the three years during which the pair bore the burden of the Gloucestershire bowling their side were fourth in the Championship. In 1939 they were third, Goddard for the third time in five years taking 200 wickets.

When first-class cricket was resumed after the war Goddard was forty-five – an age at which most county players have long since retired to the chimney-corner to dream of their past glories. But if time had deprived Goddard's hand of any of its cunning, so much was not apparent from the ring-side, nor was it reflected in his figures, which reveal that in the two seasons 1946 and 1947 he took 415 wickets – more than in any other two successive years – for 17.38 runs each. In 1948 he was somewhat less dominant, and it was freely whispered that his day was done. Yet a year later he came out virtually top of the national bowling averages, while in 1950, his last full season, he would assuredly have taken 150 wickets once again had he not missed several matches through indisposition.

Considering his phenomenal achievements in county cricket, Goddard's appearances in Test matches were on a very modest scale; in this respect his experience was curiously similar to that of A. P. Freeman. Like Parker, he played only once against Australia. Twice he went to South Africa with MCC teams. He met with little success in 1930-31; but in 1938-39 he played in three Tests, and in the first, at Johannesburg, did the hat-trick. In England, apart from his one appearance against Australia, he played twice against New Zealand in 1937 and twice against West Indies in 1939. In the second innings of New Zealand at Old Trafford in 1937 he took six wickets for 29.

On good pitches Goddard, with his accuracy and subtle nuances of flight, exacted respect from the best of batsmen. When the turf was worn or sticky he was at times unplayable. Delivering the ball from a height of some eight feet, he could make it rise from a length to the batsman's knuckles, while his long fingers spun it venomously towards the waiting short-legs. Though his stock delivery was the off-break, he occasionally turned a little from leg – a phenomenon which he himself was at a loss to explain. As a batsman he took himself seriously, and excelled in those situations in which nerve and character count for at least as much as pure technique.

To Goddard the bowler all batsmen were his sworn enemies. He had in him something of that tigerish quality which was also possessed by O'Reilly and which reached its finest flower in George Gibson Macaulay. For him no day could be too long, no captain's demands too great. His appeal, which was an urgent imperative, reflected no dishonesty of purpose but merely a perennial keenness and exuberance which accounted in no small measure for his long immunity to the passage of the years. But now at last his season has ended; and for a while the cricket field will seem a poorer place.

GLOUCESTERSHIRE v HAMPSHIRE

Played at Bristol, June 21, 23, 24, 1958

Hampshire won by five wickets. The fine medium-fast bowling of Shackleton, who took thirteen wickets for 106 in the match, proved the deciding factor. Only Young and Mortimore played him with assurance. On lively turf on the opening day, Shackleton, in his last spell with the new ball, sent back five men for 17 runs and finished with nine for 59. The controlled pace of Smith and Brown discomfited Hampshire, and Gloucestershire led by 112, but more splendid bowling by Shackleton, supported admirably by Heath, turned the tables for the visitors. Hampshire, in the end, found themselves needing 233 to win and with Marshall setting the pace with a century in just over two hours they successfully finished their task early on the last morning.

Gloucestershire

D. M. Young b Burden	72 – b Heath	1
D. Carpenter b Shackleton	2 – c Ingleby-Mackenzie b Heath	7
R. B. Nicholls c Sainsbury b Shackleton	17 – b Heath	10
C. A. Milton lbw b Shackleton	1 – b Shackleton	27
G. M. Emmett c Sainsbury b Shackleton	4 – lbw b Shackleton	0
J. B. Mortimore b Shackleton	55 – c Pitman b Shackleton	21
A. S. Brown lbw b Shackleton	20 – b Shackleton	12
D. R. Smith lbw b Shackleton	6 – b Heath	3
G. G. M. Wiltshire b Shackleton	6 – c Harrison b Heath	5
B. J. Meyer not out	15 – not out	21
C. Cook c and b Shackleton	0 – b Heath	6
L-b 3	3 B 4, l-b 3	7

1/5 2/41 3/43 4/51 5/123   201   1/1 2/14 3/26 4/27 5/59   120
6/173 7/174 8/180 9/201   6/74 7/83 8/83 9/92

Hampshire

R. E. Marshall b Smith	5 – c Carpenter b Mortimore	122
J. R. Gray b Brown	4 – c Meyer b Brown	24
H. Horton lbw b Brown	1 – c Meyer b Cook	35
R. W. C. Pitman not out	39 – not out	13
H. M. Barnard b Brown	1 – c Smith b Mortimore	3
A. C. D. Ingleby-Mackenzie c Emmett b Smith	9 – c Wiltshire b Mortimore	21
P. J. Sainsbury b Smith	6 – not out	3
L. Harrison c Milton b Mortimore	12	
D. Shackleton b Brown	1	
M. Heath b Mortimore	0	
M. D. Burden b Brown	5	
B 6	6 B 8, l-b 4	12

1/6 2/9 3/10 4/11 5/28   89   1/70 2/185 3/189   (5 wkts) 233
6/42 7/67 8/78 9/81   4/195 5/220

Hampshire Bowling

	Overs	Mdns	Runs	Wkts	Overs	Mdns	Runs	Wkts
Shackleton	31.4	8	59	9	27	11	47	4
Heath	24	3	52	—	24.4	10	53	6
Burden	21	6	56	1				
Gray	9	1	25	—	2	—	13	—
Sainsbury	5	3	6	—				

Gloucestershire Bowling

	Overs	Mdns	Runs	Wkts	Overs	Mdns	Runs	Wkts
Smith	16	3	32	3	14	2	59	
Brown	17.1	10	25	5	19	5	42	1
Wiltshire	7	2	17	—	5	1	22	—
Mortimore	5	1	9	2	19.4	6	50	3
Cook					24	9	48	1

Umpires: T. W. Spencer and T. J. Bartley.

GLOUCESTERSHIRE v HAMPSHIRE

Played at Bristol, May 9, 11, 12, 1959

Hampshire won by two wickets. Fine medium-fast bowling by Shackleton, who took nine for 81 in the first innings, and delightful free hitting by Marshall who scored 150, deservedly brought their side the honours, but they won with only four minutes to spare. Needing 144 in two hours and forty minutes, Hampshire had to struggle against the unchanged medium-fast attack of Smith and Brown, but Harrison's steadiness settled the issue. Harrison, with four catches at the wicket, played a big part in Shackleton's success on the opening day. Lively and accurate, with deceptive swing, Shackleton took six of the first seven wickets for 11 runs out of 35 before Allen and Smith hit boldly. Marshall's grand innings, marked by powerful and stylish driving, took him a little under three and a half hours, and included one 6 and twenty-one 4s. He and Gray, with their opening partnership of 214, established a new record for Hampshire for the first wicket.

Gloucestershire

D. M. Young c Harrison b Shackleton	5	– lbw b Shackleton	2
D. Carpenter c Harrison b Shackleton	3	– c Sainsbury b Burden	36
R. B. Nicholls c Harrison b Heath	2	– c Shackleton b Heath	10
T. W. Graveney b Shackleton	5	– b Heath	46
D. G. Hawkins lbw b Shackleton	2	– c and b Sainsbury	25
J. B. Mortimore c Harrison b Shackleton	14	– c and b Shackleton	45
A. S. Brown lbw b Shackleton	0	– lbw b Shackleton	24
D. R. Smith c Gray b Shackleton	49	– lbw b Heath	6
D. A. Allen b Shackleton	62	– not out	52
B. J. Meyer not out	26	– c Burden b Sainsbury	19
C. Cook c Burden b Shackleton	1	– b Burden	16
		B 4, l-b 4, n-b 1	9

1/7 2/10 3/10 4/15 5/30   169   1/2 2/25 3/90 4/112 5/143   290
6/30 7/35 8/128 9/151   6/186 7/195 8/205 9/253

Hampshire

R. E. Marshall st Meyer b Cook	150	– b Smith	10
J. H. Gray c Nicholls b Mortimore	62	– c Meyer b Smith	33
H. Horton st Meyer b Mortimore	11	– c and b Brown	7
R. W. C. Pitman lbw b Cook	13	– lbw b Smith	16
D. O. Baldry c Mortimore b Cook	4	– b Brown	12
A. C. D. Ingleby-Mackenzie b Smith	19	– c Meyer b Smith	10
P. J. Sainsbury c Meyer b Smith	6	– c Carpenter b Brown	16
L. Harrison b Smith	0	– not out	20
D. Shackleton c Nicholls b Brown	1	– c Young b Brown	12
M. Heath not out	11	– not out	0
M. D. Burden b Brown	17		
B 7, l-b 15	22	B 2, l-b 8	10

1/214 2/227 3/243 4/253 5/265   316   1/20 2/37 3/55 4/82   (8 wkts) 146
6/282 7/282 8/287 9/289   5/88 6/112 7/120 8/142

Hampshire Bowling

	Overs	Mdns	Runs	Wkts	Overs	Mdns	Runs	Wkts
Shackleton	31.2	8	81	9	39	14	68	3
Heath	19	5	54	1	38	9	104	3
Gray	4	2	6	—	19	8	37	—
Sainsbury	14	5	28	—	10	4	16	2
Burden					27	9	56	2

Gloucestershire Bowling

	Overs	Mdns	Runs	Wkts	Overs	Mdns	Runs	Wkts
Smith	16	—	71	3	27	8	57	4
Brown............	13.2	5	27	2	27	6	79	4
Mortimore	47	15	104	2				
Cook.............	45	20	68	3				
Allen............	5	1	24	—				

Umpires: R. S. Lay and D. J. Wood.

GLOUCESTERSHIRE v LANCASHIRE

Played at Gloucester, July 4, 6, 7, 1959

Lancashire won by 111 runs. They held the whip hand from the start and, despite a century by Milton and two good innings by Graveney, Gloucestershire were convincingly beaten. Barber and Wharton, in an opening partnership of 104, and Grieves, who drove powerfully, batted well for Lancashire on the first day. Milton, patient yet severe on anything loose, hit thirteen 4s, but Gloucestershire were 61 behind on the first innings. Allen, flighting his off-spinners cleverly, helped to bring a breakdown in Lancashire's second innings after another good beginning by Barber and Wharton, and Gloucestershire were set to make 237 in just over three hours. Graveney resisted gallantly, but Dyson finished the match by taking the last four wickets for 12 runs. Clayton, the Lancashire wicket-keeper, dismissed nine men in the match.

Lancashire

R. W. Barber c Meyer b Smith	74	– c Young b Allen	79
A. Wharton c Meyer b Allen....................	48	– b Allen	31
J. D. Bond c Milton b Cook	24	– run out	3
K. Grieves c Brown b Smith	68	– b Allen	3
C. Washbrook lbw b Smith.....................	39	– b Allen	28
B. Booth b Brown	4	– c Hawkins b Allen	0
J. Dyson c Young b Cook.....................	8	– not out	0
G. Clayton b Brown	3	– c Milton b Cook	12
M. J. Hilton st Meyer b Brown	5	– b Allen	4
J. B. Statham b Brown	28	– c Graveney b Allen..........	6
K. Higgs not out	6	– c Allen b Cook	0
B 12, l-b 1, w 5, n-b 1	19	B 8, l-b 1...............	9

1/104 2/138 3/171 4/268 5/275   326   1/76 2/117 3/120 4/120 5/126   175
6/275 7/281 8/291 9/293   6/142 7/169 8/173 9/174

Gloucestershire

D. M. Young b Statham	8	– c Clayton b Statham............	0
C. A. Milton c Wharton b Higgs................	115	– st Clayton b Hilton..............	19
C. T. M. Pugh c Clayton b Higgs	0	– not out	1
T. W. Graveney c Clayton b Higgs.............	48	– c Clayton b Statham..........	60
R. B. Nicholls c Booth b Statham	33	– c Washbrook b Dyson	1
D. G. Hawkins b Higgs......................	8	– b Statham	15
D. A. Allen c Clayton b Statham	3	– lbw b Hilton	5
A. S. Brown not out	17	– c Booth b Dyson.............	8
D. R. Smith c Hilton b Dyson.................	6	– c Statham b Dyson...........	4
B. J. Meyer c Clayton b Higgs	5	– not out	4
C. Cook c Clayton b Higgs....................	6	– c Clayton b Dyson	0
B 2, l-b 9, w 5	16	B 4, l-b 4...............	8

1/24 2/25 3/127 4/214 5/222   265   1/0 2/3 3/31 4/54 5/94   125
6/225 7/227 8/243 9/247   6/103 7/113 8/117 9/121

Gloucestershire Bowling

	Overs	Mdns	Runs	Wkts	Overs	Mdns	Runs	Wkts
Smith	32	8	65	3	7	1	23	—
Brown............	36.1	7	82	4	3	1	9	—
Allen.............	29	11	67	1	22.2	9	66	7
Cook.............	33	13	77	2	23	7	68	2
Hawkins	3	1	16	—				

Lancashire Bowling

	Overs	Mdns	Runs	Wkts	Overs	Mdns	Runs	Wkts
Statham	30	9	61	3	11	3	13	3
Higgs	28.2	6	56	6	4	2	6	—
Dyson............	31	17	47	1	14.3	6	23	4
Hilton	15	6	44	—	19	12	35	2
Barber...........	5	1	13	—	9	1	29	—
Booth	5	—	28	—	3	—	11	—

Umpires: W. F. Price and H. Yarnold.

GLOUCESTERSHIRE v YORKSHIRE

Played at Bristol, August 22, 24, 25, 1959

Gloucestershire won by an innings and 77 runs. Without their Test players, Yorkshire were out-played and their dismissal in the first innings for 35 settled the issue. Graveney, back to his best form after injury, drove cleanly and helped Gloucestershire recover from a shaky start, and with Mortimore hitting aggressively Yorkshire faced a substantial total. Their amazing collapse on a pitch which had sweated proved so startling that Brown and Smith, bowling unchanged, shot out their rivals in seventy-five minutes, with the last six batsmen all registering "ducks." Both medium-fast bowlers made the ball swing in the air and move disturbingly off the pitch, and Brown achieved the remarkable analysis of seven wickets for 11 runs in eleven overs. Bolus alone reached double figures and when Yorkshire followed on he justified his promotion to number one as partner to Taylor by defying his opponents for nearly four hours, but he received little protracted support and Smith and Brown once more dominated proceedings. Yorkshire, 141 for seven at the close of the second day, were beaten after an hour's cricket next morning.

Gloucestershire

D. M. Young c Bolus b Platt.............	20	D. A. Allen run out....................	16
C. A. Milton c Bolus b Platt.............	15	D. R. Smith not out....................	49
R. B. Nicholls lbw b Close	3	B. J. Meyer not out	23
T. W. Graveney b Birkenshaw	67	B 6, l-b 5	11
D. G. Hawkins st Binks b Close	13		
J. B. Mortimore c Binks b Taylor	76	1/33 2/38 3/38 4/96 (8 wkts dec.) 294	
A. Brown b Birkenshaw	1	5/150 6/162 7/198 8/223	

C. Cook did not bat.

Yorkshire

W. B. Stott b Smith	1	– b Smith		2
K. Taylor b Brown	7	– b Brown		8
D. E. V. Padgett c Meyer b Brown	4	– hit wkt b Allen		12
D. B. Close lbw b Smith	3	– b Mortimore		1
J. B. Bolus not out	12	– lbw b Brown		91
H. D. Bird b Brown	0	– run out		5
J. Birkenshaw b Brown	0	– b Smith		10
D. Wilson b Smith	0	– c Nicholls b Smith		9
J. R. Burnet lbw b Brown	0	– not out		22
J. G. Binks c Meyer b Brown	0	– b Smith		11
R. K. Platt b Brown	0	– b Brown		4
B 4, l-b 3, n-b 1	8	B 4, l-b 2, w 1		7

1/14 2/16 3/22 4/22 5/22   35   1/27 2/44 3/96 4/97 5/109   182
6/25 7/30 8/33 9/35   6/136 7/136 8/157 9/175

Yorkshire Bowling

	Overs	Mdns	Runs	Wkts
Platt	29	10	59	2
Close	42	10	115	2
Taylor	18	7	26	1
Wilson	21	8	34	—
Birkenshaw	18	4	49	2

Gloucestershire Bowling

	Overs	Mdns	Runs	Wkts	Overs	Mdns	Runs	Wkts
Smith	11	3	16	3	35	11	68	4
Brown	10.5	5	22	7	27.5	11	54	3
Mortimore					28	17	19	1
Cook					5	—	15	—
Allen					16	7	19	1

Umpires: D. Davies and J. F. Crapp.

GLOUCESTERSHIRE v SURREY

Played at Gloucester, August 26, 27, 1959

Surrey won by 89 runs, taking 12 points in a vital match which destroyed Gloucestershire's hopes of winning the Championship. Spin bowlers were masters on turf which allowed the ball to turn and lift disconcertingly, and the skill of Laker and Lock, who between them took nineteen wickets, decided the fortunes of an exciting match. Coming events were foreshadowed when Allen and Cook disposed of Surrey on the opening day in three and a half hours, and 45 by Edrich, who stayed till sixth out at 93, was a very creditable effort. Surrey wasted no time in calling on their spin bowlers, and Gloucestershire, in their turn, were nonplussed and cheaply dismissed. Only Graveney stayed long. The day's batting failures were not finished. Cook snatched two wickets with his first two deliveries in the second innings and Surrey were 39 ahead at the close with eight wickets standing.

Bold stroke-play by Barrington, whose first scoring stroke was a 6 off Cook, steadied Surrey on the second morning and Gloucestershire found themselves needing 161 to win. A. V. Bedser once more put his faith in Laker and Lock. Given the new ball they proved so devastating that Gloucestershire lost their first seven wickets for 26 and despite a little spirited hitting by Smith and Allen the issue on a pitch which had become dry and dusty was quickly settled. Laker finished with eleven wickets for 80 runs and Lock eight for 69.

Surrey

J. H. Edrich b Cook	45	– c Milton b Allen 14
A. B. D. Parsons c Meyer b Smith	7	– c Milton b Cook 0
K. F. Barrington c Milton b Smith	12	– c Milton b Cook 49
M. J. Stewart lbw b Allen	7	– c Brown b Mortimore 29
D. G. W. Fletcher c Brown b Allen	0	– b Mortimore 0
R. Swetman c Smith b Cook	13	– c Brown b Mortimore 11
D. Gibson c Nicholls b Allen	8	– b Cook 0
E. A. Bedser not out	23	– c Milton b Cook 8
G. A. R. Lock lbw b Cook	1	– c Young b Cook 16
J. C. Laker c Smith b Allen	0	– lbw b Mortimore 3
A. V. Bedser b Allen	11	– not out 0
L-b 3	3	L-b 1 1

1/17 2/35 3/45 4/45 5/70   **130**   1/0 2/0 3/58 4/77 5/79   **131**
6/92 7/109 8/110 9/119   6/102 7/111 8/111 9/131

Gloucestershire

D. M. Young c Stewart b Laker	8	– b Laker 6
C. A. Milton c Stewart b Laker	12	– b Lock 6
R. B. Nicholls c A. Bedser b Lock	2	– c Stewart b Laker 1
T. W. Graveney c and b Lock	31	– b Lock 0
D. G. Hawkins c Swetman b Lock	0	– st Swetman b Laker 0
J. B. Mortimore c Parsons b Laker	13	– c A. Bedser b Lock 0
A. S. Brown b Laker	0	– c Lock b Laker 5
D. A. Allen c Lock b Laker	16	– not out 18
D. R. Smith c Barrington b Lock	2	– lbw b Laker 28
B. J. Meyer c Edrich b Lock	17	– run out 0
C. Cook not out	0	– c Edrich b Laker 0
		B 6, l-b 1 7

1/13 2/22 3/22 4/32 5/45   **101**   1/7 2/13 3/13 4/13 5/13   **71**
6/45 7/82 8/82 9/84   6/22 7/26 8/66 9/71

Gloucestershire Bowling

	Overs	Mdns	Runs	Wkts	Overs	Mdns	Runs	Wkts
Smith	17	5	37	2				
Brown	3	1	5	—				
Mortimore	18	14	9	—	23	14	28	4
Allen	19.5	8	43	5	13	6	36	1
Cook	15	6	33	3	27.3	12	66	5

Surrey Bowling

	Overs	Mdns	Runs	Wkts	Overs	Mdns	Runs	Wkts
A. Bedser	2	—	7	—				
Gibson	1	1	—	—				
Laker	21	7	53	5	15	6	27	6
Lock	23.2	13	32	5	15	6	37	3
E. Bedser	4	—	9	—				

Umpires: C. S. Elliott and D. Davies.

GLOUCESTERSHIRE v YORKSHIRE

(C. A. Milton's Benefit)

Played at Bristol, June 21, 22, 23, 1961

Gloucestershire won by eight wickets. They were the better team all through, and their combination of accurate medium-fast bowling and skilful spin-bowling proved too much for the visitors. Allen bowled his off-spinners particularly well, taking eight for 62 in the match. Mortimore supplemented his good bowling with firm stroke-play which brought him 57, the highest score of the match. Wilson was Yorkshire's soundest batsman. The game had to go to a third day because Gloucestershire, after claiming the extra half-hour and disposing of Yorkshire's last wicket, could only score 23, out of the 26 they needed to win, in the remaining eighteen minutes. The last day's play consisted of one ball. All the players changed into flannels for the rather farcical closing stage. Bainbridge bowled the one delivery needed and Bernard, whose name had been drawn out of a hat to accompany Nicholls to the wicket, off-drove it to the boundary.

Yorkshire

J. B. Stott b A'Court	16	– b Allen		30
J. B. Bolus b A'Court	26	– b A'Court		4
D. E. V. Padgett c Mortimore b Cook	37	– lbw b Mortimore		13
D. B. Close b Brown	13	– c A'Court b Allen		4
K. Taylor b Brown	0	– lbw b Mortimore		0
*J. V. Wilson c Bernard b Allen	53	– c Milton b Allen		30
K. Gillhouley c Hawkins b Allen	0	– b Cook		13
A. B. Bainbridge lbw b Allen	0	– lbw b Allen		5
†J. G. Binks b Cook	0	– b Cook		8
B. Turner not out	3	– not out		3
M. Ryan b Cook	0	– b Allen		0
B 4, l-b 2, n-b 1	7	B 9, l-b 2		11

1/33 2/62 3/85 4/85 5/130   **155**   1/7 2/20 3/25 4/25 5/66   **121**
6/137 7/143 8/152 9/152   6/83 7/107 8/107 9/119

Gloucestershire

R. B. Nicholls c and b Gillhouley	19	– not out		12
D. Carpenter c Binks b Gillhouley	32	– st Binks b Gillhouley		1
D. G. Hawkins lbw b Gillhouley	35			
*C. A. Milton c Gillhouley b Bainbridge	29			
J. R. Bernard lbw b Gillhouley	4	– not out		4
A. S. Brown b Ryan	31			
J. B. Mortimore c sub b Bainbridge	57			
D. A. Allen b Turner	6			
†B. J. Meyer c Close b Ryan	3	– b Bainbridge		9
D. G. A'Court c and b Gillhouley	16			
C. Cook not out	0			
B 13, l-b 6	19	L-b 1		1

1/41 2/62 3/103 4/109 5/142   **251**   1/4 2/23   **(2 wkts) 27**
6/171 7/190 8/199 9/231

Gloucestershire Bowling

	Overs	Mdns	Runs	Wkts	Overs	Mdns	Runs	Wkts
A'Court	22	5	37	2	6	4	12	1
Brown	15	6	30	2	4	1	8	—
Bernard	5	3	9	—				
Cook	25	15	38	3	16	8	24	2
Mortimore	20	12	19	—	15	7	19	2
Allen	11	7	15	3	20.3	7	47	5

Yorkshire Bowling

	Overs	Mdns	Runs	Wkts	Overs	Mdns	Runs	Wkts
Ryan............	20	2	55	2				
Turner...........	14	6	30	1				
Taylor...........	13	5	21	—				
Gillhouley........	42	19	70	5	4	1	13	1
Bainbridge	45	24	56	2	4	2	13	1

Umpires: J. Arnold and W. F. Price.

GLOUCESTERSHIRE v DERBYSHIRE

Played at Gloucester, July 5, 6, 7, 1961

Drawn. Most of the excitement – apart from a hat-trick by A'Court on the first day – came in the closing stages after Gloucestershire had been left to make 223 to win. With just under an hour left and with six wickets in hand, the home county were baulked by a heavy rainstorm. Play was held up for almost half an hour then Gloucestershire, going all out regardless of wickets to make the runs, reached 190 for eight, with Young unable to bat through injury. It seemed likely at this stage that Derbyshire would win, but Cook and Meyer safely played through the remaining nine deliveries from Rhodes and Buxton. Johnson was Derbyshire's best batsman. His second-innings century contained many forceful drives and cuts.

Derbyshire

C. Lee lbw b A'Court	25	– lbw b Cook...................	31
I. W. Hall c Meyer b Brown	11	– c Meyer b Smith	28
H. L. Johnson b Brown......................	3	– b Brown	122
*D. B. Carr b A'Court	17	– c sub b Brown.................	59
W. F. Oates lbw b A'Court....................	1	– b A'Court....................	13
D. C. Morgan b A'Court......................	0	– b Cook	11
I. R. Buxton b A'Court......................	0	– c Milton b Cook	3
†G. O. Dawkes c Young b A'Court.............	28	– retired hurt	7
E. Smith b Smith...........................	16	– c sub b Cook.................	0
T. J. P. Eyre not out	33	– c Milton b Cook	4
H. J. Rhodes c Milton b Brown................	20	– not out	0
B 1, l-b 9	10	B 2, l-b 3, w 1, n-b 1	7

1/28 2/40 3/40 4/43 5/43   164   1/50 2/79 3/227 4/247 5/266   285
6/43 7/86 8/87 9/123   6/279 7/279 8/285 9/285

Gloucestershire

R. B. Nicholls c Dawkes b Rhodes	13	– c Carr b Buxton	44
D. Carpenter c Hall b Buxton..................	14	– b Eyre.......................	5
D. G. Hawkins b Buxton......................	2	– lbw b Morgan	20
*C. A. Milton b Rhodes......................	48	– run out	65
D. M. Young c and b Buxton	6		
A. S. Brown c Morgan b Eyre..................	56	– run out	40
J. B. Mortimore b Rhodes.....................	31	– c Morgan b Buxton............	3
†B. J. Meyer not out	32	– not out	1
D. R. Smith c Dawkes b Carr..................	21	– b Buxton.....................	2
D. G. A'Court c Morgan b Carr................	1	– b Rhodes.....................	2
C. Cook c Eyre b Carr	0	– not out	0
L-b 1, n-b 2	3	B 4, l-b 4	8

1/23 2/27 3/36 4/43 5/119   227   1/13 2/73 3/73 4/176   (8 wkts) 190
6/170 7/174 8/217 9/221   5/184 6/187 7/187 8/190

Gloucestershire Bowling

	Overs	Mdns	Runs	Wkts	Overs	Mdns	Runs	Wkts
Smith	24	5	66	1	29	7	63	1
A'Court	20	3	50	6	33	8	81	1
Brown.	18.3	7	34	3	15	6	43	2
Milton.	1	—	4	—				
Cook.					26.5	12	41	5
Mortimore					24	10	50	—

Derbyshire Bowling

	Overs	Mdns	Runs	Wkts	Overs	Mdns	Runs	Wkts
Rhodes	38	11	63	3	15	5	44	1
Eyre	11	4	22	1	12	5	23	1
Buxton	21	9	48	3	15	3	45	3
Morgan.	19	7	29	—	13	4	39	1
Smith	9	1	25	—				
Carr	17.2	4	37	3	7	—	31	—

Umpires: W. E. Phillipson and H. E. Hammond.

GLOUCESTERSHIRE v KENT

Played at Bristol, August 29, 30, 31, 1962

Gloucestershire won by five wickets. The game, which produced two not out centuries by Milton and some fine batting by Cowdrey and Mortimore, had an exciting conclusion, for Milton hit the winning run and completed his second hundred off what would, in any case, have been the last ball of the match. The final day yielded 467 runs for the loss of only five wickets. Cowdrey, with a superb display of driving, pulling and cutting, hit twenty-four 4s in 148 and set his rivals to make 247 for victory in two hours and fifty minutes. Milton and Mortimore helped to carry their side to success in a lively fifth wicket stand of 133 in an hour and a quarter. Windows, with accurate bowling in the first innings which brought him seven wickets for 59, played his part in giving Gloucestershire an early advantage.

Kent

P. E. Richardson c Nicholls b Windows	54	– c Pugh b Smith	13
D. Nicholls b Windows.	10	– b Brown	11
R. C. Wilson b Windows.	60	– b Mortimore	30
*M. C. Cowdrey c Mortimore b Brown	66	– not out	148
B. W. Luckhurst b Windows.	15	– not out	86
†A. W. Catt lbw b Brown	0		
A. L. Dixon c White b Windows.	2		
M. E. Denness b Brown	13		
A. Brown lbw b Windows.	1		
D. Baker c sub b Windows	8		
J. Melville not out	4		
B 4, l-b 5, n-b 1	10	B 1, l-b 7, n-b 1	9

1/43 2/80 3/158 4/212 5/212   243   1/22 2/32 3/64   (3 wkts dec.) 297
6/212 7/217 8/225 9/231

Gloucestershire

D. M. Young lbw b Dixon	23	– c Wilson b Baker 38
R. B. Nicholls c and b Melville	0	– c Cowdrey b Brown 0
C. A. Milton not out	110	– not out 102
*C. T. M. Pugh lbw b Dixon	0	– c Dixon b Luckhurst........... 13
R. C. White c Catt b Dixon	18	– b Baker...................... 0
J. B. Mortimore b Dixon	86	– b Baker...................... 80
A. S. Brown b Dixon	0	– not out 3
A. R. Windows c Richardson b Melville	1	
†B. J. Meyer c Cowdrey b Baker	0	
D. R. Smith c Denness b Brown	37	
C. Cook b Brown	3	
B 10, l-b 5, w 1	16	B 6, l-b 8............... 14

1/4 2/55 3/55 4/103 5/222   **294**   1/4 2/77 3/77   (5 wkts) **250**
6/222 7/223 8/244 9/286   4/110 5/243

Gloucestershire Bowling

	Overs	Mdns	Runs	Wkts	Overs	Mdns	Runs	Wkts
Smith	9	—	22	—	9	2	17	1
Brown	32	7	68	3	21	5	61	1
Mortimore	12	4	21	—	21	2	76	1
Windows	31	15	59	7	18	5	61	—
Cook	19	11	36	—	24	9	68	—
Milton	6	1	27	—				
Nicholls					1	—	5	—

Kent Bowling

	Overs	Mdns	Runs	Wkts	Overs	Mdns	Runs	Wkts
Brown	21.4	3	53	2	12	3	37	1
Melville	22	11	54	2				
Baker	24	5	85	1	20	4	92	3
Dixon	33	14	86	5	7	1	38	—
Nicholls					4	—	18	—
Luckhurst					13	2	51	1

Umpires: J. Arnold and W. F. Price.

HAMPSHIRE

HAMPSHIRE v KENT

Played at Southampton, May 27, 29, 30, 1950

A tie. The match ended dramatically. When Knott, the last Hampshire batsman, joined Cannings ten minutes before lunch on the last day, 22 were needed for victory. Seven runs were added before the interval and afterwards runs came mainly by singles until Knott levelled the scores with a late cut for two. Next ball Knott fell to a slip catch. This was the first tie since the system of scoring was altered in 1948, whereby a side leading on first innings in a tied match took eight points and their opponents four. Previously each obtained six. Kent, put in on a pitch taking spin, were saved from disaster by Evans, Hearn and Fagg, the only men to reach double figures. Hampshire started well, but collapsed, and their lead was restricted to 18. Kent were unlucky when Ames, in his second innings, after scoring 55 faultlessly, hurt his back while running and retired. Hampshire, needing 153, lost two wickets for 17, but Arnold gave a good display and after his run out came the crucial struggle with its exciting finish.

Kent

A. E. Fagg b Knott	20	– c McCorkell b Shackleton	2
A. H. Phebey lbw b Dare	3	– b Cannings	2
L. E. G. Ames c Walker b Knott	8	– retired hurt	55
P. Hearn b Dare	30	– lbw b Shackleton	6
L. J. Todd c Walker b Knott	9	– run out	22
T. G. Evans b Shackleton	71	– lbw b Knott	31
A. C. Shirreff c Eagar b Dare	0	– b Knott	44
D. G. Clark c Arnold b Knott	9	– c Gray b Knott	2
R. R. Dovey c and b Cannings	3	– c McCorkell b Knott	0
D. V. P. Wright not out	0	– not out	0
F. Ridgway b Shackleton	0	– b Knott	0
L-b 9	9	B 4, l-b 2	6
	162		**170**

Hampshire

N. McCorkell lbw b Wright	42	– c Shirreff b Ridgway	8
N. H. Rogers c Clark b Dovey	20	– c Shirreff b Dovey	23
G. Hill c Phebey b Wright	20	– b Shirreff	2
J. Arnold c Evans b Wright	0	– run out	52
J. R. Gray c Evans b Dovey	0	– c Evans b Shirreff	5
C. Walker lbw b Wright	46	– c Fagg b Wright	12
E. D. R. Eagar c Ridgway b Wright	11	– b Dovey	1
D. Shackleton c and b Wright	8	– c Clark b Shirreff	13
R. Dare lbw b Dovey	11	– c sub b Wright	1
V. H. D. Cannings c Evans b Dovey	3	– not out	10
C. J. Knott not out	5	– c Fagg b Wright	9
B 2, l-b 4, n-b 8	14	B 2, l-b 11, n-b 3	16
	180		**152**

Hampshire Bowling

	Overs	Mdns	Runs	Wkts	Overs	Mdns	Runs	Wkts
Shackleton	5.3	1	12	2	18	2	37	2
Cannings	5	1	17	1	17	5	43	1
Knott	28	9	49	4	17.3	4	46	5
Dare	24	5	67	3				
Hill	8	2	8	—	14	3	38	—

Kent Bowling

	Overs	Mdns	Runs	Wkts	Overs	Mdns	Runs	Wkts
Ridgway	13	1	33	—	10	3	26	1
Shirreff	3	1	4	—	11	3	27	3
Wright	31.4	10	91	6	21.2	5	49	3
Dovey...........	22	9	38	4	25	11	34	2

Umpires: H. G. Baldwin and F. S. Lee.

HAMPSHIRE v KENT

Played at Southampton, May 31, June 2, 1952

Hampshire won by 156 runs. Caught on a rain-affected pitch off which the ball rose alarmingly or skidded through, Kent were dismissed twice during a day in which twenty-nine wickets fell. Saturday's play, limited to three hours because of the weather, was notable for the sustained accuracy of Martin and Dovey and the slip fielding of Fagg. The real drama, however, occurred after the week-end when Kent collapsed against the fast-medium bowling of Shackleton and Cannings. Nine wickets went down for 18 before Martin, with 6 and 4 provided the only note of defiance. Although Hampshire, in turn, faltered at first, a fourth stand between Gray and Harrison enabled Eagar to declare 247 ahead. Evans batted courageously in what always seemed a lost cause, and with Shackleton and Cannings, who bowled unchanged in both innings, again in hostile mood, Kent's second venture was over in ninety minutes. Fieldsmen shared the dismissal of all but five of the 38 wickets which tumbled during less than two days' play.

Hampshire

N. H. Rogers c Evans b Martin..................	4	– c Murray Wood b Martin.........	4
C. Walker c Fagg b Dovey.....................	14	– c Fagg b Dovey	7
L. Harrison b Dovey..........................	20	– c Mayes b Martin...............	45
J. R. Gray c Fagg b Dovey.....................	23	– not out	61
A. W. H. Rayment c Evans b Martin	37	– c Evans b Martin	3
E. D. R. Eagar c Fagg b Dovey	14	– c Fagg b Hellmuth	11
R. O. Prouton b Martin........................	3	– c Edrich b Martin	6
G. Hill c Fagg b Dovey........................	3	– c O'Linn b Martin...............	4
D. Shackleton c and b Martin..................	6	– st Evans b Hellmuth	1
R. Dare c Fagg b Dovey.......................	0	– not out	0
V. H. D. Cannings not out	4		
B 4, l-b 3	7	W 1, n-b 1...............	2

1/2 2/37 3/38 4/69 5/107   135   1/12 2/18 3/26 4/88   (8 wkts dec.) 144
6/118 7/125 8/125 9/125   5/95 6/120 7/135 8/136

Kent

A. E. Fagg c Cannings b Shackleton	0	–	c Eagar b Shackleton		16
P. Hearn not out	12	–	b Cannings		6
T. G. Evans c Cannings b Shackleton	2	–	c Walker b Shackleton		34
S. O'Linn c Gray b Cannings	0	–	c Eagar b Shackleton		1
R. Mayes c Prouton b Shackleton	1	–	b Cannings		3
B. R. Edrich c Dare b Shackleton	2	–	c Gray b Shackleton		0
W. Murray Wood c Walker b Cannings	0	–	c Cannings b Shackleton		18
L. Hellmuth c Eagar b Shackleton	0	–	c Eagar b Shackleton		0
R. R. Dovey c Cannings b Shackleton	0	–	c Gray b Cannings		0
D. V. P. Wright c Gray b Cannings	1	–	c Prouton b Cannings		4
J. W. Martin b Cannings	14	–	not out		8
			L-b 1		1

1/3 2/5 3/6 4/11 5/15   32   1/20 2/34 3/35 4/38 5/41   91
6/16 7/17 8/17 9/18   6/66 7/72 8/75 9/81

Kent Bowling

	Overs	Mdns	Runs	Wkts	Overs	Mdns	Runs	Wkts
Martin	32	9	61	4	20	3	62	5
Dovey	31	9	67	6	15	1	50	1
Wright					3	—	19	—
Hellmuth					8	3	11	2

Hampshire Bowling

	Overs	Mdns	Runs	Wkts	Overs	Mdns	Runs	Wkts
Shackleton	9	2	22	6	12.4	1	45	6
Cannings	8.1	2	10	4	12	1	45	4

Umpires: G. S. Mobey and H. G. Baldwin.

HAMPSHIRE v SURREY

Played at Bournemouth, September 2, 3, 1953

Surrey won by nine wickets. They celebrated their feat of winning the Championship for the second year running by outplaying Hampshire, who were beaten with a day to spare. Hampshire experienced the worst of the conditions, for, having lost the toss, they batted first on a rain-affected pitch which was ideally suited to Lock, the England left-arm slow bowler. He had all the batsmen guessing and took eight wickets for 26, the best figures of his career. Surrey also found runs difficult to obtain, particularly off Burden, an off-break bowler from Southampton, making his second county appearance. Burden did most to limit Surrey's lead to 69, but Hampshire lost half their side while clearing these arrears. Lock again proved the most successful bowler and he finished with the excellent match analysis of 51 overs 29 maidens 69 runs, 13 wickets. He also took a remarkable one-handed diving catch off his own bowling when he dismissed Rayment for the second time in the match.

Hampshire

N. H. Rogers c Surridge b Lock	39	–	lbw b Laker	24
D. E. Blake c Surridge b Laker	7	–	run out	3
G. Hill c Surridge b Lock	3	–	lbw b Laker	7
L. Harrison b Lock	0	–	b Lock	0
J. R. Gray b Laker	0	–	not out	39
A. W. H. Rayment c and b Lock	1	–	c and b Lock	7
D. Cartridge c McIntyre b Lock	0	–	st McIntyre b Lock	0
E. D. R. Eagar c May b Lock	0	–	c Lock b Laker	9
D. Shackleton c Laker b Lock	0	–	c McIntyre b Lock	21
R. Dare c Surridge b Lock	20	–	c Clark b Lock	4
M. D. Burden not out	7	–	b Clark	0
B 1, l-b 4	5		B 7, l-b 6	13

1/21 2/24 3/24 4/29 5/34   82   1/3 2/29 3/41 4/42 5/64   127
6/38 7/38 8/39 9/71   6/73 7/73 8/123 9/127

Surrey

D. G. W. Fletcher b Shackleton	0	–	c Shackleton b Burden	5
T. H. Clark c Gray b Burden	15	–	not out	33
P. B. H. May lbw b Burden	35	–	not out	15
B. Constable run out	20			
R. Subba Row b Burden	20			
A. J. McIntyre b Burden	21			
J. C. Laker c Cartridge b Dare	9			
W. S. Surridge c Eagar b Dare	0			
G. A. R. Lock c Hill b Burden	23			
A. V. Bedser not out	2			
P. J. Loader b Burden	1			
B 4, n-b 1	5		B 4, l-b 2	6

1/3 2/55 3/58 4/92 5/97   151   1/27   (1 wkt)   59
6/117 7/117 8/135 9/148

Surrey Bowling

	Overs	Mdns	Runs	Wkts	Overs	Mdns	Runs	Wkts
Bedser	7	4	6	—	9	4	9	—
Loader	4	2	8	—	1	1	—	—
Laker	19	6	37	2	38	15	57	3
Lock	17	8	26	8	34	21	43	5
Clark					4.3	2	5	1

Hampshire Bowling

	Overs	Mdns	Runs	Wkts	Overs	Mdns	Runs	Wkts
Shackleton	9	3	25	1	4	1	12	—
Gray	5	4	1	—	4	2	5	—
Dare	24	9	50	2	6.2	1	22	—
Burden	20.2	1	70	6	7	1	14	1

Umpires: F. S. Lee and H. G. Baldwin.

HAMPSHIRE v GLOUCESTERSHIRE

Played at Bournemouth, August 31, September 2, 1957

Hampshire won by an innings and 28 runs. Gloucestershire collapsed in extraordinary fashion to the seam bowling of Shackleton and Cannings, the match ending abruptly on the second evening. Facing arrears of 67 they were routed in eighty-five minutes, five wickets falling at 35. Cannings took six of the first seven wickets in twelve overs on a pitch which never recovered from a soaking the previous day. That Hampshire established a first innings lead was due mainly to a cheerful partnership between Ingleby-Mackenzie (two 6s and eight 4s) and Sainsbury. They put on 65 in less than forty minutes.

Gloucestershire

G. M. Emmett c Gray b Cannings	11	– b Cannings	11
D. M. Young c Harrison b Sainsbury	41	– b Shackleton	5
R. B. Nicholls c Harrison b Cannings	0	– c Harrison b Cannings	2
T. W. Graveney c Sainsbury b Burden	10	– b Cannings	4
C. A. Milton c Sainsbury b Shackleton	27	– c Sainsbury b Cannings	8
D. G. Hawkins c Sainsbury b Burden	1	– lbw b Shackleton	0
A. S. Brown not out	13	– b Cannings	0
J. Mortimore lbw b Shackleton	15	– lbw b Cannings	0
D. R. Smith c Harrison b Shackleton	0	– not out	0
C. Cook lbw b Shackleton	0	– b Shackleton	0
B. D. Wells c Marshall b Shackleton	0	– b Shackleton	4
L-b 2, n-b 1	3	L-b 5	5

1/21 2/21 3/40 4/92 5/93   121   1/19 2/21 3/27 4/27 5/35   39
6/93 7/121 8/121 9/121   6/35 7/35 8/35 9/35

Hampshire

R. E. Marshall c Brown b Cook	12
J. R. Gray c and b Mortimore	35
H. Horton c Brown b Mortimore	14
E. D. R. Eagar b Mortimore	10
R. W. C. Pitman lbw b Wells	11
A. C. D. Ingleby-Mackenzie c Hawkins b Cook.	59
P. J. Sainsbury lbw b Wells	22
L. Harrison b Cook	2
D. Shackleton c Milton b Cook	3
V. H. D. Cannings b Smith	0
M. D. Burden not out	6
B 11, l-b 2, w 1	14

1/23 2/63 3/78 4/89 5/91   188
6/156 7/179 8/179 9/180

Hampshire Bowling

	Overs	Mdns	Runs	Wkts	Overs	Mdns	Runs	Wkts
Shackleton	21	9	36	5	12.4	8	15	4
Cannings	12	7	16	2	12	4	19	6
Burden	19	6	53	2				
Sainsbury	15	10	13	1				

Gloucestershire Bowling

	Overs	Mdns	Runs	Wkts
Smith	15	2	33	1
Brown	7	6	5	—
Cook	13.3	6	31	4
Wells	26	10	61	2
Mortimore	18	4	44	3

Umpires: P. A. Gibb and E. Davies.

HAMPSHIRE v WORCESTERSHIRE

Played at Portsmouth, June 20, 22, 23, 1959

Drawn. The batting of Kenyon dominated the match and Hampshire would have been in a sorry state but for Gray. After a useful start the later men struggled. Kenyon spent long spells on the defensive, but scored his 229 out of 337, batting six and a half hours and hitting two 6s and thirty-three 4s. This was his second double century on the Portsmouth ground. Hampshire started their second innings 160 behind, and with six wickets down for 117 they seemed in trouble. Ingleby-Mackenzie came to the rescue with a dogged innings lasting three hours and forty minutes. He received valuable support from Flood, who retired after a blow on the head but later returned, and his innings cheated Worcestershire of victory. They required 101 to win in half an hour, a task that proved impossible.

Hampshire

R. E. Marshall c Booth b Flavell	28	– c Booth b Aldridge 8
J. R. Gray c and b Flavell	89	– c Dews b Pearson 28
H. Horton c Booth b Aldridge	23	– c Richardson b Aldridge 10
D. O. Baldry b Pearson	34	– b Flavell 14
R. Flood c Booth b Pearson	0	– b Flavell 37
A. C. D. Ingleby-Mackenzie c Aldridge b Pearson	7	– c Booth b Flavell 127
L. Harrison c Dews b Pearson	1	– b Aldridge 13
A. Wassell b Flavell	0	– c Booth b Pearson 2
D. Shackleton c Dews b Aldridge	20	– c Booth b Flavell 1
V. H. D. Cannings b Flavell	11	– b Aldridge 13
M. Heath not out	10	– not out 1
L-b 4, n-b 3	7	L-b 3, w 1, n-b 2 6

1/40 2/103 3/160 4/160 5/174   230   1/21 2/37 3/56 4/74 5/110   260
6/176 7/179 8/203 9/209   6/117 7/176 8/182 9/225

Worcestershire

D. Kenyon c Ingleby-Mackenzie b Heath	229	– not out 13
L. Outschoorn lbw b Shackleton	14	
R. G. A. Headley lbw b Cannings	22	
D. W. Richardson b Cannings	0	
R. G. Broadbent c Horton b Cannings	44	
G. Dews b Heath	2	– not out 24
R. Booth not out	44	
D. N. F. Slade c Gray b Heath	3	
D. B. Pearson b Cannings	2	
J. Flavell c Wassell b Cannings	4	
K. J. Aldridge b Cannings	17	
B 4, l-b 1, n-b 4	9	L-b 5 5

1/37 2/112 3/112 4/215 5/253   390   (No wkt) 42
6/337 7/358 8/361 9/365

Worcestershire Bowling

	Overs	Mdns	Runs	Wkts	Overs	Mdns	Runs	Wkts
Flavell	23.1	1	99	4	31.2	4	81	4
Aldridge	19	2	58	2	23	6	55	4
Pearson	22	5	53	4	29	2	97	2
Slade	4	2	13	—	4	—	21	—

Hampshire Bowling

	Overs	Mdns	Runs	Wkts	Overs	Mdns	Runs	Wkts
Shackleton	45	17	100	1	3	—	15	—
Cannings	26	9	66	6	3	—	22	—
Heath	41	5	147	3				
Gray............	6	1	25	—				
Baldry...........	14	4	43	—				

Umpires: P. A. Gibb and A. E. Fagg.

HAMPSHIRE v OXFORD UNIVERSITY

Played at Bournemouth, July 4, 6, 7, 1959

Drawn. Despite a magnificent century by Alan Smith, the Oxford captain – his second of the match – the University failed to score the 332 runs needed to win on the last day in four hours. Hampshire were put out for 169 in their first innings, due chiefly to the fine bowling of Corran. Smith's chanceless 145 in Oxford's first knock occupied nearly four hours and enabled his team to lead by 79. Hampshire scored at a fast rate in their second innings, Marshall hitting 133 at nearly a run a minute. On the final day the Hampshire bowlers proved too accurate for most of the University batsmen.

Hampshire

R. E. Marshall c Smith b Corran................	10	– c Burki b Raybould	133
B. R. S. Harrison c Jowett b Green..............	29	– c Smith b Corran	52
H. Horton b Corran	8	– b Green.................	98
R. Flood lbw b Sayer	8	– lbw b Raybould	39
D. A. Livingstone c Smith b Raybould............	37	– c Duff b Corran	14
A. C. D. Ingleby-Mackenzie b Corran	25	– c Smith b Sayer................	9
A. Wassell c Duff b Corran.....................	23	– c Burki b Sayer.................	0
B. S. V. Timms b Corran.......................	9	– b Sayer.......................	0
D. W. White b Corran.........................	0	– b Green.......................	27
V. H. D. Cannings b Raybould.................	9	– b Green.......................	2
M. D. Burden not out	0	– not out	19
B 7, l-b 1, n-b 3	11	B 6, l-b 10, n-b 1	17

1/12 2/29 3/39 4/94 5/110　　　　　　　169　　1/182 2/196 3/255 4/289　　　　　410
6/137 7/156 8/160 9/169　　　　　　　　　　　5/312 6/314 7/314 8/369 9/371

Oxford University

A. C. Smith b Cannings	145	– b Cannings	124
D. M. Green b Wassell	32	– lbw b White	0
A. A. Baig c Timms b Burden..................	0	– b Harrison	0
J. Burki b Cannings..........................	22	– st Timms b Wassell.............	50
C. A. Fry lbw b Cannings.....................	0	– c Marshall b Burden............	55
M. A. Eagar lbw b Cannings...................	0	– lbw b Cannings.................	7
R. L. Jowett c Livingstone b White..............	17	– c Timms b White	8
A. R. Duff lbw b Cannings....................	9	– not out	1
J. G. Raybould c Horton b Cannings	1	– not out	1
A. J. Corran not out	16		
D. M. Sayer c and b White	5		
L-b 1............................	1	L-b 4.................	4

1/75 2/76 3/183 4/183 5/183　　　　　　248　　1/1 2/100 3/109 4/203　　　(7 wkts) 250
6/216 7/226 8/226 9/239　　　　　　　　　　　5/230 6/248 7/248

Oxford University Bowling

	Overs	Mdns	Runs	Wkts	Overs	Mdns	Runs	Wkts
Sayer	16	2	35	1	27	2	67	3
Corran	22	4	60	6	39	7	111	2
Raybould	15.4	3	47	2	21	1	103	2
Green	9	4	16	1	20.5	7	71	3
Burki............					7	1	23	—
Duff					5	—	18	—

Hampshire Bowling

	Overs	Mdns	Runs	Wkts	Overs	Mdns	Runs	Wkts
Cannings	31	13	67	6	13	4	31	2
White	27.5	6	96	2	16	3	48	2
Burden	22	7	49	1	19	3	81	1
Wassell..........	11	3	35	1	12	3	52	1
Harrison.........					11	3	34	1

Umpires: H. G. Baldwin and L. H. Gray.

HAMPSHIRE v LEICESTERSHIRE

Played at Southampton, August 22, 24, 25, 1959

Hampshire won by seven wickets. Watson, the Leicestershire captain, broke a bone in his left hand soon after the start and took no further part in the match. Although Hampshire faced a moderate total they, too, found scoring difficult on a pitch that took spin. Gray was their sheet anchor, and he hit nine 4s while making 45. Sainsbury bowled well in Leicestershire's second innings, half his overs being maidens, and he finished the match with six wickets for 42. Needing 120 to win, Hampshire scored the runs with ease. Gray was again their best batsman and he became the third player in the side to reach 2,000 runs. His 68 not out contained fifteen 4s.

Leicestershire

M. R. Hallam c Harrison b Shackleton............	7	– c Sainsbury b Shackleton	13
W. Watson retired hurt	1	– absent hurt	
D. Kirby c Sainsbury b Shackleton..............	5	– c Gray b Burden...............	24
L. R. Gardner b White	40	– c Harrison b Burden.............	19
J. van Geloven run out	21	– c Barnard b Sainsbury	27
A. C. Revill c and b White	23	– c Barnard b Sainsbury	37
G. W. Birch c Harrison b Sainsbury.............	11	– b Sainsbury....................	14
R. C. Smith c Shackleton b Burden..............	9	– c and b White	25
C. T. Spencer c White b Sainsbury	10	– b Sainsbury....................	0
J. S. Savage c Gray b Shackleton	11	– c Marshall b White	1
G. A. Hickinbottom not out	0	– not out	4
L-b 3, w 1, n-b 1	5	L-b 2..................	2

1/12 2/19 3/72 4/89 5/104   143   1/20 2/45 3/77 4/87 5/131   166
6/115 7/119 8/139 9/143   6/140 7/148 8/155 9/166

Hampshire

R. E. Marshall b Spencer	16	– c Revill b Savage	20
J. R. Gray c Spencer b van Geloven	45	– not out	68
H. Horton c sub b Savage	12	– c Hickinbottom b Savage	22
D. O. Baldry c Savage b Smith	25	– b Savage	0
H. M. Barnard c Hallam b Savage	45	– not out	5
A. C. D. Ingleby-Mackenzie lbw b Smith	5		
P. J. Sainsbury c Spencer b Savage	9		
L. Harrison c Revill b Smith	1		
D. Shackleton c Gardner b van Geloven	12		
D. W. White not out	5		
M. D. Burden c Hallam b Spencer	0		
B 13, n-b 2	15	B 1, l-b 2, n-b 2	5

1/27 2/60 3/98 4/125 5/135   190   1/48 2/103 3/103   (3 wkts) 120
6/160 7/169 8/173 9/186

Hampshire Bowling

	Overs	Mdns	Runs	Wkts	Overs	Mdns	Runs	Wkts
Shackleton	21.3	12	24	3	18	8	29	1
White	16	1	41	2	10.4	1	26	2
Gray	9	8	3	—	3	3	—	—
Baldry	5	2	8	—				
Burden	19	5	58	1	23	7	71	2
Sainsbury	8	6	4	2	30	15	38	4

Leicestershire Bowling

	Overs	Mdns	Runs	Wkts	Overs	Mdns	Runs	Wkts
Spencer	21.3	8	44	2	4	—	16	—
van Geloven	21	3	52	2	3	—	26	—
Savage	25	10	49	3	19.4	8	41	3
Kirby	3	2	1	—	3	1	4	—
Smith	16	8	29	3	17	8	28	—

Umpires: J. H. Parks and A. E. Fagg.

HAMPSHIRE v YORKSHIRE

Played at Portsmouth, May 21, 23, 24, 1960

Yorkshire won by an innings and 61 runs. Magnificent bowling by Trueman which followed hundreds by Close and Bolus proved too much for Hampshire. Bolus and Close shared a third-wicket partnership of 151 and Close hit four 6s and eight 4s in two hours. Bolus spent much longer over his maiden hundred and altogether he batted five and a half hours for his not out 146 (fifteen 4s). Hampshire played steadily to score 140 for two wickets and then Trueman, taking the new ball, finished the innings with a spell of 10–5–11–6. Following-on 208 behind, Hampshire fared even worse. Horton, who played courageously, alone defied Trueman who captured six more wickets for a match analysis of twelve wickets for 62 runs.

Yorkshire

W. B. Stott b Sainsbury	47
K. Taylor c Sainsbury b Burden	35
J. B. Bolus not out	146
D. B. Close c Harrison b Heath	102
P. J. Sharpe c Livingstone b Heath	36
D. Wilson b Heath	8
F. S. Trueman c Gray b Shackleton	13
M. Ryan st Harrison b Shackleton	2
*J. V. Wilson not out	5
B 1, l-b 3, w 1	5

1/62 2/106 3/257   (7 wkts dec.) 399
4/345 5/363 6/384 7/389

†J. G. Binks and M. J. Cowan did not bat.

Hampshire

J. R. Gray c D. Wilson b Close	54	– b Trueman	3
R. E. Marshall c Binks b D. Wilson	70	– c Bolus b Trueman	8
H. Horton c Binks b Trueman	26	– not out	68
D. O. Baldry c Binks b Trueman	16	– b Trueman	2
D. A. Livingstone c Stott b Trueman	2	– lbw b Close	23
*A. C. D. Ingleby-Mackenzie b Trueman	9	– c sub b Close	7
P. J. Sainsbury run out	0	– c sub b Taylor	20
†L. Harrison b Trueman	0	– lbw b Trueman	5
D. Shackleton c Sharpe b Cowan	1	– c and b Trueman	0
M. Heath lbw b Trueman	1	– c Binks b Trueman	8
M. D. Burden not out	1	– run out	0
B 1, l-b 6, w 1, n-b 3	11	L-b 3	3

1/118 2/140 3/166 4/176 5/179   191   1/3 2/18 3/20 4/30 5/76   147
6/179 7/179 8/185 9/190   6/86 7/130 8/139 9/147

Hampshire Bowling

	Overs	Mdns	Runs	Wkts	Overs	Mdns	Runs	Wkts
Shackleton	42	11	98	2				
Heath	28	1	125	3				
Baldry	1	—	8	—				
Burden	33	11	84	1				
Sainsbury	23	8	63	1				
Marshall	4	1	16	—				

Yorkshire Bowling

	Overs	Mdns	Runs	Wkts	Overs	Mdns	Runs	Wkts
Ryan	2	2	—	—				
Trueman	21	7	34	6	19.3	9	28	6
Cowan	23	6	34	1	14	4	36	—
D. Wilson	27	12	49	1	19	10	30	—
Close	21	5	59	1	21	5	45	2
Taylor	2	1	4	—	4	2	5	1

Umpires: H. G. Baldwin and D. J. Wood.

HAMPSHIRE IN 1961

Hampshire carried off the County Championship crown for the first time in their history after a long and exciting battle with Yorkshire and Middlesex. Sixty-six years of fruitless striving for the honour terminated at Bournemouth on 1 September when victory over Derbyshire put Hampshire beyond reach of Yorkshire, the 1960 Champions.

Hampshire, who had finished runners-up to Surrey in 1958 – the first season in which Ingleby-Mackenzie captained the side – dropped to eighth and twelfth in the succeeding summers and many people thought that they would not be serious contenders in 1961. Splendid team work and spirit, however, together with the almost complete disappearance of weaknesses in the middle batting and spin bowling led to their unexpected success. . . .

Ingleby-Mackenzie, who has always been known for his views on "brighter" cricket, revealed a hitherto unknown talent for master strategy. The experimental law which did not allow the follow-on called for intelligent declarations and in this sphere the Hampshire captain excelled. He balanced perfectly the ability of his batsmen – especially Marshall – to score quickly with his bowling strength. It was on this that Hampshire's success was almost entirely based. Had Ingleby-Mackenzie made any serious mistakes, the county might not have been in the running.

HAMPSHIRE v SUSSEX

Played at Portsmouth, August 2, 3, 4, 1961

Hampshire won by six wickets. A hat-trick by White late on the second day sealed Sussex's fate. In the last over of the evening, the young Hampshire fast bowler captured the wickets of Parks, Thomson and Smith with successive balls, and then had Cooper caught two deliveries later. White finished with five for 21 in 25 overs and Hampshire, left 143 to win, raced to victory in two hours.

Sussex

A. S. M. Oakman c Harrison b Shackleton	3	– run out 61
R. J. Langridge c Harrison b Gray	10	– c Sainsbury b Heath 38
*E. R. Dexter c Baldry b Shackleton	4	– not out 31
K. G. Suttle b Gray	27	– c Barnard b Shackleton ... 20
†J. M. Parks c Shackleton b Gray	25	– b White 19
D. V. Smith c Harrison b Shackleton	35	– b White 0
L. J. Lenham lbw b Shackleton	10	– lbw b White 5
G. C. Cooper not out	14	– c Horton b White 0
N. I. Thomson c Marshall b Gray	0	– c Harrison b White 0
R. V. Bell c Sainsbury b Gray	1	– c Harrison b Shackleton .. 0
D. L. Bates c Sainsbury b Shackleton	11	– lbw b Shackleton 0
L-b 1	1	B 5, l-b 1 6

1/8 2/12 3/36 4/65 5/84   141   1/65 2/83 3/104 4/138 5/179   180
6/106 7/115 8/116 9/120   6/179 7/179 8/179 9/180

Hampshire

R. E. Marshall b Dexter	2	– b Bell 51
J. R. Gray c Parks b Smith	16	– c Oakman b Bates 34
H. Horton c and b Bates	35	– lbw b Bell 2
D. A. Livingstone c Bell b Dexter	42	– not out 32
P. J. Sainsbury lbw b Dexter	7	– lbw b Dexter 17
D. O. Baldry c Parks b Thomson	10	– not out 7
H. M. Barnard c Bell b Dexter	18	
†L. Harrison c Bell b Bates	10	
D. Shackleton c Parks b Dexter	1	
D. W. White c Suttle b Bates	23	
M. Heath not out	5	
B 4, l-b 4, w 2	10	

1/3 2/30 3/68 4/82 5/99   179   1/83 2/85 3/91 4/135   (4 wkts) 143
6/128 7/146 8/148 9/153

Hampshire Bowling

	Overs	Mdns	Runs	Wkts	Overs	Mdns	Runs	Wkts
Shackleton	26.5	10	45	5	26.4	9	51	3
White	11	2	26	—	24	12	21	5
Heath	8	1	13	—	22	6	60	1
Gray	22	5	56	5				
Baldry					12	1	34	—
Sainsbury					8	4	8	—

Sussex Bowling

	Overs	Mdns	Runs	Wkts	Overs	Mdns	Runs	Wkts
Thomson	25	7	43	1	7	—	30	—
Dexter	23	6	63	5	10	3	39	1
Bates	17.5	8	33	3	11	2	29	1
Smith	8	1	30	1				
Bell					11.4	1	45	2

Umpires: H. G. Baldwin and H. B. Hammond.

HAMPSHIRE v DERBYSHIRE

Played at Bournemouth, August 30, 31, September 1, 1961

Hampshire made certain of becoming County Champions when they won by 140 runs. Marshall and Gray gave them a good start on a perfect pitch with an opening partnership of 120. The middle order wasted much of the advantage and half the side were out for 182, but with the last three wickets putting on 76 Hampshire reached 306. Derbyshire replied with spirit. Lee went with only nine scored, but Johnson, in partnerships of 93 with Gibson and 110, in just over an hour, with Oates, put them on top. The West Indian thrashed the Hampshire attack hitting a 6 and nineteen 4s in his 112 made in two and three-quarter hours. Derbyshire gained a lead of 12. Then Marshall, Sainsbury and Barnard hit splendidly and enabled Ingleby-Mackenzie to declare, leaving the opposition 252 to win in three hours, ten minutes. Shackleton, although receiving little help from the pitch, broke the back of the Derbyshire batting in a grand spell of controlled pace-bowling. He took the first four wickets and finished with six for 39 in 24 overs, Hampshire winning with just under an hour to spare.

Hampshire

R. E. Marshall c Lee b Smith	76	– c Lee b Morgan 86
J. R. Gray run out	78	– b Rhodes 4
H. Horton c Taylor b Jackson	13	– lbw b Rhodes 0
D. A. Livingstone c Lee b Smith	7	– c Johnson b Smith 11
P. J. Sainsbury c Rhodes b Smith	1	– c Lee b Smith 73
H. M. Barnard c Rhodes b Morgan	19	– c Taylor b Smith 61
*A. C. D. Ingleby-Mackenzie b Richardson	30	– st Taylor b Smith 5
†L. Harrison lbw b Morgan	35	– b Jackson 0
A. Wassell c Taylor b Jackson	13	
D. Shackleton not out	27	– not out 2
D. W. White b Morgan	0	– not out 13
B 1, l-b 4, w 1, n-b 1	7	B 4, l-b 3, w 1 8

1/120 2/145 3/160 4/166 5/182   306   1/8 2/16 3/40 4/141   (8 wkts dec.) 263
6/229 7/230 8/256 9/304   5/240 6/247 7/248 8/250

Derbyshire

C. Lee run out	5	– c Harrison b Shackleton	4
I. Gibson b Sainsbury	46	– lbw b Shackleton	3
H. L. Johnson c Gray b Wassell	112	– b Shackleton	14
W. F. Oates c Harrison b Shackleton	89	– b Shackleton	2
D. Millner b Shackleton	14	– c and b Wassell	17
D. C. Morgan b Wassell	13	– c Gray b Wassell	3
E. Smith c Barnard b Shackleton	0	– b Shackleton	9
G. W. Richardson c Horton b Wassell	6	– b Shackleton	0
†R. W. Taylor not out	12	– c Livingstone b Sainsbury	48
H. J. Rhodes b Wassell	9	– c and b Sainsbury	11
H. L. Jackson c Ingleby-Mackenzie b Wassell	4	– not out	0
B 4, l-b 4	8		

1/9 2/102 3/212 4/248 5/273   318   1/4 2/17 3/23 4/24 5/35   111
6/274 7/285 8/297 9/314   6/48 7/52 8/52 9/104

Derbyshire Bowling

	Overs	Mdns	Runs	Wkts	Overs	Mdns	Runs	Wkts
Jackson	24	9	44	2	14	5	25	1
Rhodes	22	4	48	—	18	8	19	2
Richardson	11	1	35	1	9	2	34	—
Lee	8	2	30	—				
Morgan	20.3	3	79	3	21	5	59	1
Smith	28	8	63	3	25	3	87	4
Oates					2	—	18	—
Gibson					2	—	13	—

Hampshire Bowling

	Overs	Mdns	Runs	Wkts	Overs	Mdns	Runs	Wkts
Shackleton	39	15	70	3	24	10	39	6
White	10	3	22	—	3	1	5	—
Gray	7	2	19	—				
Wassell	42.1	13	132	5	24	10	62	2
Sainsbury	14	3	67	1	3.2	—	5	2

Umpires: H. Yarnold and A. E. Rhodes.

HAMPSHIRE v YORKSHIRE

Played at Bournemouth, September 2, 4, 5, 1961

Yorkshire won by 58 runs. The off-break bowling of Illingworth proved decisive and swept Yorkshire, the deposed Champions, to victory. Illingworth took twelve wickets in the match for 102 runs. Hampshire's fast bowlers, White and Shackleton, proved ineffective and Yorkshire built on a fine opening partnership of 141 between Stott and Bolus, whose century occupied nearly four hours. During a rain-interrupted second day, Hampshire passed 100 for the loss of only three wickets, but at 125 Illingworth changed the course of the game by dismissing Livingstone, Barnard and Ingleby-Mackenzie in four balls. He finished the innings with seven for 39, Hampshire falling 128 behind. Yorkshire scored quickly on Tuesday and left their opponents 245 to win in three hours twenty minutes. There was always hope for Hampshire while Marshall remained, but when he was out for 109 with forty-five minutes left, Illingworth, bowling with guile and accuracy, soon finished the innings.

Yorkshire

W. B. Stott c Harrison b Wassell	75	– c Wassell b Shackleton	11
J. B. Bolus b Wassell	100	– c Ingleby-Mackenzie b Shackleton	6
D. E. V. Padgett st Harrison b Sainsbury	22	– c Ingleby-Mackenzie b Shackleton	13
D. B. Close b Sainsbury	12	– not out	25
P. J. Sharpe not out	23		
R. Illingworth c and b Wassell	4		
*J. V. Wilson c Harrison b Sainsbury	3		
F. S. Trueman c Shackleton b Sainsbury	4	– not out	51
†J. G. Binks not out	39		
B 2, l-b 4	6	B 4, l-b 6	6

1/141 2/199 3/213   (7 wkts dec.) 288   1/18 2/22 3/49   (3 wkts dec.) 116
4/213 5/217 6/220 7/224

K. Gillhouley and M. Ryan did not bat.

Hampshire

R. E. Marshall c Wilson b Trueman	14	– run out	109
J. R. Gray c Binks b Close	48	– c Close b Illingworth	0
H. Horton b Illingworth	17	– c Binks b Illingworth	8
D. A. Livingstone st Binks b Illingworth	19	– c Close b Gillhouley	1
P. J. Sainsbury c Binks b Illingworth	27	– c Ryan b Trueman	10
H. M. Barnard c Close b Illingworth	0	– b Close	26
*A. C. D. Ingleby-Mackenzie c Binks b Illingworth	0	– b Close	10
†L. Harrison c Close b Illingworth	13	– c Bolus b Illingworth	1
A. Wassell c Sharpe b Trueman	7	– not out	12
D. Shackleton not out	2	– c Stott b Illingworth	3
D. W. White b Illingworth	0	– c Wilson b Illingworth	0
B 4, l-b 9	13	B 4, l-b 2	6

1/24 2/83 3/87 4/125 5/125   160   1/4 2/50 3/53 4/77 5/120   186
6/125 7/133 8/152 9/158   6/134 7/136 8/170 9/186

Hampshire Bowling

	Overs	Mdns	Runs	Wkts	Overs	Mdns	Runs	Wkts
Shackleton	21	5	47	—	13	3	54	3
White	11	1	54	—	12	—	52	—
Wassell	55	24	116	3				
Gray	10	2	24	—				
Sainsbury	36	21	41	4				

Yorkshire Bowling

	Overs	Mdns	Runs	Wkts	Overs	Mdns	Runs	Wkts
Trueman	26	7	43	2	15	5	34	1
Ryan	12	3	22	—				
Gillhouley	1	1	—	—	12	4	53	1
Illingworth	22	9	39	7	26.3	7	63	5
Close	9	—	43	1	10	1	30	2

Umpires: J. F. Crapp and H. E. Hammond.

HAMPSHIRE v NORTHAMPTONSHIRE

Played at Bournemouth, August 25, 27, 28, 1962

Northamptonshire won by 131 runs. The match was a triumph for the brothers Watts. Jim hit 145 in just over three hours on the first day, adding 86 in fifty minutes with Peter for the sixth wicket. In the Northamptonshire second innings he scored 78 not out after three batsmen had been dismissed for 11. Peter took thirteen wickets in the game for 140 with his leg breaks and googlies, his analysis in the Hampshire second innings – seven for 77 – being his best, Jim's innings of 145 was his highest score in first class cricket.

Northamptonshire

M. Norman c Barnard b Sainsbury	89	– b Shackleton	4
C. Milburn lbw b Shackleton	21	– lbw b Shackleton	0
R. M. Prideaux lbw b Shackleton	6	– run out	25
A. Lightfoot lbw b Sainsbury	43	– c Sainsbury b Shackleton	0
P. J. Watts b Sainsbury	145	– not out	78
D. Ramsamooj c Timms b Baldry	17	– not out	28
P. D. Watts c Gray b Sainsbury	41		
J. D. F. Larter b Burden	20		
J. G. Williamson not out	1		
B 5, l-b 2	7		

1/36 2/52 3/139 4/195   (8 wkts dec.) 390   1/0 2/11 3/11   (4 wkts dec.) 135
5/274 6/360 7/388 8/390   4/51

*†K. V. Andrew and M. H. J. Allen did not bat.

Hampshire

J. R. Gray c Prideaux b P. D. Watts	22	– c P. D. Watts b Williamson	7
H. Horton b Allen	40	– lbw b P. D. Watts	23
H. M. Barnard c Andrew b P. D. Watts	51	– c P. J. Watts b P. D. Watts	23
D. A. Livingstone lbw b Allen	0	– lbw b P. D. Watts	59
P. J. Sainsbury c sub b Allen	9	– c Andrew b P. D. Watts	56
D. O. Baldry c sub b Allen	19	– c Andrew b Ramsamooj	4
*A. C. D. Ingleby-Mackenzie b P. D. Watts	15	– c Milburn b Allen	14
†B. S. V. Timms b P. D. Watts	6	– c Larter b P. D. Watts	4
D. Shackleton c Lightfoot b P. D. Watts	2	– c Norman b P. D. Watts	14
A. T. Castell not out	0	– c Norman b P. D. Watts	9
M. D. Burden c Norman b P. D. Watts	4	– not out	3
B 1, l-b 3	4	B 2, l-b 2, w 2	6

1/46 2/108 3/117 4/122 5/131   172   1/8 2/42 3/71 4/136 5/155   222
6/160 7/166 8/168 9/168   6/179 7/187 8/204 9/215

Hampshire Bowling

	Overs	Mdns	Runs	Wkts	Overs	Mdns	Runs	Wkts
Shackleton	29	11	70	2	13	9	15	3
Baldry	17	4	47	1	8	1	28	—
Burden	48	14	126	1	17	3	46	—
Sainsbury	38.4	15	89	4	4	—	15	—
Castell	15	3	51	—	9	1	31	—

Northamptonshire Bowling

	Overs	Mdns	Runs	Wkts	Overs	Mdns	Runs	Wkts
Larter	5	2	4	—				
Williamson	10	1	17	—	5	—	16	1
P. J. Watts	9	5	15	—	5	1	14	—
Allen	34	12	69	4	34	13	69	1
P. D. Watts	30.5	10	63	6	36.3	11	77	7
Ramsamooj					13	5	40	1

Umpires: W. E. Phillipson and J. S. Buller.

HAMPSHIRE v SURREY

Played at Southampton, August 29, 30, 31, 1962

Drawn. A remarkable ninth wicket partnership between Livingstone and Castell robbed Surrey of a large lead after they had declared at 363 for nine, Constable having scored a fine century in two and a quarter hours. Hampshire lost eight wickets for 128, but Livingstone, dropped before he had scored, went on in magnificent style to hit 200 – his highest innings in first class cricket – including three 6s and twenty-two 4s in nearly five hours. He and Castell (76) added 230 beating the previous best stand for that wicket – 197 by C. P. Mead and W. R. Shirley, before both were out at 358, six short of the Surrey total. With Lock and Jefferson hitting 78 in twenty minutes, Surrey declared their second innings leaving Hampshire 264 to win at 93 an hour. Five wickets fell for 74, four of them to Tindall, before Baldry and Sainsbury stopped the collapse, but Hampshire were well short of their target at the close. Surrey's hopes of winning the County Championship disappeared in this match.

Surrey

*M. J. Stewart c Sainsbury b Shackleton	3	– c Barnard b Baldry	6
J. H. Edrich c Barnard b Burden	84	– c Morton b Burden	60
A. B. D. Parsons c Livingstone b Sainsbury	22	– c Horton b Burden	34
K. F. Barrington c Livingstone b Sainsbury	26	– c Shackleton b Burden	45
B. Constable lbw b Shackleton	124	– b Sainsbury	20
R. A. E. Tindall lbw b Shackleton	29	– c Timms b Burden	3
†A. Long c Sainsbury b Shackleton	32	– c Ingleby-Mackenzie b Sainsbury	2
G. A. R. Lock run out	12	– not out	34
R. I. Jefferson b Shackleton	12	– not out	44
D. A. D. Sydenham not out	5		
B 10, l-b 4	14	B 4, l-b 6	10

1/9 2/66 3/131 4/157   (9 wkts dec.) 363   1/21 2/86 3/136   (7 wkts dec.) 258
5/252 6/323 7/334 8/353 9/363   4/173 5/173 6/178 7/180

P. J. Loader did not bat.

Hampshire

J. R. Gray c Long b Lock	15	– b Tindall	23
H. Horton b Lock	21	– c Lock b Tindall	37
H. M. Barnard c Edrich b Lock	0	– b Tindall	8
D. A. Livingstone c Stewart b Sydenham	200	– b Tindall	1
P. J. Sainsbury lbw b Jefferson	12	– b Tindall	28
D. O. Baldry b Jefferson	0	– c Tindall b Lock	90
*A. C. D. Ingleby-Mackenzie c Stewart b Jefferson	12	– c sub b Lock	6
†B. S. V. Timms lbw b Lock	4	– not out	1
D. Shackleton c Stewart b Tindall	11	– not out	0
A. T. Castell c Jefferson b Lock	76		
M. D. Burden not out	0		
B 2, l-b 3, n-b 2	7	B 12, l-b 3	15

1/37 2/37 3/38 4/57 5/59   358   1/60 2/61 3/67 4/74   (7 wkts) 209
6/87 7/103 8/128 9/358   5/74 6/187 7/205

Hampshire Bowling

	Overs	Mdns	Runs	Wkts	Overs	Mdns	Runs	Wkts
Shackleton	30.1	11	50	5	16	3	30	—
Baldry	23	3	93	—	12	2	40	1
Burden	37	12	75	1	21.4	4	103	4
Sainsbury	38	13	94	2	13	—	75	2
Castell	6	2	37	—				

Surrey Bowling

	Overs	Mdns	Runs	Wkts	Overs	Mdns	Runs	Wkts
Loader	15	4	33	—	2	—	13	—
Sydenham.........	12.3	2	22	1	2	—	4	—
Lock	46	10	149	5	25	8	66	2
Jefferson	33	10	59	3	13.4	2	29	—
Tindall	18	3	61	1	19	6	61	5
Barrington	6	—	27	—	6	2	21	—

Umpires: L. H. Gray and D. J. Wood.

KENT

KENT v LEICESTERSHIRE

Played at Tunbridge Wells, July 3, 4, 5, 1946

Kent won by eight wickets at ten minutes past three, within twenty minutes of the time arranged for drawing stumps. Heavy rain in the night prevented play on Thursday until twenty past three, but the pitch was not so much affected as the outfield and Todd, showing splendid form, increased his Wednesday's 55, made out of 118 for six wickets, to 133 and carried out his bat. At the wicket four hours and a half he hit only nine 4s, but the ball travelled slowly on the soft turf. Always sure in timing the ball Todd made his left-handed strokes without a fault, and after completing his century he scored a run a minute. He turned the fortune of the game, after a keen struggle on the first day. Wright bowled extremely well and Dovey, at much the same pace, kept the Leicestershire batsmen still more on the defensive. This was Kent's third consecutive victory in ten days.

Leicestershire

L. G. Berry c Spencer b Wright	25	– c Wright b Harding	1
G. Lester c Ames b Wright	31	– b Wright	5
F. T. Prentice b Wright	2	– b Dovey	31
M. Tompkin lbw b Wright	21	– c Evans b Wright	12
A. Riddington c Evans b Wright	9	– lbw b Wright	21
V. E. Jackson c Valentine b Dovey	45	– c and b Wright	38
T. Chapman c Todd b Wright	26	– b Dovey	8
A. W. Abbott b Dovey	0	– b Dovey	5
J. E. Walsh not out	17	– b Dovey	8
P. Corrall c Spencer b Wright	4	– c Todd b Dovey	7
J. Sperry c Valentine b Dovey	4	– not out	5
L-b 4	4	L-b 1	1
	188		142

Kent

L. J. Todd not out	133	– b Jackson	7
T. A. Pearce lbw b Walsh	7	– lbw b Lester	18
L. E. G. Ames b Walsh	16	– not out	38
T. Spencer b Walsh	5		
B. H. Valentine b Lester	2	– not out	0
A. H. Phebey lbw b Lester	0		
T. G. Evans st Corrall b Walsh	22		
A. W. H. Mallett c Walsh b Sperry	29		
D. V. P. Wright c Prentice b Sperry	10		
N. W. Harding st Corrall b Jackson	19		
R. R. Dovey b Sperry	5		
B 10, l-b 6, w 1	17	L-b 2, w 1	3
	265	(2 wkts)	66

Kent Bowling

	Overs	Mdns	Runs	Wkts	Overs	Mdns	Runs	Wkts
Harding	8	1	12	—	7	2	13	1
Mallett	17	3	39	—	10	4	15	—
Wright	31	9	80	7	29	6	69	4
Dovey	25.5	6	49	3	26	6	44	5
Todd	2	—	4	—				

Leicestershire Bowling

	Overs	Mdns	Runs	Wkts	Overs	Mdns	Runs	Wkts
Sperry	13.2	3	30	3	4	—	13	—
Abbott	3	—	8	—				
Jackson	26	10	54	1	6	2	12	1
Walsh	32	3	94	4				
Riddington	7	3	6	—	8.1	1	16	—
Lester	9	3	22	2	3	1	6	1
Prentice	9	—	34	—	3	—	16	—

KENT v ESSEX

Played at Maidstone, July 24, 26, 27, 1948

Drawn. Fagg in making two centuries in the match recalled his performance against Essex at Colchester in 1938 when he set up a record with 200 in each innings. Todd helped in a stand of 180, their eighth three-figure partnership of the season. Fagg scored his 136 out of 240 in three hours forty minutes, hitting a dozen 4s, nine in his first 50, and carried his bat through Kent's second innings in which Peter Smith claimed nine wickets, several batsmen getting out in efforts to force the game. Dodds and Avery, whose first innings stand realised 123, gave Essex another good start in the effort to obtain 337 necessary for victory in four hours. A chipped finger bone compelled Wright to give up bowling, but when eight wickets were down for 225 Kent looked sure of victory. Then two chances from Vigar and one from Wade went astray and these batsmen played out time.

Kent

L. J. Todd c Dodds b P. Smith	67	– lbw b P. Smith	29
A. E. Fagg lbw b R. Smith	136	– not out	117
L. E. G. Ames c Avery b Bailey	24	– b P. Smith	0
B. H. Valentine c P. Smith b Bailey	0	– c Bailey b P. Smith	24
P. Hearn c Bailey b P. Smith	33	– c Wade b P. Smith	5
D. G. Clark c Pearce b P. Smith	6	– c Dodds b P. Smith	24
E. Crush c Pearce b Price	44	– b P. Smith	4
R. R. Dovey b Price	30	– b R. Smith	10
D. V. P. Wright not out	7	– hit wkt b P. Smith	5
R. G. Downton not out	1	– st Wade b P. Smith	1
F. Ridgway (did not bat)		– c Insole b P. Smith	0
B 2, l-b 2, w 1	5	B 9, l-b 2	11
(8 wkts dec.)	353		230

Essex

T. C. Dodds run out	72	– c Dovey b Ridgway	21
A. V. Avery lbw b Wright	61	– c Downton b Hearn	38
T. E. Bailey c Downton b Wright	7	– c Fagg b Dovey	4
F. H. Vigar c Downton b Wright	19	– not out	13
R. Horsfall lbw b Wright	12	– b Dovey	0
T. N. Pearce c Crush b Ridgway	18	– st Downton b Hearn	78
D. J. Insole c Fagg b Crush	10	– c Downton b Ridgway	3
R. Smith b Ridgway	11	– b Dovey	32
P. Smith c Fagg b Wright	18	– c Downton b Dovey	42
T. H. Wade c Ames b Dovey	6	– not out	28
E. Price not out	2		
B 5, l-b 5, n-b 1	11	B 10, l-b 5	15
	247	(8 wkts)	274

Essex Bowling

	Overs	Mdns	Runs	Wkts	Overs	Mdns	Runs	Wkts
Bailey	20	5	60	2	6	—	24	—
R. Smith	31	5	102	1	42	7	87	1
Price	22	6	59	2				
P. Smith	38	7	100	3	37	3	108	9
Vigar	8	2	27	—				

Kent Bowling

	Overs	Mdns	Runs	Wkts	Overs	Mdns	Runs	Wkts
Wright	28.3	4	102	5	3	—	6	—
Ridgway	18	3	55	2	16	5	29	2
Crush	20	3	59	1	13	1	32	—
Dovey	22	12	20	1	42	10	97	4
Hearn					23	1	95	2

Umpires: A. Skelding and C. N. Woolley.

KENT v LEICESTERSHIRE

Played at Maidstone, July 20, 21, 22, 1949

Kent won by 209 runs. An opening stand of 251 by Todd and Fagg completely changed the aspect of affairs after Leicestershire had gained a lead of 92. It was the highest partnership achieved by this pair for Kent, surpassing their 230 against Northamptonshire at Tunbridge Wells in 1948. First to leave, Fagg batted three hours twenty-five minutes and hit fourteen 4s. Todd showed his most attractive form and, besides hitting his first century of the season, made the highest score of his long career. His only chance was when 166; staying four hours ten minutes, he hit one 6 and twenty-one 4s. Despite gruelling heat, Wright bowled with some pace down the slope. He took fifteen wickets for 163 runs. As Clark developed influenza, Ames captained Kent on the last day.

Kent

L. J. Todd c Riddington b Sperry	9	– b Jackson	174
A. E. Fagg run out	58	– c Symington b Sperry	124
L. E. G. Ames b Sperry	6	– c Walsh b Symington	2
P. Hearn b Symington	3	– not out	52
B. Edrich lbw b Lester	16	– c Riddington b Prentice	40
T. G. Evans c Jackson b Walsh	17	– b Jackson	13
D. G. Clark c Munden b Walsh	10		
E. Crush b Sperry	51		
R. R. Dovey b Symington	38		
D. V. P. Wright not out	0		
F. Ridgway b Symington	0		
B 8, l-b 8	16	B 8, l-b 4	12

224   (5 wkts dec.) 417

Leicestershire

L. G. Berry lbw b Wright	69	– c Edrich b Wright	15
G. Lester c Fagg b Ridgway	0	– lbw b Wright	29
F. T. Prentice b Wright	64	– c Edrich b Wright	37
M. Tompkin lbw b Wright	38	– c Ames b Dovey	8
V. E. Jackson lbw b Wright	46	– c Evans b Wright	3
A. Riddington b Dovey	6	– b Wright	13
S. J. Symington not out	54	– b Wright	0
V. Munden c Ames b Wright	0	– lbw b Wright	0
J. E. Walsh c Hearn b Edrich	10	– c Fagg b Wright	0
P. Corrall b Wright	18	– not out	3
J. Sperry b Edrich	1	– c Ames b Wright	0
B 6, l-b 3, n-b 1	10	B 2, l-b 5, n-b 1	8
	316		**116**

Leicestershire Bowling

	Overs	Mdns	Runs	Wkts	Overs	Mdns	Runs	Wkts
Sperry	24	6	61	3	24	4	102	1
Symington	14.5	6	22	3	18	3	70	1
Walsh	18	2	70	2	9	—	36	—
Lester	7	—	31	1	3	—	22	—
Jackson	6	1	17	—	25	3	75	2
Riddington	4	—	7	—	14	—	63	—
Prentice					8.4	2	21	1
Munden					2	—	16	—

Kent Bowling

	Overs	Mdns	Runs	Wkts	Overs	Mdns	Runs	Wkts
Ridgway	21	3	61	1	4	1	9	—
Crush	17	3	41	—	6	1	17	—
Wright	29	5	112	6	16	3	51	9
Dovey	27	8	70	1	13	4	31	1
Edrich	5.1	1	22	2				

Umpires: E. Robinson and K. McCanlis.

KENT v WARWICKSHIRE

Played at Maidstone, July 23, 25, 26, 1949

Drawn. One of the best matches of a memorable season was splendidly handled by two professional captains, Ames and Dollery, and they carried off the batting honours. After Todd was bowled by the first ball of the game, a stand of 137 by Fagg and Ames held up Warwickshire. A defiant partnership of 152 by Taylor and Dollery contributed mainly to the visitors gaining first innings points, despite the late arrival of Kardar on the second day. He had been to Oxford for one of his final exams. In a superb display of hitting on a wearing pitch Ames made 160 in three hours, his chief strokes earning one 6 and twenty-two 4s. After he left, Pritchard performed the hat-trick when dismissing Phebey, Crush and Ufton, who was making his début for Kent. Ames set Warwickshire to score

277 in three hours, and, thanks to a great innings by Dollery, who hit one 6 and eighteen 4s in a stay of less than two hours they kept pace with the clock. Eleven minutes remained when Dollery was fifth out at 262. Wolton, Pritchard and Grove all went at 263, and the last over arrived with Warwickshire still wanting five with two wickets left. From the first ball Taylor was caught, and from the next one Bromley survived a chance of stumping. Then Bromley and Spooner each took a single. They ran a leg-bye from the fifth, and all Spooner could do with the last ball was to hit it back along the ground to the bowler. So stumps were pulled up with only a single separating the sides.

Kent

L. J. Todd b Pritchard	0	– b Grove	10
A. E. Fagg c Dollery b Kardar	68	– c Spooner b Pritchard	24
L. E. G. Ames b Kardar	69	– c Pritchard b Kardar	160
P. Hearn c Spooner b Grove	59	– st Spooner b Kardar	19
A. H. Phebey c Townsend b Grove	1	– b Pritchard	44
B. R. Edrich b Pritchard	18	– lbw b Grove	12
D. G. Ufton not out	27	– c Grove b Pritchard	0
E. Crush c Spooner b Pritchard	7	– c sub b Pritchard	0
R. R. Dovey c Spooner b Pritchard	0	– not out	3
D. V. P. Wright b Grove	6		
J. W. Martin c Pritchard b Grove	0	– c Wolton b Kardar	14
B 2, l-b 6, n-b 2	10	L-b 10, w 1, n-b 3	14
	265	**(9 wkts dec.)**	**300**

Warwickshire

K. A. Taylor lbw b Wright	89	– c Martin b Dovey	2
F. C. Gardner c Hearn b Edrich	24	– c Hearn b Wright	27
A. Townsend c Martin b Wright	1	– c Phebey b Wright	16
J. S. Ord c Ufton b Wright	10	– c and b Wright	25
H. E. Dollery c Crush b Wright	95	– c Ufton b Martin	118
R. T. Spooner not out	37	– not out	6
A. V. Wolton b Dovey	4	– b Martin	26
P. H. Bromley c Hearn b Wright	4	– not out	1
C. W. Grove b Dovey	4	– c sub b Dovey	0
T. L. Pritchard b Dovey	0	– b Dovey	1
A. H. Kardar absent	0	– run out	40
B 5, l-b 15, w 1	21	B 4, l-b 7, w 1, n-b 1	13
	289	**(9 wkts)**	**275**

Warwickshire Bowling

	Overs	Mdns	Runs	Wkts	Overs	Mdns	Runs	Wkts
Pritchard	31	2	96	4	26	2	97	4
Grove	29.3	10	52	4	19	4	79	2
Townsend	15	3	32	—	8	—	32	—
Kardar	22	7	60	2	20.3	3	78	3
Bromley	6	2	15	—				

Kent Bowling

	Overs	Mdns	Runs	Wkts	Overs	Mdns	Runs	Wkts
Martin	26	7	59	—	21	2	89	2
Crush	15	2	43	—	4	—	16	—
Wright	38	11	96	5	15	—	77	3
Edrich	9	1	24	1	6	—	27	—
Dovey	21.4	8	46	3	15	1	53	3

Umpires: E. Robinson and K. McCanlis.

KENT v HAMPSHIRE

Played at Canterbury, July 30, August 1, 1949

Kent won by an innings and 28 runs. After fielding five hours fifty minutes while Kent scored 413 for eight wickets, Hampshire made 23 without loss on Saturday, but on Monday between eleven o'clock and a few minutes after seven they were dismissed twice, twenty wickets falling for an aggregate of 362 runs. Todd hit fourteen 4s during four and a half hours of admirable batting. Ames, in scoring 80 out of 142 in two hours twenty minutes, hit nine 4s and with Davies in aggressive form, 129 runs came for the third wicket before Todd left soon after tea. Davies got his 99 at one a minute, drives, cuts and leg hits bringing him twelve 4s. He fell to a good catch by Blake, a smart wicket-keeper playing his third match for Hampshire, who shaped well as a left-handed batsman. Wright carried off the bowling honours with eleven wickets for 170. In dismissing Eagar, Walker and Shackleton he did his seventh hat-trick in first-class cricket, and Eagar's wicket in the second innings was his 100th of the season. Davies, captaining Kent in the absence of D. Clark, indisposed, set a splendid example in the field and used his bowlers discreetly. Dovey could not be included in the strong Kent side after appearing in 76 consecutive matches for the county. On Monday, when over 14,000 people were present, the teams were introduced to the Duke of Edinburgh, who was accompanied on the field by Lord Harris, Kent Club President, and Lord Cornwallis, Lord Lieutenant of Kent.

Kent

L. J. Todd lbw b Shackleton 129	T. G. Evans c Blake b Shackleton. 27
A. E. Fagg b Shackleton. 12	E. Crush not out . . . `. 7
L. E. G. Ames c Blake b Shackleton. 80	D. V. P. Wright not out. 5
J. G. W. Davies c Blake b Bailey. 99	
H. A. Pawson c Knott b Dean 19	B 6, l-b 5, n-b 1 12
P. Hearn b Knott 8	
B. R. Edrich c Eagar b Bailey 15	(8 wkts dec.) 413

J. W. Martin did not bat.

Hampshire

D. E. Blake c Hearn b Crush.	16	– c Edrich b Wright.	16
N. H. Rogers c Fagg b Wright	13	– c Martin b Wright.	45
G. Dawson c Hearn b Wright.	22	– b Davies	34
J. Bailey c Fagg b Martin	22	– c Martin b Wright.	32
E. D. R. Eagar c Crush b Wright	37	– c Davies b Wright.	5
J. Arnold not out.	50	– c Pawson b Crush.	10
C. Walker lbw b Wright	0	– lbw b Wright.	6
D. Shackleton b Wright.	0	– c Evans b Martin	13
R. Carty b Davies	10	– b Wright.	4
T. A. Dean b Davies.	0	– not out	5
C. J. Knott c Wright b Davies.	19	– c Evans b Martin	1
B 4, l-b 7, w 1, n-b 1	13	B 1, l-b 6, w 3, n-b 2	12
	202		**183**

Hampshire Bowling

	Overs	Mdns	Runs	Wkts
Shackleton	28	4	74	4
Carty	13	1	50	—
Walker	18	2	60	—
Knott	21	8	52	1
Dean.	21	2	90	1
Bailey	20	2	75	2

Kent Bowling

	Overs	Mdns	Runs	Wkts	Overs	Mdns	Runs	Wkts
Martin.	11	3	12	1	12.2	2	22	2
Crush	13	—	39	1	12	4	23	1
Wright	25	7	81	5	23	3	89	6
Edrich.	11	1	24	—	6	—	23	—
Davies.	11.4	4	33	3	17	9	14	1

Umpires: A. R. Coleman and H. G. Baldwin.

KENT v MIDDLESEX

Played at Canterbury, August, 3, 4, 5, 1949

Middlesex won by 107 runs. Having twice declared for the loss of ten wickets in the two innings, Middlesex won the match after an exciting finish at twenty minutes past five. Heavy rain on the day before the match did not make the pitch difficult, though the ball was apt to lift from a good length, and Mann preferred not to enforce the follow-on when 151 ahead because the turf showed signs of wear. By a curious coincidence Middlesex in their first innings scored exactly the aggregate for which Hampshire were twice dismissed on the Monday. Brown surpassed all the other batsmen in the match by playing his first innings of 200. At the wicket five hours ten minutes, he hit twenty-one 4s in a thoroughly good display, marked by hard drives, sure pulls and neat late cuts. He outpaced Robertson while 152 runs came in two hours twenty-five minutes, but the most brilliant batting for Middlesex was by Edrich and Denis Compton, who added 169 in an hour and three-quarters during two spells on Thursday and Friday. Todd and Fagg started with stands of 72 and 63, but Davies played the best innings for Kent, hitting a 6 and ten 4s before failing in a risky run when striving after the impossible, and Evans hit splendidly until Robins judged a difficult catch at long-on – a fitting finish to a very successful Festival Week. This completed a remarkable bowling achievement by Young, whose figures in the match were 68.5 overs, 25 maidens 119 runs 13 wickets.

Middlesex

J. D. Robertson c Davies b Wright	71	– b Wright	22
S. M. Brown lbw b Dovey	200	– c Hearn b Dovey	24
W. J. Edrich c Davies b Todd	39	– not out	84
D. C. S. Compton c Mallett b Dovey	32	– c Mallett b Dovey	88
R. W. V. Robins b Dovey	4		
F. G. Mann c Davies b Edrich	8		
L. Compton b Dovey	1		
H. Sharp not out	1	– not out	7
J. Sims not out	1		
B 4, l-b 1	5	B 16, l-b 5, w 1, n-b 2	24
(7 wkts dec.)	362	(3 wkts dec.)	249

J. A. Young and L. Gray did not bat.

Kent

L. J. Todd c Edrich b Young	68	– lbw b Sharp	57
A. E. Fagg b Young	41	– c and b Young	21
L. E. G. Ames lbw b Young	1	– lbw b Young	28
J. G. W. Davies b Young	15	– run out	72
H. A. Pawson b Young	33	– c D. Compton b Sims	20
P. Hearn lbw b Young	15	– b Young	16
B. Edrich b Young	7	– c and b D. Compton	0
A. W. H. Mallett c L. Compton b D. Compton	14	– c Sharp b Young	3
T. G. Evans c Young b D. Compton	4	– c Robins b Young	61
R. R. Dovey c Robins b D. Compton	4	– c Sims b Young	1
D. V. P. Wright not out	0	– not out	3
B 7, l-b 1, n-b 1	9	B 8, l-b 2, n-b 1	11
	211		**293**

Kent Bowling

	Overs	Mdns	Runs	Wkts	Overs	Mdns	Runs	Wkts
Mallett	31	6	74	—	16	3	48	—
Todd	12	3	47	1	6	2	8	—
Dovey	25	8	72	4	24	4	74	2
Wright	22	2	82	1	14	2	65	1
Davies	16	2	51	—	3	—	7	—
Edrich	8	—	31	1	8	—	23	—

Middlesex Bowling

	Overs	Mdns	Runs	Wkts	Overs	Mdns	Runs	Wkts
Edrich	9	2	32	—	4	1	9	—
Gray	11	5	17	—	2	—	14	—
Sims	13	1	42	—	14	2	59	1
Young	29	12	47	7	39.5	13	72	6
D. Compton	16.1	1	64	3	25	3	93	1
Sharp					3	—	21	1
Robins					2	—	14	—

Umpires: A. R. Coleman and H. G. Baldwin.

KENT v SURREY

Played at Blackheath, July 15, 17, 18, 1950

Kent won by 156 runs. In gaining their first victory for sixteen years in the traditional Blackheath fixture, Kent were indebted to the splendid bowling of Dovey, whose eight wickets for 23 in the first Surrey innings was easily the best performance of his career. On rain-affected turf, Dovey made the ball turn into the batsmen so sharply that many of his victims fell to leg-side catches. Fagg and Clark increased Kent's lead by 65 before the first wicket fell, and Dovey and Martin joined in another enterprising last-wicket stand, so that Surrey were set to make 338 to win. Fishlock and Clark hit 96 for the fourth wicket, but the remaining batsmen were again helpless against Dovey.

Kent

A. E. Fagg c Surridge b Bedser	24	– lbw b Parker	44
D. G. Clark c McIntyre b Bedser	7	– c and b Lock	58
L. E. G. Ames c Lock b Bedser	14	– lbw b Laker	1
P. Hearn run out	30	– c McIntyre b Parker	3
A. H. Phebey c Lock b Parker	34	– c McIntyre b Parker	11
T. G. Evans c and b Parker	24	– lbw b Laker	12
R. Mayes c Barton b Parker	6	– b Lock	5
B. Edrich lbw b Parker	0	– b Lock	5
R. R. Dovey not out	12	– b Surridge	18
D. V. P. Wright b Laker	0	– hit wkt b Lock	0
J. W. Martin c Barton b Surridge	35	– not out	33
L-b 3	3	B 9, l-b 1, n-b 1	11
	189		**201**

Surrey

L. B. Fishlock c Edrich b Dovey	13	– c Phebey b Dovey	77
T. H. Clark c Evans b Martin	0	– b Wright	54
B. Constable c Evans b Dovey	2	– run out	8
J. F. Parker c Clark b Dovey	0	– c Fagg b Dovey	0
M. R. Barton c Phebey b Dovey	2	– c Edrich b Dovey	12
G. J. Whittaker c and b Wright	14	– b Wright	0
G. A. R. Lock lbw b Dovey	5	– not out	0
A. J. McIntyre b Dovey	7	– lbw b Dovey	4
J. C. Laker not out	4	– lbw b Martin	1
A. V. Bedser b Dovey	1	– lbw b Dovey	17
W. S. Surridge c Phebey b Dovey	0	– lbw b Wright	3
B 3, l-b 2	5	B 3, l-b 2	5
	53		**181**

Surrey Bowling

	Overs	Mdns	Runs	Wkts	Overs	Mdns	Runs	Wkts
Bedser	13	2	31	3	11	2	43	—
Surridge	12.3	—	42	1	7.2	1	24	1
Parker	23	8	32	4	11	3	22	3
Lock	15	5	33	—	14	6	40	4
Laker	24	11	48	1	28	7	61	2

Kent Bowling

	Overs	Mdns	Runs	Wkts	Overs	Mdns	Runs	Wkts
Martin	18	7	24	1	23	9	34	1
Dovey	19.2	12	23	8	29	9	52	5
Wright	2	1	1	1	16.4	3	59	3
Edrich					10	—	31	—

Umpires: H. W. Parks and T. Spencer.

KENT v MIDDLESEX

Played at Canterbury, August 9, 10, 11, 1950

Kent won by four wickets within seven minutes of half-past three, the latest time for drawing stumps. During a great effort for his side, Ames made the hundredth century of his first-class career and put victory within reach. Going in on Fagg's failure without a run scored, Ames played a grand innings. Often running to drive while getting 131 runs out of 211 in two hours, Ames fell to that risk, Moss holding a hard drive close to the ground in the deep field. He hit two 6s and seventeen 4s. Hearn shared a stand that realised 110 in seventy-five minutes, and, with Pawson very free, 85 runs came in thirty-five minutes. Pawson hit seven 4s before Warr bowled him and Mallett, but an on-boundary by Dovey brought victory. Middlesex began the match with a stand of 99, and Robertson and Dewes started their second innings by scoring 80. Fagg hit a dozen 4s in his 88 and was run out unluckily. He and Pawson added 106, and the Oxford Blue saw Kent in the lead after hitting fourteen 4s during nearly three hours' sound batting which made the first declaration possible. Edrich responded after an unfinished stand of 115 with Brown, and then came the grand climax to this splendid sporting cricket. Evans received a blow on his right hand while batting and Ames kept wicket in the Middlesex second innings.

Middlesex

J. D. Robertson st Evans b Wright	40	– b Dovey 54
J. G. Dewes c Evans b Wright	60	– c Pawson b Dovey 32
W. J. Edrich b Ridgway	6	– not out 77
H. P. Sharp b Dovey	62	– c Clark b Wright 21
S. M. Brown b Wright	19	– not out 51
L. H. Compton b Wright	7	
F. J. Titmus c Evans b Ridgway	9	
J. M. Sims c Fagg b Ridgway	13	
J. J. Warr b Wright	4	
J. A. Young b Dovey	14	
A. E. Moss not out	7	
B 4, l-b 4	8	B 6 6
	249	**(3 wkts dec.) 241**

Kent

A. E. Fagg run out	88	– c L. Compton b Warr 0
D. G. Clark c L. Compton b Warr	6	– run out 3
L. E. G. Ames c L. Compton b Warr	4	– c Moss b Young 131
P. Hearn st L. Compton b Sims	17	– b Young 30
H. A. Pawson not out	103	– b Warr 57
T. G. Evans c Sims b Warr	6	
A. Woollett c Young b Warr	10	– not out 0
A. W. H. Mallett not out	15	– b Warr 9
R. R. Dovey (did not bat)	–	not out 5
L-b 4, w 1	5	B 4 4
	(6 wkts dec.) 254	**(6 wkts) 239**

D. V. P. Wright and F. Ridgway did not bat.

Kent Bowling

	Overs	Mdns	Runs	Wkts	Overs	Mdns	Runs	Wkts
Ridgway	31	9	86	3	22	8	59	—
Mallett	20	5	58	—	27	8	65	—
Dovey	19.5	4	36	2	20	4	64	2
Wright	30	8	61	5	11	2	47	1

Middlesex Bowling

	Overs	Mdns	Runs	Wkts	Overs	Mdns	Runs	Wkts
Warr	26	8	67	4	11	1	57	3
Moss	21	4	76	—	5	2	18	—
Sims	16	2	53	1	14	1	53	—
Young	14	8	15	—	19	3	90	2
Titmus	11	2	38	—	0.5	—	4	—
Edrich					1	—	13	—

Umpires: J. T. Bell and H. Elliott.

KENT v DERBYSHIRE

Played at Folkestone, July 25, 26, 27, 1951

Derbyshire won by 177 runs. Ridgway the Kent fast bowler, made the game memorable by dismissing four batsmen with consecutive balls in the Derbyshire first innings – the first time the feat had been accomplished in England since 1937 and anywhere since the war. After taking the new ball at 204, Ridgway in his second over broke a fourth wicket stand of 159 by bowling Revill with his first delivery. Kelly, Rhodes and Gladwin followed to catches at first-slip, backward short-leg and wicket-keeper respectively. Despite these shocks Carr stood firm and he completed a fine century with the help of twelve 4s. Though less spectacular than Ridgway, Gladwin was equally effective when Kent batted. A stand of 106 between Edrich and Kimmins took the score to 190 for five but the last five wickets fell – four to Gladwin – for the addition of a single. Carr was again in magnificent batting form and, when Willatt declared with a lead of 312 was within six of a second hundred. Against the leg-breaks and googlies of Rhodes, Kent gave a poor display.

Derbyshire

C. S. Elliott c Fagg b Ridgway	0	– b Ridgway	22
A. Hamer c Davies b Wright	23	– b Ridgway	4
G. L. Willatt b Kimmins	20	– c Evans b Jose	10
A. C. Revill b Ridgway	75	– c Davies b Dovey	42
D. B. Carr not out	103	– not out	94
J. Kelly c Fagg b Ridgway	0	– c Evans b Cowdrey	40
A. E. G. Rhodes c Cowdrey b Ridgway	0	– not out	21
C. Gladwin c Evans b Ridgway	0		
G. Dawkes lbw b Ridgway	3		
T. A. Hall run out	6		
L. Jackson b Jose	0		
B 4, l-b 4, w 2	10	B 16, l-b 13, w 1	30
	240	**(5 wkts dec.)**	**263**

Kent

A. E. Fagg b Gladwin	3	– c Willatt b Jackson	2
J. G. W. Davies c Willatt b Gladwin	1	– c Dawkes b Rhodes	12
P. Hearn c Revill b Jackson	38	– c Elliott b Rhodes	36
M. C. Cowdrey c Dawkes b Jackson	26	– c Revill b Rhodes	35
B. R. Edrich c Elliott b Gladwin	72	– c Kelly b Carr	18
T. G. Evans c Carr b Gladwin	7	– c Willatt b Jackson	10
S. E. A. Kimmins c Willatt b Jackson	39	– lbw b Rhodes	0
R. R. Dovey b Gladwin	0	– b Rhodes	5
D. V. P. Wright b Gladwin	0	– st Dawkes b Rhodes	12
A. D. Jose not out	1	– lbw b Jackson	0
F. Ridgway c Carr b Gladwin	0	– not out	0
B 1, l-b 1, w 2	4	B 4, l-b 1	5
	191		**135**

Kent Bowling

	Overs	Mdns	Runs	Wkts	Overs	Mdns	Runs	Wkts
Ridgway	22	5	44	6	9	1	24	2
Jose	16.5	2	61	1	12	1	46	1
Kimmins	6	2	15	1	7	1	29	—
Wright	12	1	46	1	12	3	48	—
Dovey	15	5	20	—	15	2	50	1
Edrich	3	1	22	—	2	—	15	—
Cowdrey	2	—	22	—	3	—	10	1
Davies					6	1	11	—

Derbyshire Bowling

	Overs	Mdns	Runs	Wkts	Overs	Mdns	Runs	Wkts
Jackson..........	21	4	62	3	10	3	18	3
Gladwin..........	26.5	7	55	7	11	2	32	—
Hall..............	9	4	27	—	5	2	12	—
Rhodes...........	10	1	32	—	16.4	2	57	6
Hamer	6	2	4	—				
Carr	1	—	7	—	3	—	11	1

Umpires: J. T. Bell and C. H. Welch.

KENT v ESSEX

Played at Blackheath, July 28, 30, 31, 1951

Drawn. After two days of complete batting supremacy, Martin and Dovey upset Essex in an incredible finish. Needing 126 to win in 45 minutes, Essex lost wickets rapidly in their attempts to force the pace, then were equally unsuccessful when seeking to "put up the shutters." With ten minutes remaining, seven wickets were down but, though surrounded by fieldsmen, Avery and Vigar denied Kent further reward. Previously Fagg demonstrated once more his partiality for Essex bowling by hitting 178 out of 327 in over six hours. Essex retaliated through Gibb and Horsfall who shared a third partnership of 343 — a new Essex record. Gibb occupied five hours twenty minutes but the aggressive Horsfall spent only four and a half hours over his first double century, which included twenty-six 4s.

Kent

A. E. Fagg b Insole	178	– c Vigar b R. Smith	54
J. G. W. Davies c Greensmith b R. Smith	6	– c Greensmith b Preston	5
P. Hearn c P. Smith b Insole	16	– b P. Smith	27
H. A. Pawson c Gibb b Preston	30	– c Gibb b Greensmith	36
B. R. Edrich c Greensmith b Preston	41	– c Eve b Greensmith	9
R. Mayes c Gibb b Preston	1	– c Gibb b R. Smith	31
D. G. Clark c Eve b P. Smith	22	– c Preston b Greensmith	27
T. G. Evans c P. Smith b Insole	6	– c Insole b Greensmith	15
L. Hellmuth b P. Smith	3	– c Gibb b R. Smith	5
R. R. Dovey not out	6	– b R. Smith	7
J. W. Martin c Vigar b Insole	11	– not out	0
B 14, l-b 3, w 1, n-b 1	19	B 3, l-b 1, n-b 1	5
	339		**221**

Essex

T. C. Dodds c Edrich b Martin	30	– c Fagg b Martin	0
A. V. Avery b Edrich	34	– not out	4
P. A. Gibb c Clark b Hellmuth	141	– c Evans b Martin	0
R. Horsfall c Hellmuth b Edrich	206	– c Evans b Dovey	0
R. Smith st Evans b Edrich	7	– c Fagg b Dovey	0
T. P. B. Smith not out	4	– c Hellmuth b Martin	0
D. J. Insole (did not bat)		– c Hellmuth b Dovey	3
S. C. Eve (did not bat)		– b Dovey	5
F. H. Vigar (did not bat)		– not out	0
B 4, l-b 7, w 1, n-b 1	13	W 1	1
	(5 wkts dec.) **435**		(7 wkts) **13**

W. Greensmith and K. C. Preston did not bat.

Essex Bowling

	Overs	Mdns	Runs	Wkts	Overs	Mdns	Runs	Wkts
Preston	24	4	74	3	15	2	36	1
R. Smith	29	8	80	1	29.1	9	60	4
Insole	18.2	5	53	4	6	2	13	—
P. Smith	35	12	64	2	28	10	57	1
Greensmith	10	2	49	—	20	8	31	4
Dodds					3	—	19	—

Kent Bowling

	Overs	Mdns	Runs	Wkts	Overs	Mdns	Runs	Wkts
Martin	35	5	105	1	9	5	4	3
Dovey	39	8	98	—	8	5	8	4
Davies	10	3	20	—				
Hellmuth	31	8	86	1				
Edrich	20.3	4	60	3				
Hearn	8	1	38	—				
Pawson	2	—	15	—				

Umpires: F. Chester and F. S. Lee.

KENT v SURREY

Played at Blackheath, July 11, 13, 14, 1953

Drawn. Surrey were given an excellent start by Loader, the fast-medium bowler, who followed his twelve wickets in the previous match with thirteen for 113. Twice dismissing batsmen with following deliveries, he appeared likely to take all ten wickets in Kent's first innings, but Wright ran himself out. Loader relied on accurate length and direction. He gained little assistance from a pitch on which May, and to some extent Fletcher, later scored with freedom. Each reached his century with the help of sixteen 4s and Surrey finished the day 180 ahead. Kent eventually faced arrears of 239 and with half their side out for 49 defeat looked imminent. Then Witherden, who stayed five hours for his maiden century, and Murray Wood added 143, only fourteen short of Kent's record eighth wicket stand. Mainly through their efforts Surrey were left to score 85 to win, but rain prevented further cricket. In the absence of Surridge, Surrey's fielding fell far below its usual standard.

Kent

A. H. Phebey c McIntyre b Loader	5	– c Fletcher b Loader	14
A. F. Woollett lbw b Loader	2	– lbw b Cox	2
P. Hearn b Loader	0	– c Fletcher b Loader	27
D. G. Ufton b Loader	10	– c Fletcher b Loader	0
B. R. Edrich b Loader	0	– c Cox b Loader	3
E. G. Witherden not out	26	– not out	125
F. Ridgway c McIntyre b Loader	8	– b Clark	19
R. R. Dovey b Loader	0	– c and b Constable	8
W. Murray Wood b Loader	0	– c May b Clark	93
D. V. P. Wright run out	6	– c McMahon b Cox	10
J. C. T. Page lbw b Loader	0	– b Cox	16
B 2, l-b 4	6	L-b 6	6

1/8 2/8 3/11 4/13 5/30   63   1/10 2/44 3/45 4/46 5/49   323
6/56 7/56 8/56 9/62   6/92 7/125 8/268 9/282

Surrey

D. G. W. Fletcher b Dovey............115	K. Barrington not out................. 15
E. A. Bedser lbw b Wright 14	
B. Constable st Ufton b Witherden........ 5	B 6, l-b 5, w 1 12
P. B. H. May c and b Wright 116	
T. H. Clark c and b Wright............. 9	1/29 2/38 3/251 (5 wkts dec.) 302
R. Subba Row not out................. 16	4/265 5/275

A. J. McIntyre, D. F. Cox, J. W. McMahon and P. J. Loader did not bat.

Surrey Bowling

	Overs	Mdns	Runs	Wkts	Overs	Mdns	Runs	Wkts
Loader	16	3	28	9	41	8	85	4
Cox..............	12	3	21	—	33	5	86	3
McMahon.........	5	2	5	—	17	6	39	—
Bedser............	8	6	3	—	21	7	33	—
Clark					20	6	42	2
Constable					5	2	18	1
Subba Row........					3	—	14	—

Kent Bowling

	Overs	Mdns	Runs	Wkts
Ridgway..........	5	2	9	—
Dovey............	28	6	59	1
Wright	29	4	94	3
Witherden.........	21	5	77	1
Page	7	1	37	—
Hearn	3	1	14	—

Umpires: W. F. Price and E. Cooke.

KENT v MIDDLESEX

Played at Canterbury, August 5, 6, 7, 1953

Middlesex won by 99 runs. They were always in command. Edrich and Denis Compton retrieved a bad start with confident attacking batting, but rain caused first a long interruption then an early close to the day. More rain in the night brought much different conditions on the second day. On a lively pitch Middlesex hit out freely, adding 69 in an hour while losing seven wickets before declaring. Smith, who maintained his usual consistent length, took five of these in 31 deliveries. Kent adopted tactics similar to their opponents, but, although the innings contained twenty 4s, few of the batsmen survived for long against the spin of Titmus and Young. More Middlesex aggression raised the day's aggregate to 356 in just over five hours, during which twenty-two wickets fell. Eight successive strokes in the fifth-wicket stand of Thompson and Dewes went to the boundary. On the last day Cowdrey played a valiant innings for Kent and alone countered the sharply turning ball with certainty. Young brought his match analysis to fourteen for 115. His second innings analysis was his best of the season.

Middlesex

J. D. Robertson run out	8	– b Mallett	0
S. M. Brown b Mallett	5	– c Shirreff b Smith	5
W. J. Edrich c Phebey b Smith	63	– lbw b Page	18
D. C. S. Compton b Page	72	– c Mallett b Page	39
J. G. Dewes c Evans b Smith	22	– not out	48
A. Thompson c Mayes b Smith	26	– st Evans b Smith	48
D. Bennett b Smith	5	– c Fagg b Smith	5
L. H. Compton lbw b Smith	0	– not out	4
F. J. Titmus c Mallett b Page	1		
J. A. Young not out	0		
B 4, 1-b 10	14	B 2, 1-b 6	8

1/14 2/29 3/155 4/161   (9 wkts dec.) 216   1/7 2/7 3/58   (6 wkts dec.) 175
5/198 6/212 7/212 8/215 9/216   4/77 5/158 6/170

A. E. Moss did not bat.

Kent

A. E. Fagg c L. Compton b Titmus	5	– st L. Compton b Young	34
A. H. Phebey c Moss b Young	16	– c Edrich b Young	3
A. F. Woollett c D. Compton b Young	49	– st L. Compton b Titmus	5
M. C. Cowdrey c Moss b Titmus	28	– not out	52
R. Mayes c Robertson b Young	0	– c L. Compton b Young	0
T. G. Evans c Dewes b Young	13	– b Young	17
A. C. Shirreff b Titmus	12	– b Young	0
G. Smith lbw b Titmus	1	– c Robertson b Young	0
W. Murray Wood c Bennett b Young	1	– c Bennett b Young	8
A. W. H. Mallett c Brown b Young	0	– c Dewes b Young	23
J. C. T. Page not out	0	– b Titmus	0
L-b 4	4	B 13, 1-b 8	21

1/12 2/50 3/76 4/82 5/110   129   1/43 2/52 3/56 4/65 5/93   163
6/122 7/124 8/125 9/129   6/95 7/95 8/109 9/161

Kent Bowling

	Overs	Mdns	Runs	Wkts	Overs	Mdns	Runs	Wkts
Shirreff	23	8	51	—				
Smith	18.1	6	37	5	16	3	57	3
Mallett	17	4	51	1	16	6	45	1
Page	17	3	57	2	13	1	65	2
Cowdrey	1	—	6	—				

Middlesex Bowling

	Overs	Mdns	Runs	Wkts	Overs	Mdns	Runs	Wkts
Moss	4	2	4	—		1	6	—
Bennett	3	1	8	—	3	—	17	—
Young	17	6	55	6	20	6	60	8
Titmus	17.2	4	54	4	20.2	6	59	2
D. Compton	1	—	4	—				

Umpires: T. J. Bartley and W. T. Jones.

KENT v ESSEX

Played at Gillingham, June 25, 27, 28, 1955

Kent won by five wickets with three minutes remaining. The game was rendered memorable by the performances of Insole and Cowdrey. Each hit two separate hundreds in a match for the first time and Insole became the first player to reach 1,000 runs. On an awkward pitch, Insole saved Essex in the first innings, he and Greensmith adding 142 for the eighth wicket. In turn Cowdrey (fourteen 4s) helped Kent to a lead of 35 and a declaration. Then Insole shared with Gibb in a stand of 117 and enabled Essex to declare and leave Kent to get 206 in two and a quarter hours. Despite the loss of three men for 28, Kent kept up with the clock and Cowdrey and Hearn in a partnership of 152 in an hour and a quarter, virtually decided the issue.

Essex

T. C. Dodds c Smith b Spanswick	21	– c Smith b Spanswick 25
G. Barker c Ufton b Spanswick	10	– c Fagg b Spanswick 8
P. A. Gibb c Hearn b Page	38	– lbw b Smith 53
R. Ralph c Spanswick b Smith	1	– not out 2
D. J. Insole c Spanswick b Page	111	– c Phebey b Smith 118
R. Horsfall b Page	17	– c Ufton b Spanswick 0
M. Bear c Ufton b Page	0	– not out 19
R. Smith b Smith	8	– c Wilson b Page 12
W. T. Greensmith not out	63	
G. Smith c Cowdrey b Smith	1	
K. C. Preston lbw b Page	11	
B 1, l-b 4	5	L-b 2, w 1 3

1/29 2/32 3/33 4/81 5/113   286   1/30 2/33   (6 wkts dec.) 240
6/113 7/126 8/268 9/269   3/41 4/158 5/171 6/237

Kent

A. E. Fagg c Gibb b Greensmith	49	– lbw b Preston 15
A. H. Phebey c Insole b R. Smith	0	– b Preston 6
R. C. Wilson b Ralph	52	– c Dodds b R. Smith 7
M. C. Cowdrey not out	115	– not out 103
P. Hearn c Gibb b Ralph	3	– b Preston 60
J. Pettiford run out	30	
A. L. Dixon b R. Smith	32	– b Ralph..................... 10
D. G. Ufton not out	35	
G. Smith (did not bat)		– not out 0
L-b 4, w 1	5	B 2, l-b 6 8

1/0 2/92 3/110 4/114   (6 wkts dec.) 321   1/9 2/28 3/28   (5 wkts) 209
5/174 6/270   4/180 5/205

J. Spanswick and J. C. T. Page did not bat.

Kent Bowling

	Overs	Mdns	Runs	Wkts	Overs	Mdns	Runs	Wkts
Spanswick	18	4	48	2	18	3	75	3
Smith	33	15	75	3	26	4	62	2
Page	41.2	11	110	5	21	3	82	1
Pettiford	17	7	39	—				
Dixon	3	1	9	—	3	—	9	—
Cowdrey					2	—	9	—

Essex Bowling

	Overs	Mdns	Runs	Wkts	Overs	Mdns	Runs	Wkts
Preston	21	4	69	—	11.1	1	57	3
R. Smith	22	4	56	2	4	—	19	1
Ralph	33	7	80	2	8	1	33	1
Insole	5	—	18	—				
Greensmith	27	5	58	1	10	1	36	—
G. Smith	16	7	35	—	3	—	18	—
Dodds					8	1	38	—

Umpires: H. G. Baldwin and E. Cooke.

KENT v WORCESTERSHIRE

Played at Dover, August 17, 18, 19, 1955

Worcestershire won by 52 runs in a match dominated by two outstanding bowling performances. Wright shattered Worcestershire's first innings on an excellent batting pitch, but even his magnificent effort was surpassed by that of Flavell. Bowling very fast and straight he demoralised the Kent batsmen in taking nine for 30 – the best bowling figures of the season. Kent were all out in an hour and three-quarters, but hit back effectively before the first day ended by taking four more wickets for 49 runs. They were checked next morning by Horton and then Flavell celebrated with his highest first-class score in a valuable last-wicket stand. Kent needed only 256, but their hopes fell when Berry sent back Fagg, Phebey and Allan cheaply. A good innings by Wilson was not enough to prevent Worcestershire achieving the "double" at their expense.

Worcestershire

D. Kenyon lbw b Wright	21	– c Catt b Smith	28
L. Outschoorn c Phebey b Wright	39	– c Fagg b Sayer	7
R. G. Broadbent c Sayer b Wright	9	– b Smith	6
M. J. Horton b Wright	16	– b Allan	62
G. Dews lbw b Wright	8	– c Wright b Pettiford	33
D. W. Richardson c Catt b Allan	1	– c Catt b Smith	0
R. O. Jenkins b Wright	2	– c Wilson b Wright	1
H. Yarnold not out	0	– c Pretlove b Allan	0
G. H. Chesterton b Wright	4	– not out	6
R. Berry b Allan	5	– b Allan	0
J. Flavell c Sayer b Wright	4	– c Allan b Wright	29
B 9, l-b 1	10	B 8, l-b 5, w 1	14

1/56 2/70 3/79 4/95 5/100	119	1/39 2/46 3/47 4/49 5/132	186
6/106 7/111 8/111 9/115		6/137 7/145 8/145 9/146	

Kent

A. E. Fagg lbw b Flavell	0	– c Richardson b Berry 14
A. H. Phebey lbw b Flavell	16	– lbw b Berry 20
R. C. Wilson b Flavell	11	– c Dews b Flavell 73
J. Pettiford b Flavell	13	– b Berry 30
J. F. Pretlove c Yarnold b Flavell	0	– run out 4
J. M. Allan b Flavell	3	– c Chesterton b Berry........... 11
A. F. Brazier c Broadbent b Chesterton	4	– c Broadbent b Chesterton........ 10
A. W. Catt b Flavell	0	– not out 17
G. Smith c Yarnold b Flavell	0	– b Chesterton 5
D. V. P. Wright not out	3	– c Outschoorn b Chesterton....... 13
D. M. Sayer b Flavell	0	– b Flavell 2
		L-b 4 4

1/0 2/20 3/34 4/36 5/42 6/47　　　　　　50　　1/29 2/34 3/69 4/137 5/147　　　203
7/47 8/47 9/50　　　　　　　　　　　　　　　　6/164 7/164 8/179 9/201

Kent Bowling

	Overs	Mdns	Runs	Wkts	Overs	Mdns	Runs	Wkts
Smith	7	2	25	—	22	6	53	3
Sayer	5	—	22	—	11	1	35	1
Allan............	25	15	26	2	25	12	56	3
Wright	21.5	11	36	8	11.2	5	21	2
Pettiford					3	1	7	1

Worcestershire Bowling

	Overs	Mdns	Runs	Wkts	Overs	Mdns	Runs	Wkts
Flavell...........	13.4	3	30	9	24	2	78	2
Chesterton	13	6	20	1	19	3	61	3
Berry............					24	13	40	4
Jenkins					4	1	5	—
Horton					6	3	15	—

Umpires: F. S. Lee and A. E. Pothecary.

KENT v NOTTINGHAMSHIRE

Played at Gravesend, June 2, 4, 5, 1956

Drawn in most exciting circumstances. Nottinghamshire made a spirited attempt to score 168 in seventy-five minutes and when Ridgway began the final over they were only 10 short of victory with three wickets left. Dooland and Winfield fell in the chase for runs and the last ball could have won the match for either side. Smales tried a big hit without success, the ball missed the stumps and the game was over. Nottinghamshire took a firm grip on the opening day, finishing 76 behind with one wicket down. Leary alone attacked Dooland with confidence, hitting seventeen 4s in his highest Championship innings and making his runs out of 124. Simpson batted in his most attractive style, all but 11 of his runs coming from boundary strokes, but after Giles had seen them comfortably in the lead Nottinghamshire lost their last five wickets for 22. Kent gave a more resolute display in their second innings.

Kent

M. C. Cowdrey c Rowe b Jepson	33	– c Walker b Smales	15
A. H. Phebey b Dooland	34	– b Dooland	6
R. C. Wilson c Poole b Dooland	5	– c Rowe b Dooland	58
S. E. Leary st Rowe b Dooland	91	– c Rowe b Jepson	33
J. Pettiford b Stocks	22	– b Dooland	30
A. L. Dixon c Rowe b Dooland	6	– c Poole b Dooland	20
D. G. Ufton st Rowe b Dooland	3	– lbw b Dooland	20
A. F. Brazier st Rowe b Dooland	6	– not out	22
F. Ridgway b Smales	0	– c Winfield b Dooland	26
D. J. Halfyard not out	16	– c Winfield b Dooland	0
J. C. T. Page c Giles b Dooland	1	– b Dooland	8
L-b 1	1	B 10, l-b 9	19

1/67 2/67 3/86 4/157 5/180   218   1/9 2/40 3/47 4/74 5/116   257
6/190 7/200 8/201 9/205   6/161 7/186 8/215 9/247

Nottinghamshire

R. T. Simpson c Ufton b Pettiford	83	– c and b Ridgway	10
R. J. Giles st Ufton b Dixon	136	– c Leary b Page	55
K. Smales c Ufton b Page	20	– not out	1
M. Winfield c sub b Halfyard	2	– run out	0
C. J. Poole c Wilson b Halfyard	2	– c Page b Halfyard	32
F. W. Stocks c Leary b Page	40	– b Dixon	12
B. Dooland b Dixon	6	– c Dixon b Ridgway	6
A. K. Walker b Page	1	– c Ridgway b Page	23
A. Jepson c Wilson b Page	14	– c Brazier b Ridgway	11
E. J. Martin c Phebey b Dixon	0	– b Page	6
E. J. Rowe not out	0	– not out	0
L-b 4	4	B 5, l-b 3	8

1/141 2/212 3/223 4/225 5/286   308   1/10 2/71 3/90   (9 wkts) 164
6/292 7/294 8/294 9/298   4/135 5/139 6/150 7/158
                                   8/162 9/164

Nottinghamshire Bowling

	Overs	Mdns	Runs	Wkts	Overs	Mdns	Runs	Wkts
Walker	10	—	36	—	6	1	17	—
Jepson	16	5	40	1	13	4	28	1
Dooland	35.3	11	83	7	40.3	15	110	8
Stocks	5	1	19	1	5	1	12	—
Smales	21	10	39	1	39	18	71	1

Kent Bowling

	Overs	Mdns	Runs	Wkts	Overs	Mdns	Runs	Wkts
Ridgway	17	7	27	—	12	—	75	3
Halfyard	28	7	89	2	5	—	40	1
Brazier	4	1	16	—				
Pettiford	15	9	28	1				
Leary	5	1	28	—				
Page	23.3	5	94	4	3	—	18	3
Dixon	12	7	22	3	3	—	23	1

Umpires: E. Cooke and A. J. B. Fowler.

KENT v SURREY

Played at Blackheath, July 7, 9, 10, 1956

Surrey won by an innings and 173 runs. Kent were completely outplayed by Surrey for the second time in a week, the match being notable chiefly for the bowling of Lock and the batting of Clark and May. In excellent conditions, Clark batted masterfully on the first day in hitting the biggest score of his career. Most of his twenty-nine 4s came from crisp off-drives. May, who helped to add 174 in two hours, batted far more convincingly than when scoring a century against Kent a week earlier, much of his stroke-play being superb. Week-end rain added to Kent's plight. On the Monday, when Surridge declared first thing, Lock received enough help from the turf to shatter Kent's moderate batting. Only Cowdrey and to a lesser extent Phebey could counter his biting leg-spin and when Kent followed-on even these two succumbed quickly. By the close Lock was in sight of all ten wickets for the first time and this he achieved the following morning by dismissing the last four batsmen without conceding a run. His sixteen wickets in the match for 83 runs made his figures for the two games with Kent twenty-six for 143.

Surrey

T. H. Clark b Ridgway 191	E. A. Bedser not out 11
M. J. Stewart c Fagg b Wright 13	
K. Barrington c Ridgway b Wright........ 32	L-b 8....................... 8
P. B. H. May not out....................128	
P. C. E. Pratt c Phebey b Page 21	1/47 2/145 3/319 4/360 (4 wkts dec.) 404

R. Swetman, W. S. Surridge, G. A. R. Lock, A. V. Bedser and P. J. Loader did not bat.

Kent

A. H. Phebey b Lock..........................	22	– b Lock	12
M. C. Cowdrey c Swetman b A. Bedser	49	– lbw b Lock	8
R. C. Wilson c Barrington b Lock................	2	– b Lock	32
T. G. Evans b Loader	1	– c and b Lock..................	19
A. E. Fagg c Stewart b Lock....................	2	– c A. Bedser b Lock.............	21
A. L. Dixon c May b Lock	13	– b Lock	2
D. G. Ufton b Lock..........................	0	– not out	17
F. Ridgway c Surridge b Lock	6	– c Stewart b Lock.............	7
D. J. Halfyard c Pratt b A. Bedser	1	– c Barrington b Lock	0
J. C. T. Page not out	1	– b Lock	0
D. V. P. Wright c Loader b A. Bedser.............	2	– b Lock	0
L-b 2.............................	2	B 6, l-b 5, n-b 1............	12

1/55 2/63 3/64 4/67 5/91	101	1/20 2/29 3/60 4/84 5/101 130
6/91 7/91 8/96 9/98		6/104 7/130 8/130 9/130

Kent Bowling

	Overs	Mdns	Runs	Wkts
Ridgway	15	3	53	1
Halfyard..........	28	4	104	—
Wright	25	3	85	2
Page	25	2	107	1
Dixon	9	—	44	—
Cowdrey..........	1	—	3	—

Surrey Bowling

	Overs	Mdns	Runs	Wkts	Overs	Mdns	Runs	Wkts
Loader	16	6	38	1	8	3	7	—
A. Bedser	11	—	28	3	16	5	41	—
Lock	21	12	29	6	29.1	18	54	10
E. Bedser	3	2	4	—	18	10	16	—

Umpires: Harry Elliott (Derbyshire) and W. F. Price.

KENT v WORCESTERSHIRE

Played at Folkestone, July 10, 11, 12, 1957

Kent won by 128 runs. For their first victory since the opening match of the season, Kent were heavily indebted to three players. Phebey and Wilson gave the batting an excellent start in each innings and Halfyard again bowled excellently in gaining the best match-figures of his career. Having returned the best analysis of the season with nine for 39 against Glamorgan the previous week, Halfyard recorded the first hat-trick by dismissing Booth, Horton and Jenkins with successive balls in Worcestershire's first innings. Flavell also found the pitch responsive to his lively seam attack in causing Kent's first innings breakdown. Phebey provided the backbone of the innings by staying nearly four and a half hours. Despite a splendid fighting display by Kenyon, Worcestershire had little chance of avoiding defeat on the last day when the ball kicked viciously off rain-damaged turf. Halfyard again bowled unchanged and finished with thirteen wickets for 94 runs.

Kent

A. H. Phebey c Horton b Flavell................	111	– c P. Richardson b Horton........	38
R. C. Wilson lbw b Horton....................	43	– c D. Richardson b Horton........	45
J. F. Pretlove b Jenkins......................	7	– lbw b Horton..................	1
M. C. Cowdrey c Dews b Jenkins..............	4	– not out......................	47
S. E. Leary c Horton b Flavell................	5	– c Kenyon b Flavell.............	19
J. Pettiford c Horton b Flavell................	0	– not out......................	14
D. G. Ufton not out........................	25		
A. L. Dixon c Booth b Flavell................	0		
D. J. Halfyard b Flavell......................	0		
D. V. P. Wright c Booth b Flavell............	3		
J. C. T. Page b Flavell......................	12		
L-b 3............................	3	B 4, w 1................	5
1/107 2/126 3/132 4/147 5/149	**213**	1/84 2/86 (4 wkts dec.)	**169**
6/187 7/187 8/187 9/191		3/93 4/139	

Worcestershire

D. Kenyon b Halfyard......................	4	– b Halfyard....................	79
P. E. Richardson c Ufton b Halfyard..........	47	– c Cowdrey b Halfyard...........	6
G. Dews not out..........................	47	– c Wilson b Page...............	12
D. W. Richardson c Leary b Halfyard..........	0	– c Page b Halfyard..............	2
R. G. Broadbent c Pretlove b Wright..........	6	– c Wilson c Halfyard............	7
M. J. Horton c Ufton b Halfyard..............	0	– c Phebey b Halfyard............	5
R. Booth c Cowdrey b Halfyard..............	0	– c Ufton b Halfyard.............	2
R. O. Jenkins c Leary b Halfyard............	0	– c Wilson b Page...............	4
R. Berry c Cowdrey b Halfyard..............	4	– c Pretlove b Page..............	2
J. Flavell run out..........................	5	– c Leary b Page................	0
L. Coldwell c Leary b Wright................	0	– not out......................	4
B 2, l-b 9, w 1, n-b 1................	13	L-b 4, w 1..............	5
1/4 2/64 3/64 4/88 5/98	**126**	1/20 2/53 3/64 4/84 5/89	**128**
6/98 7/102 8/106 9/119		6/104 7/109 8/124 9/124	

Worcestershire Bowling

	Overs	Mdns	Runs	Wkts	Overs	Mdns	Runs	Wkts
Flavell	21.3	6	46	7	11	1	50	1
Coldwell	17	3	45	—	4	—	15	—
Horton	16	6	46	1	25	9	62	3
Berry	12	4	22	—	23	10	37	—
Jenkins	21	8	51	2				

Kent Bowling

	Overs	Mdns	Runs	Wkts	Overs	Mdns	Runs	Wkts
Halfyard	20	5	45	7	26.1	12	49	6
Dixon	7	1	30	—	4	—	23	—
Wright	12.1	3	38	2				
Page					22	7	51	4

Umpires: T. J. Bartley and T. W. Spencer.

KENT v LEICESTERSHIRE

Played at Gillingham, July 2, 3, 4, 1958

Kent won by 52 runs. Heavy rain followed by hot sunshine caused remarkable transformations in the fortunes of both sides on the first two days. Kent, put in to bat, made a confident start when play began after tea, but once the sun took its effect on the pitch, Boshier, Spencer and Savage made the ball perform remarkable tricks and Kent lost their last nine wickets for 38 runs. Leicestershire fared even worse. Superb spells of bowling by Halfyard, who did the hat-trick, and Ridgway toppled them for 39. Six wickets were down for 37 when Halfyard claimed his three victims. In successive balls he had Julian caught at slip, bowled Smith and brilliantly caught and bowled Spencer. On a much easier pitch Kent went for runs in their second innings and a well-judged declaration by Phebey, the acting captain, gave Halfyard and Page just enough time to dismiss Leicestershire. The last wicket fell ten minutes from the close. The only real threat to Kent was Revill, who was at his aggressive best.

Kent

A. H. Phebey b Boshier	9	– st Julian b Savage	36
J. Prodger c Julian b Spencer	14	– c and b Smith	14
R. C. Wilson c Julian b Boshier	9	– c Revill b Smith	9
J. F. Pretlove c Julian b Savage	5	– c Lester b Boshier	51
S. E. Leary c Revill b Savage	0	– st Julian b Smith	0
J. Pettiford c Revill b Boshier	4	– b Smith	45
A. W. Catt c Watson b Boshier	6	– c Hallam b Smith	3
D. J. Halfyard c and b Savage	0	– c Diment b Boshier	2
F. Ridgway c Hallam b Savage	4	– c Phillips b Smith	0
A. Brown not out	4	– not out	10
J. C. T. Page c Diment b Boshier	2		
L-b 4	4	B 9, l-b 7	16

1/23 2/23 3/35 4/41 5/41   61   1/42 2/64 3/74   (9 wkts dec.) 186
6/47 7/47 8/51 9/59   4/74 5/161 6/172
                                     7/175 8/175 9/186

Leicestershire

M. R. Hallam c Pettiford b Ridgway	10	– c Ridgway b Halfyard		10
W. Watson c Catt b Halfyard	8	– c Leary b Halfyard		18
E. F. Phillips c Catt b Ridgway	2	– c Prodger b Page		1
A. C. Revill c Prodger b Ridgway	0	– c Catt b Halfyard		53
G. Lester b Halfyard	9	– b Brown		18
R. A. Diment b Ridgway	5	– c Pettiford b Halfyard		10
R. Julian c Leary b Halfyard	0	– c Pretlove b Halfyard		3
J. S. Savage c Catt b Ridgway	0	– c Ridgway b Page		6
R. C. Smith b Halfyard	0	– c Phebey b Page		11
C. T. Spencer c and b Halfyard	0	– c and b Page		7
B. S. Boshier not out	2	– not out		5
B 1, n-b 2	3	B 7, l-b 4, n-b 3		14

1/18 2/19 3/19 4/31 5/35 6/37   39   1/24 2/25 3/55 4/94 5/115   156
7/37 8/37 9/37   6/124 7/129 8/131 9/147

Leicestershire Bowling

	Overs	Mdns	Runs	Wkts	Overs	Mdns	Runs	Wkts
Spencer	8	3	15	1	1	—	6	—
Boshier	16	3	30	5	24	7	49	2
Savage	8	4	12	4	31	12	64	1
Smith					35.1	15	51	6

Kent Bowling

	Overs	Mdns	Runs	Wkts	Overs	Mdns	Runs	Wkts
Halfyard	12	5	21	5	26	8	81	5
Page	3	1	4	—	15.1	4	36	4
Ridgway	8.1	5	11	5	5	3	8	—
Brown					6	1	17	1

Umpires: L. H. Gray and R. S. Lay.

KENT v MIDDLESEX

Played at Gravesend, May 23, 25, 26, 1959

Middlesex won by 109 runs. Not even the sternest critic of modern cricket would have faulted this match. It produced two maiden centuries, one of the fastest hundreds of the season, sixes in abundance, and an astonishing scoring spree by Middlesex on the last day. Hooker's superb 137 included three 6s and twenty-six 4s, 122 in boundaries, and Kent subsequently won a thrilling tussle for first-innings points. Even these performances were eclipsed on the third day when in two hours before lunch Middlesex made 216 for two wickets. Gale raced to his century in eighty-seven minutes, and Russell, like his colleague Hooker, went on to complete a maiden hundred. Kent, set 294 to win in three hours, never recovered from a poor start but held out until five minutes from the end of extra time.

Middlesex

R. A. Gale c Cowdrey b Page..................	26 –	c Halfyard b Page..............106
W. E. Russell b Pettiford....................	61 –	c Pretlove b Halfyard............120
J. D. Robertson b Pettiford..................	0 –	run out....................... 10
P. H. Parfitt st Evans b Dixon.................	32 –	c Leary b Halfyard.............. 6
R. W. Hooker c Halfyard b Page ....137 –		c Phebey b Page............... 4
R. A. White c Pretlove b Dixon................	0	
F. J. Titmus c Halfyard b Page................	90 –	b Halfyard 20
R. V. C. Robins not out....................	13 –	c Pretlove b Page 11
H. W. Tilly (did not bat)...................	–	not out 8
J. J. Warr (did not bat)...................	–	not out 9
B 1, l-b 2, n-b 1...................	4	L-b 6.................. 6

1/83 2/84 3/89 4/194   (7 wkts dec.) 363   1/188 2/216 3/248   (7 wkts dec.) 300
5/198 6/331 7/363   4/252 5/252 6/281 7/284

K. B. Day did not bat.

Kent

A. H. Phebey c Day b Warr..................	32 –	b Tilly..................... 13
R. C. Wilson b Robins	6 –	b Warr 0
D. J. Halfyard b Warr.....................	12 –	st Day b Titmus 0
S. E. Leary c Robertson b Tilly...............	20 –	lbw b Warr 7
M. C. Cowdrey c Day b Parfitt..............	83 –	c White b Parfitt............. 50
J. F. Pretlove b Warr.....................	0 –	not out 21
J. Pettiford not out	95 –	c Hooker b Robins 21
A. Dixon c White b Warr	83 –	c Parfitt b Titmus 36
T. G. Evans b Warr.....................	10 –	b Tilly.................. 6
R. Wilkinson not out.....................	3 –	c White b Titmus 10
J. C. T. Page (did not bat).................	–	b Warr 5
B 14, l-b 11, w 1	26	B 12, l-b 2, w 1 15

1/10 2/28 3/66 4/124   (8 wkts dec.) 370   1/0 2/11 3/26 4/100 5/100   184
5/124 6/191 7/339 8/356   6/106 7/120 8/131 9/171

Kent Bowling

	Overs	Mdns	Runs	Wkts	Overs	Mdns	Runs	Wkts
Halfyard..........	28	10	100	—	25	3	112	3
Wilkinson.........	18	8	49	—	4	—	29	—
Page	22.1	5	76	3	21	4	104	3
Pettiford	29	8	81	2				
Dixon	10	4	53	2	7	—	49	—

Middlesex Bowling

	Overs	Mdns	Runs	Wkts	Overs	Mdns	Runs	Wkts
Warr.............	37	16	62	5	20.5	5	47	3
Tilly	32	9	67	1	8	3	29	2
Robins	12	2	49	1	10	5	33	1
Russell	3	—	18	—				
Titmus	23	5	69	—	12	4	35	3
Hooker	11	1	49	—				
Parfitt	7	—	23	1	4	—	24	1
Gale	1	—	7	—	2	1	1	—

Umpires: R. S. Lay and D. J. Wood.

KENT v WORCESTERSHIRE

Played at Maidstone, July 22, 23, 24, 1959

Kent won by five wickets, taking 12 points from a game dictated to a large extent by the seam bowlers. Halfyard, of Kent, was the most successful, taking fifteen wickets for 117 runs altogether and nine for 61 in the second innings, when his persistent accuracy proved too much for the batsmen. Dews scored the only century of the match in two hours fifty minutes and, hitting sixteen 4s, helped Worcestershire to recover from a poor start. A stand of 173 in three and a half hours by Wilson and Leary enabled Kent to make a good reply and in their second innings the youthful Wilkinson found that aggressive tactics paid at a time when Kent were struggling to get 118 to win.

Worcestershire

D. Kenyon lbw b Halfyard	2	– c Wilkinson b Halfyard 5
L. Outschoorn b Sayer	31	– lbw b Halfyard 12
M. J. Horton c Phebey b Brown	34	– b Halfyard 11
D. W. Richardson c Leary b Halfyard	3	– c Leary b Halfyard 56
R. G. Broadbent lbw b Halfyard	23	– lbw b Halfyard 7
G. Dews c Leary b Halfyard	114	– lbw b Halfyard 0
R. Booth lbw b Halfyard	39	– not out 13
D. N. F. Slade c Jones b Halfyard	12	– b Sayer 12
D. B. Pearson b Brown	0	– c Evans b Halfyard 9
K. J. Aldridge b Sayer	1	– c Jones b Halfyard 4
J. Flavell not out	0	– b Halfyard 10
L-b 5, n-b 1	6	B 4, l-b 1, n-b 5 10

1/9 2/40 3/59 4/81 5/123   265   1/9 2/34 3/34 4/53 5/77   149
6/248 7/253 8/258 9/265   6/77 7/ 00 8/132 9/140

Kent

A. H. Phebey run out	4	– b Pearson 26
R. C. Wilson c Slade b Flavell	91	– b Horton 18
D. J. Halfyard c Booth b Flavell	0	
S. E. Leary c Richardson b Flavell	95	– c Aldridge b Horton 11
A. W. Catt lbw b Flavell	23	– c Broadbent b Pearson 1
P. H. Jones c Dews b Pearson	24	– b Pearson 6
R. Wilkinson not out	17	– not out 35
T. G. Evans b Flavell	12	– not out 4
D. Sayer b Pearson	5	
A. Brown not out	10	
B 5, l-b 8, n-b 3	16	B 15, l-b 2 17

1/14 2/20 3/193 4/222   (8 wkts dec.) 297   1/49 2/55 3/67   (5 wkts) 118
5/253 6/253 7/267 8/286   4/71 5/111

J. C. T. Page did not bat.

Kent Bowling

	Overs	Mdns	Runs	Wkts	Overs	Mdns	Runs	Wkts
Sayer	22.2	—	85	2	13	1	50	1
Halfyard	28	10	56	6	21.3	10	61	9
Brown	18	3	61	2	7	1	24	—
Wilkinson	6	1	19	—				
Page	11	1	32	—	2	1	4	—
Jones	6	3	6	—				

Worcestershire Bowling

	Overs	Mdns	Runs	Wkts	Overs	Mdns	Runs	Wkts
Flavell............	34	8	93	5	7	—	16	—
Aldridge..........	22	5	59	—	5	3	12	—
Pearson...........	21	3	65	2	16	5	36	3
Slade.............	11	5	29	—				
Horton	19	9	35	—	13.5	3	37	2

Umpires: H. G. Baldwin and L. H. Gray.

KENT v DERBYSHIRE

(J. Pettiford's Benefit)

Played at Canterbury, August 5, 6, 7, 1959

Derbyshire won by 99 runs. Two brilliant hundreds by Carr, the Derbyshire captain, dominated the match. He took out his bat in the first innings, having played with complete assurance against the pace of Ridgway, Halfyard and Brown on a green pitch. During his stay of four hours Carr hit twenty-eight 4s and off-drove and hooked especially well. Wilson, the Kent left-hander, although batting with a runner because of a strained leg, was the best performer in their first innings against a well-varied attack, but his side fell 25 behind. Carr again played splendidly while others faltered, especially during a spell when Pettiford, the beneficiary, who bowled his leg-breaks accurately, took four wickets in three overs. Carr, batting three hours and hitting eighteen 4s, was last out. Kent needed 217 and they collapsed before the fiery but inaccurate left-arm bowling of Richardson and the more controlled pace of Jackson. Dour defence and sparkling stroke-play from Dixon, who hit fourteen 4s, held them up for a time, but Kent were dismissed in under two and a half hours.

Derbyshire

A. Hamer c Evans b Brown	15	– st Evans b Pettiford	34
I. W. Hall c Evans b Ridgway..................	0	– lbw b Ridgway	8
W. F. Oates c Evans b Ridgway	4	– lbw b Pettiford	0
D. B. Carr not out...........................	156	– b Halfyard	109
H. L. Johnson c Halfyard b Brown	5	– c Wilkinson b Pettiford...........	0
D. C. Morgan c Wilkinson b Dixon	41	– b Pettiford.....................	1
I. Buxton b Pettiford	2	– b Ridgway	11
G. O. Dawkes lbw b Ridgway...................	15	– run out	0
G. W. Richardson c Evans b Halfyard	0	– b Pettiford.....................	16
E. Smith c Phebey b Ridgway	2	– run out	6
H. L. Jackson b Halfyard	15	– not out	0
L-b 2...........................	2	L-b 5, w 1	6

1/5 2/13 3/48 4/56 5/154   257   1/11 2/91 3/93 4/95 5/95   191
6/175 7/208 8/209 9/214   6/133 7/133 8/144 9/191

Kent

A. H. Phebey c Hall b Richardson	7	– lbw b Richardson	2
R. C. Wilson c Carr b Smith	73	– b Richardson	0
S. E. Leary st Dawkes b Carr	35	– c Morgan b Jackson	2
M. C. Cowdrey c and b Smith	15	– c Hall b Richardson	4
J. Pettiford lbw b Jackson	27	– b Smith	23
R. W. Wilkinson c Jackson b Carr	8	– c Carr b Jackson	1
T. G. Evans c Dawkes b Richardson	13	– b Richardson	6
A. L. Dixon c and b Buxton	5	– c Dawkes b Richardson	65
D. J. Halfyard b Richardson	4	– b Richardson	8
F. Ridgway b Jackson	26	– not out	1
A. Brown not out	4	– b Richardson	0
L-b 9, w 5, n-b 1	15	B 2, l-b 2, w 1	5

1/45 2/107 3/133 4/146 5/162   232   1/2 2/4 3/8 4/10 5/14   117
6/178 7/193 8/197 9/222   6/27 7/95 8/112 9/117

Kent Bowling

	Overs	Mdns	Runs	Wkts	Overs	Mdns	Runs	Wkts
Ridgway	19	6	52	4	17	5	64	2
Halfyard	23.4	6	74	2	11.2	1	46	1
Brown	14	3	54	2	11	1	42	—
Pettiford	16	1	51	1	16	6	33	5
Dixon	7	1	24	1				

Derbyshire Bowling

	Overs	Mdns	Runs	Wkts	Overs	Mdns	Runs	Wkts
Jackson	31	11	45	2	12	5	26	2
Richardson	21	4	68	3	14	6	31	7
Buxton	13	3	32	1				
Morgan	6	1	13	—	4	—	25	—
Carr	9	3	24	2	5	2	15	—
Smith	17	8	35	2	7	2	15	1

Umpires: J. H. Parks and D. J. Wood.

KENT v NOTTINGHAMSHIRE

Played at Folkestone, September 2, 3, 4, 1959

Kent, who won by an innings and 98 runs taking 14 points, owed much to Brown, their Nottingham-born fast bowler. He took four Nottinghamshire second-innings wickets in five balls and had a match analysis of nine for 82. Only Norman Hill and Springall played him with any assurance on the first day and Nottinghamshire were all out shortly before tea. Phebey and Wilson began with an opening stand of 134 for Kent and Dixon, aided by aggressive batting from the tail-enders, boosted the lead to 259. Nottinghamshire never looked likely to save the match. Brown dismissed Maurice Hill, Simpson, Poole and Norman Hill in five balls at 83, the last eight wickets contributing only 97 and Kent completed a fine victory shortly before lunch on the third day.

Nottinghamshire

N. Hill c Cowdrey b Brown	47	– c Pettiford b Brown	0
G. Millman c Cowdrey b Page	6	– b Pettiford	52
H. M. Winfield lbw b Pettiford	16	– b Page	6
M. Hill c Jones b Brown	3	– c Cowdrey b Brown	7
R. T. Simpson c Cowdrey b Pettiford	1	– lbw b Brown	0
C. J. Poole c Catt b Brown	6	– c Phebey b Brown	0
J. D. Springall b Brown	29	– c Jones b Page	31
T. Atkinson c Catt b Brown	0	– b Pettiford	23
J. Cotton b Ridgway	8	– not out	20
T. Siddons run out	4	– c Jones b Page	8
M. Morgan not out	6	– b Pettiford	5
N-b 1	1	B 4, l-b 5	9

1/31 2/61 3/67 4/68 5/73   127   1/44 2/64 3/83 4/83 5/83   161
6/81 7/81 8/98 9/110   6/83 7/114 8/147 9/156

Kent

A. H. Phebey c Cotton b Siddons	87	F. Ridgway c Winfield b Morgan	4
R. C. Wilson c Simpson b Morgan	71	A. Brown b Morgan	19
P. H. Jones run out	14	J. C. T. Page not out	4
M. C. Cowdrey c Millman b Morgan	7		
J. Pettiford lbw b Atkinson	28	B 1, l-b 11	12
A. L. Dixon b Atkinson	82		
A. W. Catt st Millman b Morgan	34	1/134 2/175 3/183 4/191 5/288	386
R. W. Wilkinson c Cotton b Morgan	24	6/317 7/358 8/361 9/366	

Kent Bowling

	Overs	Mdns	Runs	Wkts	Overs	Mdns	Runs	Wkts
Ridgway	15	6	28	1	5	1	26	—
Brown	19.2	3	49	5	18	7	33	4
Wilkinson	2	—	9	—				
Page	10	6	17	1	14	6	35	3
Pettiford	15	6	23	2	20.4	5	58	3

Nottinghamshire Bowling

	Overs	Mdns	Runs	Wkts
Cotton	34	11	70	—
Atkinson	30	12	92	2
Morgan	39	13	130	6
Springall	6	—	27	—
Siddons	29	11	55	1

Umpires: J. H. Parks and W. E. Phillipson.

KENT v WORCESTERSHIRE

Played at Tunbridge Wells, June 15, 1960

Kent won by an innings and 101 runs, taking 14 points from the first match to be completed in a day since 1953. The pitch, grassless and soft at first, dried under a hot sun, leaving crusty edges on the indentations made when the ball dug in earlier. No two deliveries behaved alike; many rising sharply, some keeping low and nearly all deviating to an unaccustomed degree. Worcestershire, not the strongest of batting sides, floundered against Brown and Halfyard, both of whom needed to do little more than turn over their arms. The pitch did the rest.

An enterprising innings by Jones, who hit two 6s and nine 4s in scoring 73 in one hour thirty-five minutes, helped Kent to a reasonable total while the pitch was drying out.

Worcestershire commenced their first innings at ten minutes to four and, with tea intervening, were all out at 5.25 after batting seventy-five minutes. Six wickets were down for nine runs and there never seemed a chance of them hitting the 38 needed to avoid the follow on. Slade, with two 4s off successive balls from Brown, became top scorer with nine, and six extras bolstered the total to 25, the lowest since Hampshire were dismissed by Derbyshire for 23 in August 1958 and only one run better than the lowest in Worcestershire's history.

Brown, six for twelve, and Halfyard, four for seven, bowled throughout and continued to demolish Worcestershire when they went in again 162 behind. The second innings stretched ten minutes into the extra half-hour – one hour thirty-five minutes in all – mainly because of the determination of Broadbent who stayed for one hour ten minutes and a bold front by Slade and Booth, whose dismissal was indicative of the pitch, described afterwards by Cowdrey as "disgraceful". The ball flew off one of the many patches on to the top of the bat, struck Booth on the cheek bone and produced a catch.

Kent

P. E. Richardson b Flavell	23	D. J. Halfyard st Booth b Gifford	0
A. H. Phebey b Gifford	16	A. Brown b Gifford	1
*M. C. Cowdrey c Broadbent b Pearson	17	P. Shenton not out	7
R. C. Wilson c Headley b Flavell	0		
S. E. Leary st Booth b Slade	23	B 7, l-b 2, n-b 1	10
P. H. Jones c Broadbent b Slade	73		
A. L. Dixon c Dews b Pearson	17	1/41 2/43 3/43 4/68 5/104	187
†A. W. Catt st Booth b Gifford	0	6/151 7/154 8/161 9/179	

Worcestershire

R. G. A. Headley b Halfyard	0	– c Wilson b Halfyard	0
J. B. Sedgley c Leary b Brown	7	– c Richardson b Brown	2
A. H. Spencer b Brown	0	– c Leary b Brown	4
D. W. Richardson b Brown	0	– b Halfyard	2
R. G. Broadbent b Halfyard	0	– c Catt b Halfyard	22
*G. Dews lbw b Brown	0	– b Brown	0
†R. Booth b Brown	2	– c Shenton b Halfyard	7
D. N. F. Slade b Halfyard	9	– c Leary b Shenton	11
N. Gifford not out	0	– c Brown b Shenton	4
D. B. Pearson b Halfyard	0	– c Cowdrey b Halfyard	2
J. Flavell b Brown	1	– not out	0
B 1, l-b 5	6	B 5, l-b 1, w 1	7

1/6 2/7 3/8 4/9 5/9 6/9   25   1/0 2/6 3/7 4/17 5/18   61
7/24 8/24 9/24   6/40 7/51 8/51 9/61

Worcestershire Bowling

	Overs	Mdns	Runs	Wkts
Flavell	18	8	25	2
Pearson	16	7	35	2
Slade	18	5	54	2
Gifford	17	5	63	4

Kent Bowling

	Overs	Mdns	Runs	Wkts	Overs	Mdns	Runs	Wkts
Halfyard	9	4	7	4	13	4	20	5
Brown	8.1	5	12	6	8	2	22	3
Shenton					4.5	—	12	2

Umpires: T. J. Bartley and J. S. Buller.

KENT v WARWICKSHIRE

Played at Blackheath, June 10, 12, 13, 1961

Warwickshire won by 154 runs taking 12 points, thanks largely to Bridge, their off-spinner, who took five Kent second innings wickets for two runs on a rain-affected pitch. At the start conditions favoured the bat. Sayer (five for 42) struck three surprise blows, but a fourth-wicket stand of 104 between Horner and Kennedy paved the way for Hitchcock, who hit two 6s and fourteen 4s, to make 105 not out. For Kent, Richardson and Prideaux shared an opening partnership of 132, but when rain intervened Phebey closed the Kent innings 154 behind. A third declaration left Kent 231 to win in three hours and immediately the drying pitch encouraged the bowlers. Dixon and Jones batted soundly before Bridge, introduced at 45 for four, proved unplayable. His figures read 5.1–4–2–5 and Kent were hustled to defeat in an hour and a half.

Warwickshire

K. Ibadulla b Sayer	16	– c Ufton b Halfyard	2
N. F. Horner c Leary b Dixon	74	– c Richardson b Halfyard	15
W. J. Stewart c Ufton b Sayer	0	– c and b Sayer	7
T. W. Cartwright b Sayer	6	– not out	36
J. M. Kennedy c Ufton b Halfyard	45		
R. E. Hitchcock not out	105	– not out	12
*†A. C. Smith c Ufton b Sayer	50		
J. D. Bannister c Ufton b Sayer	5		
W. B. Bridge not out	11		
B 7, l-b 4, w 1	12	B 4	4

1/25 2/25 3/37 4/141   (7 wkts dec.) 324   1/11 2/18 3/37   (3 wkts dec.) 76
5/151 6/250 7/260

A. Wright and R. G. Thompson did not bat.

Kent

P. E. Richardson lbw b Hitchcock	76	– c Hitchcock b Bannister	1
R. M. Prideaux not out	67	– lbw b Wright	6
*A. H. Phebey not out	23	– b Bannister	3
R. C. Wilson (did not bat)		– c and b Bannister	0
A. L. Dixon (did not bat)		– b Bridge	18
P. H. Jones (did not bat)		– c Cartwright b Bridge	35
D. J. Halfyard (did not bat)		– c and b Bridge	0
S. E. Leary (did not bat)		– b Bannister	6
†D. G. Ufton (did not bat)		– lbw b Bridge	0
D. M. Sayer (did not bat)		– b Bridge	3
D. Baker (did not bat)		– not out	2
L-b 4	4	B 2	2

1/132   (1 wkt dec.) 170   1/7 2/7 3/13 4/58 5/58   76
                          6/65 7/65 8/71 9/71

Kent Bowling

	Overs	Mdns	Runs	Wkts	Overs	Mdns	Runs	Wkts
Halfyard	31	8	87	1	13	1	42	2
Sayer	24	7	42	5	12	3	50	1
Jones	23	7	56	—				
Dixon	29	8	81	1				
Baker	15	4	46	—				

Warwickshire Bowling

	Overs	Mdns	Runs	Wkts	Overs	Mdns	Runs	Wkts
Thompson	10	1	29	—	2	1	3	—
Bannister	9	2	23	—	13	4	41	4
Hitchcock.........	7	3	24	1				
Bridge............	21	14	35	—	5.1	4	2	5
Ibadulla	9	4	31	—				
Wright	3	—	15	—	5	1	28	1
Cartwright	1	—	9	—				

Umpires: John Langridge and W. F. Price.

KENT v SURREY

Played at Blackheath, July 1, 3, 4, 1961

Drawn. The temperature during this match varied from over 90 degrees on Saturday to a wintry recording on Monday but the cricket remained consistent, with 1230 runs scored for the loss of 23 wickets. Two batsmen on each side, Richardson and Wilson for Kent and Edrich and Barrington for Surrey, scored centuries, with Richardson hitting twenty-four 4s in surpassing his previous highest for Kent. Early on the last day Wilson and Cowdrey, who fell six short of a hundred, put on 196 in two and a quarter hours, which gave an adequate indication of the continued supremacy of bat over ball, but even so Surrey did not sustain an all out effort to win after Cowdrey, with the third declaration, left them to score 260 at 90 an hour.

Kent

P. E. Richardson c Willett b Gibson 171	– b Gibson	8
R. M. Prideaux c Barrington b Gibson 5	– c Barrington b Gibson	21
R. C. Wilson b Bedser. 74	– c Swetman b Loader. 117
*M. C. Cowdrey c Lock b Gibson 34	– c May b Gibson	94
S. E. Leary lbw b Lock 5		
P. H. Jones b Bedser 24	– not out	0
A. L. Dixon b Gibson 34	– not out	5
†D. G. Ufton not out. 30		
D. J. Halfyard b Bedser. 11		
B 4, l-b 6, n-b 2 12	B 8, l-b 5, n-b 3	16

1/19 2/169 3/239 4/250   (8 wkts dec.) 400   1/13 2/60   (4 wkts dec.) 261
5/303 6/343 7/378 8/400   3/256 4/256

A. Brown and D. Baker did not bat.

Surrey

M. J. Stewart c Wilson b Halfyard 7	– b Halfyard	67
J. H. Edrich b Halfyard. 113	– lbw b Jones.	30
K. F. Barrington c Wilson b Baker 121	– lbw b Halfyard	38
*P. B. H. May b Halfyard. 50	– c Wilson b Jones.	0
B. Constable lbw b Brown. 33	– not out	5
M. D. Willett not out. 29	– not out	22
†R. Swetman c and b Baker 14		
G. A. R. Lock c Halfyard b Dixon 9		
B 14, l-b 6, w 2, n-b 4 26	B 2, l-b 3	5

1/8 2/240 3/292 4/325   (7 wkts dec.) 402   1/58 2/130 3/139   (4 wkts) 167
5/361 6/385 7/402   4/139

E. A. Bedser, D. Gibson and P. J. Loader did not bat.

Surrey Bowling

	Overs	Mdns	Runs	Wkts	Overs	Mdns	Runs	Wkts
Loader	19	2	70	—	12	2	42	1
Gibson	22	5	83	4	17	8	30	3
Willett...........	3	—	29	—				
Lock.............	24	—	98	1	26	6	87	—
Bedser...........	23.1	3	81	3	13	2	50	—
Barrington	6	1	27	—	5	—	36	—

Kent Bowling

	Overs	Mdns	Runs	Wkts	Overs	Mdns	Runs	Wkts
Halfyard..........	38	10	89	3	15	3	58	2
Brown............	25	6	68	1	12	1	46	—
Baker	27	3	98	2	3	—	16	—
Dixon	10	—	43	1				
Jones............	27	4	78	—	16	5	42	—

Umpires: W. H. Copson and A. Jepson.

KENT v SUSSEX

Played at Tunbridge Wells, June 16, 18, 19, 1962

Sussex won by an innings and 21 runs. The match was a triumph for Dexter, their captain, who hit a century and took ten wickets for 109, and Suttle, who scored the first double century of his career. Only Wilson (84) and Jones (35) defied Dexter who after taking six wickets for 63 shared a fourth wicket stand of 205 in two hours and a half with Suttle. Dexter (two 6s and sixteen 4s) hit powerfully all round the wicket. Suttle went on to reach 204 not out, and Sussex declared with a lead of 206. Then Dexter (four for 46), and Bates (five for 78) brought about another Kent downfall and they were beaten shortly before lunch on the third day.

Kent

P. E. Richardson b Bates.......................	13	– c Parks b Bates.................	15
†A. W. Catt c Parks b Thomson.................	5	– c Foreman b Bates.............	6
R. C. Wilson c Parks b Dexter	84	– c Oakman b Dexter	61
*M. C. Cowdrey c Parks b Bates	17	– c Langridge b Bates..............	15
S. E. Leary c Suttle b Dexter..................	3	– c Bell b Dexter	5
B. W. Luckhurst c Parks b Dexter	0	– c Parks b Dexter.................	42
A. L. Dixon b Dexter	9	– b Dexter	8
P. H. Jones c Suttle b Dexter..................	35	– c Bell b Bates	15
D J. Halfyard c Parks b Bates..................	13	– c Langridge b Bates..............	4
A. Brown c Cooper b Dexter	0	– c Oakman b Thomson	1
D. M. Sayer not out	0	– not out	6
B 6, l-b 1, w 1	8	L-b 5, w 1, n-b 1..........	7

1/13 2/21 3/41 4/46 5/56   187   1/21 2/27 3/43 4/76 5/126   185
6/66 7/137 8/153 9/162   6/134 7/152 8/160 9/161

Sussex

A. S. Oakman c Leary b Brown	1	G. C. Cooper b Brown	11
R. J. Langridge c Jones b Brown..........	3	D. J. Foreman not out................	15
K. G. Suttle not out....................204		B 6, l-b 10, w 1	17
†J. M. Parks c Catt b Sayer	17		
*E. R. Dexter c Cowdrey b Dixon 113		1/2 2/13 3/58 (6 wkts dec.) 393	
L. J. Lenham c Catt b Dixon.............	12	4/263 5/311 6/363	

N. I. Thomson, R. V. Bell and D. L. Bates did not bat.

Sussex Bowling

	Overs	Mdns	Runs	Wkts	Overs	Mdns	Runs	Wkts
Thomson	16	9	18	1	30	11	52	1
Bates	23	4	81	3	27	7	78	5
Dexter	18.3	2	63	6	16.4	3	46	4
Suttle	1	—	13	—				
Cooper	3	2	4	—				
Bell					1	—	2	—

Kent Bowling

	Overs	Mdns	Runs	Wkts
Halfyard	30	7	90	—
Brown	33	3	115	3
Sayer	15	1	53	1
Jones	13	2	57	—
Leary	2	—	6	—
Dixon	15	3	41	2
Luckhurst	9	4	14	—

Umpires: T. Drinkwater and H. G. Baldwin.

KENT v ESSEX

Played at Dover, July 14, 16, 17, 1962

Drawn. Kent taking four points somewhat gratuitously. Essex were 191 for four and only 18 runs behind when Bailey declared an hour after the resumption of the last day. Richardson replied by leaving Essex to score 168 in two hours to win – a task beyond them. On the first day rain held up the start until half past two and prevented cricket before tea on the second day. It also gave the slow bowlers a chance. Laker took full advantage with some fine variations which brought him thirteen wickets for 159 runs in the match. He turned the ball just enough to worry the more experienced batsmen and had the lesser players completely at sea. Sympathy was felt for Denness, a young Scot, in having to face Laker in both innings on his début in Championship cricket.

Kent

*P. E. Richardson c Preston b Laker	69	– c Bear b Greensmith	36
J. Prodger c and b Greensmith	22	– lbw b Laker	4
R. C. Wilson st Taylor b Laker	24	– c Preston b Laker	4
S. Leary b Laker	19	– b Laker	43
B. Luckhurst b Bailey	19	– c Preston b Laker	12
M. Denness lbw b Laker	0	– c Preston b Laker	3
P. H. Jones b Bailey	0	– lbw b Bailey	0
†A. W. Catt c Preston b Laker	22	– c Bear b Laker	20
A. L. Dixon c Edmeades b Laker	18	– c Bear b Bailey	16
D. J. Halfyard c and b Laker	6	– not out	9
D. M. Sayer not out	0	– not out	1
L-b 10	10	L-b 1	1

1/48 2/95 3/125 4/150 5/150   209   1/10 2/32 3/52   (9 wkts dec.) 149

6/157 7/164 8/202 9/203   4/73 5/97 6/98 7/119 8/139 9/145

Essex

G. Barker lbw b Jones	11	– lbw b Sayer	10
M. J. Bear c Luckhurst b Halfyard	15	– c Catt b Sayer	17
G. J. Smith c Halfyard b Sayer	17	– c sub b Halfyard	27
B. R. Knight b Halfyard	79	– not out	71
*T. E. Bailey not out	53	– c Luckhurst b Jones	6
W. T. Greensmith not out	14	– b Sayer	0
†B. Taylor (did not bat)		– c and b Halfyard	4
K. C. Preston (did not bat)		– run out	0
R. A. G. Luckin (did not bat)		– not out	0
L-b 2	2	L-b 3	3

1/14 2/42 3/44 4/158   (4 wkts dec.) 191   1/19 2/30 3/83   (7 wkts) 138
                                            4/91 5/91 6/129 7/130

B. Edmeades and J. C. Laker did not bat.

Essex Bowling

	Overs	Mdns	Runs	Wkts	Overs	Mdns	Runs	Wkts
Bailey	17	3	42	2	13	5	14	2
Preston	8	1	23	—	5	—	16	—
Laker	29.4	7	73	7	28	5	86	6
Greensmith	18	4	61	1	10	3	32	1

Kent Bowling

	Overs	Mdns	Runs	Wkts	Overs	Mdns	Runs	Wkts
Halfyard	27.2	9	53	2	18	1	81	2
Sayer	18	4	46	1	9	1	20	3
Jones	24	9	68	1	16	7	34	1
Luckhurst	2	—	15	—				
Dixon	4	1	7	—				
Leary					1	1	—	—

Umpires: H. E. Hammond and R. S. Lay.

LANCASHIRE

LANCASHIRE v MIDDLESEX

Played at Manchester, May 25, 27, 28, 1946

Lancashire won by seven wickets. A century in each innings by Denis Compton, Washbrook's 182, and splendid bowling by Pollard made this game extremely attractive. Compton's feat had only twice previously been equalled at Old Trafford, by J. T. Tyldesley and Percy Holmes. In the first innings he batted just under three hours, in the second two hours and three-quarters, showing complete mastery throughout. Price, playing his second county match, joined Washbrook with eight wickets down for 206 and they added 138. Washbrook batted without a flaw for nearly five and a half hours and hit fourteen 4s. For the first time in his career Pollard obtained fourteen wickets in a match. On the third morning he dismissed three men for eight runs. Lancashire then lost three leading batsmen for 35 but, with rain causing delays, Ikin and Edrich hit off the remaining 102, the last 50 coming at two a minute in a race against time.

Middlesex

J. Robertson c Brierley b Pollard	20	– lbw b Ikin	35
S. M. Brown c Ikin b Pollard	16	– c Edrich b Pollard	11
L. Muncer c Brierley b Pollard	23	– b Price	9
D. Compton b Pollard	124	– st Brierley b Price	100
R. W. V. Robins c Howard b Roberts	61	– b Pollard	38
J. Sims c Edrich b Pollard	2	– c Brierley b Pollard	0
R. Routledge b Pollard	4	– c Edrich b Price	4
M. Etherington b Pollard	0	– b Pollard	3
J. Young b Pollard	0	– b Pollard	0
H. D. King not out	13	– c Brierley b Pollard	15
R. A. Shaddick st Brierley b Price	1	– not out	0
L-b 5, n-b 4	9	L-b 9, w 1, n-b 3	13
	273		**228**

Lancashire

C. Washbrook c and b Compton	182	– b Young	0
W. Place c Etherington b Sims	25	– c Routledge b Etherington	12
J. T. Ikin lbw b Sims	19	– not out	55
N. Howard b Sims	4	– b Young	3
G. A. Edrich lbw b Sims	1	– not out	54
A. Wharton lbw b Shaddick	22		
T. L. Brierley b Shaddick	22		
J. A. Fallow b Sims	4		
R. Pollard c Robertson b Sims	0		
E. Price c Muncer b Compton	54		
W. B. Roberts not out	12		
B 14, l-b 5, n-b 1	20	B 12, l-b 1	13
	365	**(3 wkts)**	**137**

Lancashire Bowling

	Overs	Mdns	Runs	Wkts	Overs	Mdns	Runs	Wkts
Pollard	31	3	127	8	28.3	5	89	6
Roberts	31	5	62	1	25	10	45	—
Ikin	5	1	21	—	10	1	38	1
Price	8.4	—	38	1	22	8	43	3
Wharton	2	—	16	—				

Middlesex Bowling

	Overs	Mdns	Runs	Wkts	Overs	Mdns	Runs	Wkts
Etherington.......	11	1	29	—	9	1	41	1
Routledge........	6	2	18	—	2.2	—	5	—
Shaddick..........	20	2	59	2	4	1	14	—
Sims	50	7	135	6	5	—	28	—
Young............	27	5	62	—	10	2	22	2
Robins	5	—	19	—				
Compton	8.2	1	23	2	2	—	6	—
Robertson					1	—	8	—

LANCASHIRE v SUSSEX

Played at Manchester, May 28, 29, 30, 1947

Lancashire won by 130 runs. An opening partnership of 350 in three hours fifty minutes by Washbrook and Place dwarfed everything else in the match. This fell only 18 short of the Lancashire first wicket record set up by A. C. MacLaren and R. H. Spooner in 1903. Washbrook hit a 7, a 6 and twenty-one 4s, and Place, less free, nine 4s. Each gave one chance. The brothers Langridge took batting honours for Sussex, who looked likely to gain first innings lead till Pollard caused a breakdown.

Lancashire

C. Washbrook c John Langridge b Nye	1	– not out	204
W. Place c John Langridge b Cox	55	– not out	134
J. T. Ikin lbw b Cox	56		
B. P. King c Bartlett b J. Oakes	3		
G. A. Edrich c C. Oakes b Carey	51		
K. Cranston c Parks b Carey	44		
W. E. Phillipson c and b Carey	6		
E. H. Edrich b Carey	21		
R. G. Garlick st Griffith b Cox	13		
R. Pollard c C. Oakes b Carey	0		
W. B. Roberts not out	4		
B 1, l-b 2, n-b 1	4	L-b 8, w 2, n-b 2	12
	258	(No wkt dec.)	**350**

Sussex

John Langridge lbw b Roberts	62	– c Cranston b Pollard	10
C. Oakes c G. Edrich b Cranston	14	– c Phillipson b Ikin	32
James Langridge c E. Edrich b Pollard	31	– lbw b Pollard	82
G. Cox c Roberts b Phillipson	26	– c and b Ikin	0
H. Parks c E. Edrich b Pollard	26	– lbw b Ikin	7
H. T. Bartlett c E. Edrich b Pollard	7	– b Roberts	59
S. C. Griffith b Ikin	6	– c Garlick b Roberts	11
J. Oakes not out	44	– lbw b Ikin	10
J. Duffield c Cranston b Ikin	8	– not out	11
P. A. D. Carey b Pollard	8	– c Place b Ikin	0
J. K. Nye c G. Edrich b Pollard	5	– c E. Edrich b Roberts	0
B 4, l-b 11, n-b 3	18	L-b 1	1
	255		**223**

Sussex Bowling

	Overs	Mdns	Runs	Wkts	Overs	Mdns	Runs	Wkts
Nye	17	2	50	1	14	—	62	—
Carey	19	5	62	5	17	1	64	—
Duffield	9	—	27	—	7	—	44	—
C. Oakes	7	—	27	—	8	1	38	—
Cox	13	2	34	3	16	4	37	—
J. Oakes	8	1	18	1	14	1	77	—
James Langridge	5	—	36	—	2	—	9	—
Bartlett					1	—	7	—
John Langridge					1	1	—	—

Lancashire Bowling

	Overs	Mdns	Runs	Wkts	Overs	Mdns	Runs	Wkts
Phillipson	12	2	39	1	13	4	45	—
Pollard	30.1	9	56	5	20	5	53	2
Cranston	23	6	53	1	10	2	23	—
Roberts	11	4	29	1	15	7	18	3
Garlick	9	1	33	—	2	—	4	—
Ikin	8	—	27	2	25	5	79	5

Umpires: B. Flint and P. Holmes.

LANCASHIRE v YORKSHIRE

Played at Manchester, July 31, August 2, 3, 1948

Drawn. The match was memorable for the feat of Lester, who equalled the 28-year-old record of P. Holmes by scoring a century in each innings of a "Roses" game. Altogether the encounter produced five three-figure scores. Lester's first innings display was rather overshadowed by the brilliance of Hutton, who made 104 out of 184 before a fierce thunderstorm flooded the ground. Lester batted three hours and a quarter for his 125 and hit eighteen 4s while Greenwood was bowling extremely well. Lancashire lost two wickets for 12, but Washbrook hit a 6 and twenty-one 4s during three hours and a quarter. Ikin helped to add 244, putting Lancashire on the way to the lead. Lester's second hundred, made in 110 minutes, was marked by superb driving and vigorous pulls. Yardley preferred that Yorkshire should continue batting rather than declare and the match petered out. On the Bank Holiday a collection for Washbrook's benefit realised £212 16s.

Yorkshire

L. Hutton c Washbrook b Greenwood	104	– c Brierley b Greenwood	7
H. Halliday b Greenwood	5	– c Ikin b Pollard	16
J. V. Wilson c Brierley b Ikin	25	– not out	29
N. W. D. Yardley c Howard b Greenwood	28	– c Roberts b Pollard	15
W. Watson lbw b Pollard	1	– not out	1
E. Lester not out	125	– c Place b Ikin	132
A. Coxon b Roberts	14		
T. F. Smailes c Roberts b Greenwood	30	– st Brierley b Roberts	31
R. Aspinall c and b Pollard	5		
J. H. Wardle c Brierley b Greenwood	0		
D. V. Brennan c Brierley b Greenwood	7		
B 10, l-b 3, n-b 2	15	B 5, l-b 4, w 1	10
	359		**(5 wkts) 241**

Lancashire

C. Washbrook c Watson b Smailes	156	K. Cranston not out	44
W. Place c Brennan b Smailes	5	N. D. Howard not out	14
G. A. Edrich c Yardley b Smailes	0	B 1, l-b 6, n-b 1	8
J. T. Ikin st Brennan b Wardle	106		
T. L. Brierley c Aspinall b Wardle	28	(5 wkts dec.)	361

A. Wharton, P. Greenwood, R. Pollard and W. B. Roberts did not bat.

Lancashire Bowling

	Overs	Mdns	Runs	Wkts	Overs	Mdns	Runs	Wkts
Pollard	41	10	103	2	14	1	58	2
Greenwood	22.4	5	68	6	7	—	29	1
Cranston	9	—	40	—	8	—	30	—.
Roberts	32	12	72	1	17	1	67	1
Ikin	17	3	58	1	2	—	7	1
Wharton	1	—	3	—	5	1	23	—
Edrich					5	3	5	—
Washbrook					6	5	1	—
N. D. Howard					3	2	2	—
Place					1	—	9	—

Yorkshire Bowling

	Overs	Mdns	Runs	Wkts
Aspinall	25.4	9	73	—
Coxon	24	7	63	—
Smailes	28	6	92	3
Yardley	11	2	27	—
Wardle	27	2	98	2

Umpires: C. N. Woolley and A. Lockett.

LANCASHIRE v SUSSEX

Played at Manchester, May 7, 9, 10, 1949

Sussex won by 95 runs. The match proved notable for the feat of John Langridge, who became the sixth player to score two hundreds in a game on the ground. His first innings lasted five hours and a quarter and his second two hours less. Charles Oakes helped him in two three-figure partnerships. None of the Lancashire bowlers was really effective, although Grieves, an Australian all-rounder, making his county début, took three wickets for 22 in one spell of nine overs. An excellent 124 by the left-handed Wharton enabled

Lancashire to make a sound reply, but when left to score 285 in three hours only Washbrook showed confidence against purposeful bowling, and the last wicket fell with eight minutes remaining.

Sussex

John Langridge b Grieves	115	– b Wharton	129
D. V. Smith c Wilson b Pollard	6	– b Pollard	24
C. Oakes c Place b Wharton	48	– not out	80
H. T. Bartlett c Washbrook b Pollard	5		
G. Cox lbw b Ikin	54		
James Langridge c Place b Grieves	22		
J. Oakes c Place b Roberts	27	– not out	0
S. C. Griffith c Pollard b Grieves	16		
A. E. James c Ikin b Greenwood	21		
G. T. Hurst b Pollard	9		
J. Cornford not out	3		
B 7, l-b 4	11	B 4, l-b 2, n-b 1	7
	337	**(2 wkts dec.)**	**240**

Lancashire

C. Washbrook lbw b Cox	35	– c J. Oakes b James Langridge	87
W. Place b Cornford	2	– c Griffith b Cornford	8
J. T. Ikin lbw b Hurst	19	– b Hurst	13
G. A. Edrich b Cornford	22	– c James b Hurst	0
A. Wharton c and b J. Oakes	124	– c and b C. Oakes	22
N. D. Howard b Cox	6	– c Bartlett b James Langridge	0
K. Grieves c Griffith b Cornford	43	– b C. Oakes	4
P. Greenwood b Cornford	10	– c John Langridge b C. Oakes	13
R. Pollard c Cox b J. Oakes	16	– c John Langridge b James Langridge	27
W. D. Roberts not out	1	– b J. Oakes	1
A. Wilson c and b J. Oakes	0	– not out	8
B 10, l-b 5	15	B 1, l-b 5	6
	293		**189**

Lancashire Bowling

	Overs	Mdns	Runs	Wkts	Overs	Mdns	Runs	Wkts
Pollard	32	8	68	3	20	4	69	1
Greenwood	30.1	11	76	1	13	1	62	—
Grieves	33	9	80	3	8	3	23	—
Roberts	38	20	49	1	23	12	42	—
Ikin	12	2	28	1	6	—	26	—
Wharton	6	1	25	1	5	1	11	1

Sussex Bowling

	Overs	Mdns	Runs	Wkts	Overs	Mdns	Runs	Wkts
Cornford	22	6	66	4	8	2	23	1
J. Oakes	11.4	3	36	3	5	2	12	1
Hurst	17	2	44	1	12	—	51	2
Cox	17	5	35	2	8	1	23	—
James	10	1	35	—				
James Langridge	25	6	62	—	13.3	2	38	3
C. Oakes					17	8	36	3

Umpires: E. Cooke and A. R. Coleman.

LANCASHIRE v YORKSHIRE
Played at Manchester, June 4, 6, 7, 1949

Match drawn. Hutton, by scoring a double hundred, equalled the feats of Leyland and Spooner, the only others to accomplish this performance in a "Roses" match. He batted faultlessly for six hours fifty minutes and his most productive hits were three 6s, a 5 and nineteen 4s. Halliday, missed twice, helped in a second-wicket partnership of 163. Following the early loss of Washbrook, Lancashire made indifferent progress against the accurate bowling of Close, Mason and Hutton, eight wickets being down before the follow-on was avoided. Hutton again batted in masterly fashion, and when Yorkshire declared with a lead of 317 his match aggregate was 292 for once out. Yorkshire seemed likely to win when four men were dismissed for 65, but Grieves, dropped four times, thwarted them in a fifth stand of 69 with Wharton. He hit four 6s and eight 4s.

Yorkshire

L. Hutton c Grieves b Greenwood	201	– not out	91
F. A. Lowson st Wilson b Lomax	0	– c Howard b Grieves	23
H. Halliday b Ikin	69		
E. Lester b Roberts	2	– c Wilson b Grieves	12
W. Watson c Wilson b Lomax	16		
N. W. D. Yardley c and b Lomax	0	– c Washbrook b Grieves	15
D. B. Close run out	8	– not out	21
A. Coxon not out	26		
D. V. Brennan not out	0		
B 1, l-b 3	4	B 2, n-b 4	6

(7 wkts dec.) 326   (3 wkts dec.) 168

A. Mason and F. Trueman did not bat.

Lancashire

C. Washbrook b Close	17	– c Coxon b Mason	29
W. Place c and b Hutton	33	– c Brennan b Mason	6
J. T. Ikin lbw b Mason	4	– c Coxon b Hutton	7
A. Wharton c and b Hutton	14	– not out	73
N. D. Howard c and b Mason	18	– c Trueman b Hutton	9
K. Grieves b Hutton	34	– b Close	69
P. Greenwood not out	21	– not out	16
J. G. Lomax lbw b Mason	10		
R. Pollard c and b Close	6		
W. B. Roberts c Coxon b Close	12		
A. Wilson st Brennan b Mason	0		
B 6, l-b 2	8	B 14, l-b 2, n-b 2	18

177   (5 wkts) 227

Lancashire Bowling

	Overs	Mdns	Runs	Wkts	Overs	Mdns	Runs	Wkts
Pollard	31	6	67	—	7	2	28	—
Lomax	27	5	84	3	6	1	26	—
Greenwood	26	8	59	1	4	—	24	—
Roberts	35	19	59	1	7	—	28	—
Grieves	22	10	42	—	10	—	56	3
Ikin	8	2	11	1				

Yorkshire Bowling

	Overs	Mdns	Runs	Wkts	Overs	Mdns	Runs	Wkts
Trueman.........	9	3	16	—	7	1	27	—
Coxon...........	6	—	17	—	5	2	14	—
Close............	28	10	67	3	20	7	52	1
Mason...........	35.3	19	46	4	31	14	55	2
Hutton	15	5	23	3	16	6	52	2
Halliday					5	2	9	—

Umpires: D. Davies and T. J. Bartley.

LANCASHIRE v GLOUCESTERSHIRE

Played at Manchester, June 8, 9, 10, 1949

Gloucestershire won by nine wickets, Goddard, the Gloucestershire off-spin bowler, well supported in the field, played a leading part in this victory, which was completed in the first hour of the final day. His control of length and flight earned him thirteen wickets for 111. Only Washbrook, who demonstrated the importance of correct footwork and timing, showed any certainty against Goddard. Graveney, Allen and Lambert all batted soundly for Gloucestershire, and in doing so emphasised the hesitant stroke play of the Lancashire batsmen on an easy-paced pitch.

Lancashire

C. Washbrook c Crapp b Goddard..............	47	– lbw b Cook....................	63
W. Place c Crapp b Milton	6	– c Allen b Goddard	26
A. Wharton c Crapp b Bailey	15	– c Goddard b Cook	16
N. D. Howard b Goddard.....................	7	– b Goddard	1
J. T. Ikin c Crapp b Goddard	31	– b Goddard	8
K. Grieves c Graveney b Goddard	37	– b Cook	0
P. Greenwood lbw b Goddard.................	0	– c Graveney b Goddard.........	19
R. Pollard st Wilson b Cook	20	– b Goddard	1
W. B. Roberts b Goddard.....................	17	– st Wilson b Goddard	8
M. Hilton c Crapp b Cook	15	– c Milton b Goddard	9
A. Wilson not out	0	– not out	0
B 2, l-b 6, n-b 1	9	L-b 4...................	4
	204		**155**

Gloucestershire

G. M. Emmett c Howard b Pollard..............	1		
A. E. Wilson c Washbrook b Roberts	26	– c Pollard b Roberts	5
J. F. Crapp c Washbrook b Greenwood..........	34	– not out	9
T. W. Graveney b Greenwood	51		
B. O. Allen c Grieves b Roberts	65	– not out	40
G. Lambert c Place b Roberts..................	61		
C. A. Milton b Grieves	2		
Sir D. Bailey c Washbrook b Roberts............	1		
L. M. Cranfield st Wilson b Grieves	33		
T. W. Goddard hit wkt b Grieves	13		
C. Cook not out	0		
B 13, l-b 2, n-b 4	19		
	306		**(1 wkt) 54**

Gloucestershire Bowling

	Overs	Mdns	Runs	Wkts	Overs	Mdns	Runs	Wkts
Lambert	20	5	57	—	6	1	24	—
Milton............	7	1	24	1	4	—	16	—
Bailey	4	1	18	1				
Goddard..........	27	11	54	6	28.5	6	57	7
Cook.............	11	1	42	2	26	9	54	3

Lancashire Bowling

	Overs	Mdns	Runs	Wkts	Overs	Mdns	Runs	Wkts
Pollard	17	5	39	1				
Roberts..........	39	14	84	4	8	2	25	1
Hilton	13	4	33	—	4.3	—	14	—
Grieves	18.3	6	52	3				
Greenwood........	25	7	55	2	3	—	15	—
Ikin	5	—	24	—				

Umpires: W. H. Ashdown and F. S. Lee.

LANCASHIRE v NOTTINGHAMSHIRE

Played at Manchester, July 9, 11, 12, 1949

Match drawn. A remarkable opening partnership of 318 between Keeton and Simpson, lasting five and a quarter hours, transcended everything else in this match. It was their fourth three-figure stand in successive games. Simpson, hitting beautifully in front of the wicket, claimed one 6 and twenty-one 4s among his scoring strokes. He spent six and three-quarter hours at the crease. Keeton, more restrained, reached the boundary nine times. There was an unfortunate start to the Lancashire innings, Place breaking a bone in his hand when struck by a ball from Woodhead, but Wharton and Grieves scored 132 in two hours for the third wicket. Wharton, fortunate to be missed twice, hit fourteen 4s. Simpson did not enforce the follow-on, and Lancashire, left to score 243 in just over two hours, found the task quite beyond them.

Nottinghamshire

W. W. Keeton b Berry 134				
R. T. Simpson b Pollard 238				
H. Winrow b Ikin	1	– not out	30
C. J. Poole c Berry b Pollard.................	73	– not out	33
F. W. Stocks c Ikin b Pollard	7		
A. Jepson not out	32		
E. Martin not out............................	1	– c Barlow b Pollard	5
B 12, l-b 3, n-b 3	18	B 7	7

(5 wkts dec.) 504	(1 wkt dec.) 75

H. J. Butler, E. A. Meads, F. G. Woodhead and A. Richardson did not bat.

Lancashire

W. Place retired hurt	30	
J. T. Ikin lbw b Woodhead	15	– not out 57
G. A. Edrich lbw b Butler	0	– not out 56
A. Wharton c Butler b Woodhead	119	
K. Grieves b Woodhead	69	
N. D. Howard c and b Jepson	19	– b Jepson 6
P. Greenwood b Jepson	21	
A. E. Barlow c Meads b Butler	13	
R. Pollard c Keeton b Woodhead	1	
R. Berry c Meads b Simpson	12	
R. Tattersall not out	19	
B 5, l-b 14	19	
	337	**(1 wkt) 119**

Lancashire Bowling

	Overs	Mdns	Runs	Wkts	Overs	Mdns	Runs	Wkts
Pollard	35	3	117	3	8	3	21	1
Greenwood	29	5	83	—	7	3	5	—
Berry	29	6	71	1	1	—	3	—
Grieves	18	—	57	—	7	3	17	—
Tattersall	30	3	102	—	11	7	10	—
Ikin	20	6	56	1	5	—	12	—

Nottinghamshire Bowling

	Overs	Mdns	Runs	Wkts	Overs	Mdns	Runs	Wkts
Butler	25	7	49	2	4	—	10	—
Jepson	24	5	58	2	5	—	6	1
Richardson	18	3	46	—	4	2	2	—
Winrow	2	—	19	—	3	—	21	—
Woodhead	36	11	94	4				
Simpson	17	6	41	1	11	1	56	—
Stocks	2	—	11	—	11	3	24	—

Umpires: W. H. Ashdown and A. R. Coleman.

LANCASHIRE v SUSSEX

Played at Manchester, July 12, 1950

Lancashire won by an innings and 87 runs. For the third time since 1925, when Somerset were victims, a match at Old Trafford ended in one day. Afterwards James Langridge, Sussex professional captain, asserted that the pitch was not fit for three-day games, but he admitted that Lancashire were better equipped to exploit the conditions. During the day thirty wickets fell for 391 runs, and with Sussex in a hopeless plight at the end of the normal period the captains agreed on extra time to complete the match. Hilton, Lancashire's slow left-arm bowler, did his best work for the county, returning match figures of eleven wickets for 50 runs. Greenwood, with off-breaks, took nine for 67. Although John Langridge carried his bat and J. Oakes hit two 6s and five 4s, six players failed to score and Sussex were dismissed in 105 minutes before lunch. J. Oakes also bowled well, but Edrich and Barlow batted forcefully for Lancashire, who gained a lead of 138. Sussex again fell to pieces in their second innings, being put out in seventy minutes.

Sussex

John Langridge not out	48	– c Barlow b Greenwood	1
D. S. Sheppard b Hilton	7	– st Barlow b Hilton	2
C. Oakes lbw b Greenwood	4	– lbw b Greenwood	1
G. Cox c Edrich b Hilton	2	– st Barlow b Hilton	11
D. V. Smith b Hilton	0	– c Edrich b Hilton	14
James Langridge c Edrich b Hilton	0	– c Grieves b Hilton	3
J. Oakes b Greenwood	35	– b Greenwood	2
A. E. James c Wharton b Hilton	0	– b Greenwood	0
R. T. Webb c Edrich b Greenwood	0	– st Barlow b Greenwood	0
J. H. Cornford c Barlow b Greenwood	0	– b Hilton	3
D. J. Wood c Edrich b Hilton	0	– not out	5
B 3, l-b 2	5	B 4, l-b 4, n-b 1	9
	101		**51**

Lancashire

C. Washbrook c Webb b J. Oakes	21	A. Barlow c Smith b James Langridge	42
W. Place c John Langridge b J. Oakes	28	M. J. Hilton c and b James Langridge	10
G. A. Edrich c Webb b James	89	R. Tattersall not out	3
K. Grieves b J. Oakes	0	R. Berry b James	4
N. D. Howard lbw b C. Oakes	17	B 6	6
A. Wharton lbw b J. Oakes	19		
P. Greenwood b J. Oakes	0		**239**

Lancashire Bowling

	Overs	Mdns	Runs	Wkts	Overs	Mdns	Runs	Wkts
Greenwood	15	6	43	4	11	3	24	5
Hilton	18	8	32	6	10.1	3	18	5
Berry	3	1	21	—				

Sussex Bowling

	Overs	Mdns	Runs	Wkts
Wood	4	—	10	—
Cornford	3	—	11	—
J. Oakes	25	3	107	5
James Langridge	22	2	75	2
C. Oakes	7	1	27	1
James	4.5	2	3	2

Umpires: J. J. Hills and A. E. Pothecary.

FIFTY YEARS OF LANCASHIRE CRICKET [1951]

By Neville Cardus

I first saw Lancashire playing cricket one dull day in July 1899. I am at a loss to say why I went to Old Trafford at the age of nine, just as I am at a loss to explain where my gate-money came from. I wasn't interested in cricket then; my passion was football, which we played on the rough fields of Moss Side, with coats for goalposts. My heroes were Billy Meredith and Bloomer – I firmly believed that Bloomer had once split a goalpost in halves with a kick from just beyond the half-way line. I lived five miles at least from Old Trafford and, as I say, it remains a mystery that I should have entered Old Trafford in July 1899, in time to see G. L. Jessop come to the wicket to join C. L. Townsend, who scored 91, and very tall he looked, and graceful.

UNDER THE SPELL

Jessop left no indelible impression on me this time but I remember a beautiful innings by F. H. B. Champain, and with the naïve love of a boy to play upon words, I thought he was perfectly named. The only thing I remember about Lancashire from my introduction to the county is that one of the bowlers was named Lancaster, which also seemed appropriate to my dawning sense of the wonder of words and English.

Next year, 1900, I fell entirely under the spell of the game and of Lancashire cricket, once and for all and for ever. I saw – my second match! – Johnny Briggs take all the ten wickets against Worcestershire. After the ninth had fallen to him. Mold bowled wide; but for many overs Johnny couldn't pitch a ball in the danger zone. He was so excited; he bounced about as though uncontrolled and uncontrollable.

WHITSUN AT OLD TRAFFORD

My next match at Old Trafford took place on Whit-Monday 1900, and it was not Yorkshire. Believe it or not, Kent were playing Lancashire at Whitsun in 1900, when matches began on Mondays and Thursdays – so that often the great grounds of England – Old Trafford, Trent Bridge, Headingley, The Oval and Lord's – might any one of them be standing vacant on a sunny Saturday, the game having come to the end, or lost all interest, on the second day, the Friday. There's richness for you! ... Well, on Bank Holiday at Whitsun 1900, I arrived at Old Trafford at nine in the morning, paid my sixpence, and got a front bench directly facing the pavilion. At twelve o'clock Lancashire took the field, and C. J. Burnup and Alex Hearne began Kent's innings. Mold bowled from the Stretford end, Briggs from the Old Trafford end – a very fast bowler and a very slow bowler, each using the new ball (and there wouldn't be another new ball available or permissible until the Kent innings was finished, or until the "old" ball had been – as John Gunn once put it to me – "knock'd in two").

In quick time Mold and Briggs began to ruin the Kent innings. Briggs bowled Hearne for 2; Mold shattered all the stumps of W. H. Patterson for 1; Mold uprooted a stump defended by B. D. Bannon for 0 – 11 for 3 and I gloated. I always liked to watch cricket alone these early years; I could wallow better in my passions with nobody to intrude. Mold's speed was so terrific that the Kent batsmen apparently couldn't see the ball. With all of a boy's patriotic heartlessness, I derided the helplessness of Hearne, Bannon and Patterson; and my ridicule and lust were intensified when J. R. Mason came in and played forward and missed Mold three or four times, absolutely beaten, obviously "out any minute".

A GREAT INNINGS

At the other end of the wicket, a little man was putting his bat both to Briggs and Mold in a way I didn't like at all; his name, as I say, was C. J. Burnup. But there was no need to worry about him – surely! – because Mold was about to send one or two or all three of

J. R. Mason's wickets flying this coming over. The truth is that Mason and Burnup stayed in for nearly three hours and added 110 or thereabouts, and that after Mason had been caught at the wicket off Mold for 68, another Kent amateur named T. T. N. Perkins, cut and drove with an ease and elegance which utterly spoiled my holiday; he scored 88. At half-past six a disconsolate Lancashire boy rising eleven, walked all the way home, down Shrewsbury Street, past Brooks' Bar, all the way on foot to Rusholme, wondering why Mold had allowed such disappointments to occur . . . Kent had batted all day – 408 or so for 7 or 8, and C. J. Burnup was out in the last over, or almost the last, of the afternoon: "c Smith b Cuttell 200", an enormous total for one batsman – and such a small and modest one – in those days when the currency of batsmanship was not yet inflated but remained on the gold standard. I looked up this match in the newspapers the other day and found that memory had not played me false in a single important fact. One account of this day's play said, describing Burnup's innings, "it was a valuable effort, and though slow at periods, an occasional lack of enterprise on Mr. Burnup's part was excusable in view of Kent's bad start". "Slow at periods" – 200 compiled in a little more than five and a half hours by a batsman not regarded one of the country's "dashers", and, moreover, after a furious and successful onslaught by Mold! It would be regarded a quickish innings to-day, if played uphill.

I received compensation next day for this bitter taste of adversity on Bank Holiday. I saw Johnny Briggs make a half-century in each of Lancashire's innings; he slashed skimming drives over cover-point's head, and frequently he "blocked" a ball and pretended to risk a run, "chancing it", to use the period's expression. Such cricket would be regarded reprehensible from any famous contemporary England cricketer.

I was lucky to begin my long years of devoted attention at Old Trafford with three such grand games. Of course it was but seldom I could "repair" to the great ground where not so long ago the run stealers had flickered to and fro. My pocket-money didn't run to sixpence a week. But I devoured the cricket scores and rejoiced in the "cricket edition", and was afraid to turn to the "close of play" scores. One evening I read in the stop-press: "R. H. Spooner b Wilson 0". R. H. Spooner was my favourite cricketer, and whenever he failed much of the savour went out of my life, not to say the purpose. But next evening, or the evening after, a worse blow befell me. Again I turned to the "close of play" score and there, in cold print, was this announcement: "R. H. Spooner b Wilson 0", – a "pair of spectacles" for him. I hadn't the heart, that summer evening, to play cricket with my schoolmates. I wandered the streets blighted.

MAJESTIC BATSMEN

It is commonly thought that Lancashire cricket has always expressed North-country dourness and parsimony. This is an error. In 1904 Lancashire won the County Championship without losing a match; and until an August staleness afflicted the team, the rate of scoring by Lancashire averaged 70 to 80 – some days 100 – an hour. No county has boasted three batsmen going in Nos 1, 2 and 3 possessing more majesty than A. C. MacLaren's, more style and ripple of strokes than R. H. Spooner's, more broadsword attack and brilliance that Johnny Tyldesley's. In 1904 and 1905 the Lancashire XI was usually chosen from A. C. MacLaren, R. H. Spooner, J. T. Tyldesley, L. O. S. Poidevin, James Hallows, Sharp, Cuttell, W. Findlay, A. H. Hornby, Kermode, W. Brearley; and there were in these early 1900s Harold Garnett, and Heap, Huddleston and Worsley. The team was undefeated, not only in 1904 but until half-way through the summer of 1905, and then Surrey overwhelmed them at Aigburth. The "unbeaten certificate" – to quote the metaphorical language of the Press of those years – was twice threatened in 1904, by Yorkshire at Leeds: a century by Tyldesley saved the day, and he batted more than four hours for it, one of the few slow innings of his life.

Again – I seem to remember – Surrey were winning easily at The Oval on a Saturday in 1904 – the third day, before lunch – but during the interval sun baked a wet turf and Huddleston's off breaks were unplayable. Given a "sticky" pitch, Huddleston was a very dangerous spinner, but not the equal of "Razor" Smith of Surrey, who could make the ball go the other way as well. Brearley was equal to the physical feat of bowling all day; he was nearly as dangerous to limb off the field as on it when he prodded you in the chest punctuating his story of what he had done to Victor Trumper. He was known to push people the whole length of the bar in the Long Room at Lord's, leaving their drinks far away, completely isolated.

DANGEROUS PITCH

Poidevin, from Sydney, would have played for Australia had he not settled as a doctor of medicine in Manchester. James Hallows, left-handed batsman and bowler, had rare gifts but poor health. He might easily have become one of the greatest of all-round England players; he was nearly that as it was. Cuttell at his best would to-day be one of the first choices for an England XI. MacLaren, Spooner, Tyldesley, and Brearley all played for England in 1905; and Jack Sharp joined them in the English rubber of 1909. In 1901, the wicket at Old Trafford was so dangerous that Sharp took 100 wickets in a season and C. B. Fry extracted from the turf some pebbles or foreign bodies which subsequently were exhibited to the public in the window of Johnny Tyldesley's sports shop in Deansgate; we looked at them in silent wonder like people who gape in the geological museum. Incredible that during this same season Tyldesley scored 3,000 runs, playing half his innings on this rude, rough turf at an average of 55 and more. I doubt if any batsman alive or dead has so strongly as this established his genius.

So far, I have been recalling the MacLaren epoch in Lancashire cricket. There was not one recognised and accredited "stone-waller" in the XI, for Albert Ward – beautiful in forward movement, whether scoring or not – belonged to a vintage preceding the Championship summer of 1904 – and Makepeace came later. There was a subsequent A. H. Hornby period of some ebullience and insecurity, with A. Hartley sound as a rock and the skipper himself chafing on the leash for a drive over the rails. But hereabouts the bowling lost the axe-edge. Harry Dean persevered, and Frank Harry, off-spinner, was a willing horse. During the MacLaren supremacy the Lancashire attack had enjoyed rare resources, from the "sticky" wicket terrors of Webb, who but for a sceptical view of himself might have scaled the heights, to Brearley, Dean and Kermode, not forgetting William Cook, who round about 1905 would have glorified the England attack with his fast bowling, but preferred the leagues.

Now comes a gap in my memory's frieze. In 1912, 1913 and 1914 I was playing as a professional at Shrewsbury School, and temporarily lost sight of doings at Old Trafford. I am vague about these three seasons; others and earlier ones I can live again in my mind's eye to a detail, as though they all happened only last year. In 1919 I picked up the broken thread, and this time I found myself *actually* paid to watch and delight in Lancashire cricket, as correspondent of the *Manchester Guardian*.

In 1919, a season of two-day games, Old Trafford discovered Charles Hallows, nephew of James, another superb left-handed batsman – one might easily have served as England's reply to Warren Bardsley. Cecil Parkin as far back as 1914 had flickered a will o' the wisp light on one or two fields now rose to more than fame as a magnificent bowler; he won the love of that public that revels in a "character"; he was a combination of Springheel Jack, merry-andrew and, on a damaged pitch, a master of a breakback quick as the execution blade. His "googly" was his mocking cap-and-bells. "Lol" Cook maintained the classical tradition of length; James Tyldesley exploited fast in-swingers to a leg-trap, and Richard Tyldesley persuaded many batsmen to "feel" for leg-spin real and imaginary.

TRIPLE CHAMPIONS

Myles Kenyon prepared the way to a Lancashire renaissance. Then, under the firm, shrewd and humour-loving leadership of Leonard Green, Lancashire supassed even the Yorkshire of the Rhodes-Robinson dynasty or "rump". For three consecutive years

Lancashire led the County Championship – 1926, 1927 and 1928 – and again in 1930 thanks a good deal to E. A. McDonald, most beautiful of fast bowlers of our time with his silent curving sinuous run to the crease, most deadly in pace and abrupt rise to the batsman's wrists and – now and then – higher still.

The batting policy was set by Makepeace; if the toss were won, the plan was to stay there all day for 300 at least and to wear enough sheen from the pitch for McDonald. On "sticky" turf nobody has excelled Makepeace in the art of passive resistance with the "dead" bat, left-hand lightly gripping top of the handle. But, at a pinch, Makepeace would reveal resource and strokes. At Trent Bridge in 1920, Lancashire lost two wickets for next to nothing against Barratt, bowling formidably on a "green" pitch; the accredited stroke-players were out, so Makepeace was obliged to attend to the necessary job of making the runs. He was not defeated until after tea, for 152, scored in three hours fifty minutes, with eighteen fours. His left side and chest were black and blue from bruises.

The Lancashire "ca canny" batting tactics told of the change in the economy and social life of Lancashire county at large. Gone the old Manchester cosmopolitan opulence and the piles of "brass" in the hinterland, symbolised by the great amateurs, MacLaren, Spooner and the Brearleys, the Hollinses, and by Tyldesley, Sharp, and the rest. The county in the 1920s lived "near the bone", and Lancashire cricket more than hinted of this transformation. The team became notorious as a spoiler of cricket festivals; at Eastbourne and Cheltenham, retired colonels turned pale when they heard that Lancashire "were batting". At Old Trafford or in Yorkshire at Bank Holiday time, a Yorkshire innings was quite skittish compared to one by Lancashire. But there was organised technique during the Makepeace regime; the scoring was slow "on principle", not because these fine players couldn't have scored quicker had they chosen.

GOOD COMPANIONS

There was vast humour in it all; travel round the country with Lancashire in these years was an education in shrewd cricket sense as well as a revelation of North-country nature. Peter Eckersley, and later Lister, controlled a great if mixed company because they understood character as much as cricket. Under Eckersley, the County Championship was won once more in 1934. Ernest Tyldesley added aggression to Makepeace's Fabianism though he could, given the cue, be obstinate enough. At his best he was amongst not only the prolific run-getters of the period; he was one of the artists as well.

To-day Lancashire cricket is again – or was last year – in the ascendancy, sharing the honours with Surrey. There is surely an even more lustrous future ahead, for youth is there in plenty, commanded by a captain who every day gains strength as batsman and strategist. Few counties have so persistently honoured a proud tradition. A noble array of names can readily be chosen from Lancashire men fit to stand against Australia for England, chosen from teams of the last fifty years, teams of my time, in a match imagined, and because not ever to be played in Time and Space, is seen in immortal sunshine – and cloud – at Old Trafford: A. C. MacLaren, R. H. Spooner, Tyldesley (J. T.), Tyldesley (E.), Washbrook, Oldfield, H. G. Garnett (or W. Findlay) wicket-keeper, Jack Sharp, Parkin, Dean and Brearley. And I have been compelled to leave out – Heaven forgive me! – Makepeace, Cuttell, the two Hallows, "Dick" Tyldesley, A. H. Hornby, Heap. I don't include McDonald because he was an Australian. And I am not forgetting Barnes, unearthed by MacLaren. Though he played at least one whole season for Lancashire – I saw him lay low the might of Surrey at Old Trafford in 1902 on a perfect wicket, until Vivian Crawford took charge of him, backed-up by Captain H. S. Bush – Barnes can hardly be said ever to have belonged to Lancashire. Barnes was a man born to possess, not to be possessed. And if I omit Tattersall from my Lancashire team representative of the best in the country over the span of half a century, it is not from want of enthusiasm about his talent, and not because I am unaware that in 1950 he was the most successful and omnivorous bowler since Arthur Mold (a Northamptonshire man, by the way), but because, being young, Tattersall has not yet had the chance to fix immovably his claims on the attention of history. That he will do so, we can be pretty sure, is only a matter of time.

LANCASHIRE v DERBYSHIRE

Played at Manchester, June 4, 5, 6, 1952

Lancashire won by 83 runs. Splendid bowling by Hilton made the victory possible. His left-arm spinners accounted for four batsmen for 15 runs in Derbyshire's first innings, and on the last day he exploited a rain-affected pitch to such good purpose that although Derbyshire made a stubborn effort to save the game they were beaten with ten minutes to spare. Yet commendable as was Hilton's match performance of ten for 49, the main honours went to Jackson, the Derbyshire fast-medium bowler. On the first day he was in action for the greater part of five hours and fully earned the best figures of his career – nine wickets for 60. Gladwin, who spoiled Jackson's chances of taking all ten, bowled well later in the game, but Derbyshire's batting, at times cautious in the extreme, fell below standard. The Lancashire batsmen, and Edrich in particular, were more at ease under the conditions and gave their attack the support necessary to win a fiercely contested game.

Lancashire

J. T. Ikin c Hamer b Jackson	48	– c Kelly b Gladwin 7
S. Smith b Jackson	0	– c Rhodes b Gladwin 20
G. A. Edrich c Dawkes b Gladwin	73	– c Elliott b Gladwin 14
A. Wharton c Revill b Jackson	10	– c Dawkes b Rhodes 56
K. Grieves lbw b Jackson	47	– c Elliott b Jackson 1
N. D. Howard c Dawkes b Jackson	6	– c Morgan b Jackson 1
J. G. Lomax lbw b Jackson	11	– c Carr b Gladwin 9
M. J. Hilton lbw b Jackson	22	– c Dawkes b Jackson 4
J. B. Statham b Jackson	1	– b Gladwin 24
A. Wilson b Jackson	3	– not out 4
R. Tattersall not out	0	
B 2, n-b 1	3	B 1, n-b 1 2

1/1 2/101 3/123 4/167 5/186   **224**   1/11 2/30 3/63   (9 wkts dec.) **142**
6/187 7/204 8/208 9/223   4/69 5/71 6/77 7/100
                                   8/130 9/142

Derbyshire

C. S. Elliott c Grieves b Lomax	32	– c Edrich b Hilton 2
A. Hamer c Ikin b Lomax	38	– c Howard b Hilton 4
G. L. Willatt b Statham	3	– c Hilton b Tattersall 32
A. C. Revill not out	42	– st Wilson b Hilton 8
D. B. Carr c Edrich b Hilton	10	– c Grieves b Tattersall 3
J. Kelly c Smith b Lomax	10	– c and b Hilton 14
D. C. Morgan b Statham	13	– run out 9
G. Dawkes c and b Hilton	7	– not out 2
A. E. G. Rhodes c Wharton b Hilton	0	– c Ikin b Hilton 32
C. Gladwin lbw b Statham	0	– c Wharton b Hilton 1
L. Jackson c Grieves b Hilton	0	– c Edrich b Tattersall 0
B 3, l-b 7	10	B 7, l-b 4 11

1/74 2/79 3/86 4/105 5/133   **165**   1/5 2/10 3/50 4/53 5/58   **118**
6/152 7/163 8/163 9/164   6/77 7/92 8/106 9/117

Derbyshire Bowling

	Overs	Mdns	Runs	Wkts	Overs	Mdns	Runs	Wkts
Jackson	32.2	9	60	9	22	10	33	3
Gladwin	29	12	60	1	29	5	89	5
Morgan	14	3	42	—	2	—	8	—
Rhodes	12	3	44	—	6	3	10	1
Hamer	4	—	11	—				
Carr	1	—	4	—				

Lancashire Bowling

	Overs	Mdns	Runs	Wkts	Overs	Mdns	Runs	Wkts
Statham	22	3	50	3	8	4	10	—
Lomax	24	10	43	3	1	—	2	—
Wharton..........	4	—	12	—				
Ikin.............	2	1	1	—	2	—	6	—
Tattersall	25	8	34	—	24	10	55	3
Hilton............	10.5	4	15	4	27	14	34	6
Grieves					1	1	—	—

Umpires: A. E. Boulton-Carter and W. T. Jones.

LANCASHIRE v YORKSHIRE

Played at Manchester, August 2, 4, 5, 1952

Drawn. Seldom has there been such an exciting finish to a "Roses" match. With half an hour left, Lancashire were 157 for seven wickets when Trueman and Burgin took the new ball. Trueman dismissed Statham and Tattersall, and ten minutes remained when the last man, Berry, joined Parr. Amid tremendous enthusiasm they defied all efforts to dislodge them, Parr having stayed gallantly for an hour. Those present on Saturday were given little indication of the excitement to follow, for after rain prevented play until four o'clock Hutton and Lowson were content to stay. But a crowd of 20,000 had ample compensation on Monday, when twenty-three wickets fell for 234 runs. Berry perplexed the batsmen on a drying pitch, taking six wickets for 52, but Yorkshire's struggle was nothing compared with that of Lancashire, who were dismissed for their lowest total against Yorkshire at Old Trafford since 1909. Burgin, with accurate in-swingers in his first "Roses" encounter, and Trueman shared the wickets. A declaration left Lancashire to score 299 in three and three-quarter hours. They never appeared likely to get the runs, but for a long time danger of defeat looked equally remote. Then batsmen attempted suicidal strokes and the game swung in Yorkshire's favour, culminating in the dramatic finish already described.

Yorkshire

L. Hutton c Lomax b Tattersall	57	– lbw b Berry.....................	16
F. A. Lowson c and b Tattersall	40	– c Parr b Statham.............	9
H. Halliday c Grieves b Berry...................	2	– b Tattersall...................	4
E. Lester c Ikin b Berry.......................	0	– c Howard b Tattersall.........	20
W. Watson c Grieves b Statham................	49	– c and b Tattersall	7
D. B. Close c Grieves b Berry...................	2	– c Berry b Tattersall............	61
N. W. D. Yardley c Place b Berry...............	12	– c Parr b Lomax.................	10
J. H. Wardle c Howard b Tattersall	9	– c Edrich b Lomax.............	4
D. V. Brennan lbw b Berry	1	– not out	14
E. Burgin c Parr b Berry	4	– not out	2
F. S. Trueman not out........................	23		
W 1.................................	1	B 8, l-b 3, w 4, n-b 1	16

1/98 2/98 3/99 4/100 5/106   200   1/23 2/34   (8 wkts dec.) 163
6/118 7/131 8/135 9/145   3/36 4/51 5/88 6/126
                                  7/132 8/142

Lancashire

J. T. Ikin b Trueman	0	– c Wardle b Close	41
J. G. Lomax b Burgin	0	– c Close b Burgin	0
G. A. Edrich c Close b Burgin	4	– c Halliday b Wardle	40
W. Place c Brennan b Trueman	1	– c Trueman b Close	11
K. Grieves b Burgin	10	– c Watson b Wardle	16
N. D. Howard c Hutton b Burgin	20	– c Watson b Wardle	14
A. Wharton c Watson b Burgin	14	– lbw b Halliday	15
F. D. Parr b Trueman	5	– not out	9
J. B. Statham b Trueman	0	– b Trueman	0
R. Tattersall lbw b Trueman	0	– b Trueman	0
R. Berry not out	0	– not out	1
B 8, n-b 3	11	B 12, l-b 4, n-b 3	19

1/4 2/9 3/13 4/15 5/45   65   1/0 2/69 3/94   (9 wkts) 166
6/46 7/64 8/64 9/64   4/99 5/131 6/131 7/157
                               8/157 9/165

Lancashire Bowling

	Overs	Mdns	Runs	Wkts	Overs	Mdns	Runs	Wkts
Statham	17.5	4	35	1	17	3	53	1
Lomax	20	6	29	—	6	3	13	2
Tattersall	26	7	77	3	21	4	65	4
Wharton	5	1	6	—				
Berry	18	6	52	6	7	—	16	1

Yorkshire Bowling

	Overs	Mdns	Runs	Wkts	Overs	Mdns	Runs	Wkts
Trueman	10.2	5	16	5	20	6	42	2
Burgin	12	3	20	5	11	3	24	1
Wardle	2	1	8	—	28	13	57	3
Close					8	3	17	2
Halliday					8	6	7	1

Umpires: A. E. Pothecary and Harry Elliott (Derbyshire).

LANCASHIRE v SOMERSET

Played at Manchester, July 22, 23, 1953

Lancashire won by nine wickets. When the teams met at Bath in June one day sufficed for a decision; this time Lancashire were again supreme, victory coming during the extra half hour on the second day. Somerset never recovered from a wretched start after being sent in on a rain-affected pitch. Gimblett, who hit one 6 and ten 4s, alone countered the popping left-arm slows of Berry, and although Smith gave Gimblett some assistance in the second innings, Berry finished with thirteen wickets for 124 runs. Lancashire also had their uncomfortable moments, for Langford, the Somerset 17-year-old-off-spinner, sent back the first three batsmen, Washbrook, Ikin and Edrich, at a personal cost of 22, but a fine sixth-wicket partnership of 111 by Place and Wharton put them in a winning position.

Somerset

H. Gimblett lbw b Berry	53	– lbw b Berry	48
D. L. Kitson c Edrich b Berry	7	– c and b Berry	12
R. Smith c Grieves b Tattersall	3	– c Edrich b Berry	47
J. Lawrence c Washbrook b Berry	15	– b Berry	0
H. T. F. Buse c Edrich b Tattersall	2	– b Berry	0
J. Baker not out	17	– c Parr b Smith	10
H. W. Stephenson c Howard b Berry	4	– c Wharton b Ikin	7
B. G. Brocklehurst b Tattersall	0	– hit wkt b Berry	16
T. A. Hall c and b Berry	13	– not out	15
B. Langford c Grieves b Berry	7	– lbw b Tattersall	1
C. G. Mitchell lbw b Berry	0	– b Tattersall	0
B 4, l-b 2	6	L-b 1	1

1/18 2/27 3/73 4/78 5/86   127   1/32 2/75 3/75 4/75 5/96   157
6/90 7/90 8/115 9/127   6/110 7/135 8/152 9/157

Lancashire

C. Washbrook b Langford	7	– c Stephenson b Hall	2
J. T. Ikin c Lawrence b Langford	16	– not out	22
G. A. Edrich b Langford	12	– not out	24
W. Place not out	74		
K. Grieves c and b Langford	15		
N. D. Howard c Stephenson b Lawrence	34		
A. Wharton not out	69		
B 5, l-b 4	9	L-b 1	1

1/21 2/28 3/39 4/72   (5 wkts dec.) 236   1/2   (1 wkt) 49
5/125

R. Tattersall, R. Berry, F. D. Parr and C. S. Smith did not bat.

Lancashire Bowling

	Overs	Mdns	Runs	Wkts	Overs	Mdns	Runs	Wkts
Smith	4	2	7	—	7	5	5	1
Wharton	3	1	6	—				
Berry	28.1	12	58	7	36	15	66	6
Tattersall	28	4	50	3	23.5	6	49	2
Ikin					14	5	36	1

Somerset Bowling

	Overs	Mdns	Runs	Wkts	Overs	Mdns	Runs	Wkts
Buse	16	3	27	—	5	—	14	—
Langford	37	12	92	4				
Mitchell	11	1	28	—				
Lawrence	17	4	46	1				
Hall	13	3	26	—	6	1	18	1
Baker	2	1	8	—	1	—	6	—
Gimblett					1	—	5	—
Brocklehurst					0.2	—	5	—

Umpires: P. Corrall and Harry Elliott (Derbyshire).

LANCASHIRE v NOTTINGHAMSHIRE

Played at Manchester, August 26, 27, 1953

Lancashire won by ten wickets. Remarkable cricket on a treacherous pitch featured the last county match at Old Trafford and the luck of the toss played a major part. Howard won it and Nottinghamshire, after a favourable start, went from 42 for no wicket to 50 for seven in twenty-five minutes. Tattersall, with off-spinners, took all seven in nineteen deliveries without conceding a run, and, despite several dropped catches, he finished with nine for 40, the best analysis of his career. Lancashire fared even worse against Stocks and Dooland, who bowled unchanged, and they were dismissed for less than 100 for the only time during the summer. When Nottinghamshire, holding a lead of 20, batted again the pitch had improved, but they lost seven men in increasing their advantage to 107 before stumps were drawn at the end of the first day. Conditions later proved ideal and Lancashire eventually won in leisurely fashion. Their only setback was an injury to Washbrook, who was struck on the head by a return from long leg.

Nottinghamshire

J. D. Clay c Ikin b Tattersall	28	– lbw b Berry	8
E. Martin b Tattersall	13	– b Statham	15
A. G. Baxter c Grieves b Tattersall	0	– c Grieves b Tattersall	1
J. Hardstaff c Hilton b Tattersall	1	– lbw b Statham	9
F. W. Stocks b Tattersall	0	– b Statham	35
C. J. Poole c Grieves b Tattersall	18	– c and b Tattersall	11
B. Dooland b Tattersall	0	– lbw b Tattersall	8
J. Kelly c Grieves b Tattersall	0	– b Tattersall	0
A. Jepson c Hilton b Berry	33	– not out	6
A. J. Underwood b Tattersall	11	– c Grieves b Tattersall	8
E. Rowe not out	2	– b Statham	0
B 2, l-b 2	4	B 1, l-b 2, n-b 1	4

1/42 2/42 3/43 4/44 5/44   110   1/15 2/33 3/46 4/47 5/56   105
6/44 7/50 8/79 9/104   6/86 7/86 8/94 9/105

Lancashire

C. Washbrook c Stocks b Dooland	5	– retired hurt	35
J. T. Ikin c Dooland b Stocks	2	– not out	60
E. Place lbw b Dooland	0		
K. Grieves c Dooland b Stocks	0		
A. Wharton b Stocks	38	– not out	25
N. D. Howard b Stocks	10		
J. Hilton b Stocks	0		
J. B. Statham c and b Dooland	14		
R. Berry c Hardstaff b Dooland	9		
R. Tattersall not out	3		
A. Wilson b Dooland	0		
B 8, l-b 1	9	L-b 6	6

1/15 2/15 3/15 4/15 5/34   90   (No wkt) 126
6/34 7/73 8/87 9/87

Lancashire Bowling

	Overs	Mdns	Runs	Wkts	Overs	Mdns	Runs	Wkts
Statham	9	6	8	—	15	6	35	4
Wharton	2	1	4	—				
Tattersall	17.3	10	40	9	22	11	33	5
Berry	16	5	54	1	12	3	33	1

Nottinghamshire Bowling

	Overs	Mdns	Runs	Wkts	Overs	Mdns	Runs	Wkts
Dooland	16	6	43	5	15	4	38	—
Stocks............	15	6	38	5	16	4	41	—
Kelly.............					11	3	26	—
Hardstaff					5.1	2	15	—

Umpires: E. A. Roberts and T. J. Bartley.

LANCASHIRE v LEICESTERSHIRE

Played at Manchester, July 14, 16, 17, 1956

Lancashire won by ten wickets and became the first team to win a first-class match without losing a wicket. Only Wharton, who was in scintillating form on Monday, and Dyson batted. Their first innings partnership of 166 runs took about three hours and they finished the match by scoring 66 runs in fifty minutes. Leicestershire struggled against a varied attack after a blank Saturday through rain. On a drying pitch van Geloven took over an hour for 14 and Palmer two hours for 24. Lester and Hallam were helped by lax fielding when Leicestershire batted again but they alone reached double figures. Seven wickets fell for 27 runs in one period of fifty minutes.

Leicestershire

G. Lester c Statham b Wharton	2	– c Jordan b Greenhough	52
M. R. Hallam c Pullar b Statham	13	– c Collins b Hilton	42
J. van Geloven b Greenhough...................	14	– c Jordan b Statham............	3
M. Tompkin lbw b Statham	0	– c Dyson b Hilton	8
C. H. Palmer c Edrich b Hilton..................	24	– b Statham....................	1
V. E. Jackson c Collins b Statham	7	– c Wharton b Hilton............	2
R. A. Diment c Pullar b Hilton	12	– lbw b Greenhough	0
V. S. Munden c Grieves b Greenhough...........	0	– b Hilton	6
J. Firth b Statham............................	14	– c Jordan b Hilton	1
R. L. Pratt b Hilton...........................	9	– b Statham....................	0
J. Goodwin not out	5	– not out	0
B 2, l-b 3, n-b 3	8	B 5, n-b 2	7

1/7 2/17 3/22 4/34 5/49   108   1/59 2/78 3/94 4/95 5/102   122
6/75 7/75 8/75 9/85   6/115 7/116 8/117 9/122

Lancashire

A. Wharton not out...........................	87	– not out	33
J. Dyson not out	75	– not out	31
B 1, l-b 1, n-b 2	4	B 1, n-b 1	2

(No wkt) 166   (No wkt) 66

G. A. Edrich, K. Grieves, G. Pullar, R. Collins, M. J. Hilton, J. Jordan, J. B. Statham, T. Greenhough and R. Tattersall did not bat.

Lancashire Bowling

	Overs	Mdns	Runs	Wkts	Overs	Mdns	Runs	Wkts
Statham	17.3	7	32	4	15.1	3	36	3
Wharton..........	6	2	10	1	3	—	8	—
Hilton............	16	9	19	3	26	17	23	5
Greenhough	27	16	29	2	16	6	41	2
Tattersall	5	2	7	—	8	5	7	—
Collins	4	2	3	—				

Leicestershire Bowling

	Overs	Mdns	Runs	Wkts	Overs	Mdns	Runs	Wkts
Goodwin.........	10	—	41	—	7	1	36	—
Pratt............	7	—	37	—	6	1	19	—
Palmer	11	5	22	—	5	—	9	—
Jackson..........	16	7	37	—				
Munden	6	—	25	—				

Umpires: C. S. Elliott and F. W. Shipston.

LANCASHIRE v NOTTINGHAMSHIRE

Played at Liverpool, July 18, 19, 20, 1956

Drawn. Lancashire made an unusual, but justified declaration in an attempt to force a win. Leading by 121 runs on the first innings, Edrich, the acting captain, could not enforce the follow-on but he did the next best thing by declaring after Hilton had been caught off the first ball of Lancashire's second innings. This left his bowlers ninety-five minutes in which to dismiss Nottinghamshire, who themselves required to score 122 to win. At the close three wickets remained and Nottinghamshire were 29 runs short of the target. Lancashire had been sent in to bat. They made a reasonable score and then routed Nottinghamshire in two hours forty minutes for 86 on a drying pitch after the second day had been lost through rain.

Lancashire

J. Dyson lbw b Jepson........................	59			
R. W. Barber lbw b Walker....................	5			
G. A. Edrich lbw b Dooland	49			
K. Grieves c Walker b Kelly...................	16			
G. Pullar lbw b Jepson	41			
P. Marner b Dooland	10			
R. Collins lbw b Walker	9	– not out	0
M. J. Hilton not out..........................	0	– c Poole b Walker	0
J. Jordan not out	0			
B 15, l-b 3	18			

1/5 2/107 3/121 4/150   (7 wkts dec.) 207   1/0   (1 wkt dec.) 0
5/191 6/207 7/207

J. B. Statham and T. Greenhough did not bat.

Nottinghamshire

R. J. Giles c Statham b Hilton..................	19	– c sub b Hilton..................	19
N. Hill b Statham	2	– not out	2
J. Kelly c Edrich b Collins.....................	7	– b Statham	15
M. Winfield c Jordan b Greenhough.............	17	– not out	5
F. W. Stocks b Hilton	8	– c Collins b Hilton	16
M. Hill b Statham	3		
C. J. Poole c and b Greenhough	3	– b Statham......................	3
B. Dooland lbw b Statham	1	– st Jordan b Hilton..............	11
A. K. Walker not out	8	– c Jordan b Statham.............	1
K. Smales b Greenhough	1		
A. Jepson b Statham..........................	10	– b Hilton	12
B 2, l-b 1, n-b 4	7	B 2, l-b 2, w 1, n-b 4	9

1/21 2/22 3/35 4/45 5/62   86   1/30 2/41 3/41   (7 wkts) 93
6/62 7/67 8/69 9/73   4/64 5/67 6/82 7/82

Nottinghamshire Bowling

	Overs	Mdns	Runs	Wkts	Overs	Mdns	Runs	Wkts
Walker	11	8	7	2	0.1	—	—	1
Jepson...........	16	6	34	2				
Smales	26	9	54	—				
Dooland	24	6	44	2				
Kelly............	21	10	31	1				
Stocks...........	5	2	19	—				

Lancashire Bowling

	Overs	Mdns	Runs	Wkts	Overs	Mdns	Runs	Wkts
Statham	14.2	10	12	4	14	4	18	3
Marner	4	1	8	—	3	—	21	—
Hilton............	22	14	27	2	11	3	42	4
Collins	6	3	10	1				
Greenhough	14	5	22	3	3	1	3	—

Umpires: E. Davies and R. S. Lay.

LANCASHIRE v SURREY

(A. Wharton's Benefit)

Played at Manchester, May 28, 29, 30, 1958

Surrey won by 177 runs. Outplayed throughout by the champions, Lancashire collapsed in humiliating style on the last day and were dismissed for 27, only two runs more than the lowest total in their history, 25 against Derbyshire at Old Trafford in 1871. May, who with Barrington added 145 for the fourth wicket, batted five hours for his masterly 174, which included one 6 and twenty-one 4s. He fought a duel with Statham, who bowled with pace and accuracy for long spells. Surrey's well-blended attack of pace and spin ensured them a comfortable lead and bonus points, and when rain livened the turf on the last day, Lancashire were overwhelmed. Set to make 205 in three hours five minutes by May's lunch-time declaration, they lost six men for 15 in face of Gibson's lively pace, and then the spin of Laker and Lock accounted for the remaining batsmen.

Surrey

T. H. Clark b Statham.......................	2	– lbw b Statham.................	6
M. J. Stewart c Wilson b Statham..............	18	– c Wilson b Higgs	11
D. G. W. Fletcher c Marner b Higgs.............	2	– c Statham b Higgs	1
P. B. H. May b Statham	174	– not out	42
K. F. Barrington st Wilson b Hilton	74	– c sub b Higgs	14
E. A. Bedser c Marner b Statham	8	– not out	5
A. J. McIntyre b Higgs	0		
G. A. R. Lock lbw b Higgs	8		
J. C. Laker c Hilton b Statham	14		
D. Gibson b Statham	0		
P. J. Loader not out...........................	11		
B 2, l-b 1	3	B 4	4

1/4 2/11 3/49 4/194 5/223   314   1/12 2/18   (4 wkts dec.) 83
6/224 7/250 8/273 9/273   3/30 4/60

Lancashire

R. W. Barber b Loader	37	– c McIntyre b Gibson	1
A. Wharton lbw b Bedser	48	– c Stewart b Gibson	5
G. Pullar c McIntyre b Loader	8	– c McIntyre b Gibson	5
C. Washbrook lbw b Lock	6	– run out	0
K. Grieves b Loader	26	– c McIntyre b Gibson	2
P. Marner c May b Gibson	47	– c and b Lock	2
M. J. Hilton c Barrington b Gibson	2	– c Barrington b Lock	2
A. Wilson c McIntyre b Bedser	8	– c Stewart b Lock	1
J. B. Statham c Gibson b Lock	4	– c Fletcher b Laker	3
K. Higgs not out	2	– c Stewart b Laker	6
R. Tattersall c Stewart b Bedser	3	– not out	0
L-b 1, n-b 1	2		
	193		**27**

1/85 2/91 3/97 4/102 5/140
6/165 7/180 8/188 9/188

1/6 2/7 3/7 4/12 5/15
6/15 7/20 8/20 9/27

Lancashire Bowling

	Overs	Mdns	Runs	Wkts	Overs	Mdns	Runs	Wkts
Statham	30.1	3	78	6	16	5	24	1
Higgs	30	1	112	3	15	2	55	3
Tattersall	20	4	67	—				
Hilton	16	5	34	1				
Wharton	2	—	18	—				

Surrey Bowling

	Overs	Mdns	Runs	Wkts	Overs	Mdns	Runs	Wkts
Loader	30	7	65	3	8	4	7	—
Gibson	20	2	43	2	11	8	8	4
Lock	29	12	44	2	9.2	6	11	3
Laker	13	5	20	—	6	5	1	2
Bedser	19.1	12	19	3				

Umpires: T. J. Bartley and C. S. Elliott.

LANCASHIRE v WARWICKSHIRE

Played at Blackpool, July 29, 30, 31, 1959

Drawn. The match was made memorable by two splendid centuries from Stewart, the Warwickshire opening batsman, who hit the record number for first-class cricket of seventeen 6s in the match. His ten in the first innings fell one short of a record for a single innings. Lancashire, whose captain, Wharton, batted excellently in each innings, made runs freely on the first day before the first of two declarations. Stewart and Smith, adding 141 for the third wicket, made a spectacular reply. Stewart batted three and a quarter hours and hit twelve 4s in addition to his 6s, but still Warwickshire fell 57 behind. Pullar and Wharton batted splendidly in Lancashire's second innings, and when Warwickshire were set to make 280 in two hours and forty minutes, Stewart again drove fiercely, hitting seven 6s and twelve 4s.

Lancashire

G. Pullar run out	31	– c Smith b Hitchcock	84
A. Wharton c Hill b Bridge	88	– not out	122
D. M. Green c Hitchcock b Bridge	88		
K. Grieves b Bridge	24	– c Fox b Hitchcock	1
P. J. Marner c Horner b Bannister	77	– c Horner b Bannister	4
J. D. Bond not out	38	– not out	1
M. J. Hilton c Smith b Bannister	34	– run out	0
J. Dyson not out	7		
B 2	2	B 4, l-b 5, n-b 1	10

1/97 2/130 3/177   (6 wkts dec.) 389   1/183 2/183   (4 wkts dec.) 222
4/290 5/325 6/370   3/185 4/204

G. Clayton, K. Higgs and T. Greenhough did not bat.

Warwickshire

N. F. Horner c Clayton b Greenhough	39	– b Higgs	10
W. J. Stewart c Hilton b Higgs	155	– c Dyson b Green	125
A. Townsend run out	1	– c Green b Higgs	80
M. J. K. Smith c Pullar b Dyson	76	– b Higgs	9
T. W. Cartwright lbw b Greenhough	11	– c Marner b Higgs	1
R. E. Hitchcock c Clayton b Dyson	42	– b Green	14
J. D. Bannister c Wharton b Greenhough	1	– not out	3
W. B. Bridge not out	6	– not out	0
G. H. Hill c Pullar b Dyson	0		
J. G. Fox b Greenhough	0		
O. S. Wheatley c Wharton b Greenhough	0		
L-b 1	1	L-b 5	5

1/97 2/103 3/244 4/279 5/287   332   1/24 2/183 3/201   (6 wkts) 247
6/296 7/332 8/332 9/332   4/207 5/241 6/245

Warwickshire Bowling

	Overs	Mdns	Runs	Wkts	Overs	Mdns	Runs	Wkts
Wheatley	24	4	70	—	20	6	54	—
Bannister	29	10	65	2	14	5	34	1
Bridge	47	22	102	3	18	5	60	—
Hill	35	9	128	—				
Cartwright	3	—	22	—	8	1	26	—
Hitchcock					10	2	38	2

Lancashire Bowling

	Overs	Mdns	Runs	Wkts	Overs	Mdns	Runs	Wkts
Higgs	35	8	77	1	24	5	76	4
Green	10	2	42	—	17	2	64	2
Dyson	15	4	53	3	2	—	34	—
Greenhough	36.4	8	77	5				
Hilton	16	4	66	—	7	1	40	—
Marner	6	1	16	—	3	—	28	—

Umpires: J. S. Buller and C. S. Elliott.

LANCASHIRE v YORKSHIRE

(R. Tattersall and M. J. Hilton Joint Benefit)

Played at Manchester, July 30, August 1, 2, 1960

Lancashire won by two wickets, taking 12 points and so completed their first "Roses" double since 1893. They achieved victory in a tense finish when Dyson turned the last ball of the match, sent down by Trueman, to the on-boundary. Splendid bowling by Statham and Higgs dismissed Yorkshire for a moderate total on the first day, despite a sound innings by Close. Lancashire took the lead with only one wicket down, due to a second-wicket stand of 121 by Barber and Wharton, but so keenly did Yorkshire bowl and field that Lancashire were denied bonus points. Following a heavy storm just after lunch on the second day, Lancashire lost their last six wickets for 39 runs against Trueman and Ryan, who were able to make the ball fly. Statham again troubled Yorkshire, and only Sharpe and the two Wilsons effectively resisted, so that Lancashire were set to make 78 in two hours. Sustained hostility from Trueman and Ryan made the task far from easy and when Greenhough was bowled by the second ball of Trueman's last over, five runs were still needed. Two singles and two leg-byes led to the dramatic climax. During the three days 74,000 spectators saw the match.

Yorkshire

W. B. Stott c Marner b Higgs	1	– c Collins b Statham	5
K. Taylor b Higgs	19	– b Higgs	8
D. E. V. Padgett lbw b Greenhough	21	– lbw b Statham	6
D. B. Close b Statham	63	– lbw b Statham	9
P. J. Sharpe lbw b Statham	16	– lbw b Statham	46
R. Illingworth lbw b Statham	7	– c Clayton b Dyson	9
*J. V. Wilson b Statham	13	– c Clayton b Greenhough	20
D. Wilson lbw b Statham	0	– not out	32
F. S. Trueman not out	3	– lbw b Barber	4
†J. G. Binks b Higgs	4	– b Higgs	1
M. Ryan b Higgs	0	– b Barber	3
B 1, l-b 5, n-b 1	7	L-b 5, n-b 1	6

1/1 2/20 3/64 4/93 5/113   **154**   1/8 2/18 3/19 4/28 5/36   **149**
6/146 7/146 8/147 9/154   6/63 7/89 8/121 9/143

Lancashire

*R. W. Barber c Trueman b D. Wilson	71	– run out	11
G. Pullar c Taylor b Close	11	– b Ryan	14
A. Wharton c J. Wilson b Trueman	83	– c Padgett b Ryan	4
J. Dyson b Trueman	15	– not out	5
K. Grieves lbw b Ryan	5	– c Binks b Ryan	27
P. Marner run out	4	– b Trueman	0
R. Collins b Trueman	0	– b Ryan	2
†G. Clayton c Close b Trueman	28	– not out	15
T. Greenhough c Sharpe b Ryan	0	– b Trueman	0
J. B. Statham c J. Wilson b Ryan	0	– c Binks b Ryan	0
K. Higgs not out	3		
B 4, l-b 1, w 1	6	L-b 3	3

1/26 2/157 3/172 4/187 5/191   **226**   1/16 2/27 3/31 4/32   **(8 wkts) 81**
6/195 7/199 8/199 9/203   5/43 6/43 7/72 8/73

Lancashire Bowling

	Overs	Mdns	Runs	Wkts	Overs	Mdns	Runs	Wkts
Statham	23	7	43	5	24	13	23	4
Higgs	17.2	6	48	4	16	7	35	2
Greenhough	15	2	46	1	16	6	43	1
Dyson............	5	2	10	—	10	6	12	1
Barber............	1	1	—	—	7.3	—	30	2

Yorkshire Bowling

	Overs	Mdns	Runs	Wkts	Overs	Mdns	Runs	Wkts
Trueman..........	28	5	65	4	16	4	28	2
Ryan.............	33	9	69	3	15	4	50	5
Close.............	12	3	23	1				
D. Wilson	13	7	35	1				
Illingworth	16	6	28	—				

Umpires: John Langridge and J. S. Buller.

LEICESTERSHIRE

LEICESTERSHIRE v SOMERSET

Played at Melton Mowbray, June 1, 3, 4, 1946

Somerset beat Leicestershire by 58 runs. Leicestershire fared well on the first day, thanks to Walsh and Prentice, but on Monday their last nine wickets fell for 90 runs, and, despite a keen struggle, they could not recover, although Walsh, the Australian slow left-arm bowler, again in fine form, made his match record thirteen wickets for 107 runs. Lee, Gimblett and Mitchell-Innes batted steadily for Somerset, while Caesar, a Bath amateur making his début for the county, gave valuable aid with the ball, notably in the last stage when Lawrence, the Yorkshireman, finished the match summarily.

Somerset

F. S. Lee c Corrall b Prentice	27	– lbw b Walsh	44
H. Gimblett c Sperry b Prentice	66	– c Berry b Walsh	37
N. S. Mitchell-Innes b Sperry	23	– b Sperry	37
C. J. P. Barnwell b Walsh	9	– b Riddington	12
H. T. F. Buse c Corrall b Prentice	28	– run out	1
J. Lawrence b Walsh	0	– b Walsh	1
A. T. M. Jones lbw b Walsh	1	– st Corrall b Walsh	3
W. H. R. Andrews lbw b Walsh	0	– st Corrall b Walsh	6
W. T. Luckes b Walsh	24	– b Walsh	1
W. C. Caesar not out	5	– b Walsh	7
R. G. Peters b Walsh	3	– not out	2
B 19, l-b 5, n-b 1	25	B 4, l-b 7	11
	211		**162**

Leicestershire

L. G. Berry lbw b Andrews	36	– lbw b Caesar	15
G. Watson c Buse b Andrews	3	– lbw b Andrews	26
F. T. Prentice b Andrews	63	– b Andrews	5
M. Tompkin b Andrews	9	– b Caesar	75
V. E. Jackson c Jones b Andrews	1	– b Caesar	2
A. Riddington st Luckes b Lawrence	4	– c Luckes b Caesar	25
J. H. Howard st Luckes b Caesar	7	– st Luckes b Lawrence	0
J. E. Walsh b Caesar	3	– st Luckes b Lawrence	1
P. Corrall not out	8	– b Lawrence	19
J. Sperry c Jones b Andrews	4	– st Luckes b Lawrence	0
G. Udal lbw b Andrews	0	– not out	2
B 1, l-b 2	3	B 2, l-b 1, n-b 1	4
	141		**174**

Leicestershire Bowling

	Overs	Mdns	Runs	Wkts	Overs	Mdns	Runs	Wkts
Sperry	22	6	60	1	8	—	28	1
Udal	9	1	27	—	5	2	13	—
Jackson	17	8	26	—	4	—	19	—
Walsh	20	4	51	6	25	8	56	7
Prentice	15	4	22	3	11	1	27	—
Riddington					12	6	8	1

Somerset Bowling

	Overs	Mdns	Runs	Wkts	Overs	Mdns	Runs	Wkts
Andrews..........	28.5	9	66	7	18	1	55	2
Peters.............	6	1	18	—				
Buse..............	20	6	39	—	3	—	11	—
Caesar...........	7	2	11	2	23	4	59	4
Lawrence.........	3	1	4	1	12	1	45	4

LEICESTERSHIRE v SURREY

Played at Leicester, June 12, 13, 14, 1946

Surrey won by 202 runs. Scoring two centuries in a match for the third time in his career, Fishlock, the left-hander, dominated the Surrey batting, and, with Gover too much for the Leicestershire batsmen, the home county suffered a sound beating. Fishlock in his first innings hit a 6 and eight 4s; much more free in the second, he hit two 6s and eleven 4s. All ten Leicestershire wickets in their first innings were clean bowled, and only Jackson, with two steady efforts, caused Surrey any trouble. Gover's speed and length earned eleven wickets for 87 runs.

Surrey

L. B. Fishlock b Riddington 129	– c Prentice b Sperry..............112
R. J. Gregory st Corrall b Walsh 44	– b Walsh 30
H. S. Squires lbw b Jackson 0	– lbw b Walsh 1
T. H. Barling lbw b Walsh....................... 5	– lbw b Walsh 0
J. F. Parker c Corrall b Sperry 7	– b Evans....................... 22
E. A. Bedser b Evans........................... 0	– c Jackson b Walsh 8
G. S. Mobey not out 19	– b Sperry 10
A. McIntyre b Riddington....................... 24	– st Corrall b Evans............. 11
E. A. Watts b Jackson.......................... 0	– run out 2
N. H. Bennett b Riddington 1	– b Evans....................... 0
A. R. Gover b Riddington....................... 1	– not out 3
B 12, l-b 2 14	B 6, l-b 7 13
	244		212

Leicestershire

L. G. Berry b Gover 0	– lbw b Gover 27
F. T. Prentice b Gover.......................... 4	– c Squires b Parker............. 18
J. Howard b Gover 1	– b Gover....................... 28
M. Tompkin b Gover 21	– c Parker b Squires............. 3
A. Riddington b Gover 0	– b Squires...................... 1
V. E. Jackson b Gover 44	– not out 46
T. A. Chapman b Parker......................... 8	– b Gover....................... 23
J. Walsh b E. A. Bedser........................ 15	– b Watts....................... 3
P. Corrall b Gover............................. 0	– lbw b Gover 2
M. Evans b Parker............................. 0	– b Watts....................... 3
J. Sperry not out 0	– b Watts....................... 0
B 1, n-b 1........................... 2	L-b 3, w 1, n-b 1 5
	95	L-b 3, w 1, n-b 1	159

Leicestershire Bowling

	Overs	Mdns	Runs	Wkts	Overs	Mdns	Runs	Wkts
Sperry.............	23	3	53	1	16	4	40	2
Evans.............	12	3	21	1	13.1	3	30	3
Jackson...........	26	12	34	2	17	7	26	—
Walsh.............	28	2	94	2	14	—	76	4
Riddington........	18.3	8	26	4	9	1	27	—
Prentice...........	1	—	2	—				

Surrey Bowling

	Overs	Mdns	Runs	Wkts	Overs	Mdns	Runs	Wkts
Gover.............	14.5	3	31	7	25	3	56	4
Watts.............	8	—	26	—	17.3	5	49	3
Parker............	10	—	34	2	14	3	24	1
E. A. Bedser.......	4	3	2	1	3	—	5	—
Squires...........					10	3	20	2

LEICESTERSHIRE v SUSSEX

Played at Leicester, August 14, 15, 16, 1946

Leicestershire won by five wickets. The Australians, Walsh and Jackson, played a big part in a creditable victory. They took 18 wickets between them of which Walsh claimed 14, and Jackson batted very well, his second effort, while 123 runs were obtained, winning the match. Riddington played soundly in helping to get the last 72. James Langridge was in fine all-round form for Sussex. Besides bowling his left-hand slows with tantalising skill, he batted admirably while his colleagues could do little. On rain-affected turf several batsmen escaped when making false strokes.

Sussex

John Langridge lbw b Jackson	2	– st Corrall b Walsh	19
H. W. Parks c Howard b Jackson	39	– c Lester b Walsh	15
P. D. S. Blake b Riddington	2	– b Jackson	27
G. Cox c and b Walsh	11	– lbw b Walsh	10
James Langridge st Corrall b Walsh	2	– not out	81
C. Oakes lbw b Walsh	0	– lbw b Walsh	21
S. C. Griffith b Riddington	43	– c Lester b Jackson	0
R. G. Hunt st Corrall b Walsh	31	– b Walsh	0
H. E. Hammond lbw b Walsh	5	– lbw b Walsh	5
P. Carey not out	5	– b Walsh	3
J. Cornford lbw b Walsh	3	– b Walsh	6
B 8, l-b 7	15	B 11, l-b 6, w 1	18
	158		**205**

Leicestershire

L. G. Berry c John Langridge b Cox	32	– lbw b Oakes ... 9
F. T. Prentice lbw b Oakes	11	– c Blake b James Langridge ... 49
G. Lester b Oakes	27	– c Hammond b James Langridge ... 17
M. Tompkin lbw b Oakes	19	– c Hammond b James Langridge ... 21
G. Watson b Oakes	14	– lbw b Oakes ... 0
V. E. Jackson c Oakes b James Langridge	21	– not out ... 68
A. Riddington st Griffith b Hammond	11	– not out ... 30
T. A. Chapman b James Langridge	0	
J. Howard c and b James Langridge	8	
J. E. Walsh c Carey b James Langridge	14	
P. Corrall not out	2	
B 3, l-b 4	7	B 1, l-b 2, w 1, n-b 5 ... 5
	166	**(5 wkts) 199**

Leicestershire Bowling

	Overs	Mdns	Runs	Wkts	Overs	Mdns	Runs	Wkts
Jackson	24	9	30	2	25	9	52	2
Riddington	12	1	22	2	10	2	22	—
Walsh	23.5	3	91	6	34.5	6	90	8
Lester					18	11	13	—
Prentice					4	1	10	—

Sussex Bowling

	Overs	Mdns	Runs	Wkts	Overs	Mdns	Runs	Wkts
Carey	9	3	21	—	7	—	27	—
Hammond	15	5	25	1	9	1	28	—
Cornford	5	2	14	—	7	2	14	—
Oakes	24	5	51	4	27.3	7	74	2
James Langridge	26.2	8	41	4	33	15	43	3
Cox	3	—	7	1	4	2	8	—

LEICESTERSHIRE v KENT

Played at Leicester, August 24, 26, 27, 1946

Leicestershire won by 259 runs. Another great bowling performance by Walsh, whose spin and guile tied up the Kent batsmen in both innings, helped Leicestershire to their biggest win of the season. In the first innings, he was almost unplayable on a drying pitch, his first five wickets costing only 19 runs, and in the match he took 14 for 107. Vigorous driving by Berry, and two good displays from Lester gave high merit to Leicestershire's batting. Lester also did valuable work with the ball, and Ridgway, fast-medium, showed to advantage for Kent.

Leicestershire

L. G. Berry lbw b Ridgway	96	– c Levett b Crush	8
F. T. Prentice c Levett b Davis	11	– c Dovey b Davies	39
G. Lester b Dovey	47	– not out	82
M. Tompkin c Levett b Crush	6	– c Dovey b Ridgway	51
W. A. Smith c Crush b Ridgway	1	– c Levett b Davies	6
V. E. Jackson not out	39		
G. Watson c and b Ridgway	16	– c Harding b Ridgway	7
A. Riddington b Ridgway	0		
J. E. Walsh b Ridgway	0	– not out	11
P. Corrall lbw b Crush	5		
J. Sperry b Crush	0		
B 5, l-b 4, n-b 1	10	B 4, l-b 12, n-b 5	21
	231	**(5 wkts dec.)**	**225**

Kent

L. J. Todd c Smith b Walsh	19	– b Lester	9
J. G. W. Davies b Walsh	11	– b Lester	12
L. E. G. Ames c and b Walsh	7	– lbw b Walsh	11
B. H. Valentine st Corrall b Walsh	2	– lbw b Walsh	0
H. A. Pawson b Walsh	25	– st Corrall b Lester	19
E. Crush b Walsh	4	– b Walsh	12
A. J. B. Marsham c and b Lester	8	– st Corrall b Walsh	16
W. H. V. Levett lbw b Walsh	0	– b Walsh	6
N. W. Harding not out	7	– st Corrall b Lester	0
R. R. Dovey b Walsh	0	– c Riddington b Walsh	3
F. Ridgway lbw b Lester	10	– not out	1
B 3, l-b 2	5	B 8, l-b 1, w 1	10
	98		**99**

Kent Bowling

	Overs	Mdns	Runs	Wkts	Overs	Mdns	Runs	Wkts
Harding	3	—	11	—	3	—	19	—
Crush	11	4	19	3	17	5	43	1
Davies	30	10	74	1	18	6	38	2
Marsham	5	1	20	—	2	—	10	—
Dovey	31	15	45	1	24	10	43	—
Ridgway	17	4	44	5	16	3	39	2
Ames	7	4	8	—	4	—	12	—
Todd					2	2	—	—

Leicestershire Bowling

	Overs	Mdns	Runs	Wkts	Overs	Mdns	Runs	Wkts
Sperry	4	2	7	—	3	1	9	—
Jackson	14	5	21	—	4	2	5	—
Riddington	4	—	7	—				
Walsh	15	3	54	8	19.5	2	53	6
Lester	4.3	3	4	2	20	9	22	4

LEICESTERSHIRE v GLAMORGAN

Played at Leicester, August 28, 30, 1948

Leicestershire won by an innings and 38 runs. Leicestershire finished the season on a triumphant note by completing the double at the expense of the county champions – the only side to perform this feat. They owed most for their success to Walsh, the Australian leg-break and googly bowler, who claimed a match analysis of 14 for 86 runs. On an easy-paced pitch Glamorgan bowlers, supported by brilliant fielding, dismissed Leicestershire for a moderate total, six wickets falling for 15 runs directly after tea. Prentice was caught splendidly at slip. Walsh, who caused Glamorgan's downfall at Cardiff, worried all the batsmen with skilful variation of length and break and the visitors were dismissed twice on Monday. Excellent fielding helped in these remarkable collapses, good catches near the boundary and smart wicket-keeping by Corrall being of special value.

Leicestershire

L. G. Berry c Watkins b Muncer	26
G. Lester b Griffiths	40
F. T. Prentice c Dyson b Watkins	99
G. Watson c H. Davies b Jones	46
V. E. Jackson lbw b Wooller	6
M. Tompkin c and b Jones	0
A. Riddington c Watkins b Wooller	0
J. E. Walsh lbw b Wooller	0
V. Munden b Watkins	14
P. Corrall run out	12
J. Sperry not out	4
B 5, l-b 8, n-b 4	17
	264

Glamorgan

E. Davies c Tompkin b Lester	36	– hit wkt b Walsh	17
A. H. Dyson hit wkt b Munden	19	– c Munden b Jackson	30
W. G. A. Parkhouse c Corrall b Walsh	10	– st Corrall b Walsh	5
W. E. Jones c Munden b Walsh	10	– lbw b Walsh	12
A. Watkins c and b Lester	8	– b Walsh	0
W. Wooller run out	0	– c Munden b Walsh	1
L. B. Muncer c Jackson b Walsh	1	– c Prentice b Jackson	22
J. Eaglestone c Tompkin b Walsh	4	– b Walsh	4
J. Pleass b Walsh	4	– not out	6
H. Davies st Corrall b Walsh	14	– st Corrall b Walsh	4
W. H. Griffiths not out	0	– b Walsh	0
B 6, l-b 2	8	B 10, l-b 1	11
	114		112

Glamorgan Bowling

	Overs	Mdns	Runs	Wkts
Wooller	33	9	61	3
Griffiths	19	3	57	1
Watkins	25.1	7	61	2
Muncer	29	8	57	1
Jones	7	2	11	2

Leicestershire Bowling

	Overs	Mdns	Runs	Wkts	Overs	Mdns	Runs	Wkts
Sperry	11	6	6	—	5	1	16	—
Jackson	15	2	30	—	12	4	23	2
Munden	6	3	8	1				
Walsh	20.3	7	46	6	14.5	2	40	8
Lester	10	3	16	2	7	—	22	—

Umpires: E. Robinson and G. M. Lee.

LEICESTERSHIRE v SOMERSET

Played at Leicester, May 28, 30 31, 1949

Somerset won by 18 runs. The game ended excitingly with the Leicestershire tail-end batsmen trying boldly for victory while a storm approached. Immediately after the last wicket fell there was heavy rain. Buse, who showed strong leg-side play and hit seven 4s, held together the first Somerset innings. Tompkin and Jackson, with a fourth-wicket stand of 73, helped Leicestershire to gain first innings points. Gimblett quickly put Somerset back into a favourable position of making his first 35 in twenty-two minutes and dominating an opening partnership of 102 with Hill. Rogers and Wellard added 49 for the last wicket. An impressive century by Berry, who carried his bat through the second Leicestershire innings, failed to bring success. Tremlett bowled extremely well.

Somerset

H. Gimblett c Berry b Symington	26	– lbw b Jackson 82
E. Hill c and b Symington	11	– c Tompkin b Jackson 41
G. E. S. Woodhouse c Walsh b Jackson	10	– b Walsh 0
M. Coope b Jackson	15	– c Symington b Walsh 35
F. L. Angell lbw b Walsh	1	– c Corrall b Sperry........... 19
H. T. F. Buse not out	66	– b Walsh 14
M. F. Tremlett b Jackson	9	– c Chapman b Lester 6
S. S. Rogers c Chapman b Lester	13	– not out 42
J. Lawrence c and b Walsh	4	– c Sperry b Symington....... 0
H. W. Stephenson b Walsh	17	– b Sperry 3
A. W. Wellard b Sperry	22	– c Prentice b Jackson......... 22
B 5, l-b 4, n-b 1	10	L-b 9, w 1, n-b 1 11
	204	**275**

Leicestershire

L. G. Berry c Wellard b Buse	29	– not out 109
G. Lester c Tremlett b Wellard	1	– c Stephenson b Buse 4
F. T. Prentice lbw b Wellard	4	– b Tremlett.................. 16
M. Tompkin st Stephenson b Lawrence	57	– c Wellard b Tremlett........ 11
V. E. Jackson c Stephenson b Wellard	42	– c Buse b Gimblett........... 46
G. S. Watson c and b Wellard	16	– c Buse b Lawrence 12
S. J. Symington st Stephenson b Lawrence	4	– b Tremlett.................. 0
T. Chapman lbw b Lawrence	4	– b Lawrence 3
J. E. Walsh not out	43	– c Lawrence b Wellard......... 25
P. Corrall run out	5	– c Lawrence b Buse 2
J. Sperry st Stephenson b Wellard	16	– b Tremlett.................. 0
B 3, l-b 1	4	B 5, w 1, n-b 2 8
	225	**236**

Leicestershire Bowling

	Overs	Mdns	Runs	Wkts	Overs	Mdns	Runs	Wkts
Sperry	13.2	2	23	1	15	2	48	2
Symington	11	2	40	2	8	1	55	1
Jackson	20	5	40	3	31.1	9	68	3
Walsh	26	7	64	3	28	4	83	3
Lester	10	2	27	1	3	1	10	1

Somerset Bowling

	Overs	Mdns	Runs	Wkts	Overs	Mdns	Runs	Wkts
Wellard..........	30.2	9	38	5	24	6	56	1
Buse	23	4	80	1	22	4	56	2
Tremlett	7	1	25	—	23.4	6	50	4
Lawrence	21	3	78	3	22	2	62	2
Gimblett					2	1	4	1

Umpires: E. Cooke and H. G. Baldwin.

LEICESTERSHIRE v NOTTINGHAMSHIRE

Played at Loughborough, June 11, 13, 14, 1949

Leicestershire won by an innings and 24 runs. Walsh, with his unorthodox left-arm spin bowling, sorely tried Nottinghamshire, although the pitch favoured batsmen. He achieved a hat-trick by dismissing two men at the close of the Nottinghamshire first innings and another with his first ball in the second innings. Keeton and Hardstaff began the match with a stand of 59; then Nottinghamshire batted uncertainly against Walsh. Leicestershire scored freely off an attack lacking in spin bowling. Prentice and Jackson added 212 for the fourth wicket and Watson helped Prentice to put on 117 for the fifth. Hooking strongly, Prentice hit thirty-three 4s during his third century in consecutive matches and made his best score in first-class cricket.

Nottinghamshire

W. W. Keeton b Jackson	22	– c Jackson b Walsh	18
R. T. Simpson c and b Walsh	46	– b Walsh	54
H. Winrow b Walsh	3	– b Lester.....................	73
J. Hardstaff lbw b Walsh......................	36	– c and b Lester................	51
R. Giles b Jackson...........................	20	– b Walsh	6
J. D. Clay b Walsh	3	– b Walsh	6
W. A. Sime b Walsh	10	– b Walsh	0
A. Jepson b Jackson	22	– st Corrall b Walsh	25
E. G. Woodhead c Munden b Walsh.............	5	– c Prentice b Walsh	0
E. A. Meads c Berry b Walsh	1	– not out	10
A. Richardson not out........................	0	– c Jackson b Walsh	0
B 5, l-b 2	7	B 11, l-b 2	13

175   256

Leicestershire

L. G. Berry b Richardson	16	J. E. Walsh c Clay b Sime...............	23
G. Lester b Woodhead	15	S. J. Symington b Jepson..............	27
F. T. Prentice st Meads b Sime 191		V. Munden not out	16
M. Tompkin c Meads b Woodhead........	5	B 27, l-b 8, n-b 4	39
V. E. Jackson c sub b Woodhead	82		
G. Watson c Clay b Sime	41	(8 wkts dec.) 455	

P. Corrall and J. Sperry did not bat.

Leicestershire Bowling

	Overs	Mdns	Runs	Wkts	Overs	Mdns	Runs	Wkts
Sperry............	8	2	26	—	4	1	9	—
Symington	5	1	10	—	4	—	35	—
Jackson...........	27	11	71	3	7	2	27	—
Walsh.............	24.2	6	61	7	32.2	5	103	8
Lester					25	6	69	2

Nottinghamshire Bowling

	Overs	Mdns	Runs	Wkts
Jepson............	35.3	3	123	1
Woodhead	40	13	82	3
Richardson........	25	7	67	1
Sime	17	2	79	3
Simpson	6	3	13	—
Winrow...........	7	—	27	—
Hardstaff	11	2	25	—

Umpires: H. Elliott and E. Robinson.

LEICESTERSHIRE v MIDDLESEX

(P. Corrall's Benefit)

Played at Leicester, July 2, 4, 5, 1949

Middlesex won by 100 runs. A splendid match worked up to a climax in which Sims and Young, the Middlesex spin bowlers, snatched a remarkable victory for their side. When a Leicestershire victory seemed assured they made a ninth-wicket stand of 107 in fifty minutes, and then shared the wickets in a collapse of their opponents. In the first Middlesex innings Denis Compton produced brilliant strokes, batting for 100 minutes before being run out by a fine throw from Chapman when trying to gain the single needed for a century. Berry laid the foundations for the big Leicestershire score with sound batting, and Tompkin, Jackson and Walsh consolidated the innings with splendid play against an attack which remained keen. Jackson hit fourteen 4s, his late cutting being most attractive. Although Sharp and Edrich put on 132 in a second-wicket partnership, the eighth Middlesex second innings wicket fell when they were only 73 ahead. Then came the intervention of Sims and Young. Corrall, in his benefit game, helped in the dismissal of six men in the second Middlesex innings.

Middlesex

J. D. Robertson c Walsh b Symington	37	– c Berry b Symington............	3
H. Sharp lbw b Symington	31	– st Corrall b Walsh	56
W. J. Edrich st Corrall b Walsh	9	– c Corrall b Jackson 113	
D. C. S. Compton run out.....................	99	– c Corrall b Sperry..............	8
F. G. Mann b Walsh.........................	5	– c Corrall b Sperry..............	0
A. Thompson c Munden b Symington	65	– c Walsh b Sperry	0
R. W. V. Robins c Walsh b Jackson	16	– st Corrall b Lester..............	21
L. Compton c and b Sperry....................	36	– st Corrall b Lester..............	5
J. Sims not out............................	30	– b Walsh	61
J. A. Young c Sperry b Jackson	0	– b Walsh	28
L. Gray b Jackson..........................	0	– not out	5
B 1, l-b 4	5	B 32, l-b 1..............	33
	333		**333**

Leicestershire

L. G. Berry b Sims	70	– lbw b Sims 25
G. Lester b Sims	18	– c L. Compton b Young........... 6
F. T. Prentice c Edrich b D. Compton	16	– lbw b Sims 12
M. Tompkin c L. Compton b Gray	94	– lbw b Young 17
V. E. Jackson b Gray	143	– c Robertson b Young 3
J. E. Walsh c and b Robins	82	– c Thompson b Sims 5
S. J. Symington lbw b Robins	1	– b Sims...................... 21
T. Chapman b Sims	20	– b Sims...................... 2
V. Munden not out	12	– st L. Compton b Sims........... 0
P. Corral (did not bat)		– not out 0
J. Sperry (did not bat)		– c L. Compton b Sims 0
B 5, l-b 12, n-b 2	19	

(8 wkts dec.) 475   91

Leicestershire Bowling

	Overs	Mdns	Runs	Wkts	Overs	Mdns	Runs	Wkts
Sperry	27	6	89	1	28	5	84	3
Symington	25	4	90	3	8	3	18	1
Walsh	19	—	109	2	14.4	1	62	3
Jackson	9.1	1	31	3	22	1	74	1
Munden	3	—	9	—				
Lester					20	6	62	2

Middlesex Bowling

	Overs	Mdns	Runs	Wkts	Overs	Mdns	Runs	Wkts
Edrich	14	3	32	—	3	—	13	—
Gray	27.2	4	66	2	4	—	15	—
Sims	41	8	139	3	10.3	—	38	7
D. Compton	24	1	130	1	1	—	3	—
Young	23	8	47	—	9	2	22	3
Sharp	6	3	16	—				
Robins	6	1	26	2				

Umpires: W. H. Ashdown and E. Robinson.

NOTES BY THE EDITOR, 1950

SILLY POINT ENCROACHING

When Barnes, the Australian, received a severe injury from a hard hit, it seemed likely that fieldsmen would take care how they placed themselves standing at silly mid-off or mid-on; but what approaches a transgression of cricket's immaculate reputation for fair play has been seen at Lord's and other places without arousing much notice. An objection by Prentice, of Leicestershire, to Goddard, of Gloucestershire, standing too near the line of bowling in the match at Leicester in August, caused the fieldsman to move back a few yards. This occurrence suggests emphatically that the MCC, through the Rules Committee, should set out clearly how near a fieldsman may stand to the line of the ball. Perhaps the simplest plan would be an instruction to umpires to see that the rules as to "impeding" a batsman or fieldsman is carried out in the strictest manner possible. A bad example may be copied by keen scholars, and I can recall such a case in an Eton and Harrow match. A slow left-arm bowler from the practice end at Lord's might have delivered the ball, when fairly directed at the stumps, within a few feet of the fieldsman's head.

LEICESTERSHIRE v LANCASHIRE

Played at Leicester, August 29, 30, 31, 1951

Drawn. Although rain curtailed play, Leicestershire came very near to victory. Sperry, the left-arm fast-medium bowler, gained his best figures of the season during the Lancashire first innings, when only Place batted convincingly. The last four wickets fell at the final total, Sperry taking three in four balls. Tompkin and Jackson, both driving with assurance, gave Leicestershire a substantial lead, but, with the second day lost owing to rain, a finish seemed unlikely. Then the last seven Lancashire second innings wickets fell in fifty minutes while only two runs – both leg-byes – were scored. Leicestershire needed 29 to win in ten minutes, but after five minutes heavy rain ended the match.

Lancashire

C. Washbrook c Lester b Wooler	9	– lbw b Sperry	9
N. D. Howard b Sperry	4	– lbw b Wooler	6
W. Place b Sperry	77	– st Firth b Jackson	31
G. A. Edrich lbw b Sperry	16	– c Jackson b Munden	12
K. Grieves b Jackson	19	– b Wooler	31
A. Wharton lbw b Walsh	25	– c Lester b Jackson	0
J. G. Lomax b Sperry	8	– c Firth b Munden	0
R. Tattersall b Wooler	3	– lbw b Jackson	0
M. J. Hilton b Sperry	0	– c Lester b Munden	0
J. B. Statham not out	0	– c Wooler b Jackson	0
A. Wilson b Sperry	0	– not out	0
B 1, w 1	2	L-b 2	2
	163		**91**

Leicestershire

G. A. Smithson c Grieves b Statham	21	– not out	2
L. G. Berry b Statham	0		
M. Tompkin c Tattersall b Hilton	94	– run out	2
C. H. Palmer c Howard b Statham	9		
V. E. Jackson c Howard b Hilton	61		
V. Munden c and b Hilton	8		
J. Walsh c Wilson b Tattersall	14		
G. Lester c Grieves b Tattersall	1		
J. Firth b Tattersall	1		
C. Wooler b Tattersall	2		
J. Sperry not out	0		
B 4, l-b 11	15	B 1	1
	226	**(1 wkt)**	**5**

Leicestershire Bowling

	Overs	Mdns	Runs	Wkts	Overs	Mdns	Runs	Wkts
Wooler	15	3	39	2	10	3	28	2
Sperry	12.3	3	22	6	8	5	10	1
Jackson	24	13	30	1	24.1	14	21	4
Munden	4	2	12	—	16	10	15	3
Walsh	18	3	58	1	3	—	15	—

Lancashire Bowling

	Overs	Mdns	Runs	Wkts	Overs	Mdns	Runs	Wkts
Statham	13	2	43	3	1	—	4	—
Wharton	5	1	18	—	0.1	—	—	—
Lomax	3	1	7	—				
Tattersall	31.2	8	67	4				
Hilton	28	4	76	3				

Umpires: T. W. Spencer and W. F. Price.

LEICESTERSHIRE v MIDDLESEX

Played at Leicester, May 24, 26, 27, 1952

Leicestershire won by seven wickets – a splendid performance after Middlesex had scored heavily in the first innings of the match. Denis Compton, leading Middlesex, batted with delightful freedom after Robertson, who shared a first-wicket stand of 140 with Brown, had shown classical style for over four hours. Not to be outdone, Leicestershire also attacked the bowling on the second day, Tompkin and Palmer in particular scoring at a great pace. Tompkin reached three figures in two hours, driving superbly. Middlesex continued the brisk batting in their second innings, but lost wickets quickly against the clever spin bowling of Walsh and Jackson. Left to make 211 in three and a half hours, Leicestershire won with forty-five minutes to spare. Tompkin again drove powerfully and became the first Leicestershire player for five years to score two centuries in a match.

Middlesex

J. D. Robertson c Smithson b Goodwin	162	– b Walsh 34
S. M. Brown c Jackson b Walsh	77	– c Jackson b Spencer 19
W. J. Edrich b Goodwin	23	– c Palmer b Jackson 69
D. C. S. Compton not out	109	– c Firth b Spencer 21
H. P. Sharp c Firth b Jackson	7	– c Hallam b Jackson 14
W. Knightley-Smith c Jackson b Goodwin	2	– c Jackson b Walsh 42
D. Bennett not out	16	– st Firth b Walsh 0
J. M. Sims (did not bat)		– lbw b Walsh 4
J. T. Murray (did not bat)		– lbw b Jackson 3
J. A. Young (did not bat)		– b Jackson 0
A. E. Moss (did not bat)		– not out 0
B 2, l-b 5, n-b 4	11	B 4, l-b 4, n-b 1 9

1/40 2/225 3/298   (5 wkts dec.) 407   1/32 2/73 3/156 4/156 5/161   215
4/316 5/334   6/173 7/187 8/211 9/211

Leicestershire

G. Lester b Young	52	– c Knightley-Smith b Compton 43
M. Hallam lbw b Compton	25	– run out 17
M. Tompkin c Sims b Compton	156	– not out 107
C. H. Palmer lbw b Moss	56	– b Sharp 12
V. E. Jackson lbw b Young	25	– not out 13
G. A. Smithson c Murray b Young	30	
V. Munden not out	36	
J. Firth not out	8	
B 14, l-b 9, w 1	24	B 15, l-b 2, w 3 20

1/57 2/131 3/246   (6 wkts dec.) 412   1/27 2/123 3/161   (3 wkts) 212
4/326 5/334 6/371

J. E. Walsh, T. Spencer and J. Goodwin did not bat.

Leicestershire Bowling

	Overs	Mdns	Runs	Wkts	Overs	Mdns	Runs	Wkts
Goodwin.........	28	7	108	3	18	1	57	—
Spencer..........	16	3	49	—	15	2	59	2
Walsh............	27	2	103	1	11	3	40	4
Jackson..........	18	3	64	1	12	4	36	4
Palmer	10	4	16	—				
Lester	15	2	49	—	4	—	14	—
Munden	3	1	7	—				

Middlesex Bowling

	Overs	Mdns	Runs	Wkts	Overs	Mdns	Runs	Wkts
Moss.............	16	3	57	1	2	1	5	—
Bennett..........	11	1	39	—	2	—	15	—
Compton	28	1	114	2	14	2	48	1
Sims	15	—	60	—	8	1	21	—
Young...........	38	16	76	3	21	6	52	—
Sharp	9	3	42	—	8	1	13	1
Robertson........					3	—	17	—
Brown...........					3	—	7	—
Knightley-Smith....					0.5	—	14	—

Umpires: F. Chester and W. T. Jones.

LEICESTERSHIRE v SURREY

(J. E. Walsh's Benefit)

Played at Leicester, May 21, 23, 24, 1955

Surrey won by seven wickets. Despite remarkable all-round cricket from Palmer, Surrey, although behind on first innings, won comfortably. On drying turf Leicestershire began well on the first day, but the left-arm spin of Lock brought about a collapse. Then Palmer, bowling medium pace with great accuracy and bringing the ball back sharply off the seam, so severely troubled the Surrey batsmen that he took eight wickets before conceding a run. He hit the stumps seven times. Alec Bedser and Lock troubled Leicestershire in their second innings, but Tompkin and Palmer resisted strongly. Palmer, defending skilfully, stayed for four hours, but all his efforts went for nought, for in the last innings May, Clark and Constable carried Surrey to victory. Palmer conceded only one run in thirteen overs in the second innings.

Leicestershire

G. Lester b Clark	22	– b Bedser		4
M. R. Hallam b Laker	39	– b Bedser		7
M. Tompkin c and b Lock	19	– c McIntyre b Bedser		50
C. H. Palmer c Laker b Clark	1	– b Bedser		64
G. A. Smithson c Stewart b Lock	4	– lbw b Lock		0
V. E. Jackson c Stewart b Lock	2	– c Pratt b Bedser		2
V. S. Munden b Lock	4	– lbw b Bedser		6
J. E. Walsh b Lock	3	– b Lock		20
J. Firth not out	7	– b Lock		0
C. T. Spencer c May b Laker	0	– st McIntyre b Lock		0
B. Boshier c Bedser b Lock	0	– not out		0
B 7, l-b 5, n-b 1	13	B 8, l-b 3, n-b 1		12

1/68 2/74 3/75 4/98 5/99   114   1/20 2/21 3/98 4/101 5/106   165
6/100 7/104 8/109 9/114   6/116 7/151 8/153 9/165

Surrey

T. H. Clark b Spencer	7	– b Spencer	44
D. G. W. Fletcher b Palmer	7	– b Boshier	8
P. B. H. May b Palmer	28	– b Munden	84
B. Constable c Lester b Palmer	0	– not out	49
M. J. Stewart b Palmer	0	– not out	5
R. C. E. Pratt b Palmer	7		
A. J. McIntyre b Palmer	0		
J. C. Laker b Spencer	14		
W. S. Surridge b Palmer	0		
G. A. R. Lock b Palmer	4		
A. V. Bedser not out	2		
L-b 7, n-b 1	8	B 10, l-b 3	13

1/10 2/42 3/42 4/42 5/55   77   1/18 2/98 3/181   (3 wkts) 203
6/56 7/61 8/61 9/67

Surrey Bowling

	Overs	Mdns	Runs	Wkts	Overs	Mdns	Runs	Wkts
Bedser	12	6	14	—	32	14	53	6
Surridge	6	—	18	—	5	1	7	—
Lock	18.2	7	37	6	29.2	13	41	4
Laker	22	7	24	2	24	9	35	—
Clark	9	5	8	2	10	5	17	—

Leicestershire Bowling

	Overs	Mdns	Runs	Wkts	Overs	Mdns	Runs	Wkts
Spencer	11.2	3	19	2	26	6	61	1
Boshier	4	—	13	—	15	2	44	1
Munden	4	1	15	—	16.4	5	35	1
Jackson	4	3	1	—	23	8	42	—
Palmer	14	12	7	8	13	12	1	—
Walsh	7	3	14	—				
Lester					1	—	7	—

Umpires: J. S. Buller and J. J. Hills.

LEICESTERSHIRE v NOTTINGHAMSHIRE

Played at Leicester, June 23, 25, 26, 1956

Nottinghamshire won by nine wickets, a victory well merited by superior all-round cricket. On a damp pitch on the first day, Leicestershire struggled against good seam bowling by Walker, Jepson and K. Poole, but on the second day Nottinghamshire batted consistently, achieving a lead of 170. They virtually assured themselves of victory when Walker, the left-arm pace bowler, achieved a hat-trick by dismissing Lester, Tompkin and Smithson with the first three balls of the Leicestershire second innings. Hallam figured in a remarkable incident for he was given out by the square leg umpire when the wicket-keeper standing back threw down the wicket, only to be recalled because the bowler's umpire had already called "over". Leicestershire fought back, but could only leave their opponents a simple task for victory.

Leicestershire

Batsman	1st innings	R	2nd innings	R
G. Lester	c C. Poole b Jepson	13	lbw b Walker	0
M. R. Hallam	b Jepson	30	c Clay b Smales	52
M. Tompkin	lbw b K. Poole	56	b Walker	0
C. H. Palmer	c Stocks b Walker	21	c Stocks b Dooland	48
V. E. Jackson	lbw b Walker	6	c Smales b Walker	18
G. A. Smithson	b Dooland	11	c C. Poole b Walker	0
V. S. Munden	c C. Poole b K. Poole	3	c Smales b Walker	51
J. Firth	b Walker	16	b Dooland	35
C. T. Spencer	b Dooland	1	b Jepson	11
R. Smith	b Jepson	1	not out	0
B. Boshier	not out	0	st C. Poole b Dooland	1
	B 8, l-b 1, w 1	10	B 3, l-b 2, w 1	6

1/31 2/56 3/87 4/103 5/134   168   1/0 2/0 3/0 4/44 5/92   222
6/150 7/151 8/152 9/168   6/135 7/204 8/221 9/221

Nottinghamshire

Batsman	1st innings	R	2nd innings	R
R. J. Giles	c Spencer b Palmer	16	lbw b Boshier	0
J. D. Clay	lbw b Boshier	8	not out	41
P. F. Harvey	c Boshier b Munden	61	not out	11
C. J. Poole	c Boshier b Smith	40		
F. W. Stocks	c Firth b Palmer	24		
R. T. Simpson	c Smithson b Palmer	73		
K. J. Poole	c Firth b Boshier	13		
B. Dooland	lbw b Palmer	29		
A. K. Walker	c Hallam b Lester	50		
K. Smales	not out	7		
A. Jepson	b Lester	0		
	B 8, l-b 8, n-b 1	17	L-b 1	1

1/24 2/24 3/111 4/146 5/172   338   1/0   (1 wkt) 53
6/211 7/263 8/308 9/338

Nottinghamshire Bowling

	Overs	Mdns	Runs	Wkts	Overs	Mdns	Runs	Wkts
Walker	24.1	12	32	3	23	4	75	5
Jepson	21	7	36	3	24	6	69	1
K. Poole	16	5	46	2				
Dooland	19	8	44	2	28.5	16	43	3
Smales					12	7	8	1
Stocks					13	5	21	—

Leicestershire Bowling

	Overs	Mdns	Runs	Wkts	Overs	Mdns	Runs	Wkts
Spencer	15	—	59	—	5	—	14	—
Boshier	24	2	89	2	8	1	30	1
Palmer	27	17	24	4				
Smith	28	11	57	1	2	—	8	—
Jackson	18	8	34	—				
Munden	9	4	25	1				
Lester	5.4	—	33	2				

Umpires: Harry Elliott (Derbyshire) and R. S. Lay.

LEICESTERSHIRE v GLAMORGAN

Played at Leicester, May 30, June 1, 2, 1959

Leicestershire won by eight wickets. Hallam, the Leicestershire opening batsman, completely dominated the match by making 367 for once out. He hit his second double hundred within a fortnight and then went on to score the fastest century so far this summer when Leicestershire were left just under three hours to get 269 to win. Hallam flayed the bowling to such an extent that he reached three figures in seventy-one minutes. He hit twenty-seven 4s during his first stay of five and a half hours and followed with one 6 and twelve 4s in his fastest hundred. Hallam's 210 not out was the highest post-war score by a Leicestershire player. In addition, he became the first Leicestershire batsman to obtain two double hundreds in a season. Best performance for Glamorgan came from Watkins, who hit his first hundred of the summer with a precise display lasting almost three and a half hours. Then he added 32 in nine minutes.

Glamorgan

W. G. A. Parkhouse c Smith b van Geloven	17	– c Julian b Boshier 50
B. Hedges c Hallam b van Geloven	53	– c Phillips b Savage 33
J. Pressdee c Spencer b van Geloven	0	– b van Geloven 38
L. N. Devereux lbw b van Geloven	38	– c Burch b van Geloven 56
A. J. Watkins c Revill b Spencer	132	– b van Geloven 59
P. Walker c Smith b Spencer	12	– b van Geloven 0
W. Wooller c Savage b Smith	14	– not out 9
D. J. Ward c Watson b Boshier	12	– c Hallam b Boshier 11
J. E. McConnon b Boshier	5	– not out 11
D. L. Evans not out	12	
B 11, l-b 16	27	L-b 4 4

1/44 2/44 3/94 4/133   (9 wkts dec.) 322   1/56 2/112 3/129   (7 wkts dec.) 271
5/166 6/190 7/247 8/253 9/322   4/215 5/215 6/244 7/254

D. J. Shepherd did not bat.

Leicestershire

M. R. Hallam not out	210	– c Evans b Walker 157
J. van Geloven c Pressdee b Watkins	19	– c Shepherd b Walker 37
E. F. Phillips lbw b Walker	13	
A. C. Revill lbw b Wooller	30	– not out 15
W. Watson b Walker	19	– not out 59
G. W. Burch c Hedges b Ward	11	
R. Julian not out	19	
L-b 2, w 2	4	B 1, l-b 2 3

1/51 2/102 3/184   (5 wkts dec.) 325   1/158 2/247   (2 wkts) 271
4/215 5/257

R. C. Smith, C. T. Spencer, J. S. Savage and B. S. Boshier did not bat.

Leicestershire Bowling

	Overs	Mdns	Runs	Wkts	Overs	Mdns	Runs	Wkts
Spencer	24.4	1	97	2	17	3	53	—
Boshier	21	3	53	2	12	1	32	2
van Geloven	24	3	82	4	14	2	47	4
Savage	13	2	45	—	13	2	67	1
Smith	7	2	18	1	18	4	68	—

Glamorgan Bowling

	Overs	Mdns	Runs	Wkts	Overs	Mdns	Runs	Wkts
Walker	30	11	61	2	12	—	78	2
Wooller..........	32	7	80	1	16	1	92	—
Watkins	14	2	36	1	7	—	40	—
Shepherd.........	12	1	36	—	14	1	53	—
McConnon........	8	3	33	—				
Pressdee	2	—	7	—				
Ward	10	—	40	1	1.3	—	5	—
Devereux	10	2	28	—				

Umpires: C. S. Elliott and W. F. Price.

LEICESTERSHIRE v YORKSHIRE

Played at Leicester, July 29, 30, 31, 1959

Yorkshire won by 78 runs. Though Watson produced a great display for the visit of his native county, carrying his bat for 79 out of a total of 132, the Yorkshire batting as a whole proved more dependable. After sound innings by Padgett and Close, Burnet was able to ask Leicestershire to make 309 – a feat beyond their capabilities, but seventeen minutes of extra time were needed before the last wicket fell. In Leicestershire's second innings Hallam, when 36, completed 10,000 runs in first-class cricket.

Yorkshire

W. B. Stott b Palmer..........................	18	– c Burch b Spencer.................	27
K. Taylor b van Geloven.......................	27		
D. E. V. Padgett c Hallam b Savage.............	53	– not out	89
D. B. Close c Burch b van Geloven.............	57	– c Smith b Palmer	21
J. V. Wilson c Spencer b Kirby..................	6	– c Hallam b Savage	4
R. Illingworth c Burch b Kirby.................	0	– not out	63
J. R. Burnet c Burch b Savage	3		
F. S. Trueman lbw b Spencer	16		
J. G. Binks b Kirby...........................	13		
D. Wilson c Watson b Savage..................	9		
R. K. Platt not out	0		
B 10, l-b 5, n-b 1	16	B 11, l-b 6, n-b 1..........	18

1/27 2/85 3/111 4/130 5/130   218   1/30 2/75 3/103   (3 wkts dec.) 222
6/174 7/184 8/199 9/216

Leicestershire

W. Watson not out	79	– c Binks b Trueman	20
D. Kirby b Trueman..........................	1	– c sub b Close	15
M. R. Hallam c D. Wilson b Platt...............	1	– run out	57
L. R. Gardner lbw b Platt.....................	2	– c D. Wilson b Trueman	4
C. H. Palmer c Close b Illingworth.............	24	– b D. Wilson	13
J. van Geloven c sub b Illingworth	5	– c Burnet b D. Wilson	3
G. W. Burch b Close	0	– c Trueman b Close.............	15
R. C. Smith c Illingworth b Trueman	5	– c sub b Close	30
C. T. Spencer b Platt.........................	6	– b Platt......................	32
J. S. Savage b Platt..........................	4	– b Platt......................	29
G. A. Hickinbottom b Close....................	0	– not out	0
B 1, l-b 2, n-b 2	5	B 9, n-b 3	12

1/1 2/4 3/6 4/66 5/80   132   1/40 2/76 3/76 4/82 5/110   230
6/83 7/97 8/105 9/120   6/119 7/159 8/160 9/223

Leicestershire Bowling

	Overs	Mdns	Runs	Wkts	Overs	Mdns	Runs	Wkts
Spencer	26	5	48	1	17	2	49	1
van Geloven	30	5	87	2	13	1	55	—
Palmer	11	7	5	1	10	3	15	1
Savage	23.4	10	48	3	8	2	31	1
Kirby	13	6	14	3	10	—	31	—
Smith					3	—	23	—

Yorkshire Bowling

	Overs	Mdns	Runs	Wkts	Overs	Mdns	Runs	Wkts
Trueman	23	10	25	2	16	4	54	2
Platt	20	5	61	4	19.1	7	47	2
Close	13.3	4	18	2	13	1	55	3
Illingworth	13	3	23	2	18	5	43	—
D. Wilson					11	3	19	2

Umpires: A. E. Fagg and A. Copson.

LEICESTERSHIRE v LANCASHIRE

Played at Leicester, May 21, 23, 1960

Lancashire won by 122 runs. Statham, the England fast bowler, was the match winner for Lancashire who raced to victory in just over a day and a half. Statham who gained fourteen wickets for 58 put his county on the road to victory on the first day when twenty-four wickets fell to four pace bowlers on a damp, sometimes vicious pitch. Statham took seven of them at a personal cost of 17 runs. Though Boshier struck damaging blows for Leicestershire with his well-controlled medium pace, Wharton and Grieves with a third stand of 53 helped Lancashire to a reasonable score in the circumstances. Then Statham "scythed" through the home batting, Leicestershire being all out for 37, their lowest total since the war. Lancashire finished the first day 191 ahead with half their wickets standing and they added another 34 before Statham swept through the opposition again.

Lancashire

G. Pullar b Boshier	4	– lbw b Boshier ... 12
*A. Wharton b Boshier	25	– c Savage b Spencer ... 23
J. Dyson b Spencer	0	– lbw b Spencer ... 7
K. Grieves c Hallam b Boshier	29	– c Julian b Boshier ... 26
P. Marner c and b Boshier	24	– c Gardner b Boshier ... 19
B. Booth c Revill b Spencer	3	– c Savage b Boshier ... 0
†G. Clayton b Boshier	1	– c Savage b Spencer ... 10
T. Greenhough b Boshier	9	– not out ... 19
J. B. Statham b Spencer	20	– b Pratt ... 0
R. Tattersall not out	8	– b Pratt ... 0
C. Hilton b Spencer	4	– b Pratt ... 0
B 5, l-b 5, n-b 1	11	B 4, l-b 1, n-b 3 ... 8

1/5 2/6 3/59 4/64 5/76   138   1/23 2/36 3/45 4/77 5/77   124
6/77 7/89 8/104 9/130   6/99 7/117 8/118 9/124

Leicestershire

M. R. Hallam b Statham	6	– hit wkt b Statham	41
H. D. Bird retired hurt	1	– absent hurt	0
*W. Watson c Clayton b Hilton	1	– b Statham	22
L. R. Gardner lbw b Statham	2	– b Statham	1
A. C. Revill b Statham	2	– not out	19
B. Cromack b Hilton	5	– b Statham	0
†R. Julian c Clayton b Statham	7	– b Greenhough	9
R. L. Pratt c Clayton b Statham	1	– b Statham	7
C. T. Spencer c Marner b Statham	0	– b Greenhough	0
J. S. Savage not out	6	– b Statham	0
B. Boshier b Statham	2	– b Statham	0
B 4	4	B 2, l-b 1, n-b 1	4

1/6 2/11 3/14 4/20 5/22 6/22　　　　37　　1/59 2/68 3/69 4/69 5/81　　　103
7/22 8/35 9/37　　　　　　　　　　　　　6/94 7/94 8/103 9/103

Leicestershire Bowling

	Overs	Mdns	Runs	Wkts	Overs	Mdns	Runs	Wkts
Spencer	18.3	2	51	4	19	4	50	3
Boshier	19	5	39	6	16	5	46	4
Pratt	9	1	37	—	8.3	1	20	3

Lancashire Bowling

	Overs	Mdns	Runs	Wkts	Overs	Mdns	Runs	Wkts
Statham	10	2	17	7	18.4	7	41	7
Hilton	9	1	16	2	7	—	30	—
Marner					1	—	4	—
Tattersall					3	1	12	—
Greenhough					8	5	12	2

Umpires: R. S. Lay and A. E. Rhodes.

LEICESTERSHIRE v HAMPSHIRE

Played at Coalville, May 25, 26, 27, 1960

Drawn. This match proved the maxim that nothing can be taken for granted in cricket. It seemed certain when the final day began that Hampshire would need little time to press on to victory. But Leicestershire saved a match which had looked to be irretrievably lost. They did so by a magnificent ninth-wicket partnership of 125 between Gardner and his captain, Watson, who on the first day had rallied the side by making 110. Watson batted with a cracked rib heavily strapped, after being unable to go in on the second day when his county crashed to 52 for eight and still wanted 30 more runs to avoid an innings defeat. In the end Hampshire were left to get 110 in forty minutes and the loss of four wickets for 25 soon brought their challenge to an end. Earlier Gray (150 not out) and Horton (105) dominated the cricket when Hampshire, declaring with only four wickets down, established a first-innings lead of 82.

Leicestershire

M. R. Hallam b Heath	10	– b Shackleton	0
*W. Watson c Livingstone b Shackleton	110	– c and b Sainsbury	76
H. D. Bird b Heath	0	– c Sainsbury b Heath	0
L. R. Gardner c Harrison b Shackleton	34	– lbw b Burden	78
A. C. Revill c Livingstone b Heath	58	– c Marshall b Heath	8
B. Cromack c Harrison b Shackleton	13	– c Harrison b Shackleton	3
R. L. Pratt lbw b Shackleton	11	– lbw b Shackleton	2
†R. Julian lbw b Shackleton	37	– b Heath	3
C. T. Spencer c and b Baldry	7	– b Shackleton	7
J. S. Savage run out	2	– c Harrison b Heath	6
B. S. Boshier not out	0	– not out	0
L-b 3	3	B 6, 1-b 2	8

1/23 2/23 3/91 4/196 5/225   285   1/0 2/0 3/8 4/23 5/25   191
6/226 7/255 8/274 9/283   6/28 7/35 8/52 9/177

Hampshire

R. E. Marshall c Spencer b Pratt	52	– not out	11
J. R. Gray not out	150	– c Watson b Spencer	0
H. Horton c Spencer b Boshier	105	– c Pratt b Spencer	8
D. O. Baldry c Julian b Savage	13	– b Boshier	5
D. A. Livingstone c Spencer b Savage	0	– c Spencer b Pratt	0
*A. C. D. Ingleby-Mackenzie not out	33	– not out	2
B 1, 1-b 7, n-b 6	14	B 4, 1-b 1	5

1/96 2/269 3/299 4/303   (4 wkts dec.) 367   1/0 2/8 3/15 4/25   (4 wkts) 31

P. J. Sainsbury, †L. Harrison, D. Shackleton, M. Heath and M. D. Burden did not bat.

Hampshire Bowling

	Overs	Mdns	Runs	Wkts	Overs	Mdns	Runs	Wkts
Shackleton	39.5	16	62	5	38	29	33	4
Heath	26	4	90	3	33	10	91	4
Baldry	8	3	26	1	3	1	14	—
Sainsbury	29	12	60	—	13.4	8	20	1
Burden	15	4	44	—	21	12	25	1

Leicestershire Bowling

	Overs	Mdns	Runs	Wkts	Overs	Mdns	Runs	Wkts
Spencer	25	6	59	—	3	—	11	2
Boshier	27	5	99	1	3	1	5	1
Savage	40	6	104	2	3	1	9	—
Pratt	23	6	69	1	2	1	1	1
Cromack	9	3	22	—	1	1	—	—

Umpires: R. Aspinall and R. S. Lay.

LEICESTERSHIRE v SOMERSET

Played at Leicester, June 8, 9, 10, 1960

Leicestershire won by an innings and 48 runs. A second century in successive innings by van Geloven and a maiden hundred by Gardner put Leicestershire on the road to their first **win in 21 Championship matches.** Leicestershire were able to declare after their unbroken third-wicket partnership and Pratt and Spencer continued the splendid work by making Somerset follow-on 233 behind on a rain-affected pitch. Somerset offered more stubborn resistance at the second attempt but the task was too great. Julian, taking five catches in the Somerset first innings, equalled a Leicestershire wicket-keeping record set up by Corrall against Warwickshire at Hinckley in 1932.

Leicestershire

M. R. Hallam c Palmer b Biddulph	71
H. D. Bird b Biddulph	3
J. van Geloven not out	157
L. R. Gardner not out	100
B 5, l-b 2, w 1	8

1/11 2/121   (2 wkts dec.) 339

*W. Watson, B. Cromack, R. L. Pratt, †R. Julian, C. T. Spencer, J. S. Savage and P. N. Broughton did not bat.

Somerset

R. Virgin c Julian b Spencer	11	– c Spencer b Broughton	9
J. M. Lawrence c Julian b Pratt	14	– c Pratt b Broughton	0
P. B. Wight c Julian b Pratt	36	– b Spencer	30
C. L. McCool c Pratt b Spencer	1	– b Spencer	13
C. Greetham run out	14	– b Spencer	0
G. L. Keith run out	2	– c Hallam b Savage	23
K. E. Palmer c Julian b Pratt	3	– c Broughton b Spencer	46
B. Langford c Pratt b Spencer	1	– b Savage	0
*†H. W. Stephenson c Julian b Pratt	16	– lbw b Savage	39
A. Whitehead c Spencer b Pratt	0	– c Savage b Broughton	15
K. D. Biddulph not out	2	– not out	6
L-b 1, n-b 5	6	B 1, l-b 2, n-b 1	4

1/25 2/40 3/60 4/65 5/82   106   1/7 2/10 3/25 4/25 5/61   185
6/83 7/84 8/97 9/97   6/83 7/83 8/131 9/169

Somerset Bowling

	Overs	Mdns	Runs	Wkts
Biddulph	21	3	73	2
Palmer	21	2	56	—
Greetham	16	4	37	—
Whitehead	29	10	71	—
McCool	5	1	15	—
Langford	33	14	53	—
Lawrence	8	3	26	—

Leicestershire Bowling

	Overs	Mdns	Runs	Wkts	Overs	Mdns	Runs	Wkts
Broughton	13	5	24	—	26.3	8	42	3
Spencer	22	11	32	3	25	10	53	4
Pratt	21	5	44	5	11	3	27	—
van Geloven					7	1	21	—
Savage					19	8	38	3

Umpires: N. Oldfield and R. Aspinall.

LEICESTERSHIRE v ESSEX

Played at Hinckley, June 25, 27, 1960

Essex won by an innings and 27 runs. A stubborn innings by Bailey on a pitch which took spin throughout laid the foundations of this two-day win for Essex. Bailey stayed just over four hours for 91 not out, finishing on a defiant note with a six in reply to barrackers of his wearing-down policy. He was helped in a fifth-wicket stand of 97 by Bear and the only other resistance to Savage's off-spin came from Barker. Leicestershire made a fair reply but their innings ended in startling fashion for in twenty-five minutes the last six wickets went down while the score stayed at 109. Leicestershire, following-on 154 behind, again had no answer to their tormentors, Preston and Phelan, who between them took 17 wickets in the match.

Essex

G. Barker b Savage	63
G. J. Smith b Savage	18
†B. Taylor c Spencer b Savage	1
L. A. Savill c Spencer b Cromack	8
*T. E. Bailey not out	91
M. Bear c Spencer b van Geloven	31
W. T. Greensmith b Savage	0
B. R. Knight b Savage	18
P. J. Phelan b Cromack	3
K. C. Preston lbw b Savage	1
Dr C. B. Clarke not out	12
B 6, l-b 10, n-b 1	17

1/62 2/73 3/89   (9 wkts dec.) 263
4/97 5/194 6/195 7/227 8/236 9/237

Leicestershire

M. R. Hallam c Bear b Preston	8	– c Taylor b Preston		19
H. D. Bird c Savill b Preston	42	– lbw b Phelan		10
J. van Geloven c Phelan b Preston	7	– c Phelan b Preston		19
L. R. Gardner b Phelan	12	– b Bailey		30
*W. Watson c Taylor b Phelan	26	– not out		22
B. Cromack b Bailey	4	– b Preston		8
P. D. Munden b Phelan	0	– b Phelan		0
R. L. Pratt b Phelan	0	– lbw b Preston		0
†R. Julian b Bailey	0	– lbw b Phelan		4
C. T. Spencer c and b Phelan	0	– b Phelan		0
J. S. Savage not out	0	– b Preston		14
B 9, l-b 1	10	N-b 1		1

1/33 2/60 3/63 4/104 5/109   109   1/24 2/32 3/78 4/82 5/100   127
6/109 7/109 8/109 9/109   6/101 7/104 8/112 9/112

Leicestershire Bowling

	Overs	Mdns	Runs	Wkts
Spencer	11	3	34	—
Pratt	19	4	33	—
van Geloven	22	6	41	1
Savage	45	16	80	6
Cromack	20	8	45	2
Munden	2	—	13	—

Essex Bowling

	Overs	Mdns	Runs	Wkts	Overs	Mdns	Runs	Wkts
Bailey	6.2	3	12	2	12	5	19	1
Knight	6	3	6	—	3	1	13	—
Preston	20	9	33	3	21.4	10	26	5
Phelan	20	9	33	5	20	3	68	4
Clarke	4	—	15	—				

Umpires: H. G. Baldwin and N. Oldfield.

LEICESTERSHIRE v GLAMORGAN

Played at Leicester, May 24, 25, 1961

Leicestershire won by one wicket. In a wonderful finish Spencer made the winning hit with the last pair at the crease. Yet again the seam bowlers had a rich haul and in well under two full days' cricket 39 wickets tumbled for 470 runs. Glamorgan were put in by Hallam, deputy captain, and their innings lasted only 55 overs, Pratt, medium-fast, gaining seven wickets for 47. Julian, the wicket-keeper, took five catches off his bowling and just missed a sixth. Leicestershire began badly, but Pratt and Julian once again dominated the cricket, this time in a stand of 59 for the eighth wicket which helped their county to a lead of nine runs. Glamorgan failed a second time, on this occasion to van Geloven and Spencer, but Wheatley, who took thirteen for 115 in the match, kept Leicestershire on tenterhooks until Spencer on-drove him to the boundary for the winning hit.

Glamorgan

W. G. A. Parkhouse c P. Munden b Pratt	7	– c Hallam b Spencer	19
A. Rees c Julian b Pratt	47	– lbw b Spencer	11
P. M. Walker b Spencer	8	– b van Geloven	25
A. J. Watkins c Wharton b Spencer	8	– b van Geloven	26
J. Pressdee c Julian b Pratt	5	– c Wharton b van Geloven	12
D. J. Ward c Julian b Pratt	12	– b Spencer	2
J. E. McConnon c van Geloven b Pratt	7	– c Wharton b van Geloven	0
J. B. Evans c Julian b Pratt	15	– b van Geloven	8
†D. L. Evans not out	7	– lbw b Spencer	0
*O. S. Wheatley c Julian b Pratt	0	– c Hallam b Spencer	3
D. J. Shepherd c Savage b Spencer	1	– not out	1
N-b 1	1	B 4, l-b 4	8

1/7 2/26 3/42 4/52 5/77   118   1/20 2/54 3/74 4/94 5/101   115
6/85 7/106 8/111 9/113   6/101 7/105 8/107 9/111

Leicestershire

*M. R. Hallam c D. Evans b Wheatley	14	– c McConnon b Wheatley	20
A. Wharton c Walker b Wheatley	3	– c Ward b J. Evans	0
J. van Geloven lbw b J. Evans	2	– b Wheatley	49
L. R. Gardner c Walker b Wheatley	7	– b J. Evans	0
P. A. Munden b Wheatley	21	– b Wheatley	0
D. F. Munden b Wheatley	1	– b J. Evans	0
B. Cromack b J. Evans	3	– c Parkhouse b Wheatley	9
R. L. Pratt c Watkins b Wheatley	39	– b Wheatley	8
†R. Julian c Walker b Watkins	18	– c McConnon b Wheatley	5
C. T. Spencer not out	11	– not out	15
J. S. Savage c D. Evans b Wheatley	0	– not out	0
B 4, l-b 4	8	B 2, l-b 1	3

1/12 2/19 3/19 4/26 5/28 6/31   127   1/13 2/19 3/27   (9 wkts) 110
7/57 8/116 9/120   4/27 5/38 6/67 7/84 8/94 9/101

Leicestershire Bowling

	Overs	Mdns	Runs	Wkts	Overs	Mdns	Runs	Wkts
Spencer	21.1	5	50	3	22	9	49	5
Pratt	24	8	47	7	10	2	32	—
van Geloven	10	1	20	—	13.3	1	26	5

Glamorgan Bowling

	Overs	Mdns	Runs	Wkts	Overs	Mdns	Runs	Wkts
J. Evans	15	8	30	2	18	2	47	3
Wheatley	20	2	68	7	24.3	9	47	6
Walker	3	—	8	—				
Shepherd	2	—	5	—				
Watkins	4	1	8	1	7	2	13	—

Umpires: C. S. Elliott and A. Jepson.

LEICESTERSHIRE v LANCASHIRE

Played at Leicester, June 24, 26, 27, 1961

Drawn. A new Leicestershire record for the second wicket overshadowed all else in a game which ended tamely after an enterprising start. Watson and Wharton, playing against his former county, followed their record third-wicket partnership against Somerset with a new second-wicket record figure of 287. Each of the left-handers hit twenty-one 4s in their centuries. A declaration that left Lancashire forty minutes batting speedily led to a success for Spencer and Lancashire were eventually dismissed 158 behind. Though rain interrupted Leicestershire's second innings Watson was able to set Lancashire to get 299 runs in 235 minutes but it was soon obvious they lacked the ability to get the runs.

Leicestershire

*W. Watson c and b Hilton	158	– c Grieves b Higgs	47
M. R. Hallam b Higgs	8	– not out	69
A. Wharton b Barber	135		
L. R. Gardner lbw b Hilton	14	– c Marner b Howard	1
J. van Geloven not out	32	– b Higgs	7
J. Birkenshaw c Howard b Hilton	0	– not out	9
R. L. Pratt lbw b Higgs	4		
†R. Julian b Higgs	0		
C. T. Spencer not out	0		
B 2, l-b 4, w 1, n-b 1	8	L-b 7	7

1/10 2/297 3/316 4/335   (7 wkts dec.) 359   1/86 2/94 3/107   (3 wkts dec.) 140
5/337 6/358 7/358

J. S. Savage and B. S. Boshier did not bat.

Lancashire

*R. W. Barber lbw b Spencer	0	– b Pratt	18
B. Booth c Hallam b Spencer	49	– c Julian b Boshier	39
A. Bolton b Boshier	16	– not out	0
P. Marner c Watson b Savage	40	– b Boshier	11
K. Grieves b Pratt	18	– c and b Birkenshaw	37
J. D. Bond not out	54	– not out	41
G. Houlton b Savage	2		
†G. Clayton c Watson b Pratt	12		
K. Higgs c and b Savage	0		
K. Howard b Savage	0		
C. Hilton c Julian b Boshier	2		
B 1, l-b 7	8	B 4, l-b 6	10

1/7 2/62 3/78 4/125 5/131   201   1/34 2/67 3/76   (4 wkts) 156
6/141 7/172 8/179 9/191   4/148

Lancashire Bowling

	Overs	Mdns	Runs	Wkts	Overs	Mdns	Runs	Wkts
Hilton	19	2	64	3	7	—	23	—
Higgs	25	5	86	3	20	2	87	2
Marner	7	—	23	—	4	—	9	—
Howard	31	13	59	—	12	6	14	1
Barber	17	5	64	1				
Booth	7	1	22	—				
Grieves	8	1	33	—				

Leicestershire Bowling

	Overs	Mdns	Runs	Wkts	Overs	Mdns	Runs	Wkts
Spencer	17	6	44	2	13	3	24	—
Boshier	18.4	6	45	2	10	1	26	2
Savage	28	16	32	4	7	5	13	—
van Geloven	5	—	19	—	7	2	19	—
Pratt	23	3	53	2	18	2	48	1
Birkenshaw					8	4	16	1

Umpires: D. Davies and L. H. Gray.

LEICESTERSHIRE v CAMBRIDGE UNIVERSITY

Played at Loughborough, July 5, 6, 7, 1961

Cambridge University won by six wickets. In a game full of incident, the feat of Pearson, the University fast-medium bowler, of taking all ten Leicestershire second innings wickets for 78 overshadowed everything else. A Freshman from Downside, Pearson was only the second Cambridge player to take all ten. In 1890 S. M. J. Woods, who later played for **England, took ten for 69 against Thornton's XI at Cambridge.** Leicestershire began well with Hallam making his first century of the season in just under three and a half hours, but a brilliant opening partnership of 185 by Craig and Goodfellow paved the way for Cambridge to declare 54 ahead. Later, thanks to Pearson, they were left to get only 107 runs for victory. Craig gave another superb display and in the match scored 181 for once out.

Leicestershire

*M. R. Hallam lbw b Kirby	115	– b Pearson	64
D. F. Munden c Brearley b Kirby	18	– b Pearson	5
S. Jayasinghe lbw b Willard	2	– b Pearson	41
L. R. Gardner c Craig b Reddy	26	– c Brearley b Pearson	0
J. Birkenshaw b Willard	61	– b Pearson	5
*J. Mitten b Willard	16	– b Pearson	0
R. L. Pratt b Kirby	3	– c Brearley b Pearson	12
C. T. Spencer b Brodrick	21	– c Goodfellow b Pearson	11
R. Barratt b Kirby	17	– c Brearley b Pearson	5
J. S. Savage b Kirby	0	– not out	9
B. S. Boshier not out	0	– c Willard b Pearson	6
L-b 4	4	L-b 2	2

1/59 2/74 3/112 4/198 5/232   283   1/27 2/79 3/79 4/95 5/95   160
6/245 7/247 8/281 9/281   6/109 7/131 8/137 9/154

Cambridge

E. J. Craig c Munden b Barratt	101	– not out	80
A. Goodfellow b Savage	81	– lbw b Savage	17
J. M. T. Wilcox c Mitten b Pratt	21	– c Spencer b Savage	0
A. R. Lewis c Boshier b Barratt	55		
N. S. K. Reddy run out	3	– c Spencer b Savage	9
†J. M. Brearley not out	24	– not out	0
*D. Kirby not out	30		
M. J. L. Willard (did not bat)		– c Spencer b Savage	1
B 13, l-b 9	22	L-b 2	2

1/185 2/199 3/250   (5 wkts dec.) 337   1/61 2/61 3/85 4/105   (4 wkts) 109
4/264 5/292

R. H. Thomson, P. D. Brodrick and A. J. Pearson did not bat.

Cambridge Bowling

	Overs	Mdns	Runs	Wkts	Overs	Mdns	Runs	Wkts
Pearson	16	—	48	—	30.3	8	78	10
Willard	38	9	96	3	19	6	41	—
Kirby	32	6	76	5	11	1	30	—
Brodrick	22.5	12	35	1				
Reddy	7	2	24	1	2	1	9	—

Leicestershire Bowling

	Overs	Mdns	Runs	Wkts	Overs	Mdns	Runs	Wkts
Spencer	23	3	42	—	8	1	25	—
Boshier	19	4	60	—	8	1	19	—
Pratt	13	3	27	1				
Savage	26	10	44	1	8	2	30	4
Barratt	31	9	95	2	7.1	3	44	—
Birkenshaw	14	3	47	—				

Umpires: F. Jakeman and R. Aspinall.

LEICESTERSHIRE v SOMERSET

Played at Loughborough, July 8, 10, 11, 1961

Leicestershire won by 41 runs. For the third successive innings Hallam was the sheet anchor for the early Leicestershire batting and later the Yorkshireman, Birkenshaw, occupied a similar role. The total was not unduly substantial until rain, which washed out the second day, put a different complexion on the game. Stephenson declared the Somerset innings 178 behind and Leicestershire responded by batting only briefly a second time. Hallam set Somerset to get 200 in two and a half hours. For a time the outcome was in the balance until Savage turned the game in Leicestershire's favour with some deadly off-spin. He did the hat-trick when capturing the wickets of Stephenson, Palmer and Langford and finished with six for 72.

Leicestershire

*M. R. Hallam lbw b C. Atkinson	93	– not out	16
A. Wharton lbw b Palmer	1	– lbw b Alley	3
J. van Geloven c Langford b Alley	34	– not out	1
L. R. Gardner c Palmer b Lomax	0		
D. F. Munden c Lomax b Greetham	23		
J. Birkenshaw not out	81		
R. L. Pratt c G. Atkinson b C. Atkinson	7		
†R. Julian c Stephenson b C. Atkinson	7		
C. T. Spencer c Stephenson b Greetham	7		
J. S. Savage c Langford b C. Atkinson	6		
B. S. Boshier c Greetham b Hall	13		
B 3, l-b 3, n-b 1	7	L-b 1	1

1/5 2/94 3/95 4/136 5/179   279   1/15   (1 wkt dec.) 21
6/198 7/208 8/215 9/234

Somerset

B. Roe c Julian b Boshier	0	– c Gardner b Savage	50
G. Atkinson lbw b Spencer	0	– b Savage	25
P. B. Wight not out	45	– run out	22
W. E. Alley lbw b Boshier	9	– b Savage	10
J. G. Lomax run out	4	– c Wharton b Boshier	3
C. Greetham c van Geloven b Boshier	7	– c Spencer b Boshier	4
K. E. Palmer b Boshier	20	– c Spencer b Savage	1
*†H. W. Stephenson c Munden b Boshier	2	– c Wharton b Savage	27
C. R. M. Atkinson not out	13	– lbw b Birkenshaw	8
B. Langford (did not bat)		– c Hallam b Savage	0
G. Hall (did not bat)		– not out	0
N-b 1	1	B 2, l-b 6	8

1/0 2/0 3/11 4/24   (7 wkts dec.) 101   1/47 2/97 3/109 4/113 5/134   158
5/38 6/68 7/70   6/140 7/150 8/150 9/150

Somerset Bowling

	Overs	Mdns	Runs	Wkts	Overs	Mdns	Runs	Wkts
Palmer	23	4	55	1				
Hall	10.4	1	42	1	4	1	14	—
Alley	18	4	33	1	4	1	6	1
Lomax	10	—	34	1				
C. Atkinson	22	3	71	4				
Greetham	14	2	37	2				

Leicestershire Bowling

	Overs	Mdns	Runs	Wkts	Overs	Mdns	Runs	Wkts
Spencer...........	13	5	32	1	7	—	22	—
Boshier...........	16	4	54	5	14	5	25	2
Pratt.............	4	1	14	—				
Savage					17	4	72	6
van Geloven					4	—	23	—
Birkenshaw........					1	—	8	1

Umpires: F. Jakeman and W. F. Price.

LEICESTERSHIRE v MIDDLESEX

Played at Leicester, August 2, 3, 4, 1961

Middlesex won by 28 runs. A fine century by Parfitt who put on 173 with Gale for the second wicket, soon gave Middlesex a commanding position. Wharton hit a century in each innings for Leicestershire, but they could not make up a first-innings deficit of 80. Wharton reached his first hundred of the match by hitting Bick for 6 and in the same over he hit another 6 in an attempt to deny Middlesex bonus points, but he failed by 0.02 of a run. After some steady bowling by van Geloven and Kirby had caused Middlesex to be dismissed in their second innings for 149, Leicestershire wanted 230 to win. They had a good chance while Wharton remained. Hitting fifteen 4s he scored 108 out of 178 in just under three hours, being run out after colliding with Savage when going for a second run. Then the initiative passed to Middlesex for whom Bedford, their captain, bowled his leg-breaks so well that he took five wickets for 77.

Middlesex

R. A. Gale c Gardner b Savage..................	71	– c Broughton b van Geloven 28
W. E. Russell lbw b Broughton.................	6	– b van Geloven................. 25
P. H. Parfitt b van Geloven.....................101		– c Hallam b Spencer.............. 0
E. A. Clark c Cross b Kirby	15	– c Hallam b Kirby 36
F. J. Titmus c Cross b van Geloven	63	– b Kirby...................... 18
D. Bennett b van Geloven......................	37	– b van Geloven................. 2
†J. T. Murray b van Geloven	8	– b van Geloven................. 0
R. W. Hooker not out........................	7	– lbw b van Geloven 2
D. A. Bick (did not bat)........................		– not out 2
*P. I. Bedford (did not bat)		– c van Geloven b Kirby.......... 10
A. E. Moss (did not bat)		– b Kirby...................... 16
B 3, l-b 15, n-b 1	19	B 3, l-b 7............... 10

1/16 2/189 3/192 4/223   (7 wkts dec.) 327   1/55 2/56 3/68 4/113 5/116   149
5/298 6/316 7/327   6/116 7/119 8/120 9/133

Leicestershire

*M. R. Hallam c Murray b Bennett	11	– c Parfitt b Bennett	11
D. Kirby b Bennett	7	– b Hooker	32
A. Wharton c Gale b Hooker	129	– run out	108
J. S. Savage c Titmus b Moss	1	– not out	4
J. van Geloven c Clark b Moss	4	– c and b Bedford	6
L. R. Gardner lbw b Bennett	3	– c Murray b Bennett	1
G. Cross b Hooker	27	– c Parfitt b Bedford	9
†R. Julian c Murray b Bick	29	– c Clark b Bedford	3
C. T. Spencer c Hooker b Bennett	24	– c Gale b Bedford	5
R. Barratt lbw b Titmus	8	– b Bedford	20
P. Broughton not out	1	– b Titmus	0
B 1, l-b 2	3	B 1, l-b 1	2

1/13 2/26 3/27 4/33 5/42   247   1/11 2/86 3/93 4/102 5/149   201
6/82 7/144 8/197 9/225   6/157 7/166 8/194 9/200

Leicestershire Bowling

	Overs	Mdns	Runs	Wkts	Overs	Mdns	Runs	Wkts
Spencer	20	2	63	—	13	—	57	1
Broughton	21	3	61	1				
van Geloven	29	8	80	4	22	5	59	5
Savage	24	10	43	1				
Barratt	6	2	22	—				
Kirby	10	—	39	1	10	3	23	4

Middlesex Bowling

	Overs	Mdns	Runs	Wkts	Overs	Mdns	Runs	Wkts
Moss	19	5	54	2	14	2	42	—
Bennett	22	5	68	4	12	2	27	2
Hooker	9.3	1	42	2	6	1	22	1
Titmus	17	6	40	1	12.1	3	31	1
Bick	16	5	40	1				
Bedford					17	2	77	5

Umpires: W. E. Phillipson and W. H. Copson.

LEICESTERSHIRE v GLOUCESTERSHIRE

Played at Leicester, August 23, 24, 25, 1961

Gloucestershire won by 17 runs. Centuries by Nicholls, for Gloucestershire, and Hallam, for Leicestershire, dominated the early cricket, but Nicholls received better support than Hallam, who became the third Leicestershire player since the war to carry his bat through a completed innings. Six of Hallam's partners failed to score. Set to get 306 in four hours, Leicestershire fought gallantly, but Allen bowled Gloucestershire to victory with thirteen minutes to spare, taking seven wickets for 78 in the innings and twelve for 126 in the match. Watson, Kirby, Pratt and Julian made splendid efforts to turn the issue in Leicestershire's favour.

Gloucestershire

R. B. Nicholls c Wharton b Boshier	121	– c Kirby b Spencer	2
D. Carpenter c Julian b Pratt	14	– b Savage	51
*C. T. M. Pugh b van Geloven	0	– c Julian b Pratt	21
D. M. Young c Savage b Boshier	55	– b Savage	47
D. G. Hawkins b Spencer	5	– c Hallam b Pratt	59
A. S. Brown lbw b Spencer	50	– not out	47
D. A. Allen b Boshier	8	– b Savage	8
†B. J. Meyer b Boshier	1	– not out	1
D. R. Smith not out	3		
D. G. A'Court not out	7		
B 2, l-b 21, w 2	25	B 5, l-b 6	11

1/33 2/34 3/159 4/186   (8 wkts dec.) 289   1/13 2/70   (6 wkts dec.) 247
5/248 6/264 7/266 8/280   3/86 4/146 5/164 6/244

C. Cook did not bat.

Leicestershire

M. R. Hallam not out	152	– b Brown	9
D. Kirby b Smith	21	– c Cook b Allen	63
A. Wharton c Pugh b A'Court	32	– c Smith b Allen	24
*W. Watson b A'Court	0	– c Meyer b Smith	69
J. van Geloven b Allen	11	– lbw b Allen	27
J. Birkenshaw c Smith b Allen	0	– st Meyer b Allen	7
R. L. Pratt b Allen	0	– b Allen	42
†R. Julian b Allen	0	– not out	32
C. T. Spencer b Smith	0	– c Nicholls b Allen	8
J. S. Savage c Brown b Allen	9	– b Allen	2
B. S. Boshier b Smith	0	– c Meyer b Brown	2
L-b 5, w 1	6	B 1, l-b 1, w 1	3

1/51 2/112 3/124 4/156 5/156   231   1/19 2/77 3/108 4/185 5/196   288
6/162 7/184 8/189 9/230   6/201 7/266 8/276 9/283

Leicestershire Bowling

	Overs	Mdns	Runs	Wkts	Overs	Mdns	Runs	Wkts
Spencer	21	2	61	2	12	1	34	1
Boshier	24	4	64	4	21	5	48	—
van Geloven	26	5	63	1	3	—	10	—
Pratt	28	8	56	1	11	3	28	2
Savage	4	—	20	—	23	3	102	3
Birkenshaw					3	—	14	—

Gloucestershire Bowling

	Overs	Mdns	Runs	Wkts	Overs	Mdns	Runs	Wkts
Brown	13	3	37	—	10.2	1	50	2
Smith	28.2	3	86	3	26	3	86	1
A'Court	14	3	39	2	8	—	29	—
Cook	8	3	15	—	8	—	42	—
Allen	10	2	48	5	25	6	78	7

Umpires: R. S. Lay and R. Aspinall.

LEICESTERSHIRE v SOMERSET

Played at Ashby-de-la-Zouch, June 30, July 2, 3, 1962

Somerset won by seven wickets. Alley, the Somerset all-rounder, dominated the game as bowler, batsman and even part-time wicket-keeper when Stephenson aggravated a thumb injury. To crown his efforts Alley made the winning stroke when Somerset were left to score 125 to win. The pitch, which had been found to be a yard too long, proved ideal for Alley's medium paced swing and he captured six wickets for 42. Then Alley rallied his side after they had lost five men for 70 and saw them into the lead during a partnership of 78 with Greetham. Wharton batted stubbornly when Leicestershire batted a second time, but apart from Bird he received little support and Somerset were left with an easy task.

Leicestershire

M. R. Hallam lbw b Alley	19	– lbw b Alley	26
H. D. Bird b Hall	1	– not out	26
A. Wharton lbw b Alley	19	– c C. Atkinson b Greetham	58
S. Jayasinghe c and b Hall	27	– b Greetham	19
*D. Kirby b Alley	0	– c Lomax b Hall	11
J. van Geloven b Hall	1	– lbw b Alley	17
J. Birkenshaw b Alley	36	– c Alley b Hall	5
†R. Julian b Alley	6	– b Hall	17
C. T. Spencer b Langford	26	– c Wight b Alley	10
J. S. Savage not out	3	– c Lomax b C. Atkinson	7
R. J. Barratt b Alley	0	– c Langford b C. Atkinson	4
B 5, l-b 1	6	B 2, l-b 3	5

1/15 2/29 3/64 4/64 5/65   144   1/82 2/92 3/108 4/123 5/123   205
6/76 7/89 8/138 9/143   6/145 7/170 8/186 9/199

Somerset

G. Atkinson b Spencer	6	– not out	47
B. Roe lbw b Spencer	1	– c Hallam b van Geloven	0
P. B. Wight b van Geloven	15	– c Julian b Spencer	4
M. Kitchen c Julian b Spencer	15		
J. G. Lomax c van Geloven b Spencer	19		
W. E. Alley lbw b van Geloven	44	– not out	26
C. Greetham c Wharton b Spencer	82		
C. R. M. Atkinson c Wharton b van Geloven	2	– c sub b Savage	45
B. Langford c Hallam b Savage	20		
*†H. W. Stephenson not out	7		
G. Hall c Hallam b Spencer	0		
B 5, l-b 8. n-b 1	14	B 4, l-b 1. n-b 1	6

1/3 2/16 3/30 4/67 5/70 6/148   225   1/2 2/61 3/65   (3 wkts) 128
7/151 8/207 9/221

Somerset Bowling

	Overs	Mdns	Runs	Wkts	Overs	Mdns	Runs	Wkts
Hall	19	1	70	3	16	2	55	3
Alley	22.5	7	42	6	33	10	53	3
Greetham	2	—	7	—	22	9	35	2
Lomax	1	—	13	—				
Langford	1	—	6	1	14	3	51	—
C. Atkinson					5	2	6	2

Leicestershire Bowling

	Overs	Mdns	Runs	Wkts	Overs	Mdns	Runs	Wkts
Spencer...........	34.1	6	62	6	14	2	33	1
van Geloven	41	10	108	3	13	1	28	1
Savage	4	—	13	1	15	6	35	1
Kirby	13	3	28	—				
Barratt					7	2	22	—
Hallam					0.1	—	4	—

Umpires: W. F. Price and W. E. Phillipson.

MIDDLESEX

MIDDLESEX v DERBYSHIRE

Played at Lord's, June 1, 3, 4, 1946

Drawn. Rain ruined a game that otherwise would have provided an exciting climax, Derbyshire finishing 86 behind with nine wickets to fall. It was impossible to start until 3 o'clock on the second day, and then Middlesex collapsed before the cleverly flighted slow bowling of Carr and Gladwin. Their last six wickets fell for nine runs. Although losing four wickets for 26 runs, Derbyshire managed to gain first innings points. Vaulkhard, mainly by vigorous pulls, scored 76 out of 104 in ninety minutes. Edrich played two fine innings for Middlesex.

Middlesex

D. Compton lbw b Rhodes	7	– b Rhodes	1
S. M. Brown c Vaulkhard b Gladwin	20	– c Carr b Copson	34
R. W. V. Robins c Elliott b Rhodes	16	– run out	25
W. J. Edrich c Worthington b Carr	73	– not out	51
J. D. Robertson c Vaulkhard b Gladwin	26	– c Smith b Carr	31
L. Muncer c Revill b Carr	0	– b Carr	0
J. Sims c Smith b Carr	0	– not out	0
L. Gray b Gladwin	0		
H. D. King run out	8		
J. Young b Gladwin	0		
I. A. R. Peebles not out	1		
N-b 2	2	B 2, l-b 1	3
	153	**(5 wkts dec.)**	**145**

Derbyshire

D. Smith c King b Young	2	– not out	33
T. S. Worthington b Young	3	– c Edrich b Gray	14
C. S. Elliott lbw b Gray	11	– not out	7
A. Townsend b Young	1		
P. Vaulkhard st King b Sims	76		
A. Revill b Sims	12		
G. F. Hodgkinson c Robertson b Gray	32		
D. B. Carr b Compton	0		
A. E. Rhodes b Sims	0		
C. Gladwin not out	14		
B 1, l-b 1, n-b 2	4	B 2, l-b 1	3
	(9 wkts dec.) 155	**(1 wkt)**	**57**

W. Copson did not bat.

Derbyshire Bowling

	Overs	Mdns	Runs	Wkts	Overs	Mdns	Runs	Wkts
Copson	12	4	30	—	8	—	38	1
Rhodes	11	1	29	2	6	—	41	1
Gladwin	12.3	5	34	4	5	—	18	—
Worthington	6	1	15	—				
Carr	19	4	43	3	10	1	45	2

Middlesex Bowling

	Overs	Mdns	Runs	Wkts	Overs	Mdns	Runs	Wkts
Gray.............	17.2	5	31	2	9	1	19	1
Young............	23	11	39	3	4	—	18	—
Peebles..........	2	—	10	—	6	1	16	—
Sims.............	12	—	47	3				
Compton	8	1	24	1	1	—	1	—

MIDDLESEX v SURREY

Played at Lord's, August 24, 26, 27, 1946

Middlesex won by ten wickets. Notwithstanding an admirable effort by Barling, Surrey could not atone for a poor first innings in which the same batsman surpassed his colleagues. Middlesex, after losing their opening batsmen for 33, were put on the high road to victory by Denis Compton and Edrich in a stand of 296 made in three hours and three-quarters. Compton batted four hours forty minutes for his highest score of the season while the total rose by 421; he hit twenty-one 4s. Edrich, fortunate in two early escapes, hit sixteen 4s. Compton hit four consecutive 4s off Gover, who then took five wickets for 30 runs in a remarkable finish to a hard day's work. Edrich did far best in the varied Middlesex attack. About 15,000 people saw the cricket on Monday.

Middlesex

J. D. Robertson b Gover.......................	21	– not out	34
S. M. Brown b A. V. Bedser	10	– not out	14
W. J. Edrich c Mobey b E. A. Bedser	.147		
D. Compton c Bennett b Gover	.235		
R. W. V. Robins c Squires b Gover..............	30		
A. Thompson c Squires b Gover................	15		
J. P. Mann c E. A. Bedser b Gover	9		
L. Compton c Watts b A. V. Bedser	0		
W. F. Price not out	9		
J. Sims lbw b Gover	1		
J. Young not out	6		
B 7, l-b 5, n-b 4	16	L-b 1.................	1

(9 wkts dec.) 499   (No wkt) 49

Surrey

L. B. Fishlock b L. Compton	1	– b L. Compton.................	26
E. A. Bedser b Edrich	2	– c D. Compton b L. Compton	58
R. J. Gregory b Edrich	9	– b Robins.................	26
T. H. Barling c Price b Sims	60	– c Robertson b Edrich	.122
H. S. Squires c D. Compton b Robins............	23	– b Edrich	23
A. J. McIntyre b Edrich	3	– lbw b Robertson	31
G. S. Mobey b Edrich	2	– c Brown b Edrich	4
N. H. Bennett b Edrich	21	– b Young.................	53
E. A. Watts st Price b Robins..................	2	– c L. Compton b Young...........	8
A. V. Bedser not out	8	– b Sims.....................	20
A. R. Gover c Robertson b Robins..............	5	– not out	1
B 7, l-b 7	14	B 15, l-b 7, w 1	23

150   395

Surrey Bowling

	Overs	Mdns	Runs	Wkts	Overs	Mdns	Runs	Wkts
Gover	28	3	122	6	5	1	16	—
A. V. Bedser	30	3	93	2	4	1	10	—
Watts	22	5	74	—				
E. A. Bedser	22	1	93	1				
Squires	18	2	75	—				
Gregory	4	—	26	—				
Fishlock					3	2	1	—
McIntyre					2	—	11	—
Bennett					1	—	6	—
Barling					1	—	4	—

Middlesex Bowling

	Overs	Mdns	Runs	Wkts	Overs	Mdns	Runs	Wkts
Edrich	17	2	52	5	31	6	101	3
L. Compton	10	3	14	1	21	5	41	2
Sims	19	4	44	1	22	1	68	1
D. Compton	5	3	4	—	5	1	24	—
Robins	5.5	—	22	3	26	1	72	1
Young					21.5	7	57	2
Robertson					6	3	9	1

MIDDLESEX v SOMERSET

Played at Lord's, May 10, 12, 13, 1947

Somerset won by one wicket. Fortune frequently changed in a very interesting struggle. Edrich, when first playing as an amateur, revealed the best attributes in batting. Seventh out at 207, after a faultless display lasting three hours and a quarter, he hit ten 4s. By taking four wickets for five runs in six overs on the second morning, Edrich helped materially in Middlesex leading by 97. Tremlett, on his first appearance for Somerset, surpassed this bowling effort. Tall, fairly fast, with good action, Tremlett bowled at the stumps with some off-break and began by sending back five men in five overs for eight runs. This startling work, supported by Wellard, left Somerset the task of getting only 176, but they lost five wickets for 101 on Monday, and next morning the pitch, slightly affected by rain, made run-getting extra difficult. Luckes and Hill added 38 before both left, but, joined by Hazell, Tremlett showed confidence without rashness, and lunch was taken with 16 wanted. Despite a close-set field, defence still prevailed until Tremlett lifted an almost straight drive into the members' stand, and, with two 3s to the on, he finished the match. The Middlesex team lined up and cheered as their successful opponents went to the pavilion.

Middlesex

J. D. Robertson b Tremlett	39	– b Buse	30
S. M. Brown lbw b Wellard	7	– b Wellard	0
W. J. Edrich c Luckes b Buse	102	– c Lawrence b Wellard	3
D. C. S. Compton c Woodhouse b Buse	6	– b Tremlett	25
J. Eaglestone b Buse	0	– c Lawrence b Tremlett	4
F. G. Mann b Buse	27	– b Tremlett	0
A. Thomson c Wellard b Tremlett	5	– b Tremlett	0
L. H. Compton b Tremlett	11	– b Tremlett	0
J. Sims c and b Buse	3	– not out	6
J. A. Young not out	6	– c Luckes b Wellard	1
L. Gray c Hazell b Buse	5	– run out	4
B 19, l-b 1	20	B 1, l-b 4	5
	231		**78**

Somerset

F. S. Lee c D. Compton b Young	28	– c Robertson b Young	38
H. Gimblett b Edrich	25	– b Edrich	13
H. T. F. Buse lbw b Gray	1	– c L. Compton b Gray	3
G. E. S. Woodhouse b Edrich	7	– b Edrich	21
R. J. O. Meyer c Robertson b Sims	1	– b Gray	4
J. Lawrence c Mann b Sims	30	– b Young	19
E. Hill b Edrich	0	– c Edrich b Young	17
W. T. Luckes c Edrich b Gray	9	– c L. Compton b Gray	26
A. W. Wellard b Edrich	17	– b Edrich	5
M. F. Tremlett c Gray b Sims	5	– not out	19
H. Hazell not out	0	– not out	8
B 1, l-b 9, w 1	11	B 4, l-b 1	5
	134		**(9 wkts) 178**

Somerset Bowling

	Overs	Mdns	Runs	Wkts	Overs	Mdns	Runs	Wkts
Buse	33	8	52	6	4	2	14	1
Wellard	22	4	49	1	16.3	7	20	3
Tremlett	24	5	47	3	14	3	39	5
Hazell	4	—	13	—				
Lawrence	12	2	40	—				
Meyer	4	1	10	—				

Middlesex Bowling

	Overs	Mdns	Runs	Wkts	Overs	Mdns	Runs	Wkts
Gray	24	10	25	2	29.2	7	51	3
Edrich	16	3	46	4	22	8	47	3
Young	11	6	12	1	34	14	48	3
Sims	15.4	4	40	3	7	—	27	—

Umpires: A. R. Coleman and J. J. Hills.

MIDDLESEX v KENT

Played at Lord's, August 13, 14, 15, 1947

Kent won by 75 runs. They triumphed five minutes from the end of extra time after one of the most exciting struggles of the season. Kent scored so freely when holding a first innings lead of 72 that they were able to set Middlesex the task of getting 397 to win at more than

90 an hour. When four wickets fell for 135 an easy victory for Kent seemed in sight, particularly as Wright was bowling in superb form. Then Denis Compton found a good partner in Mann, and in ninety-seven minutes the score raced along by 161 before Wright broke the threatening stand. During the partnership most of the Kent fieldsmen were placed on the boundary. Compton hit nineteen 4s in his thirteenth century of the season. He played one of his finest innings. Upon Compton's dismissal, when he attempted another big hit, Kent again set an attacking field for Wright and Davies, who accounted for the last five wickets in thirty-seven minutes for 25 runs. In each innings Wright kept a remarkably accurate length and troubled most of the batsmen with variations of leg-breaks and googlies, which brought him eleven wickets for 194 runs. Robertson hit his fifth century in successive matches for Middlesex in the first innings, when Edrich was next highest scorer with 28. All through Kent batted much more consistently. Their biggest stand was 157 by Ames and Valentine for the third wicket in the second innings.

Kent

L. J. Todd b Sims	62	– b Hever 7
A. E. Fagg b Young	66	– c L. Compton b Gray 6
L. E. G. Ames c L. Compton b Sims	8	– c D. Compton b Young 69
B. H. Valentine b Gray	61	– c Gray b D. Compton 92
J. G. W. Davies c L. Compton b Sims	4	– lbw b Young 11
G. F. Anson lbw b Sims	25	– c Mann b Young 51
T. G. E. Evans lbw b D. Compton	18	– c Robertson b D. Compton 56
R. R. Dovey run out	7	– not out 10
D. V. P. Wright b Hever	36	– c Edrich b Young 11
F. Ridgway b D. Compton	0	
N. Harding not out	5	
B 5, l-b 4	9	B 5, l-b 6 11
	301	**(8 wkts dec.) 324**

Middlesex

S. M. Brown c Valentine b Harding	0	– b Harding 5
J. D. Robertson c Evans b Wright	110	– lbw b Harding 12
W. J. Edrich b Dovey	28	– c and b Wright 31
D. C. S. Compton b Wright	16	– c Davies b Wright 168
R. W. V. Robins c Harding b Wright	24	– b Davies 21
F. G. Mann c Fagg b Wright	1	– b Wright 57
L. H. Compton c Harding b Wright	6	– st Evans b Wright 7
J. Sims b Dovey	7	– b Davies 7
L. Gray c Todd b Wright	7	– not out 4
J. A. Young c Fagg b Wright	17	– c Evans b Davies 0
N. G. Hever not out	8	– b Davies 2
L-b 2, w 2, n-b 1	5	L-b 4, n-b 3 7
	229	**321**

Middlesex Bowling

	Overs	Mdns	Runs	Wkts	Overs	Mdns	Runs	Wkts
Gray	17	3	44	1	19	3	70	1
Hever	10.1	2	32	1	15	3	37	1
Robertson	3	1	12	—				
Young	16	8	24	1	38.2	12	65	4
D. Compton	24	2	87	2	31	10	86	2
Robins	2	—	6	—	3	—	18	—
Sims	19	—	87	4	12	1	37	—

Kent Bowling

	Overs	Mdns	Runs	Wkts	Overs	Mdns	Runs	Wkts
Harding	5	1	22	1	13	—	56	2
Wright	33.2	5	92	7	24	3	102	4
Dovey............	28	5	59	2	20	2	69	—
Ridgway..........	13	1	46	—	5	—	29	—
Davies............	2	—	5	—	19	3	58	4

Umpires: H. G. Baldwin and A. R. Coleman.

COMPTON AND EDRICH [1948]

By R. C. Robertson-Glasgow

They go together in English cricket, as Gilbert and Sullivan go together in English opera. Nor is the analogy so careless as you might suppose. It may be allowable that each or any of these four has been surpassed as executant in his own sphere; that would develop an argument to make any Paper Controller clutch his scanty reserves. But it should not be doubted that, in the art of giving pleasure to an English audience, both pairs lack rival.

In cricket of the first class both D. C. S. Compton and W. J. Edrich have, Providence favouring, at least ten years to go of play and struggle and alliance. As a pair they have yet, at the hour of writing, to quell the fiercest Test attack, in the sense that Hobbs and Sutcliffe quelled it; or as Bradman and Ponsford lorded it over English bowlers here in 1934. In summer, 1947, they scored between them over 2,000 runs against South Africa. To Tuckett and his fellow-bowlers, Compton and Edrich became the daily task and, maybe, the nightly vision. In the matter of Australia, fulfilment is awaited.

But, in that territory which lies outside the microcosm of numerals, already they are kings; benevolent kings appointed and acclaimed by like-minded subjects; champions in the fight against dullness and the commercial standard. In their cricket, it is what they are that matters far more than what they have done. They stand, in these eyes at least, for something which has no place prepared in the books of score and record. They are the mirror of hope and freedom and gaiety; heroic in the manner of the heroes of school stories; the inspiration, and quarry, of the young, because, in a game that threatens to become old in the saddest sense, they do not outgrow the habit, the ideals, the very mistakes of youth.

Most cricketers enjoy doing well, though I could name great ones who had a queer way of showing their enjoyment. But Compton and Edrich are of that happy philosophy which keeps failure in its place by laughter, like boys who fall on an ice-slide and rush back to try it again. They give the impression, whether batting, bowling or fielding, that they are glad enough merely to be cricketing for Middlesex or England – "Fate cannot harm me, I have played to-day." And they seem to be playing not only in front of us and for us, but almost literally with us. Their cricket is communicative. We are almost out of breath at the end of an over by Edrich. We scratch our heads perplexedly at a googly from Compton which refuses to work. We smile with something near to self-satisfaction when, with easy vehemence, he persuades a length-ball from the leg stump to the extra-cover boundary.

That such players should break records is inevitable rather than relevant. Numbers can be such silly things. They excite many and prove nothing, or nothing that matters. Sinatra has had more listeners than Caruso, Clark Gable more letters of homage than Sir Henry Irving. But *homo*, however *sapiens*, cannot feed on artistry alone, and, in cricket, the record-hunt inspires us with as pleasant an insanity as ever took John Peel from the first viewhalloo to the death in the morning.

In summer 1947, records made by the great Surrey and English pair T. Hayward and J. B. Hobbs, were knocked down. Compton's 18 centuries in a season beat Hobbs's 16 centuries in a season of twenty-two years before; his 3,816 aggregate beat Hayward's 3,518 scored in 1906. And Hayward was also beaten by Edrich with 3,539. Very well done, too. But let us not therefrom deduce comparisons of skill; for, if we were to try anything in this line, we should have to bring up the subject of modern and ancient bowling, and that would lead us not only far from our brief but also to an inescapable, if unpalatable, conclusion. Let us, rather, flatter by inconclusiveness, and meditate on the analogy that Blackpool with 2,000,000 holiday-makers would not necessarily be an improvement upon Blackpool with 1,468,749.

Touching upon this question of records, I received at the end of summer, 1947, a letter from an Australian, a friend of cricket and of mine. "As one of Compton's admirers," he wrote, "and doubtless all who see or meet him get that way, I hardly expected him to score 18 hundreds in a season. I thought him too good a player for that sort of thing. Am I right in assuming that Denis played his usual cricket and the 18 hundreds just happened in the process?" Well, my Sydney friend *is* right, or very nearly.

Compton cannot help it. He has the habit of batting, as the sun has the habit of journeying from east to west; and the fielders are his satellites. Hardest-worked of them, and most perplexed, is cover-point. Other batsmen of our time have been severer on the stroke. Walter Hammond could leave the nimblest cover motionless or just flickering as by token, could use cover's toecaps as an echoing junction for the boundary; but Compton uses cover-point as a game within a game, tantalises him with delayed direction and vexes him with variety. He is for ever seeking fresh by-products of the old forward stroke and has not yet, I fancy, come to the end of experiment. He finds it so amusing and so profitable. He outruns the traditional and discovers new truth. Compton is the axiom of tomorrow.

They say his feet are wrong. So, once, were Whistler's hands. They turn up the diagrams and manuals and grumble about the direction of his left leg. But why legs and feet only? I saw him, last summer at Lord's, playing strokes to Kent's Douglas Wright, when his body went one way, his arms the other way, and the ball the same way, past the fielders. It was genius; also contortionism. Dan Leno should have been batting at the other end. Nervo and Knox should have been in the umpires' coats, and Cinquevalli in the scorers' hutch. But, praise be, Compton has limitations, or pretends to have them. He uses the straight and near-straight drive less than most masters. Perhaps such strokes are too obvious; too easy, almost. They interfere with the jokes he hurls round cover-point. Again, he has a playful weakness for the short-arm sweep of the slow leg-break towards square-leg and long-leg, leading the bowler on to not always frustrated hope of timing error from inconsistency of bounce.

Compton has genius, and, if he knows it, he doesn't care. Edrich has talent; or, more truly, he started with a number of talents and has increased them into riches. Compton, in essence, has not altered from the lad of just eighteen who scored 100 not out at Northampton in 1936 while numbers ten and eleven, Sims and Peebles, admired and defended at the other end. His whereabouts in artistry cannot be doubted. His effect silences question. But Edrich has, as they say, gone through it. He rose, half fell, and rose again, to a place higher and less slippery. The cost and the lesson are expressed in his concentration. With bat and ball he is an all-in cricketer; no funny stuff here; no holidays of mind or body. Compton is poetry; Edrich is prose, robust and clear. Far more than Compton, Edrich uses the practical and old-fashioned methods and areas of attack. He likes the straight hit, and that pull-drive which gave old E. M. Grace so many runs and "W.G." so many moments of reflective beard-stroking. Old-fashioned, too, is Edrich's high back-lift in preparation for stroke. He gives the idea of a height and a reach beyond fact. But also he is a hooker, nearly as vicious as his great forerunner, Pat Hendren.

In bowling, though Compton uses the left arm and Edrich the right, they are alike in improvement by use. Edrich began as a muscular slinger, as a but moderate advance on village heroics; then he grew into knowledge of swerve and variety. He is never done with.

DENIS COMPTON IN 1947 (Aged 29)

BATTING

	Tests	County Champ.	Other Matches	Totals	Runs v S. Africa	100s
May	—	363	469	832	303	3
June	436	157	11	593	436	2
July	151	484	—	646	151	4
August	166	1,029	—	1,195	166	7
September	—	—	550	550	131	2
Totals	753	2,033	1,030	3,816	1,187	18

BOWLING

	Tests				County Champ.				Other Matches				Totals			
	O.	M.	R.	W.	O.	M.	R.	W.	O.	M.	R.	W.	O.	M.	R.	W.
May	—	—	—	—	16	4	48	2	22	3	63	2	38	7	111	4
June	58	22	98	4	67	20	159	11	—	—	—	—	125	42	257	15
July	30	3	104	1	99.1	9	351	15	1.1	0	6	1	130.2	12	461	17
August	15	4	61	0	253.2	47	862	28	—	—	—	—	268.2	51	923	28
September	—	—	—	—	7	2	20	1	67	4	281	8	74	6	301	9
Totals	103	29	263	5	442.3	82	1,440	57	90.1	7	350	11	635.4	118	2,053	73

W. J. EDRICH IN 1947 (Aged 31)

BATTING

	Tests	County Champ.	Other Matches	Totals	Runs v S. Africa	100s
May	—	558	200	758	200	4
June	296	257	—	553	296	2
July	256	707	84	1,047	256	3
August	—	735	—	735	—	2
September	—	—	446	446	118	1
Totals	552	2,257	730	3,539	870	12

BOWLING

	Tests				County Champ.				Other Matches				Totals			
	O.	M.	R.	W.	O.	M.	R.	W.	O.	M.	R.	W.	O.	M.	R.	W.
May	—	—	—	—	170.1	38	428	31	21	2	91	2	191.1	40	519	33
June	46	14	117	4	75	12	163	5	9	0	37	1	130	26	317	10
July	88.5	19	253	12	78	9	239	7	19	4	48	1	185.5	32	540	20
August	—	—	—	—	55.5	12	137	4	—	—	—	—	55.5	12	137	4
September	—	—	—	—	—	—	—	—	—	—	—	—	—	—	—	—
Totals	134.5	33	370	16	379	71	967	47	49	6	176	4	562.4	110	1,513	67

TOM HAYWARD'S BATTING IN 1906 (Aged 35)

	County Championship	Other Matches	Totals	100s
April	—	121	121	—
May	600	70	670	2
June	756	241	997	6
July	874	114	988	4
August	562	—	562	1
September	22	158	180	—
Totals	2,814	704	3,518	13

Hayward did not bowl in first-class cricket in 1906.

Others of his kind blaze away for an hour or two, then die into ashes or a mere harmless flicker; but Edrich, near the end of an else fruitless day, flies flat into the attack and unlooses the unanswerable ball. Compton's slow left-hand bowling has about it a certain casual humour. He brings unrehearsed jokes on to the legitimate stage. He can bowl in a Test as if he were trying things out on a friend in the nets. He is still among the joys and errors of experiment. Anything may yet happen.

Both are magnificent fielders and throwers. Edrich has been allotted specialist work in the slips; Compton more often ranges the boundaries, where he may join, for moments of leisure, in that talk which is the salt and salad of cricket.

Both are fitting adornments and exponents of a game that was meant not as an imitation of, but as a refreshment from, the worldly struggle.

MIDDLESEX v SOMERSET

Played at Lord's, May 19, 20, 21, 1948

Middlesex won by ten wickets. The match was memorable for a stand of 424 between W. J. Edrich and Denis Compton, which beat all third wicket records in first-class cricket except the 445 by W. N. Carson and P. E. Whitelaw for Auckland v Otago at Dunedin, New Zealand, in January 1937. They stayed together four hours until Mann declared with fifty minutes of the first day still to be played. Steady bowling and keen fielding kept both batsmen comparatively quiet in the early stages of their association, but after tea 209 runs came in seventy minutes. Compton making 139. In his highest first-class innings to date Compton hit three 6s and thirty-seven 4s. Edrich hit one 6 and eighteen 4s. Somerset scored freely, but lost wickets steadily on the second day, when Middlesex claimed an extra half-hour without finishing the match, and forty-five minutes play became necessary on the final day.

Middlesex

J. D. Robertson c Hazell b Buse	21	– not out	22
S. M. Brown c Mitchell-Innes b Buse	31		
W. J. Edrich not out	168		
D. Compton not out	252		
L. Compton (did not bat)		– not out	7
B 4, w 2	6		
(2 wkts dec.) 478		**(No wkt) 29**	

F. G. Mann, R. W. V. Robins, H. Sharp, J. Sims, J. A. Young and L. Gray did not bat.

Somerset

H. Gimblett b Gray	6	– b Gray	29
E. Hill c L. Compton b Gray	3	– st L. Compton b D. Compton	69
M. Coope c L. Compton b Sims	31	– lbw b Sims	59
N. S. Mitchell-Innes b D. Compton	65	– lbw b Sims	8
G. E. S. Woodhouse lbw b D. Compton	15	– c Edrich b D. Compton	8
H. T. F. Buse c D. Compton b Young	7	– c L. Compton b Young	59
M. F. Tremlett c Robins b Gray	40	– c Edrich b Robins	20
W. T. Luckes c Sharp b Young	0	– c Edrich b Sims	27
A. W. Wellard c and b Edrich	3	– c Brown b Robins	14
H. Hazell not out	4	– lbw b Robins	5
P. A. O. Graham b Gray	12	– not out	4
B 4, l-b 4	8	B 5, l-b 3	8
194		**310**	

Somerset Bowling

	Overs	Mdns	Runs	Wkts	Overs	Mdns	Runs	Wkts
Wellard...........	39	4	158	—				
Tremlett	15	2	50	—	3	—	9	—
Graham	8	—	40	—	2.2	—	20	—
Buse	33	9	107	2				
Hazell...........	19	4	56	—				
Coope...........	6	—	61	—				

Middlesex Bowling

	Overs	Mdns	Runs	Wkts	Overs	Mdns	Runs	Wkts
Gray............	14	3	27	4	14	5	25	1
Young...........	13	8	14	2	19	7	41	1
Sims	19	2	61	1	29.4	9	78	3
Edrich...........	9	2	29	1	3	—	20	—
D. Compton	15	4	55	2	19	3	69	2
Robins					17	2	69	3

Umpires: H. Elliott and P. T. Mills.

MIDDLESEX v SUSSEX
(Denis Compton's Benefit)
Played at Lord's, June 4, 6, 7, 1949

Drawn. Although early rain delayed the start until two o'clock, the match proved a great success financially. On Whit-Monday the gates were closed before lunch, and altogether during the three days 55,000 people were present, of whom 49,194 passed through the turnstiles. Denis Compton won the toss and took a wicket in his first over. Strong hitting by the left-hander, Smith, and Griffith marked the opening day. On Monday, Denis Compton celebrated the occasion by playing one of the best innings of his distinguished career. He took great pains until he became accustomed to the pace of the pitch. His hitting to the on was splendid, and when he reached 103 in two and three-quarter hours his 4s numbered seven. Afterwards Denis treated the packed crowd to a magnificent exhibition of driving and hit thirteen more 4s, his last 79 coming in forty-four minutes. When he left, his brother Leslie punished the tired bowlers mercilessly and hit ten 4s. By staying four and a half hours on the final day, John Langridge deprived Middlesex of any chance of victory, and in the closing stages Jack Oakes drove Young for four 6s and also hit six boundaries, while making 53 in twenty-five minutes. Compton's benefit realised £12,200, easily a Middlesex record.

Sussex

John Langridge lbw b Gray....................	1	– c L. Compton b Sims	139
D. V. Smith b Young.........................	85	– b Edrich	0
C. Oakes b Young............................	25	– c L. Compton b Young..........	52
H. T. Bartlett c Young b Edrich	4	– c Edrich b Young	31
G. Cox c Edrich b D. Compton	17	– lbw b Young..................	20
James Langridge b Gray.......................	40	– lbw b D. Compton	20
S. C. Griffith not out	68	– c L. Compton b Sims	5
J. Oakes c D. Compton b Young	1	– st L. Compton b Sims...........	53
A. E. James c L. Compton b Young	7	– not out	31
J. Cornford run out..........................	14	– not out	15
J. Wood b Sims..............................	0		
B 2, l-b 5	7	B 5, l-b 3...............	8
	269		**(8 wkts) 374**

Middlesex

J. D. Robertson b Cornford 1	A. Thompson st Griffith b Wood 3
S. M. Brown c J. Oakes b James Langridge . 66	L. Compton not out 59
W. J. Edrich c John Langridge b James 21	J. Sims not out....................... 19
D. C. S. Compton c Bartlett b Cornford....182	B 7, w 1.................... 8
F. G. Mann b Cornford................. 26	—
H. Sharp c James Langridge b Wood 35	(7 wkts dec.) 420

J. A. Young and L. Gray did not bat.

Middlesex Bowling

	Overs	Mdns	Runs	Wkts	Overs	Mdns	Runs	Wkts
Edrich...........	16	2	39	1	18	3	65	1
Gray.............	22	7	32	2	16	7	28	—
Young............	30	9	69	4	31	11	123	3
Sims	14	—	58	1	38	3	111	3
D. Compton	17	3	64	1	13	3	39	1

Sussex Bowling

	Overs	Mdns	Runs	Wkts
Cornford.........	26	9	71	3
Wood	24	7	82	2
James	32	8	85	1
C. Oakes..........	29	3	98	—
John Langridge.....	1	—	4	—
James Langridge....	11	—	56	1
Cox.............	4	—	16	—

Umpires: A. Skelding and H. Elliott.

MIDDLESEX v WORCESTERSHIRE

Played at Lord's, August 13, 15, 16, 1949

Middlesex won by five wickets. Although weakened by the Fourth Test, Middlesex nearly always held the initiative, mainly because of splendid work by the spin bowlers, Sims, Young and Robins, who between them claimed seventeen of the Worcestershire wickets. With Leslie Compton opening the bowling, Worcestershire's first-wicket pair scored 67, but when the slow attack took over on a pitch responsive to spin a collapse followed. In a spell of six overs Sims dismissed three men for five runs. A sound innings by Dewes and the attacking policy of Robins, who hit five 4s in his first 22 runs, helped Middlesex to gain a lead of 128. Then Worcestershire made a determined bid to save the game, Cooper, Palmer, Ainsworth and Howorth all playing patient cricket. Ainsworth never relaxed his concentration in an innings lasting three and a quarter hours, and he and Howorth added 71 for the seventh wicket before Warr broke the partnership with a splendid catch at forward short-leg. Ainsworth's dismissal marked the end of Worcestershire's resistance, and Middlesex, left 150 minutes to score 137, hit off the runs with twenty-five minutes to spare.

Worcestershire

E. Cooper c Warr b Sims	54	– c Mann b Young	49
D. Kenyon c L. Compton b Young	29	– c Robertson b Young	12
R. E. Bird b Sims	1	– b Robins	4
C. H. Palmer run out	0	– c Robertson b Young	39
M. L. Y. Ainsworth c Brown b Sims	19	– c Warr b Sims	72
L. Outschoorn lbw b Sims	0	– c and b Sims	28
R. O. Jenkins c Robertson b Sims	12	– lbw b Young	10
R. Howorth lbw b Robins	17	– c L. Compton b Warr	34
H. Yarnold c L. Compton b Robins	7	– b Warr	0
R. T. D. Perks c Robins b Sims	6	– c Robertson b Sims	5
P. F. Jackson not out	1	– not out	0
B 1, l-b 13	14	B 3, l-b 7, n-b 1	11
	160		**264**

Middlesex

J. D. Robertson lbw b Perks	17	– c Yarnold b Howorth	31
S. M. Brown c Kenyon b Perks	45	– c Perks b Palmer	9
J. G. Dewes b Perks	81	– lbw b Howorth	39
F. G. Mann c Outschoorn b Howorth	24	– c Kenyon b Jackson	21
H. Sharp c Yarnold b Jackson	1	– st Yarnold b Howorth	7
R. W. V. Robins c Kenyon b Jenkins	30	– not out	0
A. Thompson st Yarnold b Jenkins	4	– not out	13
L. Compton lbw b Jenkins	33		
J. Sims c Howorth b Jenkins	32		
J. Young not out	8		
J. J. Warr b Jenkins	0		
L-b 8, w 4, n-b 1	13	B 14, l-b 3	17
	288	**(5 wkts)**	**137**

Middlesex Bowling

	Overs	Mdns	Runs	Wkts	Overs	Mdns	Runs	Wkts
Warr	17	3	39	—	24	6	60	2
L. Compton	7	2	16	—				
Young	12	5	15	1	45	22	75	4
Sims	28	9	60	6	48.3	17	83	3
Robins	8	1	14	2	11	1	33	1
Sharp	4	3	2	—	3	1	2	—

Worcestershire Bowling

	Overs	Mdns	Runs	Wkts	Overs	Mdns	Runs	Wkts
Perks	35	8	92	3	10	—	46	—
Palmer	7	1	16	—	6	2	11	1
Howorth	32	7	61	1	13.1	2	40	3
Jenkins	20	3	64	5				
Jackson	18	4	42	1	10	1	23	1

Umpires: A. E. Pothecary and S. J. Staples.

MIDDLESEX v SURREY

Played at Lord's, August 20, 22, 23, 1949

Surrey won by 52 runs. In completing the double against Middlesex, Surrey owed much to the Bedser twins. In an opening stand of 107 with Fishlock, Eric batted splendidly before becoming the first of three men dismissed by Denis Compton in fifteen balls. Two thrilling catches by Denis Compton while falling also helped in a Surrey breakdown partially retrieved by Alec Bedser's successful hitting. The early Middlesex batsmen found trouble in the off-breaks of Eric Bedser, who took the first five wickets for 59 runs, but Robins, Leslie Compton and Young played big parts in a notable recovery. Robins, with whom Compton added 68 in fifty minutes, hit two 6s and four 4s, and Young and Warr put on 41 in half an hour for the last wicket, but, chiefly through a period of 103 in seventy minutes between Squires and Constable, Surrey finished the second day 68 in front with six wickets left. The last day was packed with excitement. Rain, which prevented a start before lunch, affected the pitch so much that as the turf dried out the ball lifted alarmingly. Parker and Barton made 60 together before the ball began to bite. Then the last five wickets fell for 22. Middlesex needed 147 to win, but the good-length medium-fast bowling of Alec Bedser put them to rout. Batting became more a matter of chance than ability, and Robertson did well to hold out for seventy minutes. In accomplishing his best performance of the season Alec Bedser received good assistance from Parker, who concentrated on keeping down runs.

Surrey

L. B. Fishlock c L. Compton b Warr	59	– lbw b Young	22
E. A. Bedser b D. Compton	57	– c Edrich b Young	13
H. S. Squires c Brown b D. Compton	30	– c Edrich b Sims	57
B. Constable c and b D. Compton	3	– lbw b Warr	50
J. F. Parker c D. Compton b Sims	21	– b Warr	42
M. R. Barton c Edrich b D. Compton	10	– c Warr b Young	40
A. J. McIntyre run out	17	– c L. Compton b Warr	4
J. C. Laker c L. Compton b Sims	8	– c Edrich b Young	14
A. V. Bedser not out	31	– c Edrich b Young	0
W. S. Surridge c Edrich b Sims	17	– b Warr	0
G. A. R. Lock lbw b D. Compton	3	– not out	0
L-b 3	3	B 1, l-b 3	4
	259		**246**

Middlesex

J. D. Robertson c Laker b E. A. Bedser	45	– c Surridge b A. V. Bedser	35
S. M. Brown b E. A. Bedser	49	– run out	0
W. J. Edrich c and b E. A. Bedser	4	– c Parker b A. V. Bedser	0
D. C. S. Compton b E. A. Bedser	0	– c Parker b A. V. Bedser	4
J. Sims c and b E. A. Bedser	37	– c McIntyre b Parker	1
J. G. Dewes c Squires b Laker	27	– c E. A. Bedser b A. V. Bedser	0
F. G. Mann st McIntyre b E. A. Bedser	28	– b A. V. Bedser	23
R. W. V. Robins b Surridge	47	– c Barton b A. V. Bedser	3
L. Compton c and b Laker	42	– c Parker b A. V. Bedser	15
J. A. Young b E. A. Bedser	43	– b A. V. Bedser	8
J. J. Warr not out	14	– not out	2
B 15, l-b 4, n-b 4	23	L-b 1, n-b 2	3
	359		**94**

Middlesex Bowling

	Overs	Mdns	Runs	Wkts	Overs	Mdns	Runs	Wkts
Edrich	8	1	25	—	11	2	30	—
Warr	13	3	41	1	16	6	30	4
Sims	27	2	71	3	11	2	42	1
Young	11	3	21	—	29	10	66	5
D. Compton	30.4	2	98	5	24	6	60	—
Robins					3	—	14	—

Surrey Bowling

	Overs	Mdns	Runs	Wkts	Overs	Mdns	Runs	Wkts
A. V. Bedser	25	9	55	—	15.5	2	42	8
Surridge	11	3	47	1	2	—	18	—
Laker	42	10	102	2	3	1	18	—
Lock	18	8	33	—				
E. A. Bedser	28.2	7	99	7				
Parker					10	4	13	1

Umpires: F. Chester and F. S. Lee.

MIDDLESEX v DERBYSHIRE

Played at Lord's, August 24, 25, 26, 1949

Middlesex won by three wickets. By winning this match, their last in the competition, Middlesex became sure of sharing the County Championship. For most of the game it appeared probable that Mann's decision to put in Derbyshire to bat on a soft pitch would go against Middlesex, but in the end a splendid innings by Denis Compton, ably supported by Robins, gained 12 points. On the first day the pitch dried only slowly, and Elliott and Smith began with a stand of 57. Revill batted soundly for three hours. Middlesex lost Robertson and Brown for 26, and on the second day Copson, Gladwin and Jackson all made the ball lift, so that apart from solid batting by Dewes and hard hitting by Robins, nobody shaped well. With Warr bowling fast and well, Derbyshire lost six second innings wickets for 50, but Revill again displayed great determination. The Derbyshire fast-medium bowlers got down five second innings Middlesex wickets for 36 before Denis Compton and Robins added 90 in seventy minutes. Then Leslie Compton helped to add 53 for the seventh wicket. Denis Compton, batting three hours forty minutes, hit nine 4s. The equanimity of the Lord's Pavilion was disturbed when Gladwin, after being run out by his partner, accidentally put his bat through the dressing-room window.

Derbyshire

C. S. Elliott c D. Compton b Young	14	– lbw b Warr	7
D. Smith c D. Compton b Young	44	– b Warr	1
M. Fredericks c Robertson b D. Compton	12	– lbw b Sims	2
L. Johnson c Warr b Young	0	– lbw b Young	6
A. C. Revill not out	25	– c L. Compton b Edrich	62
A. E. Rhodes lbw b Young	36	– c Robertson b Warr	5
D. C. Brooke-Taylor c Brown b Young	3	– c L. Compton b Warr	4
C. Gladwin c Robins b D. Compton	5	– run out	12
G. Dawkes c D. Compton b Warr	28	– c Edrich b Young	0
W. H. Copson c L. Compton b Warr	0	– c Mann b Warr	0
L. Jackson b Edrich	4	– not out	1
B 5, 1-b 4	9	B 1, 1-b 2	3
	228		**103**

Middlesex

J. D. Robertson c Dawkes b Gladwin	9	– b Copson	0
S. M. Brown c Revill b Copson	0	– c Revill b Gladwin	1
J. G. Dewes c Fredericks b Jackson	39	– b Jackson	12
W. J. Edrich c and b Gladwin	13	– c Smith b Gladwin	1
D. C. S. Compton c Dawkes b Copson	18	– not out	97
F. G. Mann c Smith b Jackson	0	– c Dawkes b Jackson	0
R. W. V. Robins b Copson	45	– c Smith b Rhodes	50
L. Compton run out	0	– b Gladwin	18
J. Sims b Copson	2	– not out	10
J. Young run out	9		
J. J. Warr not out	0		
L-b 4	4	B 4, l-b 2, n-b 1	7
	139		**(7 wkts) 196**

Middlesex Bowling

	Overs	Mdns	Runs	Wkts	Overs	Mdns	Runs	Wkts
Edrich	11.4	2	38	1	8.4	3	15	1
Warr	24	6	44	2	22	5	36	5
Young	39	12	80	5	9	6	6	2
D. Compton	26	10	57	2				
Sims					23	6	43	1

Derbyshire Bowling

	Overs	Mdns	Runs	Wkts	Overs	Mdns	Runs	Wkts
Copson	12.2	1	50	4	12	4	31	1
Gladwin	23	11	28	2	21	7	54	3
Jackson	26	7	57	2	23	3	67	2
Rhodes					12	2	37	1

Umpires: H. W. Parks and F. Chester.

MIDDLESEX v SUSSEX

Played at Lord's, May 27, 29, 30, 1950

Drawn. In turn each side gained a big advantage before Sussex were finally engaged in a struggle to avoid defeat. Sussex did well on the opening day to dismiss half the Middlesex team for 181. Sharp showed marked restraint for three and a quarter hours, but Thompson altered matters with a grand display of driving which brought him 80 (ten 4s) in two hours. Sims helped him add 82 quickly, but C. Oakes finished the innings by taking four wickets for 12 runs. On Sunday, D. Compton complained of knee trouble and not only did he take no further part in the match, but a few days later he underwent an operation which kept him out of cricket until the end of July. When six Sussex wickets fell for 129 they faced the danger of a follow-on, but their captain, James Langridge, who was not dismissed in either innings, was never in trouble and the last four wickets yielded 128. Going in again Middlesex lost half their side for 52, but Edrich turned their fortunes. He took over three hours to reach 50, doubled his score in thirty-five minutes, and altogether batted four and a quarter hours. His driving was superb and he hit one 6 and nineteen 4s. He and Sims added 131. Sheppard batted stylishly for Sussex who wanted 297 in three hours twenty minutes. At first they went for the runs, but again James Langridge came to the rescue. When 22 he was missed at second slip and that mistake probably cost Middlesex victory.

Middlesex

J. D. Robertson st Webb b James Langridge	21	– c C. Oakes b James 4
H. P. Sharp c and b James	84	– b Cornford 10
W. J. Edrich b Oakman	6	– not out 152
D. C. S. Compton b James	50	
A. Thompson c and b C. Oakes	80	– b Cornford 9
L. H. Compton b C. Oakes	9	– b Cornford 0
F. J. Titmus c Parks b James Langridge	11	– run out 11
J. M. Sims c James Langridge b C. Oakes	35	– lbw b J. Oakes 44
J. A. Young c John Langridge b C. Oakes	7	– not out 4
P. I. Bedford c James b C. Oakes	10	
L. H. Gray not out	0	
B 1, l-b 5	6	
	319	**(6 wkts dec.) 234**

Sussex

D. V. Smith c L. Compton b Gray	0	– b Sims........................ 3
John Langridge b Gray	5	– c and b Sims.................. 53
D. S. Sheppard c L. Compton b Sims	34	– c L. Compton b Titmus 70
C. Oakes c Bedford b Young	40	– b Sims........................ 21
James Langridge not out	92	– not out 31
J. Oakes c L. Compton b Young	11	– c Edrich b Sims. 38
A. E. James b Sims	5	– b Gray 10
J. M. Parks c Bedford b Gray	33	– lbw b Titmus.................. 6
A. S. Oakman c L. Compton b Gray	4	– b Sims....................... 6
R. T. Webb lbw b Bedford	18	– not out 5
J. H. Cornford run out	9	
L-b 5, n-b 1	6	B 2, l-b 6, w 1, n-b 1 10
	257	**(8 wkts) 253**

Sussex Bowling

	Overs	Mdns	Runs	Wkts	Overs	Mdns	Runs	Wkts
Cornford	21	3	66	—	31	9	73	1
James	27	11	47	2	33	14	70	—
J. Oakes	14	2	41	—	9	3	28	1
James Langridge	30	11	67	2	13	1	28	—
Oakman	10	1	36	1	2	2	—	—
C. Oakes	22	3	56	5	15	4	35	—

Middlesex Bowling

	Overs	Mdns	Runs	Wkts	Overs	Mdns	Runs	Wkts
Gray	22	5	53	4	6	1	8	1
Edrich	13	3	31	—	5	2	9	—
Sims	33.4	6	104	2	33	3	114	5
Young	25	10	43	2	9	5	19	—
Bedford	7	1	20	1	6	1	35	—
Titmus					18	4	58	2

Umpires: W. H. Ashdown and F. Chester.

MIDDLESEX v NORTHAMPTONSHIRE

Played at Lord's, August 23, 24, 25, 1950

Drawn. The feature of this match, which rain seriously interrupted, was an opening stand of 203 by Brookes and Oldfield on the opening day when Northamptonshire scored 365 for six wickets. Delightful drives earned Brookes most of his runs, and batting five hours ten minutes he hit one 5 and thirteen 4s. Oldfield excelled with the cut. Apart from this pair, Northamptonshire showed little initiative. Two heavy downpours restricted play on the second day to less than two hours, and subsequently the off-breaks of Garlick and the left-arm slows of Broderick provided problems for Middlesex. Robertson and Edrich batted skilfully on the rain-affected pitch and their partnership realised 129. Each county was captained by a professional – D. Compton, leading Middlesex for the first time, and Brookes.

Northamptonshire

D. Brookes lbw b Sims	160		
N. Oldfield lbw b Young	92		
L. Livingston c Laws b Warr	20		
F. Jakeman b Warr	13	– b Dewes	0
D. Barrick lbw b Young	12	– not out	0
V. Broderick lbw b Edrich	24		
A. E. Nutter b Sims	3		
R. W. Clarke b Sims	28		
R. G. Garlick run out	3		
J. Webster b Young	10		
K. Fiddling not out	0	– not out	4
B 12, l-b 11	23	B 1, w 1	3
	388	**(1 wkt)**	**7**

Middlesex

J. D. Robertson lbw b Garlick	56	D. Bennett b Garlick	0
J. G. Dewes lbw b Nutter	4	J. J. Warr st Fiddling b Garlick	4
W. J. Edrich c Jakeman b Garlick	57	M. L. Laws not out	1
D. C. S. Compton b Garlick	26	J. A. Young c Garlick b Broderick	0
H. P. Sharp c Webster b Broderick	72	B 16, l-b 17, w 1, n-b 1	35
D. L. Newman c Webster b Broderick	18		
J. M. Sims b Nutter	23	**296**	

Middlesex Bowling

	Overs	Mdns	Runs	Wkts	Overs	Mdns	Runs	Wkts
Warr	28	5	75	2				
Edrich	15	1	56	1	1	—	4	—
Bennett	4	—	19	—				
Young	45.1	17	61	3				
Sims	27	4	85	3				
D. Compton	19	2	66	—				
Sharp	3	—	3	—				
Dewes					2	2	—	1

Northamptonshire Bowling

	Overs	Mdns	Runs	Wkts
Nutter	26	3	55	2
Webster	13	5	23	—
Clarke	15	1	48	—
Garlick	45	17	58	5
Broderick	27.3	11	55	3
Barrick	7	—	22	—

Umpires: D. Davies and T. J. Bartley.

MIDDLESEX v SUSSEX
(S. M. Brown's Benefit)
Played at Lord's, May 23, 25, 26, 1953

Middlesex won by 101 runs. Large crowds, who enjoyed glorious weather and gave generously to the collections for Brown's benefit were rewarded by rich entertainment to which the beneficiary made one of the chief contributions. In a second-wicket century stand with Edrich he cut and hooked powerfully. The position was ideal for Denis Compton, who celebrated his 35th birthday with a sparking innings (seventeen 4s). After reaching 100, Compton added 40 in the next twenty minutes before Edrich declared. Bennett shared an unbroken stand of 131 in an hour and a half. The Sussex left-hander, Suttle, the pick of a splendid fielding side, made his first appearance at Lord's noteworthy by a thoroughly pleasing innings full of rapid footwork and punishing strokes. He met the bowling at its best just after Bennett, with the new ball, had taken three wickets in four overs. Supported by the steadiness of Oakman and James Langridge, Suttle dominated the cricket. His hits included one 6 and fourteen 4s. Apart from Brown, who again hit strongly, Middlesex batted quietly before a declaration which set Sussex 202 to get in two and a quarter hours. The spin of Young and Denis Compton put them in trouble. In his last game at Lord's James Langridge scored 67 without being dismissed in either innings.

Middlesex

J. D. Robertson run out	11		
S. M. Brown b James	68	– c Wood b Oakman	54
W. J. Edrich c Sheppard b Oakman	48	– c and b Oakman	14
D. C. S. Compton not out	143	– c Webb b James	16
A. Thompson b Oakman	8	– b James	39
H. P. Sharp b James	29	– c Sheppard b Oakman	39
D. Bennett not out	36	– b James	29
L. H. Compton (did not bat)		– b James	28
F. J. Titmus (did not bat)		– not out	14
J. A. Young (did not bat)		– not out	0
B 9, n-b 1	10	L-b 1	1

1/14 2/132 3/132 4/144   (5 wkts dec.) 353   1/85 2/98 3/111   (7 wkts dec.) 234
5/222   4/153 5/194 6/207 7/234

A. E. Moss did not bat.

Sussex

D. S. Sheppard c L. Compton b Titmus	46	– c sub b Young	32
John Langridge c Titmus b Moss	91	– b Bennett	7
G. Cox b Bennett	34	– b Bennett	1
A. S. Oakman lbw b Titmus	34	– st L. Compton b D. Compton	0
J. M. Parks b Bennett	0	– lbw b Young	15
K. G. Suttle c L. Compton b Bennett	114	– c Sharp b D. Compton	14
James Langridge not out	50	– not out	17
D. J. Wood st L. Compton b Bennett	1	– c Bennett b D. Compton	4
D. L. Bates b Moss	0	– b Moss	1
A. E. James (did not bat)		– c Young b D. Compton	1
R. T. Webb (did not bat)		– lbw b Young	0
B 10, l-b 5, n-b 1	16	B 6, l-b 1, w 1	8

1/96 2/175 3/179 4/179   (8 wkts dec.) 386   1/15 2/19 3/53 4/59 5/61   100
5/274 6/369 7/385 8/386   6/73 7/74 8/74 9/88

Sussex Bowling

	Overs	Mdns	Runs	Wkts	Overs	Mdns	Runs	Wkts
Wood...........	16	3	41	—	9	—	31	—
Bates............	19	5	48	—	6	2	23	—
James...........	36	6	94	2	34	12	79	4
Oakman.........	41	13	107	2	31	7	100	3
Parks...........	4	—	14	—				
Cox.............	10	3	39	—				

Middlesex Bowling

	Overs	Mdns	Runs	Wkts	Overs	Mdns	Runs	Wkts
Moss............	30	7	92	2	10	2	23	1
Bennett..........	21	3	59	4	6	4	9	2
D. Compton......	28	4	78	—	15.1	5	37	4
Titmus..........	37	11	81	2				
Young...........	18	6	48	—	11	3	23	3
Robertson........	5	2	12	—				

Umpires: H. G. Baldwin and J. J. Hills.

MIDDLESEX v ESSEX

Played at Lord's, July 1, 2, 3, 1953

Middlesex won by 141 runs. Individual performances featured in a game in which Edrich scored his second century of the season against Essex. He put Middlesex in a sound position with a valiant innings lasting nearly five and a half hours. Ten 4s came in his first 50 runs and altogether he hit thirty-one boundaries. Then Bailey played as gallant, if not as profitable, an innings. With the ball rising head high, he showed great courage for three hours, refusing to be daunted by a blow on the left arm which eventually led to a visit to hospital and his retirement from the game. This left Essex without a man to combat spin during their second innings, when Denis Compton took five for 58, his best of the summer. He was helped by his brother Leslie, who caught four men and stumped two.

Middlesex

S. M. Brown c Ralph b Preston..................	26	– c Horsfall b Preston............. 1
H. P. Sharp c Ralph b Bailey	13	– b Smith...................... 85
W. J. Edrich c Ralph b Bailey..................	211	– c Gibb b Preston............... 2
D. C. S. Compton lbw b Greensmith	12	– b Preston 54
A. Thompson b Preston	6	– b Smith...................... 13
D. Bennett b Bailey..........................	37	– c Smith b Preston............. 18
F. J. Titmus c Gibb b Insole	30	– not out 16
L. H. Compton b Bailey	2	– not out 12
J. J. Warr not out	0	
B 2, l-b 4	6	B 4, l-b 2................ 6

1/35 2/64 3/115 4/128   (8 wkts dec.) 343   1/4 2/14   (6 wkts dec.) 207
5/234 6/341 7/343 8/343   3/100 4/127 5/176 6/180

J. A. Young and A. E. Moss did not bat.

Essex

P. A. Gibb c L. Compton b D. Compton	47	– c L. Compton b Bennett	41
F. H. Vigar b Bennett	20	– lbw b D. Compton	12
T. E. Bailey b Moss	84	– absent hurt	0
R. Horsfall c D. Compton b Young	52	– c L. Compton b D. Compton	1
D. J. Insole c Sharp b Titmus	0	– c L. Compton b Bennett	0
W. T. Greensmith not out	26	– st L. Compton b D. Compton	9
L. Savill b Moss	2	– c D. Compton b Titmus	48
R. Smith c Moss b Warr	0	– c L. Compton b D. Compton	6
R. Ralph b Warr	8	– st L. Compton b D. Compton	22
K. C. Preston c Warr b Moss	0	– lbw b Titmus	1
P. Cousens b Moss	1	– not out	2
B 5, l-b 8, w 2	15	B 4, l-b 8	12

1/52 2/87 3/173 4/173 5/207   255   1/58 2/58 3/58 4/60 5/72   154
6/208 7/218 8/247 9/247   6/90 7/132 8/141

Essex Bowling

	Overs	Mdns	Runs	Wkts	Overs	Mdns	Runs	Wkts
Bailey	21.5	3	75	4				
Preston	23	1	83	2	16	2	67	4
Smith	17	2	59	—	19	3	89	2
Ralph	3	—	5	—				
Cousens	9	—	32	—	5	1	23	—
Greensmith	22	5	54	1	10	1	22	—
Vigar	2	—	9	—				
Insole	8	2	20	1				

Middlesex Bowling

	Overs	Mdns	Runs	Wkts	Overs	Mdns	Runs	Wkts
Moss	22.2	6	56	4	9	—	32	—
Warr	20	1	72	2	8	3	20	—
Bennett	8	2	22	1	12	4	21	2
Titmus	16	3	34	1	4.4	1	11	2
D. Compton	9	1	37	1	17	2	58	5
Young	14	5	19	1				

Umpires: A. Skelding and F. Chester.

MIDDLESEX v WORCESTERSHIRE

Played at Lord's, May 12, 13, 14, 1954

Middlesex won by 30 runs. Centuries by Edrich and D. Compton, a grand bowling performance by Perks, and the determination of the players to beat depressing conditions contributed towards an exciting game. Powerful hooking featured the batting of Edrich, but until Compton took command in the second Middlesex innings no other batsman was master of the bowling. Perks made full use of heavy atmosphere, but Compton often jumped down the pitch to drive or pull him. Rain began early in Worcestershire's attempt to make 282 to win, but the captains agreed to play on. When Kenyon and Outschoorn scored 159 together in just over two hours, Worcestershire hopes ran high, but in an unchanged spell of two hours and three-quarters Moss turned the game by taking seven wickets for 77.

Middlesex

J. D. Robertson b Flavell	44	– c Bird b Perks	3
S. M. Brown b Flavell	2	– c Bird b Perks	8
W. J. Edrich c Horton b Flavell	141	– b Perks	0
D. C. S. Compton b Grove	14	– c Flavell b Grove	113
D. Bennett c Yarnold b Flavell	16	– c Grove b Perks	5
A. Thompson c Flavell b Grove	9	– run out	9
H. P. Sharp c Dews b Perks	7	– b Flavell	11
F. J. Titmus b Perks	0	– c Outschoorn b Perks	38
L. H. Compton c Broadbent b Perks	5	– c Broadbent b Grove	6
J. A. Young b Flavell	21	– b Perks	0
A. E. Moss not out	12	– not out	0
B 2, l-b 3, n-b 2	7	B 1	1

1/20 2/75 3/101 4/138 5/167   278   1/4 2/6 3/13 4/23 5/55   194
6/191 7/191 8/208 9/248   6/85 7/187 8/190 9/190

Worcestershire

D. Kenyon b Moss	23	– b Moss	77
L. Outschoorn b Moss	34	– c L. Compton b Moss	88
G. Dews c Robertson b Young	26	– c Edrich b Young	12
R. E. Bird c and b Young	14	– b Moss	5
R. G. Broadbent b D. Compton	26	– c D. Compton b Moss	8
L. N. Devereux c L. Compton b D. Compton	37	– c L. Compton b Moss	4
M. Horton c Bennett b Moss	11	– c Sharp b Young	19
H. Yarnold b D. Compton	3	– b Moss	0
C. W. Grove b Moss	11	– b Moss	19
R. T. D. Perks st L. Compton b D. Compton	2	– c Moss b Young	14
J. Flavell not out	0	– not out	0
B 3, l-b 1	4	L-b 5	5

1/45 2/62 3/93 4/98 5/159   191   1/159 2/170 3/180 4/181 5/188   251
6/173 7/175 8/182 9/191   6/209 7/209 8/235 9/251

Worcestershire Bowling

	Overs	Mdns	Runs	Wkts	Overs	Mdns	Runs	Wkts
Perks	19	3	66	3	23	4	76	6
Flavell	18.3	1	98	5	10	—	40	1
Grove	31	4	85	2	21	4	51	2
Devereux	8	2	22	—	6	1	16	—
Horton					3	1	10	—

Middlesex Bowling

	Overs	Mdns	Runs	Wkts	Overs	Mdns	Runs	Wkts
Moss	19	2	54	4	32.3	6	101	7
Bennett	9	2	29	—	4	—	20	—
D. Compton	16.1	1	70	4	5	—	16	—
Young	10	5	18	2	37	15	66	3
Titmus	4	—	16	—	14	1	43	—

Umpires: J. J. Hills and E. A. Roberts.

DENIS COMPTON: THE CAVALIER [1958]

By Neville Cardus

Denis Compton counts amongst those cricketers who changed a game of competitive and technical interest to sportsmen into a highly individual art that appealed to and fascinated thousands of men and women and boys and girls, none of whom possessed a specialist clue, none of whom could enter into the fine points of expert skill. He lifted cricket into an atmosphere of freedom of personal expression. The score-board seldom told you more than half the truth about what he was doing on the field of play. In an age increasingly becoming standardised, with efficiency the aim at the expense of impulse – for impulse is always a risk – Compton went his unburdened way, a law to himself.

Most cricketers, even some of the greatest, need the evidence of the score-board to demonstrate their gifts over by over; if they are not scoring, if they are compelled by steady bowling or by force of adverse circumstances to fall back on the textbook, they are certain, in such moments, to wear out the patience of all who are not vehemently partisans, or students of academic zeal and watchfulness.

Even a Sir Leonard Hutton or a Peter May needs to do well to convince the lay onlooker that he is really worth watching for hours. Compton fascinated all lovers of cricket, informed or uninformed, whether he was making runs or not, or whether he was taking wickets or not.

In fact, whenever Compton seemed seriously in trouble and under the necessity to work hard he was then even a more arresting spectacle than usual. As we watched him groping and lunging and running out of his ground before the ball was released, we were more than ever aware that here was no merely talented cricketer; here was one under the sway and in the thrall of incalculable genius. For it is certain that Compton often was as much in the dark as the rest of us as to why and how he came by his own personal achievements, how he added to a fundamentally sound technical foundation an unpredictable inspiration, as though grace descended on him.

Once in Australia he ran into a new bowler of curious variations of spin; I think the bowler was Iverson. Compton was momentarily visited by one of his moods of eccentric fallibility. He played forward as though sightless; he played back as though wanting to play forward. He apparently didn't quite know where he was or with what he was coping. At the other end of the wicket a comparative newcomer was batting steadily, but runs were not being scored quickly enough. So the young novice approached Compton between overs for instructions. "You go on just as you are," was Denis's advice. "You're playing well. I'll get on with the antics."

At his greatest – which is really to say most days in a season – he made batting look as easy and as much a natural part of him as the way he walked or talked. Versatility of stroke-play; swift yet, paradoxically, leisurely footwork; drives that were given a lovely lightness of touch by wristy flexion at the last second; strokes that were born almost before the bowler himself had seen the ball's length – all these were the signs of the Master. Yet the word "Master" in all its pontifical use was not applied to him but, in his period, reserved for Sir Leonard. The reason is that Compton's cricket always looked young, fresh and spontaneous. The resonant term "Master" implies a certain air of age and pompousness, a Mandarin authority and poise.

When cricket was begun again, after the Hitler war, Compton in his wonderful years of 1946-1947 expressed by his cricket the renewed life and hopes of a land and nation that had come out of the dark abyss. In a period still sore and shabby and rationed, Compton spread his happy favours everywhere. The crows sat in the sun, liberated from anxiety and privation. The strain of long years of affliction fell from all shoulders as Compton set the ball rolling or speeding or rippling right and left, as he leaned to it and swept it from the off round the leg boundary, as he danced forward or danced backwards, his hair tousled beyond the pacifying power of any cream or unguent whatsoever ... yes, the crowd sunned themselves as much in Compton's batting as in the beneficial rays coming from the blue sky. Men and women, boys and girls, cheered him to his century, and ran every one of his runs with him.

As I say, his batting was founded on sound first principles – nose on the ball, the body near to the line. But he was perpetually rendering acquired science and logic more and more flexible. He was a born improviser. Once a beautiful spinner from Douglas Wright baffled him all the way. He anticipated a leg-break, but it was a "googly" when it pitched. To adjust his future physical system at the prompting of instinct working swift as lightning, Compton had to perform a contortion of muscles which sent him sprawling chest-flat on the wicket. But he was in time to sweep the ball to the long-leg boundary.

It is not enough to remember his brilliance only, his winged victories, his moments of animation and fluent effortless control. He has, in the face of dire need, played defensively with as tenaciously and as severely a principled skill as Hutton commanded at his dourest. Compton's 184 for England at Trent Bridge in 1948 must go down in history among the most heroically Spartan innings ever played. . . . England batted a second time 344 behind, and lost Washbrook and Edrich for 39. Compton and Hutton then staved away disaster until 150 was reached, and Hutton was bowled.

In a dreadful light Compton defended with terrific self-restraint against Miller at his fiercest. It is possible the match might have been snatched by him from the burning. Alas, at the crisis, a vicious "bumper" from Miller rose shoulder high. Compton instinctively hooked, thought better of it too late, slipped on the greasy turf, and fell on his wicket. For six hours and fifty minutes he mingled defence and offence in proportion. He did not, merely because his back was to the wall, spare the occasional loose ball. At Manchester, in the same rubber of 1948, Compton again showed us that there was stern stuff about him, the ironside breastplate as well as the Cavalier plume. He was knocked out by Lindwall. Stitches were sewn into his skull and, after a rest, he came back when England's score was 119 for five. He scored 145 not out in five hours twenty minutes.

These two superbly heroic innings, in the face of odds, may be taken as symbolical of a life and career not all sunshine and light heart, although Compton has lavished plenty of both on us. Nature was generous with him at his cradle; she gave him nearly everything. Then in his prime and heyday she snatched away his mainspring, she crippled him with many summers of his genius still to come.

In his fortieth year he is as young at heart and as richly endowed in batsmanship as at any time of his life. There are ample fruits in his cornucopia yet – if it were not for "that knee"! Still, we mustn't be greedy. He has shared the fruits of the full and refreshing cornucopia generously with us. He will never be forgotten for his precious gifts of nature and skill, which statistics have no power to indicate let alone voice. Perhaps there is more of him to come. It is hard to believe that nature is any readier than we ordinary mortals are to see him at last reposing with the authentic "Old Masters". Whatever his future, our hearts won't let him go. Thank you, Denis!

MIDDLESEX v HAMPSHIRE

Played at Lord's, May 7, 9, 10, 1960

Middlesex won by one wicket. They gained a dramatic victory with their last pair together. Murray ending the match with a 6 off Shackleton into the main grandstand. Hampshire failed badly before good bowling by Bennett, Moss and Titmus on the first day and Middlesex also struggled against Shackleton, but gained a lead of 100. Hampshire lost seven wickets before clearing the arrears, then Livingstone played the highest innings of the match. The others were worried by good bowling from Bennett on a lively pitch. Middlesex had the entire third day to get 81 to win, yet failed so badly against Shackleton and Heath that the first six wickets went for 35. When Moss, the last man, joined Murray eight were needed and Hampshire could have won. Marshall, at slip, missed Moss before Murray made the winning hit.

Hampshire

R. E. Marshall c Titmus b Bennett	27	– c White b Bennett	1
J. R. Gray lbw b Bennett	13	– c Titmus b Bennett	6
H. Horton c Parfitt b Moss	5	– c Parfitt b Warr	33
D. O. Baldry c Warr b Bennett	0	– c Parfitt b Bennett	1
D. A. Livingstone c Russell b Titmus	6	– c Murray b Moss	66
*A. C. D. Ingleby-Mackenzie c Bennett b Titmus	4	– c Murray b Warr	0
P. J. Sainsbury c Parfitt b Titmus	10	– c Murray b Hooker	14
†L. Harrison c Murray b Bennett	1	– b Hooker	2
M. Heath not out	0	– b Bennett	8
D. Shackleton c Clark b Moss	11	– c Titmus b Bennett	34
M. D. Burden c Russell b Moss	0	– not out	9
B 4, n-b 1	5	L-b 4, n-b 2	6

1/41 2/44 3/44 4/56 5/60   82   1/2 2/15 3/21 4/48 5/50   180
6/70 7/71 8/71 9/82   6/91 7/93 8/146 9/167

Middlesex

W. E. Russell c Harrison b Shackleton	14	– c Marshall b Heath	3
R. A. White c Livingstone b Shackleton	22	– lbw b Shackleton	2
R. W. Hooker lbw b Shackleton	0	– c Harrison b Shackleton	26
E. A. Clark b Baldry	31	– lbw b Shackleton	5
P. H. Parfitt c Horton b Heath	1	– c Gray b Heath	16
F. J. Titmus lbw b Shackleton	49	– c Marshall b Heath	0
D. Bennett c Baldry b Heath	15	– c Gray b Heath	0
†J. T. Murray c Sainsbury b Shackleton	13	– not out	24
M. J. Smith not out	17	– b Shackleton	0
*J. J. Warr hit wkt b Heath	9	– c Harrison b Shackleton	4
A. E. Moss c Harrison b Shackleton	1	– not out	2
B 8, l-b 2	10		

1/20 2/41 3/41 4/48 5/97   182   1/3 2/9 3/10   (9 wkts) 82
6/128 7/155 8/158 9/179   4/31 5/35 6/35 7/63
                                8/63 9/73

Middlesex Bowling

	Overs	Mdns	Runs	Wkts	Overs	Mdns	Runs	Wkts
Moss	13.5	6	32	3	26	9	59	1
Warr	9	2	13	—	11	3	29	2
Bennett	12	4	20	4	17.3	—	48	5
Titmus	8	4	12	3	11	3	19	—
Hooker					4	1	19	2

Hampshire Bowling

	Overs	Mdns	Runs	Wkts	Overs	Mdns	Runs	Wkts
Shackleton	33.1	12	46	6	19.4	6	35	5
Heath	30	9	72	3	19	3	47	4
Gray	5	—	19	—				
Baldry	13	4	19	1				
Burden	6	3	16	—				

Umpires: H. G. Baldwin and W. E. Phillipson.

MIDDLESEX v SURREY

Played at Lord's, August 13, 15, 16, 1960

Middlesex won by eight wickets. For the first time since 1948 they completed the double over Surrey. Another close finish took place, Middlesex winning with twenty-three minutes to spare. Edrich hit a splendid 125 on the first day, batting four and a half hours (twenty-two 4s). Barrington helped him add 134. Middlesex were indebted to a partnership of 125 between S. E. Russell and Parfitt. Warr declared one run ahead and Surrey lost seven men for 79 before Gibson and Lock put on 71 in thirty-five minutes. Middlesex needed 162 in two hours thirty-five minutes and Gale and S. E. Russell saw them through safely. Alec Bedser received a standing ovation from 12,000 people on the first day in recognition of his last appearance as a professional at Lord's.

Surrey

M. J. Stewart c Titmus b Warr	17	– c Hooker b Moss	20
J. H. Edrich c Moss b Warr	125	– c Murray b Moss	5
D. G. W. Fletcher c Murray b Bennett	11	– run out	1
K. F. Barrington c Gale b Titmus	67	– lbw b Moss	13
A. B. D. Parsons c S. Russell b Drybrough.........	8	– c Parfitt b Gale	22
E. A. Bedser c Murray b Moss	2	– c Hale b Titmus	15
†R. Swetman c Gale b Bennett	23	– c and b Gale	2
D. Gibson c Murray b Hooker	12	– lbw b Drybrough	37
G. A. R. Lock c Titmus b Hooker	4	– not out	35
*A. V. Bedser not out	1	– b Moss	3
P. J. Loader b Bennett........................	1	– c Murray b Bennett..........	1
B 5, l-b 4, w 1	10	B 7, l-b 1	8

1/23 2/48 3/182 4/206 5/236   281   1/17 2/18 3/34 4/41 5/73   162
6/242 7/268 8/279 9/279   6/79 7/79 8/150 9/161

Middlesex

W. E. Russell lbw b A. Bedser..................	0	– c Swetman b Gibson..........	17
R. A. Gale c A. Bedser b Lock	31	– not out	86
C. D. Drybrough c Swetman b Lock	34		
S. E. Russell c Stewart b A. Bedser.............	82	– c Edrich b Gibson..............	36
P. H. Parfitt c Lock b A. Bedser	62	– not out	8
F. J. Titmus b A. Bedser	7		
†J. T. Murray c Swetman b Gibson	29		
D. Bennett not out...........................	12		
R. W. Hooker not out	11		
B 9, l-b 2, w 3	14	B 8, l-b 6, n-b 1	15

1/5 2/56 3/79 4/204   (7 wkts dec.) 282   1/42 2/120   (2 wkts) 162
5/224 6/231 7/267

*J. J. Warr and A. E. Moss did not bat.

Middlesex Bowling

	Overs	Mdns	Runs	Wkts	Overs	Mdns	Runs	Wkts
Moss............	22	6	35	1	22	7	45	4
Warr............	20	8	44	2	11	6	11	—
Titmus	23	5	66	1	7	—	25	1
Hooker..........	8	1	36	2	3	1	7	—
Bennett..........	14	4	41	3	5.1	3	8	1
Drybrough	18	4	49	1	6	2	17	1
Gale					9	1	41	2

Surrey Bowling

	Overs	Mdns	Runs	Wkts	Overs	Mdns	Runs	Wkts
Loader	22	10	36	—	9	—	27	—
A. Bedser	25	6	63	4	9	—	26	—
Gibson	17	4	47	1	11	—	34	2
E. Bedser	20	6	41	—	3	—	31	—
Lock.............	23	8	49	2	8	1	24	—
Barrington	10	2	32	—	0.2	—	5	—

Umpires: J. S. Buller and P. A. Gibb.

MIDDLESEX v SURREY

Played at Lord's, August 12, 14, 15, 1961

Surrey won by 29 runs. On a worn and dusty pitch which developed a bad patch, the skill of Lock and Bedser gained Surrey a deserved victory. Hooker, with medium-fast variations brought about Surrey's first-day downfall, including the dismissal of May for a duck. At one stage Hooker sent back four men for six runs in 14 balls. Bedser, with accurately pitched off-breaks, showed his power for Surrey on the second day when Middlesex fared little better. Then Titmus upset Surrey after Barrington and Willett had shared a stand of 135. Once more May was out for a duck – the first time he had been dismissed for a "pair" – and Middlesex were left to make 231 in just under five hours. Gale, Titmus and Murray batted attractively, but May depended on the experience of his spinners and was fully justified. They bowled for the last two hours. Lock backed his guileful bowling with brilliant fielding. Such was the state of the pitch that six times in the last innings the ball beat the bat and wicket-keeper for four byes.

Surrey

M. J. Stewart c Hooker b Moss.................	2	–	b Moss	0
J. H. Edrich b Titmus	47	–	c Drybrough b Titmus	67
K. F. Barrington c Murray b Hooker	17	–	b Drybrough..................	78
*P. B. H. May c Drybrough b Hooker	0	–	b Titmus.....................	0
B. Constable b Hooker	6	–	b Titmus.....................	13
M. D. Willett b Hooker.......................	0	–	c Hooker b Titmus	49
†R. Swetman lbw b Hooker	7	–	c Murray b Bennett.............	5
G. A. R. Lock c Clark b Titmus	26	–	lbw b Titmus..................	18
E. A. Bedser b Bennett	0	–	c Bedford b Titmus.............	1
D. A. D. Sydenham b Bennett..................	1	–	b Titmus.....................	7
P. J. Loader not out..........................	1	–	not out	8
B 6, l-b 7	13		B 10, l-b 3	13

1/6 2/36 3/38 4/44 5/44   120   1/0 2/135 3/135 4/153 5/183   259
6/64 7/118 8/118 9/118   6/215 7/236 8/243 9/246

Middlesex

R. A. Gale c Willett b Loader	33	– run out	42
W. E. Russell b Bedser	34	– lbw b Lock	5
P. H. Parfitt c Willett b Bedser	29	– c and b Lock	1
E. A. Clark b Bedser	4	– st Swetman b Bedser	5
F. J. Titmus c Stewart b Loader	9	– st Swetman b Bedser	53
D. Bennett b Lock	6	– c and b Lock	6
†J. T. Murray c Loader b Lock	0	– c May b Lock	43
R. W. Hooker c Edrich b Bedser	20	– c Lock b Bedser	6
*P. I. Bedford lbw b Loader	3	– b Bedser	5
C. D. Drybrough not out	11	– c Stewart b Bedser	4
A. E. Moss c Loader b Bedser	0	– not out	1
		B 26, l-b 4	30

1/62 2/69 3/75 4/86 5/98   149   1/27 2/31 3/36 4/125 5/130   201
6/98 7/122 8/132 9/144   6/142 7/161 8/179 9/199

Middlesex Bowling

	Overs	Mdns	Runs	Wkts	Overs	Mdns	Runs	Wkts
Moss	7	4	6	1	11	7	11	1
Bennett	12.4	2	31	2	19	2	72	1
Hooker	17	8	30	5	13	—	42	—
Drybrough	16	10	31	—	25	8	53	1
Titmus	5	2	9	2	37.2	19	39	7
Bedford					5	—	29	—

Surrey Bowling

	Overs	Mdns	Runs	Wkts	Overs	Mdns	Runs	Wkts
Loader	25	6	66	3	9	2	25	—
Sydenham	11	4	16	—	8	3	9	—
Lock	7	4	9	2	33	8	66	4
Bedser	20.2	2	58	5	36.5	9	71	5

Umpires: John Langridge and A. E. Rhodes.

NORTHAMPTONSHIRE

NORTHAMPTONSHIRE v GLOUCESTERSHIRE

Played at Peterborough, June 12, 13, 1946

Gloucestershire won by nine wickets. Wickets tumbled so quickly against spin bowlers, exploiting a pitch damaged by rain, that at the end of the first day Gloucestershire needed only 18 runs for victory with an innings to play. Thirty batsmen were dismissed during the day for 227 runs. For Gloucestershire, Goddard (thirteen for 61) and Cook (six for 33) carried constant danger to Northamptonshire. Merritt also bowled cleverly, and Gloucestershire lost five wickets for 48, but Cranfield, in the highest innings of the match, helped them to a lead of 22. Only half an hour's play was necessary next morning.

Northamptonshire

P. Davis c Lambert b Goddard	25	– b Goddard	4
H. W. Greenwood b Scott	2	– c Scott b Cook	1
E. W. Whitfield b Goddard	4	– lbw b Cook	8
J. E. Timms c Scott b Goddard	8	– lbw b Goddard	0
W. Barron c Wilcox b Cook	30	– b Cook	7
R. Robinson c Scott b Goddard	1	– b Cook	9
W. E. Merritt b Goddard	8	– lbw b Goddard	0
W. Nevell lbw b Goddard	0	– b Goddard	0
P. Murray Willis c Wilson b Cook	0	– b Goddard	5
R. J. Partridge b Goddard	0	– lbw b Goddard	0
E. W. Clark not out	1	– not out	0
B 2, l-b 1, n-b 1	4	B 1, l-b 4	5
	83		**39**

Gloucestershire

B. O. Allen c Partridge b Merritt	10	– not out	11
A. G. S. Wilcox c Greenwood b Merritt	13	– st Greenwood b Merritt	1
W. L. Neale c and b E. W. Clark	0	– not out	7
J. F. Crapp b E. W. Clark	12		
G. M. Emmett st Greenwood b Merritt	7		
A. E. Wilson st Greenwood b Merritt	15		
L. M. Cranfield not out	38		
C. J. Scott c E. W. Clark b Merritt	0		
G. Lambert b Partridge	2		
T. W. Goddard lbw b Merritt	5		
C. Cook c Barron b Merritt	0		
B 1, l-b 1, n-b 1	3		
	105	(1 wkt)	**19**

Gloucestershire Bowling

	Overs	Mdns	Runs	Wkts	Overs	Mdns	Runs	Wkts
Lambert	5	—	10	—				
Scott	5	2	5	1	4	2	4	—
Goddard	13	—	38	7	16	6	23	6
Cook	12.3	5	26	2	12.2	8	7	4

Northamptonshire Bowling

	Overs	Mdns	Runs	Wkts	Overs	Mdns	Runs	Wkts
E. W. Clark	17	7	24	2				
Partridge.........	10	2	15	1				
Merritt	20.3	2	63	7	5	1	10	1
Robinson					4.2	2	9	—

NORTHAMPTONSHIRE v MIDDLESEX

Played at Northampton, August 7, 8, 9, 1946

Middlesex won by an innings and 201 runs. A great all-round performance by Edrich overshadowed all else in their overwhelming victory. Following an opening stand of 141 by Robertson and Brown, Edrich hit four 6s and twenty-three 4s in an enterprising display for 222 not out, lasting only three hours and a half. A. Thompson helped him add 221 for the fifth wicket. Making the ball go through at a good pace Edrich followed his splendid batting by dismissing the first six Northamptonshire batsmen, but a determined seventh-wicket stand of 92 between Merritt and Webster prevented an utter rout. In the follow-on Young bowled skilfully, his left-arm slows causing a complete collapse. In one spell of three overs Young took five wickets, including a hat-trick, for eight runs.

Middlesex

J. D. Robertson c Nevell b Merritt 64	W. F. Price run out 1
S. M. Brown c Barron b Merritt 92	J. Sims not out 8
W. J. Edrich not out 222	B 5, l-b 5, w 1, n-b 1 12
D. Compton c Barron b Merritt 38	
R. W. V. Robins lbw b Merritt 0	───
A. Thompson c Merritt b Whitfield....... 77	(6 wkts dec.) 514

L. Gray, J. A. Young and R. A. Shaddick did not bat.

Northamptonshire

D. Brookes c Price b Edrich	6 – b Gray	24
P. Davis b Edrich	28 – b Edrich	2
E. W. Whitfield c Robertson b Edrich............	6 – c Robins b Young.............	7
J. E. Timms c Compton b Edrich	7 – c Shaddick b Young	2
W. Barron c Price b Edrich....................	2 – b Shaddick	25
H. W. Greenwood c Price b Edrich..............	13 – c Robertson b Young	5
J. Webster c Compton b Gray	24 – b Young	0
W. E. Merritt run out	73 – c Gray b Young	0
R. J. Partridge c Young b Edrich	4 – not out	30
W. Nevell b Gray	9 – b Shaddick	19
E. W. Clark not out.........................	0 – run out	15
B 2, l-b 1, n-b 2	5	B 6, l-b 1...............	7
	177		136

Northamptonshire Bowling

	Overs	Mdns	Runs	Wkts
E. W. Clark	15	1	53	—
Partridge.........	10	—	59	—
Webster	19	—	90	—
Nevell............	17	1	87	—
Merritt	26	1	134	4
Timms	3	—	15	—
Whitfield.........	9	—	39	1
Davis	4	—	25	—

Middlesex Bowling

	Overs	Mdns	Runs	Wkts	Overs	Mdns	Runs	Wkts
Gray............	15.2	4	28	2	9	—	30	1
Edrich...........	26	6	69	7	9	—	23	1
Shaddick.........	3	—	5	—	9	1	28	2
Sims	10	3	28	—				
Young...........	4	1	8	—	13	3	38	5
Robins	3	1	18	—				
Compton	3	—	16	—	4	2	10	—

NORTHAMPTONSHIRE v NOTTINGHAMSHIRE

Played at Peterborough, May 22, 24, 1948

Northamptonshire won by ten wickets. The cleverly flighted left-arm spin bowling of Broderick, who took thirteen wickets for 60 runs, proved the deciding factor in Northamptonshire's first win over their rivals for 38 years. Only Sime, Simpson and Hardstaff did much in the first Nottinghamshire innings, and in the second the batting was even more uncertain. Davis, very painstaking, and Oldfield batted soundly for Northamptonshire, who, after leading by 95, needed only 12 to win.

Nottinghamshire

W. W. Keeton c Timms b Clarke	4	– c Garlick b Broderick	30
W. A. Sime b Garlick	30	– b Broderick....................	15
R. T. Simpson b Broderick	32	– c Oldfield b Nutter	4
J. Hardstaff c Fiddling b Garlick.............	27	– run out	1
F. W. Stocks b Broderick	0	– lbw b Broderick	3
H. Winrow b Broderick.......................	21	– c Bennett b Garlick.............	32
P. Harvey b Garlick	1	– c Fiddling b Broderick	4
H. J. Butler c Bennett b Broderick.............	7	– c Fiddling b Broderick	8
A. Jepson c Brookes b Broderick	1	– st Fiddling b Broderick..........	0
F. G. Woodhead c Timms b Broderick..........	2	– not out	1
E. A. Meads not out	1	– b Broderick...................	0
B 9...............................	9	B 6, l-b 2................	8
	135		**106**

Northamptonshire

D. Brookes b Butler..........................	17	– not out	7
P. Davis b Jepson	61	– not out	5
W. Barron b Butler	8		
N. Oldfield c Meads b Jepson	41		
J. E. Timms st Meads b Harvey	15		
K. Fiddling b Butler	5		
A. E. Nutter b Jepson	27		
A. C. L. Bennett c Meads b Jepson..............	0		
V. Broderick c Hardstaff b Jepson	5		
R. G. Garlick lbw b Jepson....................	5		
R. W. Clarke not out.........................	29		
B 9, l-b 5, n-b 3	17		
	230		(No wkt) **12**

Northamptonshire Bowling

	Overs	Mdns	Runs	Wkts	Overs	Mdns	Runs	Wkts
Clarke............	8	1	29	1	9	3	13	—
Nutter............	7	2	22	—	10	1	32	1
Broderick	26.4	10	31	6	18	9	29	7
Garlick	26	8	44	3	19	7	24	1

Nottinghamshire Bowling

	Overs	Mdns	Runs	Wkts	Overs	Mdns	Runs	Wkts
Butler	29	7	59	3				
Jepson............	31.4	4	69	6				
Winrow..........	13	4	25	—				
Woodhead	17	5	37	—				
Harvey	9	3	23	1				
Sime					1	—	6	—
Simpson					1	—	1	—
Hardstaff					0.4	—	5	—

Umpires: J. Smart and J. T. Bell.

NORTHAMPTONSHIRE v WARWICKSHIRE

Played at Northampton, June 12, 14, 15, 1948

Warwickshire won by 45 runs. Pritchard, the New Zealand fast bowler, who took thirteen wickets for 153, proved the match-winner but Northamptonshire fought hard before going down. The clever spin bowling of C. B. Clarke worried Warwickshire in their first innings, but Pritchard turned the tables. Few could withstand his well-directed bowling, and at one period he claimed seven wickets for 21 runs. Dollery and Spooner, by stylish stroke-play increased Warwickshire's advantage, and Northamptonshire found themselves needing 305 runs to win. Their cause seemed hopeless when five men were disposed of for 70, and although Childs-Clarke and Broderick, with a plucky stand of 116, raised hopes, Pritchard finished the game by taking the last four wickets. Broderick's century was his first for the county.

Warwickshire

W. A. Hill b Garlick 24	– c Fiddling b R. W. Clarke.........	9
F. C. Gardner b C. B. Clarke 28	– c Fiddling b Nutter..............	8
K. A. Taylor b C. B. Clarke 33	– retired hurt	0
H. E. Dollery hit wkt b C. B. Clarke............ 31	– b Nutter	58
J. S. Ord c Broderick b C. B. Clarke............ 40	– st Fiddling b Broderick..........	17
R. T. Spooner lbw b C. B. Clarke 3	– b Nutter	46
A. Townsend b Broderick...................... 5	– not out	33
D. Taylor lbw b Nutter 4	– c Nutter b Garlick	3
C. W. Grove b Nutter......................... 1	– b Nutter	35
T. L. Pritchard not out 13	– b R. W. Clarke.................	7
W. E. Hollies lbw b C. B. Clarke............... 0	– lbw b R. W. Clarke.............	0
B 6, 1-b 2, w 2 10	B 8, 1-b 5...............	13
	192	229

Northamptonshire

D. Brookes c Townsend b Grove	5	– c Spooner b Pritchard	5
K. Fiddling c Dollery b Pritchard	9	– b Pritchard	0
N. Oldfield not out	58	– lbw b Grove	4
W. Barron lbw b Hollies	11	– c Spooner b Grove	15
E. Davis lbw b Pritchard	3	– b Hollies	5
V. Broderick b Pritchard	0	– c and b Pritchard	135
A. E. Nutter b Pritchard	3	– c Townsend b Hollies	12
A. W. Childs-Clarke c Taylor b Pritchard	1	– run out	31
R. G. Garlick b Pritchard	0	– not out	4
C. B. Clarke c Grove b Pritchard	10	– b Pritchard	8
R. W. Clarke c Hollies b Pritchard	12	– c Hollies b Pritchard	13
B 2, l-b 1, n-b 2	5	B 19, l-b 6, n-b 2	27
	117		**259**

Northamptonshire Bowling

	Overs	Mdns	Runs	Wkts	Overs	Mdns	Runs	Wkts
R. W. Clarke	6	2	11	—	23.5	5	59	3
Nutter	9	3	13	2	23	7	44	4
Garlick	27	8	54	1	12	2	35	1
Broderick	38	12	55	1	16	6	22	1
C. B. Clarke	27.4	8	49	6	18	2	56	—

Warwickshire Bowling

	Overs	Mdns	Runs	Wkts	Overs	Mdns	Runs	Wkts
Pritchard	24.3	5	43	8	35.5	3	110	5
Grove	18	4	43	1	24	10	37	2
Hollies	13	5	21	1	31	6	70	2
D. Taylor	3	—	5	—	3	—	6	—
Townsend					6	1	9	—

Umpires: B. Flint and A. Skelding.

NORTHAMPTONSHIRE v LEICESTERSHIRE

Played at Northampton, July 31, August 2, 3, 1948

Leicestershire won by 182 runs. Once more rain intervened at an unfavourable time for Northamptonshire, and with Walsh spinning the ball in puzzling manner they never appeared likely to hit off the 277 needed for victory or hold out for the three hours. Besides Walsh, who returned match figures of thirteen for 108, Berry and Prentice played a big part in Leicestershire's success, their stand of 154 in the second innings turning the fortunes of the game after Northamptonshire, through good medium-fast bowling by Webster and bright batting by Oldfield, led by 33. Tompkin also batted well.

Leicestershire

L. G. Berry c Fiddling b Webster	26	– b R. W. Clarke	92
G. Watson b R. W. Clarke	13	– b Nutter	18
F. T. Prentice lbw b Webster	22	– c Fiddling b Nutter	78
M. Tompkin lbw b Nutter	5	– not out	84
V. E. Jackson b R. W. Clarke	16	– b Nutter	2
G. Lester hit wkt b R. W. Clarke	3		
W. B. Cornock not out	14	– c Fiddling b Webster	8
J. E. Walsh c Nutter b Webster	8	– not out	10
V. Munden c Nutter b Webster	1		
P. Corrall b Nutter	4		
J. Sperry c Fiddling b Nutter	0		
B 9, l-b 3, n-b 3	15	B 13, n-b 4	17
	127	**(5 wkts dec.)**	**309**

Northamptonshire

D. Brookes b Sperry	1	– c Watson b Sperry	6
P. Davis c Prentice b Walsh	16	– run out	4
N. Oldfield c Cornock b Munden	66	– c sub b Sperry	4
W. Barron b Walsh	17	– c Cornock b Walsh	18
V. Broderick b Walsh	0	– c Cornock b Walsh	15
A. E. Nutter c Corrall b Walsh	22	– lbw b Walsh	4
J. Webster run out	2	– b Walsh	5
A. W. Childs-Clarke b Walsh	1	– lbw b Walsh	9
R. W. Clarke b Walsh	9	– c sub b Walsh	15
K. Fiddling b Walsh	7	– not out	4
R. G. Garlick not out	15	– b Sperry	0
B 4	4	B 10	10
	160		**94**

Northamptonshire Bowling

	Overs	Mdns	Runs	Wkts	Overs	Mdns	Runs	Wkts
Nutter	10.5	2	27	3	28	7	89	3
R. W. Clarke	17	2	57	3	29	6	74	1
Webster	18	4	28	4	26	9	55	1
Broderick					24	10	59	—
Garlick					12	5	15	—

Leicestershire Bowling

	Overs	Mdns	Runs	Wkts	Overs	Mdns	Runs	Wkts
Sperry	8	3	20	1	10.1	3	14	3
Cornock	8	2	21	—	4	1	9	—
Walsh	25	5	66	7	26	9	42	6
Jackson	10	1	20	—	15	5	13	—
Munden	14	1	29	1	8	5	6	—

Umpires: H. G. Baldwin and W. H. Ashdown.

NORTHAMPTONSHIRE v SURREY

Played at Northampton, May 18, 19, 20, 1949

Drawn. Much fine cricket, with Whittaker playing two splendid innings and Clarke taking thirteen wickets, kept the crowd entertained, but a thunderstorm ended the game on the last day when an interesting finish seemed in prospect. On the first day Whittaker, in a display of powerful driving, hit nine 6s – three off successive balls from Broderick – and eight 4s, and in the second innings he hit two more 6s and brought his aggregate for the match to 237 for once out. Good bowling on a drying pitch gave Surrey a first innings lead of 102, and Northamptonshire, despite some more excellent medium-fast bowling by Clarke, were left to make 311. They had eight men out for 224 but just as extra time was entered upon the storm stopped play.

Surrey

E. A. Bedser c Fiddling b Clarke	2	– b Clarke	18
L. B. Fishlock lbw b Clarke	3	– b Nutter	0
M. R. Barton c Barron b Clarke	18	– c Nutter b Clarke	32
G. J. Whittaker c Fiddling b Clarke	148	– not out	89
J. F. Parker c Barron b Clarke	21	– lbw b Clarke	0
A. J. McIntyre c and b Clarke	0	– b Clarke	37
B. Constable b Broderick	21	– b Nutter	0
J. C. Laker b Brown	38	– c and b Clarke	2
E. A. Watts b Clarke	10	– c Fiddling b Nutter	13
G. A. R. Lock not out	11	– c Brookes b Clarke	7
J. W. McMahon lbw b Nutter	0		
B 7, l-b 8, w 1, n-b 4	20	B 7, l-b 3	10
	292	**(9 wkts dec.)**	**208**

Northamptonshire

D. Brookes c Laker b Watts	21	– c Barton b Parker	28
P. Davis b Parker	3	– lbw b Watts	10
N. Oldfield b Parker	29	– c Barton b Parker	40
V. Broderick b Watts	15	– b Laker	19
F. Jakeman c Parker b Watts	10	– lbw b Laker	5
F. R. Brown b Lock	51	– lbw b Lock	44
J. E. Timms c Lock b Laker	12	– c Parker b McMahon	28
W. Barron c and b Lock	4	– c Laker b Parker	33
A. E. Nutter st McIntyre b Lock	15	– not out	5
R. W. Clarke not out	17	– not out	16
K. Fiddling c Parker b Lock	2		
B 8, l-b 3	11	B 14, l-b 6	20
	190	**(8 wkts)**	**248**

Northamptonshire Bowling

	Overs	Mdns	Runs	Wkts	Overs	Mdns	Runs	Wkts
Nutter	39	14	74	1	23	8	44	3
Clarke	38	10	88	7	34.5	5	102	6
Brown	18	3	57	1	4	1	8	—
Broderick	7	1	42	1	18	4	44	—
Timms	5	2	11	—				

Surrey Bowling

	Overs	Mdns	Runs	Wkts	Overs	Mdns	Runs	Wkts
Watts	24	7	73	3	8	—	34	1
Parker	21	5	48	2	27	6	66	3
Laker	13	4	31	1	25	6	65	2
Lock	10.3	3	27	4	14	1	36	1
McMahon					9	2	27	1

Umpires: A. Skelding and H. Elliott.

NORTHAMPTONSHIRE v YORKSHIRE

Played at Wellingborough, August 6, 8, 9, 1949

Drawn. A great not-out double century by Hutton reduced almost everything else to insignificance. After playing himself in, he exploited nearly all the strokes with astonishing ease and assurance and during a stay of six and a half hours scarcely made a mistake. His chief hits were thirty-two 4s. There were several three-figure stands during the match, which produced much entertaining cricket. Only one wicket fell on the last day, when Yorkshire declared with a lead of 169. Then Brookes hit his first century against his native county, and he and Oldfield, defying all the bowlers in confident fashion, made 208 for the best Northamptonshire partnership of the season without being separated.

Northamptonshire

D. Brookes c Wilson b Leadbeater	14	– not out	104
N. Oldfield run out	79	– not out	77
W. Barron lbw b Wardle	64		
D. Barrick lbw b Wardle	14		
F. Jakeman hit wkt b Wardle	5		
F. R. Brown c Brennan b Close	79		
V. Broderick b Coxon	55		
A. E. Nutter c Coxon b Close	2		
R. G. Garlick c Hutton b Close	11		
R. W. Clarke not out	7		
K. Fiddling b Coxon	6		
B 10, l-b 7, n-b 1	18	B 19, l-b 7, w 1	27
	354		**(No wkt) 208**

Yorkshire

L. Hutton not out	269	J. H. Wardle b Brown	21	
F. A. Lowson st Fiddling b Garlick	55	E. Leadbeater lbw b Garlick	3	
J. V. Wilson b Brown	3	A. Coxon not out	65	
E. Lester b Nutter	31			
W. Watson c Nutter b Garlick	13	B 28, l-b 7	35	
N. W. D. Yardley b Broderick	11			
D. B. Close run out	17	**(8 wkts dec.) 523**		

D. V. Brennan did not bat.

Yorkshire Bowling

	Overs	Mdns	Runs	Wkts	Overs	Mdns	Runs	Wkts
Coxon	27	11	51	2	6	1	11	—
Yardley	10	2	18	—	2	—	6	—
Leadbeater	31	7	109	1	17	4	61	—
Close	35	9	77	3	17	8	31	—
Wardle	37	9	81	3	28	9	59	—
Lester					2	—	6	—
Watson					2	—	7	—

Northamptonshire Bowling

	Overs	Mdns	Runs	Wkts
Nutter	24	4	61	1
Clarke	12	2	43	—
Brown	38	5	126	2
Garlick	48	7	175	3
Broderick	22	4	83	1

Umpires: A. E. Pothecary and W. H. Ashdown.

NORTHAMPTONSHIRE v KENT

Played at Northampton, May 17, 18, 19, 1950

Northamptonshire won by 187 runs. Superior all-round form entitled them to victory. Brookes put them on the road to success by carrying his bat through the first innings for 166. A wide range of polished strokes brought him one 5 and fourteen 4s. Oldfield, Livingston and Brown also did well with the bat before Wright took five wickets for 11 runs in a remarkable spell. Ames batted best for Kent, but only a plucky effort by Shirreff prevented a follow-on. Livingston drove with power while 115 runs were added in an hour, and Northamptonshire set Kent to get 321 for victory. Fine fast-medium left-arm bowling by Clarke started a collapse from which there was no recovery.

Northamptonshire

D. Brookes not out	166	– b Shirreff	3
N. Oldfield b Ridgway	56	– c Evans b Ridgway	48
L. Livingston c Hearn b Shirreff	46	– b Dovey	87
W. Barron c Fagg b Wright	41	– c Evans b Dovey	36
F. R. Brown c Evans b Wright	4		
F. Jakeman b Wright	0	– not out	2
V. Broderick c Evans b Todd	6		
R. W. Clarke lbw b Wright	2		
R. G. Garlick b Wright	5		
A. E. Nutter c Todd b Dovey	3		
K. Fiddling c Ames b Todd	7		
B 5, l-b 5, n-b 1	11	B 7, l-b 3, n-b 1	11
	347	**(4 wkts dec.)**	**187**

Kent

A. E. Fagg run out	43	– c Fiddling b Clarke	23
A. H. Phebey c and b Brown	11	– b Clarke	22
L. E. G. Ames run out	60	– lbw b Clarke	4
P. Hearn c Nutter b Garlick	7	– b Clarke	9
L. J. Todd c and b Garlick	1	– run out	23
T. G. Evans lbw b Brown	17	– c Nutter b Brown	34
A. C. Shirreff not out	34	– c Garlick b Brown	0
D. G. Clark c Fiddling b Nutter	11	– lbw b Brown	0
R. R. Dovey b Nutter	6	– b Clarke	9
D. V. P. Wright b Nutter	6	– b Broderick	1
F. Ridgway lbw b Brown	1	– not out	2
B 6, l-b 9, n-b 2	17	B 4, l-b 2	6
	214		**133**

Kent Bowling

	Overs	Mdns	Runs	Wkts	Overs	Mdns	Runs	Wkts
Ridgway	22	2	81	1	18	2	84	1
Shirreff	22	1	80	1	10	3	28	1
Dovey	23	5	59	1	9	—	31	2
Wright	25	4	62	5	6	—	33	—
Todd	14.3	2	54	2				

Northamptonshire Bowling

	Overs	Mdns	Runs	Wkts	Overs	Mdns	Runs	Wkts
Nutter............	22	4	58	3	11	3	32	—
Clarke............	20	4	57	—	15.1	3	41	5
Brown............	21.3	2	50	3	8	2	17	3
Garlick...........	26	12	32	2	8	2	11	—
Broderick					9	3	26	1

Umpires: B. Flint and A. R. Coleman.

NORTHAMPTONSHIRE v ESSEX

Played at Northampton, July 14, 16, 17, 1951

Drawn. The match was notable for the innings of 258 not out by Jakeman, a record individual score for Northamptonshire, surpassing the 257 by Bakewell and Brookes. Jakeman delighted the holiday crowd with his fierce hitting. He drove and cut in grand style and his runs, made in five hours and twenty minutes, included four 6s and thirty-five 4s. Apart from chances at 99 and 237, his display was faultless. Broderick and Nutter shared with him in century partnerships. Insole and Gibb, who hit sixteen 4s in the second innings, were the most successful Essex batsmen, and Greensmith earned praise for steady leg-break bowling.

Essex

T. C. Dodds b Nutter	55	– b Brice 2
A. V. Avery c Fiddling b Brice	33	– b Starkie 33
P. A. Gibb c Fiddling b Broderick	27	– st Fiddling b Barrick 138
R. Horsfall b Broderick	7	– b Liddell 69
D. J. Insole b Broderick	71	– c Fiddling b Jakeman 67
R. Smith b Brice	29	– c Fiddling b Starkie.... 16
F. H. Vigar b Nutter	1	– b Jakeman 13
E. A. Stanley b Nutter	0	– not out 7
W. T. Greensmith b Starkie	29	– not out 0
T. P. B. Smith not out	19	
K. C. Preston b Starkie	0	
B 2, l-b 3, n-b 2	7	B 8, l-b 3, n-b 1 12
	278	**(7 wkts) 357**

Northamptonshire

D. Brookes c P. Smith b Preston	7	G. Brice b Greensmith	8
N. Oldfield c Gibb b Preston	18	S. Starkie b Greensmith	0
E. Davis b Preston	0	A. Liddell not out	7
F. Jakeman not out	258		
D. Barrick b Greensmith	28	B 11, w 1, n-b 2	14
V. Broderick lbw b Greensmith	48		
A. E. Nutter b Insole	39	**(8 wkts dec.) 427**	

K. Fiddling did not bat.

Northamptonshire Bowling

	Overs	Mdns	Runs	Wkts	Overs	Mdns	Runs	Wkts
Nutter............	26	4	80	3	23	7	52	—
Liddell...........	19	1	68	—	13	1	60	1
Brice.............	21	2	73	2	16	1	68	1
Broderick	30	15	42	3	11	3	14	—
Starkie	3	1	8	2	32	9	82	2
Barrick					14	—	61	1
Jakeman					3	1	8	2

Essex Bowling

	Overs	Mdns	Runs	Wkts
Preston...........	24	4	71	3
R. Smith..........	27	2	140	—
P. Smith	30	7	100	—
Greensmith........	26	6	68	4
Insole	8.1	1	34	1

Umpires: F. Chester and H. G. Baldwin.

NORTHAMPTONSHIRE v ESSEX

Played at Northampton, July 12, 14, 15, 1952

Drawn. This remarkable match of high scoring was played on a pitch which gave bowlers no encouragement and Avery, Brookes and Barrick each scored double hundreds. Avery batted faultlessly for five and three-quarter hours and hit twenty-three 4s in making the highest score of his career. Gibb shared with him a second-wicket stand of 294. Essex, in their turn, were given a thankless task in the field while Brookes and Barrick made the record Northamptonshire partnership for any wicket – 347 in five and a half hours. Barrick, like Avery, reached his highest score, and mainly by perfectly timed drives and pulls hit thirty-three 4s. Brookes, never perturbed and at ease against pace and spin bowling, defied Essex for nine hours until Brown declared after lunch on the third day. Essex, 104 behind, batted sedately for the rest of the time. Called to keep wicket because three other men were unavailable, Reynolds, a 20-year-old soldier in the Northamptonshire Regiment, allowed only six byes and altogether gave a praiseworthy display.

Essex

A. V. Avery c Barrick b Starkie	224	– not out	62
T. C. Dodds c Oldfield b Clarke	2	– b Brice	56
P. A. Gibb b Brown	132	– c and b Starkie	14
R. Horsfall c Reynolds b Clarke	6	– b Barrick	13
D. J. Insole c and b Broderick	18		
T. E. Bailey c Jakeman b Broderick	1		
K. C. Preston c Broderick b Starkie	4		
F. Rist b Broderick	18		
F. H. Vigar b Starkie	9	– not out	3
W. T. Greensmith not out	4	– st Reynolds b Barrick	4
B 2, l-b 5, w 1, n-b 2	10	B 4, l-b 2	6

1/6 2/300 3/313 4/384   (9 wkts dec.) 428   1/87 2/112 3/139 4/149   (4 wkts) 158
5/386 6/396 7/402 8/418 9/428

C. J. M. Kenny did not bat.

Northamptonshire

D. Brookes not out	204	F. R. Brown c Vigar b Rist	38
V. Broderick b Preston	7		
E. Davis b Greensmith	22	B 7, l-b 3, w 3, n-b 5	18
N. Oldfield b Preston	6		
F. Jakeman b Kenny	26	1/18 2/69 3/76 (6 wkts dec.)	532
D. Barrick c Rist b Greensmith	211	4/125 5/472 6/532	

B. Reynolds, G. Brice, S. Starkie and R. W. Clarke did not bat.

Northamptonshire Bowling

	Overs	Mdns	Runs	Wkts	Overs	Mdns	Runs	Wkts
Brown	34	7	94	1	3	2	1	—
Clarke	28	6	88	2	7	1	37	—
Brice	19	1	88	—	9	—	47	1
Starkie	28	3	99	3	13	3	29	1
Broderick	15	—	49	3	8	1	14	—
Barrick					4	—	17	2
Jakeman					3	—	7	—

Essex Bowling

	Overs	Mdns	Runs	Wkts
Bailey	24	2	79	—
Preston	34	5	89	2
Kenny	39	3	116	1
Insole	24	4	95	—
Greensmith	32	5	109	2
Vigar	4	—	18	—
Rist	4.1	2	8	1

Umpires: T. Spencer and G. S. Mobey.

NORTHAMPTONSHIRE v MIDDLESEX

Played at Peterborough, May 2, 4, 5, 1953

A tie. The fourteenth tie in first-class cricket since the First World War resulted in each side receiving six points, the match being the first to be affected by the new points ruling for tied games. After a poor display in their first innings when batsmen mostly found the fast left-arm bowling of Clarke so difficult that only two reached double figures, Middlesex gained encouragement from a valiant century by Denis Compton. Chiefly through his outstanding performance Northamptonshire were set 227 to win. When their eighth wicket fell Northamptonshire needed only two runs to win, but Leslie Compton stumped Starkie when the scores were level. Then Young needed only one ball to dispose of Fiddling, so that with the last two wickets falling for one run the teams were on equal terms. A splendid fighting innings by Barrick, who remained unbeaten, nearly brought success for Northamptonshire.

Middlesex

J. D. Robertson st Fiddling b Nutter	4	– c Clarke b Brown	16
S. M. Brown b Clarke	6	– b Nutter	42
W. J. Edrich c Livingston b Brown	55	– b Nutter	50
D. C. S. Compton c Fiddling b Clarke	2	– st Fiddling b Starkie	100
A. Thompson c Fiddling b Clarke	5	– b Brown	30
D. Bennett b Clarke	0	– b Brown	35
F. J. Titmus lbw b Clarke	0	– lbw b Brown	1
L. H. Compton c Clarke b Tribe	0	– lbw b Tribe	10
J. J. Warr c Tribe b Brown	15	– c Fiddling b Brown	11
J. A. Young not out	7	– not out	7
A. E. Moss lbw b Brown	0	– b Brown	2
B 2	2	B 7, l-b 1	8

1/7 2/15 3/30 4/37 5/39   96   1/56 2/66 3/177 4/244 5/246   312
6/49 7/54 8/82 9/96   6/247 7/269 8/288 9/304

Northamptonshire

D. Brookes run out	53	– c Moss b Warr	4
N. Oldfield b Young	31	– c Robertson b Moss	4
L. Livingston b Moss	8	– c L. Compton b Moss	12
F. Jakeman c L. Compton b Young	1	– c L. Compton b Moss	5
D. Barrick c and b Moss	4	– not out	80
G. E. Tribe b Warr	45	– b Moss	56
F. R. Brown c D. Compton b Edrich	9	– b Bennett	34
A. E. Nutter b Bennett	1	– b Moss	8
R. W. Clarke c Brown b Moss	14	– b Edrich	8
S. Starkie b Warr	3	– st L. Compton b Young	0
K. Fiddling not out	1	– b Young	0
B 5, l-b 6, n-b 1	12	B 10, l-b 3, n-b 2	15

1/57 2/70 3/71 4/76 5/130   182   1/8 2/8 3/13 4/39 5/150   226
6/139 7/140 8/170 9/181   6/189 7/202 8/225 9/226

Northamptonshire Bowling

	Overs	Mdns	Runs	Wkts	Overs	Mdns	Runs	Wkts
Nutter	10	3	21	1	22	5	46	2
Clarke	22	9	31	5	15	6	42	—
Brown	8.5	2	23	3	37.5	15	71	6
Tribe	9	2	19	1	17	—	62	1
Starkie					36	9	83	1

Middlesex Bowling

	Overs	Mdns	Runs	Wkts	Overs	Mdns	Runs	Wkts
Moss	18	2	61	3	31	9	68	5
Warr	9	3	13	2	14	1	38	1
Young	18	8	42	2	21.1	12	18	2
Titmus	8	2	14	—				
Bennett	9	2	22	1	16	1	35	1
Edrich	10	4	18	1	2	2	—	1
D. Compton					16	1	52	—

Umpires: K. McCanlis and H. Palmer.

NORTHAMPTONSHIRE v KENT

Played at Northampton, August 26, 27, 28, 1953

Kent won by four runs. Ten minutes of extra time remained when a misunderstanding between Nutter and Oldfield, their last two batsmen, resulted in defeat for Northamptonshire. Oldfield, who went in with an injured arm, attempted to snatch a quick single, but Nutter, whose batting seemed likely to bring success for Northamptonshire, hesitated and was easily run out. Brown's first century of the season for Northamptonshire deservedly brought cheers from the crowd. Making some mighty hits, Brown punished Dovey for 20 in one over, and his 101 in two hours included three 6s and thirteen 4s. Kent were indebted to Hearn and Wright for outstanding performances. When four men were out for 36, Hearn remained undaunted, and 132, his best score for the county, occupied nearly three and a half hours. Skilfully flighted leg-breaks earned Wright a match analysis of ten wickets for 157.

Kent

A. E. Fagg b Clarke	26	– st Reynolds b Brown	38
A. H. Phebey c Reynolds b Nutter	11	– b Tyson	23
A. F. Woollett c Reynolds b Clarke	20	– b Brown	5
P. Hearn lbw b Brown	27	– st Reynolds b Brown	132
A. C. Shirreff b Broderick	38	– c Brown b Tyson	0
T. G. Evans b Brown	10	– c Brown b Nutter	32
B. R. Edrich c Nutter b Broderick	6	– lbw b Nutter	2
F. Ridgway not out	10	– c Davis b Tyson	21
A. W. H. Mallett c Reynolds b Tyson	8	– b Nutter	33
R. R. Dovey b Clarke	0	– b Tribe	5
D. V. P. Wright b Nutter	1	– not out	1
B 2, l-b 9, n-b 5	16	B 15, l-b 7	22

1/23 2/59 3/70 4/117 5/132   **173**   1/53 2/65 3/91 4/91 5/145   **314**
6/150 7/151 8/167 9/168   6/154 7/216 8/272 9/312

Northamptonshire

D. Brookes hit wkt b Wright	63	– lbw b Shirreff	16
V. Broderick b Mallett	32	– c Ridgway b Wright	9
E. Davis lbw b Wright	1	– c Hearn b Wright	15
B. C. Reynolds c Edrich b Wright	12	– b Shirreff	6
N. Oldfield b Wright	0	– not out	0
G. E. Tribe c Fagg b Mallett	0	– c Phebey b Wright	41
F. R. Brown c Phebey b Wright	101	– lbw b Mallett	48
D. G. Greasley not out	33	– lbw b Mallett	2
A. E. Nutter b Mallett	0	– run out	26
F. H. Tyson b Ridgway	18	– c Ridgway b Wright	6
R. W. Clarke lbw b Shirreff	21	– c Edrich b Wright	4
B 13, l-b 7	20	B 4, l-b 4, n-b 1	9

1/53 2/56 3/78 4/80 5/85   **301**   1/32 2/36 3/42 4/54 5/136   **182**
6/165 7/242 8/243 9/274   6/144 7/149 8/168 9/172

Northamptonshire Bowling

	Overs	Mdns	Runs	Wkts	Overs	Mdns	Runs	Wkts
Tyson	9	5	13	1	11	3	38	3
Clarke	18	5	37	3	7	1	26	—
Nutter	14	6	24	2	15	2	53	3
Brown	20	6	35	2	31	10	77	3
Tribe	17	2	45	—	24	8	76	1
Broderick	5	4	3	2	7	1	22	—

Kent Bowling

	Overs	Mdns	Runs	Wkts	Overs	Mdns	Runs	Wkts
Ridgway..........	13	1	46	1	4	1	8	—
Shirreff...........	9	—	35	1	13	2	35	2
Mallett	28	5	82	3	13	3	41	2
Wright	24	8	77	5	19	3	80	5
Dovey...........	9	2	41	—	4	2	9	—

Umpires: H. Elliott (Lancashire) and A. E. Pothecary.

NORTHAMPTONSHIRE v GLOUCESTERSHIRE

Played at Kettering, July 2, 4, 5, 1955

Gloucestershire won by 154 runs. Fine batting by Young and Graveney for Gloucestershire, and Brookes, the home captain, was the feature of a keen match. Young scored a century in each innings, and Graveney narrowly failed to join the ranks of those who have scored a hundred before lunch. The Gloucestershire score passed 250 for two in under three hours, but the later batsmen failed against Tribe. Brookes, despite bruised ribs which gave him considerable pain, shared a stand of 106 with Arnold, this being Northamptonshire's third century opening partnership in successive innings, but after Arnold left only Broderick gave the captain useful assistance. Gloucestershire's declaration did not give Graveney the chance of following Young's example of scoring two hundreds in the match, but the England batsman was rewarded by the best bowling figures when Northamptonshire batted again. Northamptonshire were handicapped by Tyson's absence, and an injury to Subba Row, who cut his hand over the week-end and took no further part in the match.

Gloucestershire

D. M. Young b Tribe...........................121	– not out 117
C. C. Milton lbw b Hogan...................... 10	– b Clarke 29
T. W. Graveney c Arnold b Wild 101	– not out 75
J. F. Crapp c and b Tribe 32	
G. M. Emmett c Clarke b Tribe 12	
G. E. Lambert not out......................... 45	
J. Mortimore c Andrew b Clarke 5	
P. Rochford lbw b Tribe 2	
C. Cook c Reynolds b Tribe 7	
B. D. Wells run out 1	
F. P. McHugh st Andrew b Tribe 8	
B 9, l-b 9, n-b 1 19	B 5, l-b 2............... 7

1/17 2/198 3/272 4/286 5/287   363   1/67   (1 wkt dec.) 228
6/310 7/321 8/341 9/350

Northamptonshire

D. Brookes c Graveney b McHugh	95	– c Milton b Wells	20
P. Arnold b McHugh	56	– c Milton b Lambert	0
L. Livingston c Milton b Lambert	22	– c Wells b Lambert	0
B. Reynolds b Lambert	0	– b Graveney	50
G. E. Tribe b Mortimore	9	– c Wells b Mortimore	51
V. Broderick c Young b Lambert	36	– lbw b Wells	1
K. V. Andrew b McHugh	32	– c Milton b Graveney	14
J. Wild b Lambert	4	– c Emmett b Graveney	0
R. Hogan c Rochford b Lambert	4	– lbw b Wells	0
R. W. Clarke not out	18	– not out	0
R. Subba Row absent hurt	0	– absent hurt	0
B 2, l-b 5, w 1	8	B 3, l-b 14	17

1/106 2/138 3/146 4/163 5/219 284 1/7 2/9 3/59 4/61 5/97 153
6/228 7/241 8/251 9/284 6/142 7/142 8/145 9/153

Northamptonshire Bowling

	Overs	Mdns	Runs	Wkts	Overs	Mdns	Runs	Wkts
Clarke	27	9	56	1	15	1	57	1
Hogan	14	1	67	1	11	2	62	—
Tribe	25	3	116	6	13	—	37	—
Broderick	22	7	67	—	8	1	34	—
Wild	12	3	38	1	6	—	31	—

Gloucestershire Bowling

	Overs	Mdns	Runs	Wkts	Overs	Mdns	Runs	Wkts
Lambert	34	9	81	5	12	4	23	2
McHugh	32	6	87	3	11	7	14	—
Wells	13	3	20	—	19	5	66	3
Graveney	6	1	20	—	5.5	2	18	3
Cook	18	6	35	—	2	—	5	—
Mortimore	19	7	33	1	7	2	10	1

Umpires: E. A. Roberts and K. McCanlis.

NORTHAMPTONSHIRE v KENT

Played at Northampton, August 20, 22, 23, 1955

Drawn. After a run of six successive victories, Northamptonshire were lucky to escape defeat. At the close they were 79 behind, with only one wicket left. Allan, the Oxford Blue, was in excellent batting form for the visitors. He hit a century in each innings, and in the second shared a stand of 173 with Phebey, whose 122 was his highest score in first class cricket. Extras, contributed no fewer than 73 – more than any single batsman – to Northamptonshire's first innings total. Sunburn seriously impeded Catt's movements, and he found difficulty in taking Wright, who spun the ball sharply. In the Northamptonshire second innings the Kent captain made a determined attempt to bowl his side to victory, with six for 32, but Webster survived the final over.

Kent

A. E. Fagg c Tribe b Webster	3	– b Webster	15
A. H. Phebey b Tribe	16	– c Reynolds b Tribe	122
J. M. Allan not out	121	– c Broderick b Greasley	105
R. C. Wilson c Livingston b Tribe	24	– st Livingston b Subba Row	26
J. Pettiford c Brookes b Tribe	4	– not out	40
P. Hearn c Webster b Subba Row	27	– not out	37
B. E. Disbury lbw b Tribe	0		
A. Dixon c Greasley b Tribe	11		
A. W. Catt b Tribe	4		
J. Spanswick st Livingston b Subba Row	0		
D. V. P. Wright st Livingston b Subba Row	0		
B 5, l-b 3	8	B 8, l-b 4	12

1/5 2/23 3/104 4/116 5/172   218   1/23 2/62 3/235   (4 wkts dec.) 357
6/177 7/205 8/217 9/218   4/293

Northamptonshire

D. Brookes c Phebey b Dixon	26	– lbw b Wright	15
P. Arnold c and b Disbury	1	– c Fagg b Spanswick	3
L. Livingston b Dixon	62	– b Disbury	19
R. Subba Row c Phebey b Allan	33	– c Allan b Wright	6
B. Reynolds run out	47	– c Fagg b Wright	30
D. G. Greasley lbw b Wright	23	– lbw b Wright	0
G. E. Tribe c Allan b Pettiford	0	– c Disbury b Wright	28
V. Broderick c Fagg b Allan	55	– not out	8
F. H. Tyson c Dixon b Allan	36	– b Wright	0
J. Wild c Disbury b Allan	17	– b Pettiford	2
J. Webster not out	1	– not out	0
B 48, l-b 23, w 2	73	B 1, l-b 9, w 1	11

1/3 2/76 3/103 4/212 5/212   374   1/20 2/38 3/80 4/80 5/89   (9 wkts) 122
6/239 7/263 8/322 9/366   6/94 7/105 8/105 9/116

Northamptonshire Bowling

	Overs	Mdns	Runs	Wkts	Overs	Mdns	Runs	Wkts
Tyson	16	3	37	—	17	4	39	—
Webster	13	5	25	1	9	—	38	1
Tribe	27	5	76	6	26	6	84	1
Broderick	15	8	23	—	22	3	59	—
Subba Row	10.5	3	22	3	10	3	35	1
Wild	8	—	27	—	17	4	53	—
Greasley					7	—	37	1

Kent Bowling

	Overs	Mdns	Runs	Wkts	Overs	Mdns	Runs	Wkts
Spanswick	13	3	43	—	6	—	26	1
Disbury	4	2	16	1	7	1	33	1
Allan	22	7	81	4				
Dixon	23	4	61	2				
Wright	22	8	58	1	12	6	32	6
Pettiford	16	6	42	1	10	4	20	1

Umpires: G. S. Mobey and J. J. Hills.

NORTHAMPTONSHIRE v SURREY

Played at Northampton, June 5, 6, 7, 1957

Surrey won by ten wickets. The match was made memorable by Stewart holding seven catches during the Northamptonshire second innings. No fielder in first-class cricket other than a wicket-keeper had previously taken so many during a single innings, and only twice had even a wicket-keeper held seven. On rain-affected turf, Stewart fielded very close to the accurate bowling of Alec Bedser, Lock and Laker. He took six catches at backward short-leg and one in the gully. None was really difficult. Apart from aggressive driving by Barrick, Northamptonshire struggled against keen bowling on a good pitch during their first innings. Surrey, too, had to earn runs, but they batted consistently, with May in particularly good form. Their lead of 98 proved most valuable when rain livened the pitch and made conditions possible for Stewart's catching feat.

Northamptonshire

D. Brookes c Lock b A. Bedser	7	– c Lock b A. Bedser	6
B. L. Reynolds b Loader	2	– c Stewart b A. Bedser	26
L. Livingston b A. Bedser	0	– c Stewart b A. Bedser	0
D. W. Barrick c McIntyre b Lock	86	– c Barrington b A. Bedser	33
A. Lightfoot lbw b Laker	29	– c Stewart b Lock	5
G. E. Tribe b E. Bedser	22	– c Stewart b Lock	11
J. S. Manning b E. Bedser	0	– c Stewart b Laker	10
K. V. Andrew run out	6	– not out	12
F. H. Tyson not out	34	– c Stewart b Laker	4
M. H. J. Allen b A. Bedser	5	– c McIntyre b Lock	0
H. R. A. Kelleher b Laker	13	– c Stewart b Lock	0
B 2, l-b 6, n-b 1	9	B 4	4

1/9 2/9 3/9 4/86 5/145   213   1/11 2/11 3/52 4/59 5/71   111
6/145 7/147 8/161 9/184   6/87 7/95 8/98 9/101

Surrey

D. G. W. Fletcher c Manning b Tribe	37	– not out	8
M. J. Stewart c Andrew b Manning	24	– not out	6
B. Constable b Allen	42		
P. B. H. May c Kelleher b Tyson	96		
K. F. Barrington b Kelleher	10		
E. A. Bedser c Livingston b Tyson	46		
A. J. McIntyre b Tribe	27		
G. A. R. Lock st Andrew b Tribe	0		
J. C. Laker c Manning b Tribe	11		
P. J. Loader c Brookes b Tribe	4		
A. V. Bedser not out	0		
B 7, l-b 7	14		

1/58 2/78 3/157 4/212 5/224   311   (No wkt) 14
6/269 7/281 8/299 9/310

Surrey Bowling

	Overs	Mdns	Runs	Wkts	Overs	Mdns	Runs	Wkts
Loader	26	9	54	1	9	2	26	—
A. Bedser	26	6	58	3	16	5	43	4
Laker	13.3	10	14	2	12	6	14	2
Lock	23	10	45	1	9.2	1	20	4
E. Bedser	16	2	33	2	1	—	4	—

Northamptonshire Bowling

	Overs	Mdns	Runs	Wkts	Overs	Mdns	Runs	Wkts
Tyson	25.4	8	47	2				
Kelleher	22	7	39	1				
Manning	26	10	81	1	1.5	1	8	—
Tribe	26	3	73	5				
Allen	20	8	57	1	1	—	6	—

Umpires: F. S. Lee and A. Skelding.

UPS AND DOWNS OF NORTHAMPTONSHIRE [1958]

By James D. Coldham

Northamptonshire County Cricket Club grew naturally out of the Northampton Town Club which was formed in 1820 and by 1850 was the most powerful in the county. Some of the members were drawn from outlying districts, and in the latter year the local Press began referring loosely to this Town Club as "Northamptonshire". The venue was the Northampton Race Course, an expanse of 120 acres and for generations a public right-of-way, jealously guarded by the Freemen and townspeople.

In the 'seventies representative cricket was at a low ebb and, as the outcome of a discussion on July 3, 1878, during the annual North versus South Northants match at Kettering, a Public Meeting at the George Hotel, Kettering, on July 31 considered "the best means of placing the County Club on a footing of equality with other counties". As it was realised that "Northamptonshire" had never been properly organised and was really a town club supported by few of the gentry, a Committee was elected *representing all parts of the County*, the Earl Spencer remaining President. Other notable officials were Sir Herewald Wake, a member of MCC, the Hon. and Rev. J. Marsham of the eminent Kent family, and Mr Fred Tebbutt, proprietor of a shoe business and energetic Honorary Secretary, who arranged more ambitious fixtures.

From 1881 until 1885, of thirty-five matches eighteen were won and eight lost. Essex and MCC were defeated; the first game (in 1884) at Wellingborough School saw Warwickshire worsted by an innings. Eighteen of Northamptonshire met the Australians in 1880 and two years later the County played them (with the aid of Alfred Shaw) on equal terms; both ventures were lost.

Tom Bowley, Joe Potter and Tom Alley secured 458 wickets. A schoolmaster, G. J. Gulliver, hit the first century, 103, off MCC at Lord's in 1884; and five brothers Kingston batted zestfully. Eight of them appeared between 1874 and 1909.

NEW COUNTY GROUND

As a small body of Freemen claimed that they possessed the freehold of the Race Course, the expansion of County Cricket there was impossible. Once a brewer's dray was driven deliberately across the pitch prepared by the Yorkshire-born groundsman, who gave the driver a good thrashing and asked the Committee for a small rise in pay.

In 1885 a ploughed field of ten acres of Abington Parish was purchased from Sir R. Loyd Lindsay (afterwards Lord Wantage) by the new "Northamptonshire County Cricket and Recreation Grounds Company, Ltd.", Sir Herewald Wake and Mr Joseph Hill, Squire of Wollaston, advancing £2,000 for the site. The first match at the present County Ground was on May 14, 16, 1886, when Surrey Club and Ground won by six wickets.

Northamptonshire did not flourish as the best professionals were lured to more prosperous counties, Arthur Mold, for instance, joining Lancashire and playing for England; the membership was about 300; the County families remained aloof; finance was always a worry.

THE MINOR COUNTIES CHAMPIONSHIP

Wellingborough School and the local Leagues produced some talented players, and in 1896 a rebuilt side entered the Minor Counties Championship. Between 1899 and 1904 they enjoyed substantial success, twice winning the title outright and twice tying for first place. No matches were lost between July 1898 and July 1901.

The genial Reptonian, Tom Horton, was captain and he was assured of class batting from the impetuous C. J. T. Pool, more solidity from W. H. Kingston, and ballast down to number eleven. Besides scoring prolifically, G. J. Thompson and W. East carried the attack. From 1898 until 1904 ninety-one games brought them 964 wickets. Thompson was the greatest all-rounder ever produced by Northamptonshire; East was a capable and accurate medium pacer and dour batsman.

GEORGE THOMPSON

An Old Wellingburian, George Thompson, first appeared in 1895 at the age of seventeen, and bowled and batted the County into first-class cricket. With his complete double circle of the arm action, he was above medium pace and brought the ball off the ground with plenty of life and spin. His length was superb. As a batsman he tended to be over-cautious, but when conditions warranted he would hit hard and often. Close in he held many catches. In Minor County days he scored 5,174 runs, average 35.93, and took 751 wickets at 14.01 runs each; and from 1905 until 1922 his figures were 8,322 runs, average 23.57, and 1,078 wickets at 18.88 runs each. The first Northants player to represent England against Australia – at Birmingham in 1909 – Thompson came second to Hobbs with an average of 33.37 in the Tests in South Africa that winter, besides taking 23 wickets.

Promotion came in 1905, and no one worked harder for it than the open-handed and enthusiastic President, Lord Lilford, and the Honorary Secretary, the gifted Mr A. J. Darnell, a household name in Law, Politics and Sport.

During the first four seasons irresolute and unenterprising batting were the bane, excepting such as C. J. T. Pool's 166 at Worcester, Dr H. C. Pretty's 200 in as many minutes at Chesterfield, and Thompson's not out 103 at Fenner's after Cambridge had routed them for 57 and replied with 405, all in 1906. Top class spinners were specially feared. In 1907 Blythe of Kent took seventeen wickets in one day; and when at Ashley Down the County sank to a new low – 12 all out – before Gloucestershire's Dennett, a telegram to the captain, E. M. Crosse, read: "Bring the Boys Home – Mother".

Thompson and East virtually monopolised the attack until 1908 when W. "Bumper" Wells, who could make the ball fly disagreeably, earned a regular place. They commanded respect. At The Oval in 1906 Surrey were dismissed on a plumb pitch for 96; the same year Thompson secured fifteen for 167 against Leicestershire at Northampton. It was heartening to beat Lancashire by one wicket at Northampton; and Northants did *not* finish last in those years.

NEW BLOOD

Composed almost entirely of local men, the team received an enlivening "shot in the arm" from outside. Fresh natives like the Denton twins, J. S. and W. H., both sound run-getters, F. "Fanny" Walden, a mighty atom of cricket and soccer, and stout W. A. Buswell, a cheerful 'keeper, were joined by four bold batsmen, R. A. Haywood and C. N. Woolley from Kent, John Seymour from Sussex and versatile S. G. Smith, the outstanding West Indian all-rounder who was, moreover the first high-class left-hander Northamptonshire possessed.

HALCYON DAYS

After a poor start in 1909, eight of nine consecutive matches were won, the bowling of Smith and Thompson, who each took a hundred wickets and were admirably contrasted, being supported by increasingly offensive batting and lively fielding. Despite a drop from seventh to tenth place in 1910, S. G. Smith notched a thousand runs; at Sheffield, Yorkshire were beaten for the first time by five wickets, G. A. T. Vials contributing a sparkling 100. With Gloucestershire at Northampton 1,391 runs were scored for thirty-six wickets, including a mighty 204 by Smith. At Portsmouth, Northants were in dire straits until Smith and Thompson added 232. In 1911 only once was a total of 300 exceeded against the attack; and the batting advanced in all the rightful qualities. Against Gloucestershire at home Thompson and Haywood hit 222 in two and a half hours; the same pair put on 236 at Dewsbury. East's seven for 11 at the expense of Lancashire compensated somewhat for two collapses. Kent, however, were overcome at Tonbridge by 135 runs, Thompson securing twelve wickets; and everyone pulled well to beat Yorkshire at Northampton by 44 runs.

In the wet 1912 Northants finished a close second to Yorkshire. Ten matches were won and one lost out of eighteen. A reasonable assumption is that if rain had not curtailed play on August 7, Yorkshire (103 and 105 for seven wickets) could have been beaten by Lancashire (347) and Northants (211 for eight wickets declared) could have upset Leicestershire (96 and 96 for six wickets) – and Northamptonshire would have displaced Yorkshire! The success was due to the determination of the captain, Vials, the collective power resulting from constant association – only twelve appeared in the County matches – and excellent, well-varied bowling. Vials headed the batting with an average of 28.26; Smith took 84 wickets at 12.15 runs each and Thompson 106 at 14.59 each.

RUMPUS AT LORD'S

All was not well with County Cricket and early in 1913 A. J. Darnell, a pioneer of the Saturday start, proposed to the Advisory Committee of MCC that matches be restricted to two days and there be a system of promotion and relegation. Lord Hawke, who favoured a smaller Championship, complained that Northamptonshire were taking too much of a lead. After a rumpus at Lord's, Lord Harris stilled the troubled waters and Mr Darnell apologised for having unintentionally caused antipathy – and a few days later Yorkshire were beaten at Leeds by 20 runs, Smith (the new captain) and Thompson collecting eighteen wickets.

Northants finished fourth, winning thirteen games. Batsmen made great strides, four reaching four figures – Haywood 1,453, Smith 1,424, W. H. Denton 1,055 and J. S. Denton 1,007 – and Thompson mustered 902 runs. Between them, Thompson and Smith secured 255 wickets. At Bristol, 516 was compiled in little over five hours, this orgy being led by Smith and Haywood, who in two hours added 216 for the third partnership. At Leyton, W. H. Denton carried out his bat for a solid 230. At Horsham, Thompson and Smith, who each took ten wickets, bowled unchanged.

S. G. Smith's "swan-song" in 1914 brought him 1,193 runs, average 41.13, and 99 wickets at 16.63 runs apiece. Again, his chief helper was Thompson. Despite a fall to ninth place, the County continued strongly all round. Against Sussex at Brighton their 557 for six wickets, declared, remains the highest ever; Smith stole the honours with 177, adding 180 with Thompson. Fifty-five matches had been won in six great years, but financially the club was as certain of instability as the Liberal Party was of power.

In 1919 S. G. Smith was domiciled in New Zealand and Thompson wounded and ill; the head and the right arm were gone. Under a succession of captains the County struggled. 1921 found Haywood glorious with 1,909 runs, average 42.42, including eight centuries; it was a severe blow when he departed that autumn. Financial losses resulted in two general meetings battling over Reconstruction; V. W. C. Jupp of Sussex and England was appointed Secretary and Stephen Schilizzi emerged as a benefactor of the practical "Cricket is a business" School.

In February 1923 a prominent local agriculturalist, Alfred Cockerill, who had spent £10,000 in acquiring the County Ground, gave it to the club to be preserved for sport for ever; a unique gift. That year, however, Northants finished last for the first time.

JUPP THE CORNERSTONE

V. W. C. Jupp was qualified in 1924. The following summer he scored 1,143 runs and took 110 wickets; it was the cornerstone of the most successful season between the wars when nine encounters brought victory and eleventh place was attained. The short, broad and increasingly rotund Jupp threw himself into the fight against odds. Secretary for eleven years, captain for six, a nimble-footed batsman on all sorts of wickets and a grand adaptable off- and leg-spinner, he scored 13,635 runs, average 30.44, and collected 1,078 wickets, average 22.31; six times he achieved the "double" for the County before he gave up in 1938.

In the 'twenties other remarkable exponents included Woolley, by now reliant on economy of effort at number one; "Fanny" Walden, at his best when the need was greatest; A. P. R. Hawtin, a stylish and confident stroke-maker; Ben Bellamy, second best wicket-keeper-batsman in the country; "Bumper" Wells, veteran fast bowler and hard hitter; length specialist A. E. Thomas, "the William Attewell of Northants cricket"; two class batsmen in H. F. Bagnall and W. W. Timms; and E. W. "Nobby" Clark, a fast left-hander with a beautiful action who touched a peak that few others of his generation reached. Eighteen seasons brought him 1,097 wickets at 21.31 runs apiece, and eight appearances for England.

The measure of the weakness was revealed to the full against Yorkshire, although Jupp, Wells, Thomas and Clark sometimes bowled wonderfully well against the strongest county.

THE ARRIVAL OF BAKEWELL

In 1930 the Australians were spun out at Northampton for 93, but Northants finished at the foot of the table. Things became worse, and although in September 1931, a Special General Meeting assented to the continuance of the club, thorough-going retrenchment was advocated.

Northants commenced 1933 by overwhelming West Indies by an innings and 62 runs; though they finished disappointingly, A. H. Bakewell shone brightly. He became the first to reach 2,000 in all matches in a season, which included 246 against Nottinghamshire at Northampton and 257 against Glamorgan at Swansea in successive innings. A great future was being forecast for him. Making his début in 1928, he impressed immediately with his brilliancy at short-leg; later his stroke-play won him his place for England. A better batsman than he looked, in an effort of 30 he would produce every stroke in the game, his off-driving being particularly exhilarating. Returning from Chesterfield after the last match of 1936, in which he batted superbly for 241 not out, Bakewell was injured in a tragic car smash; his career was finished and Northants, who would soon be bereft of Jupp and Clark, could ill-afford to lose him.

SNOWDEN'S FEATS

A. W. Snowden, an amateur opening batsman from Peterborough, made his début against New Zealand in 1931 at the age of 17; he scored his first fifty against India and his maiden century against Australia. He captained the county at the age of 18 and before he was 21 he and Bakewell achieved a feat which was then without parallel by compiling two opening stands of over 100 on the same day against Warwickshire at Edgbaston. Unfortunately business claimed him soon after he came of age.

Between May 1935 and May 1939, 101 matches failed to produce a victory. It was a shocking patch, but several players epitomised "Courage": J. E. Timms, a well-equipped and defiant cavalier batsman and relisher of any fight with high-bouncing bowlers; young Dennis Brookes, already looking an England batsman with his upstanding stance and style of purest simplicity; R. J. Partridge, swinging the new ball appreciably and spurred on by his thankless task; New Zealander, K. C. James, maintaining his international reputation behind the stumps; and a born leader, R. P. Nelson, the powerful left-handed Cambridge Blue, taking charge in 1938 and bringing the County finally out of the slough of despond in May 1939, when Leicestershire were vanquished at Northampton by an innings and 193 runs.

R. P. Nelson was killed, alas in 1940; but Northamptonshire's Elder Statesman, A. P. R. Hawtin, and an enthusiastic captain, P. E. Murray Willis, kept the club in the news. Matches were played *each* war summer, and this shire which had finished seventeenth eight times between 1919 and 1939 did more for the game than any other.

The opening match in 1946 was appropriately at Lord's with Middlesex; at the close the Middlesex last pair were together and 23 runs were needed. There was a heightened tone about Northamptonshire's cricket; subsequent results disappointed. One recalls pleasurably the opening stands of Brookes and Percy Davis; left-handed Barron, so full of promise; the comeback of "Nobby" Clark, for five overs the fastest in the land; Timms at cover; and slow left-hander Vincent Broderick, a young England hope; but few matches ended in their favour. A strong leader was required.

F. R. BROWN ERA

In 1949 F. R. Brown of Cambridge, Surrey and England, who was living at Daventry, took the reins, and a "New Look" transformed the County. He understood the game thoroughly; at his elbow were a revitalised Executive and a playing staff rich in numbers and prowess. Winning ten matches in 1949, Northants jumped to sixth place; in 1952 they finished eighth. Skipper from 1949 to 1953, Brown, when freed from representative calls, scored with his pugnacious approach 4,331 runs, average 30.94, and took 391 wickets, average 23.23, while reshaping the seam, leg-break and googly departments. His right-hand man was the Yorkshireman Brookes; when at Headingley in 1953 Yorkshire were defeated for the first time in forty years, he was both acting-captain and century-maker. These years saw two pre-war Lancastrians in Norman Oldfield, overflowing with neat strokes and scorer in 1949 of 2,192 runs, average 49.81, and Albert Nutter, a hostile opening bowler; F. Jakeman who, by fierce left-handed hitting in 1951, made 558 runs in four consecutive innings before dismissal, including 258 not out off Essex at Northampton; Frank Tyson, the fastest bowler in the country; Australians "Jock" Livingston, a left-handed batsman and ubiquitous fieldsman of sheer delight, and George Tribe of Herculean all-round feats; and Desmond Barrick, who hits the ball harder than most.

NOTABLE PERSONALITIES

As captain since 1954 the quiet, knowledgeable and shrewd Brookes has proved even more successful than Brown. No longer is the Northampton pitch easy paced and a nightmare to all bowlers alike; decisive results have increased. Since 1955, Surrey have been beaten four times; and Northants rose from seventh in 1954 and 1955 to fourth in 1956, and to second in 1957 – the most successful campaign in their history, with 218 points from 28 matches, of which 15 were won. The battery of left-handed spinners, including one Tribe who accomplished the "double" for the sixth successive year, and the "Typhoon" that did *not* fizzle out into a gentle zephyr, together with a grand 'keeper in Andrew who created a new Northants record (68 victims), were the men-of-the-season. The potential is tremendous; the best has not yet been seen of the Cambridge Blue, Raman Subba Row, who in 1955 broke fresh ground in hitting 260 not out against Lancashire at Northampton, and several young bowlers who may well beat Tribe's record of 175 wickets taken the same year. Through it all remains Dennis Brookes, who first appeared in 1934, and is the sheet-anchor in a side of quick scorers. No one has amassed more runs for the county: 26,075, average 36.52, which includes 257 off Gloucestershire at Bristol in 1949; or more centuries: 63; or more runs in a season: 2,198, average 51.11 in 1952.

No reference to Northamptonshire cricket would be complete without mention of Leo Bullimer who was for 51 years the county scorer until retiring in 1950. His efforts in raising funds did much to keep Northamptonshire going during some of their worst financial crises.

A CONTROVERSY

Why do Northamptonshire engage so many players from outside (especially from overseas)? The answer is plain. A small county without either the population or resources of Yorkshire, Northamptonshire, nevertheless, possess a public with the palate for good cricket – and cricketers. Therefore, while talent scouts comb the county and trials are held regularly, experts from elsewhere are encouraged to become specially registered. Financial backing? That go-ahead modern firm, British Timken, is prepared to offer winter employment, something that redounds to the honour and skill of the present-day professional; and there is a football competition, organised by the county's eleven-year-old Supporters Club which, whatever else one may think of it, makes football serve the needs of cricket. The county have 2,000 members; 63,000 odd if one includes those who support this competition.

Heading for the title of "Champion County", Northamptonshire consider they are doing a real service to English cricket by making so many excellent craftsmen available for our delectation.

NORTHAMPTONSHIRE v WORCESTERSHIRE
(D. Brookes's Benefit)

Played at Northampton, July 26, 28, 1958

Northamptonshire won by four wickets. Once more Tribe spun his side to victory, their sixth in successive matches. He took nine wickets for 43 runs in Worcestershire's second innings, the best figures of his career, and thirteen for 99 in the match. Only Horton and the 17-year-old Slade were not puzzled by the left-arm slow bowling of Tribe and Manning in the first innings and Kenyon saved a complete rout in the second. He hit 56, including nine 4s, out of 71 before dislodging a bail with his trousers when pulling Tribe. Gloomy weather on Saturday did not please the beneficiary Brookes, who was out cheaply, but first Arnold and later Lightfoot batted well in helping Northamptonshire to lead by 32 runs on the first innings. In their second innings Northamptonshire, needing 88 to win, owed much to Barrick for fine attacking batting.

Worcestershire

D. Kenyon c Allen b Tyson	8	– hit wkt b Tribe	56
L. Outschoorn c Andrew b Manning	8	– b Tribe	13
M. J. Horton b Manning	26	– c Andrew b Tribe	8
D. W. Richardson b Manning	12	– b Tribe	4
R. G. Broadbent b Tribe	10	– c Reynolds b Tribe	9
G. Dews b Tribe	12	– c Arnold b Allen	7
R. Booth st Andrew b Tribe	3	– c Barrick b Tribe	7
D. Slade not out	36	– st Andrew b Tribe	1
K. J. Aldridge lbw b Manning	3	– st Andrew b Tribe	0
R. Berry b Tribe	4	– not out	4
J. Flavell b Manning	4	– st Andrew b Tribe	1
B 3	3	B 5, l-b 4	9

1/14 2/16 3/34 4/57 5/73	129	1/33 2/78 3/84 4/85 5/98	119
6/81 7/86 8/105 9/118		6/100 7/105 8/109 9/116	

Northamptonshire

D. Brookes c Booth b Aldridge	7	– lbw b Slade	8
P. Arnold c Flavell b Berry	43	– lbw b Horton	10
B. Reynolds c Aldridge b Horton	20	– c Dews b Horton	0
D. W. Barrick run out	13	– c Dews b Slade	41
A. Lightfoot b Horton	41	– c Outschoorn b Slade	10
G. E. Tribe c and b Aldridge	0	– b Slade	4
M. Norman b Horton	16	– not out	3
J. S. Manning c Richardson b Slade	1	– not out	12
F. H. Tyson not out	11		
K. V. Andrew c Broadbent b Horton	0		
M. H. J. Allen c Richardson b Horton	8		
L-b 1	1	L-b 2	2

1/23 2/69 3/78 4/101 5/102   161   1/16 2/16 3/64 4/69   (6 wkts) 90
6/141 7/142 8/144 9/149   5/73 6/76

Northamptonshire Bowling

	Overs	Mdns	Runs	Wkts	Overs	Mdns	Runs	Wkts
Tyson	8	2	12	1	4	1	9	—
Lightfoot	2	—	10	—	2	—	3	—
Manning	23	8	42	5	9	2	31	—
Tribe	23	5	56	4	21.2	9	43	9
Allen	6	3	6	—	14	6	24	1

Worcestershire Bowling

	Overs	Mdns	Runs	Wkts	Overs	Mdns	Runs	Wkts
Flavell	5	2	10	—	2	—	4	—
Aldridge	12	1	42	2	1	—	3	—
Slade	21	11	21	1	18.3	8	35	4
Horton	25	8	52	5	22	12	33	2
Berry	17	7	35	1	3	1	13	—

Umpires: D. J. Wood and P. A. Gibb.

NORTHAMPTONSHIRE v MIDDLESEX

Played at Northampton, June 24, 25, 26, 1959

Drawn. They were given an excellent start by Brookes and Arnold with an opening partnership of 109 and always looked the more impressive side. Brookes when 45 reached 30,000 runs, a notable landmark in his long career, and he went on to score his seventy-first century as well as his second in three days. Middlesex struggled after rain delayed the resumption three and a half hours on the second day, mainly because of some grand fielding. McGibbon and Manning ran out Hooker and Titmus with splendid throws, and Subba Row and Tribe took excellent catches. Middlesex declared 120 behind in order to keep the game alive but the final task set them, 219 in one hour fifty minutes, was not attempted after Robertson had fallen to McGibbon's first ball.

Northamptonshire

D. Brookes c Robertson b Hurst	147	– not out		55
P. Arnold c Parfitt b Moss	64	– lbw b Titmus		24
D. W. Barrick c and b Titmus	25	– c Murray b Robins		9
R. Subba Row run out	21	– c Bennett b Titmus		1
P. J. Watts b Bennett	30	– not out		2
G. E. Tribe not out	28			
J. S. Manning not out	1			
L-b 6	6	B 6, n-b 1		7

1/109 2/173 3/214   (5 wkts dec.) 322   1/43 2/70 3/71   (3 wkts dec.) 98
4/271 5/316

P. D. Watts, K. V. Andrew, J. G. Williamson and L. McGibbon did not bat.

Middlesex

J. D. Robertson c Subba Row b Tribe	37	– c Williamson b McGibbon		0
W. E. Russell c Andrew b Williamson	8	– c Andrew b Tribe		11
P. H. Parfitt c Tribe b P. D. Watts	39	– c Andrew b Williamson		7
R. W. Hooker run out	0	– not out		13
A. C. Walton lbw b Manning	8	– c Manning b P. D. Watts		9
F. J. Titmus run out	27	– not out		10
J. T. Murray not out	46			
D. Bennett b P. D. Watts	0			
R. V. C. Robins c Subba Row b Manning	4			
A. E. Moss not out	21			
B 9, l-b 2, w 1	12			

1/23 2/70 3/75 4/92   (8 wkts dec.) 202   1/0 2/10 3/20 4/29   (4 wkts) 50
5/112 6/136 7/140 8/148

R. J. Hurst did not bat.

Middlesex Bowling

	Overs	Mdns	Runs	Wkts	Overs	Mdns	Runs	Wkts
Moss	22	2	81	1	6	—	17	—
Bennett	12	1	47	1	3	—	24	—
Titmus	25	7	54	1	15	2	37	2
Robins	21	6	57	—	12	2	12	1
Hurst	34	12	76	1	1	—	1	—
Parfitt	1	—	1	—				

Northamptonshire Bowling

	Overs	Mdns	Runs	Wkts	Overs	Mdns	Runs	Wkts
McGibbon	18	5	29	—	4	2	3	1
Williamson	10	2	31	1	3	1	9	1
Tribe	29	8	73	1	11	2	24	1
Manning	26	12	36	2	4	3	4	—
P. D. Watts	16	9	21	2	8	3	10	1

Umpires: C. S. Elliott and F. S. Lee.

NORTHAMPTONSHIRE v MIDDLESEX

Played at Kettering, July 27, 28, 29, 1960

Middlesex won by an innings and 14 runs. Until Moss, the Middlesex pace bowler, began a rout on the last day, neither side gained any marked advantage. Middlesex led on first innings by 72, mainly because of a fine century (two 6s and eight 4s) by Gale, his first of the summer. He saw Drybrough, White and Hooker all dismissed by Scott, a left-arm slow bowler, in eleven balls without cost but found a capable partner in Parfitt. Moss took two wickets before the close of the second day, but with Northamptonshire only 47 behind the match still looked fairly open. Then came the debacle. Another six batsmen were out to Moss for 13 runs in thirteen overs and with Titmus taking the last two wickets, Northamptonshire were routed for 58. Finding more pace in the pitch than any other bowler during the match, Moss dismissed three batsmen at 43 and with final figures of eight for 31 he achieved his best performance.

Northamptonshire

M. Norman b Drybrough	62	– c Titmus b Moss	7
B. Reynolds run out	24	– c Murray b Moss	8
P. Arnold c Murray b Drybrough	53	– c Murray b Moss	18
P. J. Watts b Drybrough	4	– c and b Moss	9
*D. W. Barrick c Parfitt b Moss	18	– lbw b Moss	2
B. Crump not out	46	– lbw b Moss	0
M. Scott c Murray b Warr	3	– c Parfitt b Moss	0
F. H. Tyson c Murray b Warr	2	– c sub b Moss	4
M. H. J. Allen c Murray b Moss	2	– b Titmus	1
†K. V. Andrew b Moss	7	– b Titmus	2
J. D. F. Larter b Drybrough	1	– not out	3
B 1, l-b 2	3	L-b 4	4

1/49 2/139 3/143 4/146 5/182   225 1/15 2/16 3/30 4/43 5/43 58
6/191 7/193 8/196 9/220   6/43 7/44 8/53 9/53

Middlesex

W. E. Russell b Allen	26	D. Bennett c Watts b Larter	54
R. A. Gale c Norman b Tyson	101	†J. T. Murray c and b Allen	7
C. D. Drybrough b Scott	9	*J. J. Warr c Andrew b Larter	0
R. A. White c Andrew b Scott	0	A. E. Moss not out	4
R. W. Hooker c Andrew b Scott	0	B 11, l-b 6	17
P. H. Parfitt c Larter b Crump	78		297
F. J. Titmus b Tyson	1		

1/60 2/79 3/87 4/87 5/183
6/190 7/243 8/284 9/286

Middlesex Bowling

	Overs	Mdns	Runs	Wkts	Overs	Mdns	Runs	Wkts
Moss	27	6	60	3	21	7	31	8
Warr	14	3	26	2	4	3	5	—
Titmus	25	8	46	—	11.1	7	9	2
Drybrough	29.5	14	53	4	13	11	9	—
Bennett	6	—	16	—				
Hooker	5	3	14	—				
Gale	1	—	7	—				

Northamptonshire Bowling

	Overs	Mdns	Runs	Wkts
Larter	17	3	40	2
Tyson	23	2	73	2
Allen	20	6	36	2
Crump	31	13	50	1
Scott	35	12	81	3

Umpires: J. H. Parks and W. H. Copson.

NORTHAMPTONSHIRE v DERBYSHIRE

Played at Northampton, May 20, 22, 23, 1961

Northamptonshire won by 129 runs. The bowlers held the upper hand throughout, with Allen, left-arm slow, doing most to bring about victory. He took his eight wickets in Derbyshire's first innings at a cost of 19 runs during a spell of 71 balls and his full analysis of eight for 48 was his best to that time. Match figures of thirteen for 98 reflected his influence on the match. Rhodes also bowled creditably on a pitch not normally helpful to fast bowlers. The best performance with the bat again came from Williamson, who hit his third score of over 50 inside a week just at a time when Northamptonshire needed runs on the first day. Subsequently, Hall and Lee put on 90 for Derbyshire's first wicket in reply to a total of 251. Then Allen started his fine spell during a second day in which 25 wickets fell for 323 runs and Derbyshire never looked like scoring the 263 they needed to win.

Northamptonshire

M. Norman b Rhodes	24	– c Dawkes b Rhodes	55
B. L. Reynolds c Dawkes b Richardson	24	– c Hall b Rhodes	0
D. Ramsamooj c Richardson b Berry	20	– b Rhodes	0
*R. Subba Row c Dawkes b Rhodes	9	– b Smith	37
P. J. Watts c Rhodes b Berry	33	– c Rhodes b Smith	19
B. Crump c Dawkes b Rhodes	12	– c Berry b Rhodes	2
P. D. Watts c Rhodes b Smith	24	– c Hall b Smith	31
J. G. Williamson not out	70	– c Dawkes b Rhodes	2
M. H. J. Allen b Richardson	2	– lbw b Smith	5
†K. V. Andrew b Rhodes	24	– not out	6
J. D. F. Larter b Buxton	0	– not out	0
B 3, l-b 3, n-b 3	9	B 4, n-b 2	6

1/38 2/63 3/79 4/87 5/108   251   1/12 2/12 3/73 4/113 5/115   163
6/138 7/172 8/211 9/250   6/119 7/130 8/151 9/162

Derbyshire

I. W. Hall b Allen	27	– b Allen	18
C. Lee b Allen	61	– b P. D. Watts	22
*D. B. Carr lbw b P. D. Watts	0	– b Allen	0
D. Millner c Ramsamooj b Allen	16	– c Allen b P. D. Watts	0
R. Swallow lbw b Allen	10	– b Larter	4
I. R. Buxton c Williamson b Allen	1	– c Subba Row b Allen	22
†G. O. Dawkes not out	27	– c Reynolds b P. D. Watts	37
E. Smith b Allen	0	– c P. D. Watts b Allen	20
G. W. Richardson b Allen	1	– c P. J. Watts b Allen	6
H. J. Rhodes b Allen	2	– not out	0
R. Berry c Crump b Larter	4	– c Andrew b P. D. Watts	1
B 2, n-b 1	3	L-b 1, w 2	3

1/90 2/91 3/99 4/107 5/116   152   1/11 2/47 3/47 4/47 5/51   133
6/119 7/119 8/125 9/131   6/104 7/109 8/126 9/132

Derbyshire Bowling

	Overs	Mdns	Runs	Wkts	Overs	Mdns	Runs	Wkts
Rhodes	26	8	71	4	16	3	48	5
Richardson	18	3	55	2	9	2	23	—
Buxton	16	6	25	1	7	1	12	—
Berry	22	9	43	2	14	7	33	—
Smith	22	9	48	1	23.1	10	41	5

Northamptonshire Bowling

	Overs	Mdns	Runs	Wkts	Overs	Mdns	Runs	Wkts
Larter............	19.5	5	59	1	5	—	26	1
Williamson........	9	3	21	—	4	2	2	—
Allen.............	28	13	48	8	21	7	50	5
P. D. Watts.......	14	7	21	1	20.3	6	52	4

Umpires: J. H. Parks and R. S. Lay.

NORTHAMPTONSHIRE v SURREY

Played at Northampton, June 3, 5, 1961

Surrey won by 256 runs, taking 14 points from their first Championship victory of the season. They completed the match on the evening of the second day by dismissing Northamptonshire for 61 in ninety-seven minutes through the combined efforts of Gibson, Bedser and Lock. Gibson dismissed Norman, Ramsamooj and Subba Row, the same three batsmen who in the first innings had figured in his hat-trick, the first of the season. Then Northamptonshire had escaped complete rout through the efforts of Milburn, a 19-year-old 17-stone opening batsman playing in only his second county game. He hit one 6 and eleven 4s. All this came after Surrey scored 326. Andrew dismissed his 500th victim when he held Stewart off the second ball of the game but subsequently Edrich (eighteen 4s) and Barrington led the run getting with a second-wicket stand of 135 in two hours ten minutes.

Surrey

M. J. Stewart c Andrew b Larter.................	0 – not out 42
J. H. Edrich c Ramsamooj b Watts...............107 – c Crump b Lightfoot............. 69
K. F. Barrington b Ashenden 57
*P. B. H. May c Watts b Allen 30
B. Constable c Andrew b Ashenden 39
M. D. Willett c Milburn b Watts 7
†R. Swetman st Andrew b Allen................. 41
G. A. R. Lock b Ashenden 10
E. A. Bedser c Crump b Ashenden 8
D. Gibson not out............................ 4
D. A. D. Sydenham b Allen 9
B 5, w 1, n-b 8...................... 14	B 4, l-b 1............... 5

1/0 2/135 3/183 4/219 5/228   326 1/116   (1 wkt dec.) 116
6/263 7/283 8/313 9/313

Northamptonshire

M. Norman c May b Gibson...................	4 – c Stewart b Gibson............. 2
C. Milburn c Lock b Bedser	63 – c Swetman b Sydenham 0
D. Ramsamooj b Gibson	0 – c Lock b Gibson............... 19
*R. Subba Row c Willett b Gibson	0 – c Swetman b Gibson........... 2
A. Lightfoot c Swetman b Gibson................	12 – c Lock b Bedser 16
B. Crump c Swetman b Sydenham	8 – c Swetman b Lock............. 12
P. D. Watts b Gibson	7 – c May b Bedser............... 3
M. H. J. Allen c Swetman b Lock	0 – c Edrich b Bedser 1
†K. V. Andrew lbw b Lock	21 – c Stewart b Bedser 0
M. Ashenden b Gibson	4 – st Swetman b Lock............. 0
J. D. F. Larter not out........................	1 – not out 1
L-b 2, n-b 1, w 2	5 B 4, l-b 1............... 5

1/4 2/8 3/8 4/41 5/76   125 1/0 2/10 3/12 4/31 5/51   61
6/92 7/95 8/107 9/119   6/51 7/54 8/54 9/55

Northamptonshire Bowling

	Overs	Mdns	Runs	Wkts	Overs	Mdns	Runs	Wkts
Larter	17	5	44	1	6	2	14	—
Ashenden	20	2	77	4	7	2	27	—
Lightfoot.	15	5	29	—	6.3	1	7	1
Watts	14	1	54	2				
Allen.	31	9	67	3	10	3	34	—
Crump	14	5	41	—	10	2	29	—

Surrey Bowling

	Overs	Mdns	Runs	Wkts	Overs	Mdns	Runs	Wkts
Gibson	20	6	50	6	8	2	15	3
Sydenham.	11	3	26	1	7	—	27	1
Bedser.	13	10	9	1	8.3	5	4	4
Lock	25.3	13	35	2	7	4	10	2

Umpires: J. Arnold and H. J. Baldwin.

NOTTINGHAMSHIRE

NOTTINGHAMSHIRE v DERBYSHIRE

Played at Nottingham, August 17, 19, 20, 1946

Drawn. Derbyshire began badly, but Vaulkhard – whose 264 was the highest individual innings of the season – with the aid of Denis Smith completely altered the aspect of affairs. Vaulkhard, formerly a Nottinghamshire player, had never before completed a century. Twice missed before reaching three figures, he hit two 6s and thirty-one 4s during just over seven hours at the wicket. Smith, also in fine form, helped him add 328. Only Hardstaff and Heane batted well for Nottinghamshire, who were in trouble when following-on, but rain limited play to fifty minutes on the last day.

Derbyshire

A. E. Alderman c Heane b Jepson	4
A. Townsend b Butler	19
C. S. Elliott b Woodhead	9
P. Vaulkhard b Butler	264
D. Smith lbw b Jepson	146
A. Revill b Woodhead	6
E. Marsh run out	13
A. E. Rhodes b Butler	2
G. F. Hodgkinson c Harris b Jepson	21
C. Gladwin not out	14
B 8, l-b 22, w 1	31

(9 wkts dec.) 529

W. H. Copson did not bat.

Nottinghamshire

W. W. Keeton b Gladwin	1	
C. B. Harris c Alderman b Copson	10	
R. T. Simpson b Rhodes	38	– not out 10
J. Hardstaff lbw b Gladwin	65	
G. F. H. Heane c and b Gladwin	63	– not out 0
G. L. Willatt c Smith b Gladwin	41	– c Smith b Gladwin 1
F. W. Stocks c Smith b Copson	4	
A. Jepson c Elliott b Marsh	7	
H. J. Butler b Copson	2	
E. A. Meads not out	6	
F. G. Woodhead b Gladwin	0	
B 16, l-b 10, w 2	28	

265   (1 wkt) 11

Nottinghamshire Bowling

	Overs	Mdns	Runs	Wkts
Butler	42.2	5	126	3
Jepson.	36	5	123	3
Woodhead	46	10	141	2
Stocks.	4	—	10	—
Harris	40	9	98	—

Derbyshire Bowling

	Overs	Mdns	Runs	Wkts	Overs	Mdns	Runs	Wkts
Copson	30	5	83	3	4	1	7	—
Gladwin	32.5	13	58	5	5	2	4	1
Rhodes	20	4	58	1	1	1	—	—
Revill	15	2	33	—				
Marsh	4	1	5	1				

NOTTINGHAMSHIRE v WARWICKSHIRE

Played at Nottingham, May 8, 10, 11, 1948

Nottinghamshire won by eight wickets. In a thrilling race against time they scored at three runs a minute and knocked off 76 with seven minutes to spare. A grand innings by Hardstaff, who batted four and three-quarter hours for 182 not out and hit nineteen 4s, and century stands between Keeton and Harris and Harris and Hardstaff assured Nottinghamshire of a good total. Harris missed his hundred after a stay of four hours ten minutes. A century in each innings by Ord failed to save Warwickshire. Missed before scoring, Ord batted four and three-quarter hours in the first innings and just over three hours when Warwickshire followed-on 200 behind.

Nottinghamshire

W. W. Keeton b Townsend	67	– c Spooner b Grove	32
C. B. Harris c and b Hollies	92		
R. T. Simpson b Hollies	2	– b Grove.	0
J. Hardstaff not out	182	– not out	3
R. Giles c Spooner b Pritchard	14		
H. Winrow run out	9		
W. A. Sime c Grove b Hollies	26	– not out	38
A. Jepson c Dollery b Pritchard	29		
H. J. Butler b Grove	3		
F. G. Woodhead b Pritchard.	0		
E. A. Meads run out	0		
B 7, l-b 4	11	B 4	4
	435	**(2 wkts)**	**77**

Warwickshire

Batsman	1st innings	2nd innings
R. T. Spooner c Meads b Woodhead	13	lbw b Woodhead	10
K. A. Taylor lbw b Woodhead	5	b Butler	0
J. S. Ord not out	107	c Woodhead b Winrow	101
H. E. Dollery b Jepson	40	c Meads b Butler	53
A. V. Wolton lbw b Jepson	11	c and b Winrow	25
A. Townsend c Meads b Winrow	15	not out	56
F. R. Mitchell b Winrow	0	b Butler	0
C. W. Grove b Butler	14	b Winrow	6
V. H. D. Cannings b Woodhead	10	b Jepson	5
T. L. Pritchard b Woodhead	4	c Meads b Butler	9
W. E. Hollies c and b Jepson	1	lbw b Winrow	2
B 11, l-b 3, n-b 1	15	B 3, l-b 5	8
	235		**275**

Warwickshire Bowling

	Overs	Mdns	Runs	Wkts	Overs	Mdns	Runs	Wkts
Pritchard	30	3	84	3	4.5	—	40	—
Grove	20.5	2	68	1	4	—	33	2
Hollies	46	5	124	3				
Townsend	17	1	66	1				
Cannings	19	—	82	—				

Nottinghamshire Bowling

	Overs	Mdns	Runs	Wkts	Overs	Mdns	Runs	Wkts
Butler	26	8	46	1	21	3	57	4
Jepson	32.3	12	51	3	26	7	69	1
Woodhead	23	11	37	4	22	6	54	1
Winrow	39	15	86	2	27.2	11	56	4
Sime					6	2	12	—
Harris					4	—	11	—
Giles					2	—	2	—
Hardstaff					1	—	6	—

Umpires: A. R. Coleman and G. M. Lee.

NOTTINGHAMSHIRE v NORTHAMPTONSHIRE

Played at Nottingham, May 28, 30, 31, 1949

Nottinghamshire won by three wickets. The match was a personal triumph for Hardstaff, who hit a hundred in each innings and scored 214 without being dismissed. His first effort was careful and he took over four hours to reach his hundred. In the second innings, when Nottinghamshire were set to get 243 in 155 minutes, Hardstaff reached three figures at a run a minute and Nottinghamshire won with ten minutes to spare. Both sides batted carefully in the first innings, Nottinghamshire declaring with a lead of 14 after a splendid fight for the lead. A well-played hundred by Brookes enabled Northamptonshire to declare, but their bowlers wilted before the Nottinghamshire onslaught.

Northamptonshire

D. Brookes lbw b Jepson	10	– c and b Jepson	106
N. Oldfield run out	29	– b Woodhead	64
W. Barron c Meads b Harris	6	– c Poole b Harvey	14
E. Davis c Harris b Harvey	31	– not out	6
V. Broderick c Hardstaff b Harvey	34		
F. R. Brown c Hardstaff b Woodhead	33	– c Harvey b Woodhead	42
F. Jakeman b Harris	46	– not out	13
A. E. Nutter b Jepson	1		
R. W. Clarke b Harris	10		
C. B. Clarke not out	2		
K. Fiddling c Stocks b Harris	3		
B 5, l-b 1	6	B 8, l-b 3	11
	211	**(4 wkts dec.)**	**256**

Nottinghamshire

R. T. Simpson b Broderick	29	– c Brookes b R. W. Clarke	18
C. B. Harris c C. B. Clarke b Broderick	24	– c Brown b R. W. Clarke	23
E. A. Meads c and b Broderick	0		
F. G. Woodhead c Nutter b R. W. Clarke	1	– b Brown	1
H. Winrow b R. W. Clarke	6	– c Davis b Broderick	17
J. Hardstaff not out	100	– not out	114
C. J. Poole c Brown b R. W. Clarke	11	– c Brown b Broderick	2
F. W. Stocks c R. W. Clarke b Broderick	48	– c Fiddling b Brown	17
J. D. Clay not out	0	– not out	17
A. Jepson (did not bat)		– c Brookes b Brown	26
L-b 6	6	B 3, l-b 6, w 1	10
	(7 wkts dec.) 225		**(7 wkts) 245**

P. F. Harvey did not bat.

Nottinghamshire Bowling

	Overs	Mdns	Runs	Wkts	Overs	Mdns	Runs	Wkts
Jepson	22	1	69	2	26	4	83	1
Woodhead	19	8	32	1	27	1	66	2
Harris	35	10	63	4	6	2	6	—
Harvey	20	5	41	2	26	3	72	1
Stocks					3	—	18	—

Northamptonshire Bowling

	Overs	Mdns	Runs	Wkts	Overs	Mdns	Runs	Wkts
Nutter	10	4	16	—				
R. W. Clarke	31.1	10	78	3	9	—	40	2
C. B. Clarke	20	3	49	—				
Broderick	39	18	44	4	22	—	96	2
Brown	21	10	32	—	19.5	1	99	3

Umpires: A. R. Coleman and A. Lockett.

NOTTINGHAMSHIRE v SURREY

Played at Nottingham, June 4, 6, 7, 1949

Nottinghamshire won by eight wickets. For the second home match running they hit off the runs required to win at a tremendous rate. Set to get 206 in two hours they actually obtained 209 in ninety-seven minutes. Fishlock hit a hundred in each innings for Surrey, but his efforts were not enough. Simpson twice batted brilliantly for Nottinghamshire. In the first innings he scored a double hundred in four hours forty minutes and hit twenty-seven 4s. When Nottinghamshire began their final task Simpson and Hardstaff gave them a great start by scoring 120 in fifty-five minutes. Sime carried on the big hitting and obtained three 6s and six 4s in 58 made in thirty-six minutes.

Surrey

L. B. Fishlock b Jepson	111	– c sub b Woodhead	118
D. G. W. Fletcher run out	56	– c Winrow b Harvey	28
H. S. Squires lbw b Sime	2	– c Meads b Woodhead	43
G. J. Whittaker b Harris	13	– st Meads b Woodhead	1
J. F. Parker b Sime	1	– not out	7
M. R. Barton c Harris b Jepson	14	– not out	2
A. J. McIntyre c Simpson b Harris	43	– st Meads b Sime	0
E. A. Bedser c and b Harvey	25		
J. C. Laker b Jepson	11		
A. V. Bedser not out	8		
J. W. McMahon c Winrow b Harris	2		
L-b 8, n-b 4	12	B 7, l-b 3	10
	298	**(5 wkts dec.)**	**209**

Nottinghamshire

R. T. Simpson not out	200	– run out	46
C. B. Harris c McIntyre b Squires	48		
H. Winrow b A. V. Bedser	16		
J. Hardstaff not out	32	– c A. V. Bedser b E. A. Bedser	74
J. D. Clay (did not bat)		– not out	27
W. A. Sime (did not bat)		– not out	58
B 2, l-b 1, n-b 3	6	B 4	4
	(2 wkts dec.) 302		**(2 wkts) 209**

F. W. Stocks, A. Jepson, P. F. Harvey, F. G. Woodhead and E. A. Meads did not bat.

Nottinghamshire Bowling

	Overs	Mdns	Runs	Wkts	Overs	Mdns	Runs	Wkts
Jepson	38	9	98	3	13	1	46	—
Woodhead	19	8	27	—	22	4	69	3
Harris	34.3	13	55	3				
Clay	3	1	9	—				
Sime	24	10	30	2	9	—	35	1
Harvey	22	4	67	1	12	1	49	1

Surrey Bowling

	Overs	Mdns	Runs	Wkts	Overs	Mdns	Runs	Wkts
A. V. Bedser	24	3	78	1	12	2	56	—
Parker	15	2	55	—	6.3	—	42	—
Laker	24	6	50	—	4	—	23	—
McMahon	13	1	40	—	5	—	37	—
E. A. Bedser	17	6	38	—	9	1	47	1
Squires	18.4	5	35	1				

Umpires: G. M. Lee and W. Ashdown.

NOTTINGHAMSHIRE v LEICESTERSHIRE

Played at Nottingham, June 15, 16, 17, 1949

Nottinghamshire won by nine wickets. Yet again they easily beat the clock after being set what looked to be a difficult task. Leicestershire began with an opening stand of 107 between Berry and Lester, but collapsed. Bold hitting by Walsh helped in a recovery. Simpson, missed first ball, stayed just over four hours for 143 which included seventeen 4s, but despite this effort Nottinghamshire led by only 16. Lester played another good innings for Leicestershire, who declared and set Nottinghamshire to score 279 in 145 minutes. Simpson and Poole won the match during an unbroken second wicket stand of 251 in ninety-seven minutes. Poole, in that time, obtained 154 with the help of twenty-one 4s. Simpson, who hit a hundred in each innings for the first time in his career, took a hundred minutes over his second century.

Leicestershire

L. G. Berry c Meads b Butler	50	– c Meads b Jepson	30
G. Lester b Woodhead	68	– not out	122
F. T. Prentice b Butler	31	– b Jepson	83
M. Tompkin c Meads b Butler	4	– b Sime	45
V. E. Jackson lbw b Jepson	1	– not out	10
G. Watson run out	12		
J. E. Walsh c Poole b Sime	57		
S. J. Symington c Meads b Sime	34		
V. Munden lbw b Jepson	8		
P. Corrall not out	10		
J. Sperry b Jepson	1		
B 4, l-b 11, w 1	16	B 2, l-b 2	4
	292	**(3 wkts dec.)**	**294**

Nottinghamshire

W. W. Keeton lbw b Lester	31	– run out	17
R. T. Simpson b Sperry	143	– not out	102
H. Winrow c Corrall b Sperry	27		
J. Hardstaff b Walsh	14		
C. J. Poole c Symington b Walsh	8	– not out	154
J. D. Clay not out	57		
W. A. Sime b Walsh	16		
A. Jepson b Walsh	2		
H. J. Butler b Walsh	0		
E. A. Meads c Lester b Sperry	1		
F. G. Woodhead b Walsh	2		
B 4, l-b 1, w 2	7	B 3, l-b 2, w 1	6
	308	**(1 wkt)**	**279**

Nottinghamshire Bowling

	Overs	Mdns	Runs	Wkts	Overs	Mdns	Runs	Wkts
Butler	24	5	47	3	4	2	7	—
Jepson	29.1	5	67	3	28	4	114	2
Woodhead	26	6	69	1	22	6	75	—
Sime	32	8	70	2	21	5	55	1
Winrow	7	—	23	—	11	1	39	—

Leicestershire Bowling

	Overs	Mdns	Runs	Wkts	Overs	Mdns	Runs	Wkts
Sperry............	29	6	70	3	7	—	50	—
Symington	9	2	32	—	3	—	24	—
Walsh............	34.2	2	125	6	7	—	53	—
Jackson...........	16	5	25	—	9	—	68	—
Lester	12	1	36	1	5	—	48	—
Munden	7	1	13	—	4	—	30	—

Umpires: F. S. Lee and K. McCanlis.

NOTTINGHAMSHIRE v HAMPSHIRE

Played at Nottingham, June 10, 12, 13, 1950

Drawn. Hampshire's prospects were bright when Cannings, their right-arm fast-medium bowler, shattered the wickets of Clay, Giles and Hardstaff at a personal cost of two runs, but they reckoned without Harris. This experienced player stayed all day for 169 and finally carried his bat for 239, which included two 5s and thirty-one 4s. Formidable as Nottinghamshire's total of 401 seemed, Hampshire passed it for the loss of six wickets. The stand of 199 by McCorkell and Rogers fell only five short of the county's record opening partnership. Arnold, like McCorkell and Rogers, occupied more than four hours for his century, but he and Shackleton brought more life to the game when they added 101 in ninety-five minutes.

Nottinghamshire

C. B. Harris not out 239	A. Jepson c McCorkell b Walker 0
J. D. Clay b Cannings.................. 4	E. A. Meads c Harrison b Knott.......... 31
R. Giles b Cannings 0	C. S. Matthews lbw b Cannings 6
J. Hardstaff b Cannings 2	H. J. Butler lbw b Gray................. 42
W. A. Sime b Carty.................... 0	B 5, l-b 11, n-b 1.............. 17
F. W. Stocks b Shackleton 48	___
F. Stinchcombe lbw b Knott............. 12	401

Hampshire

N. McCorkell b Jepson.................109	E. D. R. Eagar b Stocks 26
N. H. Rogers b Matthews...............100	D. Shackleton run out.................. 46
L. Harrison b Jepson................... 3	V. H. D. Cannings not out 6
J. Arnold not out.....................107	B 26, l-b 17.................. 43
J. R. Gray c Jepson b Stinchcombe........ 3	___
C. Walker c Meads b Butler 25	(7 wkts) 468

R. Carty and C. J. Knott did not bat.

Hampshire Bowling

	Overs	Mdns	Runs	Wkts
Shackleton	56	14	120	1
Cannings	52	19	96	4
Carty	9	1	38	1
Knott	25	7	91	2
Walker	16	9	31	1
Gray.............	1.3	—	8	1

Nottinghamshire Bowling

	Overs	Mdns	Runs	Wkts
Butler	35	10	79	1
Jepson.	29	8	68	2
Matthews	21	8	41	1
Stinchcombe.	32	7	119	1
Stocks.	35	9	75	1
Harris	32	14	32	—
Clay	7	4	10	—
Hardstaff	2	1	1	—

Umpires: H. L. Parkin and E. Robinson.

NOTTINGHAMSHIRE v NORTHAMPTONSHIRE

Played at Nottingham, June 27, 28, 29, 1951

Drawn. In yet another match of huge scoring, 1,045 runs were made for only thirteen wickets. From the start batsmen held the upper hand, Brookes and Oldfield making 150 for the opening Northamptonshire stand. The two left-handers, Livingston and Jakeman, followed with 187 for the third wicket. Jakeman, batting two and a half hours, hit two 6s and thirteen 4s; Livingston batted four hours and hit fourteen 4s. Nottinghamshire lost two wickets for 24, but Giles and Hardstaff, acting captain, made 226 together. The next wicket produced an even bigger partnership, Hardstaff and Stocks putting on 263. Hardstaff, batting nearly eight hours, hit twenty-seven 4s, and Stocks hit one 6 and eighteen 4s in nearly five hours.

Northamptonshire

D. Brookes c Richardson b Harvey 71	V. Broderick c Meads b Oscroft 15	
N. Oldfield c Butler b Stocks. 66	G. Brice not out. 15	
L. Livingston c and b Harvey 120	R. W. Clarke not out. 7	
F. Jakeman st Meads b Smales 102	B 26, l-b 5, w 3 34	
E. Davis c Giles b Richardson 68		
F. R. Brown c Meads b Harvey 0	(7 wkts dec.) 498	

S. Starkie and K. Fiddling did not bat.

Nottinghamshire

W. W. Keeton c Starkie b Clarke 10	K. Smales c Fiddling b Jakeman. 7	
R. Giles c Oldfield b Starkie 92	E. A. Meads not out 1	
C. J. Poole c Clarke b Brice 10		
J. Hardstaff c Broderick b Starkie. 247	B 7, l-b 9, w 4 20	
F. W. Stocks c Clarke b Starkie 151		
P. F. Harvey not out 9	(6 wkts) 547	

A. Richardson, H. J. Butler and E. Oscroft did not bat.

Nottinghamshire Bowling

	Overs	Mdns	Runs	Wkts
Butler	13	3	36	—
Richardson	30	7	96	1
Oscroft	21	4	79	1
Harvey	38	6	113	3
Smales	23	8	79	1
Stocks.	24	6	61	1

Northamptonshire Bowling

	Overs	Mdns	Runs	Wkts
Clarke.........	30	3	106	1
Brice..........	23	2	106	1
Brown.........	39	8	110	—
Starkie	42	11	102	3
Broderick	50	14	101	—
Jakeman	1	—	2	1

Umpires: F. S. Lee and C. H. Welch.

NOTTINGHAMSHIRE v GLAMORGAN

Played at Nottingham, June 30, July 2, 3, 1951

Drawn. So slowly did Glamorgan score on the first day that Simpson, the Nottinghamshire captain, bowled an over of lobs as a protest and, following this incident Glamorgan lost four wickets for 11 runs. E. Davies, the left-hander, played a sound innings and hit fifteen 4s during a stay of four hours, but Wooller and Jones were very unenterprising. On the second day Nottinghamshire batted even more dourly, but lost wickets steadily against accurate medium-pace bowling by Hever, Watkins and Wooller. Though following-on 158 behind, they easily staved off defeat with much improved batting. Poole drove fiercely for three and a half hours, hitting one 6 and eighteen 4s.

Glamorgan

E. Davies b Stocks 110	B. L. Muncer not out................. 46
P. B. Clift b Harvey................... 19	J. McConnon lbw b Farr............. 1
W. G. A. Parkhouse lbw b Jepson 36	H. G. Davies c Simpson b Richardson 45
W. E. Jones c Harvey b Farr............. 20	N. G. Hever lbw b Farr................. 1
A. J. Watkins lbw b Jepson.............. 24	B 11, l-b 4 15
W. Wooller c Meads b Harvey 13	———
S. Montgomery c Meads b Farr 0	330

Nottinghamshire

W. W. Keeton lbw b Watkins.................. 40	– lbw b Hever 0
R. T. Simpson c Clift b Wooller 8	– b Watkins.................... 30
C. J. Poole c Clift b Hever..................... 1	– c Watkins b Montgomery........135
R. Giles b Wooller........................... 2	– lbw b McConnon 7
F. W. Stocks b Watkins 51	– lbw b Parkhouse............. 35
C. B. Harris c H. Davies b Watkins 29	
P. F. Harvey not out.......................... 29	– not out 28
A. Jepson c and b Wooller 1	– c Watkins b Clift............. 21
B. H. Farr b Hever 2	
E. A. Meads c Clift b Watkins 4	– hit wkt b H. Davies............. 2
A. Richardson b Hever....................... 1	– not out 0
B 3, l-b 1 4	B 2 2
172	(7 wkts) 260

Nottinghamshire Bowling

	Overs	Mdns	Runs	Wkts
Jepson.........	30	6	79	2
Richardson........	30	11	58	1
Farr	19	2	65	4
Stocks..........	30	21	31	1
Harvey	35	13	71	2
Harris.........	13	8	9	—
Simpson	1	—	2	—

Glamorgan Bowling

	Overs	Mdns	Runs	Wkts	Overs	Mdns	Runs	Wkts
Hever	17.3	4	37	3	10	2	26	1
Wooller.	30	10	60	3	10	4	27	—
Watkins	25	6	62	4	9	3	24	1
Muncer.	6	2	9	—	4	—	31	—
McConnon					17	2	48	1
E. Davies					9	2	20	—
Jones.					6	1	11	—
Parkhouse.					3	—	22	1
Montgomery.					4	—	11	1
Clift					5	1	18	1
H. Davies					3	—	20	1

Umpires: E. Paynter and J. J. Hills.

NOTTINGHAMSHIRE v KENT

Played at Nottingham, May 9, 11, 12, 1953

Drawn. Batsmen dominated matters to such extent on an easy pitch that although Nottinghamshire followed-on 194 behind they were never in serious danger of defeat. Fagg batted seven and a half hours for the highest score by any batsman during the summer and hit thirty-two 4s. He did not give a chance, but Mayes, who helped in a partnership of 236, was missed first ball. Simpson played two brilliant innings for Nottinghamshire, reaching three figures in less than two hours in the second. Giles, who recovered well from an anxious start, took an hour longer over his century. Dooland did not make a happy start to his Championship career at Trent Bridge on this unresponsive surface.

Kent

A. E. Fagg not out 269	W. Murray Wood b Stocks.	5
A. H. Phebey lbw b Goonesena 56	R. R. Dovey not out	8
P. Hearn c Dooland b Butler. 5	L-b 4	4
T. G. Evans c and b Jepson. 51		
R. Mayes c Meads b Butler. 93	1/88 2/101 3/184	(6 wkts dec.) 507
B. R. Edrich c Meads b Butler. 16	4/420 5/452 6/468	

D. V. P. Wright, F. Ridgway and J. C. T. Page did not bat.

Nottinghamshire

R. T. Simpson lbw b Wright	84 – c Ridgway b Edrich 157
F. W. Stocks c Wright b Page.	63 – b Ridgway 7
R. Giles c Evans b Page	12 – not out 132
J. Hardstaff lbw b Wright	11 – not out 40
C. J. Poole c Fagg b Ridgway.	77
J. D. Clay lbw b Ridgway	22
G. Goonesena b Wright	9
H. J. Butler c Phebey b Wright	22
B. Dooland not out	10
A. Jepson c Evans b Page.	0
E. A. Meads b Page.	0
B 1, n-b 2.	3	B 4 4

1/144 2/162 3/163 4/181 5/241   313   1/21 2/260   (2 wkts) 340
6/265 7/287 8/313 9/313

Nottinghamshire Bowling

	Overs	Mdns	Runs	Wkts
Butler............	35	6	76	3
Jepson............	33	11	77	1
Dooland..........	26	—	97	—
Stocks............	20	2	73	1
Goonesena........	30	4	121	1
Giles.............	7	2	32	—
Simpson..........	9	—	27	—

Kent Bowling

	Overs	Mdns	Runs	Wkts	Overs	Mdns	Runs	Wkts
Ridgway..........	22	2	73	2	11	1	41	1
Dovey............	30	4	73	—	21	3	82	—
Page.............	21.5	3	66	4	7	—	48	—
Wright...........	24	4	84	4	11	2	35	—
Murray Wood......	4	1	14	—	8	1	25	—
Hearn............					12	—	61	—
Edrich...........					16	1	44	1

Umpires: A. Skelding and H. Elliott (Lancashire).

NOTTINGHAMSHIRE v ESSEX

Played at Nottingham, May 19, 20, 21, 1954

Nottinghamshire won by an innings and 88 runs. They were indebted to the superb bowling of Dooland, who in each innings surpassed the previous best performance of his career. Avery, defending with great skill, fought virtually unaided against the Australian's leg-breaks and googlies on the first day and carried his bat through an innings lasting three hours twenty minutes. Hardstaff, who hit his first century for two years, Poole, Giles and Stocks helped Nottinghamshire to a lead of 205.

Essex

A. V. Avery not out...........................	92	– lbw b Dooland	13
T. C. Dodds lbw b Jepson......................	12	– lbw b Jepson..................	15
T. E. Bailey b Jepson.........................	9	– c Clay b Dooland..............	0
R. Horsfall b Dooland.........................	3	– c Poole b Dooland	9
D. J. Insole b Dooland	1	– b Dooland....................	5
F. H. Vigar c Simpson b Dooland...............	13	– b Dooland....................	2
W. T. Greensmith c Jepson b Dooland...........	0	– c Jepson b Dooland	11
R. Smith c Clay b Dooland.....................	14	– b Dooland....................	26
B. Taylor b Dooland..........................	0	– c Underwood b Stocks..........	25
J. A. Bailey b Dooland	0	– b Dooland....................	3
K. C. Preston b Dooland.......................	2	– not out	4
L-b 8................................	8	B 3, l-b 1................	4

1/14 2/26 3/53 4/55 5/79   154   1/21 2/31 3/32 4/56 5/67   117
6/84 7/134 8/140 9/142   6/71 7/82 8/97 9/112

Nottinghamshire

R. T. Simpson b T. Bailey	10	J. Kelly b T. Bailey	22
J. D. Clay lbw b T. Bailey	6	A. J. Underwood c and b Preston	27
C. J. Poole c Taylor b J. Bailey	41	E. J. Rowe not out	0
J. Hardstaff c Insole b Preston	112		
F. W. Stocks st Taylor b Greensmith	50	B 1, l-b 7, n-b 1	9
R. J. Giles c J. Bailey b Greensmith	67		
B. Dooland b J. Bailey	14	1/15 2/36 3/72 4/163 5/253	359
A. Jepson st Taylor b Greensmith	1	6/305 7/307 8/312 9/359	

Nottinghamshire Bowling

	Overs	Mdns	Runs	Wkts	Overs	Mdns	Runs	Wkts
Jepson	18	3	50	2	11	3	33	1
Underwood	7	1	17	—	2	—	3	—
Dooland	28.3	9	39	8	19	6	44	8
Stocks	13	5	26	—	9	5	28	1
Kelly	5	1	14	—				
Giles					1	—	5	—

Essex Bowling

	Overs	Mdns	Runs	Wkts
T. Bailey	24	4	61	3
Smith	30	9	65	—
Preston	23.2	4	64	2
J. Bailey	16	3	57	2
Greensmith	25	3	94	3
Insole	3	1	9	—

Umpires: T. J. Bartley and T. Spencer.

NOTTINGHAMSHIRE v LANCASHIRE

Played at Nottingham, July 9, 11, 12, 1955

Nottinghamshire won by 32 runs, Smales ending the match by performing the first hat-trick of his career. Rowe helped him to dismiss Hilton and Moore and with the first ball of his next over Smales bowled Smith. Nottinghamshire scored freely on the opening day, Giles hitting one 6 and seventeen 4s in his second century of the season against Lancashire and, despite a stubborn innings by Ikin, they gained a big lead. After more bright batting, Simpson set Lancashire the reasonable task of scoring 265 at a run a minute. Ikin and Washbrook began with a partnership of 95 in an hour and a quarter but once they were parted Smales and Goonesena held the upper hand.

Nottinghamshire

R. T. Simpson c Ikin b Tattersall	44	– c Grieves b Tattersall	13
J. D. Clay c and b Dyson	87	– c and b Hilton	26
R. J. Giles st Grieves b Hilton	115	– c Edrich b Tattersall	1
F. W. Stocks c Washbrook b Hilton	56	– not out	53
K. J. Poole c and b Ikin	13	– c Edrich b Tattersall	6
G. Goonesena c Hilton b Tattersall	28	– b Hilton	14
B. Dooland b Tattersall	16	– c Edrich b Hilton	23
E. J. Martin not out	3	– b Tattersall	1
M. Wood b Tattersall	4		
K. Smales not out	3	– not out	5
E. J. Rowe (did not bat)		– c sub b Tattersall	9
B 4	4	B 6, l-b 1	7

1/79 2/181 3/288 4/311   (8 wkts dec.) 373   1/29 2/33 3/45 4/56   (8 wkts dec.) 158
5/331 6/357 7/364 8/370   5/89 6/91 7/114 8/144

Lancashire

J. T. Ikin b Dooland	114	– c and b Dooland	57
J. Dyson c and b Dooland	31	– c Stocks b Goonesena	13
G. A. Edrich c Rowe b Smales	1	– c Rowe b Goonesena	21
C. Washbrook c Stocks b Dooland	12	– lbw b Smales	53
A. Wharton hit wkt b Goonesena	11	– c and b Goonesena	5
K. Grieves b Goonesena	31	– c Simpson b Goonesena	14
C. S. Smith c Wood b Dooland	28	– b Smales	36
J. Jordan c and b Dooland	13	– c Stocks b Smales	0
M. J. Hilton b Smales	0	– st Rowe b Smales	11
F. W. Moore not out	1	– c Rowe b Smales	0
R. Tattersall c Simpson b Smales	2	– not out	0
B 16, l-b 6, n-b 1	23	B 8, l-b 13, n-b 1	22

1/44 2/59 3/80 4/101 5/146   267   1/95 2/124 3/130 4/166 5/166   232
6/220 7/255 8/256 9/262   6/197 7/198 8/227 9/227

Lancashire Bowling

	Overs	Mdns	Runs	Wkts	Overs	Mdns	Runs	Wkts
Smith	15	2	53	—	4	1	15	—
Moore	15	1	54	—	2	—	8	—
Tattersall	29	6	78	4	25	10	59	5
Hilton	39	9	107	2	19	6	61	3
Dyson	21	8	42	1	4	—	8	—
Ikin	7	1	35	1				

Nottinghamshire Bowling

	Overs	Mdns	Runs	Wkts	Overs	Mdns	Runs	Wkts
Wood	12	3	38	—	2	—	7	—
Poole	8	1	19	—	2	—	7	—
Dooland	31	11	60	5	28	5	71	1
Smales	33.5	13	61	3	23.1	10	37	5
Goonesena	20	7	46	2	27	4	88	4
Stocks	8	1	20	—				

Umpires: F. Chester and E. A. Roberts.

NOTTINGHAMSHIRE v LEICESTERSHIRE

Played at Nottingham, May 13, 14, 15, 1959

Nottinghamshire won by four wickets. Set to score 240 in two hours twenty minutes on the last day – a rate of 103 an hour – Nottinghamshire reached their objective in the last over of extra time. It was particularly appropriate that Norman Hill, who went in late in the second innings because of a strained thigh, should make the winning hit in view of his fine performance earlier in the game, but the batsman who made victory possible was Eric Martin. He lashed a whirlwind highest score of his career and in the process hit one 6 and nineteen 4s. The dour battle for first-innings points, fought out on a batsman's paradise, lasted almost two days, and was highlighted only by N. Hill's century.

Leicestershire

M. R. Hallam b Davison	8	– lbw b Forman	21
J. van Geloven b Jepson	75	– c Millman b Forman	59
W. Watson c Millman b Davison	72	– c Jepson b Springall	58
A. C. Revill run out	23	– c N. Hill b Forman	13
E. F. Phillips c M. Hill b Forman	33	– b Springall	2
G. W. Burch b Cotton	61	– c Simpson b M. Hill	30
R. Julian c Forman b Cotton	5	– not out	34
C. T. Spencer not out	10		
R. C. Smith not out	2	– not out	19
L-b 9, w 2, n-b 2	13	B 5, l-b 2	7

1/13 2/116 3/171   (7 wkts dec.) 302   1/43 2/54 3/87   (6 wkts dec.) 243
4/189 5/260 6/279 7/298   4/114 5/181 6/206

J. S. Savage and B. S. Boshier did not bat.

Nottinghamshire

R. T. Simpson c Savage b van Geloven	28	– c Phillips b Spencer	13
N. Hill c Revill b Boshier	128	– not out	4
E. J. Martin c Watson b Savage	60	– not out	133
M. Hill run out	8	– b Spencer	13
C. J. Poole b Spencer	5	– c Spencer b van Geloven	24
J. D. Springall not out	37	– c Revill b Savage	2
G. Millman b Smith	25	– run out	3
A. Jepson not out	4	– c van Geloven b Savage	42
B 4, l-b 5, n-b 2	11	L-b 6, n-b 1	7

1/60 2/187 3/205   (6 wkts dec.) 306   1/18 2/45 3/124   (6 wkts) 241
4/215 5/236 6/297   4/198 5/222 6/223

I. Davison, P. R. Forman and J. Cotton did not bat.

Nottinghamshire Bowling

	Overs	Mdns	Runs	Wkts	Overs	Mdns	Runs	Wkts
Cotton	22	3	66	2	7	2	13	—
Davison	21	6	43	2	7	—	21	—
Jepson	24	9	40	1				
Springall	23	3	63	—	16	4	32	2
Forman	25	5	77	1	22	3	64	3
M. Hill					24	2	99	1
Simpson					0.3	—	7	—

Leicestershire

	Overs	Mdns	Runs	Wkts	Overs	Mdns	Runs	Wkts
Spencer..........	23	3	71	1	12.2	—	61	2
Boshier..........	23	5	50	1	5	—	47	—
van Geloven.......	31	6	76	1	13	2	56	1
Savage	19.5	2	56	1	10	—	70	2
Smith	12	3	42	1				

Umpires: T. W. Spencer and N. Oldfield.

NOTTINGHAMSHIRE v SURREY

Played at Nottingham, May 16, 18, 19, 1959

Drawn. John Edrich, the 21-year-old Surrey left-hand opening batsman, achieved the remarkable performance of hitting a century in each innings in only his second Championship appearance after Simpson, the Nottinghamshire captain, had mystified a large Saturday crowd by putting in his opponents on a perfect pitch. On the last day, Surrey, captained by Alec Bedser in the absence of May, were barracked for delaying their declaration. Edrich took three hours fifty minutes to reach his maiden century, but together with Willett he provided the Surrey first innings with a firm backbone. Nottinghamshire also found run-making comparatively easy after Surrey declared and, thanks to Simpson, Winfield and Springall, came within 21 of the champions' total. A stand of 221 by Edrich (one 6 and sixteen 4s) and Barrington (nineteen 4s) was the feature of the third day, when Nottinghamshire, left only two hours twenty minutes to score 273, never attempted the task.

Surrey

J. H. Edrich c Millman b Forman.................	112	– c Forman b Cotton..............	124
M. J. Stewart c Winfield b Springall	23	– c Davison b Cotton	5
K. F. Barrington c Poole b Springall..............	4	– not out	113
B. Constable b Davison......................	39		
M. D. Willett b Jepson	72	– not out	4
E. A. Bedser run out	30		
R. Swetman not out..........................	35		
G. A. R. Lock c Millman b Forman	5		
J. C. Laker not out	20		
B 1, l-b 4, w 2, n-b 3	10	B 1, l-b 3, w 1	5

1/46 2/66 3/128 　　　　　　(7 wkts dec.) 350　1/25 2/246 　　　　　　(2 wkts dec.) 251
4/215 5/263 6/302 7/322

P. J. Loader and A. V. Bedser did not bat.

Nottinghamshire

R. T. Simpson c Willett b A. Bedser	103	– c A. Bedser b Barrington	33
E. J. Martin b A. Bedser	10	– c Stewart b Lock	6
H. M. Winfield run out	98	– not out	44
M. Hill c E. Bedser b Loader	43		
C. J. Poole c and b Loader	2	– not out	21
J. D. Springall not out	60		
G. Millman c Loader b Laker	3		
A. Jepson st Swetman b A. Bedser	6		
P. R. Forman run out	2		
J. Cotton b Laker	1		
I. Davison b Loader	0		
L-b 1	1	B 4, l-b 1, w 2	7
	329		**(2 wkts) 111**

1/12 2/189 3/228 4/243 5/275
6/280 7/297 8/307 9/328

1/16 2/60

Nottinghamshire Bowling

	Overs	Mdns	Runs	Wkts	Overs	Mdns	Runs	Wkts
Cotton	21	2	61	—	21	4	67	2
Davison	19	1	56	1	17	4	44	—
Jepson	23	5	83	1	21	5	65	—
Springall	21	4	60	2	3	—	23	—
Forman	19	4	80	2	6	1	47	—
Poole					1	1	—	—

Surrey Bowling

	Overs	Mdns	Runs	Wkts	Overs	Mdns	Runs	Wkts
Loader	30	8	62	3	3	—	10	—
A. Bedser	30	12	58	3	2	—	3	—
Barrington	11	1	36	—	13	1	33	1
Laker	27	8	94	2				
Lock	13	2	40	—	19	4	39	1
E. Bedser	12	2	38	—				
Willett					6	1	19	—

Umpires: W. E. Phillipson and N. Oldfield.

NOTTINGHAMSHIRE v CAMBRIDGE UNIVERSITY

Played at Nottingham, June 13, 15, 16, 1959

Nottinghamshire won by 179 runs. The feature of this match was the appearance of Keith Miller, the Australian Test cricketer, who played as a guest for Nottinghamshire and scored 62 and 102 not out. Miller figured in a fine fourth-wicket partnership of 128 with Hall in Nottinghamshire's first innings and also took two wickets for nine runs when Cambridge batted late on the first day. On the Monday Miller was even more belligerent and hit his brilliant century (two 6s and thirteen 4s) in two hours five minutes while sharing a stand of 169 with Winfield. Cambridge, set 361 to win, made a spectacular start and had 180 on the board for the loss of only three men. Then Matthews and Jepson took the new ball and the remaining seven wickets went down for 24.

Nottinghamshire

R. T. Simpson c Howland b Douglas-Pennant	3	– c Green b Bernard	29
N. Hill c Green b Wheelhouse	7	– b Willard	43
H. M. Winfield b Douglas-Pennant	8	– not out	77
K. R. Miller c Willard b Coghlan	62	– not out	102
M. Hall lbw b Willard	72		
C. Forbes c Reddy b Hurd	36		
J. D. Springall c Willard b Hurd	77		
G. Millman c Howland b Willard	3		
A. Jepson not out	1		
M. Morgan st Howland b Willard	6		
C. S. Matthews c Reddy b Hurd	0		
L-b 9	9	B 8	8

1/5 2/13 3/23 4/151 5/155   284   1/67 2/90   (2 wkts dec.) 259
6/273 7/276 8/276 9/283

Cambridge University

E. M. Rose c Hall b Miller	8	– c Millman b Matthews	11
H. C. Blofeld c Millman b Matthews	2	– c Hill b Forbes	38
D. J. Green c Winfield b Morgan	32	– lbw b Jepson	11
N. S. K. Reddy lbw b Miller	0	– b Morgan	30
T. B. L. Coghlan run out	3	– b Jepson	1
M. J. L. Willard b Forbes	44	– c Hall b Matthews	91
J. R. Bernard c Springall b Morgan	13	– c Millman b Matthews	7
C. B. Howland run out	38	– c Millman b Matthews	3
A. Wheelhouse b Matthews	11	– not out	2
S. Douglas-Pennant c Hall b Morgan	1	– b Jepson	1
A. Hurd not out	7	– c Matthews b Jepson	1
L-b 1	1	B 3, l-b 5	8

1/10 2/10 3/14 4/24 5/66   160   1/23 2/107 3/171 4/181 5/189   204
6/98 7/102 8/143 9/152   6/198 7/199 8/199 9/202

Cambridge University Bowling

	Overs	Mdns	Runs	Wkts	Overs	Mdns	Runs	Wkts
Wheelhouse	22	3	63	1	9	—	45	—
Douglas-Pennant	21	5	52	2	11	—	45	—
Coghlan	19	4	41	1	13	3	55	—
Hurd	22.2	5	85	3	20	5	64	—
Bernard	6	2	20	—	4	—	14	1
Willard	8	3	10	3	12	6	28	1
Green	1	—	4	—				

Nottinghamshire Bowling

	Overs	Mdns	Runs	Wkts	Overs	Mdns	Runs	Wkts
Miller	12	4	35	2				
Matthews	19.5	6	38	2	25	5	54	4
Morgan	19	8	40	3	23	10	40	1
Forbes	13	4	40	1	28	10	60	1
Jepson	2	—	6	—	21	7	27	4
Springall					6	2	15	—

Umpires: H. Elliott and D. J. Wood.

NOTTINGHAMSHIRE v LANCASHIRE

Played at Nottingham, July 18, 20, 21, 1959

Nottinghamshire won by seven wickets. They owed much to Norman Hill who scored a hundred in each innings. Wharton, Grieves and Bond, all of whom batted attractively, were the architects of Lancashire's 258 and despite Norman Hill's splendid century which contained one 6 and eleven 4s, Nottinghamshire, baffled by Greenhough, forfeited first-innings lead. Lancashire quickly consolidated their advantage. Bond, who was dismissed only once in the match for 177, scored his maiden hundred in three and three-quarter hours and Nottinghamshire were set 305 to win in three hours fifty-five minutes. Again Hill came to the rescue and with Winfield (nineteen 4s) laid the foundation for victory. Hill, who earlier in the season failed to score against Lancashire, was awarded his county cap.

Lancashire

G. Pullar b Matthews	18	– c Haynes b Atkinson	19
A. Wharton c Springall b Morgan	64	– not out	16
D. M. Green hit wkt b Springall	11	– b Matthews	67
K. Grieves c Millman b Atkinson	40	– c Millman b Morgan	21
P. J. Marner c and b Morgan	5	– run out	49
J. D. Bond c Haynes b Morgan	76	– not out	101
R. Collins b Morgan	11		
G. Clayton c Millman b Atkinson	28		
J. B. Statham c Jepson b Morgan	1		
T. Greenhough c N. Hill b Atkinson	0		
K. Higgs not out	0		
L-b 4	4	B 1, l-b 2	3

1/34 2/65 3/121 4/131 5/141 258 1/35 2/139 3/171 (4 wkts dec.) 276
6/166 7/257 8/257 9/258 4/251

Nottinghamshire

N. Hill b Collins	101	– c Grieves b Higgs	102
G. Millman lbw b Statham	3	– c Bond b Collins	23
A. Jepson c Marner b Higgs	20		
H. M. Winfield b Greenhough	2	– c Grieves b Green	102
J. D. Springall lbw b Greenhough	52	– not out	45
R. T. Simpson c Bond b Greenhough	6	– not out	29
M. Haynes b Collins	13		
R. C. Vowles not out	20		
T. Atkinson c Pullar b Greenhough	2		
M. Morgan c Bond b Greenhough	0		
C. S. Matthews b Marner	7		
B 1, l-b 1, w 1, n-b 1	4	B 3, l-b 1	4

1/19 2/64 3/67 4/154 5/170 230 1/65 2/199 3/244 (3 wkts) 305
6/192 7/201 8/212 9/212

Nottinghamshire Bowling

	Overs	Mdns	Runs	Wkts	Overs	Mdns	Runs	Wkts
Matthews	23	4	71	1	22.1	1	74	1
Jepson	18	7	55	—	17	5	28	—
Atkinson	24	8	36	3	23	4	62	1
Springall	7	1	21	1				
Morgan	28.1	10	63	5	24	6	89	1
Vowles	6	2	8	—	6	—	20	—

Lancashire Bowling

	Overs	Mdns	Runs	Wkts	Overs	Mdns	Runs	Wkts
Statham	6	2	12	1				
Higgs	23	1	61	1	23	1	89	1
Greenhough	37	11	98	5	20	—	92	—
Collins	23	10	55	2	8	—	58	1
Wharton..........	1	1	—	—	1.2	—	15	—
Marner	0.1	—	—	1	6	1	18	—
Green					8	1	29	1

Umpires: L. H. Gray and R. S. Lay.

NOTTINGHAMSHIRE v SURREY

Played at Nottingham, June 4, 6, 7, 1960

Surrey won by eight wickets. Superb spin bowling by Lock (ten for 147) and E. Bedser (seven for 87) put Surrey back in the game after their attack had been thoroughly mastered by N. Hill and Poole on the first day. Hill, who batted five hours twenty minutes and hit two 6s and seventeen 4s, made the highest score of his career and with Poole (three 6s and fifteen 4s) shared a fifth-wicket stand of 191 in two and a half hours. Edrich, the Surrey left-hand opening batsman who hit two centuries in the corresponding match in 1959, again showed his liking for Trent Bridge and the bowling by scoring 120, but Nottinghamshire led on first innings by 67. Lock and Bedser then took command and despite M. Hill's defiant 51 Surrey required only 169 to win. Stewart and Fletcher put them in sight of victory with a second-wicket stand of 106.

Nottinghamshire

N. Hill c Parsons b E. Bedser 171	– run out	4
H. M. Winfield c Lock b Loader................. 0	– c Swetman b Lock	15
†G. Millman c and b Lock 19	– b E. Bedser	1
M. Hill c Stewart b Lock....................... 3	– c and b E. Bedser	51
*R. T. Simpson c Edrich b E. Bedser 5	– c Loader b Lock	11
C. J. Poole c Edrich b Lock.....................109	– b Lock	3
J. D. Springall c Swetman b E. Bedser 38	– c Lock b E. Bedser	4
R. C. Vowles c Barrington b Lock 2	– c Stewart b Lock..............	1
J. Cotton c Barrington b E. Bedser 2	– not out	2
I. Davison lbw b Lock......................... 0	– c Stewart b Lock..............	1
B. D. Wells not out 2	– c Barrington b Loader	7
B 6, l-b 5 11	L-b 1...................	1

1/3 2/58 3/91 4/96 5/287   362   1/4 2/41 3/56 4/71 5/82   101
6/345 7/358 8/358 9/360   6/89 7/91 8/91 9/92

Surrey

M. J. Stewart c M. Hill b Wells	37	– c Simpson b Cotton	75
J. H. Edrich c Wells b Vowles	120	– c Millman b Cotton	14
D. G. W. Fletcher b Cotton	11	– not out	62
K. F. Barrington c N. Hill b Wells	1	– not out	13
A. B. D. Parsons c Simpson b Vowles	20		
†R. Swetman c Vowles b Wells	39		
E. A. Bedser lbw b Cotton	0		
G. A. R. Lock b Cotton	2		
D. Gibson not out	34		
*A. V. Bedser b Wells	4		
P. J. Loader c Davison b Cotton	8		
B 4, l-b 7, n-b 4, w 4	19	L-b 6	6

1/81 2/135 3/138 4/189 5/211   295   1/31 2/137   (2 wkts) 170
6/221 7/223 8/271 9/282

Surrey Bowling

	Overs	Mdns	Runs	Wkts	Overs	Mdns	Runs	Wkts
Loader	20	3	60	1	12.4	2	28	1
A. Bedser	19	5	54	—	6	1	19	—
Gibson	3	—	14	—				
Lock	30	8	103	5	15	5	44	5
E. Bedser	33.2	12	80	4	9	4	9	3
Barrington	7	1	40	—				

Nottinghamshire Bowling

	Overs	Mdns	Runs	Wkts	Overs	Mdns	Runs	Wkts
Cotton	28	4	49	4	12	4	34	2
Davison	25	9	47	—	8	—	31	—
Vowles	19	1	55	2	7	—	33	—
Wells	38	12	100	4	10	2	38	—
Springall	10	3	25	—	6	1	24	—
Simpson					1	—	4	—

Umpires: N. Oldfield and J. F. Crapp.

NOTTINGHAMSHIRE v SUSSEX

Played at Nottingham, June 25, 27, 28, 1960

Sussex won by one run, the match finishing amid scenes of great excitement. Thanks to a timely 102 not out from Simpson, Nottinghamshire gained a first-innings lead of 62 before declaring, but the real tension was saved for the last day. Suttle completed his first century of the season and, with Shepperd contributing 50, Sussex declared at 276 for five, setting Nottinghamshire 215 to win at 83 an hour. Clay scored a sound 66, but a major collapse followed and at 140 for eight with only forty minutes left Nottinghamshire's chances looked hopeless. Springall and Millman added 43 in twenty minutes for the ninth wicket, and Springall and Atkinson, the last pair, also prospered. In desperation Shepperd took the new ball and Thomson began his last over with Nottinghamshire needing five runs. The first ball produced a single, the second and fourth one leg-bye, and off the fifth Atkinson was given out lbw.

Sussex

L. J. Lenham c Millman b Cotton	20	– run out	23
A. S. M. Oakman c Springall b Atkinson	39	– b Davison	15
K. G. Suttle c Millman b Davison	32	– not out	111
*Rev. D. S. Shepperd b Atkinson	15	– c Cotton b Atkinson	50
D. V. Smith b Wells	13	– lbw b Wells	0
G. C. Cooper c Millman b Cotton	5	– not out	35
A. Buss b Wells	0		
N. I. Thomson b Cotton	37	– c Poole b Wells	22
R. V. Bell c Millman b Atkinson	1		
†R. T. Webb b Davison	14		
D. L. Bates not out	0		
L-b 1	1	B 4, l-b 9, w 7	20

1/43 2/89 3/103 4/113 5/122   177   1/28 2/58 3/157   (5 wkts dec.) 276
6/124 7/128 8/134 9/177   4/168 5/196

Nottinghamshire

J. D. Clay lbw b Thomson	13	– c Bates b Cooper	66
H. M. Winfield c Shepperd b Buss	7	– c Shepperd b Bates	22
†G. Millman b Buss	12	– c Cooper b Bates	16
M. Hill c Cooper b Buss	39	– st Webb b Bell	9
*R. T. Simpson not out	102	– run out	5
C. J. Poole c Webb b Bell	22	– b Bates	2
J. D. Springall c Bell b Smith	34	– not out	65
T. Atkinson c and b Bell	8	– lbw b Thomson	7
J. Cotton (did not bat)		– c Buss b Bell	8
I. Davison (did not bat)		– b Cooper	0
B. D. Wells (did not bat)		– c Oakman b Cooper	10
L-b 1, n-b 1	2	L-b 3	3

1/12 2/20 3/36 4/95   (7 wkts dec.) 239   1/58 2/89 3/96 4/98 5/115   213
5/156 6/228 7/239   6/124 7/124 8/140 9/183

Nottinghamshire Bowling

	Overs	Mdns	Runs	Wkts	Overs	Mdns	Runs	Wkts
Cotton	25	9	50	3	21	4	57	—
Davison	16.1	4	27	2	18	5	34	1
Atkinson	32	9	71	3	28	8	73	1
Wells	10	5	25	2	30	8	92	2
Springall	5	3	3	—				

Sussex Bowling

	Overs	Mdns	Runs	Wkts	Overs	Mdns	Runs	Wkts
Thomson	25	7	57	1	6.5	1	21	1
Buss	25	4	58	3	5	—	16	—
Bell	25	6	56	2	17	1	79	2
Bates	21	5	55	—	12	4	35	3
Smith	3	1	11	1	3	—	24	—
Cooper					5	—	35	3

Umpires: H. Elliott and A. E. Fagg.

NOTTINGHAMSHIRE v MIDDLESEX

Played at Nottingham, June 24, 26, 27, 1961

Middlesex won by 28 runs. Parfitt, their 24-year-old left-hander, hit two centuries in contrasting style – one occupying four and a half hours and the other only one and three-quarter hours. On Saturday Middlesex soon lost three wickets before Parfitt added 98 with Hooker and 128 with Titmus enabling Bedford to declare at 324 for six. This time, Hooker and Titmus, in their capacity as bowlers, helped to dismiss Nottinghamshire for 125. Then Middlesex, with a lead of 199, went for runs quickly. Parfitt, promoted in the order hit fifty in half an hour and accounted for 101 out of 144 before Nottinghamshire attempted to get 344 in five hours. They fared well thanks to Simpson (71), Poole (82) and Vowles (44) who were the principal performers in a fighting recovery which kept the issue in the balance until the last wicket fell fifteen minutes from time.

Middlesex

R. A. Gale c Millman b Corran	3	– c Simpson b Vowles	18
W. E. Russell b Davison	3		
P. H. Parfitt c Wells b Corran	105	– not out	101
E. A. Clark c Millman b Corran	23	– not out	22
R. W. Hooker b Vowles	54		
F. J. Titmus b Corran	78		
D. Bennett not out	27		
M. J. Smith not out	20		
L-b 9, w 2	11	L-b 2, w 1	3

1/7 2/11 3/42 4/140   (6 wkts dec.) 324   1/66   (1 wkt dec.) 144
5/268 6/288

*P. I. Bedford, †M. O. C. Sturt and A. E. Moss did not bat.

Nottinghamshire

J. D. Clay c Hooker b Moss	3	– run out	13
†G. Millman c Smith b Bennett	6	– c Parfitt b Titmus	0
C. Forbes b Hooker	10	– b Moss	16
*R. T. Simpson c Hooker b Titmus	25	– b Hooker	71
C. J. Poole not out	37	– c and b Moss	82
H. M. Winfield c and b Titmus	4	– b Titmus	19
M. Hill c Gale b Hooker	6	– c Titmus b Bennett	21
R. C. Vowles c Hooker b Bennett	0	– run out	44
A. G. Corran c Bedford b Titmus	6	– c Titmus b Hooker	11
I. Davison c Sturt b Hooker	14	– not out	14
B. D. Wells b Titmus	2	– c Russell b Moss	19
B 11, l-b 1	12	B 3, l-b 1, w 1	5

1/8 2/10 3/37 4/55 5/63   125   1/28 2/28 3/37 4/155 5/187   315
6/76 7/80 8/97 9/122   6/220 7/268 8/275 9/290

Nottinghamshire Bowling

	Overs	Mdns	Runs	Wkts	Overs	Mdns	Runs	Wkts
Corran	31	5	99	4	14	—	53	—
Davison	19	2	81	1	14	—	36	—
Vowles	20	3	61	1	11	2	43	1
Forbes	16	3	51	—	1	1	—	—
Wells	20	9	21	—	1.3	—	9	—

Middlesex Bowling

	Overs	Mdns	Runs	Wkts	Overs	Mdns	Runs	Wkts
Moss.............	13	4	20	1	21.3	5	81	3
Bennett...........	18	4	28	2	17	4	35	1
Hooker...........	17	6	30	3	18	4	45	2
Titmus	17.5	6	35	4	28	5	83	2
Bedford..........					6	—	28	—
Smith					12	5	38	—

Umpires: A. E. Fagg and H. Yarnold.

NOTTINGHAMSHIRE v NORTHAMPTONSHIRE

Played at Nottingham, July 1, 3, 4, 1961

Nottinghamshire won by 127 runs. Dilley, the Northamptonshire right-arm medium-fast bowler playing his first county game for two seasons, performed the hat-trick on the first day when he dismissed Poole, Winfield and Wells. By then Nottinghamshire, despite being put in, were well established. Winfield, who added 151 for the second wicket with Millman (99) batted five hours twenty minutes, and Simpson — another participant in a century stand — brought a splash of colour with a breezy 66. Northamptonshire, barracked for their tedious progress, never looked likely to contest the lead, but were given a chance of victory in the closing stages, when set 277 at 87 an hour. Although Lightfoot performed admirably, wickets fell quickly and Wells bowled Larter, the last man with the fourth ball of the final over of extra time.

Nottinghamshire

N. Hill c Andrew b Larter......................	0	– b Dilley......................	29
H. M. Winfield c Andrew b Dilley................	103	– b Larter......................	4
†G. Millman c Reynolds b Lightfoot	99	– c Allen b Larter	32
*R. T. Simpson c Andrew b Larter	66	– run out	0
C. J. Poole c Subba Row b Dilley	12	– c Andrew b Larter	56
M. Hill c Scott b Lightfoot	26	– b Scott	14
B. D. Wells c Subba Row b Dilley	0		
I. Davison c Watts b Lightfoot	7	– not out	5
C. Forbes not out	18	– lbw b Allen....................	16
A. J. Corran not out	1	– not out	5
B 3, l-b 5, n-b 3	11	B 2, l-b 1, w 1	4

1/0 2/151 3/268 4/285   (8 wkts dec.) 343   1/9 2/38 3/50 4/53   (7 wkts dec.) 165
5/290 6/290 7/309 8/341   5/132 6/143 7/153

P. Oakden did not bat.

Northamptonshire

M. Norman c Millman b Davison	25	– c Winfield b Davison	7
B. L. Reynolds c Oakden b Davison	31	– c Millman b Davison	8
*R. Subba Row b Wells	45	– b Wells	24
D. Ramsamooj b Forbes	3	– run out	4
P. J. Watts b Davison	66	– lbw b Wells	8
M. E. Scott b Davison	2	– c Winfield b Corran	8
†K. V. Andrew c Millman b Forbes	29	– c Poole b Corran	0
A. Lightfoot c Poole b Forbes	14	– c Poole b Corran	76
M. H. J. Allen c Davison b Oakden	7	– c Poole b Wells	0
M. R. Dilley lbw b Oakden	0	– not out	12
J. D. F. Larter not out	0	– b Wells	0
B 3, l-b 7	10	B 2	2

1/48 2/59 3/76 4/131 5/140   232   1/11 2/20 3/27 4/56 5/77   149
6/200 7/225 8/228 9/229   6/83 7/100 8/122 9/148

Northamptonshire Bowling

	Overs	Mdns	Runs	Wkts	Overs	Mdns	Runs	Wkts
Larter	20	5	67	2	18	6	44	3
Dilley	26	3	71	3	16	—	54	1
Lightfoot	23	1	80	3				
Watts	5	—	13	—				
Allen	23	7	78	—	12	2	46	1
Scott	14	4	23	—	8	5	17	1

Nottinghamshire Bowling

	Overs	Mdns	Runs	Wkts	Overs	Mdns	Runs	Wkts
Corran	27	9	46	—	22	10	39	3
Davison	26	6	59	4	9	2	35	2
Oakden	17.4	4	49	2	3	1	2	—
Forbes	24	7	45	3	10	—	36	—
Wells	22	13	23	1	27.4	15	35	4

Umpires: D. Davies and H. Yarnold.

NOTTINGHAMSHIRE v SUSSEX

Played at Worksop, July 5, 6, 7, 1961

Sussex won by nine wickets. Two opening batsmen, N. Hill (Nottinghamshire) and Oakman (Sussex) scored maiden double hundreds during a protracted tussle for first-innings lead. In fact 700 runs were scored in the first two days for the loss of seven wickets. Hill, a strong on-side player, completed 1,000 runs during his six-hour innings, and altogether hit four 6s and twenty 4s. He was missed when 121. Oakman, dropped at 23, made his 229 not out (five 6s and twenty-eight 4s) in five hours and Sussex declared one run ahead. Only Poole played Buss and Smith confidently a second time and Sussex were left 166 to win. Oakman, 295 runs in the match, and Langridge began with 99 and Sussex romped home.

Nottinghamshire

N. Hill not out	201	– b Buss	4
H. M. Winfield c Parks b Buss	19	– b Smith	12
†G. Millman b Cooper	53	– b Smith	0
M. Hill b Suttle	14	– lbw b Buss	28
C. J. Poole b Buss	22	– c Cooper b Smith	68
*J. D. Clay not out	30	– c Smith b Buss	4
C. Forbes (did not bat)		– c Oakman b Thomson	33
I. Davison (did not bat)		– lbw b Smith	9
A. J. Corran (did not bat)		– b Buss	1
B. D. Wells (did not bat)		– b Buss	0
M. Morgan (did not bat)		– not out	0
B 8, l-b 3	11	B 6, l-b 1	7

1/94 2/199 3/236   (4 wkts dec.) 350   1/8 2/8 3/14 4/73 5/73   166
4/270   6/153 7/165 8/166 9/166

Sussex

R. J. Langridge run out	11	– not out	55
A. S. M. Oakman not out	229	– c Corran b Wells	66
L. J. Lenham c Winfield b Wells	30	– not out	38
K. G. Suttle b Wells	15		
†J. M. Parks not out	57		
B 2, l-b 4, w 1, n-b 2	9	L-b 7	7

1/29 2/178 3/206   (3 wkts dec.) 351   1/99   (1 wkt) 166

*D. V. Smith, G. C. Cooper, N. I. Thomson, A. Buss, R. V. Bell and D. L. Bates did not bat.

Sussex Bowling

	Overs	Mdns	Runs	Wkts	Overs	Mdns	Runs	Wkts
Thomson	24	3	52	—	12	5	22	1
Buss	30	5	100	2	30	12	70	5
Smith	10	6	20	—	22.4	9	62	4
Bates	17.4	2	59	—				
Bell	20	2	74	—				
Cooper	10	—	30	1				
Suttle	5	1	4	1	3	1	5	—

Nottinghamshire Bowling

	Overs	Mdns	Runs	Wkts	Overs	Mdns	Runs	Wkts
Corran	33	8	88	—	11	2	27	—
Davison	17	2	71	—	11	2	33	—
Forbes	20	2	70	—	8	1	18	—
Morgan	9	1	57	—	6.3	2	27	—
Wells	24	8	56	2	16	4	46	1
M. Hill					4	3	8	—

Umpires: J. F. Crapp and W. F. Price.

SOMERSET

SOMERSET v CAMBRIDGE UNIVERSITY

Played at Bath, June 26, 27, 28, 1946

Somerset won by an innings and 36 runs. Fine aggressive batting by Gimblett and excellent bowling by Wellard were the chief features in the cricket. A wet wicket delayed the start, but, despite clever slow bowling by Mills, Gimblett mastered the attack so completely that he made 114 out of 151 in ninety-five minutes, hitting six 6s and thirteen 4s by powerful drives, hooks and pulls. Wellard, with slow off-breaks, completely baffled the University batsmen, of whom only Conradi in the first innings and Trapnell in the second showed much resistance. In all, Wellard took thirteen wickets for 97 runs.

Somerset

F. S. Lee c Bodkin b Mills	14
H. Gimblett b Mills	114
J. Lawrence c Bodkin b Mills	12
F. Castle c Willatt b Mills	17
H. E. Watts st Mischler b Mills	26
H. T. F. Buse not out	27
H. D. Burrough b Mills	15
A. W. Wellard c Conradi b Lacy-Scott	9
E. F. Longrigg not out	36
B 3, 1-b 1, n-b 2	6

(7 wkts dec.) 276

W. T. Luckes and W. H. Andrews did not bat.

Cambridge University

G. L. Willatt c Gimblett b Andrews	5	– b Wellard	20
D. G. Lacy-Scott c Gimblett b Wellard	2	– c Gimblett b Lawrence	15
P. E. Bodkin c Burrough b Wellard	5	– c Lawrence b Wellard	0
N. M. Mischler c Gimblett b Andrews	2	– c Gimblett b Wellard	2
G. M. Shuttleworth b Wellard	0	– b Lawrence	0
T. W. Tyrwhitt-Drake c Longrigg b Wellard	1	– b Wellard	25
J. Pepper c Burrough b Wellard	0	– b Lawrence	7
E. R. Conradi not out	50	– c Luckes b Wellard	13
B. M. W. Trapnell st Luckes b Lawrence	6	– b Castle	37
J. M. Mills b Wellard	18	– c Burrough b Wellard	0
B. S. Hobson lbw b Wellard	0	– not out	16
B 3	3	B 6, 1-b 7	13
	92		148

Cambridge University Bowling

	Overs	Mdns	Runs	Wkts
Lacy-Scott	18	2	62	1
Hobson	9	5	19	—
Trapnell	11	2	54	—
Mills	28	4	100	6
Bodkin	8	1	35	—

Somerset Bowling

	Overs	Mdns	Runs	Wkts	Overs	Mdns	Runs	Wkts
Wellard..........	18.5	6	35	7	25	6	62	6
Andrews..........	10	4	16	2	7	2	8	—
Lawrence	6	1	32	1	16	5	41	3
Buse	3	1	6	—	9	4	8	—
Castle					4.1	—	16	1

SOMERSET v MIDDLESEX

Played at Taunton, July 13, 15, 16, 1946

Somerset won by an innings and 52 runs. A merciless onslaught by the Somerset batsmen, particularly Gimblett, who made the highest score of his career, produced 472 for eight wickets on the first day. Gimblett, in his first double century, gave only one chance at 72. Blending skilful defence with masterly cutting and driving, he hit a 6 and thirty-one 4s while batting five hours twenty minutes for 231 out of 371. Three wickets fell for 46 runs, Gray using good speed, but Woodhouse, with experience at Marlborough and Cambridge, on first appearing for Somerset, helped to add 200. After sound batting by Buse and Longrigg, Wellard hit four 6s. Brown and Robertson put up 100 in sixty-five minutes, but Wellard dismissed them both and Compton in one spell for nine runs. Following-on for the first time, Middlesex suffered their heaviest defeat of the season. They were handicapped on a drying pitch after night rain, yet their last seven wickets realised 156 runs. Robertson again batted well in a stay lasting altogether two hours twenty minutes.

Somerset

F. S. Lee c Price b Gray 16		A. W. Wellard c Robertson b Robins 56
H. Gimblett c Robertson b Robins 231		W. H. Andrews c Price b Edrich.......... 1
J. Lawrence c Price b Gray.............. 1		W. T. Luckes b Gray 14
C. J. P. Barnwell c Thompson b Gray...... 0		H. Hazell not out..................... 1
G. E. S. Woodhouse b Edrich............ 70		B 12, l-b 9 21
H. T. F. Buse c Price b Robins 40		
E. F. Longrigg not out................. 72		(9 wkts dec.) 523

Middlesex

J. D. Robertson b Wellard..................... 44	– c Hazell b Buse................. 79
S. M. Brown b Wellard 60	– b Wellard 13
W. J. Edrich st Luckes b Buse.................. 4	– b Andrews 8
D. Compton c Longrigg b Wellard.............. 7	– lbw b Buse 42
R. W. V. Robins b Buse 5	– c Gimblett b Wellard 0
A. Thompson run out 0	– c Luckes b Wellard............. 5
L. Muncer st Luckes b Buse.................. 13	– c Lee b Buse.................. 18
W. F. Price c Barnwell b Lawrence.............. 24	– b Lawrence................... 26
J. Sims st Luckes b Hazell.................... 21	– c Buse b Hazell................ 10
L. Gray st Luckes b Lawrence 0	– c Wellard b Hazell 26
J. Young not out 13	– not out 30
B 8, l-b 6 14	B 1, l-b 7, n-b 1........... 9
205	266

Middlesex Bowling

	Overs	Mdns	Runs	Wkts
Gray............	39	8	110	4
Edrich...........	28	5	100	2
Sims	20	1	80	—
Robins	29	4	86	3
Young...........	44	13	99	—
Compton	3	—	24	—
Robertson........	2	—	3	—

Somerset Bowling

	Overs	Mdns	Runs	Wkts	Overs	Mdns	Runs	Wkts
Wellard..........	26	2	85	3	24	4	84	3
Andrews.........	5	—	23	—	13	—	57	1
Buse	25	9	55	3	11	3	24	3
Lawrence	7	2	16	2	14	4	55	1
Hazell...........	3.4	—	12	1	18	7	37	2

SOMERSET v SUSSEX

Played at Weston-super-Mare, August 4, 5, 6, 1948

Sussex won by six wickets. James Langridge, the Sussex left-handed all-rounder, achieved a splendid bowling performance in claiming match figures of fourteen wickets for 129 runs. Keeping a splendid length, he often made the ball turn and lift awkwardly. In the second innings, after an opening stand of 74 between Hill and Woodhouse, Langridge brought about such a collapse that the last nine wickets went for 71. Langridge three times claimed two wickets with successive deliveries, and at one stage dismissed four men with five balls. John Langridge, too, played a big part in the Sussex success, contributing two very sound innings. Wellard bowled slow off-breaks splendidly in the first Sussex innings on a pitch which consistently assisted spin bowlers. Gimblett went in late in the second innings because of a chest strain.

Sussex

John Langridge lbw b Wellard	53	– b Hazell	67
H. W. Parks c Hazell b Lawrence	16	– c Wellard b Lawrence	12
P. D. S. Blake lbw b Wellard	43	– b Lawrence	11
C. Oakes c Hazell b Wellard	16	– c Wellard b Lawrence	51
James Langridge c sub b Hazell	8	– not out	11
G. Cox c Lawrence b Wellard	40	– not out	0
G. H. G. Doggart c Lawrence b Wellard	12		
H. T. Bartlett c Buse b Wellard	21		
R. T. Webb not out	9		
J. Wood c Tremlett b Hazell	8		
J. Cornford b Hazell	0		
B 6, l-b 2, w 1	9	B 5, l-b 3	8
	235		160

Somerset

H. Gimblett c John Langridge b Cox	20	– not out	7
E. Hill lbw b Cox	11	– c Doggart b James Langridge	40
M. Coope st Webb b James Langridge	27	– c Doggart b James Langridge	0
H. T. F. Buse lbw b Oakes	40	– c Parks b James Langridge	14
H. E. Watts st Webb b Cornford	67	– st Webb b James Langridge	0
G. E. S. Woodhouse c Bartlett b James Langridge	36	– c John Langridge b James Langridge	35
J. Lawrence c Doggart b James Langridge	0	– c John Langridge b James Langridge	9
M. F. Tremlett c Parks b James Langridge	7	– c Doggart b James Langridge	19
W. T. Luckes c Bartlett b James Langridge	0	– c Doggart b James Langridge	5
A. W. Wellard c Doggart b James Langridge	36	– c Cornford b Wood	13
H. Hazell not out	0	– b Wood	0
B 5	5	L-b 2, n-b 1	3
	249		**145**

Sussex Bowling

	Overs	Mdns	Runs	Wkts	Overs	Mdns	Runs	Wkts
Wood	6	2	19	—	24.2	10	45	2
Cornford	18	11	20	1	9	4	9	—
Cox	18	6	48	2	8	1	22	—
Oakes	21	1	88	1	3	2	5	—
James Langridge	28.4	8	68	6	30	13	61	8
Doggart	1	—	1	—				

Somerset Bowling

	Overs	Mdns	Runs	Wkts	Overs	Mdns	Runs	Wkts
Wellard	39	12	80	6	16	4	26	—
Tremlett	17	5	32	—	7	2	11	—
Lawrence	21	4	46	1	22.4	5	59	3
Hazell	45.2	21	68	3	21	7	39	1
Buse					4	1	17	—

Umpires: F. Chester and B. Flint.

SOMERSET v YORKSHIRE

Played at Taunton, August 21, 23, 24, 1948

Drawn. Somerset fell only eleven runs short of victory with five wickets in hand in a game considerably shortened by rain. No play was possible on the opening day, and on the Monday Yardley's policy of sending in his opponents did not succeed, for Somerset, aided by steady batting from Buse and the Yorkshire-born Coope, batted consistently. Lawrence, also a Yorkshireman, upset his native county in their first innings with leg-breaks and googlies, taking four wickets in five balls, including a "hat-trick". Yorkshire followed-on 116 behind, but sound batting by the left-hander Watson enabled them to avoid defeat.

Somerset

H. Gimblett c Smailes b Wardle	42	– b Foord	11
M. M. Walford b Coxon	21	– run out	0
H. E. Watts b Robinson	22	– b Coxon	5
H. T. F. Buse c Brennan b Foord	56		
G. E. S. Woodhouse b Robinson	10	– not out	2
M. Coope c Brennan b Robinson	53	– c Robinson b Foord	7
M. F. Tremlett run out	15	– c Yardley b Foord	8
J. Lawrence c Coxon b Wardle	14		
A. W. Wellard c Lester b Robinson	9	– not out	14
W. T. Luckes b Robinson	4		
H. Hazell not out	2		
B 1, l-b 4	5	L-b 1, w 4, n-b 3	8
	253	**(5 wkts)**	**55**

Yorkshire

L. Hutton run out	45	– b Tremlett	28
H. Halliday c Lawrence b Hazell	23	– c Luckes b Wellard	1
W. Watson lbw b Lawrence	1	– b Coope	63
N. W. D. Yardley b Tremlett	34	– c sub b Tremlett	9
E. Lester st Luckes b Lawrence	0	– b Buse	0
A. Coxon lbw b Wellard	20	– c Wellard b Coope	31
T. F. Smailes b Lawrence	6	– c Tremlett b Wellard	36
J. H. Wardle c Walford b Lawrence	6	– b Coope	4
D. V. Brennan b Lawrence	1	– b Tremlett	5
C. W. Foord c Tremlett b Lawrence	0	– not out	0
E. P. Robinson not out	0	– b Buse	0
L-b 1	1	B 1, l-b 1, w 2	4
	137		**181**

Yorkshire Bowling

	Overs	Mdns	Runs	Wkts	Overs	Mdns	Runs	Wkts
Coxon	17	4	32	1	7	1	24	1
Foord	14	4	58	1	6	—	23	3
Wardle	23.1	8	77	2				
Robinson	36	13	64	5				
Smailes	7	2	17	—				

Somerset Bowling

	Overs	Mdns	Runs	Wkts	Overs	Mdns	Runs	Wkts
Wellard	15	5	18	1	12	2	27	2
Tremlett	11	2	36	1	16.4	3	58	3
Hazell	21	8	44	1	11	2	36	—
Buse	5	3	3	—	12	2	27	2
Lawrence	16.2	3	35	6				
Coope					10	2	29	3

Umpires: H. Cruice and T. J. Bartley.

SOMERSET v HAMPSHIRE

Played at Taunton, May 21, 23, 24, 1949

Somerset won by 212 runs. Scoring a century in each innings for the first time in his career, Gimblett was the real architect of victory for Somerset, whose players gained the "£5 a win" bonus for the first time. Coope helped Gimblett, who altogether hit 242 for once out, in a partnership of 143 in ninety minutes, but Somerset also owed much to their slow bowlers Lawrence and Hazell, as well as to the pace of Tremlett. At one stage Hazell took three wickets without a run being hit off eleven balls. Hampshire's batting fell below standard, but Ransom, their right-arm fast-medium bowler, merited the award of his county cap.

Somerset

H. Gimblett lbw b Ransom	115	– not out ... 127
E. Hill c Rayment b Shackleton	13	– b Shackleton ... 40
G. E. S. Woodhouse c Rayment b Walker	10	– b Ransom ... 12
N. S. Mitchell-Innes c Walker b Ransom	4	– b Shackleton ... 9
M. Coope c Arnold b Knott	23	– c Eagar b Shackleton ... 71
H. T. F. Buse c Walker b Shackleton	53	
M. F. Tremlett b Ransom	2	– not out ... 5
J. Lawrence c Walker b Hill	4	
W. T. Luckes c McCorkell b Knott	6	
A. W. Wellard b Ransom	0	
H. L. Hazell not out	8	
B 3, l-b 1	4	
	242	**(4 wkts dec.) 264**

Hampshire

J. Arnold b Lawrence	44	– c Buse b Hazell ... 30
N. H. Rogers c Mitchell-Innes b Tremlett	11	– c Woodhouse b Hazell ... 37
N. McCorkell c Lawrence b Tremlett	20	– c and b Hazell ... 0
E. D. R. Eager b Lawrence	7	– c Wellard b Hazell ... 0
C. Walker st Luckes b Lawrence	0	– c Wellard b Tremlett ... 13
G. Hill st Luckes b Lawrence	6	– lbw b Tremlett ... 1
A. W. H. Rayment c and b Lawrence	16	– c Wellard b Lawrence ... 10
J. Bailey st Luckes b Wellard	0	– c Tremlett b Wellard ... 39
D. Shackleton not out	17	– c Luckes b Tremlett ... 3
V. J. Ransom st Luckes b Lawrence	2	– c Hill b Wellard ... 0
C. J. Knott c Tremlett b Wellard	14	– not out ... 0
B 2, l-b 7, w 2, n-b 2	13	B 7, l-b 1, w 1, n-b 2 ... 11
	150	**144**

Hampshire Bowling

	Overs	Mdns	Runs	Wkts	Overs	Mdns	Runs	Wkts
Ransom	33	8	84	4	29	2	99	1
Shackleton	21.1	4	45	2	27	5	84	3
Walker	26	5	62	1	14	2	43	—
Knott	9	2	27	2				
Hill	16	8	20	1	4	1	13	—
Rayment					2	—	25	—

Somerset Bowling

	Overs	Mdns	Runs	Wkts	Overs	Mdns	Runs	Wkts
Wellard	26	7	54	2	13.5	4	29	2
Buse	10	3	19	—	3	—	11	—
Tremlett	16	8	29	2	13	6	19	3
Lawrence	19	6	31	6	19	3	37	1
Hazell	4	1	4	—	25	12	37	4

Umpires: A. R. Coleman and B. Flint.

SOMERSET v SUSSEX

Played at Weston-super-Mare, August 15, 16, 1951

Somerset won by 362 runs. A characteristic century by Gimblett infused new life into the Somerset team, who gave their best all-round display of the season. Two 6s and fifteen 4s afforded ample evidence of Gimblett's hitting powers. Rogers also put plenty of power behind his strokes and claimed five 6s and five 4s. Marlar, the Cambridge Blue, persevered with off-spinners, taking seven wickets for 105. Robinson, of similar style, was even more successful for Somerset. He dismissed eight batsmen for 47 and only a polished innings by Doggart, who remained unbeaten, enabled Sussex to avert the follow-on. Gimblett, Tremlett and Stephenson stood out in Somerset's second innings, but Robinson remained their central figure. He captured seven wickets for 31 and a match record of fifteen for 78 was the best of his career.

Somerset

H. Gimblett c Oakman b Marlar	103	– lbw b Oakman	58
H. E. Watts c Webb b Marlar	31	– c Wood b James	25
J. Lawrence hit wkt b Marlar	33	– c John Langridge b James Langridge.	25
M. F. Tremlett b Marlar	6	– c Wood b Marlar	70
H. T. Buse c Webb b Marlar	10	– c Wood b James Langridge	32
J. Sainsbury lbw b Marlar	0	– b Marlar	16
S. S. Rogers c Doggart b James Langridge	58	– b Marlar	6
H. W. Stephenson st Webb b James Langridge	1	– not out	53
J. Redman c Doggart b James Langridge	8	– not out	35
H. L. Hazell c John Langridge b Marlar	0		
E. P. Robinson not out	2		
B 6, w 1, n-b 1	8	B 17, l-b 1	18
	260	**(7 wkts dec.)**	**338**

Sussex

John Langridge b Robinson	14	– c Rogers b Redman	0
D. S. Sheppard c Gimblettt b Robinson	7	– c Gimblett b Redman	24
G. H. G. Doggart not out	61	– b Robinson	24
G. Cox lbw b Robinson	5	– c Gimblett b Robinson	10
C. Oakes st Stephenson b Hazell	3	– c Gimblett b Robinson	0
James Langridge lbw b Robinson	1	– c Hazell b Robinson	22
A. S. Oakman b Robinson	0	– c Gimblett b Robinson	4
A. E. James b Robinson	2	– not out	12
D. J. Wood run out	2	– lbw b Robinson	0
R. G. Marlar b Robinson	6	– b Robinson	8
R. T. Webb c Lawrence b Robinson	0	– b Hazell	7
B 10, l-b 5	15	B 6, l-b 3	9
	116		**120**

Sussex Bowling

	Overs	Mdns	Runs	Wkts	Overs	Mdns	Runs	Wkts
Wood	5	2	13	—	4	—	32	—
James	14	7	30	—	21	7	44	1
Oakman	12	2	69	—	15	2	50	1
Marlar	33	6	105	7	28	5	116	3
James Langridge	18.2	7	35	3	24	7	78	2

Somerset Bowling

	Overs	Mdns	Runs	Wkts	Overs	Mdns	Runs	Wkts
Buse	6	4	8	—	5	1	22	—
Redman	5	2	12	—	7	2	29	2
Robinson	18.1	6	47	8	13	3	31	7
Hazell	18	7	34	1	15.4	6	29	1

Umpires: A. E. Pothecary and H. G. Baldwin.

SOMERSET v WORCESTERSHIRE

Played at Taunton, August 22, 23, 24, 1951

Worcestershire won by three wickets. Once more Tremlett made the highest score for Somerset in the first innings, and completed 2,000 runs for the first time. Jenkins varied leg-spinners in subtle fashion, taking his last four wickets for three runs. Kenyon, with this third century in successive matches, gave an impressive performance for Worcestershire and became the second player in the match to reach 2,000 runs. In Somerset's second innings Gimblett rose to great heights, his not out 174 occupying five hours forty minutes. Set 214 to win in just under two hours, Worcestershire kept pace with the clock, and a fairly even struggle produced a thrilling finish. When Buse delivered the last ball of the day six runs were required for victory, and Wyatt, Worcestershire's captain, made a great hit into the pavilion to give his side success.

Somerset

H. Gimblett c Broadbent b Perks	0	– not out	174
F. L. Angell st Yarnold b Jenkins	29	– c Yarnold b Wyatt	6
H. E. Watts b Perks	17	– c Yarnold b Howorth	74
M. F. Tremlett c Richardson b Howorth...........	63	– c Jenkins b Perks	41
H. T. F. Buse c Outschoorn b Jenkins...........	7	– b Perks	3
S. S. Rogers lbw b Jenkins.....................	35	– c Yarnold b Perks..............	7
J. Lawrence c Kenyon b Jenkins.................	35	– b Howorth	4
H. W. Stephenson c Wyatt b Jenkins	20	– b Howorth	1
J. Redman c Richardson b Jenkins	3	– b Jenkins....................	28
H. L. Hazell c Wyatt b Jenkins	7		
E. P. Robinson not out	2		
L-b 10. n-b 3	13	B 6, l-b 2, n-b 4	12
	231	**(8 wkts dec.)**	**350**

Worcestershire

D. J. Kenyon b Buse........................	138	– c Rogers b Redman	16
E. Cooper b Buse	6	– c Stephenson b Lawrence	38
L. Outschoorn retired hurt	37		
R. E. S. Wyatt b Hazell......................	13	– not out	9
R. Broadbent lbw b Lawrence.................	91	– c Redman b Robinson	47
P. E. Richardson c Lawrence b Hazell	27	– not out	1
N. H. Whiting st Stephenson b Lawrence	2	– b Lawrence..................	5
R. O. Jenkins c Stephenson b Lawrence	24	– b Buse	25
R. T. D. Perks b Robinson	21	– c Gimblett b Lawrence	8
R. Howorth not out.........................	2	– run out	58
B 5, w 1, n-b 1	7	B 4, l-b 3	7
(8 wkts dec.)	**368**	**(7 wkts)**	**214**

H. Yarnold did not bat.

Worcestershire Bowling

	Overs	Mdns	Runs	Wkts	Overs	Mdns	Runs	Wkts
Perks............	19	3	58	2	30	3	96	3
Wyatt...........	8	1	30	—	8	3	23	1
Jenkins..........	25.2	3	81	7	26.3	2	84	1
Howorth.........	19	5	45	1	35	8	79	3
Whiting..........	4	2	4	—	8	2	28	—
Broadbent........					6	—	28	—

Somerset Bowling

	Overs	Mdns	Runs	Wkts	Overs	Mdns	Runs	Wkts
Buse............	22	8	43	2	9	1	42	1
Redman.........	17	4	65	—	7	—	36	1
Robinson........	25	7	59	1	8	—	56	1
Lawrence........	33.2	2	104	3	9	—	52	3
Hazell..........	38	13	90	2	3	—	21	—

Umpires: T. J. Bartley and K. McCanlis.

SOMERSET v DERBYSHIRE

Played at Taunton, July 12, 14, 15, 1952

Drawn. Bowlers were generally helpless on a perfect pitch, but Derbyshire, facing the formidable total of 426, accomplished a splendid feat when they took first innings points. Yet Gimblett was the star performer by hitting a century in each innings. He drove, hooked and cut in brilliant style, and Tordoff, the left-hander, gave a valuable display in helping him to put on 200 for the second wicket. Derbyshire were not quite so enterprising, but a great fighting innings by Elliott helped most to gain the lead. He batted nearly six and a half hours, hitting seventeen 4s, and shared a fourth stand of 158 with Kelly.

Somerset

H. Gimblett c Jackson b Smith 146	– c Smith b Elliott 116
G. G. Tordoff st Dawkes b Morgan 89	– c Dawkes b Revill.............. 23
H. W. Stephenson b Jackson.................... 8	– c Morgan b Smith.............. 34
M. F. Tremlett c Morgan b Rhodes............. 60	– not out 16
H. T. F. Buse c Elliott b Smith 31	– not out 1
D. L. Kitson c Gladwin b Rhodes............... 16	– run out 4
S. S. Rogers b Morgan 21	
J. Lawrence not out........................... 17	– c Revill b Smith 0
J. Redman not out............................ 12	
B 4, l-b 18, n-b 4 26	B 4, l-b 2, n-b 2 8

1/25 2/225 3/290 4/330   (7 wkts dec.) 426   1/66 2/133   (5 wkts dec.) 202
5/364 6/392 7/392   3/164 4/164 5/194

E. P. Robinson and H. L. Hazell did not bat.

Derbyshire

C. S. Elliott c Robinson b Lawrence.......168	C. Gladwin not out 11
A. Hamer c Hazell b Buse.............. 0	G. Dawkes not out 1
G. L. Willatt lbw b Lawrence 34	
A. C. Revill c Hazell b Buse 68	
J. Kelly b Buse 93	B 12, l-b 12, w 1, n-b 1 26
D. C. Morgan c Hazell b Redman 18	
A. E. G. Rhodes st Stephenson b Redman .. 8	1/4 2/67 3/205 (7 wkts dec.) 427
	4/363 5/403 6/405 7/415

E. Smith and L. Jackson did not bat.

Derbyshire Bowling

	Overs	Mdns	Runs	Wkts	Overs	Mdns	Runs	Wkts
Jackson............	36	6	68	1	5	1	12	—
Gladwin..........	30	7	101	—	4	3	4	—
Rhodes...........	29	4	97	2	11	3	23	—
Morgan..........	10	2	35	2	7	2	18	—
Smith	27	7	93	2	16	2	61	2
Hamer	3	—	6	—				
Revill					12	—	57	1
Elliott					2	—	15	1
Willatt...........					2	—	4	—

Somerset Bowling

	Overs	Mdns	Runs	Wkts
Redman	18	4	38	2
Buse	26	7	70	3
Hazell............	29	7	73	—
Robinson	41	14	88	—
Lawrence	54	17	111	2
Tordoff..........	6	—	21	—

Umpires: P. Corrall and W. F. Price.

SOMERSET v LANCASHIRE

(H. T. F. Buse's Benefit)

Played at Bath, June 6, 1953

Lancashire won by an innings and 24 runs. A newly-laid pitch brought financial disaster for Buse, the match ending before six o'clock on the first day when thirty wickets fell for 292 runs. Tattersall, the England and Lancashire off-spin bowler, carried everything before him, taking thirteen for 69. His seven victims in the first innings, when not one Somerset player reached double figures, were all caught. The best stand of the match for the losers came in their second innings, Redman and Langford adding 35 in a plucky final partnership. Ironical as it seemed, Buse proved Somerset's central figure with the ball. Although hit for 18 in one over, he dismissed six batsmen for 41 runs. Lancashire, who lost half their side for 46, were put in a winning position by Marner and Wharton, whose fierce hitting brought 70 for the sixth stand in twenty-five minutes. Four times Marner cleared the boundary with huge hits for six.

Somerset

H. Gimblett run out.	0	– c Wharton b Tattersall	5
J. Lawrence c Ikin b Tattersall	8	– c Wharton b Statham	0
R. Smith c Place b Tattersall	9	– b Statham	0
M. F. Tremlett c Statham b Tattersall	4	– b Statham	1
H. T. F. Buse c Grieves b Tattersall	5	– c Grieves b Tattersall	3
H. W. Stephenson c Marner b Tattersall	8	– b Tattersall	14
B. G. Brocklehurst c Marner b Hilton	2	– c Hilton b Tattersall	2
D. P. T. Deshon c Edrich b Tattersall	0	– c Wharton b Statham	9
S. S. Rogers st Parr b Hilton	7	– c Grieves b Tattersall	0
J. Redman c Place b Tattersall	1	– not out	27
B. Langford not out	7	– b Tattersall	8
B 2, l-b 2	4	B 1, l-b 9	10

1/12 2/13 3/17 4/22 5/34 6/40   55   1/3 2/3 3/5 4/7 5/26   79
7/40 8/47 9/47   6/27 7/36 8/37 9/44

Lancashire

C. Washbrook lbw b Buse	20	F. D. Parr not out	15
J. T. Ikin c Tremlett b Buse	8	J. B. Statham c Tremlett b Langford	6
W. Place lbw b Buse	11	R. Tattersall c Stephenson b Buse	2
G. A. Edrich c Brocklehurst b Buse	2		
K. Grieves c Tremlett b Lawrence	2	B 4, l-b 4	8
A. Wharton b Redman	21		
P. Marner b Redman	44		158
M. J. Hilton b Buse	19		

1/22 2/33 3/41 4/44 5/46
6/116 7/117 8/140 9/155

Lancashire Bowling

	Overs	Mdns	Runs	Wkts	Overs	Mdns	Runs	Wkts
Statham	8	4	14	—	10	4	13	4
Tattersall	12.4	4	25	7	11.3	2	44	6
Hilton	5	1	12	2	2	—	12	—

Somerset Bowling

	Overs	Mdns	Runs	Wkts
Buse	12.4	3	41	6
Redman	6	1	32	2
Smith	1	—	8	—
Langford	3	—	18	1
Lawrence	8	2	31	1
Tremlett	2	—	20	—

Umpires: A. E. Boulton-Carter and J. S. Buller.

SOMERSET v KENT

Played at Bath, June 10, 11, 12, 1953

Somerset won by 153 runs. Their victory proved a great personal triumph for Langford, a 17-year-old off-spin bowler, who took fourteen wickets for 156. Making his second appearance for Somerset, he turned the ball to a steady length, and few played him with confidence. Wright and Page, Kent spin bowlers, almost routed Somerset in their first innings, and eventually Kent gained a lead of 55. Then Gimblett rallied Somerset with a fighting innings of 146, he and Buse, who also hit a convincing century, adding 190 for the third-wicket stand. A declaration set Kent 361 to win, but after a century partnership for the second wicket by Woollett and Edrich their batting broke down. In a devastating spell of fifteen overs Langford obtained six wickets for 27. Struck over the left eye while fielding close to the bat, Tremlett was so badly injured that he did not appear again for Somerset during the season.

Somerset

H. Gimblett b Ridgway	6	– c Edrich b Wright ... 146
J. Lawrence b Wright	15	– c Fenner b Wright. ... 65
R. Smith st Fenner b Page	14	– run out ... 2
M. F. Tremlett c Phebey b Wright	15	– absent hurt ... 0
H. T. F. Buse c Edrich b Page	0	– b Wright ... 102
H. W. Stephenson c Ufton b Page	0	– c Murray Wood b Page ... 19
B. G. Brocklehurst b Wright	39	– c Ridgway b Page ... 29
S. S. Rogers not out	11	– b Page ... 9
C. F. Davey c and b Wright	0	– not out ... 17
J. Redman b Page	9	– b Page ... 0
B. Langford st Fenner b Page	5	– not out ... 3
B 4, l-b 4, n-b 1	9	B 17, l-b 7 ... 24

1/12 2/37 3/37 4/37 5/37 6/93   123   1/97 2/118   (8 wkts dec.) 416
7/100 8/100 9/113   3/308 4/341 5/368 6/390
                                7/399 8/399

Kent

A. H. Phebey lbw b Buse	1	– c Stephenson b Lawrence ... 19
A. F. Woollett c Gimblett b Langford	34	– hit wkt b Lawrence ... 73
B. R. Edrich c Rogers b Langford	7	– c Lawrence b Langford ... 54
D. G. Ufton c Lawrence b Langford	21	– c Brocklehurst b Langford ... 23
R. Mayes b Langford	17	– c Gimblett b Langford ... 13
M. D. Fenner c Brocklehurst b Langford	11	– c Gimblett b Lawrence ... 3
R. R. Dovey st Stephenson b Lawrence	31	– b Langford ... 4
W. Murray Wood b Langford	16	– c Lawrence b Langford ... 1
D. V. P. Wright c Gimblett b Langford	13	– lbw b Langford ... 2
F. Ridgway c Gimblett b Langford	13	– c sub b Lawrence ... 1
J. C. T. Page not out	0	– not out ... 3
B 10, l-b 4	14	B 10, l-b 1, n-b 1 ... 12

1/5 2/30 3/67 4/68 5/92   178   1/48 2/150 3/158 4/192 5/195   208
6/115 7/145 8/145 9/174   6/199 7/200 8/202 9/203

Kent Bowling

	Overs	Mdns	Runs	Wkts	Overs	Mdns	Runs	Wkts
Ridgway	7	3	15	1	3	—	15	—
Dovey	7	1	11	—	18	2	55	—
Wright	17	6	53	4	39	1	163	3
Page	16.1	6	35	5	33	4	126	4
Murray Wood					7	3	25	—
Edrich					2	—	8	—

Somerset Bowling

	Overs	Mdns	Runs	Wkts	Overs	Mdns	Runs	Wkts
Buse	17	11	21	1	18	6	23	—
Langford	41	12	96	8	39	12	60	6
Lawrence	24	5	47	1	35	7	91	4
Redman					4	3	4	—
Smith					6	1	18	—

Umpires: J. J. Hills and E. A. Roberts.

SOMERSET v NORTHAMPTONSHIRE

Played at Taunton, July 18, 20, 21, 1953

Drawn. The best ever ninth-wicket stand against Northamptonshire enabled Somerset to take first innings points. When their eighth wicket fell they were 129 behind, but Gimblett and Hall added 130 without being separated, and Somerset declared with a lead of one run. Gimblett, as usual, was the mainstay and there were no real blemishes in the fiftieth century of his career. Unbeaten after nearly six hours, he hit his third hundred in successive matches against Northamptonshire. Livingston showed his liking for the Somerset bowlers by making his fifth century against them since 1950. Near the end bowlers enjoyed more success, and Somerset, worried by Clark's fast left-arm deliveries, narrowly escaped defeat.

Northamptonshire

D. Brookes c Lawrence b Mitchell	10	– lbw b Langford ... 43
N. Oldfield c Lawrence b Hall	31	– b Mitchell ... 90
L. Livingston b Buse	106	– not out ... 65
D. Barrick st Stephenson b Lawrence	18	
F. Jakeman c Gimblett b Lawrence	2	
B. C. Reynolds st Stephenson b Lawrence	64	
F. R. Brown c Hall b Langford	40	– not out ... 13
V. Broderick b Langford	8	
G. E. Tribe not out	19	
A. Lightfoot lbw b Langford	0	
R. W. Clarke c Smith b Lawrence	0	
B 16, l-b 11, w 1, n-b 1	29	B 8, l-b 3 ... 11

1/23 2/82 3/135 4/145 5/196 6/266   327   1/85 2/209   (2 wkts dec.) 222
7/297 8/317 9/326

Somerset

H. Gimblett not out	167	– c Livingston b Brown ... 42
D. L. Kitson b Clarke	15	– c Tribe b Clarke ... 5
R. Smith b Clarke	4	– b Clarke ... 10
J. Lawrence lbw b Brown	23	– b Brown ... 4
H. T. F. Buse c Livingston b Tribe	13	– c Tribe b Clarke ... 2
H. W. Stephenson c and b Tribe	9	– b Clarke ... 0
J. Baker lbw b Brown	8	– not out ... 26
B. G. Brocklehurst b Tribe	1	– b Brown ... 3
B. Langford c Reynolds b Tribe	3	– not out ... 4
T. A. Hall not out	69	– c Reynolds b Clarke ... 8
B 14, l-b 2	16	B 3 ... 3

1/20 2/50 3/126 4/154   (8 wkts dec.) 328   1/9 2/55 3/55   (8 wkts) 107
5/164 6/181 7/188 8/198   4/57 5/62 6/80 7/83 8/103

C. G. Mitchell did not bat.

Somerset Bowling

	Overs	Mdns	Runs	Wkts	Overs	Mdns	Runs	Wkts
Hall	21	1	73	1	10.4	—	57	—
Mitchell	18	4	50	1	10	3	32	1
Buse	14	1	57	1	5	1	15	—
Baker	2	—	8	—	5	—	26	—
Lawrence	29.5	9	62	4	11	—	48	—
Langford	20	3	48	3	13	4	33	1

Northamptonshire Bowling

	Overs	Mdns	Runs	Wkts	Overs	Mdns	Runs	Wkts
Clarke............	27.5	5	91	2	17	1	51	5
Brown............	33	9	76	2	15	7	21	3
Lightfoot.........	23	5	52	—	7	1	21	—
Tribe.............	34	8	79	4	9	5	11	—
Broderick	7	4	14	—				

Umpires: W. T. Jones and K. McCanlis.

SOMERSET v SURREY

Played at Weston-super-Mare, August 10, 11, 1955

Surrey won by an innings and 100 runs. The Somerset batsmen were no match for Surrey's bowlers on a spiteful pitch. Surrey did well to score 227, but they owed most to May who gave a delightful display against the lifting and turning ball. Then came a dramatic breakdown, Somerset being dismissed for the lowest total of the season. They found Lock and A. Bedser almost unplayable. Lock did the hat-trick for the first time in his career when he dismissed McMahon and Lobb at the end of the first innings and Angell with his first ball when Somerset followed on 191 behind. Only an hour and a quarter was needed on the second day, Lock and A. Bedser again routing the home county Lock took ten for 54 in the match and A. Bedser nine for 46.

Surrey

T. H. Clark c Tremlett b Lomax.......... 6	W. S. Surridge c Tordoff b Lobb......... 22
M. J. Stewart c Angell b Tordoff.......... 14	P. J. Loader c Tordoff b McMahon 17
P. B. H. May c Angell b McMahon 93	A. V. Bedser not out 1
R. Constable c Lomax b McMahon 1	
K. Barrington c Tremlett b McMahon 1	L-b 1...................... 1
E. A. Bedser c Angell b McMahon 31	
A. J. McIntyre c Angell b McMahon 4	1/6 2/42 3/47 4/61 5/135 227
G. A. R. Lock lbw b Lobb 36	6/139 7/170 8/190 9/226

Somerset

F. L. Angell c Surridge b A. Bedser..............	1 – c May b Lock.............. 0
G. G. Tordoff c Lock b A. Bedser................	13 – c Loader b A. Bedser........ 19
J. Lawrence b Loader	1 – c McIntyre b Lock.............. 9
M. F. Tremlett c Lock b A. Bedser	11 – c Clark b Lock.............. 26
G. L. Williams c May b A. Bedser	0 – c Surridge b Lock.............. 1
P. B. Wight c McIntyre b Lock................	5 – c Lock b A. Bedser.............. 7
M. Walker c May b Lock	0 – b A. Bedser.............. 0
J. G. Lomax not out	1 – c Clark b Lock.............. 13
H. W. Stephenson c McIntyre b A. Bedser	0 – c Constable b A. Bedser........ 1
J. W. McMahon b Lock	0 – c Clark b Lock.............. 5
B. Lobb st McIntyre b Lock ...'.............	0 – not out 0
B 4.............................	4 – B 9, l-b 1.............. 10

1/10 2/15 3/21 4/21 5/31   36   1/0 2/32 3/32 4/38 5/45   91
6/35 7/35 8/35 9/36   6/49 7/64 8/74 9/91

Somerset Bowling

	Overs	Mdns	Runs	Wkts
Lobb	20.3	3	64	2
Lomax	9	3	16	1
McMahon	29	11	79	6
Tordoff	7	3	14	1
Lawrence	2	1	10	—
Walker	9	—	43	—

Surrey Bowling

	Overs	Mdns	Runs	Wkts	Overs	Mdns	Runs	Wkts
A. Bedser	9	3	14	5	14	5	32	4
Loader	6	1	13	1				
Lock	3.5	2	15	4	13.4	3	49	6

Umpires: E. Davies and J. J. Hills.

SOMERSET v HAMPSHIRE

Played at Weston-super-Mare, August 17, 18, 1955

Hampshire won by 264 runs. Remarkable bowling by Shackleton gave them their decisive victory. He accomplished one of the best performances in the history of the game in taking eight wickets for four runs in 11.1 overs in the first innings and he followed with six for 25 when Somerset batted again. Rain before the start and during lunch restricted the first day's play when Hampshire did fairly well until the spin took effect. Then Hilton did the hat-trick for the first time, dismissing Harrison, Shackleton and Burden. The pitch was extremely awkward and the Somerset batsmen were helpless. They were all out in 74 minutes and Hampshire, leading by 117, scored readily. Rayment made his only hundred of the season and Horton and Harrison helped in good stands. Somerset, needing 363, again failed dismally, only Stephenson offering resistance with a hard-hit 52.

Hampshire

J. R. Gray c Lawrence b Hilton	43	– b McMahon	4
R. E. Marshall c Stephenson b Yawar Saeed	5	– c Lobb b Yawar Saeed	12
H. Horton c Lawrence b Hilton	43	– b Tordoff	59
A. W. H. Rayment c Lawrence b McMahon	12	– c Tordoff b McMahon	104
N. H. Rogers c Williams b Hilton	2	– c Williams b Tordoff	10
H. M. Barnard b McMahon	19	– b McMahon	5
L. Harrison c Williams b Hilton	9	– not out	35
P. J. Sainsbury not out	13		
D. Shackleton st Stephenson b Hilton	0		
M. D. Burden b Hilton	0	– b Hilton	4
V. H. D. Cannings c Hilton b McMahon	0		
B 8	8	B 7, l-b 5	12

1/11 2/78 3/91 4/94 5/126   154   1/12 2/16   (7 wkts dec.) 245
6/136 7/149 8/149 9/149   3/107 4/127 5/136 6/239
                                     7/245

Somerset

G. G. Tordoff b Shackleton	0	– c Marshall b Shackleton	0
G. L. Williams c Rogers b Shackleton	2	– c Burden b Shackleton	2
J. Lawrence lbw b Shackleton	0	– c Gray b Sainsbury	4
M. F. Tremlett c Gray b Shackleton	8	– b Shackleton	0
P. B. Wright c Marshall b Shackleton	2	– c and b Burden	10
J. G. Lomax c Rogers b Sainsbury	0	– c Rayment b Shackleton	20
H. W. Stephenson not out	18	– c Horton b Sainsbury	52
Yawar Saeed c Barnard b Shackleton	0	– c Barnard b Shackleton	0
J. Hilton b Shackleton	0	– b Shackleton	0
J. W. McMahon run out	1	– not out	9
B. Lobb c Rayment b Shackleton	0	– c Burden b Sainsbury	0
L-b 6	6	L-b 1	1

1/0 2/0 3/3 4/10 5/10 6/20   37   1/0 2/3 3/4 4/16 5/16   98
7/20 8/26 9/27   6/81 7/81 8/81 9/89

Somerset Bowling

	Overs	Mdns	Runs	Wkts	Overs	Mdns	Runs	Wkts
Lobb	11	4	23	—	6	1	12	—
Yawar Saeed	7	2	16	1	5	—	14	1
Hilton	24	7	49	6	12.2	—	50	1
McMahon	27.3	10	58	3	32	2	122	3
Lomax					2	1	2	—
Tordoff					11	1	33	2

Hampshire Bowling

	Overs	Mdns	Runs	Wkts	Overs	Mdns	Runs	Wkts
Shackleton	11.1	7	4	8	16	7	25	6
Cannings	4	2	5	—	4	2	3	—
Sainsbury	7	2	22	1	13.4	—	63	3
Burden					2	—	6	1

Umpires: A. Skelding and J. S. Buller.

SOMERSET v NOTTINGHAMSHIRE

Played at Weston-super-Mare, August 6, 7, 8, 1958

Somerset won by nine wickets. They were indebted to Lomax for a splendid all-round performance. Nottinghamshire failed against the spin of Langford and Bryant, but Somerset would have fared little better without Lomax, who hit fourteen 4s and shared a stand of 54 with Palmer. The only criticism which can be made of his innings was that he was at fault when two of his partners were run out. Poole and Simpson led a spirited counter-attack when Nottinghamshire went in again 81 behind, but Lomax ended the innings by performing the hat-trick in a spell of four wickets for one run. Then Lomax rounded off a fine match by scoring 53 in under an hour when Somerset needed 132 to win.

Nottinghamshire

R. T. Simpson b Langford	10	– c and b Langford		51
N. Hill lbw b Palmer	13	– c Tremlett b Bryant		28
M. Hall b Palmer	2	– c Lomax b Langford		0
M. Hill c and b Langford	16	– b Langford		2
C. J. Poole c McCool b Langford	32	– c Bryant b Lomax		81
G. Goonesena lbw b Langford	0	– c McCool b Bryant		0
K. Smales c Wight b Bryant	3	– c McCool b Lomax		19
T. Atkinson b Bryant	3	– c Silk b Lomax		2
A. Jepson c Silk b Langford	3	– c Lomax b Palmer		7
C. S. Matthews c McCool b Bryant	3	– c McCool b Lomax		0
G. Millman not out	0	– not out		7
B 3, l-b 1	4	B 12, l-b 2		14

1/19 2/21 3/25 4/76 5/76   89   1/69 2/104 3/128 4/128 5/143   211
6/77 7/83 8/86 9/86   6/191 7/192 8/193 9/193

Somerset

W. E. Alley b Smales	14	– not out	55
J. G. Lomax c M. Hill b Smales	80	– c Millman b Smales	53
P. B. Wight c and b Goonesena	14	– not out	24
C. L. McCool c Jepson b Goonesena	12		
D. W. R. Silk run out	14		
G. M. Tripp run out	0		
M. F. Tremlett st Millman b Smales	0		
K. E. Palmer b Jepson	27		
B. Langford b Smales	0		
P. Eele not out	3		
E. Bryant not out	1		
L-b 5	5		

1/34 2/49 3/67 4/100   (9 wkts dec.) 170   1/71   (1 wkt) 132
5/101 6/105 7/159 8/164 9/169

Somerset Bowling

	Overs	Mdns	Runs	Wkts	Overs	Mdns	Runs	Wkts
Lomax	4	1	7	—	10	3	15	4
Alley	6	2	8	—	16	4	18	—
Palmer	6	2	7	2	13	2	37	1
Langford	16	5	33	5	33	8	80	3
Wight	3	—	14	—	5	2	13	—
Bryant	10.1	4	16	3	13	3	25	2
McCool					5	1	9	—

Nottinghamshire Bowling

	Overs	Mdns	Runs	Wkts	Overs	Mdns	Runs	Wkts
Jepson	10	3	20	1	10	2	31	—
Atkinson	5	—	17	—	3	—	20	—
Smales	34	18	55	4	15	7	34	1
Goonesena	25	4	70	2	3	—	16	—
Matthews	1	—	3	—	7	—	25	—
Simpson					0.5	—	6	—

Umpires: H. Elliott and N. Oldfield.

SOMERSET v LANCASHIRE

Played at Weston-super-Mare, August 13, 14, 15, 1958

Somerset won by 89 runs. Spin bowlers ran riot on a rain-damaged pitch and the only batting of note came from Silk and Palmer in the Somerset second innings. Their stand of 112, allied to the bowling of Langford, decided the issue. Statham, the only successful pace bowler, and Tattersall, turned the Somerset first innings into a procession; Langford returned the compliment. His nine for 26 was the best performance of his career, and in one spell of thirteen balls he took four wickets for nine runs. Somerset lost six wickets for 57, then Silk and Palmer came together and for the first time batsmen gained the upper hand. Their partnership lasted an hour and forty minutes, Silk hitting four 6s and eight 4s, and Palmer eight 4s. They were particularly severe on Hilton. Palmer was rewarded with his county cap. Lancashire needed 144 to win with time to spare, but never looked like getting the runs. Langford took six more wickets for a remarkable match analysis of 15 for 54, making his figures for the Weston festival 35 wickets for 279 runs in three matches.

Somerset

W. E. Alley lbw b Tattersall	11	– c Grieves b Tattersall 12
J. G. Lomax c Hilton b Tattersall	6	– c Wharton b Hilton............ 8
D. R. W. Silk lbw b Statham	2	– c Statham b Hilton.............. 77
P. B. Wight b Statham	1	– c Grieves b Tattersall 5
C. L. McCool b Tattersall	11	– c Pullar b Hilton.............. 8
G. M. Tripp b Statham	11	– c Wharton b Tattersall 0
M. F. Tremlett b Statham	0	– c Marner b Tattersall 4
K. E. Palmer c Hilton b Tattersall	7	– c Hilton b Tattersall 56
B. Langford b Tattersall	4	– c and b Hilton................ 0
P. J. Eele c Wilson b Statham	1	– not out 5
E. Bryant not out	0	– lbw b Hilton 1
L-b 6	6	L-b 1 1

1/16 2/19 3/20 4/21 5/45 6/45   60   1/21 2/21 3/33 4/43 5/53   177
7/51 8/55 9/58   6/57 7/169 8/171 9/171

Lancashire

A. Wharton c Silk b Langford	34	– c Tremlett b Alley............ 9
R. W. Barber c McCool b Langford	13	– c Tremlett b Langford.......... 8
G. Pullar c and b Langford	1	– c Tremlett b Langford.......... 8
P. Marner lbw b Langford	0	– c Tremlett b Langford.......... 8
C. Washbrook lbw b Langford	1	– lbw b Langford................ 6
K. Grieves c Tripp b Bryant	9	– c Lomax b Langford........... 0
A. Bolton b Langford	2	– lbw b Wight 0
M. J. Hilton b Langford	21	– c Bryant b Wight 0
J. B. Statham b Langford	0	– b Langford 5
A. Wilson c Bryant b Langford	3	– not out 4
R. Tattersall not out	0	– c Palmer b Wight 6
B 1, l-b 4	5	B 5 5

1/37 2/47 3/47 4/53 5/58 6/62   89   1/15 2/19 3/27 4/37 5/37   59
7/72 8/72 9/89   6/44 7/44 8/44 9/59

Lancashire Bowling

	Overs	Mdns	Runs	Wkts	Overs	Mdns	Runs	Wkts
Statham	22	7	32	5	16	5	34	—
Wharton	4	1	5	—				
Tattersall	18.3	12	13	5	33	14	46	5
Hilton	1	—	4	—	10	4	85	5
Bolton					1	—	11	—

Somerset Bowling

	Overs	Mdns	Runs	Wkts	Overs	Mdns	Runs	Wkts
Lomax	2	—	9	—				
Alley	7	2	25	—	7	—	13	1
Langford	13.4	7	26	9	18	8	28	6
Bryant	8	2	24	1				
Palmer	1	1	—	—				
Wight					11.2	6	13	3

Umpires: C. S. Elliott and R. S. Lay.

THE STORY OF SOMERSET [1959]

By Eric Hill

Born at Taunton on July 9, 1923, Eric Hill made his début for Somerset as an amateur at Lord's in 1947. An opening batsman, he later turned professional and received his county cap in 1949. Now his time is fully occupied as a journalist.

Somerset have never been one of the fashionable counties, but from their very beginning they were "The Team of Surprises". Even their birth took place away from home, in Devon, for it was immediately after a match between the Gentlemen of Devonshire and the Gentlemen of Somersetshire that a meeting was held at Sidmouth on Wednesday, August 18, 1875, with the Rev. A. C. Ainslie in the chair. Mr. E. Western, of Fullands, Taunton, was requested to act as secretary and he is looked upon as the founder of the now flourishing county club. A circular letter was sent by him from Ilfracombe to likely patrons and included the following four resolutions passed at that inaugural meeting:

1. There shall be no county ground.
2. The club shall depend upon its support by voluntary contributions.
3. County matches shall be played on any ground in the county that may be selected by the Committee.
4. A president, vice-president, treasurer and secretary by nomination, and a committee consisting of nine gentlemen, three from each division of the county shall be appointed.

FIRST CAPTAIN

The first captain was the Rev. Stirling Cookesley Voules, born at Middle Chinnock, near Crewkerne, an Oxford Blue from 1863 to 1866, who was then Rector of Rise, Hull, in Yorkshire, and formerly a master of Rossall School. The new club experienced various changes of fortune, but progress was made when the freehold of the present ground and headquarters at Taunton was secured in 1886. Down the years many wonderful matches and notable performances in the annals of first-class cricket have been seen there.

It was at Taunton in 1895 that Archie MacLaren hit 424, the highest individual score ever made in England, for Lancashire against Somerset. Previously, in 1892, H. T. Hewett and Lionel Palairet had engaged the then best first-wicket partnership, 346, for Somerset at the expense of Yorkshire. At Taunton, too, in 1925, Jack Hobbs hit two centuries in the same match, to exceed W. G. Grace's record of 126 hundreds.

"SAMMY" WOODS

Through this diverting chronicle of flickering fortune, colourful characters have liberally spread their talents over the pleasant rural grounds that abound in Somerset. From the early days when the lion-hearted S. M. J. Woods, a massive all-rounder from Australia, allied his enormous talents to the graceful attributes of that prince of stylists, the aforesaid

L. C. H. Palairet, Somerset's ambition has always been to play cricket for fun. They knew their limitations but from the time of their acceptance as a first-class county in 1891 their form was quite unpredictable.

The first season in the highest grade was a pointer. Quickly, the wisdom of their newly won promotion was held in doubt; the giants, Surrey, bowled them out at The Oval for 37 in each innings to win by the mammoth margin of an innings and 375 runs, but Somerset proceeded to end a long unbeaten run by Kent. They beat Yorkshire at Bradford, avenged the Surrey debacle, and perhaps best of all they succeeded against their neighbouring rivals, Gloucestershire.

Probably what stamped Somerset most as a shock team were their performances at the turn of the century. From 1900 to 1903 they beat Yorkshire three times. In two of those seasons Yorkshire, who were champions, admitted defeat only twice, and each time their colours were lowered by Somerset. The 1901 match at Leeds was the most famous and in fact the score-card still adorns most pavilions Somerset way. At the end of the first day after Rhodes, Haigh and Hirst had skittled Somerset for 87, the story goes that at the Mayoral dinner a civic dignitary offered £100 to the club if Somerset won. L. C. Braund and L. C. H. Palairet, both out for 0 in the first innings, each made 100, putting on 222 in only two hours twenty minutes and the final total reached 630. Then Braund, one of the best all-rounders of all time, joined forces with B. Cranfield and the mighty Northerners were humbled for a paltry total of 130. "We never got the £100," said Woods, "but I won £10 on the game as I took ten to one that Palairet would make a hundred." Palairet's off-side play was a by-word of the day.

"Sammy" Woods was a real character. As a fast bowler and a hitter he made vivid contributions to the game. Born at Glenfield, near Sydney, and educated at Brighton, he captained Cambridge University in 1890 and had the unusual distinction of playing for Australia against England and for England against South Africa. K. S. Ranjitsinhji, in his Jubilee book, suggested that although Woods's bowling was going off a bit in 1897 it was still good enough to beat the Players for years to come, and added, "there is no better man to go in when the pitch is bad or things are going wrong, although he does sometimes play forward to a straight ball with his eyes turned full on the square-leg umpire – a stroke he repudiates and never fails to use successfully once or twice an innings." This remarkable man scored 12,000 runs and took 500 wickets for Somerset. In those days Woods shared most of the Somerset bowling with Braund, one of the first leg-breakers, and E. J. Tyler, a slow left-hander. Besides his prowess as a cricketer, Woods earned equal fame in the Rugby football world. As a forward he gained thirteen caps for England between 1890 and 1895. His quick breaking and relentless tackling set a new style and nowadays he is regarded as the "Father" of wing-forwards.

From 1901, Braund performed the double three consecutive seasons and played 23 times for England, going on three tours to Australia. Tyler took 869 wickets in his career. He and J. C. White shared the distinction of being the only Somerset bowlers who have taken all ten wickets in an innings. It was in 1895 that his ten for 49 in 35 overs put out Surrey at Taunton.

DIFFICULT YEARS

After their encouraging and spectacular start, Somerset faded as the 1914-18 war approached. The increasing burden began to tell on the old players. Nevertheless, some staunch professional stiffening was forthcoming in the persons of E. Robson and A. E. Lewis, both all-rounders. Robson's fine career spanned thirty years and gave Somerset 12,000 runs and 1,200 wickets. At the age of 51 he gained Somerset the surprise victory of the 1922 season when in the last over of a tense match with Middlesex at Weston-super-Mare he made the winning hit for 6 by lifting the ball clean out of the ground. This feat earned him £50 from an anonymous donor.

We have jumped ahead. Interest waned when the county three times finished last in the Championship between 1910 and 1913, but there were at least two silver linings. W. T.

Greswell, a lively pace-bowler who had discovered the knack of the inswinger, was home from Ceylon and took 100 wickets in 1912; next year came J. C. White a farmer from Stogumber, who announced his ability to bowl left arm slow to a perfect length with subtle variation of flight by taking 96 wickets at less than 20 runs each. He was to serve Somerset sublimely.

After the war Somerset, as in the past, relied heavily on an influx of gaily-capped amateurs from the Universities, where John Daniell, the new captain, was always active. Here again was a rumbustious character; an International Rugby forward who became a legend with cricketing beliefs and vocabulary to match. A born leader, Daniell made two centuries in a match with Essex in his 47th year (1925). He is credited with one classic story. When he approached the New Zealander T. C. Lowry about playing for Somerset, he was told that the birthplace was Wellington. Quickly realising there is a town of the same name seven miles from county headquarters, Daniell is said to have closed the deal to the satisfaction of MCC.

THE HEYGATE INCIDENT

Somerset were involved in an extraordinary finish with Sussex at Taunton in their very first home match after the war – the experimental two-day season of 1919. Sussex needed a single to win when their ninth wicket fell. Some of the Somerset fielders thought the match was over as H. J. Heygate, the number eleven, was suffering from rheumatism and the effects of a war wound. He had not fielded and was not expected to bat. Indeed, he had not changed, wickets having gone down so suddenly, but wearing a blue lounge suit he limped out to bat. There was a friendly consultation between the captains, H. L. Wilson and J. C. White, but so slow had been his progress that the umpires, A. E. Street and F. G. Roberts, decided he had exceeded his two minutes and pulled up the stumps, declaring the result a tie. This decision was upheld by MCC after widespread comment on the most controversial situation which had occurred since Taunton became a cricket centre.

Somerset finished fifth in 1919, but in the early 'twenties, when White, Robson and J. J. Bridges virtually carried the bowling, amateurs of standing were too often unavailable, but occasionally they strengthened the side, especially in August. Notable performers were four opening batsmen, J. C. W. MacBryan, who played for England in 1924, P. R. Johnson, and the twins A. E. S. and A. D. E. Rippon. M. D. Lyon, another University recruit, was a high-class wicket-keeper and a batsman of decided attacking inclination. His great day came during the 1926 Australian match. Somerset, set to make 302 in three hours forty minutes, began badly, but Lyon, with a burst of sustained hitting, gathered 136 in two and three-quarter hours and took them to within 57 of becoming the only side, other than England, to beat the touring team.

FOUR PLAY FOR GENTLEMEN

From 1924 to 1931 Somerset were never higher than thirteenth in the table, but still the amateur strain was rich. R. C. Robertson-Glasgow, a delightful personality and clever seam bowler from Oxford University, reinforced the attack. Later he gave pleasure to many with his writings on the game. MacBryan, White, Lyon and Robertson-Glasgow all appeared at Lord's in 1924 for the Gentlemen against the Players.

During a long and honourable span – 1909 to 1937 – White took for his county over 2,000 wickets and scored 11,375 runs, including 100 wickets each season from 1919 to 1932. His effortless bowling played a decisive part in England retaining the Ashes in 1928–29. Carrying on the Somerset tradition of longevity, White was 37 years old during this tour and although by repute his power of spin was slight, this opinion has been repudiated by M. D. Lyon, one of a splendid line of wicket-keepers beginning with the Rev. A. P. Wickham and A. E. Newton. Newton was actually wheeled to the pitch to keep most creditably for Somerset Stragglers on his 75th birthday. Later, W. T. Luckes and H. W. Stephenson, from Stockton-on-Tees, shone behind the stumps.

Following J. C. White in the captaincy came R. A. Ingle, who hit two centuries in the same match against Middlesex, and E. F. Longrigg, a talented left-handed batsman. For many years Somerset constantly took the field with nine or ten amateurs, but in the late 'twenties, when fewer of them could afford to spend so much time away from business, the county was compelled to rely more on professionals.

In passing, it is well to note that the increasing emphasis on professional players brought in its train more administrative problems. One of the most successful and highly regarded of Somerset's secretaries was A. F. Davey, who was appointed from seventy-nine applicants in 1923. A happy and useful association with Somerset ended in 1932, when Mr Davey gave his undoubted organising abilities to Surrey. Two of his early assistants are still intimately connected with the club. They are T. Tout, the present scorer, and E. H. C. Wood, the secretary of the Somerset Supporters' Club.

WELLARD THE HITTER

The County found the schoolboy's dream cricketer when they engaged A. W. Wellard, a Kentish man born at Southfleet. His native county had seen him in action, yet never encouraged him, but for Somerset he made his presence felt as a fast bowler and fearless hitter in his first year, 1929, when his wickets numbered 131. That was the start of a wonderful career which gave him 11,000 runs and over 1,500 wickets. As many as 3,000 of his runs were obtained from 6s. He also developed off-spinners to augment his great-hearted pace-bowling. The brothers Lee, right-handed J. W. and left-handed F. S., now a famous umpire, formed a successful opening partnership with Frank continuing his invaluable contribution after the war. A. (Tom) Young, another doughty performer with a bat and ball and like Wellard a wonderful slip-field, made sure that the years would not find the county wanting for typical Somerset cricketers.

Opening the attack with Wellard was W. H. R. Andrews, a classic type of inswinger who aims the half-volley at the off-stump and relies on movement not position of delivery from the return crease. With Luckes behind the stumps Somerset could call on a most useful nucleus of professional craftsmen. This team often shocked the big boys. Witness 1936, when having beaten the ultimate champions, Derbyshire, in two days at Ilkeston, they went on to complete an astonishing double at Wells, by a single wicket. In a relatively low-scoring match, Wellard took nine wickets for 136 and scored 103 runs. With Somerset in trouble when they needed 271 to win, Wellard, dropped at one, punished Armstrong for five successive 6s in the same over, hit two more 6s, and ended with 86 out of 102 in sixty-two minutes. Two years later, on the same ground, Wellard repeated his prodigious effort at the expense of the noted Frank Woolley of Kent, off whom he made 31 in an over, again including five consecutive 6s.

When one mentions prolific Somerset hitters the name of G. F. Earle must be included. Tall and proportionately broad, he was not a stylist and came to the fore as a fast bowler for Harrow against Eton in 1908 and three following years, including "Fowler's match". He made fleeting appearances for Somerset and no one hit the ball higher or farther. He never wasted time on preliminaries but believed in attacking the bowling.

HAROLD GIMBLETT'S DÉBUT

Somerset were fortunate in having a professional ready to step into J. C. White's shoes in H. L. Hazell of Brislington. He gave many years of splendid service, but the most memorable event of the 1930s as far as this county was concerned with the début of Harold Gimblett – born in a small triangle of West Somerset which includes the birthplaces of White and Greswell. Gimblett was a late choice to play against Essex at Frome in 1935. Batting number eight and played mainly as a bowler and lively fielder, he astonished the world and tested credibility by making 123, with three 6s and seventeen 4s, reaching the quickest hundred of the year in sixty-three minutes. It was a début to confound the pundits, and his illustrious career marked by only three international caps and no MCC tour, ended in 1954 when 21,142 runs of the highest calibre had flowed from him at the average rate of 36 an innings.

Gimblett, whom many averred was not a natural opening bat, hit no fewer than 265 sixes, something no other regular number one has ever accomplished. Gimblett holds almost all the Somerset batting records. Among them one finds his 310 against Sussex at Eastbourne in 1948, and a wonderful 184 against Kent on a turning Gravesend pitch which gave Somerset an unexpected win. His uninhibited and powerful shots often gave lustre to many an otherwise dull first day and even first over. Cricket was the poorer for his retirement due to ill-health. His international career hardly started after a characteristic not out 67 against India at Lord's in 1936. The complement to his remarkable first century was the hundred he made in his benefit match against Northamptonshire at Glastonbury in 1952. Gimblett scored forty-nine centuries for the county and one on the Commonwealth tour of India. Twice he hit two hundreds in the same match.

In the period before the last war, Wellard performed the conventional cricketer's double on three occasions and Andrews did it twice, and as war approached, Somerset flickered entertainingly, in tradition, on either side of the middle of the table.

MORE UNIVERSITY INFLUENCE

The 1939 war made few inroads on Somerset's strength. With J. Lawrence, a googly bowler and useful batsman from Yorkshire, the only regular addition to the staff, Somerset made full use of their preponderance of skill and experience in 1946. Under E. F. Longrigg, who had been captain since 1938, when another Somerset all-rounder in H. T. F. Buse had joined the staff, the side reached a record fourth position in the table, with twelve Championship victories. The seal was set on a magnificent season of rehabilitation when they scored over 500 in successive innings at Taunton against India, Middlesex and Yorkshire, winning the first two matches with an innings to spare. Also, it was pleasant to note the return of the University influence in the form of M. M. Walford, a triple Blue and batsman whose immaculate technique and temperament made him a leading scorer in August for several seasons. Other gifted amateurs appeared in the team to give occasional strength in R. J. O. Meyer, H. E. Watts, F. Castle. Meyer took over in 1947 when Longrigg retired from the captaincy.

Meyer was another character in the Somerset mould, but unfortunately he had been away during his most productive years. A splendid all-rounder, he had an unhappy season, partly through a series of severe back ailments, and as his side aged, replacements of the necessary calibre were not forthcoming.

True, the nucleus of the professional staff was far from finished, but although G. E. S. Woodhouse, a solid batsman from Dorset, led them to ninth position in 1949 and S. S. Rogers, a Londoner, helped them to seventh in 1950, the old strength was slowly fading away.

TREMLETT'S MATCH

Of the considerable younger brigade given trials, M. F. Tremlett alone had really arrived. Tremlett started work in the county office on leaving school in 1938 and he made a marvellous contribution to winning his first match at Lord's in 1947 by taking eight wickets and making the winning hit with number eleven at the other end. A natural all-rounder, Tremlett went with MCC to West Indies in 1948 and to South Africa the following winter, but not with the happiest results, especially as far as his bowling was concerned. Efforts of coaches to improve him met with exactly the opposite results.

H. W. Stephenson had also impressed greatly as a wicket-keeper – he narrowly missed the 1950 tour of Australasia – but by this time Somerset were becoming woefully weak in fast bowling and class batting. Gimblett compiled 2,063 runs in 1949, a Somerset record which Tremlett took in 1951, but the future looked bleak. In turn S. S. Rogers, B. G. Brocklehurst and G. G. Tordoff were given the captaincy while Somerset collected four consecutive wooden spoons. In 1953, the members of the club were roused into action. After a highly unusual public outcry, a determined effort resulted in numerous players being recruited from far and wide. The critics called Somerset the "League of Nations", but the policy of going abroad for talent was regarded as a temporary measure while the county was scoured for home-bred material to be developed in the new indoor coaching school at Taunton.

OUT OF THE DOLDRUMS

E. P. Robinson, a very successful off-spinner, whose best years had been spent in the triumphant Yorkshire pre-war side, had come and gone, but B. Langford, a local product, P. B. Wight, J. G. Lomax and J. W. McMahon had all shown considerable potential. At last, in 1956, when the amateur cupboard seemed finally bare of leaders, M. F. Tremlett was appointed the first professional captain. He was lucky enough to have a former Australian Test player, C. L. McCool, in the ranks, and the year was marked by a slight move away from the last position in the table to fifteenth. Bryan Lobb, the rangy pace-bowler from Warwickshire, had come in and J. W. McMahon's two distinctive methods of left-arm slow bowling proved useful. In 1957, with Tremlett striking tremendous form late in the season, and showing untutored but majestic straight hitting to its best advantage, Somerset rose to eighth position in the table. Last summer their monumental effort of resuscitation was rewarded with third place, the best in their history.

This achievement, in contrast to some recoveries of the past, was heightened in value by success of a number of young players who had been on the staff since the stormy controversial days of 1953. Gradually prospects like G. Atkinson, K. Palmer, B. Roe and P. J. Eele were given a taste of cricket at its best in company with the experienced elders. Now there are plenty of contestants eager to show their fitness for the roles filled by their illustrious predecessors.

FINANCIAL AID

One thing has always run true to form in Somerset cricket history. That is the desperate struggle against financial disaster. Nowadays this has been greatly relieved by the activities and energy of an enthusiastic supporters' club. Unlike similar organisations, this one does not give block grants to the county. Instead, money is provided for specific objects, such as players' houses, stands, youth coaching, pitch dryers, local club ground funds and County second eleven expenses. In this connection, an example of the increased awareness of the problems of running a first-class team lies in the very successful County 2nd XI. In 1954 only six games were played. In 1959 a schedule of 23 matches has been arranged for them. Meanwhile the County Club continues their strenuous endeavours to balance the working profit and loss account, which it has not done for some years.

HAPPY ATMOSPHERE

Somerset, with a small population and minimum of industry, cannot call upon many amateurs these days, but the side, with such bright players as W. E. Alley, a left-hander, who made a great mark at the age of 38 with his all-round work in the past two years, Wight, McCool, Tremlett and Stephenson enables Somerset to live up to and even exceed the reputation gained so long ago. The happy-go-lucky atmosphere of a few years ago is still there, but now it has the essential backing of applied talent. There is plenty of life, both old and new, in Somerset cricket, and one knows that Sammy Woods would chuckle at the help received from three of his countrymen in lifting his old county out of the depths of despair into the sunny heights. And he, who was one of the heroes of Somerset entry into first-class cricket, would indeed be grateful to see at least one of his deathless phrases borne into continual practice by the modern Somerset heroes. "Draws?" he once muttered mutinously. "Draws? They're only for bathing in." This outlook on the game has given Somerset one of the most respected names in county cricket over the past 67 years.

SOMERSET v LANCASHIRE

Played at Taunton, June 25, 27, 28, 1960

Somerset won by 8 runs, with only twelve minutes left for play. Lancashire's bid to score 323 in four hours twenty-five minutes was magnificent. When the last pair Higgs and Tattersall, came together 47 were needed in forty-five minutes and despite many bowling changes it appeared for a time that they might turn the tables, but the huge task proved just too much for them. Two grand innings by Wight (100 and 90) and a century by McCool, put Somerset in a strong position during the first two days, but an unfortunate injury while batting to Alley, who took four wickets in Lancashire's first innings, weakened the attack considerably on the last day.

Somerset

G. G. Atkinson b Dyson	27	– lbw b Greenhough	29
R. Virgin b Higgs	3	– lbw b Greenhough	8
P. B. Wight c Booth b Dyson	100	– c Clayton b Marner	90
C. L. McCool c Grieves b Dyson	20	– b Higgs	100
C. Greetham b Dyson	12	– c Clayton b Higgs	8
W. E. Alley c Grieves b Dyson	12	– retired hurt	2
B. Langford c Tattersall b Greenhough	3	– b Higgs	24
†*H. W. Stephenson c Dyson b Greenhough	19	– lbw b Greenhough	34
F. Herting not out	16	– b Higgs	0
A. Whitehead lbw b Dyson	0	– not out	2
K. D. Biddulph st Clayton b Dyson	6	– c Clayton b Greenhough	2
L-b 3	3	L-b 2	2

1/7 2/87 3/127 4/148 5/168   221   1/25 2/52 3/228 4/228 5/246   301
6/175 7/190 8/203 9/205   6/297 7/297 8/297 9/301

Lancashire

A. Wharton c Stephenson b Alley	24	– b Langford	81
B. Booth c McCool b Alley	15	– lbw b Biddulph	0
J. Dyson not out	66	– b Greetham	47
K. Grieves c Whitehead b Alley	21	– c Biddulph b Whitehead	39
P. Marner c Virgin b Whitehead	42	– c Herting b Biddulph	12
*R. W. Barber c Alley b Whitehead	9	– c McCool b Langford	11
A. Bolton c Alley b Whitehead	2	– c Langford b Whitehead	44
†G. Clayton c McCool b Whitehead	0	– b McCool	30
T. Greenhough b Langford	0	– st Stephenson b McCool	4
K. Higgs c Atkinson b Alley	5	– not out	23
R. Tattersall c McCool b Biddulph	8	– lbw b Biddulph	14
B 4, l-b 3, w 1	8	B 5, l-b 3, w 1	9

1/32 2/47 3/87 4/135 5/153   200   1/9 2/82 3/167 4/173 5/188   314
6/155 7/155 8/162 9/187   6/211 7/271 8/271 9/276

Lancashire Bowling

	Overs	Mdns	Runs	Wkts	Overs	Mdns	Runs	Wkts
Higgs	12	3	39	1	23	5	51	4
Marner	5	2	9	—	9	2	22	1
Tattersall	17	6	21	—	12	4	41	—
Greenhough	28	8	59	2	28	6	79	4
Dyson	24.5	4	83	7	8	—	42	—
Barber	7	3	7	—	12	2	47	—
Booth					4	—	17	—

Somerset Bowling

	Overs	Mdns	Runs	Wkts	Overs	Mdns	Runs	Wkts
Biddulph..........	13.1	4	34	1	17.3	5	39	3
Herting...........	4	—	16	—	14	1	67	—
Alley.............	24	6	45	4				
Langford..........	27	16	35	1	23	7	72	2
McCool	8	3	15	—	5	—	28	2
Whitehead	9	2	47	4	13	—	54	2
Greetham					12	1	45	1

Umpires: J. F. Crapp and W. F. Price.

SOMERSET v CAMBRIDGE UNIVERSITY

Played at Taunton, June 29, 30, July 1, 1960

Cambridge University won by six wickets. Neither side possessed any really penetrating bowlers and consequently there were seven centuries and three declarations on the perfect Taunton pitch. Somerset's first three batsmen, Atkinson, Virgin and Wight, all scored centuries on the first day and Prideaux, Lewis and Willard did the same for the University, Howland declaring two runs behind early on the third morning. After some quick scoring by Wight and Virgin, Stephenson left Cambridge two hours fifty-five minutes in which to score 266 to win. Prideaux, who hit his second century of the game in two and a quarter hours, shared an opening stand of 137 in eighty-one minutes with Lewis, and Bernard brought victory to Cambridge with a cover boundary in the final over. For the first time in cricket history, there were four separate three-figure opening partnerships in a match.

Somerset

G. G. Atkinson c and b Kirby...................	103	– c Willard b Hurd...............	50
R. Virgin c Lewis b Hurd	113	– c Kirby b Hurd	70
P. B. Wight c Kirby b Brodie	105	– c Howland b Hurd...............	99
C. Greetham c Howland b Willard...............	61	– c Atkins b Hurd	5
M. Kitchen c Howland b Brodie.................	0	– c Kirby b Willard...............	15
G. L. Keith c Prideaux b Coghlan................	20		
J. M. Lawrence not out........................	6		
*†H. W. Stephenson c Howland b Coghlan	0		
F. Herting (did not bat)......................		– not out	10
L-b 6, w 1, n-b 3	10	B 9, l-b 4, w 1	14

1/172 2/265 3/376   (7 wkts dec.) 418   1/112 2/149   (5 wkts dec.) 263
4/383 5/411 6/413 7/418   3/174 4/253 5/263

H. Sully and E. Bryant did not bat.

Cambridge University

R. M. Prideaux c Atkinson b Bryant..............	102	– c Stephenson b Greetham........	106
A. R. Lewis c Wight b Herting	106	– st Stephenson b Lawrence	71
M. J. L. Willard not out......................	101	– lbw b Herting	33
D. Kirby lbw b Lawrence	12	– c Stephenson b Greetham.........	9
N. S. K. Reddy c Atkinson b Virgin	75	– not out	17
J. R. Bernard not out.........................	15	– not out	27
B 4, w 1...........................	5	B 4, l-b 1...............	5

1/198 2/220 3/259   (4 wkts dec.) 416   1/137 2/211   (4 wkts) 268
4/388   3/215 4/235

G. Atkins, *†C. B. Howland, T. B. L. Coghlan, J. B. Brodie and A. Hurd did not bat.

Cambridge University Bowling

	Overs	Mdns	Runs	Wkts	Overs	Mdns	Runs	Wkts
Brodie............	23	2	99	2				
Coghlan..........	14.2	4	48	2	13	1	38	—
Willard...........	19	5	58	1	11.5	1	66	1
Hurd.............	31	6	110	1	24	3	99	4
Kirby............	14	2	60	1	10	1	35	—
Atkins...........	6	1	33	—	1	—	11	—

Somerset Bowling

	Overs	Mdns	Runs	Wkts	Overs	Mdns	Runs	Wkts
Herting...........	31	7	81	1	17	1	82	1
Greetham.........	33	12	75	—	18.3	1	80	2
Lawrence.........	12	3	41	1	8	—	38	1
Sully.............	21	6	59	—	10	1	46	—
Bryant...........	41	13	107	1	4	—	17	—
Virgin............	6	—	48	1				

Umpires: A. Jepson and W. F. Price.

SOMERSET v GLAMORGAN

Played at Bath, July 13, 14, 15, 1960

Drawn. A magnificent third-wicket partnership of 300 between Atkinson and Wight on the first day was the feature of the match. The stand was a record for Somerset, beating L. C. H. Palairet and C. A. Bernard's 262 made in 1900. It was also the highest score of Atkinson's career, and in his innings of five and three-quarter hours he hit one 6 and seventeen 4s. Facing a total of 401 for three, declared, Glamorgan made a painstaking attempt to avoid the follow-on, but failed by five runs. Heavy rain on the final day delayed play until two o'clock and on an easy-paced pitch the Somerset bowlers did not possess the penetration needed to dismiss determined batsmen.

Somerset

G. G. Atkinson c Harris b McConnon.....190	C. L. McCool not out.................. 15
R. Virgin lbw b Walker................. 29	B 2, l-b 1, w 1................ 4
A. A. Baig c Wooller b Watkins.......... 8	
P. B. Wight not out...................155	1/57 2/72 3/372 (3 wkts dec.) 401

M. F. Tremlett, K. E. Palmer, *†H. W. Stephenson, B. Langford, A. Whitehead and K. D. Biddulph did not bat.

Glamorgan

A. Harris b McCool.......................... 23	– c Langford b Baig...............	93
B. Hedges c McCool b Palmer.................. 7	– b McCool.....................	48
W. G. Davies c Stephenson b Langford........... 64	– c Stephenson b Langford........	12
P. M. Walker c Tremlett b McCool............... 23	– c Atkinson b Palmer............	0
A. J. Watkins lbw b Langford.................. 30	– not out......................	1
J. Pressdee c Stephenson b Biddulph............. 42	– not out......................	0
*W. Wooller run out.......................... 18		
D. J. Ward b Palmer.......................... 6		
J. E. McConnon c Stephenson b Palmer........... 0		
†W. Whitehill lbw b Biddulph................... 3		
D. J. Shepherd not out........................ 6		
B 16, l-b 5, w 3, n-b 1................. 25	B 9, l-b 4, w 4............	17

1/20 2/48 3/82 4/138 5/167	247	1/1 2/36	(4 wkts) 171
6/204 7/222 8/226 9/240		3/152 4/171	

Glamorgan Bowling

	Overs	Mdns	Runs	Wkts
Wooller..........	20	3	72	—
Davies...........	15	3	46	—
Watkins	18	5	44	1
Walker	34	6	99	1
Ward	13	3	31	—
Shepherd.........	15	—	47	—
McConnon.......	16	3	58	1

Somerset Bowling

	Overs	Mdns	Runs	Wkts	Overs	Mdns	Runs	Wkts
Biddulph..........	17.5	7	35	2	6	4	11	—
Palmer	15	5	17	3	10	4	12	1
McCool	31	10	77	2	18	8	49	1
Langford..........	41	23	60	2	25	17	25	1
Whitehead	12	4	33	—	10	3	29	—
Wight					8	3	19	—
Baig					2	1	1	1
Tremlett					2	1	8	—

Umpires: W. E. Phillipson and T. J. Bartley.

SOMERSET v HAMPSHIRE

Played at Frome, May 6, 8, 9, 1961

Hampshire won by 18 runs. Fine off-spin bowling by Burden throughout the game on a pitch that was always receptive to the slow men played a major part in Hampshire success. On the first day, rain made conditions very unpleasant and Hampshire scored only 57 for two before the weather halted the proceedings. On Monday, Burden took five Somerset wickets for one run in a remarkable spell of 31 balls. He finished with eight for 38, the best performances of his career. Hampshire, also in difficulties against Palmer, could leave a task of only 172, but again Burden proved the undoing of Somerset. He captured four more wickets and despite a final partnership of 40 between Langford and Latham, Somerset were finally thwarted by White when he removed Latham.

Hampshire

R. E. Marshall b Latham......................	9 – b Palmer....................	9
J. R. Gray lbw b Langford	35 – c Stephenson b Palmer......	1
H. Horton b Latham..........................	0 – lbw b Langford..............	49
D. A. Livingstone c Keith b Latham..............	31 – b C. Atkinson	2
P. J. Sainsbury c Palmer b Langford.............	0 – b Langford...................	16
H. M. Barnard lbw b Langford.................	13 – b Latham...................	16
*A. C. D. Ingleby-Mackenzie lbw b Palmer	22 – b Palmer...................	8
†L. Harrison not out.........................	20 – b Langford.................	6
D. Shackleton c and b Langford.................	4 – c Lawrence b Palmer.........	1
D. W. White b Palmer........................	14 – not out	3
M. D. Burden c C. Atkinson b Palmer	2 – b Palmer...................	0
B 3, l-b 3, n-b 1	7 B 1, l-b 4...............	5

1/21 2/21 3/62 4/68 5/83   157   1/10 2/13 3/22 4/52 5/97   116
6 95 7/117 8/124 9/153   6/99 7/107 8/113 9/115

Somerset

G. Atkinson b Burden	36	– st Atkinson b Sainsbury	19
J. M. Lawrence b White	4	– run out	17
P. B. Wight lbw b Burden	15	– c White b Burden	11
W. E. Alley b Burden	9	– c and b Sainsbury	0
G. L. Keith b Burden	6	– c Harrison b Sainsbury	20
C. Greetham lbw b Burden	0	– b Burden	18
K. E. Palmer not out	11	– lbw b Burden	0
C. R. M. Atkinson b Burden	0	– lbw b Burden	0
*†H. W. Stephenson b Burden	1	– run out	8
B. Langford c Horton b Burden	7	– b White	39
M. Latham b Sainsbury	5	– not out	21
B 2, l-b 2, n-b 4	8		

1/18 2/47 3/63 4/74 5/74 6/75   102   1/29 2/44 3/47 4/47 5/66   153
7/75 8/81 9/95   6/66 7/66 8/87 9/113

Somerset Bowling

	Overs	Mdns	Runs	Wkts	Overs	Mdns	Runs	Wkts
Palmer	17.2	7	22	3	17.5	7	19	5
Latham	24	7	60	3	6	1	13	1
Langford	24	6	63	4	26	13	50	3
Alley	7	5	5	—				
C. Atkinson					13	4	29	1

Hampshire Bowling

	Overs	Mdns	Runs	Wkts	Overs	Mdns	Runs	Wkts
Shackleton	5	1	11	—	3	—	6	—
White	9	—	17	1	5	—	19	1
Burden	21	9	38	8	30	11	70	4
Sainsbury	16.5	5	28	1	31	17	58	3

Umpires: P. A. Gibb and N. Oldfield.

SOMERSET v SURREY

Played at Taunton, June 7, 8, 9, 1961

Somerset won by four wickets. Alley became the first Somerset player to score two not out centuries in a match, his second taking the county to victory with four minutes to spare. Batsmen were always dominant on a perfect pitch. May having stood down from the first Test against Australia, was in fine form and after passing 150 he declared at 358 for four. Somerset easily headed the Surrey total, although at a slower rate, thanks to hundreds from Alley and White. Alley, using powerful strokes all round the wicket, spent only four hours twenty minutes over his 183 which included two 6s and twenty-four 4s. He and Wight put on 297 for the third wicket. A dazzling display by Tindall, who reached his hundred in ninety-six minutes, enabled Surrey to leave Somerset to score 271 in three hours to win. Alley reached his second century in an hour and a half with his seventeenth 4 appropriately won the match.

Surrey

M. J. Stewart c Lomax b Biddulph	16	– c Stephenson b Biddulph	24
A. B. D. Parsons c C. Atkinson b Lomax	38	– c Stephenson b C. Atkinson	76
M. D. Willett b Biddulph	73	– c Stephenson b Biddulph	21
*P. B. H. May not out	153	– c G. Atkinson b Biddulph	5
B. Constable lbw b C. Atkinson	5	– c C. Atkinson b Langford	13
R. A. E. Tindall not out	71	– not out	100
†R. Swetman (did not bat)		– not out	19
B 1, l-b 1	2	B 4, l-b 11	15

1/28 2/73 3/184 4/193   (4 wkts dec.) 358   1/46 2/78   (5 wkts dec.) 273
                                                 3/100 4/128 5/201

G. A. R. Lock, E. A. Bedser, D. Gibson and P. J. Loader did not bat.

Somerset

G. Atkinson lbw b Lock	25	– lbw b Loader	7
B. Roe c Parsons b Lock	11	– b Loader	42
P. B. Wight c and b Gibson	125	– b Lock	25
W. E. Alley not out	183	– not out	134
J. G. Lomax c Constable b Lock	3	– c Stewart b Bedser	31
*†H. W. Stephenson lbw b Lock	0	– not out	8
J. M. Lawrence not out	10		
C. R. M. Atkinson (did not bat)		– b Bedser	5
K. E. Palmer (did not bat)		– b Gibson	8
L-b 4	4	B 4, l-b 7, w 1	12

1/35 2/36 3/333   (5 wkts dec.) 361   1/16 2/56 3/152   (6 wkts) 272
4/340 5/340   4/216 5/226 6/241

B. Langford and K. D. Biddulph did not bat.

Somerset Bowling

	Overs	Mdns	Runs	Wkts	Overs	Mdns	Runs	Wkts
Biddulph	24	4	84	2	19	4	54	3
Palmer	17	4	58	—	13	—	35	—
Alley	12	3	50	—	2	1	11	—
Lomax	13	5	37	1	2.1	—	4	—
C. R. M. Atkinson	22	2	68	1	26	4	83	1
Langford	14	2	59	—	21	6	71	1

Surrey Bowling

	Overs	Mdns	Runs	Wkts	Overs	Mdns	Runs	Wkts
Loader	20	5	72	—	11	—	48	2
Gibson	27	4	79	1	7.1	—	34	1
Willett	2	1	12	—				
Lock	28.2	10	64	4	24	2	101	1
Bedser	19	3	66	—	16	4	65	2
Tindall	7	1	30	—	4	—	12	—
Constable	6	—	34	—				

Umpires: D. Davies and A. E. Fagg.

SOMERSET v LEICESTERSHIRE

Played at Taunton, June 17, 19, 20, 1961

Drawn. Watson and Wharton broke a 57-year-old Leicestershire record for the third wicket of 291 between A. E. Knight and J. H. King against MCC with an unfinished partnership of 316 on the second day. Watson hit 217 not out in his brilliant innings which lasted five hours. Wharton's century was his first for Leicestershire. The Somerset batsmen had struggled against the varied Leicestershire attack during the first day and Watson declared on the second evening with a lead of 125. Savage and Birkenshaw, both off-spinners, troubled Somerset at their second attempt, but resolute batting by Wight, Palmer and C. R. M. Atkinson enabled them to avoid defeat.

Somerset

G. Atkinson lbw b Boshier	10	–	c Birkenshaw b Specer	6
B. Roe b Van Geloven	24	–	lbw b Savage	46
P. B. Wight b Spencer	6	–	c Julian b Birkenshaw	77
W. E. Alley c Hallam b Van Geloven	41	–	c Julian b Savage	6
J. G. Lomax c Boshier b Savage	40	–	c and b Birkenshaw	24
M. Kitchen c and b Birkenshaw	19	–	c sub b Spencer	36
*†H. W. Stephenson c Birkenshaw b Savage	19	–	c Savage b Birkenshaw	4
C. R. M. Atkinson b Spencer	38	–	b Van Geloven	44
K. E. Palmer not out	20	–	not out	64
B. Langford c Julian b Boshier	13	–	c Gardiner b Birkenshaw	17
K. D. Biddulph b Spencer	0	–	not out	14
B 4, 1-b 5	9		B 4, 1-b 3	7

1/15 2/26 3/61 4/120 5/124   **239**   1/16 2/96 3/126 4/138 5/194   **345**
6/152 7/179 8/215 9/234   6/212 7/288 8/295 9/318

Leicestershire

M. R. Hallam c Lomax b Palmer	8
*W. Watson not out	217
H. D. Bird c Stephenson b Palmer	4
A. Wharton not out	120
B 1, 1-b 14	15

1/20 2/48   (2 wkts dec.) **364**

L. R. Gardner, J. Van Geloven, J. Birkenshaw, †R. Julian, C. T. Spencer, J. S. Savage and B. S. Boshier did not bat.

Leicestershire Bowling

	Overs	Mdns	Runs	Wkts	Overs	Mdns	Runs	Wkts
Spencer	24	8	49	3	28	8	72	2
Boshier	23	7	48	2	17	5	52	—
Van Geloven	22	6	62	2	22	6	58	1
Savage	22	11	53	2	37	25	23	2
Birkenshaw	6	2	18	1	44	12	128	4
Bird					4	—	5	—

Somerset Bowling

	Overs	Mdns	Runs	Wkts
Biddulph	23	6	79	—
Palmer	23	2	85	2
C. R. M. Atkinson	22	7	63	—
Langford	32	3	95	—
Lomax	10	4	27	—

Umpires: J. F. Crapp and H. E. Hammond.

SURREY

SURREY v OLD ENGLAND

Played at The Oval, May 23, 1946

Drawn. The King and some 15,000 enthusiasts attended the one-day match arranged to celebrate the Centenary of the Surrey County Club and of Kennington Oval as a cricket ground. Surrey faced a side comprising ten old England players and Brooks, former Surrey wicket-keeper, the one member of the eleven without the honour of Test match experience. Altogether the caps gained by the ten players and the umpires, Hobbs and Strudwick, numbered 370. On one of the finest days of the summer the cricket proved full of interest. Runs always came fast and there were three stands of over a hundred. Gregory and Squires put on 111 for Surrey; Woolley and Hendren hit up 102, and Hendren and Jardine 108 for Old England in a splendid effort to hit off the runs after Bennett, the new Surrey captain, declared. Fender was prominent in the field, making a neat catch and taking two wickets with successive balls. The most exhilarating cricket came after the fall of Sandham and Sutcliffe for two runs. Woolley, at the age of 59, drove with the same ease that delighted crowds before and after the 1914-18 war. Hendren showed all his old cheery forcing play until just before time he lifted a catch off Surrey's most famous recruit — A. V. Bedser, already marked for England honours. To stay two and three-quarter hours and hit eight 4s at the age of 57 was a great feat by Hendren. D. R. Jardine, wearing his Oxford Harlequin cap, was as polished as ever in academic skill.

The King, Patron of Surrey, accompanied by officials of the club, went on the ground, where all concerned in the game were introduced to him with the happiest of greetings. The band of the East Surrey Regiment was in attendance, and after the game a dance in the pavilion long room completed the festive occasion.

Surrey

R. J. Gregory b Fender	62	E. A. Bedser c Brooks b Allom	23
L. B. Fishlock c Fender b Freeman	25	E. A. Watts not out	13
H. S. Squires b Holmes	68		
T. H. Barling lbw b Fender	0	B 5, l-b 1	6
J. F. Parker c and b Allom	12		
A. J. McIntyre not out	39	(6 wkts dec.)	248

N. H. Bennett, G. J. Whittaker and G. S. Mobey did not bat.

Old England

H. Sutcliffe lbw b Watts	1	P. G. H. Fender not out	12
A. Sandham c A. V. Bedser b Watts	1	D. J. Knight not out	2
F. E. Woolley c McIntyre b A. V. Bedser	62	B 3, l-b 2, n-b 1	6
E. Hendren c Barling b A. V. Bedser	94		
D. R. Jardine b Parker	54	(5 wkts)	232

M. W. Tate, E. R. T. Holmes, M. J. C. Allom and E. W. J. Brooks did not bat.

Old England Bowling

	Overs	Mdns	Runs	Wkts
Tate	8	1	26	—
Allom	17	2	76	2
Freeman	15	3	58	1
Holmes	8	1	36	1
Fender	8	—	46	2

Surrey Bowling

	Overs	Mdns	Runs	Wkts
A. V. Bedser	21	3	45	2
Watts	18	3	83	2
Parker	15	—	51	1
Squires	7	—	29	—
E. A. Bedser	4	2	3	—
McIntyre	2	—	11	—
Gregory	1	—	4	—

Umpires: J. B. Hobbs and H. Strudwick.

A GREAT DAY AT THE OVAL

In a letter to *The Times*, Mr P. G. H. Fender, captain of "Old England", wrote:

"May I express to the thousands of enthusiasts who gave 'Old England' such a wonderful reception at The Oval the sincere heartfelt thanks of all those who were privileged to play in that side? There are many others who should have played, and we realise that we were the lucky ones, and that the tribute was to the game rather than to a few individuals.

"More than once while we were fielding a thought came to my mind that the warmth of the welcome, the size and the enthusiasm of the great crowd, and, above all, the presence of His Majesty, seemed to convey a message to all the younger generation of cricketers, not only in this country, but all over the world. A message telling them that where cricket is concerned, public memory, in spite of the old adage, is not short; a message to inspire all young cricketers, and to urge them to achievements in the game greater even than their wildest dreams conjured up.

"Such a welcome as was given to 'Old England', collectively and individually, must surely be a public assurance that those who can carve for themselves a little niche in the greatest of games can always be sure of a warm place in the hearts of all lovers of cricket."

SURREY v OLD ENGLAND

Played at The Oval, June 12, 1947

Drawn. In a grand day's entertainment Surrey knocked up their 315 in two and a half hours, and the veterans only just failed to beat the clock. O'Connor, the Eton coach, at the age of 47 batted as skilfully as ever, but more surprising was the energy and fitness of Charles Parker, 62 years old, and Hitch, 61. Hitch took two wickets, scored 51, and gave a lesson in stealing singles. The wicket-keeping of Duckworth also delighted everyone. Nine 6s in Surrey's innings earned £495; England's total represented £305; and a collection of £98 brought in altogether £898 for the Surrey Centenary Fund exclusive of gate takings. Field-Marshall Lord Montgomery, born at St Mark's vicarage overlooking the ground, the guest of honour, shook hands with both teams on the field.

Surrey

E. A. Bedser lbw b Stephenson	23
D. G. W. Fletcher b Stephenson	30
H. S. Squires st Duckworth b Fender	62
T. H. Barling st Duckworth b Hitch	41
E. R. T. Holmes c Gover b Hitch	66
A. J. McIntyre not out	45
G. J. Whittaker c Fender b O'Connor	48
E. A. Watts not out	0
(6 wkts dec.)	315

J. C. Laker, A. V. Bedser, J. W. McMahon did not bat.

Old England

A. Sandham b Watts	21
J. O'Connor st McIntyre b Squires	100
R. E. S. Wyatt lbw b Squires	14
J. G. W. Davies lbw b Squires	35
J. W. Hitch c Fletcher b McMahon	51
P. G. H. Fender c A. Bedser b McMahon	43
G. Duckworth b McMahon	4
J. W. A. Stephenson c McIntyre b McMahon	3
C. W. L. Parker not out	20
A. R. Gover not out	7
L-b 7	7
(8 wkts)	305

A. E. R. Gilligan did not bat.

Old England Bowling

	Overs	Mdns	Runs	Wkts
Hitch	10	1	62	2
Gover	3	—	11	—
Parker	12	—	101	—
Stephenson	6	1	34	2
Davies	4	—	18	—
Fender	8	—	72	1
Wyatt	3	1	11	—
O'Connor	1	—	6	1

Surrey Bowling

	Overs	Mdns	Runs	Wkts
Watts	20	4	68	1
Laker	11	1	33	—
McMahon	19	4	59	4
Squires	16	1	103	3
E. A. Bedser	5	—	35	—

Umpires: J. B. Hobbs, H. Strudwick, A. Peach and E. G. Hayes.

SURREY v MIDDLESEX

Played at The Oval, August 9, 11, 12, 1947

Middlesex won by an innings and 11 runs after giving a display worthy of potential Champions. Denis Compton achieved the best all-round performance of his career by hitting 137 not out and taking twelve wickets for 174 runs. The only regret on the opening day, when Middlesex scored their 537, was that Brown should be bowled for 98 after helping Robertson in an opening stand of 211. Both men batted faultlessly, paving the way for Edrich and Compton to add 287 in two and three-quarter hours without being separated. The Surrey bowling was never loose, and Compton was content with nine 4s compared with eighteen by Edrich. Torn tendons in the right arm, damaged when bowling in the previous match, prevented Edrich fielding on the second day when before tea Surrey scored freely. Squires, Holmes and McIntyre all played brilliantly. Then came a collapse before the slow left-arm unorthodox over-the-wicket bowling of Denis Compton which brought Middlesex victory before lunch on the third day. Both wicket-keepers, L. Compton and McIntyre, bowled. Altogether 54,000 people, of whom 47,000 paid, saw this match. The gates were closed by three o'clock on Saturday when 30,000 were present.

Middlesex

S. M. Brown b Surridge.	98
J. D. Robertson c and b E. Bedser	127
W. J. Edrich not out	157
D. C. S. Compton not out	137
B 8, l-b 4, n-b 6	18

(2 wkts dec.) 537

F. G. Mann, R. W. V. Robins, A. Thompson, L. Compton, J. Sims, L. Gray and J. Young did not bat.

Surrey

L. B. Fishlock c L. Compton b Gray	16	– c L. Compton b D. Compton	44
D. G. W. Fletcher lbw b D. Compton	42	– b Young	8
H. S. Squires st L. Compton b D. Compton	98	– b Robins	20
T. H. Barling c L. Compton b Sims	16	– b D. Compton	44
J. F. Parker c and b D. Compton	15	– run out	12
E. R. T. Holmes b Sims	61	– b D. Compton	2
A. J. McIntyre c Robins b D. Compton	51	– c and b D. Compton	0
E. A. Bedser c Robertson b Sims	16	– lbw b Compton	10
W. S. Surridge c Mann b D. Compton	1	– c D. Compton b Robins	23
A. V. Bedser not out	3	– c and b D. Compton	14
A. R. Gover c Mann b D. Compton	4	– not out	5
B 4, l-b 5, w 2	11	B 6, l-b 4	10
	334		192

Surrey Bowling

	Overs	Mdns	Runs	Wkts
Gover	17	—	84	—
A. V. Bedser	20	3	67	—
Surridge	18	2	77	1
Parker	21	3	83	—
Squires	17	—	95	—
E. A. Bedser	19	—	82	1
Holmes	3	—	13	—
McIntyre	3	—	18	—

Middlesex Bowling

	Overs	Mdns	Runs	Wkts	Overs	Mdns	Runs	Wkts
Gray	20	4	55	1	8	2	14	—
L. Compton	8	1	32	—				
Sims	27	5	100	3	17	2	47	—
D. Compton	27.3	4	94	6	24.5	6	80	6
Robins	3	—	11	—	8	1	18	2
Young	15	4	31	—	7	2	23	1

Umpires: J. Smart and C. N. Woolley.

SURREY v MIDDLESEX
(H. S. Squires' Benefit)

Played at The Oval, August 7, 9, 10, 1948

Middlesex won a low-scoring game by one wicket. Mann put Surrey in, and on a rain-damaged pitch exactly to his liking Young, the slow left-hander, proved almost unplayable, his match analysis being 14 wickets for 97. Fishlock saved Surrey from a feeble first total by faultlessly hitting 74 out of 120 when play was possible at half-past three on the first day. Rain again interfered seriously on Monday, permitting play for only two hours forty minutes during which spin bowlers turned the ball appreciably. On a remarkable last day 23 wickets fell for 273 runs. Middlesex fared lamentably and found themselves 38 behind on the first innings. Then Young again went to work and Middlesex required 142 to win in as many minutes. Half the team fell for 39 before Mann and Robins turned the tide with an adventurous stand of 62 added in half an hour, and Sims used his experience at such a critical stage in a way that decided the issue; he scored 36 of the last 41 runs and made the winning hit nine minutes from time. Fortune favoured him, for he was twice dropped when ten runs were needed with the last pair together.

Surrey

L. B. Fishlock b Young	82	– b Young	11
E. A. Bedser c Robins b Young	2	– absent ill	0
H. S. Squires c Gray b Young	10	– c D. Compton b Young	12
M. R. Barton b L. Compton b Young	5	– c Sims b Young	6
J. F. Parker c Edrich b Young	11	– lbw b D. Compton	30
E. R. T. Holmes hit wkt b D. Compton	5	– c Robins b Young	0
J. C. Laker c Robertson b Young	0	– c Dewes b D. Compton	17
A. V. Bedser c Mann b Young	11	– c L. Compton b Young	1
G. S. Mobey c and b D. Compton	0	– b Young	0
W. S. Surridge not out	16	– c Brown b Young	19
J. W. McMahon lbw b D. Compton	17	– not out	0
B 4, l-b 3	7	B 6, l-b 1	7
	156		103

Middlesex

J. D. Robertson c Mobey b McMahon	16	– c Laker b A. Bedser	17
F. G. Mann c Surridge b A. Bedser	2	– c Surridge b McMahon	29
W. J. Edrich b E. Bedser b Laker	19	– c Fishlock b Surridge	4
D. C. S. Compton b McMahon	14	– c Parker b A. Bedser	4
R. W. V. Robins lbw b McMahon	21	– c Mobey b McMahon	38
J. G. Dewes c Surridge b A. Bedser	14	– c Parker b Laker	4
S. M. Brown c Barton b Laker	5	– lbw b A. Bedser	4
L. H. Compton c Parker b Laker	5	– b Laker	2
J. Sims b Laker	15	– not out	36
J. A. Young c McMahon b A. Bedser	4	– c McMahon b Laker	0
L. Gray not out	1	– not out	0
B 1, l-b 1	2	L-b 4	4
	118		**(9 wkts) 142**

Middlesex Bowling

	Overs	Mdns	Runs	Wkts	Overs	Mdns	Runs	Wkts
Edrich	6	1	8	—	2	—	9	—
Gray	16	4	17	—	4	—	13	—
Young	39	15	50	7	21.1	8	47	7
D. Compton	28	8	64	3	19	7	27	2

Surrey Bowling

	Overs	Mdns	Runs	Wkts	Overs	Mdns	Runs	Wkts
A. V. Bedser	14	5	25	3	14.1	5	25	3
Surridge	6	—	20	—	8	1	23	1
McMahon	11	3	20	3	7	1	25	2
Laker	13.1	—	51	4	14	—	65	3

Umpires: P. T. Mills and H. Cruice.

SURREY v MIDDLESEX

(L. B. Fishlock's Benefit)

Played at The Oval, July 29, 31, August 1, 1950

Surrey won by ten wickets. The reappearance of Denis Compton after being kept out of cricket for two months by his injured knee increased the interest in the always attractive visit of Middlesex, and on the three days 48,530 people paid £4,326 gate money, ensuring Fishlock a worthy reward for his splendid services. He marked the occasion by scoring 133 for once out, so helping materially in the victory which came to Surrey at three o'clock on Tuesday. Fishlock made his 111 out of 205 in four hours ten minutes, hitting thirteen 4s, and he was out to a grand catch, Warr holding a hard low drive with his right hand at mid-on. Constable was out unluckily, his leg touching the stumps when he hit a boundary. McIntyre, twelve 4s, and Laker followed by adding 102, the best stand of the innings. Denis Compton surpassed Fishlock's performance by scoring 140 for once out.

The 85th century of his first-class career came in three hours twenty minutes, and altogether he batted three hours and three-quarters while the total was increased by 168; he hit twelve 4s by perfect timing and avoided unnecessary risks. On the last day chief honours fell to Laker with eight wickets for 57, the batting breaking down after an opening stand of 78. On Saturday a collection for Fishlock realised £354.

Surrey

L. B. Fishlock c Warr b Bennett	111	– not out	22
E. A. Bedser c L. Compton b Warr	0	– not out	6
P. B. H. May b Sims	22		
J. F. Parker lbw b Warr	6		
M. R. Barton lbw b Young	32		
B. Constable hit wkt b Sims	38		
A. J. McIntyre c Sharp b Warr	85		
J. C. Laker c L. Compton b Sims	44		
A. V. Bedser c L. Compton b Warr	21		
W. S. Surridge c L. Compton b Sims	16		
G. A. R. Lock not out	7		
B 4, l-b 12, w 2, n-b 1	19		
	401	**(No wkt)**	**28**

Middlesex

J. D. Robertson c McIntyre b Surridge	29	– c Surridge b A. Bedser	32
J. G. Dewes run out	17	– c Surridge b Laker	56
H. P. Sharp c and b A. Bedser	8	– c Lock b Laker	0
D. C. S. Compton not out	115	– c Constable b Lock	25
S. M. Brown c Parker b Lock	36	– c Lock b Laker	13
L. H. Compton b Laker	3	– c McIntyre b Laker	10
D. Bennett run out	4	– c Lock b Laker	7
J. M. Sims b Lock	3	– lbw b Laker	8
F. J. Titmus c A. Bedser b Surridge	7	– lbw b Laker	0
J. J. Warr b Parker	0	– not out	30
J. A. Young b Parker	0	– b Laker	11
B 2, l-b 2, n-b 3	7	B 4, l-b 1, n-b 2	7
	229		**199**

Middlesex Bowling

	Overs	Mdns	Runs	Wkts	Overs	Mdns	Runs	Wkts
Warr	35	9	79	4				
Bennett	22	3	68	1				
Titmus	23	6	59	—	2	—	21	—
Sims	27.4	7	91	4				
Young	31	10	52	1	1.2	—	7	—
D. Compton	6	—	23	—				
Sharp	4	—	10	—				

Surrey Bowling

	Overs	Mdns	Runs	Wkts	Overs	Mdns	Runs	Wkts
A. Bedser	20	7	48	1	15	3	37	1
Surridge	25	5	72	2	9	1	21	—
Parker	15.1	6	17	2	4	—	30	—
Laker	16	3	38	1	23.4	9	57	8
Lock	16	7	29	2	15	4	42	1
Constable	8	—	18	—	4	1	5	—

Umpires: D. Davies and J. J. Hills.

SURREY v LANCASHIRE

Played at The Oval, May 5, 7, 8, 1951

Drawn. Although rain prevented play on the first day and cold weather made conditions unpleasant for the rest of the match, the joint champions of 1950 played with such spirit that they nearly obtained a definite result. Ikin, the Lancashire left-hander, batted magnificently on the rain-affected pitch, carrying his bat after four and a half hours of intense concentration during which he hit fourteen 4s. Ikin "farmed" the bowling so skilfully that he made 68 of the last 70 runs in the Lancashire total. Apart from Whittaker, who hit boldly, the Surrey batsmen found the pace and lift of Statham troublesome, but the game changed when Surridge, also finding the pitch helpful, caused a Lancashire collapse in their second innings. Left to make 137 runs in sixty-five minutes, Surrey hit strongly, but lost wickets quickly against the off-breaks of Tattersall, and in the end were forced to defend in order to stave off defeat.

Lancashire

C. Washbrook c Surridge b Parker	29	– c McIntyre b Surridge	13
J. T. Ikin not out	125	– b Surridge	15
G. A. Edrich c McIntyre b Parker	0	– b A. Bedser	0
W. Place c Surridge b A. Bedser	12	– c McIntyre b Surridge	1
N. D. Howard c Barton b A. Bedser	22	– c Barton b Surridge	7
K. Grieves c McIntyre b Laker	4	– lbw b Surridge	2
A. Wharton run out	1	– c Laker b Surridge	21
M. J. Hilton b E. Bedser	0	– c Surridge b A. Bedser	1
R. Tattersall b E. Bedser	0	– c Parker b Surridge	1
F. D. Parr c McIntyre b Surridge	0	– not out	10
B. Statham c Surridge b A. Bedser	1	– c Barton b A. Bedser	2
B 1, l-b 2	3	B 2, l-b 1	3
	197		**76**

Surrey

L. B. Fishlock b Statham	4	– c Ikin b Tattersall	22
E. A. Bedser b Tattersall	7	– c Edrich b Tattersall	1
B. Constable c Grieves b Tattersall	7	– b Statham	14
M. R. Barton b Edrich b Hilton	20	– not out	2
J. F. Parker lbw b Wharton	26	– c Ikin b Tattersall	10
G. J. Whittaker c Place b Hilton	51	– c Place b Tattersall	17
A. J. McIntyre lbw b Statham	4	– c Statham b Hilton	3
J. C. Laker c Parr b Statham	7	– not out	2
A. V. Bedser lbw b Statham	0	– c Howard b Tattersall	0
W. S. Surridge c Grieves b Statham	4		
G. A. R. Lock not out	0		
B 3, l-b 3, n-b 1	7	B 3, l-b 9	12
	137	**(7 wkts)**	**83**

Surrey Bowling

	Overs	Mdns	Runs	Wkts	Overs	Mdns	Runs	Wkts
A. Bedser	25.5	9	54	3	17.1	7	19	3
Surridge	12	1	40	1	22	7	49	7
Laker	33	15	58	1	7	4	5	—
Parker	11	4	19	2				
E. Bedser	13	4	23	2				

Lancashire Bowling

	Overs	Mdns	Runs	Wkts	Overs	Mdns	Runs	Wkts
Statham	15	4	35	5	6	—	18	1
Wharton	5	2	5	1	2	—	23	—
Tattersall	16	2	57	2	7	2	26	5
Hilton	15.3	5	43	2	3	—	4	1

Umpires: F. Chester and A. E. Pothecary.

SURREY v YORKSHIRE

Played at The Oval, July 14, 16, 17, 1951

Drawn. This match was memorable for the performance of Hutton in completing his century of centuries. After Surrey had broken down when the pitch gave a little help to bowlers, Hutton and Lowson took charge and at the end of the first day their unfinished stand had realised 112. Hutton then wanted 39 runs for his hundred and on Monday 15,000 people turned up. They were not disappointed and Hutton achieved his objective with a stroke worthy of the occasion – a superb drive off Wait sped past cover-point to the boundary. Altogether the opening partnership produced 197 and Hutton, who batted faultlessly for four hours forty minutes, hit twelve 4s. Wilson drove finely, his not out 114 containing three 6s and ten 4s. Surrey looked in a hopeless position when they batted again 275 behind, but Yorkshire dropped vital catches and finally found themselves wanting 43 in twenty minutes. In a hectic scramble for runs, they paid the penalty for hitting recklessly at every ball, and although they raced to and from the pavilion gate the task was beyond them.

Surrey

M. R. Barton c Wilson b Yardley	14	– b Wardle......................	39
E. A. Bedser b Appleyard	22	– c Brennan b Leadbeater	8
B. Constable b Appleyard......................	16	– c Wilson b Appleyard.............	47
L. B. Fishlock lbw b Trueman..................	11	– st Brennan b Wardle.............	89
J. F. Parker b Appleyard......................	8	– b Appleyard	4
T. H. Clark c Brennan b Yardley	47	– c Brennan b Trueman............	15
A. J. McIntyre c Brennan b Wardle	8	– b Leadbeater.................	32
J. C. Laker c Wilson b Yardley..................	2	– lbw b Wardle	13
A. V. Bedser not out	11	– not out	27
G. A. R. Lock b Trueman......................	1	– c Wilson b Leadbeater	23
O. J. Wait b Trueman	4	– c Wardle b Leadbeater	0
B 5, l-b 4, n-b 3	12	B 8, l-b 4, w 4, n-b 4	20
	156		**317**

Yorkshire

L. Hutton b Lock	151	– c Constable b A. Bedser	5
F. A. Lowson c and b Parker	84	– c Lock b A. Bedser.............	10
J. V. Wilson not out..........................	114	– not out	5
W. G. Keighley b Wait	45	– run out	1
W. Watson not out	16	– run out	1
N. W. D. Yardley (did not bat)..................		– c Fishlock b Wait	1
J. H. Wardle (did not bat).....................		– b Wait......................	2
E. Leadbeater (did not bat)....................		– not out	0
B 4, l-b 9, w 4, n-b 4	21	L-b 4, n-b 1.............	5
	(3 wkts dec.) 431		**(6 wkts) 30**

D. V. Brennan, R. Appleyard and F. S. Trueman did not bat.

Yorkshire Bowling

	Overs	Mdns	Runs	Wkts	Overs	Mdns	Runs	Wkts
Trueman..........	19	2	52	3	22	7	26	1
Appleyard.........	21	8	53	3	23	5	54	2
Yardley...........	20	6	28	3	3	—	10	—
Wardle	9	3	11	1	32	8	83	3
Leadbeater					49.2	16	112	4
Hutton					3	—	12	—

Surrey Bowling

	Overs	Mdns	Runs	Wkts	Overs	Mdns	Runs	Wkts
A. Bedser	38	5	106	—	3	—	17	2
Wait	19	2	65	1	3	—	8	2
Parker............	15	4	38	1				
Laker	35	10	71	—				
Lock.............	22	6	58	1				
E. Bedser	13	2	46	—				
Clark	9	1	26	—				

Umpires: F. S. Lee and H. Elliott.

SURREY v KENT

Played at The Oval, July 12, 14, 15, 1952

Surrey won by two wickets. So marked was the tension in the final minutes that the crowd rose to their feet and a burst of cheering broke out as Surridge made the winning hit with the clock pointing to a shade after half-past six. The events of the last innings showed that against a side prepared to accept the challenge Murray Wood's declaration which set Surrey 188 to win in ninety-two minutes gave Kent at least an even chance. Although wickets fell frequently, Surrey pursued their aggression to the end without regard to the risk of defeat. They required 128 in the last hour, 50 with seventeen minutes to go, and 26 when the eighth wicket went eight minutes from time. Surridge, the next man in, scored from eight of the nine balls bowled to him, but before he slashed Dovey over extra cover for the final stroke he and Clark were missed in the deep. With less than a minute left and the game still open, Kent raced into position and Dovey hurriedly bowled the first ball to ensure another over. After sending in Kent on a pitch damp through over-night rain, Surridge was mainly instrumental in their cheap dismissal. His analysis was his best in first-class cricket [sic]. May, who made his first century at The Oval, excelled with cleanly hit cover-drives and cuts. The versatility and accuracy of Dovey with swing and spin was properly reflected in his bowling success for Kent. Typically robust play by Evans and five hours of solid defence by O'Linn pulled Kent round, but after the departure of Evans Kent looked to be concentrating so much on saving the game that the declaration caused a surprise.

Kent

A. E. Fagg c McIntyre b A. Bedser	0	– c Parker b A. Bedser 10
A. H. Phebey b A. Bedser	29	– lbw b Surridge 3
T. G. Evans c McIntyre b Surridge	9	– st McIntyre b A. Bedser 92
S. O'Linn b A. Bedser	3	– not out 111
A. C. Shirreff b Surridge	75	– lbw b Laker 20
R. Mayes b Surridge	11	– c McIntyre b A. Bedser 5
B. R. Edrich c McIntyre b Surridge	41	– lbw b Lock 31
W. Murray Wood c Lock b Surridge	0	– c May b Constable 4
R. R. Dovey b Surridge	2	– b A. Bedser 0
D. V. P. Wright not out	8	– lbw b Lock 4
J. C. T. Page c Parker b Surridge	9	– not out 5
L-b 3, n-b 2	5	B 21, l-b 9, n-b 5 35

1/0 2/13 3/18 4/69 5/100   192   1/12 2/48   (9 wkts dec.) 320
6/143 7/147 8/153 9/176   3/143 4/182 5/194 6/275
                                        7/288 8/291 9/320

Surrey

E. A. Bedser lbw b Page	3	– c O'Linn b Page 20
D. G. W. Fletcher c Fagg b Page	12	– c and b Shirreff 52
P. B. H. May c Evans b Dovey	124	– c O'Linn b Page 29
B. Constable c Dovey	22	– c O'Linn b Page 17
J. F. Parker c Mayes b Wright	19	– b Page 1
T. H. Clark c Fagg b Dovey	42	– not out 24
A. J. McIntyre c O'Linn b Dovey	43	– c and b Shirreff 0
J. C. Laker c Fagg b Dovey	23	– c and b Shirreff 15
A. V. Bedser b Dovey	3	– b Shirreff 14
W. S. Surridge c Mayes b Dovey	14	– not out 16
G. A. R. Lock not out	15	
B 1, l-b 4	5	L-b 1, n-b 1 2

1/5 2/36 3/74 4/122 5/205   325   1/29 2/75 3/95 4/97   (8 wkts) 190
6/262 7/275 8/278 9/297   5/104 6/125 7/144 8/162

Surrey Bowling

	Overs	Mdns	Runs	Wkts	Overs	Mdns	Runs	Wkts
A. Bedser	32	9	67	3	35	6	89	4
Surridge	30.2	7	80	7	27	5	73	1
Laker	9	2	21	—	29	11	50	1
Lock	22	14	19	—	19	1	56	2
E. Bedser					11	5	9	—
Constable					6	2	8	1

Kent Bowling

	Overs	Mdns	Runs	Wkts	Overs	Mdns	Runs	Wkts
Page	27	2	105	2	11	—	48	4
Shirreff	31	5	83	—	15	—	106	4
Wright	16	4	50	1				
Dovey	31.1	5	82	7	4.2	—	34	—

Umpires: K. McCanlis and E. Cooke.

NOTES BY THE EDITOR, 1953

SURREY CHAMPIONS

After an interval of 38 years Surrey finished Champions and no one could challenge their right to the title. In W. S. Surridge, their new captain, they possessed an exuberant personality who by his own fine example in the field extracted the very best from all his men. It was only at the end of the previous season that Col R. S. Rait Kerr urged the counties to throw off their lethargy and make their cricket "eager, quick and full of action". Surrey certain answered the call, and their enterprise was fully rewarded, as they equalled the feat of the brilliant Yorkshire pre-war team that gained 20 Championship victories in 28 matches in 1938 and 1939. In some quarters it was suggested that the Surrey total of 256 points was the highest ever obtained under the present system of 12 points for a win. Yorkshire not only achieved that number in 1938, but in 1939 surpassed it with 260. It was significant that at the Surrey celebration dinner in December, Surridge thanked H. Lock, the groundsman, for providing pitches which gave the bowler a fair chance. For years officials, players and writers have linked the problem of keen attractive cricket with the preparation of the turf. It is to be hoped that this year's Test matches will not be ruined because all life has been extracted from the pitch in the effort to ensure the contests lasting the full five days.

HOBBS'S HUNDREDS

Before leaving Surrey, I must place on record not only the remarkable reception Jack Hobbs was given at the Championship dinner, but also the really wonderful tributes he received from almost the whole of the English press and the BBC when he reached his 70th birthday on December 16. Hobbs himself remained as modest as ever, but he did remark "They are making more fuss now than when I beat W.G." The *Daily Express* approached me with a view to recognising as first class three of the hundreds he made for the Maharajah of Vizianagram's XI in Ceylon in 1930. After consulting MCC, I came to the conclusion that it would be unwise to alter cricket records that have been accepted for over twenty years. In arriving at this decision I was guided mainly by a ruling of the Imperial Cricket Conference in 1947, when, in reaching agreement in regard to the definition of a first-class match, the six countries concerned stated: "This will not have retrospective effect." The wisdom of that ruling of six years ago is clearly shown in this question of Hobbs's 100s. If three were added to make his number 200, there might be a clamour for the records of other players to be changed, perhaps even to the extent of deducting some of the hundreds which were recognised in the past (not Hobbs) but according to present-day standards would not come in the first-class category. Hobbs himself is against any tampering with the established figures.

SURREY v WARWICKSHIRE

Played at The Oval, May 16, 1953

Surrey won by an innings and 49 runs. Members rose as one when the triumphant Surrey team walked from the field having begun their Championship programme with victory in a day. The last and only time that a first-class match had been completed in one day at The

Oval was in 1857. Special applause was accorded to A. Bedser who took twelve wickets for 35 runs, and Laker, who performed the hat-trick. Bedser bowled magnificently when play commenced at noon. Unable to obtain a proper foothold on the wet turf, he attacked the leg stump at below normal pace, and, helped by fine catches, he equalled his previous best analysis of eight for 18. Surrey also found the pitch treacherous, but, chiefly through a sound innings by Constable, they took the lead with only two wickets down. The score then went from 50 for two to 81 for seven, and only the aggressiveness of Surridge, who hit three 6s in four balls from Hollies, Laker and Lock enabled them to gain a substantial lead. Lock became the second highest scorer before a blow above the right eye led to a visit to hospital and his retirement from the game. Laker was called into the attack for the first time when Warwickshire batted again and he began the final rout by achieving the first hat-trick of the season. Warwickshire, batting for ten minutes of the extra half hour, were all out in seventy minutes, five minutes less than in their first innings. No Warwickshire batsman was bowled during a day in which 29 wickets fell for 243 runs – a fact that emphasised Surrey's excellent fielding.

Warwickshire

F. C. Gardner c Laker b A. Bedser	7	– c Laker b A. Bedser	7
T. W. Cartwright lbw b A. Bedser	0	– lbw b Laker	9
Don Taylor c Fletcher b A. Bedser	0	– lbw b A. Bedser	20
R. T. Spooner c Whittaker b A. Bedser	16	– c and b Laker	0
H. F. Dollery c Lock b A. Bedser	8	– c Surridge b Laker	0
R. E. Hitchcock c Whittaker b Lock	3	– c A. Bedser b Laker	0
A. Townsend c McIntyre b Lock	7	– run out	0
R. Weeks not out	0	– c Surridge b A. Bedser	0
C. W. Grove c Fletcher b A. Bedser	3	– c Constable b Laker	10
K. R. Dollery c Brazier b A. Bedser	0	– not out	0
W. E. Hollies c Laker b A. Bedser	0	– c sub b A. Bedser	0
L-b 1	1	B 2, l-b 3, n-b 1	6

1/3 2/3 3/8 4/27 5/30   45   1/20 2/22 3/26 4/26 5/26   52
6/36 7/42 8/45 9/45   6/32 7/32 8/49 9/52

Surrey

E. A. Bedser b K. Dollery	5	W. S. Surridge b Grove	19
D. G. W. Fletcher c Townsend b Weeks	13	A. V. Bedser not out	5
B. Constable c Grove b K. Dollery	37	G. A. R. Lock retired hurt	27
T. H. Clark c K. Dollery b Hollies	2		
A. F. Brazier c Townsend b Hollies	6		
G. J. Whittaker b K. Dollery	0	L-b 4, n-b 1	5
A. J. McIntyre c and b K. Dollery	9		
J. C. Laker c H. Dollery b Hollies	18		146

1/5 2/27 3/50 4/61 5/65
6/77 7/81 8/108 9/119

Surrey Bowling

	Overs	Mdns	Runs	Wkts	Overs	Mdns	Runs	Wkts
A. Bedser	13.5	4	18	8	13.4	7	17	4
Surridge	6	1	17	—				
Lock	7	2	9	2				
Laker					13	6	29	5

Warwickshire Bowling

	Overs	Mdns	Runs	Wkts
Grove	10.1	3	29	1
K. Dollery	11	4	40	4
Weeks	8	1	24	1
Hollies	10	4	48	3

Umpires: L. Gray and E. Cooke.

NOTES BY THE EDITOR, 1954

SIR JOHN BERRY HOBBS

Cricket and particularly the professional player was honoured when in June the Queen bestowed the order of Knighthood on Jack Hobbs, the great England and Surrey batsman. Hobbs, always modest and a model sportsman, has worn his honours gracefully. When one looks back and recalls men who have enjoyed every minute of their cricket, Hobbs comes readily to mind. It is his approach to the game which is needed in this hard-headed age.

SURREY v WORCESTERSHIRE

Played at The Oval, August 25, 26, 1954

Surrey won by an innings and 27 runs by half-past twelve on the second day, thus making sure of their third successive Championship. They won in little over five hours of cricket. Play began at two o'clock on Wednesday. In a hundred minutes Worcestershire, sent in on a rain-affected pitch, were dismissed for the lowest score in first-class cricket since 1947. Against Laker and Lock, their last seven wickets fell for five runs. Surridge declared with an hour remaining and a lead of 67. His bowlers took two wickets for 13 overnight and next day they spent only an hour in finishing the game. The aggregate of 157 runs was the smallest ever recorded in any completed Championship match. Lock's figures were remarkable.

Worcestershire

D. Kenyon c Surridge b Bedser	8	– c Stewart b Lock 0
P. E. Richardson c May b Bedser	0	– c McIntyre b Laker 9
L. Outschoorn b Laker	9	– c Lock b Laker 3
R. G. Broadbent c Laker b Lock	3	– c McIntyre b Laker 1
N. Hughes run out	0	– hit wkt b Bedser 2
L. N. Devereux not out	2	– retired hurt 1
R. O. Jenkins c Stewart b Lock	1	– c Laker b Bedser 1
H. Yarnold c Barrington b Lock	1	– not out 14
R. T. D. Perks c Barrington b Laker	0	– b Bedser 2
J. Flavell c Constable b Lock	0	– c Clarke b Laker 3
J. R. Ashman c and b Lock	0	– c Bedser b Loader 2
L-b 1	1	L-b 1, n-b 1 2

1/1 2/16 3/20 4/20 5/21   25   1/0 2/5 3/13 4/16 5/16   40
6/23 7/25 8/25 9/25   6/18 7/23 8/26 9/40

Surrey

T. H. Clark c Richardson b Perks 10	K. Barrington not out 10
M. J. Stewart c Flavell b Perks 11	W 1 1
P. B. H. May not out 31	
B. Constable c and b Ashman 29	1/12 2/31 3/77 (3 wkts dec.) 92

A. J. McIntyre, J. C. Laker, W. S. Surridge, A. V. Bedser, G. A. R. Lock and P. J. Loader did not bat.

Surrey Bowling

	Overs	Mdns	Runs	Wkts	Overs	Mdns	Runs	Wkts
Bedser............	9	4	12	2	6	3	7	3
Loader	6	3	5	—	2.4	1	3	1
Laker	8	3	5	2	17	9	25	4
Lock.............	5.3	4	2	5	10	7	3	1

Worcestershire Bowling

	Overs	Mdns	Runs	Wkts
Perks.............	12	1	43	2
Flavell...........	3	1	17	—
Ashman	8	3	29	1
Devereux	1	—	2	—

Umpires: F. S. Lee and E. Cooke.

SURREY v GLAMORGAN

Played at The Oval, May 11, 13, 1957

Surrey won by an innings and 166 runs. This was their first Championship match since the retirement of Surridge, and fortunate to bat first before week-end rain made the conditions ideal for Laker and Lock, they dismissed Glamorgan twice on the second day in the space of three and a half hours. The pitch was damp enough to help the Glamorgan bowlers on the opening day, but after tea McIntyre used the cut and cover drive with devastating effect. Beside hitting twelve 4s he drove Wooller for 6, scoring his 96 in just over two hours. Glamorgan were unfortunate when Parkhouse split his chin hooking Loader, for after this mishap only Devereux and Watkins withstood the Surrey spin bowlers. Lock finished with twelve wickets for only 34 runs. As usual, Surrey fielded brilliantly close to the wicket and they dismissed Glamorgan the second time in sixty-five minutes. May's run-out caused much controversy. The Surrey captain thought Hedges had held the ball when he dived towards the stumps from mid-on, but the ball was under Hedges as he lay on the ground. Hedges signalled no catch, but May had arrived at the pavilion end where Barrington had not moved. Wooller, the Glamorgan captain, broke the stumps at the vacant end.

Surrey

T. H. Clark c Pressdee b W. G. Davies..... 12	J. C. Laker c Pressdee b Wooller 5
M. J. Stewart b H. D. Davies 1	D. F. Cox not out 9
B. Constable c H. G. Davies b Wooller..... 16	P. J. Loader run out................... 1
P. B. H. May run out.................. 10	
K. F. Barrington c Watkins b McConnon... 52	B 2, l-b 4 6
E. A. Bedser c Pressdee b Shepherd 22	
A. J. McIntyre c Watkins b H. D. Davies... 96	1/1 2/28 3/46 4/48 5/102 259
G. A. R. Lock c Watkins b Pressdee....... 29	6/127 7/167 8/205 9/256

Glamorgan

W. G. A. Parkhouse retired hurt	20	– absent hurt	0
W. G. Davies b Lock	1	– lbw b Lock	4
B. Hedges c Barrington b Lock	4	– c Lock b Laker	1
L. N. Devereux c Stewart b Lock	22	– c Barrington b Laker	8
A. J. Watkins c Stewart b Laker	7	– not out	11
W. Wooller c Loader b Lock	2	– c Cox b Lock	1
J. Pressdee lbw b Lock	0	– c Stewart b Lock	0
J. McConnon c Clark b Lock	0	– lbw b Lock	0
H. G. Davies c Barrington b Laker	0	– c Stewart b Lock	0
H. D. Davies c Stewart b Laker	0	– c Constable b Lock	0
D. J. Shepherd not out	4	– b Laker	0
L-b 1, n-b 1	2	B 4, l-b 2	6

1/16 2/25 3/56 4/56 5/58   62   1/5 2/6 3/10 4/22 5/25   31
6/58 7/58 8/58 9/62   6/25 7/25 8/29 9/31

Glamorgan Bowling

	Overs	Mdns	Runs	Wkts
H. D. Davies	18.4	3	51	2
Watkins	13	1	32	—
W. G. Davies	7	1	18	1
Wooller	24	5	60	2
Shepherd	20	6	53	1
McConnon	5	1	13	1
Pressdee	3	—	26	1

Surrey Bowling

	Overs	Mdns	Runs	Wkts	Overs	Mdns	Runs	Wkts
Loader	13	5	22	—				
Cox	2	—	8	—				
Laker	12.2	7	10	3	11.3	7	11	3
Lock	20	13	20	6	11	6	14	6

Umpires: W. F. Price and D. J. Wood.

SURREY v WARWICKSHIRE

Played at The Oval, May 17, 19, 20, 1958

Surrey won by an innings and 80 runs. With M. J. K. Smith, their captain, playing for MCC, Warwickshire were no match for Surrey, and in particular Loader. On a pitch giving the batsmen at least an equal chance, Loader brought the game to a close before lunch on the third day by taking nine second innings wickets for 17 runs, his best figures. Whether such an analysis also reflected his best performance is doubtful, for the batsmen possessed neither the skill nor the fight to combat intelligent pace bowling. The limitations of the recognised batsmen were seen clearly in the first innings when the tail-enders contributed 95 of the 162 runs. In between, Surrey also found runs difficult to score against bowlers inclined to pitch a shade short, though May gave another excellent display, notably to the off, once he had his eye in. He was finally run out through splendid fielding in the covers by Horner.

Warwickshire

F. C. Gardner c Clark b Laker	22	– c May b Loader	25
N. F. Horner c May b Gibson	1	– c Barrington b Loader	13
C. W. Leach c McIntyre b Loader	26	– c McIntyre b Loader	0
B. E. Fletcher c Lock b Laker	3	– lbw b Loader	0
R. E. Hitchcock b Loader	0	– c Bedser b Lock	0
K. Ibadulla b Loader	11	– c McIntyre b Loader	0
R. T. Spooner c Lock b Laker	14	– b Loader	0
E. Leadbeater c Bedser b Lock	20	– b Loader	0
H. J. Latham c Gibson b Lock	26	– c sub b Loader	1
R. G. Carter b Lock	22	– not out	2
R. G. Thompson not out	13	– b Loader	4
B 3, l-b 1	4	B 4, l-b 6	10

1/2 2/48 3/49 4/51 5/63   162   1/20 2/20 3/20 4/41 5/44   63
6/67 7/77 8/123 9/132   6/48 7/48 8/56 9/57

Surrey

T. H. Clark c Spooner b Latham	33
D. G. W. Fletcher c Horner b Carter	13
B. Constable c Leadbeater b Ibadulla	59
P. B. H. May run out	73
K. F. Barrington c Carter b Ibadulla	1
E. A. Bedser lbw b Thompson	17
A. J. McIntyre c Gardner b Latham	18
G. A. R. Lock c Gardner b Ibadulla	56
J. C. Laker c Spooner b Ibadulla	20
D. Gibson not out	7
B 1, l-b 7	8

1/48 2/48 3/169   (9 wkts dec.) 305
4/182 5/183 6/208 7/233 8/272 9/305

P. J. Loader did not bat.

Surrey Bowling

	Overs	Mdns	Runs	Wkts	Overs	Mdns	Runs	Wkts
Loader	22	8	37	3	15.5	6	17	9
Gibson	10	4	17	1	12	4	18	—
Laker	20	4	49	3	6	2	14	—
Lock	16.5	5	45	3	2	1	4	1
Bedser	4	1	10	—				

Warwickshire Bowling

	Overs	Mdns	Runs	Wkts	Overs	Mdns	Runs	Wkts
Thompson	28	9	61	1				
Latham	30	4	81	2				
Carter	27	1	62	1				
Leadbeater	11	1	41	—				
Ibadulla	15.2	2	43	4				
Leach	6	3	9	—				

Umpires: F. S. Lee and D. J. Wood.

SURREY v NORTHAMPTONSHIRE

Played at The Oval, June 4, 5, 6, 1958

Drawn. Northamptonshire taking two points, the first points of the season conceded by Surrey. A long struggle for first innings lead was a story of records but little entertainment. The match had lasted fifteen and three-quarter hours when Northamptonshire, who occupied nine hours of the time, went ahead. Stewart, with his first century of the season, and Constable batted particularly well for Surrey and at the close of the first day the score was 324 for four. McIntyre, captain in the absence of May, who, like Loader, Lock and Laker, was playing for England, chose to bat on for three-quarters of an hour next day on an excellent pitch, presumably in the hope of forcing a follow-on. With Northamptonshire 18 for three and then 95 for five, such an eventuality seemed likely but Surrey had to wait another six and three-quarter hours and 376 runs before breaking the sixth-wicket stand. That partnership, between the former Surrey player Subba Row, leading his side at The Oval for the first time, and Lightfoot, created a record for any Northamptonshire wicket. Subba Row's 300 was the highest individual score for the county, as well as equal to the previous highest made against Surrey, and Lightfoot reached his maiden century, which took six hours twenty-three minutes and contained fourteen 4s. In all, Subba Row batted for nine hours twenty-six minutes and hit forty-two 4s. This is the only instance of an individual hitting a treble century against Surrey at The Oval.

Surrey

T. H. Clark c Reynolds b Manning	71	A. J. McIntyre not out	18
M. J. Stewart b Lightfoot	118		
D. G. W. Fletcher c and b Lightfoot	0	L-b 4, n-b 5	9
B. Constable c Brookes b Lightfoot	73		
K. F. Barrington not out	62	1/144 2/156 (5 wkts dec.)	378
E. A. Bedser c Tyson b Lightfoot	27	3/218 4/280 5/328	

R. C. E. Pratt, R. Swetman, D. Gibson and D. A. D. Sydenham did not bat.

Northamptonshire

D. Brookes lbw b Sydenham	4	K. V. Andrew c and b Barrington	8
P. Arnold b Sydenham	6	F. H. Tyson not out	14
B. L. Reynolds b Sydenham	6	M. H. J. Allen not out	1
D. W. Barrick c Barrington b Gibson	44		
R. Subba Row b Clark	300	B 9, l-b 1, w 3, n-b 2	15
G. E. Tribe c Constable b Gibson	5		
A. Lightfoot c Swetman b Clark	119	1/7 2/15 3/18 4/89 (9 wkts)	529
J. S. Manning c Barrington b Clark	7	5/95 6/471 7/492 8/507 9/520	

Northamptonshire Bowling

	Overs	Mdns	Runs	Wkts
Tyson	32	8	93	—
Lightfoot	35	9	96	4
Tribe	26	5	78	—
Allen	19	7	40	—
Manning	25	9	62	1

Surrey Bowling

	Overs	Mdns	Runs	Wkts
Gibson	51	12	152	2
Sydenham	36	7	109	3
Bedser	60	39	65	—
Pratt	35	11	77	—
Barrington	22	6	63	1
Clark	10	—	48	3

Umpires: T. W. Spencer and E. Davies.

FROM DR GRACE TO PETER MAY [1959]

By Herbert Strudwick

H. Strudwick played in 28 Test Matches for England between 1909 and 1926. In all first-class cricket, he dismissed 1,493 batsmen and he held 1,253 catches – both world records.

They say that all good things must come to an end. Sad though it is to me, my official connection with Surrey, which began in 1897, finished last season when, after being wicket-keeper for 30 years and scorer for a similar period, I made way for a younger man. In bidding good-bye to The Oval, known the world over for the great cricketers it has produced and the exciting games it has staged, I cannot sufficiently thank the Surrey Club and the committees I have served under for all those years for giving me so much help and showing me so much kindness.

I feel, too, that I owe a debt to a lady, a Miss Wilson, daughter of the Vicar of Mitcham, where I was born on January 28, 1880. She used to supervise the choir-boys' cricket matches in which, when I was about ten years old, I took part. It was my habit to run in from cover to the wicket to take returns from the field and I apparently did this well enough to prompt her to say one day: "You ought to be a wicket-keeper". From that time I became a stumper and I was sufficiently good at the job to play for Surrey for 25 years and to keep for England 28 times at a period when Australia and South Africa were our only Test opponents.

I have known nearly all the famous cricketers of the twentieth century, from Dr W. G. Grace to Peter May, the present Surrey and England captain. One recollection I have of Grace was when I played for Surrey against London County at the Old Crystal Palace ground in 1902. On the day that "W. G." bowled me for my second "duck" of the match, Southampton and Sheffield United were fighting out the F.A. Cup Final, also at the Crystal Palace. As I passed the Doctor on my way out, he said to me: "Why didn't you tell me you got a duck in the first innings, youngster? I would have given you one to get off the mark." "Never mind, sir," I said. "I want to see the second-half of that Cup Final." And away I scampered.

The young professional of to-day has a much easier time than when I began, of that I am sure. First of all, he has a fixed wage guaranteed all the year round, differing, I presume, according to the ability of the player. My first wage was £1 per week – no match fees – for four months during the summer, expenses, train-fare and 2s. 6d. a day for lunch. Tea was free, and how we enjoyed it. If we could not get lunch on the ground, we went to a pub, for there was always one close by. There we had either arrowroot biscuit and cheese or a large piece of bread and cheese. That cost 9d. or 1s. 0d., so we made 1s. 6d. on our lunch allowance – which was then quite a lot of money.

As there were nearly 40 on the staff and a lot of amateurs came in for the club matches, we had only a few games each summer until we got a place in the second eleven. Now the staff numbers only about 24 and it is something of a job to find enough players. We spent most of our time bowling to members. Doing this from half-past eleven till half-past six was a much more tiring job than playing. That is a thing of the past, for now there are very few members, who take a net. They used to place coins on top of the stumps, and these went to the bowlers who hit the stumps. Needless to day, the senior professionals took the "half-crown batsmen", leaving the sixpenny ones to the youngsters.

The chief enjoyment is when a team goes off to play in some club games, and the boys are not only playing most days now, but earning good money because few amateurs are available, more's the pity.

When I went to The Oval for a trial in 1896, I went behind in the nets and received a smack on the head from a fast ball from Len Braund. They told me I was too young to be taken on, but I came back and in the first trial in 1898 Braund, who was bowling slow leg-breaks, suddenly whipped in a very fast ball wide of the off-stump and split the joint of my first finger. I stood close up to the stumps and had never played on so fast a pitch or taken a bowler who did that sort of thing. With three wicket-keepers already on the staff, I thought this might mean the end of my engagement, but H. Wood and C. Marshall were getting on in years and, Fred Stedman being eight years older than I was, I felt there was some hope.

There was no ceremony about the arrival of a new member of the ground staff. I received no introduction to any of the players, just told my duties and where to find the young players' room. I was lucky to find three Mitcham men already there, two brothers, A. and W. Baker, and W. Montgomery, and they took me in hand. All have passed over now, worse luck, for they were charming fellows.

After seeing a few matches, I made up my mind to go all out to get into the county side. The new Pavilion was nearly finished in the year I started, 1898, and there were two large rooms for the players, one upstairs for those who had played in the first and second teams and the other downstairs for the rest. There were also separate doors to get on to the ground. I once went upstairs and ran into Tom Hayward, who demanded: "Who are you?" I told him and he said: "You have the advantage of me and your place is downstairs."

Being very shy, I felt that this was a bad start for me, but it did not break my spirit, and the will to win and get up those stairs was stronger than ever. Little did I then dream that I should be using that room for nearly 60 years.

The great Surrey players of that day were a tough lot and it was hard work to get under their skins. Until you reached their level you were lucky to get an answer if you spoke to them! I played with a number of them before I finished and they were grand chaps. I always used to feel sad when the old ones left and that is why I took on the scoring job when I finished playing in 1927. I did not want to leave the boys; and after 60 years I feel the same.

Certain incidents stick in the mind. I remember once missing Carpenter, of Essex, when he was 29. "Sorry about that," said Carpenter sympathetically. So was I, for he was 199 when he gave his next chance — and this time I held it.

Then there was the occasion of my first Gentlemen and Players match when I asked Albert Trott how I could find his fast ball, which he disguised so well. "You'll soon find it", Albert told me. It was some time before he bowled it and when he did it just missed the leg-stump and hit me full toss on the left foot. I was hopping round in great pain when Albert came up to me. "You found it all right then", he said.

I had just received my invitation to tour Australia with the MCC team of 1911 when I shared a hansom cab with Bill Lockwood to Lord's, where we were to play Middlesex. Bill said to me: "Matey, I'm going to Australia with you this winter." I said: "Are you, Bill? That's good." He said: "You watch me bowl to-day." At that time we were going over Vauxhall Bridge when the horse stumbled and landed on its knees. Off went the two cricket bags, and I remarked that that was not a good start. However, Bill got nine wickets that day — but he did not go to Australia.

Slow bowlers always employed a deep field, or two if the batsmen were quick on their feet and able to get out to the ball. Nottingham marl spread over the table after the end of each season was taken into the pitches by rain and weather. This made the surface fine in hard weather, but very nasty after rain, and matches were often finished by lunch-time on the second day, for there was then no covering of the pitch and only a bag of sawdust protected the bowlers' footholes.

I remember a match at Packer's Ground at Bristol when we were batting on the second day and, following overnight rain, Charlie Parker, the Gloucestershire left-hander, went on to bowl. The rain had penetrated through the sawdust and as Parker attempted to deliver the ball, he slipped and fell. "I can't bowl on that," said Charlie, and the game was held up for twenty minutes while the groundsmen and umpires got to work with rakes and shovels to improve the foothold. At the end of the match Gloucestershire wanted quite a few runs with one wicket to fall. This could have been far different had the pitch been covered.

In my younger days cricket was the only summer sport, except for golf and lawn-tennis, which were too expensive for the average chap. So most people played cricket and the majority of spectators understood the finer points of the game and appreciated good bowling besides good batting and fielding. For that reason crowds of that time showed more patience than those of to-day. They were content to watch and enjoy cricket, knowing full well that the bowler was doing his best to get the batsman out and not to give him runs. Another thing, cricket received more space in the newspapers and it was given to good news and not to how many 4s a batsman hit and how long he batted. I wish that reporters would be more free with praise instead of finding so much to criticise in the best game in the world.

More amateurs played 60 years ago than now. In 1899 Surrey had seven at different times, Gloucestershire seven, Somerset eight, Middlesex seven, Kent eight, Essex six, Hampshire five, and so on. Now the amateurs cannot spare the time and so have taken up golf. As long as I can remember, Surrey have had an amateur captain and I hope they will always find one good enough to take over. They are lucky to have such a fine player as Mr May to lead them and to captain England.

I think there were more first-class players in every county in my time than nowadays and the strength of the sides was more equal. One finds it difficult to realise that Nottinghamshire were at the bottom of the Championship table last summer. I did not like to see it, for when I first started they were a very powerful team. Then there are the changes in the Laws – larger stumps, new Lbw Law, different scoring of points and the changing of the ball. At one time, no change of the ball was permitted unless it lost its shape. Later a new ball was allowed when 200 runs had been scored, but only in recent years have the number of overs bowled counted as an alternative. It began with experiments in 1947 with 55 overs, later changed to 65 overs and now 75 overs.

I recall Mr Fender once bowling a ball which went very wide of the leg-stump for four byes. "What's the idea, skipper?" I asked him. He replied: "I want to get the new ball." "Right," I said, "you bowl some long hops and full-pitches and they'll soon get the runs. I'm going to stand back. But," I added, "I don't see why they should get 200. Bowl 'em out!"

I was naturally delighted when I got my first game with Surrey's first team, against the West Indies in 1900, though I had the feeling that a better man in Fred Stedman was standing down. Wicket-keepers used to have to put up with a good deal of knocking about then, for it was not always possible to gauge how the ball would come to you and our equipment was not what it is now. Stedman used to protect his chest with a copy of the South Western Railway time-table and on one occasion, after receiving a specially heavy blow, he remarked to a team-mate: "I shall have to catch a later train tonight. That one knocked off the 7.30!"

I was never at any time nervous on the field and I always did my best. A wicket-keeper needs patience because he cannot make his own chances. He must expect a catch from every ball and not a stumping chance which will make him snatch at it. If he catches the ball, he can soon break the wicket if the batsman is out of his ground. Once when I went out to bat against Somerset their wicket-keeper, W. Hill, said to me: "I've been out here all day and haven't had a chance of a catch or a stumping." I said: "Don't worry, you will." "No," he said, "I have given it up." I gave him two chances – and he missed both!

I liked to save every run possible. I often used to chase the ball to the boundary if it were played on the leg-side where no fieldsman was placed. On one occasion when we were playing Kent, Lockwood was standing at point a long way back, so that the batsman, by pushing the ball towards him, was able to steal quite a number of singles. So at length I moved right up to the stumps, and as the bowler delivered the ball, dashed out towards point, picked up the ball and ran out A. P. Day. If the batsman had missed his stroke, the ball would have gone for four byes! Another thing, I often used to take catches in front of the wicket – sometimes almost off the bat – especially when "Razor" Smith made the ball jump.

Though the performance of winning seven Championships in successive seasons might be considered to give them pride of place, it is an open question whether the present side is the best Surrey have had, for there were some very fine teams in the past. The batting has not been too strong for the last two seasons, and that may have helped them, because they wasted no time over unnecessary runs. I do not think they have ever had a better bowling side. How the 1906 team would have shaped on the Oval pitch today with the larger stumps and the new Lbw law it is hard to say. The batsmen were better, but they might not have got so many runs under changed conditions. I think the bowlers would have done better than they used to.

The captain who began this run of Championship successes, Mr Surridge, did great work in moulding the team to catch and field as he did, especially close in on the leg-side. What a tonic to bowlers that meant. The bowling of Alec Bedser, Jim Laker, Tony Lock and Peter Loader, backed up by such wonderful catching by Mr Surridge, Michael Stewart, Lock and Ken Barrington has been beyond praise. The last year that Mr Surridge captained the side, 1956, Surrey looked as if they had no chance of the title and some of the players said as much to the skipper. "We'll win it yet," said Mr Surridge. That is the secret: the will to win. To be without four of your best players, especially bowlers who are hard to find, for ten matches and still finish at the top is a magnificent achievement. Mind you, I don't think Surrey's performance could have been done years ago when there were so many strong counties.

It is difficult to say who is the best batsman I have seen. So many have appealed to me at different times. I feel that I must give first place to Sir Jack Hobbs for his play on all wickets and against all types of bowling. He is the only batsman about whom I felt that he would not get out till he wanted to. Generally he threw his wicket away after scoring a century. I remember G. A. Faulkner after an England tour in South Africa, saying to Jack: "I only bowled you one googly." "Why," said Jack, "I didn't know you bowled one." Faulkner said: "You hit the first one I bowled for four. If you didn't know it, how did you know it would turn from the off?" "I didn't," answered Jack. "I watched it off the pitch." Yes, Jack had shots all off the wicket to different parts of the field.

K. S. Ranjitsinhji was the most polished batsman in my experience. His perfect leg-glide was one of his favourite strokes, even off the middle stump. He played fast bowling with the greatest of ease, placing the bowlers to all quarters of the compass. I believe that he could have made as many runs as he wanted to. I remember once when he was plumb lbw to Tom Richardson and given not out, he went on to make 200. Then he deliberately skied a ball from McDonell for Richardson to catch. During the time he was at Cambridge, he used whenever possible to engage Bill Lockwood and Richardson to bowl to him.

Sir Don Bradman I consider the best run-getter of my time. He never seemed to tire, he had all the other batsmen's shots – and a few of his own. He was also the best fielder I have seen. When he was fielding deep on the leg-side during a Test at The Oval, I did not seen any batsman run more than a single from a ball played anywhere near him, and his return to the wicket-keeper was a full toss right over the stumps. There have been lots of great batsmen from Australia, but never one as good.

One of the best forcing batsman England have ever had was Walter Hammond. He could play strokes all round the wicket, and his favourite drive through the covers was a joy to watch. I recall in 1928, when we were playing Gloucestershire at Cheltenham, that Mr Fender was forced to place a cover-point, two extra-covers and a mid-off, and still Hammond found a way past them without giving them a chance to stop the ball. In that match he hit 139 in the first innings and 143 in the second and held ten catches. He was also a very fine bowler and could field anywhere. Nobody is taught to hit like him nowadays. I do wish cricket instructors would teach their pupils the way to hit the ball, the way to play back and force it off the back foot, instead of forward, forward and again forward.

Another great batsman was Victor Trumper, a hard hitter who was a delight to watch. How I would have loved to see Bradman and Trumper batting together. Tom Hayward, too, was a demon against fast bowling. He once made four separate centuries in a week. I was lucky enough to be in with him when he made one of them at Nottingham. When I went in he said to me: "Run for the fifth ball or the sixth." If it happened to be the fifth ball and I had a chance to get a run, he refused the call. After he got his 100, I was run out! He used to help pick the side and would come down to the Surrey dressing-room and say to Razor Smith: "I bet you half a crown you are playing." Although Razor knew he was selected, he always took the bet. I once said to Razor: "You know you are playing. They can't leave you out." Razor grinned and said: "I know when I am well off." Hayward did the "double" one year and then gave up bowling when he began to make big scores.

Mr May is now occupying the place once filled by Jack Hobbs and Tom Hayward and is England's leading batsman with powerful shots all round. When he goes to the wicket he is out to make runs and stands up nearly straight ready to hit the first ball, if it wants hitting, not prepared to play forward for the first few overs. A four off the first ball is the best tonic to make one feel at home and relaxed. Against Nottinghamshire at The Oval last season Jepson, the fast bowler, was bowling when May went in. The first ball he received May hit over the bowler's head for six. There was a look of astonishment on Jepson's face as he watched it go. The next delivery was hit in the same direction for four. Only a class player could do that. Mr May, besides being a great cricketer, is a most charming man.

Sir Leonard Hutton was another outstanding batsman, though not the dashing player that Bradman was. Hutton had plenty of patience, but never a loose ball passed him and his cover-point shots were perfect.

What a joy to watch was Denis Compton. I wish a few more batsmen would use their feet as he did and play the strokes he did; there would be no half-empty grounds. Edrich and Compton were a great pair and the only two who received constant mention by the Press after the war. "Patsy" Hendren was another who gave much pleasure to the crowds, whether batting or fielding, and what a lovely companion.

There are so many I would like to mention, worthy men all. Frank Woolley, the best and hardest-hitting of left-handers I have seen. He stood straight up, very seldom playing forward, but his shots off the back foot and his powerful drives delighted everybody except the bowlers. In his day he was among our best all-rounders.

Andy Sandham, Jack Hobbs's opening partner for such a long time, was unlucky in having so great a player at the other end, for no player was more adept at finding an opening for a run off the fifth or sixth ball than Jack. Andy always expected it and was ready to run.

Turning to bowlers, I regard Tom Richardson as the fastest and best of men of pace. Years ago, when Surrey were playing at Nottingham, I saw Bill Lockwood, whom many thought was the best but not the fastest. Bill was sitting in a wheeled chair and I asked him whom he thought was the best and fastest bowler he had seen. "There's only one in it", he replied. "Tom Richardson," I said: "What about yourself?" Bill shook his head. "I wasn't in the same parish as Tom, never mind the same street," he said. I think J. M. Gregory and E. A. McDonald, the two fastest men from Australia I ever saw, were on a par with Richardson and Lockwood.

Maurice Tate, Alec Bedser, G. G. Macaulay, C. Kelleway and F. R. Foster stand out among fast-medium bowlers. Foster, left-arm, was a bit faster than the others and very quick off the pitch. The first time I kept wicket to him was in a trial match at Lord's. The first ball he bowled swung right across the pitch to outside the leg-stump, turned sharply and went over the top of the off-stump, leaving the batsman and me stone cold and hitting the sight-screen with a bang. James Seymour, the batsman, had half turned to play the ball to leg. I said to him: "It looks as if there will be 50 byes before lunch, but I'm not going to stand back to him." Nor did I. In the first match at Sydney in 1911 I gave Foster the signal to bowl one outside the leg-stump for me to try and stump Duff, who I thought might move his right foot in making his shot. Instead of bowling the ball I wanted, Foster sent it very wide outside the off-stump and four byes resulted. The second time I signalled, I made sure he saw what I meant. This time he bowled the ball straight to Frank Woolley at first slip. Then I realised he did not intend to give me the chance which he might have allowed had "Tiger" Smith, his own county's wicket-keeper, been behind the stumps.

One incident about Maurice Tate lingers in my memory. In his first Australian tour, 1924, Maurice bowled two overs, of eight balls per over, to Ponsford in the opening Test at Sydney. Ponsford tried to play at every ball, but each time he missed. He turned to me and said: "I've never played against such bowling in all my life." I said: "It doesn't look as though you have. You ought to have been out sixteen times!" Then "Horseshoe" Collins schemed it so that he should face Tate, and defended solidly till the Sussex bowler tired. The tactics worked, for Ponsford went on to get 110.

Sidney Barnes was the best of the medium-pace bowlers in my day, but the Australian W. J. O'Reilly followed him pretty closely. As regards slow bowlers, there were so many as good as each other. There were the left-handers Rhodes, Blythe, Verity, Woolley and Parker and numerous right-handers, with "Tich" Freeman, of Kent, at the top.

In my day the premier wicket-keepers were A. A. Lilley, G. MacGregor, H. Martin, E. J. Smith, F. H. Huish, D. Hunter, W. Storer, J. C. Hubble, G. Duckworth and L. E. G. Ames. G. J. V. Weigall, the old Cambridge and Kent player, told me one day: "I have found the best wicket-keeper-batsman England will ever have." When I asked him the name of this player, he said: "Leslie Ames". How right he was. There will never be another like Ames, who during his career hit 37,245 runs in addition to his vast number of victims. Kent have been extremely fortunate in their wicket-keepers, Huish, Hubble, Ames and Godfrey Evans all being in the very top class.

I have never seen a better wicket-keeper than Evans, but I class W. A. Oldfield, the Australian, H. B. Cameron, of South Africa, and Lilley as his equal. These men, who stood close up to the wicket to all bowling, had splendid records and did their work without any fuss. Each was quick in putting down the wicket when the occasion arose and none could be excelled when it came to taking catches. Evans does all these things equally well, and his happy disposition allows him to enjoy every minute on the field. Full of energy and enthusiasm, he makes everything difficult look easy – though he tries to make the easy ones appear difficult! Yes, Evans is a great provider of entertainment for the crowd, and is an inspiration to his team-mates, especially the bowlers, to whom he must give considerable confidence to do their utmost.

It is my opinion that games are won on the field, and not in the dressing-rooms. A captain cannot plan his campaign overnight – how he will use his bowlers and from which end they should operate, and so forth. We hear so much about "seamers' wickets" nowadays. I don't know what the term means, but I notice that if the wicket is one considered favourable to "seamers", the fast bowlers keep going till they are dead beat and cannot come back again when wanted. I do not like the captain who looks at the clock when going out to field and says to himself: "11.30. First change 12.30". It takes two fast bowlers an hour to bowl 16 overs between them, and if one gets a wicket in his seventh or eighth over, he has to send down another three or four.

This is where the good captains make their mark. I name three I consider superior to all others: A. B. Sellers, W. S. Surridge and P. G. H. Fender. Sellers welded his team into the best fielding combination I ever encountered. His placing of the field was wellnigh perfect. Always on the alert himself, he saw that the men under him were constantly on their toes. He changed his bowlers more often than any other captain I have known and with great success. I have seen a bowler get a wicket and be taken off next over, and the man who replaced him would at once succeed in disposing of a batsman. Was it luck? I don't think so. It was the captain's wicket. Sellers's heart and soul were in the game and he was out to win every time. He was a live wire on the field, never giving up, and if a player did not follow his example he was soon out of the side. I like his type, all out till the match is over.

Mr Surridge possessed the same gifts and drive. This new Lbw Law and two of the best slow bowlers of today gave him the opportunity which he took with both hands. He did more than anybody to make Laker and Lock what they are today. His placing of three fieldsmen within a few yards of the bat on the leg-side gave the batsmen little chance against Laker's off-spinner and I believe was the reason why MCC restricted the number of fieldsmen in those positions. There is no doubt that these close-in fieldsmen won matches and the Championship for Surrey.

Mr Fender was one of the finest captains who never was asked to lead England. A grand all-rounder, he would, I am sure, have won one or two Championships had the pitches been what they are today instead of the cast-iron affairs of his time, coupled with the larger stumps, new Lbw Law and the third-day declarations. The rule those days was that if you could not win you must try and save the game. I could not see any county giving Surrey a chance to win if they could avoid it.

Only once can I recall this happening and that was at Leicester. When we were coming in for tea, Mr Fender asked his rival captain, Major G. H. S. Fowke, if he intended to declare. "I don't think so," said the Major. Returning from tea, he saw Mr A. Jeacocke sitting at the dressing-room door with his pads on. "What are you doing?" asked the Major in surprise. "You have declared, haven't you?" said Jeacocke. "No," replied Major Fowke, "but I suppose I had better do so now." And Surrey won the match, Mr Fender's winning hit for 6 sending the ball through the dressing-room door. Many of the Leicestershire members were so annoyed about this that they threatened to resign. I said to one of them: "Why are you grumbling? You've seen one of the best afternoon's cricket you will ever see. Suppose it had been Leicestershire who had won?" "Ah, but it wasn't Leicestershire," he said.

It is nothing in these days for a team to declare in both innings. There was a craze before the war, when rain left only one day for play, for one side to go in, be given four runs and declare. The other side followed suit and the result really depended on the second innings. Surrey did this at Cardiff and lost the match.

There is no reason why a professional should not make an able captain. Alec Bedser, H. E. Dollery and George Emmett all showed their ability in this direction. They knew the game inside out and it was their job. No one talks more about the game than a professional cricketer. At the same time there are certain responsibilities, such as choosing the team. The professional is not a member of the club and therefore has no vote. He will be given the names of twelve or thirteen players and he has to leave out one or two men, a thing he does not like to do because they are all his pals. So he develops a conscience. If he is a bowler, he will choose the worst end to bowl from, probably against the wind. If he over-rides his conscience, he will pick the better end! Temperament plays a big part in cricket. The amateur captain, as a member of the club, has very little to worry about. He can seek the advice of the senior professional, and the odd chat with the players helps to ease the tension of a match. Yes, I am all in favour of the amateur skipper, providing that he has a sound knowledge of the game and is a reasonably good cricketer.

Sometimes I am asked how modern cricket compares with that of those far-off days. Frankly I cannot see much difference except that in my time the batsmen found it easier to score faster. The ball came more quickly on to the bat and got up stump-high from the hard pitches, giving them the chance to make more shots. The bowlers concentrated more on or outside the off-stump and those of fast and fast-medium pace had only two men on the on-side – a mid-on and a deep fine-leg.

The bowlers when I first played always tried to bowl just outside the off-stump. Dick Lilley, the Warwickshire wicket-keeper, used to hold his hands out for the bowler to bowl to in Australia.

SURREY v YORKSHIRE

(G. A. R. Lock's Benefit)

Played at The Oval, June 18, 20, 21, 1960

Yorkshire won by nine wickets. The fiery fast bowling of Trueman, who took fourteen wickets for 123 and in each innings sent back three men in five balls, was the deciding factor on a firm pitch. In the first innings he disposed of Tindall, Willett and Gibson in five deliveries with the score 93, and in the second repeated the feat at the expense of Barrington, Willett and Gibson when the total stood at 218. Trueman's speed and judicious use of the yorker and bouncer kept all his rivals on tenterhooks. Yorkshire lacked Stott and Taylor through injury, but Padgett and Close made up for the handicap with splendid centuries. Partners in a third-wicket stand of 226, both drove well, Close so powerfully that he hit Lock three times straight into the pavilion – once sending the ball clean through an open window. Close, who batted five and a half hours, hit twenty-two 4s besides four 6s. Surrey, shown the way by Stewart and Parsons, fared much better in their second innings and Lock gained some compensation for the harsh treatment of his left-arm spin bowling by gallantly hitting eight boundaries. Yorkshire were left to make only two runs to win, but only a quarter of an hour of extra time remained when they achieved their victory. The match receipts, including a collection of £409 10s., were £2,257.

Surrey

M. J. Stewart b Trueman	9	– c and b Trueman	78
A. B. D. Parsons lbw b Trueman	23	– c Binks b Trueman	45
D. G. W. Fletcher c Sharpe b Platt	42	– c Trueman b Close	11
K. F. Barrington c J. Wilson b Close	4	– b Trueman	62
R. A. E. Tindall b Trueman	14	– b Illingworth	38
M. D. Willett c Platt b Trueman	0	– c J. Wilson b Trueman	0
D. Gibson c Binks b Trueman	0	– c Binks b Trueman	0
G. A. R. Lock b Trueman	12	– b Trueman	44
†A. J. McIntyre c Illingworth b Platt	6	– c Binks b Platt	14
*A. V. Bedser c Sharpe b Trueman	6	– c and b Trueman	2
P. J. Loader not out	2	– not out	0
B 1, l-b 2, n-b 2	5	B 11, l-b 1, n-b 6	18

1/12 2/61 3/70 4/93 5/93   123   1/81 2/118 3/173 4/218 5/218   312
6/93 7/102 8/112 9/119   6/218 7/277 8/305 9/312

Yorkshire

J. B. Bolus c McIntyre b Gibson	28	– not out	4
P. J. Sharpe c McIntyre b Loader	9	– run out	0
D. E. V. Padgett c Stewart b Gibson	117	– not out	0
D. B. Close c Tindall b Loader	198		
R. Illingworth not out	55		
*J. V. Wilson not out	18		
B 5, l-b 4	9		

1/18 2/56 3/282 4/403   (4 wkts dec.) 434   1/0   (1 wkt) 4

D. Wilson, F. S. Trueman, †J. G. Binks, R. K. Platt and M. J. Cowan did not bat.

Yorkshire Bowling

	Overs	Mdns	Runs	Wkts	Overs	Mdns	Runs	Wkts
Trueman..........	21.5	5	41	7	36.1	16	82	7
Platt.............	14	5	26	2	20	11	31	1
Cowan...........	5	—	14	—	20	4	49	—
Illingworth........	5	3	7	—	27	17	41	1
Close.............	11	3	30	1	17	4	60	1
D. Wilson					23	13	31	—

Surrey Bowling

	Overs	Mdns	Runs	Wkts	Overs	Mdns	Runs	Wkts
Loader...........	27	3	106	2				
Bedser...........	29	4	63	—				
Gibson...........	22	2	76	2				
Lock.............	35	3	127	—				
Barrington	18	3	53	—				
Fletcher					1	1	—	—
Stewart...........					0.1	—	4	—

Umpires: T. W. Spencer and F. S. Lee.

SURREY v WARWICKSHIRE

Played at The Oval, July 6, 7, 8, 1960

Drawn. Not for a long time had batsmen been to such advantage at Kennington as in this match. Horner and Ibadulla seized the opportunity to break all Warwickshire partnership records by scoring 377 in five hours twenty minutes before Wheatley declared. Their previous best opening stand was 333 by J. F. Byrne and S. P. Kinneir against Lancashire at Edgbaston in 1905. Horner hit twenty-eight 4s and Ibadulla twenty-one, both excelling with the cut and drive, and both made their best scores in first-class cricket. Edrich then hit his highest score, taking five hours and ten minutes for 154 (twenty-five 4s). At the end of the second day Surrey were 323 for four wickets and they took just over seven and a half hours to gain the lead. Tindall played most attractively, getting ten 4s in his not out 68 before heavy rain prevented further cricket.

Warwickshire

N. F. Horner not out....................203
K. Ibadulla not out 170
      L-b 4....................... 4

(No wkt) 377

A. Townsend, R. E. Hitchcock, B. E. Fletcher, J. M. Kennedy, D. Amiss, J. D. Bannister, †J. G. Fox, G. H. Hill and *O. S. Wheatley did not bat.

Surrey

M. J. Stewart c Fox b Bannister 21
J. H. Edrich c Wheatley b Hill 154
D. G. W. Fletcher c Fox b Hill 27
A. B. D. Parsons c and b Hill 75
R. A. E. Tindall not out................. 68
†R. Swetman c Bannister b Wheatley...... 24

E. A. Bedser c Kennedy b Amiss 8
A. T. C. Allom not out 0
    B 15, l-b 2, w 1, n-b 1 19

1/40 2/110 3/286   (6 wkts) 396
4/297 5/363 6/384

G. A. R. Lock, *A. V. Bedser and D. A. D. Sydenham did not bat.

Surrey Bowling

	Overs	Mdns	Runs	Wkts
A. Bedser	28	5	87	—
Sydenham	23	3	80	—
Allom	12	2	53	—
Lock	23	1	82	—
E. Bedser	23	3	71	—

Warwickshire Bowling

	Overs	Mdns	Runs	Wkts
Bannister	36	9	78	1
Wheatley	27	7	66	1
Townsend	16	1	42	—
Amiss	19	3	49	1
Hitchcock	8	2	21	—
Hill	35	11	97	3
Ibadulla	23	10	24	—

Umpires: T. W. Spencer and W. H. Copson.

SURREY v SUSSEX

Played at The Oval, July 11, 12, 13, 1962

Sussex won by 10 runs. The result was a triumph for Dexter, the Sussex captain, who was the inspiration of his side in every respect. By taking seven wickets for 38, Dexter limited Surrey's first innings lead to 26. Next, while his own batsmen were labouring for runs – Sheppard spent one and three-quarter hours for 24 – Dexter with glorious strokes made 94 in two and a quarter hours, hitting two 6s and twelve 4s. Next day, Surrey needed 227 to win in five hours and with Barrington and May taking part in a stand of 122 they seemed to be romping home. When only 30 more runs were required they had seven wickets left, but with Dexter and Bell sharing the attack four wickets fell in the course of six balls while only a single was scored. First, Barrington was run out; next Langridge held Willett in the gully off Dexter and then Storey and Lock left to successive deliveries, both caught in identical fashion off Bell by Dexter at short mid-off. After that debacle, Surrey could not check the landslide and their last six wickets slumped for 19 runs. So Sussex gained a notable victory with forty minutes to spare and Dexter was duly rewarded some days later when MCC honoured him with the captaincy of the team to tour Australia.

Sussex

Rev. D. S. Sheppard c Storey b Sydenham	4	– c Storey b Lock 24
R. J. Langridge c Barrington b Storey	29	– lbw b Loader 1
K. G. Suttle c Willett b Sydenham	4	– run out 17
*E. R. Dexter c May b Loader	27	– b Loader 94
†J. M. Parks c Long b Loader	29	– c Edrich b Loader 18
D. V. Smith c Tindall b Loader	0	– c Long b Storey 17
A. S. M. Oakman c Storey b Lock	19	– c Long b Loader 12
N. I. Thomson c Tindall b Sydenham	6	– not out 39
A. Buss not out	29	– c Long b Storey 17
R. V. Bell c Loader b Lock	0	– b Loader 3
D. L. Bates c and b Lock	10	– c Long b Sydenham 6
N-b 1	1	B 3, l-b 1 4

1/13 2/21 3/56 4/77 5/77   158   1/7 2/39 3/57 4/100 5/133   252
6/96 7/116 8/122 9/122   6/181 7/186 8/227 9/243

Surrey

M. L. Stewart c Langridge b Dexter 70	– c Parks b Dexter................	13
J. H. Edrich c Parks b Buss..................... 29	– c Oakman b Thomson	0
M. D. Willett c Smith b Dexter 16	– c Langridge b Dexter	14
G. A. R. Lock c and b Bates.................... 5	– c Dexter b Bell	0
K. F. Barrington c Suttle b Thomson 5	– run out	89
*P. B. H. May c Parks b Dexter 14	– c Oakman b Suttle	80
R. A. E. Tindall c Sheppard b Dexter 19	– c Oakman b Dexter	12
S. J. Storey c Parks b Dexter.................... 0	– c Dexter b Bell	0
†A. Long not out............................ 14	– c Buss b Bell	4
D. A. D. Sydenham b Dexter 2	– c Oakman b Thomson	0
P. J. Loader b Dexter 0	– not out	0
B 6, l-b 3, w 1 10	B 3, l-b 1................	4

1/60 2/96 3/101 4/114 5/138   184   1/1 2/32 3/154 4/197 5/198   216
6/163 7/163 8/172 9/184   6/198 7/198 8/212 9/216

Surrey Bowling

	Overs	Mdns	Runs	Wkts	Overs	Mdns	Runs	Wkts
Loader	19	7	39	3	28.4	4	97	5
Sydenham.........	17	6	37	3	23	8	38	1
Storey............	10	2	50	1	10	5	30	2
Lock.............	12.1	5	31	3	25	9	66	1
Tindall					6	2	17	—

Sussex Bowling

	Overs	Mdns	Runs	Wkts	Overs	Mdns	Runs	Wkts
Thomson	21	1	56	1	18.2	7	32	2
Bates.............	23	7	53	1	11	4	22	—
Buss	10	4	19	1	10	2	25	—
Dexter...........	17.4	7	38	7	19	4	58	3
Bell.............	3	2	8	—	21	6	62	3
Suttle					6	2	13	1

Umpires: J. F. Crapp and H. Yarnold.

SURREY v SOMERSET

Played at The Oval, July 18, 19, 20, 1962

Drawn. With Stewart and Edrich on duty for the players at Lord's and Lock unfit, Surrey went through a mixed experience. On May sending in Somerset to bat, Loader and Sydenham gained three wickets cheaply, but Roe, Lomax and Stephenson averted a complete breakdown. Next day Surrey, in turn, found batting difficult and Alley, at the age of 43, varied his swing so skilfully that he took eight wickets for 65, the best analysis of his career. Somerset again underwent early shocks and again they recovered before setting Surrey to get 280 in two hours and forty minutes. In an exhilarating opening stand Parsons and Barrington scored 51 in just over half an hour, but Barrington played on and Willett hit his wicket. So Surrey gave up the chase before rain brought about a premature finish.

Somerset

G. Atkinson c Long b Sydenham	5	– lbw b Sydenham	1
B. Roe lbw b Sydenham	69	– c Long b Loader	2
P. B. Wight c Sydenham b Loader	9	– b Sydenham	6
W. E. Alley c Long b Loader	0	– not out	54
J. G. Lomax c May b Sydenham	42	– c and b Tindall	60
C. Greetham c Tindall b Sydenham	5	– b Loader	60
*†H. W. Stephenson c Sydenham b Tindall	46	– c Willett b Sydenham	34
C. R. M. Atkinson c Tindall b Storey	20	– not out	33
B. Langford not out	11		
K. E. Palmer c Parsons b Loader	9		
G. Hall lbw b Loader	0		
B 4, l-b 2	6	L-b 5	5

1/5 2/20 3/20 4/116 5/132   222   1/3 2/3   (6 wkts dec.) 255
6/135 7/191 8/203 9/222   3/17 4/113 5/149 6/202

Surrey

A. B. D. Parsons c Stephenson b Alley	16	– not out	60
K. F. Barrington lbw b Alley	48	– b Alley	34
M. D. Willett c Lomax b Alley	7	– hit wkt b Hall	1
*P. B. H. May b Alley	1	– not out	26
B. Constable c Langford b Alley	2		
R. A. E. Tindall c Stephenson b Alley	18		
S. J. Storey c Atkinson b Alley	2		
R. I. Jefferson c Alley b Hall	14		
†A. Long c Stephenson b Hall	48		
P. J. Loader b Alley	29		
D. A. D. Sydenham not out	7		
B 1, l-b 5	6	B 3, w 5	8

1/35 2/63 3/69 4/72 5/81   198   1/51 2/56   (2 wkts) 129
6/87 7/108 8/118 9/159

Surrey Bowling

	Overs	Mdns	Runs	Wkts	Overs	Mdns	Runs	Wkts
Loader	20	6	48	4	27	6	65	2
Sydenham	22	4	67	4	28	12	39	3
Jefferson	21	2	51	—	18	5	66	—
Storey	17	2	31	1	16	5	48	—
Tindall	9	2	19	1	16	9	31	1
Willett					3	2	1	—

Somerset Bowling

	Overs	Mdns	Runs	Wkts	Overs	Mdns	Runs	Wkts
Palmer	12	—	36	—				
Hall	20.4	2	59	2	8	1	31	1
Alley	34	13	65	8	8	2	29	1
Greetham	14	7	32	—				
C. Atkinson					13	1	37	—
Langford					9	5	10	—
G. Atkinson					3	—	14	—

Umpires: F. Jakeman and R. S. Lay.

SUSSEX

SUSSEX v GLAMORGAN

Played at Horsham, June 1, 3, 1946

Glamorgan won by an innings and 103 runs. Sussex collapsed in remarkable fashion, being twice dismissed within four hours. Matthews and Judge, maintaining a capital pace and magnificently supported in the field, disposed of them for the smallest total in a County Championship match during the season, and when they followed on 230 behind Matthews and the spin bowlers, Emrys Davies and Clay, caused their downfall. The Glamorgan batting, though unattractive, proved solid after the loss of two wickets for 14 runs. Dyson, missed when 20, helped W. E. Jones add 70, and Porter played a valuable innings. The teams were presented to Field-Marshal Viscount Montgomery before the game.

Glamorgan

A. H. Dyson b J. Oakes	42
E. Davies c James Langridge b Carey	4
W. Wooller c Cox b Carey	0
W. E. Jones c John Langridge b Cornford	55
G. Lavis c Bartlett b Carey	22
A. Porter run out	69
E. C. Jones b Cornford	15
H. Davies b Cornford	3
J. C. Clay b Cornford	10
A. D. G. Matthews lbw b Nye	19
P. F. Judge not out	10
B 8, l-b 5, n-b 3	16
	265

Sussex

John Langridge b Judge	3	– lbw b Matthews	2
H. Parks c H. Davies b Judge	0	– c Wooller b Clay	14
C. Oakes c E. Davies b Matthews	2	– lbw b Clay	29
G. Cox c Dyson b Matthews	4	– c Wooller b E. Davies	27
James Langridge c Lavis b Matthews	7	– b Clay	1
H. T. Bartlett b Judge	2	– b E. Davies	18
S. C. Griffith b Matthews	0	– c H. Davies b Matthews	21
J. Oakes lbw b Matthews	0	– c Porter b E. Davies	2
P. A. D. Carey lbw b Judge	7	– b Matthews	3
J. K. Nye c E. Jones b Matthews	5	– c and b E. Davies	0
J. Cornford not out	1	– not out	0
B 1, l-b 3	4	B 8, l-b 2	10
	35		127

Sussex Bowling

	Overs	Mdns	Runs	Wkts
Nye	24	7	47	1
Carey	35.4	8	78	3
J. Oakes	15	2	45	1
James Langridge	22	5	43	—
Cornford	22	7	36	4
C. Oakes	1	1	—	—

Glamorgan Bowling

	Overs	Mdns	Runs	Wkts	Overs	Mdns	Runs	Wkts
Matthews	11.1	4	13	6	10	4	10	3
Judge	11	5	18	4	4	—	14	—
Wooller..........					7	1	28	—
Clay					14	2	32	3
E. Davies					12.5	3	33	4

SUSSEX v NORTHAMPTONSHIRE

Played at Eastbourne, August 21, 22, 23, 1946

Drawn. Brookes earned great batting distinction when bowlers were generally masters. For the first time in his career he reached three figures in each innings, and he also completed 2,000 runs for the season. On the first day he was last out after three and a half hours during which he gave only one difficult chance. When Northamptonshire went in again leading by 65, he took out his bat at the end of a faultless innings lasting four hours and a quarter. His driving was specially good. Also he fielded with his customary dash and so was active throughout the playing hours. Sussex required 329 to win, but rain prevented cricket on the last day till half past three and destroyed the possibility of a definite result. John Langridge and Parks scored 113 for the opening stand.

Northamptonshire

D. Brookes b Darwall-Smith....................	112	– not out	154
P. Davis c Parks b Nye.......................	8	– b Nye	8
H. W. Greenwood b Nye	3	– c John Langridge b Cox	10
J. E. Timms b Cox............................	25	– c Oakes b James Langridge	22
W. Barron b Nye.............................	4	– c Darwall-Smith b James Langridge.	1
J. Webster run out............................	0	– b Nye	6
W. R. F. Chamberlain c J. N. Bartlett b James Langridge.	7	– b James Langridge	4
W. E. Merritt b Darwall-Smith	7	– c James Langridge b Nye	16
R. J. Partridge b Darwall-Smith	0	– not out	26
W. Nevell c Griffith b Darwall-Smith	9		
E. W. Clark not out...........................	0		
B 5, l-b 4, n-b 2	11	B 12, l-b 3, n-b 1..........	16
	186	**(7 wkts dec.) 263**	

Sussex

John Langridge b Clark	2	– c Partridge b Merritt............	61
H. W. Parks c Chamberlain b Partridge	2	– lbw b Webster.................	55
P. D. S. Blake c Greenwood b Clark.............	6	– not out	15
G. Cox b Partridge	18	– not out	31
James Langridge c Davis b Clark	3		
C. Oakes c Brookes b Merritt	59		
H. T. Bartlett b Partridge	1		
S. C. Griffith b Clark.........................	3		
R. F. H. Darwall-Smith not out..................	16		
J. K. Nye b Merritt	5		
J. N. Bartlett b Nevell	0		
B 5, l-b 1	6	B 8, l-b 1, w 1	10
	121	**(2 wkts) 172**	

Sussex Bowling

	Overs	Mdns	Runs	Wkts	Overs	Mdns	Runs	Wkts
Nye.............	20	4	38	3	27.2	2	80	3
Darwall-Smith	22.1	3	72	4	23	3	68	—
Cox.............	5	—	14	1	7	—	18	1
James Langridge....	23	4	39	1	25	6	44	3
Oakes...........	5	1	12	—	7	—	19	—
J. N. Bartlett.......					7	—	18	—

Northamptonshire Bowling

	Overs	Mdns	Runs	Wkts	Overs	Mdns	Runs	Wkts
Clark	14	2	45	4	6	1	13	—
Partridge.........	10	7	6	3	9	1	21	—
Webster	5	2	17	—	15	3	29	1
Nevell...........	6.5	2	19	1	10	2	23	—
Merritt	6	1	28	2	9	—	50	1
Timms					5	1	17	—
Brookes					1	—	9	—

SUSSEX v LEICESTERSHIRE

Played at Hove, May 22, 24, 25, 1948

Leicestershire won by nine wickets. The game provided a triumph for the Australian left-arm spin bowler, Walsh, who took 15 wickets for 100 runs. John Langridge and Parks gave Sussex a good start with a stand of 88, but afterwards only James Langridge, who defended sternly for three hours, achieved much against Walsh. Jackson, acting captain, rendered invaluable service to Leicestershire during a stay of four hours. Awaiting safe scoring opportunities, he hit nine 4s, and, thanks to him, Leicestershire led by 15 runs. Sussex began their second innings badly and, Walsh presenting increasing difficulty, they could not recover. Rain threatened to rob Leicestershire of victory, but Lester and Prentice, after a delay of two hours, speedily hit off the runs.

Sussex

John Langridge b Walsh	39	– lbw b Sperry	9
H. W. Parks lbw b Walsh	46	– c Corrall b Cornock	6
D. V. Smith b Walsh	4	– c Walsh b Jackson	28
G. Cox c Riddington b Sperry	24	– c Corrall b Walsh	10
James Langridge not out	64	– lbw b Walsh	5
H. T. Bartlett c Lester b Jackson	15	– b Walsh	5
C. Oakes lbw b Walsh	7	– lbw b Walsh	6
J. Oakes b Walsh	6	– b Walsh	11
P. A. D. Carey b Walsh	5	– c and b Walsh	2
R. T. Webb st Corrall b Walsh	7	– not out	3
J. Cornford b Walsh	0	– b Walsh	0
B 13, l-b 7	20	B 9, l-b 2	11
	237		**96**

Leicestershire

G. Lester c Smith b Carey	6	– not out		28
A. Riddington b Cox	25	– c J. Oakes b Cornford		4
F. T. Prentice c Bartlett b James Langridge	47	– not out		46
M. Tompkin c John Langridge b Cornford	7			
V. E. Jackson c and b C. Oakes	97			
G. S. Watson c John Langridge b Cornford	35			
W. B. Cornock b C. Oakes	18			
T. A. Chapman b C. Oakes	0			
J. E. Walsh c Carey b James Langridge	3			
P. Corrall not out	0			
J. Sperry b C. Oakes	0			
B 9, l-b 4, w 1	14	B 4		4
	252		**(1 wkt)**	**82**

Leicestershire Bowling

	Overs	Mdns	Runs	Wkts	Overs	Mdns	Runs	Wkts
Sperry	24	5	46	1	17	5	29	1
Cornock	18	5	28	—	10	6	19	1
Jackson	30	16	45	1	16	13	10	1
Walsh	35	8	73	8	21.5	9	27	7
Lester	6	1	25	—				

Sussex Bowling

	Overs	Mdns	Runs	Wkts	Overs	Mdns	Runs	Wkts
Carey	21	5	54	1	13	4	29	—
Cornford	27	5	66	2	11	3	29	1
Cox	13	7	18	1	1	—	4	—
J. Oakes	9	1	38	—	3	—	8	—
James Langridge	23	13	26	2				
C. Oakes	14.3	1	36	4	1	—	4	—
Smith					1	—	4	—

Umpires: J. J. Hills and F. S. Lee.

SUSSEX v NORTHAMPTONSHIRE

Played at Horsham, June 9, 10, 11, 1948

Drawn. On a drying pitch Sussex collapsed and followed-on 219 behind, but they saved the game without difficulty. Brookes, with his third successive century against Sussex on their own soil, took nearly all the batting honours for Northamptonshire. In first, he was last to leave after a stay of six hours and a half. Strong in off-driving, he placed the ball cleverly and hit fifteen 4s, but was missed twice. Broderick, slow left-arm, then achieved the best performance of his career. In the follow-on, John Langridge and Parks obtained 86 for the opening stand. Blake, strong on the leg-side, followed with a stand of 100 with Bartlett, and Griffith, scoring his first century in first-class cricket in England, hit five 6s and seven 4s during 110 minutes of powerful stroke-play. Left ninety minutes to get 200 for victory, Northamptonshire, after losing two men for 14, fell back upon defence.

Northamptonshire

D. Brookes c Carey b James	179	– c Blake b Carey	5
P. Davis b Cornford	9	– not out	26
N. Oldfield run out	54	– c Blake b Carey	0
J. E. Timms run out	0	– b Oakes	3
W. Barron c John Langridge b Carey	0	– not out	0
A. E. Nutter b Carey	11		
V. Broderick c John Langridge b Carey	10		
A. W. Childs-Clarke b Oakes	18		
R. G. Garlick b John Langridge	10		
K. Fiddling b James	23		
R. W. Clarke not out	4		
B 11, l-b 10, w 2, n-b 1	24	B 5, w 4	9
	342	**(3 wkts)**	**43**

Sussex

John Langridge c and b Garlick	28	– c R. W. Clarke b Broderick	56
H. W. Parks c Fiddling b Broderick	29	– c Fiddling b R. W. Clarke	34
C. Oakes c Fiddling b Broderick	13	– c Brookes b Nutter	6
G. Cox lbw b Broderick	0	– c R. W. Clarke b Nutter	3
James Langridge c Oldfield b Broderick	8	– c Fiddling b Nutter	31
P. D. S. Blake c Childs-Clarke b Broderick	3	– c R. W. Clarke b Garlick	77
H. T. Bartlett c Garlick b Broderick	25	– c Fiddling b Nutter	55
S. C. Griffith b Broderick	2	– not out	106
P. A. Carey c Childs-Clarke b Broderick	5	– b R. W. Clarke	11
A. E. James not out	2	– b Garlick	6
J. Cornford st Fiddling b Broderick	2	– not out	1
B 5, l-b 1	6	B 16, l-b 14, w 2	32
	123	**(9 wkts dec.)**	**418**

Sussex Bowling

	Overs	Mdns	Runs	Wkts	Overs	Mdns	Runs	Wkts
Carey	34	9	89	3	7	4	10	2
Cornford	29	7	82	1	4	1	6	—
Cox	12	2	23	—				
James Langridge	22	6	34	—	3	—	7	—
James	25	11	39	2	3	—	6	—
Oakes	21	4	43	1	3	2	5	1
John Langridge	4	—	8	1				

Northamptonshire Bowling

	Overs	Mdns	Runs	Wkts	Overs	Mdns	Runs	Wkts
R. W. Clarke	9	2	21	—	34	3	97	2
Nutter	7	—	29	—	41	13	57	4
Broderick	25.4	10	35	9	46	10	119	1
Garlick	20	12	32	1	31	10	90	2
Timms					8	2	23	—

Umpires: E. Robinson and C. N. Woolley.

SUSSEX v LANCASHIRE

Played at Horsham, June 12, 14, 15, 1948

Lancashire won by an innings and 64 runs, fully using the advantage of batting first. Place, if not always comfortable, enjoyed the distinction of completing his second century in two days, capital drives bringing him twelve 4s during three and a half hours. Ikin and Wharton, less enterprising, made valuable runs. Sussex lost half their wickets for 78, and, despite some improvement, they followed-on 196 behind. Hilton bowled his slows so cleverly that he sent down 68 balls before conceding a run. Cranston, of greater pace, caused the trouble in the second innings, when Smith and Griffith again made gallant efforts to stem the tide of disaster.

Lancashire

W. Place b Oakes	111
T. L. Brierley b Carey	23
G. A. Edrich lbw b Cornford	27
J. T. Ikin b James	61
E. H. Edrich lbw b James	0
A. Wharton not out	69
N. Howard st Griffith b Cox	26
K. Cranston c Griffith b Cox	1
R. Pollard not out	14
B 17, l-b 2, w 1, n-b 2	22
(7 wkts dec.)	354

W. B. Roberts and M. J. Hilton did not bat.

Sussex

John Langridge b Wharton	12	– c Ikin b Cranston	13
H. W. Parks c E. Edrich b Cranston	19	– c Place b Cranston	4
C. Oakes b Wharton	23	– b Cranston	10
G. Cox b Pollard	12	– c Place b Pollard	5
James Langridge c Hilton b Pollard	4	– c E. Edrich b Cranston	3
P. D. S. Blake lbw b Hilton	12	– c E. Edrich b Pollard	10
D. V. Smith b Pollard	29	– b Hilton	37
S. C. Griffith c Place b Hilton	27	– c G. Edrich b Cranston	32
A. E. James b Hilton	7	– b Hilton	0
P. A. D. Carey run out	5	– b Cranston	12
J. Cornford not out	0	– not out	2
B 4, l-b 1, n-b 3	8	B 1, l-b 3	4
	158		132

Sussex Bowling

	Overs	Mdns	Runs	Wkts
Carey	33	3	115	1
Cornford	23	5	51	1
Cox	19	5	39	2
James	17	5	43	2
Oakes	22	6	57	1
James Langridge	16	4	27	—

Lancashire Bowling

	Overs	Mdns	Runs	Wkts	Overs	Mdns	Runs	Wkts
Pollard	28	10	61	3	28	11	46	2
Cranston	22	6	47	1	23.1	7	58	6
Wharton	13	5	20	2	2	1	5	—
Hilton	16.1	11	10	3	8	1	17	2
Ikin	2	—	9	—				
Roberts	1	—	3	—	2	1	2	—

Umpires: D. Hendren and E. Robinson.

SUSSEX v SOMERSET

Played at Eastbourne, August 18, 19, 20, 1948

Drawn. An innings of real merit by Gimblett, who hit his highest score in first-class cricket and set up a record for a Somerset batsman with 310 runs, overshadowed all else in a game that yielded 1,097 runs for 19 wickets. Gimblett, who offered difficult chances when 45 and 115, drove with great power on an easy-paced pitch, and in his stay of nearly seven hours and three-quarters he hit two 6s and thirty-seven 4s. Walford shared with him in an opening stand of 180, and Coope helped him in fifth partnership realising 210 in two hours and a half. These runs came after Sussex had found run-getting easy. John Langridge and Parks put up 87, and James Langridge (eleven 4s) made 100 in three hours of skilful all-round scoring. Oakes helped him add 89, and Sussex declared at lunch-time on the second day, but, thanks to Gimblett, Somerset easily gained first-innings points.

Sussex

John Langridge b Tremlett	78		
H. W. Parks c Woodhouse b Hazell	46		
G. H. G. Doggart c Luckes b Wellard	32	– c Wellard b Coope	21
C. Oakes c Walford b Hazell	58		
James Langridge c Tremlett b Hazell	100		
S. C. Griffith c Luckes b Hazell	36	– c Wellard b Woodhouse	1
G. Cox b Hazell	28	– not out	14
P. D. S. Blake b Wellard	16	– not out	42
H. T. Bartlett not out	18		
J. Wood c Luckes b Buse	5		
J. Cornford not out	1		
B 11, l-b 5	16	W 1	1
	(9 wkts dec.) 434		**(2 wkts) 79**

Somerset

H. Gimblett c Wood b Cox	310	M. F. Tremlett run out	29
M. M. Walford c John Langridge b Wood	71	A. W. Wellard c Parks b Cox	24
H. E. Watts b Cornford	11	J. Lawrence not out	0
H. T. Buse c Griffith b James Langridge	7	B 12, l-b 11, w 1	24
G. E. S. Woodhouse b Doggart	19		
M. Coope b James Langridge	89	**(8 wkts dec.) 584**	

W. T. Luckes and H. L. Hazell did not bat.

Somerset Bowling

	Overs	Mdns	Runs	Wkts	Overs	Mdns	Runs	Wkts
Wellard	31	3	109	2				
Tremlett	28	4	89	1				
Buse	28	7	65	1				
Lawrence	26	5	73	—				
Hazell	29	6	82	5				
Gimblett					4	—	18	—
Woodhouse					4	—	8	1
Coope					6	1	25	1
Walford					3	—	12	—
Watts					3	—	15	—

Sussex Bowling

	Overs	Mdns	Runs	Wkts
Wood	37	11	104	1
Cornford.	32	10	75	1
Cox.	15	2	46	2
Oakes	31	3	121	—
James Langridge. . . .	50	10	136	2
John Langridge.	8	1	26	—
Bartlett	2	—	12	—
Doggart	8	1	40	1

Umpires: D. Hendren and P. T. Mills.

SUSSEX v GLOUCESTERSHIRE

Played at Eastbourne, August 21, 23, 24, 1948

Gloucestershire won by an innings and 26 runs. They started with a stand of 108 by Barnett (one 6, nine 4s) and Emmett, but lost the next five wickets for 55 runs. Then Allen played a great innings; driving faultlessly for nearly three hours and a half, he hit a 6 and nineteen 4s. Scott and Lambert helped him in partnerships that realised 82 and 148. Wood, left-arm fast-medium, deserved a better analysis, four catches being missed off him. Six Sussex batsmen were out, all lbw, for 153, and though Oakes (one 6, thirteen 4s) and Bartlett (one 6, ten 4s) put on 107 in ninety minutes, they could not prevent a follow-on 165 behind. This time, with conditions in his favour, Goddard, with off-breaks, caused a rapid collapse. At times he was unplayable, and in one spell of 10.3 overs (seven maidens) he dismissed six men for three runs.

Gloucestershire

C. J. Barnett c and b Oakes. 59	C. J. Scott lbw b Wood. 47
G. M. Emmett c Cornford b Wood. 63	G. Lambert b Wood 68
T. W. Graveney st Webb b James Langridge 3	T. W. Goddard run out. 7
J. F. Crapp c and b Oakes. 8	C. Cook not out 5
B. O. Allen lbw b Oakes 148	B 13, l-b 14 27
A. E. Wilson c Webb b Wood. 0	
L. M. Cranfield c Parks b Wood. 8	443

Sussex

John Langridge lbw b Goddard. 40	– c Allen b Goddard	22
H. W. Parks lbw b Lambert 9	– c Allen b Lambert.	5
G. H. G. Doggart lbw b Cook. 23	– b Scott	12
C. Oakes c Scott b Lambert 98	– c and b Goddard.	20
James Langridge lbw b Goddard 20	– c Cranfield b Goddard	12
G. Cox lbw b Cook. 0	– b Goddard	0
P. D. S. Blake lbw b Goddard. 1	– c Allen b Goddard	0
H. T. Bartlett c Emmett b Scott. 78	– c Graveney b Goddard.	8
R. T. Webb b Goddard. 0	– not out	16
D. J. Wood run out. 2	– b Goddard	9
J. Cornford not out. 0	– c Lambert b Cook	28
L-b 4, w 1, n-b 2 7	B 7	7
278	139

Sussex Bowling

	Overs	Mdns	Runs	Wkts
Wood	40.2	5	123	5
Cornford.	26	2	88	—
Cox.	8	1	53	—
C. Oakes.	18	5	49	3
James Langridge....	28	4	103	1

Gloucestershire Bowling

	Overs	Mdns	Runs	Wkts	Overs	Mdns	Runs	Wkts
Lambert	12	1	22	2	5	—	12	1
Scott	24	3	57	1	6	—	30	1
Goddard.	29.1	5	115	4	19	7	50	7
Cook.	22	3	69	2	17.5	6	40	1
Cranfield.	4	2	2	—				
Barnett	1	—	6	—				

Umpires: A. Skelding and C. Smart.

SUSSEX v YORKSHIRE

Played at Hove, June 22, 23, 24, 1949

Yorkshire, with quarter of an hour remaining, won by five wickets a game made memorable by the performance of Hutton in scoring, for the second time in his career, two separate hundreds in a match. When his side were left two hours and a half to get 247, Hutton paved the way to victory by hitting 100 inside two hours, with ten 4s as the chief figures of a faultless display. As in the first innings, when, on his 33rd birthday, he stayed nearly four hours and hit a 6 and nineteen 4s, he drove, cut and pulled splendidly. For Sussex, C. Oakes, in the first innings, and Cox and J. Oakes in the second, carried off the batting honours. C. Oakes hit a 6 and twelve 4s; Cox (sixteen 4s) and J. Oakes (a 6 and twelve 4s) put on 113 together.

Sussex

John Langridge c Close b Trueman	8	– lbw b Yardley	24
S. C. Griffith lbw b Trueman	20	– lbw b Yardley	15
C. Oakes b Close	112	– c Sutcliffe b Robinson	22
James Langridge b Close	0	– lbw b Robinson	19
G. Cox c Brennan b Yardley	10	– not out	121
H. T. Bartlett b Robinson	10	– b Robinson	19
J. Oakes lbw b Robinson	41	– b Mason	79
K. Suttle not out	43	– b Trueman	27
A. E. James b Close	17	– b Trueman	0
J. Cornford b Trueman	1	– not out	6
D. J. Wood b Close	5		
B 16, l-b 2	18	B 11, l-b 15, w 1	27
	285	(8 wkts dec.)	**359**

Yorkshire

L. Hutton c Suttle b Cornford.................165	– c C. Oakes b J. Oakes...........100
F. A. Lowson c Griffith b Cornford.............. 36	– b Cornford.................... 24
J. V. Wilson b Cornford....................... 44	– not out...................... 26
E. Lester c Griffith b James.................... 41	– c John Langridge b Cornford...... 0
W. H. H. Sutcliffe b James..................... 28	– run out...................... 29
N. W. D. Yardley c Griffith b James Langridge..... 1	– b J. Oakes.................... 42
D. B. Close c Cox b Wood..................... 44	– not out...................... 24
D. V. Brennan run out......................... 2	
E. P. Robinson b James Langridge............... 0	
A. Mason c James b James Langridge............ 22	
F. S. Trueman not out......................... 0	
B 12, l-b 1, w 2..................... 15	L-b 2................... 2
398	(5 wkts) 247

Yorkshire Bowling

	Overs	Mdns	Runs	Wkts	Overs	Mdns	Runs	Wkts
Trueman..........	20	3	64	3	34	7	84	2
Close.............	21.4	3	57	4	26	4	82	—
Yardley...........	13	4	39	1	26	9	56	2
Robinson.........	23	6	66	2	24	6	63	3
Mason............	14	5	41	—	21	7	47	1

Sussex Bowling

	Overs	Mdns	Runs	Wkts	Overs	Mdns	Runs	Wkts
Wood............	29	3	104	1	9	—	64	—
Cornford.........	31	7	81	3	8	—	41	2
Cox.............	5	1	10	—	7	—	32	—
James...........	29	7	88	2	6	—	34	—
C. Oakes.........	8	—	28	—				
John Langridge.....	1	—	4	—				
J. Oakes..........	7	—	27	—	8	1	32	2
James Langridge....	12.1	1	41	3	10	—	42	—

Umpires: C. N. Woolley and S. J. Staples.

SUSSEX v DERBYSHIRE

Played at Worthing, July 2, 4, 5, 1949

Drawn. The batting of John Langridge, who for the second time in the season put together two centuries in a match, saved Sussex. In the first innings, when Cox helped him to add 150 for the fourth wicket, he batted just over four hours and hit eighteen 4s. When Sussex faced arrears of 171, he was severely handicapped by a strained back and did not go in till the fall of the fifth wicket. Missed when 14, he gave no other chance in his tenth three-figure innings of the summer and hit nineteen boundaries during a stay of three hours and three-quarters. Bartlett, C. Oakes and James Langridge also batted well in this innings. For Derbyshire, Rhodes (twelve 4s), Johnson (a 6 and twelve 4s), Skinner and Gladwin played enterprising cricket, taking full advantage of fielding lapses.

Sussex

John Langridge run out	146	– not out	146
S. C. Griffith lbw b Jackson	12	– c D. Smith b Gladwin	33
C. Oakes c Marsh b Gladwin	5	– c Skinner b Marsh	79
James Langridge c Revill b Gladwin	2	– c D. Smith b Rhodes	46
G. Cox b Copson	50	– c Revill b Gladwin	0
H. T. Bartlett b Gladwin	11	– c Revill b Johnson	50
J. Oakes b Rhodes	9	– lbw b Gladwin	28
K. Suttle lbw b Jackson	2	– not out	12
A. E. James lbw b Rhodes	1		
J. Cornford not out	0		
D. J. Wood c Elliott b Rhodes	0		
B 1, l-b 6	7	B 11, l-b 2, n-b 2	15
	245		**(6 wkts) 409**

Derbyshire

C. S. Elliott lbw b C. Oakes	17	G. Dawkes c Suttle b C. Oakes	15
E. Marsh lbw b Cornford	4	C. Gladwin not out	44
A. Revill c J. Oakes b Cornford	4	W. H. Copson c Bartlett b Cornford	28
D. Smith c Suttle b James Langridge	57	L. Jackson b James Langridge	24
L. Johnson b C. Oakes	77	L-b 15	15
A. E. Rhodes c Griffith b C. Oakes	68		
D. A. Skinner b James Langridge	63		**416**

Derbyshire Bowling

	Overs	Mdns	Runs	Wkts	Overs	Mdns	Runs	Wkts
Copson	17	4	82	1	20	6	57	—
Gladwin	22	5	58	3	28	8	73	3
Jackson	27	10	39	2	18	4	45	—
Rhodes	12.4	1	42	3	32	4	98	1
Johnson	2	—	12	—	13	1	58	1
Skinner	1	—	5	—	8	—	22	—
Marsh					8	2	30	1
Revill					4	2	11	—

Sussex Bowling

	Overs	Mdns	Runs	Wkts
Wood	24	4	80	—
Cornford	29	5	74	3
James	12	2	27	—
C. Oakes	29	6	88	4
James Langridge	33.5	7	114	3
Cox	5	1	18	—

Umpires: A. E. Pothecary and H. G. Baldwin.

SUSSEX v GLOUCESTERSHIRE

Played at Worthing, July 5, 6, 7, 1950

Gloucestershire won by an innings and 102 runs, thanks largely to a splendid bowling performance by Goddard. They were fortunate to bat first when the pitch proved of easy pace. Graveney over-shadowed his colleagues with the highest innings of his career. In five hours and a quarter he gave no definite chance and by powerful drives and pulls hit twenty-one 4s. He and Crapp put on 165 in two hours and three-quarters, and Wilson helped to add 70. On the second day Goddard, ably seconded by Cook, the left-hander, got to work with his off-breaks on rain-affected turf, and five Sussex men were out for 83.

J. Oakes (two 6s, ten 4s) and Suttle joined in a resolute stand of 80, but Sussex followed-on 184 behind. On the last day, following a long delay through overnight rain, Goddard proved almost unplayable, taking his last five wickets in eleven overs for a single run and bringing his match analysis to thirteen wickets for just over seven runs each.

Gloucestershire

G. M. Emmett lbw b Wood 9	G. E. Lambert c Wood b James 3
D. M. Young c Smith b James Langridge . . . 30	C. J. Scott c James Langridge b Cornford . . 0
T. W. Graveney c Wood b James 201	T. W. Goddard b Cornford 4
J. F. Crapp c John Langridge b James 58	C. Cook not out 5
B. O. Allen c Wood b C. Oakes 3	B 11, l-b 4 15
C. A. Milton c Webb b Wood 13	———
A. E. Wilson c C. Oakes b James 42	383

Sussex

John Langridge c Crapp b Cook 32	– lbw b Goddard 2
D. V. Smith c Crapp b Goddard 11	– b Goddard 10
C. Oakes c and b Cook 13	– c Scott b Goddard 21
G. Cox c Wilson b Goddard 22	– lbw b Goddard . . . . , . 23
James Langridge lbw b Goddard 0	– not out 18
J. Oakes c Milton b Goddard 77	– lbw b Goddard 0
K. Suttle c Allen b Goddard 26	– c Lambert b Goddard 0
A. E. James b Cook 0	– c Emmett b Cook 1
R. T. Webb not out 7	– c Crapp b Cook 5
J. H. Cornford b Cook 0	– c Cook b Goddard 1
D. J. Wood run out 5	– b Goddard 0
B 5, l-b 1 6	N-b 1 1
———	———
199	82

Sussex Bowling

	Overs	Mdns	Runs	Wkts
Wood	20	2	67	2
Cornford.	31.2	4	91	2
James	36	7	82	4
J. Oakes	11	2	38	—
James Langridge. . . .	14	2	33	1
C. Oakes.	16	1	57	1

Gloucestershire Bowling

	Overs	Mdns	Runs	Wkts	Overs	Mdns	Runs	Wkts
Lambert	9	3	25	—	3	1	5	—
Scott	8	4	8	—	5	3	5	—
Milton.	1	1	—	—				
Goddard.	34	17	58	5	29	14	37	8
Cook.	30.5	11	102	4	26	14	34	2

Umpires: H. G. Baldwin and A. Lockett.

SUSSEX v MIDDLESEX

Played at Hove, August 5, 7, 8, 1950

Middlesex won by 24 runs in what would in any event have been the final over of an exciting struggle. Dewes carried off chief batting honours for Middlesex, scoring two centuries in the match. On the first day he cut and drove faultlessly for three hours and a half, hitting fifteen 4s and completing 2,000 runs for the season. He and the cautious Robertson made 123 for the opening stand, but against an attack weakened by the absence through injury of Cornford, the last seven wickets fell to 50 runs. Two partnerships were chiefly responsible for Sussex gaining a lead of 62. Sheppard (nine 4s) and Doggart pulled and drove splendidly in adding 128 for the second wicket, and C. Oakes (one 6, six 4s) and James Langridge (five 4s) put on 94 for the sixth. Dewes, again making no mistake in a stay of two hours fifty minutes and hitting one 6 and fourteen 4s, and Compton, who, missed when 41, obtained twelve 4s in an entertaining innings, did most to enable Middlesex to set Sussex 286 to win in three hours. John Langridge and Sheppard started with 109 in eighty-five minutes, and Langridge (eight 4s) batted freely for two hours, but efforts to maintain the necessary scoring rate cost wickets and the match.

Middlesex

J. D. Robertson c C. Oakes b James	41	– c James b Wood	42
J. G. Dewes c Webb b Wood	128	– c Wood b James	101
H. P. Sharp c and b James Langridge	23	– b J. Oakes	30
D. C. S. Compton c John Langridge b Wood	12	– st Webb b Cox	80
R. S. Cooper c John Langridge b Cox	18	– lbw b J. Oakes	8
L. H. Compton c C. Oakes b Cox	4	– c Smith b James	19
R. W. V. Robins c Doggart b Wood	0	– c and b James	36
J. M. Sims lbw b Cox	3	– c J. Oakes b Cox	5
J. J. Warr b C. Oakes	15	– not out	19
J. A. Young b Cox	3		
L. H. Gray not out	1		
B 6, l-b 3	9	B 1, l-b 6	7
	257	**(8 wkts dec.)**	**347**

Sussex

John Langridge lbw b Sims	11	– c Gray b Warr	93
D. S. Sheppard lbw b Robins	81	– c D. Compton b Gray	48
G. H. G. Doggart b Robins	57	– c Robertson b Warr	29
G. Cox c Robertson b D. Compton	3	– c Robertson b Young	10
D. V. Smith c Robertson b D. Compton	4	– st L. Compton b Young	4
C. Oakes lbw b Young	58	– c L. Compton b Warr	31
James Langridge not out	69	– b Robins	20
J. Oakes c and b Warr	12	– run out	6
A. E. James c Gray b Robins	16	– st L. Compton b Robins	5
R. T. Webb (did not bat)		– c Robertson b Robins	4
D. J. Wood (did not bat)		– not out	4
B 1, l-b 4, w 1, n-b 2	8	B 5, w 1, n-b 1	7
	(8 wkts dec.) 319		**261**

Sussex Bowling

	Overs	Mdns	Runs	Wkts	Overs	Mdns	Runs	Wkts
Wood	23	3	64	3	18	2	58	1
James	17	5	32	1	24	6	98	3
Cox	25.4	12	44	4	10.1	2	41	2
C. Oakes	12	1	28	1	13	—	59	—
J. Oakes	16	4	52	—	23	5	80	2
James Langridge	8	1	24	1				
Doggart	1	—	4	—	1	—	4	—

Middlesex Bowling

	Overs	Mdns	Runs	Wkts	Overs	Mdns	Runs	Wkts
Warr..............	30	6	74	1	12	—	42	3
Gray.............	20	4	50	—	14	—	75	1
Sims	24	6	63	1				
D. Compton.......	22	6	65	2	4	—	12	—
Young...........	21	11	38	1	21	4	79	2
Robins	11.2	5	21	3	10.2	2	46	3

Umpires: E. Cooke and H. L. Parkin.

SUSSEX v HAMPSHIRE

Played at Eastbourne, August 23, 24, 25, 1950

Hampshire won by 59 runs. Yet again Sussex lost after leading on the first innings. On the last day the pitch helped bowlers to such an extent that nineteen wickets fell for an aggregate of 136 runs. In this period James Langridge, left-arm slow, took five wickets in eight overs for four runs, making his match record twelve for 86, and Knott, with off-breaks, did most to dispose of Sussex for the lowest total of the season in County Championship engagements by dismissing five men for one run apiece. Hampshire, sent in to bat, were saved on the first day by Rogers. Driving strongly, Rogers overshadowed all his colleagues for four hours and a quarter and, without giving a chance, hit twenty 4s. Sussex began badly, but Cox drove and hit to leg skilfully for four hours and a quarter, obtaining twelve 4s. Bridger tried hard to check a Hampshire second innings breakdown and Sussex were set 98 to get, a task which, light enough on paper, proved well beyond their powers.

Hampshire

N. H. Rogers c C. Oakes b James................137	– c John Langridge	
	b James Langridge.	10
Rev. J. R. Bridger c Cornford b James Langridge.... 19	– c James Langridge b James	55
A. W. H. Rayment st Webb b James Langridge..... 31	– lbw b James Langridge...........	5
N. McCorkell c J. Oakes b James Langridge 1	– c John Langridge	
	b James Langridge.	2
C. Walker c John Langridge b James Langridge..... 1	– c Cox b James Langridge.........	0
J. R. Gray c Smith b James.................... 7	– c Webb b Cornford.............	4
G. Hill st Webb b James Langridge.............. 4	– c Smith b James Langridge.......	0
D. Shackleton c Doggart b James Langridge 0	– b Cornford	6
V. H. D. Cannings not out 10	– b J. Oakes..................	19
R. Dare st Webb b James Langridge............. 16	– c Sheppard b J. Oakes	1
C. J. Knott b James......................... 1	– not out	1
L-b 1, w 1 2	B 10, l-b 1, n-b 1.........	12
229		115

Sussex

John Langridge b Shackleton	0	– c McCorkell b Cannings	2
D. S. Sheppard c Rogers b Knott	23	– c McCorkell b Cannings	5
G. H. G. Doggart b Shackleton	4	– b Knott	14
G. Cox b Cannings	121	– run out	6
D. V. Smith c McCorkell b Shackleton	39	– c McCorkell b Knott	0
C. Oakes c Dare b Knott	18	– c Dare b Knott	0
James Langridge c Rogers b Shackleton	25	– lbw b Knott	1
J. Oakes c Rayment b Shackleton	8	– run out	8
A. E. James c Walker b Shackleton	0	– not out	1
R. T. Webb not out	0	– lbw b Knott	0
J. Cornford (did not bat)		– lbw b Shackleton	0
B 4, l-b 5	9	B 1	1

(9 wkts dec.) 247   38

Sussex Bowling

	Overs	Mdns	Runs	Wkts	Overs	Mdns	Runs	Wkts
Cornford	20	8	18	—	18	8	34	2
James	27.1	12	65	3	20.2	13	30	1
J. Oakes	11	—	36	—	7	—	20	2
C. Oakes	4	—	12	—				
James Langridge	35	13	67	7	19	11	19	5
Cox	9	3	28	—				
Doggart	2	1	1	—				

Hampshire Bowling

	Overs	Mdns	Runs	Wkts	Overs	Mdns	Runs	Wkts
Shackleton	25	6	58	6	10.5	3	18	1
Cannings	14.2	6	35	1	10	4	14	2
Knott	25	5	64	2	7	4	5	5
Dare	17	2	62	—				
Hill	4	—	19	—				

Umpires: W. H. Ashdown and J. T. Bell.

SUSSEX v SOMERSET

Played at Hove, June 7, 9, 10, 1952

Sussex won by 55 runs. While most batsmen found the pace of the pitch disconcerting, John Langridge, on the first day, proved a notable exception. Carrying his bat through an innings of three and a half hours, he put together his 69th century for Sussex, so eclipsing the record of 68 held by C. B. Fry since before the First World War. Despite missed catches and brisk batting by Tremlett (one 6, seven 4s), Sussex gained a lead of 28, for Oakman finished the innings by performing the first hat-trick of his career. Sussex established a strong position when Parks hit 52 in seventy-five minutes, but the last six wickets fell for 40, Lawrence taking three of them in one over. Against the bowling of Cornford, James and Oakman, Somerset never looked like getting the 174 necessary to win.

Sussex

John Langridge not out	111	– c Stephenson b Buse	11
C. Oakes b Buse	5	– c Tremlett b Buse	21
G. Cox b Tremlett	20	– c Lawrence b Robinson	17
J. M. Parks c Tremlett b Mitchell	15	– c Brocklehurst b Lawrence	52
D. V. Smith b Mitchell	4	– c Gimblett b Robinson	21
James Langridge st Stephenson b Lawrence	2	– c Tremlett b Lawrence	5
A. S. Oakman c Stephenson b Lawrence	18	– c Gimblett b Lawrence	2
A. E. James c Stephenson b Tremlett	1	– c Stephenson b Lawrence	0
R. T. Webb b Lawrence	0	– run out	3
D. J. Wood b Tremlett	1	– c and b Lawrence	5
J. H. Cornford c Gimblett b Buse	6	– not out	3
B 5, 1-b 3	8	B 4, 1-b 1	5

1/31 2/68 3/108 4/116 5/127   191   1/31 2/42 3/83 4/105 5/126   145
6/159 7/162 8/162 9/168   6/128 7/128 8/134 9/139

Somerset

H. Gimblett b Wood	11	– c James b Wood	13
F. L. Angell lbw b Cornford	6	– b Cornford	0
H. W. Stephenson b James	34	– lbw b Oakman	27
J. Lawrence st Webb b Cornford	5	– c Cornford b James	0
D. L. Kitson c James Langridge b Cornford	25	– b Oakman	4
M. F. Tremlett c Oakman b James	50	– b Oakman	22
H. T. F. Buse c Parks b James	9	– b Cornford	2
S. S. Rogers c Wood b Oakman	5	– c Wood b James	13
B. G. Brocklehurst c Wood b Oakman	10	– b James	14
C. G. Mitchell b Oakman	0	– not out	6
E. P. Robinson not out	0	– b Oakman	7
B 8	8	B 8, 1-b 2	10

1/13 2/27 3/40 4/73 5/116   163   1/1 2/15 3/26 4/51 5/64   118
6/145 7/152 8/163 9/163   6/69 7/79 8/96 9/111

Somerset Bowling

	Overs	Mdns	Runs	Wkts	Overs	Mdns	Runs	Wkts
Mitchell	18	5	38	2	3	—	12	—
Buse	16	4	22	2	13	4	41	2
Tremlett	20	1	64	3				
Robinson	5	—	17	—	37	18	40	2
Lawrence	17	4	42	3	21.1	8	47	5

Sussex Bowling

	Overs	Mdns	Runs	Wkts	Overs	Mdns	Runs	Wkts
Cornford	22	7	48	3	17	6	46	3
Wood	23	8	56	1	8	5	9	1
James	11	5	13	3	10	4	24	3
Oakes	4	2	13	—				
Oakman	5.4	—	25	3	18.1	8	29	3

Umpires: H. L. Parkin and Harry Elliott (Derbyshire).

SUSSEX v LANCASHIRE

Played at Hove, August 17, 18, 19, 1955

Sussex won by 87 runs. To the batting of Sheppard and the off-break bowling of Marlar who, in taking nine wickets for 46 runs in the Lancashire second innings achieved the best performance of his career, went most honours. In the match Marlar dismissed fifteen batsmen for 119 runs. Sheppard played admirably on the opening day, his stand of 110 with Doggart and one of 57 by Webb and Thomson retrieving a bad start. Apart from Washbrook, who displayed marked skill for two and three-quarter hours, none of the Lancashire batsmen dealt effectively with Marlar. Leading by 71, Sussex would have collapsed against the off-spin of Tattersall but for Sheppard who, because of a leg injury, employed a runner. Marlar dispelled any Lancashire hopes of scoring 193 to win by disposing of three men in his second over.

Sussex

J. Langridge c Barber b Wharton	13	– b Wharton	1
D. V. Smith c Wilson b Moore	11	– c Wilson b Wharton	4
A. S. M. Oakman st Wilson b Wharton	12	– b Wharton	0
J. M. Parks c Wilson b Moore	2	– lbw b Tattersall	15
D. S. Sheppard lbw b Standring	65	– c Collins b Tattersall	61
G. H. G. Doggart b Tattersall	51	– c Edrich b Tattersall	9
K. G. Suttle c Wilson b Tattersall	11	– lbw b Standring	2
R. T. Webb not out	49	– c Moore b Tattersall	18
N. I. Thomson c Wilson b Standring	32	– not out	10
R. G. Marlar c Barber b Moore	25	– c Washbrook b Moore	0
A. E. James run out	2	– b Tattersall	0
B 1, l-b 1	2	B 1	1

1/18 2/35 3/38 4/40 5/150   275   1/5 2/6 3/9 4/41 5/59   121
6/156 7/166 8/223 9/258   6/62 7/91 8/91 9/120

Lancashire

A. Wharton c Webb b Smith	26	– c Smith b Marlar	16
S. Smith b Marlar	9	– c Suttle b Marlar	19
G. A. Edrich b Langridge b Marlar	23	– c Langridge b Marlar	17
G. Pullar c Smith b Marlar	11	– c Smith b Marlar	5
C. Washbrook c Doggart b James	94	– c Suttle b Marlar	0
R. W. Barber c Doggart b Marlar	0	– b Marlar	6
R. Collins lbw b James	23	– c Suttle b Marlar	24
K. B. Standring c Webb b Marlar	0	– c Langridge b Marlar	2
F. W. Moore run out	7	– b James	16
A. Wilson b Marlar	2	– c Oakman b Marlar	0
R. Tattersall not out	0	– not out	0
B 2, l-b 7	9		

1/31 2/55 3/64 4/87 5/113   204   1/35 2/38 3/38 4/69 5/80   105
6/150 7/161 8/181 9/204   6/83 7/91 8/105 9/105

Lancashire Bowling

	Overs	Mdns	Runs	Wkts	Overs	Mdns	Runs	Wkts
Wharton	21	4	52	2	13	3	40	3
Moore	28	6	74	3	18.2	8	34	1
Standring	15	2	42	2	8	5	7	1
Tattersall	27	7	79	2	20	11	30	5
Collins	8.3	3	18	—	7	4	9	—
Barber	1	—	8	—				

Sussex Bowling

	Overs	Mdns	Runs	Wkts	Overs	Mdns	Runs	Wkts
Thomson	19	7	31	—	4	—	12	—
James	28.3	5	56	2	28	13	45	1
Smith	16	5	35	1	2	1	2	—
Marlar	33	10	73	6	23.2	8	46	9

Umpires: G. S. Mobey and J. J. Hills.

SUSSEX v GLAMORGAN

Played at Hove, May 16, 17, 18, 1956

Drawn. Apparently hoping that a well-grassed pitch would help seam bowlers, Wooller sent Sussex in to bat when winning the toss. Actually Glamorgan had to wait three hours forty minutes for their first success, Smith and Oakman meanwhile scoring 241 runs together. Both scored chiefly by strokes in front of the wicket, Smith hitting sixteen 4s and Oakman, whose 178 was the highest innings of his career, obtaining twenty 4s. Then Wooller and Watkins, fast-medium, dismissed eight more batsmen for 138 before Marlar declared. Glamorgan set themselves to defend from the start of their innings, but Smith, left-arm medium, gained his best analysis in first-class cricket and was mainly responsible for them following on 315 behind. This time Wooller stayed six and a half hours for 79, he and Parkhouse occupying five hours over an opening stand of 135. With no possibility of a definite result, all the Sussex team, including Webb, the wicket-keeper, bowled on the closing day. Glamorgan averted defeat but their dull methods caused some bitter criticism.

Sussex

D. V. Smith c Parkhouse b Pressdee......142	N. I. Thomson b Watkins 2
A. S. M. Oakman c Hedges b Wooller 178	R. T. Webb not out.................... 4
A. A. K. Lawrence c Pressdee b Wooller ... 3	A. E. James not out................... 10
J. M. Parks c Wooller b Watkins 2	
G. Potter b Watkins 2	B 5, l-b 5 10
K. G. Suttle c Horsfall b Wooller 18	
R. H. Wilson b Wooller................. 2	1/241 2/273 3/282 (9 wkts dec.) 379
R. G. Marlar c and b Watkins........... 6	4/294 5/346 6/352 7/362 8/364 9/364

Glamorgan

W. Wooller b Smith..........................	8 – not out 79	
W. G. A. Parkhouse c Oakman b James..........	8 – c Lawrence b Thomson 71	
B. Hedges c Thomson b James	0 – not out 42	
W. E. Jones lbw b Marlar	7	
A. J. Watkins lbw b Smith...................	9	
R. Horsfall c Webb b Smith	2	
L. N. Devereux b Smith	2	
J. Pressdee not out........................	10	
H. G. Davies b Smith	10	
D. J. Shepherd b Smith	3	
H. D. Davies absent hurt...................	0	
B 5.................................	5	B 4, l-b 4 8

1/12 2/12 3/24 4/32 5/38   64   1/135   (1 wkt) 200
6/39 7/44 8/56 9/64

Glamorgan Bowling

	Overs	Mdns	Runs	Wkts
H. D. Davies	5	—	20	—
Watkins	32	7	105	4
Wooller	28	6	105	4
Shepherd	21	3	79	—
Pressdee	20	3	60	1

Sussex Bowling

	Overs	Mdns	Runs	Wkts	Overs	Mdns	Runs	Wkts
Thomson	12	8	10	—	33	13	61	1
James	18	13	10	2	32	17	34	—
Smith	19	9	29	6	23	10	39	—
Marlar	12	5	10	1	24	17	13	—
Oakman					9	7	8	—
Parks					6	—	11	—
Wilson					2	2	—	—
Suttle					2	1	2	—
Potter					2	—	13	—
Lawrence					3	1	6	—
Webb					2	1	5	—

Umpires: E. Cooke and H. G. Baldwin.

SUSSEX v GLAMORGAN

Played at Hove, May 9, 11, 12, 1959

Sussex won by six wickets, taking 12 points to two by Glamorgan, who seemed to have placed themselves beyond defeat on the first day, but were thwarted by Parks who scored 242 runs without being dismissed. Watkins, strong in pulling, and Parkhouse put on 100 together for Glamorgan, and Wooller, who latterly required a runner, and Devereux shared in a partnership of 168. Apart from Parks, who hit firmly all round, the Sussex batsmen did not shine against accurate bowling and fine fielding. When Glamorgan batted again 107 ahead, Parkhouse and Watkins joined in another big stand, adding 99, and paved the way to a second declaration. Set to get 320, Sussex got home with twenty minutes to spare, thanks to Parks whose splendid all-round hitting earned him four 6s and sixteen 4s while he made 157 in two hours fifty minutes. Parks and Cooper finished the match with an unfinished stand of 137 in seventy minutes.

Glamorgan

W. G. A. Parkhouse c Parks b Bell	65	– c Oakman b James	100
B. Hedges b Thomson	0	– lbw b Thomson	24
J. Pressdee b Thomson	10	– c Parks b Thomson	8
P. Walker c Parks b Thomson	0	– b Thomson	0
A. J. Watkins c Oakman b Marlar	53	– c Marlar b James	61
L. N. Devereux not out	90	– not out	12
W. Wooller c Parks b Thomson	93		
J. E. McConnon c Cooper b Thomson	4	– not out	4
D. L. Evans b Marlar	0		
D. J. Shepherd b Marlar	4		
B 4, l-b 5, n-b 1	10	L-b 2, n-b 1	3

1/1 2/23 3/23 4/123   (9 wkts. dec.) 329   1/84 2/97 3/97   (5 wkts. dec.) 212
5/147 6/315 7/319 8/319 9/329   4/196 5/196

F. Clarke did not bat.

Sussex

A. S. M. Oakman c Parkhouse b Watkins	32	– run out	30
L. J. Lenham c Devereux b Watkins	5	– c Parkhouse b Walker	48
K. G. Suttle c Watkins b Walker	14	– lbw b Walker	7
J. M. Parks not out	85	– not out	157
D. V. Smith b Clarke	7	– c McConnon b Shepherd	23
G. C. Cooper c Parkhouse b Clarke	0	– not out	55
N. I. Thomson c McConnon b Walker	16		
R. V. Bell c McConnon b Clarke	7		
A. E. James c Walker b Pressdee	15		
D. L. Bates b Watkins	17		
R. G. Marlar lbw b Watkins	3		
B 15, l-b 5, n-b 1	21	L-b 1, n-b 1	2

1/45 2/61 3/71 4/83 5/83   222   1/54 2/74 3/91   (4 wkts) 322
6/106 7/115 8/187 9/210   4/185

Sussex Bowling

	Overs	Mdns	Runs	Wkts	Overs	Mdns	Runs	Wkts
Thomson	30	8	97	5	20	2	71	3
Bates	16	1	66	—	9	—	42	—
James	23	6	57	—	9	—	37	2
Smith	5	—	15	—				
Marlar	15.5	3	42	3	10	—	28	—
Bell	11	6	22	1	6	—	31	—
Oakman	9	3	14	—				
Suttle	2	—	6	—				

Glamorgan Bowling

	Overs	Mdns	Runs	Wkts	Overs	Mdns	Runs	Wkts
Clarke	27	8	77	3	15	5	65	—
Watkins	17.5	8	38	4	12	2	50	—
Walker	25	7	67	2	22.1	4	84	2
Pressdee	5	1	19	1				
Shepherd					27	2	74	1
McConnon					7	—	47	—

Umpires: H. G. Baldwin and A. E. Fagg.

SUSSEX v SOMERSET

Played at Eastbourne, July 4, 6, 7, 1959

Sussex won by six wickets. Set to get 221 at 90 an hour, Sussex fell behind the clock, and 136 were needed in eighty-five minutes, but Parks, batting with a broken left thumb, and Dexter took them to victory with seventeen minutes to spare. The pitch always favoured batsmen. McCool, who scored 60 in boundaries, and Wight mastered the bowling in Somerset's first innings. Oakman (one 6, twenty 4s) and Dexter (one 6, fifteen 4s) ensured Sussex gaining the lead, though Whitehead, slow left-arm, well deserved his analysis of six wickets for 74.

Somerset

Batsman	1st	2nd
G. G. Atkinson c Oakman b Thomson	79	– lbw b Dexter — 0
J. G. Lomax b Dexter	9	– b James — 32
P. B. Wight run out	106	– c and b Marlar — 74
C. L. McCool c Oakman b Dexter	108	– c and b Marlar — 0
C. Greetham lbw b Thomson	17	– b James — 56
W. E. Alley b James	25	– c Oakman b Marlar — 13
M. F. Tremlett c Dexter b James	7	– b James — 27
P. J. Eele c Oakman b James	12	– c and b Marlar — 2
B. Langford b Thomson	0	– c Smith b James — 7
J. Harris not out	1	– not out — 0
B 5, l-b 2, n-b 1	8	B 11, l-b 4 — 15

1/27 2/157 3/290   (9 wkts dec.) 372   1/5 2/109 3/161   (9 wkts dec.) 226
4/323 5/329 6/343 7/361   4/161 5/183 6/216 7/219
8/370 9/372   8/223 9/226

A. Whitehead did not bat.

Sussex

Batsman	1st	2nd
A. S. M. Oakman c Alley b Lomax	163	– b Harris — 5
L. J. Lenham b Lomax	7	
K. G. Suttle c and b Whitehead	50	– lbw b Alley — 4
E. R. Dexter not out	117	– not out — 91
D. V. Smith c Eele b Whitehead	10	– c Eele b Lomax — 20
D. J. Mordaunt c and b Whitehead	0	– c Lomax b Whitehead — 27
D. J. Preston c Atkinson b Whitehead	1	
N. I. Thomson c Atkinson b Whitehead	5	
R. G. Marlar st Eele b Whitehead	18	
J. M. Parks (did not bat)		– not out — 61
B 5, l-b 2	7	B 4, l-b 7, w 1, n-b 1 — 13

1/30 2/137 3/286 4/326   (8 wkts dec.) 378   1/23 2/29 3/39 4/85   (4 wkts) 221
5/326 6/336 7/355 8/378

A. E. James did not bat.

Sussex Bowling

	Overs	Mdns	Runs	Wkts	Overs	Mdns	Runs	Wkts
Thomson	29	3	86	3	6	3	19	—
Dexter	19	1	56	2	3	—	20	1
James	24.3	7	69	3	27.1	5	62	4
Smith	14	3	49	—				
Preston	16	5	41	—	8	4	20	—
Marlar	9	1	44	—	31	3	90	4
Suttle	4	—	19	—				
Oakman					2	2	—	—

Somerset Bowling

	Overs	Mdns	Runs	Wkts	Overs	Mdns	Runs	Wkts
Harris	13	4	37	—	3	1	19	1
Lomax	22	3	60	2	8	2	22	1
Alley	7	—	34	—	11	1	46	1
McCool	15	4	53	—	3	—	12	—
Langford	23	7	81	—	10	2	36	—
Whitehead	28	6	74	6	10	—	71	1
Greetham	7	—	32	—				
Tremlett					0.1	—	2	—

Umpires: D. Davies and H. Elliott.

SUSSEX v SURREY

Played at Hove, May 28, 30, 31, 1960

Sussex won by an innings and 39 runs, taking 14 points in their first victory over Surrey for seven years. After A. V. Bedser won the toss, Surrey collapsed on a green top, six men being out for 56 before E. A. Bedser, Gibson and Lock came to the rescue. Then Dexter and Parks gave a delightful exhibition, continuing their big stand on the second day until it had yielded 222 runs. Very big crowds were present on the first and second days in the hope of seeing Dexter complete his 1,000 runs before the end of May, but though he hit one 6 and eighteen 4s while making 135 out of 250 in three and a quarter hours, he was still 123 runs short of his objective. Parks hit one 6 over the sight-screen and fifteen 4s, getting his dazzling 155 in four hours. Patient batting by Swetman and Parsons, who put on 128, held up Sussex for two and a quarter hours, but Bates and Buss, who had always used the new ball to good purpose, took it at 225 for four wickets and Sussex won with two and a half hours to spare.

Surrey

M. J. Stewart b Bates	30	– c Buss b Thomson	46
J. H. Edrich c Parks b Thomson	12	– c Oakman b Buss	21
D. G. W. Fletcher c Buss b Mordaunt	6	– lbw b Dexter	21
K. F. Barrington c Foreman b Mordaunt	0	– b Thomson	0
A. B. D. Parsons c Parks b Bates	0	– c Parks b Buss	62
†R. Swetman b Bates	4	– c Dexter b Buss	72
E. A. Bedser c Oakman b Buss	45	– b Bates	2
D. Gibson c Cooper b Bates	20	– b Buss	1
G. A. R. Lock c Mordaunt b Suttle	33	– c and b Buss	5
*A. V. Bedser not out	2	– not out	4
P. J. Loader c Parks b Buss	0	– b Bates	1
L-b 6	6	B 11, w 6, n-b 2	19
	158		**254**

1/17 2/50 3/50 4/50 5/50
6/56 7/104 8/153 9/157

1/67 2/67 3/68 4/98 5/226
6/243 7/243 8/248 9/253

Sussex

A. S. M. Oakman c Swetman b Lock	26	G. C. Cooper c Swetman b Gibson	17
L. J. Lenham c Swetman b Loader	23	B 4, l-b 3	7
*E. R. Dexter c Swetman b Loader	135		
†J. M. Parks c Fletcher b E. Bedser	155	1/36 2/64 3/286 (5 wkts dec.)	451
K. G. Suttle not out	88	4/378 5/451	

D. J. Mordaunt, D. J. Foreman, N. I. Thomson, A. Buss and D. L. Bates did not bat.

Sussex Bowling

	Overs	Mdns	Runs	Wkts	Overs	Mdns	Runs	Wkts
Thomson	9	3	18	1	24	8	43	2
Buss	16.4	1	51	2	22	8	55	5
Bates	16	6	34	4	19.1	5	59	2
Mordaunt	10	2	29	2	9	4	11	—
Suttle	13	6	20	1	9	4	19	—
Dexter					11	4	20	1
Cooper					6	2	28	—

Surrey Bowling

	Overs	Mdns	Runs	Wkts
Loader	24	3	71	2
A. Bedser	26	4	81	—
Gibson	18.3	1	73	1
Lock.............	33	5	113	1
Barrington	15	—	60	—
E. Bedser	14	2	46	1

Umpires: H. G. Baldwin and A. Jepson.

SUSSEX v MIDDLESEX

Played at Hove, July 30, August 1, 2, 1960

Sussex won by 202 runs. The game, which was a personal triumph for Dexter – who scored 183 and took seven wickets – had a remarkable conclusion. Middlesex, set to make 329 to win in five hours, were 121 for six when a storm held up play. Cricket was recommenced with an hour remaining and Dexter, who had taken three wickets for a single just before the stoppage, sent back two more of his rivals with consecutive balls at the same score. Then Warr, suffering from a strained groin, Hooker and Moss, with runs not mattering to them, played dead bats to Dexter, Thomson and Bates and altogether 82 deliveries were sent down without a run coming before Hooker pushed Thomson to cover for a single. When Dexter had Warr brilliantly caught at backward short leg, his spell figures were six for one in eight overs and Sussex won with thirteen minutes to spare. Dexter's 157 in the first innings was a sound yet attractive effort lasting five hours and including nineteen 4s. Like Smith, his partner in a fifth-wicket stand of 181, the Sussex captain drove with power and grace. A pulled muscle prevented Moss bowling in the second innings.

Sussex

A. S. M. Oakman c Murray b Bennett 13	– c White b Hooker	13
L. J. Lenham b Warr........................... 4	– c Murray b Hooker............	5
*E. R. Dexter b Drybrough.....................157	– b Titmus	26
†J. M. Parks b Bennett 0	– c Murray b Bennett...........	21
K. G. Suttle c Parfitt b Hooker 9	– c White b Hooker	21
D. V. Smith c Parfitt b Bennett 80	– not out	65
G. H. G. Doggart not out 39	– not out	20
Nawab of Pataudi not out..................... 18		
B 2, l-b 5, w 1 8	L-b 9, w 1	10

1/6 2/26 3/27 4/42   (6 wkts dec.) 328   1/18 2/19 3/67   (5 wkts dec.) 181
5/223 6/294   4/67 5/136

N. I. Thomson, R. V. Bell and D. L. Bates did not bat.

Middlesex

Batsman		1st		2nd	
W. E. Russell c Dexter b Bates		5	– c Bell b Dexter		11
R. A. Gale run out		14	– b Bates		33
R. A. White c Dexter b Thomson		3	– lbw b Dexter		27
R. W. Hooker c Doggart b Thomson		15	– not out		5
P. H. Parfitt c Parks b Thomson		49	– b Bates		13
F. J. Titmus run out		56	– c Bates b Dexter		27
D. Bennett c Suttle b Smith		4	– b Dexter		0
†J. T. Murray b Bates		16	– c Parks b Dexter		1
C. D. Drybrough c Bell b Smith		0	– c Parks b Dexter		0
*J. J. Warr c Bates b Thomson		12	– c Bell b Dexter		0
A. E. Moss not out		6	– c Parks b Thomson		0
N-b 1		1	B 5, l-b 3, n-b 1		9

1/17 2/23 3/26 4/45 5/136   181
6/147 7/150 8/150 9/175

1/27 2/52 3/68 4/119 5/120   126
6/120 7/121 8/121 9/121

Middlesex Bowling

	Overs	Mdns	Runs	Wkts	Overs	Mdns	Runs	Wkts
Moss	10	1	31	—				
Warr	20	5	49	1				
Bennett	21	2	58	3	20	2	65	1
Hooker	19	4	58	1	20	7	70	3
Titmus	20	3	48	—	10	4	23	1
Drybrough	16	1	65	1	4	2	2	—
Gale	3	—	11	—	1	—	11	—

Sussex Bowling

	Overs	Mdns	Runs	Wkts	Overs	Mdns	Runs	Wkts
Thomson	26.1	11	50	4	22.1	13	26	1
Bates	24	6	57	2	13	4	50	2
Dexter	7	—	24	—	18	11	24	7
Suttle	1	1	—	—	3	2	6	—
Smith	9	1	27	2	5	1	11	—
Bell	8	2	22	—				

Umpires: W. E. Phillipson and Harry Elliott.

NOTES BY THE EDITOR, 1961

ENGLISH ATTENDANCES SLUMP

In 1947 the total attendances – exclusive of members – at county matches reached 2,300,910. In 1960 the figures fell to 1,046,104, a decrease of 323,569 compared with 1959, and these were the lowest figures since the war with the exception of 1958 (983,820). Daily attendances for county matches in 1960 fell on every day of the week compared with 1959, Saturday showing the biggest decrease (137,344) and Monday (74,817) the next greatest.

THE DEXTER TOUCH

That the presence of only one personality in a match can make all the difference was illustrated by the experience of Sussex last summer. They possessed that most gifted batsman, Ted Dexter, who captained them for the first time, and their membership went up by 1,200 and their gates by £2,000. There are some people who argue that runs are more difficult to make in this second half of the twentieth century than in the Golden Era before 1914. They say that the bowling is more astute, the fielding better and field-placing more skilful. They point to the catches held close to the bat these days, but I did not see many men standing close to the bat when Dexter was in full cry. The plodders and the prodders have allowed the fielders to creep nearer; they soon disperse to safer regions when a genuine batsman appears. There are too many county professionals who reckon they have done a satisfactory job if they scrape 1,200 runs in a season for an average of about 30.00. They pay no heed to the way they make their runs and it is time they were clearly told that unless they are prepared to think of making the occasional hundred in two and a half to three hours, their services will no longer be required. The decline in professional batsmanship since the War is one of the main reasons for the alarming fall in public support. Another is the counter-attraction of T.V. and sound radio.

SUSSEX v OXFORD UNIVERSITY

Played at Hove, July 1, 3, 4, 1961

Sussex won by 183 runs. Oxford were handicapped by the absence of Pataudi and Waters, injured in a car crash on the Saturday evening, and Fry was allowed to keep wicket in the Sussex second innings. Oakman and Langridge put the county in a strong position with a stand of 117 and Lenham (thirteen 4s) drove well, but Potter, maintaining a capital length, caused a breakdown. Baig (thirteen 4s) drove and hooked well and Green batted steadily for Oxford, but Sussex led by 103. Brisk batting by Oakman (two 6s, thirteen 4s) led to a second Sussex declaration which left the University 300 to win, a task they never appeared likely to achieve.

Sussex

A. S. M. Oakman c Pataudi b Drybrough	63	– not out	102
R. J. Langridge c Green b Duff	63	– c sub b Potter	9
L. J. Lenham c Pataudi b Potter	65	– c Duff b Green	28
D. J. Foreman b Piachaud	0	– run out	31
†J. M. Parks c Waters b Potter	21	– not out	14
*D. V. Smith b Green	29		
G. C. Cooper c Baig b Potter	0		
P. R. Ledden b Potter	7		
M. Buss not out	21		
D. L. Bates c Pithey b Potter	5		
F. R. Pountain not out	22		
L-b 3	3	B 8, l-b 3, w 1	12

1/117 2/148 3/165   (9 wkts dec.) 299   1/25 2/77 3/161   (3 wkts dec.) 196
4/201 5/230 6/230 7/244
8/256 9/267

Oxford University

D. R. Worsley c Oakman b Smith	1	– c Foreman b Smith	29
D. B. Pithey b Smith	3	– c Parks b Pountain	19
A. R. Duff c Parks b Bates	16	– lbw b Smith	6
†R. H. C. Waters retired hurt	0	– absent hurt	0
D. M. Green c Foreman b Smith	59	– c Lenham b Smith	26
A. A. Baig not out	80	– c Parks b Pountain	0
C. D. Drybrough c Langridge b Pountain	16	– c Oakman b Smith	2
J. D. Piachaud b Bates	3	– b Bates	9
I. C. Potter c Cooper b Smith	2	– b Bates	10
T. R. Jakobsen c Pountain b Bates	10	– not out	7
*Nawab of Pataudi absent hurt	0	– absent hurt	0
B 5, l-b 1	6	B 4, l-b 4	8

1/1 2/4 3/53 4/103 5/132   196   1/36 2/40 3/56 4/64 5/80   116
6/152 7/159 8/196   6/95 7/95 8/116

Oxford University Bowling

	Overs	Mdns	Runs	Wkts	Overs	Mdns	Runs	Wkts
Jakobsen.........	22	4	49	—	21	5	39	—
Potter	29	7	65	5	21	3	62	1
Green	14	4	48	1	11	1	35	1
Drybrough	18	6	39	1	3	—	13	—
Duff	15	5	45	1	1	1	—	—
Piachaud.........	22	8	50	1				
Pithey...........					7	2	35	—

Sussex Bowling

	Overs	Mdns	Runs	Wkts	Overs	Mdns	Runs	Wkts
Bates............	23	5	66	3	15.5	9	22	2
Smith	23	5	72	4	16	—	58	4
Pountain.........	12	3	52	1	10	3	28	2

Umpires: R. S. Lay and D. J. Wood.

SUSSEX v NORTHAMPTONSHIRE

Played at Hove, August 9, 10, 11, 1961

Drawn. Reynolds (two 6s, fourteen 4s) batted soundly on the opening day and more ready run-getting by Ramsamooj and Crump enabled Subba Row to declare. With the exception of Oakman and Smith, Sussex batted moderately against the pace of Dilley who, in dismissing Lenham, Suttle and Dexter, performed his second "hat-trick" of the summer. When Northamptonshire went in again leading by 176 Norman (sixteen 4s) and Subba Row put on 115 together before a second declaration. Set to get 421 to win, Sussex saved the game without difficulty, Oakman (twelve 4s) and Lenham (thirteen 4s) joining in an unbroken stand of 154 on a pitch which always played easily.

Northamptonshire

M. Norman c Parks b Bell......................	30	– b Suttle........................	115
B. L. Reynolds b Smith.........................	109	– c and b Suttle.................	21
P. J. Watts c Lenham b Cooper	21	– b Pountain	22
*R. Subba Row c Parks b Smith.................	35	– lbw b Suttle....................	65
A. Lightfoot c Parks b Dexter..................	4	– not out	4
D. Ramsamooj c Oakman b Bell	54	– not out	0
B. Crump not out	74		
G. Williamson b Pountain......................	11	– b Smith.........................	14
M. R. Scott not out	1		
B 11, l-b 4, n-b 1	16	B 1, l-b 1, n-b 1...........	3

1/89 2/132 3/199   (7 wkts dec.) 355   1/65 2/94 3/209   (5 wkts dec.) 244
4/210 5/214 6/310 7/348   4/228 5/240

†K. V. Andrew and M. R. Dilley did not bat.

Sussex

A. S. M. Oakman c Andrew b Dilley	58	– not out	102
R. J. Langridge lbw b Dilley	0	– c Andrew b Watts	25
L. J. Lenham c Andrew b Dilley	14	– not out	85
K. G. Suttle b Dilley	3		
*E. R. Dexter c Andrew b Dilley	0		
†J. M. Parks c Ramsamooj b Watts	14		
D. V. Smith b Williamson	56		
G. C. Cooper b Williamson	0		
N. I. Thomson not out	21		
R. V. Bell b Williamson	0		
F. R. Pountain c Subba Row b Dilley	6		
B 5, l-b 2	7	L-b 4	4

1/8 2/68 3/74 4/74 5/81   179   1/62   (1 wkt) 216
6/130 7/133 8/158 9/158

Sussex Bowling

	Overs	Mdns	Runs	Wkts	Overs	Mdns	Runs	Wkts
Thomson	9	4	8	—	5	1	18	—
Dexter	16	4	44	1	10	2	26	—
Pountain	15	3	51	1	23	5	79	1
Bell	47	13	154	2				
Cooper	16	7	36	1				
Suttle	7	4	10	—	8	2	37	3
Smith	15	3	36	2	20	4	81	1

Northamptonshire Bowling

	Overs	Mdns	Runs	Wkts	Overs	Mdns	Runs	Wkts
Dilley	22.1	5	74	6	4	1	21	—
Williamson	21	5	60	3	10	2	32	—
Lightfoot	9	4	16	—	6	1	9	—
Watts	8	3	22	1	10	3	31	1
Subba Row					2	—	10	—
Scott					18	5	50	—
Crump					10	2	20	—
Reynolds					4	—	19	—
Norman					3	—	15	—
Ramsamooj					2	—	5	—

Umpires: J. Arnold and R. Aspinall.

SUSSEX v LEICESTERSHIRE

Played at Worthing, August 30, 31, September 1, 1961

Leicestershire won by 62 runs. The match provided a triumph for Hallam who, cutting specially well, put together two centuries in the match and scored 346 runs without being dismissed. He overshadowed everybody else in both Leicestershire innings. On the opening day he hit thirty-two 4s, he and Birkenshaw adding 175. Despite a partnership of 111 between Langridge and Suttle, Sussex fell 69 behind and Hallam (nineteen 4s), sharing stands of 136 with Bird and 112 with Gardner, was able to declare a second time. Set to get 326 to win in three hours thirty-five minutes, Sussex made a brave effort, thanks to Lenham, Suttle and Parks, but never looked like succeeding.

Leicestershire

*M. R. Hallam not out	.203	– not out	.143
H. D. Bird b N. Thomson	0	– lbw b Doggart	65
A. Wharton c Parks b N. Thomson	0	– c and b Doggart	4
L. R. Gardner c Langridge b Snow	18	– not out	40
J. van Geloven c Langridge b Pountain	8		
J. Birkenshaw c Parks b N. Thomson	95		
R. L. Pratt b Smith	7		
†R. Julian b N. Thomson	2		
C. T. Spencer not out	33		
B 5, l-b 4, w 1	10	B 3, l-b 1	4

1/3 2/5 3/51 4/66   (7 wkts dec.) 376   1/136 2/144   (2 wkts dec.) 256
5/241 6/266 7/309

J. S. Savage and B. S. Boshier did not bat.

Sussex

A. S. M. Oakman c Julian b Boshier	10	– c and b Pratt	20
R. J. Langridge c Hallam b Savage	95	– c van Geloven b Boshier	5
L. J. Lenham b Boshier	17	– st Julian b Birkenshaw	43
K. G. Suttle c Hallam b Savage	65	– c Julian b Birkenshaw	55
†J. M. Parks c Julian b Pratt	32	– c Julian b Birkenshaw	47
G. H. G. Doggart c Wharton b Savage	37	– lbw b Savage	6
*D. V. Smith c Hallam b Savage	0	– c Hallam b Savage	0
R. H. Thomson b van Geloven	21	– st Julian b Birkenshaw	1
N. I. Thomson lbw b Savage	0	– b Birkenshaw	20
F. R. Pountain b Boshier	12	– c Hallam b Savage	27
J. A. Snow not out	15	– not out	35
L-b 2, n-b 1	3	L-b 4	4

1/13 2/65 3/176 4/201 5/227   307   1/20 2/28 3/101 4/154 5/154   263
6/234 7/275 8/275 9/280   6/166 7/166 8/197 9/220

Sussex Bowling

	Overs	Mdns	Runs	Wkts	Overs	Mdns	Runs	Wkts
N. Thomson	23	5	79	4	8	2	16	—
Smith	22	5	76	1	18	1	71	—
Pountain	22	1	79	1				
Snow	16	1	76	1	4	—	19	—
Oakman	7	1	32	—	11	2	35	—
Suttle	7	1	24	—	11.3	1	36	—
Doggart					24	4	75	2

Leicestershire Bowling

	Overs	Mdns	Runs	Wkts	Overs	Mdns	Runs	Wkts
Spencer	15	3	54	—				
Boshier	16	1	64	3	6	—	20	1
Pratt	7	3	10	1	6	—	29	1
Savage	40	12	89	5	20	5	85	3
van Geloven	9	2	39	1				
Birkenshaw	16	2	48	—	19.5	—	124	5

Umpires: W. E. Phillipson and W. F. Price.

WARWICKSHIRE

WARWICKSHIRE v NOTTINGHAMSHIRE

Played at Birmingham, July 24, 25, 1946

Nottinghamshire won by seven wickets. The match was made memorable by a brilliant bowling performance, Hollies taking all ten wickets very cheaply in the Nottinghamshire first innings. Following a disappointing Warwickshire display, in which only Fantham with his first fifty for the county achieved much, Hollies carried all before him. Keeton and Harris opened with a stand of 47; then Hollies, changing ends, was unplayable. He did not receive any help from his colleagues, seven batsmen being bowled and the other three lbw. Warwickshire again failed and Nottinghamshire, thanks to a good stand between Harris and Hardstaff, easily obtained the 149 required to win although Hollies in 31 overs bowled twenty maidens.

Warwickshire

P. Cranmer c Heane b Woodhead	1	– b Jepson	1
R. Sale c Heane b Woodhead	30	– lbw b Jepson	7
R. H. Maudsley b Jepson	0	– c Meads b Heane	22
H. E. Dollery c Simpson b Butler	2	– b Heane	25
J. M. Mills c Jepson b Butler	16	– c Meads b Heane	16
K. A. Taylor b Butler	37	– b Jepson	18
J. S. Ord c Heane b Butler	0	– b Butler	12
W. E. Fantham lbw b Heane	51	– b Butler	1
F. Mitchell lbw b Jepson	13	– b Butler	0
C. C. Goodway not out	9	– not out	5
W. E. Hollies c Jepson b Heane	2	– b Jepson	4
B 6, l-b 3	9	B 1, l-b 1	2
	170		**113**

Nottinghamshire

W. W. Keeton b Hollies	40	– run out	4
C. B. Harris b Hollies	10	– not out	80
R. T. Simpson lbw b Hollies	14	– b Maudsley	6
J. Hardstaff lbw b Hollies	0	– c Goodway b Hollies	41
T. B. Reddick b Hollies	1	– not out	19
G. F. H. Heane lbw b Hollies	4		
F. W. Stocks not out	37		
A. Jepson b Hollies	7		
H. J. Butler b Hollies	8		
E. A. Meads b Hollies	0		
F. G. Woodhead b Hollies	8		
B 4, l-b 2	6		
	135		**(3 wkts) 150**

Nottinghamshire Bowling

	Overs	Mdns	Runs	Wkts	Overs	Mdns	Runs	Wkts
Butler	25	9	49	4	13	4	19	3
Jepson	20	7	40	2	20.3	6	43	4
Woodhead	13	3	24	2	12	6	17	—
Harris	1	1	—	—				
Heane	23.4	10	48	2	19	8	32	3

Warwickshire Bowling

	Overs	Mdns	Runs	Wkts	Overs	Mdns	Runs	Wkts
Mitchell..........	6	2	19	—	5	2	10	—
Maudsley........	7	3	19	—	7	1	22	1
Hollies	20.4	4	49	10	31	20	29	1
Fantham..........	20	3	42	—	10	1	36	—
Mills.............					18	4	46	—
Dollery..........					2	1	7	—

WARWICKSHIRE v WORCESTERSHIRE

Played at Birmingham, July 29, 31, August 1, 1950

Worcestershire won by 166 runs. They benefited in their first innings from mistakes in the field, and Kenyon, surviving an early chance, batted three hours twenty minutes. Kardar bowled accurate left-arm slows, and Warwickshire fell in sensational fashion before Jackson, whose devastating off-breaks earned five wickets in eight overs, five maidens, for four runs. Warwickshire, though 154 behind, were not forced to follow-on. Dews, missed before scoring, and Howorth added 97 in Worcestershire's second innings, but Pritchard and Hollies did fine work with the ball for Warwickshire before Howorth excelled by taking four wickets in six balls without conceding a run, the last three giving him a "hat-trick".

Worcestershire

E. Cooper lbw b Hollies	42	– c Spooner b Hollies	27
D. J. Kenyon b Pritchard	77	– c Maudsley b Pritchard	2
R. E. Bird c Spooner b Pritchard	13	– c Kardar b Pritchard	0
R. E. S. Wyatt lbw b Kardar	16	– c Dollery b Pritchard	5
G. Dews c Maudsley b Kardar	2	– b Thompson	58
R. Howorth c Gardner b Kardar	25	– c Bromley b Hollies	47
L. Outschoorn run out	16	– not out	13
R. O. Jenkins b Hollies	4	– c Kardar b Hollies	0
H. Yarnold c Maudsley b Kardar	2	– lbw b Hollies	0
R. T. D. Perks c Wolton b Kardar	6	– b Kardar	8
P. F. Jackson not out	0	– c Gardner b Kardar	0
B 5, l-b 8, w 1, n-b 3	17	B 9, l-b 3, n-b 2	14
	220		**174**

Warwickshire

F. C. Gardner lbw b Jackson	19	– lbw b Jackson	33
R. T. Spooner b Wyatt	5	– b Jenkins	34
J. B. Guy c Yarnold b Wyatt	0	– c Jackson b Jenkins	6
R. H. Maudsley b Jackson	17	– b Perks	18
H. E. Dollery b Jackson	0	– b Jackson	1
A. V. Wolton b Jackson	0	– not out	42
A. H. Kardar c Jackson b Jenkins	2	– st Yarnold b Jackson	14
P. H. Bromley b Jackson	5	– c Yarnold b Howorth	6
T. L. Pritchard c Wyatt b Jenkins	6	– c Kenyon b Howorth	0
W. E. Hollies b Jenkins	7	– c Bird b Howorth	0
R. G. Thompson not out	0	– lbw b Howorth	0
L-b 2, n-b 3	5	L-b 3, n-b 5	8
	66		**162**

Warwickshire Bowling

	Overs	Mdns	Runs	Wkts	Overs	Mdns	Runs	Wkts
Pritchard.........	22	2	58	2	23	5	56	3
Thompson	13	4	36	—	14	5	20	1
Hollies	32	16	41	2	24	14	42	4
Kardar	26	10	49	5	19.4	5	34	2
Bromley	5	1	19	—	5	2	8	—

Worcestershire Bowling

	Overs	Mdns	Runs	Wkts	Overs	Mdns	Runs	Wkts
Perks.............	6	—	19	—	11	1	45	1
Wyatt............	7	3	11	2	4	2	9	—
Jenkins...........	11.5	3	27	3	14	4	40	2
Jackson..........	8	5	4	5	25	8	42	3
Howorth.........					14	6	18	4

Umpires: F. S. Lee and H. Elliott.

WARWICKSHIRE v GLAMORGAN

Played at Birmingham, July 11, 12, 1951

Warwickshire won by an innings and 68 runs. Magnificent fast bowling by Pritchard swept Warwickshire to their second two-day win in three matches, his fourteen wickets bringing his total in four games to thirty-six. On a "green" pitch, Glamorgan had no answer to the speed of Pritchard and Grove and, after an opening stand of 31, nine wickets fell for 29. In their last ten overs the Warwickshire pair sent back seven batsmen for six runs. Pritchard bowled the last two with successive balls and, after Warwickshire batted, he dismissed Emrys Davies with his first ball in the Glamorgan second innings. Needing 225 to save an innings defeat, Glamorgan never recovered from this setback. Jones struggled valiantly to hold the innings together but found little support. The Glamorgan attack was handicapped by an injury to McConnon, who pulled a muscle, and Spooner batted attractively for his third century of the season. Hitchcock showed characteristic freedom.

Glamorgan

E. Davies c Townsend b Grove................	17	– c Gardner b Pritchard	0
P. B. Clift c Weeks b Pritchard..................	12	– b Pritchard....................	12
W. G. A. Parkhouse c Townsend b Grove	0	– c Townsend b Pritchard..........	7
W. E. Jones lbw b Pritchard....................	17	– not out	92
A. J. Watkins b Pritchard......................	6	– c Dollery b Pritchard...........	4
W. W. Wooller c Spooner b Grove...............	5	– c Spooner b Pritchard...........	0
B. Hedges lbw b Pritchard	0	– c and b Hollies	16
B. L. Muncer not out.........................	0	– c Spooner b Pritchard...........	15
J. McConnon c Spooner b Grove	0	– absent hurt	0
H. G. Davies b Pritchard	1	– c Spooner b Pritchard...........	2
N. G. Hever b Pritchard......................	0	– c Spooner b Pritchard...........	3
W 2..............................	2	L-b 4, n-b 2..............	6
	60		**157**

Warwickshire

F. C. Gardner c H. Davies b Hever 2	T. L. Pritchard c Wooller b Hever 9
R. T. Spooner c H. Davies b Watkins. 102	R. Weeks b Hever. 1
J. S. Ord c Jones b McConnon 16	C. W. Grove run out. 4
A. V. Wolton run out 0	W. E. Hollies not out. 6
H. E. Dollery c Watkins b E. Davies 19	L-b 5, w 2 7
R. E. Hitchcock c H. Davies b Watkins 90	—
A. Townsend not out 29	(9 wkts dec.) 285

Warwickshire Bowling

	Overs	Mdns	Runs	Wkts	Overs	Mdns	Runs	Wkts
Pritchard.	15.5	3	38	6	21.5	2	55	8
Grove	15	6	20	4	19	6	30	—
Weeks.					15	2	34	—
Hollies					19	10	28	1
Hitchcock					2	—	4	—

Glamorgan Bowling

	Overs	Mdns	Runs	Wkts
Hever	19	4	49	3
Wooller.	13	1	38	—
Watkins	21	6	54	2
McConnon	16	3	64	1
E. Davies	18	5	45	1
Muncer	10	4	17	—
Jones.	6	2	11	—

Umpires: F. Chester and F. S. Lee.

WARWICKSHIRE v SUSSEX

Played at Birmingham, June 18, 19, 20, 1952

Warwickshire won by nine wickets. Helped by a strong cross wind and a "green" pitch, Grove moved the ball disconcertingly at a lively pace and troubled all the batsmen. He took the first eight wickets and the last, Hollies claiming the other, and finished with the best figures of his career. Conditions were less helpful to bowlers when Warwickshire batted two and a half hours after the match began, with the result that Sussex found themselves facing arrears of 205. Cox and Smith shared a stubborn third-wicket stand, but with seven wickets down for 164 the game looked likely to end in two days. Plucky resistance by Suttle, Webb and Wood, however, ensured a third morning's play during which Warwickshire hit off the runs for the loss of Ord and Horner, who retired after being struck in the groin. Cornford took his 1,000th wicket in first-class cricket when he dismissed Hitchcock.

Sussex

John Langridge b Grove	2	– c Spooner b Pritchard	12
C. Oakes lbw b Grove	18	– c Spooner b Pritchard	6
G. Cox b Grove	21	– lbw b Grove	26
A. S. Oakman b Grove	1	– b Pritchard	28
D. V. Smith c Spooner b Grove	23	– b Hollies	38
N. I. Thomson b Grove	5	– c and b Pritchard	7
K. Suttle c Spooner b Grove	2	– c Dollery b Bromley	33
A. E. James not out	3	– c Spooner b Grove	8
R. T. Webb c Spooner b Grove	1	– not out	33
D. J. Wood c Pritchard b Hollies	5	– c Spooner b Grove	12
J. H. Cornford c Dollery b Grove	0	– run out	0
L-b 5	5	B 8, l-b 18, n-b 1	27

1/9 2/39 3/48 4/50 5/58   **86**   1/22 2/25 3/92 4/100 5/136   **230**
6/64 7/77 8/81 9/86   6/139 7/164 8/192 9/228

Warwickshire

F. C. Gardner c Suttle b Wood	98	– not out	9
R. T. Spooner b Wood	7	– not out	8
J. S. Ord b Wood	29	– c James b Wood	9
N. F. Horner b Wood	9	– retired hurt	0
H. E. Dollery c and b James	13		
R. E. Hitchcock c Suttle b Cornford	20		
P. H. Bromley b Thomson	34		
R. Weeks b James	16		
C. W. Grove c Smith b Oakman	24		
T. L. Pritchard b Oakman	29		
W. E. Hollies not out	1		
B 6, l-b 4, n-b 1	11	L-b 3	3

1/26 2/87 3/111 4/132 5/161   **291**   1/21   **(1 wkt) 29**
6/200 7/227 8/259 9/259

Warwickshire Bowling

	Overs	Mdns	Runs	Wkts	Overs	Mdns	Runs	Wkts
Pritchard	7	2	25	—	25.5	5	58	4
Grove	19.1	3	39	9	26	6	48	3
Hollies	13	9	17	1	26	12	47	1
Weeks					14	4	26	—
Bromley					8	1	24	1

Sussex Bowling

	Overs	Mdns	Runs	Wkts	Overs	Mdns	Runs	Wkts
Cornford	26	1	78	1				
Wood	27	2	61	4	5	—	16	1
James	29	12	61	2				
Thomson	18	1	57	1	4	1	4	—
Oakman	6.4	2	23	2				
John Langridge					1	1	—	—
Smith					1	—	6	—

Umpires: H. Palmer and J. S. Buller.

WARWICKSHIRE v GLOUCESTERSHIRE

Played at Birmingham, June 12, 13, 14, 1957

Warwickshire won by six wickets. Two separate hundreds by Graveney, who also became the first to complete 1,000 runs for the season, failed to save Gloucestershire. On the opening day Graveney made 106 out of 130 in just under two hours, a display rich in graceful strokes. Hollies, bowling with great steadiness, took six wickets. The Warwickshire innings was dominated by the monumental patience of Gardner who stayed five and three-quarter hours, hitting a 6 and twenty-three 4s. Graveney's second century was even more impressive than his first. He showed exceptional skill against the turning ball skilfully delivered by Hollies and timed his strokes so well that 80 of his runs came in boundaries. When Warwickshire went in again wanting 119, Gloucestershire opened with their spinners, but though they gained early successes another admirable innings by Gardner saw Warwickshire through to victory.

Gloucestershire

G. M. Emmett b Hollies	52	– c Spooner b Ibadulla	25
D. M. Young c Smith b Hollies	29	– lbw b Hollies	18
W. Knightley-Smith c Spooner b Hollies	4	– c Singh b Ibadulla	16
T. W. Graveney c Townsend b Carter	106	– not out	101
R. B. Nicholls c Cartwright b Hollies	14	– lbw b Ibadulla	8
J. Mortimore c Townsend b Ibadulla	2	– c Townsend b Ibadulla	4
B. J. Meyer c Spooner b Carter	13	– lbw b Bannister	8
G. G. M. Wiltshire b Bannister	18	– c Townsend b Singh	14
D. R. Smith c Smith b Hollies	15	– c Smith b Singh	14
C. Cook not out	2	– lbw b Hollies	0
B. D. Wells hit wkt b Hollies	13	– lbw b Hollies	6
L-b 2	2	B 4, l-b 2, n-b 1	7

1/81 2/85 3/86 4/160 5/185   270   1/45 2/51 3/89 4/99 5/103   221
6/215 7/222 8/240 9/257   6/138 7/175 8/193 9/200

Warwickshire

F. C. Gardner c Knightley-Smith b Cook	163	– not out	73
N. F. Horner c Graveney b Cook	29	– run out	4
M. J. K. Smith c Smith b Graveney	59	– c Young b Wells	0
A. Townsend b Graveney	0	– c and b Mortimore	12
T. W. Cartwright c Graveney b Wiltshire	22	– b Mortimore	2
R. T. Spooner c Meyer b Wiltshire	10	– not out	27
K. Ibadulla c Meyer b Wells	20		
S. Singh lbw b Cook	37		
R. G. Carter c Smith b Cook	8		
J. D. Bannister c Wiltshire b Cook	1		
W. E. Hollies not out	0		
B 17, l-b 7	24	L-b 1	1

1/38 2/170 3/170 4/229 5/239   373   1/18 2/21 3/63 4/69   (4 wkts) 119
6/286 7/357 8/367 9/373

Warwickshire Bowling

	Overs	Mdns	Runs	Wkts	Overs	Mdns	Runs	Wkts
Bannister	15	3	67	1	12	2	29	1
Carter	13	1	53	2	11	4	30	—
Townsend	8	3	15	—				
Ibadulla	19	7	33	1	29	11	48	4
Hollies	25.5	4	62	6	43	18	66	3
Singh	12	1	38	—	20	6	41	2

Gloucestershire Bowling

	Overs	Mdns	Runs	Wkts	Overs	Mdns	Runs	Wkts
Smith	20	3	62	—				
Wiltshire	13	1	50	2				
Cook.............	41	13	86	5	13	3	30	—
Wells............	37	8	89	1	14	1	48	1
Mortimore	13	3	35	—	11	—	28	2
Graveney	8	1	27	2				
Emmett..........					1	—	8	—
Nicholls					0.1	—	4	—

Umpires: T. J. Bartley and W. Place.

WARWICKSHIRE v SURREY
(A. V. Wolton's Benefit)
Played at Birmingham, May 9, 11, 12, 1959

Warwickshire won by six wickets after Alec Bedser, the Surrey captain, had twice declared. The main honours of this exciting match during which only nineteen wickets fell, went to the batsmen who thoroughly enjoyed themselves on a pitch that remained easy throughout. For Surrey, Barrington hit two centuries, his 186 being the highest of his career. M. J. K. Smith was in great form for Warwickshire and he, too, hit a century. Smith declared as soon as Warwickshire were ahead and then came a big stand by Stewart and Barrington. Warwickshire wanted 234 in two hours thirty-five minutes and more spirited batting by Horner and Cartwright saw them home, Townsend clinching the issue with fifteen minutes to spare when he hit Laker for 6 into the Members' stand.

Surrey

D. G. W. Fletcher b Hill	32	– b Wheatley	13
M. J. Stewart c Townsend b Wheatley	12	– c Horner b Ibadulla	79
K. F. Barrington c Gardner b Ibadulla	186	– not out	118
R. C. E. Pratt c Townsend b Wheatley	4	– b Cartwright..................	22
B. Constable b Hill	20		
E. A. Bedser c and b Ibadulla	65		
R. Swetman not out	20		
L-b 5	5	L-b 3..................	3

1/30 2/68 3/72   (6 wkts dec.) 344   1/21 2/180 3/235   (3 wkts dec.) 235
4/110 5/285 6/344

D. Gibson, J. C. Laker, A. V. Bedser and P. J. Loader did not bat.

Warwickshire

F. C. Gardner lbw b Laker	20		
N. F. Horner lbw b Loader	25	– run out	98
K. Ibadulla c Swetman b Gibson	39		
T. W. Cartwright c Stewart b E. Bedser	56	– not out	74
M. J. K. Smith not out........................	130	– c Pratt b A. Bedser	5
A. V. Wolton c Pratt b Laker	49	– c Gibson b Laker	2
A. Townsend b Laker	0	– not out	12
R. T. Spooner not out	18	– c A. Bedser b Laker	35
B 4, l-b 5	9	L-b 8..................	8

1/29 2/57 3/109   (6 wkts dec.) 346   1/28 2/101 3/184 4/207   (4 wkts) 234
4/184 5/302 6/302

G. H. Hill, R. G. Carter and O. S. Wheatley did not bat.

Warwickshire Bowling

	Overs	Mdns	Runs	Wkts	Overs	Mdns	Runs	Wkts
Carter............	22	3	79	—	10	1	47	—
Ibadulla	32.4	7	82	2	16	5	53	1
Wheatley	25	5	65	2	21	9	48	1
Hill..............	28	6	87	2	23	6	69	—
Cartwright	18	8	26	—	8.2	1	15	1

Surrey Bowling

	Overs	Mdns	Runs	Wkts	Overs	Mdns	Runs	Wkts
Loader	21	2	71	1	6	—	34	—
A. Bedser	16	5	42	—	10	—	40	1
Laker	34	9	94	3	12.5	—	77	2
E. Bedser	21	8	46	1	9	—	34	—
Gibson	17.4	—	63	1	8	1	41	—
Barrington	9	2	21	—				

Umpires: W. H. Copson and A. E. Rhodes.

WARWICKSHIRE v COMBINED SERVICES

Played at Birmingham (Mitchell and Butler's ground), May 27, 28, 1959

Warwickshire won by nine wickets. The match was remarkable for the play of Stewart and Bannister. Both put up the best performances of the season in first-class cricket at this date, Stewart by scoring the fastest hundred in eighty-five minutes and Bannister by capturing all ten wickets in Combined Services' first innings. Stewart hit five 6s and nineteen 4s and his innings occupied only two hours twenty-five minutes. Bannister was the third Warwickshire player to take all ten wickets, the others being E. Hollies against Nottinghamshire in 1946, and H. Howell against Yorkshire in 1923, both at Edgbaston.

Warwickshire

K. Ibadulla c Fawkes b Tordoff .... 46 – not out 17
W. J. Stewart c Jones b Meakin ....151 – b Meakin 0
T. W. Cartwright c Hardy b Meakin.............. 9 – not out 0
B. E. Fletcher c Fawkes b Meakin 0
R. E. Hitchcock not out 60
M. J. K. Smith not out........................ 58
         B 1, l-b 2, w 1 4

1/167 2/200 3/200   (4 wkts dec.) 328   1/1   (1 wkt) 17
4/207

W. B. Bridge, G. H. Hill, J. G. Fox, J. D. Bannister and R. G. Carter did not bat.

Combined Services

A. Jones c Ibadulla b Bannister	20	– b Carter	0
B. Roe c Hitchcock b Bannister	10	– b Bannister	17
D. S. Williams c Fox b Bannister	0	– c Cartwright b Carter	34
R. Langridge c Fox b Bannister	4	– c Ibadulla b Bannister	5
G. G. Tordoff lbw b Bannister	15	– c Ibadulla b Bridge	75
E. M. P. Hardy c Cartwright b Bannister	0	– c Bridge b Bannister	15
J. H. Deighton c Carter b Bannister	0	– c sub b Hill	25
J. Fawkes c Ibadulla b Bannister	4	– lbw b Bridge	24
P. J. Phelan c Fox b Bannister	41	– b Bridge	0
D. Meakin not out	14	– b Bridge	16
R. Pratt c Ibadulla b Bannister	0	– not out	5
B 4, l-b 1, w 1	6	B 10, l-b 1, n-b 1, w 1	13

1/25 2/27 3/32 4/35 5/39 114 1/6 2/24 3/38 4/85 5/123 229
6/47 7/50 8/68 9/114 6/146 7/183 8/196 9/210

Combined Services Bowling

	Overs	Mdns	Runs	Wkts	Overs	Mdns	Runs	Wkts
Pratt	25	2	94	—	2	1	11	—
Meakin	17	3	52	3	1.4	—	6	1
Phelan	11	—	69	—				
Tordoff	17	—	82	1				
Deighton	6	—	17	—				
Langridge	2	—	10	—				

Warwickshire Bowling

	Overs	Mdns	Runs	Wkts	Overs	Mdns	Runs	Wkts
Bannister	23.3	11	41	10	17	8	43	3
Carter	12	2	31	—	12	3	33	2
Cartwright	2	1	4	—				
Ibadulla	9	4	32	—	5	2	21	—
Hill					23	9	67	1
Hitchcock					8	4	16	—
Bridge					21.5	10	36	4

Umpires: N. Oldfield and D. Davies.

WARWICKSHIRE v NORTHAMPTONSHIRE

Played at Birmingham, August 1, 3, 4, 1959

Drawn. Northamptonshire broke down after a fine second-wicket partnership of 159 between Norman and P. J. Watts. Norman's hundred was his first in county cricket. M. J. K. Smith was the only Warwickshire batsman who dealt competently with a Northamptonshire attack in which Tyson bowled well. His magnificent 142 not out (eighteen 4s and three 6s) enabled him to break a county record, taking his aggregate ahead of R. E. S. Wyatt's total of 2,630 in 1929. Set to score 289 to win, Warwickshire were content to play out time after losing three wickets for 57.

Northamptonshire

M. Norman c Horner b Ibadulla	109	– c Wolton b Bannister	40
R. Subba Row c Cartwright b Bannister	13	– b Bannister	29
P. J. Watts lbw b Bridge	63	– c Fox b Bannister	4
D. Brookes c Fox b Ibadulla	4	– c Smith b Cartwright	49
A. Lightfoot b Bannister	14	– c Ibadulla b Bridge	42
G. E. Tribe c Townsend b Wheatley	10	– not out	50
P. D. Watts c Horner b Wheatley	9	– c Townsend b Cartwright	0
J. S. Manning b Bannister	8	– b Bridge	20
K. V. Andrew not out	4	– not out	29
F. H. Tyson b Bannister	2		
J. G. Williamson not out	4		
B 12, l-b 4, w 1	17	B 8, l-b 2	10

1/42 2/201 3/201 4/215   (9 wkts dec.) 257   1/66 2/72 3/77 4/160 (7 wkts dec.) 273
5/225 6/234 7/239 8/251 9/253   5/183 6/183 7/224

Warwickshire

N. F. Horner b Tyson	22	– c Andrew b Tribe	60
W. J. Stewart c P. D. Watts b Tyson	8	– c Andrew b Williamson	0
A. Townsend b Williamson	14	– b Manning	10
M. J. K. Smith not out	142	– c Williamson b Manning	10
A. V. Wolton lbw b Tribe	36	– not out	70
T. W. Cartwright c Andrew b Williamson	2	– b Tribe	33
K. Ibadulla b Tyson	1	– not out	2
J. D. Bannister b Tyson	3		
W. B. Bridge b Williamson	0		
J. G. Fox lbw b Tribe	4		
O. S. Wheatley b Tyson	10		
B 4, l-b 6	10	B 5, l-b 2, w 1	8

1/9 2/46 3/48 4/110 5/125   252   1/2 2/37 3/57 4/123   (5 wkts) 193
6/126 7/148 8/149 9/174   5/174

Warwickshire Bowling

	Overs	Mdns	Runs	Wkts	Overs	Mdns	Runs	Wkts
Wheatley	23	7	41	2	9	1	18	—
Bannister	29	7	72	4	28	6	66	3
Cartwright	12	2	45	—	29	7	80	2
Townsend	5	1	20	—	1	—	2	—
Ibadulla	19	9	33	2	13	6	25	—
Bridge	12	4	29	1	29	6	72	2

Northamptonshire Bowling

	Overs	Mdns	Runs	Wkts	Overs	Mdns	Runs	Wkts
Tyson	27.5	10	59	5	7	1	26	—
Lightfoot	14	1	49	—	3	—	19	—
Williamson	20	4	51	3	4	2	7	1
Tribe	11	—	63	2	17	2	51	2
P. D. Watts	4	2	20	—	8	1	29	—
Manning					10	—	47	2
Subba Row					2	1	3	—
Brookes					1	—	3	—

Umpires: C. S. Elliott and J. S. Buller.

WARWICKSHIRE v YORKSHIRE

Played at Birmingham, August 20, 22, 23, 1960

Yorkshire won by nine wickets. Two left-handers, Cowan and Stott, each recorded the best performances of their careers and virtually won the match by themselves. Stott scored 186 in six and a quarter hours after Warwickshire had collapsed after being put in to bat. He hit twenty-two 4s and he offered only one chance, at 102. When Warwickshire batted a second time, Cowan ran through the side after taking the second new ball at 129. He broke a stubborn third-wicket partnership of 101 between Stewart and Hitchcock and finished off the innings by bowling the last two batsmen with successive deliveries. Cowan's figures with the new ball were 10.2–7–11–7 and he took nine for 43 in the innings.

Warwickshire

N. F. Horner c Illingworth b Close	11	– lbw b Cowan	19
K. Ibadulla b Close	21	– c J. Wilson b Cowan	5
W. J. Stewart b Taylor	20	– c Close b Cowan	60
R. E. Hitchcock c Binks b Ryan	3	– b Ryan	42
T. W. Cartwright b Ryan	5	– lbw b Cowan	0
D. Amiss c and b Ryan	30	– c J. Wilson b Cowan	3
†A. C. Smith c Binks b Cowan	51	– not out	22
J. D. Bannister c D. Wilson b Cowan	17	– c Binks b Cowan	1
A. Wright c Binks b Ryan	4	– b Cowan	0
R. G. Carter lbw b Cowan	2	– b Cowan	2
*O. S. Wheatley not out	2	– b Cowan	0
B 5, l-b 1, w 1	7	B 7, l-b 1	8

1/27 2/54 3/54 4/60 5/65   173   1/22 2/29 3/130 4/134 5/134   162
6/148 7/152 8/163 9/170   6/138 7/144 8/148 9/162

Yorkshire

W. B. Stott c Wheatley b Carter	186	– c Cartwright b Smith	10
J. B. Bolus c Smith b Cartwright	56	– not out	15
P. J. Sharpe lbw b Cartwright	1	– not out	14
D. B. Close run out	14		
K. Taylor c Smith b Bannister	0		
R. Illingworth c Smith b Wheatley	2		
*J. V. Wilson c Smith b Bannister	5		
D. Wilson c Horner b Wheatley	1		
†J. G. Binks b Amiss	21		
M. Ryan b Carter	3		
M. J. Cowan not out	0		
B 4, l-b 2	6	L-b 2	2

1/152 2/154 3/179 4/179 5/186   295   1/18   (1 wkt) 41
6/193 7/194 8/253 9/278

Yorkshire Bowling

	Overs	Mdns	Runs	Wkts	Overs	Mdns	Runs	Wkts
Ryan	21	5	44	4	26	9	48	1
Cowan	20.1	4	44	3	27.2	11	43	9
Close	19	6	27	2	6	3	13	—
Taylor	10	3	26	1	14	3	33	—
Illingworth	15	11	13	—	15	11	9	—
D. Wilson	3	1	12	—	10	8	8	—

Warwickshire Bowling

	Overs	Mdns	Runs	Wkts	Overs	Mdns	Runs	Wkts
Bannister	25	8	46	2	3	—	10	—
Wheatley	39	7	66	2	3	—	6	—
Wright	22	3	66	—				
Cartwright	21	6	58	2				
Carter............	14.1	6	23	2				
Amiss	9	2	26	1				
Hitchcock.........	1	—	4	—				
Smith					3.5	—	5	1
Ibadulla					2	—	13	—
Horner					1	—	5	—

Umpires: A. Jepson and John Langridge.

WARWICKSHIRE v SOMERSET

Played at Nuneaton, May 13, 15, 16, 1961

Warwickshire won by 47 runs. Somerset's Australian all-rounder, Alley, had the extraordinary experience of scoring 221 not out in the fourth innings and yet finished on the losing side. Set to score 389 for victory, Somerset started badly and had lost two wickets for 23 when Alley went to the wicket. He was never troubled by the bowling, reached his hundred with twenty-nine scoring strokes in an hour and twenty minutes and his double hundred, which included six 6s and thirty-one 4s, in under four hours. Apart from C. Atkinson, who helped to add 99 for the seventh wicket, Alley was unable to find anyone to stay with him long enough for his team to win. On a fast pitch, Warwickshire totalled 265 through the efforts of Stewart, M. J. K. Smith and Ibadulla, who were the only three batsmen to reach double figures. In reply, Somerset did not recover after Thompson had taken five of the first six wickets for 23 runs. An opening partnership of 136 by Ibadulla and Ratcliffe and another good innings by Smith enabled Warwickshire to declare and despite Alley's brilliant innings Somerset failed to reach their target.

Warwickshire

K. Ibadulla lbw b Palmer	50	– c C. Atkinson b Langford......... 68
D. P. Ratcliffe b Palmer	3	– c Keith b Lomax................ 62
W. J. Stewart c G. Atkinson b Lomax	95	– c Lomax b Langford............ 10
*M. J. K. Smith c Greetham b Palmer	92	– st Stephenson b Langford........ 82
T. W. Cartwright c G. Atkinson b Lomax	0	– b Langford 21
R. E. Hitchcock c Stephenson b Lomax	4	– not out 4
†A. C. Smith b Biddulph......................	5	– not out 11
W. B. Bridge b Palmer	5	
J. D. Bannister b Palmer......................	2	
R. G. Carter c Stephenson b Biddulph	0	
R. G. Thompson not out......................	4	
L-b 4, n-b 1	5	B 8, l-b 5............... 13

1/6 2/118 3/204 4/210 5/222   265   1/136 2/136 3/162   (5 wkts dec.) 271
6/243 7/250 8/259 9/260   4/243 5/254

Somerset

G. Atkinson lbw b Bannister	37	– c A. Smith b Bridge	27
J. G. Lomax c Cartwright b Thompson	6	– b Thompson	7
P. B. Wight b Thompson	5	– b Bannister	6
W. E. Alley c Cartwright b Bannister	9	– not out	221
G. L. Keith b Thompson	4	– c and b Carter	6
C. Greetham b Thompson	0	– c A. Smith b Bridge	1
B. Langford c Bannister b Thompson	0	– lbw b Thompson	1
K. E. Palmer c M. Smith b Bannister	5	– lbw b Hitchcock	13
C. R. M. Atkinson b Bridge	32	– c A. Smith b Bridge	33
*†H. W. Stephenson c Hitchcock b Bridge	39	– c Ratcliffe b Bannister	18
K. D. Biddulph not out	5	– c Hitchcock b Bannister	5
B 6	6	B 1, l-b 2	3

1/8 2/26 3/41 4/46 5/50   148   1/16 2/23 3/89 4/112 5/143   341
6/50 7/59 8/80 9/140   6/176 7/275 8/325 9/326

Somerset Bowling

	Overs	Mdns	Runs	Wkts	Overs	Mdns	Runs	Wkts
Biddulph	22	3	70	2	7	1	28	—
Palmer	20.2	5	47	5	7	1	20	—
C. Atkinson	10	2	32	—	4	1	11	0
Alley	18	6	38	—	12	1	57	—
Lomax	23	7	50	3	14	3	38	1
Greetham	4	—	23	—				
Langford					30	4	104	4

Warwickshire Bowling

	Overs	Mdns	Runs	Wkts	Overs	Mdns	Runs	Wkts
Bannister	26	8	43	3	26.4	5	88	3
Thompson	27	5	56	5	17	8	35	2
Cartwright	7	1	28	—	3	1	7	—
Bridge	4.1	—	15	2	33	9	121	3
Carter					14	1	67	1
Hitchcock					3	1	20	1

Umpires: J. S. Buller and D. Davies.

WARWICKSHIRE v MIDDLESEX

Played at Birmingham, June 17, 19, 20, 1961

Middlesex won by six wickets. A magnificent century by M. J. K. Smith, who went in after two wickets had fallen for eleven runs, dominated the Warwickshire first innings. He batted for two hours and twenty-six minutes and hit nineteen 4s before he was caught off Hooker, who, in a spell of eight overs, took four wickets for nineteen runs. Middlesex also owed a great deal to one man. Their opening batsman, W. E. Russell, stayed for over five hours and scored thirteen 4s in his 134. Apart from Horner and M. J. K. Smith, Warwickshire disappointed when they batted a second time. Horner hit 64 in boundaries, including six 4s off successive deliveries from Titmus. In the Middlesex second innings, Clark, awarded his county cap during the match, also decided that aggression was the best policy on a wearing pitch and hit two 6s and six 4s in under an hour.

Warwickshire

N. F. Horner c Hooker b Moss	0	– c Titmus b Hooker	85
K. Ibadulla c Murray b Titmus	38	– c Hooker b Bennett	18
W. J. Stewart c Clark b Bennett	4	– c Parfitt b Hurst	15
*M. J. K. Smith c Parfitt b Hooker	102	– c Bennett b Moss	63
T. W. Cartwright c Murray b Hooker	0	– b Hooker	2
R. E. Hitchcock c Parfitt b Hooker	5	– c Hooker b Titmus	0
†A. C. Smith c Hooker b Titmus	0	– c Parfitt b Hooker	10
J. D. Bannister c Russell b Hooker	9	– c Bedford b Moss	2
W. B. Bridge b Titmus	13	– b Moss	9
A. Wright run out	4	– c Murray b Moss	7
R. G. Thompson not out	0	– not out	0
B 2, l-b 1	3	L-b 6	6

1/0 2/11 3/125 4/136 5/149   178   1/38 2/93 3/157 4/159 5/160   217
6/149 7/149 8/173 9/178   6/199 7/201 8/201 9/208

Middlesex

R. A. Gale c Bridge b Bannister	15	– c Ibadulla b Bridge	16
W. E. Russell st A. Smith b Thompson	134	– c A. Smith b Bannister	5
P. H. Parfitt c A. Smith b Thompson	1	– lbw b Bannister	13
E. A. Clark c M. Smith b Bridge	15	– c sub b Ibadulla	59
R. W. Hooker st A. Smith b Cartwright	10	– not out	31
F. J. Titmus c M. Smith b Bridge	15	– not out	2
D. Bennett lbw b Bridge	6		
†J. T. Murray b Bannister	36		
R. J. Hurst c A. Smith b Bannister	0		
*P. I. Bedford c A. Smith b Thompson	16		
A. E. Moss not out	8		
B 8, l-b 3	11	B 2, l-b 2	4

1/25 2/26 3/75 4/100 5/131   267   1/11 2/34 3/62 4/118   (4 wkts) 130
6/147 7/212 8/212 9/240

Middlesex Bowling

	Overs	Mdns	Runs	Wkts	Overs	Mdns	Runs	Wkts
Moss	12	7	18	1	15.5	7	38	4
Bennett	8	1	17	1	8	—	15	1
Hooker	17.4	8	42	4	19	10	37	3
Titmus	22	9	53	3	21	4	72	1
Hurst	12	2	45	—	14	4	43	1
Parfitt					1	—	6	—

Warwickshire Bowling

	Overs	Mdns	Runs	Wkts	Overs	Mdns	Runs	Wkts
Bannister	25	9	48	3	14	4	25	2
Thompson	21.1	4	59	3	14	8	23	—
Bridge	31	10	81	3	5	—	29	1
Wright	15	1	39	—	3	1	17	—
Cartwright	5	2	8	1				
Ibadulla	10	3	21	—	2	1	4	1
Hitchcock					5	1	16	—
A. Smith					2.5	—	12	—

Umpires: R. S. Lay and A. E. Rhodes.

WORCESTERSHIRE

WORCESTERSHIRE v NORTHAMPTONSHIRE

Played at Kidderminster, July 6, 8, 9, 1946

Drawn. An easy-paced pitch on the small Kidderminster ground enabled batsmen to hold the upper hand throughout a match which produced 1,223 runs while only 21 wickets fell. An aggregate of 297 for once out by Cooper and an innings of 200 by Brookes emphasised the punishment of bowlers. Cooper batted nearly six hours for his 191; he hit twenty 4s and completed a thousand runs for the season. He and Howorth added 218. After the visitors had done remarkably well in gaining a first innings lead, Cooper scored 106 in a little over two hours, hitting fourteen 4s, and he was not out when the match was abandoned. Brookes and Davis opened the Northamptonshire innings with 243 – the best stand ever made for their county. Brookes got his 200 in 275 minutes, his square cuts and drives being specially good; Davis hit well in front of the wicket.

Worcestershire

E. Cooper b C. B. Clarke	191	– not out	106
A. P. Singleton b C. B. Clarke	25	– c Greenwood b Nevell	41
R. Howorth c Greenwood b Nevell	89	– not out	65
R. E. S. Wyatt b Nevell	44		
R. E. Bird lbw b C. B. Clarke	3		
E. H. Perry b C. B. Clarke	5		
N. H. Humphries lbw b Whitfield	16		
A. F. T. White c Barron b Nevell	59		
S. Buller not out	21		
R. T. D. Perks c C. B. Clarke b Nevell	7		
P. F. Jackson b C. B. Clarke	0		
B 10, l-b 7	17	B 4, l-b 3	7
	477	**(1 wkt)**	**219**

Northamptonshire

D. Brookes c Bird b Howorth	200	W. Nevell c Bird b Singleton	0
P. Davis c Perry b Perks	105	R. J. Partridge b Perks	25
E. W. Whitfield b Perks	0	C. B. Clarke c Buller b Perks	26
J. E. Timms c Bird b Perks	48	E. W. Clark not out	6
W. Barron c Bird b Perks	0	B 12, l-b 14, w 2, n-b 6	34
H. W. Greenwood b Jackson	29		
P. E. Murray Willis c Singleton b Howorth	54		**527**

Northamptonshire Bowling

	Overs	Mdns	Runs	Wkts	Overs	Mdns	Runs	Wkts
E. W. Clark	33	2	116	—	4	1	17	—
Partridge	31	7	88	—	5	1	9	—
C. B. Clarke	36.1	9	114	5	9	1	50	—
Nevell	33	5	103	4	8	—	40	1
Whitfield	5	1	13	1	9	1	32	—
Davis	4	—	26	—	3	—	10	—
Timms					6	—	16	—
Barron					5	1	38	—

Worcestershire Bowling

	Overs	Mdns	Runs	Wkts
Perks............	31.5	2	125	6
Perry............	10	—	58	—
Howorth.........	34	9	82	2
Jackson..........	37	8	104	1
Singleton.........	23	3	76	1
Wyatt...........	6	—	26	—
Humphreys.......	2	—	22	—

WORCESTERSHIRE v R.A.F.

Played at Worcester, May 19, 20, 21, 1948

Worcestershire won by 190 runs. The Service gave a creditable performance, but the skilful leg-break and googly bowling of Jenkins, who took thirteen wickets for 161, proved too much for them. Worcestershire, trying some young players, were impressed by the free stroke-play of Whiting on his first appearance as a professional, and the fast-medium bowling of Everton, who swung the ball away in disconcerting style. Cockle, the RAF leg-spin bowler, caused the home batsmen a good deal of worry. Lyttelton, Lumsden and Jenkins all played attractive cricket.

Worcestershire

N. Whiting lbw b Cockle.......................	17	– not out 155
M. Young c Shirreff b Rayment	23	– st Parr b Cockle 40
D. Kenyon c Parr b Rayment...................	18	– c Parr b Cockle................. 47
G. Dews c Shirreff b Cockle	44	– not out 30
Hon. C. J. Lyttelton lbw b Shirreff	89	
R. Jenkins not out...........................	82	
A. F. T. White c Wilson b Cockle................	51	
R. T. D. Perks lbw b Cockle	0	
H. Yarnold c Shirreff b Cockle	0	
G. Everton b Shirreff........................	15	
P. F. Jackson b Wilson	1	
B 1, l-b 3, n-b 3	7	B 9, l-b 4............... 13

347   (2 wkts dec.) 285

RAF

W. E. Payton b Jenkins.......................	26	– c Lyttelton b Jenkins............ 43
J. F. Roberts c Yarnold b Everton...............	59	– absent injured.................. 0
F. S. R. Johnson b Jenkins	0	– b Jenkins..................... 0
I. J. M. Lumsden lbw b Everton	71	– b Jackson 70
L. R. White c Kenyon b Everton................	11	– b Jackson 2
A. C. Shirreff b Jenkins......................	15	– lbw b Jenkins 11
F. D. Parr c Lyttelton b Jenkins	30	– b Jackson 0
A. F. Godwin c Yarnold b Jenkins	18	– st Yarnold b Jenkins............ 6
A. Rayment st Yarnold b Jenkins...............	0	– c and b Jenkins................ 18
R. G. Wilson not out........................	23	– st Yarnold b Jenkins............ 6
D. F. Cockle b Jenkins	8	– not out 7
B 8, l-b 1, n-b 2	11	B 6, l-b 1............... 7

272   170

RAF Bowling

	Overs	Mdns	Runs	Wkts	Overs	Mdns	Runs	Wkts
Wilson	18.1	3	48	1	22	2	71	—
Shirreff	27	5	90	2	14	2	39	—
Cockle	37	5	115	5	39	11	104	2
Rayment..........	13	1	66	2	8	—	38	—
Godwin...........	5	1	21	—	3	—	20	—

Worcestershire Bowling

	Overs	Mdns	Runs	Wkts	Overs	Mdns	Runs	Wkts
Perks.............	23	5	59	—	4	—	10	—
Everton..........	19	3	54	3	2	—	11	—
Jackson..........	23	14	21	—	19	7	37	3
Jenkins	29.1	9	84	7	21.1	4	77	6
Lyttelton..........	6	—	43	—	3	—	22	—
Dews.............					1	—	6	—

Umpires: S. Buller and E. Cooper.

WORCESTERSHIRE v WARWICKSHIRE

Played at Dudley, August 21, 23, 24, 1948

Drawn. In a close finish Worcestershire, with their last man in, wanted 24 to win. They were set to make 269 in 230 minutes, and for getting within sight of success owed much to Ainsworth, who hit his first county century in about two and a half hours. Donnelly gave an equally attractive display in Warwickshire's first innings. Unusual circumstances attached to the New Zealander's exhibition. One of the not-out batsmen on the Saturday, Donnelly, arrived ten minutes late on Monday and had to ask permission of the Worcestershire captain to resume after Ord's dismissal. Dollery helped Donnelly in a three-figure partnership.

Warwickshire

R. H. Maudsley b Jackson	11	– b Palmer......................	11
K. A. Taylor b Perks..........................	24	– c Yarnold b Perks.............	15
J. S. Ord c Ainsworth b Perks..................	37	– c Jenkins b Howorth............	53
M. P. Donnelly b Perks.......................	96	– c Cooper b Palmer	11
H. E. Dollery lbw b Jackson	28	– not out	45
A. Wolton c Yarnold b Perks	2		
R. T. Spooner st Yarnold b Howorth	22		
A. Townsend c Cooper b Howorth...............	4		
C. W. Grove c Howorth b Jackson...............	1		
T. L. Pritchard not out	0		
W. E. Hollies lbw b Howorth	0		
L-b 5, n-b 6	11	B 2, l-b 2, n-b 1	5
	236	(4 wkts dec.)	140

Worcestershire

E. Cooper c Spooner b Townsend	21	– b Pritchard	15
D. Kenyon c Townsend b Pritchard	0	– b Hollies	0
C. H. Palmer lbw b Hollies	10	– b Grove	52
M. L. Ainsworth b Pritchard	15	– b Pritchard	100
R. Jenkins c Spooner b Hollies	19	– lbw b Hollies	6
R. Howorth b Maudsley	4	– c Pritchard b Hollies	19
L. Outschoorn c Hollies b Maudsley	11	– b Grove	18
A. F. T. White b Hollies	11	– c Townsend b Pritchard	0
R. T. D. Perks b Hollies	9	– run out	24
H. Yarnold b Pritchard	5	– not out	0
P. F. Jackson not out	0	– not out	0
L-b 2, n-b 1	3	B 4, l-b 5, w 1, n-b 1	11
	108		**(9 wkts) 245**

Worcestershire Bowling

	Overs	Mdns	Runs	Wkts	Overs	Mdns	Runs	Wkts
Perks	41	10	89	4	16	3	42	1
Palmer	19	6	57	—	16	4	34	2
Jackson	27	7	58	3	3	—	17	—
Howorth	6.4	1	13	3	6.3	—	31	1
Jenkins	2	1	8	—	4	1	11	—

Warwickshire Bowling

	Overs	Mdns	Runs	Wkts	Overs	Mdns	Runs	Wkts
Pritchard	16	2	38	3	26	6	72	3
Grove	4	2	3	—	19	1	68	2
Hollies	16.3	5	37	4	27	3	73	3
Townsend	1	—	10	1				
Maudsley	6	—	17	2	6	1	21	—

Umpires: G. M. Lee and E. Robinson.

WORCESTERSHIRE v YORKSHIRE

Played at Worcester, June 15, 16, 17, 1949

Yorkshire won by 35 runs. Worcestershire had not defeated Yorkshire twice in a season for forty years, but after their success at Sheffield they came very near to completing the feat in this match. Yorkshire started disastrously, losing Hutton and Halliday to Perks without a run scored. Moreover, five wickets were down for 59 before Wilson, the tall left-hander, and Yardley checked the collapse with a stand of 93. Wilson showed splendid judgment in driving and cutting. Worcestershire, too, lost wickets cheaply to an attack lacking Coxon and Aspinall (injured), and only Bird looked at ease against the out-swingers of Close. When Yorkshire batted again 73 ahead, Hutton once more failed to score, and with Perks virtually unplayable in his opening spell five men were out for 29. Worcestershire could not press home their initial ascendancy, and Yardley, Sutcliffe and Close inspired a recovery. Left to obtain 251 runs on a wearing pitch, Worcestershire were always struggling, though had Jenkins found a partner to stay with him the result might have been different. As it was, Perks enlivened the end with a characteristic display of hitting. In 1936, at Stourbridge, Worcestershire also dismissed Hutton twice for nought.

Yorkshire

L. Hutton lbw b Perks	0	– b Perks	0
F. A. Wilson lbw b Jenkins	12	– c Kenyon b Perks	7
H. Halliday b Perks	0	– b Wyatt	12
J. V. Wilson lbw b Perks	84	– b Perks	6
W. H. H. Sutcliffe b Jenkins	0	– c Yarnold b Howorth	20
W. Watson c Outschoorn b Howorth	7	– c Cooper b Perks	0
N. W. D. Yardley lbw b Perks	68	– c Wyatt b Jackson	72
D. B. Close not out	26	– c and b Jenkins	47
E. P. Robinson b Perks	1	– c Yarnold b Jenkins	11
D. V. Brennan b Jenkins	9	– not out	0
A. Mason b Jenkins	0	– b Jenkins	0
L-b 3	3	L-b 2	2
	210		**177**

Worcestershire

E. Cooper b Yardley	6	– lbw b Yardley	2
D. Kenyon c Brennan b Close	5	– c Mason b Close	34
R. O. Jenkins hit wkt b Mason	10	– c Halliday b Yardley	40
R. E. S. Wyatt b Mason	11	– b Robinson	0
R. E. Bird c Halliday b Close	44	– c Hutton b Robinson	27
R. Howorth c Hutton b Close	6	– c Halliday b Close	24
L. Outschoorn lbw b Close	21	– c Halliday b Mason	5
A. F. T. White b Close	9	– b Close	6
R. T. D. Perks c Brennan b Close	2	– b Robinson	51
H. Yarnold c and b Yardley	0	– b Robinson	12
P. F. Jackson not out	4	– not out	1
B 17, l-b 2	19	B 10, l-b 2, w 1	13
	137		**215**

Worcestershire Bowling

	Overs	Mdns	Runs	Wkts	Overs	Mdns	Runs	Wkts
Perks	28	6	75	5	19	6	43	4
Wyatt	10	5	18	—	9	1	25	1
Jackson	13	1	31	—	12	—	49	1
Jenkins	20	5	54	4	10	—	38	3
Howorth	17	4	29	1	9	2	20	1

Yorkshire Bowling

	Overs	Mdns	Runs	Wkts	Overs	Mdns	Runs	Wkts
Close	24.2	3	47	6	25	9	45	3
Yardley	24	15	26	2	13	7	10	2
Halliday	5	2	4	—				
Mason	12	1	31	2	28	15	37	1
Robinson	13	7	10	—	29.4	9	78	4
Sutcliffe					2	—	6	—
Hutton					11	3	26	—

Umpires: T. J. Bartley and A. E. Pothecary.

WORCESTERSHIRE v MIDDLESEX

Played at Worcester, July 23, 25, 26, 1949

Middlesex won by an innings and 54 runs. Robertson, by hitting the highest score of his career, the highest individual score for Middlesex and the largest individual total recorded in England since 1938, put Middlesex in an unassailable position in this match which had an important bearing on the County Championship. Never at fault, Robertson showed excellent judgment in going out to punish the slow bowlers, and his two 6s and thirty-nine 4s were the result of well-timed drives and wristy cuts. He figured in huge stands with Allen, Dewes, Mann and Robins, Middlesex scoring at nearly 100 an hour. Splendid leg-break bowling by Sims and Robins put Middlesex within sight of victory by the end of the second day, and although Cooper, Palmer, Outschoorn, Howorth and Yarnold all provided spirited resistance when Worcestershire followed-on 435 runs behind, they only delayed the inevitable.

Middlesex

J. D. Robertson 331	R. W. V. Robins c Cooper b Bird 59
S. M. Brown b Palmer.................. 3	
J. G. Dewes b Perks 45	B 14, l-b 5, n-b 3 22
F. G. Mann c Bird b Palmer 65	
G. O. Allen b Palmer.................. 98	(5 wkts dec.) 623

H. Sharp, L. Compton, J. Sims, J. A. Young and L. Gray did not bat.

Worcestershire

D. Kenyon c Robertson b Sims.................. 32	– hit wkt b Robins	23
E. Cooper c Robins b Allen..................... 10	– b Young	68
C. H. Palmer st Compton b Young............... 13	– lbw b Young	40
R. E. Bird not out 44	– b Sharp......................	4
R. O. Jenkins lbw b Robins.................... 8	– c Compton b Sims	27
R. Howorth c and b Robins 0	– c Compton b Gray.............	23
L. Outschoorn st Compton b Robins 0	– not out	94
A. F. T. White b Sims 9	– b Sims.......................	18
H. Yarnold st Compton b Sims.................. 21	– b Young......................	61
R. T. D. Perks c Robins b Sims.................. 28	– lbw b Gray....................	0
P. F. Jackson c Mann b Sims ....\. 14	– c Robins b Gray................	1
B 5, l-b 2, w 2 9	B 10, l-b 5, w 6, n-b 1	22
188		381

Worcestershire Bowling

	Overs	Mdns	Runs	Wkts
Perks.............	24	7	92	1
Palmer	30	8	119	3
Jenkins	30	4	153	—
Howorth..........	24	5	99	—
Jackson...........	23	1	104	—
Bird..............	4.3	—	34	1

Middlesex Bowling

	Overs	Mdns	Runs	Wkts	Overs	Mdns	Runs	Wkts
Allen.............	7	—	26	1	11	1	34	—
Gray.............	4	—	15	—	13.1	1	26	3
Young............	12	4	48	1	56	26	75	3
Sims	19.4	3	54	5	39	5	128	2
Robins	11	1	36	3	26	2	85	1
Sharp					11	5	11	1

Umpires: B. Flint and A. E. Pothecary.

WORCESTERSHIRE v HAMPSHIRE

Played at Worcester, August 3, 4, 5, 1949

Worcestershire won by one wicket. Set to score 166 in two and a half hours, Worcestershire seemed assured of a comfortable victory when, at the fall of the third wicket, they required only 49 runs. Their confidence was quickly dispelled by the bowling of Knott, off-spin, and Shackleton, fast-medium, who dismissed the next five batsmen for 36 runs, and thirteen runs were needed when Howorth, ninth in, joined Jenkins. Fielders clustered near the bat as the pair fought for runs, and the total remained at 159 for four overs before Jenkins hooked Knott for 4 in the last over of the day. He was out next ball, and with the last man at the crease, Howorth won the match by driving Knott's fifth delivery to the boundary. During Hampshire's first innings Perks surpassed the record aggregate of 1,523 wickets for the county, established by Fred Root. Yarnold kept wicket splendidly and shared in the dismissal of nine batsmen, six of them in the second innings.

Hampshire

N. McCorkell c Yarnold b Howorth	55	– c Yarnold b Howorth	35
N. H. Rogers lbw b Perks	6	– st Yarnold b Jenkins	15
G. Dawson b Jenkins	47	– st Yarnold b Jenkins	9
J. Bailey b Perks	14	– st Yarnold b Jenkins	35
E. D. R. Eagar c Yarnold b Perks	25	– lbw b Palmer	42
J. Arnold not out	37	– c Bird b Jenkins	21
D. E. Blake b Perks	17	– b Jenkins	3
C. Walker hit wkt b Palmer	4	– c Ainsworth b Palmer	31
J. R. Gray st Yarnold b Jenkins	0	– not out	22
D. Shackleton c Outschoorn b Perks	8	– c Yarnold b Perks	2
C. J. Knott c Howorth b Jenkins	13	– c Yarnold b Jenkins	1
B 6, l-b 3, n-b 3	12	B 13, l-b 14, n-b 2	29
	238		**245**

Worcestershire

E. Cooper b Shackleton	115	– c Eagar b Walker	0
D. Kenyon c Eagar b Bailey	79	– c Rogers b Knott	72
C. H. Palmer run out	19	– b Shackleton	7
R. E. S. Wyatt b Walker	2	– c McCorkell b Bailey	53
R. E. Bird c Shackleton b Walker	9	– lbw b Knott	8
M. L. Y. Ainsworth c Blake b Shackleton	1	– b Knott	1
L. Outschoorn lbw b Shackleton	1	– lbw b Shackleton	2
R. O. Jenkins st Blake b Bailey	30	– run out	10
R. Howorth lbw b Shackleton	39	– not out	7
R. T. D. Perks b Shackleton	0	– b Shackleton	2
H. Yarnold not out	0	– not out	0
B 12, l-b 10, n-b 1	23	B 3, l-b 2	5
	318		**(9 wkts) 167**

Worcestershire Bowling

	Overs	Mdns	Runs	Wkts	Overs	Mdns	Runs	Wkts
Perks	28	5	83	5	24	10	50	1
Palmer	22	7	47	1	15	7	23	2
Wyatt	3	1	9	—				
Jenkins	16.4	3	65	3	37.3	6	92	6
Howorth	26	15	22	1	25	10	38	1
Outschoorn					2	1	9	—
Bird					2	—	4	—

Hampshire Bowling

	Overs	Mdns	Runs	Wkts	Overs	Mdns	Runs	Wkts
Shackleton	36	7	75	5	17	4	36	3
Walker	20	7	44	2	4	—	25	1
Gray	4	—	13	—				
Knott	30	7	75	—	21.5	2	73	3
Bailey	38	13	88	2	9	2	28	1

Umpires: H. Elliott and E. Robinson.

WORCESTERSHIRE v SURREY

Played at Worcester, August 27, 29, 30, 1949

Worcestershire won by 109 runs. This match will be remembered especially for the remarkable feat of Jenkins, the Worcestershire leg-break and googly bowler, who performed the "hat-trick" in each Surrey innings. The only other occasion Jenkins had taken three wickets with consecutive deliveries was also against Surrey at The Oval the previous year. On the first day Surridge upset the Worcestershire batsmen with his fast-medium bowling, half the side being out for 24. Palmer and Wyatt improved the position, but A. V. Bedser, using the new ball, brought the innings to an abrupt close. Surrey began confidently and seemed likely to gain a commanding advantage until Jenkins changed the whole aspect and restricted their lead to 38. Worcestershire maintained the ascendancy, largely through the sound batting of Cooper and Kenyon, who shared a three-figured opening stand, and Surrey, set to score 217, could not cope with the turning ball when the effects of the roller had gone. Jenkins and Howorth dismissed the last six batsmen with the total unchanged at 107.

Worcestershire

E. Cooper b Surridge	10	– c Squires b Lock	60
D. Kenyon b Surridge	3	– b E. A. Bedser	51
L. Outschoorn b Surridge	1	– b E. A. Bedser	7
C. H. Palmer run out	59	– b A. V. Bedser	35
M. L. Y. Ainsworth b Surridge	0	– c McIntyre b Lock	0
R. E. Bird c McIntyre b A. V. Bedser	4	– b Lock	0
R. E. S. Wyatt c McIntyre b Surridge	40	– c Lock b A. V. Bedser	48
R. O. Jenkins c Parker b A. V. Bedser	9	– c McIntyre b A. V. Bedser	11
R. Howorth b A. V. Bedser	0	– c Surridge b Laker	31
H. Yarnold b A. V. Bedser	5	– not out	0
R. T. D. Perks not out	10	– c Parker b A. V. Bedser	0
W 1	1	B 8, l-b 1, n-b 2	11
	142		**254**

Surrey

L. B. Fishlock c Cooper b Jenkins	43	– c Bird b Jenkins	43
E. A. Bedser b Perks	25	– lbw b Wyatt	9
H. S. Squires b Jenkins	24	– b Perks	7
B. Constable b Perks	0	– c Yarnold b Perks	13
J. F. Parker c Yarnold b Jenkins	57	– c Outschoorn b Howorth	31
M. R. Barton lbw b Howorth	4	– c and b Jenkins	1
A. J. McIntyre c Outschoorn b Jenkins	13	– st Yarnold b Jenkins	0
J. C. Laker c Jenkins b Howorth	7	– c Outschoorn b Howorth	0
A. V. Bedser b Jenkins	0	– c and b Jenkins	0
W. S. Surridge c Perks b Jenkins	0	– c and b Jenkins	0
G. A. R. Lock not out	4	– not out	0
B 1, l-b 2	3	L-b 3	3
	180		**107**

Surrey Bowling

	Overs	Mdns	Runs	Wkts	Overs	Mdns	Runs	Wkts
A. V. Bedser	14	4	23	4	25	6	52	4
Surridge	16	1	53	5	17	3	47	—
Parker.	6	3	4	—	4	1	10	—
Laker	17	4	42	—	20	12	21	1
Lock	14	9	15	—	35	15	65	3
E. A. Bedser	4	2	4	—	24	9	48	2

Worcestershire Bowling

	Overs	Mdns	Runs	Wkts	Overs	Mdns	Runs	Wkts
Perks.	24	11	38	2	13	5	18	2
Wyatt	7	2	22	—	9	4	16	1
Jenkins	27	4	112	6	15.3	2	54	5
Howorth	10.1	7	5	2	14	7	16	2

Umpires: E. Cooke and D. Hendren.

WORCESTERSHIRE v NOTTINGHAMSHIRE

Played at Worcester, July 25, 26, 27, 1951

Worcestershire won by nine wickets. This match not only produced the best batting performance of the season, but one of the most notable in the whole history of cricket. Worcestershire were set to score 131 in forty minutes – a task which many county sides would not have considered possible – and they responded with such a dynamic display that they hit off the runs with five minutes to spare. Kenyon struck a challenging note with his first scoring stroke, a hook for 6 off Farr, and he and Dews scored 54 runs in five overs. At the fall of Kenyon's wicket, Jenkins ran to the crease and in the subsequent assault on the bowlers he overtook Dews, making 47 runs in fifteen minutes. When the match had been won excited spectators dashed on to the field to congratulate the batsmen and also to applaud the sporting way in which Simpson, the Nottinghamshire captain, had made sure that no time was wasted in changing the field between overs.

Nottinghamshire

W. W. Keeton c Howorth b Perks	34	– b Perks	33
R. Giles c and b Jenkins	16	– st Yarnold b Howorth.	21
C. J. Poole c Bird b Jenkins.	62	– c Perks b Howorth	10
F. W. Stocks b Perks.	0	– c Yarnold b Flavell	6
R. T. Simpson c Kenyon b Perks	3	– lbw b Howorth	19
J. D. Clay c Yarnold b Jenkins	43	– c Outschoorn b Howorth	96
P. F. Harvey c Yarnold b Perks	5	– c Outschoorn b Jenkins	1
H. R. Cox c Broadbent b Perks.	64	– c and b Jenkins.	5
K. Smales b Perks.	16	– b Flavell	38
B. H. Farr not out.	32	– c Yarnold b Howorth	37
E. A. Meads c Yarnold b Perks.	9	– not out	2
B 4, l-b 11, n-b 1	16	B 2, l-b 5, w 1, n-b 4	12
	300		**280**

Worcestershire

D. J. Kenyon c Stocks b Farr	70	– b Smales	38
E. Cooper c Meads b Farr	3		
L. Outschoorn b Farr	106		
R. Broadbent b Harvey	54		
R. E. Bird c Meads b Farr	80		
G. Dews c Smales b Cox	12	– not out	43
R. O. Jenkins b Harvey	66	– not out	47
R. Howorth lbw b Smales	10		
H. Yarnold c Harvey b Farr	24		
R. T. D. Perks not out	15		
B 8, l-b 1, w 1	10	B 1, l-b 1, w 1	3
(9 wkts dec.) 450		**(1 wkt) 131**	

J. Flavell did not bat.

Worcestershire Bowling

	Overs	Mdns	Runs	Wkts	Overs	Mdns	Runs	Wkts
Perks	29	4	111	7	19	1	76	1
Flavell	13	1	67	—	14	2	50	2
Jenkins	36	8	89	3	42	8	100	2
Howorth	11	5	17	—	30	15	42	5

Nottinghamshire Bowling

	Overs	Mdns	Runs	Wkts	Overs	Mdns	Runs	Wkts
Farr	36	8	96	5	3	—	32	—
Cox	40	11	118	1	2	—	21	—
Harvey	40	12	110	2				
Smales	20	8	65	1	2	—	15	1
Stocks	12	7	23	—	3.1	1	41	—
Simpson	17	6	28	—	2	—	19	—

Umpires: K. McCanlis and A. E. Boulton-Carter.

WORCESTERSHIRE v DERBYSHIRE

Played at Stourbridge, July 23, 24, 1952

Derbyshire won by an innings and 57 runs. Gladwin, their in-swing bowler, was deadly on a pitch which had not been used for a county match for three years. Aided by brilliant catching in the leg-trap and also on the boundary, he took eleven wickets on the last day and returned the remarkable match figures of 16 wickets for 84 runs. His nine for 41 in the second innings was the best analysis of his career. Lobban, Worcestershire's new fast bowler from Jamaica, enjoyed success on the first day when, after taking the new ball with the total 201 for two, he sent back six men – five clean-bowled – in twelve overs. His effectiveness enhanced the value of Elliott's sound innings, which lasted three and three-quarter hours, but Worcestershire's hopes were soon dashed by the almost unplayable pace and swing of Gladwin, who took the first five wickets for 25 runs.

Derbyshire

C. S. Elliott c Richardson b Lobban 122	C. Gladwin b Lobban 4
A. Hamer lbw b Devereux 28	G. Dawkes not out 18
J. Kelly c Bird b Jenkins 30	L. Jackson b Lobban. 0
A. C. Revill b Lobban 25	
D. B. Carr c and b Perks 19	L-b 9, n-b 1 10
P. Vaulkhard b Lobban. 0	
D. C. Morgan b Lobban 3	1/51 2/142 3/207 4/220 5/220 274
A. E. G. Rhodes c and b Perks 15	6/232 7/247 8/254 9/254

Worcestershire

D. Kenyon c Morgan b Gladwin.	19	– b Gladwin	5
P. E. Richardson c Kelly b Gladwin	13	– c Morgan b Gladwin	20
L. Outschoorn hit wkt b Gladwin	6	– c Carr b Gladwin	11
R. E. Bird c Dawkes b Gladwin	1	– b Gladwin.	18
R. Broadbent c Morgan b Gladwin.	4	– c Hamer b Gladwin	12
N. H. Whiting c Morgan b Gladwin	0	– c Kelly b Gladwin.	4
R. O. Jenkins c Kelly b Rhodes.	9	– c Kelly b Gladwin.	12
L. N. Devereux c Hamer b Rhodes.	7	– c Hamer b Gladwin	12
H. Yarnold c Revill b Rhodes	19	– c and b Gladwin	0
R. T. D. Perks c Morgan b Gladwin	6	– c Carr b Rhodes	17
K. Lobban not out.	1	– not out	1
B 8, l-b 2, w 1	11	B 7, l-b 2.	9

1/19 2/35 3/36 4/45 5/52   96   1/17 2/37 3/38 4/69 5/70   121
6/63 7/65 8/83 9/93   6/88 7/88 8/91 9/120

Worcestershire Bowling

	Overs	Mdns	Runs	Wkts
Perks.	23	4	62	2
Lobban	14.3	2	52	6
Jenkins	27	8	78	1
Devereux	22	2	49	1
Whiting.	9	2	17	—
Bird.	3	—	6	—

Derbyshire Bowling

	Overs	Mdns	Runs	Wkts	Overs	Mdns	Runs	Wkts
Jackson.	7	1	17	—	3	—	5	—
Gladwin	18	3	43	7	22.4	8	41	9
Morgan.	1	—	2	—	2	—	9	—
Rhodes	11	4	23	3	22	9	57	1

Umpires: H. L. Parkin and W. F. Price.

WORCESTERSHIRE v SUSSEX

Played at Dudley, June 17, 18, 19, 1953

Worcestershire won by four wickets. Twice batting on drying turf, Sussex could do little with the leg-breaks and googlies of Jenkins, who took fifteen wickets for 122 runs. After scoring 70 without loss during the ninety-five minutes cricket possible on the first day, Sussex were all out for another 122. Worcestershire also found runs hard to get, but they took the lead with six wickets down and declared three ahead. Then Jenkins again wrought havoc until Sheppard in turn closed his innings. Worcestershire, left an hour and a half in which to score 166, won with six minutes to spare. Dews, promoted to open the innings, drove hard, hitting three 6s and seven 4s in eight-five minutes. Kenyon, who became the first player to complete 1,000 runs, helped put on 86 in forty-three minutes.

Sussex

D. S. Sheppard st Yarnold b Jenkins	53	– c Broadbent b Jenkins	41
John Langridge c Yarnold b Jenkins	30	– c Bird b Jenkins	42
G. Cox b Jenkins	0	– c Dews b Jenkins	20
C. Oakes c Devereux b Jenkins	7	– c Bird b Jenkins	3
J. M. Parks c Yarnold b Jenkins	32	– b Perks	11
K. G. Suttle lbw b Perks	5	– b Jenkins	8
A. S. Oakman b Jenkins	11	– b Jenkins	12
N. I. Thomson c Bird b Jenkins	0	– st Yarnold b Jenkins	16
A. E. James c Broadbent b Devereux	5	– not out	8
D. J. Wood c and b Jenkins	19	– b Devereux	4
R. T. Webb not out	26	– not out	0
L-b 3, w 1	4	B 3	3

1/81 2/81 3/84 4/99 5/104   192   1/76 2/99 3/106   (9 wkts dec.) 168
6/124 7/124 8/141 9/155   4/107 5/115 6/135 7/145
                                       8/158 9/165

Worcestershire

D. Kenyon b Oakman	53	– c and b Oakman	42
P. E. Richardson b James	16	– not out	9
R. G. Broadbent c Langridge b Thomson	48	– c Langridge b James	0
R. E. Bird b Thomson	34	– b James	0
G. Dews not out	16	– not out	89
J. R. Ashman c Parks b Thomson	0		
R. T. D. Perks c Cox b Oakman	0	– c Parks b Oakman	11
R. O. Jenkins not out	13	– st Webb b James	4
L. N. Devereux (did not bat)	–	c Webb b Oakman	10
B 3, l-b 12	15	L-b 2	2

1/52 2/88 3/160   (6 wkts dec.) 195   1/86 2/95 3/101   (6 wkts) 167
4/163 5/163 6/165   4/101 5/128 6/158

H. Yarnold and J. Flavell did not bat.

Worcestershire Bowling

	Overs	Mdns	Runs	Wkts	Overs	Mdns	Runs	Wkts
Perks	31	10	58	1	10	1	25	1
Flavell	6	1	12	—	3	1	11	—
Ashman	9	2	25	—	5	—	34	—
Devereux	13	5	31	1	13	3	35	1
Jenkins	28.3	7	62	8	22	2	60	7

Sussex Bowling

	Overs	Mdns	Runs	Wkts	Overs	Mdns	Runs	Wkts
Wood	7	1	19	—	3	—	20	—
Thomson	18	9	28	3	3	—	22	—
Oakman	33	14	61	2	11	—	62	3
James	34	14	57	1	10.4	1	61	3
Oakes	6	2	15	—				

Umpires: T. Spencer and A. E. Pothecary.

WORCESTERSHIRE v YORKSHIRE

Played at Worcester, August 26, 27, 28, 1953

Drawn. Fine batting by Lowson, who in nearly six hours hit his highest innings, made the first day notable. Firm driving and attractive cutting featured an innings including thirty-six 4s. Kenyon stayed in for the whole of the second day and for three-quarters of an hour the following morning, passing the previous best Worcestershire individual score against Yorkshire. With runs coming so freely a definite finish never appeared likely.

Yorkshire

L. Hutton lbw b Perks	4	– c Flavell b Ashman	72
F. A. Lowson not out	259	– b Devereux	39
J. V. Wilson b Devereux	34	– b Devereux	28
E. Lester c Yarnold b Flavell	4	– not out	88
R. Illingworth c Devereux b Flavell	41		
W. Watson lbw b Flavell	0	– not out	67
N. W. D. Yardley c Yarnold b Flavell	12		
R. Booth not out	53		
B 4, l-b 4, w 1, n-b 4	13	N-b 3	3

1/6 2/99 3/123   (6 wkts dec.) 420   1/57 2/121 3/161   (3 wkts dec.) 297
4/236 5/236 6/263

J. H. Wardle, C. W. Foord and W. E. N. Holdsworth did not bat.

Worcestershire

D. Kenyon not out	238	L. N. Devereux lbw b Wardle	51
P. E. Richardson b Foord	7	R. T. D. Perks b Wardle	14
J. R. Ashman b Foord	0	H. Yarnold not out	10
G. Dews b Foord	0	B 10, l-b 27, n-b 3	40
R. E. Bird c and b Wardle	16		
L. Outschoorn lbw b Wardle	38	1/12 2/13 3/12 4/33 (8 wkts dec.) 421	
R. G. Broadbent c and b Wardle	7	5/133 6/169 7/336 8/376	

J. Flavell did not bat.

Worcestershire Bowling

	Overs	Mdns	Runs	Wkts	Overs	Mdns	Runs	Wkts
Perks	31	7	83	1	18	6	47	—
Flavell	24	1	89	4	7	—	28	—
Outschoorn	11	2	32	—				
Devereux	32	6	105	1	22	4	75	2
Ashman	22	4	98	—	19	1	77	1
Richardson					8	1	39	—
Bird					5	1	11	—
Dews					2	—	13	—
Broadbent					2	1	4	—

Yorkshire Bowling

	Overs	Mdns	Runs	Wkts
Foord	21	3	80	3
Wardle	76	29	136	5
Illingworth	38	14	64	—
Holdsworth	21	2	76	—
Yardley	16	4	25	—

Umpires: A. E. Boulton-Carter and P. Corrall.

WORCESTERSHIRE v LEICESTERSHIRE

Played at Stourbridge, July 24, 25, 26, 1957

Worcestershire won by an innings and 73 runs. They established a commanding position almost from the start. Flavell took a wicket at four and when Horton came on to allow the fast bowler to change ends, his off-breaks proved so effective that the next four wickets fell to him in 17 balls at a cost of five runs. Then, after a shower, Coldwell, fast-medium, performed the first hat-trick of his career, and although Gardner batted resolutely, Leicestershire could not recover. They collapsed again after Dews, who hit seventeen 4s in his first century of the summer, Broadbent and Horton helped Worcestershire to a lead of 210. On a drying pitch, Horton conceded only 37 runs in 42.4 overs, 24 of them maidens, and took five wickets. He finished with match figures of nine wickets for 48 runs.

Leicestershire

G. Lester lbw b Flavell	4	– b Jenkins	46
M. R. Hallam b Horton	6	– st Booth b Jenkins	41
J. van Geloven st Booth b Horton	6	– c Outschoorn b Horton	2
C. H. Palmer c Outschoorn b Horton	0	– b Flavell	6
L. R. Gardner c Flavell b Coldwell	50	– st Booth b Jenkins	3
V. S. Munden c Dews b Horton	2	– not out	21
J. Firth lbw b Coldwell	13	– c Lester b Jenkins	0
J. Savage c Booth b Coldwell	0	– b Horton	0
R. Smith c Booth b Coldwell	0	– c Outschoorn b Horton	13
C. T. Spencer b Coldwell	6	– c Coldwell b Horton	0
B. Boshier not out	0	– b Horton	0
B 1, l-b 2	3	B 1, w 4	5

1/4 2/12 3/12 4/21 5/29   90   1/76 2/81 3/92 4/97 5/110   137
6/55 7/55 8/55 9/89   6/110 7/110 8/129 9/129

Worcestershire

D. Kenyon b Savage	15	J. Lister c Munden b van Geloven	7
L. Outschoorn b Spencer	5	J. Flavell not out	5
G. Dews c Palmer b Savage	115	B 1, l-b 2	3
R. G. Broadbent c Firth b Spencer	66		
M. J. Horton not out	70	1/7 2/27 3/173 (6 wkts dec.) 300
R. Booth c Firth b Munden	14	4/234 5/265 6/288

R. Berry, R. O. Jenkins and L. Coldwell did not bat.

Worcestershire Bowling

	Overs	Mdns	Runs	Wkts	Overs	Mdns	Runs	Wkts
Flavell	14	1	58	1	10	2	19	1
Coldwell	11.5	5	18	5	4	1	7	—
Horton	12	8	11	4	42.4	24	37	5
Berry	1	1	—	—	4	2	7	—
Jenkins					35	11	62	4

Leicestershire Bowling

	Overs	Mdns	Runs	Wkts
Spencer	21	—	64	2
Boshier	17	4	41	—
Savage	30	9	75	2
Smith	29	14	59	—
Palmer	7	1	22	—
Munden	10	5	20	1
van Geloven	4	—	16	1

Umpires: John Langridge and H. G. Baldwin.

WORCESTERSHIRE v YORKSHIRE

Played at Worcester, July 27, 29, 30, 1957

Yorkshire won by seven wickets. When the last day commenced with Yorkshire only 56 ahead on first innings with three wickets left, there seemed little to suggest the victory ahead. Success was made possible by the accurate off-spin of Illingworth, who utilised a spot on otherwise placid turf. He took nine wickets for 42 runs, his best performance, and Yorkshire, left to score 67 in an hour, won with seven minutes to spare. The previous day Illingworth showed excellent batting form. Watson, much less enterprising, took more than three and a half hours over 80.

Worcestershire

D. Kenyon b Illingworth	47	– b Illingworth ... 28
L. Outschoorn b Illingworth	32	– lbw b Illingworth. ... 60
G. Dews c Taylor b Appleyard	21	– lbw b Illingworth. ... 6
D. W. Richardson st Binks b Wardle	20	– st Binks b Wardle ... 13
R. G. Broadbent b Pickles	14	– c Stott b Illingworth ... 16
M. J. Horton c Binks b Wardle	38	– c Close b Illingworth. ... 12
R. Booth st Binks b Appleyard	2	– b Illingworth ... 11
R. O. Jenkins b Appleyard	26	– not out ... 7
R. Berry b Illingworth	12	– c Wilson b Illingworth ... 8
J. Flavell c and b Pickles	3	– st Binks b Illingworth ... 0
L. Coldwell not out	0	– c Stott b Illingworth ... 1
B 9, l-b 6, n-b 7	22	B 9, l-b 1 ... 10

1/72 2/85 3/128 4/128 5/172   237   1/57 2/71 3/107 4/127 5/132   172
6/179 7/189 8/206 9/217   6/147 7/154 8/168 9/168

Yorkshire

W. B. Stott c Jenkins b Flavell	21	– b Berry ... 5
K. Taylor c Richardson b Berry	27	– lbw b Berry ... 8
J. V. Wilson c Booth b Horton	38	– c Jenkins b Coldwell ... 1
D. B. Close b Jenkins	38	– not out ... 41
W. Watson c and b Jenkins	80	– not out ... 9
R. Illingworth c Broadbent b Richardson	58	
W. H. H. Sutcliffe lbw b Berry	27	
J. H. Wardle b Coldwell	1	
J. G. Binks st Booth b Jenkins	19	
R. Appleyard c Berry b Jenkins	23	
D. Pickles not out	0	
B 2, l-b 4, w 4, n-b 1	11	L-b 3, n-b 1 ... 4

1/25 2/79 3/91 4/133 5/223   343   1/13 2/14 3/18   (3 wkts) 68
6/291 7/292 8/317 9/330

Yorkshire Bowling

	Overs	Mdns	Runs	Wkts	Overs	Mdns	Runs	Wkts
Pickles	14	2	35	2	4	—	25	—
Appleyard	23	5	63	3	3	—	18	—
Illingworth	23	10	49	3	32	15	42	9
Close	10	1	34	—	6	2	26	—
Wardle	24	14	34	2	31	16	51	1

Worcestershire Bowling

	Overs	Mdns	Runs	Wkts	Overs	Mdns	Runs	Wkts
Flavell............	11	3	31	1				
Coldwell..........	27	7	73	1	8	1	21	1
Berry.............	23	3	73	2	7.5	—	43	2
Horton	23	12	57	1				
Jenkins	16.4	3	68	4				
Richardson........	8	1	30	1				

Umpires: P. A. Gibb and T. J. Bartley.

WORCESTERSHIRE v SUSSEX

Played at Worcester, August 24, 26, 27, 1957

Drawn. Parks, released from his duties as twelfth man in the Test, hit a century in each innings for the first time. His second hundred, which took only two and a half hours, came at an opportune time, for Sussex were 76 for five and only 78 runs on. Parks hit fourteen 4s in his first innings, during which he retired hurt after being struck on the knee. Suttle, who helped to add 110 runs in ninety minutes for the seventh wicket, also reached three figures. So did Kenyon, of Worcestershire, who completed 2,000 runs for the seventh time in ten years. He spent two and a half hours over his first 50, reached 100 in another forty-five minutes and then occupied over an hour in adding 19. Despite a last wicket stand of 42, Worcestershire failed to gain the lead by three runs. Flavell, their fast bowler, took eleven wickets for 155 runs in the match.

Sussex

D. V. Smith c Booth b Flavell...................	12	– c Booth b Flavell..............	6
L. J. Lenham b Jenkins.......................	51	– lbw b Flavell..................	6
K. G. Suttle c and b Flavell...................103		– c Booth b Flavell................	25
J. M. Parks lbw b Flavell.....................101		– not out 100	
G. H. G. Doggart b Jenkins	9	– c Booth b Coldwell...........	9
Nawab of Pataudi b Flavell...................	0	– c Kenyon b Flavell...........	23
R. T. Webb b Jenkins	0	– not out	14
N. I. Thomson b Flavell	7		
A. E. James b Flavell........................	0	– b Flavell.....................	4
R. G. Marlar c Flavell b Jenkins	20		
D. L. Bates not out	2		
B 1, l-b 5, w 1	7	B 1, l-b 2...............	3

1/42 2/82 3/114 4/115 5/116   312   1/7 2/20 3/32   (6 wkts dec.) 190
6/133 7/243 8/243 9/309   4/49 5/76 6/143

Worcestershire

D. Kenyon c Doggart b Thomson. 119	– not out	29
L. Outschoorn c Nawab of Pataudi b Bates 0	– b Bates	0
G. Dews c Doggart b Bates. 30	– c and b Bates	24
D. W. Richardson st Webb b Smith 22	– not out	6
R. G. Broadbent st Webb b Marlar. 27		
M. J. Horton c Doggart b Bates 43		
R. Booth b Bates. 6		
R. O. Jenkins c Webb b Bates. 2		
R. Berry not out 26		
J. Flavell b Bates. 9		
L. Coldwell run out. 10		
B 4, l-b 11, n-b 1 16	L-b 4.	4

1/2 2/52 3/103 4/185 5/218   310   1/3 2/47   (2 wkts) 63
6/243 7/249 8/256 9/268

Worcestershire Bowling

	Overs	Mdns	Runs	Wkts	Overs	Mdns	Runs	Wkts
Flavell.	28	5	68	6	24	2	87	5
Coldwell	15	2	70	—	24	5	63	1
Jenkins	30	4	103	4	2	—	12	—
Berry.	15	5	40	—	4.2	—	25	—
Horton	6	1	24	—				

Sussex Bowling

	Overs	Mdns	Runs	Wkts	Overs	Mdns	Runs	Wkts
Thomson	24	6	49	1	6	—	27	—
Bates.	30	8	99	6	9	1	18	2
Smith	14	6	26	1				
Marlar	29.2	12	72	1	1	—	3	—
Suttle	12	2	32	—				
Parks	1	—	1	—				
James	7	5	15	—				
Lenham					2	—	11	—

Umpires: A. Skelding and D. Davies.

WORCESTERSHIRE v DERBYSHIRE

Played at Kidderminster, June 14, 16, 17, 1958

Worcestershire won by nine wickets. Derbyshire began well with an opening stand of 91 followed by free hitting from Morgan who, in for nearly three hours, registered ten 4s. Then the bowlers took command, the last five wickets falling for 77 runs. For Worcestershire, Outschoorn (one 6, fifteen 4s) hit his first century of the season, he and Horton (one 6, thirteen 4s) adding 131 runs. Only nine runs were needed for the lead at the fall of the third wicket but, with the help of three catches at the wicket, Jackson achieved the hat-trick and four wickets went down for six runs. So Worcestershire's lead was restricted to 76. A Derbyshire collapse against the fast bowling of Flavell followed, and Worcestershire needed no more than 42 to win.

Derbyshire

A. Hamer c P. Richardson b Berry	69	– c Morris b Flavell		12
C. Lee c Morris b Coldwell	34	– c Berry b Flavell		11
J. Kelly c Broadbent b Pearson	9	– c Horton b Flavell		8
D. C. Morgan c Pearson b Berry	91	– c Morris b Coldwell		40
D. B. Carr run out	1	– b Flavell		1
H. L. Johnson c Morris b Berry	5	– c Morris b Flavell		6
G. O. Dawkes c Morris b Flavell	13	– lbw b Flavell		6
H. J. Rhodes b Flavell	14	– run out		1
E. Smith c Broadbent b Berry	1	– b Flavell		2
C. Gladwin lbw b Flavell	0	– c Morris b Coldwell		14
H. L. Jackson not out	0	– not out		2
B 2, l-b 6, n-b 2	10	B 8, l-b 5, n-b 1		14

1/91 2/105 3/131 4/143 5/170   247   1/14 2/23 3/50 4/64 5/88   117
6/197 7/246 8/246 9/247   6/88 7/89 8/94 9/105

Worcestershire

P. E. Richardson lbw b Jackson	24	– c Morgan b Rhodes		2
L. Outschoorn run out	113	– not out		16
M. J. Horton c Morgan b Rhodes	91	– not out		20
D. W. Richardson c Carr b Jackson	9			
R. G. Broadbent c Dawkes b Jackson	5			
G. Dews not out	45			
R. Morris c Dawkes b Jackson	0			
D. B. Pearson c Dawkes b Jackson	0			
R. Berry b Rhodes	14			
L. N. Coldwell c Dawkes b Rhodes	0			
J. Flavell c Hamer b Smith	17			
N-b 5	5	L-b 4		4

1/71 2/202 3/239 4/239 5/245   323   1/3   (1 wkt) 42
6/245 7/245 8/283 9/291

Worcestershire Bowling

	Overs	Mdns	Runs	Wkts	Overs	Mdns	Runs	Wkts
Pearson	11	1	48	1	5	1	12	—
Flavell	16	2	40	3	21	5	43	7
Coldwell	29	6	57	1	12.5	1	29	2
Berry	41.5	17	66	4	6	4	14	—
Horton	8	3	26	—	5	2	5	—

Derbyshire Bowling

	Overs	Mdns	Runs	Wkts	Overs	Mdns	Runs	Wkts
Jackson	31	10	53	5	5	1	14	—
Gladwin	19	5	85	—				
Rhodes	26	2	74	3	5	—	23	1
Carr	4	—	25	—				
Smith	14.3	3	51	1				
Morgan	10	3	30	—				
Johnson					0.1	—	1	—

Umpires: J. F. Crapp and J. B. Bowes.

WORCESTERSHIRE v GLOUCESTERSHIRE

Played at Worcester, May 25, 26, 27, 1960

Gloucestershire won by 31 runs. Throughout batsmen were tied down by an accurate attack on a pitch that gave bowlers little encouragement. First Smith, the Gloucestershire pace man, and then Slade of Worcestershire with left-arm slows, brought indiscretions by their nagging accuracy and though Worcestershire, left four hours twenty minutes to score 214 to win, looked to have ample time, the earlier cricket suggested that they had a hard fight ahead. So it proved and despite a sound stand of 65 between Dews and Booth after five wickets fell for 35, they were beaten with fifteen minutes left for play. Gloucestershire thus gained their first victory of the season to celebrate the birth of a son to their captain, Graveney, earlier in the day.

Gloucestershire

D. M. Young c Spencer b Slade	45	– c Headley b Pearson	29
C. T. M. Pugh b Flavell	0	– lbw b Slade	28
*T. W. Graveney c Spencer b Aldridge	35	– c Slade b Aldridge	11
R. B. Nicholls c Booth b Pearson	29	– c Booth b Slade	15
C. A. Milton b Slade	14	– not out	64
D. A. Allen c Booth b Flavell	1	– b Aldridge	12
J. B. Mortimore c Booth b Slade	25	– lbw b Flavell	3
A. S. Brown b Slade	11	– c Booth b Aldridge	0
D. R. Smith c Headley b Pearson	26	– c Booth b Flavell	7
†B. J. Meyer c Kenyon b Flavell	11	– c Booth b Pearson	1
C. Cook not out	14	– absent ill	0
L-b 2, n-b 1	3	L-b 5, n-b 1	6

1/3 2/79 3/81 4/82 5/102   214   1/62 2/68 3/90 4/113 5/135   176
6/130 7/157 8/159 9/198   6/149 7/152 8/171 9/176

Worcestershire

*D. Kenyon c Brown b Smith	3	– c Meyer b Mortimore	22
R. G. A. Headley run out	41	– b Brown	0
D. W. Richardson c Allen b Smith	64	– c Meyer b Smith	0
D. N. F. Slade b Mortimore	13	– lbw b Mortimore	8
A. H. Spencer c Milton b Mortimore	19	– c Milton b Smith	6
G. Dews c Meyer b Smith	19	– c Meyer b Mortimore	53
J. B. Sedgley c Meyer b Smith	1	– b Mortimore	3
†R. Booth c Meyer b Smith	0	– c Nicholls b Brown	64
D. B. Pearson b Smith	4	– c Meyer b Brown	11
K. J. Aldridge not out	5	– c and b Brown	1
J. Flavell c Meyer b Brown	1	– not out	11
L-b 7	7	B 1, l-b 2	3

1/9 2/100 3/126 4/134 5/155   177   1/1 2/2 3/29 4/29 5/35   182
6/162 7/162 8/171 9/174   6/100 7/116 8/161 9/165

Worcestershire Bowling

	Overs	Mdns	Runs	Wkts	Overs	Mdns	Runs	Wkts
Flavell	20.2	8	38	3	25	8	45	2
Aldridge	18	4	61	1	25	8	41	3
Pearson	18	3	53	2	17.1	7	39	2
Slade	26	12	59	4	34	18	45	2

Gloucestershire Bowling

	Overs	Mdns	Runs	Wkts	Overs	Mdns	Runs	Wkts
Brown...........	29	11	52	1	17.3	4	45	4
Smith ...:......	30	7	71	6	19	8	24	2
Mortimore	27	13	42	2	30	13	48	4
Cook.............	3	1	5	—				
Nicholls					1	1	—	—
Graveney					17	1	62	—

Umpires: N. Oldfield and L. H. Gray.

WORCESTERSHIRE v CAMBRIDGE UNIVERSITY

Played at Worcester, June 25, 27, 1960

Worcestershire won by an innings and eight runs. Gifford, a 21-year-old Lancashire-born left-arm slow bowler playing in only his second match, took ten wickets for 59 runs and looked a useful batsman while scoring 35. Sent in on a turning pitch, Cambridge collapsed after scoring 67 for two during the morning. Their remaining eight wickets fell for 69 runs, Gifford taking four for 20 in twelve overs during this period. With the off-spinner, Hurd, dismissing five of the first six batsmen for 28 runs, Worcestershire were in trouble, too, until Richardson, hooking and driving well, raced to 50 in sixty-five minutes with the help of eleven 4s. On Monday, Gifford faced the new ball confidently for an hour and later again showed the limitations of the Cambridge batsmen on a pitch taking spin. With persistent accuracy he took six wickets for 18 runs.

Cambridge University

R. M. Prideaux b Horton	30	– run out	17
A. R. Lewis b Rumsey	9	– lbw b Gifford	19
M. J. L. Willard c Broadbent b Standen	31	– b Rumsey	12
D. Kirby b Aldridge	10	– b Gifford	13
J. R. Bernard c Horton b Aldridge	12	– c Headley b Aldridge	8
G. Atkins b Gifford	15	– c Booth b Aldridge	5
E. M. Rose c Booth b Standen	0	– c Broadbent b Gifford	7
*†C. B. Howland c Standen b Gifford	10	– b Gifford	16
J. B. Brodie c Headley b Gifford	3	– c Davies b Gifford	7
S. Douglas-Pennant not out	4	– not out	4
A. Hurd c Headley b Gifford	8	– c Broadbent b Gifford	0
B 4	4	B 4, l-b 4	8

1/12 2/60 3/80 4/83 5/102   136   1/33 2/33 3/42 4/48 5/66   116
6/102 7/119 8/123 9/127   6/71 7/90 8/105 9/116

Worcestershire

*D. Kenyon b Hurd	38
M. J. Horton c Prideaux b Douglas-Pennant	3
R. G. A. Headley c Rose b Hurd	20
D. W. Richardson c Lewis b Brodie	57
R. G. Broadbent c Kirby b Hurd	0
T. E. Davies c Prideaux b Hurd	6
J. A. Standen b Hurd	2
†R. Booth c Lewis b Willard	48
F. E. Rumsey c Prideaux b Douglas-Pennant	28
N. Gifford c Brodie b Willard	35
K. J. Aldridge not out	3
B 16, l-b 1, w 1, n-b 2	20

1/6 2/59 3/106 4/106 5/116   260
6/124 7/154 8/203 9/247

Worcestershire Bowling

	Overs	Mdns	Runs	Wkts	Overs	Mdns	Runs	Wkts
Aldridge	16	7	16	2	10	—	39	2
Rumsey	8	1	22	1	9	3	12	1
Gifford	21.5	8	41	4	15.5	7	18	6
Horton	17	6	34	1	12	5	20	—
Standen.	10	4	19	2	11	5	19	—

Cambridge University Bowling

	Overs	Mdns	Runs	Wkts
Brodie.	23	5	66	1
Douglas-Pennant . . .	14	5	26	2
Hurd.	40	18	91	5
Bernard.	4	—	21	—
Kirby	16	8	22	—
Willard	5.4	3	14	2

Umpires: W. H. Copson and R. Aspinall.

WORCESTERSHIRE v GLAMORGAN

Played at Stourbridge, June 29, 30, July 1, 1960

Worcestershire won by seven wickets. Parkhouse, captain of Glamorgan, batted pluckily with a swollen finger following a blow in the previous match. He hit eleven 4s playing many strokes one-handed before he retired with 80 and went for an X-ray. This having revealed no fracture, he returned and added another boundary towards Glamorgan's 255. A. Jones (one 6 and eleven 4s) and Parkhouse added 139 runs. Worcestershire lost three wickets for 50 runs and would have been four for 50 had J. Jones held on to a catch at long-leg. Having thus escaped, Kenyon went on to hit 201 (one 6 and thirty-one 4s) in just under five hours and with Dews put on 187 for the sixth wicket. Because of the injury to Parkhouse, Walker opened for Glamorgan when they went in 100 behind and with 68 (one 6 and eleven 4s) out of 81 scored in an hour, helped to improve the position. Parkhouse also stayed for ninety minutes before he became one of six batsmen caught by Broadbent, but insufficient runs were scored to leave Worcestershire a task of any consequence.

Glamorgan

*W. G. A. Parkhouse b Flavell	84	– c Broadbent b Slade	22
B. Hedges c Aldridge b Flavell	1	– b Rumšey	10
A. Jones b Rumsey	72	– c Broadbent b Flavell	1
P. M. Walker c Booth b Horton	5	– c Kenyon b Rumsey	68
A. J. Watkins c Booth b Aldridge	32	– c Broadbent b Slade	16
A. Rees c Broadbent b Flavell.	13	– c Broadbent b Horton.	14
J. E. McConnon lbw b Aldridge	26	– c Kenyon b Horton.	44
J. B. Evans b Flavell	2	– c Broadbent b Slade	0
†W. Whitehill c Booth b Aldridge.	6	– c Broadbent b Flavell	3
J. Jones b Flavell	0	– not out	0
D. J. Shepherd not out.	0	– lbw b Horton	28
B 4, l-b 10	14		

1/9 2/164 3/172 4/217 5/217   255   1/50 2/75 3/81 4/103 5/111   206
6/227 7/238 8/243 9/255   6/115 7/168 8/169 9/199

Worcestershire

*D. Kenyon c A. Jones b Walker	201	– c Whitehill b McConnon	26
M. J. Horton b J. Jones	1	– c Whitehill b J. Jones	15
R. G. A. Headley b J. Jones	2	– not out	37
D. N. F. Slade c Walker b J. Jones	21		
D. W. Richardson c Parkhouse b Evans	35	– c Whitehill b Shepherd	19
R. G. Broadbent c A. Jones b Evans	1	– not out	7
G. Dews not out	85		
†R. Booth not out	6		
B 1, l-b 2	3	B 2, l-b 1	3

1/2 2/16 3/50   (6 wkts dec.) 355   1/19 2/51 3/84   (3 wkts) 107
4/134 5/144 6/331

F. E. Rumsey, K. J. Aldridge and J. Flavell did not bat.

Worcestershire Bowling

	Overs	Mdns	Runs	Wkts	Overs	Mdns	Runs	Wkts
Flavell	21	7	37	5	18	4	58	2
Aldridge	26.5	3	92	3	9	—	42	—
Rumsey	16	1	44	1	13	4	22	2
Slade	15	7	31	—	14	6	40	3
Horton	15	6	37	1	23.1	8	44	3

Glamorgan Bowling

	Overs	Mdns	Runs	Wkts	Overs	Mdns	Runs	Wkts
Evans	29	4	111	2	6	1	25	—
J. Jones	26	2	102	3	8	3	17	1
Walker	13	2	46	1	7	2	19	—
Shepherd	18	3	66	—	5.1	—	15	1
Watkins	6	1	27	—				
McConnon					9	3	22	1
Hedges					1	—	6	—

Umpires: R. Aspinall and J. F. Crapp.

WORCESTERSHIRE v MIDDLESEX

Played at Worcester, August 20, 22, 23, 1960

Middlesex won by ten wickets. They gave a sound all-round display and retained the initiative throughout after W. E. Russell (fourteen 4s) and Gale set them off with an opening stand of 105 in the same number of minutes. Worcestershire were soon in trouble against the fast bowling of Warr, who had a cross-wind to help his swing. He took the first six wickets for 17 runs. Then Titmus with off-spin claimed three for eight and he again caused trouble when Worcestershire followed-on 263 behind. During the course of the second day he bowled 66 overs and taking eight wickets for 84 completed his fifth double in six seasons. Altogether he took eleven for 97 in the match.

Middlesex

W. E. Russell c Richardson b Gifford	89	– not out	2
R. A. Gale b Slade	46	– not out	26
S. E. Russell c Slade b Gifford	30		
P. H. Parfitt c Gifford b Coldwell	30		
F. J. Titmus st Booth b Gifford	4		
†J. T. Murray c and b Horton	39		
D. Bennett not out	73		
T. W. Higginson b Slade	0		
R. W. Hooker run out	5		
C. D. Drybrough c Slade b Flavell	4		
B 3, l-b 2	5		

1/105 2/161 3/170   (9 wkts dec.) 325   (No wkt) 28
4/186 5/211 6/270 7/281
8/293 9/325

*J. J. Warr did not bat.

Worcestershire

*D. Kenyon b Warr	4	– b Titmus	35
M. J. Horton b Warr	1	– c Murray b Titmus	73
N. Gifford b Warr	6	– not out	2
D. N. F. Slade c Murray b Warr	10	– c Hooker b Titmus	38
R. G. A. Headley lbw b Titmus	21	– b Titmus	51
D. W. Richardson c Gale b Warr	4	– lbw b Titmus	9
G. Dews lbw b Warr	2	– st Murray b Gale	27
A. H. Spencer b Titmus	4	– b Titmus	6
†R. Booth c Higginson b Drybrough	2	– c Hooker b Drybrough	26
L. J. Coldwell c Gale b Titmus	6	– c Drybrough b Titmus	3
J. Flavell not out	0	– c Gale b Titmus	4
L-b 2	2	B 11, l-b 3, w 1	15

1/5 2/6 3/13 4/24 5/38   62   1/68 2/131 3/155 4/182 5/204   289
6/40 7/54 8/55 9/61   6/204 7/276 8/276 9/283

Worcestershire Bowling

	Overs	Mdns	Runs	Wkts	Overs	Mdns	Runs	Wkts
Flavell	24.5	4	75	1				
Coldwell	17	3	55	1				
Slade	44	18	79	2				
Horton	23	9	60	1	5	—	22	—
Gifford	20	7	51	3	5	4	2	—
Kenyon					0.1	—	4	—

Middlesex Bowling

	Overs	Mdns	Runs	Wkts	Overs	Mdns	Runs	Wkts
Warr	13	7	17	6	7	2	21	—
Bennett	8	2	21	—	5	1	15	—
Titmus	12	8	8	3	65.2	31	89	8
Hooker	1	—	8	—				
Drybrough	6.3	4	6	1	40	16	75	1
Gale					26	10	46	1
Parfitt					3	—	10	—
W. Russell					9	3	18	—

Umpires: T. J. Bartley and R. S. Lay.

WORCESTERSHIRE v YORKSHIRE

Played at Worcester, September 3, 5, 6, 1960

Drawn, no decision. With Yorkshire already Champions nothing was at stake and with cricket limited to just over half the playing time of the second day, this was just as well. Yorkshire were trapped on a drying pitch when sent in, but D. Wilson in a bright display hit one 6 and six 4s in helping to boost a meagre total. When Booth stumped Close he had taken a hand in 100 dismissals during the season, a feat accomplished previously for Worcestershire only by Yarnold, an umpire in this match. Worcestershire, favoured by better conditions, were within 45 runs of the lead with six wickets left when rain prevented further play.

Yorkshire

W. B. Stott b Horton	18	F. S. Trueman c Davies b Rumsey	17
J. B. Bolus b Slade	3	†J. G. Binks c Rumsey b Flavell	1
D. E. V. Padgett st Booth b Slade	1	M. J. Cowan not out	0
D. B. Close st Booth b Gifford	19		
P. J. Sharpe b Slade	4	B 3, l-b 2	5
R. Illingworth lbw b Horton	6		
*J. V. Wilson c Booth b Gifford	6	1/14 2/22 3/24 4/39 5/47	125
D. Wilson b Flavell	45	6/55 7/95 8/122 9/124	

Worcestershire

*D. Kenyon c and b Illingworth	31	N. Gifford not out	0
M. J. Horton c Close b Illingworth	7	L-b 1	1
R. G. A. Headley c Padgett b D. Wilson	28		
D. W. Richardson c Cowan b Close	14	1/28 2/51 3/76 4/81 (4 wkts)	81

G. Dews, T. Davies, †R. Booth, D. N. F. Slade, F. E. Rumsey and J. Flavell did not bat.

Worcestershire Bowling

	Overs	Mdns	Runs	Wkts
Flavell	7.2	3	11	2
Rumsey	9	1	23	1
Slade	24	14	27	3
Horton	15	7	28	2
Gifford	18	9	31	2

Yorkshire Bowling

	Overs	Mdns	Runs	Wkts
Trueman	5	2	16	—
Cowan	3	1	7	—
Illingworth	18	8	26	2
D. Wilson	14.3	7	27	1
Close	3	2	4	1

Umpires: A. Jepson and H. Yarnold.

WORCESTERSHIRE v YORKSHIRE

Played at Worcester, June 3, 5, 6, 1961

Yorkshire won by one wicket. Spectators at this casualty-stricken match will long remember the plucky effort of Don Wilson. The end of Yorkshire's unbeaten record in the championship looked imminent when nine wickets tumbled to a combination of pace and spin with 36 runs still required. Then Wilson, with his left arm in plaster from the elbow to the knuckles because of a fractured thumb, joined Platt with twenty-five minutes to play. Though the pain quickly prompted him to bat one-handed, Wilson swept Gifford twice for 4 and when Flavell took the new ball five minutes from the end with 22 runs still needed, he immediately struck three boundaries and a two with one-handed drives. This over also brought four byes. Then Platt took a single off Coldwell and the crowd rose to cheer when Wilson straight drove to the boundary to complete a thrilling finish. He hit 29 in a last-wicket stand of 37.

Yorkshire had to fight hard all the time in face of some excellent bowling. They lost half their side for 136 in the first innings, at which point Trueman helped them recover by hitting eight 4s while scoring 43 in a stand of 50 with his captain. Later when left to score 190 for victory they were 86 for seven before Illingworth, pressed into service though not fully fit, and Binks added 60 in fifty-five minutes as a prelude to Wilson's game effort. Worcestershire had their casualties, too. Kenyon went for an X-ray after being struck on the left wrist by a ball from Trueman and Broadbent was reduced to a hobble by a pulled hamstring.

Worcestershire

*D. Kenyon c J. V. Wilson b Trueman	30	– c J. V. Wilson b Bainbridge	34
M. J. Horton b Platt	13	– c Binks b Trueman	6
R. G. A. Headley st Binks b Close	61	– c Binks b Trueman	49
D. W. Richardson c Close b Illingworth	23	– c sub b Close	5
G. Dews c Stott b Illingworth	47	– b Bainbridge	14
R. G. Broadbent b Illingworth	5	– b Trueman	4
†R. Booth lbw b Illingworth	6	– run out	31
J. A. Standen b Close	0	– b Bainbridge	23
N. Gifford not out	6	– not out	12
L. J. Coldwell c and b Close	4	– b Trueman	25
J. A. Flavell c J. V. Wilson b Close	2	– c Padgett b Platt	1
B 14, l-b 8, w 5, n-b 3	30	B 11, l-b 1, n-b 1	13

1/44 2/48 3/106 4/155 5/192   227   1/19 2/58 3/109 4/127 5/166   227
6/209 7/211 8/211 9/219   6/166 7/173 8/174 9/205

Yorkshire

W. B. Stott c Dews b Horton	46	– c Standen b Flavell	5
J. B. Bolus c Standen b Gifford	54	– b Coldwell	5
D. E. V. Padgett c Booth b Horton	6	– c sub b Flavell	7
D. B. Close c sub b Horton	11	– c sub b Flavell	15
R. Illingworth c Headley b Horton	5	– lbw b Coldwell	42
*J. V. Wilson run out	49	– lbw b Horton	16
F. S. Trueman b Coldwell	43	– c Flavell b Gifford	7
A. B. Bainbridge c Standen b Horton	24	– b Horton	0
†J. G. Binks c Richardson b Flavell	19	– b Flavell	46
R. K. Platt not out	0	– not out	7
D. Wilson (did not bat)	–	– not out	29
B 4, l-b 4	8	B 8, l-b 4	12

1/100 2/108 3/119 4/119   (9 wkts dec.) 265   1/6 2/14 3/32 4/36   (9 wkts) 191
5/136 6/186 7/224 8/257 9/257   5/75 6/86 7/86 8/146 9/154

Yorkshire Bowling

	Overs	Mdns	Runs	Wkts	Overs	Mdns	Runs	Wkts
Trueman	14	4	33	1	27	9	50	4
Platt	15	5	43	1	17.3	6	43	1
Illingworth	29	13	47	4				
D. Wilson	2	1	13	—				
Bainbridge	18	8	34	—	31	16	52	3
Close	9.1	3	27	4	14	4	69	1

Worcestershire Bowling

	Overs	Mdns	Runs	Wkts	Overs	Mdns	Runs	Wkts
Flavell...........	16	4	38	1	24	10	45	4
Coldwell.........	10	4	22	1	10.4	7	17	2
Gifford	40	18	74	1	34	15	80	1
Horton	44	18	110	5	19	7	37	2
Standen..........	5	1	13	—				

Umpires: T. W. Spencer and F. Jakeman.

WORCESTERSHIRE v OXFORD UNIVERSITY

Played at Worcester, June 21, 22, 1961

Worcestershire won by an innings and nine runs, completing the match half an hour before lunch on the second day. The University batsmen had no answer to Flavell and Carter, who made his county début after giving up a school teaching appointment in York for a summer cricket engagement. Flavell, moving the ball back sharply off the seam, hit the wicket four times in taking seven for 26 as Oxford were shot out for 68. Then Dews, captain in the absence of Kenyon, hit one 6 and thirteen 4s in helping Worcestershire lead by 105 before declaring. Next Carter obtained an unusual amount of life out of the pitch with his fast-medium bowling. He took four of the first five wickets at a cost of eight runs. Only three Oxford batsmen reached double figures in the two innings, and seven fell without scoring.

Oxford

D. R. Worlsey lbw b Flavell	5	– c Richardson b Carter	1
D. B. Pithey c Horton b Flavell................	44	– c Elliott b Flavell...............	6
A. A. Baig b Flavell.........................	2	– c Dews b Carter	7
D. M. Green c Davies b Standen................	2	– b Carter	0
C. A. Fry b Standen	3	– c Elliott b Carter..............	1
*C. D. Drybrough c Horton b Flavell...........	0	– c Sedgley b Horton...........	56
†R. H. C. Waters b Flavell	0	– c Richardson b Gifford...........	10
A. R. Duff not out..........................	8	– b Horton.....................	4
I. C. Potter b Flavell	0	– not out	5
T. R. Jakobsen c Horton b Standen	0	– c Richardson b Horton..........	0
E. W. Anderson b Flavell	0	– b Gifford....................	2
L-b 3, n-b 1	4	L-b 3, w 1..............	4

1/12 2/33 3/40 4/50 5/51   68   1/7 2/7 3/8 4/10 5/23   96
6/51 7/60 8/60 9/61   6/79 7/85 8/89 9/89

Worcestershire

J. B. Sedgley c Duff b Jakobsen	11	J. W. Elliott not out....................	18
M. J. Horton c Worsley b Potter..........	1		
R. G. A. Headley c Drybrough b Green	17	L-b 5	5
D. W. Richardson b Green	35		
T. E. Davies c Pithey b Anderson........	6	1/16 2/20 3/68 (5 wkts dec.) 173	
*G. Dews not out	80	4/73 5/99	

J. A. Standen, N. Gifford, J. A. Flavell and R. G. M. Carter did not bat.

680 *Wisden Anthology 1940-1963*

Worcestershire Bowling

	Overs	Mdns	Runs	Wkts	Overs	Mdns	Runs	Wkts
Flavell	15.5	6	26	7	18	7	36	1
Carter	5	1	23	—	17	4	46	4
Standen	10	2	15	3				
Gifford					9.5	9	2	2
Horton					5	2	8	3

Oxford University Bowling

	Overs	Mdns	Runs	Wkts
Jakobsen	16	2	42	1
Potter	19	7	29	1
Drybrough	5	3	17	—
Green	15	4	34	2
Anderson	13	8	21	1
Pithey	4	1	25	—

Umpires: J. S. Buller and H. Yarnold.

WORCESTERSHIRE v MIDDLESEX

Played at Worcester, August 9, 10, 11, 1961

Worcestershire won by 15 runs. Spin brought Worcestershire their fourteenth victory of the season. Horton, off-breaks, and Gifford, left-arm slow, took 17 wickets between them, both exposing weaknesses in the Middlesex batting against the turning ball. This was particularly evident on the last day when Middlesex, needing 137 to win, were dismissed for 121 after being 58 for three at lunch. Gifford was awarded his county cap after the match. In contrast, Middlesex found pace more rewarding. Moss narrowly missed a hat-trick in the Worcestershire first innings, taking four wickets for five runs in one period with the new ball, and he took three of the first four second-innings wickets for eleven runs, Murray holding a catch in each instance. Late inswing caused many hurried strokes.

Worcestershire

*D. Kenyon b Moss	25	– lbw b Bennett	1
M. J. Horton b Titmus	64	– c Murray b Moss	0
R. G. A. Headley c Bedford b Moss	38	– c Murray b Moss	14
D. W. Richardson c Titmus b Moss	58	– c Murray b Moss	0
R. G. Broadbent b Titmus	2	– b Drybrough	38
G. Dews b Titmus	15	– st Murray b Titmus	24
†R. Booth b Moss	10	– not out	46
J. A. Standen b Bennett	9	– b Drybrough	13
N. Gifford not out	2	– lbw b Titmus	0
L. J. Coldwell b Moss	0	– lbw b Titmus	4
J. A. Flavell b Moss	4	– b Moss	0
B 5, l-b 4, w 1	10	L-b 1	1

1/36 2/114 3/140 4/146 5/182   237   1/1 2/9 3/9 4/26 5/71   141
6/220 7/229 8/231 9/231   6/83 7/118 8/125 9/133

Middlesex

R. A. Gale lbw b Coldwell	19	– st Booth b Horton	26
W. E. Russell lbw b Horton	26	– c Broadbent b Flavell	9
P. H. Parfitt c Broadbent b Gifford	2	– c Broadbent b Horton	16
E. A. Clark b Flavell	46	– c Coldwell b Horton	11
F. J. Titmus c Horton b Gifford	72	– b Horton	5
D. Bennett c Broadbent b Horton	32	– st Booth b Gifford	10
†J. T. Murray not out	20	– b Horton	4
R. W. Hooker b Gifford	12	– c and b Gifford	4
*P. I. Bedford c Booth b Horton	0	– c Standen b Gifford	4
C. D. Drybrough c Broadbent b Gifford	1	– not out	1
A. E. Moss b Horton	2	– c Kenyon b Horton	24
B 4, l-b 6	10	B 7	7

1/36 2/49 3/59 4/111 5/206   242   1/11 2/37 3/49 4/60 5/75   121
6/206 7/233 8/238 9/239   6/80 7/85 8/96 9/96

Middlesex Bowling

	Overs	Mdns	Runs	Wkts	Overs	Mdns	Runs	Wkts
Moss	22	8	47	6	21.3	7	48	4
Bennett	18	5	47	1	9	1	35	1
Hooker	24	7	44	—				
Titmus	26	11	64	3	21	7	48	3
Drybrough	5	3	8	—	11	7	9	2
Bedford	8	2	17	—				

Worcestershire Bowling

	Overs	Mdns	Runs	Wkts	Overs	Mdns	Runs	Wkts
Flavell	22	5	50	1	8	3	12	1
Coldwell	20	5	41	1	2	—	10	—
Gifford	18	10	25	4	25	9	52	3
Horton	26	3	100	4	20.4	9	40	6
Standen	6	—	16	—				

Umpires: C. S. Elliott and F. Jakeman.

WORCESTERSHIRE v SOMERSET

Played at Worcester, June 16, 18, 19, 1962

Worcestershire won by 264 runs. Somerset went into the match with victory over Pakistan to encourage them but their bowlers were completely mastered. In five hours, ten minutes Worcestershire had 520 runs on the board and Horton and Graveney by adding 314 together surpassed the previous best third wicket stand for Worcestershire, 306 by W. V. Fox and L. G. Crawley against Northamptonshire at Worcester in 1923. Horton made his highest score, hitting thirty-six 4s while batting for four and three-quarter hours. Kenyon (sixteen 4s) just missed a century before lunch, being bowled eight minutes before the interval. Graveney (one 6 and twenty-one 4s) stayed three and a quarter hours for his fifth three-figure innings of the summer. All this exhilarating batting was too much for Somerset. They could not cope with the accurate in-swing bowling of Coldwell in their first innings and the same player wrecked any little chance they may have had of saving their face on the last day. He bowled both Wight and Alley for "ducks", a feat appropriately followed by the news that he had been selected for his first Test. The match was over by lunch.

Worcestershire

*D. Kenyon b Palmer	97	– b Palmer	31
M. J. Horton run out	233	– c Stephenson b Palmer	38
R. G. A. Headley run out	0	– c and b Palmer	14
T. W. Graveney not out	164	– b Palmer	15
D. W. Richardson not out	10	– c Palmer b Alley	10
R. G. Broadbent (did not bat)		– st Stephenson b Alley	0
†R. Booth (did not bat)		– not out	25
J. A. Standen (did not bat)		– c Greetham b Alley	18
L. J. Coldwell (did not bat)		– not out	1
B 10, l-b 6	16	B 2, l-b 1	3

1/167 2/167 3/481   (3 wkts dec.) 520   1/62 2/73 3/90 4/98   (7 wkts dec.) 155
5/99 6/111 7/144

N. Gifford and J. A. Flavell did not bat.

Somerset

G. G. Atkinson lbw b Coldwell	3	– lbw b Flavell	1
B. Roe c Booth b Flavell	42	– c Richardson b Horton	11
P. B. Wight c Booth b Coldwell	45	– b Coldwell	0
W. E. Alley c Booth b Coldwell	8	– b Coldwell	0
M. Kitchen b Coldwell	7	– c and b Horton	19
C. Greetham b Standen	28	– lbw b Horton	9
J. G. Lomax c Graveney b Coldwell	65	– c Kenyon b Gifford	22
C. R. M. Atkinson c Richardson b Horton	2	– b Gifford	10
B. Langford b Horton	45	– not out	7
*†H. W. Stephenson c Coldwell b Horton	0	– b Gifford	45
K. E. Palmer not out	8	– c Headley b Gifford	9
B 12, l-b 3, w 1, n-b 1	17	B 3, l-b 5	8

1/4 2/81 3/95 4/106 5/113   270   1/2 2/25 3/26 4/26 5/75   141
6/143 7/150 8/233 9/237   6/84 7/97 8/118 9/123

Somerset Bowling

	Overs	Mdns	Runs	Wkts	Overs	Mdns	Runs	Wkts
Palmer	19	4	87	1	21	1	92	4
Alley	16	—	72	—	21	7	60	3
Langford	34	5	140	—				
C. Atkinson	16	1	81	—				
Greetham	16	1	97	—				
Wight	5	—	27	—				

Worcestershire Bowling

	Overs	Mdns	Runs	Wkts	Overs	Mdns	Runs	Wkts
Flavell	21	5	67	1	8	1	21	1
Coldwell	18.1	4	47	5	11	4	27	2
Gifford	16	7	41	—	16.2	9	29	4
Horton	24	7	68	3	15	4	51	3
Standen	13	—	30	1	1	—	5	—

Umpires: C. S. Elliott and L. H. Gray.

WORCESTERSHIRE v NOTTINGHAMSHIRE

Played at Worcester, September 1, 3, 4, 1962

Worcestershire won by eight wickets. They needed this victory to put them on top of the table with an advantage of ten points and though in the event Yorkshire won their last game and so supplanted them, this in no way detracted merit from their win or denied them the right to celebrate with champagne at the close of the game. The end came with rain threatening again after thunderstorms twice left pools all over the ground and brought players as well as groundstaff scampering out to manhandle the drying equipment.

Between the hold-ups, Kenyon and Graveney steered Worcestershire home with a stand of 145 in ninety-five minutes. The target was 192, and what would have happened had Kenyon not been dropped without a run on the board inside the last twelve minutes of the second day can be only conjecture. As it was, Kenyon hit 103 in two and a half hours. Excitement held commendably large crowds throughout. Nottinghamshire were 32 for five before Gill led a recovery, being helped by Millman, who again in the second innings foiled Coldwell and Carter with his second fifty of the match. Worcestershire themselves looked in trouble when, replying to a first innings score of 193, they were 118 for six, but the bowlers came to their rescue with the bat. Even so, the ninth pair were together before the lead was established.

Nottinghamshire

N. Hill c Graveney b Coldwell	0	– c Standen b Coldwell	41
A. Gill b Slade	61	– c Slade b Carter	0
H. M. Winfield b Coldwell	7	– b Carter	0
M. Hill lbw b Coldwell	4	– c Graveney b Coldwell	24
C. J. Poole run out	0	– b Slade	19
R. Bilbie b Carter	3	– b Standen	35
C. Forbes c Booth b Gifford	19	– b Carter	17
†G. Millman not out	51	– lbw b Coldwell	63
*A. J. Corran b Horton	38	– c Graveney b Coldwell	33
J. Cotton lbw b Carter	4	– not out	14
B. D. Wells b Carter	0	– b Coldwell	2
B 1, l-b 5	6	B 2, l-b 1	3

1/0 2/16 3/22 4/22 5/32   193   1/2 2/2 3/31 4/78 5/84   251
6/88 7/96 8/180 9/193   6/118 7/141 8/226 9/237

Worcestershire

*D. Kenyon c Gill b Cotton	7	– not out	103
M. J. Horton c Millman b Cotton	6	– b Corran	1
D. W. Richardson c Corran b Forbes	56	– c Gill b Corran	15
T. W. Graveney c Corran b Forbes	19	– not out	62
A. Ormrod lbw b Forbes	0		
†R. Booth lbw b Wells	12		
D. N. F. Slade c Corran b Forbes	40		
J. A. Standen b Wells	40		
N. Gifford b Wells	21		
L. J. Coldwell c Corran b Wells	37		
R. G. N. Carter not out	1		
B 9, l-b 5	14	B 6, l-b 6	12

1/8 2/19 3/81 4/85 5/106   253   1/2 2/48   (2 wkts) 193
6/118 7/182 8/188 9/251

Worcestershire Bowling

	Overs	Mdns	Runs	Wkts	Overs	Mdns	Runs	Wkts
Coldwell	20	2	63	3	21.2	1	87	5
Carter	14.2	3	38	3	21	7	51	3
Gifford	17	6	33	1	6	1	25	—
Standen	3	—	14	—	14	5	27	1
Slade	8	—	19	1	12	4	18	1
Horton	10	3	20	1	22	11	40	—

Nottinghamshire

	Overs	Mdns	Runs	Wkts	Overs	Mdns	Runs	Wkts
Cotton	17	6	54	2	18	1	36	—
Corran	10	2	46	—	18	4	50	2
Wells	30.4	10	85	4	6	2	25	—
Forbes	24	2	54	4	13	2	57	—
Poole					0.4	—	13	—

Umpires: P. A. Gibb and F. C. Gardner.

YORKSHIRE

YORKSHIRE v SUSSEX

Played at Leeds, June 29, 30, July 1, 1949

Drawn. Heavy atmosphere prompted Yardley to put Sussex in to bat. After their modest score, batsmen prevailed so completely that 962 more runs came for the loss of ten wickets. Hutton made the match noteworthy by raising his aggregate for a month to 1,293, the best recorded by any batsman, surpassing the 1,281 credited to Hammond in August 1936. Wilson and Lester put on 208 for Yorkshire's third wicket; the left-hander hit nineteen 4s during nearly five hours, and Lester in his first century of the season hit eighteen 4s, mostly drives, during two hours forty minutes. Close hit three 6s, a 5 and four 4s. Facing arrears of 339 Sussex lost two wickets for 43, and Charles Oakes left at 116, but James Langridge and Cox, in great form, added 326 runs in five and a half hours without further success for the Yorkshire attack in which all but Firth the wicket-keeper took part on the hard, easy-paced pitch. James Langridge batted six hours and three-quarters, gave two chances and hit fourteen 4s. Cox scored his 212 in five hours twenty minutes without a mistake and hit thirty-six 4s.

Sussex

John Langridge c Firth b Coxon	30	– lbw b Coxon	33
A. E. James b Close	4	– b Coxon	9
C. Oakes b Coxon	14	– c Coxon b Robinson	38
James Langridge c Hutton b Coxon	9	– not out	133
G. Cox c Firth b Close	18	– not out	212
H. T. Bartlett not out	51		
J. Oakes b Close	13		
K. Suttle lbw b Coxon	2		
R. T. Webb c Robinson b Coxon	1		
J. Cornford b Close	17		
J. Wood c Firth b Close	2		
B 13, l-b 3, n-b 4	20	B 10, l-b 4, n-b 3	17
	181	**(3 wkts)**	**442**

Yorkshire

L. Hutton c C. Oakes b James	80	D. B. Close c Cox b Wood	44
F. A. Lowson lbw b James Langridge	61	E. P. Robinson c James b Wood	9
J. V. Wilson not out	157		
E. Lester st Webb b James Langridge	112		
G. A. Smithson run out	2	B 8, l-b 5, w 1	14
N. W. D. Yardley c John Langridge b James Langridge	41	**(7 wkts dec.)**	**520**

A. Coxon, J. Firth and A. Mason did not bat.

Yorkshire Bowling

	Overs	Mdns	Runs	Wkts	Overs	Mdns	Runs	Wkts
Coxon.	24	2	56	5	30	6	79	2
Close.	17.5	5	73	5	20	7	51	—
Yardley.	11	1	32	—	8	2	23	—
Robinson					46	23	73	1
Hutton					20	7	46	—
Mason.					33	10	86	—
Lester					7	4	11	—
Wilson					4	—	16	—
Smithson.					3	—	27	—
Lowson.					2	—	13	—

Sussex Bowling

	Overs	Mdns	Runs	Wkts
Wood	35	9	111	2
Cornford.	28	6	70	—
James	37	9	100	1
J. Oakes	19	5	85	—
James Langridge. . . .	27	6	89	3
C. Oakes.	8	2	31	—
Cox.	3	—	20	—

Umpires: A. R. Coleman and A. Lockett.

YORKSHIRE v MCC

Played at Scarborough, August 31, September 1, 2, 1949

Drawn. Rain fell during the night after Yorkshire batted all the first day, but the entirely protected pitch remained favourable to run-getting and bowlers seldom caused trouble on easy-paced turf. Of several personal performances of high merit the most noteworthy was that of Hutton, who, by scoring 199 in the match, raised his season's aggregate to 3,145. Hutton made his 147 out of 245 in two hours fifty minutes and hit three 6s and eighteen 4s, all splendid strokes. Close exceeded a thousand runs so completing "the double", in his first season of county cricket at the age of 18; Coxon and Wardle each took his hundredth wicket, and Cranston on his first appearance of the season played his highest innings in important cricket. Broderick showed surprising form with the bat in a stand of 127; Dawkes hit freely and Young gave the necessary aid for MCC to gain the lead, a remarkable achievement on the second day after the loss of four wickets for 16 and the fall of the seventh at 193. Compton played finely at the most critical period; he hit a 6 and fourteen 4s. Heavy sea mist at times on the second day blew across the ground without causing any serious inconvenience though contrasting strangely with bright sunshine which prevailed generally during the match. After the third declaration MCC wanted 212 for victory with ninety minutes remaining, but against Coxon and Wardle in their best form runs did not come easily.

Yorkshire

L. Hutton c Wyatt b Compton	147	st Dawkes b F. R. Brown	52
F. A. Lowson run out	58	st Dawkes b Young	89
J. V. Wilson b Edrich	58	c S. Brown b Compton	19
D. B. Close c S. M. Brown b Young	44	not out	46
E. Lester c Wyatt b Edrich	9		
G. A. Smithson c Dawles b Young	23		
N. W. D. Yardley not out	58		
A. Coxon lbw b Young	0		
J. H. Wardle c Pearce b Young	0		
D. V. Brennan not out	17		
B 4, l-b 11	15	B 4, l-b 2	6

(8 wkts dec.) 429   (3 wkts dec.) 212

E. P. Robinson did not bat.

MCC

S. M. Brown b Coxon	4	lbw b Coxon	24
F. R. Brown lbw b Close	1	b Coxon	6
W. J. Edrich run out	0	b Wardle	24
D. C. S. Compton c Brennan b Wardle	127	c Brennan b Coxon	0
R. E. S. Wyatt c Hutton b Coxon	0		
T. N. Pearce run out	27	not out	4
F. G. Mann lbw b Robinson	8	c Hutton b Wardle	8
K. Cranston not out	156		
V. Broderick run out	53	not out	41
G. Dawkes c Wilson b Wardle	31		
J. A. Young not out	11		
B 8, l-b 1, n-b 3	12	L-b 1, w 1	2

(9 wkts dec.) 430   (5 wkts) 109

MCC Bowling

	Overs	Mdns	Runs	Wkts	Overs	Mdns	Runs	Wkts
Edrich	15	1	78	2	9	2	26	—
Cranston	19	4	62	—	3	—	21	—
F. R. Brown	26	7	119	—	10	1	64	1
Young	34	10	89	4	12.4	1	30	1
Broderick	7	1	25	—	4	—	19	—
Compton	8	—	41	1	5	—	36	1
Wyatt					2	—	10	—

Yorkshire Bowling

	Overs	Mdns	Runs	Wkts	Overs	Mdns	Runs	Wkts
Coxon	40	3	140	2	10	—	29	3
Close	16	1	60	1	2	—	7	—
Yardley	8	2	13	—				
Wardle	52	17	110	2	12	3	29	2
Robinson	28	6	77	1	7	2	31	—
Hutton	4	—	18	—				
Wilson					3	—	9	—
Lowson					1	—	2	—

Umpires: H. Elliott and A. R. Coleman.

YORKSHIRE v MCC

Played at Scarborough, September 1, 3, 4, 1951

Drawn. This was another triumph for Appleyard, who, in his last match of the season, captured the eleven wickets he required to take his aggregate to 200. When eight MCC second innings wickets were down he needed to take the last two to reach this figure. He succeeded in one over. Appleyard's first innings analysis was his best in first-class cricket. By aggressive batting, Yorkshire built up a big lead. Seven 6s, three by Wardle off Brown, were hit, and Watson's strokes included twelve 4s. In taking his second wicket, Brown reached career figures of 10,000 runs and 1,000 wickets. MCC gave an improved display in the second innings.

MCC

R. T. Simpson c and b Appleyard	17	– c Leadbeater b Trueman........... 5
W. J. Edrich b Appleyard	21	– c Hutton b Appleyard............ 32
P. B. H. May c Wilson b Appleyard	0	– c Halliday b Trueman 56
G. H. G. Doggart b Wardle	31	– lbw b Wardle 28
D. J. Insole c Leadbeater b Appleyard	14	– run out 45
T. E. Bailey b Wardle	31	– st sub b Wardle............... 28
F. R. Brown c Watson b Appleyard	5	– c and b Wardle................ 28
S. C. Griffith b Appleyard	11	– b Wardle.................... 6
R. Tattersall c Trueman b Appleyard	10	– c Trueman b Appleyard 5
T. A. Hall c Leadbeater b Appleyard	2	– c Yardley b Appleyard 3
K. C. Preston not out	0	– not out 0
B 9, l-b 2, w 4, n-b 1	16	B 29, l-b 6, n-b 2......... 37
	158	**273**

Yorkshire

L. Hutton b Hall	10	
H. Halliday b Brown	36	– not out 10
J. V. Wilson b Tattersall	0	– c and b Edrich 4
E. Lester c Preston b Tattersall	66	
W. Watson b Tattersall	70	
N. W. D. Yardley c Preston b Tattersall	40	
J. H. Wardle c May b Tattersall	43	
D. V. Brennan lbw b Brown	4	
E. Leadbeater lbw b Brown	0	– not out 11
R. Appleyard b Brown	12	
F. S. Trueman not out	24	
B 11, l-b 6, w 9, n-b 2	28	W 4.................... 4
	333	**(1 wkt) 29**

Yorkshire Bowling

	Overs	Mdns	Runs	Wkts	Overs	Mdns	Runs	Wkts
Trueman	7	2	11	—	20	6	39	2
Yardley	4	2	3	—	3	—	10	—
Appleyard	33	6	76	8	45.5	12	105	3
Wardle	25.1	12	34	2	25	10	57	4
Halliday	1	—	2	—	1	—	4	—
Leadbeater	4	—	16	—	11	2	21	—

MCC Bowling

	Overs	Mdns	Runs	Wkts	Overs	Mdns	Runs	Wkts
Preston	13	2	36	—				
Hall..............	13	2	48	1	3	1	7	—
Tattersall	35	10	122	5				
Brown...........	20.1	4	62	4				
Bailey	20	6	37	—				
Edrich............					3	—	9	1
Insole					2	1	8	—
Doggart					2	1	1	—

Umpires: H. Elliott and E. Robinson.

YORKSHIRE v MCC

Played at Scarborough, September 3, 4, 5, 1952

Drawn. Hutton and May each scored two separate hundreds in a splendid match. Hutton's first century took less than two and a half hours. He received consistent support, but MCC did even better. May and Graveney were in great form during their stand of 187. May's glorious strokes brought three 6s and twenty-five 4s and he took only just over three hours to score 174. May and Cowdrey spent no more than forty-five minutes adding 106. Another brilliant display came from Hutton, and MCC were set to score 245 in two and a half hours. Except for May they were forced to fight hard to save the game. May's second century was completed in the last over of the match.

Yorkshire

L. Hutton c Graveney b Smith 103	– b Smith......................	137
F. A. Lowson lbw b Bailey	30 – st Evans b Bedser	36
J. V. Wilson c Simpson b Insole	38 – c Insole b Cowdrey.............	23
E. Lester c Evans b Robins....................	36 – c Cowdrey b Simpson...........	39
W. Watson lbw b Robins	10 – c Insole b Smith	34
H. Halliday b Bailey	50 – not out	10
D. B. Close c Edrich b Bedser...................	14 – b Bedser	6
N. W. D. Yardley b Bedser.....................	21
J. H. Wardle c Evans b Bedser	7 – b Bedser	4
D. V. Brennan b Bailey.......................	0
E. Burgin not out...........................	4
L-b 5, n-b 1......................	6	L-b 2..................	2

1/86 2/158 3/207 4/209 5/226   319   1/90 2/146 3/213   (7 wkts dec.) 291
6/258 7/296 8/304 9/306   4/254 5/259 6/279 7/291

MCC

R. T. Simpson b Yardley	5	– c Halliday b Yardley	10
D. J. Insole c Hutton b Yardley	10	– c Hutton b Wardle	39
P. B. H. May c Wardle b Yardley	174	– not out	100
T. W. Graveney c Lowson b Yardley	88	– b Burgin	3
W. J. Edrich c Hutton b Yardley	2	– c Yardley b Halliday	6
M. C. Cowdrey not out	51	– c Watson b Halliday	15
T. G. Evans c Hutton b Yardley	10	– c Watson b Wardle	7
T. E. Bailey not out	19	– not out	5
R. Smith (did not bat)		– c Yardley b Halliday	1
R. W. V. Robins (did not bat)		– b Wardle	9
B 4, l-b 2, n-b 1	7	B 5, l-b 5, n-b 1	11

1/4 2/17 3/204   (6 wkts dec.) 366   1/30 2/66 3/81 4/82   (8 wkts) 206
4/217 5/323 6/334   5/122 6/133 7/160 8/187

A. V. Bedser did not bat.

MCC Bowling

	Overs	Mdns	Runs	Wkts	Overs	Mdns	Runs	Wkts
Bedser	30	3	73	3	18.3	3	51	3
Bailey	27.2	2	80	3	12	1	42	—
Smith	15	1	68	1	11	—	70	2
Edrich	7	1	32	—	5	1	21	—
Insole	8	2	20	1	2	—	8	—
Robins	11	1	40	2	7	—	29	—
Cowdrey					7	—	35	1
Simpson					5	1	33	1

Yorkshire Bowling

	Overs	Mdns	Runs	Wkts	Overs	Mdns	Runs	Wkts
Burgin	19.2	5	44	—	12	2	41	1
Yardley	24	3	106	6	7	—	30	1
Halliday	10	—	61	—	14	—	72	3
Wardle	18	2	75	—	11	—	43	3
Close	11	—	73	—				
Watson					1	—	9	—

Umpires: A. Skelding and Harold Elliott (Lancashire).

YORKSHIRE v SUSSEX

Played at Hull, June 2, 3, 5, 1954

Yorkshire won by an innings and 20 runs. The all-round skill of Wardle served Yorkshire well. Going on in the first innings with Sussex 30 for one, Wardle in the next two and a half hours took the remaining nine wickets. Had all chances been held, his figures would have been even better. Lowson, Wilson and Watson batted soundly enough for Yorkshire to finish the first day on terms with eight wickets left, and next day, with Wardle (eleven 4s) hitting hard and then revelling in a crumbling pitch, they pressed home their advantage. The last morning's cricket consisted of two overs, Wardle finishing with match figures of 16 wickets for 112.

Sussex

J. Langridge b Wardle	33	– lbw b Trueman 5
D. V. Smith c Hutton b Trueman	4	– c Hutton b Wardle 6
G. H. G. Doggart c Lowson b Wardle	28	– b Appleyard 5
J. M. Parks c Watson b Wardle	2	– lbw b Wardle 35
K. G. Suttle b Wardle	17	– b Wardle....................... 2
A. S. Oakman c Wilson b Wardle	45	– lbw b Trueman 40
N. I. Thomson st Booth b Wardle	4	– b Wardle....................... 1
A. E. James lbw b Wardle	0	– st Booth b Wardle 39
R. G. Marlar b Wardle	14	– b Wardle..................... 17
R. T. Webb not out	0	– c Illingworth b Wardle 8
D. J. Wood b Wardle	0	– not out 9
B 2, l-b 5	7	B 2, l-b 8, n-b 1 11

1/8 2/67 3/69 4/74 5/111   154   1/11 2/15 3/21 4/24 5/99   178
6/123 7/129 8/150 9/154   6/99 7/100 8/132 9/163

Yorkshire

L. Hutton b Wood	1	R. Booth c James b Wood 23
F. A. Lowson lbw b Oakman	33	F. S. Trueman run out.................. 1
J. V. Wilson c James b Marlar	75	R. Appleyard not out 10
W. Watson run out	48	
N. W. D. Yardley b Marlar	35	B 11, l-b 6 17
D. B. Close c Webb b Thomson	34	
R. Illingworth b Thomson	9	1/2 2/75 3/148 (9 wkts dec.) 352
J. H. Wardle not out	66	4/195 5/206 6/241 7/252 8/325 9/332

Yorkshire Bowling

	Overs	Mdns	Runs	Wkts	Overs	Mdns	Runs	Wkts
Trueman	20	6	45	1	13	1	26	2
Appleyard	15	5	33	—	32	4	59	1
Yardley	3	1	7	—				
Wardle	25.4	11	48	9	25	13	64	7
Close	4	1	14	—	4	—	18	—

Sussex Bowling

	Overs	Mdns	Runs	Wkts	Overs	Mdns	Runs	Wkts
Wood	19	1	57	2				
Thomson	27	9	64	2				
James	16	4	45	—				
Marlar	32	8	90	2				
Oakman	37	12	79	1				

Umpires: W. F. Price and W. T. Jones.

YORKSHIRE v NORTHAMPTONSHIRE

Played at Bradford, May 7, 9, 1955

Yorkshire won by 78 runs. A rain-damaged pitch, ideally suited to spin bowlers, produced astonishing cricket, the game being over in seven and a half hours of actual playing time. Tribe, the Northamptonshire slow left-arm bowler, had the mixed experience of accomplishing the best match performance of his career, but being on the losing side. His full figures were 15 wickets for 75 runs, including nine for 45 in the second innings. After leading by 33, Yorkshire lost eight batsmen in their second innings for 60 before play ended on Saturday. Much depended on the conditions on Monday. Fortunately for Yorkshire the pitch remained almost unplayable and Northamptonshire never looked like scoring the 138 they needed to win.

Yorkshire

F. A. Lowson st Andrew b Broderick	22	– c Brookes b Tribe	7
W. H. H. Sutcliffe b Tribe	13	– c Barrick b Tribe	8
J. V. Wilson c Subba Row b Tribe	20	– b Bribe	0
D. B. Close b Tribe	15	– lbw b Tribe	0
W. Watson c Andrew b Broderick	2	– c and b Tribe	32
E. Lester st Andrew b Broderick	3	– c Clarke b Broderick	11
N. W. D. Yardley lbw b Broderick	5	– c Clarke b Tribe	10
J. H. Wardle lbw b Tribe	8	– c Clarke b Tribe	7
R. Booth c Tyson b Tribe	3	– lbw b Tribe	0
F. S. Trueman c Tyson b Tribe	0	– c Tyson b Tribe	21
R. Appleyard not out	0	– not out	2
B 3	3	L-b 6	6

1/27 2/57 3/73 4/73 5/76   94   1/8 2/8 3/8 4/17 5/36   104
6/82 7/91 8/91 9/94   6/47 7/55 8/59 9/85

Northamptonshire

D. Brookes b Appleyard	8	– b Wardle	7
P. Arnold c Close b Trueman	0	– lbw b Appleyard	5
L. Livingston c Lester b Appleyard	19	– b Appleyard	1
D. Barrick b Wardle	7	– c Watson b Wardle	4
R. Subba Row c Lowson b Appleyard	0	– c Booth b Wardle	15
G. E. Tribe b Appleyard	12	– c Appleyard b Wardle	6
V. Broderick c Lowson b Wardle	0	– run out	3
F. H. Tyson not out	8	– c Lowson b Appleyard	1
S. Starkie c Wilson b Wardle	1	– b Appleyard	3
K. V. Andrew b Appleyard	0	– not out	2
R. W. Clarke c Lowson b Appleyard	0	– b Appleyard	2
L-b 6	6	B 2, l-b 6, n-b 2	10

1/5 2/26 3/37 4/37 5/41   61   1/10 2/11 3/18 4/34 5/43   59
6/41 7/51 8/52 9/61   6/48 7/50 8/50 9/55

Northamptonshire Bowling

	Overs	Mdns	Runs	Wkts	Overs	Mdns	Runs	Wkts
Tyson	5	3	2	—	2	—	2	—
Clarke	3	—	13	—				
Broderick	15	5	46	4	21	8	51	1
Tribe	13.1	—	30	6	19.2	5	45	9

Yorkshire Bowling

	Overs	Mdns	Runs	Wkts	Overs	Mdns	Runs	Wkts
Trueman	2	—	12	1	3	—	6	—
Appleyard	11.5	4	25	6	13.1	4	23	5
Wardle	11	6	18	3	12	2	20	4

Umpires: E. Cooke and Harry Elliott (Derbyshire).

YORKSHIRE v WARWICKSHIRE

Played at Sheffield, May 25, 26, 27, 1955

Yorkshire won by five wickets despite a remarkable bowling performance by Bannister for Warwickshire. After sharing a partnership of 60 with Townsend, Bannister caused a complete collapse. His nine wickets for 35 runs, the best achievement of his career, included the hat-trick when he dismissed Wilson, Yardley and Lester. Bannister's previous best, eight for 54, was also against Yorkshire in 1954. Leading by 75, Warwickshire again struggled, but they set Yorkshire to get 217 to win. A fine third wicket stand of 118 between Watson and Close decided the match. Close played many excellent forcing strokes and Watson's patience proved invaluable. He stayed five hours twenty minutes.

Warwickshire

R. T. Spooner lbw b Close	14	–	c Lowson b Wardle	27
N. F. Horner b Trueman	4	–	b Wardle	12
A. V. Wolton c Booth b Trueman	13	–	b Trueman	12
T. W. Cartwright b Trueman	27	–	b Trueman	4
H. E. Dollery b Close	5	–	c Booth b Appleyard	32
A. Townsend lbw b Wardle	40	–	b Appleyard	14
R. E. Hitchcock b Trueman	9	–	lbw b Trueman	3
J. D. Bannister c Booth b Appleyard	23	–	c Lowson b Appleyard	16
I. M. King c and b Wardle	1	–	lbw b Wardle	3
R. G. Thompson b Trueman	7	–	not out	3
W. E. Hollies not out	0	–	b Wardle	0
L-b 1, w 2, n-b 2	5		B 4, l-b 8, n-b 3	15

1/4 2/23 3/44 4/64 5/66   **148**   1/18 2/46 3/68 4/99 5/110   **141**
6/80 7/140 8/140 9/142   6/111 7/126 8/130 9/134

Yorkshire

F. A. Lowson lbw b Bannister	8	–	b Thompson	26
W. Watson b Bannister	24	–	not out	64
J. V. Wilson b Bannister	17	–	c Spooner b Bannister	3
D. B. Close lbw b Thompson	1	–	b Hollies	85
E. Lester c and b Bannister	1	–	c Cartwright b Hollies	12
N. W. D. Yardley c Townsend b Bannister	0	–	lbw b Hollies	7
R. Illingworth b Bannister	7	–	not out	15
J. H. Wardle b Bannister	1			
R. Booth c Cartwright b Bannister	8			
F. S. Trueman b Bannister	4			
R. Appleyard not out	0			
L-b 2	2		B 2, l-b 3, n-b 1	6

1/28 2/41 3/50 4/52 5/52   **73**   1/44 2/47 3/165   **(5 wkts) 218**
6/53 7/61 8/62 9/70   4/179 5/192

Yorkshire Bowling

	Overs	Mdns	Runs	Wkts	Overs	Mdns	Runs	Wkts
Trueman	18.4	4	35	5	20	6	57	3
Appleyard	17	6	35	1	23	7	38	3
Close	17	1	59	2	4	2	15	—
Wardle	8	4	14	2	7.5	3	16	4

Warwickshire Bowling

	Overs	Mdns	Runs	Wkts	Overs	Mdns	Runs	Wkts
Thompson	16	3	36	1	32	4	90	1
Bannister	15.2	5	35	9	31	5	58	1
Hollies					24	13	26	3
Townsend					3	10	15	—
King					8	1	23	—

Umpires: A. Skelding and H. Elliott (Lancashire).

YORKSHIRE v NOTTINGHAMSHIRE

Played at Scarborough, August 10, 11, 12, 1955

Yorkshire won by nine wickets. The fast bowling of Trueman played a leading part in the success. In the first innings he did the hat-trick for the second time against Nottinghamshire, sending back Giles, Stocks and C. Poole. His other hat-trick was at Trent Bridge in 1951. A useful innings by K. Poole and hard hitting by Jepson enabled Nottinghamshire to recover slightly. Yorkshire also found run-getting difficult, but Illingworth batted three and a quarter hours in fine style and Binks helped him add 92 for the ninth wicket stand, which put Yorkshire ahead. At the close of the second day Nottinghamshire led by one run with eight wickets left, but they were out in another forty-five minutes. Trueman accomplished his best performance of the season in taking seven for 23. Yorkshire needed only 18 to win.

Nottinghamshire

R. T. Simpson c Illingworth b Wardle	28	– c Wardle b Trueman	44
J. D. Clay c Sutcliffe b Ryan	1	– c Wilson b Ryan	11
R. J. Giles c Binks b Trueman	17	– b Trueman	30
F. W. Stocks c Wilson b Trueman	0	– c Illingworth b Trueman	0
C. J. Poole c Lowson b Trueman	0	– b Wardle	2
K. J. Poole c Wardle b Close	43	– c Wardle b Trueman	2
G. Goonesena b Wardle	23	– b Wardle	3
B. Dooland c Yardley b Wardle	0	– not out	1
K. Smales c Binks b Ryan	23	– c Binks b Trueman	1
A. Jepson not out	52	– b Trueman	6
E. J. Rowe b Ryan	2	– b Trueman	0
B 1, l-b 11, w 1, n-b 1	14	L-b 1, n-b 4	5

1/7 2/34 3/34 4/34 5/61   203   1/34 2/89 3/89 4/92 5/92   105
6/117 7/119 8/135 9/201   6/97 7/97 8/99 9/105

Yorkshire

W. H. H. Sutcliffe b K. Poole	30	– b Smales	3
D. B. Close c Clay b Smales	36	– not out	7
J. V. Wilson c K. Poole b Goonesena	13		
D. E. V. Padgett b Jepson	16		
F. A. Lowson c Dooland b Jepson	11		
R. Illingworth c K. Poole b Smales	94		
N. W. D. Yardley b K. Poole	19		
J. H. Wardle c C. Poole b Smales	5		
F. S. Trueman c Clay b Goonesena	11		
J. G. Binks not out	42	– not out	8
M. Ryan b Goonesena	0		
L-b 13, n-b 1	14		

1/54 2/74 3/92 4/102 5/111   291   1/5   (1 wkt) 18
6/156 7/163 8/198 9/290

Yorkshire Bowling

	Overs	Mdns	Runs	Wkts	Overs	Mdns	Runs	Wkts
Trueman	27	7	71	3	18.2	7	23	7
Ryan	9.3	—	22	3	10	2	15	1
Yardley	8	1	16	—				
Wardle	21	7	55	3	13	3	37	2
Close	4	—	25	1	4	1	13	—
Illingworth					9	6	12	—

Nottinghamshire

	Overs	Mdns	Runs	Wkts	Overs	Mdns	Runs	Wkts
Jepson............	29	15	47	2				
K. Poole..........	21	4	59	2	3.4	—	14	—
Dooland..........	33	7	86	—				
Smales...........	18	10	33	3	3	1	4	1
Goonesena........	17.2	5	52	3				

Umpires: P. Corrall and T. Spencer.

THE STORY OF YORKSHIRE [1955]

By J. M. Kilburn

The history of cricket, its records and its honours are bound up with the deeds of Yorkshire and Yorkshire players. Founded in 1863, Yorkshire were one of the original nine counties considered first-class when the Championship was formed in 1873. They took twenty years to win the title for the first time, since when they have been almost regular contenders. Twenty-two summers have ended with the White Rose at the top. No other county can match this tale of success. Here is a tribute to men who have put Yorkshire in the forefront of the cricket world.

Yorkshire County cricket is not to be identified with any one Yorkshire centre. The administrative offices are in Leeds and only Headingley of the Yorkshire grounds is now granted a Test match, but there would be prompt and fierce protest from every Riding were any individual claims put forward for distinction as the home of Yorkshire cricket. The county club owns no ground, though it has financial interest in several. Home fixtures are spread as widely as circumstances and accommodation allow; playing resources are discovered and developed everywhere.

SHEFFIELD INFLUENCE

This distribution of favour has its origins in the early history of the county's cricket when a narrow conception of resources and interests found little favour. The Kent secretary of 1864 remarked that it was difficult to know who were the proper parties to get up Yorkshire county matches, and some years passed after the formal foundation of the county club before its authority was accepted with much grace, or indeed accepted at all, outside the Sheffield area. Perhaps the difference of outlook was more an illustration of characteristic wariness than of protest against local leadership, because the original Sheffield resolution of formation did envisage an unlimited membership with subscriptions "to provide funds for the playing of first-class matches in Sheffield and other centres". Moreover, when the first side was chosen it contained cricketers from Huddersfield, Bradford, Ripon and the North Riding as well as from Sheffield.

Storms soon blew into the life of the young Yorkshire club and in 1865 there was a secession by five of the leading players, less through any quarrel with their own management than because of personal ill-feeling between players of the North and the South. Yorkshire, governed wholly from Sheffield, resolved to play and lose rather than abandon their venture, and determination preserved existence. Prodigals returned, new talent came forward and Yorkshire established themselves as a force in the cricketing land. In 1867 seven engagements were undertaken and in these matches fifty-one wickets went to George Freeman and thirty to Tom Emmett. The highest total of any opposing innings was Lancashire's 159. George Freeman was accounted the finest fast bowler of the day by his contemporaries, who included W. G. Grace and Richard Daft, and though his career was short he left an imperishable name.

Tom Emmett lasted longer, playing from 1866 to 1888, carrying Yorkshire through the period of establishment of the County Championship and holding a principal part in a company that included Alan Hill as Freeman's successor in fast bowling; George Pinder, the wicket-keeper who was beyond compare in his time; Ephraim Lockwood, sturdiest of batsmen whose bucolic appearance belied his talent; George Ulyett, a bowler who fell in love with batting and was indulged in his fancy; and Peate and Peel, leaders of that long line of left-arm slow bowlers giving cause for so much Yorkshire gratitude.

THE DISCIPLINED YORKSHIRE

The potentialities in such a collection of players was beyond doubting. The results were wholly unworthy. The side remained a collection of individuals without common purpose or spur. In 1893 endurance reached its limit, and a complete reorganisation of the committee was accepted. The change was wise and profitable, though its justice at the particular moment might be questioned. The new Yorkshire, the disciplined Yorkshire, began to satisfy themselves.

There can be no doubt that much of the spirit inculcated into the Yorkshire side during the 1890s came directly from the leadership of Lord Hawke. It was his declared ambition to win for Yorkshire cricket not only admiration but respect, and he took some drastic steps to ensure that his teams became acceptable everywhere for their conduct both on the field and off. Lord Hawke could never be classed as an outstanding player. Experience gave him usefulness as a batsmen in the lower half of the order and in his younger days he was certainly not a handicap to his team in the field, but other qualities than playing ability were needed to raise him to the eminence he attained on the fields and in the councils of cricket.

Those qualities were an abiding affection for his cause, which was Yorkshire cricket, and a happy understanding of the men who played under his captaincy. As a captain Lord Hawke was a martinet; in course of time firmness could have been seen as obstinacy, depending upon the viewpoint, and his major interest tended to become paramount. Yet there can be no denying that in developing Yorkshire cricket Lord Hawke did rare service to cricket in its widest sphere. He set standards that have survived him and he took cricket to Australia, India, Canada, United States, South Africa, West Indies and the Argentine. He was captain of Yorkshire from 1883 to 1910 and President of the club from 1898 until his death in 1938.

By his influence alone Lord Hawke could have changed the character of the Yorkshire team, but he could not have achieved the historic results for ever to be associated with his name without help from players of unimpeachable quality. Lord Hawke's time was the time of George Hirst and Wilfred Rhodes; of Tunnicliffe and Brown and David Denton; of Wainwright and Peel; of F. S. Jackson and T. L. Taylor and Ernest Smith; of Haigh and Hunter. He who gave such memorable service was himself well served.

TRIPLE CHAMPIONS

The peak of Yorkshire playing success under the captaincy of Lord Hawke came in the seasons of 1900-01-02 when the championship was won so comprehensively that the wonder of the time was not a Yorkshire victory but a Yorkshire failure to complete victory. In those three years only two championship matches were lost, both of them to Somerset, and some of the victories provided staggering figures. Nottinghamshire were dismissed for 13; against Worcestershire, Yorkshire were all out for 99 and still had margin to win by an innings. There seemed no end to the triumphs, and a new conception of cricketing power was created. Yorkshire have had benefit ever since. They have believed in themselves, and they have undoubtedly impressed that belief upon their opponents.

However great a part the determination to win and the strong team-spirit may have played in Yorkshire's establishment as one of the most successful of all cricketing counties, the essential basis of rare technical quality must not be overlooked. Yorkshire have enjoyed the service of a succession of players to be ranked among the very highest, players as familiar by repute in Sydney as in Sheffield. There was never a more dominating cricketer than F. S. Jackson; never a cricketer more respected for his wisdom and skill than Wilfred Rhodes; never a cricketer to capture the heart and the imagination and the affections more firmly than George Herbert Hirst.

Jackson was a player by the light of nature, gifted in the rhythm of movement, scarcely needing practice to attain perfection of form. He bowled with economy of effort and batted with graceful efficiency. He knew his own abilities and was surprised at personal failure because he counted it unreasonable. The more demanding the occasion the more likely his success, and his Test match record against Australia is incomparable.

GENIUS OF RHODES

Wilfred Rhodes has no parallel in cricket, in either the county or the international story. In his first season he established himself as one of the world's leading bowlers; twelve years later he was opening the innings for England; at the age of 48 he was playing again for England, an invaluable all-rounder. He was a cricketing genius; as a bowler with the genius that comes as a gift from the gods, and as a batsman with the genius that is the infinite capacity for taking pains. He was born wise in cricketing ways. In more than thirty years on the first-class fields his principles of the game were never outmoded. Whilst Wilfred Rhodes was playing nobody ever ventured the opinion that Rhodes's type of bowling would not take wickets in current conditions. Results spoke only too clearly for themselves throughout a career that linked the batsmanship of Grace with that of Bradman.

HIRST THE WARRIOR

George Hirst became the epitome of Yorkshire cricket, the happy warrior that every Yorkshire cricketing knight-at-arms would wish to be. It was part of Hirst's nature that the greater the need of the occasion the greater the response to be called from him. Often enough his innings was brief or his bowling comparatively unsuccessful when no particular demand was laid upon him, but in time of crisis he was the most trustworthy of all his contemporaries as either batsmen or bowler. He seldom failed when a failure would have been fatal to his side, and this fighting spirit, presented always with the broad, bold facets of a noble character, brought him the affection and admiration of the whole county, and, indeed, of all the cricketing world. Yorkshire cricket will always accept George Hirst as its representative, anywhere in any age. His public esteem was reflected in his benefit match which brought him, in 1904, the then enormous return of £3,700. His playing stature rests on the performances of perhaps the most amazing individual feat in cricket history; in 1906 he scored over 2,000 runs and took over 200 wickets in the first-class season. His batting average was 45.86 and his bowling average 16.50.

Hirst and Rhodes remained Yorkshire's leading players for many years after the disintegration of the great side of the early 1900s and they helped the county to Championship victories in 1905, 1908 and 1912. Hirst was still playing – and whenever he played he was a significant force – in the improvisation of 1919, but Rhodes went on alone into the second period of dominance which began in 1922 and persisted for four seasons. In that era Yorkshire played 122 Championship matches, won 81 of them and lost only six. In general the performances were as remarkable as the figures, for Yorkshire were ruthless conquerors crushing their enemies so thoroughly that they came to regard the five-day week as an expectation rather than a privilege. In 1923 they won 25 of their 32 championship matches, and 13 of the 25 were won with an innings to spare.

Such achievements suggest, and rightly suggest, powerful batting resources, but it was the bowling strength in all conditions that made the side so formidable. Rhodes after his period of concentration upon batsmanship returned to full honour as a bowler; Waddington blazed across the cricketing sky; Macaulay and Emmott Robinson were surprised and disappointed if they did not take 100 wickets in a season; and Roy Kilner rapidly established himself, not as a rival to Rhodes, but complementary to him in the slow left-arm attack. As often as not Kilner bowled over the wicket, where Rhodes invariably bowled round in the classical tradition.

Success did not bring Yorkshire universal popularity. They were acknowledged cricketing masters of the counties, but they were not always on the happiest of terms with some of their rivals. The very fixity of their purpose, the grim determination of their methods cost them some affection, and there were one or two occasions when the pressure in the boiler of neighbourly goodwill ran dangerously high. Naturally enough, the bowling fires were the first to fade. When Lancashire took over the Championship in the late 1920s Yorkshire preserved their formidable batting, but awaited the arrival of new bowling of the necessary vitality. When they found it, the batting of Sutcliffe, Holmes, Oldroyd, Leyland, and their company guaranteed all the scope needed for the winning of more Championships.

HOLMES AND SUTCLIFFE

Holmes and Sutcliffe developed the most successful of all opening partnerships in county cricket. They came together experimentally and began inauspiciously, for the first time they opened the innings together the scoreboard quickly showed 0 for one, but their individual technical skill allied to the indefinable sympathy that grew between them soon made their association safe and their achievements historic. They put up a century partnership 69 times for Yorkshire and 74 times in all, and in 1932 they took the world's record opening partnership from their distinguished predecessors. Tunnicliffe and Brown made 554 against Derbyshire in 1898; Holmes and Sutcliffe made 555 against Essex. Curiously enough both these enormous stands were contrived with one of the batsmen under physical handicap. At Chesterfield, Tunnicliffe chose to sit up all night rather than risk unsatisfactory hotel accommodation, and he batted throughout the next day with a sandwich as his only sustenance because of catering confusion at the ground. At Leyton, Holmes was suffering from lumbago and in obvious pain throughout the long innings.

Holmes played for Yorkshire from 1913 to 1933 and therefore saw the beginning but not the end of the wonders of the 1930s. Sutcliffe's career extended from war to war, and he was a member of the teams that won the Championship seven times in the nine seasons from 1931 to 1939. He was always an outstanding member because he scarcely ever knew a year of personal failure and because his was a personality that could never be overlooked.

Sutcliffe's batsmanship has been accounted of limited range, but no question of its efficiency has been raised. No question could be raised while memories last and scoreboards remain to be read. Sutcliffe's limitations were mainly self-imposed. He restricted himself because restriction best served his purpose. He batted in the light of circumstances. His problems were the problems of the moment, each to be treated as it arose and instantly dismissed upon solution. The sum of his achievements represents the adequacy of his exposition. For Yorkshire, and for England, he rendered imperishable service.

By 1930 Yorkshire had found the bowling they sought as the basis for a great team, and to Bowes and Verity, Wilfred Rhodes and Emmott Robinson hastened to pass on the legacy of accumulated wisdom and intensity of purpose. The training was invaluable, the material for instruction more than adequate. Bowes, Verity and Macaulay, with Smailes and Ellis Robinson in subsequent support, and Sutcliffe, Leyland, Mitchell, Barber and eventually Hutton, brought Yorkshire to glories as great as they had ever known. They became a living legend in all the cricketing lands. They toured Jamaica as a county side, and had Australian wish been granted they would have toured Australia, too.

THE SELLERS ERA

It was not, of course, in the mere possession of individuals beyond the ordinary that Yorkshire found their strength. Great players do not necessarily establish great teams. Yorkshire had great players in the 1930s and they established a great team primarily because they were prepared to devote their special talents to a common cause. The character of the side became something more than the agglomerated characters of the members. Yorkshire cricket given to be the over-riding concern of every player and the personal achievement was the common satisfaction. The origin of this outlook lay far back in history but its development, or its renaissance, at least, was the contribution of A. B. Sellers who took over the captaincy in 1933 and held office for fifteen seasons. Perhaps Lord Hawke did more than Sellers in that there was more to do, but neither Lord Hawke nor any other Yorkshire leader brought greater devotion or persistent efficiency to the task in hand.

Sellers drew loyalty because he gave loyalty. He maintained unswervingly the principle that team interests were paramount, and his principles were so clearly illustrated that they could not escape the notice of established player or newcomer. The Yorkshire of Brian Seller's time would have been unmistakable in multi-coloured caps and disguised by beards. They carried their character on to every field they visited.

AGGRESSIVE FIELDING

Much was asked. Bowling had to be justifiable in cricket strategy; mere bowling and hoping for the best was not acceptable. Fielding had to be a positive ally to bowling. It was not enough to wait in likely places for catches to come; catches had to be created where none would have existed without courage, and confidence in the ability of colleagues. Yorkshire did not invent the "aggressive field" in the 1930s but they advanced its position in cricket. Their performances and their principles stood as the standard for the time and it is doubtful if the standard has ever been higher. In the nine seasons between 1931 and 1939 Yorkshire were County Champions seven times and there is no knowing how long their dominance would have continued but for the interruption of the Second World War. When cricket came again the greatness had gone. Sutcliffe and Wood passed into retirement; Bowes was no longer a fast bowler after four years in prison camps; Verity died of wounds in Italy. In 1946 the remainder of the old guard reassembled to win yet another Championship but their success contained the sunset gleam. Leyland and Turner brought their first-class careers to an end, Bowes and Smailes followed in the next season or two and Sellars himself handed on the torch of leadership in 1948, though he gave help when his appointed successor, Norman Yardley, was involved in Test match captaincy and selectorial duties.

Recent years have been spent in reconstruction; and in the inevitable experiment Yorkshire have missed both success and satisfaction. The Championship was shared with Middlesex in 1949 and second position has been attained three times in the past four seasons, but 1953 saw a humiliating descent into the bottom half of the table and the optimism of spring has rarely been matched in the reflections of autumn. Perhaps the essential lack has been a direct link between the old Yorkshire and the new. Players joining the side since 1946 could not acquire tradition by first-hand observation. They knew only their own way of playing cricket, the current way, and time was required for adjustment in a world inclined to be casual in reaction against the taut living of war.

PROBLEMS FOR YARDLEY

Yorkshire made mistakes in selectorial judgment as well as in playing technique and they had therefore to extend the period of experiment beyond the term expected. Yardley found himself with as difficult a task as any current county captain, for he had played long enough to appreciate needs and desires but could find no illustration of intentions for the newcomers.

Young Yorkshiremen did not know quite what was expected of them and were short of a yardstick for comparison. Social circumstances were a handicap to every county and a particular trial to Yorkshire who have long expected their young players to fit into a given pattern, of proven worth. Yardley's success in captaincy has been limited by the lack of understanding and ambition in some of his players, but he has done invaluable work in keeping the good name of Yorkshire cricket at the highest level.

Another era of playing distinction comparable with those of the past still remains speculative. There are players of immense potentiality now wearing the Yorkshire cap and it is to be presumed that Appleyard, Close and Trueman among others have not yet reached the peak of their careers; but character has yet to be confirmed in the side as a whole, and there are obvious shortcomings to be eradicated before a good team can turn itself into a great one. The Yorkshire enthusiasm stands as high as ever; the Yorkshire ambition is in no way diminished. Cricket is an integral part of the Yorkshire scene and the club has never been in more flourishing financial condition. Len Hutton's genius in batsmanship remains a beacon to guide the struggling and a vicarious pride to every compatriot. Yorkshiremen need only be true to their inheritance to find the cricketing satisfactions they desire.

LEN HUTTON: THE MASTER [1956]

By Neville Cardus

Len Hutton was the only batsman of his period to whom we could apply the term "Old Master", referring in his case not to his number of years but to the style and vintage of his cricket. He followed in the succession of the classic professional batsmen who each went in first for his county and for England: Shrewsbury, Hayward, Hobbs and Sutcliffe – though Sutcliffe wore his classicism with a subtly Sutcliffian difference.

As Old Masters go, Hutton was young enough; the sadness is that physical disability put an end to his career in its prime. He had all the classic points of style when, not much more than 19, he came to Lord's in 1936 and scored fifty-five. I then wrote of him in this strain of Cassandrian prophecy: "Here is a young cricketer who is already old in the head and destined to enliven many a Lancashire and Yorkshire match of the future".

If by means of some Time-machine capable of television we could today see a picture of Hutton batting twenty years ago, and one taken of him during his maturity, we would notice no fundamental difference in technique. We would see that his cricket had grown in experience and finish, that is all. Like the music of Bach, Hutton's batsmanship in its evolution from an early to a late period presented no marked divisions; it was never raw, unprincipled or embryonic. He batted grammatically from the start, choosing his strokes as carefully as a professor of logic his words.

Even when he first played for Yorkshire, beginning with 0, he seemed to begin an innings to a plan, building the shape and the duration of it to a blue-print in his mind, and to a time-table. But once in the greenest of his salad days he fell into error. He opened a Yorkshire innings on Saturday at Bradford with Arthur Mitchell, dourest and most unsmiling of the clan. After a characteristically Yorkshire investigation of the state of the wicket, the state of the opposition bowling, the state of mind the umpires were in, the state of the weather and barometer, and probably the state of the Bank of England itself, Mitchell and Hutton began to score now and then.

Young Hutton was feeling in form, so after he had played himself in he decided to cut a rising ball outside the off-stump. Remember that he was fresh to the Yorkshire scene and policies. He actually lay back and cut hard and swiftly, with cavalier flourish. He cut under the ball by an inch, and it sped bang into the wicket-keeper's gloves. And Mitchell, from the other end of the pitch, looked hard at Hutton and said, "That's no . . . use!" This was probably Hutton's true baptism, cleansing him of all vanity and lusts for insubstantial pageantry and temporal glory.

He observed the classical unities; that is to say, he did not venture beyond reliable and established limitations of batsmanship learned in the traditional school. Geometrical precision in the application of bat to ball, each movement of the feet considered until the right position was found almost instictively, not bringing him merely to the ball and, as far as possible and if necessary over it, but also with body at the proper balance.

Never, or hardly ever, did Hutton play a thoughtless innings; his mind usually seemed to move a fraction of time in advance of his most rapid footwork and sudden tensions of limb, sinew and nerve. It is, of course, wrong to suppose that Hutton was at any time a batsman slow in his mental and physical reactions at the crease.

The score-board may have told us that he was not getting runs feverishly, but the vigilance of Hutton was eternal; the concentration in him was so intense that it frequently exhausted his not robust physique much sooner than did the more obvious toil and burden of the day. In the most austerely defensive Hutton innings we could feel a mental alertness; purpose in him suffered no weariness.

And whether or not he was putting into practice his wide repertoire of strokes, he was the stylist always; rarely was he discovered in an awkward position at the crease, rarely was he bustled or hurried. Once at Kennington Oval, Lindwall knocked Hutton's cap off in a Test Match. Such an outrage could be equalled in a cricketer's imagination only by supposing that Alfred Mynn's tall hat was ever likewise rudely removed.

On a bowler's wicket, when the ball's spin was angular and waspish in turn, he could maintain his premeditated technical responses, often using a "dead" bat, the handle held so loosely that when the ball came into contact with the blade's middle it was as though against a drugged cushion: the spin was anaesthetised into harmlessness.

But Hutton was, when grace descended upon him, a versatile and handsome stroke player. Old Trafford will remember that in 1948 he made a century of a brilliance which, in the circumstances – Bank Holiday and a Lancashire v Yorkshire match – was almost pagan.

He drove Lindwall with Spooneresque charm and panache at Brisbane in December 1950; at Lord's in the Test Match of 1953, he played one of the most regal and most highly pedigreed innings ever seen in an England and Australia Test Match on that hallowed ground. And he has contributed to a festival at Scarborough.

If Hutton had lived and played in the Lord Hawke epoch, when even Test cricketers in England had somehow to adapt themselves and their skill to matches limited to three days, he would have been a different batsman in his tempo and mental approach. But he could not possibly have been greater.

Any artist or master of craft is an organism in an environment; he is very much what circumstances and atmosphere make of him. His very greatness consists in how fully he can sum up the technique of his day as he finds it, and how representative he is of his day's spirit. MacLaren, lordly and opulent at the crease, was a representative man and cricketer in a lordly opulent period; Hutton's cricket has been as true as MacLaren's to the Zeitgeist, to the feeling, temper and even to the economy of the age which shaped his character and his skill, both conceived as much as in integrity as in joy.

As a captain he was shrewd but courteous; he knew the game's finest points, and though never likely to give anything away, was too proud to take anything not his due. Sometimes he may have allowed thoughtfulness to turn to worry; but this is a natural habit in the part of the world which Hutton comes from.

Hutton certainly showed that a professional cricketer can wear the robes of leadership in the field of play with dignity. At first, no doubt, he appeared at the head of his troops not wearing anything like a Caesarian toga, but rather the uniform of a sergeant-major. But he moved up in rank and prestige until he became worthy of his command and defeated Australia twice in successive rubbers, wresting one from the enemy at the pinch and looting the other after a series of Tests which were, if I may be free with my allusions and metaphors, the Australians' Austerlitz.

One of Hutton's most winning characteristics — and his personality is extremely attractive — is his smile, a smile with a twinkle in it. He had many occasions in his distinguished career on which to indulge this smile, many provocations to it, and he never missed the joke. A Yorkshireman has his own idea of humour, and Hutton, as great or famous as any Yorkshireman contemporary with him, relished his laugh all the more because very often it came last.

YORKSHIRE v GLOUCESTERSHIRE

Played at Leeds, June 18, 19, 20, 1958

Drawn. No decision. Bad weather returned to Yorkshire, no play being possible on the second and third days. This made thirteen blank days in the season already for them, eleven within the county. The cricket on the first day was full of interest, leading features being a hat-trick and an opening stand of 151 between Stott and Taylor. Both batted splendidly against steady bowling on a docile pitch. Wiltshire, the Gloucestershire medium-paced bowler, finished the Yorkshire innings by dismissing Binks, Ryan and Cowan with successive balls and his seven for 52 was easily the best performance of his career. Yorkshire lost their last seven wickets for 83. Gloucestershire batted for the last twenty-five minutes and that ended play in the match.

Yorkshire

W. B. Stott b Wiltshire 96	J. G. Binks b Wiltshire 3
K. Taylor c Brown b Wiltshire 72	M. Ryan b Wiltshire 0
D. E. V. Padgett b Wiltshire 0	M. J. Cowan lbw b Wiltshire. 0
D. B. Close b Wiltshire 16	
J. V. Wilson c Brown b Cook 2	L-b 5, n-b 1 6
J. B. Bolus c Carpenter b Brown. 39	
J. R. Burnet c Brown b Smith 6	1/151 2/151 3/180 4/183 5/195 263
J. H. Wardle not out 23	6/218 7/257 8/263 9/263

Gloucestershire

D. M. Young not out 18
D. Carpenter retired hurt 6
B. J. Meyer not out 1

(No wkt) 25

R. B. Nicholls, D. Hawkins, G. M. Emmett, A. S. Brown, J. B. Mortimore, D. R. Smith, G. G. M. Wiltshire and C. Cook did not bat.

Gloucestershire Bowling

	Overs	Mdns	Runs	Wkts
Smith	26	8	66	1
Brown.	31	5	69	1
Mortimore	12	5	33	—
Wiltshire.	29.5	12	52	7
Cook.	18	5	37	1

Yorkshire Bowling

	Overs	Mdns	Runs	Wkts
Cowan	4	—	22	—
Ryan.	3	1	3	—

Umpires: W. H. Copson and J. S. Buller.

THE WARDLE CASE

The dismissal of J. H. Wardle by Yorkshire three days after he had been chosen by MCC to go to Australia and the action taken later by MCC in withdrawing their invitation to him became a national topic. It was during the match between Yorkshire and Somerset at Sheffield on July 30 [1958] that Mr J. H. Nash, the Yorkshire secretary, announced:

"The Yorkshire Committee have informed J. H. Wardle that they will not be calling on his services after the end of the season."

Wardle was selected for the match against Lancashire at Old Trafford, August 2, 4 and 5, but while the players were waiting for play to begin, rain having caused a delay, the Yorkshire captain, J. R. Burnet, made the following statement:

"J. H. Wardle has requested that he stand down from the match because of comments he intends to make about his colleagues in a newspaper article to be published while the match is in progress. He has been given permission to stand down and has left the ground."

The articles duly appeared in the *Daily Mail* and on August 4 Mr R. Aird, secretary of MCC, announced: "The differences between the Yorkshire CCC and J. H. Wardle have up till now been considered a domestic affair, but owing to the Press publicity now being given to the matter, the MCC Committee will consider the situation at their next meeting on August 19."

Meanwhile the Yorkshire CCC Committee met again at Bradford on August 11, when Mr J. H. Nash issued the following statement:

"The Yorkshire County Cricket Club Committee regret the unpleasant publicity given to their decision to dispense with the services of J. H. Wardle after the present season. In past years Wardle has been warned on several occasions that his general behaviour on the field and in the dressing rooms left much to be desired. As no improvement was shown this year, the decision to dispense with his services was made, as it was unanimously considered that it was essential to have discipline and a happy and loyal team before any lasting improvement could be expected in the play of the Yorkshire XI.

It is felt that the recent articles published in the *Daily Mail* fully justify the committee's decision. Wardle broke his contract when he wrote these articles without first obtaining permission, and the committee are therefore terminating his engagement forthwith. The committee emphatically reaffirm their high regard for the services of Mr J. R. Burnet and his predecessors in the captaincy, for the loyalty and restraint shown by players in the trying circumstances and for the valued work the former players give so helpfully in acting as cricket coaches."

The full MCC Committee interviewed Wardle during their meeting at Lord's on August 19, after which Mr. R. Aird, the MCC secretary, announced:

"The committee of MCC have considered certain articles contributed by J. H. Wardle to a national newspaper since the date of his selection for the forthcoming Australian tour. They have also considered a report received from the Yorkshire County Cricket Club, many of the details of which were not available to the selection committee at the time when the team was chosen.

The committee considered that the publication by Wardle in the press of the criticisms of his county captain, his county committee and some of his fellow players in the form and at the time that he published them did a grave disservice to the game. They believe that the welfare of cricket as a whole in terms of loyalty and behaviour must override all other considerations. After an interview with Wardle and after very careful consideration of all aspects of the question, the MCC Committee have reached the decision that the invitation to him to go with the MCC team to Australia must be withdrawn."

Wardle received invitations from some counties to join them and on August 13 he informed Nottinghamshire that he was prepared to play for them. Consent of Yorkshire and MCC would have been necessary for the purpose of special registration. A month later Wardle announced that he had finished with county cricket and had signed a two-year contract with Nelson, the Lancashire League club. He had been assisting Rishton, another Lancashire League club, since leaving Yorkshire. Later, Wardle went to Australia to comment on the MCC tour for the *Daily Mail*.

NOTES BY THE EDITOR, 1959

WHEN TROUBLES BEGAN

When the seventeen names were announced for the Australian tour, many of us were of the opinion that MCC had chosen one of the strongest sides ever to be sent overseas. I am afraid that since then those ideas have been completely shattered. To my mind England's troubles began when the MCC Committee found it necessary to withdraw their invitation to Wardle. That was a bold decision and one which MCC took in the best interests of the game; but in the first place they should never have been placed in that embarrassing position. Yorkshire must shoulder the blame, for no sooner had they informed MCC that Wardle would be available to tour Australia than the county decided to dispense with his services.

Wardle's name having been withdrawn, the selectors then committed an error in not producing an immediate replacement. They had decided to take seventeen players; yet a few weeks later they reckoned Laker and Lock could shoulder the slow bowling alone.

NOTES BY THE EDITOR, 1960

YORKSHIRE'S PROFESSIONAL CAPTAIN

For the first time for many years, Yorkshire now have a professional captain in J. V. Wilson, who has been appointed to succeed J. R. Burnet. Thirty-five years ago the late Lord Hawke said some strong things about professional captains and during the course of time the leadership of Yorkshire has been linked with them, whereas he was expressing his opinion about England.

In the summer of 1924, C. Parkin, then at his zenith, criticised A. E. R. Gilligan, the England captain, for not calling upon him to bowl on the third morning of the Edgbaston Test when South Africa, dismissed by Gilligan and Tate for 30, followed on. Parkin wrote disparagingly about Gilligan's captaincy in general and said he would never play for England again. At the Yorkshire annual meeting in the following January, Lord Hawke touched on this matter and said:

"Pray God no professional will ever captain the England side. I love professionals, every one of them, but we have always had an amateur skipper. If the time comes when we are to have no more amateurs captaining England, well, I don't say England will become exactly like League football, but it will be a thousand pities, and it will not be for the good of the game."

Lord Hawke did not live to see Leonard Hutton, a Yorkshire professional, restore England's post-war cricket fortunes, nor to learn of the knighthood Hutton received for his services to cricket.

In the early years of his long reign as captain of Yorkshire (1883-1909) Lord Hawke was often helped by Louis Hall, a professional who at one time was termed assistant-captain and led Yorkshire throughout the summer of 1885 when Lord Hawke was away.

I also wonder what Lord Hawke's reaction would have been to recent suggestions that the present time may be the twilight of the amateur. It is seriously suggested that all players should be termed "Cricketers" and that there should be no distinction between amateur and professional. In the past I may have thought along these lines, but when one remembers the great work done by B. H. Lyon for Gloucestershire, R. W. V. Robins for Middlesex, A. B. Sellers and J. R. Burnet for Yorkshire, and W. S. Surridge and P. B. H. May for Surrey, surely, no matter what the financial set-up, English cricket, and particularly county cricket, cannot afford to lose the amateur. His very independence contributes to the welfare of the game and therefore to the well-being of the professional. Look what M. C. Cowdrey, D. B. Carr, E. R. Dexter, D. J. Insole, T. E. Bailey, M. J. K. Smith, A. C. D. Ingleby-Mackenzie have meant to their sides. True, there are capable professionals who command respect from their men, but I would not like to see the amateur disappear entirely from the English scene.

YORKSHIRE v NOTTINGHAMSHIRE

Played at Middlesbrough, May 9, 11, 12, 1959

Yorkshire won by 194 runs. After losing half their side for 99 at the start, they completely dominated the rest of the match. Wilson and Burnet led the recovery with a stand of 61. Nottinghamshire broke down before the speed of Trueman and Ryan. Leading by 85, Yorkshire were given a great send-off to their second innings. Taylor and Stott sharing a stand of 161. Taylor, driving powerfully, reached his century in an hour and fifty-five minutes, including three 6s and fifteen 4s. He punished Forman for 4, 6, 6, 4, 4, off five successive balls in one over. Needing 323 to win, Nottinghamshire lost Simpson overnight and the match ended just before lunch on the third day. Don Wilson, the slow left-hander, helped the rapid finish by achieving the only hat-trick of the season and the first of his career when dismissing Millman, Morgan and Davison.

Yorkshire

W. B. Stott c Poole b Jepson	26	– c Simpson b Morgan	65
K. Taylor run out	19	– c Jepson b Morgan	103
D. E. V. Padgett c N. Hill b Cotton	10	– not out	39
D. B. Close c Forman b Davison	2	– c Forman b Morgan	0
J. V. Wilson c Morgan b Cotton	76	– c Martin b Forman	1
R. Illingworth c Jepson b Davison	11	– not out	22
J. R. Burnet c Forman b Morgan	47		
F. S. Trueman c M. Hill b Morgan	26		
J. G. Binks b Cotton	8		
D. Wilson c Millman b Cotton	8		
M. Ryan not out	4		
B 1	1	B 5, w 2	7

1/45 2/45 3/48 4/69 5/99   238   1/161 2/181   (4 wkts dec.) 237
6/160 7/192 8/209 9/233   3/181 4/188

Nottinghamshire

R. T. Simpson c Binks b Trueman	56	– b Illingworth	7
N. Hill b Trueman	6	– b Close	58
E. J. Martin b Trueman	0	– lbw b Trueman	7
M. Hill lbw b Trueman	34	– b Illingworth	26
C. J. Poole c Binks b Ryan	4	– b D. Wilson	11
G. Millman b Ryan	8	– c Burnet b D. Wilson	0
A. Jepson b Trueman	27	– b Illingworth	12
M. Morgan b Trueman	0	– c Trueman b D. Wilson	0
P. R. Forman c J. Wilson b Ryan	4	– c Trueman b Ryan	6
I. Davison b Trueman	0	– c J. Wilson b D. Wilson	0
J. Cotton not out	1	– not out	0
B 5, l-b 8	13	L-b 1	1

1/15 2/15 3/97 4/108 5/108   153   1/25 2/39 3/70 4/95 5/106   128
6/126 7/135 8/142 9/152   6/116 7/128 8/128 9/128

Nottinghamshire Bowling

	Overs	Mdns	Runs	Wkts	Overs	Mdns	Runs	Wkts
Cotton	17.1	4	55	4	16	3	67	—
Davison	19	7	61	2	8	3	21	—
Jepson	18	5	40	1	11	1	42	—
Forman	12	1	49	—	9	—	53	1
Morgan	8	2	32	2	12	2	47	3

Yorkshire Bowling

	Overs	Mdns	Runs	Wkts	Overs	Mdns	Runs	Wkts
Trueman	25	6	57	7	13	2	31	1
Ryan	21	6	47	3	9	1	25	1
Illingworth	6	—	23	—	12.2	6	20	3
D. Wilson	5	—	13	—	13	6	31	4
Close	2	2	—	—	5	1	20	1

Umpires: Harry Elliott and T. W. Spencer.

YORKSHIRE v NORTHAMPTONSHIRE

Played at Sheffield, May 28, 30, 31, 1960

Yorkshire won by six wickets. Trueman accomplished the best match performance of his career, taking fourteen wickets, seven in each innings. He began by causing a Northamptonshire breakdown on a fast pitch, but the middle batsmen improved the position. Yorkshire also struggled against Tyson, but after losing three wickets for 52, they recovered through Taylor, J. V. Wilson and Illingworth. Northamptonshire, 36 behind, did much better for a time, but Trueman quickly ran through the tail. Subba Row remained unbeaten for 90. Yorkshire, needing 198 in four hours, won with an hour to spare. Close and Bolus put on 81 for the third wicket.

Northamptonshire

M. Norman b Trueman	17	– c Binks b Trueman	16
B. Reynolds b Trueman	6	– lbw b Close	50
P. J. Watts c Close b Hatton	7	– c Close b Hatton	6
*R. Subba Row c Binks b Taylor	22	– not out	90
D. W. Barrick b Trueman	38	– b D. Wilson	30
A. Lightfoot lbw b Trueman	16	– c J. Wilson b Trueman	23
F. J. Tyson c Close b Taylor	26	– c Close b Trueman	0
M. H. J. Allen c Binks b Trueman	0	– b Trueman	3
P. D. Watts c Illingworth b Trueman	14	– b Trueman	4
†K. V. Andrew not out	20	– b Trueman	3
M. Ashenden b Trueman	1	– b Trueman	0
L-b 2	2	B 6, l-b 6	8

1/19 2/24 3/34 4/76 5/103   169   1/20 2/87 3/117 4/130 5/201   233
6/108 7/108 8/138 9/157   6/201 7/205 8/213 9/233

Yorkshire

W. B. Stott c Norman b Tyson	8	– c Barrick b Allen	30
K. Taylor lbw b Ashenden	75	– lbw b Tyson	1
J. B. Bolus b Tyson	1	– st Andrew b Allen	59
D. B. Close lbw b Tyson	0	– not out	83
R. Illingworth c Reynolds b Tyson	31	– c Andrew b Allen	7
*J. V. Wilson c Norman b Allen	48	– not out	16
D. Wilson b Tyson	0		
F. S. Trueman c P. J. Watts b Tyson	12		
†J. G. Binks st Andrew b Allen	17		
M. J. Cowan st Andrew b Allen	0		
A. G. Hatton not out	4		
L-b 7, n-b 2	9	L-b 2	2

1/40 2/46 3/52 4/114 5/116   205   1/7 2/57 3/138   (4 wkts) 198
6/116 7/139 8/197 9/197   4/176

Yorkshire Bowling

	Overs	Mdns	Runs	Wkts	Overs	Mdns	Runs	Wkts
Trueman	21.2	3	60	7	29.3	7	65	7
Cowan	16	4	44	—	23	3	53	—
Hatton	14	3	42	1	13	2	33	1
Taylor	10	4	21	2	6	2	15	—
Illingworth					14	10	4	—
D. Wilson					19	9	36	1
Close					9	3	19	1

Northamptonshire Bowling

	Overs	Mdns	Runs	Wkts	Overs	Mdns	Runs	Wkts
Tyson	27	4	57	6	17	3	53	1
Ashenden	12	4	28	1				
P. D. Watts	14	6	41	—	15	1	64	—
Allen	22.5	13	47	3	25	8	58	3
Lightfoot	4	—	23	—				
P. J. Watts					6	2	16	—
Subba Row					1	—	5	—

Umpires: J. S. Buller and T. W. Spencer.

THE UNIVERSITIES

CAMBRIDGE UNIVERSITY

CAMBRIDGE UNIVERSITY v LANCASHIRE

Played at Cambridge, May 1, 3, 4, 1948

Drawn. Heavy rain allowed play only on Monday, when the cricket was notable for the brilliant batting of G. H. G. Doggart, a Freshman, who created an English record by scoring 215 not out – the highest innings by any batsman on his début in first-class cricket. The feat was all the more notable because K. Cranston, the Lancashire captain, put the University in. Doggart, at the wicket for nearly six hours, hit a 5 and eighteen 4s. He was ably supported by Insole, who helped to add 116 in eighty minutes, the stand stopping a collapse.

Cambridge University

J. M. Mills b Pollard	7
J. G. Dewes c Place b Cranston	0
G. H. G. Doggart not out	215
G. M. Shuttleworth st Barlow b Roberts	12
T. E. Bailey c Barlow b Roberts	3
D. J. Insole b Pollard	66
B. C. Elgood lbw b Cranston	25
B. J. K. Pryer c Ikin b Cranston	10
R. D. Pearsall b Cranston	0
F. B. Barnes st Barlow b Roberts	22
W. H. Griffiths b Greenwood	0
B 18, l-b 8	26
	386

Lancashire

C. Washbrook not out	6
W. Place not out	10
(No wkt)	16

K. Cranston, N. D. Howard, J. T. Ikin, G. A. Edrich, A. Wharton, P. Greenwood, A. Barlow, R. Pollard and W. B. Roberts did not bat.

Lancashire Bowling

	Overs	Mdns	Runs	Wkts
Pollard	32	5	91	2
Cranston	30	3	93	4
Greenwood	31.4	8	80	1
Roberts	28	6	63	3
Ikin	7	1	33	—

Cambridge University Bowling

	Overs	Mdns	Runs	Wkts
Bailey	3	1	12	—
Griffiths	3	1	4	—

Umpires: F. S. Lee and H. Palmer.

CAMBRIDGE UNIVERSITY v YORKSHIRE

Played at Cambridge, May 11, 12, 13, 1949

Yorkshire won by nine wickets. Yorkshire gave a trial to three young players, Lowson, an opening batsman, Close, an all-rounder, and Trueman, a spin bowler. All gave the county much assistance during the season, and Close, aged 18, played for England. The best performance on this occasion was by Lowson, whose innings on the last day helped Yorkshire to victory shortly after lunch. Halliday also contributed to the win by some adventurous batting. The University started well, but their bowlers gave little support.

CAMBRIDGE UNIVERSITY v ESSEX

Played at Cambridge, May 7, 9, 10, 1949

Drawn. The feature of the march was an unfinished partnership of 429 in five hours ten minutes between Dewes and Doggart, the highest second-wicket stand in English cricket and only 26 short of the world record. Each batsman made his highest score to date in first-class cricket; Dewes hit twenty-one boundaries; Doggart a 5 and twenty-five 4s. The University attack also came in for punishment, and three declarations could not bring about a result. Dodds, aggressive from the start, played the best Essex innings.

Cambridge University

J. G. Dewes not out	204	– not out	58
R. J. Morris b R. Smith	8	– b Bailey	14
G. H. G. Doggart not out	219	– b Vigar	8
J. H. H. Anton (did not bat)		– b Bailey	19
A. C. Burnett (did not bat)		– not out	24
B 4, l-b 2, w 2, n-b 2	10	B 14, n-b 5	19
(1 wkt dec.)	441	(3 wkts dec.)	142

D. J. Insole, M. H. Stevenson, O. B. Popplewell, P. J. Hall, B. J. K. Pryer and P. A. Kelland did not bat.

Essex

T. C. Dodds lbw b Hall	86	– b Hall	0
G. H. West run out	55	– b Pryer	8
S. J. Cray st Popplewell b Morris	7	– b Doggart	51
F. H. Vigar lbw b Pryer	37	– c Hall b Pryer	36
W. B. Morris lbw b Insole	65	– c Popplewell b Kelland	68
T. E. Bailey lbw b Insole	28	– not out	14
T. N. Pearce c and b Insole	5	– not out	19
R. Smith c Burnett b Insole	3	– c Insole b Pryer	19
W. J. Dines not out	1		
B. Taylor b Kelland	2		
B 4, l-b 6, w 5	15	B 4, l-b 2, w 1	7
(9 wkts dec.)	304	(6 wkts)	222

Essex Bowling

	Overs	Mdns	Runs	Wkts	Overs	Mdns	Runs	Wkts
Bailey	25	5	91	—	12	2	41	2
R. Smith	26	4	81	1	17	4	38	—
Price	32	3	110	—	10	2	22	—
Vigar	16	—	71	—	12	3	22	1
Morris	10	2	33	—				
Dines	11	—	42	—				
Dodds	1	—	3	—				

Cambridge University Bowling

	Overs	Mdns	Runs	Wkts	Overs	Mdns	Runs	Wkts
Hall..............	30	5	74	1	7	1	18	1
Kelland..........	18.3	6	50	1	9	2	28	1
Stevenson........	30	17	47	—	2	—	4	—
Morris...........	20	10	45	1	11	3	32	—
Pryer............	17	4	37	1	21	2	76	3
Doggart	8	2	17	—	5	—	21	1
Insole	8	1	19	4	2	—	14	—
Dewes...........					2	—	22	—

Umpires: F. S. Lee and H. Palmer.

CAMBRIDGE UNIVERSITY v HAMPSHIRE

Played at Cambridge, June 7, 8, 9, 1950

Match drawn. A splendid innings by May and centuries by Stevenson, his first at Fenner's, and Dewes gave Cambridge an exceptional score. May played his highest innings which enabled him to share with Sheppard the distinction of recording a double century in his first year at the University. He and Dewes added 209 and Stevenson and May made an exhilarating 233 in two hours five minutes. Hill did not bowl because of an injured finger, but he looked set for a century when the game finished with the county 32 runs behind. Dewes, acting captain, put on to bowl all his side apart from the wicket-keeper Popplewell.

Cambridge University

J. G. Dewes c and b McCorkell 101	T. U. Wells b Ransom.................	3
D. S. Sheppard c Harrison b Ransom...... 9	B 10, l-b 7, n-b 1	18
P. B. H. May not out................... 227		
M. H. Stevenson lbw b Dare............. 109	(4 wkts dec.) 467	

A. G. J. Rimell, W. I. D. Hayward, O. B. Popplewell, G. H. C. Griffith, G. A. Robertson and P. A. Kelland did not bat.

Hampshire

N. McCorkell c May b Robertson 52	R. Carty c and b Rimell	43
N. H. Rogers c Kelland b Robertson 0	R. Dare c May b Wells	51
J. R. Gray c Popplewell b Kelland 13	V. J. Ransom c May b Wells..............	15
J. Arnold b Rimell..................... 87	C. J. Knott not out	11
L. Harrison b Dewes................... 22	B 21, l-b 6, w 9, n-b 5	41
A. W. H. Rayment lbw b Sheppard 14		
G. Hill not out........................ 86	(9 wkts) 435	

Hampshire Bowling

	Overs	Mdns	Runs	Wkts
Ransom	28	4	85	2
Carty	23	5	77	—
Gray.............	12	2	30	—
Knott	23	3	68	—
Dare	29	3	94	1
Hill..............	2	1	1	—
McCorkell	14	2	73	1
Arnold	2	—	21	—

Cambridge University Bowling

	Overs	Mdns	Runs	Wkts
Kelland...........	37	6	74	1
Robertson.........	21	6	53	2
Hayward	40	13	75	—
Rimell............	50	25	65	2
Griffith	22	5	64	—
May	2	1	1	—
Wells.............	10	1	25	2
Dewes............	8	3	13	1
Stevenson.........	12	5	18	—
Sheppard	2	—	6	1

Umpires: F. S. Lee and K. McCanlis.

CAMBRIDGE UNIVERSITY v MIDDLESEX

Played at Cambridge, June 6, 7, 8, 1951

Drawn. No more thrilling finish could have been possible for Middlesex, after being set to score at the rate of nearly 100 an hour, were within one run of victory with their last pair together. The match was memorable also for the batting of the Cambridge pair, Sheppard and May, who shared a stand of 215 in the first innings. May (fifteen 4s) hit his third century in four innings, and Sheppard became the first player of the season to hit two hundreds in a match. His second display, which lasted only two hours twenty minutes and included thirteen 4s, was more impressive than the first. That occupied five and a half hours. The opening stand with Mathews realised 167, Middlesex accepted the challenge and, after Robertson and Brown gave their side a splendid start, Edrich hit his first 100 of the summer in under two hours.

Cambridge University

D. S. Sheppard b Sharp.......................143	– b Bennett	.125
K. P. A. Mathews b McCorquodale 19	– run out	45
P. B. H. May c Compton b Sharp................120	– not out	18
T. U. Wells b Sharp........................... 20		
M. H. Stevenson c Compton b Sharp 12	– b Bennett	4
R. J. Morris not out........................... 11		
R. G. Marlar c Brown b Young................. 14		
O. B. Popplewell not out 13		
B 1, l-b 4, n-b 2 7	B 6, l-b 5, w 1	12

(6 wkts dec.) 359   (3 wkts dec.) 205

R. Subba Row, O. J. Wait and M. N. Morgan did not bat.

Middlesex

J. D. Robertson lbw b Wait	16 – b Morgan	84
S. M. Brown c Morgan b Wait	68 – b Marlar	48
W. J. Edrich st Popplewell b Marlar	6 – b Wait	101
H. P. Sharp c May b Wait	14 – c Morris b Stevenson	9
D. Bennett c Sheppard b Subba Row	19 – c May b Marlar	1
D. L. Newman c Wait b Stevenson	21 – not out	21
A. Thompson run out	50 – b Morgan	6
J. L. Swann retired hurt	29 – not out	1
L. H. Compton not out	3 – b Wait	29
J. A. Young b Marlar	9 – c Wells b Marlar	11
A. McCorquodale b Subba Row	0 – c May b Wait	1
B 5, l-b 2, n-b 2	9	B 1, l-b 6, n-b 1	8
	244	**(9 wkts) 320**

Middlesex Bowling

	Overs	Mdns	Runs	Wkts	Overs	Mdns	Runs	Wkts
McCorquodale	19	6	53	1	12	2	58	—
Bennett	11	—	31	—	6.5	1	31	2
Edrich	14	2	45	—	11	2	42	—
Young	30	20	39	1	20	6	49	—
Swann	24	2	90	—				
Sharp	19	3	94	4	3	—	13	—

Cambridge University Bowling

	Overs	Mdns	Runs	Wkts	Overs	Mdns	Runs	Wkts
Wait	35	10	75	3	21	4	84	3
Morgan	16	4	38	—	17	1	81	2
Marlar	36	6	85	2	21	1	100	3
Stevenson	11	5	13	1	9	—	37	1
Subba Row	12.4	3	24	2	2	—	10	—

Umpires: F. S. Lee and T. J. Bartley.

CAMBRIDGE UNIVERSITY v ESSEX

Played at Cambridge, May 7, 8, 9, 1952

Drawn. A closely-fought match ended with Cambridge needing 12 runs to win and three wickets left. Centuries by Sheppard and May and a hat-trick by Marlar, the first at Fenner's for many years, formed the features of the University cricket, but Essex were the more consistent side. On a pitch affected by rain, the county lost their first eight wickets cheaply, but recovered. Sheppard batted four hours for 113 and Cambridge were well placed until their last five wickets fell for five runs. Dodds and Gibb put on 95 for the second Essex wicket before Marlar dismissed Gibb, Smith and Insole with successive balls. Cambridge needed 232 to win in two and a half hours. Sheppard again batted well, and May showed his best form for the first time in the season.

Essex

T. C. Dodds c Sheppard b Subba Row	50	– c Moore b Warr	56
A. V. Avery lbw b McCarthy	0	– lbw b McCarthy	4
P. A. Gibb b McGinty	46	– c McGinty b Marlar	62
R. Horsfall lbw b McCarthy	10	– not out	56
D. J. Insole lbw b Warr	19	– st Alexander b Marlar	0
T. E. Bailey b McGinty	9	– not out	14
R. Smith b McCarthy	5	– lbw b Marlar	0
F. H. Vigar not out	41		
W. T. Greensmith lbw b Warr	9		
C. J. M. Kenny c Sheppard b Subba Row	16		
K. C. Preston b Marlar	30		
L-b 6, n-b 1	7	B 2, l-b 3	5

1/1 2/84 3/107 4/108 5/122 242 1/8 2/103 (5 wkts dec.) 197
6/137 7/144 8/160 9/195   3/158 4/158 5/158

Cambridge University

D. S. Sheppard lbw b Bailey	113	– c Insole b Greensmith	64
M. H. Bushby st Gibb b Greensmith	27	– b Kenny	13
P. B. H. May b Bailey	1	– not out	104
G. G. Tordoff c and b Smith	31	– c Kenny b Greensmith	13
N. H. Moore c Gibb b Greensmith	13	– c Bailey b Greensmith	1
R. Subba Row c Gibb b Kenny	16		
J. J. Warr run out	1	– b Preston	1
F. C. M. Alexander b Bailey	1	– c Dodds b Bailey	13
R. McGinty b Kenny	0	– not out	0
R. G. Marlar run out	1	– c Bailey b Greensmith	5
C. N. McCarthy not out	1		
B 1, n-b 2	3	B 5, l-b 1	6

1/64 2/75 3/139 4/162 5/203 208 1/35 2/105 3/166 (7 wkts) 220
6/205 7/205 8/206 9/207   4/174 5/180 6/208 7/214

Cambridge University Bowling

	Overs	Mdns	Runs	Wkts	Overs	Mdns	Runs	Wkts
McCarthy	32	5	38	3	14	3	27	1
Warr	16	3	55	2	19	4	55	1
Marlar	22.1	4	67	1	26	4	83	3
McGinty	19	7	36	2	8	2	27	—
Subba Row	9	2	39	2				

Essex Bowling

	Overs	Mdns	Runs	Wkts	Overs	Mdns	Runs	Wkts
Preston	14	2	36	—	11	1	42	1
Bailey	18	6	24	3	12	5	32	1
Kenny	15	3	34	2	8	—	35	1
Smith	17	3	42	1	11	—	42	—
Greensmith	13	1	40	2	12	1	63	4
Vigar	11	3	29	—				

Umpires: F. S. Lee and H. Palmer.

CAMBRIDGE UNIVERSITY v SUSSEX

Played at Cambridge, April 30, May 1, 2, 1958

Sussex won by eight wickets with eight minutes to spare. Apart from Dexter, the captain, who hit twenty 4s in his 114, and Green, who shared a third wicket stand of 154 in the first innings, the University batsmen failed against a keen attack. Sussex, aided by an aggressive 162 from Doggart, the former Cambridge captain, led by 57 runs. When half the University's second innings wickets fell for 98 victory for Sussex seemed merely routine, but the later batsmen, particularly Rutherford, fought back well. Sussex were left to score 148 in two hours twenty-five minutes on a wearing pitch, but Oakman, Suttle and Parks were rarely in difficulty.

Cambridge University

I. M. McLachlan b Thomson	0	– b Thomson	0
D. J. Green b Marlar	75	– lbw b Thomson	1
J. M. Watson c Doggart b James	2	– c Bell b Oakman	31
E. R. Dexter c Lenham b Suttle	114	– c and b Thomson	14
R. M. Prideaux run out	30	– c Bell b Oakman	48
R. M. James c Oakman b James	27	– c Suttle b Marlar	16
C. D. White not out	7	– c and b Marlar	7
C. B. Howland b Smith	10	– b Oakman	26
O. S. Wheatley b Smith	0	– c Bell b Oakman	12
J. R. Rutherford lbw b Smith	0	– not out	37
A. Hurd (did not bat)		– b Thomson	8
B 5, l-b 5	10	L-b 4	4

1/0 2/7 3/161 4/209   (9 wkts dec.) 275   1/0 2/1 3/21 4/87 5/98   204
5/258 6/259 7/275 8/275 9/275   6/109 7/134 8/154 9/185

Sussex

D. V. Smith c Howland b Wheatley	15		
L. J. Lenham st Howland b James	64	– c James b Hurd	16
A. S. M. Oakman c Howland b Rutherford	11	– b James	52
J. M. Parks lbw b Wheatley	10	– not out	28
G. H. G. Doggart not out	162		
K. G. Suttle c James b McLachlan	11	– not out	46
N. I. Thomson b Dexter	16		
A. E. James c Hurd b Wheatley	6		
R. T. Webb c Rutherford b Dexter	3		
R. G. Marlar c Green b Dexter	6		
R. V. Bell not out	16		
L-b 9, n-b 3	12	B 7, l-b 1	8

1/37 2/57 3/70 4/147   (9 wkts dec.) 332   1/60 2/82   (2 wkts) 150
5/190 6/232 7/245 8/260 9/270

Sussex Bowling

	Overs	Mdns	Runs	Wkts	Overs	Mdns	Runs	Wkts
Thomson	20	7	47	1	20	8	47	4
James	27	6	70	2	16	10	11	—
Smith	12.3	3	37	3	6	4	13	—
Bell	6	2	18	—	11	3	31	—
Oakman	22	4	47	—	29.3	13	41	4
Marlar	8	1	26	1	22	9	53	2
Suttle	7	2	20	1				
Parks					1	—	4	

Cambridge Bowling

	Overs	Mdns	Runs	Wkts	Overs	Mdns	Runs	Wkts
Wheatley	21	7	59	3	6	—	22	—
Rutherford	13	2	60	1	6	—	23	—
Dexter............	10	2	30	3	7	3	17	—
James	19	2	60	1	16.4	3	50	1
Hurd.............	23	4	66	—	10	1	30	1
McLachlan	12	2	45	1				

Umpires: F. S. Lee and H. Palmer.

CAMBRIDGE UNIVERSITY v FREE FORESTERS

Played at Cambridge, May 20, 22, 23, 1961

Cambridge won by eight wickets. Free Foresters failed completely against the fast bowling of Douglas-Pennant and Weedon, a Freshman from Harrow, who bowled unchanged. The University proved that there was nothing wrong with the pitch and maiden centuries by Craig (seventeen 4s) and Brearley (twelve 4s) enabled Douglas-Pennant to declare with a lead of almost 300. Howland, the previous season's Cambridge captain, and Cook dominated Free Foresters' second innings. Howland raced to his century in one hundred minutes and altogether batted for two and a quarter hours. Cook's innings lasted five and a half hours. The University had little difficulty in scoring the 109 runs for victory. Yates and Brearley shared the wicket-keeping for Cambridge. Brearley kept on the final day and held two catches.

Free Foresters

D. E. Bale b Douglas-Pennant	7	– b Douglas-Pennant............	4
G. W. Cook c Yates b Weedon..................	11	– c Craig b Weedon..............	140
D. J. Green c Yates b Douglas-Pennant	6	– b Weedon	14
J. H. Hardstaff b Weedon......................	16	– c Yates b Howard..............	36
P. C. Hatch c Craig b Douglas-Pennant	14	– c and b Howard	9
†C. B. Howland not out	14	– b Weedon	124
*F. R. Brown c and b Weedon	8	– b Harper.....................	14
R. V. C. Robins b Weedon	1	– c Brearley b Weedon	16
A. T. C. Allom b Douglas-Pennant.............	10	– b Howard	0
J. K. Hall b Douglas-Pennant..................	0	– c Brearley b Weedon	22
C. J. M. Kenny b Douglas-Pennant	2	– not out	0
L-b 5	5	B 1, l-b 1...............	2

1/9 2/25 3/25 4/51 5/55   94   1/8 2/29 3/76 4/96 5/283   381
6/63 7/69 8/84 9/84   6/320 7/355 8/356 9/380

Cambridge University

E. J. Craig lbw b Hall	112	– st Blake b Brown	22
A. Goodfellow b Brown	58	– c Brown b Allom	32
†J. M. Brearley c sub b Cook	101	– not out	42
J. H. Minney c Howland b Hall.................	33	– not out	11
N. J. Harper b Allom	1		
P. D. Brodrick b Hall	49		
†K. Yates not out	0		
B 5, l-b 7, w 1	13	W 1, n-b 1...............	2

1/118 2/217 3/275 4/284   (6 wkts dec.) 367   1/44 2/80   (2 wkts) 109
5/367 6/367

Cambridge University Bowling

	Overs	Mdns	Runs	Wkts	Overs	Mdns	Runs	Wkts
Douglas-Pennant ...	19.2	3	43	6	19	3	66	1
Weedon	19	4	46	4	35.4	2	114	5
Brodrick					30	13	60	—
Howard					36	15	100	3
Harper					11	2	39	1

Free Foresters Bowling

	Overs	Mdns	Runs	Wkts	Overs	Mdns	Runs	Wkts
Hall.............	29	4	78	3	14	1	45	—
Allom	29	7	81	1	11	2	23	1
Kenny............	19	4	62	—				
Brown............	16	4	52	1	13	5	25	1
Robins	3	—	20	—	2	—	5	—
Cook.............	13	—	61	1				
Green					2.3	—	9	—

Umpires: D. Davies and A. E. Rhodes.

OXFORD UNIVERSITY

OXFORD UNIVERSITY v LANCASHIRE

Played at Oxford, May 15, 16, 17, 1946

Oxford won by 76 runs. Donnelly and Maudsley in partnerships of 218 and 134, after making 171 together against India, carried off chief honours with the bat. Donnelly hit a 6 and twenty-three 4s, three 6s and twelve 4s, in his two brilliant innings. He missed a third consecutive century by skying a catch when forcing the game. Maudsley, playing in sound style, helped the New Zealand left-hander master the good Lancashire attack, and on the first day, when rain caused two interruptions, lost his wicket in attempting a big hit. Macindoe bowled a good length with life on a drying pitch, and Bartlett made the ball turn in his prolonged spell which helped largely in the victory. Washbrook took part in two stands for 117 with Philipson and 84 with Place. In the two Lancashire innings the England opening batsmen supplied the only case of bowled.

Oxford University

R. Sale b Phillipson	0	– c Ikin b Roberts	16
J. D. Cairns c Brierley b Garlick	17	– b Roberts	14
J. O. Newton-Thompson c and b Ikin	27	– b Roberts	14
M. P. Donnelly c Ikin b Pollard	139	– c Fallows b Pollard	95
R. H. Maudsley c Ikin b Pollard	92	– b Pollard	45
H. E. Webb c Brierley b Ikin	13	– c Pollard b Roberts	1
D. F. Henley c Edrich b Roberts	19	– not out	0
G. A. Wheatley not out	42	– b Pollard	4
D. H. Macindoe c Cooper b Phillipson	0		
B. H. Travers c Edrich b Phillipson	0		
J. N. Bartlett b Garlick	8		
B 5, l-b 8, n-b 4	17	B 1, l-b 1, n-b 2	4
	374		**193**

Lancashire

C. Washbrook lbw b Travers	67	– b Travers	55
W. Place c Sale b Macindoe	0	– c Henley b Macindoe	89
J. T. Ikin c Maudsley b Macindoe	10	– c Macindoe b Bartlett	6
W. E. Phillipson c Macindoe b Bartlett	49	– lbw b Macindoe	27
G. A. Edrich c Wheatley b Macindoe	23	– c Bartlett b Macindoe	1
T. L. Brierley c Donnelly b Macindoe	24	– c Bartlett b Macindoe	3
S. F. Cooper c Wheatley b Macindoe	6	– not out	20
J. A. Fallows c Sale b Macindoe	15	– c and b Bartlett	3
R. G. Garlick c Newton-Thompson b Bartlett	8	– c Henley b Bartlett	27
R. Pollard not out	6	– lbw b Bartlett	20
W. B. Roberts run out	0	– c Webb b Bartlett	4
B 5, l-b 13, w 3	21	B 5, l-b 2	7
	229		**262**

Lancashire Bowling

	Overs	Mdns	Runs	Wkts	Overs	Mdns	Runs	Wkts
Phillipson	19	3	90	3	8	2	25	—
Pollard	28	3	139	2	17	2	73	3
Garlick	17.1	7	50	2	2	—	7	—
Ikin	20	3	52	2	3	—	35	—
Roberts	12	3	26	1	21.1	5	49	4

Oxford University Bowling

	Overs	Mdns	Runs	Wkts	Overs	Mdns	Runs	Wkts
Macindoe	31	10	61	6	30	5	85	4
Henley	12	2	44	—	2	—	14	—
Travers	19	7	43	1	15	2	42	1
Bartlett	15	5	22	2	33	3	102	5
Webb	1	—	5	—				
Newton-Thompson .	7	1	33	—				
Donnelly					2	—	12	—

OXFORD UNIVERSITY v GLOUCESTERSHIRE

Played at Oxford, May 1, 3, 4, 1948

Drawn. A. H. Kardar, the Indian Test player, showed good form with both bat and ball in the University's opening game. Oxford started badly, but a third-wicket parnership of 110 in ninety-five minutes by Pawson and Keighley stemmed the collapse. Kardar then played a delightful innings of well-timed strokes, and when the County batted he varied his left-arm slows skilfully and took five wickets for 47. Only Emmett, who carried his bat for 104 out of 156, played him confidently. The University fared very badly when they batted again, but rain prevented play on the last day.

Oxford University

W. G. Keighley c Allen b Goddard	59	– c Crapp b Lambert	13
N. C. F. Bloy b J. K. Graveney	7	– b Lambert	3
C. B. Van Ryneveld b J. K. Graveney	4	– not out	8
H. A. Pawson b Goddard	58	– c Scott b J. K. Graveney	3
A. H. Kardar c J. K. Graveney b Cook	58	– c Cook b Scott	0
D. B. Carr b Cook	19	– c Allen b Scott	3
P. A. Whitcombe b Goddard	8	– b Scott	6
A. W. H. Mallett run out	1	– c Emmett b J. K. Graveney	3
B. H. Travers lbw b Cranfield	24	– c Wilson b Lambert	8
H. B. Robinson not out	48	– not out	0
W. W. Davidson c Allen b Cook	15		
B 2, l-b 2	4	B 1, l-b 3	4
	305		**(8 wkts) 51**

Gloucestershire

G. M. Emmett not out	104	J. K. Graveney b Travers	1
T. W. Graveney c Travers b Whitcombe ...	0	C. J. Scott b Travers	4
B. O. Allen c Robinson b Mallett	1	T. W. Goddard st Davidson b Kardar	1
J. F. Crapp c Mallett b Kardar	23	C. Cook b Kardar	5
L. M. Cranfield c Robinson b Van Ryneveld	5	B 5, l-b 1, w 1, n-b 2	9
A. E. Wilson b Kardar	0		
G. Lambert st Davidson b Kardar	3		**156**

Gloucestershire Bowling

	Overs	Mdns	Runs	Wkts	Overs	Mdns	Runs	Wkts
Lambert	6	1	16	—	13	4	30	3
J. K. Graveney	9	2	17	2	6	2	7	2
Scott	4	—	27	—	5	2	5	3
Goddard	33	8	109	3				
Cook	36.1	8	106	3	1	—	5	—
Cranfield	7	—	26	1				

Oxford University Bowling

	Overs	Mdns	Runs	Wkts
Mallett	19	6	40	1
Whitcombe	5	2	11	1
Robinson	6	1	15	—
Kardar	27.4	14	47	5
Van Ryneveld	2	—	5	1
Travers	10	2	29	2

Umpires: F. Chester and D. Hendren.

OXFORD UNIVERSITY v SUSSEX

Played at Oxford, June 16, 17, 18. 1954

Drawn. Doggart, the Sussex captain and Cambridge captain of 1950, gained the honours in a high-scoring match by hitting a century in each innings. Altogether he batted throughout seven hours and reached the boundary seventeen times in the first innings and thirteen times in the second. On a perfect pitch, Allan and Cowdrey replied with centuries for Oxford, each hitting twenty 4s and Allen two 6s, and after three declarations the University were left to score 238 to win in two and a half hours. They made a gallant attempt without ever nearing success, and finally Walshe and Allan defended dourly to save the game.

Sussex

J. Langridge c Allan b Jowett	32	– not out	10
D. S. Sheppard lbw b Arenhold	0	– c Fellows-Smith b Arenhold	19
G. H. G. Doggart c Fasken b Arenhold	140	– c Marsland b Arenhold	105
D. V. Smith c Smith b Cowdrey	20	– lbw b Arenhold	1
G. Potter c Walshe b Birrell	54	– not out	28
G. Cox c Allan b Birrell	50	– c Fellows-Smith b Jowett	73
D. Foreman c Marsland b Allan	15	– c Fasken b Fellows-Smith	5
A. S. Oakman not out	21	– c and b Jowett	0
B 7, l-b 3	10	B 3, l-b 2, w 5, n-b 1	11

1/1 2/89 3/151 4/235   (7 wkts dec.) 342   1/1 2/30   (6 wkts dec.) 252
5/290 6/313 7/342   3/171 4/185 5/190 6/226

G. Cogger, D. J. Wood and R. T. Webb did not bat.

Oxford University

M. J. K. Smith c Sheppard b Oakman	24	– b Wood	0
J. M. Allan c Oakman b Doggart	153	– not out	15
C. C. P. Williams c Langridge b Potter	25	– c Webb b Cogger	4
M. C. Cowdrey c Webb b Potter	140	– c Webb b Oakman	46
H. B. Birrell b Wood	7	– c Webb b Oakman	64
G. P. Marsland not out	7	– b Oakman	1
J. P. Fellows-Smith (did not bat)	–	c Langridge b Potter	22
J. A. Arenhold (did not bat)	–	run out	3
D. K. Fasken (did not bat)	–	c and b Oakman	6
A. P. Walshe (did not bat)	–	not out	24
L-b 1	1	B 1	1

1/52 2/101 3/313   (5 wkts dec.) 357   1/0 2/9 3/102   (8 wkts) 186
4/344 5/357   4/106 5/119 6/128 7/142 8/148

Oxford Bowling

	Overs	Mdns	Runs	Wkts	Overs	Mdns	Runs	Wkts
Arenhold	13	1	42	2	17	4	64	3
Fasken	18	5	53	—	10	1	39	—
Jowett	15	1	70	1	18	8	39	2
Fellows-Smith	15	2	38	—	23	9	54	1
Allan	21.5	8	48	1	15	5	45	—
Cowdrey	9	3	22	1				
Birrell	12	1	59	2				

Sussex Bowling

	Overs	Mdns	Runs	Wkts	Overs	Mdns	Runs	Wkts
Wood	27	13	71	1	11	5	16	1
Cogger	16	3	57	—	7	—	39	1
Oakman	29	14	61	1	13	4	25	4
Potter	14	2	61	2	19	3	89	1
Foreman	12	3	33	—				
Doggart	9	4	39	1				
Cox	11	—	34	—	3	—	16	—

Umpires: D. Hendren and H. G. Baldwin.

OXFORD UNIVERSITY v KENT

Played at Oxford, June 4, 5, 6, 1958

Kent won by 164 runs. Most of the excitement in this match of fluctuating fortunes was crammed into a brief spell between tea and the close on the first day. Kent had crawled to 167 for six when Sayer enlivened the proceedings with a hat-trick against his own county. He took the wickets of Catt, Ridgway and Brown with successive balls and Kent were all out for 172. The fact that they scored so many was due to Pretlove and Pettiford, who added 84 for the fifth wicket. But the fun had not yet ended. The Oxford opening pair began by making 23 together; then Ridgway removed Smith, Eagar and Corran with successive balls – the second hat-trick in an amazing day's play. Oxford, 50 behind on first innings, were set 258 to win, but failed by a considerable margin. For Sayer, however, the match was a personal triumph. He finished with an analysis of 11 for 91.

Kent

A. H. Phebey c Piachaud b Corran	16	– lbw b Sayer	3
R. C. Wilson c Piachaud b Sayer	8	– c Piachaud b Corran	53
J. Prodger b Corran	1	– b Sayer	63
J. F. Pretlove lbw b Corran	57	– c and b Burki	31
S. E. Leary c Eagar b Sayer	21	– c Smith b Raybould	19
J. Pettiford run out	43	– not out	10
A. L. Dixon b Sayer	11	– c Smith b Sayer	11
A. W. Catt b Sayer	4	– b Sayer	2
F. Ridgway c Dyson b Sayer	0	– b Sayer	2
A. Brown b Sayer	0	– not out	7
J. C. T. Page not out	0		
B 8, l-b 3	11	B 6	6

1/23 2/24 3/29 4/62 5/146   **172**   1/6 2/120   (8 wkts dec.) **207**
6/163 7/167 8/167 9/167   3/120 4/147 5/169 6/186
7/189 8/197

Oxford University

A. C. Smith b Ridgway	11	– b Page	45
J. Burki b Page	43	– lbw b Ridgway	10
M. A. Eagar b Ridgway	0	– b Page	0
A. J. Corran b Ridgway	0	– c Ridgway b Page	1
R. L. Jowett c Dixon b Pettiford	17	– lbw b Page	12
E. M. Dyson not out	21	– b Page	4
G. D. Roynon run out	2	– st Catt b Pettiford	0
D. Piachaud b Ridgway	6	– b Pettiford	7
J. G. Raybould b Ridgway	0	– not out	1
R. G. Woodcock b Ridgway	0	– b Pettiford	5
D. Sayer lbw b Ridgway	1	– b Pettiford	2
B 14, l-b 2, n-b 5	21	B 6	6

1/23 2/23 3/23 4/64 5/88   **122**   1/23 2/72 3/72 4/75 5/84   **93**
6/98 7/110 8/110 9/110   5/84 6/84 7/84 8/89 9/90

Oxford Bowling

	Overs	Mdns	Runs	Wkts	Overs	Mdns	Runs	Wkts
Sayer	57	11	44	6	27	8	47	5
Corran	26	5	62	3	11	4	38	1
Burki	11	7	9	—	12	3	43	1
Jowett	10	2	26	—				
Raybould	1	—	1	—	14	3	39	1
Piachaud	14	9	19	—	2	—	11	—
Woodcock					9	5	23	—

Kent Bowling

	Overs	Mdns	Runs	Wkts	Overs	Mdns	Runs	Wkts
Ridgway	21.2	8	42	7	7	4	7	1
Brown	14	7	18	—	4	1	12	—
Page	19	10	26	1	14	7	14	5
Pettiford	9	4	15	1	12.4	2	43	4
Leary					3	—	11	—

Umpires: W. Jones and A. E. D. Smith.

OXFORD UNIVERSITY v FREE FORESTERS

Played at Oxford, June 4, 6, 1960

Oxford won by an innings and 104 runs. The Free Foresters never looked worthy of first-class status. Oxford established a commanding position through some forceful play by the Nawab of Pataudi and Fry, each of whom hit a hundred, and shared a third-wicket partnership of 191. Then Smith, the Oxford captain, gave himself a rest from wicket-keeping and, bowling in-swingers at a little above medium pace, took five Foresters wickets for 32 runs, causing his opponents to follow-on 289 behind. Although Purves offered stubborn resistance Smith again caused a collapse and the game ended in two days. Smith finished with nine wickets for 77.

Oxford University

*A. C. Smith b Livock	9	D. B. Pithey c Purves b Fasken	17
D. M. Green run out	50	T. R. Jakobsen not out	0
A. A. Baig retired hurt	61		
Nawab of Pataudi c Livock b Parkes	113	B 2, l-b 4, w 2, n-b 2	10
†C. A. Fry b Allom	100		
E. M. Dyson not out	68	1/35 2/102 3/293 (6 wkts dec.)	414
F. W. Neate c Metcalfe b Allom	6	4/372 5/386 6/420	

J. D. Piachaud and I. C. Potter did not bat.

Free Foresters

S. G. Metcalfe lbw b Piachaud	18	– b Piachaud	21
J. H. Purves b Pithey	32	– c Green b Pithey	69
R. D. Montgomerie b Piachaud	1	– b Jakobsen	15
M. L. Y. Ainsworth c Green b Piachaud	0	– c Fry b Smith	0
M. F. J. Checksfield c Fry b Smith	11	– c Jakobsen b Pithey	42
A. T. C. Allom b Smith	30	– c Dyson b Smith	5
†O. B. Popplewell c Potter b Smith	30	– b Pithey	2
*P. A. Whitcombe c Fry b Smith	0	– c Pataudi b Pithey	0
M. Livock c Pataudi b Piachaud	9	– b Smith	12
D. K. Fasken not out	0	– not out	14
J. L. Parkes b Smith	0	– b Smith	0
B 8, l-b 4, n-b 2	14	B 2, l-b 2, n-b 1	5

1/37 2/46 3/46 4/56 5/95   145   1/36 2/88 3/89 4/148 5/151   185
6/107 7/116 8/139 9/145   6/159 7/159 8/159 9/185

Free Foresters Bowling

	Overs	Mdns	Runs	Wkts
Livock	19	2	95	1
Fasken	27	7	74	1
Whitcombe	14	4	49	—
Parkes	13	—	61	1
Metcalfe	19	1	68	—
Allom	22	4	77	2

Oxford University Bowling

	Overs	Mdns	Runs	Wkts	Overs	Mdns	Runs	Wkts
Potter	7	4	7	—	7	1	16	—
Jakobsen	7	5	3	—	13	4	33	1
Green	4	—	12	—	9	3	21	—
Piachaud	24	11	44	4	5	3	2	1
Pithey	12	—	33	1	27	12	59	4
Smith	10	1	32	5	27	11	45	4
Dyson					1	—	4	—

Umpires: F. S. Lee and J. H. Parks.

OXFORD UNIVERSITY v YORKSHIRE
Played at Oxford, May 10, 11, 12, 1961

Drawn. The Nawab of Pataudi took a place in cricket history by scoring a century in each innings off the Yorkshire attack, for the young Indian batsmen was only the tenth player ever to have achieved the feat. Small and slim, but possessing perfect timing, the Oxford University captain twice saved his side when they appeared to be on the verge of surrendering to the County champions. Yorkshire, after declaring their first innings at 286 for four, removed the first three University batsmen for 41 on the opening day. Pataudi, however, refused to be daunted even when two more wickets fell quickly on the second morning, and reached his hundred in just under two and a half hours. The situation was similar after Oxford University were left to score 235 to win in three and a half hours. Three wickets fell cheaply, but once again Pataudi was in magnificent fettle. He hit twelve 4s in his 50 and finished with eighteen boundaries in his century, scored with strokes to all parts of the field. Towards the end of his two-hour 16-minute innings there was not a Yorkshire fielder within 30 yards of his bat, but despite his efforts the University still fell 54 short of their task with five wickets left and the extra half an hour unclaimed.

Yorkshire

W. B. Stott run out	62	– c Baig b Pithey 10
J. B. Bolus c Duff b Thompson	10	– c Fry b Pithey 20
K. Taylor c Waters b Duff	85	– c and b Pithey 0
D. E. V. Padgett c Duff b Drybrough	33	– b Pithey 53
D. B. Close not out	54	– not out 39
P. J. Sharpe not out	35	– c and b Drybrough 4
R. Illingworth (did not bat)		– b Pithey 0
*J. V. Wilson (did not bat)		– c Baig b Jakobson 0
†J. G. Binks (did not bat)		– c and b Duff 41
D. Wilson (did not bat)		– c Waters b Drybrough 25
F. S. Trueman (did not bat)		– c Fry b Drybrough 22
B 4, l-b 3	7	B 4 4

1/28 2/139 3/196 4/196   (4 wkts dec.) 286   1/21 2/23 3/26 4/34 5/73   218
6/95 7/99 8/135 9/214

Oxford University

D. R. Worsley c Trueman b Close	8	– c Close b Trueman 8
D. B. Pithey b Trueman	20	– c Binks b Trueman 11
A. A. Baig lbw b Close	9	– c Stott b Illingworth 5
A. R. Duff c Binks b Trueman	6	
*Nawab of Pataudi b Taylor	106	– not out 103
C. A. Fry c Stott b Trueman	5	– c Binks b D. Wilson 26
C. D. Drybrough c Sharpe b D. Wilson	44	– c Binks b Trueman 5
F. W. Neate b D. Wilson	5	– not out 7
†R. H. C. Waters c Sharpe b Illingworth	37	
T. R. Jakobson run out	20	
N. P. Thompson not out	0	
B 2, l-b 8	10	– B 4, l-b 1 5

1/21 2/35 3/41 4/43 5/71   270   1/14 2/25   (5 wkts) 170
6/197 7/202 8/207 9/270   3/25 4/127 5/140

Oxford University Bowling

	Overs	Mdns	Runs	Wkts	Overs	Mdns	Runs	Wkts
Jakobson	22	7	61	—	11	5	15	1
Thompson	15	5	46	1	6	3	9	—
Pithey	33	6	71	—	39	23	61	5
Drybrough	32	8	75	1	35	11	99	3
Duff	8	1	26	1	9	1	30	1

Yorkshire Bowling

	Overs	Mdns	Runs	Wkts	Overs	Mdns	Runs	Wkts
Trueman.........	22	7	52	3	16	7	27	3
Close............	26	11	58	2	11	3	40	—
Taylor...........	19	3	52	1				
D. Wilson........	21	10	52	2	16	4	51	1
Illingworth	20.3	4	46	1	20	8	47	1

Umpires: N. Oldfield and A. E. Fagg.

OXFORD UNIVERSITY v GLOUCESTERSHIRE

Played at Oxford, May 2, 3, 4, 1962

Gloucestershire won by an innings and 65 runs. Cricket history was made in this match when the Gloucestershire opening batsmen, Young and Nicholls, achieved the highest partnership recorded for the county, 395, and made their own best scores. The Indian Test cricketer, Abbas Ali Baig had played an innings of great charm in making 127 (fifteen 4s) and the University declared with only seven wickets down. Then came Gloucestershire's tremendous reply which carried them into the lead and Pugh was able to declare 179 on. Oxford failed in their second innings although Baig once more showed his class.

Oxford University

D. R. Worsley b Andrew.......................	20	– lbw b Allen....................	4
D. B. Pithey c Mortimore b Brown...............	33	– lbw b Smith....................	15
A. A. Baig b Brown...........................	127	– c Brown b Mortimore..........	50
E. Marsh c Mortimore b Brown	3	– lbw b Smith....................	1
*C. D. Drybrough run out	23	– b Smith.......................	4
M. A. Baig b Mortimore.......................	10	– b Mortimore...................	12
K. B. H. Stevens c Pugh b Mortimore.............	0	– b Smith.......................	4
J. L. Cuthbertson not out	59	– c Brown b Mortimore..........	15
†N. L. Majendie not out	2	– b Allen	1
J. D. Martin (did not bat)		– c Brown b Allen	1
R. F. Jackson (did not bat)		– not out	2
B 4, l-b 8	12	B 1, l-b 4...............	5

1/37 2/68 3/78 4/120   (7 wkts dec.) 289   1/21 2/21 3/28 4/32 5/64   114
5/143 6/153 7/264   6/80 7/103 8/110 9/111

Gloucestershire

D. M. Young c Majendie b Martin	198
R. B. Nicholls c Stevens b Pithey	217
*C. T. M. Pugh not out..................	28
B 12, l-b 13	25

1/395 2/468   (2 wkts dec.) 468

D. Carpenter, J. B. Mortimore, A. S. Brown, D. A. Allen, D. R. Smith, †B. J. Meyer, F. J. Andrew and C. Cook did not bat.

Gloucestershire Bowling

	Overs	Mdns	Runs	Wkts	Overs	Mdns	Runs	Wkts
Smith	15	1	71	—	21	6	56	4
Andrew.	6	3	7	1				
Allen.	38	19	81	—	27.3	13	28	3
Brown.	24	8	73	3	3	3	—	—
Mortimore	22	5	45	2	24	13	23	3
Cook.					2	1	2	—
Nicholls					1	1	—	—

Oxford University Bowling

	Overs	Mdns	Runs	Wkts
Jackson.	19	3	74	—
Martin.	33	6	104	1
Pithey	29.2	6	107	1
Drybrough	24	3	82	—
M. A. Baig	9	1	34	—
Cuthbertson	7	1	32	—

Umpires: F. S. Lee and J. Arnold.

OTHER MATCHES

OXFORD v CAMBRIDGE

Played at Lord's, July 6, 8, 9, 1946

Oxford won by six wickets. The first official match between the Universities since 1939 gave good reason for satisfaction, just as did the 1919 revival of the fixture after the first world war. Oxford then won by 45 runs, thanks to a grand innings by Miles Howell, and again the efforts of one batsman accounted largely for the result. M. P. Donnelly, with the experience of having played for New Zealand against England in 1937, created a personal record for a Test player in scoring a century in the 'Varsity match when a freshman. In the previous season by scoring 133 and 39, this fine left-handed batsman was mainly responsible for the Dominions beating England, despite two centuries by W. R. Hammond; and at the age of 28 he held a distinct advantage over the other players, apart from his captain, D. H. Macindoe, who, by virtue of his bowling when a freshman in 1937, appeared that season for Gentlemen against Players. R. Sale, a blue in 1939, was another Oxonian above the age usually associated with University players. His sound left-handed play saved Oxford from a serious breakdown when batting late on Saturday, and, curiously enough, another left-hander did well, notably on Monday when play proceeded until half-past seven in the effort to finish the match. This was Bloy, who made the winning stroke on Tuesday morning when the 11 runs then required were obtained in fifteen minutes for the loss of Maudsley, very neatly caught close to the ground at short square leg.

Mischler, a sound player, besides earning high commendation for his wicket-keeping, was highest scorer after Bodkin won the toss; he checked a lamentable start, three wickets having fallen for 19 runs. Travers, medium to fast right hand, began by bowling 13 overs, 8 maidens, for 17 runs and two wickets, but Bartlett, the slow left hander with mixed spin, sending down an occasional fastish ball, did best work by taking four of the last five wickets in two spells between which Travers beat Pepper with a fine ball, also from the Nursery end.

Griffiths, the Cambridge fast bowler, with seven fieldsmen, including Mischler, in a semicircle about five yards behind the wicket, proved menacing rather than dangerous, and Donnelly, going in at 47, soon hit him three times to the boundary. Sale left at 70 to a good gulley catch and then another left-handed partnership took the total to 99 at seven o'clock.

On Monday morning, with the pitch unimpaired, though the ball sometimes lifted appreciably, Donnelly reigned supreme; in an hour and three-quarters he added 113 to his not out 29 before an extra fast ball, that looked to turn a little down the slope, sent his off stump flying. To Griffiths fell the distinction of completing the most enjoyable feature of the match in this dramatic fashion, and from the pavilion end he took three of the last four Oxford wickets. No words would exaggerate the beauty and effectiveness of Donnelly as a batsman in this perfect innings of 142 scored out of 194 during two hours and 55 minutes at the crease. Of moderate height and build Donnelly played the left-handed game in a manner comparable to the best we have known. Never looking in doubt or difficulty, he usually played forward in defence, and his watchful back play made the forcing stroke look simple, as he invariably kept the ball on the turf as it sped away from his bat. Some drives off, on and straight, were grand. The hook, genuine leg hit and cut were done with equal facility and his figures included a 5, all run for a leg hit off Trapnell, first thing on Monday, and nineteen 4s. No one scored more than 19 while Donnelly was at the wicket and he retired amidst an ovation.

As Oxford required only 68 for victory when they began their second innings at 25 minutes past six, it was arranged that play should proceed until half-past seven, and

Donnelly, facing Griffiths from the pavilion end, cut a ball into second slip's hands in an obvious attempt to force the pace, but the match remains memorable for his grand batting.

About 15,000 people saw the cricket on Saturday, over 12,000 paying for admission, and some 8,000 on Monday, the ground looking almost gay with promenaders during the intervals, so recalling pre-war memories. It is noteworthy that four of the winning side came from the Dominions.

Cambridge

G. L. Willatt (*Repton and St Catharine's*)
c Newton-Thompson b Travers. 9 – c Newton-Thompson b Travers 6
D. G. Lacy-Scott (*Marlborough and Peterhouse*)
c Rumbold b Travers. 0 – c Travers b Macindoe........... 11
P. E. Bodkin (*Bradfield and Caius*) lbw b Macindoe . 3 – c Maudsley b Travers............ 2
N. M. Mischler (*St Paul's and St Catharine's*)
b Sutton. 42 – lbw b Bartlett 16
G. M. Shuttleworth (*Queen Elizabeth Grammar
School and King's*) c Wheatley b Bloy. 33 – lbw b Bartlett 16
J. Pepper (*The Leys and Emmanuel*) b Travers ..... 33 – b Bartlett...................... 3
E. R. Conradi (*Oundle and Caius*) b Bartlett .... 12 – c Maudsley b Sutton............ 22
B. M. W. Trapnell (*UCS and St John's*) b Bartlett .. 41 – c Wheatley b Sutton............ 8
J. M. Mills (*Oundle and Corpus Christi*) not out .... 10 – c Bartlett b Macindoe........... 11
B. S. Hobson (*Taunton and St Catharine's*)
b Bartlett. 2 – b Travers 6
W. H. Griffiths (*Charterhouse and St John's*)
lbw b Bartlett. 0 – not out 0
B 10, l-b 5, n-b 1 .... 16 B 21, l-b 4, n-b 1 26
——— ———
201 127

Oxford

R. Sale (*Repton and Oriel*) c Conradi b Trapnell .... 42 – c Mischler b Mills.............. 10
J. S. Rumbold (*St Andrew's Coll., New Zealand
and Brasenose*) b Griffiths. 9 – lbw b Mills 10
R. H. Maudsley (*Malvern and Brasenose*) b Trapnell 3 – c Shuttleworth b Trapnell......... 15
M. P. Donnelly (*Canterbury Univ., New Zealand
and Worcester*) b Griffiths.142 – c Hobson b Griffiths............. 1
N. C. F. Bloy (*Dover and Brasenose*) b Bodkin .... 19 – not out 26
J. O. Newton-Thompson (*Diocesan Coll.,
Rondebosch, S. Africa and Trinity*) b Griffiths. 4 – not out 1
G. A. Wheatley (*Uppingham and Balliol*) c Conradi
b Trapnell. 10
B. M. Travers (*Sydney Univ. and New College*)
lbw b Griffiths. 8
D. H. Macindoe (*Eton and Christ Church*)
c Mischler b Griffiths. 13
M. A. Sutton (*Ampleforth and Worcester*)
st Mischler b Bodkin. 6
J. N. Bartlett (*Chichester and Lincoln*) not out...... 1
B 1, l-b 2, n-b 1 .... 4 B 4, l-b 2 6
——— ———
261 (4 wkts) 69

Oxford Bowling

	Overs	Mdns	Runs	Wkts	Overs	Mdns	Runs	Wkts
Macindoe	26	11	52	1	29	18	30	2
Travers...........	26	16	30	3	12.5	4	27	3
Maudsley	1	—	3	—				
Sutton............	18	4	39	1	8	1	28	2
Bloy	12	1	49	1				
Bartlett	11	5	12	4	24	15	16	3

Cambridge Bowling

	Overs	Mdns	Runs	Wkts	Overs	Mdns	Runs	Wkts
Griffiths	28.4	7	84	5	13	5	18	1
Lacy-Scott	8	2	23	—				
Trapnell	24	12	41	3	6.5	1	19	1
Mills	18	1	52	—	4	—	10	2
Bodkin	13	7	40	2	4	—	16	—
Hobson..........	2	—	17	—				

CLIFTON v TONBRIDGE

Played at Lord's, July 29, 30, 1946

Tonbridge won by two runs. Reputed to be the youngest player to appear in a match at Lord's, 13 year-old Michael Cowdrey, in his first match for Tonbridge, contributed largely to the success of his side. When Tonbridge were sent in to bat on a drying pitch, Cowdrey scored one more than the runs made by his colleagues and in the second innings raised his aggregate to 119. A right-arm spin bowler, mainly with leg break, he proved deadly in the Clifton second innings and with Kirch, medium, supported by smart fielding, dismissed the last five Clifton batsmen for 33 runs, so snatching a victory. Exton, with length and spin, excelled as a bowler, taking 14 wickets for 125.

Tonbridge

D. S. Kemp lbw b Exton........................	25	– st Lindsay b Exton	44
G. Bowler b Exton	28	– b Exton........................	0
M. C. Cowdrey c Lindsay b Exton	75	– c Lindsay b Exton	44
D. K. Horton c Green b Penny..................	3	– st Lindsay b Bird	51
J. Wrightson c Lindsay b Penny.................	0	– c Ritchie b Exton	1
G. McNicol c Penny b Exton	0	– c Lindsay b Ritchie	6
A. J. Turk b Penny	0	– c Bishop b Exton	8
M. J. Bickmore c Lindsay b Penny	16	– b Exton........................	0
J. D. Bickmore c Bishop b Exton	1	– not out	10
J. F. MacMillan b Exton.......................	1	– b Exton........................	2
P. N. Kirch not out..........................	0	– b Exton........................	1
B 2, l-b 2, w 3	7	B 5, l-b 3..............	8
	156		**175**

Clifton

T. S. Penny c Cowdrey b MacMillan	25	– absent........................	0
P. M. Crawford c MacMillan b M. J. Bickmore	57	– st Wrightson b Cowdrey.........	17
M. L. Green c Wrightson b Cowdrey	56	– st Wrightson b Cowdrey.........	6
R. N. Exton b M. J. Bickmore..................	9	– st Wrightson b Cowdrey.........	28
M. F. Bishop not out.........................	44	– not out	45
R. K. Green c Turk b Cowdrey.................	0	– b M. J. Bickmore	1
D. B. Bird b Cowdrey........................	5	– lbw b Cowdrey.................	2
D. C. Dickinson b Kirch......................	8	– b Kirch	8
R. A. M. Whyte b Kirch......................	0	– b Kirch	0
J. V. Ritchie b Kirch	0	– c Horton b Cowdrey............	0
R. T. M. Lindsay b Kirch	0	– b Kirch	0
B 7, l-b 1, w 2	10	B 6, w 2	8
	214		**115**

Clifton Bowling.—Ritchie 0 for 14 and 1 for 36; Exton 6 for 64 and 8 for 61; Dickinson 0 for 21 and 0 for 39; Bird 0 for 18 and 1 for 15; Penny 4 for 32 and 0 for 16.

Tonbridge Bowling.—Kirch 4 for 20 and 3 for 21; MacMillan 1 for 41 and 0 for 7; M. J. Bickmore 2 for 26 and 1 for 20; Cowdrey 3 for 58 and 5 for 59; Bowler 0 for 33; McNichol 0 for 26.

MIDDLESEX (CHAMPION COUNTY) v REST OF ENGLAND

Played at The Oval, September 13, 15, 16, 17, 1948

Middlesex won by nine wickets. For only the third time were the Champion County successful over Rest of England. Yorkshire were winners in 1905 and 1935, the last occasion on which the game took place. The match provided further personal triumphs for Compton and Edrich, who concluded their remarkable season in superb style. Compton, despite a heavily strapped knee which restricted his freedom, played his highest innings in England and was only three short of the 249 he made for Holkar against Bombay in the Indian Championship final of 1944-45. Edrich followed Compton in beating Hayward's record aggregate. Middlesex began by losing three wickets for 53, but Compton and Edrich added 138 before Compton retired through a recurrence of his knee trouble. He resumed on Monday and in all he and Edrich put on 210 and made 426 between them out of the Middlesex total of 543. Compton hit thirty 4s, Edrich a 6 and twenty-one 4s. The Rest lost Washbrook first ball and Place also failed to score. Steady batting by Emmett and a bright display from Evans failed to save the follow-on. Emmett again showed good form, but only Washbrook and Yardley of the others did much and Middlesex were set a simple task. Only fifty minutes' play was necessary on the last day.

Middlesex

S. M. Brown c Evans b A. V. Bedser	4	– not out	8
J. D. Robertson c Evans b A. V. Bedser	3	– lbw b Wright	0
W. J. Edrich st Evans b Goddard	180	– not out	13
F. G. Mann st Evans b Wright	33		
D. C. S. Compton st Evans b Goddard	246		
R. W. V. Robins c Butler b Goddard	33		
A. Thompson c Cranston b Howorth	1		
W. F. Price c A. V. Bedser b Goddard	3		
J. Sims run out	17		
J. Young not out	9		
B 6, l-b 4, n-b 4	14		

(9 wkts dec.) 543   (1 wkt) 21

L. Gray did not bat.

Rest of England

Batsman	Runs		Runs
C. Washbrook c Robins b Gray	0	– b Sims	61
W. Place lbw b Gray	0	– run out	3
R. Howorth st Price b D. Compton	30	– c Robertson b Gray	3
G. M. Emmett c Price b Gray	89	– b D. Compton	43
N. W. D. Yardley b D. Compton	0	– lbw b Young	71
K. Cranston c Price b Gray	18	– b Robins	22
T. G. Evans lbw b Young	70	– c Thompson b D. Compton	15
A. V. Bedser not out	13	– b Young	23
D. V. P. Wright lbw b Young	0	– c Sims b Gray	29
T. W. Goddard st Price b D. Compton	8	– c and b Gray	14
H. J. Butler b D. Compton	0	– not out	2
B 12, l-b 6	18	B 21, l-b 9, w 1	31
	246		**317**

Rest of England Bowling

	Overs	Mdns	Runs	Wkts	Overs	Mdns	Runs	Wkts
Butler	24	4	54	—				
A. V. Bedser	37	10	93	2				
Wright	23	2	97	1	4.2	2	9	1
Goddard	46.3	6	179	4				
Howorth	37	7	106	1				
Cranston					5	1	12	—

Middlesex Bowling

	Overs	Mdns	Runs	Wkts	Overs	Mdns	Runs	Wkts
Gray	18	6	47	4	17.3	4	36	3
Young	29	6	71	2	27	5	77	2
Sims	7	1	29	—	10		41	1
Robins	8	1	24	—	5	—	21	1
D. Compton	18.4	2	57	4	16	1	84	2
Thompson					9	1	27	—

Umpires: F. Chester and H. G. Baldwin.

H. D. G. LEVESON-GOWER'S XI v MCC SOUTH AFRICAN TOURING TEAM

Played at Scarborough, September 4, 6, 7, 1948

Drawn. Although entirely covered throughout each night, the pitch was soft enough for Yardley to expect it to become difficult, but the sun never shone and, given first innings, the team chosen for the tour in South Africa batted all Saturday. Hutton played admirably for two hours, but Denis Compton took the honours with 135 made in less than three hours, three 6s and twelve 4s being his chief strokes. On Monday he did the best bowling, and next day he again excelled in making his second century of the match. Going in when Hutton left at 64, Compton began with 50 at one a minute, and then thrashed the bowling, making 75 in thirty-five minutes before lunch, during which Mann declared. At the crease eighty-five minutes, Compton hit three 6s and fifteen 4s in his not out 125 – 260 in the match for once out. F. R. Brown distinguished himself in his unaccustomed place as opening batsman when seldom playing first-class cricket by scoring 123 out of 197 in two hours thirty-five minutes; he hit two 6s and thirteen 4s. Like Compton, he drove very hard, and his second effort ended at 73 when trying a big hit. Yardley, with aid from Wooller, staved off likely defeat for his side on a wretched day of wind and gloom.

MCC South African Team

L. Hutton c Wooller b Laker	73	– b Brown	35
R. T. Simpson c Pritchard b Brown	24	– b Brown	19
J. F. Crapp c and b Laker	9	– c Wooller b Laker	23
D. C. S. Compton b Laker	135	– not out	125
C. H. Palmer b Brown	1	– b Pritchard	32
F. G. Mann c and b Brown	1	– not out	0
T. G. Evans c Edrich b Wooller	32	– run out	2
M. F. Tremlett c Cranston b Laker	35		
A. V. Bedser c Dewes b Laker	8		
C. Gladwin run out	6		
J. A. Young not out	0		
B 21, l-b 2	23	L-b 1, n-b 2	3
	347	**(5 wkts dec.)**	**239**

H. D. G. Leveson-Gower's XI

J. G. Dewes c Evans b Gladwin	4	– st Evans b Young	33
F. R. Brown b Tremlett	123	– b Tremlett	47
T. N. Pearce c and b Young	29	– c Tremlett b Young	15
M. P. Donnelly b Bedser	27	– run out	36
R. E. S. Wyatt b Bedser	24	– c and b Compton	7
N. W. D. Yardley b Bedser	15	– not out	49
K. Cranston st Evans b Compton	8	– b Compton	19
W. Wooller lbw b Compton	20	– c Simpson b Gladwin	31
E. H. Edrich run out	4	– lbw b Gladwin	0
J. C. Laker c Evans b Compton	10		
T. L. Pritchard not out	4		
L-b 2, w 1, n-b 2	5	B 10, l-b 11, n-b 1	22
	273	**(8 wkts)**	**259**

H. D. G. Leveson-Gower's XI Bowling

	Overs	Mdns	Runs	Wkts	Overs	Mdns	Runs	Wkts
Pritchard	16	2	54	—	14	4	30	1
Wooller	17	4	45	1	11	1	54	—
Cranston	16	4	56	—	4	—	22	—
Brown	24	3	72	3	13	1	58	2
Laker	27.1	2	97	5	12	2	72	1

MCC South African Team Bowling

	Overs	Mdns	Runs	Wkts	Overs	Mdns	Runs	Wkts
Bedser	29	4	84	3	13	—	35	—
Gladwin	19	2	65	1	9	1	49	2
Tremlett	8	—	41	1	7	1	11	1
Young	16	5	45	1	23	4	77	2
Palmer	2	1	5	—				
Compton	11.3	2	28	3	12	1	65	2

Umpires: H. Elliott and H. G. Baldwin.

EAST v WEST

Played at Kingston-on-Thames, September 8, 9, 10, 1948

East won by 233 runs. Stylish batting by Pawson and skilful bowling by Sims, who took all ten wickets for the first time in his career, brought plenty of excitement. Pawson took only twenty-five minutes over his second fifty runs. The feat of Sims on the last day when West were set to score 403 to win was surprising in view of the previous supremacy by batsmen. Cleverly varying his flight and spin, Sims troubled everyone. Before lunch he disposed of seven men for 69, and with Pawson, his captain, going on at the other end, he soon made his triumph complete. Brown, substitute wicket-keeper when McIntyre was hurt, stumped two men.

East

L. J. Todd lbw b Jenkins	36	– c Cooper b Howorth	107
T. C. Dodds b Jenkins	50	– c and b Jenkins	46
T. H. Barling b Lambert	73	– c Wilson b Jenkins	13
S. M. Brown b Jenkins	11	– st Wilson b Jenkins	8
H. A. Pawson c and b Lambert	128	– c Tremlett b Howorth	51
A. J. McIntyre b Tremlett	14	– b Howorth	9
R. Smith b Lambert	4	– run out	3
T. P. B. Smith c Wilson b Lambert	32	– c Crapp b Cook	40
J. Sims not out	30	– not out	6
R. R. Dovey c Emmett b Jenkins	5	– not out	7
L. Gray c Cook b Jenkins	2		
B 3, l-b 3, w 1	7	B 10, l-b 3, n-b 1	14
	392	**(8 wkts dec.)**	**304**

West

G. M. Emmett lbw b R. Smith	15	– b Sims	35
F. Cooper c McIntyre b Gray	53	– c Gray b Sims	16
R. Jenkins c Pawson b Sims	26	– c Barling b Sims	8
A. E. Wilson c Todd b Sims	16	– b Sims	2
R. Howorth c Todd b P. Smith	11	– not out	37
J. F. Crapp c and b R. Smith	77	– b Sims	28
M. F. Tremlett c McIntyre b Sims	31	– st McIntyre b Sims	32
A. E. Nutter c Todd b R. Smith	32	– b Sims	0
G. Lambert c Pawson b P. Smith	16	– b Sims	0
B. H. Lyon c Dodds b Gray	12	– st Brown b Sims	10
C. Cook not out	1	– st Brown b Sims	2
B 1, l-b 3	4	B 7, l-b 2	9
	294		**179**

West Bowling

	Overs	Mdns	Runs	Wkts	Overs	Mdns	Runs	Wkts
Nutter	14	—	74	—	2	—	6	—
Lambert	23	3	103	4	7	—	32	—
Tremlett	10	—	80	1	4	—	25	—
Jenkins	25	4	84	5	19	1	93	3
Howorth	2	—	6	—	29	2	106	3
Lyon	2	—	21	—				
Cook	2	—	17	—	5	—	28	1

East Bowling

	Overs	Mdns	Runs	Wkts	Overs	Mdns	Runs	Wkts
R. Smith	11	—	56	3	4	1	13	—
Gray	25	6	59	2	9	1	16	—
Sims	16	1	82	3	18.4	2	90	10
Dovey	8	1	36	—				
T. P. B. Smith	13.4	3	57	2	8	1	36	—
Pawson					6	1	15	—

Umpires: S. H. Hipple and G. Mobey.

ROYAL NAVY v ROYAL AIR FORCE

Played at Lord's, July 22, 23, 1949

Drawn. Batsmen dominated the match after a deplorable start by the Navy. They lost seven men for 91, but May, who scored 220 runs without being dismissed, found an admirable partner in Hodges, and their unfinished stand produced 192 runs. After the RAF lost Roberts for 26, Payton and Murray engaged in another unfinished partnership of 165 before Shirreff, although his team were 92 behind, declared. The Navy left their opponents to score 247 in two hours, but stubborn batting by Shirreff and Greensmith thwarted them. There were three declarations.

Royal Navy

Surg. Cdr C. H. P. Pearson b Greensmith	12	– b Shirreff	2
Lt Cdr (E) A. L. Thackara c Ford b Greensmith	22	– b Shirreff	49
Lt M. L. Y. Ainsworth c Roberts b Bedford	10	– lbw b Greensmith	4
Writer P. B. H. May not out	162	– not out	58
Lt Cdr J. E. Manners lbw b Greensmith	0	– c Ford b Cockle	26
Lt (S) J. M. Vernon c Bedford b Greensmith	6	– c Francis b Cockle	11
A/b K. Hamilton c Wilson b Greensmith	0		
S/A A. G. Coomb b Shirreff	2		
Cdr (E) J. Hodges not out	58		
B 6, l-b 4, n-b 1	11	L-b 3, n-b 1	4

(7 wkts dec.) 283   (5 wkts dec.) 154

Lt J. D. Sayer and Lt Cdr (S) R. Martin did not bat.

Royal Air Force

Sq Ldr Rev. W. W. Payton not out	107	– c May b Sayer	32
Wing Cdr J. F. Roberts c Sayer b Martin	6	– b Coomb	6
A/c M. Murray not out	76	– lbw b Sayer	29
A/c W. Greensmith (did not bat)		– not out	21
Flt Lt A. C. Shirreff (did not bat)		– not out	21
Sq Ldr R. G. Wilson (did not bat)		– b Martin	3
B 1, l-b 1	2	B 8, l-b 2	10

(1 wkt dec.) 191   (4 wkts) 122

A/c B. E. Disbury, A/c G. C. Francis, Wing Cdr W. R. Ford, Flt Sgt D. F. Cockle and A/c I. Bedford did not bat.

Royal Air Force Bowling

	Overs	Mdns	Runs	Wkts	Overs	Mdns	Runs	Wkts
Wilson	25	5	84	—	6	4	8	—
Shirreff	26	7	56	1	15	2	37	2
Greensmith........	34	14	73	5	13	3	41	1
Cockle	11	7	11	—	22.5	4	64	2
Bedford...........	10	1	48	1				

Royal Navy Bowling

	Overs	Mdns	Runs	Wkts	Overs	Mdns	Runs	Wkts
Coomb	19	5	55	—	9	—	25	1
Martin............	19	2	35	1	8	2	23	1
Sayer	15	3	34	—	9	1	26	2
Hodges...........	8	1	19	—	5	1	16	—
Vernon...........	9	1	26	—	5	1	18	—
Ainsworth........	4	—	13	—	1	—	4	—
Manners..........	2	—	7	—				

Umpires: D. H. Tregear and W. F. Simpson.

ENGLAND v THE REST

(Test Trial)

Played at Bradford, May 31, June 1, 1950

England won by an innings and 89 runs. One of the most remarkable representative matches on record finished before lunch on the second day. Such was the mastery of the bowlers on drying turf that in seven hours and fifty minutes of playing time thirty wickets fell for 369 runs, of which Hutton made nearly one-quarter. Although the desperate struggle for runs provided keen interest for spectators, the selectors could have learned little not already known to them. Yardley put in The Rest on winning the toss, and the off-breaks of Laker caused so complete a rout that in 110 minutes they were all out for the lowest total in a match of representative class. The previous smallest score was 30, made by South Africa against England at Port Elizabeth in 1896 and at Edgbaston 1924. On the ground, five miles from his birthplace on which he had enjoyed many League triumphs for Saltaire, Laker dominated the scene. He took two wickets in his first over and a third before conceding a run; in his fifth over he dismissed four more men before being edged for a second single, and he brilliantly caught and bowled the last man. His full analysis was: 14 overs, 12 maidens, 2 runs, 8 wickets. He spun the ball skilfully, his length was immaculate and his direction perfect. The young batsmen opposed to Laker did not possess the ripe experience needed to cope with his skill under conditions so suited to his bowling. England obtained a lead of 202, chiefly through superlative batting by Hutton, ably assisted by Edrich, against bowling of moderate quality apart from that of Berry, the left-hander, and Jenkins with leg spin. Berry did not lose accuracy even when Hutton used every possible means to knock him off his length. Hutton, who made 85 out of 155 in two hours, gave a dazzling display of batsmanship on a difficult pitch. Laker again met with early success in The Rest second innings; but Hollies caused chief damage. He turned the ball sharply and varied flight and pace well. Eric Bedser and Spooner made 42 in the only stand. On the sporting Bradford turf the Australians in 1948 and the West Indies earlier in 1950 also were made to look very ordinary.

The Rest

D. J. Kenyon c Evans b Laker	7	– lbw b Hollies	9
D. S. Sheppard lbw b Bailey	4	– b Laker	3
G. H. G. Doggart c Bailey b Laker	2	– st Evans b Hollies	12
P. B. H. May c Hutton b Laker	0	– b Laker	2
D. B. Carr c Bailey b Laker	0	– st Evans b Hollies	2
E. A. Bedser lbw b Laker	3	– c Evans b Hollies	30
R. T. Spooner b Laker	0	– c Yardley b Bedser	22
R. O. Jenkins not out	0	– c Bedser b Hollies	3
R. Berry b Laker	0	– c Yardley b Bedser	16
F. S. Trueman st Evans b Bedser	1	– not out	0
L. Jackson c and b Laker	5	– st Evans b Hollies	1
B 3, l-b 1, w 1	5	B 4, l-b 6, n-b 3	13
	27		**113**

England

L. Hutton b Trueman	85	T. G. Evans run out	1
R. T. Simpson st Spooner b Berry	26	J. C. Laker not out	6
W. J. Edrich lbw b Jenkins	46	A. V. Bedser c Jackson b Jenkins	5
J. D. Robertson c Sheppard b Berry	0	W. E. Hollies st Spooner b Berry	4
J. G. Dewes c Doggart b Berry	34	L-b 1, n-b 1	2
N. W. D. Yardley c Trueman b Jenkins	13		
T. E. Bailey c Spooner b Berry	7		**229**

England Bowling

	Overs	Mdns	Runs	Wkts	Overs	Mdns	Runs	Wkts
Bailey	6	4	3	1	5	2	6	—
Bedser	9	3	12	1	9	2	22	2
Laker	14	12	2	8	18	4	44	2
Hollies	7	5	5	—	22.4	13	28	6

The Rest Bowling

	Overs	Mdns	Runs	Wkts
Jackson	12	3	38	—
Bedser	13	—	60	—
Jenkins	10	—	38	3
Berry	32	10	73	5
Trueman	9	3	18	1

Umpires: W. H. Ashdown and H. Elliott.

GENTLEMEN v PLAYERS

Played at Lord's, July 26, 27, 28, 1950

Drawn. A match worthy of the traditions of its title became specially memorable because of two features. One was the gloriously thrilling finish. The Players accepted the challenge of a declaration by Brown which set them 253 to win in two and a half hours so spiritedly that with twenty minutes left and seven wickets in hand they required 36. From this point such a transformation occurred that in seventeen minutes six more batsmen were out, three the victims of a hat-trick by Knott. When Hollies, the last man, joined Wright five balls remained and eleven runs were needed for victory. Amidst tense excitement Hollies managed to keep the last deliveries out of his wicket and away from the clutching hands of the ten fieldsmen crouched in a circle only a few yards from the bat.

A superb display by Brown, reminiscent of H. T. Bartlett's magnificent innings in the 1938 game, also placed the contest above the ordinary. On the opening day, after his side had been put in, Brown launched a remarkable attack on the bowling. His fierce driving recalled memories of bygone days. So completely was he the master that he scored all but nine of the 131 runs made in the 110 minutes he batted. He hit sixteen 4s and celebrated his century with a six into the pavilion. Other good innings for the Gentlemen were those of Dewes and Doggart. Dewes, in an unusually free mood, put much power into his hits, which included one 6 and ten 4s, and Doggart charmed by his varied stroke-play.

Just as Brown pulled round the Gentlemen, so Dollery, the Player's captain, rescued his side after four wickets, three in succession to Brown, went down for 71. Dollery never looked in difficulty and he cut, drove or hooked with strength and expert placing. He received good assistance from Bedser in a seventh-wicket stand of 116. As soon as the Gentlemen team left the field upon Dollery's declaration on the second day Brown was invited to captain the side to Australia during the winter, and by the time his team began batting he was sitting in Committee discussing the first cricketers to be picked for the tour. Simpson and Dewes opened the Gentlemen second innings with a stand of 103, and Doggart and Insole also batted well, as did Parkhouse a second time for the Players. Of the bowlers, Wright showed good form, Tattersall kept a tantalisingly accurate length with off-breaks rolled rather than spun, and Knott grasped his opportunities cleverly when the Players were racing for runs in the final dramatic overs.

Gentlemen

R. T. Simpson c and b Bedser	10	– lbw b Hollies 69
J. G. Dewes c Washbrook b Tattersall	94	– b Tattersall 48
G. H. G. Doggart b Wright	75	– lbw b Wright 36
D. B. Carr b Tattersall	0	– c Bedser b Wright 17
D. J. Insole c Evans b Wright	4	– not out 38
N. W. D. Yardley run out	5	
T. E. Bailey c Parkhouse b Bedser	5	
F. R. Brown b Tattersall	122	– not out 22
J. J. Warr b Wright	2	
D. V. Brennan b Hollies	0	
C. J. Knott not out	1	
B 5, l-b 2	7	B 1, l-b 3, n-b 1 5
	325	**(4 wkts dec.) 235**

Players

H. Gimblett lbw b Brown	23	– c Knott b Bailey 14
C. Washbrook c Insole b Bailey	0	– c and b Brown 43
W. G. A. Parkhouse b Brown	29	– c Brown b Knott 81
D. J. Kenyon lbw b Brown	5	– c Brennan b Bailey 54
H. E. Dollery c Brennan b Doggart	123	– c Yardley b Knott 20
T. G. Evans b Bailey	19	– st Brennan b Knott 9
D. Shackleton c Simpson b Knott	25	– c Insole b Knott 2
A. V. Bedser c Dewes b Knott	59	– b Bailey 10
R. Tattersall lbw b Doggart	12	– st Brennan b Knott 0
D. V. P. Wright not out	6	– not out 2
W. E. Hollies not out	1	– not out 0
B 2, l-b 4	6	B 2, l-b 5 7
	(9 wkts dec.) 308	**(9 wkts) 242**

Players Bowling

	Overs	Mdns	Runs	Wkts	Overs	Mdns	Runs	Wkts
Bedser...........	23	2	77	2	12	—	41	—
Shackleton	18	3	51	—	13	—	60	—
Tattersall	16.4	6	38	3	10	—	35	1
Hollies	23	8	49	1	12	1	43	1
Wright	25	4	103	3	9	—	51	2

Gentlemen Bowling

	Overs	Mdns	Runs	Wkts	Overs	Mdns	Runs	Wkts
Bailey	25	6	65	2	14	2	59	3
Warr............	21	5	66	—	8	1	38	—
Yardley..........	10	1	23	—	4	—	13	—
Brown...........	28	3	63	3	10	—	59	1
Knott	21	2	63	2	11	—	66	5
Carr	2	—	11	—				
Doggart	4	1	11	2				

Umpires: K. McCanlis and A. Skelding.

UNDER THIRTY-TWO v OVER THIRTY-TWO

Played at Hastings, September 6, 7, 8, 1950

Under Thirty-two won by six wickets. The younger players batted attractively on the opening day, Dodds, Carr, Doggart and Jenkins all scoring readily. Dodds drove splendidly during a stay of three hours; he hit one 6 and five 4s. E. Davies, the Glamorgan left-hander, dominated the second day's play. He carried his bat through the first innings of the older men, which lasted just over three and a half hours. With powerful drives and well-timed strokes to leg he hit twelve 4s. When his side followed-on Davies made 52 in an opening stand of 64 with John Langridge; he hit ten 4s. Palmer drove and hit to leg well in a steady innings lasting two and three-quarter hours, refusing to be tempted by the spin bowlers, of whom Tattersall did especially well. The fast bowling of Perks, who took two wickets in his opening over without a run scored, worried the Over Thirty-two batsmen before they achieved their modest second innings task.

Under Thirty-two

J. G. Dewes b Perks	23	– c McCorkell b Perks	11
T. C. Dodds c Edrich b Surridge	93	– not out	4
G. H. G. Doggart b Palmer	46	– b Perks	0
D. B. Carr c McCorkell b Perks	56	– not out	1
P. Hearn c McCorkell b Knott	29		
M. F. Tremlett c Surridge b Davies	30	– b Perks	0
D. Shackleton lbw b Knott	4		
R. O. Jenkins c Davies b Cox	54		
H. W. Stephenson not out	21		
R. W. Clarke (did not bat)		– b Perks	25
B 7, l-b 9	16	B 4, l-b 2	6
	(8 wkts dec.) 372		(4 wkts) 47

R. Tattersall did not bat.

Over Thirty-two

John Langridge b Shackleton	2	– c Clarke b Carr	15
E. Davies not out	107	– c Dewes b Carr	52
N. McCorkell run out	8	– b Tattersall	4
C. H. Palmer lbw b Carr	15	– not out	71
G. Cox b Jenkins	2	– c Clarke b Jenkins	17
G. A. Edrich b Tattersall	0	– c Clarke b Jenkins	14
James Langridge c Doggart b Tattersall	28	– lbw b Carr	6
B. L. Muncer c Dewes b Tattersall	3	– lbw b Tattersall	9
W. S. Surridge run out	0	– b Shackleton	18
R. T. D. Perks b Tattersall	7	– c Doggart b Jenkins	14
C. J. Knott b Tattersall	0	– b Shackleton	1
B 6, w 1, n-b 1	8	B 17	17
	180		**238**

Over Thirty-two Bowling

	Overs	Mdns	Runs	Wkts	Overs	Mdns	Runs	Wkts
Perks	22	3	76	2	10.2	4	28	4
Surridge	10	2	36	1	6	2	12	—
Knott	25	5	73	2	3	2	1	—
Davies	19	3	59	1				
Muncer	10	—	52	—				
Palmer	13	5	33	1				
Cox	4.1	—	16	1				
James Langridge	4	—	11	—				

Under Thirty-two Bowling

	Overs	Mdns	Runs	Wkts	Overs	Mdns	Runs	Wkts
Shackleton	17	2	44	1	10.3	1	53	2
Clarke	3	—	12	—	5	—	31	—
Jenkins	18	2	44	1	17	—	42	3
Tattersall	28.5	9	45	5	25	8	46	2
Carr	7	1	27	1	14	3	47	3
Doggart					1	—	2	—

Umpires: F. Chester and H. W. Parks.

GENTLEMEN v PLAYERS

Played at Lord's, July 18, 19, 20, 1951

Players won by 21 runs. This match was worthy of its great tradition, for after a skilfully timed declaration by Compton the last Gentlemen's wicket fell with only three minutes left. F. R. Brown was chosen to captain the Gentlemen, but injury kept him away. Then the leadership was passed to Yardley, but a few minutes before the match was due to begin he gave the honour to Howard so that he could gain experience of handling a representative side before taking the MCC team to India. The Players also underwent a change of captain. Officially Hutton was in charge, but owing to a severely bruised back he batted number six and did not field.

Magnificent batting by the Middlesex pair, Robertson and Compton, was the feature of the opening day. For two and a half hours Robertson, who hit ten 4s, dominated the cricket with clean drives, hooks and cuts. The came Compton in his most devastating mood. Often he walked yards down the pitch to drive and, hitting one 6 and seventeen 4s, he made his chanceless 150 out of 232 in three and a half hours. With Marlar the only recognised slow bowler in the side, Howard was compelled to keep him on for long spells and he responded by maintaining an almost faultless length with his off-breaks.

The second day was memorable for the superb hundred by May for the Gentlemen. The 21-year-old Cambridge Blue saw his side through a most difficult position. He came in when Simpson and Sheppard had left for 53 and with the lunch interval near he scored only two in his first half-hour. In a hard battle Edrich and May put on 51, but the Gentlemen did not prosper until May was joined by his old Light Blue captain, Insole.

It was Insole who took the initiative against some really good bowling by the four England professionals, Tattersall, Hilton, Statham and Bedser. Some perfect drives past cover by Insole seemed to inspire May and he proceeded to hit cleanly in front of the wicket. The stand yielded 94, but not until he was joined by Brennan did May reach his hundred by driving Hilton and Ikin each for three. May offered to chances off Hilton when 28 and 93, but his was a grand display. He batted four hours ten minutes and hit one 5 and thirteen 4s.

Howard declared first thing on Friday morning and Compton accepted the challenge, the Players scoring 188 in three hours. Compton again hit splendidly and Watson for the second time in the match helped him in a three-figure stand.

The Gentlemen wanted 244 in two and three-quarter hours – an average of 90 an hour – but Compton, having batted the preceding hundred and ten minutes knew exactly the state of the pitch. He gave Bedser and Statham only one over each before he rubbed the new ball in the dust and called on Tattersall and Hilton. Despite the turning ball, the batsmen went boldly after the runs. Sheppard and Edrich each drove Tattersall for 6, and with 50 appearing in half an hour the issue was open.

Suddenly Compton switched to Ikin, and he changed the outlook by dismissing both Sheppard and Edrich. With that danger removed, Bedser came back at 112 and he stayed at the pavilion end until the match was decided ninety minutes later. When Hilton in one over disposed of Yardley and Howard, six wickets were down for 138, so that with sixty-five minutes remaining the Players appeared to be in sight of an easy victory.

Then Divecha, the Indian, hit fearlessly and, enjoying some luck, he claimed six 4s while making 32 out of 45 in twenty-five minutes. Again Insole shaped splendidly. Consequently, when the extra half-hour was taken, 55 runs were still needed with three wickets standing, but Bedser was too much for Brennan and Warr. Finally, Compton not only brought back Ikin specially to attack Marlar, but snatched a win for his side by catching him at slip.

Players

J. T. Ikin b Warr	0	– lbw b Edrich	34
J. D. Robertson lbw b Yardley	80	– run out	20
T. W. Graveney st Brennan b Marlar	87	– c Brennan b Marlar	3
*D. C. S. Compton c Yardley b Divecha	150	– not out	74
W. Watson b Edrich	33	– not out	49
L. Hutton b Divecha	19		
T. G. Evans b Divecha	6		
A. V. Bedser c Brennan b Warr	4		
R. Tattersall c Insole b Divecha	17		
J. B. Statham st Brennan b Divecha	6		
M. J. Hilton not out	0		
B 2, l-b 5, n-b 2	9	B 7, l-b 1	8

1/3 2/101 3/141 4/252 5/301   361   1/37 2/57 3/63   (3 wkts dec.) 188
6/311 7/332 8/336 9/361

Gentlemen

R. T. Simpson b Statham	6	– b Tattersall	16
D. S. Sheppard c Watson b Hilton	31	– lbw b Ikin	39
W. J. Edrich c Robertson b Hilton	36	– b Ikin	36
P. B. H. May not out	119	– b Bedser	24
D. J. Insole c Robertson b Hilton	50	– not out	44
N. W. D. Yardley b Compton	17	– c Graveney b Tattersall	4
*N. D. Howard c Robertson b Compton	1	– st Evans b Tattersall	0
R. V. Divecha lbw b Ikin	2	– c Robertson b Bedser	32
D. V. Brennan lbw b Ikin	13	– c Statham b Bedser	3
J. J. Warr st Evans b Ikin	11	– b Bedser	17
R. G. Marlar (did not bat)		– c Compton b Ikin	2
B 12, l-b 3	15	B 4, l-b 6	10

1/11 2/53 3/104 4/198   (9 wkts dec.) 301   1/23 2/78 3/109 4/122 5/137   227
5/238 6/240 7/245 8/287 9/301   6/138 7/183 8/211 9/219

Gentlemen Bowling

	Overs	Mdns	Runs	Wkts	Overs	Mdns	Runs	Wkts
Warr	32	6	100	2	12	2	34	—
Divecha	21.4	4	81	5	10	1	47	—
Yardley	18	4	47	1	8	—	30	—
Edrich	20	5	43	1	8	2	25	1
Marlar	33	11	81	1	18	5	44	1

Players Bowling

	Overs	Mdns	Runs	Wkts	Overs	Mdns	Runs	Wkts
Bedser	18	5	39	—	15	1	53	4
Statham	14	5	23	1	3	—	7	—
Hilton	43	18	90	3	18	3	67	—
Tattersall	25	5	62	—	12	—	53	3
Compton	11	—	40	2				
Ikin	14.4	5	32	3	8.4	—	37	3

Umpires: H. Elliott and W. F. Price.

SOUTH v NORTH

Played at Kingston-on-Thames, September 1, 3, 4, 1951

North won by four wickets. The match was a personal triumph for Gladwin, the Derbyshire fast-medium bowler. With everything pointing to a draw he changed the situation by taking nine South second innings wickets for 64 runs in 13.4 overs, the best performance of his career. Because of rain, only two hours' play was possible on the first day, when Brown, batting number three, looked completely at ease. He continued aggressively on Monday, reaching a century in just under two hours. Altogether he hit three 6s and fifteen 4s. Brown was again the most successful batsman in the second innings, when in two overs he hit 26 of the 64 runs conceded by Gladwin.

South

Batsman	1st	2nd
H. Gimblett c Grieves b Wharton	7	c Hilton b Gladwin — 0
G. M. Emmett b Wharton	3	c Wharton b Gladwin — 10
S. M. Brown st Livingston b Gladwin	114	c Howard b Gladwin — 50
M. F. Tremlett b Gladwin	0	c Hilton b Gladwin — 12
E. A. Bedser c Rhodes b Hilton	49	c Howard b Gladwin — 23
A. J. Watkins c Howard b Wharton	4	b Gladwin — 2
J. F. Parker c Place b Gladwin	8	lbw b Wharton — 2
B. A. Barnett not out	64	c Howard b Gladwin — 2
L. H. Compton b Gladwin	17	b Gladwin — 0
J. M. Sims lbw b Gladwin	0	not out — 3
G. A. R. Lock not out	3	c Place b Gladwin — 0
B 6, l-b 2	8	L-b 1, n-b 1 — 2
	(9 wkts dec.) 277	**106**

North

Batsman	1st	2nd
D. Brookes c and b Parker	14	c Parker b Bedser — 13
N. Oldfield b Lock	32	b Watkins — 7
L. Livingston lbw b Lock	37	c Watkins b Bedser — 14
D. J. Kenyon c Bedser b Sims	8	b Lock — 4
W. Place c Parker b Lock	29	not out — 19
N. D. Howard c Compton b Sims	0	b Lock — 10
K. Grieves c Compton b Watkins	45	lbw b Bedser — 3
A. Wharton c Watkins b Bedser	21	not out — 11
A. E. G. Rhodes lbw b Lock	47	
C. Gladwin c and b Watkins	32	
M. J. Hilton not out	20	
B 7, l-b 6, w 1	14	B 2, l-b 3 — 5
	299	**(6 wkts) 86**

North Bowling

	Overs	Mdns	Runs	Wkts	Overs	Mdns	Runs	Wkts
Gladwin	30	4	118	5	13.4	1	54	9
Wharton	12	3	27	3	13	1	40	1
Hilton	26	6	96	1				
Rhodes	5	—	28	—				

South Bowling

	Overs	Mdns	Runs	Wkts	Overs	Mdns	Runs	Wkts
Parker	6	—	36	1	3	—	8	—
Watkins	19	5	52	2	6	4	11	1
Lock	36	8	115	4	11	2	37	2
Sims	18	3	50	2				
Bedser	13	4	32	1	8.5	2	25	3

Umpires: G. S. Mobey and W. F. Price.

NORTH v SOUTH

Played at Kingston-upon-Thames, September 6, 8, 9, 1952

The South won by an innings and 79 runs. Hopes of a close match were dashed by the weather, for week-end rain so affected the pitch that the North were soon forced to follow-on 174 behind and the match barely extended to the third day. Nevertheless, the spectators who braved the cold on the Saturday were given an exhibition of carefree hitting by the South batsmen, particularly the Surrey players, Whittaker and Surridge. In a dazzling display of only two hours Whittaker hit his only century of the summer, and it contained six 6s, one 5 and nine 4s. Surridge also thrashed the bowling, taking three successive 6s off Ikin. Apart from Poole, Ikin and Edrich, who defended stubbornly against the turning ball, the Northern batsmen were always struggling against Bedser, Sims and Muncer. Splendid fielding aided the bowlers in their task. Surridge, at slip and short leg, set a fine example by holding seven catches on the second day.

South

E. A. Bedser c Howard b Hilton 29	G. E. Lambert c Hilton b Ikin 7
S. M. Brown lbw b Jackson............... 21	W. S. Surridge c Edrich b Ikin 26
B. Constable c Yarnold b Jackson 49	J. M. Sims not out 9
P. A. Gibb c Howard b Warr 20	
L. B. Fishlock c Jackson b Ikin........... 37	B 6, l-b 5 11
A. Thompson c Poole b Jackson......... 42	
G. J. Whittaker c Oldfield b Ikin.........103	1/29 2/86 3/123 4/126 5/195 375
B. L. Muncer lbw b Hilton 21	6/214 7/266 8/309 9/344

North

D. Brookes c Bedser b Surridge	2	– b Lambert..................... 3
J. T. Ikin b Bedser............................	48	– c Surridge b Bedser........... 29
N. Oldfield c Surridge b Lambert	9	– c Gibb b Surridge 1
G. A. Edrich c Muncer b Bedser.................	48	– c Whittaker b Muncer.......... 42
C. J. Poole c Surridge b Bedser.................	50	– c Surridge b Bedser........... 0
N. D. Howard b Sims	7	– c Surridge b Muncer........... 0
J. G. Lomax c Surridge b Bedser...............	19	– b Muncer 0
M. J. Hilton c Surridge b Sims	2	– c Constable b Muncer.......... 5
H. Yarnold c Whittaker b Sims.................	1	– b Muncer 12
J. J. Warr not out	5	– c Thompson b Bedser.......... 1
L. Jackson b Sims...........................	1	– not out 1
B 9...............................	9	L-b 1................. 1

1/3 2/22 3/91 4/136 5/169	201	1/14 2/17 3/49 4/49 5/50 95
6/173 7/189 8/191 9/200		6/52 7/58 8/83 9/90

North Bowling

	Overs	Mdns	Runs	Wkts
Jackson...........	23	5	82	3
Warr.............	24	4	70	1
Lomax	10	3	23	—
Ikin..............	28.4	3	140	4
Hilton............	20	8	49	2

South Bowling

	Overs	Mdns	Runs	Wkts	Overs	Mdns	Runs	Wkts
Lambert	14	3	20	1	10	2	21	1
Surridge	7	—	18	1	9	1	23	1
Muncer...........	13	3	35	—	11.3	2	28	5
Bedser............	19	4	50	4	11	1	22	3
Sims	12.2	—	69	4				

Umpires: G. S. Mobey and J. J. Hills.

GENTLEMEN v PLAYERS

Played at Lord's, July 17, 18, 19, 1957

Drawn. The Players, set to make 291 in three and three-quarter hours, looked likely to succeed when the needed 91 in the last hour with seven wickets in hand, but in the event they had to fight to play out time. Sheppard, in only his second first-class game of the summer, quickly settled down with Peter Richardson after a delayed start. Further rain curtailed the first day to two hours' play, and after another delay on the second day, wickets tumbled on a lifting pitch. Trueman, Laker and Hollies caused the last nine wickets of the Gentlemen to fall for 71 runs, but the amateur fast-medium bowlers, Warr, Smith and Dexter, were even more effective. Dexter, the Cambridge Blue, who had previously taken only 18 wickets in first-class cricket, gave particular trouble, and the Players, with nine wickets down, declared at their lowest score for well over a hundred years. Then the pitch rolled out easier, and aggressive batting by Insole, who hit Laker for 20 in one over, enabled May to declare. Smith, who batted two and a quarter hours and hit thirteen 4s, and Gardner laid a sound foundation with a stand of 145, but Dexter again brought about a collapse of the middle batting, and in the end Trueman and Hollies were left to play out the last ten minutes. Denis Compton captained the Players in his last season as a professional.

Gentlemen

P. E. Richardson hit wkt b Trueman	47	– c Evans b Hollies	13
Rev. D. S. Sheppard c Smith b Trueman	55	– c Compton b Trueman	24
D. J. Insole c Trueman b Tyson	21	– not out	79
P. B. H. May c Graveney b Trueman	5	– c Trueman b Laker	8
M. C. Cowdrey b Trueman	6	– lbw b Hollies	8
E. R. Dexter b Laker	13	– st Evans b Smith	13
G. Goonesena b Hollies	6		
C. S. Smith c Compton b Hollies	0		
J. J. Warr st Evans b Laker	0	– st Evans b Laker	13
R. G. Marlar run out	4		
E. B. Lewis not out	9		
B 2, l-b 1	3	B 4, l-b 5	9
	169	**(6 wkts dec.)**	**167**

1/87 2/113 3/131 4/131 5/138
6/152 7/156 8/156 9/156

1/34 2/41 3/79
4/87 5/110 6/167

Players

D. V. Smith c Richardson b Dexter	19	– c May b Goonesena	102
T. H. Clark c Goonesena b Smith	0	– b Smith	10
F. C. Gardner b Smith	0	– c Lewis b Goonesena	48
T. W. Graveney c Goonesena b Warr	6	– run out	24
D. C. S. Compton c Cowdrey b Dexter	6	– c Lewis b Dexter	26
D. W. Richardson c Lewis b Dexter	0	– lbw b Dexter	2
T. G. Evans c Smith b Dexter	7	– c May b Dexter	4
F. H. Tyson c Goonesena b Dexter	0	– b Smith	2
J. C. Laker c May b Warr	7	– c Lewis b Warr	5
F. S. Trueman not out	1	– not out	3
W. E. Hollies (did not bat)		– not out	1
		B 6, l-b 7, w 1, n-b 1	15
	(9 wkts dec.) 46	**(9 wkts)**	**242**

1/0 2/0 3/11 4/24
5/30 6/33 7/33 8/38 9/46

1/11 2/156 3/169 4/207
5/217 6/225 7/225 8/230 9/234

Players Bowling

	Overs	Mdns	Runs	Wkts	Overs	Mdns	Runs	Wkts
Trueman	18	8	38	4	10	2	25	1
Tyson	15	4	51	1	9	1	37	—
Hollies	18	6	39	2	10	1	26	2
Laker	18	6	38	2	18	5	54	2
Smith					2.5	—	16	1

Gentlemen Bowling

	Overs	Mdns	Runs	Wkts	Overs	Mdns	Runs	Wkts
Warr............	10.2	4	23	2	20	7	63	1
Smith	5	1	15	2	16	7	31	2
Dexter...........	5	2	8	5	12	2	47	3
Marlar					3	—	25	—
Goonesena					13	2	61	2

Umpires: A. E. Pothecary and W. F. Price.

IRELAND v SCOTLAND

Played at Dublin, July 27, 29, 1957

Ireland won by 38 runs with a day to spare. Exceptional spin bowling and wicket-keeping marked this match in which the highest individual score was 30. Frank Fee, the 23-year-old off-spinner, achieved an Irish record in taking nine wickets for 26 runs. He finished with twelve for 60 and Livingstone, specialising in leg-breaks, took eleven wickets for 51 for Scotland. He owed much to the competency of Brown who equalled the world's wicket-keeping record with seven victims in one innings.

Ireland

S. F. Bergin b Barr	13	– c Brown b Lawrence............	17
K. Quinn st Brown b Livingstone	25	– c Brown b Wilson..............	2
A. Finlay b Lawrence	24	– st Brown b Livingstone.	9
L. A. Warke c Dudman b Livingstone	1	– c Brown b Wilson..............	4
J. S. Pollock c Dudman b Barr	21	– b Livingstone	17
W. I. Lewis c Barr b Wilson	10	– c Brown b Livingstone..........	4
A. P. Hollick b Livingstone....................	0	– b Roberts	0
G. W. Fawcett c Wilson b Livingstone	9	– st Brown b Livingstone..........	3
I. B. J. Wilson st Brown b Livingstone	7	– c Aitchison b Livingstone........	4
F. Fee c Cosh b Livingstone	7	– not out	9
E. H. Bodell not out..........................	9	– st Brown b Roberts.............	0
B 1, l-b 3, w 1, n-b 8	13	B 1, l-b 1, n-b 2...........	4

1/27 2/54 3/59 4/72 5/92   139   1/17 2/23 3/28 4/38 5/42   73
6/99 7/106 8/113 9/123   6/47 7/52 8/63 9/72

Scotland

R. H. E. Chisholm b Fee......................	12	– lbw b Bodell	3
L. C. Dudman b Fee	7	– c Hollick b Fee	17
Rev. J. Aitchison c Bergin b Fee	3	– b Fee.........................	30
J. N. Kemsley c Warke b Fee	3	– b Bodell......................	0
D. Barr c Warke b Fee	12	– b Bodell......................	2
S. H. Cosh b Fee...........................	0	– b Bodell......................	2
J. Brown not out	25	– c Fee b Wilson	7
J. B. Roberts c Warke b Fee	0	– c Fee b Wilson	6
D. Livingstone b Fee........................	6	– not out	16
J. S. Wilson c Fawcett b Fee.................	0	– b Wilson	1
D. R. Lawrence b Warke	10	– b Fee.........................	0
B 2, l-b 1, n-b 1	4	B 3, l-b 5...............	8

1/13 2/22 3/27 4/34 5/34   82   1/6 2/46 3/46 4/50 5/56   92
6/41 7/41 8/49 9/49   6/56 7/72 8/75 9/89

Scotland Bowling

	Overs	Mdns	Runs	Wkts	Overs	Mdns	Runs	Wkts
Wilson	14	5	23	1	9	5	22	2
Lawrence	14	4	24	1	6	1	19	1
Barr	13	2	27	2	4	2	5	—
Roberts..........	11	4	19	—	8	5	5	2
Livingstone.......	23.5	6	33	6	14	5	18	5

Ireland Bowling

	Overs	Mdns	Runs	Wkts	Overs	Mdns	Runs	Wkts
Bodell	23	6	45	—	14	6	24	4
Warke...........	3.4	1	7	1	3	—	16	—
Fee	22	12	26	9	21	7	34	3
Wilson	2	2	—	—	10	6	10	3

Umpires: J. Connerton and K. Orme.

IRELAND v MCC

Played at Dublin, September 1, 3, 4, 1956

MCC won by 22 runs. By an unfortunate oversight the report and full scores of this match were omitted from last year's *Wisden*. Two memorable bowling performances provided the main feature. Fee, the North of Ireland schoolmaster and off-spinner, took fourteen wickets, equalling the Irish record of S. S. Huey, for exactly 100 runs. In the MCC first innings Pollock held five excellent leg-side catches off the bowling of Fee. Chesterton, the MCC captain and Malvern schoolmaster, took ten wickets for 52 runs in the match with his medium-pace bowling.

MCC

W. Knightley-Smith c Pollock b Huey	27	– c Lewis b Fee	17
R. E. Bird c Neville b Warke....................	1	– c Neville b Fee	19
G. P. S. Delisle c Warke b Fee	14	– run out	23
J. M. A. Marshall c Pollock b Fee...............	12	– b Wilson.....................	10
W. Murray-Wood b Fee	6	– c Martin b Fee	0
J. P. Fellows-Smith c Pollock b Fee	27	– c Martin b Fee	28
M. H. Stevenson c Fawcett b Huey...............	12	– c Wilson b Fee	10
P. A. Whitcombe c Martin b Fee	14	– not out	4
C. B. R. Featherstonhaugh c Pollock b Fee	6	– c Pollock b Fee................	1
P. I. Bedford not out	6	– b Fee........................	20
G. H. Chesterton c Pollock b Fee................	3	– c Fawcett b Wilson.............	2
B 3, l-b 2, w 2	7	B 1, n-b 2	3

1/9 2/33 3/54 4/65 5/74   135   1/25 2/54 3/58 4/85 5/92   137
6/95 7/118 8/124 9/124   6/107 7/126 8/132 9/134

Ireland

H. Martin c Bird b Chesterton	6	– c Stevenson b Whitcombe	33
S. F. Bergin c Bird b Chesterton	10	– b Whitcombe	28
L. A. Warke b Chesterton	2	– c Bird b Chesterton	46
J. S. Pollock c Bird b Chesterton	0	– c Knightley-Smith b Whitcombe	5
P. A. Neville c Fellows-Smith b Chesterton	0	– c Bedford b Chesterton	17
W. I. Lewis run out	0	– c Bird b Chesterton	2
G. W. Fawcett c Marshall b Fellows-Smith	1	– c Bird b Fellows-Smith	7
S. S. Huey c Chesterton b Fellows-Smith	0	– b Fellows-Smith	10
I. B. J. Wilson c Bedford b Chesterton	12	– c Stevenson b Whitcombe	18
F. Fee c Stevenson b Chesterton	1	– b Fellows-Smith	7
S. W. Ferris not out	3	– not out	4
B 6, l-b 4, n-b 3	13	B 14, l-b 8, w 1, n-b 2	25

1/15 2/23 3/23 4/23 5/26   48   1/61 2/72 3/80 4/118 5/122   202
6/27 7/30 8/30 9/32   6/147 7/147 8/176 9/187

Ireland Bowling

	Overs	Mdns	Runs	Wkts	Overs	Mdns	Runs	Wkts
Ferris	6	2	8	—	4	1	15	—
Warke	4	1	11	1	3	1	5	—
Fee	24	8	56	7	28	11	44	7
Wilson	6	1	12	—	13	1	40	2
Huey	16	4	41	2	14	3	30	—

MCC Bowling

	Overs	Mdns	Runs	Wkts	Overs	Mdns	Runs	Wkts
Whitcombe	6	3	9	—	24	17	24	4
Chesterton	15.4	9	14	7	33	19	38	3
Fellows-Smith	10	6	12	2	22.4	7	43	3
Bedford					15	1	49	—
Marshall					11	4	23	—

Umpires: C. Fox and J. Connerton.

MCC v YORKSHIRE

Played at Lord's, April 30, May 1, 2, 1958

MCC won by five wickets. Swetman and Trueman were the leading figures in an interesting match in which bowlers were generally on top. Swetman, sent in as stop-gap on Thursday evening, hit the first century of his career. His 107 took three and a half hours. Yorkshire batted unevenly on the first day when Burnet, the new captain, playing in his first first-class match, was one of only four players to reach double figures. MCC looked to be getting on top but on the second morning they lost six wickets for 11 runs, four to Trueman, who did the hat-trick when dismissing Swetman, Allen and Tattersall. Yorkshire collapsed again after a useful start and MCC needed 215 to win. Milton and Swetman virtually assured success during a second wicket stand of 111 and when Swetman left only 16 were needed for victory.

Yorkshire

W. B. Stott c Swetman b Smith	39	– c Pullar b Tyson	1
F. A. Lowson c Milton b Bennett	10	– c Tattersall b Allen	34
J. V. Wilson run out	9	– c Hallam b Smith	76
D. B. Close c Hallam b Tattersall	34	– c Hallam b Allen	28
D. E. V. Padgett b Bennett	4	– b Allen	6
R. Illingworth b Bennett	0	– c Swetman b Allen	2
J. R. Burnet c Swetman b Tyson	16	– lbw b Allen	0
J. H. Wardle b Tattersall	0	– b Tyson	9
F. S. Trueman lbw b Tattersall	2	– b Bennett	40
J. G. Binks not out	5	– c Hallam b Bennett	5
D. Pickles c and b Tyson	1	– not out	1
B 1, l-b 1	2	B 2, l-b 9, n-b 2	13

1/42 2/54 3/65 4/83 5/83   **122**   1/3 2/97 3/151 4/151 5/159   **215**
6/108 7/108 8/110 9/120   6/159 7/160 8/209 9/209

MCC

M. R. Hallam c Wilson b Trueman	26	– c Binks b Trueman	10
C. A. Milton b Close	48	– c Close b Wardle	47
T. W. Graveney c Padgett b Illingworth	20	– lbw b Wardle	21
G. Pullar c Wilson b Trueman	12	– c Binks b Wardle	9
D. J. Insole b Trueman	9	– not out	13
D. Bennett b Pickles	0	– not out	1
R. Swetman c Close b Trueman	4	– b Wardle	107
F. H. Tyson b Pickles	2		
D. R. Smith not out	1		
M. H. J. Allen b Trueman	0		
R. Tattersall lbw b Trueman	0		
N-b 1	1	B 6, l-b 2, w 1	9

1/50 2/80 3/102 4/112 5/116   **123**   1/16 2/127 3/194   (5 wkts) **217**
6/116 7/121 8/123 9/123   4/199 5/208

MCC Bowling

	Overs	Mdns	Runs	Wkts	Overs	Mdns	Runs	Wkts
Tyson	13.1	6	24	2	16	2	34	2
Bennett	16	4	41	3	18	4	46	2
Smith	10	2	24	1	18	3	52	1
Tattersall	13	5	17	3	14	4	27	—
Allen	6	3	14	—	16	6	43	5

Yorkshire Bowling

	Overs	Mdns	Runs	Wkts	Overs	Mdns	Runs	Wkts
Trueman	15.1	5	41	6	16	4	39	1
Pickles	17	5	26	2	14	3	33	—
Wardle	14	5	31	—	20.2	5	57	4
Illingworth	8	2	19	1	14	1	52	—
Close	2	—	5	1	6	—	27	—

Umpires: B. L. Muncer and H. P. Sharp.

D. R. JARDINE'S XI v CAMBRIDGE UNIVERSITY

Played at Eastbourne, July 9, 10, 11, 1958

Cambridge won by 198 runs, proving overwhelmingly stronger in batting and bowling. Dexter, after spending twenty minutes over three runs, reached his hundred in an hour and fifty minutes. He hit three 6s, one 5 and fourteen 4s, and shared a stand of 170 with Cook. Pieris performed the hat-trick in his fourth over by bowling Wilenkin, having Walton caught at the wicket and Thresher taken at short-leg. Winn held up the Cambridge attack for two and a quarter hours but Jardine's XI finished 173 behind. McLachlan, 55 not out on the first day, hit nine 4s in his second innings' 63, and Jardine's XI were set to score 314 to win, a task they never looked like achieving.

Cambridge University

D. J. Green c Melluish b Fasken	26	– lbw b Wait	4
J. R. Bernard lbw b Fasken	14	– c Melluish b Robins	16
G. W. Cook lbw b Robins	68	– c Walton b Wait	0
E. R. Dexter st Melluish b Robins	110	– c Winn b Metcalfe	3
R. M. Prideaux b Wait	20	– c Winn b Robins	17
I. M. McLachlan not out	55	– c Paul b Robins	63
R. M. James c Melluish b Wait	4	– c Melluish b Robins	35
C. B. Howland not out	21	– not out	0
P. I. Pieris (did not bat)	–	– c Melluish b Wait	0
O. S. Wheatley (did not bat)	–	– b Metcalfe	0
B 5, l-b 6, w 4	15	B 2	2

1/46 2/57 3/227   (6 wkts dec.) 333   1/5 2/33 3/34 4/50   (9 wkts dec.) 140
4/228 5/271 6/287   5/82 6/137 7/140 8/140 9/140

A. Hurd did not bat.

D. R. Jardine's XI

B. C. G. Wilenkin b Pieris	11	– b Hurd	34
S. G. Metcalfe c sub b Pieris	15	– c Howland b Pieris	5
A. C. Walton c Howland b Pieris	0	– lbw b Wheatley	7
R. Thresher c Barnard b Pieris	0	– c Bernard b Hurd	10
R. V. C. Robins c Bernard b Wheatley	5	– lbw b Wheatley	4
C. E. Winn c Green b Wheatley	47	– c Pieris b Dexter	14
N. A. Paul lbw b Wheatley	20	– c Howland b McLachlan	31
A. R. B. Neame c and b McLachlan	21	– b Hurd	0
M. E. L. Melluish c Green b Wheatley	9	– b Wheatley	3
D. K. Fasken b Pieris	0	– c Hurd b McLachlan	4
A. J. Wait not out	15	– not out	1
B 12, l-b 2, n-b 3	17	L-b 1, w 1	2

1/16 2/16 3/16 4/35 5/50   160   1/6 2/12 3/12 4/21 5/47   115
6/72 7/122 8/136 9/137   6/94 7/100 8/104 9/104

D. R. Jardine's XI Bowling

	Overs	Mdns	Runs	Wkts	Overs	Mdns	Runs	Wkts
Thresher	16	2	46	—	6	—	18	—
Wait	14	2	39	2	11	4	24	3
Fasken	30	7	85	2				
Neame	18	7	46	—				
Paul	7	—	34	—				
Robins	12	2	68	2	20	5	43	4
Metcalfe					14.2	3	53	2

Cambridge Bowling

	Overs	Mdns	Runs	Wkts	Overs	Mdns	Runs	Wkts
Wheatley	22.2	4	56	4	10	2	25	3
Pieris.............	21	6	44	5	11	5	19	1
Dexter............	1	—	1	—	5	—	21	1
Bernard...........	5	1	7	—				
Hurd.............	8	1	17	—	5.5	4	15	3
James	1	—	3	—				
McLachlan	5	—	15	1	6	—	33	2

Umpires: J. Funnell and T. Medhurst.

GENTLEMEN v PLAYERS

Played at Lord's July 13, 14, 15, 1960

Drawn. In a remarkable finish the scores were level when Dexter, from long-on, threw down the middle stump as Allen and Moss were going for the second run which would have given the Players victory off the last ball of the match. Dexter's throw travelled fully 35 yards. Following a blank first day through rain, the Gentlemen batted disappointingly on a pitch that never became really difficult. At the same time the ball often went through at varying heights and paces.

The Players began slowly, Edrich taking almost an hour and a half over his first six runs. Then he found his best form and with Russell put the Players ahead for the loss of one wicket. On the last morning they carried their stand to 117 in eighty minutes and Statham declared 60 ahead. Cowdrey accepted the challenge to score quickly. Subba Row and Prideaux opened with 134 and a fine innings came from Cowdrey who declared and set the Players to score 168 in an hour and three-quarters, a rate of 96 an hour. The Players went boldly for the runs and looked to be on top until Sayer caused a collapse. The Gentlemen then had a good chance of success and the last over arrived with the Players needing 13 and two wickets left. They obtained 12 of them before the thrilling finish came. In a fine last day's play of five and a half hours, 437 runs were scored and fourteen wickets lost.

Gentlemen

R. Subba Row c Horton b Statham	11	– c Horton b Barrington	64
R. M. Prideaux lbw b Allen....................	22	– b Allen	70
E. R. Dexter c Barrington b Statham	0	– run out	7
*M. C. Cowdrey c Barrington b Moss	24	– c Murray b Jackson	48
M. J. K. Smith c Murray b Moss................	17	– not out	28
D. B. Carr not out...........................	25	– not out	2
R. W. Barber lbw b Allen	0		
†A. C. Smith c Jackson b Allen	5		
D. M. Sayer c Statham b Allen	2		
A. J. Corran c Murray b Jackson	0		
A. Hurd b Jackson	0		
L-b 2	2	B 1, l-b 7..............	8

1/20 2/24 3/49 4/60 5/84   108   1/134 2/145   (4 wkts dec.) 227
6/85 7/101 8/108 9/108   3/152 4/218

Players

J. H. Edrich b Sayer	69	– st A. Smith b Hurd	21
M. J. Stewart c A. Smith b Hurd	29	– c Corran b Dexter	27
W. E. Russell not out	55	– b Sayer	39
H. Horton not out	4	– b Sayer	0
K. F. Barrington (did not bat)		– b Sayer	32
D. E. V. Padgett (did not bat)		– b Sayer	0
†J. T. Murray (did not bat)		– c Corran b Barber	3
D. A. Allen (did not bat)		– not out	11
*J. B. Statham (did not bat)		– c and b Hurd	6
A. E. Moss (did not bat)		– run out	20
B 4, l-b 6, w 1	11	B 4, l-b 3, w 1	8

1/40 2/157   (2 wkts dec.) 168   1/38 2/40 3/63 4/120   (9 wkts) 167
5/120 6/123 7/129 8/135 9/167

H. L. Jackson did not bat.

Players Bowling

	Overs	Mdns	Runs	Wkts	Overs	Mdns	Runs	Wkts
Statham	14	5	22	2	11	2	18	—
Jackson	18.3	6	34	2	13	3	46	1
Moss	11	4	21	2	6	—	23	—
Allen	19	6	29	4	19	4	51	1
Barrington					11	—	81	1

Gentlemen Bowling

	Overs	Mdns	Runs	Wkts	Overs	Mdns	Runs	Wkts
Sayer	13	3	45	1	11	2	36	4
Corran	12	4	13	—	4	—	19	—
Dexter	3	—	12	—	2	—	7	1
Hurd	11	3	34	1	5	—	36	2
Barber	16	2	53	—	9	1	44	1
Carr					4	—	17	—

Umpires: W. F. Price and N. Oldfield.

ENGLAND XI v COMMONWEALTH XI

Played at Hastings, September 6, 7, 8, 1961

Commonwealth XI won by 41 runs. The completion of a season's tally of 3,000 runs by Alley and a splendid last innings by the retiring Subba Row made the game memorable. On the first day, Alley drove, pulled and glanced effectively in obtaining the 78 runs he needed for his target, and Sobers, Hitchcock and Hunte also batted entertainingly. Oakman, driving forcefully, scored an excellent century in reply, and Titmus, too, hit hard, but, in face of clever spin bowling by Sobers, their efforts just failed to give the England XI the lead. Jayasinghe showed his power of drive in Commonwealth's second innings and the England men were left to make 317 at 65 an hour. Despite attractive batting by Subba Row and Titmus, Commonwealth won with just over an hour and a half to spare. Subba Row, applauded all the way to the crease, fluently hit 60 in an hour and twenty minutes, then was clapped and cheered all the way to the dressing-room.

Commonwealth XI

C. Hunte c Loader b Lock	43	– b Lock ... 12
R. G. A. Headley c Mortimore b Loader	2	– c Titmus b Lock ... 12
P. B. Wight c Lock b Mortimore	27	– c Subba Row b Mortimore ... 20
W. E. Alley c Taylor b Loader	82	– b Titmus ... 15
G. Sobers b Loader	54	– c Norman b Mortimore ... 40
S. Jayasinghe c Subba Row b Titmus	2	– c Taylor b Loader ... 88
D. Ramsamooj c Norman b Loader	17	– c Norman b Oakman ... 26
R. E. Hitchcock b Loader	55	– c Constable b Jackson ... 54
*†B. Barnett c and b Mortimore	11	– b Lock ... 26
T. Dewdney not out	1	– b Jackson ... 3
W. Hall b Lock	3	– not out ... 3
B 6, l-b 5, n-b 1	12	B 5, l-b 2 ... 7

1/12 2/68 3/85 4/180 5/185   309   1/24 2/31 3/50 4/100 5/113   306
6/237 7/238 8/286 9/303   6/187 7/249 8/299 9/301

England XI

M. Norman b Hall	1	– st Barnett b Hitchcock ... 21
A. S. M. Oakman b Alley	116	– b Dewdney ... 11
W. J. Stewart c Wight b Alley	6	– c Hunte b Alley ... 43
*R. Subba Row b Alley	33	– b Hunte ... 60
B. Constable b Hitchcock	12	– c Hunte b Alley ... 7
F. J. Titmus st Barnett b Hitchcock	60	– b Hitchcock ... 64
†B. Taylor c Jayasinghe b Sobers	33	– b Sobers ... 6
J. B. Mortimore st Barnett b Sobers	13	– b Sobers ... 10
G. A. R. Lock not out	5	– c Headley b Sobers ... 7
P. J. Loader c Hitchcock b Sobers	1	– st Barnett b Hitchcock ... 24
H. L. Jackson b Sobers	1	– not out ... 2
B 7, l-b 10, n-b 1	18	B 11, l-b 7, w 2 ... 20

1/2 2/46 3/152 4/171 5/195   299   1/16 2/67 3/81 4/104 5/145   275
6/272 7/280 8/296 9/298   6/169 7/182 8/200 9/251

England XI Bowling

	Overs	Mdns	Runs	Wkts	Overs	Mdns	Runs	Wkts
Jackson	12	3	32	—	18.3	—	39	2
Loader	12	2	33	5	11	1	24	1
Mortimore	20	2	91	2	17	2	56	2
Titmus	20	2	60	1	12	1	55	1
Lock	16	2	81	2	25	3	119	3
Oakman					2	—	6	1

Commonwealth XI Bowling

	Overs	Mdns	Runs	Wkts	Overs	Mdns	Runs	Wkts
Hall	10	—	36	1	7	—	27	—
Dewdney	6	1	20	—	10	2	21	1
Alley	9	1	50	3	9	—	50	2
Hitchcock	18	—	106	2	12.1	2	68	3
Sobers	19	2	69	4	9	—	26	3
Hunte					16	2	63	1

Umpires: F. S. Lee and John Langridge.

Wisden Anthology 1940-1963

NORTH v SOUTH

Played at Blackpool, September 6, 7, 8, 1961

South won by two wickets. The highlight of the match was a century in fifty-two minutes in the South's first innings by Prideaux – the fastest in first-class cricket since 1937. He hit four 6s and sixteen 4s in his hundred and hit one more 6 and three more 4s before being bowled for 118 after an hour at the crease. After rain had restricted the first day's play to forty minutes, batsmen attacked the bowling and there was a glut of boundaries. On the second day, 685 runs were scored for the loss of twenty-three wickets. The South, set to score 280 in four and a quarter hours, won with two hours to spare, thanks to a hurricane innings by Evans, the former Kent and England wicket-keeper. He hit seven 6s and seven 4s in his not out 98 made in fifty-three minutes.

North

G. Pullar c Bedford b Smith	1	– c Knight b Marlar 9
R. Booth c Bedford b Walker	62	– b Shepherd 48
D. B. Close c Knight b Flavell.	15	– c Prideaux b Walker 0
K. Grieves c Knight b Walker.	39	– st Evans b Walker. 4
H. L. Johnson c Walker b Bedford	46	– st Evans b Walker. 76
J. T. Ikin c Walker b Bedford	3	– b Smith 22
R. Illingworth st Evans b Walker	30	– c Bedford b Walker. 66
C. Washbrook c Prideaux b Bedford	1	– st Evans b Smith. 49
H. J. Rhodes b Bedford.	0	– st Evans b Smith. 14
J. B. Statham c Smith b Bedford	15	– not out 15
†K. V. Andrew not out	2	– c Richardson b Shepherd 7
B 1, l-b 1	2	B 12, l-b 1, w 1 14

1/5 2/26 3/118 4/118 5/133   216   1/102 2/114 3/117 4/118 5/191   324
6/174 7/180 8/180 9/204   6/231 7/255 8/298 9/303

South

P. Richardson b Illingworth	21	– b Close 12
R. A. Gale st Andrew b Illingworth	15	– c Statham b Close. 71
D. Kenyon c sub b Illingworth	18	– b Illingworth. 31
R. M. Prideaux b Booth	118	– b Close 9
B. R. Knight run out	17	– b Illingworth. 2
P. M. Walker c sub b Booth	19	– c Statham b Close. 9
T. G. Evans c Booth b Grieves	7	– not out 98
D. J. Shepherd b Booth	1	– b Booth. 4
D. R. Smith not out	18	– c Close b Booth 15
P. I. Bedford not out	23	– not out 25
B 4	4	B 5, l-b 2. 7

1/32 2/57 3/66 4/118   (8 wkts dec.) 261   1/39 2/108 3/126 4/129   (8 wkts) 283
5/212 6/212 7/214 8/232   5/129 6/151 7/183 8/188

J. A. Flavell did not bat.

South Bowling

	Overs	Mdns	Runs	Wkts	Overs	Mdns	Runs	Wkts
Flavell.	5	1	14	1	5	—	16	—
Smith	4	—	21	1	10	1	35	3
Walker	22.4	6	75	3	21	5	102	5
Knight	1	—	6	—	6	1	26	—
Gale	1	—	4	—	10	1	48	—
Shepherd.	4	2	6	—	20	4	61	2
Bedford.	16	—	88	5	3	—	22	—

North Bowling

	Overs	Mdns	Runs	Wkts	Overs	Mdns	Runs	Wkts
Statham	4	1	15	—	5	1	11	—
Rhodes	7	—	24	—	6	—	20	—
Illingworth	13	3	52	3	11	2	34	2
Close.............	8	2	74	—	19.4	—	160	4
Booth	7	—	33	3	10	1	51	2
Grieves	8	—	59	1				

Umpires: N. Oldfield and W. E. Phillipson.

ENGLAND IN AUSTRALIA

ENGLAND v AUSTRALIA
Second Test Match

Played at Sydney, December 13, 14, 16, 17, 18, 19, 1946

Australia won by an innings and 33 runs. Compared with the first Test, England made two changes, Evans for Gibb as wicket-keeper and Smith for Voce. With Lindwall still unfit, Australia introduced Freer, the Victoria fast-medium bowler. Hardstaff and Meuleman were nominated again as twelfth men. When Hammond won the toss, most people expected a big score from England. The conditions were ideal, even if the pitch did prove responsive to spin. England's troubles commenced in the second over of the match, when Freer clean bowled Washbrook. I understand that as he went forward to play the ball Washbrook caught his glove against the inside of his pad. Miller, rather erratic, caused the ball to lift, but Freer was steady and accurate. Hutton and Edrich set out to repair the damage, and they fared well enough, even when Bradman introduced the two left-handers Tribe and Toshack. The second pair added 78 in one and three-quarter hours before the appearance of Johnson at 88 upset the stand. With his third delivery Johnson got Hutton taken on the leg-side by Tallon. That disaster occurred at twenty minutes to three, and in the next twenty-five minutes Australia virtually won the match when Tallon took two more catches off McCool which accounted for Compton and Hammond. So four England wickets were down for 99, McCool claiming two in less than three overs for five runs. Once again England batsmen had failed against Australian spinners. There followed a desperate stand by Edrich and Ikin. The Australians, completely on top, gave nothing away. Johnson bowled his off-breaks so magnificently that at the end of seventy minutes, when given a well-earned rest, his analysis read eleven overs, eight maidens, three runs, one wicket. The score crept to 148, when Edrich, having batted splendidly for three hours and twenty minutes, was leg-before. Yardley provided that vigilant wicket-keeper Tallon with his fourth catch, and Johnson completed a notable day's bowling by removing Smith and Evans. He might have claimed Ikin also before stumps were drawn at 219 for eight, for the Lancashire left-hander when 36 was dropped by Barnes at silly mid-off.

Bradman, who limped badly the first day, did not field on Saturday, Hassett taking over the leadership. Within half an hour England were all out, Ikin being caught at mid-off after a stay of three hours. Johnson, bowling for the first time in a Test, came out with six wickets for seven runs apiece. The Australian innings had been in progress only nine minutes when bad light, followed by an almost torrential downpour, held up the cricket for over three hours. On resuming, Edrich made the ball kick viciously, sometimes from a very short length, and at 24 Morris, turning his back to the ball, was bowled off his legs. Bradman preferred to rest his injured leg, and as soon as Johnson appeared Barnes repeatedly appealed against the light. At the fifth appeal the umpires gave way, and play ended for the day with the Australian total 27 for one wicket. All told, only ninety-three minutes of cricket was possible this second day.

Brilliant sunshine on Sunday transformed the pitch, which rolled out perfectly on Monday when cricket took place in glorious weather. Biggest crowd of the match, 51,459, saw Barnes bat all day. England put up a praiseworthy fight. Wright bowled splendidly, and the batsmen were never really comfortable in face of his mixture of leg-breaks and googlies. Bedser and Edrich also bowled well, but Smith failed to produce his State match form. Only three wickets fell this day, all to Edrich, as after Miller left at ten minutes to four, Bradman, without a runner, stayed with Barnes until the stumps were drawn with the total 252 for four wickets. Not before twenty minutes to six the following day did England break the Barnes-Bradman stand. Then, in successive overs, Bradman, who batted superbly despite a pronounced limp which must have been very painful, and Barnes were dismissed at the same total. Each hit 234, and they established a new fifth-wicket Test partnership record of 405. It was also a fifth-wicket world record for first-class cricket, and there was only one bigger in Test cricket, 451 by Bradman and Ponsford for the second wicket at Kennington Oval in 1934. Bradman batted for six and a half hours and hit twenty-four 4s. Barnes took ten hours forty minutes over his runs and hit seventeen 4s.

On the fifth day Australia forced the pace, and at last Wright gained reward for his excellent bowling when in his forty-fifth over he held a return catch from Tallon. In the next quarter of an hour Freer and the left-hander Tribe put on 42 before Bradman declared, Australia again having made their highest Test total in their own country. The innings lasted eleven hours forty minutes. Twenty-four minutes remained before lunch, and in that time Hutton launched a fierce attack against the bowling of Miller and Freer. Facing a closely set field. Hutton drove with such freedom into the open spaces that he made 37 out of 49 before he unluckily hit his wicket when facing the last ball before lunch. Actually Hutton struck the ball hard, but as the bat swung over his shoulders his glove slipped and he could not retain his grip. To show that their first innings form was all wrong, the principal England batsmen offered stubborn resistance. Edrich batted for the rest of the day and with Compton took part in their side's first Test century stand of the tour.

The last day began with England 247 for three wickets, and Edrich went on to complete his first century against Australia. Altogether he batted five hours ten minutes and hit seven 4s. Meanwhile England lost Hammond, who, mistiming McCool, was caught behind the bowler. Apart from Yardley, Australia encountered little more opposition and the match was all over by 3.15 p.m. Both Tallon and Evans kept wicket magnificently. Evans did not concede a bye in his first Test. The two double centuries by Bradman and Barnes, combined with the masterly slow bowling of Johnson and McCool, earned Australia their victory.

Only once before had England been defeated twice by an innings in successive matches, and that was in 1897-98 when A. E. Stoddart's team toured Australia. The match drew an aggregate attendance of 196,253 people, the receipts amounting to £26,544.

England

L. Hutton c Tallon b Johnson	39	– hit wkt b Miller	37
C. Washbrook b Freer	1	– c McCool b Johnson	41
W. J. Edrich lbw b McCool	71	– b McCool	119
D. Compton c Tallon b McCool	5	– c Bradman b Freer	54
W. R. Hammond c Tallon b McCool	1	– c Toshack b McCool	37
J. T. Ikin c Hassett b Johnson	60	– b Freer	17
N. W. D. Yardley c Tallon b Johnson	25	– b McCool	35
T. P. B. Smith lbw b Johnson	4	– c Hassett b Johnson	2
T. G. Evans b Johnson	5	– st Tallon b McCool	9
A. V. Bedser b Johnson	14	– not out	3
D. V. P. Wright not out	15	– c Tallon b McCool	0
B 4, l-b 11	15	B 8, l-b 6, w 1, n-b 2	17

1/10 2/88 3/97 4/99 5/148   255   1/49 2/118 3/220 4/280 5/309   371
6/187 7/197 8/205 9/234   6/327 7/346 8/366 9/369

Australia

S. G. Barnes c Ikin b Bedser	234	D. Tallon c and b Wright	30
A. Morris b Edrich	5	F. Freer not out	28
I. W. Johnson c Washbrook b Edrich	7	G. Tribe not out	25
A. L. Hassett c Compton b Edrich	34	L-b 7, w 1, n-b 2	10
K. R. Miller c Evans b Smith	40		
D. G. Bradman lbw b Yardley	234	1/24 2/37 3/96 4/169 (8 wkts dec.)	659
C. McCool c Hammond b Smith	12	5/564 6/564 7/595 8/617	

E. Toshack did not bat.

Australia Bowling

	Overs	Mdns	Runs	Wkts	Overs	Mdns	Runs	Wkts
Miller	9	2	24	—	11	3	37	1
Freer............	7	1	25	1	13	2	49	2
Toshack	7	2	6	—	6	1	16	—
Tribe............	20	3	70	—	12	—	40	—
Johnson	30.1	12	42	6	29	7	92	2
McCool	23	2	73	3	32.4	4	109	5
Barnes...........					3	—	11	—

England Bowling

	Overs	Mdns	Runs	Wkts
Bedser...........	46	7	153	1
Edrich...........	26	2	79	3
Wright	46	8	169	1
Smith	37	1	172	2
Ikin.............	3	—	15	—
Compton	6	—	38	—
Yardley..........	9	—	23	1

Umpires: J. D. Scott and G. Borwick.

ENGLAND v AUSTRALIA

Fourth Test Match

Played at Adelaide, January 31, February 1, 3, 4, 5, 6, 1947

Drawn. There were four extraordinary features about this Test. It was played in perpetual heat and dense humidity, with the temperature sometimes 105; Lindwall finished the England first innings by taking three wickets, all bowled, in four balls; and both Compton and Morris achieved the rare feat of hitting two separate hundreds. This was the first time for an Australian to accomplish this in his own country. The South Australian Cricket Association marked these performances by presenting a watch to each of the three players. England put up another brave struggle, but once again Hammond accomplished little with the bat and the bowling was not good enough. England introduced Hardstaff instead of Voce, and, with Barnes unfit, Australia played M. Harvey of Victoria. In both innings Hutton and Washbrook gave England a splendid send-off with a three-figure stand, but after tea on the opening day Edrich, Hutton and Hammond were dismissed in a disastrous thirty-five minutes before Compton and Hardstaff played out the final three-quarters of an hour. Again England were upset by the slower bowlers, and it was not surprising that Bradman did not take the new ball at 200. Third out, Hutton batted without mistake for four hours.

The second day provided plenty of thrills. Hardstaff remained with Compton until after lunch and then, trying to hook a bouncing delivery from Miller, he played-on, the stand having put on 118 in two hours thirty-five minutes. Ikin stayed while 61 were added, and, with Compton in complete control, Yardley saw 74 runs put on for the seventh wicket before the Middlesex player's great innings ended. Lindwall, after a rest and still using the old ball, held a sharp return catch from his first delivery. This was Compton's finest display so far during the tour; at the wicket four and three-quarter hours, he did not offer any kind of chance. His main scoring strokes were fifteen 4s and the feature of his play was powerful driving. Lindwall then took the new ball, and in his next over bowled both Bedser and Evans off-stump with successive deliveries; the next just missed the wicket and the fourth bowled Wright. So Lindwall captured the last four wickets in two overs while conceding only two runs. Twenty-five minutes remained, and Bedser served England splendidly by causing Harvey to play-on and then producing an almost unplayable ball that bowled Bradman for nought. Consequently Australia finished the day 24 for two wickets.

During the third day Australia made a complete recovery by adding 269 while losing only Morris – who hit his second Test century – and Hassett, who helped to put on 189 for the third partnership in nearly four hours. Bedser alone bowled well this day, as Wright, uncertain in his run, delivered many no-balls. Showing more freedom than in previous Tests, Morris drove delightfully and hit two 6s and twelve 4s. Altogether his innings lasted four and a half hours. Miller and Johnson carried the score to 293 for four wickets before the close.

The heat was again almost overwhelming on the fourth day, when Miller and Johnson carried their fifth-wicket stand to 150 before Johnson was leg-before. The high temperature was too much for Bedser, who had to rest for a period in the pavilion. Again Yardley bowled his leg theory splendidly and quietened the batsmen, but Miller became the seventh Australian to hit a century in this series. When Lindwall left, Australia, with two wickets remaining, were 37 behind, and at this point Bedser returned; but without further loss Australia went ahead. The innings closed when Edrich brilliantly ran out Toshack. Miller, who offered three chances after passing three figures, remained unbeaten, having batted attractively for four and a half hours. He hit one 6 and nine 4s. No sooner had Hutton and Washbrook opened England's second innings than a sharp thunderstorm accompanied by vivid flashes of lightning held up the game for twenty-three minutes. Lindwall and Miller each bounced the ball freely, but Hutton and Washbrook seldom missed a scoring opportunity. Their praiseworthy stand reached 96 at the close.

On the fifth day, off the first three deliveries by Lindwall, Hutton and Washbrook got four runs needed to complete their second three-figure opening stand of the match, having batted eighty-seven minutes; then disaster occurred. Tallon, standing well back, held a snick from Washbrook. Some people thought the ball was scooped off the ground. For a time Edrich shaped well, but Johnson bowled Hutton, and Toshack caused such a collapse that by 5.15 p.m. eight England wickets were down for 255. Compton alone of the recognised batsmen remained, and, shielding Evans from the bowling, he defied all Bradman's devices to remove him. At the close England were 274 for eight; Evans had not scored.

Evans again produced a splendid defence on the rare occasions Compton could not face the bowling, but within a quarter of an hour of the resumption, when Compton was 60 and the total 282, Tallon failed to stump Evans off Dooland. Had this chance been accepted, Australia must have won, but, instead England made such an excellent recovery that Hammond was able to declare. Evans was at the wicket ninety-five minutes before he got his first runs by placing Lindwall to leg for two at 309. With the last scoring stroke before lunch Compton hit Dooland through the covers for four, so completing his second hundred. He batted four hours forty minutes, hitting ten 4s, and his gallant stand with Evans realised 85 in two and a quarter hours. Of 98 balls received, Evans scored off only seven.

When one ball had been sent down after lunch Hammond applied the closure, setting Australia to make 314 in three and a quarter hours. Considering England's poor bowling resources and the experienced hitters at Australia's command, this was not an impossible task, but from the outset Bradman declined to accept the challenge. Up to a point Morris was enterprising, but Harvey, in his first Test, naturally was disinclined to take risks. He stayed one hundred minutes while helping Morris to make Australia's first three-figure opening stand of the series. Then Morris and Bradman calmly played out time, and Morris became the second Australian to hit two centuries in a Test against England, the first being W. Bardsley, another left-hander, at Kennington Oval in 1909.

Never before had two players each hit two separate hundreds in a Test; Compton earned the distinction of completing four hundreds in consecutive innings in first-class cricket. This drawn game gave Australia the rubber. The full attendance was 135,980 and the receipts £18,117.

England

L. Hutton lbw b McCool	94	– b Johnson	76
C. Washbrook c Tallon b Dooland	65	– c Tallon b Lindwall	39
W. J. Edrich c and b Dooland	17	– c Bradman b Toshack	46
W. R. Hammond b Toshack	18	– c Lindwall b Toshack	22
D. Compton c and b Lindwall	147	– not out	103
J. Hardstaff b Miller	67	– b Toshack	9
J. T. Ikin c Toshack b Dooland	21	– lbw b Toshack	1
N. W. D. Yardley not out	18	– c Tallon b Lindwall	18
A. V. Bedser b Lindwall	2	– c Tallon b Miller	3
T. G. Evans b Lindwall	0	– not out	10
D. V. P. Wright b Lindwall	0		
B 4, l-b 5, w 2	11	B 5, l-b 3, w 2, n-b 3	13

1/137 2/173 3/196 4/202 5/320   460   1/100 2/137 3/178   (8 wkts dec.) 340
6/381 7/455 8/460 9/460   4/188 5/207 6/215 7/250 8/255

Australia

M. Harvey b Bedser	12	– b Yardley	31
A. Morris c Evans b Bedser	122	– not out	124
D. G. Bradman b Bedser	0	– not out	56
A. R. Hassett c Hammond b Wright	78		
K. R. Miller not out	141		
I. W. Johnson lbw b Wright	52		
C. McCool c Bedser b Yardley	2		
D. Tallon b Wright	3		
R. Lindwall c Evans b Yardley	20		
B. Dooland c Bedser b Yardley	29		
E. Toshack run out	0		
B 16, l-b 6, w 2, n-b 4	28	B 2, n-b 2	4

1/18 2/18 3/207 4/222 5/372   487   1/116   (1 wkt) 215
6/389 7/396 8/423 9/486

Australia Bowling

	Overs	Mdns	Runs	Wkts	Overs	Mdns	Runs	Wkts
Lindwall	23	5	52	4	17.1	4	60	2
Miller	16	—	45	1	11	—	34	1
Toshack	30	12	59	1	36	6	76	4
McCool	29	1	91	1	19	3	41	—
Johnson	22	3	69	—	25	8	51	1
Dooland	33	1	133	3	17	2	65	—

England Bowling

	Overs	Mdns	Runs	Wkts	Overs	Mdns	Runs	Wkts
Bedser	30	6	97	3	15	1	68	—
Edrich	20	3	88	—	7	2	25	—
Wright	32.4	1	152	3	9	—	49	—
Yardley	31	7	101	3	13	—	69	1
Ikin	2	—	9	—				
Compton	3	—	12	—				

Umpires: J. D. Scott and G. Borwick.

MCC v SOUTH AUSTRALIA

Played at Adelaide, October 27, 28, 30, 31, 1950

MCC won by seven wickets. After more than three days and a half of cautious compilation of runs by both sides the game became charged with excitement. A declaration by Ridings left MCC 185 to win in an hour and three-quarters. They won with twenty minutes to spare. Washbrook and Simpson made 131 together in an hour and Evans finished the match in a whirl of spectacle by smiting five of the last six balls to the boundary. He batted seventeen minutes. Such tactics contrasted strongly with those generally adopted earlier and could be used in argument against suggestions that quick scoring was impracticable because of the slowness of the pitch. Brown's decision to give his opponents first innings in the hope that the turf had sweated and would be helpful to bowlers did not meet with success. The chief obstacle was Hamence who, on his last appearance before retiring, repeated his century feat in the corresponding match four years previously. Centuries by Hutton, in his initial innings of the tour, and Simpson redeemed an otherwise uninspired first innings by MCC. Both batted stylishly against good bowling, particularly that of Noblet, medium-fast. Evans kept wicket splendidly, and MCC's fielding showed considerable improvement, no doubt because the weather was much warmer than in Perth.

South Australia

R. McLean c Close b Bailey	2	– lbw b Bailey	19
N. Dansie c Washbrook b Warr	31	– b Warr	64
L. Duldig c Evans b Bailey	46	– not out	70
R. Hamence st Evans b Brown	114	– run out	7
G. Hole c Bailey b Wright	33	– not out	23
P. Ridings lbw b Wright	40		
B. Bowley c Hutton b Wright	29		
G. Langley not out	30		
G. Noblet st Evans b Brown	20		
R. Hiern st Evans b Brown	0		
J. Wilson c Evans b Wright	1		
W 1, n-b 3	4	B 1, w 1	2

1/2 2/70 3/97 4/153 5/238   350   1/50 2/119 3/140   (3 wkts dec.) 185
6/279 7/301 8/349 9/349

MCC

L. Hutton c Langley b Hiern	126	– c Langley b Noblet	1
C. Washbrook lbw b Hiern	9	– c McLean b Hole	63
R. T. Simpson c and b Noblet	119	– c Hiern b Wilson	69
J. G. Dewes b Noblet	10		
D. B. Close c Noblet b McLean	4		
T. E. Bailey b Hole	6		
F. R. Brown c Dansie b Wilson	16	– not out	13
T. G. Evans c Duldig b Noblet	38	– not out	33
J. J. Warr b Hiern	4		
D. V. P. Wright not out	5		
R. Berry not out	5		
L-b 7, w 2	9	B 1, l-b 5, n-b 1	7

1/16 2/186 3/216 4/247   (9 wkts dec.) 351   1/3 2/134 3/138   (3 wkts) 186
5/254 6/291 7/299 8/340 9/340

MCC Bowling

	Overs	Mdns	Runs	Wkts	Overs	Mdns	Runs	Wkts
Bailey	18	1	75	2	10	—	37	1
Warr.............	20	—	80	1	15	4	39	1
Wright	28	3	103	4	8	1	33	—
Berry............	12	3	33	—	13	1	40	—
Brown...........	15	1	55	3	10	1	34	—

South Australia Bowling

	Overs	Mdns	Runs	Wkts	Overs	Mdns	Runs	Wkts
Noblet...........	31	5	79	3	6	—	52	1
Hiern	20	2	64	3	5	—	46	—
Bowley	3	—	18	—				
Wilson	20	4	56	1	4.6	—	50	1
Hole	17	4	50	1	4	1	31	1
McLean	17	1	75	1				

MCC v VICTORIA

Played at Melbourne, November 3, 4, 6, 8, 1950

Drawn. The first clash between MCC batsmen and Iverson, a century by Compton for the second successive match, and a sustained spell of fast bowling by Bailey made noteworthy a game spoiled by cheerless weather. In the absence of Brown, resting an injured finger, Compton became the first professional to lead MCC in Australia. He signalised the distinction with an innings which ripened into quality after early difficulties. These were created by Iverson, who beat Compton with his first ball and should have had him stumped when five. Despite the cold and a soggy ball, Iverson worried most batsmen and his figures did less than justice. For the first time on the tour Bailey worked up to top speed. His control of length was better and he made full use of a pitch and atmosphere offering some assistance to one of his type. When half the Victoria side were out for 89, Bailey had taken all five wickets for 27, but the supporting attack could not press home the advantage. So much did the game swing that Howard and Ring added 120 in eighty minutes for the seventh wicket. By arrangement, November 7, Melbourne Cup day, was left free. On the last day rain caused an early closure.

MCC

L. Hutton lbw b Johnson.....................	32	– c Carr b Johnston.............	13
C. Washbrook c and b Johnson	40	– c Loxton b Johnson.........	32
D. S. Sheppard c McDonald b Harvey............	28	– st McDonald b Ring...........	19
D. C. S. Compton c Howard b Johnston	107	– not out	0
J. G. Dewes c McDonald b Kerr................	1	– lbw b Johnston	5
D. B. Close c Johnson b Ring.................	30	– not out	7
A. J. McIntyre b Iverson......................	6		
T. E. Bailey not out.........................	28		
J. J. Warr c Kerr b Iverson...................	23		
R. Berry c Harvey b Iverson..................	2		
W. E. Hollies not out........................	1		
L-b 7, n-b 1........................	8	L-b 2, w 1..............	3

1/61 2/89 3/146 4/153   (9 wkts dec.) 306   1/25 2/61 3/66 4/73   (4 wkts) 79
5/207 6/230 7/257 8/285 9/298

Victoria

K. Meuleman b Bailey	6	I. McDonald c Bailey b Hollies	4
R. Howard lbw b Close	139	W. A. Johnston st McIntyre b Compton	30
R. N. Harvey c Sheppard b Bailey	7	J. Iverson not out	1
A. L. Hassett b Bailey	19		
S. J. Loxton c Hutton b Bailey	4	B 4, l-b 3	7
D. Kerr c Close b Bailey	3		
I. W. Johnson run out	36	1/17 2/31 3/71 4/81 5/89	331
D. Ring c Berry b Close	75	6/161 7/281 8/287 9/325	

Victoria Bowling

	Overs	Mdns	Runs	Wkts	Overs	Mdns	Runs	Wkts
Johnston	16	2	59	1	11	1	30	2
Kerr	9	1	27	1	6	—	25	—
Johnson	27	4	77	2	6.3	1	20	1
Iverson	31	5	71	3				
Ring	14	1	49	1	2	1	1	1
Loxton	3	—	11	—				
Harvey	1	—	4	1				

MCC Bowling

	Overs	Mdns	Runs	Wkts
Warr	22	2	77	—
Bailey	22	5	54	5
Hollies	22	1	95	1
Compton	2.2	—	16	1
Close	15	2	53	2
Berry	5	—	29	—

MCC v NEW SOUTH WALES

Played at Sydney, November 10, 11, 13, 14, 1950

Drawn. The three senior batsmen, Hutton, Washbrook and Compton, saved MCC from possible rout on turf so good for batting that 1,131 runs were scored for seventeen wickets. The first two days belonged to Miller and Morris, who repeated their batting triumphs of earlier matches. Their second successive double-century stand for New South Wales was five short of the wicket record for the State against an MCC touring side. Miller, whose concentration and discretion revealed him as more mature than when in England in 1948, batted five hours and hit three 6s and fifteen 4s. He raised his season's aggregate to 616 in four innings, twice not out. A smart catch at forward short-leg from the last ball of the day ended MCC's opening stand of 92, and thereafter only Hutton and Compton faced the attack with confidence. Eight batsmen made 73 runs between them. Lindwall showed flashes of top speed, notably when bowling Hutton and Sheppard in quick succession, and Johnston flighted and spun right-arm leg-breaks with skilful variation. With Wright suffering from fibrositis and unable to bowl, MCC's attack was again collared, and New South Wales raised their match harvest to 649 for five wickets before Morris declared, leaving MCC 311 to get to win at two a minute. By extreme watchfulness and sound stroke-play, Burke carried his match total to 140 without being dismissed. MCC accepted the challenge and 143 runs came in ninety minutes before rain and bad light intervened.

New South Wales

J. Moroney c McIntyre b Bedser	23	– c Hollies b Compton	53
A. R. Morris c Hutton b Bailey	168		
K. R. Miller b Hollies	214		
J. Burke not out	80	– not out	60
R. James not out	20	– b Hollies	0
R. Benaud (did not bat)		– not out	20
B 1, l-b 1, n-b 2	4	B 1, n-b 6	7

1/52 2/317 3/455   (3 wkts dec.) 509   1/95 2/97   (2 wkts dec.) 140

R. R. Lindwall, F. Johnston, S. G. Sismey, A. Davidson and A. Walker did not bat.

MCC

L. Hutton b Lindwall	112	– c James b Lindwall	18
C. Washbrook c Morris b Johnston	50	– not out	53
R. T. Simpson c and b Johnston	7	– c Burke b Johnston	32
D. C. S. Compton c Sismey b Johnston	92	– not out	34
D. S. Sheppard b Lindwall	1		
D. B. Close st Sismey b Johnston	18		
A. J. McIntyre not out	32		
T. E. Bailey b Benaud	9		
A. V. Bedser lbw b Johnston	2		
D. V. P. Wright b Johnston	0		
W. E. Hollies run out	4		
B 4, l-b 7, n-b 1	12	B 2, l-b 3, n-b 1	6

1/92 2/112 3/218 4/224 5/276   339   1/34 2/87   (2 wkts) 143
6/301 7/324 8/327 9/327

MCC Bowling

	Overs	Mdns	Runs	Wkts	Overs	Mdns	Runs	Wkts
Bailey	14	2	54	1	7	2	16	—
Bedser	24	2	127	1	8	2	25	—
Wright	16	—	93	—				
Hollies	25	—	138	1	14	—	61	1
Close	12	—	68	—				
Compton	4	—	25	—	7	—	31	1

New South Wales Bowling

	Overs	Mdns	Runs	Wkts	Overs	Mdns	Runs	Wkts
Lindwall	17	5	57	2	5	—	46	1
Walker	17	2	30	—	8	—	46	—
Davidson	16	2	63	—	2	—	15	—
Johnston	25	—	100	6	5	—	30	1
Benaud	16.5	2	75	1				
Burke	1	—	2	—				

MCC v NEW SOUTH WALES COUNTRY TEAM

Played at Newcastle, November 17, 18, 1950

Drawn. Apart from Dewes, who made half the total, the young MCC batsmen struck bottom form together in the team's sorriest performance of the tour. Hollies, Berry and Brown spun out the local side, but MCC shaped poorly against medium-paced bowling. Their main troubles were caused by one John Bull. The pill tasted no less bitter because of that. One bright feature was the return to catching form of Parkhouse, who held two very hard chances. No play was possible on the first day.

New South Wales Country Team

R. Beattie c Sheppard b Hollies 69
K. Wood c Brown b Hollies 14
K. Hill c Close b Hollies 0
M. Hinman c Parkhouse b Hollies 0
R. McDonald c and b Brown 9
J. Mannix c Warr b Berry 18
R. Harvey st Evans b Berry 15
O. Lambert b Berry. 0

John Bull c Berry b Hollies 1
W. Pickles c Parkhouse b Berry 17
R. Roxby not out 20

B 4, l-b 2 6

1/49 2/49 3/49 4/90 5/96   169
6/124 7/124 8/125 9/142

MCC

R. T. Simpson c Mannix b Bull 23
D. S. Sheppard c and b Bull 4
W. G. A. Parkhouse lbw b Bull 0
J. G. Dewes c Roxby b Bull 71
D. B. Close lbw b Hinman 2
F. R. Brown b Roxby 17
T. G. Evans c Hinman b Bull 4
A. V. Bedser b Pickles. 1

J. J. Warr b Pickles 5
R. Berry not out 2
W. E. Hollies c Beattie b Bull 8

B 5. 5

1/23 2/24 3/33 4/37 5/81   142
6/92 7/96 8/122 9/132

MCC Bowling

	Overs	Mdns	Runs	Wkts
Warr.	3	—	17	—
Bedser.	6	—	23	—
Hollies	16	3	39	5
Berry.	9.5	1	45	4
Brown.	4	1	25	1
Close.	3	1	14	—

New South Wales Country Team Bowling

	Overs	Mdns	Runs	Wkts
Pickles	13	2	38	2
Bull.	13.2	5	24	6
Hinman.	8	2	30	1
Hill	7	4	16	—
Roxby.	8	1	29	1

NOTES BY THE EDITOR, 1951

ONE-DAY MATCH CONTROVERSY

There are mixed opinions as to how far the rules governing one-day matches apply to fixtures of two days or more which are reduced to one day owing to bad weather. In November many people were surprised that the MCC team's two-day match at Newcastle, New South Wales, was officially announced as a draw when, following a blank first day, New South Wales Country Districts XI led on the first innings by 169 runs to 142. For years many of us have regarded such rain-spoiled games as coming entirely under the one-day law, but a careful inspection of the Laws, as they are worded now, shows that only the parts covering the declaration and the follow-on are applicable in such circumstances.

In recent years in the English County Championship when a three-day match reduced to one day has not been played out the county leading on the first innings has received eight points and been credited with a win. There were two such instances last summer: Middlesex v Hampshire at Lord's and Sussex v Gloucestershire at Bristol, the visitors in each case being announced as victors and the results given in the Championship table as wins and not draws. How confused is the interpretation was shown following the two-day

Minor Counties match last June at Skewen, where after a blank day Glamorgan led Gloucestershire on the first innings. Glamorgan modestly gave the result as a draw, whereas Gloucestershire, the losers, generously conceded a victory to Glamorgan. In the Minor Counties table, which is compiled by their keen and efficient secretary, Mr Frank Crompton, the result was given as a win for Glamorgan. The Minor Counties award ten points for an outright win and ten points to the side which leads on the first innings in a one-day match. Mr Crompton told me that the Minor Counties have always regarded such cases as a win or a loss, not as a draw, and that they will continue to do so.

When the First-class Counties decided to award special points for a one-day match they did so for the express purpose of providing attraction to games ruined by rain on the first two days. The intention of awarding eight points instead of the usual four was to avoid farcical declaration and to cut down the number of drawn games. The public like to see a definite result, and if such games are going to be termed draws, even if one team takes eight points as in the case of the First-class Counties and ten points in the Minor Counties, it may be detrimental to public interest. In my opinion the MCC should consult all cricket bodies, including those overseas, and then give a definite ruling as to the procedure to be adopted.

MCC v QUEENSLAND

Played at Brisbane, November 24, 25, 27, 28, 1950

Drawn. In taking eight wickets for 216 on the first day, MCC showed all-round improvement, but if Carrigan, the century-maker, had been caught when he offered a simple chance to short-leg at 13, the whole course of the subsequent cricket might have been different. Carrigan scored most of his runs by the cut, a stroke he was always aiming to employ. Rain prevented play on the second day, and only a day and half remained when MCC began batting. With such little prospect of winning, MCC were not inclined to hurry. Against defensive bowling, they concentrated chiefly on obtaining practice for the approaching Test, and Washbrook spent five hours over 81. Dewes, whose innings was interrupted through an attack of cramp, played just as cautiously and shared with him in a stand of 108. In all, 1,036 balls were bowled by Queensland. MCC were shown a score-book containing a remarkable feat by the opposing opening batsman, McKay. Playing for Virginia School against Sherwood School in the Semi-Final of the Queensland C.A. Shield on November 10, 1939, McKay took all ten wickets for 53 and scored 367 not out.

Queensland

K. Archer lbw b Bedser	63		
K. McKay c Brown b Bedser	0		
C. Harvey lbw b Warr.	3		
A. Carrigan b Hollies	100		
C. L. McCool c Hutton b Warr.	18		
K. Jack lbw b Hollies	0		
E. Toovey not out	58	– not out	4
D. Tallon c Washbrook b Bedser	5		
V. Raymer c Washbrook b Warr	6	– b Warr	0
L. Chapman run out	38	– not out	1
L. Johnson c Brown b Close	2		
B 9, l-b 3	12		

1/4 2/23 3/143 4/188 5/188   305   1/0   (1 wkt)   5
6/188 7/200 8/216 9/297

MCC

L. Hutton b Johnson 2	A. V. Bedser b Johnson 0
C. Washbrook b Johnson 81	J. J. Warr b McCool 10
R. T. Simpson c Raymer b Johnson 13	W. E. Hollies not out 3
D. C. S. Compton c Archer b McCool 28	
J. G. Dewes c Johnson b Raymer 117	B 5, l-b 2, n-b 1 8
D. B. Close b Johnson 21	
F. R. Brown c Archer b Johnson 0	1/3 2/25 3/72 4/180 5/182 291
T. G. Evans b Raymer 8	6/200 7/215 8/215 9/252

MCC Bowling

	Overs	Mdns	Runs	Wkts	Overs	Mdns	Runs	Wkts
Warr	23	3	70	3	2	2	—	1
Bedser	23	6	40	3	1	—	5	—
Hollies	18	3	73	2				
Brown	10	1	63	—				
Close	7	—	30	1				
Compton	5	1	17	—				

Queensland Bowling

	Overs	Mdns	Runs	Wkts
Johnson	35	10	66	6
Chapman	9	—	17	—
Raymer	35.5	17	51	2
McCool	41	7	110	2
Archer	11	3	25	—
McKay	2	—	14	—

ENGLAND v AUSTRALIA

First Test Match

Played at Brisbane, December 1, 2, 4, 5, 1950

Australia won by 70 runs. How much the events of the Brisbane Test influenced the remainder of the series could be only a matter of conjecture, but certainly England were entitled to feel that their misfortune here added to their subsequent tasks. Most Australians agreed with the general view that the intervention of a typical Brisbane storm brought in its train defeat for the side which batted better, bowled better and fielded better than the winners. The realisation that on the play they were superior made defeat particularly galling for a team conceded so little chance before the cricket began.

Virtually the game was won and lost at the toss of the coin. When Brown called incorrectly to Hassett, he allowed Australia first use of a good pitch more suited to batting, even though its slow pace did not encourage forcing strokes. Yet the first day belonged to England. They surprised everybody by dismissing Australia for such a meagre total in the conditions.

Compensation for losing the toss came swiftly. From the fourth ball of the day Hutton, at backward short-leg, smartly held Moroney. That was just the tonic needed. For the rest of the innings England's fielding touched the highest class and Evans, behind the wicket, was inspired. No better catches were seen in the Tests than those by which he dismissed Harvey and Loxton. When Loxton cut Brown, the ball struck Evans hard on the glove and rebounded forward. His reaction instantaneous, Evans dived headlong and grasped the catch with his left hand inches from the turf as his body struck the ground with force. Bedser and Bailey also rose to the occasion nobly. Bedser rarely bowled a ball which did not compel the batsman's closest vigilance and he cut either way with marked nip and variation. The good-length ball which beat Hassett pitched on the middle and leg stumps and hit the top of the off. Bailey attacked each batsman to a pre-arranged plan and his life with the new ball enabled England to follow up their previous successes. Wright's figures told anything but the worth of his bowling. Until the last moment Wright had received injections to relieve fibrositis and pulled muscle trouble which made his fitness doubtful, but he produced many fine balls, several of which beat the bat and missed the wicket only because of their high bounce. Curiously his one wicket came from a long hop which caught Miller in two minds. Brown pitched his leg-breaks on a consistently accurate length.

Well as England bowled and fielded, Australia's batting was not convincing. Apart from Harvey, few of the batsmen gave the impression of being at ease. Harvey put his usual vigour into a thrilling sequence of his most spectacular left-handed strokes before being caught at the wicket on the leg side when glancing Bedser off the middle of the bat. His 74, made out of 118, contained ten sparkling 4s. Lindwall was solid and watchful, but impatience cost the wickets of at least three early batsmen.

To the end of the Australian innings the cricket was exciting enough. It became more so. A successful appeal against the light by England's new opening pair, Washbrook and Simpson – Brown decided to put Hutton at five to give strength to the middle – was the final act on that dramatic Friday.

Inside a few hours the storm broke, and cricket could not be resumed until half an hour before lunch on Monday. For thirty minutes Washbrook and Simpson provided skill and courage so far unsurpassed in the match. In that time they scored 28 runs together on a pitch just as treacherous as it played through the remainder of the day, in which twenty wickets went down for 102.

True to tradition, the pitch was the game's villain. Medium-paced bowling of good length presented a wellnigh insoluble problem. Sometimes the ball reared head high, at other times it kept horribly low. Both captains placed nearly all their fieldsmen in a circle a few yards from the bat, and twelve of the wickets resulted from catches close to the wicket.

When the back of England's innings had been broken, Brown declared. His one hope was to force Australia in again as soon as possible. Moroney, who experienced the disaster of a "pair" on his Test début, Morris and Loxton were out before a run was scored, and wickets continued to go down so quickly that Hassett retaliated by a declaration which gave England an hour and ten minutes to bat before the close. They required 193 to win. If only two or three men had been lost then their prospects might have been bright. It was not to be.

A lightning yorker by Lindwall wrecked Simpson's wicket with the first ball of the innings. There followed half an hour of sound defence by Washbrook and Dewes. Each left within a few minutes of the other, but England's most crushing blow that evening occurred in the last ten minutes when three wickets were lost. Anxiety caused at least two of these dismissals, McIntyre, for example, being run out trying a fourth run when preservation of wickets was of paramount importance. Wicket-keeper Tallon ran ten to fifteen yards before catching a bad throw-in and, with his gloved hand, hurling down the wicket.

So England entered the last day wanting 163 to win with only four wickets left. The task was hard but not hopeless, because evidence was provided at once that, although still difficult, the pitch had lost some venom. Evans helped Hutton add sixteen before he and Compton pushed successive balls from Johnston into the hands of forward short-leg. Australia were within sight of victory but it was not theirs until Hutton had given yet another exhibition of his wonderful batsmanship on tricky turf. Aided first by Brown and then by Wright, Hutton thrashed the fast bowlers majestically and played the turning or lifting ball with the ease of a master craftsman. When assisted by Wright in a last-wicket stand of 45, Hutton even looked capable of carrying England through, but Wright succumbed to temptation to hook the last ball before lunch. Hutton's was an innings to remember.

Australia

J. Moroney c Hutton b Bailey	0	– lbw b Bailey	0
A. R. Morris lbw b Bedser	25	– c Bailey b Bedser	0
R. N. Harvey c Evans b Bedser	74	– c Simpson b Bedser	12
K. R. Miller c McIntyre b Wright	15	– c Simpson b Bailey	8
A. L. Hassett b Bedser	8	– lbw b Bailey	3
S. J. Loxton c Evans b Brown	24	– c Bailey b Bedser	0
R. R. Lindwall c Bedser b Bailey	41	– not out	0
D. Tallon c Simpson b Brown	5		
I. W. Johnson c Simpson b Bailey	23	– lbw b Bailey	8
W. A. Johnston c Hutton b Bedser	1		
J. Iverson not out	1		
B 5, l-b 3, n-b 3	11	N-b 1	1

1/0 2/69 3/116 4/118 5/129   **228**   1/0 2/0 3/0 4/12   (7 wkts dec.) **32**
6/156 7/172 8/219 9/226   5/19 6/31 7/32

England

R. T. Simpson b Johnston	12	– b Lindwall	0
C. Washbrook c Hassett b Johnston	19	– c Loxton b Lindwall	6
T. G. Evans c Iverson b Johnston	16	– c Loxton b Johnston	5
D. C. S. Compton c Lindwall b Johnston	3	– c Loxton b Johnston	0
J. G. Dewes c Loxton b Miller	1	– b Miller	9
L. Hutton not out	8	– not out	62
A. J. McIntyre b Johnston	1	– run out	7
F. R. Brown c Tallon b Miller	4	– c Loxton b Iverson	17
T. E. Bailey not out	1	– c Johnston b Iverson	7
A. V. Bedser (did not bat)		– c Harvey b Iverson	0
D. V. P. Wright (did not bat)		– c Lindwall b Iverson	2
B 2, n-b 1	3	B 6, n-b 1	7

1/28 2/49 3/52 4/52   (7 wkts dec.) **68**   1/0 2/16 3/22 4/23 5/23   **122**
5/56 6/57 7/67   6/30 7/46 8/46 9/77

England Bowling

	Overs	Mdns	Runs	Wkts	Overs	Mdns	Runs	Wkts
Bailey	12	4	28	3	7	2	22	4
Bedser	16.5	4	45	4	6.5	2	9	3
Wright	16	—	81	1				
Brown	11	—	63	2				

Australia Bowling

	Overs	Mdns	Runs	Wkts	Overs	Mdns	Runs	Wkts
Lindwall	1	—	1	—	7	3	21	2
Johnston	11.2	1	35	5	11	2	30	2
Miller	10	1	29	2	7	3	21	1
Iverson					13	3	43	4

Umpires: H. Elphinston and A. Barlow.

NOTES BY THE EDITOR, 1951

BAD LIGHT PROBLEM

Of special importance because of its influence on the extraordinary Test match at Brisbane was the gruesome light in which England lost three wickets while eight runs were scored in ten minutes when almost everyone present except the umpires thought play should have ceased. The adverse decision in reply to batsmen's appeals meant a big help to

Australia on that first Monday in December during which, all told, twenty wickets fell for 130 runs. Drying turf, which made the appellation "sticky dog" almost complimentary, meant conditions scarcely possible for batting. England scored 52 for three wickets, then lost four more men for 16 before F. R. Brown declared; seven Australian wickets fell for 32, then Lindsay Hassett "followed suit," setting England to get 193. The sad finish of the day left Hutton practically our one hope, and his glorious effort (possible only for this batsman, whom I have described as unequalled on all kinds of pitches) necessitated this reference to the actual play, though my object is to call attention to a *light meter* about the size of a pocket compass which could be used by umpires to a set scale determining when light became unfit for cricket. If any uncertainty exists surely the umpires should stop play. "Give the batsman the benefit of the doubt" has been a standing instruction to the umpire as long as I can remember.

AUSTRALIA THROW DOWN THE GAUNTLET [1953]

By Neville Cardus

For the Coronation Year of 1953 we can think only by effort of the English cricketers who in 1862 sailed to Australia in a paddle-steamer virtually as missionaries to a foreign land, though they didn't look altogether missionary. They were a bewhiskered company, and after they had departed from these shores without notice and unobserved no more was heard of them until they arrived at Melbourne somewhere near Christmas.

Only twelve of them were taken: H. H. Stephenson (capt., Surrey), W. Caffyn (Surrey), G. Griffith (Surrey), W. Mortlock (Surrey), W. Mudie (Surrey), T. Sewell (Surrey), C. Lawrence (Kent), G. Bennett (Kent), T. Hearne (Middlesex), G. Wells (Middlesex), R. Iddison (Yorkshire) and E. Stephenson (Yorkshire). Twelve and no more; nobody, it seems, entertained the idea or risk of "casualties" accruing from fibrositis, wrenched muscles and what-not. Hardy pioneers. We have lived to see Test cricket go round the globe from Occident to Orient. But, none the less, it is still the privilege, prerogative and honour of Australia to throw down before us, in this country, the glove of the challenger and to say to all other comers and aspirants in the Test match tournament: "Hands off: this is mine own enemy!"

It was at Melbourne in March 1877 that the first recorded Test match was played between England and Australia; Australia batted first, and Charles Bannerman (born in Kent) opened the innings and scored the first of all Test match centuries, 165, then received a blow on the hand and retired hurt. *Absit Omen!* The England bowlers on this inaugural occasion were Alfred Shaw, Ulyett, Hill, Southerton, Armitage, Lillywhite and Tom Emmett; but it has never been reported what Emmett said about it all.

This score by Bannerman of 165 remained unbeaten in a Test match until 1884, when at Kennington Oval W. L. Murdoch amassed 211 out of an Australian grand total of 551. Already correspondence was breaking out in the newspapers protesting against the "over preparation of wickets, and the passing of the game in general to the dogs". Ten years were to elapse before Murdoch's 211 was approached in a Test match by another Australian, S. E. Gregory, who reached 201 at Sydney in one of the most astonishing games of them all.

Australia batted first and lost three wickets for 21 to Tom Richardson, who, on this tour when A. E. Stoddart was the captain, rose to unprecedented and never since surpassed heights of endurance and grandeur of speed and action. Iredale and Giffen held Richardson at bay in a menacing hour; and the spearhead of Richardson's attack was supported by Lockwood, Peel, Briggs and Brockwell. Sadly and curiously, Lockwood was a failure in Australia, and while Australia were winning through from 21 for three to 586 all out he bowled only three overs. The Australian aggregate was the highest so far to stagger human eyesight and power of computation in Test cricket.

England could naturally find comfort only in resignation. Test matches in those days were played to a finish in Australia; there was no escape from defeat for one side or the other; every ball, from the first to the last, was a nail in somebody's coffin. England lost seven for 211 in the first innings; then Johnny Briggs flashed his bat and L. H. Gay, wicket-keeper, obtained 33, so that the total amounted to 325, 261 in arrears.

Now we come to the main clue to this wonderful struggle. In 1894 the follow-on was not optional; the side with the legal, or rather illegal, deficit was obliged to bat again, the conquering fielding side had no choice but to go into the tropical Australian sun once more. So it happened now. The Australians, dead-tired from labours extending from Saturday afternoon to the following Wednesday, could scarcely be blamed if England's second innings reached 437 and left them with 177 to make for victory.

Still there was no cause for Australian worry. The wicket remained a batsman's heaven. At the end of the fifth day Australia were 113 for two; only 64 needed, a mere formality for the next morning's performing. But during the night a terrific thunderstorm flooded

Sydney. For reasons peculiar and amusing, it was not heard by Bobby Peel and Johnny Briggs. The next day dawned hot and glorious.

As Briggs and Peel journeyed to the ground, under a blue sky, the storm had apparently left not a wrack behind. But according to professional habit Johnny and Bobby, still clad in their serge and watch-chains, went into the "middle" to inspect the wicket. Bobby looked at the turf hard, stooped down knees bent and pressed it with a finger, then got up and from behind his hand whispered to Briggs, "Hey, Johnny, somebody's bin watterin wicket in neight. We'll have 'em out in a jiffy!" Australia collapsed for 166 and England won, in the face of Australia's first innings record score of 586, by ten runs. All the world wondered. It was a world capable of feeling wonder, a world unstaled by too much achievement, by too much abnormal skill cultivated by neglect of imagination and relish of risk.

Stoddart's invasion of Australia in 1894-95 belongs to the Homeric poetry of cricket. The struggle was gigantic, fought in scourging heat. After the miracle of the ten runs victory at Sydney, Giffen won the toss in the second game of the rubber after Christmas at Melbourne. On a "sticky" pitch England were shot out for 75. Nowadays a captain might act with more canniness than Giffen on this occasion; the wicket had not lost venom when the Australians themselves batted, and they could score only 123. On a good pitch England retaliated to the tune of 475, Stoddart 173 in five and a half hours, a stern act of self-discipline – for Stoddart! Australia, one down in the rubber already – and if they lost this game England would be two up and three to play – went determinedly after 428 runs necessary for her triumph.

At one period their score stood at 190 for one. Brockwell, of Surrey, a pretty harmless bowler in Australia, was visited by plenary inspiration at the pinch, broke the back of the Australian batting, and England won by 94. In England's second innings of 475 George Giffen bowled 78 overs and two balls for 155 runs and six wickets. In this match Richardson and Peel each bowled 60 overs in Australia's second innings. In the previously played Test at Sydney, Giffen had bowled 75 overs in an innings.

The climax of this rubber of 1894-95 gathered a momentum almost insupportable by lovers of the game scattered far and wide, with no radio messages to tell the news minute by minute. Australia won the third and fourth games. Two all. So on March 1 people journeyed thousands of miles to Melbourne and on a flawless turf saw Australia, first at the wicket, score 414, with no individual century but five contributions of 40 and over. In spite of one of A. C. MacLaren's finest innings, an imperial 120 until he hit his own stumps, England fell just 29 behind Australia's 414. The tug-of-war was torment to contemplate as night interrupted the action on its inevitable way to somebody's funeral. Magnificent bowling by Tom Richardson turned the scale. He took six for 104, and England would win the rubber if, in a fourth innings, 297 could be got. The beginning of the task was dreadful: Brockwell and Stoddart succumbed for 28. "The position was desperate," narrates *Wisden*, "but at this point Albert Ward and J. T. Brown made the stand which, if they never do anything more, will suffice to keep their names famous in the history of English and Australian cricket. By wonderful batting – Ward's patient defence being scarcely less remarkable than Brown's brilliant hitting – they put on 210 together, their partnership practically ensuring the success of their side." England won the rubber by six wickets; and in the depths of a London winter the *Pall Mall Gazette* performed a national service "in arranging every afternoon for cable messages, keeping people in closer touch with cricket in Australia than they had ever been before. . . ."

Mr. Roy Webber, in his monumental and valuable book on Test Cricket, expresses the opinion that Tests in Australia before 1903-04 cannot "by any stretch of imagination" be compared to those played since. Not by "any" stretch? The players in Stoddart's titanic rubber included, besides himself, MacLaren, Ward, Brown, Peel, Lockwood, F. G. J. Ford, Briggs, Richardson, G. H. S. Trott, George Giffen, Iredale, Gregory, Joe Darling, Albert Trott, Turner. Where one or two only of these names gather together in memory or history it is a Test match – even as it was only the truth spoken by Sarah Bernhardt when, taken to task for appearing in Wanamaker's store in New York, she said, "Wherever *I* act is a *theatre*".

We cannot measure one against another the cricketers of different periods; each master was great in the conditions of his day and according to his solution of the problems then presented to him. It is doubtful if a finer innings has ever been played in any Test match than Arthur Shrewsbury's 164 at Lord's against Australia in July 1886; or a more magical one than Ranjitsinhji's 154 not out when at Old Trafford in 1896 he flicked the fast bowling of Ernest Jones from the lobe of his left ear; or a more stupendous innings than Jessop's 104 at The Oval in 1902; or a more brilliant and skilful innings than J. T. Tyldesley's 62 on a sticky Melbourne pitch in 1904, made out of England's 103 all out; or a more consummately governed innings than any Test century of Jack Hobbs; or a calmer and more confident one than Sutcliffe's 161 at The Oval in 1926 begun on a bad wicket and ended by Mailey in the day's last over; or a more audacious one than Macartney's century before lunch at Leeds in 1926; or a more ruthlessly directed and inevitable innings than Bradman's triple hundred in one and the same day at Leeds in 1930; or a more far-seeing innings than Hutton's 364 at The Oval in 1938; or a nobler one than Hammond's 240 at Lord's the same season, when the whole ground, members and crowd, rose to him as he walked at the end of it up the pavilion steps; or a more heroic innings than Compton's disciplined fight in the dark against the Australians at Nottingham in 1948; or a more decisively challenging innings than Trumper's century before lunch at Old Trafford in 1902; or an innings more thrillingly and handsomely shot through and through with the romantic colours of lost causes than McCabe's 232 at Trent Bridge in 1938.

So we could continue, with no compulsion to make arbitrary comparisons. The glory of the game is that its genius, whenever it changes – as change it must if it is to survive and evolve – remains the same creative thing. Spofforth or Barnes or O'Reilly or Tate or Bedser; Grace or Hobbs; Bradman or Fry; Tyldesley or Compton; Hayward or Hammond; Albert Ward or Hutton; Lockwood or Larwood; Richardson or E. A. McDonald; Peel or Briggs; Rhodes or Verity; Oldfield or Evans; J. M. Gregory or Keith Miller; they are not competitors for renown or for our admiration. They are planets in conjunction, equal in distinction and immortality. *Amurath* unto *Amurath*. Eternal sunshine falls on them all.

Who of English batsmen can boast the highest average in Test matches against Australia? Not Hobbs, not Sutcliffe, and not Hutton. None other than "Eddie" Paynter, who in eleven innings, four times not out, scored 591 with the figures 84.42. Only Bradman is statistically his peer, with 5,028 runs, average 89.78. Prodigious! In both cases! The best bowler, English or Australian, is George Lohmann, 77 wickets at 13.01 each, followed by C. T. B. Turner, 101 wickets at 16.53 each. One of the most remarkable performances by a bowler in the same rubber is seldom remembered to-day or commented upon; I refer to J. N. Crawford's 30 wickets, average 24.73, in the Australian summer of 1907-08. Crawford was then 21 years old, and against batsmanship seldom equalled even in Australia for skill and experience and in the teeth of heavy totals he dismissed Trumper (three times), M. A. Noble (three times), Clem Hill (twice), Warwick Armstrong (five times), S. E. Gregory (twice), and Macartney (twice).

We are usually inclined to discuss, praise and remember Macartney as one of the three or four most brilliant stroke players of all time, just as we dwell on the lovely style of Woolley's batting. We forget that each at one point of his career was good enough to have been chosen to play Test cricket purely and simply as a left-arm slow spinner. At Leeds in 1909 Macartney took eleven of England's wickets in the match for 85 runs. In 1912, at The Oval, Woolley overthrew ten Australians, in two innings, for 49. The bowling of S. F. Barnes before lunch at Melbourne is, of course, historical and comprehensible; for Barnes was capable of anything. But it would be difficult to demonstrate that in all the matches played between England and Australia anybody has excelled, for endurance, skill and power, faith, service, greatness of heart and beauty of physical motion and poise, the bowling here and at the other end of the earth of Tom Richardson:

	O.	M.	R.	W.
Sydney, December 1894..............	53.5	13	181	5
Melbourne, January 1895.............	26	6	57	5
	60	10	100	2
Adelaide, January 1895	21	4	75	5
	31.2	8	89	3
Melbourne, March 1895..............	42	7	138	3
	45.2	7	104	6
Lord's, June 1896...................	11.3	3	39	6
	47	15	134	5
Old Trafford, July 1896	68	23	168	7
	42.3	16	76	6

One could go on indefinitely recalling the great matches and the great players of England and Australia over the last seventy-five years. The subject is worthy of a whole *Wisden* in itself.

MCC v NEW SOUTH WALES

Played at Sydney, November 12, 13, 15, 16, 1954

Drawn. To Cowdrey fell the distinction of hitting two centuries in the same match before he had even hit one in the County Championship. Watson, of NSW, also accomplished an unusual performance, for in only his second first-class innings he hit his maiden century in any type of cricket. Miller, winning the toss, requested MCC to bat and Crawford, a tall young fast bowler, began so well that four men left for 38 before Cowdrey and Hutton, by excellent batting, put on 163. Throughout the Australians fielded magnificently, Watson and Simpson making some grand slip catches. With Watson and Miller adding 161 together, New South Wales came within 40 of the MCC's 252 before their third wicket fell. Watson, sixth out, stayed six and a quarter hours, hitting eighteen 4s. On MCC batting again Cowdrey opened for the first time in his life, being accompanied by Wilson, Hutton going in sixth. Finally, New South Wales faced an impossible task, needing 198 in seventy-five minutes. They threw away their chance of victory when on Saturday with forty-five minutes left, De Courcy suggested to Hutton that the light was too bad to continue. It was not in Hutton's interest that his tired bowlers should be punished and he agreed to the game being stopped. After a delay of twenty-four minutes the cricket continued but soon the umpires upheld an appeal against the light.

MCC

L. Hutton c Davidson b Treanor	102	– c Simpson b Treanor 87
W. J. Edrich c Watson b Crawford	7	– c Burke b Davidson 37
R. T. Simpson c Simpson b Crawford	0	– b Crawford 21
P. B. H. May c Lambert b Treanor	1	– c de Courcy b Treanor 16
J. V. Wilson c Simpson b Miller	9	– b Crawford 0
M. C. Cowdrey c and b Davidson	110	– lbw b Crawford 103
T. G. Evans c Watson b Crawford	11	– c Simpson b Davidson 7
F. H. Tyson c Simpson b Treanor	7	– b Crawford 15
A. V. Bedser c Lambert b Davidson	0	– c Simpson b Treanor 5
P. J. Loader c and b Davidson	0	– c Burke b Treanor 16
R. Appleyard not out	0	– not out 8
L-b 2, w 1, n-b 2	5	L-b 5, w 1, n-b 5 11

1/24 2/24 3/25 4/38 5/201   252   1/0 2/39 3/69 4/158 5/226   327
6/245 7/249 8/252 9/252   6/253 7/292 8/298 9/312

New South Wales

A. R. Morris c Simpson b Bedser	26	
W. Watson lbw b Tyson	155	– c May b Loader 8
R. Benaud c May b Tyson	2	
K. R. Miller c Wilson b Bedser	86	
J. Burke lbw b Bedser	6	– not out 34
J. H. de Courcy b Appleyard	20	
R. L. Simpson c Evans b Tyson	22	– b Loader..................... 4
A. K. Davidson c Loader b Bedser	30	– not out 27
G. Lambert c Wilson b Loader	6	
J. Treanor c Wilson b Tyson	12	
P. Crawford not out	0	
B 8, l-b 4, n-b 5	17	L-b 2, n-b 3 5

1/48 2/51 3/212 4/253 5/294   382   1/16 2/29   (2 wkts)   78
6/328 7/335 8/343 9/374

New South Wales Bowling

	Overs	Mdns	Runs	Wkts	Overs	Mdns	Runs	Wkts
Crawford	17	6	51	3	19	1	86	4
Davidson	19.2	3	41	3	27	10	63	2
Treanor	16	3	64	3	25.5	6	96	4
Miller	8	—	31	1	6	1	8	—
Benaud	15	2	50	—	29	11	52	—
Burke	3	—	6	—	1	1	—	—
Simpson	2	—	4	—	3	1	11	—

MCC Bowling

	Overs	Mdns	Runs	Wkts	Overs	Mdns	Runs	Wkts
Bedser	24.5	3	117	4	4	—	13	—
Tyson	25	2	98	4	2	1	1	—
Loader	18	2	92	1	4	—	14	2
Appleyard	21	3	58	1	3	1	7	—
Cowdrey					3	—	38	—

Umpires: H. Elphinstone and H. MacKinnon.

ENGLAND v AUSTRALIA

First Test Match

Played at Brisbane, November 26, 27, 29, 30, December 1, 1954

Australia won by an innings and 154 runs at ten minutes past four on the fifth day with a day to spare. Nothing went right for the Englishmen. Before the match Evans fell ill with sunstroke and on the first morning Compton, when fielding, ran into the wooden palings, breaking a bone in the back of his left hand, but above everything else the whole course of the game probably turned on the decision of Hutton, after winning the toss, to give Australia first innings. Never before had an England captain taken such a gamble in Australia and certainly never before in a Test match had a side replied with a total of 601 after being sent in to bat.

Hutton may have made up his mind some time earlier that he would take this course if the decision rested with him. Four times already on the tour the procedure had been adopted always with satisfactory results for the fielding side and for this game England had banked on an all-speed attack of four bowlers. Hutton inspected the pitch most carefully with several of his colleagues. It looked a beauty, but he carried out his plan and although on subsequent events he could be condemned, the fact remains that besides the loss of Compton, England allowed about twelve possible chances to go astray, including one from Morris to Andrew off Bedser in the third over of the match before he scored. If the England fielding had approached any decent standard Hutton might well have achieved his objective.

Australia, who omitted Davidson from the chosen twelve and were captained for the first time by Ian Johnson, averaged just over 40 runs an hour on the first day when they scored 208 for the loss of Favell and Miller. A splendid catch near his boots by Cowdrey at square-leg removed Favell and then Miller charmed the crowd of 20,000 for eighty-five minutes before he chopped a harmless-looking ball into his stumps. So at three o'clock the two left-handers, Morris and Harvey, entered on a long partnership. Both flicked at balls outside the off stump and never during the two hours and ten minutes they were together on the first day did they establish a complete mastery over the bowling. Immediately after tea Bailey at deep long-leg gave Morris a life when he was 55 and the total 145. That mistake alone cost England dearly.

With the new ball available first thing on Saturday there was still hope, but now Morris and Harvey took absolute control and thanks to their example and enterprise Australia added 295 that day for the loss of four more wickets. Taking into consideration the length of time the fast bowlers occupied completing an over this was extremely fast scoring in present-day Test matches. Hutton realised it would be futile to persist with an attacking field. He placed his men with the idea of saving runs and Tyson cut yards off his run in order to gain accuracy: but not until mid-afternoon did England meet with their first success of the day when Cowdrey, the only slip, held a waist-high catch from a chop by Morris who, with two 6s and seven 4s, batted seven hours for his 153. The stand produced 202 in four hours ten minutes.

England had to wait another two hours for their next wicket, Harvey and Hole putting on 131 before a fine throw by Tyson from long-leg ran out Hole. Then with seven more runs added Harvey fell to a brilliant catch at backward square-leg, Bailey rolling over as he held a hard pull. Harvey's 162, made in six hours twenty minutes, was easily his highest against England and also his first hundred against them in Australia. He hit one 5 and seventeen 4s.

Archer soon gave an easy catch to gully, but more trouble came from Lindwall and Benaud for both hit with great power. Australia, 503 for six at the week-end, kept England in the field until lunch time on Monday, Lindwall continuing his sparkling hitting which brought him eleven 4s. Altogether the Australian innings lasted eleven and a half hours.

After his spell of ninety minutes with the bat on the third morning, Lindwall came out fresh and bowled superbly for an hour during which time the first four England wickets crashed for 25 runs. Not until Bailey arrived was there any sign of stability and then in two hours forty minutes he and Cowdrey added 82, Cowdrey in his first Test match hit seven splendid 4s and gave a foretaste of the great innings he was to play later in the series. The end of the third day found England 107 for five wickets and defeat was obviously only a matter of time unless rain came to the rescue.

Having made 38 in two hours forty minutes, Bailey continued the fight. He soon lost Tyson, Bedser and Andrew but Statham kept up his end for thirty-five minutes and when he left Bailey had reached 81. Against medical advice Compton decided to bat, but he was almost helpless and so Bailey, who had batted without error, hit out and was bowled. He stayed four hours twenty minutes for his highest score against Australia and besides eleven 4s he hit one 6 and one 5. When he drove Johnson for his six, Bailey won the prize of £A100 offered by a local businessman for the first English 6.

By two o'clock England followed on 411 behind and in the first hour they lost Simpson and Hutton. Simpson foolishly tried a single when Hutton was dropped by Favell in the slips off Lindwall, but Edrich and May checked the opposition in a defiant stand. They took the total to 130 at the close but next day Australia were on top again. May, playing at a short ball, was lbw when the partnership had added 124 in just under two and a half hours, and next Edrich, having shaped splendidly, especially against Lindwall, also fell to a short ball which took his middle stump when he was too soon with his hook. Edrich batted three hours ten minutes and hit one 6 and thirteen 4s. Subsequently only Bailey and Tyson gave the Australian bowlers any trouble. Scoring 111 runs in the match Bailey defended resolutely for just under six hours. In less than half an hour after tea the last four wickets fell to the spin of Benaud and Johnson, the match ending with a glorious running catch in the deep by Harvey when Statham tried to lift Benaud for 6.

The full attendance of 77,008 was below Brisbane's best of 93,143 in the 1932-33 series, but the receipts of £21,000 were easily a record for the capital city of Queensland.

Australia

L. Favell c Cowdrey b Statham	23
A. R. Morris c Cowdrey b Bailey	153
K. R. Miller b Bailey	49
R. N. Harvey c Bailey b Bedser	162
G. B. Hole run out	57
R. Benaud c May b Tyson	34
R. G. Archer c Bedser b Statham	0
R. R. Lindwall not out	64
G. R. Langley b Bailey	16
I. W. Johnson not out	24
B 11, l-b 7, n-b 1	19

1/51 2/123 3/325   (8 wkts dec.) 601
4/456 5/463 6/464 7/545 8/572

W. A. Johnston did not bat.

England

L. Hutton c Langley b Lindwall	4	– lbw b Miller	13
R. T. Simpson b Miller	2	– run out	9
W. J. Edrich c Langley b Archer	15	– b Johnston	88
P. B. H. May b Lindwall	1	– lbw b Lindwall	44
M. C. Cowdrey c Hole b Johnston	40	– b Benaud	10
T. E. Bailey b Johnston	88	– c Langley b Lindwall	23
F. H. Tyson b Johnson	7	– not out	37
A. V. Bedser b Johnson	5	– c Archer b Johnson	5
K. V. Andrew b Lindwall	6	– b Johnson	5
J. B. Statham b Johnson	11	– c Harvey b Benaud	14
D. C. S. Compton not out	2	– c Langley b Benaud	0
B 3, l-b 6	9	B 7, l-b 2	9

1/4 2/10 3/11 4/25 5/107   190   1/22 2/23 3/147 4/163 5/181   257
6/132 7/141 8/156 9/181   6/220 7/231 8/242 9/243

England Bowling

	Overs	Mdns	Runs	Wkts
Bedser............	37	4	131	1
Statham	34	2	123	2
Tyson............	29	1	160	1
Bailey	26	1	140	3
Edrich............	3	—	28	—

Australia Bowling

	Overs	Mdns	Runs	Wkts	Overs	Mdns	Runs	Wkts
Lindwall	14	4	27	3	17	3	50	2
Miller	11	5	19	1	12	2	30	1
Archer	4	1	14	1	15	4	28	—
Johnson	19	5	46	3	17	5	38	2
Benaud...........	12	5	28	—	8.1	1	43	3
Johnston..........	16.1	5	47	2	21	8	59	1

Umpires: M. J. McInnes (Adelaide) and C. Hoy (Brisbane).

ENGLAND v AUSTRALIA

Second Test Match

Played at Sydney, December 17, 18, 20, 21, 22, 1954

England won by 38 runs at twelve minutes past three on the fifth day with one day in hand. Such a victory seemed beyond any possibility when England – this time they were put in by the Australian captain, Morris – lost eight wickets for 88, but among a crop of batting failures in both teams the tail-enders made their presence felt. In addition May hit his first Test century against Australia and Neil Harvey made a supreme effort of 92 not out for his side.

The match was a triumph for pace bowlers and in particular for Tyson and Statham. Many people feared that Tyson had been seriously hurt when, batting just before lunch on the fourth day, he turned his back on a bouncer from Lindwall and it struck him on the back of the head. Temporarily, Tyson was knocked out but not only did he resume his innings but the next day he knocked out Australia, taking six wickets for 85 runs.

Tyson won the match for England because he kept his head. After his painful experience he might well have been tempted to hurl down bouncers, particularly at Lindwall, but he never did so. Possibly Lindwall expected retaliation, for Tyson yorked him as he did Burke and Hole in the same innings. The cricket at this vital stage emphasised that, above everything else in bowling, perfect length and direction win matches.

Both teams made changes compared with the first Test at Brisbane. England brought in Evans, Graveney, Wardle and Appleyard for Andrew, Compton, Simpson and Bedser, while Australia had Burke and Davidson for Ian Johnson and Miller, both injured. The omission of Bedser from the twelve on the morning of the match created a controversy, but subsequent events justified the introduction of both Appleyard and Wardle who brought variety to the attack.

Yet in this match the seam bowlers of both teams controlled the play; in fact Morris achieved what Hutton, the England captain, hoped but failed to accomplish at Brisbane, England being dismissed in four and a quarter hours. Hutton stayed two hours but the promotion of Bailey was a failure and it was not repeated in subsequent Tests.

Lindwall, rarely bowling short and swinging the ball either way while aiming persistently at the stumps, kept the hesitant opposition on tenterhooks, and Archer, Johnston and Davidson were equally menacing. The fielding, as usual, reached the best Australian traditions with Davidson outstanding. The loss of Bailey and May for 19 put Hutton completely on the defensive and in ninety minutes before lunch England mustered only 34 runs. Between lunch and tea came a dreadful collapse, five wickets falling for 60, and as Cowdrey and Appleyard soon went on resuming, nine men were out for 111. The two left-handers, Wardle and Statham, struck heartily at almost every ball and their partnership of 43 was the best of the innings.

The only enjoyable moment that day for England came with the last ball when Hutton at leg-slip caught his rival captain, Morris, leaving Australia 18 for one wicket. Next day the bowlers recovered much of the ground lost by the batsmen. At first Favell and Burke made speedy progress, paying little respect to Bailey and Statham, but on Bailey changing ends and sharing the attack with Tyson the tempo changed. Graveney held Favell at second slip, so that at lunch Australia were 88 for two wickets – and quite comfortable.

Bailey continued to bowl splendidly and with Tyson causing much trouble Australia were not only put on the defensive but in one hour fifty minutes between lunch and tea they lost four more men for the addition of 70. A daring and lucky effort by Archer saved Australia. Although constantly missing when trying to cut Tyson and more than once fortunate not to be bowled, Archer pulled Appleyard for 6 and hit six 4s, his stand of 52 in an hour with Davidson being the best of the match for Australia whose first innings occupied just over five hours.

England, having restricted their deficit to 74, went in again first thing on Monday, but at the lunch interval with Hutton, Bailey and Graveney gone for 58, it seemed that Australia might win without any serious challenge. Happily, May, who began his innings just after midday, found a worthy partner in Cowdrey and their fourth wicket stand of 116 in three and a quarter hours altered the structure of the match.

It was most heartening to see these two young amateurs, one from Oxford and the other from Cambridge, master the Australian bowling by their sureness in defence and their willingness to hit the half-volley or any loose ball. Seldom were they beaten and never did they offer the semblance of a chance until Cowdrey, trying to hit himself out of a quiet spell, attempted to drive Benaud for 6 when there were two men waiting in the deep. Powerful cover drives and hard hits to leg brought Cowdrey most of his runs. May used a wide range of strokes and compelled Morris to remove his array of leg fielders behind the wicket. His punishing strokes were beautifully timed.

With twenty-five minutes remaining before the close Edrich and May took the total to 204 for five, and May needed only two for his hundred, but Australia had the right to the new ball first thing in the morning.

Because of the wet state of the outfield Morris delayed claiming the second new ball, but May having completed his century from the second ball of the day added only three more runs in the next fifty minutes. Then at 222 Lindwall and Archer went into action with the new ball and immediately the bowlers took charge so that the position changed to 250 for nine.

May, who hit ten 4s in a stay of five hours, was bowled when playing forward to a late inswinger and in twelve overs on this fourth day Lindwall claimed three wickets for 20 runs. Wardle could not repeat his first innings performance, but the last pair, Appleyard and Statham, faced the situation calmly and, unafraid to play forward to the well-pitched up ball, they added 46 runs in fifty minutes – another invaluable late stand.

Australia wanted 223 for victory, not an unreasonable task, but at once Statham and Tyson, with more pace than Lindwall, made the ball fly nastily. In Statham's first over Edrich could not hold a hot chance from Favell. Statham gave Morris a terrible time, beating him four times in the last over before tea and removing him leg before with the seventh ball.

The interval came within twenty-five minutes of the start of the innings, giving the two England bowlers time to rest. On resuming Tyson, with his sixth ball, beat Favell by sheer pace, Edrich taking a nice catch in front of his chest, and both the opening batsmen were out for 34. That was a great start, but Harvey, after a shaky beginning, settled down. Burke did not score for nearly an hour and the pair played through the last seventy-eight minutes, seeing the total to 72 for two at nightfall.

Australia now needed 151 more runs and first thing the odds were in their favour. Though much rain fell during the night, the ground was perfect and the protected pitch played with less fire than at any stage of the match, but it was never slow. Tyson struck in the second over of the day when he yorked both Burke and Hole. Hutton did not overtax either Tyson or Statham at this stage and Bailey and Appleyard entered the attack. In the Yorkshireman's second over, Benaud hooked a skier which Tyson held and half the wickets were down for 106.

At lunch the total stood at 118 for five; Harvey 51, Archer 5, and no one cared to hazard a guess as to the ultimate result. The match was resumed at twenty minutes to two and Statham and Tyson virtually clinched the issue in the next fifty minutes when they removed Archer, Davidson, Lindwall and Langley for only 27, making Australia 145 for nine.

For some time Harvey had played a lone hand and as his partners disappeared the more brilliant he became. When Johnston arrived he and Harvey held a mid-wicket conference and obviously they agreed that Harvey should have most of the strike. Harvey hit boldly, but never chanced anything when a defensive stroke was imperative.

Johnston made some queer strokes but he lasted thirty-seven minutes, playing only 16 of 80 balls sent down during a stand which added 39. He hit runs to long leg off the back-hand until at length he flicked a catch to Evans standing back. Harvey remained unbeaten, having played one of his finest innings for Australia. For four hours twenty minutes he faced England unflinchingly, hitting nine 4s.

While justice must be done to Tyson who bowled without relief for over ninety minutes down wind in that vital spell in which his figures were 7.4 overs, 1 maiden, 41 runs, 3 wickets, England could not have won without the valuable work Statham accomplished bowling into the wind for eighty-five minutes. With ten wickets for 130 runs in the match, Tyson was England's hero, and the whole of Hutton's party faced Christmas and the New Year in a new frame of mind – optimistic that their luck had changed and that the rubber could be won. Attendance 135,350. Receipts £19,485.

England

L. Hutton c Davidson b Johnston	30	– c Benaud b Johnston.............. 28
T. E. Bailey b Lindwall	0	– c Langley b Archer.............. 6
P. B. H. May c Johnston b Archer	5	– b Lindwall..................... 104
T. W. Graveney c Favell b Johnston	21	– c Langley b Johnston 0
M. C. Cowdrey c Langley b Davidson	23	– c Archer b Benaud 54
W. J. Edrich c Benaud b Archer	10	– b Archer..................... 29
F. H. Tyson b Lindwall	0	– b Lindwall.................... 9
T. G. Evans c Langley b Archer	3	– c Lindwall b Archer 4
J. H. Wardle c Burke b Johnston	35	– lbw b Lindwall 8
R. Appleyard c Hole b Davidson	8	– not out 19
J. B. Statham not out	14	– c Langley b Johnston 25
L-b 5	5	L-b 6, n-b 4.............. 10

1/14 2/19 3/58 4/63 5/84   154   1/18 2/55 3/55 4/171 5/222   296
6/85 7/88 8/99 9/111   6/232 7/239 8/249 9/250

Australia

A. R. Morris c Hutton b Bailey	12	– lbw b Statham	10
L. Favell c Graveney b Bailey	26	– c Edrich b Tyson	16
J. Burke c Graveney b Bailey	44	– b Tyson	14
R. N. Harvey c Cowdrey b Tyson	12	– not out	92
G. B. Hole b Tyson	12	– b Tyson	0
R. Benaud lbw b Statham	20	– c Tyson b Appleyard	15
R. G. Archer c Hutton b Tyson	49	– b Tyson	8
A. K. Davidson b Statham	20	– c Evans b Statham	0
R. R. Lindwall c Evans b Tyson	19	– b Tyson	1
G. R. Langley b Bailey	5	– b Statham	6
W. A. Johnston not out	0	– c Evans b Tyson	12
B 5, l-b 2, n-b 2	9	L-b 7, n-b 3	10

1/18 2/65 3/100 4/104 5/122   228   1/27 2/34 3/77 4/77 5/106   184
6/141 7/193 8/213 9/224   6/122 7/127 8/136 9/145

Australia Bowling

	Overs	Mdns	Runs	Wkts	Overs	Mdns	Runs	Wkts
Lindwall	17	3	47	2	31	10	69	3
Archer	12	7	12	3	22	9	53	3
Davidson	12	3	34	2	13	2	52	—
Johnston	13	3	56	3	19.3	2	70	3
Benaud					19	3	42	1

England Bowling

	Overs	Mdns	Runs	Wkts	Overs	Mdns	Runs	Wkts
Statham	18	1	83	2	19	6	45	3
Bailey	17.4	3	59	4	6	—	21	—
Tyson	13	2	45	4	18.4	1	85	6
Appleyard	7	1	32	—	6	1	12	1
Wardle					4	2	11	—

Umpires: M. J. McInnes and R. Wright.

ENGLAND v AUSTRALIA

Third Test Match

Played at Melbourne, December 31, 1954, January 1, 3, 4, 5, 1955

England won by 128 runs at nineteen minutes past one on the fifth day with a day to spare. As in the previous Test, the combined speed of Tyson and Statham proved too much for Australia and again the two young amateur batsmen, Cowdrey (102) and May (91), carried the England batting on a sporting pitch which was said to have been "doctored" on the Sunday. Certainly large cracks were evident on Saturday yet on Monday these had closed and for a time the surface behaved more kindly to batsmen. The Victorian Cricket Association and the Melbourne Cricket Club held an inquiry into a report published in *The Age* alleging watering and issued the following statement:

"After a searching inquiry it is emphatically denied that the pitch or any part of the cricket ground has been watered since the commencement of the third Test match on Friday, December 31."

With Compton fit England had their strongest side (Bedser again being omitted) and Australia welcomed back Ian Johnson, their captain, and Miller, but Langley, the wicket-keeper, stood down through injury which gave Maddocks his opportunity to make his début in Test cricket.

This time Hutton, winning the toss, decided to bat, but apart from Cowdrey, Evans and Bailey, England made a sorry show. Cowdrey went in when Edrich and May had fallen for 21 and soon he saw Hutton and Compton follow, these four wickets going down in less than an hour for 41.

Then another defiant amateur, Bailey, joined Cowdrey and they checked the Australian bowlers for two hours, adding 74, following which there came a Kent partnership by Cowdrey and Evans that produced 54, before the last four wickets fell for 22. For four hours Cowdrey batted without mistake, getting his body and bat behind short rising balls which Lindwall and Miller were able to bowl off this pitch almost at will. Cowdrey specialised in perfectly-timed drives, both straight and to cover, and he forced the ball skilfully off his legs.

Miller bowled magnificently throughout the ninety minutes before lunch when his figures were 9 overs, 8 maidens, 5 runs, 3 wickets. There were only two scoring strokes against him, a cover drive for 3 by Compton and one for 2 by Cowdrey. As Miller's knee was still suspect Johnson later preferred to conserve his energy for batting. Hutton, troubled by a heavy cold, decided only at the last minute to play.

So England faced the second day knowing that yet again the bowlers must rescue them from a crisis, and thanks to Tyson and Statham ably assisted by Bailey and Appleyard the first eight Australian wickets fell for 151. Hutton used his bowlers in short spells, for the heat was stifling. As Compton could not field, having bruised his thumb when he fell to a bouncer, Wilson acted as substitute, excelling in the leg trap.

Maddocks, who had kept wicket neatly and efficiently, rallied Australia. Arriving when six men had gone for 115 he saw the total to 188 for eight at the close, having made 36 in two and a quarter hours. Maddocks batted another half-hour making top score, 47. He and Johnson added 54 and with Johnson lasting altogether two hours Australia gained a lead of 40, their last four wickets adding 116 against England's 22.

It was essential that the early England batsmen did not let down their side a second time and the arrears were cleared before a turning ball across the wicket took Edrich's off stump. So at eight minutes to three May joined Hutton and proceeded to play masterly cricket in which the straight drive predominated. There was always the possibility that he might be trapped by a "creeper", but May watched the ball intently. At 96 he saw Hutton fall to one which moved fast and low from outside the off stump. The captain had served his side well by remaining nearly two and a half hours and giving a fine example of watchfulness and concentration. With May in such form, Cowdrey preferred to take the defensive, but soon he played on, England being 159 for three at the close; May 83, Compton 10.

On the fourth day May soon left having batted three hours twenty minutes and hit eight 4s. Bailey defended for two and three-quarter hours but Evans and Wardle hit gaily, Wardle taking 16 in one over from Johnston and 14 from the next by Johnson. Actually Wardle hit 38 out of 46 in forty minutes, but this time the rest of the tail failed so that Australia were left to make 240 to win.

A superb right-hand catch by Cowdrey at forward short-leg when he disposed of Morris brought England their first success at 23, but in order to keep Miller fresh, Benaud came next and both he and Favell exercised great care until Appleyard yorked Favell. Nearly half an hour remained that day and Benaud (19) and Harvey (9) raised the total to 79 for two.

This meant that Australia still required 165, a task that seemed far from impossible. The pitch was worn and the experts predicted that England must look to Appleyard, pointing out that the conditions were made for his off spin, and probably they were right, but Tyson and Statham saw England home without Hutton having to look elsewhere for any bowling.

Sheer speed through the air coupled with the chance of a shooter at any moment left the Australian batsmen nonplussed. Tyson blazed through them like a bush fire. In seventy-nine minutes the match was all over, the eight remaining wickets crashing for 36 runs. Here are the bowling figures:

> Tyson   6.3 overs, 0 maidens, 16 runs, 6 wickets.
> Statham 6   overs, 1 maiden, 19 runs, 2 wickets.

A wonderful leg-side catch by Evans when Harvey glanced the seventh ball of the day heralded the collapse. The loss of Harvey was a terrible blow to Australia and with Benaud hooking too soon and Edrich catching Miller at slip from a ball which lifted, Tyson claimed three wickets in 21 balls in the first half-hour.

Then Statham accounted for Hole, who flashed; Maddocks played on to Tyson and in the same over Lindwall went to drive a half-volley which shot under his bat. Next Statham bowled Archer with a fast full toss and finally Evans took his third catch, this time from Johnston high with the left hand, Australia being all out in three hours and five minutes.

The full attendance for the match was 300,270. The receipts, £A47,933, were a record for any Australian match.

England

L. Hutton c Hole b Miller	12	– lbw b Archer ... 42
W. J. Edrich c Lindwall b Miller	4	– b Johnston ... 13
P. B. H. May c Benaud b Lindwall	0	– b Johnston ... 91
M. C. Cowdrey b Johnson	102	– b Benaud ... 7
D. C. S. Compton c Harvey b Miller	4	– c Maddocks b Archer ... 23
T. E. Bailey c Maddocks b Johnston	30	– not out ... 24
T. G. Evans lbw b Archer	20	– c Maddocks b Miller ... 22
J. H. Wardle b Archer	0	– b Johnson ... 38
F. H. Tyson b Archer	6	– c Harvey b Johnston ... 6
J. B. Statham b Archer	3	– c Favell b Johnston ... 0
R. Appleyard not out	1	– b Johnston ... 6
B 9	9	B 2, l-b 4, w 1 ... 7

1/14 2/21 3/29 4/41 5/115   191
6/169 7/181 8/181 9/190

1/40 2/96 3/128 4/173 5/185   279
6/211 7/257 8/273 9/273

Australia

L. Favell lbw b Statham	25	– b Appleyard ... 30
A. R. Morris lbw b Tyson	3	– c Cowdrey b Tyson ... 4
K. R. Miller c Evans b Statham	7	– c Edrich b Tyson ... 6
R. N. Harvey b Appleyard	31	– c Evans b Tyson ... 11
G. B. Hole b Tyson	11	– c Evans b Statham ... 5
R. Benaud c sub b Appleyard	15	– b Tyson ... 22
R. G. Archer b Wardle	23	– b Statham ... 15
L. Maddocks c Evans b Statham	47	– b Tyson ... 0
R. R. Lindwall b Statham	13	– lbw b Tyson ... 0
I. W. Johnson not out	33	– not out ... 4
W. A. Johnston b Statham	11	– c Evans b Tyson ... 0
B 7, l-b 3, n-b 2	12	B 1, l-b 13 ... 14

1/15 2/38 3/43 4/65 5/92   231
6/115 7/134 8/151 9/205

1/23 2/57 3/77 4/86 5/87   111
6/97 7/98 8/98 9/110

Australia Bowling

	Overs	Mdns	Runs	Wkts	Overs	Mdns	Runs	Wkts
Lindwall	13	—	59	1	18	3	52	—
Miller	11	8	14	3	18	6	35	1
Archer	13.6	4	33	4	24	7	50	2
Benaud	7	—	30	—	8	2	25	1
Johnston	12	6	26	1	24.5	2	85	5
Johnson	11	3	20	1	8	2	25	1

England Bowling

	Overs	Mdns	Runs	Wkts	Overs	Mdns	Runs	Wkts
Tyson............	21	2	68	2	12.3	1	27	7
Statham	16.3	—	60	5	11	1	38	2
Bailey............	9	1	33	—	3	—	14	—
Appleyard........	11	3	38	2	4	1	17	1
Wardle	6	—	20	1	1	—	1	—

Umpires: M. J. McInnes and C. Hoy.

ENGLAND v AUSTRALIA

Fourth Test Match

Played at Adelaide, January 28, 29, 31, February 1, 2, 1955

England won by five wickets at twenty minutes past five on the fifth day, the first four Tests all being concluded with one day to spare. This victory gave England the rubber for the first time in Australia since 1932-33, and again the fast bowlers, Tyson and Statham, who were well supported by Bailey and Appleyard, played a major part. It was the only match of the series won by the side batting last.

While England were at full strength – they relied on the side which succeeded at Melbourne – Australia left out Hole and Favell and a leg injury in a State game caused Lindwall to withdraw. Originally Morris was also omitted but he replaced Lindwall in the chosen eleven to which Davidson was added. Favell, at first named to play, was dropped and McDonald and Burke completed the side. As Langley, the local wicket-keeper, was fit there was much indignation about Maddocks being retained, but the crowd gave him a great reception and he responded by making the top score for Australia.

With the temperature hovering near 100 degrees both sides wanted to win the toss; Ian Johnson was the lucky man and when the lunch interval arrived with Australia 51 for nought trouble seemed likely for England.

In each session Hutton used Tyson and Statham in short spells. When 12 Morris offered a low chance off Statham to Hutton's left hand, otherwise there was no encouragement for the bowlers on this placid pitch until after the interval. Then Tyson made one ball rise and it touched Morris's glove in transit to Evans; so Australia's first wicket fell after one hour and fifty minutes.

McDonald (43) received a life off Statham from Compton at mid-on and next over, trying to hit himself out of a negative spell, he was taken by May. Back came Tyson and he trapped Burke at short-leg, England going to tea satisfied with Australia 119 for three.

On resuming, Bailey put in a very fine effort from the Cathedral end while Tyson and Statham attacked in turn from the Torrens river end. Harvey edged Bailey to slip, but Benaud and Miller avoiding all risks remained together for the last seventy-five minutes taking the score to 161 for four – a very fine first day for England.

With the new ball coming later Hutton gave Tyson and Statham only two overs each the next morning and switching to Appleyard he made an unsuspected and wise change. The Yorkshire off-spinner took the wickets of Benaud and Miller in the course of only three overs. Archer greeted Wardle by pulling him for 6 first ball, and on taking the new ball England soon accounted for both Archer and Davidson, making Australia 229 for eight on a perfect pitch. Here Ian Johnson joined Maddocks and by sensible batsmanship they added 92 in as many minutes, though the stand should have ended at 270 when with both batsmen at the same end Appleyard at square-leg shied the ball high over Evans.

England wilted in the heat, Evans notably missing chances, and Statham was handicapped with a sore foot caused by the removal of a toe nail a few days before the match. Hutton and Edrich relieved the tension by making the best opening stand of the series. England waged a hard fight on the third day and thanks to Hutton, Cowdrey and Compton they reached 230 for three wickets at the close.

First thing, Australia struck two swift blows, dismissing Edrich and May. Johnson put down Edrich's off stump and Archer at first slip made a wonderful low right-hand catch. Already the pitch was favouring spin, but by cultured batting Hutton and Cowdrey added 99 before Hutton also fell to an amazing catch after batting four and a half hours for 80, the best score of the match. Hutton unerringly hooked a long hop and Davidson, only a few yards from the bat at forward short-leg, turned his back, shot out his hands to protect himself and the ball stayed. Although the new ball became due forty minutes before the end of the day Johnson preferred to rely on his spinners.

On the fourth day England continued with Cowdrey 77 and Compton 44 and at once Miller and Davidson struck with the new ball, both men falling for the addition of only two runs. Cowdrey batted five hours and Compton two, but happily for England Evans hit cleanly and impudently and some steady efforts by Wardle and as usual Bailey led to a first innings advantage of 18 by mid-afternoon, the innings altogether lasting nine hours.

Some Australians felt that England were playing for a draw which would have sufficed to ensure the retention of the Ashes. In any case the initiative rested with Australia, but England's objective was outright victory.

On Australia batting a second time, Hutton gave only two overs to Statham before introducing Appleyard at 24 and this move, hailed as a touch of genius, gave England the upper hand. Exploiting worn patches caused by bowlers' footmarks, Appleyard removed Morris, Burke and Harvey in his first six overs at a personal cost of six runs and he finished the day with these figures: 10 overs, 5 maidens, 13 runs, 3 wickets, Australia's score standing at 69 for three wickets.

On this evidence alone, most people reckoned Appleyard would be unplayable next day, yet again those two demon fast bowlers, Tyson and Statham, denied him his chance. Statham, freed from pain by having a hole cut in his left boot which allowed the injured toe to move freely, staggered Australia by removing McDonald, Miller and Maddocks in his first three overs of the day between which Tyson yorked Benaud. Subsequently, Tyson accounted for Archer and Johnston so that at lunch Australia were 103 for nine. Bowling unchanged for ninety minutes, Tyson and Statham had caused six wickets to fall for 34 runs and their analyses during this breath-taking period read: Statham 7-0-12-3; Tyson 7-1-17-3.

Appleyard did not get his opportunity until after the interval and then Wardle dismissed Davidson leg before. Davidson, who alone offered any resistance, batted for seventy-five minutes. One would emphasise that Tyson and Statham broke down the opposition without delivering one bouncer and as in the other successful Tests they were forced to rely on an orthodox field as England could not afford to give away runs.

England wanted only 94 and though no one sensed any real danger Miller provided shocks when in the course of bowling 20 balls he disposed of Edrich, Hutton and Cowdrey. Next he caught May brilliantly at cover, but Compton and Bailey were equal to the situation and saw England within four runs of their objective before Bailey was lbw. So those two old campaigners, Compton and Evans, were there at the finish, Evans making the winning hit.

After the match Hutton, reviewing the series, paid tribute to Statham, Tyson, Cowdrey, May and Evans and thanked the Australian crowds for their patience when the number of overs had been restricted during the day. "Fast bowlers must take time over their overs", he said, "and I feel that as youngsters they need my help in placing the field". Commenting on the success of the fast bowlers during the later stages of the Tests, Hutton said that whereas one would have expected the spinners to succeed the habit of the ball to come through on this tour at varying heights made the fast bowlers trickier to face.

The total attendance was 165,038; receipts £25,816.

Australia

C. C. McDonald c May b Appleyard	48	– b Statham	29
A. R. Morris c Evans b Tyson	25	– c and b Appleyard	16
J. Burke c May b Tyson	18	– b Appleyard	5
R. N. Harvey c Edrich b Bailey	25	– b Appleyard	7
K. R. Miller c Bailey b Appleyard	44	– b Statham	14
R. Benaud c May b Appleyard	15	– lbw b Tyson	1
L. Maddocks run out	69	– lbw b Statham	2
R. G. Archer c May b Tyson	21	– c Evans b Tyson	3
A. K. Davidson c Evans b Bailey	5	– lbw b Wardle	23
I. W. Johnson c Statham b Bailey	41	– not out	3
W. A. Johnston not out	0	– c Appleyard b Tyson	3
B 3, l-b 7, n-b 2	12	B 4, l-b 1	5

1/59 2/86 3/115 4/129 5/175   **323**   1/24 2/40 3/54 4/69 5/76   **111**
6/182 7/212 8/229 9/321   6/77 7/79 8/83 9/101

England

L. Hutton c Davidson b Johnston	80	– c Davidson b Miller	5
W. J. Edrich b Johnson	21	– b Miller	0
P. B. H. May c Archer b Benaud	1	– c Miller b Johnston	26
M. C. Cowdrey c Maddocks b Davidson	79	– c Archer b Miller	4
D. C. S. Compton lbw b Miller	44	– not out	34
T. E. Bailey c Davidson b Johnston	38	– lbw b Johnston	15
T. G. Evans c Maddocks b Benaud	37	– not out	6
J. H. Wardle c and b Johnson	23		
F. H. Tyson c Burke b Benaud	1		
R. Appleyard not out	10		
J. B. Statham c Maddocks b Benaud	0		
B 1, l-b 2, n-b 4	7	B 3, l-b 4	7

1/60 2/63 3/162 4/232 5/232   **341**   1/3 2/10 3/18   (5 wkts) **97**
6/283 7/321 8/323 9/336   4/49 5/90

England Bowling

	Overs	Mdns	Runs	Wkts	Overs	Mdns	Runs	Wkts
Tyson	26.1	4	85	3	15	2	47	3
Statham	19	4	70	—	12	1	38	3
Bailey	12	3	39	3				
Appleyard	23	7	58	3	12	7	13	3
Wardle	19	5	59	—	4.2	1	8	1

Australia Bowling

	Overs	Mdns	Runs	Wkts	Overs	Mdns	Runs	Wkts
Miller	11	4	34	1	10.4	2	40	3
Archer	3	—	12	—	4	—	13	—
Johnson	36	17	46	2				
Davidson	25	8	55	1	2	—	7	—
Johnston	27	11	60	2	8	2	20	2
Benaud	36.6	6	120	4	6	2	10	—
Burke	2	—	7	—				

Umpires: M. J. McInnes and R. Wright.

NOTES BY THE EDITOR, 1955

HUTTON'S MEN BRING HOME THE ASHES

After waiting for twenty-two years, England have again won a rubber in Australia and retained the Ashes they retrieved at Kennington Oval in 1953. This is a great triumph for Len Hutton, the captain, and a great thing for English cricket. At last England are on top again and with so many excellent young players in the first-class counties, the team should be even stronger when Australia renew the challenge in England next year.

Twelve months ago I drew attention to the way history has repeated itself in cricket following two wars. Now the circle has been completed. After the Second World War, as after the First, Australia overwhelmed England, winning the first three Test rubbers. In each case Australia won eleven times before England broke the monopoly. Then, as now, England won back the Ashes – at The Oval – in the fourth series and retained them in convincing fashion when touring Australia.

Between 1946 and 1950 English cricket suffered many humiliations, culminating in those heavy reverses at the hands of West Indies at Lord's, Nottingham and The Oval. F. R. Brown began the England revival, since when Hutton, who succeeded him in 1952, has captained his country in twenty Tests up to that wonderful day at Adelaide. Already the Hutton era embraces five Test campaigns in which England have mastered Australia twice, India once and shared the honours with West Indies in the Carribean and with Pakistan.

SUCCESSFUL OPENING BOWLERS

I feel sure that Hutton and his fellow selectors carefully examined the reasons for victory in previous Tests in Australia before they chose the side for the most recent visit. During the past fifty years England have won the rubber only four times in the Antipodes. Each time success has depended on a great pair of opening bowlers. In 1911-12 Barnes and Foster took 66 wickets for 22.27 runs each, dismissing Australia for such totals as 184, 133, 191, 173 and 176 despite the presence of such talented batsmen as Trumper, Hill, Macartney, Bardsley and Armstrong, and England won by 4-1. In 1928-29 England again produced two wonderful pace bowlers in Larwood and Tate, who shared 35 wickets. Australia were dismissed in three innings for 122, 66 and 253, though among their batsmen were Woodfull, Ponsford, Ryder, Bradman, Kippax and Jackson. Again England won by 4-1.

In 1932-33 came the "bodyline" tour of Larwood and Voce. They took 48 wickets for 21.89, Australia, though possessing batsmen of the calibre of Woodfull, Ponsford, Bradman, Kippax, Richardson and McCabe, being put out for totals of 164, 191, 193, 175 and 182. Again the rubber ended with England winning 4-1.

In 1954-55 Statham and Tyson routed Australia. Excluding the last Test – these Notes were written immediately after the rubber was clinched at Adelaide – they took 43 wickets costing 22.65 apiece. In five innings Australia made only 228, 184, 231, 111 and 111. Small wonder that everyone expected that Hutton's men would make the rubber 4-1 at Sydney.

Australia thrived similarly after the two wars with those grand combinations, Gregory and McDonald and Lindwall and Miller. Yet two of the greatest bowlers went through unsuccessful tours because they lacked adequate help from the other end. I refer to Tate in 1924-25, when he took 38 Test wickets, and Bedser in 1950-51, when his haul was 30. Each time England lost by 4-1.

YOUTH TAKES COMMAND

This most recent struggle for the Ashes thrilled cricket lovers the world over. The issue was closer than the bare results indicate. As in England in 1953, one could rarely predict which way a match was likely to go. One day Australia looked to be on top; the next England would turn the tables. For the time being the ball has gained the mastery over the bat and generally youth, guided by the wise old head of Hutton, has taken command.

Fielding still remains an integral part of the game. When Australia scored 601 at Brisbane and won the first Test by an innings and 154 runs, England paid dearly for missed catches and there seemed to be little chance for them. Then within a month the whole outlook changed. Three days before Christmas, England won at Sydney by 38 runs – a handsome present for their friends at home – and for good measure they added a New Year's gift in the shape of victory by 128 runs at Melbourne.

Of necessity the full review of the tour together with the reports and scores of each match must await the 1956 edition, but there is no reason to hold back some observations. Let us consider England's assets. By their performances in Australia, Tyson and Statham have proved beyond all doubt that fast bowling has returned to English cricket. Tyson was mainly instrumental in those victories in Sydney and Melbourne. He took four for 45 and six for 85 at Sydney and two for 68 and seven for 27 at Melbourne, but at Brisbane his only reward for much toil was one for 160.

Why the transformation? The easy-paced pitch offered no encouragement in the first Test, but that alone does not provide the answer. In that disastrous match Tyson relied almost entirely on speed. He ran from a mark of thirty-two paces and just hurled the ball down the 22 yards. Tyson soon realised that these tearaway methods were useless in Test cricket. He needed control over length and particularly direction and to achieve these objectives he cut down and remodelled his run so that he finished with seven or eight determined, raking strides. Unlike most athletes, Tyson runs with his toes pointing outwards and he used to finish with a shuffle. That caused loss of impetus and meant that the long run was a sheer waste of energy. He learned to begin with a shuffle and then carry right through. I would not be surprised if Tyson manages sooner or later to do away entirely with the shuffle.

Tyson is a very conscientious young man. From the time the England team sailed from Tilbury he kept himself in condition running many laps round the decks of the *Orsova* before breakfast and throughout the tour he made sure he was always physically fit for the big occasion. He is the fastest bowler in cricket today and gives every promise of being a telling force in England's fortunes for some years to come.

It seems unbelievable that Lancashire turned him down on account of doubtful physique. Not only was this decision unfortunate for Lancashire, but it was unfortunate for Tyson himself. His adopted county, Northamptonshire, are not likely to provide him with the big benefit which must have come to him had he stayed in his native county. It is also to be hoped that Tyson will not wear himself out on the lifeless Northampton pitches. Now would be an appropriate time for Northamptonshire to remodel their pitches.

While Tyson was the main weapon, Statham played a vital and equally valuable part. Justice has been done to Statham in the *Five Cricketers of the Year* and it is a pleasure to record that he has since further justified himself in Australia. Whereas Statham finished virtually top of the English bowling averages in 1954 with 92 wickets at 14.13 each, Tyson came a long way down the list with 78 wickets at 21.38 each, which stresses Tyson's advance during his first tour abroad.

Supporting these two was T. E. Bailey – still England's only real all-rounder and a most valuable member of the party. It is interesting to note that England failed at Brisbane when they entered the match with only four bowlers – Bedser, Statham, Tyson and Bailey, and that victory was achieved when emphasis was placed on attack and the team met Australia with five bowlers, leaving out Bedser but including Appleyard and Wardle.

BEDSER'S REIGN OVER

The giants of cricket come and go. The rise of Tyson has apparently hastened the end of Alec Bedser's glorious career in Test cricket. One test failure sufficed to put Bedser on the shelf. Unfortunate to be stricken down with an attack of shingles at the beginning of his third MCC tour of Australia, Bedser took only one wicket for 131 runs at Brisbane and out he went – a vastly different experience from that of some batsmen who fail but still receive another chance. Bedser belongs to the truly great. One of four England bowlers who have obtained 100 wickets against Australia, he holds the record for the number of wickets taken in one series, 39, and he has dismissed more batsmen, 232, than any other bowler in Test history, besides bowling more balls than any other bowler. Bedser has always encouraged youth and many young bowlers are grateful to him for sound advice.

MAY AND COWDREY

Few people anticipated that two young amateurs would carry off the batting honours in Australia – at least during the important early months of the tour. Both Peter May and Colin Cowdrey accustomed themselves quickly to the strange conditions and lived up to the promise they showed during their University careers. While these products of the Public Schools and Oxford and Cambridge were displaying the arts of batsmanship, the failures of Hutton, Graveney, Simpson, Wilson and Compton were a sad reflection upon the methods adopted by the modern professional.

To a certain extent the change in Australian pitches accounted for the shortcomings of so many batsmen in both teams. The Australian authorities, like those in England, have made a genuine attempt to provide more helpful conditions for the bowlers. With the growing of grass on the pitches, the familiar shirt-front surface has disappeared. No longer is the turf at Sydney and Melbourne uniform. In some places there is grass and in others no grass, and consequently the ball comes through at varying heights. That is where the ordinary performer with the bat comes to grief; but May and Cowdrey have shown that by determination and concentration the high-class player can master these conditions as well as produce attractive strokes in front of the wicket.

ENGLAND IN SOUTH AFRICA

MCC TEAM v NORTH-EASTERN TRANSVAAL

Played at Benoni, December 3, 4, 1948

MCC won by an innings and 203 runs. By hitting 300 out of 399 in 181 minutes in his fourth century in five innings, Compton surpassed all his previous fast-scoring achievements. Such power and freedom did he bring into his batting that his strokes included five 6s and forty-two 4s – 198 runs from boundary hits. Compton made his first hundred in sixty-six minutes, his second in seventy-eight and his third in thirty-seven. Often he walked down the pitch before the bowler released the ball and he mixed orthodoxy with a bewildering assortment of unclassified strokes which went from the middle of the bat at lightning speed. He whipped balls pitched outside his off stump to the mid-wicket boundary and he stepped away in order to cut leg-breaks pitched outside the wicket. His was the highest score made by a visiting cricketer to South Africa, his own best to that period and only six short of the record in South African first-class cricket. Much credit was due to Simpson, who gave Compton every opportunity to take the bowling in a stand of 399, second only for an English third wicket to the Compton-Edrich partnership of 424 in May 1948. When taking the last four wickets in five balls in the North-Eastern first innings, Gladwin accomplished the only hat-trick of the tour. In the second innings Jenkins did chief damage. His match-figures were eleven for 137.

North-East Transvaal

J. Seccombe c and b Young	47	– c Compton b Tremlett	0
T. Louw c Griffith b Tremlett	5	– c Tremlett b Jenkins	14
A. Steyn c Compton b Jenkins	4	– c Griffith b Tremlett	2
K. Funston c and b Jenkins	65	– b Jenkins	13
L. Waller lbw b Jenkins	0	– lbw b Jenkins	29
R. Edwards c Mann b Jenkins	5	– c Griffith b Jenkins	15
J. Waites c Watkins b Gladwin	38	– c Compton b Jenkins	3
H. Patterson b Gladwin	2	– not out	21
J. Lindsay not out	0	– b Gladwin	0
J. Waller b Gladwin	0	– st Griffith b Jenkins	0
J. Hayward b Gladwin	0	– c Griffith b Jenkins	11
L-b 2	2	B 3, l-b 2	5
	168		113

MCC

C. Washbrook st Lindsay b J. Waller	38	M. F. Tremlett c Hayward b Funston	7
R. T. Simpson not out	130	S. C. Griffith not out	9
C. H. Palmer lbw b J. Waller	0		
D. C. S. Compton c Hayward b Funston	300	(4 wkts dec.)	484

F. G. Mann, A. Watkins, R. O. Jenkins, C. Gladwin and J. A. Young did not bat.

MCC Bowling

	Overs	Mdns	Runs	Wkts	Overs	Mdns	Runs	Wkts
Gladwin	15.3	7	27	4	12	5	16	1
Tremlett	10	2	26	1	5	2	7	2
Jenkins	15	1	82	4	13.2	1	55	7
Young	10	2	15	1	10	5	18	—
Compton	4	—	16	—	3	—	12	—

North-Eastern Transvaal Bowling

	Overs	Mdns	Runs	Wkts
Waites.............	2	—	9	—
Hayward..........	30	—	175	—
J. Waller..........	23	—	171	2
Patterson	11	—	94	—
L. Waller..........	1	—	3	—
Funston	4	—	32	2

ENGLAND v SOUTH AFRICA

First Test Match

Played at Durban, December 16, 17, 18, 20, 1948

England won by two wickets. No greater support could have been given to the contention of cricket lovers that an exciting cricket match can provide as intense a thrill as anything else in sport than by the drama of the final stages. With three balls left any one of four results remained possible. Before Bedser brought the scores level with a single from Tuckett off the sixth delivery of the last over, a draw or a tie could be visualised as easily as a victory for either side.

Gladwin hit at but missed the seventh ball. Then in a mid-wicket conference about the last ball he and Bedser decided to run in any event except the wicket being hit. Few of their England colleagues in the pavilion could bear the strain of watching as Tuckett began his run-up. As he did so the fieldsmen started to run in like sprinters towards the wicket to prevent the single which would win the match. Gladwin went into his stumps, swung his bat, but again missed his stroke. The ball struck his thigh and bounced a yard or two in front of him. From short-leg Mann pounced on the ball, but both batsmen galloped to safety. With Bedser and Gladwin executing a jubilation one-step, hundreds of people invading the pitch and some chairing off their varying heroes, there ended a Test which will provide a rich memory for everyone fortunate enough to have participated or to have watched.

By their superior batting in the worst conditions England deserved to win, but, when an hour from time six England wickets were gone for 70 in the task of making 128, the odds looked considerably in favour of South Africa. Their prospects slumped when, for three-quarters of an hour, Compton and Jenkins fought through the speed attack of McCarthy and Tuckett on a pitch from which the ball at times lifted abruptly and at others skidded through scarcely an inch off the greasy turf. At any time during this partnership England would have been justified in appealing against the light. Equally South Africa would have been within their rights in complaining that the steady rain made the ball too slippery for proper hold. The fact the neither team did so and that to the end South Africa did not resort to what would have been legitimate negative bowling tactics exemplified the grand spirit in which the Test was played. When after the dismissals of Compton, bowled by a shooter, and Jenkins, Bedser and Gladwin came together with 12 runs wanted in the last ten minutes the light was turned almost to darkness, and this probably accounted for a missed catch given by Gladwin from the first ball he received. That was the ultimate blow to South Africa.

Nothing was more unexpected than South Africa's first innings collapse. True, the pitch – the same as used for the notorious timeless Test ten years before – was of such character that at one end the ball went through lower than at the other, and Bedser and Gladwin swung late in the humid atmosphere, but the main reason for England's success was superlative fielding. The catch at short-leg by which Watkins, whose fielding largely influenced his selection, disposed of Nourse, typified a day when everything went right for England and most things wrong for South Africa.

When Nourse placed a ball to leg, Watkins dived swiftly to his right and with one hand inches from the turf grasped the catch as he rolled over. That broke the Mitchell-Nourse stand of 51 at a time when the attack looked to have been mastered. It was the turning point of the innings. Next came a brilliant throw by Washbrook, who from right angles to the wicket threw out Wade. Three fine catches by Evans and two by Compton at backward short-leg off Bedser completed England's joy day. After a single by Hutton, bad light followed by rain prevented further play.

Less than three hours' cricket was possible next day before bad light caused an early stoppage. Then came a heavy rainstorm. In the time available England lost two wickets in getting to within 17 of South Africa's total. Hutton and Washbrook began so confidently against the fast-medium bowlers that 50 came in fifty minutes, but upon the introduction of a slow attack the character of the batting changed completely. On a pitch taking spin and from which the ball continued to go through low, Mann, with left-arm slows, and Rowan (off-breaks) pinned down England's premier batsmen. Mann's two wickets in thirteen overs cost only 15 runs.

Batsmen struggled for runs even more on Saturday, which was full of dramatic incident. Before bad light brought play to an early end for the third day in succession, nineteen wickets fell for 199 runs. An important part in the day's thrilling events was caused by a changed decision by Mann on the rolling of the pitch. After a pre-breakfast inspection, Mann asked for the pitch to be rolled early to repair any damage caused by the storm, but he changed his mind before the ground staff arrived, and by delaying the rolling till just before the start ensured that the pitch would not improve.

By the time the heavy roller was put on, a dry crust had formed on the surface and, as the rolling made this crumble, the pitch became all in favour of slow bowlers. At once Nourse brought his spin attack into operation. Mann and Rowan bowled unchanged for the last two hours and three-quarters of the England innings, in which eight wickets fell for 109 runs. The ball turned a good deal and lifted quickly, but Compton was in grimly determined mood. His innings contained no sparkle, but was worth more than many a double century on turf favourable to batting.

Although England were not so well equipped in bowling to take advantage of the conditions, they dismissed four men for 90 before a stoppage for bad light occurred. In order not to handicap his batsmen still further, Nourse did not have the pitch rolled, but he alone shaped confidently against Wright, who showed a return to form. When play stopped an hour from time it was announced that no resumption would be made that evening, but Mann rightly pointed out the possibility of improvement in the light and the first statement was revoked. Even so, no further play became possible.

South Africa began the final day two runs behind with six wickets left. Fine innings by Wade and Begbie, who added 85 for the fifth wicket, raised their hopes to such an extent that although the innings closed for 129 more runs, England's chances of making 128 to win looked no more than reasonable.

Two hours and a quarter were left for play, but five minutes were lost through a knee injury to Nourse and twelve minutes because of a sharp shower. From the start there could be no mistake about England's intentions; but attempts at big hitting involved risks. Off the first ball he received from Tuckett, Washbrook was dropped on the boundary, and when, after the loss of Hutton, Mann promoted himself in the order, he was missed in the deep. In both instances the fieldsman could be excused for not holding a ball made slippery by the persistent drizzle. A superb slip catch by Mitchell, which helped 19-year-old McCarthy to his first wicket, began a remarkable change of fortunes.

McCarthy maintained pace, length and hostility in a splendid spell of eighty-five minutes, in which, by taking six wickets for 33 runs in ten overs, he brought South Africa to within an ace of victory. At no time was he other than difficult to play, but Compton and Jenkins warded off disaster while adding 45 for the seventh wicket. Unfortunately for South Africa, the wet ball presented a severe handicap to their spin bowlers, otherwise England's task might have been even harder than it was.

South Africa

E. A. Rowan c Evans b Jenkins	7	– c Compton b Jenkins	16
O. Wynne c Compton b Bedser	5	– c Watkins b Wright	4
B. Mitchell c Evans b Bedser	27	– b Wright	19
A. D. Nourse c Watkins b Wright	37	– c and b Bedser	32
W. Wade run out	8	– b Jenkins	63
D. Begbie c Compton b Bedser	37	– c Mann b Bedser	48
O. C. Dawson b Gladwin	24	– c Compton b Wright	3
A. M. Rowan not out	5	– b Wright	15
L. Tuckett lbw b Gladwin	1	– not out	3
N. Mann c Evans b Gladwin	4	– c Mann b Compton	10
C. McCarthy b Bedser	0	– b Jenkins	0
B 3, l-b 2, n-b 1	6	B 1, l-b 5	6

1/9 2/18 3/69 4/80 5/99   161   1/22 2/22 3/67 4/89 5/174   219
6/148 7/150 8/152 9/160   6/179 7/208 8/208 9/219

England

L. Hutton c McCarthy b A. Rowan	83	– c Dawson b Tuckett	5
C. Washbrook c Wade b Mann	35	– lbw b Mann	25
R. T. Simpson c Begbie b Mann	5	– c E. Rowan b McCarthy	0
D. C. S. Compton c Wade b Mann	72	– b McCarthy	28
A. Watkins c Nourse b A. Rowan	9	– b McCarthy	4
F. G. Mann c E. Rowan b A. Rowan	19	– c Mitchell b McCarthy	13
T. G. Evans c Wynne b A. Rowan	0	– b McCarthy	4
R. O. Jenkins c Mitchell b Mann	5	– c Wade b McCarthy	22
A. V. Bedser c Tuckett b Mann	11	– not out	1
C. Gladwin not out	0	– not out	7
D. V. P. Wright c Tuckett b Mann	0		
B 2, l-b 12	14	B 9, l-b 10	19

1/84 2/104 3/146 4/172 5/212   253   1/25 2/49 3/52 4/64   (8 wkts) 128
6/212 7/221 8/247 9/253   5/64 6/70 7/115 8/117

England Bowling

	Overs	Mdns	Runs	Wkts	Overs	Mdns	Runs	Wkts
Bedser	13.5	2	39	4	18	5	51	2
Gladwin	12	3	21	3	7	3	15	—
Jenkins	14	3	50	1	22.3	6	64	3
Wright	9	3	29	1	26	3	72	4
Compton	2	—	5	—	16	11	11	1
Watkins	3	—	11	—				

South Africa Bowling

	Overs	Mdns	Runs	Wkts	Overs	Mdns	Runs	Wkts
McCarthy	9	2	20	—	12	2	43	6
Dawson	3	—	16	—				
Tuckett	6	—	36	—	10	—	38	1
A. Rowan	44	8	108	4	4	—	15	—
Mann	37.4	14	59	6	2	—	13	1

ENGLAND v SOUTH AFRICA

Second Test Match

Played at Johannesburg, December 27, 28, 29, 30, 1948

Drawn. Bowlers were not sorry when the first Test match to be played on the new Ellis Park ground came to an end. From first to last ball everything was in favour of batsmen. The pitch played perfectly and in the rarefied atmosphere the ball did not swerve or swing. Not only did Hutton and Washbrook set up a Test record partnership for the first wicket with 359, but all through batsmen were so much on top that 1,193 runs were scored for the loss of only 22 wickets, four men hit centuries, four others passed 50, and on the last day no more than one wicket went down. At the end of the match the turf showed no signs of wear.

More than 35,000, the biggest crowd to watch a cricket match in South Africa, baked under a scorching sun while England's opening pair beat record after record and finished only eleven short of the best stand for any wicket in England-South Africa Tests, the 370 by W. J. Edrich and D. Compton at Lord's in 1947.

Hutton and Washbrook first concentrated on wearing down the attack, and they made 65 in 105 minutes before lunch. When the bowling had lost its sting they gradually increased their pace, and after tea runs came at a fast rate, so that 359 was reached in 290 minutes before the tiring Hutton threw away his wicket. His off and cover drives touched perfection and he scored many runs with a leg sweep. Hutton hit sixteen 4s. Washbrook, who also had showed signs of tiring, lifted a catch to long-leg in McCarthy's next over. After a quiet start Washbrook hit freely in his highest innings in Test cricket, which contained eighteen 4s. Full-blooded hooks and square-cuts predominated in his chanceless display.

Further severe punishment of the attack came in a third-wicket stand of 150 by Compton and Crapp, but attempts by the remaining batsmen to score quickly were not successful, the last seven wickets falling in seventy-five minutes for 89 runs. Like Hutton, Compton made full use of the leg sweep. His fifth century of the tour brought his average at this stage to 116 in eleven innings. The analysis did no justice to the fine spells of off-break bowling by A. Rowan, who caused the batsmen most trouble.

On a pitch still ideal for batting, England's prospects of dismissing South Africa twice looked slight. Accordingly the swift loss of Wynne and E. Rowan was a big blow to South Africa, but Mitchell, Nourse and Wade brought about a recovery, and the ease with which Tuckett and Mann batted in a ninth-wicket stand of 40 revealed the big task still facing England. South Africa's moderate total could be explained largely by a combination of England's attacking bowling and brilliant fielding, together with a series of batting blunders unlikely to occur again in the same match.

Even when Wynne was out quickly in the follow-on, chances of a definite result seemed remote. England's chief hope lay in separating E. E. Rowan and Mitchell early on the last day, but by rigid defence they removed practically all danger. Rowan, whose omission from the Third Test was known earlier in the day, stayed to the end of the match, batting altogether six hours ten minutes for the highest score made against MCC in the tour. He allowed himself no freedom till he had seen South Africa safe from defeat. The irony of the situation was apparent to all – not least to Rowan himself – but in view of the proximity of the Third Test and the large distances players had to travel the Selectors could not do otherwise than choose the side while the Second Test was in progress. The only blemish in Rowan's innings occurred when with his total 59 he gave a sharp chance to mid-off from Wright, but an injured ankle prevented Mann from getting to the ball as fast as he would have done otherwise. After Mitchell was caught at short slip, Nourse helped Rowan play out time in an unbroken partnership of 163. Sympathy could be felt for England's bowlers and fielders, who toiled for over thirteen hours in intense heat in the forlorn hope of dismissing South Africa twice.

The attendance for the match reached 75,000, a record for South African cricket.

England

L. Hutton c Wade b McCarthy.......... 158	A. V. Bedser b McCarthy.............. 12
C. Washbrook c Begbie b McCarthy 195	C. Gladwin lbw b Dawson 23
J. F. Crapp c and b Mitchell............. 56	D. V. P. Wright not out................ 1
D. C. S. Compton c Mitchell b Mann...... 114	
A. Watkins c Wade b Mann 7	B 3, l-b 10................... 13
F. G. Mann c McCarthy b Mann 7	
T. G. Evans run out 18	1/359 2/366 3/516 4/540 5/549 608
R. O. Jenkins st Wade b A. Rowan........ 4	6/550 7/570 8/576 9/602

South Africa

E. A. Rowan lbw b Bedser .... 8 – not out 156
O. Wynne lbw b Wright .... 4 – lbw b Bedser.................. 4
B. Mitchell b Gladwin......................... 86 – c Hutton b Wright 40
A. D. Nourse lbw b Wright.................... 32 – not out 56
W. W. Wade c Evans b Compton................ 85
D. Begbie c Watkins b Jenkins 5
O. C. Dawson c Watkins b Jenkins.............. 12
A. Rowan b Wright.......................... 8
L. Tuckett st Evans b Jenkins.................. 38
N. Mann st Evans b Jenkins 23
C. McCarthy not out 1
B 4, l-b 7, n-b 2..................... 13   B 9, l-b 4, n-b 1........... 14

1/12 2/17 3/96 4/191 5/204   315   1/15 2/108   (2 wkts) 270
6/220 7/234 8/273 9/313

South Africa Bowling

	Overs	Mdns	Runs	Wkts
McCarthy.........	26	1	102	3
Dawson	16.5	3	59	1
A. Rowan........	41	4	155	1
Tuckett	12	—	55	—
Mann	30	2	107	3
Begbie...........	6	—	38	—
Mitchell..........	18	1	79	1

England Bowling

	Overs	Mdns	Runs	Wkts	Overs	Mdns	Runs	Wkts
Bedser...........	22	6	42	1	17	4	51	1
Gladwin..........	20	6	29	1	16	5	37	—
Jenkins	21.4	3	88	3	19	3	54	—
Wright	26	2	104	3	14	3	35	1
Compton	10	—	34	1	13	3	31	—
Watkins	5	2	5	1	12	2	48	—

MCC TEAM v A NATAL XI

Played at Pietermaritzburg, February 19, 21, 22, 1949

Drawn. In a thrilling race with time, MCC finished only ten short of 270 which Nourse challenged them to get in just over two hours. As usual Compton revelled in the chase for victory. In his most dashing mood he hit 141 out of 217 in 99 minutes, his varied strokes including a 6 and twenty 4s. He was dismissed by a spectacular catch on the edge of the boundary in an over in which Watkins was punished for 22 runs. His seventh century of the tour beat the previous best achievement by an overseas cricketer in South Africa, and when 66 he passed the record aggregate by a touring player to the Union, the 1,489 by

J. B. Hobbs in 1913-14. These distinctions were not confirmed until three weeks later when the match received first-class status. In the first MCC innings Tremlett hit his initial century in first-class cricket. In the second he took part with Compton in a stand of 190 in under 90 minutes. For Natal XI, Nourse hit his third century in successive matches against MCC. He was free and adventurous from the start. Nourse received good assistance from de Gersigny, one of the few young aggressive batsmen met by MCC on the tour, and Dowling, a stylish left-hander. de Gersigny helped add 101 for the third wicket and Dowling 109 for the fourth.

A Natal XI

D. R. Fell c Griffith b Tremlett	9	– c Tremlett b Bedser	45
D. Turner b Bedser	4	– c and b Jenkins	18
L. de Gersigny c Watkins b Wright	77	– c Bedser b Compton	24
A. D. Nourse lbw b Wright	117	– b Palmer	76
D. F. Dowling c Crapp b Bedser	43	– lbw b Wright	13
J. Watkins c Crapp b Bedser	1	– b Palmer	42
L. Rutherford hit wkt b Jenkins	8	– not out	4
R. J. Williams c Palmer b Wright	2	– not out	19
L. Upton b Bedser	14		
A. Tayfield st Evans b Jenkins	2		
D. Dinkleman not out	1		
Extras	10	Extras	16
	288	(6 wkts dec.)	**257**

MCC

C. H. Palmer b Dinkleman	80	– c Williams b Dinkleman	29
R. T. Simpson b Tayfield	17	– lbw b Dinkleman	20
D. C. S. Compton st Williams b Tayfield	15	– c Fell b Watkins	141
J. F. Crapp lbw b Dinkleman	14		
A. Watkins c Nourse b Dinkleman	2		
M. F. Tremlett c Watkins b Tayfield	105	– not out	63
T. G. Evans c Gersigny b Dinkleman	6	– st Williams b Dinkleman	2
S. C. Griffith c Nourse b Dinkleman	1		
R. O. Jenkins c Rutherford b Tayfield	32		
A. V. Bedser not out	0		
D. V. P. Wright not out	0		
Extras	4	Extras	5
	276	(4 wkts)	**260**

MCC Bowling

	Overs	Mdns	Runs	Wkts	Overs	Mdns	Runs	Wkts
Bedser	23.4	6	70	4	14	1	44	1
Tremlett	9	2	14	1	4	—	32	—
Jenkins	15	2	78	2	10	—	75	1
Compton	8	1	34	—	8	—	37	1
Watkins	4	1	14	—				
Wright	16	4	68	3	8	2	43	1
Palmer					4	1	10	2

A Natal XI Bowling

	Overs	Mdns	Runs	Wkts	Overs	Mdns	Runs	Wkts
Watkins	7	3	25	—	4	1	43	1
Rutherford	12	4	32	—	3	1	11	—
Dinkleman	36	10	113	5	16.7	1	112	3
Tayfield	32.7	8	102	4	9	—	51	—
Upton					6	—	38	—

MCC v ORANGE FREE STATE

Played at Bloemfontein, November 9, 10, 1956

MCC won by an innings and 168 runs, gaining another overwhelming success with a day to spare. Insole, who led the side for the first time, won the toss and MCC batted on the fastest pitch they had met so far. Richardson soon fell to a catch at the wicket for the third time in succession, but Cowdrey and Oakman mastered a moderate attack and added 318 in 220 minutes, the highest partnership for the second wicket ever recorded in South Africa. Cowdrey hit twenty-one 4s while scoring 173 in four hours twelve minutes, and Oakman stayed three hours forty minutes for 150 which included one 6 and eighteen 4s. Insole declared first thing on the second morning and Orange Free State were dismissed twice in a day. Carlstein, an eighteen-year-old batsman, showed promise in each innings, and Johnstone, Fox and Kirby also made reasonable scores, but nearly everyone was baffled by the mixed spin of Wardle, who took 14 wickets for 96 runs. Insole claimed the extra half-hour and finished the match with nine minutes remaining. At the start of the OFS second innings Statham tore the fibres under his right heel.

MCC

P. E. Richardson c Kirby b Blenkinsop..... 9	T. G. Evans not out.................... 14
M. C. Cowdrey c Richardson b Blenkinsop .173	B 1, l-b 5, n-b 1.............. 7
A. S. M. Oakman c Johnstone b Blenkinsop.150	—
D. C. S. Compton c Fox b Fairbairn 32	1/19 2/337 (4 wkts dec.) 420
T. E. Bailey not out.................... 35	3/339 4/400

D. J. Insole, J. H. Wardle, J. C. Laker, J. B. Statham and P. J. Loader did not bat.

Orange Free State

S. Hanson c Evans b Statham....................	0 – b Wardle......................	19
C. Richardson b Loader	0 – b Wardle......................	19
E. Johnstone c Oakman b Wardle.................	21 – c Oakman b Wardle	3
D. Schonegevel c Bailey b Loader................	6 – lbw b Wardle	2
P. Carlstein c Wardle b Laker...................	25 – b Compton	41
S. Fox not out...............................	17 – c and b Compton	29
I. Kirby c Evans b Wardle	0 – not out	47
G. Jackson c Bailey b Wardle...................	0 – b Wardle......................	7
I. Littleford st Evans b Wardle	1 – b Wardle......................	0
D. Fairbairn st Evans b Wardle	0 – st Evans b Wardle.............	8
A. Blenkinsop c Statham b Wardle...............	0 – c Loader b Wardle	6
L-b 1	1	

1/0 2/4 3/18 4/44 5/54   71   1/30 2/40 3/41 4/106 5/113   181
6/55 7/61 8/69 9/71   6/115 7/133 8/133 9/169

Orange Free State Bowling

	Overs	Mdns	Runs	Wkts
Littleford.........	15	3	68	—
Blenkinsop	20	2	97	3
Fairbairn..........	20	—	110	1
Hanson............	10	1	30	—
Fox...............	7	—	47	—
Jackson...........	10	—	45	—
Carlstein..........	3	—	16	—

MCC Bowling

	Overs	Mdns	Runs	Wkts	Overs	Mdns	Runs	Wkts
Statham	5	—	16	1	1	1	—	—
Loader	6	1	13	2	7	2	30	—
Bailey	3	1	7	—	4	2	8	—
Laker	9	3	18	1	13	5	20	—
Wardle	7.1	1	16	6	18.2	3	80	8
Compton					10	—	43	2

Umpires: J. Laupos and G. Niddrie.

MCC v RHODESIA

Played at Salisbury, November 23, 24, 25, 1956

MCC won by an innings and 292 runs with a day remaining, their biggest success of the tour. Rhodesia, who made three changes, were no match for MCC on a pitch which gave fast bowlers a fair amount of help. After losing three wickets for 66, MCC took control. May was again in tremendous form, playing his fourth three-figure innings in succession, and Bailey shared a stand of 301 in 245 minutes. May's 206, made in four and a half hours, included two 6s and thirty-three 4s. Evans hit 50 in three-quarters of an hour and was the first of three victims in an over to Lawrence, a tall, fast-medium bowler who alone troubled the batsmen. Rhodesia were helpless against the controlled swing of Loader, and after losing their first six wickets for 11, followed on 444 behind. Loader took two wickets in his first over before twisting a knee when losing the heel of a boot. A seventh wicket stand of 50 between a promising eighteen-year-old schoolboy, Bland, and Arnott delayed MCC's triumphant progress.

MCC

M. C. Cowdrey c Coventry b Barber 20
A. S. M. Oakman c Duckworth b Paton.... 26
T. E. Bailey b Lawrence 110
D. J. Insole lbw b Lawrence 8
P. B. H. May c Coventry b Barber 206
B. Taylor c Mansell b Lawrence 46
T. G. Evans c and b Lawrence 50
J. C. Laker c Coventry b Lawrence 0
G. A. R. Lock c O'Connell-Jones
           b Lawrence. 0
F. H. Tyson not out 19
P. J. Loader c sub b Barber............. 0
           B 10, l-b 4, n-b 2 16
                                          ——
1/42 2/48 3/66 4/367 5/393   501
6/465 7/465 8/465 9/500

Rhodesia

D. O'Connell-Jones lbw b Loader............. 2 – c Bailey b Loader 0
G. Barber lbw b Tyson .... 0 – lbw b Loader................... 2
C. A. R. Duckworth lbw b Tyson............. 7 – c Insole b Bailey............. 9
D. J. Lewis lbw b Loader .... 0 – lbw b Laker................... 4
P. N. F. Mansell c Evans b Loader .... 0 – c and b Tyson.............. 12
M. Davies b Loader .... 0 – c Evans b Tyson........... 18
C. Bland c Evans b Loader.................. 19 – c and b Lock.............. 38
D. B. Arnott c Oakman b Lock............... 9 – run out 22
R. W. Coventry c Cowdrey b Loader.......... 13 – b Laker................... 7
H. Paton b Loader .... 6 – c Oakman b Laker 21
G. B. L. Lawrence not out................... 0 – not out 12
           N-b 1.............................. 1   B 3, l-b 3, n-b 1 7

1/1 2/7 3/7 4/7 5/7 6/11   57   1/4 2/6 3/13 4/23 5/47   152
7/34 8/51 9/57   6/48 7/98 8/105 9/127

Rhodesia Bowling

	Overs	Mdns	Runs	Wkts
Lawrence	35	11	104	6
Coventry	30	4	138	—
Barber	23.4	5	108	3
Paton	24	4	98	1
Mansell	9	—	37	—

MCC Bowling

	Overs	Mdns	Runs	Wkts	Overs	Mdns	Runs	Wkts
Tyson	8	2	16	2	11	4	23	2
Loader	13	3	28	7	3	1	3	2
Laker	4	2	3	—	19	6	63	3
Lock	2.4	1	9	1	12.3	4	31	1
Bailey					6	2	25	1

Umpires: H. Fox and A. Maddocks.

MCC v SOUTH AFRICAN XI

Played at Pretoria, December 7, 8, 10, 11, 1956

South African XI won by 38 runs and ended MCC's one hundred per cent record. This was also the first time MCC had lost on a turf pitch in South Africa; their first defeat in that country since 1930-31 and their first defeat outside a Test Match since 1913-14. The game was played on a football ground and the pitch had been laid only three months. It broke up on the first day and batsmen found it almost impossible to make a stroke. The South African side gained a big advantage in winning the toss, but the MCC batting, even allowing for conditions, disappointed. Spin bowlers were always in command, Tayfield and Wardle particularly enjoying themselves. A good innings by Funston turned the scales and MCC were eventually set to get 148 to win. They lost half the side for 41, and although Bailey made a great effort, staying four hours five minutes for 26, they never looked like getting the runs. An unusual incident occurred at the end of the third day when McGlew ran off the field to see Insole about extra time, and Bailey and Lock, the not out batsmen, walked in with the umpires with the rest of the fieldsmen standing their ground. The batsmen had to return, having been under a misapprehension about the rules existing for extra time.

South African XI

D. J. McGlew st Taylor b Lock	41	– lbw b Wardle	13
A. I. Taylor b Wardle	34	– lbw b Loader	2
W. R. Endean b Wardle	11	– run out	3
K. J. Funston c Bailey b Loader	10	– c and b Lock	55
C. Burger b Lock	0	– b Wardle	0
J. Watkins b Wardle	8	– b Loader	2
P. Carlstein c Richardson b Lock	4	– b Wardle	9
R. Pearce lbw b Lock	0	– b Wardle	8
H. Tayfield st Taylor b Wardle	4	– b Wardle	7
K. Gibbs not out	2	– not out	0
G. B. L. Lawrence b Statham	12	– b Wardle	1
B 3, n-b 9	12	B 9, l-b 4, n-b 1	14

1/57 2/85 3/106 4/107 5/109   138   1/6 2/10 3/63 4/63 5/68   116
6/113 7/113 8/120 9/123   6/87 7/103 8/113 9/113

MCC

P. E. Richardson c Lawrence b Tayfield	23	– b Tayfield		4
A. S. M. Oakman b Lawrence	2	– run out		6
D. J. Insole lbw b Lawrence	7	– c Funston b Lawrence		0
D. C. S. Compton b Tayfield	15	– c Lawrence b Tayfield		2
M. C. Cowdrey c Burger b Tayfield	16	– b Gibbs		13
T. E. Bailey not out	20	– c Carlstein b Tayfield		26
B. Taylor lbw b Tayfield	4	– lbw b Tayfield		6
G. A. R. Lock b Tayfield	5	– c McGlew b Tayfield		0
J. H. Wardle b Watkins	1	– lbw b Gibbs		21
P. J. Loader c McGlew b Tayfield	8	– c Watkins b Tayfield		10
J. B. Statham b Watkins	0	– not out		1
L-b 4, n-b 2	6	B 10, l-b 8		18

1/10 2/37 3/37 4/62 5/69   107   1/16 2/16 3/16 4/21 5/41   109
6/73 7/81 8/82 9/93   6/79 7/88 8/90 9/106

MCC Bowling

	Overs	Mdns	Runs	Wkts	Overs	Mdns	Runs	Wkts
Statham	10.1	1	17	1	4	1	9	—
Loader	11	3	18	1	6	1	14	2
Lock	24	8	63	4	15	5	49	1
Wardle	25	12	28	4	18.3	9	30	6

South African XI Bowling

	Overs	Mdns	Runs	Wkts	Overs	Mdns	Runs	Wkts
Lawrence	13	4	26	2	24	9	24	1
Gibbs	6	2	13	—	12	5	19	2
Tayfield	16	4	36	6	36.5	18	47	6
Watkins	9.6	2	26	2	3	2	1	—

Umpires: G. I. Fitzpatrick and G. S. Hawkins.

ENGLAND v SOUTH AFRICA

Second Test Match

Played at Cape Town, January 1, 2, 3, 4, 5, 1957

England won by 312 runs and placed themselves in a strong position to win the series. They took control almost from the start and never relaxed, finally racing to victory when South Africa collapsed badly for the second time in two Tests. Cricket history was made on the last day when the first handled ball dismissal occurred in a Test Match.

Tyson, because of tonsillitis, could not be considered for England, being replaced by Loader. McGlew, despite his shoulder trouble, captained South Africa, displacing Taylor. May won the toss for the second time and it quickly became obvious that the pitch lacked pace which, with South Africa's type of attack, proved a big handicap to them. Richardson and Bailey gave England a sound start, but soon after lunch South Africa broke the stand and, in the space of seventy minutes, three wickets, including that of May, fell for the addition of 43 runs.

The situation changed when Cowdrey joined Compton. Neither took the slightest risk, but they rarely looked in trouble. They added 67 and by the close England, with a total of 214 for four, had recovered well. Tayfield, going on fifty minutes after the start of the match, bowled unchanged at one end until the close, sending down 41 successive overs and taking three of the four wickets for 69.

England lost Insole early next morning, but South Africa's hopes of finishing the innings quickly were dashed by Cowdrey and Evans, who put on 93 in eighty-five minutes. Evans, one of the few batsmen who attempted attacking strokes, scored 62 of the runs. The next three wickets fell for 20, but Cowdrey remained, and when Statham, the last man, joined him he needed 20 for his century. At last, departing from rigid defence, Cowdrey, after being missed at long-on off Tayfield when 85, punished that bowler for 13 in an over and reached his century. One run later he was out, having batted six hours ten minutes and hit one 6 and nine 4s. His solid play helped considerably to give England their good total.

McGlew and Goddard looked safe enough when they opened the South Africa innings, but when the slow bowlers appeared the situation changed rapidly. McGlew, batting with his shoulder strapped, fell in Laker's fourth over, and although the fast-medium Loader took the next two wickets it was apparent that spin was going to decide the match. South Africa finished the second day at 51 for three and despite useful efforts from McLean and Waite they never really recovered. Laker could not get the ball to turn quickly, but Wardle, with his off-breaks and googlies, caused innumerable problems. He spun the ball a prodigious amount, although not quickly enough on the slow pitch to be really unplayable.

Although leading by 164, May did not enforce the follow-on and England built an impregnable position. When the third day ended Richardson and Bailey had scored 21 without loss and they carried their stand to 74. Adcock could not play on the fourth day because of a sore toe, and van Ryneveld, although fielding could not bowl because of a slightly fractured little finger on his right hand.

McGlew endeavoured to keep down runs and did not employ a slip or close fieldsman for either Heine or Goddard, who bowled unchanged throughout the morning and for twenty minutes after lunch. The deep defensive field succeeded in restricting England's rate of progress, but steadily the lead mounted. Compton and Cowdrey again shared a good stand and this time Cowdrey showed his wide range of strokes, scoring 61 of the 87 added in eighty-six minutes.

May declared when Compton gave a return catch in the last over before tea and South Africa were set to get 385 to win in eight hours on a pitch which made quick scoring extremely difficult. Their task was almost hopeless and from the first they decided on defensive tactics in an effort to save the game. Again Wardle was England's trump card. He bowled McGlew round his legs in his second over and quickly followed by getting Keith caught at cover.

South Africa ended the fourth day at 41 for two, and although defeat looked inevitable it came much quicker than expected. Wardle, again making the ball spin considerably, did almost as he pleased and the match ended after ninety minutes on the last day. Four wickets fell at 67 and altogether the remaining eight wickets went down for the addition of 31 runs, South Africa being out for the same total as their second innings in the First Test.

Wardle's seven for 36 were his best Test figures and his beautifully controlled and varied spin left South Africa nonplussed.

The "handled ball' incident occurred when Endean pushed out his leg outside the off stump to Laker in the second innings. The ball rose high and might well have fallen on to the stumps had not Endean thrown up a hand and diverted it. On appeal the umpire had no option but to give him out. Endean, curiously, was concerned in the previous strange Test dismissal, being the wicket-keeper when Hutton was given out "obstructing the field" at The Oval in 1951. Endean might have made a catch had not Hutton knocked away the ball when trying to protect his wicket.

England

P. E. Richardson lbw b Heine	45	– c Endean b Goddard 44
T. E. Bailey c Waite b Tayfield	34	– b Heine 28
D. C. S. Compton c McLean b Tayfield	58	– c and b Goddard 64
P. B. H. May c Waite b Tayfield	8	– c Waite b Heine 15
M. C. Cowdrey lbw b Adcock	101	– c Waite b Tayfield 61
D. J. Insole c Goddard b Adcock	29	– not out 3
T. G. Evans c McGlew b Goddard	62	– c Endean b Goddard 1
J. H. Wardle st Waite b Tayfield	3	
J. C. Laker b Adcock	0	
P. J. Loader c Keith b Tayfield	10	
J. B. Statham not out	2	
B 6, l-b 6, n-b 5	17	L-b 2, n-b 2 4

1/76 2/88 3/116 4/183 5/233   369   1/74 2/74   (6 wkts dec.) 220
6/326 7/334 8/335 9/346   3/109 4/196 5/208 6/220

South Africa

D. J. McGlew c Cowdrey b Laker	14	– b Wardle 7
T. L. Goddard c Evans b Loader	18	– c Bailey b Wardle 26
H. J. Keith c Evans b Loader	14	– c May b Wardle 4
C. B. van Ryneveld b Wardle	25	– not out 0
H. J. Tayfield run out	5	– c Evans b Wardle 4
R. A. McLean c May b Statham	42	– lbw b Laker 22
J. H. B. Waite c Evans b Wardle	49	– c Cowdrey b Wardle 2
W. R. Endean b Wardle	17	– handled ball 3
J. C. Watkins not out	7	– c and b Wardle 0
P. Heine b Wardle	0	– b Wardle 0
N. A. T. Adcock c Evans b Wardle	11	– b Laker 1
B 1, l-b 1, n-b 1	3	L-b 2, n-b 1 3

1/23 2/39 3/48 4/63 5/110   205   1/21 2/28 3/42 4/56 5/67   72
6/126 7/178 8/191 9/191   6/67 7/67 8/67 9/71

South Africa Bowling

	Overs	Mdns	Runs	Wkts	Overs	Mdns	Runs	Wkts
Heine	19	—	78	1	21	1	67	2
Adcock	22.2	2	54	3	3	—	8	—
Tayfield	53	21	130	5	12	4	33	1
Goddard	38	12	74	1	17.5	1	62	3
van Ryneveld	3	—	16	—				
Watkins					10	2	46	—

England Bowling

	Overs	Mdns	Runs	Wkts	Overs	Mdns	Runs	Wkts
Statham	16	—	38	1	8	2	12	—
Loader	21	5	33	2	7	2	11	—
Laker	28	8	65	1	14.1	9	7	2
Bailey	11	5	13	—				
Wardle	23.6	9	53	5	19	3	36	7
Compton					2	1	3	—

Umpires: D. Collins and V. Costello

ENGLAND v SOUTH AFRICA

Fourth Test Match

Played at Johannesburg, February 15, 16, 18, 19, 20, 1957

South Africa won by 17 runs and gained their first victory over England in their own country for 26 years. Never before had they beaten England in South Africa on a turf pitch. The match proved a personal triumph for Tayfield, although both sides deserve credit for making the game so exciting. The cricket followed the usual pattern of slow, cautious batting, but there was plenty of interest throughout.

Tayfield established a new record for a South African bowler in taking nine wickets in an innings of a Test Match. He also became the first South African to take 13 wickets in a Test against England.

England relied on the team which drew at Durban and South Africa made one change, Duckworth making his Test début in place of Keith. The pitch, shorn of most of its grass in contrast to the previous game on the ground, looked ideal for batting and so it proved.

Winning the toss for the first time, South Africa quickly showed their intention of going boldly for victory. Pithey did not last long, but Goddard again revealed his skill and Waite, promoted to number three, helped in the first century stand of the tour against MCC, adding 112 for the second wicket. Both were a little fortunate with snicks, but they batted well and set South Africa on the road to their good total. Waite scored faster than Goddard, who, third out, stayed four hours ten minutes.

A miss at slip by Insole off Loader cost England dearly. Insole, usually so good in the field, had not dropped a catch the entire tour, but he allowed McLean to escape when three and the hard-hitting South African stayed almost four hours. He had plenty of luck early in his innings when he was right out of touch, but later played splendidly.

On the second morning England made a good effort to swing the game, turning the overnight score of 234 for four to 251 for six, but McLean found a steady partner in van Ryneveld, who helped to add 58. McLean was run out when seven short of his second century in successive Tests. South Africa's 340 was easily the highest score against the touring team, being the first time a side had reached 300.

England began shakily, both the opening batsmen being out for 40, but Insole, promoted to number three, continued his fine form of recent weeks and May at last found something like his touch in Tests. They put on 91 before an unusual incident ended the stand. Tayfield unsuccessfully appealed against Insole for lbw. The ball went into the hands of Goddard at slip, but Insole, thinking it had gone through, started for a run. Goddard had time to run forward and remove the bails before Insole could regain his crease. This proved an unfortunate blow for England, who never mastered the attack. May, although not at his best, stayed three hours ten minutes before playing on in the last over before lunch on the third day.

Compton played a remarkable innings, being so tied down by the accuracy of Tayfield, that his score at the end of two and a half hours to tea was no more than 13. England at that point were 176 for seven and in danger of following on, but Compton improved after the interval and the tail again proved defiant. Compton remained altogether three and a half hours. The last pair, Loader and Statham, stayed forty-eight minutes and put on 24.

South Africa failed to add to their lead of 89 in the one over bowled in their innings on the third evening. The stage was set for quick scoring on the fourth day, but great-hearted accurate bowling not only prevented this but turned the game so much that England stood a reasonable chance of victory. In two hours to lunch only 51 were scored and the opening partnership of 62 by Pithey and Goddard lasted in all two hours twenty-five minutes.

Trying to make up for lost time the South Africans ran into trouble, losing five wickets for 48 in two hours between lunch and tea. Slight improvement came, but when England went in three-quarters of an hour before the close they needed 232 to win.

Bailey was out just before time and England started the last day requiring 213 at a rate of 34 an hour. This was the most exciting day of the series. England for a long time looked almost certain victors before finally collapsing. South Africa's chief hope was Tayfield. He spun the ball just enough to be difficult and, as in previous Tests, bowled most accurately to a well-placed field.

England decided on a bold policy which nearly succeeded. Richardson and Insole scored 55 in seventy-two minutes for the second wicket and Insole found another good partner in Cowdrey. Twenty-five minutes after lunch England were 147 for two and another 85 were needed, but once the stand of 82 in an hour and forty minutes ended the batting broke down.

Insole's second excellent innings of the game lasted just under three hours. The loss of May and Compton for a single between them was a blow from which England never recovered. Cowdrey made a fine, determined effort and good hitting by Wardle put England back in the picture.

At tea time the game was still open, England wanting 46 with four wickets left, but the end came fifty minutes later with Arthur Tayfield, fielding substitute for Funston, who hurt a leg, catching Loader on the long-on boundary off his brother's bowling.

Hugh Tayfield was deservedly chaired off the field. He bowled throughout the four hours fifty minutes on the final day, sending down 35 overs, and although heavily punished by the early batsmen he always looked menacing. Cowdrey, finding himself running out of partners, tried attacking him, but when he gave a return catch after staying three hours twenty minutes, the end was in sight.

After a closely fought and keen struggle South Africa went into the last Test with a chance of sharing the rubber – an excellent effort considering they were two down after two matches.

South Africa

A. Pithey c Wardle b Bailey	10	– b Laker 18
T. L. Goddard b Bailey	67	– c Evans b Bailey 49
J. H. B. Waite c Evans b Statham	61	– c Cowdrey b Statham 17
K. J. Funston c Evans b Bailey	20	– run out 23
R. A. McLean run out	93	– c Cowdrey b Statham 0
C. A. R. Duckworth c Wardle b Loader	13	– b Wardle 3
W. R. Endean b Statham	13	– c Insole b Bailey 2
C. B. van Ryneveld c Cowdrey b Laker	36	– c and b Statham 12
H. J. Tayfield c Bailey b Wardle	10	– not out 12
P. S. Heine not out	1	– c Insole b Wardle 0
N. A. T. Adcock lbw b Wardle	6	– run out 1
L-b 8, w 1, n-b 1	10	B 4, l-b 1 5

1/22 2/134 3/151 4/172 5/238   340   1/62 2/91 3/94 4/95 5/97   142
6/251 7/309 8/328 9/333   6/104 7/129 8/130 9/131

England

P. E. Richardson c Tyfield b Heine	11	– b Tayfield 39
T. E. Bailey c Waite b Adcock	13	– c Endean b Tayfield 1
D. J. Insole run out	47	– c Tayfield b Goddard 68
P. B. H. May b Adcock	61	– c Endean b Tayfield 0
D. C. S. Compton c Pithey b Heine	42	– c Goddard b Tayfield 1
M. C. Cowdrey c Goddard b Tayfield	8	– c and b Tayfield 55
T. G. Evans c Endean b Tayfield	7	– b Tayfield 8
J. H. Wardle c Goddard b Tayfield	16	– c Waite b Tayfield 22
J. C. Laker lbw b Tayfield	17	– c Duckworth b Tayfield 5
P. J. Loader c Endean b Goddard	13	– c sub b Tayfield 7
J. B. Statham not out	12	– not out 4
L-b 1, n-b 3	4	B 3, l-b 1 4

1/25 2/40 3/131 4/135 5/152   251   1/10 2/65 3/147 4/148 5/156   214
6/160 7/176 8/213 9/227   6/168 7/196 8/199 9/208

England Bowling

	Overs	Mdns	Runs	Wkts	Overs	Mdns	Runs	Wkts
Statham	23	5	81	2	13	1	37	3
Loader	23	3	78	1	13	3	33	—
Bailey	21	3	54	3	13	4	12	2
Wardle	19.6	4	68	2	14	4	29	2
Laker	15	3	49	1	7	1	26	1

South Africa Bowling

	Overs	Mdns	Runs	Wkts	Overs	Mdns	Runs	Wkts
Adcock...........	21	5	52	2	8	1	22	—
Heine	23	6	54	2	8	1	21	—
Goddard..........	25.2	15	22	1	25	5	54	1
Tayfield..........	37	15	79	4	37	11	113	9
van Ryneveld	8	—	40	—				

Umpires: J. McMenamin and B. V. Malan.

NOTES BY THE EDITOR, 1962

SOUTH AFRICA'S STATUS

The automatic disappearance of South Africa from the Imperial Cricket Conference when the country ceased to be a member of the British Commonwealth has left a complex problem. South Africa's matches against other countries can no longer be classified as Tests. They come second to Australia as England's oldest opponents, the first match having taken place at Port Elizabeth in March, 1889. Efforts are being made to find a means of restoring South Africa to membership of the Conference. This move may receive support from England, Australia and New Zealand, whom South Africa meet on the field, but it is likely to be vehemently opposed by the West Indies, India and Pakistan, who because of the colour question, have never met the Springboks at cricket. The matter will come up for discussion again when the Imperial Cricket Conference next meet at Lord's in July. Pakistan, I understand, are putting forward a novel suggestion to form a kind of "second division" to incorporate all the cricket-playing countries which are not Conference members, such as Ceylon, Malaya, Kenya, East and West Africa, Hong Kong, Singapore, Canada, the United States of America, Denmark and Holland. In the end, everything may depend upon whether or not South Africa will agree to change their ideas and consent to play against the "coloured" countries.

ENGLAND IN WEST INDIES

ENGLAND v WEST INDIES
Second Test Match

Played at Queen's Park Oval, Port of Spain, February 11, 12, 13, 14, 16, 1948

Drawn. For holding West Indies to a draw England were indebted mainly to Griffith. In the absence through illness or injury of Brookes, Place and Hardstaff, the batting was sadly weakened, and in his dilemma Allen pressed Griffith into service as opening batsman. Like a true cricketer, the Sussex amateur never allowed the responsibility to worry him. Instead, he curbed his natural impulse, did not attempt anything reckless, and pursued this course so rigidly that he gained the distinction of scoring his maiden century in first-class cricket on his first Test appearance. One cannot praise Griffith too highly for this stupendous effort. At the same time credit must be given also to Ganteaume, a 27-year-old clerk in the Trinidad Civil Service who, in the absence through injury of J. B. Stollmeyer, stepped into the breach and, like Griffith, claimed a century in his first Test. In the course of the match all four opening batsmen reached three figures. England were soon in trouble; brilliant fielding by Gaskin at cover when Griffith called for a sharp single led to Robertson being narrowly run out with only five runs on the board. Ikin, Allen and Evans all began in promising style; in fact Evans hit five grand 4s; but the end of the first day found six England wickets down for 230 with Griffith 110. Seventh to leave at 288, Griffith defied the West Indies bowling for six minutes short of six hours. His only serious error occurred when 75 with the total 157; he lifted Ferguson to long leg, where Christiani, blinded by the sun, lost sight of the ball. Griffith hit fifteen 4s with a variety of strokes, of which the cover-drive was especially attractive. Smithson helped him add 87 for the seventh wicket, and then came a fine display by Laker, who, last out, hit seven 4s in a stay of seventy minutes. Butler gave valuable support while the last stand realised 56. Daring stroke play by Carew quickly established a complete mastery over the English bowling. Wearing a chocolate-coloured felt hat and chewing gum the whole time, Carew, in an unorthodox display, used the hook and pull freely in a dazzling exhibition. Butler alone looked at all difficult, and when 8 and again at 41 Carew offered hard chances off the Nottinghamshire bowler to the slips; but at the drawing of stumps on the second day the West Indies score reached 160 without loss, with Carew 101 and Ganteaume 52. Early next day the big stand ended at 173, when Carew, whose 4s numbered sixteen, was lbw. Weekes enjoyed an early escape, being dropped at first slip off Robertson when only one, but otherwise he hit convincingly, getting six 4s before Butler bowled him with a very fine ball. Meanwhile Ganteaume maintained his defiant attitude, but by this time everyone was admiring the cultured batting of Worrell. Ganteaume duly reached 100 out of 279 in four and a half hours, but only 46 runs came in an hour, and Gomez, the West Indies captain, realised that his men were falling behind the clock. A note was sent out to Ganteaume, who promptly replied by lifting the ball to extra cover, where Ikin accepted the catch. Mainly by off-drives, Ganteaume hit thirteen 4s. Walcott did his utmost to obey his captain and force the pace, but it was Gomez himself who really pushed the score along. His fifth-wicket stand with Worrell, who claimed one 6 and nine 4s, produced 99. Whereas Worrell spent three and a quarter hours over his 97, Gomez made 62 in eighty-six minutes, West Indies raising their total to 447 for six wickets on the third day. On Saturday, Williams attempted to repeat his Barbados performance, and in sixteen minutes helped himself to seven 4s and three singles before Butler finished the innings, which gave West Indies a well-deserved lead of 135.

England's only hope was to play for a draw. Rain cut short the cricket on Saturday by two hours, leaving the outfield slow, and the bowlers used towels to dry the ball when Robertson and Griffith began the grim task. Robertson defended splendidly and Ikin kept up his end for over an hour, but three wickets fell for 70 before stumps were drawn. At one time on the final day West Indies looked likely to force a win, the seventh wicket going at 196, but Robertson received valuable assistance from Smithson, who stayed seventy-five minutes. Then Robertson duly completely his first Test hundred; he altogether stayed five and three-quarter hours before being ninth out, having hit fifteen 4s. West Indies, wanting 141 for victory in fifty-seven minutes, sent in Weekes and Walcott, with Williams number three. Weekes fell to a wonderful right-hand catch by Evans, and at no time did the batsmen look like achieving their objective. Best bowling for England was by Butler, Laker, Ikin and Howorth, but no one looked as good as Ferguson, the stocky leg-break expert, who at times tossed his deliveries skilfully in to the wind. His was a very fine performance in taking eleven wickets on the easy-paced batting wicket. Near the end Allen pulled up lame after sending down two balls in his fifth over.

England

J. D. Robertson run out.	2	– c Christiani b Ferguson	133
S. C. Griffith lbw b Worrell	140	– c Ferguson b Gomez	4
J. T. Ikin b Ferguson	21	– lbw b Ferguson	19
K. Cranston c and b Ferguson	7	– c Christiani b Williams	6
G. O. Allen c Walcott b Gaskin	36	– c Walcott b Williams	2
R. Howorth b Ferguson	14	– b Ferguson	14
T. G. Evans c Walcott b Williams	30	– st Walcott b Ferguson	21
G. A. Smithson c Goddard b Ferguson	35	– b Ferguson	35
J. C. Laker c Gaskin b Goddard	55	– c Carew b Williams	24
J. H. Wardle c Worrell b Ferguson	4	– not out	2
H. J. Butler not out	15	– b Ferguson	0
L-b 1, n-b 2	3	B 5, l-b 3, n-b 7	15

1/5 2/42 3/54 4/126 5/158   362   1/18 2/53 3/62 4/97 5/122   275
6/201 7/268 8/296 9/306   6/149 7/196 8/270 9/275

West Indies

G. A. Carew lbw b Laker	107	– not out	18
A. Ganteaume c Ikin b Howorth	112		
E. Weekes b Butler	36	– c Evans b Butler	20
F. M. Worrell c Evans b Cranston	97	– not out	28
C. L. Walcott c Butler b Howorth	20	– lbw b Allen	2
G. E. Gomez lbw b Laker	62		
R. J. Christiani c Robertson b Allen	7		
J. D. Goddard not out	9		
E. A. V. Williams c and b Allen	31	– b Butler	0
W. Ferguson b Butler	5		
B. M. Gaskin b Butler	0		
B 2, l-b 4, w 1, n-b 4	11	L-b 2, w 1, n-b 1	4

1/173 2/226 3/306 4/340 5/440   497   1/3 2/8 3/41   (3 wkts) 72
6/447 7/454 8/488 9/497

West Indies Bowling

	Overs	Mdns	Runs	Wkts	Overs	Mdns	Runs	Wkts
Gaskin	37	14	72	1	21	6	41	—
Williams	21	8	31	1	27	7	64	3
Ferguson	39	5	137	5	34.2	4	92	6
Goddard	23.3	6	64	1	9	4	11	—
Worrell	23	4	55	1	14	2	30	—
Gomez					8	2	22	1

England Bowling

	Overs	Mdns	Runs	Wkts	Overs	Mdns	Runs	Wkts
Butler	32	4	122	3	8	2	27	2
Allen.	16	—	82	2	5	—	21	1
Laker	36	10	108	2				
Cranston.	7	1	29	1	3	—	18	—
Ikin.	20	5	60	—				
Howorth.	30	3	76	2	1	—	2	—
Wardle	3	—	9	—				

Umpires: V. Guillen and B. Henderson.

THE MCC TEAM IN WEST INDIES, 1953–54

By R. J. Hayter

In the arrangement of tours Marylebone Cricket Club always has set the furtherance of friendship between man and man, country and country, as one of its main hopes and objectives. As the recognised Privy Council of cricket, MCC firmly maintain their idealistic outlook that the spirit in which the game is played carries greater importance than such transient elation or disappointment as the winning or losing of a Test Series. In days when so many attach the unhappy word prestige to nearly every international sporting event such an attitude should be encouraged rather than criticised as out-dated and unrealistic.

This made it all the more regrettable that the visit of the MCC representatives to the West Indies in the early months of 1954 aroused such controversy and uneasiness. Whatever the gains in other directions, the primary intention for the tour was not fulfilled and the circumstances of its failure were such that all those with the welfare of cricket at heart recognised that the problems arising needed to be tackled boldly but without heat.

To set out the origins and assess the responsibilities for the tension which marred so much is anything but simple. Certainly the early insistence of so many people that the "cricket championship of the world" was at stake did nothing to ease the situation. Nor did the constant emphasis upon victory which the MCC players found to be stressed by English residents in the West Indies.

A certain amount of tension was thus created before a ball had been bowled. This quickly became heightened through crowds, whose intense noise, coupled with almost ceaseless torrid heat, provided a background in which tempers too easily became frayed. At times some crowds were demonstrative and twice they became menacing.

Convinced by the happenings on the field that the general standard of umpiring in the West Indies was not adequate for Test cricket, the touring team felt that the crowd atmosphere made the work of the men in the middle even harder than it should have been. The MCC players sympathised with umpires threatened with physical violence, as marred the First and Third Tests. When, as the West Indies players admitted, the majority of disputed decisions, usually at moments of match crisis, went against MCC, they wondered how in the circumstances any umpires could remain completely calm and controlled.

To a man the MCC team recognised their responsibilities as ambassadors of sport, but, being human, the less phlegmatic did not always hide their annoyance and displeasure. In some instances only someone with the forbearance of the most highly-trained diplomat could have been expected to preserve absolute *sang-froid*. Dramatic gestures of disappointment and untactful remarks, however understandable some of them were in the heat of a moment, caused resentment among West Indies officials, umpires and others. No doubt some of the "incidents" were exaggerated, but to deny their existence or to minimise their seriousness would be only a disservice to the future welfare of the game.

In view of previous occurrences, fears were held that the last Test, which England entered requiring victory to draw the rubber, would add fuel to the flames, though these, it must be emphasised, had never extended to the players. Instead, reason prevailed and a splendid match went through without rancour. Cricket became a game again, not a battle. Even so, one pleasant game was insufficient to erase earlier memories, and anyone who followed the tour from first to last finished with two definite conclusions.

One concerned the necessity for alteration in the system of electing umpires for Tests in West Indies. As it was, in every Test England had to accept umpires from the colony in which the game was to be played. Even when Hutton in British Guiana objected to the two colony match officials standing in the Test, the West Indies Board would not agree to umpires being brought over from another island. After hearing their emphasis on the danger of creating inter-island jealousies, Hutton reluctantly agreed to two other Georgetown umpires, one of whom he had never seen in charge of a game.

A panel of umpires, drawn from all the islands, who could be inspected by the captains before the Tests began and from whom officials could be chosen for the whole series, appeared to be the only solution and one which was to be recommended emphatically. In nearly every Test series one side experiences more than an equal share of acceptedly wrong decisions, but the England team estimated that the proportions of these which went against them was in the region of seven or eight to two, a number they believed to be too much out of proportion for them not to become aggrieved.

Against this dissatisfaction had to be placed the responsibility attached to all cricketers honoured by selection for MCC. Whatever the provocation and the pinpricks, only harm can arise when MCC cricketers fall from the highest estate of conduct on the field. As many loyal West Indies people pointed out, the foundation of their own task in instilling the principles of sportsmanship into the rising generations in the islands was to cite England cricketers as the models. They said that if the models lowered their code, the effect could be far-reaching and depressing.

Only one or two of Hutton's team deserved this censure, but when even the slightest sign of disagreement became public property, as must be accepted in times when Test matches are given increasing prominence in newspaper, radio and newsreel, self-control should have been regarded as essential. Earlier and firmer handling of the most recalcitrant member, the fiery Trueman, might have avoided several situations, but, anxious not to dim the spark of Trueman's hostility and aggressiveness, Hutton probably waited too long before calling his lively colt to heel. Potentially Trueman remained a fast bowler of whom England could expect stirring deeds, but first he required to harness his temper solely to his fast bowling.

WEST INDIES v ENGLAND

First Test Match

Played at Sabina Park, Kingston, Jamaica, January 15, 16, 18, 19, 20, 21, 1954

West Indies won by 140 runs. A game of many fluctuations which roused intense excitement finally turned in favour of West Indies through a second England landslide in excellent batting conditions. Influenced by the moderate performance of the West Indies batsmen against Australia's pace attack in 1951-52 and expecting a fast pitch similar to that of the opening colony game, the England selectors picked four fast bowlers.

Instead the pitch, resembling polished marble, played appreciably slower than in the Jamaican match. England thus did well to restrict West Indies, who lacked Worrell (unfit) to 331 for six by tea time on the second day. Then came the first of their several black periods. In the next hour Gomez and McWatt took 60 runs from Statham and Trueman using the new ball. McWatt, a left-hander who struck powerfully, enjoyed remarkable luck, being missed from successive balls when 14 and altogether five times before reaching 50. Only one of the chances was easy.

Flight and change of pace, skilfully exploited by Ramadhin and Valentine, brought about an England batting debacle, but West Indies lost their first six second innings wickets for 119. Impatience at their inability to score freely against defensive bowling, some down the leg side, cost several batsmen their wickets. McWatt, more sound than in the first innings, helped Weekes (twelve 4s) in another seventh wicket recovery before a declaration which left England nine hours and a half to make 457 to win.

With the outfield extremely fast, this was not an impossible target, and Watson (sixteen 4s) and Hutton opened with a century stand notable for confidence and certain stroke-play. May took over where Hutton left off and England finished the fifth day 227 for two.

All continued well on the last day until Stollmeyer switched to negative tactics. Gomez and Kentish conceded only 23 runs in the last hour before lunch, and just before the interval May, in frustration, groped for a ball outside the leg stump. In an instant the situation changed. An hour after lunch the match was over, seven wickets having toppled in that time for 39 runs, of which the last pair, Bailey and Moss, made all but eight. Apart from that of Bailey, who batted three and a half hours in the match without being dismissed, the resistance was feeble. Kentish gained his success by accurate medium-fast bowling at or outside the leg stump to an on-side arc of seven men.

Two unhappy incidents underlined the intensity of some of the feeling of the crowd. Stollmeyer was booed on three separate occasions for not enforcing a follow-on and physical attacks, fortunately not serious, were made on the wife and son of umpire Burke, presumably because he gave out Holt when the local batsman was within six runs of a century in his first Test. In the second West Indies innings Lock was no-balled once for throwing.

West Indies

M. Frederick c Graveney b Statham	0	– lbw b Statham	30
J. B. Stollmeyer lbw b Statham	60	– c Evans b Bailey	8
J. K. Holt lbw b Statham	94	– lbw b Moss	1
E. Weekes b Moss	55	– not out	90
C. L. Walcott b Lock	65	– c Bailey b Lock	25
G. Headley c Graveney b Lock	16	– b Lock	1
G. E. Gomez not out	47	– lbw b Statham	3
C. McWatt b Lock	54	– not out	36
S. Ramadhin lbw b Trueman	7		
E. Kentish b Statham	0		
A. L. Valentine b Trueman	0		
B 9, l-b 4, w 1, n-b 5	19	B 8, l-b 6, n-b 1	15

1/6 2/140 3/216 4/234 5/286   417   1/28 2/31   (6 wkts dec.) 209
6/316 7/404 8/415 9/416   3/46 4/92 5/94 6/119

England

W. Watson b Gomez	3	– c and b Stollmeyer	116
L. Hutton b Valentine	24	– lbw b Gomez	56
P. B. H. May c Headley b Ramadhin	31	– c McWatt b Kentish	69
D. C. S. Compton lbw b Valentine	12	– b Ramadhin	2
T. W. Graveney lbw b Ramadhin	16	– c Weekes b Kentish	34
T. E. Bailey not out	28	– not out	15
T. G. Evans c Kentish b Valentine	10	– b Kentish	0
G. A. R. Lock b Ramadhin	4	– b Kentish	0
J. B. Statham b Ramadhin	8	– lbw b Ramadhin	1
F. S. Trueman c McWatt b Gomez	18	– b Kentish	1
A. E. Moss b Gomez	0	– run out	16
B 9, l-b 2, w 1, n-b 4	16	B 4, l-b 1, n-b 1	6

1/4 2/49 3/73 4/79 5/94   170   1/130 2/220 3/277 4/282   316
6/105 7/117 8/135 9/165   5/282 6/282 7/283 9/285

England Bowling

	Overs	Mdns	Runs	Wkts	Overs	Mdns	Runs	Wkts
Statham	36	6	90	4	17	2	50	2
Trueman	34.4	8	107	2	6	—	32	—
Moss	26	5	84	1	10	—	30	1
Bailey	16	4	36	—	20	4	46	1
Lock	41	14	76	3	14	2	36	2
Compton	2	1	5	—				

West Indies Bowling

	Overs	Mdns	Runs	Wkts	Overs	Mdns	Runs	Wkts
Kentish	14	4	23	—	29	11	49	5
Gomez	9.2	3	16	3	30	8	63	1
Ramadhin	35	14	65	4	35.3	12	88	2
Valentine	31	10	50	3	25	6	71	—
Headley					5	—	23	—
Walcott					2	1	4	—
Stollmeyer					3	—	12	1

Umpires: P. Burke and T. Ewart.

MCC v BRITISH GUIANA

Played at Georgetown, British Guiana, February 17, 18, 19, 20, 1954

MCC won by an innings and 98 runs. A fourth-wicket stand of 402 between Watson and Graveney dominated the match. After three wickets had fallen cheaply on a true pitch, they did much as they pleased with a moderate attack. On Hutton's order before the second day that they should soon provide opportunities for later batsmen to obtain practice, neither concentrated much longer. Had they been so minded they would have stood an excellent chance of making the other 47 needed to set up an English fourth-wicket record. Watson (two 6s and thirty-one 4s) and Graveney (one 6 and twenty-four 4s) used all the strokes. Two big innings by Christiani restored him to favour with the West Indies selectors, but, apart from the 18-year-old Thomas, few others showed much ability to deal with Wardle's flight and variations of spin. MCC were not happy with the standard of umpiring and after the game Hutton protested about either official standing in the forthcoming Test. His protest was upheld.

MCC

W. Watson c Dyer b Hector 257	G. A. R. Lock b G. Gibbs	4
L. Hutton c G. Gibbs b Hector 0	A. E. Moss c Camacho b G. Gibbs	0
P. B. H. May c Gibbons b Hector 9	F. S. Trueman c Seaforth b G. Gibbs	20
D. C. S. Compton b L. Gibbs 18		
T. W. Graveney c Christiani b L. Gibbs 231	B 2, l-b 2, n-b 1	5
K. G. Suttle run out 39		
R. T. Spooner not out 20	1/5 2/21 3/51 4/453 5/547	607
J. H. Wardle c Christiani b G. Gibbs 4	6/565 7/570 8/574 9/574	

British Guiana

G. Gibbs c Graveney b Moss	34	– b Moss		1
A. Gibbons b Wardle	38	– b Wardle		29
G. Camacho c Graveney b Wardle	24	– c Trueman b Lock		38
R. J. Christiani c Trueman b Wardle	75	– c Compton b Trueman		82
C. McWatt c and b Wardle	29	– c Graveney b Wardle		9
N. Thomas run out	26	– lbw b Wardle		30
H. Dyer run out	5	– c Trueman b Compton		5
R. Hector b Lock	13	– c Compton b Trueman		9
L. Gibbs b Wardle	1	– not out		14
S. Seaforth b Wardle	2	– b Moss		17
A. Basdeo not out	0	– c Graveney b Moss		5
B 8, l-b 7	15	B 5, n-b 3		8

1/71 2/105 3/110 4/209 5/225   262   1/8 2/53 3/65 4/95 5/171   247
6/238 7/249 8/258 9/262   6/176 7/217 8/221 9/239

British Guiana Bowling

	Overs	Mdns	Runs	Wkts
Hector	30	2	136	3
Camacho	12	1	52	—
Seaforth	22	2	82	—
L. Gibbs	41	8	126	2
Basdeo	5	—	32	—
Thomas	3	—	22	—
G. Gibbs	32	2	122	4
Christiani	6	—	30	—

MCC Bowling

	Overs	Mdns	Runs	Wkts	Overs	Mdns	Runs	Wkts
Trueman	12	3	34	—	11	3	24	2
Moss	17	8	25	1	10.5	1	45	3
Wardle	39	17	77	6	28	9	82	3
Lock	28.5	11	55	1	18	6	47	1
Compton	18	5	56	—	14	5	41	1
Graveney					6	6	—	—

Umpires: A. Rollox and G. Kippins.

WEST INDIES v ENGLAND

Third Test Match

Played at Georgetown, British Guiana, February 24, 25, 26, 27, March 1, 2, 1954

England won by nine wickets. For the first time in the series the West Indies were at full strength, but England, working together well as a team, won on their merits. A fine cricket match was marred by disgraceful crowd scenes on the fourth day.

By winning the toss for the first time in eight Tests, Hutton gave England a distinct moral advantage and, after the early loss of Watson and May, he and Compton put the side on the way to a big total. Hutton (one 6 and twenty-four 4s) played faultlessly for seven hours and three-quarters. He concentrated mainly on safety, but occasionally he produced a cover-drive, cut or leg glance which revealed his superb technique. The promotion of Wardle to provide aggression from the other end to his tiring captain brought successful results, and Bailey batted with his customary Test vigilance. Throughout a long innings the West Indies bowled and fielded excellently and, when dismissing Laker, Valentine became the youngest cricketer to take 100 Test wickets.

The vital period of the game came in the three-quarters of an hour in which West Indies batted before lunch on the third morning. In that time Statham, bowling with rare devil, dismissed Worrell, Stollmeyer and Walcott for ten runs. Stollmeyer was beaten by an inswinger which pitched on his middle and leg stumps and struck the off. Rain washed out further play for the day, but on the Saturday the West Indies collapse continued until seven men were out for 139. Of these the punishing Weekes made 94. He hit with shattering power.

Recovery came through McWatt, given lives at 141 and 158, and Holt, who went in late because of a pulled leg muscle which restricted his movement and necessitated the use of a runner. Trying for a second run which would have taken the stand to 100, McWatt was run out through a fast return by May.

Apparently disagreeing with the decision of Menzies, the umpire and groundsman, sections of the crowd hurled bottles and wooden packing-cases on to the field and some of the players were fortunate to escape injury. The President of the British Guiana Cricket Association went out and suggested to Hutton that the players should leave but Hutton preferred to remain. He wanted more wickets. His was a courageous action for which he deserved much praise. In the last over England took another wicket and early on the fifth day they enforced the follow-on.

This time Holt, although still limping, went in first. He and Stollmeyer gave the innings a sound start before Compton, at short fine-leg, dived to his right and clutched a one-hand catch from Stollmeyer. Once more Statham quickly disposed of Worrell and although Weekes and Gomez batted resolutely, England never lost grip. Towards the end of the day the ball began to turn and keep low, but generally conditions favoured batsmen. Consistently accurate bowling, two first-rate slip catches by Graveney and a surprisingly high standard of fielding all round featured England's work in the second innings.

To give practice to his younger players, Hutton changed the batting order when England wanted 73 to win. The runs came in an hour, Watson finishing the match with a 6.

England

W. Watson b Ramadhin	12	– not out	27
L. Hutton c Worrell b Ramadhin	169		
P. B. H. May lbw b Atkinson	12	– b Atkinson	12
D. C. S. Compton c Stollmeyer b Atkinson	64		
T. W. Graveney b Ramadhin	0	– not out	33
J. H. Wardle b Ramadhin	38		
T. E. Bailey c Weekes b Ramadhin	49		
T. G. Evans lbw b Atkinson	19		
J. C. Laker b Valentine	27		
G. A. R. Lock b Ramadhin	13		
J. B. Statham not out	10		
B 20, n-b 2	22	B 3	3

1/33 2/76 3/226 4/227 5/306   435   1/18   (1 wkt) 75
6/321 7/350 8/390 9/412

West Indies

F. M. Worrell c Evans b Statham	0	– c Evans b Statham		2
J. B. Stollmeyer b Statham	2	– c Compton b Laker		44
E. Weekes b Lock	94	– c Graveney b Bailey		38
C. L. Walcott b Statham	4	– lbw b Laker		26
R. J. Christiani c Watson b Laker	25	– b Bailey		11
G. E. Gomez b Statham	8	– c Graveney b Wardle		35
D. Atkinson c and b Lock	0	– b Wardle		18
C. McWatt run out	54	– not out		9
J. K. Holt not out	48	– b Lock		64
S. Ramadhin b Laker	0	– b Statham		1
A. L. Valentine run out	0	– b Wardle		0
B 8, l-b 7, w 1	16	B 2, l-b 4, n-b 2		8

1/1 2/12 3/16 4/78 5/132   251   1/79 2/96 3/120 4/168   256
6/134 7/139 8/238 9/240   5/186 6/200 7/245 8/246 9/251

West Indies Bowling

	Overs	Mdns	Runs	Wkts	Overs	Mdns	Runs	Wkts
Ramadhin	67	34	113	6	4	—	7	—
Valentine	44	17	109	1				
Gomez	32	6	75	—	5	ı	15	—
Worrell	16	5	33	—				
Atkinson	58	27	78	3	7	—	34	1
Stollmeyer	2	1	3	—				
Walcott	2	—	2	—	2	—	6	—
Weekes					2.1	—	8	—
Christiani					1	—	2	—

England Bowling

	Overs	Mdns	Runs	Wkts	Overs	Mdns	Runs	Wkts
Statham	27	6	64	4	22	3	86	2
Bailey	5	—	13	—	22	9	41	2
Laker	21	11	32	2	36	18	56	2
Wardle	22	4	60	—	12.3	4	24	3
Compton	3	1	6	—				
Lock	27.5	7	60	2	25	11	41	1

Umpires: B. Menzies and E. S. Gillette.

WEST INDIES v ENGLAND

Fourth Test Match

Played at Port-of-Spain, March 17, 18, 19, 20, 22, 23, 1954

Drawn. From the outset of the tour those who knew the nature of the Trinidad jute-matting pitch, on which no Test had reached a definite finish since it was laid down in 1934, prophesied a certain draw in the Fourth Test and at no time in the match did any other result look possible. From first to last batsmen enjoyed such advantage that in six days 1,528 runs were scored while only 25 wickets fell. The complete subjugation of bowlers took away much competitive interest and the cricket was enjoyed only by those who delight in utter dominance by batsmen.

West Indies, needing to draw to make sure of not losing the rubber, batted until just before lunch on the third day, and in doing so made their highest total in Test cricket. For the second time in their careers Weekes, Worrell and Walcott scored centuries in the same innings. Weekes, the most punishing of the three, and Worrell created a record for any wicket in the England-West Indies series with a stand of 338. England were handicapped when Statham, who had been kept specially for Test matches, pulled a rib muscle on the first morning and could not bowl again on the tour, but on such a true and easy-paced surface even he would have found difficulty in worrying batsmen.

The England innings, which lasted until shortly before the close of the fifth day, was notable for May and Compton hitting their first Test centuries since 1951. Both played a comparatively restrained game which the position thoroughly justified. Graveney narrowly missed being the sixth batsman in the match to reach 100. In an effort to force batsmen into mistakes King bowled a number of bumpers. One struck Watson on the elbow and restricted his movement. In trying to hook another Laker was hit above the left eye and had to go to hospital for the wound to be stitched. England saved any possibility of a follow-on with the last pair together, so that the sixth day's play was of exhibition character.

Play began three-quarters of an hour late on the fourth morning because of a wet patch where the ground staff, who watered and rolled the mixture of clay and sand under the matting first thing every day, had repaired a spot worn by King in bowling the previous day.

Injuries kept out Valentine and Gomez of the West Indies and Evans, the England wicket-keeper.

West Indies

J. K. Holt c Compton b Trueman	40		
J. B. Stollmeyer c and b Compton	41		
E. D. Weekes c Bailey b Lock	206	– c sub b Trueman	1
F. M. Worrell b Lock	167	– c sub b Lock	56
C. L. Walcott c and b Laker	124	– not out	51
B. Pairaudeau run out	0	– hit wkt b Bailey	5
D. Atkinson c Graveney b Compton	74	– not out	53
C. McWatt b Laker	4		
W. Ferguson not out	8	– b Bailey	44
B 6, l-b 4, w 4, n-b 3	17	L-b 2	22

1/78 2/92 3/430 4/517   (8 wkts dec.) 681   1/19 2/20   (4 wkts dec.) 212
5/540 6/627 7/641 8/681   3/72 4/111

S. Ramadhin and F. King did not bat.

England

L. Hutton c Ferguson b King	44	– not out	30
T. E. Bailey c Weekes b Ferguson	46		
P. B. H. May c Pairaudeau b King	135	– c Worrell b McWatt	16
D. C. S. Compton c and b Ramadhin	133		
W. Watson c Atkinson b Walcott	4	– c Ferguson b Worrell	32
T. W. Graveney c and b Walcott	92	– not out	0
R. T. Spooner b Walcott	19	– c Ferguson b Ramadhin	16
J. C. Laker retired hurt	7		
G. A. R. Lock lbw b Worrell	10		
F. S. Trueman lbw b King	19		
J. B. Statham not out	6		
B 10, l-b 5, w 7	22	L-b 4	4

1/73 2/135 3/301 4/314 5/424   537   1/52 2/52 3/83   (3 wkts) 98
6/493 7/496 8/510 9/537

England Bowling

	Overs	Mdns	Runs	Wkts	Overs	Mdns	Runs	Wkts
Statham	9	—	31	—				
Trueman	33	3	131	1	15	5	23	1
Bailey	32	7	104	—	12	2	20	2
Laker	47	8	154	2				
Lock	59	14	178	2	10	2	40	1
Compton	9.4	1	40	2	7	—	51	—
Graveney	3	—	26	—	5	—	33	—
Hutton					6	—	43	—

West Indies Bowling

	Overs	Mdns	Runs	Wkts	Overs	Mdns	Runs	Wkts
King	48	16	97	3				
Worrell	20	2	58	1	9	1	29	1
Ramadhin	34	13	74	1	7	4	6	1
Atkinson	32	12	60	—	4	—	12	—
Ferguson	47	17	155	1				
Stollmeyer	6	2	19	—				
Walcott	34	18	52	3				
Weekes					5	1	28	—
McWatt					4	1	16	1
Pairaudeau					1	—	3	—

Umpires: K. Woods and E. Achong.

WEST INDIES v ENGLAND
Fifth Test Match

Played at Sabina Park, Kingston, Jamaica, March 30, 31, April 1, 2, 3, 1954

England won by nine wickets. In overcoming the disadvantage of losing the toss for the fourth time in the series England accomplished their most noteworthy achievement by inflicting defeat upon such a powerful batting side and so drawing level in the rubber after being two down.

When Stollmeyer beat Hutton in the toss few would have given England much hope of victory. The pitch looked perfect and, in fact, it contained no more life than any well-prepared strip does on the first day. In the circumstances the utter collapse of the West Indies for 139 bordered on the incredible. The architect of England's bowling triumph was the vice-captain, Bailey, who, had Statham been fit to play, might well have been confined to a few overs. Instead Bailey, inspired by constant successes, beginning with a fine short-leg catch by Lock from his fifth ball, swung a little either way to a spot length and occasionally cut sharply off the seam. One such ball whipped back from the off and bowled Weekes. When Worrell, stabbing apprehensively at a fast short ball immediately following a bumper, gave a catch to short-leg, four men were out for 13 runs in forty minutes. Three fell to Bailey for five runs.

Walcott led a partial recovery, but Bailey could not be denied for long and he achieved easily his best analysis in Test cricket. As Bailey himself was first to say, he would have been pleased with figures only half as good in a county match played in similar conditions.

Straight from his bowling exertions Bailey accompanied Hutton to open the innings. They played safely through the last thirty-five minutes, and although they made only 24 runs from 24 overs before lunch on the second day they accomplished their mission of safety while the turf eased from sweating under the covers during the night.

In the effort to pull round, Stollmeyer called on his fast bowler, King, for a maximum effort. During the day King's analysis was 21-11-31-2 and he was always most difficult to play. He bowled straight and very fast, but his over-use of the bumper was not to be commended. One brought about the dismissal of Compton, who tumbled into his wicket in evading a flying ball. When, at the close, England led by only 55 with half their wickets gone, West Indies had good reason for satisfaction, but the hard work had told upon King, who strained a leg muscle and could not bowl again in the innings.

Next day the bowling, without King, contained little bite and, after more early consolidation, England went over to the attack. In two hours between lunch and tea they scored 146 runs. Once again Hutton was the bulwark of the England innings. He received able help in century stands from Evans, whose innings of two hours and twenty minutes was his longest in Test cricket, and Wardle (one 6 and nine 4s). For concentration and control, Hutton's innings of a shade under nine hours scarcely could have been excelled. Many of his twenty-three 4s – he also drove Sobers for 6 – came from his cover-drive. This, the only double century by an England captain on a tour abroad, was Hutton's nineteenth Test hundred. Considering the responsibilities and worries on his shoulders, he deserved unstinted praise.

When West Indies lost four wickets – three to Trueman, who produced some of his most accurate and hostile fast bowling of the tour – for 123, visions arose of an innings defeat, but the dependable Walcott found solid partners in Atkinson and Gomez, and England were left to make 72 to win, one more than in the Third Test. Just after reaching the 90s Walcott was struck hard on the left wrist and, although no bone was fractured, he felt such pain afterwards the he could not attempt a forcing stroke. The restriction was partly responsible for Walcott's dismissal soon after he completed his third century of the series. In an innings only little less meritorious than that of Hutton, Walcott hit twenty 4s.

Well as he bowled, Trueman followed King in the employment of too many bumpers and, like King, he received one initial "caution" from the umpire at the bowler's end as laid down in Law 46. Laker, who constantly varied his off-breaks, revelled in his chance to bowl for a long spell.

A shower towards the end of the West Indies innings left the pitch slightly moist and, after Graveney had been bowled in King's first over, Watson and May lived through a short series of adventures, but May, striking handsomely, soon made the finish certain with a day to spare. So West Indies suffered their first defeat at Sabina Park.

The match throughout was played without any of the rancour which marred some of the earlier games.

West Indies

J. K. Holt c Lock b Bailey	0	– c Lock b Trueman	8
J. B. Stollmeyer c Evans b Bailey	9	– lbw b Trueman	64
E. Weekes b Bailey	0	– b Wardle	3
F. M. Worrell c Wardle b Trueman	4	– c Graveney b Trueman	29
C. L. Walcott c Laker b Lock	50	– c Graveney b Laker	116
D. Atkinson lbw b Bailey	21	– c Watson b Bailey	40
G. E. Gomez c Watson b Bailey	4	– lbw b Laker	22
C. McWatt c Lock b Bailey	22	– c Wardle b Laker	8
G. Sobers not out	14	– c Compton b Lock	26
F. King b Bailey	9	– not out	10
S. Ramadhin lbw b Trueman	4	– c and b Laker	10
L-b 1, n-b 1	2	B 4, l-b 3, w 1, n-b 2	10

1/0 2/2 3/13 4/13 5/65 6/75   139   1/26 2/38 3/102 4/123   346
7/110 8/115 9/133   5/191 6/273 7/293 8/306 9/326

England

L. Hutton c McWatt b Walcott..................205		
T. E. Bailey c McWatt b Sobers 23		
P. B. H. May c sub b Ramadhin 30	– not out	40
D. C. S. Compton hit wkt b King 31		
W. Watson c McWatt b King................... 4	– not out	20
T. W. Graveney lbw b Atkinson 11	– b King.......................	0
T. G. Evans c Worrell b Ramadhin.............. 28		
J. H. Wardle c Holt b Sobers................... 66		
G. A. R. Lock b Sobers....................... 4		
J. C. Laker b Sobers 9		
F. S. Trueman not out........................ 0		
L-b 3 3	B 12	12

1/43 2/104 3/152 4/160 5/179 6/287   414   1/0   (1 wkt) 72
7/392 8/401 9/406

England Bowling

	Overs	Mdns	Runs	Wkts	Overs	Mdns	Runs	Wkts
Bailey	16	7	34	7	25	11	54	1
Trueman..........	15.4	4	39	2	29	7	88	3
Wardle	10	1	20	—	39	14	83	1
Lock.............	15	6	31	1	27	15	40	1
Laker	4	1	13	—	50	27	71	4

West Indies Bowling

	Overs	Mdns	Runs	Wkts	Overs	Mdns	Runs	Wkts
King	26	12	45	2	4	1	21	1
Gomez	25	8	56	—				
Atkinson..........	41	15	82	1	3	—	8	—
Ramadhin........	29	9	71	2	3	—	14	—
Sobers...........	28.5	9	75	4	1	—	6	—
Walcott..........	11	5	26	1				
Worrell	11	—	34	—	4	—	8	—
Stollmeyer........	5	—	22	—				
Weekes					0.5	—	3	—

Umpires: P. Burke and T. Ewart.

WEST INDIES v ENGLAND
First Test Match

Played at Bridgetown, Barbados, January 6, 7, 8, 9, 11, 12, 1960

Drawn. Over six days only eighteen wickets fell on a pitch which gave bowlers not the slightest help and reduced the match to an exercise in patience and stamina for batsmen. Even at the end of the game the ball scarcely turned. Statham, who slipped and fell in the rain at the end of the Barbados game, damaged a hamstring muscle and could not play. Allen received his first chance for England; Watson and Scarlett made their débuts for West Indies.

May did England a good service by winning the toss, although Pullar and Cowdrey had to withstand a fiery attack from Hall and Watson, who made liberal use of the bouncer and even with the pitch slow provided plenty of problems. Cowdrey touched a rising ball to second slip but Pullar found another good partner in Barrington. The failure of May, brilliantly caught low down at the wicket on the leg-side, came as a shock and at the end of the first day England were 188 for three. Barrington hit his first Test century, batting five and a half hours for 128 (twenty 4s) but at 303 for six England were by no means well placed. Then Dexter and Swetman changed the situation by adding 123. Dexter, in fine driving form, gave a polished display, taking out his bat for 136 (one 6, nineteen 4s) after four and three-quarter hours.

Alexander established a new West Indies wicket-keeping record by dismissing five batsmen in the innings, all catches. West Indies began their reply at lunch time on the third day and made a bad start, losing McMorris to a run-out off a no ball at six. By the end of the day England looked to be on top with West Indies 114 for three. Then came a remarkable stand, Sobers and Worrell remaining together from 4.50 p.m. on Friday until 11.40 a.m. on Tuesday, a total of nine hours thirty minutes and adding 309, the highest for any West Indies wicket against England and the best fourth-wicket stand by any country against England.

Sobers offered a difficult return catch to Trueman when seven and another to mid-on off Allen when 40. Worrell should have been caught at short mid-on when 109 off Illingworth, but these were the only blemishes during the long partnership. Both batsmen were in complete control against an attack which was almost helpless on the easy conditions. Sobers, strong all round, batted ten hours forty-seven minutes for 226 which included twenty-four 4s. Worrell, at his best when driving, stayed eleven hours twenty minutes for 197 not out (two 6s, seventeen 4s). These were the two longest innings ever played against England. By the end of the fifth day West Indies were four ahead with four wickets left, but they failed to score quickly against steady bowling and a defensive field, adding only 77 in two hours ten minutes, Worrell managing no more than 20 in that time. When the declaration came with West Indies 81 ahead only two hours forty minutes remained and rain cut this short by twenty minutes. Pullar and Cowdrey quietly kept their wickets intact.

England

G. Pullar run out	65	– not out	46
M. C. Cowdrey c Sobers b Watson	30	– not out	16
K. F. Barrington c Alexander b Ramadhin	128		
*P. B. H. May c Alexander b Hall	1		
M. J. K. Smith c Alexander b Scarlett	39		
E. R. Dexter not out	136		
R. Illingworth b Ramadhin	5		
†R. Swetman c Alexander b Worrell	45		
F. S. Trueman c Alexander b Ramadhin	3		
D. A. Allen lbw b Watson	10		
A. E. Moss b Watson	4		
B 4, l-b 6, n-b 6	16	B 7, l-b 1, w 1	9
	482	(No wkt)	71

1/50 2/153 3/162 4/251 5/291
6/303 7/426 8/439 9/478

West Indies

C. Hunte c Swetman b Barrington	42	
E. McMorris run out	0	
R. Kanhai b Trueman	40	
G. Sobers b Trueman	226	
F. M. Worrell not out	197	
B. Butcher c Trueman b Dexter	13	
W. Hall lbw b Trueman	14	

*†F. C. M. Alexander c Smith b Trueman .. 3
R. Scarlett lbw b Dexter 7

B 8, l-b 7, w 1, n-b 5 21

1/6 2/68 3/102   (8 wkts dec.) 563
4/501 5/521 6/544 7/556 8/563

C. Watson and S. Ramadhin did not bat.

West Indies Bowling

	Overs	Mdns	Runs	Wkts	Overs	Mdns	Runs	Wkts
Hall	40	9	98	1	6	2	9	—
Watson	32.4	6	121	3	8	1	19	—
Worrell	15	2	39	1				
Ramadhin	54	22	109	3	7	2	11	—
Scarlett	26	9	46	1	10	4	12	—
Sobers	21	3	53	—				
Hunte					7	2	9	—
Kanhai					4	3	2	—

England Bowling

	Overs	Mdns	Runs	Wkts
Trueman	47	15	93	4
Moss	47	14	116	—
Dexter	37.4	11	85	2
Illingworth	47	9	106	—
Allen	43	12	82	—
Barrington	18	3	60	1

Umpires: C. Jordan and J. Roberts.

WEST INDIES v ENGLAND
Second Test Match

Played at Port-of-Spain, Trinidad, January 28, 29, 30, February 1, 2, 3, 1960

England won by 256 runs after one of the most dramatic Test matches for many years. Excitement was intense throughout and it led to an unfortunate and remarkable scene on the third day. A crowd of almost 30,000, a record for any sporting event in West Indies, became so inflamed that soon after tea tempers boiled over and a few hooligans began throwing bottles on to the outfield. This started an orgy of bottle-throwing and a large part of the crowd wandered on to the playing area. Things became so bad that a riot developed. The England players were escorted from the field, though no animosity was being shown to them. No further play was possible that day. Bottles were also thrown at Georgetown on the previous MCC tour six years earlier but on that occasion the cricket was resumed after a short delay. During the match players on both sides were told to play their parts in avoiding incidents by accepting umpiring decisions without quibble and by walking immediately they were given out.

Statham, fit again, replaced Moss and West Indies brought in Solomon and Singh for McMorris and Scarlett. May won the toss again on a pitch faster than at Bridgetown, but England were soon in trouble. After doing little for half an hour Hall and Watson changed ends and unleashed a blistering attack of bumpers and short-pitched balls which sent England reeling to 57 for three with Pullar, Cowdrey and May gone. Barrington and Dexter brought a fine recovery with a stand of 142 in two hours thirty-seven minutes. At one point Hall was cautioned by the umpire, Lloyd, for excessive use of short-pitched balls in accordance with Law 46. England finished the first day with 220 runs for four wickets and next morning Barrington and Smith continued the improvement. The other umpire, Lee Kow, cautioned Watson for infringing Law 46 early in the day and after that there were only a few short balls.

Barrington batted five hours fifty minutes for his second successive Test century in his only two innings against West Indies. Smith, ninth out, stayed almost five hours for 108. Hunte and Solomon were also subjected to bouncers from Trueman and Statham when they batted for the last twenty-six minutes on the second day, but for the rest of the match there was no further trouble with this type of bowling.

On the dynamic third day West Indies broke down badly in face of England's deadly accurate fast attack. Eight wickets were down for 98 when the bottle-throwing began. The atmosphere on the last three days was calm and peaceful, England steadily built a powerful position. May did not enforce the follow-on when leading by 270 and although wickets fell steadily, a stand of 68 in fifty minutes came from Illingworth and Trueman.

May declared after an hour on the fifth morning, leaving West Indies to get 501 to win in ten hours. No side had ever scored so many in winning a Test, West Indies, somewhat naturally, tried to play for a draw. At the end of the fifth day two wickets were down for 134, but the early loss of Sobers and Worrell next morning were severe blows for them. Kanhai made a great effort, staying six hours eighteen minutes for 110 which included one 6 and nineteen 4s, but England were not to be denied and with the last three wickets falling at the same total they won with an hour and fifty minutes to spare. The attendance of almost 100,000 and the receipts were both records for a match in West Indies.

England

G. Pullar c Alexander b Watson	17	– c Worrell b Ramadhin ... 28
M. C. Cowdrey b Hall	18	– c Alexander b Watson ... 5
K. F. Barrington c Alexander b Hall	121	– c Alexander b Hall ... 49
*P. B. H. May c Kanhai b Watson	0	– c and b Singh ... 28
E. R. Dexter c and b Singh	77	– b Hall ... 0
M. J. K. Smith c Worrall b Ramadhin	108	– lbw b Watson ... 12
R. Illingworth b Ramadhin	10	– not out ... 41
†R. Swetman lbw b Watson	1	– lbw b Singh ... 0
F. S. Trueman lbw b Ramadhin	7	– c Alexander b Watson ... 37
D. A. Allen not out	10	– c Alexander b Hall ... 16
J. B. Statham b Worrell	1	
L-b 3, w 1, n-b 8	12	B 6, l-b 2, w 4, n-b 2 ... 14

1/37 2/42 3/57 4/199 5/276   382   1/18 2/79   (9 wkts dec.) 230
6/307 7/308 8/343 9/378   3/97 4/101 5/122 6/133
                                       7/133 8/201 9/230

West Indies

C. Hunte c Trueman b Statham	8	– c Swetman b Allen ... 47
J. Solomon run out	23	– c Swetman b Allen ... 9
R. Kanhai lbw b Trueman	5	– c Smith b Dexter ... 110
G. Sobers c Barrington b Trueman	0	– lbw b Trueman ... 31
F. M. Worrell c Swetman b Trueman	9	– lbw b Statham ... 0
B. Butcher lbw b Statham	9	– lbw b Statham ... 9
*†F. C. M. Alexander lbw b Trueman	28	– c Trueman b Allen ... 7
S. Ramadhin b Trueman	23	– lbw b Dexter ... 0
C. Singh run out	0	– c and b Barrington ... 11
W. Hall b Statham	4	– not out ... 0
C. Watson not out	0	– c Allen b Barrington ... 0
L-b 2, w 1	3	B 11, l-b 6, w 2, n-b 1 ... 20

1/22 2/31 3/31 4/45 5/45   112   1/29 2/107 3/158 4/159   244
6/73 7/94 8/98 9/108   5/188 6/222 7/222 8/244 9/244

West Indies Bowling

	Overs	Mdns	Runs	Wkts	Overs	Mdns	Runs	Wkts
Hall	33	9	92	2	23.4	4	50	3
Watson	31	5	100	3	19	6	57	3
Worrell	11.5	3	23	1	12	5	27	—
Singh	23	6	59	1	8	3	28	2
Ramadhin	35	12	61	3	28	8	54	1
Sobers	3	—	16	—				
Solomon	7	—	19	—				

England Bowling

	Overs	Mdns	Runs	Wkts	Overs	Mdns	Runs	Wkts
Trueman..........	21	11	35	5	19	9	44	1
Statham	19.3	8	42	3	25	12	44	2
Allen.............	5	—	9	—	31	13	57	3
Barrington	16	10	15	—	25.5	13	34	2
Illingworth	7	3	8	—	28	14	38	—
Dexter............					6	3	7	2

Umpires: E. Lee Kow and E. L. Lloyd.

WEST INDIES v ENGLAND
Third Test Match

Played at Sabina Park, Jamaica, February 17, 18, 19, 20, 22, 23, 1960

Drawn. Six days of exciting cricket ended with the result in doubt until the final quarter of an hour. Rarely has a Test match undergone so many changes of fortune and although in the end England were probably satisfied to draw, they came close to winning.

England were unchanged but West Indies brought in McMorris, Scarlett and Nurse for Worrell, Butcher and Singh. Worrell damaged an ankle just before the match. May won the toss for the third time and on a pitch resembling polished marble England made a poor showing on the first day. Again the batsmen had to withstand plenty of short-pitched bowling from Hall and Watson although bumpers were scarcer than at Trinidad. Hall, fast and menacing, caused the England breakdown and by the end of the first day he had taken five for 35 in a total of 165 for six. Cowdrey, though hit many times and badly bruised, stayed throughout the five hours for 75. During the afternoon part of a tin roof collapsed through people standing on it and several were injured.

Next day England came back well with Cowdrey and Trueman adding 45 for the eighth-wicket stand and the last three wickets putting on 107. Cowdrey, ninth out, fought splendidly for six and three-quarter hours, but he kept his strokes in check and his 114 included only eleven 4s. Hall finished with seven for 69, the best of his Test career.

West Indies ended the second day at 81 for two, Kanhai being run out when he and McMorris were at the same end. Sobers, when two, offered an awkward chance to mid-wicket off Statham and this proved a costly miss. England toiled the entire third day without a wicket, West Indies leaving off 14 ahead with eight wickets left. McMorris wore down the bowling for over five and a half hours while scoring 65 before a short ball from Statham struck him on the chest and caused his retirement with a contused lung. McMorris and Sobers put on 133 and another big stand came when Nurse replaced McMorris.

A record crowd of over 20,000 was shocked by the complete transformation which came over the game on Saturday. Sobers, who batted six hours eleven minutes and hit one 5 and twenty-one 4s, was soon out and in ninety minutes before lunch, despite their strong position, West Indies added only 38. Trying to improve the rate in the afternoon, they collapsed badly. Three wickets fell at the lunch score of 329 and in eighty-two minutes the last seven went for the addition of 24 to the interval total. McMorris, with his chest protected, resumed at the fall of the sixth wicket, but did not stay long.

England thus restricted the lead to 76 of which Cowdrey and Pullar cleared 65 by the close. The pitch developed large cracks, but played well while Cowdrey and Pullar carried their stand to 177. Both left at the same total. Cowdrey, in great form, gave one of his finest displays and missed a century in each innings by three. He drove and hooked with perfect timing. Subsequently, the ball began to shoot and turn off the cracks and England broke down, only May holding out for long. Nine wickets went for 280 by close on the fifth day but on the last morning Allen and Statham held out for a valuable forty-five minutes and West Indies needed 230 to win in four hours five minutes.

Hunte began with a flourish, scoring 40 out of 48 for one in an hour, but the turning-point came when Sobers was run out when he looked dangerous. West Indies kept after the runs, but although the pitch did not deteriorate as much as expected scoring was never easy. At tea 115 were needed with ninety minutes left, but when Kanhai was sixth out West Indies gave up the chase and England tried to get the last four wickets in the final forty-five minutes. Near the end May refused to allow a runner for Kanhai, who developed cramp and muscle trouble at the back of the leg. Later May apologised to Kanhai and Alexander for his misinterpretation of the law, though the umpires and Alexander himself were also in doubt about the position.

England

M. C. Cowdrey c Scarlett b Ramadhin	114	–	c Alexander b Scarlett	97
G. Pullar c Sobers b Hall	19	–	lbw b Ramadhin	66
K. F. Barrington c Alexander b Watson	16	–	lbw b Solomon	4
*P. B. H. May c Hunte b Hall	9	–	b Hall	45
E. R. Dexter c Alexander b Hall	25	–	b Watson	16
M. J. K. Smith b Hall	0	–	lbw b Watson	10
R. Illingworth c Alexander b Hall	17	–	b Ramadhin	6
†R. Swetman b Hall	0	–	lbw b Watson	4
F. S. Trueman c Solomon b Ramadhin	17	–	lbw b Watson	4
D. A. Allen not out	30	–	not out	17
J. B. Statham b Hall	13	–	lbw b Ramadhin	12
L-b 4, w 10, n-b 3	17		B 8, l-b 10, w 3, n-b 2	23

1/28 2/54 3/68 4/113 5/113   277   1/177 2/177 3/190 4/211   305
6/165 7/170 8/215 9/245   5/239 6/258 7/269 8/269 9/280

West Indies

C. Hunte c Illingworth b Statham	7	–	b Trueman	40
E. McMorris b Barrington	73	–	b Trueman	1
R. Kanhai run out	18	–	b Trueman	57
G. Sobers lbw b Trueman	147	–	run out	19
S. Nurse c Smith b Illingworth	70	–	b Trueman	11
J. Solomon c Swetman b Allen	8	–	not out	10
R. Scarlett c Statham b Illingworth	6	–	lbw b Statham	12
*†F. C. M. Alexander b Trueman	0	–	not out	7
S. Ramadhin b Statham	5			
C. Watson b Statham	3			
W. Hall not out	0			
B 6, l-b 7, w 1, n-b 2	16		B 9, l-b 3, w 6	18

1/12 2/56 3/299 4/329 5/329   353   1/11 2/48   (6 wkts) 175
6/329 7/341 8/347 9/350   3/86 4/111 5/140 6/152

West Indies Bowling

	Overs	Mdns	Runs	Wkts	Overs	Mdns	Runs	Wkts
Hall	31.2	8	69	7	26	5	93	1
Watson	29	7	74	1	27	8	62	4
Ramadhin	28	3	78	2	28.3	14	38	3
Scarlett	10	4	13	—	28	12	51	1
Sobers	2	—	14	—	8	2	18	—
Solomon	4	1	12	—	6	1	20	1

England Bowling

	Overs	Mdns	Runs	Wkts	Overs	Mdns	Runs	Wkts
Statham	32.1	8	76	3	18	6	45	1
Trueman..........	33	10	82	2	18	4	54	4
Dexter............	12	3	38	—				
Allen.............	28	10	57	1	9	4	19	—
Barrington	21	7	38	1	4	4	—	—
Illingworth	30	13	46	2	13	4	35	—
Cowdrey..........					1	—	4	—

Umpires: P. Burke and E. Lee Kow.

ENGLAND IN INDIA, PAKISTAN AND CEYLON

ENGLAND v INDIA

Fifth Test Match

Played at Madras, February 6, 8, 9, 10, 1952

India won by an innings and eight runs. They made history by recording their first Test victory, and they did it in emphatic style. India were the superior all-round side and they went all out for success from the first ball. Their hero was Mankad, who bowled superbly in each innings, taking twelve wickets in the match for 108. His performance of eight for 55 in the first innings has seldom been bettered in Test cricket when it is considered that the pitch gave him little assistance. Mankad's bowling inspired the whole side, the fielding being far better than in previous matches and the batting possessed a more adventurous spirit, necessary for the occasion. England disappointed badly. There was no real reason for the batting collapse in the first innings which virtually decided the match. Hopes that they could stage one of their renowned recoveries were dashed when the pitch turned difficult after the third day.

Yet again India made five changes from their previous side. Manjrekar, Nayudu, Shinde, Joshi and Adhikari stood down for Mushtaq Ali, Amarnath, Gopinath, Divecha and Sen. As originally chosen the side included Adhikari and omitted Umrigar, but a wrist injury due to a fall gave Umrigar another opportunity which he seized splendidly. Carr led England for the first time, Howard standing down with pleurisy, this being the one change from the Kanpur side.

Carr won the toss, giving England a 3-2 advantage in the series, but they were soon in difficulties, Lowson being bowled by a splendid breakback with three scored. Spooner and Graveney looked like bringing about a recovery, but the advent of Mankad at 65 changed the course of the match. Two or three times Mankad almost lured Graveney out of his ground before the batsman could resist no longer and moved forward to a ball well on the off and was stumped.

Spooner and Robertson added 60 for the next stand, but again just when England looked to be getting themselves out of trouble a wicket fell, Spooner, who stayed two hours fifty minutes, being caught at cover off Hazare's second ball. For a change, Watkins failed and Poole was never comfortable. With half the side out for 197 only two recognised batsmen, Robertson and Carr, remained. They made a good effort with a partnership of 47 before Robertson was brilliantly caught and bowled after a stay of four and a half hours. Mankad followed this by taking the last four wickets which fell for 22, three of them stumped when lured forward by the flight.

During the afternoon the death of King George VI was announced and arrangements were changed, the second day being made the rest day. Subsequently India batted consistently, with Roy again in fine form. Fourth out at 191, he scored his second century of the series and hit fifteen 4s in 111, made in three hours fifty minutes. India really took control after the fall of the fifth wicket, Phadkar and Umrigar adding 104 and Umrigar and Gopinath 93 in eighty minutes. Umrigar took out his bat for 130 after four hours thirty-five minutes, a splendid effort following a run of disappointing scores in the Tests.

England, 191 behind, survived the last quarter of an hour on the third day, but with the pitch wearing they were soon struggling next day. Robertson again batted well and made top score for the second time, Watkins showed he was still full of fight, but they were almost alone in their resistance and the match ended before tea on the fourth day. The scenes at the finish were surprisingly subdued, but the Indian officials and players were delighted at the first victory by their country at the twenty-fifth attempt to win a Test match.

England

F. A. Lowson b Phadkar	1	– c Mankad b Phadkar	7
R. T. Spooner c Phadkar b Hazare	66	– lbw b Divecha	6
T. W. Graveney st Sen b Mankad	39	– c Divecha b Ghulam Ahmed	25
J. D. Robertson c and b Mankad	77	– lbw b Ghulam Ahmed	56
A. J. Watkins c Gopinath b Mankad	9	– c and b Mankad	48
C. J. Poole b Mankad	15	– c Divecha b Ghulam Ahmed	3
D. B. Carr st Sen b Mankad	40	– c Mankad b Ghulam Ahmed	5
M. J. Hilton st Sen b Mankad	0	– st Sen b Mankad	15
J. B. Statham st Sen b Mankad	6	– c Gopinath b Mankad	9
F. Ridgway lbw b Mankad	0	– b Mankad	0
R. Tattersall not out	2	– not out	0
B 4, l-b 4, n-b 3	11	B 7, l-b 2	9

1/3 2/71 3/131 4/174 5/197 6/244 266 1/13 2/15 3/68 4/117 183
7/252 8/261 9/261   5/135 6/159 7/159 8/178 9/178

India

Mushtaq Ali st Spooner b Carr	22	R. V. Divecha c Spooner b Ridgway	12
P. Roy c Watkins b Tattersall	111	P. Sen b Watkins	2
V. S. Hazare b Hilton	20	Ghulam Ahmed not out	1
V. Mankad c Watkins b Carr	22	B 8, l-b 2	10
L. Amarnath c Spooner b Statham	31		
D. G. Phadkar b Hilton	61	1/53 2/97 3/157 (9 wkts dec.) 457	
P. Umrigar not out	130	4/191 5/216 6/320	
C. D. Gopinath b Tattersall	35	7/413 8/430 9/448	

India Bowling

	Overs	Mdns	Runs	Wkts	Overs	Mdns	Runs	Wkts
Phadkar	16	2	49	1	9	2	17	1
Divecha	12	2	27	—	7	1	21	1
Amarnath	27	6	56	—	3	—	6	—
Ghulam Ahmed	18	5	53	—	26	5	77	4
Mankad	38.5	15	55	8	30.4	9	53	4
Hazare	10	5	15	1				

England Bowling

	Overs	Mdns	Runs	Wkts
Statham	19	3	54	1
Ridgway	17	2	47	1
Tattersall	40	9	100	2
Hilton	39	13	94	2
Carr	19	2	84	2
Watkins	14	1	50	1
Robertson	5	1	18	—

Umpires: B. J. Mohoni and M. G. Vijayasarathy.

MCC v CEYLON

Played at Colombo, February 22, 23, 24, 1952

MCC won by an innings and 33 runs. Keen to re-establish themselves after their heavy defeat in the previous match, MCC took revenge against an all-Ceylon side in emphatic manner. The pitch was again lively and the pace of Statham and Ridgway proved far too much for hesitant batsmen. Even C. I. Gunesekara and de Saram, who did well for the Commonwealth, failed, scoring only eleven runs between them in four innings. Ceylon were all out in under two and a half hours for 58, the lowest total against MCC on the tour. MCC took the lead without loss, Robertson and Spooner opening with 70. Graveney gave another fine display of driving and also defended well on the second morning following overnight rain which made the pitch soft. Unbeaten after three hours five minutes for 102, Graveney recorded his sixth century of the tour. Carr declared with four men out and a lead of 212, and Ceylon looked like becoming easy victims again when four men left for 50. Improvement came, opening batsmen Rodrigo defending doggedly for three hours forty minutes while scoring 42. Leadbeater spun his leg-breaks well from a shortened run, but after getting nine men out for 134, MCC were held up for another forty minutes, the last pair, Navaratne, batting with a heavily plastered forehead following a blow in the first innings, and Nathanielsz adding 45. Thus MCC finished their first-class matches in fine style.

Ceylon

M. Rodrigo c Carr b Statham	0	– b Statham	42
C. H. Gunesekara b Leadbeater	22	– c Spooner b Leadbeater	12
F. C. de Saram b Statham	1	– c Watkins b Robertson	5
C. I. Gunesekara c Robertson b Ridgway	0	– c Hilton b Robertson	5
S. Jayasinghe b Hilton	16	– b Statham	11
S. Coomaraswamy c Spooner b Ridgway	12	– c Watkins b Leadbeater	18
B. Kasipillai c Spooner b Ridgway	2	– c Statham b Leadbeater	8
B. Navaratne b Statham	2	– not out	34
E. C. Kelaart c Leadbeater b Statham	3	– st Spooner b Leadbeater	0
T. Shanmuganatham c Carr b Ridgway	0	– c Ridgway b Leadbeater	2
E. Nathanielsz not out	0	– c Graveney b Hilton	13
		B 20, l-b 8, n-b 1	29

1/4 2/6 3/7 4/39 5/43 6/45   58   1/17 2/30 3/36 4/50 5/96   179
7/56 8/58 9/58   6/128 7/128 8/130 9/134

MCC

J. D. Robertson lbw b Nathanielsz	30	C. J. Poole not out 14
R. T. Spooner b Kelaart	57	
T. W. Graveney not out	102	B 7, l-b 6 13
D. Kenyon c Kelaart b Shanmuganatham	52	
A. J. Watkins c C. H. Gunesekara b Shanmuganatham	2	1/70 2/111 3/240 (4 wkts dec.) 270 4/248

D. B. Carr, F. Ridgway, J. B. Statham, M. J. Hilton and E. Leadbeater did not bat.

MCC Bowling

	Overs	Mdns	Runs	Wkts	Overs	Mdns	Runs	Wkts
Statham	11	7	9	4	13	8	10	2
Ridgway	10	1	20	4	9	3	21	—
Watkins	3	—	12	—	5	2	10	—
Hilton	4	—	11	1	19.3	11	31	1
Leadbeater	1	—	6	1	16	6	41	5
Robertson					10	—	27	2
Carr					6	1	10	—

Ceylon Bowling

	Overs	Mdns	Runs	Wkts
Nathanielsz........	18	1	51	1
Coomaraswamy....	4	1	16	—
Jayasinghe........	5	—	19	—
Shanmuganatham ..	22	1	71	2
Kelaart...........	22	5	70	1
C. I. Gunesekara ...	16	2	30	—

Umpires: D. S. Soyza and H. E. W. de Zylva.

MCC "A" TEAM IN PAKISTAN, 1955-56

The first MCC "A" team to undertake a tour abroad returned from Pakistan amid a storm of controversy. In order that some of the countries who seldom receive visits of full-strength sides from England should be able to keep interest alive in the intervening years, "A" tours were originated. To England it gave the opportunity of trying promising young cricketers and also of rewarding players for long and valuable service in county cricket.

On this occasion a happy band of 15 players set out early in December 1955 with little thought of trouble ahead. The party comprised D. B. Carr, A. J. Watkins, K. Barrington, D. B. Close, F. J. Titmus, G. A. R. Lock, A. E. Moss and J. M. Parks with Test match experience, P. E. Richardson, W. H. H. Sutcliffe, R. Swetman, P. J. Sainsbury, and M. J. Cowan, youngsters of whom much was expected, H. W. Stephenson and M. Tompkin, the attractive and consistent Leicestershire batsman who began his career in 1938. Carr, the captain, and Watkins had previously been in Pakistan with the MCC team in 1951-52.

For most of the tour all went well, but the difficulties arose during the third representative match against Pakistan at Peshawar. An incident, which began as a joke on the part of some of the MCC players, was magnified to such alarming proportions that a few days later it led to an offer from the MCC President, Lord Alexander of Tunis, to call off the rest of the tour.

The incident involved the ragging of one of the umpires, Idris Begh, when what was known as "the water treatment" took place. One of the standing jokes on the tour between the MCC players themselves had involved the use of cold water much in the same way as students might do in a rag. Unfortunately, some of the players did not realise that the type of humour generally accepted by most people in Britain, might not be understood in other parts of the world.

More important was the unhappy timing of the affair, for it occurred during the course of a match in which some comments had been made about umpiring decisions. The MCC players and manager made it quite clear when they returned home that the umpiring had nothing to do with their rag. They thought that Begh was a willing "victim" and, indeed, all might have passed off without comment had not other Pakistanis happened to witness the tail-end of the incident.

From then onwards events moved quickly and something that had started innocently soon got out of hand. On March 2 Lord Alexander sent two cables to Pakistan. The first was an official message from himself, as MCC President, to the President of the Pakistan Board of Control which said: "MCC are deeply concerned at the regrettable incident reported from Peshawar. Our manager's report is still awaited before the matter can be dealt with officially. Meanwhile we should like you to know that the expressions of regret and apology made on our behalf by our manager are fully endorsed."

The other cable, a personal message from Lord Alexander to General Iskander Mirza, at the time Governor-General of Pakistan, read: "I am greatly perturbed at the reports about the behaviour of our team at Peshawar. I have been waiting to receive our manager's report before writing to you, but since I have not yet received the report I hasten to tell you how much I deplore this unfortunate incident and to offer you, an old and valued friend, my own personal regrets."

General Mirza replied: "Thank you very much for your personal telegram. I am sure good relations between the MCC team and our people, if not already restored, will be restored soon. I join you in regretting the incident." General Mirza later said that Lord Alexander had offered to cancel the tour during the course of a telephone conversation. MCC confirmed this and also stated that Lord Alexander had offered to recall the team forthwith if this would be in the best interests of restoring friendly relations, and also to compensate the Pakistan Board of Control for any financial loss arising from this action. General Mirza replied that he greatly appreciated the attitude taken by the MCC but asked that the tour should be allowed to continue.

Unfortunately the damage to good relations had been done and in the last match at Karachi there came a further upset which led to D. B. Carr and Fazal Mahmood, the acting Pakistan captain, issuing a joint statement which said: "Imtiaz Ahmed, when batting, objected to some close-to-the-wicket fielders using words among themselves which upset him while he was preparing to take strike."

"He drew the attention of the MCC captain to it and asked him to stop them, which he did."

Then came an announcement from Group-Captain Cheema, the Hon. Secretary of the Pakistan Board of Control, which said: "The Board of Control have taken note of the incidents which took place on the field yesterday and which were reported in the Press. An inquiry at which Mr. Howard was present has revealed that both sides were equally at fault. In the circumstances the Board strongly feel that these incidents should be treated as closed and appeal to both teams and the public to do likewise. They sincerely hope that the public will co-operate in this matter in a truly sporting spirit and give the players on both sides a fair chance."

On March 17, when the team returned to England, Mr. Howard issued a long statement which included these points:

(1) "I hope that the adverse publicity given towards its end will not be allowed to eclipse the successes of the tour. I believe it is fair to say that the tour has been successful in its object.

(2) "The folly of the Peshawar incident has been fully realised and we also appreciate the serious repercussions at home and in Pakistan that resulted. I can assure you that our young team are bitterly sorry about it and have suffered a good deal as a result.

(3) "The incident itself was actuated by nothing more than high spirits and a sense of fun. It had no connection whatsoever with umpiring decisions made by Mr. Idris Begh.

(4) "Suggestions made in some quarters that the members of the team implicated in the affair were under the influence of alcohol are quite unfounded and completely untrue. In fact, the majority of the team are either teetotal or persons who drink very little indeed."

On March 20 the MCC Committee issued the following statement: "The MCC Committee have fully investigated the incident which occurred at Peshawar on the evening of February 26, 1956. They condemn the treatment accorded to Mr. Idris Begh. The captain, who was present at the time, should have recognised at once that this 'ragging', although initiated by nothing more than high spirits and with no harmful intent what-soever, might be regarded, as it was in many quarters, as an attack upon an umpire. The Committee are satisfied that this was not the case.

"The Committee consider that the responsibility for the incident rests entirely with the captain and he has been so informed. It is hoped that the publicity that has attended this affair may now be discontinued, both in the best interests of cricket relations between the two countries and for the sake of a team of young cricketers who, up to that time, had proved themselves loyal, conscientious and well-mannered tourists."

The following day D. B. Carr, the captain, accepted full responsibility for the "ragging" incident.

These events tended to overshadow the tour from the cricket point of view, but it could not hide the fact that Pakistan, in their short cricket history, had made rapid strides. They were the first to admit that they were fortunate to share the rubber in England in 1954, but the MCC players were soon made to realise that they were a much stronger team on their own pitches, many of them matting.

Of the four representative matches the first was drawn, Pakistan won the next two and MCC succeeded in the last. These two defeats were the only ones suffered on the tour, MCC winning seven first-class games and drawing five.

The outstanding personality was undoubtedly Lock, the Surrey slow left-arm bowler, whose 81 wickets on such a short tour was a remarkable achievement. He found the pitches completely to his liking and he enjoyed a tour of almost unbroken triumph. Moss, the Middlesex fast bowler, also did extremely well without a great deal of support. Cowan, the Yorkshire fast left-arm bowler, developed back trouble and returned home early after playing in only four matches. Until Thomson, of Sussex, was flown out as a replacement Moss had to shoulder a heavy burden.

Few of the batsmen enhanced their reputations. Exceptions were Richardson and Close, the left-handed opening pair, who often gave the side a good start, and possibly Barrington, although following his good season in England, more was expected from him.

Richardson, who hit the only two hundreds made on the tour, showed himself to be a sound, defensive batsman with plenty of determination. Swetman had played only nine first-class matches when chosen to tour, but he fully justified his selection and his wicket-keeping and batting reached a high standard. Titmus and Sainsbury were capable all-rounders, but generally the team was inconsistent in batting and relied too much on Lock and Moss in attack.

For Pakistan, Fazal Mahmood confirmed that he was one of the leading fast-medium paced bowlers in the world. Khan Mohammad, A. H. Kardar, the captain, and Shuja-ud-Din also rose to the occasion with the ball when needed. Hanif Mohammad was again their leading batsman and most support came from his brother, Wazir, Alim-ud-Din, Waqar Hassan and Imtiaz Ahmed.

CRICKET IN AUSTRALIA

AUSTRALIA v INDIA

First Test Match

Played at Brisbane, November 28, 29, December 1, 2, 3, 4, 1947

Australia won by an innings and 226 runs. Unfortunate to be caught on a treacherous pitch, India collapsed twice, and the manner of their defeat must have resulted in loss of confidence for the remaining Tests. There was nothing wrong with the conditions when Australia batted first, and, after the early loss of Brown, Bradman gave one of his superb displays. He lost Morris at 97, but completely demoralised the bowlers by punishing methods which brought runs at a terrific rate. Not a ball could be bowled until five o'clock on the second day, but the surprising attendance of 11,000 watched the hour's cricket that took place. A further downpour saturated the pitch on the Sunday, but next day the sun appeared and India's task was hopeless. Realising the awkwardness of the conditions, the Australians soon declared. Bradman took four and three-quarter hours over 185, which contained twenty 4s.

With the ball doing all manner of unexpected tricks, India, used to the fast, hard pitches in their own country, were completely baffled. Mankad and Gul Mahomed fell in the first over from Lindwall, but the most successful bowler was Toshack, who, with left-arm slow-medium deliveries, dismissed five men in nineteen balls for two runs. All out 58, India followed-on 324 behind, and before the dismal day ended for them four second innings wickets fell for 41.

More rain restricted the fourth day to an hour, and nothing could be done next day, but conditions were not quite so difficult when play re-started on Thursday, Sarwate gave a stubborn defensive display for three hours, but few of his colleagues could cope with Toshack, who again made the most of the pitch. In the match he took eleven wickets for 31 runs.

If India had won the toss the result might well have been different, for in Mankad they possessed a bowler able to exploit the conditions equally as well as Toshack.

Australia

W. A. Brown c Irani b Amarnath 11	D. Tallon not out. 3
A. R. Morris hit wkt b Sarwate 47	I. W. Johnson c Rangnekar b Mankad 6
D. G. Bradman hit wkt b Armarnath ..... .185	E. R. H. Toshack not out 0
A. L. Hassett c Gul Mahomed b Mankad... 48	B 5, l-b 1, w 1 7
K. R. Miller c Mankad b Amarnath 58	
C. L. McCool c Sohoni b Amarnath 10	1/38 2/97 (8 wkts dec.) 382
R. R Lindwall st Irani b Mankad 7	3/198 4/318 5/344 6/373 7/373 8/380

W. A. Johnston did not bat.

India

V. Mankad c Tallon b Lindwall	0	– b Lindwall	7
C. T. Sarwate c Johnston b Miller	12	– b Johnston	26
Gul Mahomed b Lindwall	0	– b Toshack	13
H. R. Adhikari c McCool b Johnston	8	– lbw b Toshack	13
G. Kishenchand c Tallon b Johnston	1	– c Bradman b Toshack	0
V. S. Hazare c Brown b Toshack	10	– c Morris b Toshack	18
K. M. Rangnekar c Miller b Toshack	1	– c Hassett b Toshack	0
S. W. Sohoni c Miller b Toshack	2	– c Brown b Miller	4
L. Amarnath c Bradman b Toshack	22	– b Toshack	5
C. S. Nayudu not out	0	– c Hassett b Lindwall	6
J. K. Irani c Hassett b Toshack	0	– not out	2
B 1, l-b 1	2	B 3, n-b 1	4

1/0 2/0 3/19 4/23 5/23   58   1/14 2/27 3/41 4/41 5/72   98
6/53 7/56 8/58 9/58   6/80 7/80 8/89 9/94

India Bowling

	Overs	Mdns	Runs	Wkts
Sohoni	23	4	81	—
Amarnath	39	10	84	4
Mankad	34	3	113	3
Sarwate	5	1	16	1
Hazare	11	1	63	—
Nayudu	3	—	18	—

Australia Bowling

	Overs	Mdns	Runs	Wkts	Overs	Mdns	Runs	Wkts
Lindwall	5	2	11	2	10.7	2	19	2
W. Johnston	8	4	17	2	9	6	11	1
Miller	6	1	26	1	10	2	30	1
Toshack	2.3	1	2	5	17	6	29	6
I. Johnson					3	1	5	—

AUSTRALIA v INDIA

Third Test Match

Played at Melbourne, January 1, 2, 3, 5, 1948

Australia won by 233 runs. Bradman added to his long list of triumphs by hitting a hundred in each innings, the first time he had accomplished the feat in a Test match. India fared reasonably well up to a point, but were again faced with ill fortune with regard to the weather.

A third-wicket stand of 169 between Bradman and Hassett assured Australia of a good total. Hassett, missed in the slips off Hazare when 31, scored as fast as his partner, and at times runs came at two a minute. Bradman scored 132 out of 260, and on his departure the bowlers met with better reward, the last six wickets falling for 105.

When Mankad and Sarwate began India's reply with a stand of 124, the position was intriguing, but the fall of two of their best batsmen, Hazare and Amarnath, to successive balls changed the character of the game. Mankad, fifth out at 198, claimed the distinction of being the first India batsman to hit a hundred against Australia. Rain overnight altered the state of the pitch, and when three of his batsmen fell cheaply Amarnath declared, although India were 103 behind. Bradman countered this move by sending in his tail-end men in the hope that conditions would ease. He must have been worried, however, when three of them fell for 13, and Barnes, one of his leading batsmen, followed at 32.

Any hopes India may have held of a complete collapse were soon dashed, for Morris and Bradman thoroughly mastered the attack and shared in an unbroken fifth partnership of 223. Bradman reached his hundred first and Morris followed suit just before the close of the day. Heavy overnight rain made the pitch responsive to spin, and Bradman, seizing his opportunity, declared. The India batsmen never looked like making a fight. Half the side fell for 60 and, despite a few good hits by Rai Singh, the end was inevitable.

Australia

S. G. Barnes b Mankad	12	– c Sen b Amarnath ... 15
A. R. Morris b Amarnath	45	– not out ... 100
D. G. Bradman lbw b Phadkar	132	– not out ... 127
A. L. Hassett lbw b Mankad	80	
K. R. Miller lbw b Mankad	29	
R. A. Hamence st Sen b Amarnath	25	
R. R. Lindwall b Amarnath	26	
D. Tallon c Mankad b Amarnath	2	
B. Dooland not out	21	– lbw b Phadkar ... 6
I. W. Johnson lbw b Mankad	16	– c Hazare b Amarnath ... 0
W. A. Johnston run out	5	– lbw b Amarnath ... 3
Extras	1	B 3, n-b 1 ... 4

1/29 2/99 3/268 4/289 5/302   394   1/1 2/11 3/13 4/32   (4 wkts dec.) 255
6/339 7/341 8/352 9/387

India

V. Mankad c Tallon b Johnston	116	– b Johnston ... 13
C. T. Sarwate c Tallon b Johnston	36	– b Johnston ... 1
Gul Mahomed c and b Dooland	12	– c Morris b Johnson ... 28
V. S. Hazare c Tallon b Barnes	17	– c Barnes b Miller ... 10
L. Amarnath lbw b Barnes	0	– b Lindwall ... 8
D. G. Phadkar not out	55	– c Barnes b Johnston ... 13
H. R. Adhikari st Tallon b Johnson	26	– c Lindwall b Johnson ... 1
Rai Singh c Barnes b Johnson	2	– c Tallon b Johnston ... 24
K. M. Rangnekar c and b Johnson	6	– c Hamence b Johnson ... 18
P. Sen b Johnson	4	– c Hassett b Johnson ... 2
C. S. Nayudu not out	4	– not out ... 0
B 9, l-b 3, n-b 1	13	B 6, l-b 1 ... 7

1/124 2/145 3/188 4/188 5/198   (9 wkts dec.) 291   1/10 2/27 3/44 4/60 5/60   125
6/260 7/264 8/280 9/284   6/69 7/100 8/107 9/125

India Bowling

	Overs	Mdns	Runs	Wkts	Overs	Mdns	Runs	Wkts
Phadkar	15	1	80	1	10	1	28	1
Amarnath	21	5	78	4	20	3	52	3
Hazare	16.1	—	62	—	11	1	55	—
Mankad	37	4	135	4	18	4	74	—
Sarwate	3	—	16	—	5	—	41	—
Nayudu	2	—	22	—				
Gul Mahomed					1	—	1	—

Australia Bowling

	Overs	Mdns	Runs	Wkts	Overs	Mdns	Runs	Wkts
Lindwall..........	12	—	47	—	3	—	10	1
Miller............	13	2	46	—	7	—	29	1
W. Johnston.......	12	—	33	2	10	1	44	4
I. Johnson........	14	1	59	4	6	—	35	4
Dooland..........	12	—	68	1				
Barnes...........	6	1	25	2				

AUSTRALIA v INDIA

Fourth Test Match

Played at Adelaide, January 23, 24, 26, 27, 28, 1948

Australia won by an innings and 16 runs. Although they gained another overwhelming success, and in so doing won the rubber, the match was a personal triumph for Hazare, who followed Bradman's example in the Third Test and hit a hundred in each innings. Against such a powerful attack as that possessed by the Australians, this was a truly remarkable performance. To balance this, however, Bradman was once again in irresistible form, hitting a double hundred. Hassett fell only two short of that figure and Barnes also completed a century.

Bradman gave Australia a big advantage when he won the toss for the third time; on a perfect pitch bowlers were helpless to check the flow of runs. Morris fell early, but Barnes and Bradman shared in a second wicket stand of 236. Apart from a chance to second slip when 61, Barnes batted faultlessly. Bradman, always the complete master, scored 201 out of 341 before leaving towards the close of the first day. More free hitting came from Hassett and Miller during a fourth-wicket partnership of 142. An interesting race developed to see whether Hassett could complete two hundred, but he was just short, taking out his bat for an excellent 198. In reaching 674, Australia made the highest score ever recorded against India and also the biggest total for any Test Match in Australia.

India made a shocking start, losing two wickets for six runs, but they fought back well. Half the side fell for 133, but Hazare found a capable partner in Phadkar, 188 runs being added. Hazare, always master of the situation, hit fourteen 4s and his partner fifteen 4s. Despite this gallant effort, India followed on 293 behind, and this time their start was even worse, two wickets falling without a run on the board. Six men were out for 139 and it looked as though India would capitulate easily, but Hazare again refused to be disturbed by the situation; he received useful help from Adhikari and 132 runs were added. Then the end soon came, the last three wickets falling for six runs. Six men failed to score in this innings, most of the batsmen finding the pace of Lindwall to much for them. Accurate attacking bowling brought Lindwall seven wickets for 38 runs.

Australia

S. G. Barnes lbw b Mankad 112	R. R. Lindwall b Rangachari 2
A. R. Morris b Phadkar 7	D. Tallon lbw b Mankad................ 1
D. G. Bradman b Hazare 201	E. R. H. Toshack lbw b Hazare 8
A. L. Hassett not out...................198	
K. R. Miller b Rangachari............... 67	B 8, l-b 6, n-b 2.............. 16
R. N. Harvey lbw b Rangachari.......... 13	
C. L. McCool b Phadkar 27	1/20 2/256 3/361 4/503 5/523 674
I. W. Johnson b Rangachari............. 22	6/576 7/634 8/640 9/641

India

V. Mankad b McCool	49	– c Tallon b Lindwall	0
C. T. Sarwate b Miller	1	– b Toshack	11
P. Sen b Miller	0	– not out	0
L. Amarnath c Bradman b Johnson	46	– b Lindwall	0
V. S. Hazare lbw b Johnson	116	– b Lindwall	145
Gul Mahomed st Tallon b Johnson	4	– b Barnes	34
D. G. Phadkar lbw b Toshack	123	– lbw b Lindwall	14
G. Kishenchand b Lindwall	10	– b Lindwall	0
H. R. Adhikari run out	21	– lbw b Miller	51
K. M. Rangnekar st Tallon b Johnson	8	– b Lindwall	0
C. R. Rangachari not out	0	– c McCool b Lindwall	0
B 18, l-b 3, n-b 1	22	Extras	22

1/1 2/6 3/69 4/124 5/133   **381**   1/0 2/0 3/33 4/99 5/139   **277**
6/321 7/353 8/359 9/375   6/139 7/271 8/273 9/273

India Bowling

	Overs	Mdns	Runs	Wkts
Phadkar	15	—	74	2
Amarnath	9	—	42	—
Rangachari	41	5	141	4
Mankad	43	8	170	2
Sarwate	22	1	121	—
Hazare	21.3	1	110	2

Australia Bowling

	Overs	Mdns	Runs	Wkts	Overs	Mdns	Runs	Wkts
Lindwall	21	5	61	1	16.5	4	38	7
Miller	9	1	39	2	9	3	13	1
McCool	28	2	102	1	4	—	26	—
Johnson	23.1	5	64	4	20	4	54	—
Toshack	18	2	66	1	25	8	73	1
Barnes	9	—	23	—	18	4	51	1
Bradman	1	—	4	—				

AUSTRALIA v SOUTH AFRICA

Second Test Match

Played at Melbourne, December 24, 26, 27, 29, 30, 1952

South Africa won by 82 runs. Their first victory over Australia for forty-two years came as reward for superior all-round cricket. Endean and Tayfield played specially notable roles, but the whole side deserved praise for two fielding performances which drew favourable comparison with some of the best teams of the past. Little indication of the events which were to lead to Australia's third defeat in thirty-three post-war Tests – all in the last eight matches – was contained in the early play. South Africa ran into immediate trouble against Miller and Lindwall, and the total only became respectable through solid rescue work by Murray, top scorer, Mansell and Tayfield.

Throughout the series South Africa gave no finer display of out-cricket than on the second day. Although their attack was depleted by the absence of Murray (fibrositis) and Watkins (strained back) they held Australia to a purely nominal lead. The stand of 84 by McDonald and Morris was Australia's first-wicket best in twenty-two Test innings but, apart from the hard-driving Miller, the middle batsmen failed against the off-breaks of Tayfield and the leg-spin of Mansell. By steady length and bowling to his field, Tayfield gave nothing away in an unchanged spell of nearly four hours, at one stage of which he took the wickets of Ring, Miller and Johnston for one run.

The spectacular catch which dismissed Morris set South Africa's standard for the innings. A drive hit Cheetham's upflung hands close to the wicket but bounced away from him. Tayfield spun round, raced after the ball, and caught it in a full-length dive. Cheetham and McGlew made other excellent catches, and Endean, with his back to the iron fence, held a drive by Miller above his head.

The last three days went all in favour of South Africa. When Lindwall and Miller used the new ball the bowling presented some menace, but Endean, Waite, who shared a second-wicket stand of 111, Funston and McLean faced them calmly. Most of the other bowling was made to look innocuous. Endean, though unattractive in style and relying chiefly on strokes behind the wicket, withstood the attack for seven and a half hours without giving a chance. His 162 not out was the second highest innings for South Africa against Australia, the best being G. A. Faulkner's 201 on the same ground in 1910-11. On account of sore feet Miller was used sparingly, but even so he caused most batting problems and when he dismissed Waite he completed his Test double of 1,000 runs and 100 wickets.

Poor light did not help Australia when they started the last innings, but more high-class bowling by Tayfield was the chief reason for their failure to score the 373 required to win. In one period of nine maiden overs he sent back Miller, Langley and Hole, and he richly merited his match record of thirteen wickets for 165. Once again Harvey stood out as Australia's best batsman and the lofted stroke which brought his innings to a close resulted from his only error of timing.

A ninth-wicket stand of 61 by Benaud and the hard-hitting Ring temporarily raised Australia's hopes, but Tayfield split the stand and, when he also brought Ring's brave innings to a close, he fittingly clinched South Africa's triumph.

South Africa

D. J. McGlew b Lindwall	46	– st Langley b Ring	13
J. H. B. Waite c Lindwall b Miller	0	– c Hole b Miller	62
W. R. Endean c Benaud b Lindwall	2	– not out	162
K. J. Funston c Ring b Miller	9	– run out	26
R. A. McLean c Lindwall b Ring	27	– lbw b Miller	42
J. E. Cheetham c Johnston b Miller	15	– lbw b Johnston	6
J. C. Watkins c Langley b Benaud	19	– b Johnston	3
P. N. F. Mansell b Lindwall	24	– b Miller	18
A. R. A. Murray c Johnston b Benaud	51	– st Langley b Ring	23
H. J. Tayfield c Langley b Miller	23	– lbw b Lindwall	22
M. G. Melle not out	4	– b Lindwall	0
B 4, l-b 3	7	B 1, l-b 5, w 4, n-b 1	11

1/2 2/9 3/27 4/63 5/93 6/112   227   1/23 2/134 3/196 4/261   388
7/126 8/156 9/207   5/284 6/290 7/319 8/353 9/388

Australia

C. C. McDonald c Fuller b Mansell	82	– c Mansell b Murray	23
A. R. Morris c and b Tayfield	43	– c Watkins b Melle	1
R. N. Harvey c Cheetham b Tayfield	11	– c Watkins b Tayfield	60
A. L. Hassett c Melle b Mansell	18	– lbw b Tayfield	21
K. R. Miller c Endean b Tayfield	52	– b Tayfield	31
G. B. Hole c Waite b Mansell	13	– b Tayfield	25
R. Benaud b Tayfield	5	– c Melle b Tayfield	45
R. R. Lindwall run out	1	– b Melle	19
D. Ring c McGlew b Tayfield	14	– c Melle b Tayfield	53
G. R. Langley not out	2	– b Tayfield	4
W. A. Johnston lbw b Tayfield	0	– not out	0
N-b 2	2	B 1, l-b 6, n-b 1	8

1/84 2/98 3/155 4/158 5/188 6/211   243   1/3 2/34 3/76 4/131   290
7/219 8/239 9/243   5/139 6/148 7/181 8/216 9/277

Australia Bowling

	Overs	Mdns	Runs	Wkts	Overs	Mdns	Runs	Wkts
Lindwall	14	2	29	3	31.5	4	87	2
Miller	21	3	62	4	22	5	51	3
Johnston.........	12	2	37	—	31	9	77	2
Ring	18	1	72	1	31	5	115	2
Benaud	6.6	1	20	2	6	—	23	—
Hole					7	—	24	—

South Africa Bowling

	Overs	Mdns	Runs	Wkts	Overs	Mdns	Runs	Wkts
Melle............	14	—	73	—	11	2	39	2
Watkins	6	1	15	—	10	2	34	—
Murray..........	3	1	11	—	23	7	59	1
Tayfield..........	29.4	9	84	6	37.1	13	81	7
Mansell..........	19	3	58	3	14	2	69	—

Umpires: H. Elphinston and M. McInnes.

VICTORIA v SOUTH AFRICANS

Played at Melbourne, January 31, February 2, 3, 4, 1953

Drawn. By scoring a century in each innings, Keith, the only left-hand batsman among the South Africans, played himself into the team for the fifth Test. His first innings contained a mixture of forceful strokes, which brought him sixteen 4s, and a degree of good fortune, but his second century was the outcome of sound batting without a real mistake. Innes, the 21-year-old Capetown University student, drove splendidly in making his first century in Australia. He began quietly but subsequently hit with full power and confidence. Hassett gave the South Africans first innings.

South Africans

D. J. McGlew c Hill b Johnston	0	– absent hurt	0
W. R. Endean c I. McDonald b Hill	22	– b Johnston	11
G. A. S. Innes c Hassett b Ring................	109	– c I. McDonald b Loxton........	7
R. A. McLean b Johnson	1	– c Johnson b Loxton	6
J. C. Watkins c R. Harvey b Ring.............	33	– c Hassett b Johnston	0
J. E. Cheetham c Johnston b Loxton..............	46	– c I. McDonald b Johnston	74
H. J. Keith c I. McDonald b Johnson	111	– not out	113
E. B. Norton lbw b Johnston..................	58	– c I. McDonald b Johnston	2
P. N. F. Mansell c Johnston b Loxton.............	4	– c I. McDonald b Loxton.........	7
E. R. H. Fuller not out	8	– c R. Harvey b Ring.............	3
M. G. Melle c R. Harvey b Johnston.............	3	– st I. McDonald b Ring	0
B 3, l-b 2, n-b 1	6	B 2, l-b 1, w 1, n-b 1	5

1/0 2/31 3/32 4/89 5/177 6/259   401   1/16 2/16 3/20 4/29 5/184   228
7/361 8/373 9/395   6/191 7/210 8/220 9/228

Victoria

C. C. McDonald c Mansell b Fuller	1		
R. Harvey c Cheetham b Mansell	47 – not out		5
A. L. Hassett c Mansell b Fuller	7		
R. N. Harvey c and b Mansell	69		
S. J. Loxton c Keith b Melle	60		
J. Chambers lbw b Mansell	4		
D. Ring c and b Mansell	3		
I. W. Johnson run out	44		
I. McDonald not out	18 – not out		12
J. C. Hill c Watkins b Mansell	3		
W. A. Johnston lbw b Mansell	0		
B 2, l-b 2	4	B 4	4

1/7 2/21 3/117 4/128 5/138 6/142   260   (No wkt) 21
7/231 8/250 9/260

Victoria Bowling

	Overs	Mdns	Runs	Wkts	Overs	Mdns	Runs	Wkts
Johnston	25.6	3	89	3	12	1	33	4
Loxton	20	3	53	2	16	2	49	3
Hill	17	3	63	1				
Johnson	34	8	95	2	14	2	50	—
Ring	23	5	83	2	10.6	2	38	2
R. Harvey	2	—	12	—	4	1	16	—
R. N. Harvey					5	—	21	—
Hassett					4	—	16	—

South Africans Bowling

	Overs	Mdns	Runs	Wkts	Overs	Mdns	Runs	Wkts
Melle	11	—	58	1				
Fuller	17	2	73	2				
Watkins	7	—	30	—	2	1	3	—
Keith	12	1	42	—	1	—	9	—
Mansell	14.3	3	53	6				
Innes					1	—	5	—

AUSTRALIA v WEST INDIES

First Test Match

Played at Brisbane, December 9, 10, 12, 13, 14, 1960

A tie. Quite apart from gaining a niche in cricket history as the first Test to end in a tie this match will always be remembered with enthusiasm because of its excellent cricket. It was played in a most sporting spirit, with the climax coming in a tremendously exciting finish as three wickets fell in the final over.

Australia, set to score 233 runs at a rate of 45 an hour for victory, crumbled before the fiery, sustained pace of Hall, and lost five wickets for 57. The sixth fell at 92. Then the drama began to build up as Davidson, the Australian all-rounder who enjoyed a magnificent match, was joined by Benaud, in a stand which added 134. They were still together half an hour before time, with 27 needed, when Hall took the new ball – a crucial stage.

In the event, however, the West Indies fieldsmen, often at fault during the match, rose to the occasion so that three of the last four batsmen to fall were run out in the desperate race against time. The first run-out came when Benaud called for a sharp single, but Solomon hit the stumps from mid-wicket to dismiss Davidson. Grout came in and took a single off Sobers, so that when the last momentous over from Hall began, six runs were needed with three wickets left.

The first ball hit Grout on the thigh and a leg-bye resulted; from the second Benaud gave a catch at the wicket as he swung mightily. Meckiff played the third ball back to the bowler, but when the fourth went through to the wicket-keeper, the batsmen scampered a run, Hall missing a chance to run out Meckiff as the wicket-keeper threw the ball to him. Grout hit the fifth ball high in the air, Hall attempted to take the catch himself, but the ball bounced out, and another run had been gained. Meckiff hit the sixth ball hard and high to leg, but Hunte cut it off on the boundary as the batsmen turned for the third run, which would have given Australia victory. Hunte threw in superbly, low and fast, and Grout was run out by a foot. So Kline came in to face the last two balls with the scores level. He played the seventh ball of the over towards square leg and Meckiff, backing up well, raced down the wicket, only to be out when Solomon again threw down the wicket with only the width of a stump as his target. So ended a match in which both sides had striven throughout for victory, with no thought of safety first.

West Indies attacked the bowling from the start of the match only to lose three men for 65 before Sobers, who hit a masterly century in just over two hours, including fifteen 4s, and Worrell mastered the bowling. Solomon, Alexander and Hall added valuable contributions to an innings which yielded 4.5 runs an over, despite much excellent pace bowling by Davidson. Australia succeeded in establishing a lead of 52, largely through the determination of Simpson and O'Neill, who made his highest Test score without reaching his very best form.

Indeed, West Indies missed several chances at vital times. More fine bowling by Davidson caused West Indies to battle hard for runs in their second innings, and they owed much to some high-class batting from Worrell for their respectable total, swelled usefully on the final morning by a last-wicket stand of 31 between Hall and Valentine.

West Indies

C. C. Hunte c Benaud b Davidson	24	– c Simpson b Mackay 39
C. Smith c Grout b Davidson	7	– c O'Neill b Davidson 6
R. Kanhai c Grout b Davidson	15	– c Grout b Davidson 54
G. Sobers c Kline b Meckiff	132	– b Davidson 14
*F. M. Worrell c Grout b Davidson	65	– c Grout b Davidson 65
J. Solomon hit wkt b Simpson	65	– lbw b Simpson 47
P. Lashley c Grout b Kline	19	– b Davidson 0
†F. C. M. Alexander c Davidson b Kline	60	– b Benaud................... 5
S. Ramadhin c Harvey b Davidson	12	– c Harvey b Simpson 6
W. Hall st Grout b Kline	50	– b Davidson.................. 18
A. L. Valentine not out	0	– not out 7
Extras	4	Extras................. 23

1/23 2/42 3/65 4/239 5/243   453   1/13 2/288 3/114 4/127 5/210   284
6/283 7/347 8/366 9/452   6/210 7/241 8/250 9/253

Australia

C. C. McDonald c Hunte b Sobers	57	– b Worrell	16
R. B. Simpson b Ramadhin	92	– c sub b Hall	0
R. N. Harvey b Valentine	15	– c Sobers b Hall	5
N. C. O'Neill c Valentine b Hall	181	– c Alexander b Hall	26
L. Favell run out	45	– c Solomon b Hall	7
K. D. Mackay b Sobers	35	– b Ramadhin	28
A. K. Davidson c Alexander b Hall	44	– run out	80
*R. B. Benaud lbw b Hall	10	– c Alexander b Hall	52
†A. W. T. Grout lbw b Hall	4	– run out	2
I. Meckiff run out	4	– run out	2
L. F. Kline not out	3	– not out	0
Extras	15	Extras	14

1/84 2/138 3/194 4/278 5/381   505   1/1 2/7 3/49 4/49 5/57   232
6/469 7/484 8/489 9/496   6/92 7/226 8/228 9/232

Australia Bowling

	Overs	Mdns	Runs	Wkts	Overs	Mdns	Runs	Wkts
Davidson	30	2	135	5	24.6	4	87	6
Meckiff	18	—	129	1	4	1	19	—
Mackay	3	—	15	—	21	7	52	1
Benaud	24	3	93	—	31	6	69	1
Simpson	8	—	25	1	7	2	18	2
Kline	17.6	6	52	3	4	—	14	—
O'Neill					1	—	2	—

West Indies Bowling

	Overs	Mdns	Runs	Wkts	Overs	Mdns	Runs	Wkts
Hall	29.3	1	140	4	17.7	3	63	5
Worrell	30	—	93	—	16	3	41	1
Sobers	32	—	115	2	8	—	30	—
Valentine	24	6	82	1	10	4	27	—
Ramadhin	15	1	60	1	17	3	57	1

Umpires: C. Hoy and C. J. Egar.

THE GREATEST TEST MATCH

AUSTRALIA AND WEST INDIES TIE AT BRISBANE

By E. M. Wellings

I was there. I saw it all. That is something that countless thousands would give much to be able to say. For it was The Greatest Test Match, The Greatest Cricket Match and surely The Greatest Game ever played with a ball. Australia v West Indies at Brisbane from December 9 to December 14 was already a great match before it bounded explosively to its amazing climax to produce the only tie in the history of Test cricket.

Some time has elapsed since the remarkable events of Hall's last over, in which the final three Australian wickets fell, five runs were made to bring the scores level and one catch dropped. But the picture of those events is more vivid now than it was at the time. Then all was confusion, for so much happened and thrill followed thrill so rapidly that everything became an exciting jumble. Even Meckiff, the last man out, was confused and thought West Indies had won by a run.

THE FINAL OVER

Six runs were wanted by Australia when Hall began what had to be the final over. The first ball hit Grout high on the leg, dropped at his feet, and he and Benaud scampered a single. Now the odds were heavily on Australia for Benaud was 52 and batting in match-winning vein. But immediately the odds were levelled. The next ball was a bouncer and Benaud aimed to hook it, as Davidson a few minutes earlier had superbly hooked a similar ball. He merely nicked it, and every West Indian leapt for joy as Alexander took the catch. So Meckiff arrived to play his first ball quietly back to Hall, and Australia needed a run off each ball.

A bye was run, and Grout skied the fifth ball just out on the leg side. Fielders converged from all directions, but Hall was the tallest and most determined, and he alone put his hands to it as the batsmen were running a single. It bounced out, and the fielders drooped in despair. The next delivery almost completed their despair, for Meckiff courageously clouted it loftily away to leg. He and Grout ran one, then another, and staked all on a third to win the match as Hunte was preparing to throw from the square-leg boundary. It was a glorious low throw, fast and true, and though Grout hurled himself at the line and skidded home on severely grazed forearms he could not counter the speed of the ball.

Umpire Hoy flung his right arm high to announce the decision immediately to everyone anxiously looking towards him, and again the West Indies leapt and flung their arms in triumph. A minute or so later umpire and fielders repeated their actions, only more so. At the fall of the last wicket the joy of the West Indies was so expressed in leaps and bounds and running about that the scene might have served for a ballet of ultramodern abandon. The man who sent them into transports of delight and tied the match was little Solomon when Kline smoothly played the seventh ball of that fateful last over towards square-leg. Meckiff at the other end was well launched on a run, but he never made it. With little more than one stump's width to aim at, Solomon threw the wicket down, as he had done some dozen minutes earlier from farther away to run out Davidson and give his side the chance to save themselves.

THREE RUN OUT

That was not the least remarkable feature of this very remarkable match. Three of the last four batsmen were run out by a fielding side whose throwing often had their wicket-keeper racing yards from the target area to retrieve the ball. At the crisis the throws straightened themselves, or perhaps they were made by the right men, for Hunte and Solomon were not often among the wild throwers.

That final over lasted nine minutes and ended four minutes after the appointed time. Not so long ago it would have been cut short at the dismissal of Grout. But for a comparatively recent law amendment, which provided for the last over being played out whatever the time, we lucky spectators would not have palpitated to the last tremendous thrill of that last tremendous over. Nor perhaps would spectators, bounding with excitement no less than the fielders, have raced across the ground to cheer and call for the heroes of the day, and repeat their cheers again and again in front of the players' pavilion.

UNFORGETTABLE SIGHT

That, like the freely expressed delight of the West Indies fielders, was an unforgettable sight. They were not so numerous as that gathered rapturously in front of The Oval pavilion in 1953, when Hutton's team at last recovered the Ashes from Australia, but the Queenslanders made up for their relative lack of numbers by their enthusiasm. We all recognised that this was more than a tied match. It was tied by teams playing in Homeric manner.

At the climax neither side made the slightest attempt to play for safety. Both were set on winning or perishing in the attempt. With three wickets standing, including that of Benaud, Australia could surely have coasted home to safety, and since they had gallantly pulled themselves up from a position of imminent defeat only two hours earlier, we could hardly have blamed them if they had. On the other side Hall, who had earlier wasted many deliveries barely within the batsman's reach, bowled straight more consistently than at any previous time in the match. Australia and West Indies played out the game in a spirit which should serve as an example to all others.

There have been other Test matches not far removed from being tied. Perhaps the most momentous was that at The Oval in 1902, when Australia were cantering home until Jessop hit a hurricane century and Hirst and Rhodes, the last pair, scored the final runs with typical Yorkshire unconcern in singles to give England the win by one wicket. Now in 1960 the Brisbane Test eclipsed that and all other close and thrilling finishes.

RIGHT EXAMPLE

From first to last the spirit of enterprise was in striking contrast to the play in most other recent Tests. Almost coinciding with it a bitter defensive contest was waged by India and Pakistan without ever any prospects of a definite result. Only two years earlier Brisbane had been the scene of the dullest ever England-Australia Test. England based their sketchy plans entirely on defensive batting and restrictive practices, and there was hardly a hint at batting enterprise until, on the last afternoon, O'Neill hit out for an Australian win. More recently West Indies and England opposed each other with nothing but negative intentions.

Test cricket had come to a sorry pass. Unpalatable though it is to admit, England developed the tight, restrictive tactics. Having then superior forces, they proved victorious for a time. It is not, therefore, surprising that others followed their lead and, in particular, sought to play England at their own game. Hence the tedium of many recent matches. Now Australia and West Indies have given a new lead, which England can neglect to follow only at the risk of grave loss of prestige.

SOBERS' CENTURY

England's recently defensive opponents in the West Indies were very different players against Australia at Brisbane. From the outset their batsmen were attacking, and they hoisted the first 50 off only 58 balls. Their batting attack was somewhat undisciplined and cost wickets, but, in the course of a magnificent stand of 174, Sobers and Worrell proved how fruitful discreet aggression can be. They were superb, and the hundred by Sobers in just over two hours, from no more than 29 overs, was the fastest Test century for many years. Sobers had the glory in his team's innings of 453, which brought runs at the rare average rate of 4.5 per eight-ball over. But Worrell was the man of great cricketing character who imposed discipline on his side's play throughout the match. In this respect Solomon's well-judged batting gave him valuable assistance.

Before the end Hall hit furiously and played amusingly. A partnership between him and Trueman would be enormous fun. Then Australia played an innings of 505 which, by comparison with that of their opponents, did not entirely commend itself to the home critics. Without that comparison, however, it would have been very well received by spectators disillusioned by other Tests. Yet O'Neill's 181, his highest Test score at the time, was not up to the standard of his innings on the same ground in 1958. In the meantime he had apparently fallen into the stultifying groove of current Test cricket.

GREAT PACE

A second West Indies innings of 284, maintained largely by Worrell and Solomon after some of the earlier batsmen had shown suicidal tendencies, left Australia 310 minutes in which to make 233. And so to the final remarkable chapter. It began with Hall, a bowler of great pace and enormous, though sometimes misplaced enthusiasm, bowling now with greater discipline and taking West Indies to the brink of success. Half Australia were out for 57, and Hall had four for 37. Then a sixth wicket fell at 92, and those watchers who lived in Sydney were planning to catch the 5.45 plane. They had to wait until the following morning.

Most batting sides, I think, would have tried to play for a draw in these circumstances. Australia did not. They had their captain at the wicket, and he and Davidson set off for victory. Davidson had already had a great match. He had taken 11 wickets and scored 44. Moreover, while the general standard of Australia's fielding was below their best standards, his own work in the field had been flawless. Now he added 80 more vigorous runs to his fine record and, after playing himself through a sticky period at the start, earned every single of them. Such was his all-round success that in normal circumstances the Test would rightly go down to history as Davidson's Match. As it is, this is to be known as The Greatest Test Match, but it was big enough to carry also a sub-title recognising Davidson's performance.

UP WITH THE CLOCK

He and Benaud batted with outstanding judgment. They played the bowling strictly on its merits and brought off some sterling strokes, among which Davidson's hook off a head-high bumper from Hall stands out as a vivid memory. And they ran like whippets. Time after time they had the West Indies hurling fiercely at their stumps and missing. It would not have mattered if the stumps had been hit, for their judgment was splendid and their understanding perfect. It was astonishing that, after all the hard work Davidson had done, he was running as keenly and as rapidly at the end as at the start. He was tremendously fit.

After tea Australia had to score just above one run a minute, which was not easy when the average tally of overs per two-hour session was around 27. But they kept well up with the clock, and with 12 minutes to go only seven were needed. The story seemed cut and dried. Australia were going to win, and Worrell would perhaps regret not having used the left-arm off-breaks and googlies of Sobers earlier. When Sobers did arrive to use spin after a spell at medium pace, Davidson and Benaud were in full blast and he could not part them.

DEADLY AIM

It was Solomon who did that when 12 minutes remained. Davidson went for an extra run. Perhaps this was the one and only time during the partnership when a direct hit by a fielder could have been effective. Solomon achieved the direct hit from some 25 yards and square with the wicket on the leg side. There followed the two other run-out wickets, and when the dust of excitement had settled there was some talk that Australia had only themselves to blame for faulty running. That is ungenerous to both sides and takes no account of the daring running of Benaud and Davidson, without which they could not have levelled the scores. The attempted runs by Grout and Meckiff in the last over were fully justified.

Post-mortems on such a match are out of place. I am happily content to have been one of the company of 4,100 who saw the thrilling and inspiring end of this greatest match. It serves as a challenge to all cricketers and calls to them to tackle their matches in the same spirit of sporting enterprise. This was essentially a sporting game, as the crowd recognised when they called for the 22 victors in the cause of cricket to show themselves on the patio of their pavilion.

NOTES BY THE EDITOR, 1961

YEAR OF CONTRASTS AND CONTROVERSY

Most lovers of cricket will look back on 1960 as "The Sad Season." It will be remembered for the rain which spoiled so many matches, for the alarming fall in attendances and for its bitter controversies – the throwing of Griffin, the sacking of Buller as a Test umpire, the withdrawal by MCC and Surrey of privileges to Laker following the publication of his book, *Over to Me*, and the Graveney dispute over the Gloucestershire captaincy. There was also the disappointing South African tour. For the fourth consecutive summer a visiting team failed to extend England in the Test matches. Indeed, for the third year running England settled the rubber in three straight matches, South Africa undergoing the same fate as India in 1959 and New Zealand in 1958. On the other side of the picture, there was the superb batsmanship of Dexter and the successful Imperial Cricket Conference at which the delegates of all seven Test match countries showed a genuine desire to tackle the various problems confronting the first-class game.

A WONDERFUL GAME

Then as this depressing year was reaching its close Australia and West Indies lit the torch to the path of brighter cricket by playing a tie at the Woolloongabba ground, Brisbane. It was the first tie in the long history of five hundred Test matches and there was scarcely a dull moment throughout the five days. I am grateful to E. M. Wellings, who was there and saw every ball bowled and every run scored, for his graphic description which precedes these Notes. He avers that this was the greatest match ever played. How was the miracle achieved in this age of so much unimaginative and negative cricket? It was achieved by Richie Benaud and Frank Worrell, the rival captains. First of all they were blessed with ideal conditions, sunshine and a perfect pitch, two importance factors. Just as important was the attitude of both men to the game. These captains insisted that the men under their command played enterprising cricket from the very first ball and they did not think of withdrawing into their shells when they ran into trouble. They still put victory as their goal and the stories of their deeds right through the series thrilled the cricket world.

RESPONSIBILITY OF CAPTAINS

Many people are anxious about the future of the first-class game. One cannot control the weather, but when it is favourable the destiny of cricket is in the hands of the captains. Benaud and Worrell have proved this truism. You can vary the Laws and do what you like, but without the goodwill of the captains all is in vain. In other words there is nothing wrong with cricket – and particularly county cricket – that the captains cannot put right. It is useless them going to Lord's in the winter and agreeing that it is essential for every county to adopt a dynamic attitude to the game from first ball to last whether batting, bowling or fielding and then deliberately ignoring the agreement on the field. And I am afraid this accusation can be levelled against some county captains. Too many excuses for poor cricket are attributed to the weather. We have always had rainy seasons in this country. The odd tropical summers like those of 1921 and 1959 come only rarely. Nowadays, the public will not risk the heavy expenditure of fares to the grounds and the price of admission when the weather is doubtful because even if the conditions are quite good for play they cannot be certain they will be entertained. The professional cricketer, and particularly the specialist batsman, should remember that he is a paid entertainer and if he fails or makes no attempt to keep the onlookers interested, the time will surely come when he will have to seek a living elsewhere. Some County Committees, too, should be more realistic and not pick players on the form shown by the weekly averages but by their actual deeds on the field.

AUSTRALIA v WEST INDIES

Fourth Test Match

Played at Adelaide, January 27, 28, 30, 31, February 1, 1961

Drawn. In a finish almost as exciting as the First Test, a defiant last-wicket partnership prevented West Indies taking the lead in the series. When Kline joined Mackay, an hour and fifty minutes remained with the West Indies total beyond reach. Two minutes later, Sobers, four yards from the bat, appealed confidently for a catch from Mackay off Worrell but it was turned down by Egar, the umpire, and the pair not only played out time but added 66 runs.

The match was full of incident. Gibbs, the West Indies off-spinner, did the hat-trick in Australia's first innings – the first against Australia this century – and Kanhai scored a hundred in each innings.

West Indies won the toss and after losing Hunte at 12 scored freely on an easy-paced pitch. The best batting came from Kanhai and Worrell who added 107 in just over an hour. Kanhai's first hundred came in a little over two hours and included two 6s and eleven 4s. Benaud kept the score in check with his accurate spin and captured five wickets for 96.

Australia also suffered a quick reverse when Favell was dismissed, but McDonald played doggedly for 71 and Simpson, after a shaky start, scored 85. Mackay never appeared comfortable and eventually was leg-before to Gibbs. Grant and Misson were the other victims in the hat-trick when Australia slumped from 281 for five to 281 for eight. Benaud appeared unperturbed and, receiving unexpected help from Hoare, took the score to 366.

The Australian bowling offered few terrors when the West Indies batted a second time and Kanhai scored his second hundred of the match. With Hunte, he put on 163 – a record second-wicket partnership for West Indies against Australia. Worrell declared and set Australia to score 460 in just over six and a half hours. Australia lost three wickets for 31 and anxiously faced the last day. Their hopes were raised by a determined stand by O'Neill and Burge, who justified his return to Test cricket. This lasted almost until lunch. Yet all seemed lost until the splendid fighting resistance of Mackay and Kline. For the last over Worrell recalled Hall to bowl to Mackay, but the Queenslander survived.

West Indies

C. C. Hunte lbw b Hoare	6	– run out	79
C. Smith c and b Benaud	28	– c Hoare b Mackay	46
R. Kanhai c Simpson b Benaud	117	– lbw b Benaud	115
G. Sobers b Benaud	1	– run out	20
*F. M. Worrell c Misson b Hoare	71	– c Burge b Mackay	53
S. Nurse c and b Misson	49	– c Simpson b Benaud	5
J. Solomon c and b Benaud	22	– not out	16
†F. C. M. Alexander not out	63	– not out	87
L. Gibbs b Misson	18		
W. Hall c Hoare b Benaud	5		
A. L. Valentine lbw b Misson	0		
Extras	13	Extras	11

1/12 2/83 3/91 4/198 5/271   393   1/66 2/229   (6 wkts dec.) 432
6/288 7/316 8/375 9/392   3/263 4/270 5/275 6/338

Australia

C. C. McDonald c Hunte b Gibbs	71	– run out	2
L. Favell c Alexander b Worrell	1	– c Alexander b Hall	4
N. C. O'Neill c Alexander b Sobers	11	– c and b Sobers	65
R. B. Simpson c Alexander b Hall	85	– c Alexander b Hall	3
P. J. Burge b Sobers	45	– c Alexander b Valentine	49
*R. Benaud c Solomon b Gibbs	77	– c and b Sobers	17
K. D. Mackay lbw b Gibbs	29	– not out	62
†A. W. T. Grout c Sobers b Gibbs	0	– lbw b Worrell	42
F. M. Misson b Gibbs	0	– c Solomon b Worrell	1
D. Hoare b Sobers	35	– b Worrell	0
L. F. Kline not out	0	– not out	15
Extras	12	Extras	13

1/9 2/45 3/119 4/213 5/221   366   1/6 2/7 3/31 4/113   (9 wkts) 273
6/281 7/281 8/281 9/366   5/129 6/144 7/203 8/207 9/207

Australia Bowling

	Overs	Mdns	Runs	Wkts	Overs	Mdns	Runs	Wkts
Hoare	16	—	68	2	13	—	88	—
Misson	17.5	2	79	3	28	3	106	—
Mackay	2	—	11	—	12	—	72	2
Benaud	27	5	96	5	27	3	107	2
Kline	21	3	109	—	12	2	48	—
Simpson	5	—	17	—				

West Indies Bowling

	Overs	Mdns	Runs	Wkts	Overs	Mdns	Runs	Wkts
Hall	22	3	85	1	13	4	61	2
Worrell	7	—	34	1	1⁷	9	27	3
Sobers	24	3	64	3	39	11	87	2
Gibbs	35.6	4	97	5	28	13	44	—
Valentine	21	4	74	—	20	7	40	1
Solomon					3	2	1	—

Umpires: C. Hoy and C. J. Egar.

AUSTRALIA v WEST INDIES

Fifth Test Match

Played at Melbourne, February 10, 12, 13, 14, 15, 1961

Australia won by two wickets. When late on the afternoon of February 15, 1961, Valentine spun a ball past batsman and wicket-keeper it was swallowed up by the crowd as they swarmed on to the Melbourne Stadium while Mackay and Martin were going through for the winning run. Thus ended an enthralling series which appropriately culminated in excitement and drama.

The drama occurred when Australia, needing 258 to win, were 254 for seven. Grout late-cut Valentine and the off-bail fell to the ground. Alexander, the wicket-keeper, did not turn round to follow the ball's flight but instead stood pointing at the broken wicket. The batsmen went through for two runs, after which the umpire at the bowler's end, Egar, went over to speak to Hoy at square leg. They decreed that Grout was not out. What caused the bail to fall off can only be conjecture but those two runs remained fact and the value of two runs at such a vital stage cannot be calculated.

The umpires' ruling brought forth some hostility from the crowd of 41,186, who, however, soon had other events to occupy their minds. Grout was eighth out without addition and at the same total the West Indies missed a chance of dismissing Martin. Hall at mid-on failed to react quickly enough to a fairly easy catch. This lapse gave Martin a single and brought the scores level. Then came that final extra.

The beginning matched the end. Though rain fell over the city two days earlier it was generally considered that the side winning the toss would bat first. But Australia had a captain brave in Benaud. With the atmosphere heavy and Hall on the other side, he sent a murmur of surprise round the ground by telling the West Indies to take first innings. In the event, Davidson, the one bowler who, it was hoped, would do most to prove Benaud right, accomplished practically nothing. Instead the spinners worried all except Kanhai and Sobers and there was no cause for complaint from Australia when at the end of the first day West Indies were 252 for eight.

A world record crowd of 90,800 saw McDonald, at his very best, and Simpson serve Australia well on Saturday with an opening partnership of 146, the best send-off for either side in the series, but at 236 for six the lead still stood 57 runs away when stumps were drawn.

Thus far the cricket had been interesting but not so engrossing as much of the play in the earlier matches. The game really began to tick again on Monday. Then the batsmen, including Harvey, who injured a leg muscle catching Kanhai, were wound in the web of Sobers and Gibbs and Australia were thankful for the aggressiveness of broad shouldered Burge in helping to finish their innings 64 ahead. Sobers went on to bowl at 124 for no wicket, half an hour before the tea interval on Saturday, and did not come off until the score stood at 335 for nine. He bowled slow at first, opened with the new ball on Monday and bowled all morning and for an hour afterwards. In all, his marathon effort lasted 41 overs and his final figures of five for 120 in 44 overs spoke eloquently of an unflagging performance.

The first-innings deficit did not worry West Indies. Indeed, it seemed to spur them to greater effort. Smith hooked the second ball from Misson over fine leg for six and he and Hunte had 50 on the board in as many minutes, so that runs soon began to count again. Kanhai sent the fieldsmen scurrying with some delightful stroke play and by the end of the third day the match had regained its even keel. West Indies were 62 runs on with eight wickets left. Some of the balance tilted Australia's way as they fought with all their natural tenacity but once more they found an "enemy" of comparable toughness in Alexander, who maintained his record of having exceeded 50 in each of the Tests. For two and a half hours he defied the bowlers. Then he was caught off Davidson, who when he had Hall taken behind the stumps brought his aggregate wickets to 33 in four Tests of the series. This catch, and three more taken during the day despite a damaged wrist, enabled Grout to match the record of helping in 23 dismissals in a rubber.

So came the final phase with Australia needing 258 for victory. Simpson began as enthusiastically as Smith, taking 24 runs off the first ten balls sent down to him, including 18 from the opening over. He was just as convincing when the spinners wrought havoc later and to him more than any other went the main accord on this final day of a memorable series. Both sides agreed before the start that an extra day should be added so as to minimise the chances of a stalemate but enterprising cricket from all made it unnecessary.

West Indies

C. Smith c O'Neill b Misson	11	– lbw b Davidson	37
C. C. Hunte c Simpson b Davidson	31	– c Grout b Davidson	52
R. Kanhai c Harvey b Benaud	38	– c Misson b Benaud	31
G. Sobers c Grout b Simpson	64	– c Grout b Simpson	21
*F. M. Worrell c Grout b Martin	10	– c Grout b Davidson	7
P. Lashley c Misson b Benaud	41	– lbw b Martin	18
†F. M. M. Alexander c McDonald b Misson	11	– c Mackay b Davidson	73
J. Solomon run out	45	– run out	36
L. Gibbs c Burge b Misson	11	– c O'Neill b Simpson	8
W. Hall b Misson	21	– c Grout b Davidson	21
A. L. Valentine not out	0	– not out	3
Extras	9	Extras	14

1/18 2/75 3/81 4/107 5/200   **292**   1/54 2/103 3/135 4/173   **321**
6/204 7/221 8/235 9/290   5/201 6/238 7/262
                                    8/295 9/304

Australia

R. B. Simpson c Gibbs b Sobers	75	– b Gibbs	92
C. C. McDonald lbw b Sobers	91	– c Smith b Gibbs	11
N. C. O'Neill b Gibbs	10	– c Alexander b Worrell	48
P. J. Burge c Sobers b Gibbs	68	– b Valentine	53
K. D. Mackay c Alexander b Hall	19	– not out	3
R. N. Harvey c Alexander b Sobers	5	– c Smith b Worrell	12
A. K. Davidson c Alexander b Sobers	24	– c Sobers b Worrell	12
*R. Benaud b Gibbs	3	– b Valentine	6
J. Martin c Kanhai b Sobers	15	– not out	1
F. M. Misson not out	12		
†A. W. T. Grout c Hunte b Gibbs	14	– c Smith b Valentine	5
Extras	20	Extras	15

1/146 2/181 3/181 4/244 5/260   **356**   1/50 2/75 3/154 4/176   **(8 wkts) 258**
6/309 7/309 8/319 9/335   5/200 6/236 7/248 8/256

Australia Bowling

	Overs	Mdns	Runs	Wkts	Overs	Mdns	Runs	Wkts
Davidson	27	4	89	1	24.7	4	84	5
Misson	14	3	58	4	10	1	58	—
Mackay	1	—	1	—	10	2	21	—
Benaud	21.7	5	55	2	23	4	53	1
Martin	8	—	29	1	10	1	36	1
Simpson	18	3	51	1	18	4	55	2

West Indies Bowling

	Overs	Mdns	Runs	Wkts	Overs	Mdns	Runs	Wkts
Hall	15	1	56	1	5	—	40	—
Worrell	11	2	44	—	31	16	43	3
Sobers	44	7	120	5	13	2	32	—
Gibbs	38.4	18	74	4	41	19	68	2
Valentine	13	3	42	—	21.7	4	60	3

Umpires: C. Hoy and C. J. Egar.

CRICKET ALIVE AGAIN

ONUS NOW ON ENGLAND AND AUSTRALIA

By Jack Fingleton

I am writing this just after the incredible tie between Australia and the West Indies in Brisbane. It would be a captious critic, indeed, who saw anything wrong in this rosy dawn of a cricket renascence – as we all hope it will be – but one must be practical and the request the Editor made to me long before this aura of brilliancy was cast over the cricket world here was this: how do the present-day methods of Australian batsmen compare with those of my own era?

My own Test-playing era was the "thirties", but a youthful mind formed some pretty strong impressions of the decade before that. I saw the Master, Jack Hobbs, bat in Sydney. I played against Macartney, the Magnificent, in Sydney club games. True, he was past his best, but to the end Macartney carried a pugnacious brilliancy about his batting.

As a lad in my teens, I walked proudly out with the veteran one day to open an innings on the Sydney Cricket Ground No. 2. "Keep your eye open for the first ball, son," he told me. I, somewhat naturally, assumed he wanted a quick single and so, avid to please, I was leading up the pitch when the ball came back like a bullet.

I dropped to the ground. So did the bowler and the umpire, all in a great flurry. The ball crashed against the picket-fence and came back towards us. I picked myself up and walked down the pitch to have words with the Great Man. "Always", he told me, "aim the first ball at the bowler here" – and he tapped the middle of his forehead. "They don't like it. It rattles them." And not only the bowler, I remember thinking.

Macartney, Bradman, J. M. Taylor, T. J. E. Andrews, Alan Kippax, Ponsford, A. A. Jackson, J. M. Gregory, Victor Richardson, Stan McCabe and Hanson Carter were the adventurous type. Not one, of course, is now playing and three, alas, are dead, but one had only to walk around the corner of the M. A. Noble stand at the Sydney Cricket Ground, see one of those I have mentioned in action and immediately recognise him. Each had his own way of playing the game; each made strokes, or used his feet (as did Bradman) in his own individual manner.

Macartney had a delicious and vigorous twirl of the wrist that took his bat inordinately high in the follow-through. He would "dab" the ball through the slips. Nobody before or since quite pulled as Bradman did. He crashed the ball, yet in doing so he managed to turn his wrists over so that the ball immediately went to earth. Nobody had the flourish of Kippax in his late-cut – many a wicket-keeper's tingling hands could testify to the lateness of the stroke. Ponsford's broad blade was the desperation of all bowlers and nothing exasperated them more than the genius he had for forcing their best balls wide of wide-on and square-leg.

Archie Jackson was a purist in the Trumper-Kippax mould. Kippax once told me of how he used to follow Trumper around Sydney's suburban ovals when he was a small boy. Kippax instinctively moulded his game on Trumper's, and Jackson, who played under Kippax's captaincy in the NSW team, obviously imitated Kippax. So the strain of Trumper ran through Australian cricket until the mid-thirties. Richardson and Gregory were of the cavalier type, ferocious hitters of the ball at their best. McCabe had his own effortless style and nobody, in my recollection, other than the wicket-keeper Carter, played that impish over-the-shoulder stroke to fine-leg from a good-length ball.

McCabe once told me that the best batting lesson he had in his life was one day at Kennington Oval in the 1930 Australian tour of England. "Jack Hobbs batted against us for half an hour and I fielded at cover," said McCabe. "I learnt more about batting in that half-hour than in the rest of my cricket career."

A graceful tribute indeed, because McCabe has played three of the greatest innings seen in Test cricket – 187 not out against the fury of Larwood and Voce in Sydney in 1932; 189 not out against South Africa on a "bumping pitch" and in a "blinding light" at

Johannesburg in 1936; and 232 against England at Nottingham in 1938. I was privileged to see all three innings. Bradman's 1930 innings at Leeds – a century before lunch, a century before tea and a century before stumps – was in the same brand of sheer brilliance.

The names I have mentioned do not exhaust the list of really good Australian batsmen I played with and against. Far from it. Those already singled out had characteristics or stroke of genius that placed them above their fellow-cricketers. The blood in their veins made them seek adventure. Cooler blood ran through Collins, Bardsley, Woodfull, Brown and Barnes, yet all of these knew triumphs of the highest order. They were more of the suspicious, respectful type. Where those of the first order were wont, so to speak, to fling their cap in the face of the bowler, these others (and I was of their ilk) were first prepared to touch their cap in respect and then set out to dominate proceedings by long occupancy and a refusal to quit. Like a canny man given a tip on the Stock Exchange, they wanted to know everything about everybody. They were suspicious by nature and often, as occasional innings shows, suspicious of their capacity to play another type of game. Nobody would doubt, however, that they forged a large piece of Australian cricket history.

The Second World War did not cut the continuity of Australian batting art. Bradman, Brown, Hassett, Miller and Barnes carried over from one period to the next. Morris, too, was just about to make his entrance when cricket was put back into the wings. England had Hutton, Compton and Edrich, for three, to tide it over the break and so the young of both countries were not lacking for champions to emulate.

Yet, at the end of a decade, one is pessimistically inclined to wonder whether any decade in Australian cricket history threw up less champions that the fifties. Harvey and Morris, both capital cricketers, were the product of the forties. Each was well entrenched as the fifties began. Benaud and Davidson I immediately accept as two all-round cricketers who would have been termed "great" in any period of the game but it is of specialist batsmen I write particularly and I am forced to the conclusion that although many were chosen, few were found. Consider this list of batsmen who have been tried over and over again in practically every cricketing country of the world without achieving a decisive position in our national team: Craig, de Courcy, Hole, Mackay, Favell, Archer (K. and R.), Burge, Burke, Rutherford and Moroney.

Only two – O'Neill and McDonald – have berths by right at the moment of writing. Simpson, a neat batsman who made his début in the middle fifties for NSW against Hutton's team, is on the verge of permanent occupancy. He, however, is no new comet flashing across the cricketing sky. He has toured South Africa; he has played Lancashire League. What we so badly want at the moment in Australia are several new batsmen cast in the classical mould.

I am not, I hope, being a carping conservative in saying this. I am conscious of Australia's rich batting heritage; and I am conscious that at the moment of writing the West Indians are giving us much more cultured batting than our own men. Sobers, Worrell, Hunte and Kanhai are the men of batting destiny in Australia at the moment. Their flashing bats are the ones our youngsters will need to emulate if we are to recapture our former batting greatness and individuality.

To write this is not to belittle Norman O'Neill. No batsmen could have wished for a more distinguished entry into England-Australia Test cricket than O'Neill two years ago at Brisbane. After days and days of intolerable boredom, O'Neill came on the last day to lift the game from the dreary depths to heights of brilliancy. His shots off the back foot were magnificent, speeding in all directions. He gave the Snooze of Brisbane the only sparkle it knew, yet for all the scores he has made lately it would be idle to pretend that O'Neill of this summer so far is batting with the surety or the wide range of strokes that he showed us only two years ago. I want to be fair to O'Neill. He has given us some glorious strokes but every now and then his batting has an odd fall from grace that Bradman and McCabe, for instance, did not know when they were in full flight.

That demon fast bowler, Wesley Hall, could be responsible for this. He has, to this time of writing, brought a flurry of uncertainty into the batting of some of our men. O'Neill has not wilted before him. Indeed, in a Sydney game for NSW, he twice in succession pulled bouncers from the tip of his nose, almost, square and furiously to the fence. These were the strokes of a great batsman and if, at other times, O'Neill seems disposed to cut and force whereas before he was full-blooded and full-faced with his bat, the explanation might be that Hall's fury has caused O'Neill to hold his bat with a tighter grip. As in golf, so in cricket. A grip should be snug, not over-tight. There is no flow of stroke from a bat that is held with clenched fingers.

McDonald, like Woodfull before him, anchors himself at the crease and refuses to yield. Possessed of a good sense of humour, McDonald, after a few onslaughts by Hall, does not now see much humour in being hit on the ribs, but he, like Mackay, suffers from lack of mobility. McDonald is a lower hand player – the left does little work. Woodfull, too, was a lower hand player. It enables one to deflect, to cut; it has most pronounced limitations on the drive. And, clenching hard with that right bottom hand, McDonald further anchors himself on his feet. He has his limitations but not in intelligence or pluck. Had he not become an opening batsman and thus impregnated with the thought of always meeting the dangerous, swinging ball, McDonald might have become more top-hand conscious and thus a freer batsman. As he is, he is no model for the young to copy as a stylist.

Mackay! Here is the oddest-looking batsman I have seen in Test cricket. His stance is odd in that he is bolt upright, his head full to the bowler, his arms out stiff from his body. When he hits the ball – and he can hit as hard as the next when he allows himself – there is no sense of the bat having been taken back or swung through. He hits, it seems, with a rigid bat. His feet rarely move – one reason why he was in such dire straits on those spinning pitches at Leeds and Old Trafford in 1956. In all things, apart from teeth that wage an incessant onslaught on chewing-gum, Mackay is immobile. He is in a cast of his own and when the cast becomes useless, it will be put aside. Strange though it might seem, I do not expect that to happen before the next tour of England.

O'Neill is top-class; Harvey is still a very good batsman, even though Hall has quickened up the tempo of his stroke-making, thus making for some indecisive moments; but, all in all, I could think of no two better Australian models for our young players than Davidson and Benaud. That is, as batsmen. This might seem very surprising. It indicates, to be true, a paucity of genius; but, in itself, it is a tribute to two very great all-rounders. Davidson's defence in the Tie of Brisbane was impeccable, foot and bat always to the ball. His strokes, too, are ideal. He plays all of them. Benaud has an odd grip with his top hand. He seems to have exaggerated even Bradman's grip with that hand, but Benaud, when attacking, is a delight to watch. He has played some of the greatest innings in cricket history – one at Lord's, one at Scarborough, one at Bradford, one Test innings in the West Indies – and if at times he has disappointed us as a batsman, one has to remember that he either has done or is faced with a terrific job of work as a bowler when he appears in a Test. I expect, however, to see him play some more great Test innings.

Why have not men like Craig and the others come on? Temperament, perhaps, or some odd little habit that has unknowingly developed. Last time I saw Craig bat I was impressed by the fact that he had allowed his right shoulder to swing around towards the bowler. This, no doubt, he incurred when he made himself into an opening batsman, as Barnes did. So many do. They are struggling as hard in the thirties as at the start of an innings because, unknowingly, their bat is swinging across the line of flight.

Favell is one of the game's greatest surprises. At 30-odd years of age, he has changed his stance from a crouch to that of a bolt, upright batsman. His feet and bat are now together. Before they were wide apart. He has had many failures – his style of play leaves a few things to chance – but Favell in full flow is a sight for any ground. He has the distinction of hitting two successive sixes in a Test – successive balls from Valentine in Brisbane.

If it is thought from the foregoing that I am not over-impressed with Australia's batting talent at the moment – one or two near-Test men just crumple when a bouncer is bowled to them – you will have guessed correctly. I cannot recall a time in our history when a Test-berth was there just for the sake of one good score. Never, I think, has it been so necessary for our Test selectors to show judgment and confidence in their team for England. They could, in fact, trip again to the hamlets of Bowral and Grenfell and choose some unknown who might emulate Bradman and McCabe. The latter, I recall, went to England without having made a first-class century. Our selectors must so choose again because I see no future in favouring those who have had so many chances, who have done so little and who have so little future ahead.

How is it that we have fallen on such poor batting days? A combination, I think, of several circumstances. Every country has its years of plenty and famine, of ebb and flow. The young Australian, with so many other attractions – so many motor cars – might now not be disposed to work so hard at a game that will not yield itself easily. Cricket must be learnt the hard way and by much application, early mornings at the nets, for instance, much study of the masters, much discussion and much experimenting. With time-wasting tactics, with too many bouncers, cricket has lost much of its appeal. Sir Jack Hobbs, in a letter, once wrote: "Why did bumpers ever have to come into cricket?" I knew what he meant. I never mind a bumper if it is to test the moral fibre of a batsman but the fifties in Australia were marked by far too many bumpers from too many bowlers. There is nothing uglier in batting than falling to earth under a bumper. Then, too, it is all so aimless. A long walk back for the bowler; a long run in; a bumper; the batsman ducks – and so on, all over again.

I think it was Doug Insole who recently wrote that captaincy had reached its highest perfection and this was one reason why runs were so difficult to score. If by this he meant dull, stodgy, defensive captaincy, I agree with him; but what particular cleverness is there in the dawdling bowler of an over; in tight field-placing; in a refusal to get on with a game? What captaincy merit is there in it when all the risks are left to the batsman and, if he does not attempt to perform miracles or suicide, he is roasted by many in the public (the slow handclap) and many in the Press-box who have not an expert appreciation of what is happening in front of them? One who has been through the mill knows the tricks and the subterfuges. In England and Australia we have put up with a lot for a long time in the belief that Test cricket covers all, even to the little personal tugs-of-war off-field that set the stage for on-field.

It is well to assess these matters because they have made the task of the modern batsman all too difficult. Seemingly, now, the captain who is prepared to experiment with a few runs to get a wicket or two is an ass. Runs must not be given away; they must not even be yielded, and so the slow leg-break bowler, he who allowed for the execution of every stroke in the game, including the hit over the fence, is an outcast. I blame that revised lbw rule, favouring the man who works the ball in from the off, very much for this, but that is another matter. It will suffice here to note that slow leg-break bowling provides three important things in cricket: (a) quick overs; (b) the opportunity to play every stroke in the game; and (c) the chance of a batsman to make a fool of himself – in other words, humour.

Englishmen like May, Cowdrey and Dexter have had to make their distinguished paths in county cricket with little chance of playing against slow leg-break bowlers. I salute them for the brilliance they have shown under handicap because those Australians I have mentioned all had the chance of footwork and stroke-play against slow bowlers. Our slow bowlers have run through the years – Hordern, Mailey, Grimmett, Hartkopf, O'Reilly (quicker paced than the others), Ward, Fleetwood-Smith, Tribe, Dooland, Walsh, Benaud, Kline and Martin. All ready to gamble with a few runs to get a wicket or two; all led by skippers who were not run-misers.

Against fast bowling and against tight field concentrations as practised by, first Yardley at Nottingham in 1948, Hutton and May, our modern Australian batsmen have had to fight much harder for their runs against England. All this considered, however, I doubt if we have two we can place with May and Cowdrey as stylists, although the latter so often denies his better parts. I consider Peter May one of the greatest batsmen I have seen. O'Neill and Harvey would be our best batsmen. I am hoping against hope that, as so often happens in Australia, we will suddenly produce at least two new men over-night because

England now has Dexter, who, seemingly, has come ahead by leaps and bounds since Australia of two years ago. He is like Benaud and Davidson, firm believers, as Bradman was, in the full face of the bat to the ball. This, I now know after years of playing and watching the game, is the most payable stroke in cricket – a minimum of risk for the maximum value. Pushes, cuts and deflections are all very well if the bowling is good but the risk in these, with the bat half-face, is pronounced and often not worth the result. Sobers is a delightful example of the full, flowing stroke, mostly top-hand. No bowler likes being driven for four. Cuts and pushes, yes, he does not mind a little bit because he always feels he will break through – but a full-blooded drive, no! "It rattles them", as Macartney said. As a boy I asked Alan Kippax once how he played his late cut. He smiled and replied, "I'm afraid I won't tell you. It's got me out too often."

I have high hopes that the flourishing bats of Sobers and his henchmen will inspire a young generation of Australians. I have high hopes, too, that the wind of change which Benaud and Worrell so bravely inspired in Brisbane, will blow on to all cricketing countries and disperse that mean, niggardly outlook on Tests which says they must be won at all costs and, if they cannot be won, they must never be lost. Had Benaud and Worrell not put that thought aside there would never have been the Brisbane Tie. Halfway through the last day both sides would have been cannily playing for another day and another Test. In Brisbane, at a time when many were lamenting that the game was dying, cricket was never more alive in its challenge, in its brilliance, in its down-to-earth honesty and the link it forged between men of different countries and different colours of skin.

In England, Jack Hobbs was celebrating his 78th birthday. "The tie in Brisbane", he said, "is the best possible birthday present I could have had". It reminded me of another of Sir Jack's birthdays. It would, I think, have been his 46th. He was led by that great Australian captain of other days, M. A. Noble, on a circuit of the Sydney Cricket Ground and the whole ground rose to him and gave him a special birthday cheer. These are the memories that linger, the touches that warm the heart. So many are just underneath the skin of this great game. So few captains and officials worry about pricking the surface for them. Cricket matches are always at their best when they are hard-fought. I have no stomach for anything else but there comes a time when the desire to win defeats itself in a dull negation of the game and its virtues. We, England and Australia, must in the near future have more confidence in each other, more trust. Often, as might have happened in Brisbane, there is as much virtue in losing as in winning if the game has been played honorably, with courage, with character and with challenge.

SHEFFIELD SHIELD

NEW SOUTH WALES v VICTORIA

Played at Sydney, January 28, 29, 31, February 1, 1949

New South Wales won by 88 runs. There was some bad batting by both sides after Hassett sent in New South Wales on a grassy pitch which did not play badly. The two fast-medium left-handers, Lambert and Johnston, upset New South Wales apart from Miller, who gave a superb display in making 99, his best innings of the season. Neil Harvey revealed his class, but with Hassett brilliantly caught on the left side by wicket-keeper Saggers, Victoria found themselves 64 behind. In the respective second innings W. A. Johnston and Walker carried all before them, each taking five wickets. Stumps with dome-shaped tops were not available for this match, and there were three instances of a ball bowled hitting the batsman's wicket without a bail being removed. This was believed to be unprecedented in Australia, Burke (bowler Lambert), Donaldson (Ring) and Saggers (played on, Johnston) were the New South Wales batsmen concerned.

New South Wales

A. R. Morris c Hassett b Lambert	1	– c McDonald b Lambert	2
J. Burke c Hassett b Johnston	37	– lbw b Johnston	1
K. R. Miller b Lambert	99	– c Ring b Lambert	7
J. Moroney lbw b Johnston	51	– c McDonald b Johnson	63
W. A. Donaldson b Lambert	0	– b Johnston	47
J. de Courcy c McDonald b Lambert	3	– lbw b Johnston	32
R. R. Lindwall c Johnson b Johnston	11	– b Johnston	0
R. A. Saggers b Lambert	2	– c and b Johnson	34
G. Powell c Ring b Johnson	7	– c McDonald b Johnson	8
F. Johnston not out	4	– b Johnston	9
A. Walker c Meuleman b Johnson	2	– not out	2
Extras	12	Extras	16
	229		**221**

Victoria

K. Meuleman lbw b Lindwall	4	– b Burke	58
R. Howard lbw b Lindwall	2	– lbw b Walker	8
A. L. Hassett c Saggers b Miller	6	– c and b Miller	27
N. Harvey c Morris b Johnston	72	– c Moroney b Walker	75
S. J. Loxton c Saggers b Walker	26	– c Moroney b Burke	3
K. Stackpole c de Courcy b Lindwall	18	– c sub b Walker	3
I. W. Johnson lbw b Walker	12	– b Walker	2
D. Ring c Moroney b Johnston	10	– not out	10
I. McDonald not out	9	– c Lindwall b Walker	0
H. Lambert lbw b Walker	1	– lbw b Lindwall	4
W. A. Johnston c de Courcy b Lindwall	1	– b Lindwall	1
Extras	4	Extras	6
	165		**197**

Victoria Bowling

	Overs	Mdns	Runs	Wkts	Overs	Mdns	Runs	Wkts
Johnston	22	4	47	3	29.7	8	62	5
Lambert	20	3	64	5	20	4	47	2
Loxton	9	1	24	—	12	4	14	—
Johnson	20.3	4	73	2	13	2	35	3
Ring	4	—	9	—	18	4	47	—

New South Wales Bowling

	Overs	Mdns	Runs	Wkts	Overs	Mdns	Runs	Wkts
Lindwall	14.3	—	42	4	13.2	—	51	2
Walker	12	—	42	3	16	1	58	5
Miller	6	—	24	1	8	—	29	1
Johnston	9	1	29	2	2	—	15	—
Powell	5	—	24	—				
Burke					9	—	38	2

SOUTH AUSTRALIA v VICTORIA

Bradman's Final Match

Played at Adelaide, March 4, 5, 7, 8, 1949

Victoria won by 271 runs. This match marked the last appearance of Sir Donald Bradman in first-class cricket. He played under the captaincy of Ridings and made 30 in scratchy fashion. His innings began on the first day and ended the next morning. Bradman twisted an ankle while fielding and could not bat in the second innings. His disappearance from the match – set aside for the benefit of A. J. Richardson, the former South Australian and Test all-rounder – quickly affected the attendance. O'Neill caused a surprise in the middle of Victoria's first innings when, bowling with the new ball, he took five wickets for seven runs in eighteen deliveries. Loxton hit well for his 135.

Victoria

C. McDonald b Noblet	1	– c Langley b O'Neill	9
R. Howard b Noblet	35	– c Noblet b McLean.............	26
K. Stackpole c Bradman b Gogler	35	– c Langley b Noblet	15
N. Harvey b McLean	41	– c and b McLean	9
S. J. Loxton lbw b O'Neill.....................	25	– lbw b Noblet	135
H. Turner b O'Neill..........................	22	– lbw b O'Neill.................	29
I. W. Johnson c Langley b O'Neill	1	– lbw b McLean	22
D. Ring b O'Neill	1	– lbw b Noblet.................	32
I. McDonald b O'Neill	2	– not out	32
J. Baird not out	13	– run out	1
W. A. Johnston c Bradman b McLean	38	– c Gogler b Noblet..............	7
Extras	17	Extras..................	11
	229		**328**

South Australia

K. Lewis c Howard b Loxton	16	– run out	20
K. Gogler c McDonald b Baird.................	6	– c Johnson b Loxton	20
R. A. Hamence b Baird......................	11	– c Stackpole b Ring	10
Sir D. G. Bradman b Johnston	30	– absent hurt	0
P. Ridings c Howard b Baird	17	– c Stackpole b Johnston..........	4
B. Bowley c Howard b Johnson	12	– st McDonald b Johnson	8
G. R. Langley c and b Johnson................	15	– run out	36
P. Bednall st McDonald b Ring................	7	– b Ring......................	3
K. O'Neill b Baird..........................	10	– c McDonald b Baird.............	3
A. R. McLean c and b Ring	10	– run out	19
G. Noblet not out	8	– not out	0
Extras	12	Extras..................	9
	154		**132**

South Australia Bowling

	Overs	Mdns	Runs	Wkts	Overs	Mdns	Runs	Wkts
O'Neill	13	2	45	5	12	1	40	2
Noblet.	14	3	39	2	26.6	7	54	4
Bowley	6	1	30	—	5	1	20	—
McLean	15.4	1	66	2	21	2	139	3
Gogler.	4	—	19	1	8	—	53	—
Ridings	4	2	13	—	5	1	11	—

Victoria Bowling

	Overs	Mdns	Runs	Wkts	Overs	Mdns	Runs	Wkts
Baird.	15	1	69	4	7	2	28	1
Johnston	14	4	28	1	23.2	10	51	1
Loxton	8	1	19	1	4	—	10	1
Ring	6.3	2	15	2	9	1	30	2
Johnson	6	3	11	2	8	6	4	1

QUEENSLAND v NEW SOUTH WALES

Played at Brisbane, October 19, 20, 22, 23, 1951

New South Wales won on first innings. Outstanding successes by the batsmen Archer and Morris, and the fast bowler, Lindwall, marked this match. On a favourable pitch Archer scored 104 and 88, showing improvement on the previous season and pressing his claims to a further opportunity in Test cricket. He gave a difficult chance off Lindwall when eight in the first innings. Morris was on the field throughout the match. He played a sheet-anchor innings, making his highest score in Shield cricket, 253 out of a total of 400, the last 50 runs coming in seventeen minutes. Lindwall, bowling accurately and at reduced pace, had a devastating burst with the new ball on the second day and finished the first innings with seven wickets for 45 runs.

Queensland

K. Archer c Kissell b Lindwall	104	– lbw b Lindwall	88
C. Harvey c Benaud b Lindwall	9	– c and b Walker	5
K. Mackay lbw b Flockton	51	– c Benaud b Burke	75
A. Carrigan c Trueman b Lindwall	6		
K. Jack run out	23	– b Lindwall	2
E. Toovey b Lindwall	63	– not out	24
C. L. McCool c Trueman b Lindwall	32	– not out	3
W. Grout c Miller b Lindwall	5	– c de Courcy b Benaud	8
V. N. Raymer b Lindwall	6		
L. Johnson not out	5		
C. Smith run out	7		
Extras	5	Extras	6
	316		**Five wkts 211**

New South Wales

A. R. Morris c Archer b Raymer	253	R. R. Lindwall c and b McCool	2
S. G. Barnes lbw b Johnson	35	R. Benaud lbw b Archer	27
K. R. Miller c Raymer b McCool	3	A. Walker b Smith	2
J. Burke b Smith	32	G. Trueman not out	6
J. de Courcy c McCool b Johnson	0	Extras	6
R. Flockton c McCool by Ramyer	25		
R. Kissell c Jack b McCool	9		**400**

New South Wales Bowling

	Overs	Mdns	Runs	Wkts	Overs	Mdns	Runs	Wkts
Lindwall	26.1	7	45	7	13	5	23	2
Walker	21	1	68	—	10	5	18	1
Miller	9	—	21	—	6	1	18	—
Benaud	17	—	64	—	17	1	79	1
Flockton.	20	—	62	1	10	1	36	—
Barnes.	5	—	21	—				
Burke	16	4	30	—	9	1	28	1
de Courcy.					1	—	1	—
Morris.					1	—	2	—

Queensland Bowling

	Overs	Mdns	Runs	Wkts
Smith	23	2	93	2
Johnson	34	10	63	2
Mackay	12	2	23	—
Raymer.	32.4	4	107	2
McCool	32	2	107	3
Archer	2	1	1	1

NEW SOUTH WALES v WESTERN AUSTRALIA

Played at Sydney, January 18, 19, 21, 1952

New South Wales won by 250 runs with a day to spare. Barnes, Moroney and Miller were dismissed early, Western Australia's opening bowlers, Price and Puckett, shaping well; but the young all-rounders, Flockton and Benaud, made a useful stand for the seventh wicket. Western Australia then collapsed against the left-handed fast-medium bowling of Davidson and the additional pace of Lindwall, their total of 50 being their lowest ever in a Shield match. New South Wales then scored freely before Lindwall and Davidson took more wickets. Carmody, facing his former State, alone gave New South Wales much trouble.

New South Wales

S. G. Barnes c Sarre b Price	0		
J. Moroney b Pucket.	7 – c Munro b Price	61
J. Burke c Dunn c Puckett.	40 – c Frankish b Price.	54
K. R. Miller c Williams b Puckett	13 – c Bennett b Langdon.	32
J. de Courcy b Price	26 – c Frankish b Puckett.	22
R. R. Lindwall b Dunn	21		
R. Benaud c Langdon b Price	34 – c Frankish b Puckett.	12
R. Flockton c Munro b Price	47 – not out	64
A. Davidson b Price	20 – b Puckett	18
A. Walker c Langdon b Puckett	11		
G. Trueman not out	0		
Extras	9	Extras	3
	228	(6 wkts dec.) 266	

Western Australia

D. Williams b Lindwall	2	– b Lindwall	1
R. Sarre c Lindwall b Davidson	14	– c Trueman b Lindwall	7
C. Bennett c Trueman b Davidson	6	– st Trueman b Benaud	20
A. Edwards c Benaud b Davidson	3	– b Lindwall	2
W. Langdon c Lindwall b Davidson	0	– c Trueman b Davidson	18
D. K. Carmody b Davidson	21	– b Lindwall	83
R. Frankish c Lindwall b Davidson	0	– run out	45
J. Munro b Walker	1	– lbw b Davidson	1
C. Puckett b Lindwall	1	– c Trueman b Benaud	6
H. Price c Trueman b Lindwall	0	– b Davidson	8
W. Dunn not out	0	– not out	0
Extras	2	Extras	3
	50		**194**

Western Australia Bowling

	Overs	Mdns	Runs	Wkts	Overs	Mdns	Runs	Wkts
Price	22	4	70	5	16	2	74	2
Dunn	14	6	36	1	10	1	46	—
Puckett	21.6	3	76	4	19	—	126	3
Langdon	3	1	13	—	2.3	—	7	1
Sarre	2	—	5	—				
Frankish	3	—	12	—	3	1	10	—
Williams	2	—	7	—				

New South Wales Bowling

	Overs	Mdns	Runs	Wkts	Overs	Mdns	Runs	Wkts
Lindwall	8	2	17	3	9	1	24	4
Walker	6	—	18	1	13	2	45	—
Davidson	9.3	3	13	6	15	5	36	3
Benaud					13.1	2	50	2
Burke					3	—	6	—
Flockton					3	—	20	—
Miller					3	—	10	—

NEW SOUTH WALES v VICTORIA

Played at Melbourne, December 22, 24, 26, 27, 1956

Tied. Craig, suffering from tonsillitis, and Burke, with a broken finger, batted for New South Wales in their second innings and helped in the first tie in the 100 years' history of inter-State cricket. On a drying pitch New South Wales needed 161 runs for victory.

When seven wickets fell for 70 they seemed sure to be beaten, but Craig and Benaud shared a stand of 75 for the eighth wicket. Craig, pale and weak, batted for thirty minutes. Victoria's heroes were the 22-year-old Kline, slow left-arm bowler, and Meckiff, tall and fast, who also played a valuable first innings. For New South Wales, Burke carried his bat through the first innings and was well supported by the 19-year-old O'Neill.

Victoria

C. C. McDonald b Benaud	50	– c Lambert b Wyatt		8
W. Lawry c Lambert b Davidson	1	– lbw b Wyatt		7
R. N. Harvey c Lambert b Treanor	46	– b Burke		22
J. Shaw lbw b Martin	26	– st Lambert b Treanor		52
K. Kendall c Watson b Benaud	8	– lbw b Treanor		21
S. J. Loxton b Benaud	26	– c sub b Treanor		0
L. Maddocks c Craig b Martin	16	– b Benaud		33
A. Dick b Benaud	0	– b Benaud		29
I. Meckiff b Wyatt	55	– b Treanor		8
L. Kline b Davidson	11	– not out		9
J. Salmon not out	0	– b Treanor		0
Extras	5	Extras		8
	244			**197**

New South Wales

S. Carroll c Dick b Meckiff	11	– b Kline		14
J. W. Burke not out	132	– c Maddocks b Meckiff		8
J. Treanor c Maddocks b Salmon	14	– c Maddocks b Meckiff		0
N. O'Neill st Maddocks b Kline	69	– c and b Kline		11
I. D. Craig lbw b Dick	3	– c Lawry b Kline		24
W. Watson c Harvey b Meckiff	16	– lbw b Kline		15
R. Benaud c Harvey b Meckiff	8	– c Shaw b Kline		63
J. Martin b Loxton	1	– c Maddocks b Meckiff		6
A. K. Davidson lbw b Kline	22	– b Meckiff		0
O. Lambert b Kline	0	– lbw Kline		5
A. Wyatt run out	0	– not out		2
Extras	5	Extras		12
	281			**160**

New South Wales Bowling

	Overs	Mdns	Runs	Wkts	Overs	Mdns	Runs	Wkts
Wyatt	9.3	—	38	1	4	2	14	2
Davidson	14	3	50	2	17	1	65	—
Treanor	16	5	50	1	10.4	2	36	5
Benaud	26	2	67	4	21	9	34	2
Martin	7	—	34	2				
Burke					13	1	40	1

Victoria Bowling

	Overs	Mdns	Runs	Wkts	Overs	Mdns	Runs	Wkts
Meckiff	21	6	65	3	21.1	6	56	4
Salmon	13	4	41	1				
Loxton	9	—	56	1	5	2	10	—
Kline	20	—	72	3	19	3	57	6
Dick	14	2	42	1	13	1	25	—

NEW SOUTH WALES v SOUTH AUSTRALIA

Played at Sydney, January 18, 20, 21, 22, 1957

New South Wales won on first innings. Rain checked their bid for outright victory on the last day when they needed 196 in a hundred and forty-three minutes. The feature of the match was the performance of the South Australia opening batsmen, Favell, who equalled a 32-year-old record for his State by scoring a century in each innings. He was particularly strong in strokes off the back foot. Benaud was the only man to cause Favell much concern. For New South Wales O'Neill shared in big stands with Burke and Craig.

South Australia

L. Favell st Lambert b Benaud	112 – run out	114
G. Stevens by Wyatt	0 – run out	32
C. Pinch c Lambert b Davidson	0 – b Davidson	80
J. Ducker c and b Benaud	13 – st Lambert b Benaud	0
G. B. Hole c Lambert b Benaud	2 – c O'Neill b Davidson	4
P. Ridings run out	0 – b Benaud	51
A. Bedford b Davidson	15 – c Treanor b Burke	25
B. Jarman b Wyatt	51 – c and b Benaud	14
J. Drennan c Davidson b Wyatt	35 – b Benaud	0
J. Beagley c Benaud b Davidson	12 – b Benaud	0
J. Wilson not out	0 – not out	0
Extras	8	Extras 13
	248	**333**

New South Wales

S. Carroll c Pinch b Drennan	0 – not out	4
J. W. Burke c and b Bedford	57	
W. Watson c Jarman b Drennan	0 – not out	2
N. O'Neill c Beagley b Wilson	127	
I. D. Craig c Stevens b Bedford	102	
R. Benaud c and b Bedford	0	
A. K. Davidson c Hole b Bedford	74	
J. Martin c and b Wilson	6	
J. Treanor c and b Wilson	3	
O. Lambert not out	0	
A. Wyatt c Stevens b Wilson	0	
Extras	17	
	386	**(No wkt) 6**

New South Wales Bowling

	Overs	Mdns	Runs	Wkts	Overs	Mdns	Runs	Wkts
Wyatt	14	2	53	3	14	2	76	—
Davidson	18.6	3	59	3	20	3	61	2
Benaud	22	5	73	3	31	10	70	5
Martin	10	—	27	—	11	2	37	—
Treanor	6	—	21	—	9	2	46	—
Burke	1	—	7	—	11.1	1	30	1

South Australia Bowling

	Overs	Mdns	Runs	Wkts	Overs	Mdns	Runs	Wkts
Pinch	1	—	2	—				
Hole	7	—	52	—				
Bedford..........	20	5	80	4				
Wilson	29.3	9	78	4				
Drennan	17	4	65	2	1	—	4	—
Beagley..........	17	3	92	—	1	—	2	—

WESTERN AUSTRALIA v SOUTH AUSTRALIA

Played at Perth, January 26, 28, 29, 30, 1957

South Australia won on first innings. On a pitch that gave little help to bowlers, batsmen were generally masters. Noteworthy performances were those by Pinch, who scored two centuries for South Australia, and Meuleman, who took out his bat for 234, the highest Sheffield Shield innings of the season, and the biggest to be scored on the Perth ground.

South Australia

L. Favell c Strauss b Slater	73	– b Strauss......................	1
G. Stevens c Shepherd b Gaunt..................	2	– c Buggins b Meuleman	80
J. Lee c Slater b Bevan	11	– not out	19
C. Pinch c Sawle b Strauss......................	110	– c and b Edwards................	100
G. B. Hole c Meuleman b Strauss................	104	– not out	26
B. Jarman b Slater............................	53		
J. Drennan c Buggins b Rutherford..............	0		
J. Beagley b Rutherford........................	0		
P. Ridings st Buggins b Slater	75		
L. Weekley c Buggins b Rutherford	1		
J. Wilson not out.............................	0		
Extras	18	Extras..................	13
	447	**(3 wkts dec.) 239**	

Western Australia

L. Sawle c Hole b Beagley.......................	20	– c Ridings b Beagley	3
J. Rutherford b Beagley.........................	15	– not out	71
R. L. Simpson lbw b Beagley	0	– not out	28
K. Meuleman not out	234		
A. Edwards c Jarman b Drennan	15		
B. Shepherd c Pinch b Drennan	0		
K. Slater c Drennan b Wilson...................	23		
B. Buggins lbw b Wilson.......................	20		
R. Strauss c Favell b Wilson....................	43		
H. Bevan b Wilson	22		
R. Gaunt c Hole b Drennan	14		
Extras	6	Extras..................	3
	412	**(1 wkt) 105**	

Western Australia Bowling

	Overs	Mdns	Runs	Wkts	Overs	Mdns	Runs	Wkts
Gaunt............	16	—	92	1	12	—	45	—
Bevan............	18	2	98	1	9	1	40	—
Strauss...........	23	2	86	2	11	3	35	1
Slater	21	4	82	3	13	5	36	—
Rutherford	9	2	20	3	18	6	34	—
Meuleman.........	1	—	17	—	3	—	15	1
Simpson	4	—	32	—	4	—	10	—
Edwards..........	1	—	2	—	4	—	11	1

South Australia Bowling

	Overs	Mdns	Runs	Wkts	Overs	Mdns	Runs	Wkts
Drennan..........	24	1	92	3	3	—	13	—
Beagley...........	18	2	77	3	3	—	27	1
Hole	19	1	60	—				
Wilson	48	17	99	4				
Weekley	14	1	78	—	3	—	31	—
Ridings					2	—	21	—
Favell					1	—	10	—

VICTORIA v SOUTH AUSTRALIA

Played at Melbourne, January 1, 2, 3, 4, 1958

Victoria won on first innings. Pinch and Hole scored centuries in South Australia's first innings, and Pinch followed with an identical score, 102, in the second innings. But Victoria surpassed the total of 356 runs, mainly through Potter and Loxton, who contributed hundreds and were together in a fifth-wicket partnership of 221. Dooland bowled 48 overs in this innings for four wickets. The South Australian captain, Hole, was injured when fielding and taken to hospital.

South Australia

D. Harris c Quick b Salmon	5	– lbw b Germaine	13
G. Stevens c Shaw b Quick	44	– c Salmon b Edwards...........	8
N. Dansie lbw b Salmon	1	– c Crompton b Salmon	3
C. Pinch st Maddocks b Germaine	102	– b Germaine..................	102
G. B. Hole c Aylett b Quick	123		
L. Head run out.............................	4	– c Maddocks b Edwards	75
B. Dooland c Edwards b Germaine	36	– not out	31
J. Ducker lbw b Huntington	14	– not out	1
A. Bedford lbw b Edwards	12	– run out	8
J. Beagley b Edwards	7		
P. Trethewey not out	4		
Extras	4	Extras.................	5
	356		**(6 wkts dec.) 246**

Victoria

A. Aylett b Trethewey	13 – not out	34
N. Crompton c and b Trethewey	18 – b Dooland	12
J. Shaw run out	34 – not out	23
I. Huntington c Trethewey b Beagley	75	
J. Potter b Dooland	115	
S. J. Loxton c Hole b Dooland	106	
L. Maddocks not out	40	
I. Quick c Stevens b Bedford	6	
J. Edwards b Dooland	0	
J. Salmon c Beagley b Dooland	0	
L. Germaine b Beagley	5	
Extras	22	Extras ... 15
	434	**(1 wkt) 84**

Victoria Bowling

	Overs	Mdns	Runs	Wkts	Overs	Mdns	Runs	Wkts
Salmon	17	—	68	2	15	1	61	1
Edwards	24.2	6	83	2	22	2	47	2
Loxton	6	—	27	—				
Huntington	5	—	21	1	2	—	4	—
Quick	27	5	81	2	22	4	72	—
Germaine	14	—	72	2	11	1	49	2
Potter					4	1	8	—

South Australia Bowling

	Overs	Mdns	Runs	Wkts	Overs	Mdns	Runs	Wkts
Beagley	23.1	4	81	2	4	2	5	—
Trethewey	28	4	90	2	5	1	11	—
Dooland	48	10	136	4	4	—	11	1
Bedford	23	2	74	1	2	—	7	—
Dansie	3	—	17	—	2	—	10	—
Hole	1	—	5	—				
Head	1	—	9	—	2	—	8	—
Harris					2	—	4	—
Stevens					4	—	12	—
Pinch					1	—	1	—

NEW SOUTH WALES v SOUTH AUSTRALIA

Played at Sydney, January 10, 11, 13, 14, 1958

South Australia won by six wickets. The New South Wales captain, Carroll, with first innings points assured, made a generous declaration at lunch time on the last day, leaving South Australia to score 237 in three and three-quarter hours to win. Their victory came with eighteen minutes to spare. The spectacular last day brought 420 runs in five and a quarter hours. South Australia fought well in the first innings and were only 14 runs short of New South Wales' total of 411. Stevens scored a century in each innings for South Australia, batting competently with neat stroke-play. O'Neill hit a brilliant century for New South Wales, for whom Saunders and Carroll began the second innings with a partnership of 181.

New South Wales

W. Saunders c Smart b Beagley	9	– st Ducker b Bedford	80
S. Carroll c Ducker b Beagley	51	– c Head b Cameron	94
W. Watson c Pinch b Smart	14	– not out	14
N. O'Neill c Harris b Beagley	125	– not out	23
B. Booth run out	9		
P. Philpott c Ducker b Cameron	97		
J. Martin c Harris b Dooland	72		
G. Rorke b Dooland	3		
A. Wyatt c Head b Dooland	6		
D. Ford not out	7		
J. O'Regan c Pinch b Smart	6		
Extras	12	Extras	11
	411	**(2 wkts dec.)**	**222**

South Australia

D. Harris lbw b Martin	15	– c Philpott b Martin	55
G. Stevens c Wyatt b Philpott	164	– b O'Neill	111
N. Dansie b Martin	10	– c Wyatt b O'Regan	27
C. Pinch c Wyatt b Rorke	38	– not out	20
L. Head st Ford b Philpott	22	– b O'Regan	0
L. Smart st Ford b Philpott	14	– not out	15
B. Dooland b Philpott	32		
R. Cameron lbw b O'Neill	10		
J. Ducker b Philpott	35		
A. Bedford not out	32		
J. Beagley c Ford b Wyatt	4		
Extras	21	Extras	9
	397	**(4 wkts)**	**237**

South Australia Bowling

	Overs	Mdns	Runs	Wkts	Overs	Mdns	Runs	Wkts
Beagley	21	2	78	3	11	—	63	—
Cameron	25	5	86	1	8	1	47	1
Smart	10	—	58	2	1	—	5	—
Dooland	39	8	121	3	8	1	49	—
Bedford	22	7	56	—	6	—	47	1

New South Wales Bowling

	Overs	Mdns	Runs	Wkts	Overs	Mdns	Runs	Wkts
Rorke	14	1	52	1	8	—	35	—
Wyatt	15.6	1	62	1	7	—	26	—
O'Regan	13	4	33	—	11	4	55	2
O'Neill	14	—	57	1	6	—	28	1
Martin	16	—	91	2	12	1	37	1
Philpott	22	2	81	5	6	—	45	—
Carroll					1	—	2	—

NEW SOUTH WALES v VICTORIA

Played at Sydney, January 25, 27, 28, 29, 1958

New South Wales won by ten wickets. The teams were the only remaining contenders for first place in the Shield table, Victoria having three more matches to play. New South Wales started badly, losing three for 58, but O'Neill played a memorable innings of 233 (thirty-eight 4s) in just over four hours. He allied dazzling stroke-play to pulverising power and roused the crowd to tremendous enthusiasm. New South Wales scored 411 runs for four wickets on the first day. Booth played a supporting role, contributing his first century in the competition to a partnership of 325 – the highest for the fourth wicket in Shield cricket. On a slow pitch taking turn, Victoria failed miserably against the spinners of Philpott and Martin in their first innings but atoned handsomely when following on 414 behind, though they could not avert defeat. Crompton, who made his best strokes to the off, and Shaw, strong in the pull, stayed together in a second-wicket stand of 211.

New South Wales

W. Saunders c Quick b Edwards	16	– not out	24
S. Carroll lbw b Edwards	33		
W. Watson c sub b Loxton	0		
N. O'Neill st Huntington b Potter	233		
B. Booth c Murray b Salmon	123	– not out	13
P. Philpott lbw b Murray	22		
J. Martin c Crompton b Murray	53		
D. Ford c Botham b Quick	19		
G. Rorke c Loxton b Quick	5		
A. Wyatt not out	7		
J. O'Regan st Botham b Quick	3		
Extras	17		
	531	(No wkt)	**37**

Victoria

N. Crompton b O'Regan	23	– b Rorke	124
R. Furlong lbw b Wyatt	1	– c Booth b Rorke	16
J. Shaw st Ford b Philpott	41	– b O'Regan	167
I. Huntington b Philpott	17	– c Philpott b Rorke	46
J. Potter b Martin	9	– b Martin	6
S. J. Loxton run out	4	– b Martin	0
B. Murray b Philpott	1	– c Watson b Philpott	18
L. Botham b Martin	0	– b Martin	16
I. Quick b Philpott	8	– b O'Regan	6
J. Edwards not out	10	– c and b Martin	14
J. Salmon b Martin	0	– not out	9
Extras	3	Extras	28
	117		**450**

Victoria Bowling

	Overs	Mdns	Runs	Wkts	Overs	Mdns	Runs	Wkts
Salmon	24	2	107	1	3.2	—	19	—
Edwards	36	6	120	2				
Loxton	7	—	46	1				
Murray	22	6	96	2				
Quick	19.4	1	111	3				
Potter	4	—	34	1	3	—	18	—

New South Wales Bowling

	Overs	Mdns	Runs	Wkts	Overs	Mdns	Runs	Wkts
Rorke	6	4	11	—	19	3	65	3
Wyatt	6	1	30	1	4	—	15	—
O'Regan	5	—	17	1	19	3	53	2
O'Neill	1	—	5	—	15	—	82	—
Martin	10.1	1	35	3	21.7	—	95	4
Philpott	10	5	16	4	26	3	112	1

NOTES BY THE EDITOR, 1960

AUSTRALIAN BOWLER'S FEAT

Geoffrey Jinkins of the North Melbourne club achieved an astounding bowling feat in a Grade One match. He was playing in the last fixture of the 1958-59 season against Prahran, the club which produced Sam Loxton. Owing to rain, no play was possible on the first day, Saturday, but on Monday North Melbourne gained an outright win by six wickets. The scores were Prahran 53 and 13; North Melbourne 52 and 15 for four wickets. In Prahran's first innings Jinkins took six wickets for 25 runs in eleven overs and in the second innings his analysis was eight wickets for no runs in 4.2 overs, a performance probably without parallel in senior cricket.

QUEENSLAND v WESTERN AUSTRALIA

Played at Brisbane, February 12, 13, 15, 16, 1960

Queensland won on first innings. Reynolds and McLaughlin put on 224 runs in fine style for Queensland's second wicket, missing by 19 runs equalling their own record for that wicket for their State. It was Reynolds' best display of the season, and his third century. Meuleman put Queensland in to bat, but the pitch proved to be dead. Lindwall and Grout reappeared for the home side after their overseas tour, and Grout created his world record of eight catches in an innings.

Queensland

S. Trimble c Hoare b O'Dwyer	37	– b Hoare	14
R. Reynolds c and b Mateljan	151	– c Buggins b Mateljan	37
J. McLaughlin c Vernon b Strauss	111	– b Hawke	5
T. Veivers c and b Strauss	31	– not out	41
†W. Grout c O'Dwyer b Hawke	23	– c Mateljan b Hoare	37
D. Bull lbw b Strauss	3		
D. Hughson not out	32		
J. Mackay c Vernon b Strauss	0		
*R. Lindwall b Hoare	1		
C. Westaway c Hawke b Strauss	9		
P. Allan c Sawle b Hawke	14		
B 1, l-b 1, n-b 3	5	B 1, n-b 1	2

1/78 2/302 3/302 4/339 5/350   417   1/27 2/32   (4 wkts dec.) 136
6/361 7/361 8/374 9/389   3/82 4/136

Western Australia

P. Wishart b Allan	25	– not out	50
L. Sawle c Grout b Mackay	6	– not out	53
M. Vernon c Grout b Veivers	78		
D. Hoare c Grout b Allan	11		
B. Shepherd c Grout b Mackay	23		
*K. Meuleman c Grout b Mackay	105		
N. Hawke c Grout b Mackay	7		
T. Mateljan c Grout b Lindwall	0		
R. Strauss b Mackay	7		
†B. Buggins not out	17		
T. O'Dwyer c Grout b Allan	12		
B 1, l-b 2, n-b 1	4	B 3, l-b 1	4

1/25 2/44 3/69 4/107 5/194   295   (No wkt) 107
6/246 7/247 8/259 9/268

Western Australia Bowling

	Overs	Mdns	Runs	Wkts	Overs	Mdns	Runs	Wkts
Hoare............	18	1	61	1	11.4	1	42	2
Hawke	28.6	2	94	2	12	1	37	1
Strauss...........	30	6	100	5	6	1	15	—
Mateljan..........	21	3	90	1	6	1	40	1
O'Dwyer..........	10	—	55	1				
Shepherd..........	2	—	12	—				

Queensland Bowling

	Overs	Mdns	Runs	Wkts	Overs	Mdns	Runs	Wkts
Lindwall..........	24	5	60	1	5	2	7	—
Allan.............	20.3	4	71	3	4	—	10	—
Mackay	29	7	83	5	7	1	19	—
Westaway.........	13	2	42	—	8	—	22	—
Veivers...........	10	4	29	1	12	2	29	—
Trimble...........	1	—	6	—				
McLaughlin					1	—	2	—
Bull..............					3	—	4	—
Reynolds..........					1	—	10	—

Umpires: L. Rowan and J. Goodwin.

CRICKET IN SOUTH AFRICA

TRANSVAAL v AUSTRALIANS

Played at Johannesburg, December 10, 12, 13, 1949

Australians won by 15 runs after one of the most exciting finishes of the tour. From the start the pitch took spin and A. Rowan baffled all the Australian batsmen by his quickly turning off breaks. Transvaal found conditions scarcely less easy but determined batting by Roothman, Winslow and A. Rowan enabled them to establish a lead of 41 before declaring. Again the Australians collapsed against A. Rowan, who captured fifteen wickets in the match for 68 runs, and Transvaal began their second innings requiring 69 for victory. In a tensely charged atmosphere the Transvaal batsmen tried valiantly to counter the capricious mood of the turf but despite a second commendable display by A. Rowan they could not cope with Johnson's cleverly flighted off-spin bowling.

Australians

A. R. Morris c Mitchell b A. Rowan	15	– lbw b Heaney	12
J. R. Moroney c Mitchell b A. Rowan	6	– c Roothman b Heaney	4
R. N. Harvey c Abernethy b A. Rowan	7	– c Winslow b A. Rowan	13
K. R. Miller c Mitchell b A. Rowan	7	– b A. Rowan	1
S. J. Loxton b A. Rowan	6	– c McLaren b Heaney	3
K. Archer not out	20	– c Mitchell b A. Rowan	15
C. L. McCool c Mitchell b A. Rowan	0	– b Heaney	18
I. W. Johnson c E. Rowan b A. Rowan	5	– b A. Rowan	1
R. A. Saggers c Winslow b A. Rowan	1	– not out	0
A. Walker st McLaren b Heaney	2	– st McLaren b A. Rowan	15
G. Noble c E. Rowan b A. Rowan	9	– c Winslow b A. Rowan	14
B 5, n-b 1	6	Byes etc.	13
	84		**109**

Transvaal

E. A. B. Rowan b Noblet	0	– c Miller b Johnson	11
J. Pickerill c Loxton b Miller	0	– lbw b Walker	0
B. Mitchell c Harvey b Noblet	17	– c Moroney b Miller	4
D. W. Begbie b Noblet	1	– lbw b Johnson	10
J. Roothman c Loxton b Johnson	36	– c Morris b Johnson	0
P. Winslow c McCool b Johnson	27	– c Morris b Johnson	0
A. M. B. Rowan c Morris b Johnson	31	– not out	15
N. N. McLaren b Noblet	1	– c Saggers b Johnson	3
M. Melle c Moroney b Miller	2	– b Noblet	5
L. J. Heaney not out	4	– b Noblet	0
T. F. Abernethy not out	3	– st Saggers b Johnson	0
N-b 3	3	Byes etc.	5
(9 wkts dec.)	**125**		**53**

Transvaal Bowling

	Overs	Mdns	Runs	Wkts	Overs	Mdns	Runs	Wkts
Melle	3	—	12	—	1	—	1	—
Heaney	18	5	47	1	19	5	46	4
A. M. B. Rowan	15.4	7	19	9	21	6	49	6

Australian Bowling

	Overs	Mdns	Runs	Wkts	Overs	Mdns	Runs	Wkts
Walker	7	4	13	—	5	2	8	1
Miller	18	4	48	2	4	2	5	1
Noblet	21.6	6	29	4	14	8	13	2
Johnson	8	—	16	3	13.3	5	22	6
Loxton	4	—	16	—				

SOUTH AFRICA v AUSTRALIA

Fourth Test Match

Played at Johannesburg, February 10, 11, 13, 14, 1950

Drawn. Having already made sure of the rubber, the Australians proceeded to consolidate their gains with powerful batting displays. Morris and Moroney set the mood for the Australian innings in an opening stand of 214, which was only 19 short of the record partnership for Australia-South Africa Tests created by J. H. Fingleton and W. A. Brown at Newlands in 1935. The left-hander Morris hit a 6 and nine 4s and Moroney's innings contained thirteen 4s. Further evidence of Australia's batting strength came from Miller and Hassett whose attractive stand added 109, and Harvey became the fifth batsman to pass fifty. South Africa's opening pair E. Rowan and Nel played the fast bowling of Lindwall and Miller quite confidently, their stand producing 84 well-made runs, but a collapse followed and six wickets were down for 148 when Fullerton and Tayfield came together. Exercising proper restraint they put on 65, and Mann helped to maintain the recovery by sharing in a partnership of 94 with Fullerton which prevented any possibility of a follow-on. By this time much of the interest had gone out of the game, although Moroney became the first Australian to score two separate hundreds in a Test match against South Africa. Harvey, too, completed three figures before being beaten by Melle, a promising fast medium bowler, who was making his Test début. Melle is a son of B. G. Von B. Melle, the old Oxford blue.

Australia

A. R. Morris c Fullerton b McCarthy	111	– c Mann b McCarthy	19
J. R. Moroney c Fullerton b Melle	118	– not out	101
K. R. Miller c Fullerton b Melle	84	– not out	33
R. R. Lindwall b Melle	5		
A. L. Hassett b McCarthy	53		
R. N. Harvey not out	56	– b Melle	100
S. J. Loxton b Melle	6		
C. L. McCool st Fullerton b Tayfield	8		
I. W. Johnson c Tayfield b Melle	3		
R. A. Saggers not out	5		
B 8, l-b 7, n-b 1	16	B 5, l-b 1	6

1/214 2/265 3/273 4/382   (8 wkts dec.) 465   1/28 2/198   (2 wkts) 259
5/392 6/418 7/437 8/440

W. A. Johnston did not bat.

South Africa

E. A. B. Rowan b Lindwall	55	N. B. F. Mann b Lindwall	52
J. Nel run out	25	M. Melle lbw b McCool	14
R. Draper c Saggers b Johnston	15	C. McCarthy not out	2
A. D. Nourse c Saggers b Lindwall	5		
D. W. Begbie c McCool b Miller	24	B 7, l-b 5, n-b 1	13
P. Winslow c and b Miller	19		—
G. M. Fullerton c Hassett b McCool	88	1/84 2/86 3/96 4/115 5/145	352
H. Tayfield c Johnson b Miller	40	6/148 7/213 8/307 9/345	

South Africa Bowling

	Overs	Mdns	Runs	Wkts	Overs	Mdns	Runs	Wkts
McCarthy	31	4	113	2	13	1	56	1
Melle	33	3	113	5	12	—	58	1
Tayfield	31	4	103	1	14	2	88	—
Mann	25	2	85	—	8	1	32	—
Begbie	7	—	35	—	3	—	19	—
Rowan					1	1	—	—
Nourse					1	1	—	—

Australia Bowling

	Overs	Mdns	Runs	Wkts
Lindwall	26	3	82	3
Johnston	29	5	68	1
Miller	28	3	75	3
Loxton	10	2	22	—
Johnson	18	4	52	—
McCool	7	—	29	2
Hassett	1	—	5	—
Harvey	3	—	6	—

SOUTH AFRICA v AUSTRALIA

Third Test Match

Played at Durban, January 24, 25, 27, 28, 29, 1958

Drawn. South Africa went close to recording the first victory in their own country against Australia, but although undoubtedly the better side in the match they contributed towards their own failure to win by surprising and unnecessarily slow batting. McGlew earned the unenviable distinction of recording the slowest century in history and although as a feat of endurance and concentration it was remarkable, it is doubtful whether South Africa benefited by it.

Gaunt, the fast-medium bowler recently flown from Australia, displaced the injured Meckiff for Australia and Heine, fit again returned to the South African side for Fuller. The pitch at Durban often helps the faster bowlers at the start of a match, but with five days ahead Craig decided to bat. Australia made a bad start and despite a good innings by Craig himself, they never recovered. Australia spend the entire first day of six hours scoring 155 for six, and next morning the last four wickets fell in 28 balls for the addition of eight runs. Adcock, bowling with fine speed and life on an unevenly grassed pitch, achieved his best Test figures, six for 43. Heine and Goddard gave him good support.

South Africa changed their opening partnership, Westcott going in first instead of Goddard. The move failed, for Westcott did not score, giving Gaunt a wicket in his first Test over. Endean soon followed, but from 28 for two South Africa slowly gained the upper hand. By the close of the second day they were only 13 behind with eight wickets left, but McGlew and Waite showed no intention of hurrying on the third day. Although losing only three wickets South Africa added no more than 168. McGlew took nine hours five minutes over his century and altogether stayed nine hours thirty-five minutes for 105. Waite also defended grimly while scoring 134 and their stand of 231 was the highest for any South Africa wicket against Australia.

Australia's fast-medium bowlers were never able to obtain the same amount of lift as Adcock and Heine. The pitch eased a good deal, but subsequently took spin, and Benaud played the leading part while the last five wickets fell in one hundred minutes on the fourth morning for 66. Grout the wicket-keeper, helped to dismiss five men in the innings which lasted thirteen hours.

Australia, 221 behind, set out to play for a draw, so the entire match brought no relief from slow scoring. McDonald and Burke wiped out 92 of the arrears before a wicket fell and Australia entered the last day with one man out for 117. Harvey and Mackay, the left-handers, removed any hope of a South African victory by determined displays on a pitch which took spin, but never broke up as expected. Australia held out for nine and a quarter hours. Rain and bad light ended a dreary match forty-two minutes early.

Australia

C. C. McDonald c Goddard b Adcock	28	– lbw b Tayfield	33
J. W. Burke c Waite b Adcock	2	– b Goddard	83
R. N. Harvey c Waite b Adcock	6	– b Adcock	68
I. D. Craig b Goddard	52	– c Goddard b Tayfield	0
R. Simpson b Goddard	17	– c Tayfield b van Ryneveld	4
K. Mackay hit wkt b Adcock	32	– not out	52
R. Benaud lbw b Adcock	5	– c Waite b van Ryneveld	20
A. K. Davidson c Waite b Heine	12	– c McGlew b Tayfield	4
W. Grout b Heine	2	– not out	3
L. Kline c Goddard b Adcock	0		
R. Gaunt not out	0		
N-b 7	7	B 19, l-b 5, n-b 1	25

1/13 2/19 3/54 4/87 5/131   163   1/92 2/170 3/179 4/221   (7 wkts) 292
6/142 7/161 8/163 9/163   5/261 6/274 7/289

South Africa

D. J. McGlew c Grout b Gaunt	105	H. J. Tayfield st Grout b Benaud	0
R. Westcott b Gaunt	0	P. Heine c Burke b Benaud	7
W. R. Endean c Simpson b Benaud	15	N. A. T. Adcock c Grout b Benaud	0
J. H. B. Waite b Davidson	134		
T. L. Goddard lbw b Davidson	45	B 2, l-b 5, n-b 1	8
K. J. Funston c Grout b Mackay	27		
C. B. van Ryneveld not out	32	1/6 2/28 3/259 4/259 5/313	384
R. A. McLean c Grout b Benaud	11	6/356 7/371 8/371 9/383	

South Africa Bowling

	Overs	Mdns	Runs	Wkts	Overs	Mdns	Runs	Wkts
Heine	17.4	4	30	2	14	1	40	—
Adcock	18	2	43	6	15	1	34	1
Goddard	23	12	25	2	42	18	62	1
Tayfield	21	7	41	—	59	25	94	3
van Ryneveld	3	—	17	—	17	1	37	2

Australia Bowling

	Overs	Mdns	Runs	Wkts
Davidson	34	8	62	2
Gaunt	27	2	87	2
Mackay	35	5	77	1
Benaud	50.7	13	114	5
Kline	17	6	36	—

CRICKET IN WEST INDIES

BARBADOS v INDIA

Played at Bridgetown, January 31, February 2, 3, 4, 5, 1953

Drawn. After following-on, the Indians were helped in their efforts to save the game by a sudden downpour. At that point, with one wicket to fall and sixty-five minutes play remaining, they stood only 48 runs ahead. The ground staff, however, neglected to cover the pitch and within twenty minutes it became so soaked that further play was impossible. Weekes followed his 207 in the First Test with another brilliant double century against the Indian bowlers. After dominating a fourth-wicket stand of 213 with Williams, he found an equally aggressive partner in Atkinson, who helped to add 155. In spite of fine batting by Umrigar, the Indians failed against Barker, a powerfully-built fast bowler, and Sobers, a 16-years-old left-arm spin bowler. Roy and Manjrekar began their second innings recovery and Umrigar again batted well.

Barbados

R. E. Marshall run out	25	J. D. Goddard not out	50
C. C. Hunte c Maka b Kannaiyaram	29	C. Depeiza b Gadkari	26
C. L. Walcott c Phadkar b Hazare	51	H. Sobers not out	7
E. D. Weekes b Roy	253	Extras	24
C. B. Williams c Umrigar b Phadkar	60		—
D. Atkinson b Roy	81	(7 wkts dec.)	606

H. King and H. Barker did not bat.

India

P. Roy lbw b Barker	4	– c and b Atkinson	89
M. L. Apte b Marshall	5	– b Barker	4
V. L. Manjrekar lbw b Marshall	44	– lbw b Sobers	154
V. S. Hazare c Depeiza b Barker	15	– b Barker	38
P. R. Umrigar b Sobers	63	– not out	96
D. G. Phadkar b Sobers	7	– b Sobers	2
D. K. Gaekwad lbw b Sobers	27	– b Sobers	13
D. H. Shodhan lbw b Sobers	0	– run out	0
C. V. Gadkari b Barker	24	– c Walcott b Barker	9
E. S. Maka b Marshall	9	– c Walcott b King	9
N. Kannaiyaram not out	0	– not out	10
Extras	11	Extras	21
	—		—
	209	(9 wkts)	445

India Bowling

	Overs	Mdns	Runs	Wkts
Phadkar	40	8	98	1
Kannaiyaram	18	2	60	1
Shodhan	20	2	87	—
Gadkari	35	2	154	1
Hazare	20	1	85	1
Manjrekar	6	—	30	—
Gaekwad	1	—	10	—
Roy	14	1	58	2

Barbados Bowling

	Overs	Mdns	Runs	Wkts	Overs	Mdns	Runs	Wkts
Barker...........	17.2	4	22	3	43	8	113	3
Atkinson..........	12	6	14	—	46	24	62	1
Marshall.........	29	8	62	3	26.4	6	77	—
King.............	12	4	29	—	15	5	34	1
Sobers...........	22	5	50	4	67	35	92	3
Walcott..........	9	5	13	—	17	7	27	—
Goddard..........	3	—	8	—	4	2	6	—
Weekes..........					9	3	13	—

WEST INDIES v INDIA

Fifth Test Match

Played at Kingston, March 28, 30, 31, April 1, 2, 4, 1953

Drawn. The match was notable for the double-hundred by Worrell and five other centuries. In the finish the West Indies, already one victory to the good, did not attempt the task of making 181 to win in 135 minutes. Roy, Umrigar and Manjrekar were India's best batsmen and Worrell, Weekes and Walcott upheld their reputations. It was the first time the three "W's" had each hit a hundred in the same innings. Valentine, Gupte and Mankad carried off bowling honours.

India scored 216 for three on the first day, Roy batting faultlessly and Umrigar driving powerfully. Next day India, after being 269 for four at lunch collapsed against the wiles of Valentine, but not before Roy and Umrigar had added 150 for the fourth wicket. West Indies, 103 for one at the close, raced to 400 for three on the third day, thanks to Worrell, who batted brilliantly for 171 not out, and Weekes, who helped him put on 197. Both were in entertaining form. On the fourth day Worrell and Walcott, by more careful methods, increased their fourth-wicket partnership to 213. Worrell, caught at mid-on when at last he lifted the ball, scored his 237 in nine and a half hours, and Walcott spent four hours for 118. Gupte, bowling his leg-breaks skilfully, and Mankad sent the last six wickets tumbling for 33, but West Indies reached their highest score in a home Test.

India, 264 behind, made 63 without loss before drawing of stumps, then, on the fifth day, a grand second-wicket stand of 237 by the patient Roy and attractive Manjrekar gave the tourists hope of saving the match. India left off 63 runs on with seven wickets in hand, but even with the unexpected fall of four wickets before lunch on the last morning they were not really in trouble.

Pairaudeau and Stollmeyer probably were ready to take risks when West Indies began their second innings, but when both were out for 15 Worrell and Weekes set the tempo for a defensive finish. Weekes passed Headley's 1929-30 record of 703 runs in a Test series in the West Indies.

India

P. Roy c Legall b King	85	– lbw b Valentine |150
M. L. Apte run out	15	– lbw b Valentine	33
G. S. Ramchand lbw b Valentine	22	– c Pairaudeau b Valentine	33
V. S. Hazare c Valentine b King	16	– c Weekes b Valentine	12
P. R. Umrigar b Valentine	117	– c Weekes b King	13
V. L. Manjrekar c Weekes b Valentine	43	– c Weekes b Gomez |118
V. Mankad lbw b Valentine	6	– c Weekes b Gomez	9
C. V. Gadkari c Legall b Valentine	0	– c Stollmeyer b Gomez	0
J. M. Ghorpade c Legall b Gomez	4	– b King	24
S. P. Gupte not out	0	– b Gomez	8
D. H. Shodhan absent ill	0	– not out	15
L-b 1, w 3	4	B 18, l-b 10, w 1	29

1/30 2/57 3/80 4/230 5/277   312   1/80 2/317 3/327 4/346 5/360   444
6/295 7/312 8/312 9/312   6/360 7/368 8/408 9/431

West Indies

B. H. Pairaudeau b Gupte	58	– run out	2
J. B. Stollmeyer b Mankad	13	– b Ramchand	9
F. M. Worrell c Hazare b Mankad	237	– c Apte b Mankad	23
E. Weekes c Gadkari b Gupte	109	– c Ghorpade b Ramchand	36
C. L. Walcott c Gadkari b Mankad	118	– not out	5
R. J. Christiani lbw b Mankad	4	– not out	1
G. E. Gomez c Hazare b Mankad	12		
R. Legall c sub b Gupte	1		
F. King st Manjrekar b Gupte	0		
A. P. H. Scott c and b Gupte	5		
A. L. Valentine not out	4		
B 7, l-b 4, w 4	15	B 15, w 1	16

1/36 2/133 3/330 4/543 5/554   576   1/11 2/15 3/82   (4 wkts)   92
6/554 7/567 8/567 9/569   4/91

West Indies Bowling

	Overs	Mdns	Runs	Wkts	Overs	Mdns	Runs	Wkts
King	34	13	64	2	26	6	83	2
Gomez	28	13	40	1	47	24	72	4
Worrell	16	6	31	—	6	2	17	—
Scott	31	7	88	—	13	2	52	—
Valentine	27.5	9	64	5	67	22	149	4
Stollmeyer	4	—	20	—	11	3	28	—
Walcott	1	—	1	—	8	2	14	—

India Bowling

	Overs	Mdns	Runs	Wkts	Overs	Mdns	Runs	Wkts
Ramchand	36	9	84	—	15	6	33	2
Hazare	17	2	47	—	2	1	1	—
Gupte	65.1	14	180	5	8	2	16	—
Mankad	82	17	228	5	22	11	26	1
Ghorpade	6	1	22	—				

Umpires: T. A. Ewart and R. C. Burke.

WEST INDIES v AUSTRALIA

Second Test Match

Played at Port of Spain, April 11, 12, 13, 14, 15, 16, 1955

Drawn. A century in each innings by Walcott, who became the third West Indies cricketer to achieve this feat in a Test match, and the return to his best form of Weekes enabled West Indies to share the honours in a game of heavy scoring. So great was public interest that on the opening day the gates were closed before the start, and a crowd estimated at 28,000 comprised the biggest ever to watch a match in the West Indies.

Rain limited the first day's cricket to eighty-five minutes in which time West Indies lost two wickets for 73. Next day Weekes and Walcott, scoring 242 together, established a new record for any West Indies wicket in a Test with Australia. Both employed powerful strokes all round. Weekes gave a masterly display for three and a half hours, hitting one 6 and twenty-four 4s, and Walcott obtained seventeen 4s. On the third morning the last five wickets fell, four of them to Lindwall, for 27 runs, and McDonald and Morris followed with sound batting. Nine bowlers tried without success to part them before the close when the total stood at 147, and despite the handicap of injuries they stayed till their stand reached 191, a record for an Australian first wicket against West Indies.

Harvey completed his second century of the series and fierce hitting came from Archer (one 6, twelve 4s) and Johnson. So Australia gained a first innings advantage of 218.

West Indies went ahead for the loss of two wickets, Walcott and Weekes adding 127 together. Walcott, whose forcing tactics took him to three figures in just over an hour and fifty minutes, hit thirteen boundaries.

The game, the first Test match to be played in Trinidad on a turf pitch, yielded 1,255 runs for the loss of twenty-three wickets.

West Indies

J. K. Holt c Johnston b Lindwall	25	– lbw b Archer	21
J. B. Stollmeyer b Lindwall	14	– b Johnson	42
C. L. Walcott st Langley b Benaud	126	– c Watson b Archer	110
E. D. Weekes c Johnson b Benaud	139	– not out	87
O. G. Smith b Benaud	0	– c Langley b Archer	0
G. Sobers c Langley b Lindwall	47	– not out	8
C. McWatt c Benaud b Miller	4		
F. King b Lindwall	2		
S. Ramadhin b Lindwall	0		
L. Butler c Johnson b Lindwall	16		
A. L. Valentine not out	4		
B 1, l-b 3, n-b 1	5	L-b 3, w 2	5

1/39 2/40 3/282 4/282 5/323   382   1/40 2/103 3/230 4/236   (4 wkts) 273
6/355 7/360 8/360 9/361

Australia

C. C. McDonald c Walcott b Valentine	110	R. R. Lindwall not out	37
A. R. Morris c King b Butler	111	G. R. Langley c King b Walcott	9
R. N. Harvey lbw b King	133	W. A. Johnston not out	1
W. Watson lbw b Ramadhin	27		
R. Benaud c Walcott b Ramadhin	5	B 5, l-b 6, w 1, n-b 2	14
K. R. Miller run out	3		
R. G. Archer c McWatt b Valentine	84	1/191 2/259 3/328 (9 wkts dec.) 600	
I. W. Johnson c McWatt b Butler	66	4/336 5/345 6/439 7/529 8/570 9/594	

Australia Bowling

	Overs	Mdns	Runs	Wkts	Overs	Mdns	Runs	Wkts
Lindwall	24.5	3	95	6	16	1	70	—
Miller	28	9	96	1	12	—	52	—
Archer	9	—	42	—	8	1	37	3
Johnston..........	7	1	28	—	7	—	31	—
Johnson	19	5	72	—	7	2	26	1
Benaud..........	17	3	44	3	12	2	52	—

West Indies Bowling

	Overs	Mdns	Runs	Wkts
Butler	40	7	151	2
King	37	7	98	1
Holt	1	1	—	—
Ramadhin.........	32	8	90	2
Valentine.........	49	12	133	2
Walcott...........	19	5	45	1
Sobers............	3	1	10	—
Smith	15	1	48	—
Stollmeyer........	5	—	11	—

Umpires: E. Lee Kow and C. Jordan.

WEST INDIES v AUSTRALIA

Fourth Test Match

Played at Bridgetown, May 14, 16, 17, 18, 19, 20, 1955

Drawn, a result which sufficed to give Australia the rubber. The match was rendered memorable by a huge partnership by Atkinson and Depeiza during the first West Indies innings. In putting on 348 they established a world's record for the seventh wicket, beating the 344 by K. S. Ranjitsinhji and W. Newham for Sussex against Essex at Leyton in 1902.

The Australian batsmen lost no time in mastering the bowling. For the third time in the series they began with a three-figure stand, Favell (thirteen 4s) and McDonald scoring 108 together. The Australian innings lasted till the third day. Miller, batting in aggressive style, hit twenty-two 4s and Archer helped him to add 206 for the sixth wicket. Lindwall (two 6s, fifteen 4s) also punished wilting bowlers, reaching his second century in Test cricket, and Langley scored readily.

Another Australian victory appeared in prospect when six West Indies batsmen were dismissed for 146, but Atkinson and Depeiza came to the rescue, defying the attack for more than a day. Atkinson, the leading personality in the stand, hit one 6 and twenty-six 4s. In the end Australia's lead was restricted to 158, and as the pitch showed signs of wear Johnson did not enforce the follow-on. Favell batted skilfully and a good innings came from Johnson, so that in the end West Indies were left to make 408 in less than three hours and fifty minutes. This was clearly beyond them, but another good innings by Walcott made them safe from defeat.

Australia

C. C. McDonald run out	46	– b Smith	17
L. Favell c Weekes b Atkinson	72	– run out	53
R. N. Harvey c Smith b Worrell	74	– c Valentine b Smith	27
W. Watson c Depeiza b Dewdney	30	– b Atkinson	0
K. R. Miller c Depeiza b Dewdney	137	– lbw b Atkinson	10
R. Benaud c Walcott b Dewdney	1	– b Sobers	5
R. G. Archer b Worrell	98	– lbw b Atkinson	28
R. R. Lindwall c Valentine b Atkinson	118	– b Atkinson	10
I. W. Johnson b Dewdney	23	– c Holt b Smith	57
G. R. Langley b Sobers	53	– not out	28
J. C. Hill not out	8	– c Weekes b Atkinson	1
B 1, l-b 2, w 4, n-b 1	8	B 9, l-b 4	13

1/108 2/126 3/226 4/226 5/233   668   1/71 2/72 3/73 4/87 5/107   249
6/439 7/483 8/562 9/623   6/119 7/151 8/177 9/241

West Indies

J. K. Holt b Lindwall	22	– lbw b Hill	49
G. Sobers c Hill b Johnson	43	– lbw b Archer	11
C. L. Walcott c Langley b Benaud	15	– b Benaud	83
E. D. Weekes c Langley b Miller	44	– run out	6
F. M. Worrell run out	16	– c Archer b Miller	34
O. G. Smith c Langley b Miller	2	– b Lindwall	11
D. Atkinson c Archer b Johnson	219	– not out	20
C. Depeiza b Benaud	122	– not out	11
S. Ramadhin c and b Benaud	10		
T. Dewdney b Johnson	0		
A. L. Valentine not out	2		
B 5, l-b 4, w 2, n-b 4	15	B 6, l-b 2, w 1	9

1/52 2/69 3/105 4/142 5/143   510   1/38 2/67 3/81 4/154   (6 wkts) 234
6/146 7/494 8/504 9/504   5/193 6/207

West Indies Bowling

	Overs	Mdns	Runs	Wkts	Overs	Mdns	Runs	Wkts
Worrell	40	7	120	2	7	—	25	—
Dewdney	33	7	125	4	10	4	23	—
Walcott	26	10	57	—				
Valentine	31	9	87	—	6	1	16	—
Ramadhin	24	3	84	—	2	—	10	—
Atkinson	48	14	108	2	36.2	16	56	5
Smith	22	8	49	—	34	12	71	3
Sobers	11.5	6	30	1	14	3	35	1

Australia Bowling

	Overs	Mdns	Runs	Wkts	Overs	Mdns	Runs	Wkts
Lindwall	25	3	97	1	8	1	39	1
Miller	22	2	112	2	21	3	66	1
Archer	15	4	44	—	7	1	11	1
Johnson	35	12	77	3	14	4	30	—
Harvey	4	—	16	—				
Watson	1	—	5	—				
Benaud	31.1	6	73	3	11	3	35	1
Hill	24	9	71	—	11	2	44	1

Umpires: E. Lee Kow and C. Jordan.

WEST INDIES v AUSTRALIA

Fifth Test Match

Played at Kingston, June 11, 13, 14, 15, 16, 17, 1955

Australia won by an innings and 82 runs a game in which more records were established. First and foremost was the performance of Walcott in hitting for the second time during the series two separate centuries in a match, a feat never before accomplished. Furthermore he became the first player to reach three figures on five occasions in a Test rubber. The Australian total, besides being the biggest ever recorded in a Test match by a team from the Commonwealth, yielded two other records – the scoring of five centuries in an innings and the highest third wicket stand in history for Australia.

By the end of the opening day West Indies appeared likely to make a better fight, for with six wickets down they had 327 runs on the board. They began badly on a pitch "full of runs", losing two wickets, including that of the new opening batsman, Furlonge for 13. Then Walcott led a recovery in which Weekes and Worrell rendered able support. Let off when 21 by Johnston, who twisted a knee in attempting the catch and did not bowl in the match, Walcott offered only one more chance, at 105, during a stay of nearly five hours. While always strong in defence, he drove, cut and pulled with great power. Weekes, who injured a thigh muscle early in his innings, hit so fiercely all round that in scoring 56 of the 82 added for the third wicket, he registered no fewer than ten boundaries. Worrell, with a discriminating display, helped Walcott to put on 110 before falling to a splendid left-handed catch on the leg side behind the wicket by Langley, who gave a capital exhibition and in the two innings allowed only eight byes. Next day Miller bowled so effectively that the remaining four wickets went down for 30 runs. Three of them fell to Miller at a cost of 15 runs, and he finished with six for 107.

Australia in turn made a poor start, losing two men for seven runs, but from that point they were the masters. McDonald and Harvey, proceeding unhurriedly, put on 295 in a little over five hours. Harvey, staying till his side stood 16 ahead, batted for seven hours five minutes and hit one 6 and twenty-four 4s. Very slow at first, Miller shared with Archer in a stand which realised 220, and there followed a dazzling display of forcing batsmanship by Benaud. So mercilessly did Benaud flog a tiring attack that, with two 6s and fifteen 4s among his figures, he reached 100 in seventy-eight minutes. Upon his dismissal Johnson declared with Australia 401 ahead.

Three West Indies wickets went down for 65, but again Walcott checked the success of bowlers. He found a steady partner in Sobers, who stayed three hours while 179 runs were added, but when they were parted such a breakdown occurred that the innings and the match were all over for another 75 runs early on the sixth day.

West Indies

J. K. Holt c Langley b Miller	4	– c Langley b Benaud	21
H. Furlonge c Benaud b Lindwall	4	– c sub b Miller	28
C. L. Walcott c Langley b Miller	155	– c Langley b Lindwall	110
E. D. Weekes b Benaud	56	– not out	36
F. M. Worrell c Langley b Lindwall	61	– b Johnson	12
O. G. Smith c Langley b Miller	29	– c and b Benaud	16
G. Sobers not out	35	– c Favell b Lindwall	64
D. Atkinson run out	8	– c Langley b Archer	4
C. Depeiza c Langley b Miller	0	– b Miller	7
F. King b Miller	0	– c Archer b Johnson	6
T. Dewdney b Miller	2	– lbw b Benaud	0
L-b 2, w 1	3	B 8, l-b 6, w 1	15

1/4 2/13 3/95 4/205 5/268   357   1/47 2/60 3/65 4/244 5/244   319
6/327 7/341 8/347 9/347   6/268 7/273 8/283 9/289

Australia

C. C. McDonald b Worrell 127
L. Favell c Weekes b King 0
A. R. Morris lbw b Dewdney 7
R. N. Harvey c Atkinson b Smith 204
K. R. Miller c Worrell b Atkinson. 109
R. G. Archer c Depeiza b Sobers 128
R. R. Lindwall c Depeiza b King 10

R. Benaud c Worrell b Smith 121
I. W. Johnson not out 27

B 8, l-b 7, w 9, n-b 1 27

1/0 2/7 3/302 4/373   (8 wkts dec.) 758
5/593 6/597 7/621 8/758

G. R. Langley and W. A. Johnston did not bat.

Australia Bowling

	Overs	Mdns	Runs	Wkts	Overs	Mdns	Runs	Wkts
Lindwall	12	2	64	2	20	5	56	2
Miller	25.2	2	107	6	19	3	58	2
Archer	11	1	39	—	26	6	68	1
Benaud	24	5	75	1	30	10	76	3
Johnson	22	7	69	—	23	10	46	2

West Indies Bowling

	Overs	Mdns	Runs	Wkts
Dewdney	24	4	115	1
King	31	1	126	2
Atkinson.	55	21	132	1
Smith	52.4	17	145	2
Worrell	45	10	116	1
Sobers.	38	12	99	1

Umpires: P. Burke and T. Ewart.

WEST INDIES v PAKISTAN

First Test Match

Played at Bridgetown, January 17, 18, 20, 21, 22, 23, 1958

Drawn. A match of high scoring apart from an unexpected collapse by Pakistan in their first innings, ended in a wave of excitement as Hanif Mohammad, the Pakistan opening batsman, fell only 28 runs short of Sir Leonard Hutton's record Test score of 364. Even so, Hanif completed the longest innings played in a first-class match. He batted for sixteen hours thirteen minutes, and hit twenty-four 4s in an innings of unflagging concentration which exceeded by nearly three hours that of Hutton in his 1938 marathon for England against Australia at The Oval.

After Pakistan followed on 473 behind, Hanif shared in four century stands with Imtiaz Ahmed, Alim-ud-Din, Saeed Ahmed and his brother, Wazir. Not until after tea on the final day was he dismissed, and by then Pakistan were safe from defeat. The West Indies' opening batsman, Hunte, also distinguished himself, for he made a sound century in his first Test, batting five hours and hitting seventeen 4s. Kanhai and Sobers gave good support, and Weekes, helped by Walcott and Smith, punished the bowling before West Indies declared. After two days in the field, Pakistan found the pace of Gilchrist and Smith's off-spin too much for them in their first innings, but Hanif's monumental display thwarted West Indies.

Nasimul Ghani, aged sixteen years 248 days, became the youngest player to appear in a Test when he took the field on the first day.

West Indies

C. Hunte c Imtiaz b Fazal	142	– not out	11
R. Kanhai c Mathias b Fazal	27	– not out	17
G. Sobers c Mathias b Mahmood	52		
E. D. Weekes c Imtiaz b Mahmood	197		
C. L. Walcott c Mathias b Kardar	43		
O. G. Smith c Mathias b Alim	78		
D. Atkinson b Mahmood	4		
E. Atkinson b Fazal	0		
F. C. M. Alexander b Mahmood	9		
A. L. Valentine not out	5		
B 9, l-b 4, w 3, n-b 6	22		

1/22 2/209 3/266   (9 wkts dec.) 579   (No wkt) 28
4/356 5/541 6/551 7/556
8/570 9/579

R. Gilchrist did not bat.

Pakistan

Hanif Mohammad b E. Atkinson	17	– c Alexander b D. Atkinson	337
Imtiaz Ahmed lbw b Gilchrist	20	– lbw b Gilchrist	91
Alim-ud-Din c Weekes b Gilchrist	3	– c Alexander b Sobers	37
Saeed Ahmed st Alexander b Smith	13	– c Alexander b Smith	65
Wazir Mohammad lbw b Valentine	4	– c Alexander b E. Atkinson	35
Wallis Mathias c Alexander b Smith	17	– lbw b E. Atkinson	17
A. H. Kardar c D. Atkinson b Smith	4	– not out	23
Fazal Mahmood b Gilchrist	4	– b Valentine	19
Nasimul Ghani run out	11	– b Valentine	0
Mahmood Hussain b Gilchrist	3	– not out	0
Haseeb Ahsan not out	1		
B 4, l-b 5	9	B 19, l-b 7, n-b 7	33

1/35 2/39 3/45 4/53 5/81   106   1/152 2/264 3/418   (8 wkts dec.) 657
6/84 7/91 8/93 9/96   4/539 5/598 6/628 7/647 8/649

Pakistan Bowling

	Overs	Mdns	Runs	Wkts	Overs	Mdns	Runs	Wkts
Fazal	61	12	145	3	2	1	3	—
Mahmood	41.2	5	153	4				
Kardar	32	5	107	1	3	1	13	—
Haseeb	22	—	84	—				
Nasimul	14	1	51	—				
Alim	2	—	17	1				
Hanif					3	1	10	—
Saeed					2	2	—	—
Wazir					1	—	2	—

West Indies Bowling

	Overs	Mdns	Runs	Wkts	Overs	Mdns	Runs	Wkts
Gilchrist	15	4	32	4	41	5	121	1
E. Atkinson	8	—	27	1	49	5	136	2
Smith	13	4	23	3	61	30	93	1
Valentine	6.2	1	15	1	39	8	109	2
D. Atkinson					62	35	61	1
Sobers					57	25	94	1
Walcott					10	5	10	—

WEST INDIES v PAKISTAN

Third Test Match

Played at Kingston, February 26, 27, 28. March 1, 3, 4, 1958

West Indies won by an innings and 174 runs. All else in this crushing defeat for Pakistan was overshadowed by the feat of Garfield Sobers, the West Indies 21-year-old left-hander, in beating the Test record individual score, 364 by Sir Leonard Hutton, made for England against Australia at The Oval nearly twenty years previously. Sobers passed him by one run and was still unbeaten when West Indies declared at the vast total of 790 for three. So elated were the crowd of 20,000 at Sabina Park that they swarmed over the field and the pitch became so damaged that the umpires ordered repairs and the last fifty-five minutes of the fourth day could not be played.

Sobers' monumental innings was his first century in Test cricket. On a perfect pitch he made strokes freely throughout, hitting thirty-eight 4s and batting for ten hours eight minutes, compared with thirteen hours twenty minutes by Hutton. Two factors greatly helped Sobers, the sadly depleted nature of the Pakistan attack, and the splendid support of Hunte, who helped him in a second-wicket stand of 446. This, the second highest stand in Test cricket, fell only five runs short of the record for any wicket, 451 by Sir Donald Bradman and W. H. Ponsford for Australia against England at The Oval in 1934.

Kardar, Pakistan's captain, went into the match with a broken finger on his left hand, yet he bowled 37 overs of his left-arm spinners against doctor's orders. Mahmood Hussain pulled a thigh muscle after only five balls in the first over of the innings, and did not bowl again; Nasimul Ghani, another left-arm bowler, fractured a thumb quite early in the long West Indies' innings. So Fazal Mahmood, who sent down a phenomenal number of overs for a bowler of his pace, and Khan Mohammad were left as the only two fit regular bowlers. Sound batting by Imtiaz Ahmed, Saeed Ahmed and Wallis Mathias gave Pakistan a good start on the first day, but a shower next day helped the seam bowlers E. Atkinson and Dewdney, who brought about a collapse. Wazir Mohammad batted gallantly in a bid to stave off defeat in the second innings, but with Mahmood Hussain and Nasimul Ghani unable to bat West Indies secured victory after only forty minutes' play on the last day.

Pakistan

Hanif Mohammad c Alexander b Gilchrist	3	– b Gilchrist	13
Imtiaz Ahmed c Alexander b Gilchrist	122	– lbw b Dewdney	0
Saeed Ahmed c Weekes b Smith	52	– c Gilchrist b Gibbs	44
Wallis Mathias b Dewdney	77	– c Alexander b Atkinson	19
Alim-un-Din c Alexander b Atkinson	15	– b Gibbs	30
A. H. Kardar c Sobers b Atkinson	15	– lbw b Dewdney	57
Wazir Mohammad c Walcott b Dewdney	2	– lbw b Atkinson	106
Fazal Mahmood c Alexander b Atkinson	6	– c Alexander b Atkinson	0
Nasimul Ghani b Atkinson	5	– absent hurt	0
Mahmood Hussain b Atkinson	20	– absent hurt	0
Khan Mohammad not out	3	– not out	0
B 2, l-b 5, n-b 1	8	B 16, l-b 3	19

1/4 2/122 3/223 4/249 5/287   328   1/8 2/20 3/57 4/105 5/120   288
6/291 7/299 8/301 9/317   6/286 7/286 8/288

West Indies

C. Hunte run out	260	C. L. Walcott not out ... 88
R. Kanhai c Imtiaz b Fazal	25	B 1, l-b 8, w 4 ... 13
G. Sobers not out	365	
E. D. Weekes c Hanif b Fazal	39	1/87 2/533 3/602 (3 wkts. dec.) 790

O. G. Smith, E. Atkinson, L. Gibbs, F. C. M. Alexander, T. Dewdney and R. Gilchrist did not bat.

West Indies Bowling

	Overs	Mdns	Runs	Wkts	Overs	Mdns	Runs	Wkts
Gilchrist	25	3	106	2	12	3	65	1
Dewdney	26	4	88	2	19.3	2	51	2
Atkinson.	21	7	42	5	18	6	36	3
Gibbs	7	—	32	—	21	6	46	2
Smith	18	3	39	1	8	2	20	—
Sobers.	5	1	13	—	15	4	41	—
Weekes.					3	1	10	—

Pakistan Bowling

	Overs	Mdns	Runs	Wkts
Mahmood.	0.5	—	2	—
Fazal.	85.2	20	247	2
Khan.	54	5	259	—
Nasimul	14	3	39	—
Kardar	37	2	141	—
Mathias.	4	—	20	—
Alim	4	—	34	—
Hanif	2	—	11	—
Saeed	6	—	24	—

NOTES BY THE EDITOR, 1959

SOBERS MAKES HIGHEST TEST SCORE

Garfield Sobers, the tall 22-year-old West Indies left-hander, also distinguished himself by scoring 365 not out in the third Test against Pakistan at Kingston on March 1, 1958 and surpassing Hutton's world record Test innings of 364 for England against Australia at The Oval in 1938. He followed with a century in each innings in the next Test and continued his Bradman-like consistency when touring India, scoring centuries in his first three Tests there. His remarkable sequence brought him 1,115 runs in six successive Tests – ten innings, four times not out.

WEST INDIES v PAKISTAN

Fourth Test Match

Played at Georgetown, March 13, 14, 15, 17, 18, 19, 1958

West Indies won by eight wickets, Sobers hitting a century in each innings. After holding West Indies to a lead of two runs, Pakistan could not prevent heavy scoring by their opponents in the second innings, which led to a comfortable win and decided the series. Rahman, a leg-break bowler sent to reinforce Pakistan's injury-hit side, made his first Test appearance only two days after arrival. Saeed Ahmed and Hanif Mohammad, in a cautious third-wicket stand, ensured that Pakistan would build up a useful total, although Gilchrist produced occasional bursts of lively fast bowling. Saeed hit one 5 and sixteen 4s in his first Test century. Sobers and Walcott thrashed the Pakistan bowlers in a brilliant second-wicket stand of 269, but the youthful left-arm slow bowler, Nasimul, troubled later batsmen in a fine spell. Sound batting by Wazir Mohammad, unlucky not to gain a century and Kardar helped Pakistan to a useful second innings score, despite steady bowling by Gibbs and Smith. Pakistan's chances suffered a heavy blow at the start of West Indies' second innings. After bowling only four overs, Fazal Mahmood, who had been struck on the knee when batting, had to go to hospital with leg trouble. Without him, the attack lacked penetration and Hunte and Kanhai began with a stand of 125 before Sobers scored his second century of the match.

Pakistan

Alim-ud-Din b Smith	30	– lbw b Smith	41
Imtiaz Ahmed c Walcott b Smith	32	– b Gibbs	7
Saeed Ahmed b Gibbs	150	– run out	12
Hanif Mohammad b Gilchrist	79	– c Madray b Gilchrist	14
Wazir Mohammad lbw b Gilchrist	7	– not out	97
Wallis Mathias b Gilchrist	16	– lbw b Gibbs	18
A. H. Kardar b Smith	26	– c Smith b Gibbs	56
Fazal Mahmood c Gibbs b Gilchrist	39	– c Alexander b Gibbs	31
S. F. Rahman b Gibbs	8	– run out	2
Nasimul Ghani b Dewdney	13	– c and b Gibbs	22
Haseeb Ahsan not out	0	– b Gilchrist	0
B 2, l-b 2, w 2, n-b 2	8	B 8, l-b 4, w 1, n-b 5	18

1/60 2/69 3/205 4/221 5/249   **408**   1/22 2/44 3/62 4/102 5/130   **318**
6/337 7/349 8/365 9/408   6/224 7/263 8/265 9/304

West Indies

C. Hunte b Fazal	5	– b Rahman	114
G. Sobers b Nasimul	125	– not out	109
C. Walcott run out	145		
E. D. Weekes c Rahman b Nasimul	41	– not out	16
O. G. Smith c sub b Haseeb	27		
R. Kanhai st Imtiaz b Nasimul	24	– c Mathias b Haseeb	62
F. C. M. Alexander c Mathias b Haseeb	2		
I. Madray c Fazal b Nasimul	2		
L. Gibbs run out	11		
R. Gilchrist c Alim b Nasimul	12		
T. Dewdney not out	0		
B 4, l-b 9, w 1, n-b 2	16	B 12, l-b 1, w 2, n-b 1	16

1/11 2/280 3/297 4/336 5/361   **410**   1/125 2/260   (2 wkts) **317**
6/370 7/384 8/389 9/410

West Indies Bowling

	Overs	Mdns	Runs	Wkts	Overs	Mdns	Runs	Wkts
Gilchrist	28	3	102	4	19.1	3	66	2
Dewdney	16.1	1	79	1	11	3	30	—
Gibbs	30	12	56	2	42	11	80	5
Sobers	16	2	47	—	17	6	32	—
Smith	25	2	74	3	44	10	80	1
Madray	10	—	42	—	6	1	12	—

Pakistan Bowling

	Overs	Mdns	Runs	Wkts	Overs	Mdns	Runs	Wkts
Fazal	25	5	74	1	4	2	12	—
Kardar	6	1	24	—	2	—	10	—
Nasimul	41.4	11	116	5	28	4	76	—
Haseeb	44	10	124	2	41	7	151	1
Rahman	17	1	56	—	17	2	43	1
Wazir					1	—	8	—
Saeed					0.1	—	1	—

CRICKET IN INDIA AND PAKISTAN

INDIA v WEST INDIES

First Test Match

Played at New Delhi, November 10, 11, 12, 13, 14, 1948

Drawn. Early on it looked as if West Indies, who won the toss, might find themselves in trouble on the turf pitch. The ball began to lift occasionally and an astute move by Amarnath, India's captain, brought quick results. He took himself off in favour of Rangachari, a round-arm bowler, whose out-swingers were so disconcerting that Rae and Stollmeyer, West Indies opening pair, soon found themselves back in the pavilion. Another shock came at 27, when Headley completely failed; Walcott and Gomez faced a critical situation.

Thanks chiefly to their courage, West Indies made a truly amazing recovery. The pitch became less difficult, and at the end of the day the fourth pair were still together. Then Walcott claimed his first Test century and Gomez needed only one run for the same achievement. Next day he got his hundred and he and Walcott were dismissed in a few minutes, but their 267 stood as a record for any partnership in West Indies Test cricket. Weekes followed with a delightful innings of 128, and Christiani reached three figures for the first time in a Test. With four century-makers, West Indies thus equalled England's record against Australia at Nottingham in 1938. When West Indies' innings ended on the third day for their highest total (631) in Tests, Rangachari claimed five wickets for 107.

More than two days remained, but West Indies found the task of dismissing India twice beyond their powers. India were saved in their first innings by a sound not-out first Test century from Adhikari, but they were forced to follow-on 177 behind. The atmosphere became tense near the end. India needed 25 to clear the arrears with only four wickets left, but in spite of Christiani's skilful slow bowling Adhikari and Sarwate batted safely through the last eighty minutes.

West Indies

A. F. Rae c Sen b Rangachari	8
J. B. Stollmeyer lbw b Rangachari	13
G. A. Headley b Rangachari	2
C. L. Walcott run out	152
G. E. Gomez st Sen b Amarnath	101
J. D. Goddard b Mankad	44
E. Weekes c Hazare b Mankad	128
R. J. Christiani c Hazare b Rangachari	107
F. J. Cameron lbw b Sarwate	2
D. Atkinson st Sen b Rangachari	45
P. Jones not out	1
Extras	28
	631

India

V. Mankad lbw b Jones	5	– b Goddard	17
K. C. Ibrahim lbw b Gomez	85	– run out	44
R. S. Modi c Rae b Cameron	63	– b Christiani	36
L. Amarnath c Christiani b Jones	62	– b Cameron	36
V. S. Hazare c Atkinson b Gomez	18	– b Christiani	7
D. G. Phadkar c Weekes b Stollmeyer	41	– c and b Christiani	5
H. R. Adhikari not out	114	– not out	29
C. T. Sarwate st Walcott b Stollmeyer	37	– not out	35
P. Sen c Walcott b Cameron	22		
C. R. Rangachari c and b Goddard	0		
K. Tarapore c Walcott b Jones	2		
Extras	5	Extras	11
	454	(6 wkts)	220

India Bowling

	Overs	Mdns	Runs	Wkts
Phadkar	18	1	61	—
Amarnath	25	3	73	1
Rangachari	29.4	4	107	5
Mankad	59	10	176	2
Tarapore	19	3	72	—
Hazare	17	1	62	—
Sarwate	16	—	52	1

West Indies Bowling

	Overs	Mdns	Runs	Wkts	Overs	Mdns	Runs	Wkts
Jones	28.4	5	90	3	10	2	32	—
Gomez	39	4	76	2	10	4	17	—
Atkinson	13	3	27	—	5	—	11	—
Headley	2	—	13	—	1	—	5	—
Cameron	27	3	74	2	27	10	49	1
Stollmeyer	15	—	80	2	10	2	23	—
Goddard	13	7	83	1	15	7	18	1
Christiani	4	—	6	—	23	—	52	3
Weekes					1	—	2	—

INDIA v WEST INDIES

Third Test Match

Played at Calcutta, December 31, 1948, January 1, 2, 3, 4, 1949

Drawn. The pitch was not entirely devoid of grass, and early on showed signs of helping India's attack. Banerjee moved the ball about at a good pace and speedily accounted for Rae and Atkinson. Then came stout opposition from Weekes and Walcott, who soon dispelled India's hopes of a collapse. Weekes revealed flawless technique, his third consecutive century of the series perhaps being even sounder than his previous efforts. West Indies were all out on the second day for 366, and India, after the early departure of Ibrahim, made a good reply. Mushtaq Ali, Modi and Hazare all batted well, India being satisfied with 204 for two wickets at the close. Next day the new ball wrecked their chance to get on top; Modi, Hazare and Amarnath left for the addition of only six runs. Goddard's off-breaks, Ferguson's leg spin, and varied deliveries by Gomez brought a complete-breakdown, eight wickets falling in an hour and three-quarters for 68. Owing to an attack of fever, Walcott retired for a time, his place behind the wicket being taken by Christiani. West Indies, going in again 94 ahead, were not happy until Weekes joined Walcott. On the fourth day the completion by Weekes of his fifth successive Test hundred and fourth of the series overshadowed everything else. The first of these two feats meant a world record by this young player. Walcott's 108 in 175 minutes was also noteworthy because he was not fit. West Indies declared at 336 for nine wickets, and India, needing 431 to win, concentrated on saving the game. Taking nearly two hours overnight for 64 without loss, they lost only three wickets during the last day, but Mushtaq Ali and Modi, the principal run-getters, were both missed in the slips after the appearance of the new ball at 204.

West Indies

A. F. Rae lbw b Banerjee	15	– run out	34
D. Atkinson b Banerjee	0	– not out	5
C. L. Walcott c Banerjee b Ghulam Ahmed	54	– c Amarnath b Mankad	108
E. Weekes c and b Ghulam Ahmed	162	– c and b Ghulam Ahmed	101
G. E. Gomez b Mankad	26	– b Ghulam Ahmed	29
G. A. Carew lbw b Mankad	11	– b Banerjee	9
J. D. Goddard not out	39	– c Banerjee b Amarnath	9
R. J. Christiani c and b Banerjee	23	– b Amarnath	22
F. J. Cameron c Mushtaq Ali b Banerjee	23	– c and b Mankad	2
W. Ferguson b Ghulam Ahmed	2	– lbw b Mankad	6
P. Jones b Ghulam Ahmed	6		
Extras	5	Extras	11
	366	**(9wkts dec.)**	**336**

India

Mushtaq Ali c Rae b Goddard	54	– lbw b Atkinson	106
K. C. Ibrahim b Gomez	1	– c Atkinson b Gomez	25
R. S. Modi b Jones	80	– c Christiani b Goddard	87
V. S. Hazare b Gomez	59	– not out	58
L. Amarnath c Christiani b Gomez	3	– not out	34
V. Mankad c Ferguson b Goddard	29		
H. R. Adhikari not out	31		
C. T. Sarwate b Goddard	0		
P. Sen lbw b Ferguson	1		
Ghulam Ahmed st Christiani b Ferguson	0		
Sunil Banerjee st Christiani b Ferguson	0		
Extras	14	Extras	15
	272	**(3 wkts)**	**325**

India Bowling

	Overs	Mdns	Runs	Wkts	Overs	Mdns	Runs	Wkts
Banerjee	30	3	120	4	21	—	61	1
Amarnath	20	6	34	—	23	4	75	2
Hazare	5	—	33	—	11	3	33	—
Ghulam Ahmed	35.2	5	94	4	25	—	87	2
Mankad	23	5	74	2	24.3	5	68	3
Sarwate	2	—	6	—	1	—	1	—

West Indies Bowling

	Overs	Mdns	Runs	Wkts	Overs	Mdns	Runs	Wkts
Jones	17	3	48	1	21	5	49	—
Gomez	32	10	65	3	29	10	47	1
Ferguson	29	8	66	3	9	—	35	—
Goddard	13	3	34	3	23	11	41	1
Cameron	7	2	12	—	30	7	67	—
Atkinson	9	—	27	—	14	3	42	1
Christiani	2	—	6	—	3	—	12	—
Carew					3	2	2	—
Walcott					3	—	12	—
Weekes					1	—	3	—

INDIA v PAKISTAN

First Test Match

Played at New Delhi, October 16, 17, 18, 1952

India won by an innings and 70 runs with a day to spare. The cleverly varied left-arm slow bowling of Mankad on a pitch responsive to spin proved too great an obstacle for Pakistan. Mankad's most deadly spell came after Nazar Mohammed and Hanif Mohammed made 64 for the opening stand. In 16 overs he took six wickets, and his final figures of eight wickets for 52 in the first innings and thirteen wickets for 131 in the match were both new records for Indian Test cricket. Ghulam Ahmed gave good support with off-spinners, but it was as a batsman in a record last-wicket stand of 109 in eighty minutes with Adhikari that he won the admiration of the crowd. Ghulam hit two 6s and five 4s. Kardar and Imtiaz Ahmed were Pakistan's only convincing batsmen against spin.

India

V. Mankad b Khan Mohammed	11	
P. Roy b Khan Mohammed	7	
V. S. Hazare b Amir Elahi	76	
V. L. Manjrekar c Nazar Mohammed b Amir Elahi	23	
L. Amarnath c Khan Mohammed b Fazal Mahmood	9	
P. R. Umrigar lbw b Kardar	25	
Gul Mohammed c Hanif Mohammed b Amir Elahi	24	
H. R. Adhikari not out	81	
G. S. Ramchand c Imtiaz Ahmed b Fazal Mahmood	13	
P. Sen c Nazar Mohammed b Kardar	25	
Ghulam Ahmed b Amir Elahi	50	
Extras	28	

1/19 2/26 3/67 4/76 5/110   372
6/180 7/195 8/229 9/263

Pakistan

Nazar Mohammed run out	27	– b Mankad	7
Hanif Mohammed c Ramchand b Mankad	51	– b Amarnath	1
Israr Ali b Mankad	1	– lbw b Mankad	9
Imtiaz Ahmed lbw b Mankad	0	– lbw b Ghulam Ahmed	41
Maqsood Ahmed c Roy b Mankad	15	– c Adhikari b Mankad	5
A. H. Kardar c Roy b Mankad	4	– not out	43
Anwar Hussain c and b Mankad	4	– lbw b Ghulam Ahmed	4
Waqar Hassan lbw b Mankad	8	– c Gul Mohammed b Ghulam Ahmed	5
Fazal Mahmood not out	21	– c and b Ghulam Ahmed	27
Khan Mohammed c Ramchand b Mankad	0	– st Sen b Mankad	5
Amir Elahi c Gul Mohammed b Ghulam Ahmed	9	– c Ramchand b Mankad	0
Extras	10	Extras	5

1/64 2/65 3/65 4/97 5/102   150   1/2 2/17 3/42 4/48 5/73   152
6/111 7/112 8/129 9/129   6/79 7/87 8/121 9/152

Pakistan Bowling

	Overs	Mdns	Runs	Wkts
Khan Mohammed	20	5	52	2
Maqsood Ahmed	6	1	13	—
Fazal Mahmood	40	13	92	2
Amir Elahi	39.4	4	134	4
Kardar	34	12	53	2

India Bowling

	Overs	Mdns	Runs	Wkts	Overs	Mdns	Runs	Wkts
Ramchand	14	7	24	—	6	1	21	—
Amarnath.........	13	9	10	—	5	2	12	1
Mankad	47	27	52	8	24.2	3	79	5
Ghulam Ahmed	22.3	6	51	1	23	7	35	4
Hazare	6	5	3	—				
Gul Mohammed	2	2	—	—				

INDIA v NEW ZEALAND

Fifth Test Match

Played at Madras, January 6, 7, 8, 10, 11, 1956

India won by an innings and 109 runs. India wound up the high-scoring series by breaking more records and gaining an overwhelming victory. Mankad and Roy, the Indian opening batsmen, mastered the New Zealand bowlers on an easy-paced pitch, and they were not parted until after lunch on the second day. They made 413, a record for Test cricket, surpassing 359 made by Hutton and Washbrook for England against South Africa at Johannesburg in 1948-49. Mankad scored 231, and passed the Indian individual Test record of 223 which he and Umrigar each made earlier in the series. India's 537 for three set up a new record total for that country, beating 498 for four declared in the first Test. The first-wicket partnership was also the best by an Indian pair in first-class cricket, exceeding 293 by V. M. Merchant and Mankad for the Indians against Sussex at Hove in 1946. New Zealand, by steady bowling and keen fielding, managed to restrict the scoring rate for long spells, and the opening stand lasted for nearly eight hours. Mankad batted eight and three-quarter hours, hitting twenty-one 4s. Gupte, with leg-breaks, and Jasu Patel, an off-break bowler playing his first Test of the series, worried New Zealand, who despite cautious batting, followed-on 328 behind. Again spin upset them, this time Mankad, with left-arm slows, proving an effective partner to Gupte.

India

V. Mankad c Cave b Moir 231	V. L. Manjrekar not out	0
P. Roy b Poore 173	B 18, l-b 11, n-b 4	33
P. R. Umrigar not out.................. 79		
G. S. Ramchand lbw b MacGibbon 21	1/413 2/449 3/537	(3 wkts dec.) 537

D. G. Phadkar, J. S. Patel, S. P. Gupte, N. S. Tamhane, A. G. Kripal Singh, and N. J. Contractor did not bat.

New Zealand

J. G. Leggat lbw b Phadkar.....................	31	– c Tamhane b Mankad............	61
B. Sutcliffe c Umrigar b Patel	47	– c and b Gupte................	40
J. R. Reid b Patel.............................	44	– c Umrigar b Gupte...........	63
J. W. Guy c Umrigar b Gupte...................	3	– st Tamhane b Gupte...........	9
S. N. McGregor c Phadkar b Gupte	10	– c Gupte b Mankad	12
A. R. MacGibbon c Phadkar b Gupte	0	– lbw b Patel	0
M. B. Poore lbw b Gupte.......................	15	– b Mankad	1
A. M. Moir c Umrigar b Patel..................	30	– c Ramchand b Mankad	1
H. B. Cave c Roy b Gupte	9	– not out	22
T. G. McMahon not out	4	– b Gupte.......................	0
J. A. Hayes absent ill.........................	0	– absent ill......................	0
B 4, l-b 10, n-b 2	16	B 1, l-b 8, n-b 1...........	10

1/75 2/109 3/121 4/141 5/155   209   1/89 2/114 3/116 4/117 5/147   219
6/165 7/190 8/201 9/209   6/151 7/219 8/219 9/219

New Zealand Bowling

	Overs	Mdns	Runs	Wkts
Hayes............	31	2	94	—
MacGibbon.......	38	9	97	1
Cave.............	44	16	94	—
Reid	7	3	10	—
Moir	26	1	114	1
Poore	31	5	95	1

India Bowling

	Overs	Mdns	Runs	Wkts	Overs	Mdns	Runs	Wkts
Phadkar	15	4	25	1	28	13	33	—
Ramchand	4	3	1	—	8	5	10	—
Gupte	49	26	72	5	36.4	14	73	4
Patel.............	45	23	63	3	18	7	28	1
Mankad	19	10	32	—	40	14	65	4

INDIA v WEST INDIES

Third Test Match

Played at Calcutta, December 31, 1958, January 1, 2, 3, 4, 1959

West Indies won by an innings and 336 runs. Rohan Kanhai batted splendidly in compiling 256, the highest score for West Indies in any Test against India. It was his first century in Test cricket, and he batted six and a half hours, hitting forty-two 4s. Butcher, who shared a fourth-wicket stand of 217 in just over three hours with Rohan Kanhai, stayed three hours and hit fifteen 4s; then Sobers and Solomon put on 160 in two hours twenty minutes without being separated. Sobers reached his third century of the series and his sixth in his last ten Test innings. By the end of the second day India had lost two wickets in scoring 29, and they followed on 490 behind. Gilchrist, whose match figures were nine wickets for 73, and Hall swept through the second innings, and West Indies won with a day and a half to spare.

West Indies

J. K. Holt c Contractor b Surendranath 5	J. Solomon not out 69	
C. Hunte c Surendranath b Gupte 23		
R. Kanhai c Umrigar b Surendranath......256	B 8, l-b 9, n-b 1 18	
O. G. Smith b Umrigar 34		
B. Butcher lbw b Ghulam Ahmed.........103	1/12 2/72 3/180 (5 wkts dec.) 614	
G. Sobers not out 106	4/397 5/454	

F. C. M. Alexander, S. Ramadhin, R. Gilchrist and W. Hall did not bat.

India

P. Roy c Solomon b Gilchrist	11 – c Alexander b Hall	0
N. Contractor lbw b Ramadhin	4 – b Gilchrist	6
J. M. Ghorpade c Alexander b Gilchrist	7 – b Sobers	16
R. B. Kenny c Alexander b Hall	16 – b Hall	0
P. R. Umrigar not out	44 – c Alexander b Hall	2
V. L. Manjrekar b Hall	0 – not out	58
D. G. Phadkar c Sobers b Gilchrist	3 – b Gilchrist	35
N. S. Tamhane c Sobers b Hall	0 – b Gilchrist	0
R. Surendranath run out	8 – c Alexander b Gilchrist	3
Ghulam Ahmed lbw b Sobers	4 – b Gilchrist	0
S. P. Gupte b Ramadin	12 – b Gilchrist	15
B 2, l-b 8, w 1, n-b 4	15	B 3, n-b 16	19

1/24 2/26 3/52 4/52 5/52   124   1/5 2/7 3/10 4/17 5/44   154
6/57 7/58 8/89 9/99   6/115 7/131 8/131 9/131

India Bowling

	Overs	Mdns	Runs	Wkts
Phadkar	43	6	173	—
Surendranath	46	8	168	2
Gupte	39	8	119	1
Ghulam Ahmed	16.1	1	52	1
Umrigar	16	1	62	1
Ghorpade	2	—	22	—

West Indies Bowling

	Overs	Mdns	Runs	Wkts	Overs	Mdns	Runs	Wkts
Gilchrist	23	13	18	3	21	7	55	6
Hall	15	6	31	3	18	5	55	3
Ramadhin	16.5	8	27	2	8	3	14	—
Smith	2	1	1	—				
Sobers	6	—	32	1	2	—	11	1

INDIA v WEST INDIES

Fifth Test Match

Played at New Delhi, February 6, 7, 8, 10, 11, 1959

Drawn. India, under the leadership of the 39-year-old Adhikari, gave their best performance of the series, yet only lack of time prevented West Indies from gaining their fourth victory. Fine batting by Borde was the outstanding feature of the match, and he failed by only four runs to equal the feat of V. Hazare, the only previous batsman to score centuries in each innings of a Test match for India. After a fine stand of 137 by Contractor and Umrigar, Borde stayed for four hours, hitting sixteen 4s and sharing a partnership of 134 with Adhikari. When West Indies batted, Umrigar and Manjrekar were absent from the field because of injuries, and Borde, too, was unable to bowl on the third day. Holt was overshadowed in a bright opening stand with Hunte, but went on to his first century of the series, paving the way for invigorating displays by the later batsmen. Holt took four and a quarter hours for his century, but Smith and Solomon reached three figures in less than three hours. West Indies declared with a lead of 229, but their drive for victory was interrupted by injuries which at various times prevented Hall, Sobers and Atkinson from bowling. Gaekwad and Roy shared a useful stand of 93 and then Borde and Adhikari steered India clear of defeat with their second century partnership of the match. Borde stayed three and a half hours before hitting his wicket in the last possible over. So West Indies, wanting only 47 to win, were denied the chance of hitting off the runs.

India

P. Roy b Gilchrist	1	– c Holt b Smith	58
N. J. Contractor lbw b Hall	92	– run out	4
P. R. Umrigar b Hall	76	– absent hurt	0
V. L. Manjrekar c Alexander b Hall	6	– not out	0
C. G. Borde c Alexander b Smith	109	– hit wkt b Gilchrist	96
D. K. Gaekwad c Holt b Gilchrist	6	– c Hunte b Smith	52
H. R. Adhikari c Alexander b Smith	63	– c sub b Smith	40
V. Mankad c sub b Gilchrist	21	– b Smith	0
N. S. Tamhane c Gilchrist b Smith	3	– hit wkt b Smith	5
S. P. Gupte b Hall	5	– b Gilchrist	0
R. Desai not out	2	– b Gilchrist	5
B 6, l-b 15, n-b 10	31	B 2, l-b 6, n-b 7	15

1/6 2/143 3/170 4/208 5/242   415   1/5 2/98 3/135 4/243 5/247   275
6/376 7/399 8/407 9/413   6/260 7/264 8/274 9/275

West Indies

C. Hunte lbw b Adhikari	92	F. C. M. Alexander run out	25
J. K. Holt c Roy b Desai	123	E. Atkinson c and b Adhikari	37
R. Kanhai lbw b Desai	40	W. Hall not out	0
B. Butcher lbw b Adhikari	71	B 2, l-b 8, w 1, n-b 1	12
O. G. Smith c Tamhane b Desai	100		
J. Solomon not out	100	1/159 2/244 3/263 (8 wkts dec.)	644
G. Sobers c Tamhane b Desai	44	4/390 5/455 6/524 7/565 8/635	

R. Gilchrist did not bat.

West Indies Bowling

	Overs	Mdns	Runs	Wkts	Overs	Mdns	Runs	Wkts
Gilchrist	30.3	8	90	3	24.2	6	62	3
Hall	26	4	66	4	13	5	39	—
Atkinson	14	4	44	—	1		4	—
Smith	40	7	94	3	42	19	90	5
Sobers	24	3	66	—				
Solomon	7	2	24	—	21	9	44	—
Butcher					6	1	17	—
Hunte					4	2	4	—

India Bowling

	Overs	Mdns	Runs	Wkts
Desai	49	10	169	4
Mankad	55	12	167	—
Gupte	60	16	144	—
Adhikari	26	2	68	3
Contractor	4	1	11	—
Borde	17	3	53	—
Roy	2	—	12	—
Gaekwad	1	—	8	—

PAKISTAN v AUSTRALIA

Third Test Match

Played at Karachi, December 4, 5, 6, 8, 9, 1959

Drawn. With Australia two wins ahead in the series and Pakistan beaten at home for the first time in a rubber, there seemed every chance of some lively cricket. In fact, play was drab for most of the time, with Pakistan taking eight hours forty-eight minutes over 287 in their first innings and eight hours over 194 in their second. Australia showed more enterprise on the matting pitch, though they needed a last-wicket stand of 50 between Davidson and Lindwall to keep their first innings deficit down to 30.

Finally, Australia were left two hours in which to score 225 to win, a task they never seriously attempted. Hanif Mohammed hit most runs, 51 in the first innings and 101 not out in nearly six hours in the second, but failed to sparkle. He batted for most of the fourth day while 104 runs were scored and was again painfully slow on the next, when Australia were without Lindwall because of a pulled groin muscle. Saeed Ahmed, dropped before scoring, hit 91. Intikhab Alam in bowling McDonald took a wicket with his first ball in Test cricket. Mr Eisenhower watched play on the fourth day and as he was the first United States President to see Test cricket, his visit may well be remembered long after this disappointing game is forgotten.

Pakistan

Hanif Mohammed lbw b Lindwall	51	– not out	101
Imtiaz Ahmad b Davidson	18	– c Harvey b Davidson	9
Saeed Ahmed c Harvey b Lindwall	91	– c Mackay b Davidson	8
Shuja-ud-Din c O'Neill b Benaud	5	– c Favell b Mackay	4
D. Sharpe c Burge b Benaud	4	– c Mackay b Lindwall	26
Ijaz Butt c Grout b Benaud	58	– run out	8
Wallis Mathias c Favell b Mackay	43	– c Davidson b Benaud	13
Intikhab Alam run out	0	– c and b Mackay	6
Fazal Mahmood c Harvey b Benaud	7	– c Benaud b Davidson	11
Mohammed Munaf not out	4	– not out	4
Munir Malik st Grout b Benaud	0		
L-b 3, n-b 3	6	L-b 2, n-b 2	4

1/36 2/124 3/143 4/149 5/181   287   1/11 2/25 3/25 4/78 (8 wkts dec.) 194
6/265 7/267 8/276 9/287   5/91 6/124 7/159 8/179

Australia

C. C. McDonald b Intikhab	19	– lbw b Munir	30
G. Stevens c Mathias b Fazal	13	– c Imtiaz b Intikhab	28
W. Grout c and b Intikhab	20		
K. Mackay c Butt b Fazal	40		
R. N. Harvey c Imtiaz b Fazal	54	– not out	13
N. O'Neill b Munir	6	– not out	7
L. Favell c Sharpe b Fazal	10		
P. Burge c Sharpe b Munaf	12		
R. Benaud c Imtiaz b Munir	18		
A. K. Davidson not out	39		
R. R. Lindwall c Imtiaz b Fazal	23		
L-b 1, n-b 2	3	L-b 3, n-b 2	5

1/29 2/33 3/82 4/106 5/122   257 1/54 2/76   (2 wkts) 83
6/145 7/174 8/184 9/207

Australia Bowling

	Overs	Mdns	Runs	Wkts	Overs	Mdns	Runs	Wkts
Davidson	26	5	59	1	34	8	70	3
Lindwall	25	6	72	2	17	10	14	1
Benaud	49.5	16	93	5	26	13	48	1
Mackay	27	8	53	1	32.4	11	58	2
O'Neill	4	1	4	—				

Pakistan Bowling

	Overs	Mdns	Runs	Wkts	Overs	Mdns	Runs	Wkts
Fazal	30.2	12	74	5	10	5	16	—
Munaf	8	—	42	1	3	—	10	—
Intikhab	19	4	49	2	6	1	13	1
Munir	22	4	76	2	9	1	24	1
Shuja	3	—	13	—	2	1	9	—
Saeed					3	—	6	—

EISENHOWER AT THE TEST

An historic day for cricket was December 8, 1959, when Mr Dwight Eisenhower, President of the United States of America, graced the third Test of the series between Pakistan and Australia at the National Stadium, Karachi. It was the first occasion that the head of the United States has witnessed a Test match and he was seen in a very happy mood applauding attractive strokes by the batsmen and good work by the fielders.

INDIA v AUSTRALIA

Second Test Match

Played at Kanpur, December 19, 20, 21, 23, 1959

India won by 119 runs. The chief architect of India's first Test victory over Australia since the two countries first met in 1947 was Patel, the Ahmedabad off-spin bowler, who took fourteen wickets for 142 runs. In the Australian first innings Patel exploited newly-laid turf and achieved an analysis of nine for 69 – India's finest Test bowling performance. Then on the last day, amid scenes of great excitement, he routed Australia a second time and took five more wickets for 55.

For Australia Davidson, the fast bowler, took 12 wickets for 124 and twice regained the initiative for his side. India collapsed alarmingly on the first day. Benaud began the slide after lunch, and Davidson pressed home the advantage when India slumped from 38 for no wicket to 152 all out. At first the India bowlers failed to gain any assistance from the pitch when Australia replied and 71 were scored before Patel dismissed Stevens. Then a remarkable transformation took place. Patel took eight wickets for 24 runs and the Australian lead was restricted to 67. Contractor (74) and his colleagues showed improved form during the India second innings and Australia were left requiring 225 for victory. McDonald, Harvey and Kline, who scored 73 between them, batted confidently enough, but the other seven – Rorke was absent ill – mustered only 20 against Patel and Umrigar and India won comfortably.

India

P. Roy b Benaud	17	– c Benaud b Davidson	8
N. J. Contractor c Jarman b Benaud	24	– c Harvey b Davidson	74
P. R. Umrigar c Davidson b Kline	6	– c Rorke b Davidson	14
A. A. Baig b Davidson	19	– c Harvey b Benaud	36
C. G. Borde c Kline b Davidson	20	– c O'Neill b Meckiff	44
G. S. Ramchand c Mackay b Benaud	24	– b Harvey	5
R. Kenny b Davidson	0	– c Jarman b Davidson	51
R. G. Nadkarni c Harvey b Davidson	25	– lbw b Davidson	46
N. S. Tamhane b Benaud	1	– c Harvey b Davidson	0
J. Patel c Kline b Davidson	4	– b Davidson	0
R. Surendranath not out	8	– not out	4
L-b 2, n-b 2	4	B 7, l-b 2	9

1/38 2/47 3/51 4/77 5/112   152   1/32 2/72 3/121 4/147 5/153   291
6/112 7/126 8/128 9/141   6/214 7/286 8/286 9/291

Australia

C. C. McDonald b Patel	53	– st Tamhane b Patel	34
G. Stevens c and b Patel	25	– c Kenny b Patel	7
R. N. Harvey b Patel	51	– c Nadkarni b Umrigar	25
N. O'Neill b Borde	16	– c Nadkarni b Umrigar	5
K. Mackay b Patel	0	– lbw b Umrigar	0
A. K. Davidson b Patel	41	– b Patel	8
R. Benaud lbw b Patel	7	– c Ramchand b Patel	0
B. Jarman lbw b Patel	1	– b Umrigar	0
L. Kline b Patel	9	– b Patel	0
I. Meckiff not out	1	– not out	14
G. Rorke c Baig b Patel	0	– absent ill	
B 9, l-b 2, n-b 4	15	B 8, l-b 4	12

1/71 2/128 3/149 4/159 5/159   219   1/12 2/49 3/59 4/61 5/78   105
6/174 7/186 8/216 9/219   6/78 7/79 8/84 9/105

Australia Bowling

	Overs	Mdns	Runs	Wkts	Overs	Mdns	Runs	Wkts
Davidson	29.1	7	31	5	57.3	22	93	7
Meckiff	8	2	15	—	18	4	37	1
Benaud	25	8	63	4	38	15	81	1
Rorke	2	1	3	—				
Kline	19	7	36	1	7	3	14	—
Mackay					10	5	14	—
Harvey					12	3	31	1
O'Neill					2	—	12	—

India Bowling

	Overs	Mdns	Runs	Wkts	Overs	Mdns	Runs	Wkts
Surendranath	4	—	13	—	4	2	4	—
Ramchand	6	3	14	—	3	—	7	—
Patel	35.5	16	69	9	25.4	7	55	5
Umrigar	15	1	40	—	25	11	27	4
Borde	15	1	61	1				
Nadkarni	2	—	7	—				

OTHER OVERSEAS MATCHES

COMMONWEALTH v INDIA

Fourth Unofficial Test

Played at Kanpur, January 14, 15, 16, 17, 18, 1950

Drawn. Commonwealth began disastrously, Oldfield and Place being out with 19 scored, but Livingston and Worrell settled down to a splendid third-wicket partnership of 151. Aided also by Tribe in a valuable eighth-wicket stand of 106, Worrell gave a magnificent display lasting six hours forty minutes, and he hit sixteen 4s. India started poorly, but Mushtaq Ali was in form and found a good fourth-wicket partner in Phadkar, who helped to add 109. Mushtaq Ali hit eleven 4s. Determined play by Adhikari and Kishenchand further improved India's position. Livingston and Worrell again shared in a century stand in the Commonwealth second innings, when they added 137 for the third wicket, and Worrell took his aggregate for the match to 306 without being out. Set to make 300 runs in roughly three hours, India lost their first four wickets for 18 runs, but Hazare and Adhikari played out time.

Commonwealth

N. Oldfield c Mantri b Hazare	0	– lbw b Hazare	13
W. Place c Hazare b Gaekwad	8	– lbw b Hazare	9
L. L. Livingston lbw b Hazare	80	– b Gaekwad	81
F. M. Worrell not out	223	– not out	83
F. Freer b Ghulam Ahmed	26		
W. Alley c Phadkar b Ghulam Ahmed	15	– not out	48
W. Langdon lbw b Phadkar	25		
G. H. Pope lbw b Hazare	0		
G. Tribe c Mantri b Ghulam Ahmed	61		
D. Fitzmaurice st Mantri b Gaekwad	1		
H. Lambert c Phadkar b Gaekwad	6		
Extras	3	Extras	3
	448	(3 wkts dec.	237

India

Mushtaq Ali b Worrell	129	– c Pope b Lambert	2
V. Mankad c and b Tribe	27	– c sub b Fitzmaurice	0
R. S. Modi b Tribe	10	– c Livingston b Fitzmaurice	8
V. S. Hazare b Tribe	6	– not out	41
D. G. Phadkar c Tribe b Freer	64	– b Freer	3
H. R. Adhikari lbw b Worrell	61	– not out	20
G. Kishenchand c Worrell b Freer	39		
P. R. Umrigar c Freer b Tribe	29		
M. K. Mantri b Tribe	1		
H. Gaekwad not out	7		
Ghulam Ahmed c and b Worrell	1		
Extras	12	Extras	10
	386	(4 wkts)	84

India Bowling

	Overs	Mdns	Runs	Wkts	Overs	Mdns	Runs	Wkts
Phadkar	20	3	49	1				
Hazare	23	4	59	3	24	2	57	2
Gaekwad	42.1	17	112	3	26	4	79	1
Ghulam Ahmed	62	17	129	3	13	—	38	—
Mankad	25	1	87	—	9	—	41	—
Umrigar	3	—	9	—	5	1	19	—

Commonwealth Bowling

	Overs	Mdns	Runs	Wkts	Overs	Mdns	Runs	Wkts
Lambert	21	4	57	—	4	1	5	1
Fitzmaurice	20	5	47	—	8	3	7	2
Tribe.............	50	13	122	5	16	7	35	—
Freer.............	36	8	80	2	10	5	12	1
Pope.............	9	1	24	—				
Worrell	24.5	7	42	3	8	6	2	—
Langdon..........	2	—	2	—	3	—	6	—
Alley.............					6	3	7	—

INDIA v COMMONWEALTH

First Unofficial Test

Played at New Delhi, November 19, 20, 21, 22, 1953

India won by an innings and 15 runs. The Commonwealth batsmen gave such a feeble display against the spin attack of Gupte and Ghulam Ahmed that India's crushing victory was gained with a day and a half to spare. There was no excuse for the touring team's collapse. Whereas their own spin bowlers were unable to command any life and assistance from the pitch on the first two days, Gupte and Ghulam Ahmed swiftly assumed a mastery over hesitant batsmen. Gupte (leg-breaks) caused most trouble in the first innings, and Ghulam Ahmed (off-spin) completed Commonwealth's rout. Both were splendidly supported behind the wicket by Tamhane, a young Bombay College student who, in his first "Test," caught three and stumped four batsmen. Simpson alone batted freely. In the first innings he hit both Gupte and Ahmed for 6, and his second innings contained ten 4s, nearly all past cover. Worrell tried hard to pull the game round with a patient innings, but his dismissal marked the end of serious resistance. Ramchand, missed twice during a stay of four and a half hours, Manjrekar and Umrigar helped to build India's formidable total.

India

P. Roy lbw b Worrell	5	Arjun Nayudu not out	10
M. L. Apte c and b Berry	30	Ghulam Ahmed st Barnett b Berry........	4
V. L. Manjrekar b Worrell	86	S. P. Gupte c Loxton b Berry	16
V. S. Hazare b Worrell	18		
P. R. Umrigar c and b Worrell	47	B 13, n-b 1...................	14
G. S. Ramchand b Berry................	119		
C. D. Gopinath run out.................	23	1/7 2/110 3/147 4/148 5/249	387
N. S. Tamhane lbw b Berry..............	15	6/297 7/346 8/357 9/361	

Commonwealth

R. T. Simpson c and b Gupte	57	– b Ghulam Ahmed	59
R. E. Marshall st Tamhane b Gupte	35	– c and b Ghulam Ahmed	8
G. M. Emmett lbw b Gupte	10	– c Tamhane b Ghulam Ahmed	4
F. M. Worrell b Ghulam Ahmed	26	– c Tamhane b Ghulam Ahmed	54
K. Meuleman b Ghulam Ahmed	24	– c Tamhane b Gupte	23
G. A. Edrich c Ramchand b Gupte	4	– lbw b Ghulam Ahmed	4
S. J. Loxton c Manjrekar b Gupte	6	– b Ghulam Ahmed	2
B. A. Barnett not out	13	– c Manjrekar b Gupte	0
S. Ramadhin b Gupte	4	– st Tamhane b Gupte	2
P. J. Loader st Tamhane b Gupte	4	– st Tamhane b Gupte	5
R. Berry b Gupte	0	– not out	2
B 4, l-b 11	15	B 2, l-b 9	11

1/90 2/113 3/113 4/152 5/163   198   1/40 2/68 3/87 4/146 5/146   174
6/169 7/185 8/192 9/198   6/162 7/163 8/163 9/169

Commonwealth Bowling

	Overs	Mdns	Runs	Wkts
Loader	16	3	45	—
Worrell	40	16	66	4
Loxton	20	3	72	—
Ramadhin	45	13	101	—
Berry	47.4	16	89	5

India Bowling

	Overs	Mdns	Runs	Wkts	Overs	Mdns	Runs	Wkts
Nayudu	4	—	9	—	4	2	6	—
Ramchand	5	2	3	—	4	2	6	4
Gupte	35.5	10	91	8	31.3	6	82	4
Ghulam Ahmed	35	11	80	2	38	21	52	6
Hazare					7	—	17	—

C. G. HOWARD'S XI v CRICKET CLUB OF INDIA PRESIDENT'S XI

Played at Brabourne Stadium, Bombay, January 5, 6, 7, 8, 1957

C. G. Howard's XI won by 152 runs. Graveney dominated the match. In the first innings he scored 153, delighting the crowd with his majestic stroke-play. After Howard's team had gained a first innings lead of 148, Graveney obtained his second century of the match and the Indians were left to score 462 to win. They made a good effort but despite a punishing hundred by Umrigar, Howard's XI gained a comfortable victory over their opponents who were handicapped through an injury to Hazare.

C. G. Howard's XI

R. T. Simpson c Modi b Ramchand	27	– b Mankad	37
A. Wharton c Hazare b Gupte	25	– c Mushtaq Ali b Borde	47
C. McCool c and b Borde	23	– lbw b Gupte	1
T. W. Graveney c Hardikar b Nadkarni	153	– c sub b Mankad	120
W. Watson c Mushtaq Ali b Mankad	21	– b Gupte	25
W. J. Edrich b Gupte	4	– st Tamhane b Gupte	58
G. Tribe c Tamhane b Gupte	8	– not out	8
B. Dooland c Tamhane b Mankad	15	– not out	6
F. S. Trueman c Mushtaq Ali b Gupte	33	– st Tamhane b Gupte	6
A. E. Moss b Nadkarni	0		
A. V. Bedser not out	0		
Extras	10	Extras	5
	319	**(7 wkts dec.)**	**313**

President's XI

Mushtaq Ali c Graveney b Trueman	13	– c Wharton b Trueman	8
V. Mankad st McCool b Dooland	27	– c Bedser b Tribe	28
P. R. Umrigar c and b Dooland	57	– b Moss	100
V. S. Hazare retired hurt	32	– absent ill	
R. S. Modi b Moss	1	– c Moss b Trueman	39
G. S. Ramchand b Tribe	8	– c Bedser b Tribe	5
M. S. Hardikar lbw b Moss	0	– c Edrich b Tribe	38
R. Nadkarni c Watson b Tribe	4	– run out	35
C. G. Borde not out	6	– b Moss	21
N. S. Tamhane c and b Dooland	0	– run out	11
S. P. Gupte c Moss b Tribe	9	– not out	10
Extras	14	Extras	14
	171		**309**

President's XI Bowling

	Overs	Mdns	Runs	Wkts	Overs	Mdns	Runs	Wkts
Umrigar	7	2	26	—				
Ramchand	18	4	50	1	6	—	14	—
Hazare	2	—	11	—				
Gupte	23.4	3	99	4	16	1	77	4
Nadkarni	11	1	33	2	15	2	43	—
Borde	5	—	18	1	9	—	59	1
Mankad	18	2	59	2	19	4	82	2
Hardikar	2	—	13	—	3	—	13	—
Modi					12	5	20	—

C. G. Howard's XI Bowling

	Overs	Mdns	Runs	Wkts	Overs	Mdns	Runs	Wkts
Trueman	13	4	29	1	17	2	66	2
Moss	13	5	13	2	16	1	48	2
Bedser	7	—	22	—	11	3	23	—
Dooland	17	3	38	3	20.1	1	65	—
Tribe	13.4	2	55	3	33	3	93	3

THE RECORD INDIVIDUAL INNINGS

Hanif's 499 at Karachi

Hanif Mohammad, Pakistan's 24-year-old opening batsman, made 499, the world's highest individual score in first-class cricket, for Karachi against Bahawalpur in the semi-final of the Quaid-e-Azam Trophy at the Karachi Parsi Institute ground on January 8, 9, 11, 12, 1959. This beat the 453 not out by Sir Donald Bradman for New South Wales against Queensland at Sydney in 1929-30.

On a coir matting pitch, Hanif scored 25 in forty minutes on the first evening, 230 in five hours on the second day and 244 in four hours fifty-five minutes on the third day. He was run out when going for his 500 off the last ball of the day. Altogether he batted ten hours thirty-five minutes and hit sixty-four 4s. Hanif played superbly, rarely putting the ball in the air, he did not offer a chance and was beaten only once, and then off the pitch. Hanif shared a stand of 259 with Wallis Mathias for the second wicket.

Hanif is one of four brothers all playing in first-class cricket. Three appeared for Karachi in this match; Wazir was captain and the other was Mushtaq.

Bahawalpur

Ijaz Hussain run out	24	– c Waqar b Mahmood	32
Zulfiqar Ahmed c Aziz b Mahmood	0	– c Aziz b Mahmood	8
Mohammad Iqbal b Ikram	20	– c Aziz b Munaf	0
Mohammad Ramzan c Wallis b Ikram	64	– lbw b Munaf	5
Ghiasuddin b Ikram	4	– c Wazir b Ikram	12
Jamil Khalid run out	12	– b D'Souza	4
Farrukh Salim c Aziz b Mahmood	3	– b Ikram	4
Riaz Mahmood b Mahmood	4	– lbw b Mushtaq	10
Asad Bhatti st Aziz b Mushtaq	21	– b Ikram	4
Tanvir Hussan not out	16	– c Aziz b D'Souza	7
Aziz Ahmed b Ikram	8	– not out	5
Extras	9	Extras	17
	185		**108**

Karachi

Hanif Mohammad run out	499	Abdul Munaf b Iqbal	18
Alim-ud-din c Zulfiqar b Aziz	32	Abdul Aziz not out	9
Waqar Hassan c Tanvir b Iqbal	37		
Wazir Mohammad st Tanvir b Jamil	31	Extras	22
Wallis Mathias run out	103		
Mushtaq Mohammad lbw b Aziz	21	(7 wkts dec.)	772

Ikram Elahi, Mahmood Hussain and Antao D'Souza did not bat.

Karachi Bowling

	Overs	Mdns	Runs	Wkts	Overs	Mdns	Runs	Wkts
Mahmood	18	4	38	3	10	2	27	2
Ikram	17	3	48	4	8	2	10	3
Munaf	8	1	23	—	9	1	29	2
D'Souza	11	2	42	—	11	3	17	2
Mushtaq	4	—	19	1	3	—	8	1
Hanif	1	—	6	—				

Bahawalpur Bowling

	Overs	Mdns	Runs	Wkts
Zulfiqar	34	5	95	—
Ramzan	19	—	83	—
Aziz	50	4	208	2
Riaz	9	—	44	—
Ghias	37	3	139	—
Jamil	23	1	93	1
Iqbal	25	3	81	2
Tanvir	3	—	7	—

Umpires: Idris Beg and Daud Khan.

In the final, a few days later, Abdul Aziz, the Karachi wicket-keeper, died while batting against Combined Services. He was struck on the heart by a slow off-break from Dildar Awan and fell. He died fifteen minutes later on the way to hospital. Play was postponed for a day.

NOTES BY THE EDITOR, 1959

Hanif's World Record

It is pleasing to record that Hanif Mohammad, the Pakistan opening batsman who showed such immense promise when he toured England in 1954 at the age of 19, set up a new world highest individual score when he hit 499 for Karachi against Bahawalpur at Karachi on January 10, 1959. I am informed by my Pakistan correspondent, Ghulam Mustafa Khan, that it was a truly brilliant display of stylish hitting, notable for the fact that Hanif consistently kept the ball on the ground and averaged nearly fifty runs an hour. He was run out off the last ball of the day. Twelve months previously Hanif batted for sixteen hours thirteen minutes, the longest innings in first-class cricket, when he scored 337 in a Test match for Pakistan against West Indies at Bridgetown. So in the space of a year he broke two records standing to the names of two Knights of cricket, Sir Donald Bradman and Sir Leonard Hutton.

A HUNDRED YEARS OF WISDEN

JOHN WISDEN'S NEW CENTURY [1951]

By The Rt Hon. Lord De L'Isle and Dudley, VC

The name of Wisden is a household word wherever cricket is played, or indeed spoken about. The centenary of the firm which still bears the name of its founder was a notable event in the annals of 1950.

Outstanding in his day as a fast bowler, despite his small stature, John Wisden ensured the survival of his name by founding the "Cricket and Cigar" shop which has grown and flourished into the great business of today with its world-wide ramifications. He reinsured his fame by starting fourteen years later *The Cricketers' Almanack*, which has become the acknowledged chronicle of cricket, the universal referee in any argument over the history of the game. The first issue ran to a mere 112 pages, compared with the 1,000 pages of the current number.

The story of John Wisden, his life and times, is set out in detail in *A Wisden Century*, written by John Hadfield in honour of the centenary. The facts may be briefly summarised.

BIRTH OF WISDEN

John Wisden was born in 1826, the son of a Brighton builder. His father died when he was still a boy, and he went to live, as a pot-boy, with Tom Box, the wicket-keeper whose fame later became a legend. With Tom Box he began to learn his cricket. He was described in the chronicles of the time as "a hungry-looking lad glad of one's sixpence for his trouble", but by 1845 he had been chosen to play for Sussex against Kent, and he made his first appearance at Lord's in the following year when Sussex played their annual match against the MCC. He took six wickets.

From 1846 until 1863 John Wisden played regularly for Sussex, and Mr H. S. Altham, in his *History of Cricket*, describes him as the mainstay of an eleven "which might almost claim the county supremacy in the interregnum between the great days of Kent and the revival of Surrey cricket at the newly opened Kennington Oval", and as "easily the smallest fast bowler who ever made history". It was not long before he came to be known as "The Little Wonder", a title given him by Bob Thoms, a famous umpire of the day, and batsmen were soon to fear his "fast and ripping" deliveries.

He performed many great feats of bowling. In 1848 he took fifteen Kent wickets and fourteen Nottinghamshire wickets; in 1849 he took thirteen wickets against MCC and Ground at Lord's, and the same number against the same opponents in the following year. His greatest performance was in 1850, when he appeared, strangely enough, for the North against the South at Lord's, and in the second innings, bowling from the pavilion end, took all ten wickets *clean bowled*, a record which still stands unequalled.

From 1852 to 1855 Wisden was professional bowler at Harrow School, where the teaching of cricket was in the hands of the Hon. Frederick Ponsonby, afterwards the 6th Earl of Bessborough. The accuracy of Wisden's bowling was of great value for coaching. It was not surprising, therefore, that Harrow School itself recognised the centenary when the

Head Master accepted a "John Wisden Prize" of a bat and a ball to be awarded annually to the boy with the best bowling analysis.

AN ENGLAND PLAYER

In 1846 Wisden was invited to join the All-England Eleven, started by William Clarke, which played a great part in popularising and raising the standard of cricket. Clarke took his eleven all over England, playing against 18s, 20s and 22s, and thus establishing the professional cricketer as a man with some prospect of a career.

For a time all went well, but Clarke was in his way a martinet, and soon several of his professionals were in rebellion against him. Wisden headed the revolt and, with his fellow-Sussex bowler, Dean, started a rival organisation called the United England Eleven. John Lillywhite, Adams and Jimmy Grundy joined them, and in August 1852 they played their first match, at Southampton, against twenty gentlemen of Hampshire.

For the next decade England's professional cricket was divided into two camps, with Wisden's United England Eleven attracting many of the greatest players of the day. After Clarke's death in 1856 George Parr became captain of the All-England Eleven and, in 1859, he and Wisden became associated as joint proprietors of a cricket ground at Leamington, and brought the two elevens together in a tour to the United States and Canada. This visit was one of Wisden's chief contributions to cricket. It set the precedent for all subsequent tours.

THE RADIANT PROPRIETOR

The House of Wisden had its beginning nine years before this tour. John Wisden, already part-proprietor with George Parr of the Leamington ground, started in 1850 Parr and Wisden's Cricket Club, with which he associated the business of sports outfitter. Five years later he moved to London and opened a "Cricket and Cigar" depot in Coventry Street, off the Haymarket. There, "radiant with watch and chain of gold", he became at once the well-to-do, courteous proprietor of a West End cricket emporium.

On Wisden's death in 1884 the business passed to his manager, Henry Luff. The latter part of the nineteenth century saw a very large growth in the popularity of all games and sports. With this expansion there naturally came an increasing demand for all kinds of sports gear. Under Luff's enterprising management the House of Wisden set out to satisfy the public's needs, from boxing gloves to badminton, from fives to footballs. The firm has never lost its impetus. In the course of time several other businesses have become absorbed into its organisation.

By its amalgamation in 1920 with the well-known Kent firm of Duke and Son, its main factory became fixed at Penshurst. Thus it is as a neighbour – but not, alas! as a cricketer – that I pay my tribute to the House of John Wisden & Co.

Fortunately, cricket has an appeal far wider than the mere playing of it. W. G. Grace occupies a place in the history of sport which is still unshaken by any rival. Don Bradman is a hero to thousands who will never hold a bat straight. It is a national game, a true reflection of our peculiar temperament. But, like a sturdy plant, it has struck its roots and thrived on a variety of soils along with a number of other growths of indigenous British origin.

AUSTRALIAN MESSAGE

It seems natural, therefore, that a message of goodwill to the firm on its centenary from the Prime Minister should have its counterpart in a similar message from the Australian Prime Minister. "Wisden and cricket are synonymous," said Mr. Menzies. So it seemed to Mr. Oliver Lyttelton, who presided at the firm's centenary luncheon and introduced the principal guest, Mr Harold Wilson, President of the Board of Trade. He, too, appeared to share the same opinion. The many great performers at the game, past and present, who rose to toast the memory of the firm's celebrated founder, at the bidding of that doyen of cricketers, Sir "Plum" Warner, bore witness to the accuracy of Mr Menzies' words.

"Wisden and cricket are synonymous." Let this message from Australia be the tribute of the whole British Commonwealth at once to a famous cricketer, to the great enterprise which he founded, and to the game of cricket wherever it is played.

NOTES BY THE EDITOR, 1951

CENTURIES BY LICENCE

Cricket functions are renowned for the high quality of the speeches they usually produce. After spending a lifetime in the game I naturally expect something brilliant and witty, and it was therefore most appropriate from my point of view that the speakers at the John Wisden & Co., Ltd., centenary luncheon in May lived up to the high tradition. This was a memorable occasion. Mr. Oliver Lyttelton, in his happiest vein, when referring to the West Indies team said: "I have it on the authority of no less a person than Mr Harold Wilson (President of the Board of Trade) that, if they won too many matches in this country, he would have seriously to consider setting up a working party to examine the low productivity of British batsmen and bowlers. And that might be followed by the setting up of a development council, and even the nationalisation of cricket itself. I warn West Indies that if they come again in a few years time they may find that centuries will only be scored with a licence, and that maidens will only be obtained with a coupon."

Of this almanack Mr Lyttelton said: "Within *Wisden's* well-known covers lie the records of our national game; and those who, like myself, turn its pages in a spirit of escapism can see in their mind's eye many of the beautiful grounds, some of them lying below the gleaming spires of our cathedrals or the smoking chimneys of our industrial life. We know that as long as we have the spirit and tradition of this game and allow them to endure, change and decay which we may discern in other nations will touch us only lightly with their dread fingers."

RUSSIAN STORY

To Mr Harold Wilson fell the task of proposing the toast of "This Wonderful Century". He confessed that he was no cricketer himself, but he remarked: "I am a Yorkshireman, and cricket is never far from a Yorkshireman's thoughts." Then he amused us with an account of the last time he played cricket. He said it was in Moscow when he was there for trade talks with the Russians. "There was one Sunday afternoon, during a lull in the negotiations, when my delegation repaired to some woods not far from Moscow. A few weeks afterwards, following the breakdown of the discussions, the Moscow Press, who seem to have observed our innocent pastime, came out with an account of the 'orgies and strange pirouettes by the lakeside of the English delegation'." Continuing his reminiscence, Mr Wilson told this story:

"My second over was interrupted by a gentleman from the NKVD or Ogpu, who was appointed to follow us around and see that we came to no harm. He stood in the middle of the pitch and remonstrated with us in a very long Russian speech which I understood came to this – that we could not do that there! He was supported by two men who came up on horseback with rifles. I persuaded him, after some negotiation, to take up his position at square leg, out of the way of even my bowling. The episode closed with the NKVD man's failure to make any attempt to catch a ball – and after that my opinion of the Russian secret police fell even lower." Mr Wilson suggested that the incident should be recorded in *Wisden* as the "only case of a catch being missed at square leg by a member of the NKVD off an off-spinner by a visiting British minister".

A HISTORY OF WISDEN [1963]

By L. E. S. Gutteridge

The year 1864 was memorable for many reasons. Paraguay was at war with Brazil. Britain was having some trouble with the Bhutanese in India and the Ashantis in West Africa. Charles Dickens produced *Our Mutual Friend*. In Manchester, photographs were taken for the first time by magnesium flashlight: the first stone of the London Embankment was laid; Clifton Suspension Bridge was opened and, after repulsing an attack on Kintang, the great General Gordon exploded 40,000 lb of powder under the walls of Nanking before recapturing it. Whilst the sound of this explosion was still reverberating, three other earth-shaking events occurred. At fifteen years of age, W. G. Grace scored 170 and 56 not out for the South Wales Cricket Club against the Gentlemen of Sussex at Brighton, overarm bowling was legalised and, most important of all *Wisden's Cricketers' Almanack* was born.

A height of five feet four inches and a weight of seven stone is not perhaps the popular image of a fast bowler. Yet, John Wisden, a Brighton builder's son, rightly known as the "Little Wonder", averaged 225 wickets a season for twelve years, took 455 wickets in 1851, and with a tremendous off-break clean bowled all ten wickets in the second innings for North v South in 1850. He was largely responsible for the tour – the first by an English team – to Canada and the United States in 1859 where he performed a double hat-trick, actually taking six wickets in six balls. He owned a tobacconist's and sports equipment store in Leicester Square. His chief rival was Lillywhite Brothers & Co. "dealers in foreign cigars, tobacco etc (unrivalled shag, highly recommended at 6s 6d) and sports equipment", whose premises were at 10, Princes Terrace, Caledonian Road, Islington. Since 1849 they had issued *The Young Cricketer's Guide* at eighteenpence a copy, falling to one shilling for the later issues. It ended in 1866, but *The Cricketer's Companion* had taken its place in 1865. A mind as cogent as John Wisden's realised the value of such a publication as an advertisement and he determined to produce his own. It became a lasting memorial of his fame. It is significant that he played his last first-class match against the MCC and Ground at Brighton in August 1863 – exactly one hundred years ago.

Books must not be classified by size and shape alone. They are subject, even as clothes are, to the decrees of fashion. There is a straining after novelty, but always a dislike of breaking with the past. There have been volumes as tall as a man and others as small as a walnut. We confess to a certain dislike of the Elephant folio. At Addison's Banquet of the Books, the folio still takes the top of the table; the twelves are below the salt, and the slim books can hardly find a place at all. *Wisden's Cricketers' Almanack*, having chosen at the outset a most perfect size for its purpose, has retained it through 100 issues, and with age its girth has increased. A natural slimming was evidenced during the lean years of two world wars, but the astonishing and wholly admirable thing is that it continued at all.

In outward appearance, few vital changes can be noticed. The paper covers gave way to a limp-cloth binding in 1938 and an alternative cloth-boards edition was commenced in 1896. In 1938 the Wisden *motif* of two top-hatted players at the wicket, appeared on the cover of the limp edition and has continued. In the paper editions 1904-5 the spelling "Almanac" is employed but this usage does not appear on the front cover nor on the cloth edition, which has "Almanack".

The first issue was published for one shilling and was available "post free for 13 stamps" – obviously penny ones. By 1874 the number of pages had increased from the 112 of 1864 to 208 and a copy was sent post free for 14 stamps. It is curious that the issue for 1875, although 32 pages larger, was available for 13 stamps post free and that this also applied to that for 1876. Changes in postal charges are not unknown today. The post free price for 1878 and 1879 was 1s 1½d and that for 1880 (234 pages with the advertisements) was 1s 2d. The price was increased to 1s 3d post free with the issue of 1886 (382 pp.). So size and postage progressed, until today the cheapest way of posting a 1,067-page Wisden costs 1s 3d.

The first advertisement was in 1867 where, on the last page, appears an illustration of John Wisden and Co.'s Patent Catapulta, "the principle of working which will be shown at 2, New Coventry Street, Leicester Square". Mr Wanostrocht, in his *Felix on the Bat* published in 1845, shows a Catapulta which was based on the principle of the siege machine of classical antiquity. Wisden's model was of an entirely different principle, the ball being propelled by a bow-like structure. In 1883, the first advertisement appears in the text and is on the verso of the title-page. Dr Johnson in 1759 said: "The trade of advertising is now so near perfection that it is not easy to propose any improvement." In 1960, Britain spent £456 million on advertising and *Wisden* itself shows a similar evolution of the art to a stage much beyond any that Johnson could have conceived. The earnest desire of the proprietors to keep the cost as low as possible meant that advertisements must increase in quantity and to a very great extent these were banished to the front and end of the actual work itself. The increasing circulation helped to lower the cost of production, but the advertisements were an absolute necessity if the price were to remain at 1s. And so it did for over half its present life, that is for 51 issues until during the First World War in 1915.

With the exception of 1868 there are only three publishers' imprints, with one minor variation. Until 1937 John Wisden and Co. were the publishers (in 1914 it became a limited liability company) and it seems that for a trial period of one year, John Wisden had a partner by name Maynard, and, for the year 1868 only, the imprint was Wisden and Maynard. Research has failed to provide any information on this short partnership. *Wisden's* publishers were blitzed during the winter of 1940 and all the records were lost, while Wisden's Mortlake factory with other records was destroyed in 1944. H. S. Altham says: "No doubt the Cabinet was unmoved, but cricketers felt it an almost personal outrage." Six printers are known to have been concerned with its production and Messrs. Balding and Mansell printed 39 consecutive issues.

A main contributory to *Wisden's* success was the founding in 1880 of the Cricket Reporting Agency. Begun by Charles Pardon, who, seven years after its foundation first undertook the Editorship of *Wisden*, the editorial work has, since the 1887 edition, been carried through by the Cricket Reporting Agency, and *Wisden's* Editor has generally been a partner in the firm. Some members of the firm have worked on *Wisden* for long periods, notably Sydney Pardon, from 1887 to 1925, Charles Stewart Caine, 1887 to 1933, S. J. Southerton, 1894 to 1935, and Hubert Preston, 1895 to 1951. Four current members with long service records are E. Eden, who began in 1922, H. Gee in 1931 and Norman Preston and Leslie Smith in 1933.

Perhaps the greatest of the editors was S. H. Pardon, who was responsible for the issues from 1891 until 1925. He would have been the first to acknowledge his debt to C. F. Pardon and E. S. Pardon. This was a great and formative period. His first issue had 420 pages and his penultimate one 1,010 pages. Every aspect of the game came under his careful scrutiny. The number of entries under Births and Deaths in 1891 was 753 and in his final issue of 1925, was 6,274. His was a cultured mind. He had definite opinions and was prepared to state them. His editorials make most interesting reading and his influence on the growth of the game throughout the world was immense. Like all great editors, he had the ability to pick the right helpers, and F. S. Ashley-Cooper's meticulously accurate and informed statistical assistance was invaluable. Hubert Preston was in the same tradition and was equally notable in other and different fields.

The present editor has shown that he too is worthy of the great traditions and has a lively sense of the best interests of the game. He is still fighting space, as all his predecessors have done, but is nevertheless allowing the publication to grow, and even the lesser-known touring teams are allowed their brief mention. At this point it should be stated that the Almanack has attained a most remarkable degree of accuracy. The possibilities of errors are incalculable. The fact is that the degree of accuracy attained over the years has been astonishing. The old adage says that there are three kinds of lies. Lies, damned lies and statistics.

Charles Dexter Cleveland in his preface to *A Complete Concordance to the Poetical*

Works of John Milton says: "I had occasion to look at Todd's *Verbal Index* in connection with *Lycidas*. I found 63 mistakes". This in a poem of 193 lines. Yet, in its day, Todd's *Verbal Index* was considered to be a literary masterpiece. The fact is that in view of the inevitably large content of statistics, *Wisden's Cricketers' Almanack* has performed with very great credit.

Wisden has attained an authoritative position that is now unrivalled. In its earlier days it met and squarely beat its competitors. Captain Bayley produced *The Cricket Chronicle* for the season 1863 which contained full scores of minor as well as important matches and the Lillywhites produced *Guides, Companions* and *Annuals* from 1849 to 1900. *Wisden* appears in the committee rooms of the whole world where cricket is played and is the final arbiter in any matter under dispute. Such is its present authority that I must remind the reader that it is published by a private firm that has no official connection with cricket's rulers. Its success has been due to its manner of presentation and to its emphasis on accuracy and detail. It is a one hundred volume history of the game, a permanent source of information to which many authors have freely admitted their indebtedness and to which many more have not.

The evolution of the growth of overseas cricket is a fascinating study and deserves an article to itself. Even the second issue of 1865 devoted 22 of its 160 pages to the doings of the Twelve in Australia under the captaincy of George Parr. In 1868, the full scores of a match played by I Zingari against the Paris Club, which IZ won very comfortably, is recorded, and in 1869 both the English Team in America and the results of the visit of the Australian Aboriginals to this country are given ample space. In 1875 an American Baseball team came to this country to demonstrate the virtues of their game and stayed for one month only. The comment generally made was that their fielding was good. Sad to record, they played a number of cricket matches as well and "the Americans having one or two good bowlers, several plucky hard-hitters, and a team of good fielders, they had the best of every match they played." When Lillywhite went on his second trip to America in 1868 with Willsher as captain, the team beat the best baseball side that America at that time could produce. In 1887, reference is made to the Tour of the Parsees and also of the visit of the West Indian Gentlemen to Canada and the United States. Australian Inter-Colonial Matches were first recorded in 1891. By 1893 the visit of an Irish team to America, and statistics prepared by Lord Harris of Cricket in India, was considered of sufficient interest to occupy valuable space, and a visit during the month of August by the Gentlemen of Holland was recorded in 1895.

It was nothing less than an editorial stroke of genius when Charles F. Pardon decided that "to signalise the extraordinary success that bowlers achieved in 1888" he would give "new portraits, specially photographed by Hawkins of Brighton, of six of the most prominent and skilful of their number". A proof of its popularity is that the demand for 1889 was so great that for the first time a second edition was necessary. The photograph is still clearly legible and unfaded after over 70 years. (Prints were substituted for actual photographs in 1915.) It became a regular feature thereafter (except for 1916 and 1917, and this for an obvious reason). In 1897, it had developed into that much-loved and delightfully argumentative feature, *Five Cricketers of the Year*. Why is it that we so rarely guess all the five in advance, and yet agree with the final choice? It was a most happy thought in 1918 to give the *Five School Bowlers of the Year*, and in the following year, the *Five Public School Cricketers of the Year*. It should be mentioned that one of the latter was A. P. F. Chapman, of Uppingham. "Though he bowls left-handed with some ability, it is also as a batsman that Chapman is chiefly distinguished . . . he ought to make his mark." It becomes most impressive on the four occasions that the Five Cricketers of the Year were dropped to find the solitary names of John Wisden, W. G. Grace, P. F. Warner and Jack Hobbs in lonely grandeur.

The beginnings of the important obituary section were in 1872 when 15 cricketers were listed as having died in 1871. These included Mr Dark, of Lord's, and the father of W. G. Grace. In 1891 a brief obituary notice was given of Charles F. Pardon and this inspired the editor to do the same for other deaths in the following year and brief biographical notices were added. Since then there have been brief and accurate summaries from various pens. Obituaries of cricketers killed in action were separated from the others during the wars.

I must confess to a certain sadness at the inevitable passing of the almanack that graced the earliest editions. 1864 commences its 12 pages of almanack by informing us that the British Museum closes on January 1st, and amongst other gratuitous information, tells us when carpets were first manufactured in Kidderminster, the date of the Battle of Lodi on the Adda in 1796 and ends with a mention of Thomas Brett, "the fastest and straightest underhand bowler ever known". In 1865 the almanack gives more cricket information than other subjects, and in 1870 it is given a new form and has only four pages. This continued until 1879 when a single page calendar was substituted. Even the calendar disappeared in 1941 and all that is left of the almanack is its mention in the title. (A twelve-page Almanack, extracted from G. D. Martineau's *Cricketer's Historical Calendar* which Sporting Handbooks Ltd will publish late in 1963, has been included in this edition.) The first issue contained a deal of delightful, but quite extraneous, matter – such as the Rules of Knur and Spell, a brief history of China, the Rules for playing the Game of Bowls, the winners of the Derby, Oaks and St Leger, and sundry other "discrete" information on Canals, British Societies, The Wars of the Roses, and Coinage. It ends with a mention of the interesting fact that a brass bell weighing 17 cwt cast at Woolwich Arsenal in 1699 was cleft by the hammer while ringing from the effect of the severe frost.

The Laws of Cricket have appeared in every edition. In the very earliest editions they followed the almanack, and until 1937 they appeared towards the beginning of the volume. From 1938 to 1947 they were to be found after the statistics and immediately before the details of matches played. From 1948 the Laws have been placed at the end. A study of their variations would in itself provide much of the history of Cricket. The laws governing bets were dropped in 1885.

Women's cricket was honoured by having its first mention in 1938. There is a detailed account with full scores of the first women's Test Match between Australia and England, by Miss V. M. M. Cox, of the Woman's Cricket Association.

In later years improvements and additions come thick and fast. Public Schools had space accorded to them as early as the second issue, where a whole page is given to the recording of the Eton v Harrow match at Lord's when over 9,000 people were present. In 1962 sixty pages are devoted to Public Schools cricket. It is fascinating to notice a C. J. Kortright playing for Tonbridge in 1887 or a T. W. Graveney with 4 innings, twice not out, 27 runs, 10 as the highest innings, and an average of 13.50 for Bristol Grammar School in 1942.

County cricket has always rightly formed a very large part of a year's issue and during the Second World War, when we lacked this important feature of our national life, we were solaced with many details of League cricket and of the Northern Universities. In 1960 room was found for the permanent inclusion of League cricket. Lists of "Blues" were commenced in 1923 at the suggestion of W. Livingstone Irwin, and Mr Ashley-Cooper drew up two tables adding the schools of the players. A list of "Blues" from 1827-1939 appeared in 1940. Statistics of many kinds are provided and the Cricket Records have been amended every year.

The reporting of matches in earlier days was quaint and typical of the period. It was always readable and never descended to the type of journalese provided by Bell's *London Life*. The reporting of matches is now factual and unlike former years, the Test match reports are initialled, thus departing from the strict anonymity that was traditional.

The first article was by W. H. Knight in 1869 and he wrote in a fresh and bright manner on the *Individual Innings of 200 or more Runs*. He is recorded as the editor in the preface of 1870. Since then, many lesser known and greater names have contributed. The Hon. Mr Justice Herbert V. Evatt – later the Prime Minister of Australia – contributed an article in 1935, and another celebrated lawyer, Lord Birkett, also appeared in 1958. Among famous cricketers contributing articles are G. O. Allen in 1938 on *A Case for More Natural Wickets*, Sir Jack Hobbs on *The Hobbs Era* and Spofforth on *Schoolboys' Bowling* in

1904. A list of all the special articles appears at the end of the Index which was produced by Mr Rex Pogson in 1944.

In certain years it was found that an insufficient number of copies of the Almanack had been published. It was decided to issue a second edition and I have seen the issues for each year from 1889 to 1901 except 1896 and 1900. It is always more costly to produce small numbers and the published price in these cases was 2s for the paper edition and in 1899 3s for the cloth. A curious situation arose in 1898. The Five Cricketers of the Year appear in one edition on the cover in a pattern of two names with one in the centre and two underneath. But another copy of the same year has a pattern 1-2-2. Further there is a variation of the same kind that has the name P. F. Warner correctly on the title-page and another that has the misprint W. P. Warner.

A list of cricket books at that time in print was given in 1938 and was dropped in 1943, to reappear in 1950 with a further list of books to be published during the year. A bibliography of cricket was written by that Sussex enthusiast, Alfred J. Gaston, in the editions of 1892, 1894, 1900 and 1923. From 1952, John Arlott has reviewed the books of the previous year except where an item was his own.

Considerable space has always been accorded to the matches of the MCC, and all decisions of legislative bodies have been fully covered. Even the dinner following the AGM was reported in 1878 (it must have been a little embarrassing for the retiring President of 1877, Lord Londesborough, to have to record that he had great satisfaction in proposing the Duke of Beaufort as his successor, but that the Duke was not present since he had misinformed him as to the day).

I have frequently been asked why the edition of 1875 is so very scarce and the simple answer can only be that fewer of them were issued. It is always a very difficult problem to estimate circulation and particularly so at the beginning of a new publication's career. The edition of 1873 was a bumper issue for its time and contained the full scores of the visit of the English Twelve to America and Canada. This will have sold well. The issue for 1874 was smaller by 28 pages and may not have had so wide a circulation, although on the basis of the previous year's demand, more copies may have been issued. It would have been normal practice to have reduced the number of copies printed for 1875. It is also interesting to note that at this period, the year of publication was given at the foot of the title-page and that the title-page gave always the same year. This is not true for 1875 which reads "John Wisden's Cricketers' Almanack for 1875" and had the date at the foot of the title-page as 1874. This implies that 1874 and 1875 were published in the same year, and although this has often been taken for a misprint, it is probably true that 1875 was issued in December 1874.

I have seen a letter addressed to an enquirer by John Wisden & Co., in 1881. It thanked the writer for his letter but regretted that 1875 was not available. It pointed out that they themselves were paying 10s for a copy, which is the equivalent of paying £10 for a 1962 copy! The 1875 edition is not, however, so scarce as the first issue of 1864. It was a great day for the enthusiast when the present publishers decided to reprint the first fifteen issues in facsimile.

As I have said, Wisden's were their own publishers until 1937. By then, as a result of the years of slump, sales had fallen to such an alarming extent that professional help was called in and the publishing of *Wisden* was passed over to J. Whitaker & Sons, Ltd, publishers of *Whitaker's Almanack*. From the 1938 edition substantial changes were made, designed to make *Wisden* easier to use and understand. The cumbrous "early Victorian survival" of a division into two parts was discarded, a new cover was designed, a complete index was provided, the Counties were set out in alphabetical order instead of, as previously, in the previous year's County Championship table order, and more illustrations were provided. Sales increased considerably, and immediately.

Whitaker's imprint as publishers stayed until the 1944 edition when the name of the publisher changed to Sporting Handbooks Ltd. (Whitaker's had purchased in 1939 a firm called Sporting Handbooks Ltd as being a more suitable imprint under which to publish *Wisden*, and Wisden's had taken a share in it, it then being jointly owned by Wisden's and

Whitaker's. The change of imprint was made with the 1944 edition, and has remained the same since then. In 1957 Whitaker's bought out the Wisden interest in Sporting Handbooks Ltd which is now a wholly-owned subsidiary of Whitaker's and continues to publish *Wisden* under agreement with John Wisden & Co. Ltd who remain the proprietors of the copyright in *Wisden*.)

The quantity printed of the early years would be fascinating to know, but it has proved impossible to trace any printing orders earlier than 1936. The following table shows the number printed in the years from 1936, and the way in which the demand for the cloth boards edition has increased is particularly notable:

Year	Quantity paper		
1936	8,500	(total, no separate cloth boards figure known)	
1937	8,000	(total, no separate cloth boards figure known)	
	limp	cloth boards	
1938	12,000	not known	
1939	12,000	not known	
1940	8,000	not known	
1941	3,200	800	(War paper restriction)
1942	4,100	900	(War paper restriction)
1943	5,600	1,400	(War paper restriction)
1944	5,600	1,400	(War paper restriction)
1945	6,500	1,500	(War paper restriction)
1946	11,000	5,000	(War paper restriction)
1947	14,000	6,000	(Restrictions eased)
1948	14,500	6,500	(Restrictions eased)
1949	21,500	10,500	(Restrictions ended)

1949 was the peak. With other consumer goods in stringently short supply, and sport one of the few outlets, sport and writing about sport boomed as never before. The boom slowly diminished, but even in 1955 the limp edition sold 15,500 copies and the cloth boards edition had increased to 11,000 copies. Today the sale is steady, averaging 11,000 of the limp edition and 10,000 of the cloth boards edition.

What a pity it is that all owners of books do not put their signatures on a fly-leaf! It is far more interesting than a bookplate and takes up less room. It is most interesting to learn who have been the previous owners and to trace them through the relevant volumes. I have, for example, seen the signatures of Haygarth, C. B. Fry, R. Daft and even Horatio Bottomley (once rightly mis-spelled Hotairio) on *Wisdens*, and perhaps even more rewarding are the signatures of such relatively little known players as W. Rashleigh. Perseverance produced the information that he played for Oxford University in 1886 and that he made 21 and 107 against Cambridge University. That he made 49 against a strong MCC side which included Studd, Hearne and Webbe and that in seven matches that year, he had 13 innings and made 343 runs. Did Rashleigh own only the one copy of *Wisden* in which his name appeared to such advantage, or was he a genuine devotee and are the rest of his volumes with his bold signature still in existence somewhere?

I have a catalogue issued by A. J. Gaston in 1899 of the library of T. Padwick. A set (1864-1898) of the Almanack was advertised for £10. One of the best cricket book catalogues ever produced was that of A Maurice & Co., of Covent Garden. It was issued in 1909 and is itself a rare item. It has no set for sale, but lists the rarer *Wisdens* at 5s each. Gaston issued a further general catalogue of cricket books in 1925 and has a bound set (1864-1924) available, at fifty guineas. Sotheby's auction in 1937 of the library of J. A. H. Catton had a set (1864-1936) and a further 11 duplicate volumes unspecified. This fetched £33. Messrs. Hodgson & Co., of Chancery Lane, auctioned a set (1864-1953) in 1954 and the price was £145. The present accepted price for a set in good condition and collated as complete is £250.

Great is bookishness and the charm of books. No doubt there are times in the lives of most reading men when they rebel against the dust of libraries. We all know the "dark hours" when the vanity of learning and the childishness of merely literary things are brought home to us in such a way as to put the pale student out of conceit with his books, and to make him turn from his best-loved authors as from a friend who has outstayed his welcome. In what a different category are a set or a run of *Wisden.* K. A. Auty, a well known Yorkshireman, who had spent the greater part of a long life in America, and whose obituary appears in *Wisden*, possessed a most notable collection of cricket books. He kept his complete set of *Wisden* under his bed. He could then, having made himself properly comfortable, forget his maturing bills and overdue argosies, dip down and take at random any volume that came to hand. He was often found perusing the same volume hours later.

TABLE I. PAGE NUMBERING

Square brackets denote unnumbered pages.   * Denotes largest issue to date.

Year	pages		Year	pages	
1864	[4] + 112	(116)	1914	iv + 252 (pt. 1) + 543 (pt. 2)	(799)
1865	[4] + 160	(164)*	1915	iv + 252 (pt. 1) + 535 (pt. 2)	(791)
1866	[4] + 196	(200)*	1916	299	
1867	[4] + 159 + 1	(164)	1917	351	
1868	[4] + 112	(116)	1918	339	
1869	[4] + 120	(124)	1919	327	
1870	152		1920	xii + 284 (pt. 1) + 431 (pt. 2)	(727)
1871	152		1921	272 (pt. 1) + 523 (pt. 2)	(795)
1872	172		1922	la-c + 320 (pt. 1) + 675 (pt. 2)	(998)*
1873	208*		1923	la-c + 360 (pt. 1) + 607 (pt. 2)	(970)
1874	180		1924	328 (pt. 1) + 683 (pt. 2)	(1011)*
1875	214 + [2]	(216)*	1925	4 + 336 (pt. 1) + 615 (pt. 2)	(955)
1876	224*		1926	12 + 340 (pt. 1) + 679 (pt. 2)	(1031)*
1877	248*		1927	350 (pt. 1) + 693 (pt. 2)	(1043)*
1878	250*		1928	352 (pt. 1) + 711 (pt. 2)	(1063)*
1879	241 + [5]	(246)	1929	308 (pt. 1) + 707 (pt. 2)	(1015)
1880	[2] + 216 + [18]	(236)	1930	320 (pt. 1) + 739 (pt. 2)	(1059)
1881	[2] + 228 + [10]	(240)	1931	336 (pt. 1) + 730 (pt. 2)	(1066)*
1882	[2] + 212 + [10]	(224)	1932	312 (pt. 1) + 722 (pt. 2)	(1034)
1883	[2] + 284 + [18]	(304)*	1933	312 (pt. 1) + 719 (pt. 2)	(1031)
1884	[2] + 268 + [18]	(288)	1934	338 (pt. 1) + 721 (pt. 2)	(1059)
1885	[2] + 290 + [20]	(312)*	1935	336 (pt. 1) + 711 (pt. 2)	(1047)
1886	[2] + 360 + [22]	(384)*	1936	356 (pt. 1) + 679 (pt. 2)	(1035)
1887	[2] + xx + 308 + [18]	(348)	1937	340 (pt. 1) + 715 (pt. 2)	(1055)
1888	[2] + xxxviii + 362 + [20]	(412)*	1938	990 + [1]	(991)
1889	[2] + xl + 356 + [22]	(420)*	1939	958	
1890	[2] + lii + 301 + [21]	(376)	1940	871	
1891	xlvi + 354 + [20]	(420)	1941	426	
1892	lxii + 330 + [20]	(412)	1942	391	
1893	liv + 376 + [18]	(448)*	1943	403	
1894	lxxiv + 390 + [24]	(488)*	1944	343	
1895	lxxviii + 386 + [14]	(478)	1945	367	
1896	lxxviii + 418 + [28]	(524)*	1946	xvi + 463	(479)
1897	lxxxii + 416 + [30]	(528)*	1947	xxxii + 715	(747)
1898	xciv + 428 + [24]	(546)*	1948	xxxii + 843	(875)
1899	cxiv + 438 + [26]	(578)*	1949	viii + 935	(943)
1900	cxii + 506 + [28]	(646)*	1950	viii + 1003	(1011)
1901	cxx + 477 + [35]	(632)	1951	xvi + 1019	(1035)
1902	cxxviii + 536 + [38]	(702)*	1952	viii + 1031	(1039)
1903	cxl + 532 + [42]	(714)*	1953	xx + 1015	(1035)
1904	cxl + 492 + [50]	(682)	1954	xx + 999	(1019)
1905	clxviii + 528 + [50]	(746)*	1955	xx + 1011	(1031)
1906	clx + 602	(762)*	1956	xxxii + 1043	(1075)*
1907	clxxviii (pt. 1) + 510 (pt. 2) + [36]	(724)	1957	xxxii + 1019	(1051)
1908	206 (pt. 1) + 574 (pt. 2)	(780)*	1958	xxxvi + 1035	(1071)
1909	208 (pt. 1) + 562 (pt. 2)	(770)	1959	xlviii + 1011	(1059)
1910	212 (pt. 1) + 534 (pt. 2)	(746)	1960	iv + 1023	(1027)
1911	216 (pt. 1) + 550 (pt. 2)	(766)	1961	viii + 1019	(1027)
1912	220 (pt. 1) + 566 (pt. 2)	(786)*	1962	iv + 1063	(1067)
1913	iv + 236 (pt. 1) + 607 (pt. 2)	(847)*	1963	xlviii + 1131	(1179)*

FACSIMILE EDITION

In 1961 a limited facsimile reprint of the issues from 1864 to 1878 was published.

PUBLISHERS

1864-1867	John Wisden and Co.
1868	Wisden and Maynard.
1869-1914	John Wisden and Co.
1915-1937	John Wisden and Co. Ltd.
1938-1943	J. Whitaker and Sons Ltd for John Wisden and Co. Ltd.
1944-1963	Sporting Handbooks Ltd for John Wisden and Co. Ltd.

COMPILERS AND EDITORS

1864-1869	It is likely that W. H. Crockford (S.B. xiv-xxviii) and W. H. Knight were concerned.

1870-1879	W. H. Knight	1934-1935	S. J. Southerton
1880-1886	George H. West	1936-1939	W. H. Brookes
1887-1890	C. F. Pardon	1940-1943	Haddon Whitaker
1891-1925	S. H. Pardon	1944-1951	Hubert Preston
1926-1933	C. S. Caine	1952-1963	Norman Preston

Note: From 1887 to today the material for *Wisden* has been compiled by the staff of the Cricket Reporting Agency, while (except for 1940-43, in the uncertainty of the early war years) the Editorial responsibility has been undertaken by one of its partners, usually the senior.

PRINTERS

1864-1886	W. H. Crockford	1936-1937	S. H. Benson Ltd
1887-1893	Not known	1938-1940	Purnell & Sons
1894-1896	Wyman & Sons	1941-1963	Unwin Brothers Ltd
1897-1935	Balding & Mansell		

No name of a printer is stated from 1887-1893. However, there appears to be no difference in the typography between the issues of 1889-1893 and those printed by Wyman from 1894-1896. It is therefore probable that Wyman were the printers from 1889 onwards. There are only minor differences in the 1887 and 1888 issues and it is possible that these were produced by a different printer. It is also quite conceivable that the printers were again Wyman. The publishers lost all their records of this period during the last war. The printer's name does not appear in the cloth-board edition from 1938 onwards, but is given in the limp cloth edition.

PRICE

1864-1895	paper	1/-		
1896-1914	paper	1/-	cloth boards	2/-
1915-1917	paper	1/6	cloth boards	2/6
1918	paper	2/-	cloth boards	3/-
1919-1920	paper	2/6	cloth boards	4/-
1921-1937	paper	5/-	cloth boards	7/6
1938-1942	limp cloth	5/-	cloth boards	7/6
1943-1946	limp cloth	6/-	cloth boards	8/6
1947	limp cloth	7/6	cloth boards	9/6
1948-1950	limp cloth	9/6	cloth boards	12/-
1951	limp cloth	10/6	cloth boards	12/6
1952-1955	limp cloth	12/6	cloth boards	15/-
1956	limp cloth	15/-	cloth boards	17/6
1957-1959	limp cloth	16/-	cloth boards	18/6
1960-1961	limp	18/6	cloth boards	21/-
1962	limp	20/-	cloth boards	22/6
1963	limp	22/6	cloth boards	25/-

No price is given on the title page from 1891-1938 and therefore nowhere on the 1938 cloth-board edition. From 1939 it reappears on the title page.

ILLUSTRATIONS

Five Cricketers of the Year appeared in the following issues: 1897, 1898, 1902-1908, 1910-1911, 1914-1915, 1922-1923, 1925, 1927-1937. From 1938 many other illustrations have been given together with the Five Cricketers of the Year, except in the issues for 1941-1946.

In other years before 1938 the following illustrations have appeared:

1889	6 Great Bowlers	1909	Lord Hawke and 4 Cricketers of the Year
1890	9 Great Batsmen		
1891	5 Wicket Keepers	1912	5 Members of MCC to Australia
1892	5 Great Bowlers	1913	John Wisden
1893	5 Batsmen of the Year	1918	5 School Bowlers of the Year
1894	5 All-round Cricketers	1919	5 Public School Cricketers of the Year
1895	5 Young Batsmen of the Year		
1896	W. G. Grace	1920	5 Batsmen of the Year
1899	5 Great Players of the Season	1921	P. F. Warner
1900	5 Cricketers of the Season	1924	5 Bowlers of the Year
1901	Mr R. E. Foster and 4 Yorkshire Cricketers	1926	J. B. Hobbs

SECOND EDITIONS

Second issues appeared from 1889-1901 except (so far as is at present known) in 1896 and 1900. They are the same as the ordinary issues save only for:—

(i)   The additional words on the front cover "Second Issue."

(ii) The price 2/- paper (3/- cloth boards from 1898) instead of the normal 1/-.

(iii) The price and words "Second Issue" on the title pages of the 1889 and 1890 issues. Despite the price announcement for cloth-bound second issues I have been unable to trace any.

STYLE OF FRONT COVER OF PAPER EDITION

1864-1869	First style (1865 slightly different from 1864)	
1870-1877	Second style.	Original version
1878-1880	Second style.	First variation
1881-1884		Second variation
1885	Third style.	Original version
1886		First version
1887	Fourth style.	Original version
1888		First variation
1889-1896		Second variation
1897-1935	Fifth style.	Original version
1936-1937		First variation. (1937 last paper issue)
1938-1962	Sixth style.	(1938 was the first limp cloth issue)

STYLE OF LETTERING ON SPINE OF PAPER EDITION

1887-1895	First appearance	
1895-1907	Slightly bolder	
1908-1935	Second style	Title vertically reading from the bottom
1936-1937	Second style. First variation	
1938-1962	Third style	

Some copies of the 1901 first (but not second) issues had 1900 on the spine, covered over with a label bearing the correct date. 1904-1905 paper spines bore the words "ALMANAC" not the usual "ALMANACK". The unusual spelling does not occur on the front cover nor on the spine of the cloth edition.

STYLE OF BRASSES ON FRONT COVER OF CLOTH BOARDS EDITION

1896-1902 First style
1903-1928 Second style
1929-1937 Second style (Variation due to change of address)
1938-1962 Third style
From 1896 to 1937 yellow paper front and back covers were bound in as end papers and faced with yellow advertisement end papers on the insides of the front and back cloth boards.

STYLE OF BRASSES ON SPINE OF CLOTH-BOARDS EDITION

1896-1937	First style	Title vertically reading from bottom
1938-1940	Second style Original version	Title horizontally; at bottom No. of issue
1941-1948	Third style	Title vertically reading from top
1949-1962	Second style First variation	Title horizontally; at bottom the publisher's name

COLOUR OF PAPER COVERS

1864-1871 Pale buff
1872-1877 Pale pink/buff
1878-1879 Glossy paper. Pale yellow/buff
1880-1882 Pale yellow/buff
1883-1886 Pale pink/buff
1887-1937 Bright yellow which fades to buff
1938-1962 Limp cloth bright yellow with little or no fading
Some war issues 1941-1945 rather brown

SIX GIANTS OF THE WISDEN CENTURY [1963]

By Neville Cardus

I have been asked by the Editor of *Wisden* to write "appreciations" of six great cricketers of the past hundred years. I am honoured by this invitation, but it puts me in an invidious position. Whichever player I choose for this representative little gallery I am bound to leave out an important name. My selection of immortal centenarians is as follows: W. G. Grace, Sir Jack Hobbs, Sir Donald Bradman, Tom Richardson, S. F. Barnes and Victor Trumper. But where – I can already hear in my imagination a thousand protesting voices (including my own) – where are "Ranji", Spofforth, Rhodes, J. T. Tyldesley, who, in one rubber v Australia, was the only professional batsman in England thought good enough to play for his country on the strength of his batting alone? Where are Macartney, Aubrey Faulkner, O'Reilly, Keith Miller, Woolley, Lindwall, Sir Leonard Hutton? And where are many other illustrious names, Australian and English?

I'll give reasons why my six have been picked. There have been, there still are, many cricketers who possess the gifts to bat brilliantly, skilfully and prosperously. There have been, there still are, many bowlers capable of wonderful and destructive arts. But there have been a few who have not only contributed handsome runs and taken worthy wickets by the hundred, but also have given to the technique and style of cricket a new twist, a new direction. These *creative* players have enriched the game by expanding in a fresh way some already established method. One or two of them have actually invented a technical trick of their own. Sadly for their posterity, they have often been the experimental unfulfilled pioneers, such as B. J. T. Bosanquet, who was the first bowler to baffle great batsmen in Test cricket by means of the "googly". J. B. King, a Philadelphian, demonstrated the potentialities of a swerving ball. My immortal six were at one and the same time masters of the old and initiators of the new.

W. G. GRACE

In recent years his great bulk has seemed to recede. Others following long after him have left his performances statistically behind. In his career he scored 54,896 runs, average 39.55. He also took 2,876 wickets, average 17.92. He scored 126 hundreds in first-class matches, a number exceeded by Sir Jack Hobbs, Hendren, Hammond, Mead, Sutcliffe, Woolley and Sir Leonard Hutton. None of these, not even Sir Jack, dominated for decades all other players, none of them lasted so long, or wore a beard of his commanding growth. In the summer of 1871 his aggregate of runs was 2,729, average 78.25. The next best batsman that year was Richard Daft, average 37.

A Hobbs, a Bradman, a Hutton, a Compton might easily any year amass more than 2,000 runs, averaging round about the 70s. But some other batsmen will be running them close, so as far as figures go, averaging 50, 60 and so on. Grace, in 1871, achieved an average which was proof that he stood alone in consistent skill, twice as skilful as the next best! His career ranged from the age of 17, in 1865, until 1908, when he was nearing sixty years. He had turned the fiftieth year of his life when for the Gentlemen v the Players at Kennington Oval he scored 82 and one of the attack he coped with magisterially was none other than S. F. Barnes, approaching his best.

All these facts and figures tell us no more of the essential "W.G." than we are told of Johann Sebastian Bach if all his fugues, cantatas, suites, and even the B Minor Mass, are added up. In a way he *invented* what we now call "modern" cricket. His national renown packed cricket grounds everywhere. He laid the foundations of county cricket economy. The sweep of his energy, his authority, and prowess, his personal presence, caused cricket to expand beyond a game. His bulk and stride carried cricket into the highways of our national life. He became a representative Victorian, a "father figure." People not particularly interested in cricket found the fact of "W.G.'s" eminence looming into their social consciousness. The Royal family (in those days too) inquired from time to time about his health – a formal request, because "W.G." was seldom, if ever, unwell. We must not remember him as the "Grand Old Man" of his closing years. He was an athlete, a champion thrower of the cricket ball, a jumper of hurdles. Yet, though I have seen portraits of him taken in early manhood, in his late teens in fact, I have never seen a portrait of a beardless "W.G." Is such a one in existence anywhere?

Ranjitsinhji wrote in his "Jubilee" book (or C. B. Fry wrote it for him) that "'W.G.' transformed the single stringed instrument into the many chorded lyre" which, translated, means that "W.G." elaborated batsmanship, combined back-and-forward play for the first time, and perfected the technique of "placing" the ball. When he began to play cricket, round-arm bowling had been the fashion for some thirty years. He inherited a technique formed from an obsolete attack and soon he was belabouring over-arm fast bowling at ease – often on rough wickets. He "murdered" the fastest stuff right and left.

He kept his left leg so close to the ball when he played forward that an old professional of the late 1900s told me (long after his retirement) that "W.G." "never let me see daylight between pads and bat. Ah used to try mi best to get 'im out on a good wicket, then suddenly summat 'give' in me, and we all knew it were hopeless." If "W.G." kept religiously to a rigid right foot in his batting, we must take it for granted, from the greatness he carved out of the game, that this principle suited all the needs and circumstances of cricket as he had to meet them. It is stupid to argue that he couldn't have scored heavily against bowlers of 1963. He mastered the bowling problems presented in *his* period. Logically, then, we can demonstrate that he would have mastered those of today.

"W.G.'s" mastery over speed compelled bowlers to think again. Thus, ironically, he was the cause of the first extensive developments of spin. A. C. M. Croome played with Grace (later he became cricket correspondent of *The Times*, one of the most learned). "The first season I saw Grace play", he wrote, "was 1876. In August he scored 318 v Yorkshire. Earlier in the week he had made 177 v Nottinghamshire, and on the previous Friday and Saturday 344 at Canterbury v Kent. He scored 1200 runs in first-class cricket during that month of August, yet he found time before September came to run up to Grimsby and score 400 not out for United South against twenty-two of the district. That would be a normal month for him if he could begin again today, knowing that even bowlers and wicket-keepers know now all about the 'second line of defence', and enjoy the advantages of true wickets, longer overs and shorter boundaries."

He conquered the entire world and range of the game – 15 centuries v the Players, so that in 18 years of his reign the Players won only seven times. He scored 1,000 runs in May 1895, within two months of his 47th birthday, scored two hundreds in one match v Kent; took 17 wickets in one and the same match v Notts; and took all ten wickets in an innings v Oxford University. He was cricket of his period personified; he was one of the eminent Victorians; he had the large girth and humanity of the foremost Englishmen of his epoch. Nobody before him, nobody following greatly in his train, has loomed to his stature or so much stood for cricket, or done as richly for it.

SIR J. B. HOBBS

Sir Jack is the only cricketer of whom we might fairly say that he directly descended from "W.G." fully-armed, like Jove. It was Hobbs who first challenged the "Old Master's" primacy as Centurion, passing his record of 126 hundreds, and going as far as 197 in first-class cricket. He commanded in his earliest years a technique inherited from "W.G." and his period, adding to it the strokes and protective method evolved from having to cope with the more or less "modern" swinging and "googly" attack. It is not generally realised that Hobbs learned to bat in an environment of technique and procedure very much like those in which "W.G." came to his high noon. The attack which Hobbs as a young man had to face day-by-day was more or less concentrated on the off-stump or just outside it. Bowlers were allowed to use only one ball through a team's innings; as a consequence they were obliged to make the best possible use of an old one by means of spin, variations of length, pace and direction, or by sheer pace. Only a few were developing back of the hand trickery in the early 1900s – Bosanquet, Vine of Sussex and Braund were three of these.

Yet in 1907 when South Africa sent a team to England containing at least four back-of-the-hand spinners – Vogler, Faulkner, Gordon White and Schwarz – Hobbs, then aged 24 and a half, was able to find the answer to the new "witchery" (as the old cricketers called it then) and teach the remedy to others. Hobbs was, of course, not the only batsman to demonstrate how the "googly" should be played. Johnny Tyldesley, Jessop, R. H. Spooner, Braund and George Gunn mastered it up to a point. But Hobbs gathered together in his method all the logical counters for the ball that "turned the other way". Moreover, on all sorts of pitches, fast, slow, "sticky" or matting, here or in Australia or in South Africa, even on the horrible spitting and kicking pitches of Melbourne after rain and hot sun, he asserted his mastery. Confronted by every manner of attack so far conceived and rendered practical by the mortal skill of bowlers in every kind of circumstance, in fine weather or foul, Hobbs reigned supreme. He must be named the Complete Batsman, the Master of all, a later "W.G." in fact.

His cricket extended from 1905 to 1934. He opened an innings for England when he was within four months of his 48th birthday. In his career he scored 61,237 runs, average 50.65. Like "W.G." he added to the batsman's armour and so, by forcing the attack to resort to fresh ideas, he gave cricket a new twist. Pad play among the Victorians was not done. It was a "caddish professional, don't you know, from Nottinghamshire, named Arthur Shrewsbury", who began to exploit pads as a second line of defence. Hobbs seldom, until towards the end, used pads merely obstructively. He perfected footwork which brought the batsman not only to the line of the ball, spin or swerve, but behind it.

We can divide the reign of Hobbs into two periods, each different in general method from the other. Before the war of 1914 he was quick on the attack on swift feet, strokes all over the field, killing but never brutal, with no strength wasted or strained, most of the strokes governed by the wrists, after the body's balance had provided the motive power. After the resumption of cricket in 1919, when he was moving towards his 37th birthday, he entered his second period, and cut out some of his most daring strokes. He ripened to a classic. His style became as serenely-poised as any ever witnessed on a cricket field, approached only by Hammond (another great player I have been obliged to omit from my Six!). The astonishing fact about Hobbs is that of the 130 centuries to his name in county cricket, 85 were scored after the war of 1914-18; that is, after he had entered "middle-age". From 1919 to 1928 his seasons' yields were as follows – the more his years increased, the more he harvested:

1919	2,594 runs, average 60.32
1920	2,827 runs, average 58.89
1921	321 runs, average 78.00
	(a season of illness)
1922	2,552 runs, average 62.24
1923	2,087 runs, average 37.38
1924	2,098 runs, average 58.16
1925	3,024 runs, average 70.32
1926	2,949 runs, average 77.60
1927	1,641 runs, average 52.93
1928	2,542 runs, average 82.00

From his 43rd to his 48th birthday Hobbs scored some 11,000 runs, averaging round about the sixties. Yet he once said that he would wish to be remembered for the way he batted before 1914. "But, Jack", his friends protested, "you got bags of runs after 1919." "Maybe", replied Hobbs, most modest of cricketers, "but they were nearly all made off the back foot."

His baptism to first-class cricket happened under the eye of and in the actual presence of "W.G." – on Easter Monday, 1905, at Kennington Oval in a match between Surrey and the Gentlemen of England. He made 18 in his first innings, tieing with Ernest Hayes for top-score. Next innings, his genius announced itself plainly: 88 in two hours. Next morning *The Times* ventured a prophecy: Hobbs had done well enough "to justify the belief that he will prove a useful addition to the Surrey XI".

The truth about his career cannot be emphasised too often. In every changing circumstance of the game, on every sort of pitch, against every form of bowling as it developed during the quarter of a century of his mastery, he went his way, calmly in control, never arrogant, full of the spring and pride of early manhood, then quietly enjoying the ripeness that is all. Twice he asserted his command on difficult turf, with the Australians hungry for a victory close at hand. Twice, with Herbert Sutcliffe, he frustrated them – at The Oval in 1926, and at Melbourne in 1928. At Melbourne, England needing 332 to win, were trapped on a Melbourne "gluepot". The general idea in the crowd and amongst cricketers was that England would do well to scrape or flash 80 or so all out. The score was 105 for one when Hobbs was leg-before. The match was won by England, Sutcliffe 135. And Hobbs was the architect.

We nearly lost him in 1921. He was attacked by acute appendicitis during the Test match v Australia at Leeds. He was rushed to the operating table. The celebrated surgeon, Sir Berkeley (later Lord) Moynihan, told Hobbs afterwards, "You couldn't have lived five hours."

I never saw him make an uneducated stroke. When he misjudged the nature of a ball he could, naturally enough, make the wrong right stroke. He not only enlarged and subtilised the art of batsmanship; he, like "W.G." widened and strengthened cricket's appeal and history. He was in his 44th year, let us remember, when he passed "W.G.'s" roll of 126 centuries. The game will retain the image of him in its Hall of Fame – the twiddle of his bat before he bent slightly, to face and look at the attack; the gentle accurate to-an-inch push for a single to get off the mark, the stroke so nicely timed that he could, had he wished, have walked it. The Trumperesque Hobbs of the pre-1914-19 days, lithe, but his slender physique, concentrated and yet graceful! Then the vintage Hobbs, the "Master" of our time, biding his own, and often getting himself out as he reached his hundred.

Every honour that the game – and the nation – could bestow came to him, not the least of all, in lasting value, the pride and affection of cricketers the world over.

TOM RICHARDSON

I choose Richardson as one of my Six, not on the supposition that he was the greatest fast bowler of the century, though certainly he was in the running. I take him as the fully-realised personification of the fast bowler as every schoolboy dreams and hopes he might one day be himself. Richardson was, in his heyday, a handsome, swarthy giant, lithe, muscular, broad of shoulder, and of apparently inexhaustible energy. He bowled fast, with a breakback obtained by body action and the swing of the upper part over the left leg at the moment of release, the right hand sweeping away nearly at a right angle to the line of flight. He could bring the ball back inches on Sam Apted's most heavily-rolled grassless stretch of turf. Herbert Strudwick loves to tell how when he first kept wicket for Surrey, Richardson pitched a very fast one rather outside the off-stump. Strudwick moved, naturally enough, towards the off, in anticipation. But the ball, beating the bat, just missed the leg-stump and went for four byes – to Strudwick's excusable amazement.

Richardson didn't "go in" for swing or seam refinements. In his period it wasn't possible for any fast bowler to do so. Only one and the same ball was at his service during the batting side's longest innings. Moreover, the seam of a cricket ball wasn't as pronounced in Richardson's day as it is in ours. We need to bear in mind this fact – that Richardson had to get through most of his thousand overs a season using an "old ball".

In the four summers of 1894-97 he bowled some five thousand eight hundred overs and – take your breath – took 1,005 wickets:

		Overs	Runs	Wickets	Average
1894	..	936.3	2,024	196	10.32
1895	..	1690.1	4,170	290	14.37
1896	..	1656.7	4,015	246	16.32
1897	..	1603.4	3,945	273	14.45

Between the English seasons of 1894 and 1895 he bowled, in Australia, 3,554 balls, taking 69 wickets at 23.42 each; and after his haul of 273 wickets at home in 1897 (and his 1,600 overs), he went to Australia again and, bowled at last to his knees, took only 54 wickets, average 29.51.

Yet on his return to England the great giant achieved an herculean revival, his season's plunder amounting to 161 wickets, average 19.54, in more than twelve hundred overs. All done, remember, or nearly all, with a seamless ball.

In his career, extending from 1892 to 1905, his performances, in statistics, work out at 2,105 wickets, average 18.42, from nearly 16,000 overs. He, like most fast bowlers of the 1890s, was expected in dry weather to bowl all day, or the better part of it. Fast bowlers of the 1890s shared the White Man's burden in hot weather, and were given rest (now and again) when the rain swamped the ground so much that they couldn't stand up. Wickets were not covered in the 1900s. At Old Trafford, in 1902, when Victor Trumper scored a century before lunch, Lockwood was unable to bowl or get a foothold until mid-afternoon. He then came on and took six for 48.

Lockwood, of course, opened the Surrey county attack with Richardson. Ranjitsinhji maintained that Lockwood was the more dangerous fast bowler of the two. "On a good wicket Tom's speed and breakback needed watching, but I knew what was coming. With Lockwood I had to keep awake for his slower ball." Lockwood was temperamental, an artist, moody. One day his fires were sullen and slow. Batsmen played him with impunity – poor innocents, cultivating their gardens on the slopes of a Vesuvius, which next day erupted.

In Australia, Lockwood was a dead failure – his Test figures for his only rubber in Australia were 124.5 overs, 31 maidens, 340 runs, five wickets. But in Australia, under the hottest suns experienced there during the century, Richardson's labours were heroic, unparalleled. Today they would probably be considered servile. In the service of Stoddart's team of 1894-95, in five Test matches he bowled more than 300 five-ball overs for 849 runs and 26 wickets. At Sydney, December 1894, when Australia scored 586, Richardson sweated and toiled for 53 overs for five wickets and 181 runs.

The greatest of his lion-hearted endeavours was at Manchester in the Test match there of 1896. He bowled 68 five-ball overs in Australia's first innings of 412. On the third and last day, Australia needed 125 to win – England having "followed on". Richardson nearly won the match. For three hours he attacked without an over's rest, taking six of the seven wickets which fell before Australia scraped home. A missed catch frustrated Richardson at the pinch. His devotion – and his will-power and stamina – is faintly indicated by his figures for the match:

110 overs 3 balls, 39 maidens, 244 runs, 13 wickets.

The one favour granted to Richardson, but hardly a compensation for bondage to an "old" ball – was the pace of the wickets he bowled on; they usually had a certain hardness and resilience. Strudwick, again, is witness; he tells that often he had to "take" Richardson standing back to him, of course, and standing "pretty well" high up, near his "middle". Richardson seldom, if ever, "bounced" a ball deliberately. He was a good-natured soul, loving a pint of ale and a good laugh at the long day's end.

In Richardson's period, bowlers exploited off theory on hard, dry pitches, hardly a fieldsman on the other side of the wicket excepting mid-on. When I was a small boy I saw J. T. Tyldesley pull square a short ball from Richardson, the only loose one on a scorching sun-streamed afternoon. The stroke dropped short of the boundary, was retrieved an inch or two from the edge and thrown back to the middle by – believe it or not – Richardson. The Surrey mid-on had seen the ball pass him and was content to "let it go". Richardson who had been attacking with his long striding run for hours had thought differently.

He was indeed the ideal fast bowler, aiming at the stumps, always on the attack. Never did he send down a defensive ball. He would have been too proud.

"He tried," A. C. MacLaren told me, "to get a wicket every ball. Honest Tom!" Let us remember him by those two words of MacLaren's tribute – "Honest Tom."

VICTOR TRUMPER

It is futile to ask "who was the greatest batsman?" There are different orders of greatness. Talent, even genius, is conditioned by the material circumstances in which it is developed. Victor Trumper was the embodiment of gallantry as he made his runs. He was a chivalrous batsman, nothing mean or discourteous in any of his movements or intentions at the wicket. "He had no style," wrote C. B. Fry of him, "but he was all style." But the most handsome compliment ever made to him, or to any other cricketer, was A. C. MacLaren's: "I was supposed to be a batsman of the Grand Manner. Compared to Victor I was as a cab-horse to a Derby winner."

His stance was relaxed, but watchful, a panther ready to spring. Yet this panther simile suggests a certain cruelty and hungriness. Trumper scored his runs generously, as though out of an abundance of them in his possession. He, so to say, *donated* runs over the field, bestowing them like precious jewels to us, to the crowd, to the bowlers even. He wasn't, as Bradman, was, a "killer". His strokes didn't stun or insult a bowler. I have seen bowlers applaud the glory of Trumper's strokes; he put them, with the rest of us, under an enchantment. Do I exaggerate? I confess that whenever I write about Trumper I am in danger of exhausting a store of superlatives. So I'll be content for the moment to quote from the formal and restrained prose of the "MCC's Cricket Scores and Biographies":

"For Trumper the English season of 1902 was a triumphal progress, and those who were fortunate to witness his amazing brilliance will never be able to forget the unrivalled skill and resource he displayed. On 'sticky' wickets he hit with freedom, whilst everybody else were puddling about the crease, unable to make headway and content if they could keep up their wickets."

The season of 1902 was the spin-bowler's dream of heaven. Rain and hot sun day by day. Wickets uncovered. When the pitch dried the ball whipped in, whipped away, reared and kept low, changing direction and pace, sometimes startling the bowlers themselves. And in 1902 Trumper had to cope with the greatest spinners the game had so far evolved – Rhodes, Blythe, Haigh, Wass (fast from leg stump to the off), Walter Mead, J. T. Hearne, S. F. Barnes, to name a few. In this year of 1902 Trumper scored 2,570 runs, average 48.49, with eleven centuries. His rate of scoring was round about 40 an hour, and 1902 was his first experience of vicious English wickets, for in 1899, his first visit to this country, the summer had been dry.

In the upstairs tea-room at Kennington Oval hangs a photo of Victor showing him jumping out to drive, yards from the crease, bat aloft behind him, the left leg prancing like a charger's in the Bayeux tapestry. A certain England batsman, vintage 1950, looked at this picture in my company and said, "Was he really any good?" "Why do you ask?" was my natural question. "Well," said this International, "just look where he is – stumped by yards if he misses."

This sceptical England batsman had never in his life been so far out of his crease. But Trumper was stumped only once in all the 89 Test innings of his career. And only five times was he lbw.

Like Hobbs, he led the way to the counter-attack of the "googly" bowling, a new problem to harass batsmen of his period. In Australia, 1910-11, against the superb South African back-of-the-hand bowlers, such as Vogler, Schwarz, Pegler and Faulkner, his Test scores in the rubber were 27 (run out), 34, 159, 214 (not out), 28, 7, 87, 31 and 74 not out – 661 runs, average 94.42. Let me quote Jack Fingleton: "He teased Percy Sherwell, the South African captain. When a fieldsman was shifted, Trumper deliberately hit the next ball where the man had been . . . Later, somebody commiserated with Sherwell at having his captaincy and his fieldsmen torn to tatters while Trumper made 214. Whereupon Sherwell said, 'Ah, don't talk about it. We have seen batting today.'"

For six balls apparently alike in pitch, or pace or spin, Trumper could produce six different strokes. His footwork was quick, graceful and effortless. With the easiest swing of the bat he could drive an extraordinary distance. His cutting and his leg glancing were performed by wrists of rare flexibility. "He played a defensive stroke," wrote C. B. Fry, "as a last resort."

At Old Trafford, in 1902, A. C. MacLaren lost the toss for England on a slow wicket which, he knew, would turn difficult by mid-afternoon. Lockwood was unable to get a sure foothold until shortly before lunch. So MacLaren's plan was, as he himself put it, "to keep Victor quiet for an hour or two". Then, with the pitch developing tantrums, Australia could be disposed of at ease. MacLaren's reserve bowlers were Rhodes, F. S. Jackson, Tate and Braund, and they were ordered to operate defensively. "I set my field with the inner and outer ring," said MacLaren. Some of the best cricket brains and skill in England concentrated to "keep Victor quiet". At lunch Australia's score was 173 for one, Trumper a century.

So easily did Trumper bat, though his rate of scoring frequently equalled Jessop's, never for a moment did he make an impression of violence or hurry. His every movement was lovely to see. Against Victoria for New South Wales at Sydney, in 1905, on a bowler's wicket, he scored 101 out of 139 in fifty-seven minutes. On a Melbourne "gluepot", in 1904, he scored 74 out of Australia's all out total of 122 v England – England's bowlers being Rhodes (who took 15 wickets in the match for 124), Hirst, Relf and Braund. In 1913, playing in a match at Goulburn for the benefit of J. A. O'Connor, Australian Test cricketer, Victor scored 231 in ninety minutes. In 1899 he scored 300 not out v Sussex in five hours. In 1902 he scored 62 out of 80 in fifty minutes v England at Sheffield. His achievements in high-class "Grade" cricket in Sydney have become historic. For his team, Paddington, in 1897 and 1898, he averaged 204, with 1,021 runs, when he was only twenty years old.

These statistics, chosen at random, tell their tale. But not by counting Victor's runs, not by looking at any "records", will you get the slightest idea of Trumper's glorious cricket. You might as well count the notes of the music of Mozart.

He was sadly on his way to a fatal illness when he came to England in 1909, for the last time, but a flash of the dauntless Victor came out at The Oval in an innings for Australia of 73, scored against D. W. Carr (googly), Barnes, Woolley, Rhodes, and Sharp. And, as we have noted, his genius burnt in wonderful flame and colour against South Africa in Australia in 1910-11. But it was burning itself out. He died, only 37 years old, in June 1915; and the Sydney streets were packed with sorrowing crowds as the funeral passed by.

He was good-looking, clean-shaven (a rare and boyish thing in those days), weighing 12 stones, and 5 feet 10 inches of height. He was, as everybody vowed who came his way, even the bowlers, a quiet but delightful companion. The gods of cricket loved him, so he died young.

S. F. BARNES

Most cricketers and students of the game belonging to the period in which S. F. Barnes played were agreed that he was the bowler of the century. Australians as well as English voted him unanimously the greatest. Clem Hill, the famous Australian left-handed batsman, who in successive Test innings scored 99, 98, 97 v A. C. MacLaren's England team of 1901-2, told me that on a perfect wicket Barnes could swing the new ball in and out "very late", could spin from the ground, pitch on the leg stump and miss the off. At Melbourne, in December 1911, Barnes in five overs overwhelmed Kelleway, Bardsley, Hill and Armstrong for a single. Hill was cleaned bowled by him. "The ball pitched outside my leg stump, safe to the push of my pads, I thought. Before I could 'pick up' my bat, my off-stump was knocked silly."

Barnes was creative, one of the first bowlers really to use the seam of a new ball and combine "swing" so subtly with spin that few batsmen could distinguish one from the other. He made a name before a new ball was available to an attack every so many runs or overs. He entered first-class cricket at a time when one ball had to suffice for the whole duration of the batting side's innings.

He was professional in the Lancashire league when A. C. MacLaren, hearing of his skill, invited him to the nets at Old Trafford. "He thumped me on the left thigh. He hit my gloves from a length. He actually said, 'Sorry, sir!' and I said, 'Don't be sorry, Barnes. You're coming to Australia with me.'" MacLaren on the strength of a net practice with Barnes chose him for his England team in Australia of 1901-2. In the first Test of that rubber, Barnes took five for 65 in 35 overs, 1 ball, and one for 74 in 16 overs. In the second Test he took six for 42 and seven for 121 and he bowled 80 six-ball overs in this game. He broke down, leg strain, in the third Test and could bowl no more for MacLaren, who winning the first Test, lost the next four of the rubber.

Barnes bowled regularly for Lancashire in 1902, taking more than a hundred wickets in the season, averaging around 20. *Wisden* actually found fault with his attack this year, stating that he needed to cultivate an "off break". In the late nineties he had appeared almost anonymously in the Warwickshire XI.

Throughout his career he remained mysteriously aloof, appearing in the full sky of first-class cricket like a meteor – declaring the death of the most princely of batsmen! He preferred the reward and comparative indolence of Saturday league matches to the daily toil of the county tourney. Here is one of the reasons of his absence from the England XI between 1902 and 1907. He didn't go to Australia as one of P. F. Warner's team of 1903-4 and took no part of the 1905 England v Australia rubber. The future historian of cricket may well gape and wonder why, in the crucial Test of 1902, Barnes didn't play for England at Manchester, where the rubber went to Australia by three runs only.

Barnes had bowled for England at Sheffield in the third and previous Test, taking six for 49 and one for 50. It is as likely as conjecture about cricket ever can be likely that had Barnes taken part in the famous Manchester Test of 1902 England wouldn't have lost the rubber by a hair's breadth.

He was in those days not an easy man to handle on the field of play. There was a Mephistophelian aspect about him. He didn't play cricket out of any "green field" starry-eyed realism. He rightly considered that his talents were worth estimating in cash values. In his old age he mellowed, yet remained humorously cynical. Sir Donald Bradman argued that W. J. O'Reilly must have been a greater bowler than Barnes because he commanded every ball developed in Barnes's day – plus the "googly". I told Barnes of Bradman's remark, "It's quite true," he said, "I never bowled the 'googly.'" Then with a glint in his eye, he added, "I never needed it."

Against Australia he took 106 wickets, average 21.58. Only Trumble and Peel have improved on these figures in Tests between England and Australia (I won't count Turner's 101 wickets at 16.53 because he bowled in conditions not known to Barnes and Trumble). Barnes had no opportunities to pick up easy victims. He played only against Australia and South Africa and, in all Test matches, his haul was 189 at 16.43 each. On matting in South Africa when South Africa's batsmanship, at its greatest, was represented by H. W. Taylor, A. D. Nourse, L. J. Tancred, J. W. Zulch, in 1913-14, he was unplayable, with 49 wickets in Tests at 10.93 each.

Yet against this fantastically swinging, bouncing, late-turning attack, "Herbie" Taylor scored 508 runs, average 50.80, perhaps the most skilful of all Test performances by a batsman. He was a man of character (and still is). At Sydney on the 1911-12 tour, J. W. H. T. Douglas opened the England attack using the new ball with Frank Foster. Barnes was furious. He sulked as he sent down 35 overs for three wickets and 107 runs (in the match he took only four for 179). England lost by 146 runs.

At Melbourne, Australia batted first and Barnes this time had the new ball. We all know with what results. Australia suffered defeat – and also in the ensuing three games. The destruction wreaked by Barnes, and on all his great days, was mostly done by the ball which, bowled from a splendid height, seemed to swing in to the leg stump then spin away from the pitch, threatening the off-stump. Barnes has assured me that he actually turned the ball by "finger twist". The wonder of his career is that he took 77 of his 106 Australian Test wickets on the wickets of Australia when they were flawless and the scourge of all ordinarily good bowlers. He clean bowled Victor Trumper for 0 at Sydney in the 1907-8 rubber, then Fielder and J. N. Crawford in the following Test, dismissed Trumper for a "pair", so Trumper was out for 0 in three successive Test innings.

Barnes remained a deadly bowler long after he went out of first-class cricket. So shrewdly did he conserve his energy that in 1928 when he was in his mid-fifties, the West Indies team of that year faced him in a club match and unanimously agreed that he was the best they had encountered in the season.

For Staffordshire, in his fifty-sixth year, he took 76 wickets at 8.21 each. Round about this period a young player, later to become famous in International company, was one of the Lancashire Second XI playing against Staffordshire. His captain won the toss and the Lancashire lads went forth to open the innings against Barnes. As this colt was no. 6 in the batting order he put on his blazer and was about to leave the pavilion to watch Barnes "from behind". But his captain told him to go back to the dressing room and "get on his pads". "But," said the colt, "I'm not in until number six and I'd like to look at Barnes." His captain insisted. The young colt returned to the dressing room. "And there", he said "there were four of us all padded up waiting. And we were all out in the middle and back again in half an hour."

Barnes had a splendid upright action, right arm straight over. He ran on easy strides, not a penn'orth of energy wasted. He fingered a cricket ball sensitively, like a violinist his fiddle. He always attacked. "Why do these bowlers today send down so many balls the batsman needn't play?" he asked while watching a Test match a few years ago. "I didn't. I never gave 'em any rest." His hatchet face and his suggestion of physical and mental leanness and keenness were part of Barnes's cricket and outlook on the game. He was relentless, a chill wind of antagonism blew from him on the sunniest day. As I say, he mellowed in full age and retirement. He came to Lord's for Test matches heading for his ninetieth year, leading blind Wilfred Rhodes about.

As we think of the unsmiling destroyer of all the batsmen that came his way, let us also remember Barnes immortalised in that lovely verse of Alan Ross:

"Then, elbows linked, but straight as sailors
On a tilting deck, they move. One, square-shouldered as a tailor's
Model, leans over whispering in the other's ear;
'Go easy, Steps here. This end bowling'
Turning, I watch Barnes guide Rhodes into fresher air,
As if to continue an innings, though Rhodes may only play by ear."

SIR DONALD BRADMAN

Sir Donald Bradman (hereinafter to be named Bradman or "The Don"), must be called the most masterful and prolific maker of runs the game has so far known. He was, in short, a great batsman. Critics have argued that he was mechanical. So is a majestically flying aeroplane. The difference between Bradman and, say, Victor Trumper as batsmen, was in fact the difference between an aeroplane and a swallow in flight. But it is nonsense to say that Bradman's batsmanship was without personality or character, or nature, or that it was in the slightest anonymous. He had a terrifically dynamic style. It was thrilling to see him gathering together his energy at the last second to hook, a stroke somehow reminding me of a boxer's swinging stunning "right".

Like all great players, he made his strokes very late. He didn't move at all until the ball was on him; then the brilliant technique shot forth concentrated energy – and the axe fell. All the strokes were at his command. After he had appeared almost for the first time in an Australian State match, J. V. Ryder, Australian captain, was asked, "How does this young Bradman bat?" And Ryder, a man of few but eloquent words, replied: "He belts the hell out of everything he can reach."

Bradman's achievements stagger the imagination. No writer of boys' fiction would dare to invent a "hero" who performed with Bradman's continual consistency. Nobody would even suspend disbelief as he read such fiction. Between 1927 and 1948 he scored 28,067 runs. (The war interrupted his genius at its high noon.) In his career as cricketer he scored these 28,067 runs with an average of 95.14, an average "for life" twice as high as that of most other master batsmen. He made 117 centuries in 338 innings, forty-three times not out – a century every third time he walked to the wicket. He scored 6,996 runs in Test matches, average 99.94. He scored 1,000 runs between April 30 and May 31 in an English season. He scored 1,000 runs in a season sixteen times. He scored 974 runs in one and the same rubber v England. He scored a triple Test match century – 309 – in a day. He scored 13 centuries in the English season of 1938. He scored six centuries in consecutive innings. He hit thirty runs in one over. He scored two centuries in the same Test match v India.

Moreover, I think he knew at the time that he was about to do these extraordinary things; for he planned everything. No cricketer has had a quicker, shrewder brain than Bradman's. At Leeds in 1934, Australia bowled England out on a beautiful turf for 200. Then, at the afternoon's fall, Australia lost three wickets for 39. That evening Bradman cancelled dinner with me, saying he was going to bed early as, next day, it would be necessary for him to score 200 "at least!" I reminded him that on his previous Test appearance at Leeds, in 1930, he had scored 334. "The law of averages is against you pulling-off another big score here tomorrow in a Test," I said. He replied: "I don't believe in the law of averages." Next day he set about scoring 304.

The extraordinary point of this innings is that until this Leeds Test, Bradman had battled in the rubber with a certain lack of concentration, as though the effects of the Jardine-Larwood "body-line" assaults on him of 1932-33 were still shaking him. At Nottingham and Lord's, he played fast bowling with a rhetorical slash, a quite wild impetuosity. Now, at Leeds, in a serious hour for Australia, he could summon back at one call the old cool, premeditated craft and foresight.

I asked him once, in Melbourne, to give me some idea of how he did it all. "Every ball for me is the first ball," then, he added, taking away my breath, "and I never think there's a possibility of anybody getting me out."

The critics say he couldn't bat on a turning pitch. Hedley Verity held the opposite opinion – from experience. It is a fact, though, that "The Don" seemed occasionally not to face up to a "sticky" pitch, *on principle*. He argued that wickets should be covered from rain, especially in his own country. It wasn't fair that a side should bat in perfect run-getting conditions one day. Then next day, the other side could be trapped on a spitting pitch.

Bradman had all the attributes needed to cope with the spinning, kicking ball – swift feet, and an eye rapid and comprehensive. Against Larwood's devastating "body-line" attack, dangerous to breastbone and skull, Bradman in the Tests scored 396 runs, average 56.57. Jardine reduced his powers temporarily by half; but no other mortal batsman could have coped with Larwood as Bradman coped with him. In spite of Larwood's velocity and menace – seven fieldsmen on the leg- or on-side – Bradman was driving or punching to the vacant off-side, bowling coming like lightning from a spot on or outside the leg stump, often rising shoulder high.

He first came to England in 1930, twenty-one years old. He began at Worcester with 236 in four and half hours, twenty-eight boundaries. To Leicester he proceeded, to score 185 not out. Then, on the soft wicket v Yorkshire, he scored 78. And a newspaper placard announced, "Bradman fails". It was in 1930 that he exhibited, I think, the most wonderful batsmanship of his life, when during the Lord's Test match he came to the wicket after Ponsford had got out. In two hours and forty minutes before half-past six, he cut, drove and hooked the England attack, to the tune of 155. J. C. White, the untouchable, was brought on immediately to keep "The Don" quiet. White's first ball, a good length, was slapped to the on-boundary, near the clock at the Nursery. Bradman leaped yards out of his crease; and the crack of his bat sent the Lord's pigeons flying in affrighted circles.

It was at Lord's, in 1938, during the MCC v Australians match that the effervescent J. W. A. Stephenson, a splendid opening bowler, appealed for lbw against Bradman, and Bradman had not yet got into double figures. Stephenson leapt skywards as he appealed. The "near thing" was negatived. If the reply had been in the affirmative, I imagine Stephenson would have been the first into and beyond the "barrier". Bradman went on to amass 278. He was ruthless. None the less, he didn't ever fail to respond to a bowler's challenge.

Nobody ever saw Bradman show mercy to a loose ball. If he went on the defensive, there was good reason. At Trent Bridge, in 1938, Australia followed-on after they had scored 411 in response to England's 658 for eight (declared). McCabe made history with a marvellous and gallant 232. But the pitch grew dusty and the closing day had a severe ordeal waiting for Bradman. Early that day Bradman wrote home to the young lady he was later to marry, telling her that a job of work had to be done, but, he guessed, all would have turned out well for Australia long before his letter reached her. Bradman then set forth to Trent Bridge and saved the day by batting nearly six hours.

Never, as I say, did he play with sterile negation. He was a Test cricketer of our contemporary temper, realistic and without cant. He reacted to the environment in which he found himself. He hadn't to play, as Trumper was obliged to play, in this country, in games limited to three days. If he didn't throw his wicket away as Trumper frequently did on reaching his hundred, the reason was that he played in a different economy of the game than Trumper ever knew. If and when Bradman stayed at the wicket all day he not only put his team in a position pretty secure from defeat but into a position from which the Australian bowlers could attack, with time to bring in victory, also he was holding the crowd in thrall.

He was a born batsman, out of a remote part of his beloved Australia, never coached academically; consequently he was free to give rein to his innate and rare gifts. He was born, too, with a good brain. Nobody has excelled Bradman's "cricket sense", his intuitions and understanding. He must be counted among Australia's cleverest, most closely calculating cricket captains.

After he had scored a triple century on a warm day at Leeds in 1930, he came from the field apparently cool, no sign of perspiration, not a buckle out of place, flannels immaculate, and, as the crowd roared him home, he seemed withdrawn and impersonal. People said that he lacked emotion. Maybe he was content to be the cause of "emotion" in others – in bowlers, for example. "Stripped to the truth", wrote Robertson-Glasgow, in a brilliant appreciation of Bradman in *Wisden*, "he was a solitary man with a solitary aim". Personally I have found in Sir Donald plenty of friendliness and humour. But, then, I was never called on to bowl or play cricket against him! Discussing him entirely from the point of view of a writer on the game, I am happy to say that he was for me a constant spur to ideas. A newspaper column couldn't contain him. He was, as far as a cricketer can be, a genius.

THE COUNTY CHAMPIONSHIP IN THE WISDEN CENTURY [1963]

By Rowland Bowen

The first year of *Wisden* – 1864 – saw also the first mention of a County Champion in the regular series. It does not matter that this was not a strictly contemporary reference – it occurred twenty-three years later when Surrey were again Champions; the earliest contemporary reference was in December 1866 when the Nottinghamshire Committee referred to their team's doings in 1865. It is no coincidence that the first of the long list of County Champions and the commencement of *Wisden* should date from the same year, for both sprang from the same cause.

There had been a steadily increasing interest in cricket over the whole kingdom from the end of the Napoleonic wars. With the rise of public interest in the game there was naturally an increase in county cricket, for, almost from the start of recorded match results, the county had been the accepted competitive unit for good-class cricket.

Even before the end of the 18th century we find occasional references to county cricket clubs in and around the chalk and homeland of cricket. After peace came, we find such clubs springing up all over these islands, in England, in Scotland, in Ireland and in Wales. How representative of their counties in the modern sense some of these clubs may have been we cannot now confidently state, though in a few cases we can be sure that they would have fully matched our modern, and somewhat different standards.

The playing standard in the more representative clubs helped to raise that of the others and, in turn, caused them to become more representative. The more remote counties came to play their neighbours, and others even more distant, and as communications became easier, they no longer confined themselves to matches against leading teams within their own borders.

In the 1840s, we find the great cricket annuals appearing, and in 1846 the first of the great touring teams organised by William Clarke, followed in 1852 by the second, formed by John Wisden himself. The boom in cricket was already on, and these two teams cashed in on it heavily and, by bringing players of the highest class to remote towns and villages, increased yet further the interest in the game and the standard of play.

By the early 1860s, the task of the great touring teams was substantially done, though their successors survived until 1883. Most of the counties now considered first class had been established and, more or less, in the form in which we now find them.

Even earlier than the 1860s there had been references to Champions – the first was to Nottinghamshire, somewhat early in the season, in May 1853 – to County Champions, or to a County Championship – it is interesting that the latter term was first used in connection with a proposed knock-out competition in 1855. The idea of designating some county as the Champions was certainly in the air; of course, a team may well be so dubbed without engaging in any actual or organised competition, but simply on its own playing merit, and it is clear that this is how the earlier Champions were acclaimed.

It was into this world that *Wisden* was born – a world in which the baby, when full grown, was to play a leading and sometimes decisive part. That same year (1864) saw another cricket annual which lasted but one issue: it was a foretaste of what *Wisden* itself was to become, but was far too early on the scene.

The increase in fixtures between counties, and especially between a few strong counties, gradually led to the sporting press collating the results and showing a table of positions: the dubbing of one successful county was no longer sufficient – people wanted to know how the counties stood in relation to each other. *Wisden* tended at this period to follow rather than to lead – the first mention of a Champion we find in *Wisden* is Yorkshire in the 1871 edition (p. 92) and it was not until the 1889 issue that we find a table, though such tables had appeared long before in other annuals. Differences of playing standards and the logic of fixture list lengths led soon to a positive differentiation between the "accepted" or "great" (i.e. the first class) counties and the rest. Yet this differentiation was flying in the face of MCC "who recognise no classification of counties; all counties are equal" as Haygarth recorded even so late as the early 1880s, and as, indeed, the counties themselves said in December 1884. Less than twelve months later the second class counties had recognised the true state of affairs by convening a meeting to discuss their own problems in November 1885.

With the edition of 1887, C. F. Pardon succeeded to the editorship of *Wisden* and almost with his very first issue raised the *Almanack* from merely being somewhat better than its contemporaries to a new exalted position where it earned the title of "The Cricketers Bible". Pardon had his own clear ideas about the classification of counties and organised competitions, and he did not hesitate to put them forward; they were somewhat better than those of the abortive Cricket Council of the late 1880s because they were pragmatic and based rather on county cricket as he knew it than on some cut-and-dried, but unworkable and unlikeable ideal scheme.

As a result of a meeting in December 1889, we find a properly recognised second-class county championship, which lasted until the end of 1893. By now the only recognition needed for the first-class competition was that of MCC itself. This came in October 1894, the year when five counties were raised to first class status. As a result, the old second class competition fell apart, and in December of the same year, the Minor Counties Competition was formed; it had only five years to wait for MCC's recognition – the major counties had waited thirty.

Elsewhere in Great Britain, the Scottish Counties Championship was formed in 1902, and the North Wales County Cricket Association by 1907. From that time onward there have been four distinct competitions (allowing for interruptions due to wars), and though no Scottish county has competed outside its own competition (there is no reason why they should not) there has been a fair degree of mobility between the other three competitions. Worcestershire, Northamptonshire and Glamorgan all moved up from the Minor Counties competition, into which Denbighshire for a while moved, but finally withdrew to the more relaxed atmosphere of Colwyn Bay. In 1959, a fresh competition was organised for the second elevens of first class counties, but several of them have dropped out and others now confine themselves to the more strictly regulated Minor Counties competition.

Considering county cricket, and specially county championship matters, rather than cricket in its wider appeal, what have been the most important changes in these one hundred years? In the beginning, the emphasis was on winning (even if put negatively, the champions being generally chosen on the basis of fewest matches lost). In certain years this led to inequitable results and other criteria were applied, but finally it was realised that the system in force showed too little difference between a draw and a victory – or between a draw and a loss. A more suitable difference was adopted officially by the counties at the end of 1889, but later pressure increased to apportion merit in drawn matches and the system used by the Minor Counties – adopted solely to offset the unfortunate effects of weather on their shorter two-day games – was imported into first-class cricket in 1911. *Wisden* said on this: "Personally I was opposed to the plan of giving points on the first innings in drawn games but I think it led to more interesting play. The most important result of the new system was that Warwickshire carried off the Championship. Under any of the old methods, Kent would have come out first and even as it was they only lost by a fraction."

Ever since, there has been a conscious or unconscious movement away from first innings points; first of all there was a reapportioning of points in a drawn game, and then there was a gradual increase in the difference between the number of points awarded for a drawn game and those for a victory, and then, more recently, "bonus" points have been awarded for a faster first innings lead.

Over the years, then, the competition has witnessed the fundamental irreconcilability of rewarding a victor appropriately and of apportioning merit in a drawn match.

There has been a parallel development in the qualifications for players. Since some had been playing for two or even three counties, stringent qualification rules for those appearing in county cricket were drawn up and finally adopted in July 1873 – by these rules MCC first recognised something special about county cricket, though not for nearly a generation, the championship itself. *Wisden* said in the 1874 issue: "The practical result was that three players played against their native counties, two against their residential counties, and one county eleven was formed by men in five different counties."

From the time of their adoption these rules have been subject to gradual whittling down and amendment: in the beginning they applied to all county cricket (the idea of a "friendly" between counties was absurd to our great grandparents) and even as late as 1889 there was an appeal to MCC concerning a county not at that time considered first class.

Now anyone may play for a county in a "friendly" and we have even reached the stage where, in the second eleven competition, a player needs no sort of qualification at all. Even in the first eleven, a player may transfer from one county, with few exceptions, with only a winter intervening. The filling up of mediocre county teams with even more mediocre players discarded from stronger county elevens is beyond question one of the factors leading to modern dreary cricket.

Thus as the *Wisden* century comes to an end, we see some signs of the wheel turning full circle: there were only a few "great" counties one hundred years ago and, if we look at the century objectively, we see that there have been only a few all the way through. Of all the first class counties now playing there are only three which attract large crowds to the grounds they visit (always excepting Bank Holiday matches) and the rest are very far behind. A further contraction in "great" matches would be no bad thing for cricket in the coming century.

SOME PRINCIPAL DATES IN COUNTY CRICKET

First mention of a county playing: Kent in 1718 (or, arguably, 1719).

First inter-county match: Surrey v Middlesex, June 1730.

First mention of a county cricket club: Oxfordshire, 1787. (In Ireland, the earliest were Carlow, 1829; and Kilkenny before 1830; in Wales, Pembrokeshire, 1830; in Scotland, Lanarkshire, by 1835).

First inter-county match in Wales: Breconshire v Monmouthshire, 10th August 1825.

First inter-county match in Scotland: East Lothian v Stirling County, 7th August 1851.

Earliest known printed county cricket club annual with scores: Shropshire, 1865.

Earliest known commercially printed county cricket annual: Nottinghamshire – Spibey's Annual Register, 1878.

First published history of a county cricket club: Derbyshire, 1897.

First history of County Cricket Championship: R. S. Holmes, January 1893.

The oldest county cricket club year-book still in continuous publication comes from Kent, first issued 1877.

DATES OF FORMATION OF COUNTY CLUBS NOW FIRST CLASS

County As hitherto accepted	First known county organisation	Present Club	
		Original date	Reorganisation, if substantial
Derbyshire 1870	November 4, 1870	November 4, 1870	—
Essex[a] 1864-5, dissolved 1866, re-formed 1876 and 1886	1830	January 14, 1876	—
Glamorgan 1888-9	1864	July 6, 1888	—
Gloucestershire[b] 1871	November 3, 1863	1871	—
Hampshire[c] 1863	April 3, 1849	August 12, 1863	July, 1879
Kent[d] 1859, re-formed 1870	August 6, 1842	March 1, 1859	December 6, 1870
Lancashire[e] 1864	January 12, 1864	January 12, 1864	—
Leicestershire[f] 1873	By August, 1820	March 25, 1879	—
Middlesex[g] 1864	December 15, 1863	December 15, 1863	—
Northamptonshire[h] About 1843, re-formed 1878	1820	1820	July 31, 1878
Nottinghamshire[j] 1859	March/April, 1841	March/April, 1841	December 11, 1866
Somerset[k] 1875, reorganised 1885	October 15, 1864	August 18, 1875	—
Surrey 1845	August 22, 1845	August 22, 1845	—
Sussex[l] 1836, re-formed 1839 and 1857	June 16, 1836	March 1, 1839	August, 1857
Warwickshire[m] 1863-4, re-formed 1882	May, 1826	January 19, 1884	—
Worcestershire 1865	1844	March 5, 1865	—
Yorkshire[n] 1863	March 7, 1861	January 8, 1863	December 10, 1891

N.B. – No attempt has been made in this list to give the dates of the first matches played by the respective counties; these, in many cases antedated a county club by up to 100 years, and in a few cases, even longer.

NOTES

[a] There is no evidence to support an alleged reorganisation in 1886.

[b] Gloucestershire were formed some time after March 14, 1871, on the demise of the Cheltenham & County of Gloucester CC and before the end of November that year.

[c] Although the club was in suspense during part of 1879, it never actually ceased to exist and there is complete continuity of officials from 1863 to the present time.

[d] In 1870 the Kent Club amalgamated with the old Beverley, Kent Club.

[e] The Manchester CC sponsored the formation of the County Club with whom it shared officials, and in which it was itself in due course merged; before the County club came into existence the Manchester CC made itself responsible for many Lancashire county matches.

[f] There is some doubt whether the 1820 club was a true Leicestershire Club and it may be there was not such a thing before September 1835 from which time there is no doubt.

[g] Though the date 1864 is commonly given, the actual meeting to convene a Middlesex Club was as given now; there had been several earlier abortive attempts to form a Middlesex Club.

[h] 1820 is a date provided by one authority for a Northamptonshire Club and is by no means impossible though it is likely that, at that date, it was not a true county club; that title came to it over the years, most probably before 1843 when Earl Spencer was first elected President. There is complete continuity all the way through to the reorganisation of 1878.

[j] The date hitherto given for Nottinghamshire is undoubtedly erroneous – for a full discussion see *The Cricketer*, June 9, 1962.

[k] There is no evidence for any special reorganisation in 1885. The 1864 club was based on Yeovil and may not have lasted much after 1865.

[l] What was formed in 1836 was a Sussex Match Fund, not a county club; it handed its functions over to the newly formed club in 1839.

[m] In 1826 the Wellbourne CC called itself the Warwickshire CC but later reverted to its earlier name. In early November 1863, it changed its name, this time to the Warwickshire CCC; this club, predominantly amateur and not truly representative of the county was re-formed in 1882 but dissolved in December 1883 to make way for the present Club.

[n] What was formed in 1861 was a Match Fund Committee which handed over to the Sheffield based and unrepresentative Yorkshire CCC in 1863, in which year another Yorkshire CCC was formed based on York. Another attempt at forming a representative county club in 1874 lasted only a few years, and it was not until the reorganisation of 1891 that the Sheffield-based club became truly representative.

THE UNIVERSITIES IN THE WISDEN CENTURY [1963]

By Robin Marlar
(Cambridge University captain, 1953)

Cricket at Oxford and Cambridge, "the two eyes of the country",* received scant attention in the first John Wisden *Cricketers' Almanack.* This stumpy son of Sussex was "no mug", as the Australians would say, either as cricketer or businessman. His first issue looked suspiciously like good advertising copy for professional cricket; particularly for the United England XI of which he was a founder member and, at that time, secretary. Only the Gentlemen and Players matches and the feats of the great peripatetic sides, the UEE and the All England XI, were given full treatment.

But in the second issue the Universities have pride of place over MCC and all the County XI's. From 1865 to 1885 the compiler varied the strength of his spotlight, sometimes giving the full scores and sometimes including them in an abbreviated form.

In 1885, the first introductory articles were included before the details of the Oxford and Cambridge matches. Oxford were given first billing because they had won the University Match of 1884, and once born this convention continued. So, too, did the articles and except for the four-year gap between 1916 and 1919 games in the Parks and at Fenner's have been fully chronicled ever since.

For this supreme service let there be Light and Dark Blue thanks.

Both University clubs had reached respectable middle age by 1864, the year of the first Almanack. The Oxford University Cricket Club was known in its early days as the Magdalen Club after its first benefactor, the Rev. H. Jenkins, Headmaster of the Magdalen Choir School. Between 1800 and 1805 he handed over an area of Cowley Common to the University cricketers.

The Cambridge club was founded in 1820 and it is clear from the earliest scorebooks that some of the matches were played on Parker's Piece, the precious plot which nurtured among others, cricket's "parfit, gentil knight", Jack Hobbs.

Originally both clubs were run by "treasurers". Cambridge had two in the first year but, subsequently, both clubs were administered by a triumvirate. The system evidently worked better at Cambridge than at Oxford. In 1839 the Oxford treasurers left it to each other to provide the 11th man for the side; in that year Cambridge beat ten of Oxford by an innings and 125 runs!

Cambridge were the first to move into a home which suited them. They rented the field they now own from F. P. Fenner in 1846. Fenner boasted that "you may put a stump where you will, measure 22 yards, and you can play a game on any part of the ground". However, there is evidence that Oxford refused to play there in the early days when one Cambridge captain was "knocked down senseless by a ball in the eye from young Lillywhite".

Fenner left Cambridge in 1861; Walter Watts took over the ground the following year and apart from an understandable lack of pace in April and May there have been few complaints since – at least not from batsmen. The present pavilion was built in 1877, largely thanks to the Rev. A. R. Ward, captain in 1854 and at that time President. A massive man – his chair remains as evidence – his idiosyncrasies included a daily breakfast of "noo-laid eggs, Noomarket sausages, salmon cutlets and champagne by Bollinger" and insistence that everyone should rhyme "bowl" with "howl". In 1892 the CUCC and the Athletic Club bought the ground, on hire purchase, from Gonville and Caius College on condition that it be "secured as an open space for ever".

THE PARKS AT OXFORD

When Cowley Common was sold by the Parish in the 1840s a number of Oxford Colleges established grounds there. The University bought the Magdalen Ground for

* Morley: *Life of Gladstone,* Vol. III, p. 486.

£2,000 at auction. But the ground was often flooded, though Oxonians regarded it as an excellent training ground because the pitches were not as good as those at Fenner's. In the mid-60s suggestions were made that the University Club and all the college clubs then playing on Cowley Common should move into the Parks. In 1881, after a petition to Convocation, supported enthusiastically by Dr Jowett, ten acres were leased *in perpetuum*. Professor Thomas Case, President of Corpus Christi College, moved mountains (and dons who tended to be bigger obstacles though less permanent ones) to acquire this superb site and it was he who planned the pavilion exactly the same distance from the wicket as at Lord's. The pitches in the Parks have varied infinitely more than those at Cambridge, but it would be a bigoted Cantab who claimed Fenner's as the better setting for a game of cricket.

The Universities first met at Lord's in 1827. Charles Wordsworth and Herbert Jenner had already played there in an Eton and Harrow match. Wordsworth was the son of a Master of Trinity College, Cambridge. With an academic father in one University and the other as his alma mater it was perhaps easier for him than for others to bring the two together on sporting occasions. In 1829, he organised the first boat race and rowed at Number Four. He badly blistered his hands and so it was perhaps hardly surprising that the next day he made 0 for the cricket team.* Later in the match he made history by becoming the first man to bag 'em in the match. Five out of the first 16 matches were played in Oxford (none in Cambridge) but from 1851 the match has always been part of the Lord's calendar.

At this stage it is important to repeat the distinction made by Mr Geoffrey Bolton in his admirable *History of the OUCC*. Amateur cricket was at its most brilliant in the Golden Age from 1870 until 1914, the year in which the Victorian world crashed in ruins. During that period the County Championship was growing in significance and in numbers and so, for that matter, was Test cricket. Thus cricketers were remembered not for their exploits at Manchester or Melbourne, but for the part they played in the University Match. In an age when intense competition was rare this match was an institution – as the Rugby match is today. To underline this point *Wisden* complained sadly that "only 11,462 paid gate-money on the first day" of the 1884 match.

FIFTY ENGLAND CAPTAINS

Differences of attitude or emphasis, such as this, are interesting but comparison of the game or of the skill of individuals in different generations is a futile exercise. However, the contribution made by University Blues to the cricket of County and Country is quite remarkable. A glance at the pinnacle proves the point. There have been 50 Captains of England in the history of Test cricket from 1876.

Four were professionals. Of the remainder, thirty won Blues: G. O. Allen, The Hon. Ivo Bligh, F. R. Brown, The Hon. F. S. G. Calthorpe, D. B. Carr, A. P. F. Chapman, M. C. Cowdrey, E. R. Dexter, F. L. Fane, R. E. Foster, C. B. Fry, A. E. R. Gilligan, A. H. H. Gilligan, Lord Harris, Lord Hawke, The Hon. F. S. Jackson, D. R. Jardine, A. O. Jones, H. D. G. Leveson Gower, F. G. Mann, F. T. Mann, P. B. H. May, Sir T. C. O'Brien, R. W. V. Robins, The Rev. D. S. Sheppard, Sir C. Aubrey-Smith, A. G. Steel, G. T. S. Stevens, Sir P. F. Warner, N. W. D. Yardley.

The list is astonishing testimony to the value of the University Clubs as a training ground for cricketing leadership. Other countries, too, have called on Blues as captains: T. C. Lowry (New Zealand), A. Melville and C. B. Van Ryneveld (South Africa), R. S. and G. C. Grant, F. C. M. Alexander (West Indies), A. H. Kardar and J. Burki (Pakistan), and perhaps most remarkable of all, the Nawabs of Pataudi, father and son (India).

Looking through the list of England captains it is clear that the last to achieve this honour without having to succumb to the discipline of six days cricket every week from April to September was G. O. Allen, who never captained his county but led England against India in 1936, MCC against Australia in 1936-37, and again in West Indies in

---

* In his history of the CUCC, W. J. Ford places the boat race *after* the cricket match.

1947-48. The selection of E. R. Dexter rather than D. S. Sheppard as captain of MCC last winter was cricket's Curzon case. The captain must belong to the mainstream of the game.

At the present time, therefore, a University player has to choose between cricket or some other career. This was not the case years ago in the days of early retirements, the Studds, the Ashtons, W. H. B. Evans whose "real heroes were Handel and William Pitt" and scores of others. The curious feature of University cricket since the second war is that very few men who had the ability to play cricket at the highest standard have, in fact, turned their backs on the game. Donnelly and Sheppard are the only post-war Blues of whom cricket lovers have seen too little since they were undergraduates.

Clearly the great University batsmen of the Golden Age were distinguished for their style *vis-à-vis* the professionals of their generation. Those of us who did not have the good fortune to see this cricket cannot really know what was this distinction. In modern times, there is less gaiety about the game, if we read the signs aright, and yet the great University batsmen of the 1950s still contrived to stand head and shoulders above their contemporaries. Sheppard, May, Cowdrey and Dexter all had, or have a grandeur quite lacking in other Englishmen of their generation. In each case this characteristic was apparent at University and May and Cowdrey began to exhibit it at school.

In University cricket the bowling, and occasionally the fielding, have fallen below the standard set by the batsmen. Mr H. S. Altham included an exhortation to University cricketers in the 1938 edition of his *History of Cricket*. "A University captain is entitled to demand the maximum effort in fielding from every member of his side . . . in this respect University XI's can fairly be expected to lead the way." Latterly fielding, which demands a high degree of concentration and specialisation close to the wicket, has been as difficult an activity to master as bowling, but University sides have usually contained some expert sprinters and throwers in the outfield. The name of C. E. Winn, the England Rugby three-quarter, comes to mind in the post-war generation.

In every decade a number of fast bowlers of the high class have broken into first-class cricket at the Universities, particularly at Cambridge. The line stretches from S. M. J. Woods to O. S. Wheatley, with A. E. R. Gilligan, G. O. Allen and K. Farnes holding centre stage. Furthermore, many of these men have been able to bat well enough to hold down a middle order place in the England XI: the Hon. F. S. Jackson and T. E. Bailey.

LE COUTEUR'S ALL-ROUND FEAT

P. R. Le Couteur, who hit 160 and took 11 Cambridge wickets in the match of 1910 when Cambridge made 189 in two innings and were beaten by an innings and 126 runs, was the first leg-break-googly bowler to run amok in the University Match. Since then I. A. R. Peebles, R. W. V. Robins, F. R. Brown and G. Goonesena have figured high amongst the list of wicket-takers for their Universities. But not many undergraduate spin bowlers have the accuracy of E. R. Wilson and it is here that the professional game has had the finer edge throughout. On the other hand the Universities have turned up some bowlers who have not fitted any conventional pattern, but who have passed the real tests as understood by that great judge A. V. Bedser – ability to get batsmen out: F. B. R. Browne, who bowled off the wrong foot, and A. R. Legard, whose leg-breaks were surprising on account of their pace and the bowler's action. Eccentricity has always been part of the University scene.

THE LONGEST PERMANENT FIXTURE

This year the University Match becomes the one first-class fixture with an unbroken annual history. Developments in cricket have their reflection in it. Two of them are particularly interesting: the attempt to discover and define a suitable delivery of the ball and changes in the Follow-on Law.

Scores in the early University Matches contain a staggering number of extras. There were 46 wides in the Cambridge total of 287 in 1839 and extras contributed three half-centuries to Cambridge and one to Oxford between 1836 and 1851. Bumpy grounds were partially responsible, of course, but when Law X was finally repealed in 1864, and over-arm bowling allowed, the number of extras declined sharply. So, too, did the significance of long stop, a vital position in the early days.

Within two decades of James Lillywhite's no-balling of Willsher the first throwing controversy had broken. As far as I can discover no University players were involved at that time but then, as now, Blues of former years played a major part in cricket administration. Lord Harris, Sir Pelham Warner once told me, was "very hot on throwing". The first University bowler to evoke startled cries was C. B. Fry, whose action was described in *Wisden* as "unfair". When the second, more severe, trouble occurred in the 1890s with Mold of Lancashire fulfilling the same role as had Crosland a few summers before, an Index of suspect actions was prepared and Fry's name was put on it.

Vigorous action at that time proved effective and there were only sporadic outbreaks of throwing until the 1950s. In 1951, C. N. McCarthy, a double jointed South African, came to England with Dudley Nourse's team and proved himself the fastest bowler in the world at that time. Frank Chester, England's leading umpire, saw him for the first time at Nottingham and wanted to call him in the first Test. At lunchtime on the first day he asked Sir Pelham Warner if he would be supported should he no-ball McCarthy; but he was not satisfied with the answers given and turned his back on the fast bowler for the rest of the game. Had that interview gone otherwise the throwing controversy of recent years might never have happened.

The following year McCarthy went up to Cambridge, and at Worcester P. Corrall, the old Leicestershire wicket-keeper, called McCarthy from square leg. McCarthy retired at the end of the season, although he has since played Minor County cricket for Dorset.

One other minor point about the legality of a ball: in the late 1940s no England bowler was fast enough, or had the knack, of bowling bouncers and so for intimidatory purposes the beamer – a high fast full toss – was invented and much used, particularly at Cambridge. The ball has gone out of favour now, though D. M. Sayer, late of Oxford, occasionally uses it. Looking back, this type of delivery should have been banned at birth by authority.

The follow-on was introduced in 1835. A team 100 runs behind on first innings was compelled to bat third. Later the margin was reduced to 80. This was the Law in 1893. In that year Prince Ranjitsinhji was in the Cambridge XI who made 182. Oxford were 95 for nine at which point they could only hope to follow-on and hope Cambridge would be caught on a "crumbler". Their last two batsmen consulted to this effect, but C. M. Wells bowled three no-ball wides, two of which got through to the boundary. "Cambridge were not quite cordially received when they returned to the pavilion", we are told.

Three years later Oxford were in similar straits but this time the Cambridge captain, F. Mitchell, decided that he did not want Oxford to bat again and ordered E. B. Shine to bowl 12 extras. This time there was no cordiality at all in the Pavilion, but instead "inconsiderate hostility", "disgraceful rowdyism" and "volleys of vulgar uproar". Mitchell's tactics boomeranged. Cambridge were upset by the demonstrations and Oxford, set to get 330, registered one of their most famous victories by four wickets. Their main destroyer was G. O. Smith who, given the last place in the Dark Blue XI, made 132. With only two wanted he was caught in the slips attempting the winning hit but his side got home by four wickets. G. O. Smith won even greater fame at Association Football as a centre-forward for England and Corinthians.

Tactics apart, the follow-on Law, as it was then framed, was clearly nonsensical, and the compulsory enforcement was removed soon after Mitchell's action. So it remained until the latest tinkering, equally stupid, but this year we may see the Law happily restored. A glance at a list of administrators of MCC and the Counties shows that Blues of former years are still to the fore in cricket's council chamber when Laws are changed.

And now a plea: in the 1860s Quidnunc and Harlequin shirts, jacket and cap were almost as popular as the Light and Dark Blue rigs and often there was a silk stripe down the trouser leg too. Gradually all this has gone. Even the Harlequin cap which D. R. Jardine made for ever famous is now left in the bag in favour of duller, plainer caps.

Certainly the sight of a "fancy-hat" tickles the fancy of most county bowlers who "pull out all the stops" in hope of a cheap wicket. Now that the amateur game is officially dead will those who are entitled to them please wear these colours – preferably right down to the stripe on the trouser-leg? Cricket needs colour.

COBDEN'S MATCH

It has been impossible in the space available to do anything but skim the ground. Impossible, for example, to capture all the conversations and the moods which gave life to 100 years of University cricket. Perhaps one match will make the point. In 1870 W. Yardley scored the first century of the series for Cambridge and F. C. Cobden performed the hat-trick with the last three balls of the match to get Cambridge home by two runs. There has never been such a match; no, not anywhere. Controversy raged about Cobden's last four-ball over. Where was the first ball played? Were the last two men clean bowled? Or was one or both bowled off their legs? As late as 1937 Mr Alfred Cochrane was writing to *The Times* about this match to remind us that the account of Yardley, the wicket-keeper, differed from that of Cobden. He claimed these three balls were three of the best he ever bowled! Maybe, by 1970, D. R. W. Silk and his captain will be arguing about words which passed between them on the last evening of the most exciting University Match played since the second war, that of 1953. Alas, *Wisden* will not be able to settle such a dispute, but if you want facts, sir, that is where you will find them. There can be no finer tribute.

CRICKET LITERATURE OF THE WISDEN CENTURY [1963]

By John Arlott

Cricket writing has grown up side by side with *Wisden*. In 1864 a small, but growing, number of writers and publishers were searching for acceptable methods of presenting the game. Now, by 1963, virtually every possible style and formula has been used and, in the intervening period, the attitude of the writers has altered as much as cricket itself.

A single example shows how great the change has been. In the first issue of *Wisden*, the editor wrote, of the Gentlemen v Players matches – "We have abstained from making any remarks concerning the individual play of any man, since, where all are so good, it would, perhaps, be invidious to single out any one as being superior to those with whom he has so often played with varied success." Compare those lines with any cricket criticism of today and the whole reversal of outlook is apparent. For better or worse, "varied success" had ceased to be an expression of gentle approval before "The Ashes" were invented. As for subject matter, the whole pattern of the County Championship, Test Matches and the spread of the game across the world lay ahead. That growth was sensed by some few, perhaps; but, even to them, the present ramifications of the game would have seemed a wild dream.

THE SCOPE OF CRICKET WRITING

The full bibliography of cricket, which is to be published by The Cricket Society, will list some 8,000 titles. No other game can remotely approach that figure, which is the measure of the unique quality of cricket in stimulating art, imagination and study. It would be stupid to protest that everything ever written about the game is of true literary value. Some half-dozen cricket books are outstanding, irrespective of the limitation of the subject. But, where cricket itself is an inherent part of merit, no such narrow choice can be made. The field stretches from the mightly marshalling of facts which is Haygarth's *Scores and Biographies* to the brief sparkle of Sir James Barrie's *Allahakbarries*; from the erudite technical exposition of C. B. Fry's *Great Batsmen*, to one of D. L. Stevenson's piquant essays on the Scottish tours of the Carlton Club. Others, like Pardon's accounts of the Australian tours of 1882 and 1884, or Thomsonby's *Cricketers in Council*, are significant because they created fresh styles in cricket books.

Cricket books may be outstanding for many different reasons, sometimes because of their excellence in isolation, sometimes because they set a trend, or make fresh information available, sometimes for their effect on playing technique, or on the understanding of the spectator.

From time to time, specific fields have become crowded. Twelve titles on the so-called "Bodyline" series between England and Australia in 1932-33 is an obvious example. In such concentrations, many books jostle for recognition which, had they appeared alone, would deserve attention.

For a quarter of a century after the first appearance of *Wisden*, cricket literature was taking shape in a fashion best appreciated in chronological order.

THE FOUNDATIONS

What had those cricket-writers of 1864 to guide them? There had been cricket publications over a hundred years earlier, but they were broadsheets, the Laws or ballad-accounts of matches, now only of antiquarian interest. There were the volumes of scores compiled by Bentley, Britcher and Epps, the instruction books of Boxall, Tyas, Clarke, Lambert and "Bat": collectors' pieces but not classics.

There had been, however, six remarkable peaks, towering above the rest of a century of intermittent effort. The first was John Nyren's *The Young Cricketer's Tutor* (1883), which, with its essays on "The Cricketers of My Time" remains as fine a book as the game has ever known. In his *Sketches of the Players* (1846), William Denison, the first cricket-reporter, recorded another generation of great players, and the "revolution" which brought in round-arm bowling. Cricket's best seller, *The Cricket Field*, by the Reverend James Pycroft, which was to run to many editions and frequent partial reprinting for another hundred years, first appeared in 1851. It blends history with opinion and anecdote in as nostalgic view of early nineteenth-century cricket.

Two of the earlier books are still much esteemed for their illustrations: *Felix on the Bat* had different coloured lithographs in each of its three editions, to accompany a text which imparted sound cricketing wisdom with dashes of period humour; and William Lillywhite's *Hand Book of Cricket*, now a rarity, is notable for its delicate aquatint portraits of players.

Finally, two years before the first *Wisden*, came volumes 1 to 4 of *Scores and Biographies*. Eleven more were to follow, in the most massive work of reference – almost 10,000 pages – ever compiled on any sport. William Haygarth devoted most of his life to what his first publisher, Frederick Lillywhite, described in the dedication as "*GRATUITOUS* EXERTIONS" in compiling "S. & B." for the cricket played between 1746 and 1878. Every cricket historian must lean heavily on Haygarth's vast research but, remarkably enough, it can still be bought at its original price of one guinea for each of its bulky volumes.

FROM 1864

Wisden was born at a time when cricket annuals were dying after one or two issues. Its chief rivals, Lillywhite's *Guide*, *Companion*, and *Annual*, cannibalized one another, and eventually petered out in 1900. Of the nineteenth-century annuals, only *Wisden*, and *The Athletic News Cricket Annual* (first issue in 1888, last in 1955), continued healthily into the twentieth.

For twenty-five years from 1864 cricket writing was in a formative stage. Most of the publications were ephemeral, but there were popular successes like Frederick Gale's *Echoes from Old Cricket Fields*, and *The Game of Cricket*, while Charles Box's *The English Game of Cricket* (1877) was the type of solid work, full of facts and antiquarian bias, that the Victorians relished. By 1890, however, the cricket-reading public had been identified and its tastes explored with clear success. Important books in that process were the original "Badminton" *Cricket*; the first "star" biography – of W. G. Grace, of course – by W. M. Brownlee; and the earliest tour accounts, varying from the semi-private, undergraduate humour of R. A. Fitzgerald's *Wickets in the West*, to the highly competent reporting of Charles F. Pardon on the tours of the 1882 and 1884 Australians, and the correspondent of *The Sporting Life* who accompanied Shaw and Shrewsbury's team in Australia.

From this point onward, chronological order loses its significance and the outstanding books fall more conveniently into their various type-groups. To list them in that fashion, as if choosing a balanced, all-round collection to go into a single bookcase, is probably the most orderly method: but it must be emphasised that it is an *exclusive* method. Many good books must be omitted for the sake of balance alone. In some few instances, particular authors have merited sections of their own.

HISTORY

Histories have been written on almost every aspect of human interest. But by no means all show the subject in perspective, catch its feeling as well as its facts, the shape of its development as well as its dates. So, when *A History of Cricket*, by H. S. Altham, appeared in 1926, rendering the game all those services, it established itself not only as authoritative, but as so eminently *right* as not to be superseded. Mr Altham, who played for Repton, Oxford University, Surrey and Hampshire, is a classical scholar. His history has sweep, the disciplined prose which is bred by study of the classics, imagination and, at times, a stirring quality stemming from the author's generous enthusiasm for his subject.

A year ago, in its fifth edition, the *History* was divided into two volumes: in the first, H. S. Altham revised his earlier work in the light of subsequent study, and ended it at 1914. In the second, E. W. Swanton (who had continued the story in some earlier editions) took over the task of setting in assimilable order the vast welter of facts about modern cricket, with its huge growth of first-class and Test play. That he did so while retaining the dignity of the original work was a considerable feat of study, compression and sympathy.

All the Test-playing countries, except Pakistan, have their definitive "hard" histories, recording major scores, facts and dates: South Africa (W. M. Luckin and Louis Duffus), New Zealand (T. W. Reese and R. T. Brittenden), West Indies (Christopher Nicole), and India (J. M. Framjee Patel, W. D. Begg and Arbi). *Australian Cricket: a History*, by A. G. Moyes, is notable for its scope, style and understanding. Shorter periods, with their own particular significance, are dealt with in *Cricket Between Two Wars*, by Sir Pelham Warner, and Test series between England and Australia in *Cricket Decade* (1946 to 1956), by J. M. Kilburn.

Some centres whose play is less exalted have produced attractive writing: *Cricket in the Fiji Islands*, by C. P. Snow; *A Century of Philadelphia Cricket*, edited by J. A. Lester, a handsome volume dealing, in effect, with all the major cricket of the United States; and *Cricket in Ireland*, by Patrick Hone, are among the most distinguished of cricket books. S. P. Foenander has written exhaustively and enthusiastically on play in Ceylon.

Anyone who studies early cricket must stand much in the debt of four archivists: "H.P.-T." (P. F. Thomas) produced six booklets collected under the title *Old English Cricket*; G. B. Buckley searched prodigiously in the files of old newspapers, published two collections of extracts and left a huge quantity of notes; H. T. Waghorn's *The Dawn of Cricket*, and *Cricket Scores 1730-1733*, probed back earlier than "S. & B."; and, more lately, H. F. & A. P. Squire have unearthed many hitherto unknown facts about early cricket in Sussex. G. D. Martineau has presented his studies in graceful essay-form in *The Field is Full of Shades*, and *Bat, Ball, Wicket and All*. The most notable research of Gerald Brodribb is in *Next Man In*, *Hit for Six*, and a memoir of Felix.

Outstanding is *The Hambledon Men*, in which E. V. Lucas reprinted Nyren, with relevant extracts from Haygarth, the Reverend John Mitford's review and other early writers, and rounded off the collection with discovery, and characteristically felicitous appreciation, of his own.

Two diverting works of period atmosphere which are apt, nowadays, to pass unregarded are Davey's *The Canterbury Cricket Week* (1865: labelled "Volume First") which is as much concerned with the performances of the "Old Stagers" as with cricket, and is illustrated with pasted-in photographs; and *Sportascrapiana*, by C. A. Wheeler, which has some lively writing on the cricket of Budd and Osbaldeston, well set against the "sporting" background of their time.

COUNTY HISTORIES

Every first-class county has, in name at least, a history: though that of Derbyshire (last edition, 1899) is scanty and out of date, while Middlesex has little more than a list of match-scores. Yorkshire are best served with three volumes, by the Rev. R. S. Holmes, A. W. Pullin and J. M. Kilburn, carrying through from 1833 to 1949. There are many books on Nottinghamshire cricket, most of them put out by that most prolific publisher of cricketana, C. H. Richards. The other counties are variably served: Leicestershire (E. E. Snow), Hampshire (H. S. Altham, E. D. R. Eagar, etc.), Lancashire (A. W. Ledbrooke), Northants (J. D. Coldham), Somerset (R. A. Roberts), Surrey (G. Ross), Sussex (J. Marshall), and Worcestershire (W. R. Chignell), are the most nearly up-to-date of these histories.

CLUB HISTORIES

The two major University clubs are admirably treated in *The Cambridge University Cricket Club, 1820-1901*, by W. J. Ford — which now requires a second volume, and *History of the O.U.C.* (1962), by Geoffrey Bolton.

Cricket clubs, from the largest to some of the most obscure, have recorded their doings in books varying in length between the two-volume leisure of the *Eton Ramblers*, or the long row of Incogniti scores, to single-sheet fold-overs with which some village teams have marked their centenaries. There probably would be no happier cricket book to give a non-cricketer than *Annals of the West Kent Cricket Club*, by Philip Norman: historical, statistical, humorous, warmly personal and naïve, in turn, it is, by any standard, companionable and diverting.

Some well-known writers contributed amusing notes to the six, now rare volumes of *The Old Broughtonians Cricket Weeks*, in which the atmosphere is as important as the convivial matches described.

There are substantial histories of the Harlequins, by a useful cricketer and poet, A. J. H. Cochrane, and of the Free Foresters. Several public schools have their own histories: *Public Schools Cricket 1901-1950*, edited by W. N. Roe, is a good general survey.

Finally reference must be made to the fact that, thanks largely to T. C. Riddell, the Greenock Club is more extensively documented that any other cricket club in the world, and that Scottish club cricket, in general, is notably well recorded.

STATISTICS

The mathematics of cricket are an important facet of the game's history. They have been an absorbing hobby for many; and have often proved valuable servants. There is little doubt that there has been too much emphasis, of late years, on unrelated figures: and most of them, understandably enough, have been inaccurate to some degree. But, when best presented, they have proved absorbing and illuminating. The first recognised statistician – Haygarth being always excepted in any judgement of researchers, annalists or recorders – was the Rev. R. S. Holmes, author of *The County Cricket Championship* (1897). The first major work of this sort was *Cricket Form at a Glance*, by Sir Home Gordon, which, in its final version, covered the scores of teams and players in cricket played in England from 1878 to 1937, and this considerable undertaking remains a basic work of reference.

The leading statistician of recent years was Roy Webber. Trained as an accountant, he never hesitated, in cases of doubt, to go to original score-books for verification and, as a result, set right many errors in scores that had been long perpetuated. He built up an appreciable filing system which was, in effect, an extension of his remarkable memory. Apart from his generally high standard of accuracy, he had an imaginative quality in relation to statistics which enabled him to present them, often, in fresh and illuminating fashions. His *Test Cricket* (two volumes), *The Book of Cricket Records*, and *The County Championship*, are standard reference, placing the onus on some subsequent mathematician of comparable ability to keep them up to date.

REFERENCE

Some few, but worth while, books of cricket reference fall outside the classification of history or statistics. *The Language of Cricket* (1938), by W. J. Lewis, is a workmanlike dictionary of cricket terms with the earliest available quotation to illustrate the use of each. A supplement to the list, by the late G. B. Buckley, was published in *The Cricket Quarterly* of January 1963. *Cricket Who's Who*, subtitled "The Cricket Blue Book", by H. V. Dorey, appeared in five partly repetitive volumes, 1909 to 1913, and remains extremely valuable on the players of that period. After *Cricket's Guide to Cricketers* (J. N. Pentelow, 1911) and some slight booklets, the next significant publication of the kind was *The Cricketer's Who's Who* (1934), compiled by S. Canynge Caple, whose revised version, published serially by the Cricket Book Society in 1946 and 1947, unfortunately ended, after five issues, at "E". The latest of this type, Roy Webber's *Who's Who in World Cricket*, appeared, in a second issue, in 1954.

Oxford and Cambridge Scores and Biographies, by J. D. Betham, is well made, but it ends at 1904, and although the author prepared notes for its continuation they have not been published. *The Australians in England* is a record, compiled by Roy Webber, of the twenty-one Australian tours of England to 1953, with averages, records, memorabilia and reviews of the tours, paying due attention to Tests but also considering other matches. S.

Canynge Caple has compiled histories and records of England's Test Matches with Australia, New Zealand, South Africa, India and West Indies.

The Laws of Cricket, detailing their history and growth, by R. S. Rait Kerr, secretary of MCC from 1936 to 1952, is an impeccable piece of scholarship. The author re-drafted the Laws of Cricket in 1947, and was prompted by this to the research which made his book definitive and complete to the date of its publication in 1950. Colonel Rait Kerr also edited with his usual precision *Cricket Umpiring and Scoring*, the admirable textbook of the Association of Cricket Umpires.

F. S. ASHLEY-COOPER

Frederick Samuel Ashley-Cooper (1877-1932), according to his bibliographer, G. Neville Weston, was the author, joint-author or editor, of 103 books or pamphlets about cricket, and *Wisden* (1933) reported that he had written 40,000 biographical and obituary notices of cricketers. Physically delicate, he spent his entire life studying and writing about cricket in a genuinely scholarly fashion. He compiled volume 15 of *Scores and Biographies* from Haygarth's notes, edited *Wisden's Cricketer's Note Book* (1900-1913) and, for five years, the periodical *Cricket*. In the case of some of his less popular monographs, he was fortunate in his publisher, the devoted C. H. Richards. Ashley-Cooper's *Nottinghamshire Cricket and Cricketers* is a characteristic example of his thoroughness and his ability to marshal and concentrate facts. Probably his best book was *Highways and Byways of Cricket*, a collection of erudite and gracious essays.

APPRECIATION

If statistics are a form of cricket history, so, at the opposing pole of understanding is the more literary and imaginative writing, generally, if not quite precisely, termed "appreciation," the evocation of character and the emotional response to the game. The writer who seeks to record this type of impact of cricket is in danger of becoming over-lush on the one hand or, but less often, dull, on the other. John Nyren – or was is Charles Cowden Clarke, who "collected and edited" the *Tutor*? – was the first who struck a wholly authentic chord. Pycroft and Gale were his subsequent disciples, and, like him, they were essentially nostalgic in approach, though at times Gale can seem antipathetic to the modern taste for the same reasons that made him relish the soubriquet of "The Old Buffer".

After them, no one adequately filled this imaginative gap for the cricket-reader until the inter-war period. Apart from Neville Cardus, the writers who did so then were "Country Vicar" with *Cricket Memories* and *Second Innings*; Dudley Carew, whose output was regrettably small for one who could write *England Over*, and *To the Wicket*; Richard Binns, author of *Cricket by Firelight*; and J. M. Kilburn, whose *In Search of Cricket* distilled much experience into small compass.

Three other authors, not generally regarded as cricket-writers, also treated of cricket briefly but in distinguished fashion during the twenties and thirties. Apart from *The Hambledon Men*, E. V. Lucas wrote occasional cricket essays and verse with his usual sensitivity, and the best of that writing was brought together by Rupert Hart-Davis in *Cricket All His Life* (1950). Robert Lynd, another of the outstanding essayists of the time, wrote some characteristically humanistic observations on the 1921 Test matches which are collected in his book *The Sporting Life*. James Thorpe's reputation was made as a *Punch* artist, but he was a keen club cricketer with a good, and earnestly read, cricket library. His book, *A Cricket Bag*, illustrated with his own drawings, is friendly, wise but never pompous, and full of cricketers' humour.

Since 1946, the Australian writer, Ray Robinson, in *Between Wickets*, *From the Boundary* and *The Happy Season* (called *Green Sprigs* in Australia), has employed a fresh and impressive style, especially effective in biographical studies. He builds up a picture through a balanced blend of observation, quotation, interview, and just so many dates and statistics as are necessary; the result is solidly satisfying.

A. A. Thomson, already an experienced novelist, used the formula of anecdote, nostalgia and king-making in several books, of which *Cricket My Pleasure* is perhaps the best, but all are friendly, generous, and written with a romantic bias. Cricket fanaticism was naïvely expressed in the little-known *Homage to Cricket*, by "Gryllus".

NEVILLE CARDUS

Neville Cardus has had, almost certainly, a more profound effect on cricket writing and, indeed, on the imaginative watching of cricket, than any one else. He was both cricket correspondent and music critic of *The Manchester Guardian* and his first collection of match-reports and essays, called simply *A Cricketer's Book*, appeared in 1922. *Days in the Sun* (1924), *The Summer Game* (1929), a superbly compressed history called *Cricket* (in "The English Heritage" series, 1930) and *Good Days* (1934), steadily extended his public and, by the time he brought out *Australian Summer*, an account of the 1936-37 Test series, he was the most admired writer, by literary and imaginative standards, that the cricket world had known. Four subsequent books, including two of autobiography, confirmed his standing. His contribution is probably best defined as putting into words the emotional and visual impressions which cricket enthusiasts had long felt but which no one before Cardus had ever been able to distill into prose. His method was effective because it was simple, he found heroes among cricketers in the way that a boy does at the time when he receives the impressions that make him believe, all his life, that the players he watched in his younger days were the finest of all. Neville Cardus brought the equipment of a first-class writer to the outlook of an enthusiast. Never presuming to argue about technique, he created an acceptable mythology of cricket, portraying the best cricketers not merely as performers but as characters. Sometimes, perhaps, they were a little more than life-size, but always credible. His brightest colours had justification because he used them to highlight significant features in the manner of the good photographer. If Woolley and Macdonald were his most memorable portraits, and if he tended, like most men, to revere the heroes of his youth, he could still see, and crystallize, the merits of such later players as Hammond, Compton, Lindwall and Miller. There can be no doubt that, even if his imitators have sometimes virtually caricatured him, Neville Cardus's style, imagery, and the bright precision of his prose will commend his books to generations of readers after he, and his subjects, have passed beyond argument.

R. C. ROBERTSON-GLASGOW

A capable University and county cricketer, R. C. Robertson-Glasgow brought to cricket reporting keen eyes and a dry wit. His collection of prose and verse, *The Brighter Side of Cricket*, is indisputably the merriest book ever written about the game. His two volumes of profiles of players – *Cricket Prints* and *More Cricket Prints*, are sharply observed and drily, but understandingly, interpreted. His autobiography, *46 Not Out*, and several books of short, light essays, emphasise the convivial approach of a happy amateur player with a deep feeling for the game, honest respect for its practitioners, and a broad appreciation of humanity. His writing is always amusing: at its best it is extremely perceptive and quite gloriously funny.

IAN PEEBLES

Any man who bowls leg-breaks and googlies at Test level needs a sense of humour. So, while Ian Peebles can analyse a game of cricket by strictly technical standards, he also observes its humours in the Jonsonian sense, and its humour in the comic sense. In his three books he adds to those merits the gift of a born raconteur, telling cricketers' stories in the perfect manner.

BIOGRAPHY AND REMINISCENCES

Biography, and even more so autobiography, can add flesh to the bare bones of cricket history as recorded in score-sheets. But in recent years the field of "star" players' autobiographies has been bedevilled by "ghosting". There is no doubt that some of the earlier life-stories of cricketers benefited from what was called "editorial assistance", sometimes provided by quite distinguished writers. But since then entire so-called autobiographies of players have been written by journalists from cuttings-books or even less, and the whole genre has tended to fall into disrepute. Nevertheless, it includes so many books of undoubted value that it must be treated with respect, albeit respect tempered with caution.

A few books by mid-Victorian cricketers are absorbing as social documents and throw revealing light on early domestic and Anglo-Australian cricket. *Kings of Cricket*, by Richard Daft, is notable for two reasons: written from close observation, it gives sound assessments of, and many anecdotes about, the great Victorian players of forty years; and the introduction, by Andrew Lang, is a quite outstanding essay. A sequel to "Kings", called *A Cricketer's Yarns*, dealing largely with the early Nottinghamshire players, was edited from Daft's notes, many years after his death, by F. S. Ashley-Cooper. *Seventy-one Not Out* is another good source-book. It is the life-story of William Caffyn, the Surrey player who was on the first two tours of Australia and, after that of 1863-64, remained to coach in Sydney and Melbourne and to take a considerable part in the development of Australian cricket. *With Bat and Ball*, by George Giffen, one of the leading early Australian cricketers, was, until the issue of A. G. Moyes's *History*, virtually the only book on the formative years there, and it is still worth reading for its atmosphere and the critical estimates of Australian players from the start of first-class play in that country.

W. G. Grace was the subject of the first "popular" biography of a cricketer and *The Memorial Biography of W. G. Grace*, edited by Lord Hawke, Lord Harris and Sir Home Gordon and issued (1919) "under the auspices of the Committee of MCC," is the most impressive tribute ever offered to any player. Some forty friends, colleagues, and opponents contributed recollections and assessments of the various periods and aspects of his career, and F. S. Ashley-Cooper provided a statistical appendix. This is an authoritative, evocative and dignified book. The many other studies of "W. G." include *W. G. Grace* ("Great Lives" series: 1934), by Bernard Darwin, whose main reputation is as a golf-writer but who often, and certainly in this case, wrote about cricket with the same felicity.

Talks With Old Yorkshire Cricketers and *Old English Cricketers*, by "Old Ebor" (A. W. Pullin), are important for their first-hand views of nineteenth-century cricket, gathered in a long series of faithful interviews with veteran players. The Yorkshire studies, by drawing attention to the financial straits of so many of these men in their old age, were largely responsible for the Yorkshire Club's subsequent efforts to give its professionals security after their playing days. A similar interview and quotation method was followed by W. A. Bettesworth in a parallel series of appreciations, largely of amateur players, originally published in *Cricket*, and brought together under the title *Chats on the Cricket Field*. Bettesworth also wrote *The Walkers of Southgate*, devoted to the famous cricketing family, which was edited by E. T. Sachs, with added recollections by a number of their contemporaries.

From 1920 onwards there had been a steady increase in the number of cricketers' life-stories, many of which make pleasant reading. C. B. Fry's *Life Worth Living*, although only partly concerned with cricket, and *Ranjitsinhji*, by Roland Wild, are entitled to places in any cricket collection. There have been, too, notable contributions from Australia. *Googlies*, by Dr H. V. Hordern, is an unassuming, easy-moving book; and *Ten for Sixty-six and All That*, by Arthur Mailey, illustrated with the author's drawings, is witty, wise, discursive and delightful. In addition to his substantial studies of *A Century of Cricketers*, *Australian Batsmen*, and *Australian Bowlers*, A. G. Moyes has written informed biographies of *Benaud* and *Bradman*. Sir Donald Bradman, however, has been most elaborately treated in *Bradman the Great*, by B. J. Wakley, an unusual form of biography, 317 pages long, recording and analysing every innings he ever played. *Masters of Cricket*, from Trumper to May, is a series of profiles written with J. H. Fingleton's characteristic vitality.

Recent autobiographies of undoubted authenticity include *Express Deliveries*, shrewd, warm, and containing some relishable anecdotes, by W. E. Bowes; *Cricket From the Middle*, life-story and views of D. J. Insole; and *A Typhoon Called Tyson*, an often vivid self-portrait by Frank Tyson. Ronald Mason has written full length biographies of two of the greatest of modern batsmen in *Jack Hobbs* and *Walter Hammond*. Sir John Hobbs was also the subject of an unusual form of appreciation in *The Perfect Batsman*, in which A. C. MacLaren, with the aid of many photographs from films, discussed "The Master's" technique.

Among many other autobiographies, of varied appeal, are those by A. A. Lilley, G. L. Jessop, Lord Hawke, F. B. Wilson, R. G. Barlow, Lord Harris, S. M. J. Woods, Godfrey Evans and Frank Laver.

A number of players have written, though not strictly in the form of autobiography, lucid accounts of their own experience of play and players; they include Trevor Bailey, P. G. H. Fender, Richie Benaud, R. E. S. Wyatt, W. G. Grace and E. H. D. Sewell.

SIR PELHAM WARNER

Only three of Sir Pelham Warner's books – the last of them *Long Innings* (1951) – were avowedly autobiographical. But all of them have been informed by his vast experience of cricket and his quite remarkable memory for the subject. In 1890 he was "chaired" off the field at Lord's after making the highest score of the match for Rugby against Marlborough and, in the next seventy years, as player (in nine different countries), cricket correspondent of the *Morning Post*, selector and administrator, he must have taken part in, and watched more first-class cricket, all over the world, than anyone else in the history of the game.

His prose is capable and straightforward, it rarely soars, but never sags, it defines, and is instinct with enthusiasm. Sir Pelham's accounts of the pre-1914 tours, in which he took part, established the modern form for such books. Partly because of its content, *England v Australia* (1911-12) remains popular, but all are eminently reliable and readable.

Lord's 1787-1945 and *Gentlemen v Players 1806-1949* are authoritative works on subjects near to Sir Pelham's heart; while *Cricket Between Two Wars* is a rounded history, largely written from personal observation. Sir Pelham founded and edited *The Cricketer*, which, since 1921, has reflected his deep love and knowledge of cricket, and consideration for its dignity.

OVERSEAS TOURS

Since Fred Lillywhite put out *The English Cricketers' Trip to Canada and the United States*, in 1860, at least 150 books, of varying sizes and quality, have been devoted to cricket tours of as widely differing significance. Some, particularly in recent years, have concentrated almost entirely on Test matches but, since 1926, eleven books under the title *The Fight for The Ashes* – distinguished by the relevant date – have fully covered the tours between England and Australia. They have been competently written by M. A. Noble, P. F. Warner, J. B. Hobbs, A. G. Moyes, Peter West, I. A. R. Peebles and R. A. Roberts.

Prior to the First World War the output of tour-books was much smaller than now and, apart from those by P. F. Warner and C. F. Pardon, only *With the MCC in Australia, 1907-08* (Philip Trevor), Conway's *Australian Cricket Annual for 1879* (with a report of the Australians in England, 1877-78), *With Stoddart's Team in Australia, 1897-8*, by K. S. Ranjitsinhji, *The Cricketing Record of Major Wharton's Tour, 1888-1889* (in South Africa) and *The Triangular Tournament* (1912), by E. H. D. Sewell are of much significance. Outside the usual formula for these books, and under the unlikely title of *Ten Thousand Miles Through India and Burma*, Cecil Headlam dealt with the social and topographical aspects, as well as the cricket, of the Oxford Authentics Eastern tour of 1902-03.

Between the two Wars, P. G. H. Fender produced four notable studies of England-Australia rubbers: *Defending The Ashes* (1920-21); *The Turn of the Wheel*

(1928-29); *The Tests of 1930*; and *Kissing the Rod* (1934). *Gilligan's Men* (1924-25), and *Those Ashes* (1296), by M. A. Noble, are written in a similar, expertly analytical fashion. Of the many accounts of the 1932-33 series, *And Then Came Larwood*, by Arthur Mailey, is admirably balanced, sage and perceptive, while in *In Quest of The Ashes*, D. R. Jardine himself gave an important close-up view, counter-balanced, to some extent, by J. H. Fingleton's *Cricket Crisis*, published as late as 1946. Neville Cardus included Test accounts in several of his books and his *Manchester Guardian* reports on the 1938 England-Australia series, not elsewhere available in book form, were included in *The Essential Neville Cardus* (1949), edited by Rupert Hart-Davies. *The Greatest Test Match* is a companionable and nostalgic account, by "John Marchant" (Harold Lake) of England winning The Ashes at The Oval in 1926.

Since 1946, a number of cricket reporters have already written more tour accounts than existed in the entire previous history of cricket. The anxiety of competing publishers to bring out these books hard on the heels of the final Test of a rubber has frequently militated against a contemplative attitude, and, as often, against complete coverage of the tour.

Nevertheless, many of them are of high quality. J. H. Fingleton, in informed, lively, and sometimes trenchant fashion, dealt at length with four tours in *Brightly Fades the Don* (1948), *Brown and Company* (1950-51), *The Ashes Crown the Year* (1953), and *Four Chukkas to Australia* (1958-59), and he devoted an entire book, *The Greatest Test of All*, to the epic tied match between Australia and West Indies in 1960. Another Australian Test player, W. J. O'Reilly, wrote observantly and with much technical insight in *Cricket Conquest* (1948), and *Cricket Task-force* (1950-51). E. W. Swanton, in addition to reprinting his *Daily Telegraph* reports in book form on several occasions, wrote more fully on major tours in *Elusive Victory* (1950-51), *West Indian Adventure* (1954), *West Indies Revisited* (1959-60) and *Report from South Africa* (1956-57). In much lighter fashion, and with happy success, M. J. C. Allom and M. J. Turnbull produced diary-form accounts of their tours with MCC in Australasia and New Zealand, 1929-30, and South Africa, 1930-31 in *The Book of the Two Maurices*, and *The Two Maurices Again*.

A. G. Moyes described several tours in Australia, but none more stimulatingly than in *With the West Indies in Australia, 1960-61*. Alan Ross writes of tours as rounded experiences, treating of the countries and the people, as well as the cricket, and using his own photographs as illustrations. His three books, covering four tours, are *Australia '55*, *Cape Summer and the Australians in England* (1956 and 1956-57), and *Through the Caribbean* (1960).

There is also much good cricket history in *The South Africans in Australia, 1952-53* (A. G. Moyes); *Silver Fern on the Veld*, R. T. Brittenden's account of the New Zealanders in South Africa, 1953-54; *Test Status on Trial – Pakistan in England, 1954*, by their captain, A. H. Kardar; *Springbok Glory* (Louis Duffus: South Africa in England, 1955); and *May's Men in Australia* (1958-59), which is unpretentiously but unmistakably a mature cricketer's view, by Alec Bedser. *A Tale of Two Tests* (Australia v West Indies at Brisbane, 1960, and England v Australia at Old Trafford, 1961), by Richie Benaud, is an absorbing and authentic close-up view of those two great matches.

TECHNIQUE

After the broadsheet-verses and scores, "how to play" was the theme, wholly or in part, of most of the early cricket books; and instruction, in varying bulk, has been published steadily ever since. If some of it is slight, it is almost all worthy, but it has an unavoidable sameness. Fortunately for the selective collector, six titles stand head and shoulders above all the rest.

Heading the list is *The MCC Cricket Coaching Book*, which in 1962 appeared in its third revised edition. It has been compiled, with infinite care and enthusiasm, by a committee of MCC, with H. S. Altham, G. O. Allen and R. W. V. Robins as prominent members. It is doubtful if any cricket book ever received more devoted or detailed attention. Every sentence has been weighed, pruned, and shaped, while the illustrations, both in line and photography, have been constantly revised until the two now tell their story as nearly perfectly as is well possible.

K. S. Ranjitsinji's *Jubilee Book of Cricket*, which owed much in planning and writing to C. B. Fry, was, to its date – 1897 – the most ambitious instructional book on cricket, with many photo-illustrations and a profound, and still impressive, text. Its legitimate descendant was *The Game of Cricket*, by many experienced hands, produced with the typical thoroughness of the Lonsdale Library.

Great Batsmen: their Methods at a Glance (1905), and *Great Bowlers and Fielders: their Methods at a Glance* (1906), were the result of a most effective collaboration. C. B. Fry brought a quick, informed and analytical mind, and his experience of *The Jubilee Book*, to the examination of the techniques of the finest cricketers in every department of the game. The books are illustrated by George W. Beldham, himself a capable county cricketer, and the earliest sporting action-photographer. Text or illustrations alone are impressive, and together they form an unequalled analysis of the methods of the players of the "Golden Age".

The Art of Cricket, by Sir Donald Bradman, is a masterly exposition of practical cricket, in terms of its marshalling, application and significance. It is concisely written with an acumen which is, at times, quite brilliant in its elucidation and definition, and the illustrations are a true complement to the text.

ANNUALS

Wisden has proved the most enduring, and internationally accepted annual publication on cricket; its successive editors have been at pains to produce a responsible and wide coverage of world cricket. This hundredth issue argues its own case with full effect.

Complete sets of its predecessors, *Denison's Cricketers' Companion* (1844 to 1847), and *Lillywhite's Guide to Cricketers* (22 editions between 1848 and 1866) are now rarities. Its main early competitors, *Lillywhite's Cricketers' Companion* (1865 to 1885), and *Lillywhite's Cricketers' Annual* (1872 to 1900), are easier to come by, and contain much information on the play and players of the time.

In this century, most daily, and several evening papers, have produced annuals of varying lengths of life. Post-war the most successful has been *The Playfair Cricket Annual* (first issue, 1948), attractively produced with generous illustrations and valuable references such as full career records of present players, and a "Who's Who" compiled by Roy Webber. From 1963 the title is being transferred to *The Cricket Annual*, the former *News-Chronicle* annual.

Overseas cricket, too, has been more regularly covered in recent years. The present annuals of the chief cricketing countries are *The Cricket Almanack of New Zealand* (since 1948), *The South African Cricket Annual* (intermittently since 1951-52), *Indian Cricket* (since 1946-47) and *The Indian Cricket Field* (since 1957-58). There is no general Australian annual, but full Sheffield Shield and Test coverage is supplied by *The New South Wales Cricket Year Book* (since 1927-28). There is no yearly record of cricket in Pakistan or the West Indies but, from the non-Test-playing countries, *The Uganda Cricketer* (since 1953) is a sturdy growth, and the cyclostyled *Canadian Cricket Association Year Book* has maintained publication since 1959.

PERIODICALS

The disappearance-rate among cricket monthly and weekly publications has been relatively as heavy as among annuals. Two, however, have lived long enough to deal with the game for over eighty years. *Cricket* – "A weekly record of the game" – first appeared in 1882 and, with a change of title to *The World of Cricket* in its final year, survived to 1914. At the beginning of the 1921 season Sir Pelham Warner founded *The Cricketer*, which, with several changes of format and issue-pattern, has continued until now. By this juncture the collector's book-case is becoming somewhat strained but, if he has ten feet of shelf-space remaining, it may accommodate, in the shape of these two publications, the contemporary recording, discussion and annotation of cricket from the day of Spofforth and the origin of "The Ashes" to Benaud and the latest England-Australian series: many years of absorbing reading for the enthusiast, and, by present price-standards, extremely cheap.

More recently two other periodicals have begun publication. *The Playfair Cricket Monthly* was started in 1960, under the editorship of Gordon Ross, with, like its annual, plenty of well-reproduced illustrations, and statistics by Roy Webber. *The Cricket Quarterly*, edited by Rowland Bowen, was begun only in 1963, and more than any other cricket magazine it is concerned with research and comment on a scholarly basis; it has a mind of its own.

PICTORIAL AND "PRESENTATION" BOOKS

After the few early copper-plate, aquatint and lithograph illustrations, cricket books boasted little more than indifferent woodcuts until C. W. Alcock edited *Famous Cricketers and Cricket Grounds* (1895), which was followed by C. B. Fry's *The Book of Cricket*. Both are folio-sized, and while the latter has more comment, the appeal of both is based on sharp reproduction of photographs of leading players of the time. Then, in the same manner, though with more text, came the two-volume *Cricket of Today*, by P. C. Standing.

The Fry-and-Beldam "Methods" and *The Jubilee Book* have been treated previously; *Cricket* (1903), edited by Horace Hutchinson, while ambitious in its text by several distinguished hands, is most notable for the excellence of its reproductions of early cricket pictures and prints.

The Noble Game of Cricket, with text by Clifford Bax, was issued in a handsome limited edition of 150 copies, of which only 100 were for sale, in 1941. It was, to be precise, a prolifically illustrated catalogue of the cricket pictures gathered by Sir Jeremiah Colman. His collection was so extensive that the book amounted, in effect, to a review of cricket art, with a number of its hundred reproductions in colour. Copies are now scarce and costly. But many of the best of its pictures and others now in the possession of MCC, are well reproduced in *The Game of Cricket* (1955), with an essay by Sir Norman Birkett and notes by Diana Rait Kerr. *A Portfolio of Cricket Prints* (1962) (introduction by Irving Rosenwater) has eight colour-reproductions of nineteenth-century aquatints and lithographs.

Cricketers of the Empire is a substantial folio which reproduces a series of drawings by A. Chevallier Taylor, in crayon, heightened with Chinese white on grey paper, of prominent cricketers of the Edwardian period.

The Book of Cricket (1952) is the legitimate successor to C. B. Fry's book of the same title. Sub-titled "A Gallery of Great Players from W. G. Grace to the Present Day", it has over two hundred photo-portraits of individual players and teams, and accompanying text by Denzil Batchelor.

Imperial Cricket (1912), edited by P. F. Warner, was typical of the "de luxe" publications of its time. An impressive list of contributors deal with cricket throughout the Empire, and it was ambitiously illustrated by photo-blocks and in photogravure.

Cricket features in the even more elaborate *Fifty Years of Sport at Cambridge and the Great Public Schools* (three volumes, edited by A. C. M. Croome), and in the "Cricket and Football" and "Past Sportsmen" volumes of *British Sports and Sportsmen* (1917). All these may now be bought for less than the original value of their luxurious bindings or of their illustrations.

HUMOUR

All humour "dates", and the early attempts at cricket humour seem laboured to the modern taste, with *Jerks in from Short Leg* ("Quid" – R. A. Fitzgerald) and *Crickety Cricket* (Moffatt) probably the best. But in recent years, apart from the writing of R. C.

Robertson-Glasgow, *The Art of Coarse Cricket*, by Spike Hughes, which is charmingly irreverent, and *The Weaving Willow*, by John Marshall, which, with its human quality, may prove more enduring, none have seemed genuinely funny.

FICTION

One cricket novel stands high above the remainder, though four others deserve serious attention. *The Cricket Match*, by Hugh de Selincourt, has been described by Sir James Barrie as "the best book written about cricket or any other game", and needs no further commendation. In it cricket seems at some points the theme, at others incidental, which means that it is the convincing background of a fully realised novel.

The Son of Grief, by Dudley Carew, is a sombre story but not, for that reason, the less discerning or convincing. *The Friendly Game* and *Malleson at Melbourne*, both by William Godfrey, are the first two novels of a projected trilogy published, under a pseudonym, by an established novelist, and the writer's experience is implicit in two well-worked-out stories.

The Devil in Woodford Wells, by the well-known dramatic critic, Harold Hobson, is an intriguing combination of deep research about Lord Frederick Beauclerk, in a well-contrived fictional setting, and is an absorbing and neglected book. Hugh de Selincourt's other books of fiction are pleasant but, by comparison with *The Cricket Match*, not more than pleasing light entertainment.

Best Cricket Stories, a collection made by E. W. Swanton, brings together most of the worth while fiction in shorter form.

VERSE

There is no single volume of cricket verse of a standard comparable with the best of its prose. Norman Gale put out several small books of lyrics with cricket themes and *For the Luncheon Interval*, by A. A. Milne, is gay, but both, though the best in their field, are lightweight. Apart from the one indisputable *poem* on the game – Francis Thompson's "At Lord's" – there have been some well-contrived pieces of verse by A. J. H. Cochrane, G. D. Martineau, E. B. V. Christian, G. Rostrevor Hamilton, W. J. Prowse, Siegfried Sassoon, Norman Nicholson, Alan Ross, Thomas Moult, Andrew Lang, Edmund Blunden and G. F. Wilson. Anyone who has read *The Book of Cricket Verse*, edited by Gerald Brodribb and the "Poetry of Cricket" section of Alan Ross's *The Cricketer's Companion* has seen all the good cricket verse, and some of lower standard.

ANTHOLOGIES

It is doubtful if there has ever been a better symposium of cricket prose than the first, which was the 1888 "Badminton" *Cricket*, a distinguished, satisfying and balanced collection of writings by many hands on the divers aspects of the game. The second (1920) "Badminton" yielded little to its predecessor, although it is tempting to single out from it E. R. Wilson's essay on bowling, because it is the only substantial venture into prose of the thoughtful bowler who was one of the wittiest and most erudite of students of cricket. *The Game of Cricket*, in the Lonsdale Library, is well produced in the thorough tradition of that series.

Bat and Ball, edited by Thomas Moult, holds a friendly balance between the technical and the popular and is an eminently readable collection. *The Cricketer's Week End Book* was edited by Eric Parker in his usual catholic fashion. Gerald Brodribb's *The Book of Cricket Verse*, and *The English Game* are anthologies which reflect their editor's care in research and representation.

Two recent, bulkily satisfying and pleasantly produced collections, planned to go in double harness, are *The Cricketer's Companion*, edited by Alan Ross, and *Great Cricket Matches*, by Handasyde Buchanan. Both are generous in scope and size and have been selected with imagination and good taste.

The Boundary Book (1962) edited by Leslie Frewin, was produced for The Lord's Taverners, and the profits were devoted to The National Playing Fields Association. The contributors and artists gave their contributions without fee and, with some gratuitous technical assistance, it was possible to produce a book which would have been impossible by the normal standards of publishing economy. The result was an opulent, entertaining collection.

BIBLIOGRAPHIES

The main bibliographies of cricket have been those by A. J. Gaston contained in *Wisden* for 1892, 1894, 1900 and 1923; A. D. Taylor (1906: with supplement published in *Cricket*, April 7th, 1907); and J. W. Goldman (1937). Studies in specialist fields have been done by G. Neville Weston, on "Bat", Nyren, and F. S. Ashley-Cooper, and Gerald Brodribb on *Cricket in Fiction*.

The definitive work, however, has been prepared by The Cricket Society, and is planned for publication by 1966.

Meanwhile, even as this issue of *Wisden* is being printed, cricket literature is flowing steadily from thought, through manuscript – or typescript – printing and binding, to render bibliographies and reviews of cricket literature out of date as soon as they are written. The very nature of the game and its people ensures that the process will continue as long as cricket itself.

OBITUARIES

ABERDARE, THE THIRD BARON (Clarence Napier Bruce), who died on October 4, 1957, aged 72, was one of the best all-round sportsmen of his time. His death was caused by drowning after his car fell over a precipice in Yugoslavia into three feet of water in a river bed. As the Hon. C. N. Bruce, he was in the Winchester XI of 1904 and would have gained his Blue at Oxford as a Freshman but for illness. Against Cambridge at Lord's in 1907 he scored only five runs, but the following year his 46 in the Dark Blues' first innings was second top score. A fine batsman who hit the ball hard with perfect timing, due mainly to splendid wristwork, he first appeared for Middlesex in 1908 and played his last match for them in 1929. In all first-class games he scored 4,316 runs, average 28.96. Against Lancashire at Lord's in 1919 he hit 149 in two hours twenty-five minutes and two seasons later again trounced the Lancashire bowling on the same ground, scoring 82 not out and helping Hendren add 50 in a quarter of an hour. In 1921 he also scored 144 against Warwickshire and 127 for Gentlemen v Players at The Oval.

He won most honours at rackets, for he was the Winchester first string in 1903-4; won the Public Schools championship in 1904; played for Oxford v Cambridge in 1905-8; won the Oxford University Silver Racket in 1907; won the Amateur Championship in 1922 and 1931; was ten times Doubles Champion; was Champion of the USA in 1928 and 1930; Singles Champion of Canada in 1928 and 1930 and Doubles Champion also in 1930. At tennis, Bruce was USA Amateur Champion in 1930 and of the British Isles in 1932 and 1938. He played eighteen times for Great Britain in the Bathurst Cup and six times won the Coupe de Paris. He carried off the MCC Gold Prize on five occasions and nine times won the Silver Prize. He also excelled at golf, playing for Oxford against Cambridge from 1905 to 1908, was a good footballer and a capital shot.

In 1937 he was appointed chairman of the National Advisory Council in connection with the Government scheme for improving the physical fitness of the nation. For twenty years he was a member of the International Olympic Executive and he played a big part in organising the 1948 Games in London. In his later years he devoted himself closely to work for the Order of St John of Jerusalem and the St John Ambulance Association, and was a member of the executive committee of the National Playing Fields Association. He succeeded to the title in 1929.

ARMSTRONG, MR WARWICK WINDRIDGE, one of the most famous Australian cricketers, died on July 13, 1947, aged 68. While a great all-round player, he remains in one's memory chiefly for his unequalled triumph in leading Australia to victory in eight consecutive Tests with England. After the first world war our cricket took a long time to settle down. During this period the England touring team, led by J. W. H. T. Douglas, lost all five matches, and the following summer Armstrong commanded Australia, who won the first three Tests and drew the other two. In that superb manner Armstrong terminated a remarkable career. Of colossal build at 42, Armstrong then weighed about 22 stone and bore himself in a way likely to cause offence, but he invariably carried his desires over all opposition and sometimes with good reason.

Born on May 22, 1879, Armstrong rose to prominence in the season of 1901-02, when he did well for Victoria before playing in the Tests of which A. C. MacLaren's team won the first and lost the other four. Armstrong headed the Australian Test averages, thanks to being not out four times. His bowling then was hardly wanted, but, coming to England under Joe Darling, he took 81 wickets at 17.50 runs each, besides scoring 1,087 runs, average 26. He surpassed these efforts on his second trip to England, making 2,002 runs, average 48.82, and taking 130 wickets at 17.60 apiece, being top of both averages. These figures constitute a record, no other visitor to England having scored 2,000 runs and taken 100 wickets in a season. His 303 not out at Bath was the highest innings hit on the tour, and his 248 not out contributed largely to victory by an innings and 189 runs over the Gentlemen at Lord's.

If not quite so successful in 1909 he scored 1,480 runs, average 46.39, and claimed 126 wickets at 16.23, being second in each table and by far the most effective bowler. He was absent from the Australian team that came over for the Triangular Tournament in 1912, but when he captained the 1921 side with such marked success he ranked third in batting and top of the bowling. With 1,405 runs, average 43.90, and 106 wickets, average 14.56, he for the third time accomplished the "cricketer's double", so equalling the record for any Australian in England established by George Giffen twenty-five years before. In four tours in England he helped Australia win the Test Rubber three times, the exception being in 1905, when F. S. Jackson won the toss in each of the five matches.

He was fortunate to lead a very powerful combination, with J. M. Gregory and E. A. McDonald, the fast bowlers, too much for England's impoverished batting, while Macartney and Bardsley headed an exceptional array of batting talent, eight men having aggregates ranging from 2,335 to 1,032, with averages from 58 to 30. The only defeats suffered by that 1921 team were at Eastbourne and Scarborough when the serious part of the tour was over. Armstrong led Australia to victory at Nottingham, Lord's and Leeds before rain ruined the Manchester match, and England recovered something of her lost prestige at The Oval.

On that occasion Warwick Armstrong acted in an extraordinary manner by way of emphasising his opinion that all Test matches should be played to a finish irrespective of time. When a draw was certain he rested his regular bowlers, went into the long field himself, an unknown position for him, and actually picked up and read a fully extended newspaper that was blown from the crowd! Clearly he was then indifferent to what happened; but he was very much alert a few weeks before at Old Trafford, where the England Captain erred over a declaration. Rain prevented play on Saturday, and so the match became an affair of two days. With England's score over 300 for four wickets the Hon. L. H. Tennyson, at ten minutes to six, went on to the field and called the players in. Ernest Tyldesley and P. G. H. Fender, the batsmen, left the field, but Armstrong demurred and sat on the turf near the stumps where he had been bowling. After a wait the Australians and umpires went to the pavilion, and Armstrong pointed out that the law, amended in 1914, showed that a closure in the circumstances of a lost first day could not be made later than an hour and forty minutes before the time for drawing stumps. It was amazing that no England official or player in the pavilion knew enough to prevent such a lamentable blunder; that the captain should be corrected by his Australian rival was a humiliating incident. The umpires, also at fault of course, were so muddled that when, after twenty minutes delay, play was resumed, Armstrong himself was allowed to commit an error by bowling the next over – two in succession.

Armstrong established a record by playing in 42 Test matches against England – one more than Clem Hill. In these games he scored 2,172 runs, average 35.03, and took 74 wickets at an average cost of 30.91. He made four Test centuries against England – all in Australia – and in ten Tests with South Africa he twice reached three figures. Altogether 46 centuries stand to his name in first-class cricket. With M. A. Noble, Armstrong put on 428 at Hove against Sussex in 1902 – still an Australian record for the sixth wicket. In Sheffield Shield matches Armstrong scored 4,993 runs, average 49.93, and took 177 wickets at 24.16 runs apiece. At Melbourne in November 1920 he made two centuries for Victoria against South Australia – 157 not out and 245. In November 1912, in the corresponding match, also at Melbourne, he scored 250, his highest innings in these tournaments.

Very tall and slim when first coming to England, Armstrong was of quite different build nineteen years later, and his massive frame made him a dominating personality as captain, quite apart from his ability with bat and ball. If appearing ungainly at the wicket because of bent knees, almost inevitable in the case of such a big man, Armstrong was a splendid stroke player, with the drive and cut most in evidence, and his defence was untiring. Bowling slows, usually round the wicket from a great height, he did not turn the ball a lot, but his leg theory was so pronounced that on occasions he sent down over after over wide of the leg stump without being punished, because he dropped the ball with what really was deceptive flight and usually very little break. Against a field cleverly placed for catches, batsmen refrained from taking risks. In fact, Armstrong was adept at keeping down runs in emergency. John Tyldesley, at The Oval in 1905, countered this, stepping back a yard and cutting the alleged leg-breaks where no fieldsman stood.

Like many cricketers, after retiring from active participation in the game, Armstrong wrote for the Press, and his caustic Test criticisms created ill-feeling of a kind which should not be associated with cricket.   H.P.

AUTY, MR KARL ANDRÉ, who died in Chicago on November 30, 1959, aged 81, was the owner of an outstanding cricket book collection. Educated at Wheelwright Grammar School, Dewsbury, and on H.M.S. Conway Training Ship, he accomplished a Military and General course at the Sorbonne, Paris, and obtained a B.Sc. at Nottingham. He was an active participant in cricket until his late sixties in New England, B.C., and in North America. In the thirties he published a weekly newspaper, *The British American*, and for some years issued a cricket annual containing full details of Chicago cricket. He was celebrated for his Christmas cards, one of which included the following information: "It is interesting to note that a Surrey (England) team on its way to play exhibition games in Paris in 1789 was at Dover ready for the crossing, but turned back when met there by their host, the Duke of Dorset, H. B. M. Ambassador, who had fled from Paris before the coming outbreak of the French Revolution. Otherwise this would have been the first team ever to leave Britain's shores to play cricket abroad, thus depriving the 1859 team of that distinction."

BEET, GEORGE, achieved his ambition of umpiring in a Test match before he died on December 13, 1946, at his home in Derby. Appointed to the umpires' list in 1929, he stood regularly, and at length was chosen for the England and India Test at Manchester in July 1946. On the way home by train from that game, Beet was taken seriously ill and rushed to Derby Infirmary for an operation. From this illness he never recovered. He made his first appearance as wicket-keeper for Derbyshire in 1910, and last played for them in 1922. Very dependable behind the sticks, he also gave useful help with the bat, and in 1919 was second in the Derbyshire averages with 24.80. For several seasons Fred Root was the Derbyshire fast bowler, and the junction of their names in many scores earned the pair the endearing name of "Beet-root". During the war George Beet and A. Fowler were the regular umpires in almost every match at Lord's. Beet in several winters went to South Africa as coach. He was sixty years old.

BLAKER, MR RICHARD NORMAN ROWSELL, M.C., died in Eltham Hospital on September 11, 1950, following an operation for peritonitis. Born on October 24, 1879, he captained Westminster School at cricket and Association football for four years, and, going to Cambridge, gained his cricket Blue in the three seasons, 1900 to 1902, being contemporary with such players as S. H. Day, F. B. Wilson, E. M. Dowson and E. R. Wilson. He also appeared as centre-forward in three Association football University matches against Oxford, being captain in 1901. For Kent, between 1898 and 1908, he gained a high reputation both as a hard-hitting batsman and a fine slip fielder. One of his best batting performances was against Gloucestershire at Catford in 1905, when he hit 120, including five 6s, out of 194 in seventy-five minutes. Against Surrey at Canterbury in 1900, he and S. H. Day put on 50 in eighteen minutes. He helped Kent to carry off the County Championship in 1906, and was President of the club when he died. He also captained the Butterflies. As a footballer, he was a frequent member of the Corinthian teams who achieved such great things in the early part of the century. In the first Great War, when a Lieutenant in the Rifle Brigade, he was awarded the Military Cross for bravery at Cambrai. His twin daughters, Barbara and Joan, known as the "Blaker Twins", were prominent members of the Kent women's cricket team and both played for England.

During the last Canterbury Week his tent was the centre of pleasant entertainment, but he showed signs of ill-health and in little more than a month passed away.

CANNON, MR JAMES, for 65 years with MCC at Lord's, died on April 20, 1949, aged 82. He started as a ball-boy for the tennis courts when 12 and held the horses for members when they visited the ground. Gradually he climbed the ladder, becoming boot-boy in the cricket dressing-rooms, and then went into the office where for many years he was chief clerk. A small, popular figure, "Jimmy" Cannon was given the title "King of Lord's", by Sir Pelham Warner. A keen gardener, he was recognised by hundreds of people by his straw-hat and button-hole of sweet-peas, rose or carnation. On his retirement in 1944, he was elected an honorary member of MCC.

CARR, MR DOUGLAS WARD, who died in a nursing home at Sidmouth on March 23, 1959, at the age of 78, was one of the most remarkable cricketers at the start of the century. He was an unknown bowler when, at the age of 37, he entered first-class cricket. Originally an ordinary fast-medium bowler, Carr developed and practised the googly, then almost unknown, and his arrival with this unorthodox type of bowling created consternation among batsmen.

In his first match that season of 1909 he took seven Oxford wickets for Kent at a cost of 95 runs. So impressed were the selectors that he was invited to play for Gentlemen against Players at The Oval and Lord's. Realising that they had discovered a bowler out of the ordinary, the selectors then chose him as one of the England party to attend Manchester for the Fourth Test Match against Australia.

Because the ground was considered too soft for his bowling, Carr was not included in the final eleven, but he won a place in the last Test at The Oval. His start was dramatic, for, opening the England attack, he dismissed S. E. Gregory, M. A. Noble and W. W. Armstrong for a combined total of 18 runs. Unfortunately for England he tired and was kept on too long. His first innings figures were five for 146 in 34 overs, and he took two for 136 in 35 overs in the second innings. Even so he showed his immense possibilities, and at the end of that season he took eight for 105 in the match and helped Lord Londesborough's XI to victory over the Australians.

Born at Cranbrook in Kent on March 17, 1872, Carr went to Sutton Valence School and then to Brasenose College, Oxford. He took part in little cricket at the University because of a football injury to his knee. He did most of his early bowling in club cricket in Kent.

Carr showed that his remarkable entry into big cricket was no mere fluke, for in 1910 he headed the Kent bowling averages. He did not join the side until the end of July, but took sixty wickets in Championship matches at an average of 12.16 runs apiece. He fully maintained his form up to 1914, when war intervened and he dropped out of first-class cricket. He enjoyed a particularly successful time in 1912, when he again headed the Kent bowling with 49 wickets for 9.59 runs each. In his brief first-class career of six years Carr took 334 wickets with an average of 16.84.

CHAPMAN, MR ARTHUR PERCY FRANK, who died in Alton Hospital, Hampshire, on September 16, 1961, aged 61, will always be remembered as a player who brought to cricket a light-hearted air seldom encountered in these days and as an England captain of great personal charm who got the best out of the men under him. He had been in ill health for some years. As a tall, polished left-handed batsman who, excelling in the off-drive and leg-side strokes, was generally willing and able to attack the bowling, he scored 16,309 runs, average 31.97, in a first-class career dating from 1920 to 1939. Of his 27 centuries, the highest and certainly one of the best was 260 for Kent against Lancashire, that season's Champions, at Maidstone in 1927. The position when he went in was far from encouraging, half the side being out for 70 runs. Yet he and G. B. Legge (101) assailed an attack including such men as E. A. McDonald, the Australian fast bowler, Richard Tyldesley and F. M. Sibbles with such vigour that in two and a half hours they put on 284 runs. Percy Chapman's 260, scored in just over three hours and containing five 6s and thirty-two 4s, typified his outlook on the game. A defensive policy was abhorrent to his nature, whether batting or fielding, and besides being a punishing though never reckless hitter, he made a name as a silly point, cover or slip of amazing speed and brilliancy.

Born at Reading, Berkshire, he was in the Uppingham eleven for four years from 1916 to 1919, being captain in the last two, and soon attracted attention with splendid performances. In 1917 he headed the school batting figures with 668 runs in 10 innings and an average of 111.33. After an indifferent start to the season, he wound up with 66, 206, 160, 81 and 114 in five innings, being not out on four occasions and run out on the other! In those days, too, he met with success as a bowler, first slow left-arm and then fast-medium. Not surprisingly, especially as he took 118 from the Essex bowling at Fenner's on his first-class début, he gained his Blue as a Freshman at Cambridge in 1920, scoring 27 against Oxford and being chosen for the Gentlemen at Lord's. Against Oxford in 1921 he obtained 45 and next season helped Cambridge to a handsome victory with a scintillating innings of 102 not out. In this latter season he took part in that famous match at Eastbourne where an England XI defeated Warwick Armstrong's hitherto unbeaten Australians by 28 runs, justifying the assertion of A. C. MacLaren, maintained throughout the summer, that he could pick a side good enough to overcome the touring team.

Chapman played with distinction for Berkshire before qualifying for Kent in 1924, and he became one of the few players to appear for England while taking part in Minor Counties' cricket. He turned out for England 26 times in all, 17 of them as captain, in which role he was only twice on the losing side. Twice he went to Australia, under A. E. R. Gilligan in 1924-25 and as leader of the 1928 side who, regarded as probably the best in fielding ever sent out, won the Test rubber by four wins to one. Though he played several good innings for his country, sharing stands of 116 with E. Hendren in 1926 and 125 with G. O. Allen in 1930, both at Lord's against Australia, he only once scored a century in a Test match. Then, in hitting 121 against Australia at Lord's in 1930, he achieved a triple performance never before accomplished, for on the same ground he had previously reached three figures in both the University and – in 1922 – the Gentlemen v Players match, a fixture in which he figured 19 times. He captained Kent from 1931 to 1936.

Tributes included:

S. C. Griffith, Assistant-Secretary, MCC: "I will always remember him for his debonair and aggressive approach to the game and as a great fielder."

Sir John Hobbs: "I well remember the surprise caused by the appointment of Percy Chapman as the England captain for the final Test against Australia at The Oval in 1926. He was only 25 and all the team liked him. He was not a disciplinarian like his predecessors and he did not hesitate to seek advice. He often talked to me about tactics on the field and he set a great example by his brilliant catching in the slips. The Australian crowds loved him during the tour of 1928-29, when he made us a happy team."

G. Duckworth, former Lancashire and England wicket-keeper: "He was a most delightful gentleman and an ideal captain. He had such a persuasive charm as a leader that you could not help trying your utmost for him."

W. J. Fairservice, former Kent player: "Percy Chapman and Frank Woolley, two left-handers, were two of the greatest cricketers in the game."

CHESTER, FRANK, who died at his home at Bushey, Hertfordshire, on April 8, 1957, aged 61, will be remembered as the man who raised umpiring to a higher level than had ever been known in the history of cricket. For some years he had suffered from stomach ulcers. Often he stood as umpire when in considerable pain, which unfortunately caused him to become somewhat irascible at times, and at the end of the 1955 season he retired, terminating a career in which he officiated in over 1,000 first-class fixtures, including 48 Test matches.

The First World War cut short his ambitions as an all-rounder for Worcestershire. In 1912, at the age of 16, he joined that county's staff and in the following season he scored 703 runs, including three centuries, average 28.12, and took with off-breaks 44 wickets, average 26.88. *Wisden* said of him that year: "Nothing stood out more prominently than the remarkable development of Chester, the youngest professional regularly engaged in first-class cricket. . . . Very few players in the history of cricket have shown such form at the age of seventeen and a half. Playing with a beautifully straight bat, he depended to a large extent on his watchfulness in defence. Increased hitting power will naturally come with time. He bowls with a high, easy action and, commanding an accurate length, can get plenty of spin on the ball. Having begun so well, Chester should continue to improve and it seems only reasonable to expect that when he has filled out and gained more strength, he will be an England cricketer."

In 1914 he put together an aggregate of 924 runs, average 27.17, with an innings of 178 not out – including four 6s from the bowling of J. W. H. T. Douglas – against Essex at Worcester, his highest. Then came the war and, in the course of service with the Army in Salonika, he lost his right arm just below the elbow. That, of course, meant no more cricket as a player for Chester; but in 1922 he became a first-class umpire and, with the advantage of youth when the majority of his colleagues were men who had retired as cricketers on the score of *Anno Domini*, he swiftly gained a big reputation. His lack of years caused him difficulty on one occasion at Northampton for a gate-man refused him admission, declining to believe that one so young could be an umpire, and suggested that he should try the ground of a neighbouring works team!

From the very beginning of his career as an umpire, he gave his decisions without fear or favour. In an article, "Thirty Years an Umpire", in the 1954 *Wisden*, Vivian Jenkins told how, when standing in his first county match, Essex v Somerset at Leyton, Chester was called on to give decisions against both captains, J. W. H. T. Douglas and J. Daniell, and did his duty according to his lights – Douglas lbw, Daniell stumped. "You'll be signing your death warrant if you go on like that", he was warned by his venerable colleague, but he went on undeterred.

Chester began the custom, now prevalent among umpires, of bending low over the wicket when the bowler delivered the ball, and his decisions were both prompt and rarely questioned. Yet the ruling which probably caused most discussion was one in which Chester was wrong. This occurred during the England v West Indies Test match at Trent Bridge in 1950, when S. Ramadhin bowled D. J. Insole off his pads. Chester contended that the batsman was leg before wicket, because he (Chester) gave his decision in the brief time before the ball hit the stumps, and as "lbw" Insole remained in the score. Soon after this, MCC added a Note to Law 34 which made it clear beyond dispute that, where a batsman is dismissed in such circumstances he is out "bowled".

Chester had some brushes with Australian touring players, whose demonstrative methods of appealing annoyed him, but nevertheless Sir Donald Bradman termed him "the greatest umpire under whom I played". Chester, for his part, rated Bradman "the greatest run-making machine I have ever known", and considered Sir John Hobbs the greatest batsman of all time on all pitches.

Throughout his long spell as an umpire Chester used, for counting the balls per over, six small pebbles which he picked up from his mother's garden at Bushey before he "stood" in his first match.

Tributes included:

Mr R. Aird, Secretary of MCC: "He was an inspiration to other umpires. He seemed to have a flair for the job and did the right thing by instinct. He was outstanding among umpires for a very long time."

Sir John Hobbs: "I played against him in his brief career and am sure he would have been a great England all-rounder. As an umpire, he was right on top. I class him with that great Australian, Bob Crockett."

F. S. Lee, the Test match umpire: "Frank was unquestionably the greatest umpire I have known. His decisions were fearless, whether the batsman to be given out was captain or not. There is a great deal for which umpires have to thank him."

DELME-RADCLIFFE, MR ARTHUR HENRY, who died on June 30, 1956, was a native of South Tedworth, Hampshire. A member of the Sherborne XI before going to Oxford, he headed the school's batting averages in 1889. Subsequently he played for Hampshire and Berkshire. While batting for Hampshire against Somerset at Southampton in August 1889, he was concerned in a curious incident. Thinking he was out stumped, Delme-Radcliffe began to walk towards the pavilion, but the appeal had not been upheld. Then a fieldsman pulled up a stump and he was given out "run out", but in the meantime the other umpire had called "over", so the batsman continued his innings.

DULEEPSINHJI, KUMAR SHRI, who died from a heart attack in Bombay on December 5, 1959, aged 54, was among the best batsmen ever to represent England and certainly one of the most popular. Ill-health limited his first-class career to eight seasons, but in that time he scored 15,357 runs, including 49 centuries, at an average of 50.11. A remarkably good slip fieldsman, he brought off 243 catches. "Duleep" or "Mr Smith", as he was affectionately known in cricket circles, was in the Cheltenham XI from 1921 to 1923, and when captain in the last year headed the batting figures with an average of 52.36, his highest innings being 162. He also met with considerable success as a leg-break bowler and in 1922 was top of the averages with fifty wickets at 13.66 runs each, but he rarely bowled after leaving school. During this time H. S. Altham, the present President of MCC, wrote of him in *Wisden*: "In natural gifts of eye, wrist and footwork he is certainly blest far above the ordinary measure ... there is no doubt about the judgment and certainty with which he takes toll of straight balls of anything but the most immaculate length. His late cutting is quite beautiful and there is a certain ease and maturity about all his batting methods that stamps him as of a different class from the ordinary school batsman." The accuracy of this estimate of his qualities was borne out when in 1925 he went up to Cambridge. He got his Blue as a Freshman, scoring 75 in the University match, and also played against Oxford in 1926 and 1928. Illness kept him out of the side for most of the 1927 season.

His career with Sussex, whom he captained in 1932, began in 1926 and he headed the county averages in every season until 1932, when doctors advised him not to take further part in cricket. In 1930 he hit 333 in five and a half hours against Northamptonshire at Hove, which still stands as the highest individual innings played for Sussex and beat the biggest put together by his famous uncle, K. S. Ranjitsinhji – 285 not out against Somerset at Taunton in 1901; three times he reached three figures in each innings of a match, 246 and 115 v Kent at Hastings in 1929, 116 and 102 not out v Middlesex and 125 and 103 not out for Gentlemen v Players, both at Lord's the next summer; and in 1931 he registered twelve centuries, four of them in successive innings.

He made twelve appearances for England and in his first against Australia at Lord's in 1930 he obtained 173. Of this display a story is told that, when Prince Duleepsinhji was at last caught in the long field from a rash stroke, his uncle remarked: "He always was a careless lad". His one tour abroad was with the MCC team in New Zealand and Australia in 1929-30, when he scored more runs than any other member of the side. A. H. H. Gilligan, the captain, rated him the best player of slow bowling on a wet pitch that he ever saw. "Duleep" had to withdraw from the team for D. R. Jardine's "body-line" tour of 1932-33.

He joined the Indian foreign service in 1949 and became High Commissioner for India in Australia and New Zealand. Upon returning to India in 1953 he was appointed chairman of the public service commission in the State of Saurashtra.

When he retired from cricket through recurring illness, *Wisden* wrote of him: "Of singular charm of character; extremely modest of his own wonderful ability; and with a love for the game which transcended his joy in all other pastimes, Duleepsinhji will always be remembered as one of the outstanding personalities during his period in first-class cricket." So he remained to the end.

Tributes included:

Sir John Hobbs: "He was an extremely popular personality and did not have an enemy on the field. He was a brilliant player."

R. Aird: "He was not only a very great cricketer, but he also possessed a charming and gentle nature which endeared him to all his many friends."

H. Sutcliffe: "There was no better man to play with. He was never out for personal glorification, his great concern being for the success of the team. He was a real joy to watch and was, above all, a first-class man."

FANE, MR FREDERICK LUTHER, who died on November 27, 1960, aged 85, was a prominent figure in cricket for some twenty years before the First World War. Owing to a similarity of initials, *Wisden* reported his death when he was 79. The man concerned was Francis L. Fane, his cousin. By a coincidence, Mr Fane's father also once read his own obituary. Educated at Charterhouse, Frederick Fane was in the XI from 1892 to 1894, and after coming down from Oxford, where he gained a Blue in 1897 and the following year, he played a good deal for Essex, being captain from 1904 to 1906. His best season for the county was that of 1906 when he scored 1,572 runs, average 34. In 1899 he put together his highest innings, 207 against Leicestershire. At Leyton in 1905, when Essex beat the Australians by 19 runs, Fane ended the match with a remarkable catch at a position approximating to deep long-stop where, with Buckenham bowling very fast, he had placed himself to save possible byes. In the 1907-8 tour of Australia, he captained the MCC side in the first three Test matches when A. O. Jones fell ill. During that tour he scored 774 runs, average 33, hitting 101 against New South Wales. Fane also went to South Africa in 1905-6 and 1909-10, to New Zealand in 1902-3 and the West Indies in 1902. Altogether he played in fourteen Test matches.

FERGUSON, MR WILLIAM HENRY, who died at Bath on September 22, 1957, aged 77, was the best-known cricket scorer in the world. For 52 years, from the time he first visited England with Joe Darling's Australian side of 1905, he acted as scorer and baggage-master for England, South Africa, West Indies, New Zealand and, naturally, Australia, in no fewer than 43 tours. In all that time his boast was that he never lost a bag. "Fergie", as he was affectionately known in the cricket world, scored in no fewer than 208 Test matches in every country where big cricket is played. He liked to relate how he first took up the job. The office in Sydney, his birthplace, where he was employed as a clerk, overlooked the harbour and he often felt the urge to travel. So in 1905 he "thought up a nice toothache", went to see his dentist, M. A. Noble, the Test batsman, and brought up the question of scoring. Amused at the ingenious method of approach, Noble put forward "Fergie's" name to the authorities, with the result that this short, slightly-built man began his travels which totalled well over half a million miles. His salary for the 1905 tour was £2 per week, from which he defrayed his expenses, and he paid his own passage.

For all his long connection with it, "Fergie" never took much active part in the game, but figures, for which he always had a passion, fascinated him, and he loved to travel. Besides actual scoring, he kept diagrams of every stroke played, with their value, by every batsman in the matches in which he was concerned, and could account for every ball bowled – and who fielded it. Touring captains, including D. G. Bradman and D. R. Jardine, employed his charts to study the strength and weaknesses of opposing batsmen.

When in England with the Australian team of 1948, "Fergie" was presented to King George VI. That summer Bradman scored 2,428 runs. Said the King: "Mr Ferguson, do you use an adding-machine when the Don is in?"

"Fergie", who received the British Empire Medal in 1951 for his services to cricket, emerged from two years' retirement to score for the West Indies last summer. A fall at an hotel in August prevented him from finishing the tour, and he spent some time in hospital, returning home only two days before his death. His autobiography, titled *Mr Cricket*, was published in May, 1957.

C. B. FRY

By Neville Cardus

Captain Charles Burgess Fry, who died at his home at Hampstead, London, on September 7, 1956, aged 84, was probably the grestest all rounder of his or any generation. He was a brilliant scholar and an accomplished performer in almost every branch of outdoor spot. Fry was the perfect amateur; he played games because he loved them and never for personal gain. He captained England in Test matches, and the Mother Country never lost under his captaincy. He played Association Football for England against Ireland in 1901; he was a full-back for Southampton in the F.A. Cup Final of 1902; and he put up a world's long jump record of 23 ft 5 in. in 1892 which stood for twenty-one years. But it was at cricket that his outstanding personality found its fullest expression. The following tribute by Mr Neville Cardus first appeared in the Manchester Guardian.

Charles Fry was born into a Sussex family on April 25, 1872, at Croydon, and was known first as an England cricketer and footballer, also as a great all-round athlete who for a while held the long-jump record, a hunter and a fisher, and as an inexhaustible virtuoso at the best of all indoor games, conversation.

He was at Repton when a boy, where at cricket he joined the remarkable and enduring roll of superb young players emanating from the school – Fry, Palairet, Ford, J. N. Crawford, to name a few. At Oxford he won first-class honours in Classical Moderations at Wadham, and it is a tribute to his calibre as a scholar and personal force that most of the obituary articles written after the death of Viscount Simon named Fry in a Wadham trinity with Birkenhead. Not the least doughty and idealistic of his many-sided achievements was as a Liberal candidate for Brighton, where he actually polled 20,000 votes long after he had ceased to live in Sussex and dominate the cricket field.

With all his versatility of mind and sinew Fry himself wished that he might be remembered, as much as for anything else, by his work in command of the training-ship *Mercury*. For forty years he and his wife directed the *Mercury* at Hamble, educating youth with a classical sense of values. He once invited the present writer to visit Hamble and see his boys play cricket and perform extracts from "Parsifal"! Hitler sent for him for advice during the building-up of the "Youth Movement" in Germany. He was a deputy for the Indian delegation to the first, third, and fourth Assemblies of the League of Nations, edited his own monthly magazine more than half a century ago, and was indeed a pioneer in the school of intelligent and analytical criticism of sport. He wrote several books, including an autobiography, and a *Key to the League of Nations*, and one called *Batsmanship*, which might conceivably have come from the pen of Aristotle had Aristotle lived nowadays and played cricket.

Fry must be counted among the most fully developed and representative Englishmen of his period; and the question arises whether, had fortune allowed him to concentrate on the things of the mind, not distracted by the lure of cricket, a lure intensified by his increasing mastery over the game, he would not have reached a high altitude in politics or critical literature. But he belonged – and it was his glory – to an age not obsessed by specialism; he was one of the last of the English tradition of the amateur, the connoisseur, and, in the most delightful sense of the word, the dilettante.

As a batsman, of course, he was thoroughly grounded in first principles. He added to his stature, in fact, by taking much thought. As a youth he did not use a bat with much natural freedom, and even in his period of pomp he was never playing as handsomely as his magnificent physical appearance seemed to suggest and deserve. He was, of course, seen often in contrast with Ranjitsinhji, who would have made all batsmen of the present day, Hutton included, look like so many plebeians toiling under the sun. Yet in his prime Fry was a noble straight-driver. He once said to me: "I had only one stroke maybe; but it went to ten different parts of the field." But in 1905, when the Australians decided that Fry could make runs only in front of the wicket, mainly to the on, and set the field for him accordingly, he scored 144 in an innings sparkling with cuts.

In his career as cricketer, he scored some 30,000 runs, averaging 50, in an era of natural wickets, mainly against bowlers of great speed or of varied and subtle spin and accuracy. From Yorkshire bowling alone he scored nearly 2,500 runs in all his matches against the county during its most powerful days, averaging 70, in the teeth of the attack of Hirst, Rhodes, Haigh, Wainwright, and, occasionally, F. S. Jackson. In 1903 he made 234 against Yorkshire at Bradford. Next summer he made 177 against Yorkshire at Sheffield, and 229 at Brighton, in successive innings. Ranjitsinhji's performances against Yorkshire were almost as remarkable as Fry's; for he scored well over 1,500 runs against them, averaging more than sixty an innings. In 1901 Fry scored six centuries in six consecutive innings, an achievement equalled by Bradman, but on Australian wickets and spread over a season. Fry's six hundreds, two of them on bowler's wickets, came one on top of the other within little more than a fortnight.

The conjunction at the creases of C. B. Fry and K. S. Ranjitsinhji was a sight and an appeal to the imagination not likely ever to be repeated: Fry, nineteenth-century rationalist, batting according to first principles with a sort of moral grandeur, observing patience and abstinence. At the other end of the wicket, "Ranji" turned a cricket bat into a wand of conjuration. Fry was of the Occident, "Ranji" told of the Orient.

Cricket can scarcely hope again to witness two styles as fascinatingly contrasted and as racially representative as Fry's and Ranjitsinhji's. Between them they evolved a doctrine that caused a fundamental change in the tactics of batsmanship, "Play back or drive". "Watch the ball well, then make a stroke at the ball itself and not at a point in space where you hope the ball will presently be." At the time that Fry was making a name in cricket most batsmen played forward almost automatically on good fast pitches, frequently lunging out full stretch. If a ball can be reached only by excessive elongation of arms and body, obviously the pitch of it has been badly gauged. Fry and Ranjitsinhji, following after Arthur Shrewsbury, developed mobile footwork.

It is a pungent comment on the strength of the reserves of English cricket half a century ago that Fry and "Ranji" were both dropped from the England team at the height of their fame. In 1901 Fry scored 3,147 runs, average 78.67: in 1903 he scored 2,683 runs, average 81.30. In 1900 Ranjitsinhji scored 3,065, average 87.57. Yet because of one or two lapses in 1902, both these great players were asked to stand down and give way to other aspirants to Test cricket.

As we consider Fry's enormous aggregates of runs summer by summer, we should not forget that he took part, during all the extent of his career, in only one Test match lasting more than three days, and that he never visited Australia as a cricketer. For one reason and another Fry appeared not more than eighteen times against Australia in forty-three Test matches played between 1899, when he began the England innings with W. G. Grace, and 1912, in which wet season he was England's captain against Australia and South Africa in the ill-fated triangular tournament. By that time he had severed his illustrious connection with Sussex and was opening the innings for Hampshire. The general notion is that Fry was not successful as an England batsman; and it is true that in Test matches he did not remain on his habitual peaks. None the less, his batting average for Test cricket is much the same as that of Victor Trumper, M. A. Noble, and J. T. Tyldesley. The currency had not been debased yet.

Until he was no-balled for throwing by Phillips – who also "called" Mold at Old Trafford – Fry was a good fast bowler who took six wickets for 78 in the University match, opened the Gentlemen's bowling against the Players at The Oval, and took five wickets. Twice he performed the hat-trick at Lord's.

He played Association football for his university, for the Corinthians, Southampton, and for England.

In his retirement he changed his methods as a writer on cricket and indulged a brisk impressionistic "columnist" style, to suit the running commentary needed by an evening paper: "Ah, here comes the Don. Walking slowly to the wicket. Deliberately. Menacingly.

I don't like the look of him. He has begun with a savage hook. He is evidently in form. Dangerously so. Ah, but he is out. . . ." Essentially he was an analyst by mind, if rather at the mercy of an impulsive, highly strung temperament. He sometimes, in his heyday, got on the wrong side of the crowd by his complete absorption in himself, which was mistaken for posing or egoism. He would stand classically poised after making an on-drive, contemplating the direction and grandeur of it. The cricket field has seen no sight more Grecian than the one presented by C. B. Fry in the pride and handsomeness of his young manhood.

After he had passed his seventieth birthday, he one day entered his club, saw his friend Denzil Batchelor, and said he had done most things but was now sighing for a new world to conquer, and proposed to interest himself in racing, attach himself to a stable, and then set up "on his own". And Batchelor summed up his genius in a flash of wit: "What as, Charles? Trainer, jockey, or horse?"

It is remarkable that he was not knighted for his services to cricket, and that no honours came his way for the sterling, devoted work he did with the training-ship *Mercury*.

Mr Hubert Preston writes: Charles Fry secured a place in the Repton XI in 1888 and retained it for the next three years, being captain in 1890 and 1891. In his last season at school his average reached nearly 50.

When he went up to Oxford, Fry was captain of the cricket and Association football XIs and president of the athletic club, acting as first string in the 100 yards and the long-jump.

He also played a good deal of Rugby football, and his friends insisted that but for an unfortunate injury he would have added a Rugger "Blue" to his other honours. Charles Fry was also a fine boxer, a passable golfer, swimmer, sculler, tennis player and javelin thrower. But it was on the cricket field that he achieved his greatest triumphs. He represented three counties – Sussex, Hampshire and Surrey – scoring altogether 30,886 runs in first-class matches, average 50.22. His total of centuries reached 94 and five times he scored two separate hundreds in a match.

Fry's best season was 1901 when his aggregate reached 3,147, average 78.67. In that summer he scored 13 hundreds and made six in successive innings – a feat equalled only by Sir Donald Bradman. In 1899, 1901, and 1903, Charles Fry hit a century for the Gentlemen against the Players at Lord's, his 232 not out in 1903 remaining the highest individual score for the Gentlemen at Headquarters.

His one three-figure Test innings against Australia was 144 at The Oval in 1905, when the rubber had already been decided. Two years later he made his only other hundred for England, 129 against the South Africans, also at The Oval. Fry shared with Vine (J.) in thirty-three opening partnerships of 100 for Sussex.

Considering the very high rank he attained among batsmen, Fry, at the outset, was a stiff ungainly performer and was still somewhat laboured in stroke-production when he went up to Oxford. But from the time he began playing for Sussex with "Ranji" his game improved. He was a natural on-side batsman with a powerful straight drive and many useful leg-side strokes.

The records contain very few details of Fry's achievements as a bowler. Yet he figured in a somewhat heated controversy in the 'nineties about "unfair deliveries". Cricket writers generally regarded him as a "thrower". Fry was equally insistent that all his deliveries were scrupulously fair.

In his writings, Fry recalled how Jim Phillips, an Australian heavy-weight slow bowler turned umpire, was sent to Hove specially to "no-ball" him.

"A bright move", commented Fry, "because, of course, I rolled up my sleeve above my elbow and bowled with my arm as rigidly straight as a poker. The great Jim, sighting himself as a strong umpire, was not deterred. Large as an elephant, he bluffly no-balled me nine times running. It was a farce and the Sussex authorities and players were very angry.

"However, I bowled often afterwards unscathed, even in Gentlemen v Players' at Lord's and in a Test match."

Outside sport, Fry's greatest work was accomplished as director of the training ship

Mercury, which he saved from extinction and to which he devoted forty-two years of unsparing effort entirely without remuneration. He was assisted by his wife, formerly Miss Beatrice Holme-Sumner, who died in 1941. In recognition of their work, Charles Fry was given the honorary rank of Captain in the R.N.R. and Mrs Fry was awarded the O.B.E.

In his absorbing autobiography, *Life Worth Living*, published in 1939, Fry told of how he "very nearly became the King of Albania". His association with Ranjitsinhji led him to occupy the position of substitute delegate for India at the Assemblies of the League of Nations at Geneva, where he composed a speech delivered by Ranji which "turned Mussolini out of Corfu".

The Albanians sent a delegation and appointed a Bishop, who bore a striking resemblance to W. G. Grace, to find "an English country gentlemen with £10,000 a year" for their King. Fry had the first qualification but not the second; but Ranji certainly could have provided the money. "If I had really pressed Ranji to promote me," said Fry, "it is quite on the cards that I should have been King of Albania yesterday, if not today."

In collaboration with his wife, he wrote the novel *A Mother's Son* which was published in 1907.

Other tributes included:

Sir Pelham Warner: "His style was stiff, but he had a cast-iron defence and played well off his pads. He put his great mental powers into improving his cricket, and that he developed into a very great batsman there can be no question. Ranjitsinhji's opinion was that he was 'the greatest of all batsmen of his time on all wickets and against every type of bowling'. ... Perhaps his greatest innings was his 129 at The Oval in 1907 against the famous South African googly bowlers – Vogler, Faulkner, Schwarz and White – on a wicket which *Wisden* says 'was never easy' and on which 'the South African bowling was very difficult and the fielding was almost free from fault'."

Sir John Hobbs: "I played with 'C. B.' in my first Test against Australia in this country. The year was 1909 and we both got blobs in the first innings. 'C. B.' persuaded Archie MacLaren, our captain, to let him go in first with me in the second innings, and we knocked off the 105 runs wanted for victory. ... Later he was my skipper and we always got on well together. He was a great raconteur, and my wife and I have spent many happy hours just listening to him. I saw him at Lord's this season."

Sir Leonard Hutton: "He was a fine judge of a cricketer and he always took the keenest interest in the progress of young players. I had a number of letters from him when I was still in the game. They were kindly, encouraging letters which contained much sound advice which I greatly appreciated."

Frank Woolley: "He was one of the most solid batsmen I ever bowled against. He had a tremendous amount of determination, especially on difficult pitches, and the patience to play the type of game required. I remember once bowling to him on a 'sticky' when the ball was turning a lot. I beat him several times in one over without getting his wicket. Next over, to my surprise, he demonstrated that I was not pitching the ball on the right spot and it was going over the stumps. That was typical of him. He was a great theorist."

H.M. KING GEORGE VI died at Sandringham on February 6, 1952. He was Patron of the Marylebone, Surrey and Lancashire clubs. When Prince Albert he performed the hat-trick on the private ground on the slopes below Windsor Castle, where the sons and grandsons of Edward VII used to play regularly. A left-handed batsman and bowler, the King bowled King Edward VII, King George V and the present Duke of Windsor in three consecutive balls, thus proving himself the best Royal cricketer since Frederick, Prince of Wales, in 1751, took a keen interest in the game. The ball is now mounted in the mess-room of the Royal Naval College, Dartmouth. King George VI, like his father, often went to Lord's when Commonwealth teams were playing there, and invariably the players and umpires were presented to His Majesty in front of the pavilion. He entertained the 1948 Australian team at Balmoral, and in his 1949 New Year's Honours Donald Bradman, the captain, received a Knighthood.

GILLINGHAM, REV. GEORGE WILLIAM, who died on June 11, 1953, after a ministry of fifty-two years, played cricket for Gentlemen of Worcestershire before the First World War. Though never attaining to first-class standards, he was a great cricket enthusiast who did much good work for Worcestershire. When becoming Rector of St Martin's, Worcester, he revived and managed the Worcestershire Club and Ground matches, and in 1923 he organised a bazaar which realised £2,300 for the County Club. From 1929 he acted for some seasons as honorary secretary to Worcestershire in order that the secretary, C. F. Walters, could play for the county. During this period when, during the winter the River Severn flooded the county ground at Worcester, Gillingham swam across the ground to gain access to the Pavilion and returned with the account books. He was author of *The Cardinal's Treasure*, a romance of the Elizabethan age, part of the proceeds from which he devoted to the Worcestershire CCC and the RSPCA. When Vicar of St Mark's, Coventry, he was for four years tenant of a condemned public house, "The Barley Mow", which he transformed into a "Holligans' Club" where boxing and Bible classes went hand-in-hand.

HARGREAVES, MR TOM KNIGHT, who died in hospital at Rotherham on November 19, 1955, aged 61, was a prominent all-rounder in Yorkshire Council cricket from 1921 till 1951. He played for Wath till he was 57, scoring many runs and proving successful as a slow bowler. A forcing batsman, he scored 191 in ninety minutes against Brampton in 1935. He brought off one of the biggest hits in cricket on one occasion when playing at the Wath Athletic Ground. A mighty six sent the ball soaring out of the ground and into a wagon of a goods-train on the nearby railway line. The ball was carried on to Scunthorpe.

HARRIS, CHARLES BOWMAR, who died in Nottingham General Hospital on August 8, 1954, aged 45, played as opening batsman for Nottinghamshire from 1928 till 1951, in which time he scored nearly 20,000 runs. A fine batsman, capable of strong hitting or dour defence, and a capable spin-bowler, he did not gain a regular place in the county side till 1931, when he got his chance as a result of a motoring accident involving three Nottinghamshire players. So well did he seize the opportunity that in twelve games he scored 456 runs, headed the county averages with 50.66 and earned his county cap. Next season, for the first of eleven times, he exceeded 1,000 runs and established himself in the eleven.

In 1933 he made 234 against Middlesex at Trent Bridge, he and W. W. Keeton sharing in a first wicket stand of 277. He and Keeton steadily became one of the best opening pairs in the country and in 1950 they joined in two three-figure partnerships against Northamptonshire at Northampton. Harris's best season was that of 1934, when he obtained 1,891 runs, average 38.59, and hit five centuries. His highest innings was 239 not out in 1950 when he carried his bat against Hampshire at Trent Bridge. His benefit match, against Yorkshire in 1949, realised £3,500 – a county record – despite the loss through rain of the opening day. Troubled by ill-health for some years, Harris appeared to have recovered when he was appointed a first-class umpire last season, but after standing in a few matches he broke down and was compelled to resign.

Well known as one of cricket's humorists, he habitually greeted the fieldsmen when going in to bat at the start of a day with the remark: "Good morning, fellow workers". On one occasion when the light was far from good, he made his way from the pavilion carrying a flare and headed straight for square-leg!

HARRIS, LIEUT.-COLONEL FRANK, who died at Tunbridge Wells on July 2, 1957, aged 91, was for thirty-five years captain of Southborough CC, for whom he first played when 16. In his younger days an enthusiastic runner, he walked from Bidborough to London on his 70th birthday because his father did the same thing and had told him that he would not be able to do so when he was 70. The journey occupied him just over thirteen hours. He served in the Royal Engineers during the First World War, being mentioned in dispatches.

HENDREN, ELIAS, who died in a London hospital on October 4, 1962, aged 73, was one of the most famous batsmen to play for Middlesex and England. Only one cricketer, Sir John Hobbs, in the whole history of the first-class game hit more centuries than Hendren's 170; only two, Hobbs and F. E. Woolley, exceeded his aggregate of runs, 57,610 scored at an average of 50.80 per innings.

"Patsy", as because of his Irish ancestry, he was affectionately known the world over, joined the Lord's ground-staff in 1905 and from his first appearance for Middlesex in 1909 he played regularly till 1937. Not always orthodox in style, this short, stockily-built batsman was celebrated for the power with which he invested his driving, for his cutting and for his courage in hooking fast bowlers. On pitches helpful to bowlers, he used his feet with consummate skill. His ability as a deep fieldsman is illustrated to some extent by the number of catches he brought off, 725, but the number of runs he saved cannot be gauged.

Apart from his achievements, "Patsy" was a "character" of a type sadly lacking in modern cricket. No game in which he was engaged could be altogether dull. If it looked like becoming so, Hendren could be relied upon at one time or another to produce some antic which would bring an appreciative chuckle from the onlookers. Furthermore, he was a first-rate mimic and wit, qualities which made him an admirable member of teams on tours, of which he took part in six – three in Australia, one in South Africa and two in the West Indies. Altogether he played in 51 Test matches, 28 of them against Australia, scoring 3,525 runs.

Of his seven centuries in Tests the highest was 205 not out against the West Indies at Port of Spain in 1930, when he and L. E. G. Ames (105) shared a fourth wicket stand of 237. "Patsy's" aggregate of 1,766, average 126.14, in that tour remains a record for a season in the West Indies. His highest innings in first-class cricket was 301 not out from the Worcestershire bowling at Dudley in 1933; on four occasions he put together a hundred in each innings of a match and he reached three-figures for Middlesex against every other first-class county. His best season was that of 1928 when he hit 3,311 runs, including 13 centuries, at an average of 70.44. In three summers he exceeded 3,000 runs; in twelve he made more than 2,000 and in ten over 1,000. Among many big partnerships with his great friend and county colleague, J. W. Hearne, that of 375 against Hampshire at Southampton in 1923 was at the time a world's record for the third wicket.

In 1933 Hendren caused something of a sensation at Lord's when he batted against the West Indies' fast bowlers wearing a special cap. Fashioned by his wife, this cap had three peaks, two of which covered the ears and temples, and was lined with sponge rubber. Hendren explained that he needed protection after being struck on the head two years earlier by the new-fashioned persistent short-pitched bouncers.

Following his retirement from the field, he succeeded Wilfred Rhodes as coach at Harrow School and for four years held a similar post with Sussex. He was elected a life member of MCC in 1949 and also served on the Middlesex Committee. In 1952 he became scorer for Middlesex, continuing till ill-health compelled him to give up in 1960. In his younger days he was a fine Association football wing forward, playing in turn for Brentford, Queen's Park Rangers, Manchester City and Coventry City, and he appeared in a "Victory" International for England in 1919.

Tributes included:

Sir John Hobbs: "Patsy was a great cricketer and a great companion. He was the life and soul of the party on all our tours. In my opinion he was as good a player as anyone. He had beautiful strokes and he did get on with the game. I do not know of any bowlers who could keep him quiet on a good pitch and he was not so bad on the stickies. He was at his best after the 1914-18 War when he and Jack Hearne carried the Middlesex side."

Mr S. C. Griffith, Secretary of MCC: "Patsy was coaching Sussex while I was Secretary of the county and I also played with him. Apart from being a great cricketer, and perhaps more important, he brought a tremendous amount of fun and happiness to everything associated with the game. We at Lord's shall miss him terribly."

HIGGS, MR GEOFFRY, the Dulwich College cricket captain of 1950, died at the age of 18 on April 29, 1951, following an injury he received while playing for the First XV on November 18, 1950. For over five months he lay paralysed in hospital. Throughout his illness he set a magnificent example of courage. In the words of the College Chaplain, the Reverend A. W. Brown, "It is easy to talk of courage and fortitude when all is going well, but it is a very different matter to exhibit those shining qualities when the test comes". Three years after entering the School, Higgs became a member of the Eleven, and in the following year he was chosen for the Athletics team. during 1950 he was made Captain of Marlowe, Captain of Athletics and Captain of Cricket, and finally gained a place in the First XV. He was made Captain of the School while in hospital.

HORNBY, MR ALBERT HENRY, who died at North Kilworth, near Rugby on September 6, 1952, aged 75, captained Lancashire from 1908 to 1914. Born on July 29, 1877, the son of A. N. ("Monkey") Hornby, of England cricket and Rugby football fame., he first appeared for the county in 1899, and during his career he scored 9,541 runs, average 24.78, with 129 against Surrey at The Oval in 1912 his highest innings. Also in 1912, Hornby (96) shared in a partnership of 245 in two and a half hours with J. Sharp (211) against Leicestershire at Old Trafford, a Lancashire seventh-wicket record which still stands. Another noteworthy performance of this free-hitting batsman occurred in 1905 when, going in No. 9, he hit 106 from the Somerset bowling at Old Trafford, he and W. Findlay who afterwards became Secretary of MCC, adding 113 in half an hour for the ninth wicket.

The following appreciation by Mr Neville Cardus appeared in the *Manchester Guardian*:

Those who were boys at Old Trafford just before the war of 1914 will wish to express gratitude for the pleasure given by the cricket of A. H. Hornby. He was no mere chip from the old block; any metaphor suggestive of solidity, woodenness, or any object or body not endowed with spirit and volition is out of place in a discussion or description of the Hornbys. Albert, like his father, played the game for fun, and would have been as ashamed to refuse the challenge of a good ball as the challenge of a stiff jump on the hunting field.

A batsman so constituted and sharing his ideas might easily seem eccentric and anachronistic nowadays. He was known as a dashing batsman. We used strange categories in those old-fashioned years so as to get our players in their right degree and pedigree. There were also stonewallers; one in every county eleven but not more than one as a rule, though Warwickshire boasted two, Quaife and Kinneir, each of whom scored his centuries at the rate of 25 runs an hour, which is the speed of our contemporary "Masters".

Albert Hornby for years was content to go in for Lancashire number seven or eight in the batting order; and usually he sustained an average of round about 23-28 an innings. Considering the quality of first-class bowling then and first-class bowling now, Hornby's figures can safely be raised in the present currency to 32 an innings. He played for the Gentlemen against the Players at Lord's in 1914, went in first, and in the second innings, in spite of a nasty wicket, scored 69 ("hitting brilliantly", says *Wisden*) against the attack of Barnes, Hitch, Tarrant, Kennedy and J. W. Hearne – and what an attack! He batted in the manner of C. S. Barnett and H. Gimblett, not as good and as well organised as either maybe, but he was in the same class. We could always be sure that if he stayed at the wicket half an hour he would for certain show us every time at least six great and thrilling strokes. Only of Gimblett can as much as this be said in 1952.

He was a gallant and purposeful captain for Lancashire, and a superb fieldsman. To this day I can see this catch near the off-side boundary at Old Trafford in June 1906; he ran yards like a hare to hold a really magnificent hit by E. W. Dillon of Kent. It was in this same match that on Whit Thursday J. T. Tyldesley scored 295 not out and was fielding at third man at six o'clock; Lancashire had made 531 at more than a hundred an hour. This was Woolley's first game in county cricket; he missed one or two catches – one of them gave Tyldesley a second innings at about 130; he was bowled by Cuttell for none and took one wicket for a hundred odd. But in Kent's second innings he drove and cut in a way that heralded the coming of a new and incomparable star.

Perhaps Hornby himself would wish to be remembered most of all at Old Trafford for his innings of 55 not out against Nottinghamshire in June 1910. On the third day – a Saturday – Nottinghamshire, all out second innings, left Lancashire 403 to get to win in five and a quarter hours. Tyldesley and Sharp attacked ruthlessly and scored 191 in two and a half hours. But there was work to do after they had both got out, and Hornby, so we thought, would not bat because of lameness. At the pinch he hobbled to the field on invisible crutches. He scarcely needed his runner; he drove right and left – off the back foot, an unusual position for any Hornby to be seen in during the act of belabouring a bowler. Lancashire won the match – 403 in a fourth innings in less than five and a quarter hours. On this occasion – and I can remember no other – the crowd rushed across the field to cheer the conquering heroes near the pavilion. One small boy remained gazing in awe at the wicket on which only a few moments ago his heroes had stood and walked and run and played. He was mightily impressed by the depth of the holes made by the bowlers. . . . O my Hornby and my Tyldesley long ago!

HUISH, FREDERICK HENRY, who died at Northiam, Sussex, on March 16, 1957, aged 87, was the first of a line of exceptional Kent wicket-keepers which L. E. G. Ames and T. G. Evans continued. First appearing for the county in 1895, he continued until the outbreak of war in 1914, accounting in the meantime for no fewer than 1,328 batsmen – 952 caught and 376 stumped. Yet, unlike Ames and Evans, he was never chosen to play for England and only once, at Lord's in 1902, for Players against Gentlemen.

It was a curious fact that while Huish, born at Clapham, was a Surrey man who played for Kent, H. Wood, from whom he learned much of his skill, was Kentish by birth and assisted Surrey. One of the ablest and least demonstrative wicket-keepers of his generation, Huish was among the few to assist in the taking of 100 wickets in a season. This performance he achieved twice, for in 1911 he obtained 100 victims (62 caught, 38 stumped) and in 1913 raised his tally to 102 (70 caught, 32 stumped). In 1911 he enjoyed his greatest triumph in a single match, when, against Surrey at The Oval, he caught one batsman and stumped nine, thus dismissing ten in the two innings. On five other occasions he disposed of eight men in a game. Four times he helped Kent to carry off the County Championship, in 1906, 1909, 1910 and 1913.

Huish showed his readiness and resource in memorable if lucky fashion in a match between Kent and the Australians at Canterbury in 1902. He was standing far back to W. M. Bradley, the famous amateur fast bowler, when R. A. Duff played a ball a few yards behind the wicket and the Australian's partner called for a run. To get to the ball, Huish had to move so far that he realised that he would not have time to gather it before the batsmen got home. Accordingly he attempted to kick it on to the stumps at his end. The ball missed its immediate objective, but Huish put so much power into his effort that the ball went on and hit the wicket at the other end before Duff could make the necessary ground.

Though not generally successful as a batsman, Huish scored 562 runs in 1906, his best innings being 93 against Somerset at Gravesend. When Huish became the Kent senior professional, he was reputed to exercise remarkable control over his colleagues. Indeed, it used to be alleged that, unless he appealed, no brother professional dared to ask for a catch at the wicket!

HYMAN, MR WILLIAM, who died in February, 1959, aged 83, earned fame as a hard-hitting batsman who, for Bath Cricket Association against Thornbury at Thornbury in 1902, hit 359 not out in 100 minutes in a total of 466 for six wickets. He was specially severe upon E. M. Grace, brother of "W. G.", whom he thirty-two times hit for 6 and punished for 62 runs in two following overs. "Billy" Hyman made 27 appearances for Somerset between 1900 and 1914, his highest innings being 110 against Sussex at Bath in 1913 when he and P. R. Johnson added 159 for the second wicket. He and his three brothers all played Association football for Radstock Town and he also turned out for Bath City and Somerset.

IREMONGER, JAMES, who died at Nottingham on March 25, 1956, aged 80, was one of the finest batsmen ever to play for Nottinghamshire. While it could not be said that he was a player of particularly graceful style, his skill as a run-getter was beyond doubt. Standing over six feet, he watched the ball closely and could hit hard in front of the wicket, being specially good in on-driving.

Though of Yorkshire birth, he came of a Nottingham family and played from 1897 till 1914 for the county, for whom he scored 16,328 runs, average 35.33, including 32 centuries. His best season was that of 1904 when, with the aid of six centuries, he scored in 34 innings 1,983 runs, average 60.09. In that summer he hit the highest of his four scores of 200 or more, 272 against Kent at Trent Bridge, in the course of which he shared three partnerships exceeding 100. He and A. O. Jones began Nottinghamshire innings with as many as 24 stands of three figures – twice in a match (134 and 144) against Surrey at The Oval in 1901 and (102 and 303) against Gloucestershire at Trent Bridge in 1904.

Iremonger was chosen for Players v Gentlemen on eight occasions, three times at Lord's and five times at The Oval, and he toured Australia with Pelham Warner's MCC Team of 1911-12 without taking part in a Test match.

Besides his ability in batting, he developed into a capital medium-pace bowler, bringing the ball down from a good height and making it break back from the off. He took 616 wickets for Nottinghamshire, average 22.25. Among his performances was the dismissal of eight Gloucestershire batsmen for 21 runs in the first innings at Trent Bridge in 1912.

Against MCC and Ground at Lord's in 1902, he was the central figure of an unusual incident. For the first time in a big match, white enamelled stumps were being used – and the enamel was not quite dry. Iremonger received a ball which moved a stump to which the bail adhered! He went on to score 100.

At the end of the 1921 season he was appointed coach to Nottinghamshire, holding that post till he retired in 1938. To him belonged much credit for the early development of that celebrated pair of England fast bowlers, H. Larwood and W. Voce.

Besides his cricketing ability, Iremonger was an Association footballer of class. During fifteen years with Nottingham Forest as left full-back, he gained England International honours three times; against Scotland and Germany in 1901 and Ireland the following season. He later served as player-coach to Notts County.

JARDINE, MR DOUGLAS ROBERT, who died in Switzerland on June 18, 1958, aged 57, was one of England's best captains and a leading amateur batsman of his time. He caught tick fever while visiting Southern Rhodesia in 1957 and thenceforward had been in poor health.

Son of M. R. Jardine, himself an Oxford Blue, Douglas Jardine was born at Bombay and educated at Winchester, where he was in the XI for three years, being captain in the last, 1919, when he headed the batting figures with 997 runs, average 66.46. Going up to New College, Oxford, he got his Blue as a Freshman and played against Cambridge in 1920, 1921 and 1923 without achieving anything out of the ordinary. He missed the 1922 University match because of a damaged knee. In 1923 he began to play for Surrey and in 1932 took over the captaincy from P. G. H. Fender.

He went to Australia in 1928-29 with the MCC team under A. P. F. Chapman, taking part in all five Test matches. To England's success by 12 runs in the fourth Test he made a big contribution when scoring 98 and sharing with W. R. Hammond in a third-wicket partnership of 262. He also enjoyed the distinction of hitting three centuries in successive innings, against Western Australia, Victoria and New South Wales.

Four years later he captained the MCC side in Australia in what was probably the most controversial tour in history. England won four of the five Tests, but it was the methods they employed rather than the results which caused so much discussion and acrimony. H. Larwood and W. Voce, the Nottinghamshire fast bowlers, exploited "leg-theory", or what came to be known as "body-line" bowling to a packed leg-side field. The Australians and others considered this means of attack placed batsmen at a grave disadvantage because they had either to risk being struck on the head or body by persistently short-pitched balls or, if they attempted to play them, were virtually certain to be caught by the close-set field.

Strongly-worded cables passed between the Australian Board of Control, who asserted that "body-line bowling has assumed such proportions as to menace the best interests of the game, making protection of the body the main consideration", and the MCC. The Australians threatened to call off the projected tour of England in 1934. MCC at length agreed that "a form of bowling which is obviously a direct attack by the bowler upon the batsman would be an offence against the spirit of the game". Jardine always defended his tactics and in a book he wrote about the tour described allegations that the England bowlers directed their attack with the intention of causing physical harm as "stupid and patently untruthful".

Finally in 1934 MCC issued a ruling: "That the type of bowling regarded as a direct attack by the bowler upon the batsman, and therefore unfair, consists in persistent and systematic bowling of fast and short-pitched balls at the batsman standing clear of his wicket". That was the end of body-line bowling.

Meanwhile in 1933, however, fast leg-theory had been employed by both England and the West Indies in the second Test match at Old Trafford. Jardine, who always held that this type of attack could be successfully countered by a resolute batsman, set out to prove the accuracy of his contention. For nearly five hours he faced the hostile pace of L. N. Constantine and E. A. Martindale and he hit 127, his first and only century in a Test match. In the process, he took much physical punishment, but "The Iron Duke", as he was sometimes called, had proved his point to his own satisfaction.

Jardine captained the MCC team in India the following winter, but thereafter his appearances on the field became fewer till in 1937 he dropped out of first-class cricket altogether. At the same time he maintained his interest in the game, being President of the Oxford University CC from 1955 to 1957 and making occasional contributions to the Press. In 1953 he became the first President of the Association of Cricket Umpires.

Six feet tall, he possessed a very strong defence and was specially skilful in on-side strokes. In 22 Test match appearances he hit 1,296 runs, average 48, and held 26 catches. During his career his runs numbered 14,821, average 46.90, the highest of his 35 centuries being 214 not out against Tasmania in 1928-29. Extremely proud of his Oxford associations, he always wore a Harlequin cap.

Tributes included:

Sir Pelham Warner: "In my humble opinion, Jardine was a very fine captain, both on and off the field, and in the committee-room he was also extremely good. If ever there was a cricket match between England and the rest of the world and the fate of England depended upon its result, I would pick Jardine as England captain every time."

Sir John Hobbs: "I played with him a lot in the Surrey side and I feel that he will be chiefly remembered as a splendid skipper. As a captain, I would rank him second only to P. G. H. Fender. He was a great batsman – how great I do not think we quite appreciated at the time. I remember that he was the first man to refer to me as 'The Master'."

W. E. Bowes: "To me and every member of the 1932-33 MCC side in Australia, Douglas Jardine was the greatest captain England ever had. A great fighter, a grand friend and an unforgiving enemy."

R. Aird: "Jardine was a great player and captain and a man of character who, like all men of character, was not liked by everybody. He did what he set out to do, as when his side won the 'Ashes' in Australia in 1932-33, even if the method he adopted did not meet with general approval. His sound, solid batting inspired confidence in his colleagues."

JEACOCKE, MR ALFRED, who died in Lewisham Hospital on September 25, 1961, aged 68, rendered able service to Surrey as a right-handed batsman between 1920 and 1929. In 1921, when J. B. Hobbs, first because of an accident and then through illness, could play in only one county game, Jeacocke formed a splendid opening partner to A. Sandham, scoring in all matches 1,056 runs, average 42.24. An enterprising batsman specially strong in driving, he hit eight centuries for Surrey, the highest being 201 not out (twenty-two 4s) against Sussex at The Oval in 1922, and altogether obtained 6,228 runs, average 28.83. A capital slip fieldsman, he held 106 catches. Among his six appearances for Gentlemen against Players was that at The Oval in 1927 when A. Kennedy, of Hampshire, took all ten wickets in the Gentlemen first innings at a cost of 37 runs. His first-class cricket in 1922 came to an abrupt end when *Wisden* records: "Jeacocke ... dropped out of the team in August under circumstances that gave rise to some friction and discussion, the MCC ruling, after an enquiry asked for by Kent, that his qualification was not valid". The reason was that the house where he lived came within the boundary of Kent; the other side of the road was in the county of Surrey! From 1929 onwards, Jeacocke confined his activities to club cricket, chiefly with Forest Hill.

JESSOP, MR GILBERT LAIRD, who died at St. George's Vicarage, Dorchester, on May 11, 1955, aged 80, was famed as the most remarkable hitter cricket has ever produced. He had lived with the Rev. Gilbert Jessop, his only child, from 1936 till his death.

Born at Cheltenham on May 19, 1874, he enjoyed a memorable career in first-class cricket which, dating from 1894 to the start of the First World War, extended over twenty years. There have been batsmen who hit the ball even harder than Jessop, notably C. I. Thornton and the two Australians, George Bonnor and Jack Lyons, but no one who did so more often or who, in match after match, scored as rapidly. Where Jessop surpassed all other hitters was in the all-round nature of his scoring. At his best, he could make runs from any ball, however good it might be. Although only 5 ft 7 ins. in height, he bent low as he shaped to play, a method which earned him the sobriquet of "The Croucher". Extraordinarily quick on his feet, he was ready to hit firm-footed if the ball were pitched well up and equally, when it was of shorter length, to dash down the pitch and drive. When executing leg-side strokes, he almost lay down and swept round with the bat practically horizontal, putting great power behind the ball as, thanks to strong, supple wrists, he also did when bringing off the square cut. Lightness of foot allied to wonderful sight made it possible for him to run out to the fastest bowlers of his time – Richardson and Mold – and at the peak of his form pull or straight-drive them with almost unerring certainty. No one ever approached him in this particular feat; indeed, nobody else could have attempted it with reasonable hope of success.

At times Jessop sacrificed his wicket through trying to hit before he got a true sight of the ball or judged the pace of the turf and, not unnaturally in view of the liberties he took with good length bowling, the ball which kept low often dismissed him. A batsman with such marvellous gifts that in half an hour he might win a game seemingly lost, he was a wonderful personality on the field and the idol of spectators who always love a fearless batsman.

Jessop's claims to distinction were not limited to the brilliancy of his run-getting. For a number of years he ranked high as a fast bowler and for a man of his pace he showed surprising stamina. Far more remarkable than his bowling, however, was his fielding, which might fairly be termed as phenomenal as his hitting and which was a matter of great pride to him. No hit proved too hard for him to stop and his gathering and returning of the ball approached perfection. In his early days he fielded at cover-point; later he specialised in the position of extra mid-off, standing so deep that with almost anyone else a run would have been a certainty. Jessop's presence deterred the boldest of batsmen from making any attempt. In short, such a fine bowler and such a superb fieldsman was he that, even without his batting ability, he would have been worth a place in almost any team. A man of engaging manners, he was a charming companion and, like most truly great men, modest to a degree.

First tried for Gloucestershire in 1894, Jessop established his reputation a year later when, among other performances, he hit 63 out of 65 in less than half an hour from the Yorkshire bowling at Cheltenham. He continued to assist Gloucestershire till the end of his first-class career and for thirteen years from 1900 he captained the side. By 1897 he had become one of the great players of the day, making 1,219 runs in first-class matches and taking 116 wickets for less than 18 runs each. In that summer he hit two particularly noteworthy innings – 140 for Cambridge University against the Philadelphians in 95 minutes and 101 out of 118 in 40 minutes against Yorkshire at Harrogate. In the course of the latter display he hit the ball six times out of the ground and some dozen times over the ropes. Until 1907 a hit over the ropes counted four; only a hit out of the ground earned six. Except in 1898 he regularly made over 1,000 runs every season until 1909, when a bad back injury sustained while fielding in the Test Match at Leeds in early July kept him out of the game for the rest of the year. In 1900 he scored 2,210 runs and took 104 wickets and next summer his aggregate amounted to 2,323, including 157 out of 201 in an hour against West Indies at Bristol.

Among his 53 centuries were five of more than 200: 286 out of 335 in 175 minutes for Gloucestershire against Sussex at Brighton, 1903 (he and J. H. Board adding 320 for the sixth wicket); 240 out of 337 in 200 minutes for Gloucestershire v Sussex at Bristol, 1907; 234 out of 346 in 155 minutes for Gloucestershire v Somerset at Bristol, 1905; 233 out of 318 in 150 minutes for An England XI v Yorkshire at Lord's 1901; and 206 out of 317 in 150 minutes for Gloucestershire v Nottinghamshire at Trent Bridge, 1904.

Four times for Gloucestershire he reached three figures in each innings of a match: 104 and 139 v Yorkshire at Bradford, 1900, when the newspapers stated that, in the two innings he cleared the ropes more than twenty times; 143 and 133 not out v Somerset at Bath, 1908; 161 and 129 v Hampshire at Bristol, 1909; and 153 and 123 not out v Hampshire at Southampton, 1911. He achieved the feat on another occasion, against Somerset in a friendly game organised for the opening of a new club pavilion. S. M. J. Woods termed this a remarkable performance on a pitch far from true and against professional bowling. Altogether in first-class cricket he hit 26,058 runs, average 32.60.

His bowling successes included eight wickets for 34 runs v Hampshire, 1898; five for 13 v Lancashire, 1895; eight for 54 v Lancashire, 1898; eight for 29 v Essex, 1900; eight for 58 v Middlesex, 1902. All these were achieved for Gloucestershire except that against Hampshire, on which occasion he was playing for Cambridge. His wickets in first-class cricket totalled 851, average 22.91.

Jessop took part in eighteen Test matches between 1899 and 1909, thirteen against Australia and five against South Africa, and would probably have appeared in others but for the back strain he suffered in 1909. He disappointed in Australia except for his fielding, and in most of the contests in England met with moderate success; but he earned undying fame in The Oval Test of 1902. There, under conditions considerably helpful to bowlers, England, set 273 to make to win, lost their first five wickets for 48. Australia looked to have the match in hand, but Jessop joined F. S. Jackson and in marvellous fashion hit 104 out of 139 in an hour and a quarter, paving the way to victory by one wicket for England. Twice he sent the ball to the roof of the Pavilion and from another big hit was caught on the Players' Balcony by H. K. Foster.

Jessop went to Cambridge in 1896 and played for the University for four seasons, being captain in 1899. He accomplished little of note against Oxford in the way of batting, two innings of over 40 being his best scores on the big occasion, but he bowled to good purpose in two of the games, taking six wickets for 65 in the first innings in 1897 and six for 126 in the first innings a year later.

Besides his cricketing ability, Jessop was an all-round athlete of note. He got his Blue as a hockey goalkeeper, but fell ill and could not play in the University match; came near getting an Association football Blue and played for The Casuals as half-back or goalkeeper. He also appeared as a wing threequarter for Gloucester RFC. He would have played billiards for Cambridge against Oxford, but was "gated" and could not take part.

In one week he made two breaks of over 150. He could run the 100 yards in 10.2 seconds and frequently entered for sports meetings. A scratch golfer, he took part in the Amateur Championship in 1914, was Secretary of the Cricketers' Golfing Society and for some years Secretary of the Edgware Club.

In addition to the visit he paid to Australia in 1901-2 under A. C. MacLaren, he went to America with the team captained by P. F. Warner in 1897, and again in 1899 when K. S. Ranjitsinhji led the side.

For Beccles School in 1895, when a master there, Jessop scored 1,058 runs, average 132, and took 100 wickets at a cost of less than two and a half runs apiece.

He served as a captain in the Manchester Regiment during the First World War from 1914 till he was invalided out with a damaged heart in 1918. Married in October 1902, he first met his bride a few months earlier during his visit to Australia. She died in 1953.

Tributes paid to Jessop include:

Sir Pelham Warner: "He was a wonderful cricketer. It was a great pleasure to play with or against him. It has been said that he was unorthodox, but no one watched the ball more closely."

Sir John Hobbs: "He was undoubtedly the most consistently fast scorer I have seen. He was a big hitter, too, and it was difficult to bowl a ball from which he could not score. He made me glad that I was not a bowler. Gilbert Jessop certainly drew the crowds, too, even more than Bradman, I should say."

JOHNSTON, COLONEL ALEXANDER COLIN, D.S.O., M.C., who died suddenly at his home at Woking on December 27, 1952, aged 68, was a leading personality in Army sport during forty years' service. Born on January 26, 1884, he played as opening batsman and leg-break bowler in the Winchester XI's of 1901 and 1902. His second match with Eton, in which he dismissed eight batsmen for 56 runs, was rendered memorable by the fact that G. A. Sandeman took all ten wickets for 22 runs in the Winchester first innings. From Winchester, Johnston went to Sandhurst, and he spent a year as a cowboy in Colorado and New Mexico before joining the Worcestershire Regiment. During the First World War he served three years in France as a member of the original Expeditionary Force, being four times wounded, five times mentioned in dispatches, and rising to the rank of Brigadier General. Though left with a permanent limp, he continued his activities as soldier and sportsman. He played cricket for Hampshire over a period of twelve years and three times appeared for Gentlemen against Players, making top score for his side in the Lord's match of 1912. In all first-class games he scored 5,996 runs, average 30.91, hitting ten centuries. He also represented the Army at Association football and hockey and played polo for Western Nigeria.

JONES, MR SAMUEL PERCY, who died at Auckland, New Zealand, on July 14, 1951, in his 90th year, was then the oldest Test cricketer and the last survivor of the side which beat England in the "Ashes" Test Match at The Oval in 1882, Australia's first victory in England.

Educated at Sydney Grammar School and Sydney University, he toured England four times, in 1882, 1886, 1888 and 1890. A sound batsman with good defence, he was also a brilliant fieldsman and useful change bowler. Before he reached the age of 20, he made a century for New South Wales against Victoria. His most successful tour was that of 1886, when he finished second in the averages and made 151 at The Oval against the Gentlemen, a feat for which he was presented in the Committee Room at Lord's with a gold watch and chain as a souvenir from Australian friends. In twelve Test Matches against England he scored 428 runs with an average of 21.40.

Having settled in Queensland, Jones toured New Zealand with that State's team in 1896-97. In 1904 he went to live in New Zealand, playing for Auckland in 1904-5 and 1905-6. He afterwards paid only one brief visit to Australia and he never saw Bradman bat.

During the 1882 Oval Test, Jones was concerned in an incident which caused great controversy. In the Australian second innings Murdoch played a ball to leg and with Jones, his partner, ran a single. The Hon. A. Lyttelton, the English wicket-keeper, chased the ball and returned it to the striker's end, where Dr W. G. Grace, who had moved up from slip, took it. Jones, apparently thinking the ball was dead, moved out of his ground to pat the soft pitch, and Grace put down the wicket, the umpire giving Jones out. Several of the Australians felt very bitter about Grace's action, and many people thought that the ball should have been considered dead, since it had settled in the hands of Grace, who might for the moment have been considered to be in the position of wicket-keeper. Others maintained that Grace's action was quite justified and within the law and spirit of cricket.

That the affair left Jones without ill-will was illustrated a few years before his death. Of W. G. Grace, whom he described as a great sportsman and cricketer, he said: "I never saw him leave alone any ball outside the off stump. He either cut or drove them".

He liked to recall his early days in cricket, comparing the comparatively meagre expenses then allowed in inter-Colonial cricket with those received by modern players. "Yet", he said, "I am game to wager that we had more real enjoyment during those times than the financed ones have today. Twice daily we practised, with no restrictions as to 'a modest quencher'. I shall always remember breakfasting at Magdalen College before our first match of the 1882 tour. Champagne cup was sent round with monotonous regularity, with old Oxford Ale as a sort of topper to the function".

KILLICK, THE REVEREND EDGAR THOMAS, who died while taking part in a cricket match between the diocesan clergy of St Albans and Coventry at Northampton on May 18, 1953, aged 46, played for Cambridge University, Middlesex and England. He first showed his ability as a sportsman while at St Paul's School, where he won his colours as a Rugby three-quarter and captained the cricket XI. In 1925 his batting average was 104.44, and the following summer he led the Public Schools fifteen against the Australians at Lord's.

H. L. Collins, the Australian captain, objected to the Schools fielding fifteen players and Killick had the unenviable duty of deciding which four had to leave the field. Happily, Collins relented and the four boys returned. Killick made 31 on a difficult pitch.

Everyone predicted that he would be an automatic choice as a Freshman for the 1927 Cambridge XI, but for some reason he failed to do himself justice and did not obtain his Blue that year. For a time during the early part of the next season it looked as if the distinction might again elude him, but an innings of 82 for Middlesex against Essex ensured him a further trial. He seized the opportunity, taking 100 off the Surrey bowlers at The Oval and 161 from the Sussex attack at Hove. He made another hundred for Cambridge v MCC at Lord's and in the 'Varsity Match hit 74 and 20.

One of his finest innings was the 206 he scored for Middlesex against Warwickshire in 1931, his opening stand with G. T. S. Stevens producing 277 runs. Curiously, this was the only time he played for the county that season. Moreover, play was possible only on the first day because of rain. He twice played for England against South Africa in 1929, going in first with H. Sutcliffe, but his appearances in first-class cricket subsequently became more infrequent because of his work. Nevertheless, he continued to play as often as possible in club matches. E. Hendren once described Killick as "the prettiest forward player since Lionel Palairet". Certainly, there was grace in his stroke-play and few batsmen executed the off-drive and square-cut with such ease of movement. As a fieldsman he delighted onlookers by his anticipation, swift running and clean picking up of the ball in the deep.

Perhaps it was not altogether surprising that he showed a natural aptitude for games, for he came from a sporting family. A brother, G. S. Killick, represented Great Britain at rowing in the Olympic Games. Another brother was a wing three-quarter, and Stanley, the youngest, also played Rugby and cricket. E. T. Killick was for a time chaplain at Harrow School. Later he became rector of Willian, near Letchworth. During the war he went to

West Africa as Senior Padre (Church of England) of the RAF West Africa Command. He had been Vicar of Bishop's Stortford since 1946.

KITTERMASTER, MR FREDERICK JAMES, who died at Rugby on July 2, 1952, aged 83, was in the Shrewsbury XI of 1887. While at King's College, Cambridge, he gained an Association football Blue as full-back in 1892 – a considerable achievement considering that in the final of the College Cup Ties he had ordered M. H. Stanbrough, the University captain, off the field! He was a master at Clifton, Uppingham and, for many years, at Rugby.

KNIGHT, ALBERT E., who died in April 1946, aged 72, was a sound batsman and an excellent field at cover-point. He did fine service for Leicestershire from 1895 to 1912, when he went to Highgate School as coach. During that period he scored nearly 20,000 runs at an average of 29.24. Knight possessed no exceptional gifts as a cricketer, but, studious and painstaking, made himself a first-rate batsman of the old style. Driving particularly well to the off and using the square-cut with good effect, he pulled or hooked scarcely at all. In 1899 – his first big year – he made 1,246 runs, and for eight consecutive seasons reached his thousand. At his best in 1903, when, sixth in the general first-class averages, his aggregate was 1,835, average 45. Among his most notable successes were 229 not out at Worcester, 144 not out at Trent Bridge, 144 at The Oval, 127 against Surrey at Leicester, and a faultless 139 for Players against Gentlemen at Lord's. Curiously enough, during that summer Leicestershire gained only one victory in the County Championship. In the autumn of 1903 Knight went to Australia in the MCC team captained by P. F. Warner. Figuring in three of the five Test matches, Knight scored 70 not out at Sydney in the fourth game of the series, and on the same ground made 104 against New South Wales, but, on the whole, scarcely realised expectations. The following summer found him again in great form with an aggregate of 1,412, an average of 40, and five separate three-figure innings to his credit, including 203 against MCC at Lord's. He wrote a book entitled *The Complete Cricketer*, grandiose in style, containing much startling metaphor.

LILLEY, BEN, who kept wicket for Nottinghamshire between 1921 and 1937, died at his home at Nottingham on August 4, 1950, aged 55. He was licensee of the Forest Tavern, Mansfield Road, Nottingham, and had been in failing health for some years. A native of Kimberley, a village in Nottinghamshire, Lilley first played for the county against Essex at Leyton in 1921, but he could not find a regular place in the team until 1925. Then, as successor to Tom Oates, he set up a Nottinghamshire record by becoming the first wicket-keeper to score over 1,000 runs in a season. He achieved the feat again in 1928. Lilley was considered one of the best wicket-keepers in the country, but Test honours eluded him. For several years he "kept" to Larwood and Voce, the England fast bowlers. He retired in 1937 following injury to a thumb. During his first-class career Lilley scored 10,479 runs, including seven centuries, made 645 catches and stumped 132 batsmen. In a Second Eleven match he scored 200 not out against a Staffordshire side including S. F. Barnes.

CHARLES MACARTNEY AND GEORGE GUNN

By Neville Cardus

Among several notable personalities who died in 1958 were two famous batsmen, Charles Macartney of Australia and George Gunn of England. Each played in his first Test at Sydney in 1907 and their careers ran parallel.

Charles Macartney and George Gunn were two great individualists amongst batsmen, alike in their determination to occupy the crease on their own terms. But they were independent with a difference. Macartney revelled in constant aggression. He played a defensive stroke as a last resort. A maiden over to him he received as a personal affront and insult. George Gunn would one day make runs quickly and as audaciously as Macartney, but he never appeared to bustle. Next day, in fact, it might happen in the same innings, he would suddenly change mood and gear, and indulge in stonewalling obviously at his own whim, no credit to the bowler. George took little notice of the scoreboard. A few days before his death he came to Lord's last summer, and he told me that he had "always batted according". It would have been beside the point if I had asked him "according to what?"

In June 1913, at Trent Bridge, Yorkshire went in first against Nottinghamshire and scored 471, leaving Nottinghamshire with only a draw to play for. Gunn scored 132 in six hours, so wilfully slow that the Yorkshire bowlers taunted him, asking, "Hast lost thi strokes, George?" And George replied, "Oh, you'd like to see some strokes, would you? Well, next innings I'll show you some." Yorkshire declared their second innings closed and Nottinghamshire's total, when rain washed out the day, was 129 for three wickets. The score-card, preserved in silk at Trent Bridge, reads as follows:

Gunn not out........................	109
Lee b Haigh........................,	4
Hardstaff run out	3
Alletson c Booth b Rhodes	0
Gunn J. not out.....................	8
Extras	5
	129

Gunn scored his 109 in 85 minutes. "I decided to play swashbuckle just to show 'em", he explained. In another match at Trent Bridge, in August 1928, Nottinghamshire, playing Kent, wanted only 157 to win on a perfect wicket on a beautiful third afternoon. There was heaps of time left and the crowd settled down to watch Gunn and Whysall jog home comfortably. But George scored exactly 100 in an hour and a half, so that the game came to an unnecessarily abrupt end, with an hour or two of sunshine wasted. I asked Gunn afterward, "Why did you hurry? And on such a lovely afternoon". "Well", he replied in his amiable, indulgent way, "when 'Dodge' (Whysall) and me were coming down pavilion stairs, a member spoke to me and said something he shouldn't have said. I can't tell you what it was, but it annoyed me. So I went and took it out of Kent bowlin'."

Macartney on the kill was as the tiger with his prey. George played with bowling, the best in the world, like cat with mouse. He didn't eat it after he'd killed it. Macartney put the attack unmercifully to the sword. In 1926 Armstrong's conquering team feared Macaulay of Yorkshire. Macartney decided to knock Macaulay out of the rubber at Leeds, the third Test, and Macaulay's first that year. A. W. Carr, captain of England, won the toss and sent Australia in on a soft but not difficult pitch. (Charles Parker, deadliest of left-arm spinners, was "drink-waiter".) Warren Bardsley fell to a slip catch off the first ball sent down by Maurice Tate and Macartney was missed by Carr in the slips off the fifth ball of the same over. Macartney, not at all interested in his good or Carr's bad luck, immediately annihilated the England attack. He scored a century before lunch, incidentally removing the menace of Macaulay once and for all out of Australia's way.

In 1921 at Trent Bridge, he scored 345 in three hours fifty minutes. He was missed when 9 in the slips by none other than our other hero – George Gunn. Macartney cut and drove with a blinding swiftness and so utterly demoralised the Nottinghamshire attack that A. W. Carr decided to make a gesture which would convey to the critics in the Pavilion some idea that he, at least, was keeping his head. He decided to change his bowlers round. "It wouldn't have mattered a damn to Charles which end Fred Barratt or Tich Richmond was bowling from, but the move would be proof that I was still in charge." He decided to bowl the odd over himself to enable the change-round. "It'll look all right in the score-sheet in all the slaughter", he thought. "A. W. Carr 1–1–0–0". If my readers will consult *Wisden* of 1922, they will discover that Carr's single over was plundered to the extent of 24 runs. "And I pitched 'em wide where I thought he couldn't possibly reach them", said Carr. No bowler, no tactics, no kind of field could tame Macartney.

In the 1926 Test at Old Trafford against Fred Root's "Leg theory" inswingers, Macartney took three hours to reach a century. Though he hit 14 boundaries in that time, he assured me afterwards that he had hated the innings. "'Rootie' knew he couldn't get me out, so he bowled wide. Only fools get out that way." He often batted in a temper. In the Triangular Tests of 1912 when England played Australia at Lord's, somebody in the dressing-room teased Charles as he was putting on his pads. "Cripes, Charlie, 'Barney' (Barnes) and Frank Foster are goin' to do it again." (It was the season following the great Barnes-Foster triumphs in Australia.) "Cripes, Charlie, 'Barney's' pitchin' 'em on the leg and only just missin' the off." When Charles went out to bat he was, so I was authoritatively informed, "livid with rage". He scored 99; D'Artagnan and Mercutio in one. Barnes took none for 74.

In Test matches Macartney scored 2,132 runs, average 41.80. George Gunn, in two rubbers, both against Australia in Australia, scored 843 runs in nineteen innings, with an average of over 44.

Only once was he invited to play for England in England – at Lord's in 1909, when he was lbw Cotter 1, and b Armstrong 0. Nobody to this day knows why George Gunn was not called into action for England in 1921 against Gregory and McDonald. He liked fast bowling and used to walk out of his crease, in leisurely fashion, to play it. "If I stayed in crease for it", he explained to me, "it come up too 'igh, because I'm not tall. So I goes out to meet it on the rise, where I can get on top." A young Lancashire wicket-keeper who had not seen George before was astounded to see him "walking-out" to McDonald. "Ah", thinks the young wicket-keeper, "if ah can stump him off 'Mac' ah'll sure get me county cap." So next ball, as George sauntered forth while McDonald was still gliding into action, the young wicket-keeper risked stealing up to the stumps. Gunn played down a nasty kicking express to his toes, then turning round, saw the young 'keeper's nose near the bails. "Good mornin', young feller", he said. "Nice day, isn't it?"

He celebrated his 50th birthday in June 1929 by scoring 164 not out against Worcestershire. He promised me, weeks in advance of the event, that he would thus celebrate it. There was nothing, in fact, that he couldn't do with a cricket bat. He once said to me, "Ever since I played the game – and I began in 'W.G.'s' time – batters have always made two big mistakes. First of all, they take too much notice of the state of the wicket, pattin' and pokin' – it only encourages bowlers. Then – and this is more serious – they take too much notice of the bowling."

Often he stonewalled with obvious self-determination, seldom because he was compelled to by the attack. "I never hurry", was his motto. "Either on the field or off it." When he made runs swiftly, he was still apparently taking his own time with ample ease and leisure to enjoy himself. He was a shortish, well-built but not at all a sturdy man, a little bandy in the legs, quizzical of eye and face, and slow and humorous in his talk. In 1906 he suffered a haemorrhage of the lungs and was obliged to winter in New Zealand. He happened to be in Australia in December 1907 when A. O. Jones's MCC team were there. He was called on for the Test matches and scored 119 in his first Test innings at Sydney. Though he seemed to improvise strokes and do all sorts of original things with the best bowlers, he was at bottom faultless of style; he owed much to instruction when young from the scrupulously classical Arthur Shrewsbury. It is true that Gunn totalled 35,190 runs in first-class cricket, average 35.90 with 62 hundreds, but statistics tell little of his genius. We might as well add up the quavers and crotchets in Rossini's operas. He was himself, delightful and lovable; and he "always batted according".

Macartney's resource and brilliance were vehement. His innings often plundered the attack savagely. His strokes might flash at times all round the wicket, but there was no yielding humour in them. He was after the blood of Englishmen. As the bowler prepared to run, Macartney would raise his bat above his head, legs apart, as though stretching himself loose for action. From under the long peak of his green Australian cap gleamed two eyes bright as a bird's. The chin was thrust out in defiance. His shoulders were square, and he also was below medium height. His arms were powerful, wrists as steel. He was not born commanding; only after hard service did he earn his nickname "The Governor-General". He was self-taught, never coached. To begin with he had few strokes at all. In his first Tests – during 1907-1908 rubber, the same in which Gunn first had international honours – Macartney's place in the order of going in varied. Twice he was seventh or eighth. He was known then less as a batsman than as a left-handed slow spinner. In England, his first trip here, he took 11 wickets for 85 against England at Leeds, in July 1909. In the same rubber, at Birmingham, in England's first innings, he went on first and in a few overs he got rid of MacLaren, bowled for 5, Hobbs lbw for 0 and C. B. Fry bowled for 0. No spinner has enjoyed so impressive a haul at so little expense. In those days his spin and length were superb.

Macartney goes down in the game's history side by side with Victor Trumper. He did not share Victor's effortless and chivalrous poise. For all his dazzling sword play and footwork, Macartney was an ironside cavalier. None the less, he belongs to the great immortal and decreasing company of cricketers who, while they are attending to the duty to their team – and the first duty of any player is to try to win – combine serious intent with personal relish, thus winning not only our admiration, but our affection, remaining warm in our memory for years.

THE MACKINNON OF MACKINNON (35th Chief of the Mackinnon Clan), the title to which MR FRANCIS ALEXANDER MACKINNON succeeded on the death of his father in 1903, passed away at his home, Drumduan, in Forres, Morayshire, on February 27, 1947. He would have been 99 years old on April 9. As it was he reached a greater age than attained by any other first-class cricketer, surpassing that of Herbert Jenner-Fust, Cambridge captain in the first match with Oxford in 1827, who died in 1904 when his exact age was 98 years 5 months and 7 days. Mackinnon was within forty days of 99 years at his passing.

Born at Acryse Park, in Kent, he went to Harrow without getting into the eleven, but at Cambridge he played in the historic match of 1870 when Cobden did the hat-trick by dismissing the last three Oxford batsmen and gaining for the Light Blues a dramatic victory by two runs. He played ten years for Kent, and in 1884, going in first, he helped, with scores of 28 and 29, in the only victory gained by a county over the Australians. Of the winning side, Mr Stanley Christopherson, President of MCC during the war years, who finished the match by taking three wickets for 12 runs, Mr M. C. Kemp, wicket-keeper, and Alec Hearne, seven wickets for 60, are three survivors of that eleven.

During that year he scored 115 against Hampshire and 102 against Yorkshire, his average being 33, second to 41 by Lord Harris. He was President of the Kent County Club in 1889.

In the winter of 1878 he went with Lord Harris to Australia. A strong batting side included only two professionals, George Ulyett and Tom Emmett, the Yorkshiremen. Mackinnon was a victim of F. R. Spofforth in a hat-trick in the only match with the full strength of Australia, who won by ten wickets.

Born on April 9, 1848, three months before W. G. Grace, he married in 1888 the eldest daughter of Admiral, First Baron Hood, the Hon. Emily Hood, who died in 1934. There survive a son and a daughter, who accompanied her father on his cricket visits to the South.

The oldest Harrovian, University Blue and Test cricketer, he was also the senior member of MCC, to which he was elected in 1870. Until the last he retained a keen interest in the game he loved so well by following the reports of the matches played by the England team in Australia.

Although he gave up County cricket sixty-two years ago, he maintained to a remarkable extent a close touch with the game, as his memory and good physique gave evidence. Using two sticks, he walked firmly, and enjoyed meeting old friends on Kent grounds as well as at Lord's. During the Tunbridge Wells Cricket Week in 1946 he watched the cricket from the Band of Brothers' tent or from the pavilion. One afternoon, accompanied by his daughter and the Marchioness of Abergavenny, he visited Rose Hill School and examined the old desk where he used to sit as a pupil eighty-nine years before. He gave a talk to the whole school, besides inspecting the Sea Scout Troop.

Several opportunities occurred for me to speak to the Mackinnon, and he related some of his experiences in the happiest way. He liked Canterbury better even than Lord's, his second love. An amusing tale was how, at The Oval when playing for Kent, Lord Harris put him to field at a particular spot – "'Mac, by that worm cast'. After some hits just out of reach, my captain said; 'You have left your cast'. 'No, George, I haven't. That's another worm's cast'."

Referring to "Cobden's Match", he said with a smile, "I really won the match, for I scored two" (the margin of victory). That was his second innings, after a useful 17 not out at a time when runs were never more difficult to get than at Lord's on the big occasion.

Among those who chatted with him in the Lord Harris Memorial garden, where he enjoyed a picnic lunch with his daughter during the University match, was the Rev. T. R. Hine Haycock, an Oxford Blue in 1883, who played for Kent when Mackinnon was finishing his active cricket career and is now 85 years old.

Mackinnon wore an I Zingari tie, and on his watch chain showed with pride a gold medallion bearing the insignia of crossed bats presented to all the team captained by Lord Harris in Australia. His wonderfully clear conversation and strong handshake revealed his hearty enjoyment in meeting any cricket acquaintance. Among the last active signs of his fondness for the game was the presentation at Canterbury of a picture of the Kent and Sussex match at Hove a hundred years ago, in which the players, among them Alfred Mynn, "the Lion of Kent", and Fuller Pilch, are wearing tall hats.

When 98 years of age, in reply to a question by telephone from London as to his health, he said: "I am going into hospital tomorrow – but only for the annual meeting at which I shall preside. I am very well in health – very well indeed. I still do a lot of work in the garden: weeds don't like me at all."   H.P.

NOTES BY THE EDITOR, 1948

OLDEST TEST PLAYER

The passing of F. A. Mackinnon raised a doubt as to who could be the oldest surviving Test player. Having heard in reply to a letter that Sir Timothy C. O'Brien was living in the Isle of Man, I found that his seniority for England was established by a matter of six days over that of Stanley Christopherson, born on November 11, 1861. But M. C. Kemp, born on September 7 of that same vintage year, seems to have become the oldest living University Blue. Actual seniority of all Test players belongs, however, to Australia, S. P. Jones, born on August 1, 1861, being strong and hearty, as my son, Norman Preston, when touring with the England team last winter, found him in Auckland, New Zealand. Sam Jones watched the cricket with keen zest, and told my son that he well remembered Charles, Sydney and Edgar Pardon. He came to England in 1882, 1886 and 1888, having first played for Australia in February 1882 at Sydney, when the England team, captained by Alfred Shaw, lost by five wickets. Talking to my son, Jones said he disliked modern batsmanship, even deploring the methods of Hobbs and Hammond compared with the old masters, Grace and Trumper. On his first visit to England he played in the historic Oval Test which Australia won by 7 runs. The sole survivor of that match, he remembers vividly how W. G. Grace, fielding point, ran him out. Of Grace, whom he described as a great sportsman and cricketer, he said, "I never saw him leave alone any ball outside the off stump. He either cut or drove them". Jones went to Auckland in 1904 as coach to the Grammar School, and stayed there, making only one visit to Sydney some twenty-three years ago. He has never seen Bradman play.

MARCHANT, MR FRANCIS, who died April 13, 1946, was closely connected with the Kent eleven over a period of twenty-three seasons – 1883 to 1905 – and captain of the side from 1890 to 1897. He was a brilliant and stylish batsman. Born at Matfield, Staplehurst, on May 22, 1864. Frank Marchant, after one term at Rugby, went to Eton, and was in the eleven there in 1882 and 1883. In his second match with Harrow at Lord's he gave a delightful display, making, mainly by cutting and square-leg hitting, 93 out of 115 in ninety-five minutes. At Cambridge he gained his Blue as a Freshman, but his cricket career at the University was rather disappointing for a player of such promise. Had he exercised a little more restraint on first going in, he must, with his gifts, have attained the highest honours. Still, he did some great things for Kent, scoring 111 out of 150 in ninety-five minutes against Yorkshire at Sheffield in 1901, and in the same year 100 out of 141 on a bad wicket in seventy-five minutes against Middlesex at Lord's. In the match with Yorkshire at Leeds in 1896 he narrowly missed two separate hundreds, making 128 in the first innings and 88 in the second. His highest score for Kent was 176 against Sussex at Gravesend in 1889, when he and G. G. Hearne (103) put on 249 for the fourth wicket.

Marchant's most famous performance was an innings of 103 for the MCC against the Australians at Lord's in 1893, when he and Flowers (130) put on 152 runs in seventy minutes.

NEWTON, MR ARTHUR EDWARD, who died at his home at Trull, Somerset on September 15, 1952, three days after his 90th birthday, was a famous wicket-keeper who continued his activities in club cricket until the age of 81. When 74, having cycled to the Taunton ground to turn out for Somerset Stragglers, he demonstrated that his ability had not seriously declined by stumping five batsmen. While at Eton in 1880 he began an association with Somerset which lasted for thirty-four years. "A.E.", as he was affectionately known to so many, helped S. M. J. Woods to take a wicket with the first ball he bowled for Somerset. This was at Edgbaston in 1886. C. W. Rock, batting for Warwickshire, missed a very fast yorker on the leg-side, and Newton stumped him brilliantly.

Born on September 12, 1862, he played against Harrow at Lord's in 1879 and the two following years. The matches of 1880 and 1881 were noteworthy for the fact that, though P. J. de Paravacini took twelve Harrow wickets on each occasion, he was twice on the losing side. When at Pembroke College, Oxford, Newton gained a Blue in 1885, and he appeared for Gentlemen against Players at The Oval in 1897, conceding only two byes in a total of 431, and at Lord's in 1902. He took part in two tours abroad. In 1885 he was a member of a team of amateurs who went to the USA under E. J. Sanders, finishing second in the batting averages, and in the winter of 1887-88 he visited Australia with G. F. Vernon's side. Cricket grounds in the Antipodes in those far-off days left much to be desired. Newton used to relate how one of his team-mates refused to field in the deep during a match in Tasmania because he had seen a snake wriggle into a hole close to where he was placed! Altogether in first-class cricket Newton caught 297 batsmen and stumped 119. Until the last ten years of his life he hunted regularly with the Taunton Vale Foxhounds and the Taunton Vale Harriers. He was a member of the MCC from 1884.

NICHOLS, MORRIS STANLEY, who died on January 26, 1961, aged 60, was, in an era of a good many all-rounders, one of the best. An Essex player from 1924 to 1939, he scored 17,789 runs, average 26.39, as a left-handed batsman strong in strokes in front of the wicket and with right-arm fast bowling took 1,834 wickets for 21.66 runs apiece. Of his 20 centuries the highest was 205 against Hampshire at Southend in 1936. He was first recommended to Essex solely as a batsman, but Percy Perrin, observing his height and strong physique, encouraged him as a pace bowler. How successful this proved is shown by the fact that in each of eleven seasons "Stan" Nichols dismissed over 100 batsmen, his best being that of 1938 when he took 171 wickets at a cost of 19.92 runs each. He could bowl for long spells without fatigue or loss of accuracy.

He enjoyed perhaps his greatest triumph as an all-rounder in 1935 when at Huddersfield he played the leading part in the overthrow by an innings and 204 runs of Yorkshire, the ultimate Champions, whose one defeat in the competition this was. In the two innings he gained an analysis of eleven wickets for 54 runs and he hit 146. Three years later at Gloucester, he played an innings of 159 and gained full bowling figures of fifteen wickets for 165 runs, his first-innings analysis being nine wickets for 37 runs in 15.2 overs. On three other occasions he took nine wickets in an innings – for 59 runs v Hampshire at Chelmsford in 1927; for 32 runs v Nottinghamshire at Trent Bridge in 1936 and for 116 runs v Middlesex at Leyton in 1930. Twice he disposed of four batsmen in four deliveries – v Sussex at Horsham in 1929 and v Lancashire at Chelmsford in 1935 – and he also achieved the "hat-trick" against Yorkshire at Leeds in 1931.

Eight times he performed the "cricketers' double" – five in succession from 1935 till the war ended his first-class career in 1939 – a number exceeded by only four men, W. Rhodes, G. H. Hirst, V. W. C. Jupp and W. E. Astill. He played fourteen times for England between 1929 and 1939, took part in MCC tours of Australasia in 1929 and India in 1933, also visited Jamaica on two occasions and appeared in nine matches for Players v Gentlemen. He played in Birmingham League cricket after the war.

As modest as he was popular, Nichols was once asked if he had found any batsman particularly difficult. He replied: "Old George Gunn, I think. He used to walk down the pitch to me, I always felt a fool trying to bowl him out."

In his footballing days a useful goalkeeper, Nichols played for Queen's Park Rangers.

O'BRIEN, SIR TIMOTHY CAREW, third Baronet, who at the time of his passing was the senior Test player in England against Australia, died in the Isle of Man on December 9, 1948, aged 87. Born in Dublin on November 5, 1861, he was educated at Downside, always a good cricket school, and he became qualified for Middlesex when at St Charles College, Notting Hill, but he did not reveal his full batting ability until going up to Oxford in 1884. Taking this step for the purpose of cricket, he fulfilled his ambition by at once being given his Blue by M. C. Kemp, his senior by about two months.

He started against the Australians and, playing a brilliant innings of 92, was largely responsible for defeating the visitors by seven wickets, the only victory gained by Oxford over an Australian team. With 72 for MCC at Lord's he showed to equal advantage and again helped to beat the Australians, but when he played for England against Australia at Manchester that season and at Lord's four years later, he did little in low scoring matches.

During a long career lasting until 1898, O'Brien was one of the most attractive and valuable amateur batsmen in the country. He used his height and powerful build with great effect in forcing the game and played many notable innings for Middlesex, MCC and Gentlemen. He went to Australia with the team captained by G. F. Vernon in 1887-88 and to South Africa with Lord Hawke's side in the winter of 1895.

Strangely enough he failed utterly in his first University match, being bowled in each innings without scoring; yet Oxford won by seven wickets, but next year, 1885, when Cambridge won by a similar margin, O'Brien made 44 and 28. By a remarkable coincidence Sir C. A. Smith, who died eleven days after O'Brien, played in the same matches. He failed to score in 1884, being twice not out, and took two wickets; next year

Smith scored 23 in a valuable last-wicket stand and with six wickets for 81 assisted materially in the Cambridge victory.

For Middlesex O'Brien scored 7,222 runs at an average of 30, with highest innings 202 against Sussex in 1895 at Hove, where he and R. Slade Lucas put on 338 in three hours twenty minutes. A more notable performance was against Yorkshire at Lord's in June 1889, when Middlesex were set to make 280 in little more than three hours and a half. For a time everything pointed to a tame finish, but with about ninety minutes left and 151 wanted, O'Brien went in and hit up a hundred in eighty minutes; the last 83 runs came in 35 minutes and Middlesex won by four wickets, ten minutes from time. This brilliant display followed 92 by O'Brien in the first innings. That match created a record for heavy scoring in England, the aggregate being 1,295 runs; there were then five balls to the over.

I saw O'Brien play a fine innings of 110 not out at Taunton against Somerset in August 1894 and Middlesex won a great match by 19 runs – that was the first occasion on which P. F. Warner appeared for Middlesex. Some years after giving up first-class cricket, O'Brien, when nearly 53 years of age, played for Lionel Robinson's eleven against Oxford at Attleborough in 1914 and scored 90 and 111 in splendid style.

Sir Timothy married in 1885 Gundrede Annette Teresa, daughter of Sir Humphrey de Trafford, and there were two sons and eight daughters of the marriage. The elder son, Timothy John Aloysius, was killed in action during the 1914-18 war, and the baronetcy passed to the younger son Robert Rollo Gillespie O'Brien. H.P.

ODD, MR MONTAGU, who died at Sutton, Surrey, on June 11, 1951, aged 82, used to make cricket bats by hand for Dr W. G. Grace at a guinea apiece. He was at work in his little shop a few days before his death.

PILKINGTON, MR CHARLES CARLISLE, the second of three brothers who played for Eton, died at The Manor, South Warnborough, on January 8, 1950, aged 73. During four years in the Eton XI he scored 427 runs, average 32.84, in the matches with Harrow and Winchester, and when captain in 1895 he took five wickets for 30 runs in Harrow's second innings. Getting his Oxford Blue as a Freshman, he helped to beat Cambridge by four wickets in his only inter-University match, which made cricket history by influencing the change in the follow-on rule to *optional*. Cambridge, led by Frank Mitchell, copying the example set three years before when F. S. Jackson was captain, gave away twelve extras, three balls being bowled deliberately to the boundary, in order to prevent the follow-on. Cambridge began badly in their second innings after a tremendous uproar all round the ground and a critical demonstration by MCC members in the pavilion. Oxford were set to score 330 in the last innings, and they won by accomplishing the heaviest task ever performed at that time in the University match. P. F. Warner, G. J. Mordaunt and H. K. Foster were out for 60 runs before Pilkington helped G. O. Smith to add 84; H. D. G. Leveson Gower, the Oxford captain, did still better by staying while 97 were put on, and the runs were obtained for the loss of six men, G. O. Smith, 132, leaving when only two were required for victory. Pilkington averaged over 36 for Oxford that season. He gave up first-class cricket when on the Stock Exchange, but in 1901 for Silwood Park he took all ten R.M.C. wickets for 25 runs at Sandhurst. I saw that 1896 game at Lord's and remember vividly all that happened. H.P.

HUBERT PRESTON

By Neville Cardus

Born on December 16, 1868, Hubert Preston died on August 6, 1960, aged 91. He spent the greater part of his life reporting Cricket and Association Football. He helped in the preparation of Wisden *from 1895 to 1951, being Editor for the last eight years.*

When I entered the Press Box at Lord's some forty years ago, Hubert Preston sat next to Sydney Pardon at the end of the front row, near the steps leading to the exit. It was a different Press Box then, far different from the large place of accountancy which today is metallic during the summers with typewriters. I doubt if Sydney Pardon would have allowed anybody to use a typewriter in his presence at Lord's or any other cricket ground.

I didn't dare go into the Lord's Press Box during my first season as a cricket writer for the *Manchester Guardian*. I was shy, provincially raw. I wrote my reports sitting on the Green Bank. I wrote them on press telegram forms, and at close of play handed them in at the telegraph office under the clock at the Nursery End.

One afternoon, Hubert Preston saw me as I sat on the Green Bank scribbling my message. "Why don't you come into the Press Box?" he said, in his own brisk, rapidly articulated way. He took me by the arm and led me up the steep iron steps. The tea interval wasn't over yet. Preston introduced me to Sydney Pardon, who then introduced me to the other members of the Press Box, some of them life-members – Stewart Caine, Harry Carson, Frank Thorogood and others. Each made a courteous bow to me; it was like a *levée*. Pardon pointed to a seat in the back row. In time, he assured me, I would graduate to a front place among the elect.

Hubert Preston was, with Pardon and Stewart Caine, the most courteous and best-mannered man ever to be seen in a Press Box on a cricket ground. Stewart Caine would actually bow to me and give me precedence into a gentlemen's lavatory. Hubert's deafness was the reason why, now and again, the aristocratic Pardon was obliged to raise his voice. Pardon once apologised to me for an occasional voice crescendo. "You know", he said, "Hubert is quite sensationally deaf". At The Oval, a match was beginning on a superlative wicket in the 1930s, a shaven lawn, reduced into an anaesthetic condition by a ten-ton roller. As we watched, we made our several comments on this batsman's paradise. "Not fair to bowlers." "Ought to be stopped, this doping." "Bound to be a draw – no life in the pitch." "Not fair to bowlers – doped – killin' the game" and so on.

Hubert, unable to hear a word of all this, sat concentrating on the cricket. Then he spoke: "This wicket is playing funny already. J. T. Hearne would have 'em all out before lunch. Too much water in the preparation." What is more, Hubert's prophecy, uttered in the silence surrounding him, was soon proven right. The wicket *did* very soon help the bowler.

Hubert was so modest, so reticent of his own talents and history, that not until his death did I learn from the obituary notices that his first job in London as a journalist was with my own paper, *The Guardian*. Or that he farmed for some time in Canada, from 1893-1895. Or that he had played cricket on the sacrosanct turf of Lord's and had performed the "hat-trick" there, for the Press v The Authors. Or that he had played soccer for Lyndhurst v The Royal Arsenal, forerunners of *the* Arsenal.

He was naturally a man of few words because of his deafness. But his sparkling eyes could talk. I have seen him chastise a poor stroke on the field of play by means of a facial expression far more eloquent than any word, written or oral. He was alive in every nerve and muscle. If responsive life had departed from his ears, the more sharply vital his other faculties seemed to grow. In no sense did he become an "old man". And though he extolled the great players of the past, he was, to the end of his career as a cricket journalist, quick to recognise young talents of quality. Almost to the last hours of a life extending from December 16, 1868, to August 6, 1960, he remained mentally active and curious. He was apparently tireless, and a continuous enjoyer of good health. His only stay in a hospital as a patient was the last two days of his life.

As a boy, cricket was at his shoulders temptingly. He began his education at a preparatory school overlooking Kennington Oval. Later he was a student at the City of London School. He joined Pardon's Cricket Reporting Agency in 1895 and was in active and faithful service for this same agency until 1951. In those days there was no radio to spread far and wide the latest cricket scores. The work of the Cricket Reporting Agency, responsible for the Press Association's sporting news, was comprehensive and exhaustive. But nothing could exhaust Hubert. He saw dynasty succeed unto dynasty at cricket – Grace and Shrewsbury, "Ranhji" and Trumper, right down the historic line, Abel, Hayward, Hobbs and Tyldesley, until the Bradman sunset. His life was full and happy. And he had the happy knowledge in his period of heavily accumulated years of knowing that his son was carrying on the good work of his life, as Editor of his beloved *Wisden*. He was loved as a man and a gentleman. And he was respected by his colleagues as a craftsman.

*   *   *   *

E. Eden writes: "H.P.", as all his friends knew him, was celebrated all over Great Britain as a journalist who, whether reporting cricket or football, wrote what he meant and meant what he wrote. He never really liked the modern tendency towards speed as opposed to accuracy, about which he was meticulous to a degree; and, among his idiosyncrasies, he insisted always that pedestrians should walk on the right-hand side of the pavement! When I first worked with him 42 years ago, he used an old-fashioned ear-trumpet. As they became available, he adopted electrical hearing-aids which occasionally led to mildly awkward situations. For instance, when a change of battery was needed, it became necessary to roar at "H.P." to make him hear. When, without one's knowledge, he attached a fresh battery, a few words above normal tones would evoke the sharp rebuke: "There's no need to shout, my boy, I'm not deaf!"

Even late in life he liked to talk about his footballing exploits, and many a less heavily built colleague suffered something of a shaking when he illustrated forcibly "how we used to charge 'em in the old days". Despite his handicap, he served for a time in the East Surrey Regiment during the First World War and inwardly he was intensely proud of the fact that he was an Honorary Freeman of the City of London though he rarely mentioned it.

Unfortunately, H.P. was not spared to learn of the exciting Test tie in Brisbane. The finish of that match would have given him much pleasure for he was the leading campaigner for the last over to be played out in a close finish irrespective of whether a wicket fell or not. I quote the following extract from his "Notes by the Editor", page 68 of the 1947 *Wisden*:

The newly arranged "Laws of Cricket", which will not come into force as finally approved until the 1948 season, clarify some details, and make one change which is specially pleasing to me. The "last over" of a match shall be played to a finish at the request of either captain. I first urged this in my Notes in the 1944 edition of *Wisden*, and each subsequent year emphasised the possible unfairness to the fielding side, so I may take some credit for bringing about this alteration which makes the balance even in a close finish on time.

Other tributes:

Sir John Hobbs: We became great friends almost as soon as I gained a footing in first-class cricket. We had a common attraction because our birthdays fell on the same day, he being my senior by 14 years. The players looked up to Hubert Preston as a genuine cricket reporter who knew the game and always did us justice.

Ronald Aird, secretary of MCC: I remember him since the early twenties. He was always so courteous and helpful over the business which we did together. His work for cricket with *Wisden* will live for all time and was a great contribution to the game. I am very grateful for having known him so well.

A. H. H. Gilligan: He was a familiar figure to us all in those far-off days when I used to play County Cricket and whether we got nought or plenty he always had a smile and a word of encouragement. If there was criticism it was always constructive.

Ian Macartney: He played a long innings with very little public recognition. The vivid and concise reporting of *Wisden* taught a generation of youngsters – the striplings of 1920 – how to write their own language, far better than any formal English lesson, without wasting words and space. The whole match was brought to life in a few lines. Gibbon and Macaulay had plenty of time to spread themselves, but S. H. Pardon and his successors are among the masters of English prose.

Leslie Deakins, secretary of Warwickshire CCC: Cricket is deeply indebted to him for his achievements on its behalf over a very long lifetime. His journalistic talents gave pleasure to those thousands of Englishmen who regularly follow the game. He could truly reflect with the late Charles Fry that his had been "Life Worth Living".

RICE, FATHER WILLIAM IGNATIUS, O.S.B., M.A., who died at Douai Abbey on April 22, 1955, aged 72, was Headmaster of Douai School from 1915 to 1952. In his younger days he played for Warwickshire during the summer holidays and for some years enjoyed the distinction of being the only monk whose cricket performances were chronicled in *Wisden*.

RUSSELL, MR ALFRED ISAAC, who died on August 20, 1961, aged 94, played as wicket-keeper and batsman for Hampshire before they acquired first-class status. For over 70 years, 50 of them as chairman, he was associated with the Deanery CC, whom he had captained. He liked to relate how once he caught an Essex batsman behind the wicket, threw the ball into the air and loudly appealed. "Not out", said the umpire. "I won't be rushed."

SELINCOURT, MR HUGH DE, author of many delightful books about cricket, died at his home near Pulborough, Sussex, on January 20, 1951. He was 72. Educated at Dulwich and University College, Oxford, Mr de Selincourt was for some years dramatic, then literary critic for London newspapers before he decided to devote his career to writing. Although his works were not confined to cricket, and there is no evidence that he was a specially accomplished player himself, he was perhaps best known for such tales as *The Cricket Match, Over* and *More Over*. These revealed particularly his love for cricket of the village-green variety.

SEWELL, MR EDWARD HUMPHREY DALRYMPLE, well known for many years as a cricket and Rugby football journalistic reporter, died on September 21, 1947, aged nearly 75. Born in India, where his father was an Army officer, he was educated at Bedford Grammar School, captaining the cricket and Rugby teams and playing for Bedfordshire County. In a curiously varied life he returned to India as a civil servant, and his very powerful hitting enabled him to make many big scores at an exceptional rate of scoring. The first batsman in India to make three consecutive hundreds, he also twice exceeded 200. Sometimes he enjoyed the advantage of having Ranjitsinhji for captain. Coming back to England, he joined the Essex County Club as a professional, and met with considerable success, notably in 1904 at Edgbaston, where, with Bob Carpenter, he shared in an opening stand of 142. He used to relate that the partnership lasted only sixty-five minutes – he was first out for 107; but, as he added, "They didn't give prizes for the fastest century in those days." The time was given officially as eighty minutes. In 1904, for London County, captained by W. G. Grace, he played his highest innings in first-class cricket, 181, against Surrey at Crystal Palace; one of his on-drives off Lockwood measured 140 yards. He punished moderate bowling in matches of minor class with merciless severity. Whitgift School suffered especially when, at Croydon for MCC, he hit up 142 out of 162 in fifty minutes, and again at The Oval, where for Wanderers he hit three 6s and nineteen 4s while scoring 108. After being a coach at The Oval, he became honorary secretary to the Buckinghamshire Club and played for the County as an amateur. He bowled medium pace with marked effect against any batsmen but the best, and fielded with dash and certainty. During recent years he attended every match of importance at Lord's, having a regular seat in the Long Room, where he was often the centre of discussions on the game he loved and knew so thoroughly. He gave practical evidence of this in several books – *From a Window at Lord's, The Log of a Sportsman* and *Who Won the Toss* being the best known. He played Rugby football for Blackheath and Harlequins; put the shot 37 feet and threw the cricket ball 117 yards at athletic sports meetings.

SHINE, MR EUSTACE BEVERLEY, C.B., who died at his home at New Milton, Hampshire, on November 11, 1952, will always hold a place in cricket history as the fast bowler who bore a leading part in bringing about an important alteration in the law governing the follow-on. Born at Port of Spain, Trinidad, on July 9, 1873, he was educated at King Edward VI School, Saffron Walden, and Selwyn College, Cambridge, where he got his Blue in 1896 and the following year. It was in the first of his appearances against Oxford that Shine became involved in an incident which had far-reaching results. By quarter to four on the second day, Oxford stood 131 behind the Cambridge first innings total of 319 with only one wicket to fall. Then, to quote *Wisden* of the time, the Cambridge captain, Frank Mitchell, "by palpably giving away runs to prevent his opponents from following-on, forced the MCC to reconsider the whole question" of a much-criticised law.

"Shine sent down three balls – two of them no-balls – to the boundary for four runs. These 12 runs deprived Oxford of the chance of following-on and immediately afterwards the Dark Blues innings closed for 202, or 117 behind. As they left the field the Cambridge eleven came in for a very hostile demonstration at the hands of the public, and inside the pavilion matters were still worse, scores of members of the MCC protesting in the most vigorous fashion against the policy that Frank Mitchell had adopted." In the end Oxford, set 330 to get, won by four wickets. At that time Law 53 read: "The side which goes in second shall follow their innings if they have scored 120 runs less than the opposite side in a three days' match, or 80 runs in a two days' match." In 1900 the law was altered, making the enforcing of the follow-on optional to the side who led by 150 on the first innings in a three-day match. After his University days Shine played occasionally for Kent between 1896 and 1899. When making his highest score (49) against Warwickshire at Tonbridge in 1897, he and F. Marchant (144 not out) added 158 for the ninth wicket in an hour. In all Shine took 129 wickets, average 24.14. A man of charming personality, he served with the Board of Agriculture from 1900 until he retired in 1933.

SKELDING, ALEXANDER, who died at Leicester on April 17, 1960, aged 73, stood as a first-class umpire from 1931 to 1958. He began his cricket career as a very fast bowler with Leicestershire in 1905, but, because he wore spectacles, was not re-engaged at the end of the season. He then joined Kidderminster in the Birmingham League and achieved such success that in 1912 the county re-signed him and he continued with them till 1929. His best season was that of 1927, when he took 102 wickets, average 20.81. Altogether he dismissed 593 batsmen at a cost of less than 25 runs each. One of the most popular personalities in the game, he always wore white boots when umpiring and he was celebrated for his sense of humour. It was his custom at the close of play to remove the bails with an exaggerated flourish and announce: "And that concludes the entertainment for the day, gentlemen."

"Alec" was the central figure in many amusing incidents. Once in response to an appeal for run out, he stated: "That was a 'photo-finish' and as there isn't time to develop the plate, I shall say not out." In another match a batsman who had been celebrating a special event the previous evening was rapped on the pad by a ball. At once the bowler asked: "How is he?" Said Alec, shaking his head sadly: "He's not at all well, and he was even worse last night." Occasionally the joke went against Alec. In a game in 1948 he turned down a strong appeal by the Australian touring team. A little later a dog ran on to the field, and one of the Australians captured it, carried it to Skelding and said: "Here you are. All you want now is a white stick!"

Asked in his playing days if he found spectacles a handicap, Alec said: "The specs are for the look of the thing. I can't see without 'em and on hot days I can't see with 'em, because they get steamed up. So I bowl on hearing only and appeal twice an over."

One of his most cherished umpiring memories was the giving of three leg-before decisions which enabled H. Fisher of Yorkshire to perform a unique "hat-trick" against Somerset at Sheffield in 1932. "I was never more sure that I was right in each case", he said afterwards, "and each of the batsmen agreed that he was dead in front".

SMITH, SIR CHARLES AUBREY, CBE, famous in the world of cricket before making a name on the stage and becoming a universal favourite on the films in comparatively recent years, died on December 20, 1948, aged 85, at Beverly Hills, California. Born in London on July 21, 1863, the son of a doctor, C. A. Smith went to Charterhouse School and bowled with such success that it came as no surprise that he gained his Blue at Cambridge when a Freshman in 1882. Four times he played at Lord's against Oxford and, by a remarkable series of coincidences, all of these matches ended with a decisive margin of seven wickets, Cambridge winning three of these interesting encounters. In the 1884 match which Oxford won, C. A. Smith was not out 0 in each innings and took two wickets for 65 runs, but in the other three games he showed his worth. In 1883 he helped C. T. Studd dismiss Oxford for 55 and in the second innings he took six wickets for 78 and Oxford just equalled the Cambridge total 215. He made four catches in the match. His last effort for the Light Blues brought six wickets for 81. His captains were the three brothers Studd and the Hon. M. B. Hawke.

He played for Sussex from 1882 until 1896, with varying regularity, and was captain from 1887 to 1889. For Gentlemen at Lord's in 1888 he and S. M. J. Woods dismissed the last four players for one run scored after A. G. Steel handed the ball to Smith. Each of the Cambridge fast bowlers took two of these wickets and Gentlemen won by five runs. In the match Woods took ten wickets for 76 and C. A. Smith five for 36.

In the previous winter he went to Australia, captaining the side organised by Shaw and Shrewsbury, and in 1888-89 he captained the first English side which went to South Africa, Major R. G. Wharton, the Australian, was manager. All the matches were against "odds" except two engagements called "English Team v Eleven of South Africa", but some years afterwards given the description "Tests". During the tour C. A. Smith took 134 wickets at 7.61 each, a modest achievement compared with the 290 wickets at 5.62 credited to John Briggs, the Lancashire left-hander. Smith stayed in South Africa for a time in partnership with M. P. Bowden, of Surrey, a member of the team, as stockbrokers. During this period he captained Transvaal against Kimberley in the first Currie Cup match in April 1890, so initiating a competition which has done much to raise the standard of cricket in South Africa.

Among C. A. Smith's best bowling performances were five wickets for eight runs for Sussex against The University at Cambridge in 1885, and seven for 16 against MCC at Lord's in 1890. A hard-hitting batsman, he scored 142 for Sussex at Hove against Hampshire in 1888.

Over six feet tall, he made an unusual run-up to deliver the ball and so became known as "Round The Corner" Smith. Sometimes he started from a deep mid-off position, at others from behind the umpire, and, as described by W. G. Grace, "it is rather startling when he suddenly appears at the bowling crease".

He maintained his love for cricket to the end. Until a few years ago he captained the

Hollywood side and visited England for the Test matches, the last time as recently as 1947, when South Africa were here.

He was knighted in 1944 in recognition of his support of Anglo-American friendship.

A very good Association outside-right, he played for Old Carthusians and Corinthians.

H.P.

SMITH, O'NEILL GORDON, who died in hospital at Stoke-on-Trent on September 9, 1959, aged 26, following injuries received in a motor-car accident in which two other West Indies players, G. Sobers and T. Dewdney, were also involved, took part in 26 Test matches between 1955 and 1959, scoring 1,331 runs, including four centuries, average 31.69. His death came as a heavy blow to the West Indies, for much had been hoped from him against P. B. H. May's MCC team last winter.

Smith's interest in cricket began at the age of seven and, such was his rapid advance, he gained a place in the team at St Alban's School, Jamaica, when nine and became captain inside three years. Later at Kingston College he progressed still further, but not till 1955 did he first appear for Jamaica. This was against the visiting Australians and he gave full evidence of his quality by playing an innings of 169, he and A. P. Binns putting on 277 for the sixth wicket. That performance earned him a place in the opening Test match and, by hitting 104 in the second innings, he joined the list of men who obtained a century on Test début. His success in three other Tests in the series was limited – indeed, he was dismissed for 0 and 0 in the second – but, with characteristic cheerfulness, he did not allow setbacks to deter him and from 1956, when he toured New Zealand, his place in the team was firmly established.

He learned to curb his natural desire to hit at practically every ball, though he never lost his punishing powers, and in England in 1957 he took 161 in the Edgbaston Test, becoming the only batsman to register a century on first appearance against both Australia and England. In the third meeting with England at Trent Bridge he made his highest Test score, 168, doing much to rescue the West Indies from what had seemed a hopeless position. "Collie" Smith was also a useful off-break bowler, having turned from pace to spin after watching J. C. Laker during the MCC tour of 1948. During the summers of 1958 and 1959 he achieved marked all-round success as professional to Burnley in the Lancashire League.

His body was taken to Jamaica where it was estimated that about 60,000 people attended the funeral.

Tributes to Smith included:

Sir Kenneth Blackburne, Governor of Jamaica: "The name of Collie Smith will long live as an example not only of a fine cricketer, but also of a great sportsman. He will provide inspiration for our youth in the future."

J. F. Dare, President of the West Indies Board of Control: "He was one of a diminishing band who play a game for the game's sake and he had a great future before him."

F. C. M. Alexander, West Indies and Jamaica captain: "His passing is a tremendous loss to those of us who came to realise what a wonderful spirit of cricket he was."

STREET, ALFRED EDWARD, who died at Budleigh Salterton on February 18, 1951, aged 80, played for Surrey from 1892 to 1898, scoring 1,304 runs, average 22.48. A useful cricketer and a friend of W. G. Grace, he might have played more regularly for the county had not Surrey during this period been specially rich in batting talent. Born at Godalming on July 7, 1871, "Jim" Street was the son of the former Surrey fast bowler, James Street. On his first appearance he created a most favourable impression by helping Hayward in a stand of 95 against the Australian touring side of 1893, and in 1895 he hit 161 not out from the Leicestershire bowling at Leicester. Twice he was concerned in "tie" matches. In 1894, when Surrey carried off the County Championship, they "tied" with Lancashire at The Oval, Street distinguishing himself by scoring 48 in a first innings of 97. Then, during a long career as a first-class umpire, during which he stood in an England v

Australia Test match, he became involved in a controversy because of what *Wisden* then described as "a regrettable incident". In the match with Somerset at Taunton in 1919 the scores stood level with one Sussex wicket to fall and the remaining batsman, Heygate, crippled with rheumatism. It was understood at the start of the innings that Heygate would not be able to bat, but as some doubt existed as to whether he would be able to go in a Somerset player appealed to Street on the ground that the two minutes time limit had been exceeded. Street thereupon pulled up the stumps and the match was officially recorded as a "tie". This incident gave rise to much discussion and was at length referred to the MCC, who upheld Street's decision.

TATE, MAURICE WILLIAM, "Chubby" to his many friends and admirers, died at his home at Wadhurst, Sussex, on May 18, 1956, aged 61. Only three weeks earlier he had umpired the opening match of the Australians' tour against the Duke of Norfolk's XI at Arundel.

Maurice Tate was the son of Fred Tate, the Sussex and England cricketer whose name will ever be associated with the 1902 Test at Old Trafford, which England lost by three runs. Fred Tate missed a vital catch and was last out when England wanted only four runs to win. In his reminiscences, published in 1934, Maurice Tate wrote that his father's greatest ambition was to see his son playing for England and retrieving his own tragic blunder. How well the son atoned for the father's misfortune! Maurice Tate began as a slow off-break bowler and had been playing some years before he developed his fast-medium action which gave him a deceptive swerve and tremendous pace off the pitch. He was probably the first bowler deliberately to use the seam and many of the best batsmen of the day regarded him as the most dangerous bowler they had ever played against.

He will be remembered as one of the greatest-hearted bowlers in the game – and one of cricket's most lovable and colourful personalities. He was an inveterate fun-maker and wherever he went he found new friends. He could go on bowling for hours, keeping an immaculate length and seeming to enjoy every moment of the game. A large and amiable man, with many of the characteristics of the true rustic, his broad grin and large feet were a "gift" to contemporary cartoonists.

Between 1912 and 1937, when he retired from the game, Tate took 2,784 wickets at an average cost of 18.12 runs. A. E. R. Gilligan, his old county and England captain, told of his "conversion" when, reviewing the history of Sussex cricket in the 1954 *Wisden*, he wrote:

"Tate, I must say at once, was the greatest bowler our county has produced. Curiously, when I first played for Sussex, Maurice used the same run-up and style of delivery as his father – a slow bowler! A sheer piece of luck caused Maurice to change his methods. Sussex had batted very badly in 1922, and when we had a day off the whole team practised at the nets. Maurice Tate bowled me several of his slow deliveries, then down came a quick one which spreadeagled my stumps. He did this three times. I went up to him and said: 'Maurice, you must change your style of bowling immediately.' My hunch paid. In the next match against Kent at Tunbridge Wells, Maurice, in his new style as a quick bowler, was unplayable. He took three wickets in four balls and eight in the innings for 67. That was the turning-point in his career.

"In the Test Trial at Lord's in 1923, he took five wickets without a run being scored from him after the Rest had made 200 for four wickets. They were out for 205. The following year Maurice and I bowled out South Africa at Birmingham for 30 – a day neither of us will ever forget. I was fortunate to take six for seven runs, and Maurice captured the other four for 12. In the second innings we shared nine wickets and England won by an innings. The tide flowed for Sussex bowlers about that time, for we had previously dismissed Surrey for 53 at The Oval, and in the Whitsuntide match at Lord's had disposed of Middlesex in their second innings for 41.

"Maurice was a member of my 1924-25 MCC team to Australia and on this tour he beat Arthur Mailey's record of 36 wickets in a Test series by taking 38. He bowled Mailey out to gain his 37th success! Besides being a great bowler, Maurice was a hard-hitting batsman with a wealth of strokes. He scored 17,518 runs (average 24.19) for the county and took 2,223 wickets (average 16.34). For seven consecutive seasons he did the "double" and in 1929 he took over 100 wickets for the county alone and scored more than 1,000 runs in first-class cricket. In fact, with the exception of 1933 when a damaged foot kept him out of the last three matches (he had taken 99 wickets), he never failed to take over 100 wickets for Sussex.

"In 1953 Alec Bedser beat Tate's Test record by taking 39 wickets in a series, and many times since I have been asked how I compare Bedser with Maurice. My answer is: 'They are two very great bowlers.' Having said that, I still think that Maurice Tate just stands out as the superior bowler of the two, bearing in mind the strength of the Australian batting in the 1924-25 series. But it is a very close thing indeed and one must not forget that Bedser had to contend with Bradman between 1946 and 1948."

Tate played in 20 consecutive Test matches against Australia and represented England in a further 19 Tests against South Africa, India and the West Indies. In all he took 155 Test wickets – a feat excelled only by A. V. Bedser and S. F. Barnes.

Tate was so consistently successful as a bowler that the quality of his batting is now often overlooked. Yet he was one of the best all-rounders of his generation. He scored 100 not out against South Africa in the Lord's Test in 1929. Eight times he completed the cricketers' double of 1,000 runs and 100 wickets in a season – and in 1923, 1924 and 1925 his "bag" of wickets topped 200. Fourteen times he took over 100 wickets in a season.

As a batsman, his best season was 1927, when he scored 1,713 runs, including five centuries. In 1922 he was the best all-rounder in the country, taking 118 wickets and scoring only 22 short of his 1,000. In 1921 he shared with Bowley a second wicket partnership of 385 against Northants – a Sussex record.

Tate was the first professional ever to captain Sussex – the honour later fell to James Langridge – and after his retirement he was elected an honorary life member of the County Club. He was also one of the former professionals similarly honoured by MCC in 1949.

When he retired from first-class cricket, Tate took over the licences of several Sussex inns and for a number of years coached the boys of Tonbridge School.

Tributes included the following:

Capt. C. B. Fry: "Tate was a very great cricketer indeed. He could make the ball swing away very late outside the off-stump, and even the best batsmen were often beaten by him. He could make the ball rear off the pitch like a snake striking. He was even more successful in Australia than in this country – in fact, he ranks with S. F. Barnes as the most successful bowler England has ever sent there."

Sir John Hobbs: "Maurice was one of the greatest bowlers of all time. It is difficult to find words to praise him sufficiently. I know from experience how difficult it was to play against him."

A. E. R. Gilligan: "His death has come as a great shock to everybody in Sussex, and in fact the whole of the cricket world. Not only was Maurice a great bowler; he was a very great sportsman. He played cricket for the real joy and fun of it. It was his life."

E. ("Patsy") Hendren: "I doubt whether we shall ever see the like of Maurice again. He was a great bowler and a great character. How they loved him in Australia! As a bowler he made the batsman play at five balls out of six. He was the finest fast-medium bowler I ever played with or against."

S. C. Griffith: "He was the best bowler of his type I have ever kept wicket to. If the modern field-placing had been in vogue when he was playing, I feel sure he would have taken hundreds more wickets. Often batsmen would get an inside edge which now would almost certainly mean a catch at short-leg. In Maurice's day, the ball used to run harmlessly down the leg-side."

Herbert Strudwick: "He was the best length bowler I ever kept wicket to and the best bowler of his pace I ever knew. There was not a quicker bowler off the wicket. I class him with Sidney Barnes and F. R. Foster as the three best bowlers I ever kept to."

TURNER, BRIGADIER ARTHUR JERVOIS, C.B., C.M.G., D.S.O. and Croix de Guerre, who died at Graffham, Sussex, on September 8, 1952, aged 74, was born at Mussorie, India, one of several cricketing sons of Major J. T. Turner, who, with other members of the Hong Kong cricket team, lost his life in the wreck of the *Bokhara* in 1892 when returning from a match with Shanghai. An all-rounder, A. J. Turner was educated at Bedford Modern School, where he gained a place in the eleven in 1892 when thirteen. He played four seasons for the school, being captain in 1895. For Woolwich and the Army he also earned a reputation as a cricketer, and after occasional appearances for Bedfordshire he assisted Essex between 1897 and 1910. In his first season of first-class cricket he hit 40 and 111 against Yorkshire at Huddersfield. He played for Gentlemen v Players at The Oval in 1898 and was invited for the Lord's match the following summer, but because of military duties could not accept. Besides his cricketing abilities, Turner was an excellent Rugby footballer and played for Blackheath and Kent. He served with the Royal Artillery in the South African War and, while on the General Headquarters Staff in France during the First World War, was four times mentioned in despatches.

TYLDESLEY, ERNEST, of Lancashire and England, died at his home at Rhos-on-Sea on May 5, 1962, aged 73.

Neville Cardus wrote in *The Guardian*:

Ernest Tyldesley, one of the most accomplished batsmen ever to play for Lancashire, was born in Lancashire, brother of one of the three greatest professional batsmen in the game's history. As a boy he played for Roe Green, which in a way was a Tyldesley club, for the famous "J.T.T." learned his cricket on the same village green. J. T. Tyldesley kept a more than brotherly eye on Ernest but turned the other way when he saw the youngster's cross-bat. "J.T.T." also tended to bring his bat along a line beginning at third man. "A straight bat's all right to a straight ball", said "J.T.T." one day, "but there are not many runs to be made by straight pushing". "J.T.T." never pushed; but Ernest seldom began an innings without one or two anxious or tentative thrusts. Once he had "seen" the ball he could be as brilliant and as punitive as he was defensively sound.

"J.T.T." was a genius, and it is to Ernest's credit that, though on his entrance into Lancashire cricket he had to survive a disheartening comparison, he never lost faith. "J.T.T." of course, constantly encouraged him. "Some day", he said, "he'll be a better bat than ever I was". Ernest certainly scored a few more runs in his career than came from the broadsword of his brother. Between 1909 and 1936 Ernest scored 38,874, average 45.46; "J.T.T.'s" portion was, between 1895 and 1932, 37,809, average 40.69.

In style they were more than different. Ernest's batting was always courteous; in his most aggressive moods, when he would hook fast bowling vividly, he rarely suggested militancy or the ruthless slayer of bowling. "Johnny" was usually on the kill. ... If a maiden over were bowled at him, "J.T.T." would gnaw a glove at the end of it. He had, with Macartney, no patience with a good attack; he felt the necessity of falling on it and demolishing it without delay. Ernest was more patient. But when the situation called for valiance Ernest could go into battle with chivalric manners concealing ruthless and belligerent purpose.

In the Test match of 1921 at Old Trafford he was the first England cricketer that year really to treat the conquering attack of Armstrong with contumely. In 1925 at Kennington Oval he played one of the most tremendously incisive, powerful, merciless, and gallant innings I have ever seen. At close of play on the second day Lancashire were apparently at Surrey's mercy. Four wickets had fallen, with 117 still needed to escape defeat by an innings. Hitch began the Surrey attack next morning at a hair-raising pace. He employed five slips. In a quarter of an hour four of those slips had been moved to the leg and on sides – defensively. Tyldesley's hooking was savage and daring; he hooked from his eyebrow. His hits to the off were no less swift and exacting. In five hours he scored 236 without a shadow of error. Lancashire saved the game easily.

Ernest's experiences in Test cricket were peculiar, making strange reading these days when all manner of inglorious Miltons are asked, almost on bended knees, to bat for England. In 1921 Tyldesley played for England at Nottingham against the ferocious McDonald and Gregory attack. He made 0 and 7, knocked out second innings by Gregory, bowled off his cheek-bone. He was recalled for the Old Trafford Test, when he scored 78 not out, and for the fifth Test at Kennington Oval where he made a pleasant 39. Not until 1926 was he again asked to play for England against Australia at Old Trafford in the fourth Test of the rubber. He scored 81; and was dropped for the concluding game of the same rubber.

He was taken to Australia, one of Chapman's team of 1928-29, but was entrusted with only one Test, in which he made 31 and 21. He was never again chosen for the England eleven against Australia. So, in five opportunities against the strongest cricket power, his record was, and remains, 0, 7, 78 not out, 39, 81, 31 and 21. In South Africa, in the Test matches there of the 1927-28 rubber, he headed England's averages – 65 an innings for 520 runs, with these scores: 122, 0, 87, 78, 62 not out, 42, 8, 100 and 21. And South Africa's attack was then composed of Nupen, Morkel, Vincent, Bissett and Hall.

In 1928 Tyldesley amassed 3,024 runs in the season, average 79.57. In 1926, when he was only once picked for the England eleven (and scored his 81), he made four centuries in successive innings, with a season's aggregate of 2,826, average 64.22, only Hobbs and Sutcliffe his statistical peers. Yet he could not hold a place in the England side. In his career he reached the century 102 times, and twice he scored two centuries in the same match.

Figures alone will give some idea to posterity of his quality. Like his brother, he had the answer to unpleasant wickets. His great cricket in South Africa was achieved on matting, against Nupen spinning viciously. In fact, he preferred a turning ball to the one that came straight through quickly enough to find a slight chink in the armour – the bat just a little out of the straight. But those of us who saw him play and knew him off the field as a friend will remember his batsmanship not only for its skill, resource, and plenty, but mainly because it was so like the man himself – modest yet firm of character, civilised in all its called-for action. He was, in a word, a gentlemanly babuean who, when he needed to assert his authority, never exceeded the privileges of class and manners.

His cricket was part and parcel of a Lancastrian of quiet charm, having a modesty that concealed the tough fibre in him of Lancashire. A year or two ago, at a painful stage of his broken health, George Duckworth went to visit him at his home. "And how are you, Ernest?" "Well, George, I was at the specialist's yesterday, and he says my eyes are in a bad way. And I've had awful pains in my thighs, and my chest's been giving me jip." Then he paused, before adding, "But, mind you, George, there's nothin' the matter with me!"

That's the Lancashire man for you, all over. We'll not forget him.

WASS, TOM, who died at Sutton-in-Ashfield on October 27, 1953, aged 79, was on his day one of the most effective bowlers of his time. Born in Sutton-in-Ashfield, a village once the most productive nursery for Nottinghamshire cricketers, on December 26, 1873, he gained an early reputation as a fast bowler in local cricket. Following a spell as professional with Edinburgh Academicals he joined Liverpool CC, and, becoming qualified by residence for Lancashire, was offered a place on the staff at Old Trafford. This Wass, originally a miner, declined, and instead gave his services to his native county, for whom he made a first-class début in 1897. Not till the following season, however, did his county career really begin, and thereafter he progressed from strength to strength.

Ability to make the ball turn from leg rendered him specially dangerous to batsmen, and no bowler of his pace was a greater menace on slow pitches. Before he gave up first-class cricket in 1920 he took 1,679 wickets, a Nottinghamshire record. In 1907 he played a leading part in helping Nottinghamshire to carry off the County Championship without suffering defeat, dismissing in that season 163 batsmen at a cost of 14.28 runs each. It was remarkable that in view of his many successes "Topsy" Wass was never chosen for England, but he appeared three times for Players against Gentlemen, at Lord's in 1908 and at The Oval in 1904 and 1908.

Twice he took sixteen wickets in a match, and on each occasion performed the feat in the course of a single day. The first was against Lancashire at Liverpool in 1901, when his figures were eight for 25 and eight for 44; the second against Essex at Trent Bridge in 1908, his analyses then being eight for 29 and eight for 74. In the first innings of Essex he at one time took six wickets for nine runs, including the hat-trick. Twice, against Surrey at The Oval in 1902 (for 91 runs) and against Derbyshire at Blackwell in 1911 (for 67 runs) he dismissed nine batsmen in an innings, and he took eight wickets in an innings no fewer than sixteen times. The best of these latter performances was eight for 13 at the expense of Derbyshire at Welbeck in 1901. At Lord's in 1907 he gained the remarkable analysis of six wickets for three runs, his victims including J. H. King, F. A. Tarrant and L. C. Braund. A moderate fieldsman, Wass also accomplished little in batting, though in 1906 at Derby he hit, with the aid of four missed catches, an innings of 56, he and J. W. Day adding 98 for the ninth wicket and so enabling Nottinghamshire to recover from a breakdown against A. W. Warren.

Generally of kindly character, Wass could be stubborn when roused. The story used to be told of how he once arrived at The Oval for a match accompanied by his wife and was told by the gateman that the lady would not be allowed in without payment. "Oh," said Wass grimly. "If this beggar doan't coom in, this beggar" – indicating himself – "doan't play!" Mrs Wass was admitted without further argument.   E.E.

WILLIAMS, MR WILLIAM, who died at his home at Hampton Wick on April 14, 1951, aged 90, was a fine all-round sportsman. Born on April 12, 1860, he was a member of MCC from 1900. In the seasons of 1885 and 1886 he appeared as wicket-keeper for Middlesex, and after an absence of 14 years returned to the county side as a bowler of leg-breaks, playing occasionally till 1905. During the winter of 1896-97 he toured the West Indies with Mr Arthur Priestley's team and, with 67 wickets at an average cost of 9.62, finished second in the bowling averages to A. E. Stoddart. He often assisted MCC and was credited with taking 100 or more wickets a season in all matches for fifty-five years. In his last summer as a player, he turned out at the age of 74 for MCC against the House of Lords and, after dismissing Lord Dalkeith, Lord Tennyson and Major L. George for 16 runs, was presented by the Marylebone Club with the ball. A good story is told of when, at the age of 65, he visited the West Indies during the tour of the Hon. F. S. G. Calthorpe's MCC Team in 1925-26. In Georgetown he challenged a West Indian friend against whom he played 30 years before to a single-wicket match for £25 a side. Winning the toss, Williams severely punished his opponent's bowling, completed a century and declared. Then, with a googly, he bowled his exhausted victim first ball.

Apart from his cricket, "Billy" Williams, as he was known to everyone for many years, was celebrated as the man who, in the early part of the century when a member of the Middlesex County Rugby Union Committee, ended a long search for a suitable site for a National Rugby Union ground by discovering a cabbage field of ten acres which has since developed into the famous Twickenham enclosure. For a long time the ground, later extended by eighteen acres, was known to Rugby football followers as "Billy William's cabbage patch". Formerly a player for the Harlequins RFC, he was a Rugby referee for 21 years. An honorary member of the Wimbledon Park Golf Club, he played a daily round until his last illness, and was a regular attendant at Lord's and at Rugby matches in the London area, particularly Richmond.

WREFORD BROWN, MR CHARLES, the amateur footballer and Soccer legislator who played first-class cricket between 1886 and 1889, died at his home in London on November 26, 1951, aged 85. A free hitter, a slow bowler with a break either way and a good field at mid-off, Wreford Brown captained Charterhouse, and in 1887 he would have been in the Oxford team against Cambridge but for an accident. He occasionally assisted Gloucestershire, the county of his birth, and he visited America with Lord Hawke's team in 1891. As a Soccer player, Wreford Brown achieved fame as a centre-half, although he could fill any position. He captained Oxford against Cambridge in 1889 and gained four caps for England, one when he led his team to notable victory against Scotland in Glasgow in 1898. He helped Old Carthusians and Corinthians. He became Vice-President of the Football Association and for many years was Chairman of the F.A. Internatioanl Selection Committee. He kept in trim even when undertaking legislative duties, and at 60 he turned out for Corinthians against Eton. Wreford Brown, who was a solicitor, made many trips abroad with F.A. teams as member in charge, and a good tale is told of him in this connection. A fine chess player, his keenness for the game led him into an embarrassing situation during one visit to the colonies. On arrival he was greeted by an old friend, a high officer of the home Association, also an enthusiastic chess player. All tour matters forgotten for the moment, the pair slipped off to a little café for a game, and there they stayed for several hours oblivious of the fact that officials were searching in vain for them and that the lunch of welcome had to go on without them.

WRIGHT, MR LEVI GEORGE, who died at Derby on January 11, 1953, four days before his 91st birthday, was one of the finest batsmen who ever appeared for Derbyshire. Probably a better player at the age of 40 than at any other period of his career, he will be best remembered for his work as a fieldsman at point. Never standing more than four or five yards from the bat, he brought off many brilliant catches.

Born at Oxford on January 15, 1862, Wright was a batsman well worth watching, though possessing no particular grace of style. Like most cricketers who learned the game before hooking and pulling came into general vogue, he played forward a lot and scored chiefly on the off-side. Strong in defence, he displayed a good deal of enterprise considering that during the whole of his career he so regularly found himself battling for a side that was nearly always struggling. First playing for Oxford City, he went to Derby as an assistant schoolmaster in 1881, appearing for Derby Midland. A year later began that association with Derbyshire which, apart from the summers of 1885 and 1886, went on without interruption till he retired at the end of the season of 1909.

His biggest scores were 195 against Northamptonshire in 1905 and 193 against Nottinghamshire in 1901, both at Derby. On five other occasions for the county he exceeded 140. He followed his score of 195 with 176 and 122 against Warwickshire at Edgbaston, so enjoying the satisfaction of playing three successive three-figure innings. Four times he represented Gentlemen against Players, and, with 1901 his best year when he registered 1,482 runs, average 32, he scored in all 15,155 runs, average 26. He was also an able Association footballer, and after giving up cricket took to bowls, a game he continued till the late eighties.

Of his fielding, E. M. Grace used to relate how on one occasion when a batsman kept poking at the ball and cocking it up, Wright crept in closer and closer till he was only a yard or so away from the striker. Soon the fieldsman thought he saw his chance of a catch. He made a grab and the crowd cheered, but it was the bat he held, not the ball!

YOUNG, MR JOHN VILLIERS, who died in hospital at Eastbourne on September 3, 1960, aged 76, was in the Eastbourne College XI from 1901 to 1904, being captain in the last two years. A fine all-rounder, he scored 947 runs and took 63 wickets in 1903. To him belonged an unusual distinction, for he played in the 1906 Cambridge Freshmen's match and in the 1907 Oxford Freshmen's match, becoming both a Cambridge Crusader and an Oxford Authentic. He played in three matches for Sussex in 1908. He was the brother of R. A. Young, the celebrated Cambridge University, Sussex and England batsman.

MISCELLANY

NO MAGIC IN FAST BOWLING [1948]

HONEST TOIL THE KEY TO SUCCESS

By C. J. Kortright

(*In an interview*)

The name of C. J. Kortright in cricket circles is almost legendary. Many people who saw him play consider he was the fastest bowler during a period which was notable for the number of speed men in England and Australia. A reference to the 1944 article in Wisden *on fast bowlers by the late Sir Stanley Jackson bears out this fact. After a career beginning in 1889, the famous Essex amateur gave up county cricket eleven years before the first World War. At 77 he is still a keen observer of cricket, and in the belief that his views on bowlers past and present will not only throw much light on our present problems but will also inspire the younger generation to take up fast bowling, the Editor persuaded him to express his opinions in the pages of* Wisden.

One of the questions my friends most frequently ask me is why there are so few fast bowlers today compared with the start of the century, and why the few there are attain comparatively small success. They seem to think there was some sort of magic about the old-time men of pace, and that I may be able to explain how it was obtained. Let me disillusion them at once. There is no magic in fast bowling; but, on the contrary, much hard work, coupled with intelligent methods, is the key to success.

I have little patience with modern bowlers who condemn "these shirt-front wickets" and ask how can they be expected to get men out when the pitch will not help. There were many such pitches in my playing days, the sort on which if we could bounce the ball bail high we thought ourselves pretty clever. Yet every county fielded two, sometimes three, genuinely fast bowlers, who were not discouraged by the wickets.

A basic principle of cricket which I feel is sometimes overlooked is that the prime object of a bowler is to get batsmen out. For this reason I do not favour the modern craze for such expressions as "in-swingers", "out-swingers", all sorts of "spins" and "swerves". Some bowlers seem to concentrate on these dubious achievements so much that they forget to keep a length and to bowl at the stumps.

A striking sign of this tendency is the present cult of off-spin bowling to a cluster of short-leg fielders, who would not have been allowed to stay in their suicidal positions by some of the old-time batsmen like Gilbert Jessop and Johnny Tyldesley. This style compares very poorly with the methods of Tom Richardson of Surrey, the finest bowler I ever saw. He used only two leg-side men, a mid-on and a deep fine-leg to save snicks, because he bowled consistently on the off-stump to that beautiful length which meant that batsmen could never leave the ball alone.

Richardson's long easy run, fine action, accuracy and speed, coupled with a little break-back from the off, made him a bowler to be feared; and another man I greatly admired was Walter Brearley, who took a much shorter run but achieved real pace through a splendid body action. Such men as these could take seven or eight wickets in an innings on plumb pitches, nearly all clean bowled, because they bowled a length, bowled with their heads, and bowled at the stumps. What is the use of "swerves" if you beat the batsman, beat the wicket-keeper, and everybody else? Bowlers like Richardson used to move the ball just that vital inch or two off the pitch, and they hit the stumps.

If England can find a real fast bowler who is willing to take a bit of advice from an old-timer, here is a wrinkle he might well remember. He should never forget to try bowling a fast yorker on the leg stump to a newly arrived batsman. It can be a deadly ball to face early in an innings; I have dismissed many top-class batsmen with it. I frequently used to advise the late Kenneth Farnes to pitch the ball farther up to the batsmen, because I considered that he wasted too much energy on pointless short deliveries, like many other modern pace bowlers.

Another encouragement which I would mention to bowlers and those aspiring to success with the ball is that they enjoy many advantages compared with those of the old days. They have a slightly smaller ball – easier to get the hand round – a wider crease, which helps in varying the angle of delivery, bigger stumps at which to aim. There is also the new leg-before-wicket law by which it is possible to get a decision from a ball pitching on the off-side of the wicket, a boon to the modern bowler. Last but by no means least among present-day benefits is the high standard of umpiring in first-class cricket, one respect in which I admit the game has made a great advance since my days.

The umpires of today are very good and impartial. They watch the ball extremely closely and know the game thoroughly, so that any bowler can feel confident that he will get any decisions he has earned.

A young bowler should not be allowed to over-tax his strength and, although there is no reason why he should not bat well, it should always be remembered that his real task is to take wickets. I remember Alfred Shaw of Nottinghamshire telling me when I was a youngster why the best bowlers so seldom make runs. He said: "After holding a bat for a long time we lose that freshness in ourselves, and that suppleness in the fingers which helps so much in bowling. So it is better not to bat too much when one will soon have to bowl."

[Shaw, between 1864 and 1897, took 2,072 wickets for 11.97 runs each, much the lowest figure of the twenty bowlers who have taken over 2,000 wickets in first-class cricket. – Editor.]

Another thing a bowler should always remember is to mark out his run and stick to it, even at practice. Too many no-balls are delivered by men who should know better, and they represent free gifts to the opposing side.

Perhaps one of the greatest differences between modern and old-time bowling lies in the attitude towards the new ball and the method of gripping it. Personally, I didn't worry a great deal about how I held the ball in relation to the seam as long as I got a firm grip on it, and I think most of my contemporaries felt the same. We wanted to be accurate, and to make the ball move a little off the pitch through finger action. For that reason, fast bowlers often roughened a new ball by rubbing it in the dirt, to obtain a good grip. Now bowlers dirty their clothes in efforts to keep the ball shiny, but I feel sure they do not control it so well.

I do not think we shall get a plentiful supply of bowling talent again until the youngsters realise that there is no easy way to become a good bowler and no secret either. The road to success lies in enthusiasm coupled with patience and willingness to devote as much time as possible to practice. I do not feel that young cricketers today are always prepared to take the trouble over their game that they should, possibly because there are so many counter-attractions.

One of the clearest recollections of my early days is the "little cricket" we played at Brentwood school. This involved creeping out through a window at four in the morning, with any sort of makeshift gear, to play against the chapel wall until seven o'clock, the official time for rising. If discovered, we were in trouble, but I thought the game well worth the risk, and I was always ready for two and a half hours of compulsory cricket practice when school was over for the day.

In those days almost invariably I was holding something to throw or bowl, if not a ball a sizeable stone, which I would hurl at a convenient tree or post. All this helped to develop a sense of distance and timing, and built up the muscles of hand, arm and shoulder. I was for ever wanting to project things farther or faster than any of my friends, and this I think accounted for the pace I was able to develop later as a bowler.

The present-day lack of enthusiasm for practice, especially in bowling and fielding, was brought home to me a few years ago when I tried to coach two youngsters in whom I was interested. They batted in the nets for about half an hour, then they wanted to be off to knock a ball about at some other game. As for bowling to somebody else or getting fielding practice – that mattered not at all.

Yet I would stress to all cricketers, especially the youngsters, that if we are to develop great bowlers again, and especially fast bowlers, there must be much greater concentration on fielding. Any bowler is so much better with the support of a keen field, and every player in any side should impose an unwritten law on himself to field well even if he can do little else. I used to enjoy Free Foresters cricket immensely because it was played in a really sporting spirit and the standard of fielding was very high.

As a final word to budding fast bowlers, let me again emphasise that you should not be afraid to pitch the ball well up, and remember the value of the yorker on the leg stump against a newcomer. The first time I hit the stumps in county cricket was with that ball, in the Essex and Surrey match at The Oval in 1892. I bowled Billy Brockwell with a fast one which hit the base of the stumps and brought the bails forward, one breaking as it flew over my head. Another of my yorkers which remains in my memory rebounded from the bottom of the stumps and went back past me almost to the boundary.

[In the match to which C. J. Kortright refers, he took in all five wickets for 71 runs, three of them bowled, but Surrey, for whom Tom Richardson gained match figures of twelve for 100, won by 195 runs. – Editor.]

My favourite story is rather hard to believe, but I vouch for its truth. Playing in a club match at Wallingford on a very small ground with a pitch perhaps best described as "sporty", I bowled a ball which rose almost straight and went out of the ground, without a second bounce. I suggest that this made me the first man to bowl a six in byes! The ball was pitched right up to the batsman and on the wicket, so that it was undoubtedly within the striker's reach, and there was no question of wides being awarded.

W. G. GRACE CENTENARY [1949]

By The Editor

When W. G. Grace passed away in 1915, Sydney Pardon, then Editor of *Wisden*, paid the highest eulogy possible to the greatest figure who ever trod the cricket field, and after the centenary of his birth one may assert confidently that no one has risen to equal fame in the world of cricket. As batsman, bowler and fielder he remains supreme, while to those who knew his attributes from watching many of his wonderful performances his position stands out with all the more clearness. My personal knowledge of his greatness by means of eyesight commenced in 1884 at The Oval Test match in which Australia scored 551. How W.G. kept wicket and caught Midwinter off the Hon. Alfred Lyttelton, who, with his pads on, bowled lobs from the Vauxhall end and finished Australia's innings by taking the last four wickets for eight runs, remains a clear picture to me. When England batted, W. L. Murdoch, the Australian captain, tried the experiment of putting on G. J. Bonnor, the six-foot-four giant, to open the bowling with the pavilion behind him. How W.G. calmly played forward and turned the good-length ball to the leg boundary was a matter of perfect timing and subtle wrist work. W.G. made 19 and then was run out. He played a ball to cover-point, and McBlackham, the brilliant wicket-keeper, fourth bearded man in the match, receiving a splendid return, whipped off the bails as Grace slid his bat over the crease. It was a sad disappointment when the umpire signalled "out". The stubborn Scotton and free-hitting Walter Read in a ninth-wicket stand of 151 saved England.

I can see the bearded giant at a distance two years later making 170 for England against Australia at The Oval on drying turf. He was second out at 216; he hit splendidly, his on-drives over the boundary from Spofforth arousing much delight. And so by various pictures on to 1895 at Gravesend, where he came to the Press tent during lunch time and wrote a telegram. To my delight, Edgar Pardon, my chief, introduced me to the Doctor, so making the occasion still more memorable to me – though unforgettable for anyone present. That was the match in which W.G. scored 257 out of 443 before being last out on the Saturday. Then after lunch Kent were dismissed for 76. Of the 106 runs which gave

Gloucestershire victory by nine wickets W.G. scored 73, while to complete the remarkable three days, during which he was on the field while every ball was bowled, he trotted from the dressing tent in his tweed tail suit and hard felt hat, carrying his heavy cricket bag to a four-wheeled cab which took him to the station. Nothing "legendary" – a word misapplied to him by some writers who cannot have seen him – about this, but honest fact. This was the first instance in first-class cricket in England of a side winning after facing a total of over 400 – Kent began the match with 470. W.G. was then 47.

Next season came another triumph – the last match in which W.G. led England to victory. In this encounter at The Oval in 1896 the dismissal of Australia by Robert Peel and J. T. Hearne for 44 established what is still a Test record for The Oval, eight less than the total for which the home country fell last season on that sad Saturday, August 14. In that innings of 44, nine wickets were down for 25 when M'Kibbin joined Hugh Trumble and hit up 16 before a grand catch at slip by Abel completed the collapse. W.G. scored 33 runs in the match, an aggregate exceeded only by F. S. Jackson, Robert Abel and Joe Darling, the Australian captain, who equalled Jackson's 47.

So we may look back with thanks to W.G. for one Test match record, and remember that when the Australians came in 1878 he decided not to give up all his time to medicine as he had intended, but to continue participation in the game taught him by his father, uncle and other relations from the time that he could run with a bat in his hands. In 1880 I felt surprise when W. L. Murdoch, with 153 not out, just beat W.G.'s score in the first England v Australia match at The Oval; and then came "The Ashes" match – a doleful day for a boy worshipper of cricket even at home as I heard the news.

These are merely memories of what I saw, and are small items in his wonderful life. From the many books on "W.G." one gathers an amazing panorama of astonishing events. In 1865 he first appeared for Gentlemen against Players at Lord's, and in this connection it is good to quote the Hon. Robert H. Lyttelton, whose tribute hangs at Lord's by the side of a small copy of the W. G. Grace picture, which is placed prominently in the National Portrait Gallery: "The Champion" in flannels, wearing the MCC red and yellow cap, as he always did on the cricket field.

WILLIAM GILBERT GRACE

1848-1915

"The greatest of the world's cricketers, as a batsman, supreme; as a bowler, great. In his prime he towered above his contemporaries. From 1850 to 1866 the Professionals won 23 out of 26 matches against the Amateurs. In the next series of 26 matches the Amateurs won 19, the Professionals 1. This remarkable change was entirely due to the black-bearded hero 'W.G.' A terror to bowlers, he was worshipped by the crowd."

Arranged as customary for the third week in July, the Gentlemen and Players match at Lord's came opportunely for celebrating the Centenary, and MCC appropriately marked the anniversary.

On entering the ground one saw that laurel leaves surrounded the panels on each side of the gates, on which the exact inscription is:

TO THE

MEMORY OF

WILLIAM GILBERT
GRACE

THE GREAT CRICKETER
1848-1915

THESE GATES WERE
ERECTED BY THE MCC
AND OTHER FRIENDS
AND ADMIRERS

"The *Great* Cricketer" was decided upon as the simplest and best description at the suggestion of Sir Stanley Jackson.

The score card was headed: "In celebration of the 100th anniversary of the birth of Dr W. G. Grace", and on the back was printed:

Dr W. G. Grace
"The Great Cricketer"
July 18th, 1848–October 23rd, 1915.

"In 44 seasons of first-class cricket – 1865 to 1908 – he scored 54,896 runs, took 2,876 wickets, and made 126 centuries.

"When only sixteen years old, he went in first and opened the bowling for the Gentlemen v Players at Lord's; on his last appearance for the Gentlemen, in 1906, at The Oval, he made 74 on his 58th birthday. In 84 matches against the Players he scored over 6,000 runs and took 271 wickets.

"In 1880 he scored 152 against Australia in the first Test Match played in this country, and was the automatic first choice and opening batsman for England until 1899.

"In 1876 he scored 839 runs in three consecutive innings against Kent, Nottinghamshire and Yorkshire; nineteen years later he made 1,000 runs in May.

"On fourteen occasions he scored a century and took 10 or more wickets in the same match.

"In prowess and personality alike he dominated the cricket field; he was the kindest of men and no Englishman was better known."

In Wheatstone Hall, Gloucester, Colonel D. C. Robinson, a former captain of the County team, presided at a meeting, and C. L. Townsend, a fine all-rounder, opened an exhibition of trophies used by W.G. and other players in memorable games. Among the company was Paish, another contemporary of Grace. Gilbert Jessop wrote that "W.G. was his hero as a boy and remained so still". Walter Hammond sent a menu card of the banquet held in 1895 to celebrate Grace's 100th century, and the Gloucestershire XI, headed by B. O. Allen, signed a letter of good wishes. As *The Times* correspondent wrote, "This exhibition shows how W. G. Grace in this century year of his birth is remembered with pride and affection."

At Bristol, where his old county met Derbyshire, the W.G. centenary was celebrated by the Duke of Beaufort, the Gloucestershire President, unveiling a memorial plaque on the Nevil Road gates, which are known as "Grace's Gates".

INTERESTING EVENTS

W. G. Grace established a name in the West Country before the Gloucestershire County Club was formed, and he first played at Lord's in 1864 for South Wales against MCC. Just 16 years of age, he was then, as stated in *Scores and Biographies*, an inch or two taller than six feet and weighed 14 stone 5 lb. He scored 50, a week after making 170 and 56 not out against Gentlemen of Sussex at Brighton. Yet it was as a bowler that he first attracted attention in first-class cricket. In 1865 at The Oval he and I. D. Walker bowled unchanged through both innings of Players of the South; W.G. took 13 wickets for 84 runs.

When 18 years of age he scored 224 not out for England against Surrey at The Oval. On the second afternoon he was allowed by V. E. Walker, the England captain, to go to Crystal Palace for the National Olympian Association 440 yards hurdle race, which he won over twenty hurdles in 70 seconds.

Also in 1866, for Gentlemen of South against Players of South, he scored 173 not out and took nine wickets for 108 runs. These performances earned him the description "The Champion".

In August 1868 he scored 130 and 102 not out for South of Thames v North of Thames at Canterbury – the first instance of two hundreds being made by a batsman in a first-class match. The season of 1871 brought wonderful performances. W.G. scored 2,739 runs in first-class matches when the over was four balls and every stroke run out except a hit out of the ground for six; he made ten centuries and twice passed 200, average 78.25; also he took 79 wickets at a cost of 17.03 each.

Besides his phenomenal batting in August 1876, when he scored consecutive innings of 344 out of 546 in six hours twenty minutes for MCC against Kent at Canterbury, 177 out of 262 in three hours ten minutes for Gloucestershire against Nottinghamshire at Clifton, and 318 not out against Yorkshire at Cheltenham, carrying his bat through the innings of 528, which lasted eight hours, he took four wickets against Kent, nine against Nottinghamshire, eight in the second innings for 69 runs, and two wickets for 48 against Yorkshire. The Sunday intervening between the first two matches was the only break in these stupendous performances. His aggregate runs for the season was 2,622, average 62.42 and he took 129 wickets at 19.05 apiece.

Regarding these wonderful innings, the tale has been handed down that the Nottinghamshire team leaving Clifton met the Yorkshiremen on their way to Cheltenham. "What did the black-bearded blighter do?" asked a Tyke, and, on being told, said, "Thank goodness, we've got a chance." The reply came next day – 318.

Next season, under less favourable batting conditions, he scored 1,474 runs and took 179 wickets at an average of 12.79. At Cheltenham, 17 Nottinghamshire wickets fell to him at a total cost of 89 runs; he finished the second innings by dismissing seven men in the course of 17 balls without conceding a run.

The match at Gravesend, to which I have referred, might be described as an *encore* to what happened ten years before. In August 1885, at Clifton, after sitting up all night in attendance on a difficult maternity case, he carried his bat through an innings of 348, scoring 221; then took six wickets for 45, and in the Middlesex follow-on five for 75.

Although a splendid athlete – he won more than seventy prizes on the track – he gradually put on weight, and was a very heavy man for his age when, in 1880, he played the only three-figure innings against the powerful Australian side captained by W. L. Murdoch in a season when run-getting generally was low.

In May 1899 W.G. left Gloucestershire because of differences with the club committee, and he captained London County at the Crystal Palace, where he scored 166 against MCC on his 56th birthday. That was his last hundred in important cricket, and in that season, 1904, he made his final appearance for MCC at Lord's.

London County Club then ceased first-class cricket, but W.G. played in various club games. It is related that on one occasion when young strangers were in his side he asked one hopeful: "Where do you go in?" "I'm always number one." "Number eleven today." "And you, my lad, where do you go in?" "Where I'm put, sir." "Then come in first with me."

W.G. was a strict disciplinarian; his presence kept everyone intent on the game, and it would be for the good of cricket if such an example was with us now. He insisted on the closest possible adherence to the laws, so preventing any attempts at sharp practice by fieldsmen to distract the batsman's attention from the bowler.

W. G. Grace, in his last match – Eltham v Grove Park on July 25, 1914 – when 66 years of age, scored 69 not out in a total of 155 for six wickets declared; the next best score was 30 not out by E. F. Tyler. Grove Park lost eight wickets for 99 and the result was a draw.

The figures given are taken from the book by F. S. Ashley-Cooper, published by John Wisden & Co. on July 18, 1916, and these quotations are worthy of inclusion in a lasting memorial of "The Champion".

F. R. Spofforth, the Australian "Demon" bowler, said: "He seems different from all other cricketers – a king apart. I never see him in the field but I am reminded of my boyish days when our schoolmaster used to join in the game and teach us the way. W. G. Grace is like a master among his pupils; there may arise pupils who will be no less skilful with the bat and ball, but they never will command the permanent and world-wide reputation of the man who first taught us to play."

Lord Harris, England captain, contemporary with Grace, wrote: "He was always a most genial, even-tempered, considerate companion, and, of all the many cricketers I have known, the kindest as well as the best. He was ever ready with an encouraging word for the novice, and a compassionate one for the man who made a mistake."

A National Testimonial organised by MCC raised £1,458, besides a handsome clock, and the presentation was made at Lord's during the "Over 30 v Under 30" match in 1879. In 1895, as an appreciation of W.G.'s "rejuvenation", the MCC initiated a "Grace Testimonial Fund", which amounted to £2,377 2s. 6d., and a National Testimonial organised by the *Daily Telegraph* produced £5,000 in shilling subscriptions.

THROWING: A SYMPOSIUM

NOTES BY THE EDITOR, 1953

THROWING

During the English summer of 1952 C. N. McCarthy and G. A. R. Lock were no-balled for throwing. The case of McCarthy occurred when he was playing for Cambridge University at Worcester and that of Lock when India played their second match with Surrey at The Oval. It was stated that the umpires concerned, P. Corrall and W. F. Price, who took this action when standing at square-leg, would report the facts to MCC, but so far there has been no indication that the rulers carried the matter further. Although the laws of cricket state that if either umpire be not entirely satisfied with the absolute fairness of a delivery he shall call and signal no-ball instantly, umpires have always been reluctant to take this extreme action. Not only do they dislike jeopardising a player's future in the game, but they know they are unlikely to receive any support from the crowd. This was borne out at The Oval, where Price was subjected to howls of disapproval from both inside and outside the pavilion. Yet in the interests of cricket I would congratulate both Price and Corrall for their efforts to see the game is conducted properly.

This is no new problem. As far back as 1888, when *Wisden* hailed the proposed formation of the first Cricket Council at Lord's, Mr Charles F. Pardon wrote: "I have watched for many years with interest, and generally with cordial sympathy, the efforts of Lord Harris to improve conditions under which the great game is played. His crusade against throwing was fully justified, and there is today very much less unfair bowling than was the case a few years ago. I have not, nor can I have, any personal feeling in this matter; my only desire is that the game should be played fairly and honourably, and that cricketers as lovers of a splendid game, should be above suspicion. . . . Prominent umpires have over and over again told me that in their opinion men upon whose style of bowling adverse criticisms have been written, were unfair, but they were not sufficiently sure of support to take the initiative in no-balling them. Now the County Cricket Council is fairly under way any transgressions should quickly be brought before the Executive, and with Lord Harris as Chairman, there need be no hesitation in doing this."

LOCK CHOSEN FOR ENGLAND

Now, sixty-five years later, we find ourselves in exactly the same position, chiefly because no one wants to shoulder the responsibility. In fairness to McCarthy and Lock, it must be stated there was not unanimity about the alleged unfairness of their actions. Certainly before the match in which each was no-balled one heard only adverse criticisms, but afterwards there was plenty of support for both men and in addition the cine-film failed to show any throw in McCarthy's action. The week before Lock was chosen for England he bowled in a needle match at The Oval against Yorkshire and must have satisfied both

N. W. D. Yardley, Chairman of the Test Selectors, and L. Hutton, the England captain, who batted against him, or they would never have given him his England cap.

Possibly a solution to the problem of dealing with throwing would be the appointment by MCC before each season of a small panel to which umpires could report suspicious cases. If the panel were satisfied there were grounds for complaint they could inform the player concerned that his action had come under their notice and that unless he adjusted his style within a certain time he might be barred from first-class cricket.

NOTES BY THE EDITOR, 1959

THROWING

During the recent MCC tour of Australia, one read constant references to the questionable bowling actions of several men who opposed P. B. H. May's team. Four of them, Meckiff, Rorke, Slater and Burke were chosen for Australia. Even some old Australian players did not mince their words in criticising these young men. What can be done to check unfair tactics?

The danger of not stamping on offenders in the past has led to the problems which now confront the authorities. They have only themselves to blame for the spread of this menace to the game. Too much responsibility is left to the umpires, who, I feel, would take action if they knew they could rely on support from the officials above them. I remember Frank Chester's experience during the first Test between England and South Africa at Trent Bridge in 1951. Chester disapproved of C. N. McCarthy's action at the beginning of England's first innings. South Africa batted almost the whole of the first two days. On the third morning Chester, who was at square-leg when McCarthy was operating, watched the bowler intently. It was quite obvious that he was studying his action. After the lunch interval, Chester rarely looked that way again.

CHESTER'S VAIN HOPE

Some time later I asked him the reason and he told me that he had gone without his lunch in order to find out whether he would receive official support if he no-balled McCarthy for throwing. He spoke to two leading members of the MCC Committee and could get no satisfaction. They were not prepared to say that MCC would uphold the umpires. In other words Chester was given the impression that, if he adopted the attitude which he knew was right according to the Laws, there was no guarantee that he would remain on the panel of Test match umpires. Naturally, Chester was not prepared to make a financial sacrifice in the interests of cricket and McCarthy continued unchecked in Test matches.

And, of course, the corollary came when anyone commented on McCarthy's action, for the South Africans replied: "He satisfied Chester. What else do you want?"

In my opinion each member-country of the Imperial Cricket Conference must be responsible for the fair delivery of each bowler selected for Test matches and for overseas tours. It is unfair and discourteous to thrust the onus on the host country. In a perfect world no dubious thrower or dragger would be allowed to stay in first-class cricket. He would be stopped long before he had made any sort of name for himself, though there have been cases when a bowler has developed an unfair action after becoming recognised as a first-class player.

SOUTH AFRICA'S DECISION

Early this year Mr A. H. Coy, President of the South African Cricket Association, was reported to have said that the number of bowlers with suspect actions had reached such proportions that the law would have to be more clearly defined. He considered that each country should ensure that such bowlers were corrected or kept out of first-class cricket and he added: "South Africa must make certain that touring teams do not include any bowler whose action is likely to cause controversy of embarrassment".

There were a few suspicious cases in England last summer. Umpires are not likely to invoke the wrath of spectators or deprive a man of his living by making open examples during the course of a match. Nevertheless umpires could report cases to Lord's and if a panel were appointed to deal with these matters, suspects could be watched. Then if the panel were satisfied with the umpires' opinions, the offenders and the counties concerned could be informed that unless such a bowler mended his ways immediately his presence in the game would no longer be tolerated.

THROWING IN THE "EIGHTIES"

Throwing is no modern trend. Ever since over-arm bowling came into fashion there have been players who have exploited it. As long ago as 1883 Lord Harris proposed an amendment to the Law concerned, that "The ball must be fairly bowled, not thrown or jerked" and that is how the law now stands. During the "eighties" Charles Pardon, then Editor of *Wisden*, came down heavily on it, and later Sydney Pardon, his youngest brother who succeeded him in the Editorship, conducted a long campaign. In the 1895 issue Sydney Pardon wrote: "Umpires, according to the laws of cricket, are the sole judges of fair and unfair play, but for reasons readily understood they have in this particular so persistently shirked their duty that, if English bowling is once and for all to be cleared from the stigma of unfairness, some steps will have to be taken by those in authority."

Two years later Mr Pardon, dealing with the tour of Harry Trott's Australian team, wrote: "Up to last season one of the special virtues of Australian bowling was its unimpeachable fairness. Despite the evil example set by many English throwers, team after team came to this country without a bowler to whose delivery exception could be taken, but unhappily things are not as they once were. . . . A fast bowler with the action of Jones or a slow bowler so open to question as McKibbin would have found no place in the earlier elevens that came to England."

"W.G.'s" BEARD SINGED

Ernest Jones, who took 121 wickets on the tour, was one of the central figures in a time-honoured story about W. G. Grace. In the Australians' opening match, against Lord Sheffield's XI at Sheffield Park, Sussex, Jones continually pitched short. He hit W.G. on the body and a little later sent a bumper sizzling through the Doctor's beard to the boundary. Down the pitch stalked the incensed "Old Man" and demanded of Trott: "Here, what's all this?" Said Trott to Jones: "Steady, Jonah". To which the bowler replied: "Sorry, Doctor, she slipped!"

Tom McKibbin, who also took over 100 wickets with spinners, was referred to in a letter to *Bell's Sporting Life* by F. R. Spofforth, himself a famous Australian player, as a bowler who hardly ever delivered a fair ball – which was outspoken comment even in those days. Spofforth suggested that a committee of first-class captains be formed and that if they found a bowler guilty of throwing, he be suspended for a week; for a second offence, he be fined and suspended and for a third, he be disqualified for the season.

Mr Pardon persevered and in the 1899 *Wisden* referred to the satisfactory results. "For the first time within my experience", he wrote, "bowlers were no-balled for throwing. C. B. Fry was no-balled by West at Trent Bridge, by Phillips at Brighton and Sherwin at Lord's; Hopkins, of Warwickshire, by Titchmarsh at Tonbridge."

The county captains did meet in 1900 and they decided to take united action "for the purpose of ridding English cricket of all throwing and dubious bowling". C. B. Fry, who had twice performed the hat-trick at Lord's, Mold, Tyler, Paish, Geeson and Quaife were all named as illegal bowlers.

THE THROWING CONTROVERSY

IMPERIAL CONFERENCE TACKLE MANY PROBLEMS

By Leslie Smith

November 3, 1960, will go down as a momentous day in cricket. It was the day when England and Australia announced details of the agreement on throwing for 1961; a day on which the Laws were partially amended to permit throwing without penalty for a period of five weeks; a day on which the very small number of offenders temporarily gained the upper hand over the vast majority and the day on which English umpires were instructed to hold in abeyance their interpretation of what constituted fair and unfair bowling. A day, in fact, which to my mind, reflected no credit on the authorities of the two senior cricketing countries.

For years throwing had become an increasing menace to the game and it was obvious that firm action had to be taken. In 1959 English umpires received a definite assurance that they would be given support in their efforts to stamp out the evil of throwing. This came in the statement issued by MCC on March 17, following a meeting of the Advisory County Cricket Committee:

"The part of Law 26 which deals with throwing and jerking has been under discussion between MCC, the county committees and captains, and the first-class umpires since the winter of 1957-58. In the autumn of last year, it was unanimously agreed by the umpires that the action of certain bowlers in this country was, on occasion, suspect. The counties concerned have undertaken to warn these bowlers. The umpires have again been assured of the fullest support of MCC, the counties and the county captains in any action they may feel it necessary to take."

Taking MCC at their word, the umpires set about their task, reluctantly but, in most cases, fearlessly. This led last season to the no-balling of Geoff Griffin, the South African, and several English bowlers. Instead of continuing with their policy, which unpleasant though it may have been, would certainly have put a quick end to throwing, at least in England, MCC, at the suggestion of Australia, partially relaxed their determination and reached the following compromise:

MCC and the English counties have agreed with the Australian Board of Control for International Cricket to the following application of Law 26 during the Australian Tour to the United Kingdom in 1961:

English umpires will be instructed not to call on the field for a suspect delivery (throwing) any Australian bowler on the 1961 tour prior to June 7, 1961. Up to that date every umpire who officiates in an Australian match and who is not entirely satisfied of the absolute fairness of a delivery of any Australian bowler will, as soon as possible after the conclusion of each match, complete a confidential report on a form to be provided and send it to the President of MCC – a duplicate copy to be sent through the Secretary of MCC to the Manager of the Australian team. From June 7, 1961, the umpires will be instructed to implement Law 26 on the field in the normal way, according to their own judgment; and the Australian bowlers will become "liable" to be called for any infringement. At no stage of the tour will a bowler be, as it were, "declared illegal" and he will be free to play as and when chosen at Australia's discretion.

In view of the new definition of a throw and the agreement referred to above, the MCC and the English counties will consider whether or not to adopt the same procedure in all first-class matches prior to June 7, 1961.

The Umpire's Report is set out thus:

CONFIDENTIAL   FORM "A"
UMPIRE'S REPORT
To the President,
MCC

I beg to report that I officiated at the match Australia v .... played on ....
(date) at ....

In my opinion the Australian bowler .... (name) infringed Law 26 (Throwing)
in this match to the following degree:

☐ Basically – that is every ball.
☐ Frequently.
☐ Occasionally.
☐ Very rarely.

(Please mark category thus ☒ and make any comments you may wish and especially
any which you think may help the bowler concerned.)

Yours faithfully,

At the Advisory County Cricket Committee on November 16, it was agreed that the
same truce period should apply to English bowlers in matches against the Australians. At
the same time the counties stated that they did not intend to have anything to do with it for
Championship matches. They were quite happy with the position as it stood.

It was difficult to see what benefits either side could derive from a five-week truce
period. If umpires thought every Australian bowler had a fair action he would not no-ball
him either in May or after June 7. On the other hand, should an umpire believe that the
action of any bowler was doubtful he would, in all honesty, have to call him in June,
irrespective of what happened in May unless his action had been changed in the meantime.
The Australians, whether they had adverse written reports in front of them or whether
umpires had taken action on the field, had the same amount of time to consider what move
they would make, if any were necessary.

Let me make it clear that I am not for a moment suggesting that English umpires are
always right or that the English interpretation of the Laws is necessarily correct. Indeed, to
do so would be to condone the very thing which is helping to damage cricket – the
increasing Nationalism and the win-at-all-costs attitude which has developed. Indeed, all
around us we can see examples of such Nationalism and the bad feeling it causes. Almost
every International sporting occasion is riddled with it and the public must be getting
heartily sick and tired of the perpetual squabbles on and off the field. Dwindling gates in
practically every major sport reflects the public reaction. First-class cricket, confined as it
is to a handful of countries within the Commonwealth, ought to rise above such pettiness.

I can well see the point of view of the Australian Board of Control. The man most
concerned was Ian Meckiff, the left-arm fast bowler, whose action had aroused
considerable controversy. Now, I have not seen Meckiff in the flesh although I have
watched him on film, both at normal speed and in slow motion. Therefore I must reserve
my final opinion although I felt that there was, at the very least, a doubt about his action.
Many of those who have seen him and whose views are not those of hot-headed
sensationalists (the favourite term used by people who see no wrong in Meckiff) are
convinced that on occasion he has thrown. They include several past and present
Australian cricketers. Meckiff was not alone in having a suspect action and one of
Australia's greatest cricketers has gone on record as claiming, cynically, that he was the
last of the fast straight-arm bowlers in that country. Keith Miller stated many times that
Meckiff's action was definitely questionable and so did Jack Fingleton, the former Test
player and a respected journalist. These were only two of the several.

But the point remained that Meckiff had not been no-balled by any umpire in Australia,
nor in South Africa, New Zealand, India and Pakistan, where he has toured. So what
could the Australian Board do? Should they not select him, purely on account of his
action, they would be condemning the umpires of five countries. On the other hand, by
choosing him they stood the risk of losing a valuable man if English umpires thought

otherwise. This was their dilemma and they saw the problem long before they had to tackle it. This may well have led to the compromise agreement, but personally I cannot approve of it. As it happened, Meckiff lost form during the West Indies' tour and he was not chosen for the visit to England. Nor was any other bowler whose action had been queried. So the compromise, after all, should be proved unnecessary. Surely, the sensible thing for the authorities of any country to do would be to free from all possible doubt in their own minds that a bowler's action was absolutely fair before sending him on tour and placing the onus on the home country. It could be that one or two bowlers in various parts of the world would have to be sacrificed, but would that not be better than ruining the entire game? Is the winning or losing of a Test series so much more important than cricket itself?

The spread of throwing in recent years has been alarming. Ten years ago I went to India, Pakistan and Ceylon with the MCC team. In India, MCC played a match at Poona where a bowler was no-balled for throwing. The umpire concerned told me that he knew for a long time that this bowler's action was unfair, but he felt it better to wait until MCC arrived before bringing it to a head! I also saw several other instances of doubtful actions, not only in the tour games themselves, but by youngsters in the nets.

In 1959-60, on my visit to West Indies, there were again instances of bent elbows among fast and off-break bowlers. Indeed, in British Guiana, one leading umpire resigned rather than give an assurance that he would not no-ball Stayers, a fast-medium bowler, for throwing. Yet Stayers played against MCC and was not called although practically every English batsman thought his action, on occasions, highly suspicious. So did I.

The attitude to this was summed up by one West Indies writer who, when I suggested that in the best interests of the game he ought to oppose such bowling, replied: "Why should we do anything while you permit Tony Lock to throw". That is nationalism and how it encroaches in cricket. He knew very well, and so did many others actively concerned in the game in West Indies, that Stayers was at least suspect. Yet because he was one of the leading bowlers in British Guiana, it was being over-looked. So a courageous umpire was kept out of the game and the man who caused the problem continued in it.

In many parts of West Indies I again saw youngsters, many of them schoolboys, using an exaggerated bent elbow, either to impart more spin on unresponsive turf or to get added lift to the ball. These youngsters were the future cricketers and unless checked ruthlessly the increase in throwing would get out of all proportions.

Take South Africa. They were fully aware of the problem and not long ago took the trouble to announce that they would never include a bowler with a suspicious action in their teams. Griffin had been called twice in their own country before they sent him to tour England. Almost inevitably he ran into trouble and the entire season was dominated by the unfortunate no-balling incidents which occurred. It also led to bitter feelings between the South African and English public. Apparently Griffin was, after Neil Adcock, the bowler considered most likely to succeed under English conditions. Again I ask – was the chance of winning Test matches worth all the unpleasantness which arose?

As for England, they have by no means been free of criticism. Tony Lock, the Surrey slow left-hander, for a long time had a suspicious action, particularly when sending down his faster ball. Indeed, he was no-balled for throwing by Fred Price in 1952, yet in 1953-54 he was chosen to tour West Indies where he was again no-balled, three times in one day against Barbados and also in the first Test at Kingston.

To Lock's credit he realised his problems and set about remedying them. Twice he changed his action completely and he obviously made a tremendous effort to put himself right. Other suspect bowlers could follow suit and stay in the game free from suspicion. Reports from Australia stated that Meckiff had smoothed out his action and that he would pass English umpires, but apparently in doing so he lost effectiveness.

Whatever the circumstances, could not their Board of Control have told their umpires that while they had complete confidence in them, there apparently was a doubt about some bowlers and in the desire to avoid further awkwardness they had decided not to risk them on tour. That is, of course, if there was any doubt at all. Somebody has to take a firm lead and England and Australia are best qualified to put the game in order.

Throwing is no new problem. It began way back before the turn of the century and continued until about 1903 when strong action eliminated it. Only one more case of no-balling for throwing occurred before 1930, but with increasing competition and as the emphasis on winning became paramount, the epidemic started again in the 1950s. In 1959 English umpires, with the assured support of MCC behind them, no-balled three bowlers. Unfortunately this "get tough" announcement was badly timed, for it happened shortly after England had lost the series in Australia and after the storm about Meckiff had broken. It was difficult to avoid the accusation of retaliation on the part of the English authorities.

In 1960 a further purge resulted in bowlers being called for throwing in twelve separate matches, one of them in Australia and the others in England. Griffin suffered most. After considerable controversy about his action in the early matches, Griffin was first called in the game against MCC at Lord's. Subsequently, he was no-balled against Not-tinghamshire and Hampshire. Despite this, he was chosen for the second Test at Lord's where he was called 11 times in all. That was the end of Griffin as a bowler on the tour, although he remained with the party and played occasionally as a batsman. It was a great pity that it had to happen to Griffin, but one could not get away from the belief that he should never have been sent on tour and placed in such a position.

The particularly unfortunate outcome was that Sid Buller, the Test umpire, became a central figure in the trouble. Buller had earned for himself a reputation as a strong and fearless umpire and had been on the Test panel since 1956. It was noticeable in the Lord's Test that McGlew, the South African captain, did not put Griffin on to bowl while Buller was standing at square leg. Despite that, Frank Lee, the other umpire, frequently called Griffin for throwing. With the match ending early on the fourth day an exhibition game took place and during this Buller, now at square-leg, called Griffin four times in his opening over. After McGlew had spoken to Buller, Griffin, was advised to finish the over underarm. With the South Africans raising an objection, Buller did not umpire again in the series. Most people were furious that an umpire should suffer because he had attempted to carry out his duties conscientiously. Fortunately in December the county captains showed their confidence in Buller and nominated him for the Umpires' Test panel against Australia in 1961. The fee he lost at the time for missing the match with South Africa was paid to him.

Umpires have a very difficult time already and when they hear of such things happening and when they are told to hold Laws in abeyance, no one should be surprised if they take the easy way out and let things slide. After all, in England, their living is at stake and if authorities cannot find the solution why should they throw themselves open to abuse and possible loss of earnings? That is a very real danger.

Throwing is only one of the problems which has bedevilled cricket in recent years and in July 1960 a highly important Imperial Cricket Conference took place at Lord's. Instead of having their usual English representatives at the annual Conference, countries sent from home. Australia were represented by their President, W. J. Dowling, and Sir Donald Bradman.

It was recalled that at the 1959 Conference, the important and difficult problem of doubtful bowling actions was discussed and the following decision was reached and recorded:

It was unanimously agreed that throwing and jerking should be eliminated from the game and that each country would do everything possible to achieve this end.

The 1960 Conference resolved to reaffirm this declaration but went further and unanimously recommended that the following experimental definition be adopted:

A ball shall be deemed to have been thrown if, in the opinion of either umpire, the bowling arm having been bent at the elbow, whether the wrist is backward of the elbow or not, is suddenly straightened immediately prior to the instant of delivery.

The bowler shall nevertheless be at liberty to use the wrist freely in the delivery action.

It is considered that the pregoing definition will result in a more uniform interpretation of what constitutes a throw and should assist greatly in achieving the object all have in mind. The question of throwing is, however, a complicated and difficult problem, especially for the umpires who are solely responsible for interpreting the Laws. The whole problem has been complicated by modern methods of publicity resulting in a danger of prejudgment.

The Conference, therefore, having reached a unanimous conclusion in a most amicable spirit, hope that all those who may be concerned with the future welfare of cricket will do all in their power to assist those whose admittedly difficult task is to adjudicate on this problem. . . .

As can be seen, the problems of cricket are many and varied, but not beyond solution. In past years the game has been upset by bodyline bowling pitches that have not been up to standard, excessive bouncers, gamesmanship, umpiring squabbles and throwing.

To some extent the Press has been blamed for sensationalising the difficulties. That may be true in a few cases, but the Press did not originate the troubles. Cricketers and legislators have done that themselves and but for publicity bad habits might continue. Personally I would have liked to have seen a far bigger outcry in the 1950s when throwing began to get a hold once more. We may not have found ourselves in this position now.

I am assured that despite the truce, which I understand has been adopted solely with the idea of avoiding the high-pressure publicity which arose over Griffin, MCC are determined to stamp out throwing. Thank goodness for that, but I still fail to see how appeasement helps.

Surely cricket authorities must realise the harm they are doing by worrying more about the result and so-called prestige than about the way cricket should be played. Only by complete sincerity and a determination by everyone to keep trouble and trouble-makers out of the game will cricket lift its head once more.

MEETINGS IN 1961

KNOCK-OUT CRICKET IN 1963

At a special meeting of the Advisory County Cricket Committee at Lord's on December 20 it was decided to inaugurate a one-day knock-out competition in 1963, with the Championship that year standardised at 28 three-day matches for each county. This followed an interim report submitted by the Committee of Inquiry studying the game as a whole.

Some counties favoured experimenting on these lines in 1962 but this was turned down because of difficulties of short notice in arrangements of fixtures and venues. Only narrowly defeated was a suggestion that instead of the knock-out competition each county should play 32 matches, 16 of them three days, the other 16 comprising two one-day matches played on successive days. No vote was taken on two proposals: (1) that each county should play 14 three-day games and also 14 on the two by one-day basis; (2) that County Cricket should remain unaltered.

The rounds in the knock-out competition would start on a Wednesday, with the games confined to one innings each side. In case of interruption through the weather, the match would carry on into Thursday or Friday, when possible from the point where it left off. These were the only points decided immediately. It was considered that, for 1963, the knock-out competition should be confined to first-class counties, with a draw after each round, but these and other points, such as grounds, dates, time limit or limited number of overs, were passed to a Sub-Committee being set up by MCC to consider the finer details.

SUNDAY CRICKET

At the same meeting, there was a general discussion on a letter received by MCC from the Home Office inviting the views of cricket on Sunday play. The counties were in favour of amending the Lord's Day Observance Act so as to allow Sunday matches at which the public would be admitted on payment. They were not prepared to commit themselves to playing first-class games on Sunday.

Earlier, at their annual meeting, the Minor Counties decided not to support organised cricket on Sunday. Only one of the twenty-three counties voted in favour.

MEETINGS IN 1962

THE GILLETTE TROPHY

The Advisory Committee accepted a block grant of £6,500 from Gillette, who will sponsor the new knock-out competition. This grant, together with Television and Broadcasting fees, to be divided equally among the 17 first-class counties. A trophy, to be known as the Gillette trophy, would also be awarded to the winners. Meritorious performances in each of the 16 games involved would warrant awards, to the man or men of the match, such awards to be made at the conclusion of each tie on the ground.

NOTES BY THE EDITOR, 1963

DISAPPEARANCE OF THE AMATEUR

To many people the abolition of the amateur status in first-class cricket provided yet another big surprise. Four years earlier MCC had conducted a full inquiry into this matter and arrived at certain conclusions which were accepted by the Advisory County Cricket Committee. Among them were the following:

> The wish to preserve in first-class cricket the leadership and general approach to the game traditionally associated with the Amateur player.
>
> The Committee rejected any solution to the problem on the lines of abolishing the distinction between Amateur and Professional and regarding them all alike as "cricketers".
>
> They considered that the distinctive status of the amateur cricketer was not obsolete, was of great value to the game and should be preserved.

The members of this Committee were: The Duke of Norfolk (chairman), H. S. Altham, G. O. Allen, M. J. C. Allom, Col. R. J. de C. Barber, F. R. Brown, E. D. R. Eagar, C. A. F. Hastilow, C. G. Howard, D. J. Insole, P. B. H. May, C. H. Palmer, Col. R. S. Rait Kerr, A. B. Sellers, Rev. D. S. Sheppard, R. Aird (secretary).

It seems strange that within four years the opinions of some people appear to have been completely reversed. We live in a changing world. Conditions are vastly different from the days of our grandparents; but is it wise to throw everything overboard?

We have inherited the game of cricket. The story of its development during the last hundred years is appropriately given full treatment in this edition of *Wisden*. Right through these hundred years the amateur has played a very important part.

In the time of Dr W. G. Grace there was talk that the amateur received liberal expenses. Whether this was true or not, I do not believe cricket, as we know it today, would be such a popular attraction, or so remunerative to the professional, without the contribution which Dr Grace and his contemporaries made as amateurs.

By doing away with the amateur, cricket is in danger of losing the spirit of freedom and gaiety which the best amateur players brought to the game.

On the other hand there is at present a source of talent which has been untapped because of the gulf between the amateur and the professional. This comprises the band of cricketers who could get away from business or other activities for periods during the summer to assist their counties if they could receive compensation for loss of salary. In other words, their employers would be willing to release them, but not to pay their salaries during their absence from work.

The passing of the amateur could have a detrimental effect in the vital matter of captaincy both at County and Test level. True, it was under a professional, Sir Leonard Hutton, that England last regained the Ashes, in 1953, and men like Tom Dollery (Warwickshire), J. V. Wilson (Yorkshire) and Don Kenyon (Worcestershire) have led their counties with distinction.

Because the amateur possessed independent status, the professionals, generally, preferred to have him as captain. Two of the most popular and most successful captains were A. B. Sellers (Yorkshire) and W. S. Surridge (Surrey). Their gifts of leadership were stronger than their batting or bowling ability. Both were great fielders, but if either had been on equal status as a "cricketer" with the professional he might well have been passed over.

Under the new set-up, one presumes there will still be players with a full-time contract while others receive match fees and a minority may still prefer to play solely for the love of the game. One can visualise smaller full-time staffs, particularly if, as many reformers desire, there is a reduction in the number of days allotted to county cricket.

Sir John Hobbs, commenting on the change, said: "It is sad to see the passing of the amateurs because it signals the end of an era in cricket. They were a great asset to the game, much appreciated by all of us because they were able to come in and play freely, whereas many professionals did not feel they could take chances. Now times are different, and I can understand the position of the amateur who has to make his living. You cannot expect him to refuse good offers outside cricket."

1879 DEFINITION

The difference between the amateur and the professional status is not a modern problem. As far back as 1879 it caused enough controversy in cricket circles for MCC to appoint a sub-committee to inquire into the Definition and Qualification of Amateur Cricketers. Their report, which follows, was adopted unanimously by the General Committee:

> We have in the first instance referred to the accounts of the last few years, in order to ascertain the amount which has been expended by the club under the long established rule that a gentleman who is invited to play in an MCC match, and would be debarred from playing by the expense to which he would be put, may, on application to the Secretary, receive his reasonable expenses; we find that the total amount paid under this rule is comparatively trifling (under £50 a year in all); that there has been no abuse of this rule, so far as MCC are concerned, at all events since the management of the finances of the club has been in its own hands (1866); and that no gentleman has been retained by the club by extra payment.
>
> We see no reason for recommending the abolition of the old established rule, but we think it is advisable that the committee should lay down distinctly the principle on which they are prepared to act, especially as regards the match, Gentlemen v Players.
>
> We are in the opinion that no Gentleman ought to make a profit by his service in the cricket field, and that for the future any cricketer taking more than his expenses in any match should not be qualified to play for the Gentlemen against the Players at Lord's but that if any gentleman should feel difficulty in joining in the match without such assistance, he should not be debarred from playing as a Gentleman by having his actual expenses defrayed.
>
> Whilst expressing our opinion that the payments by the MCC under their rule have been reasonable, we feel that we must notice statements which have been made to us that sums much in excess of actual expenses have been frequently paid to gentlemen by other clubs or individuals.
>
> We have not thought it desirable to go into this question at any length, because we hope that if the committee of the MCC should adopt our suggestion as to the above minute, and should make such minute public, that course will have the effect of checking a system which might grow into a serious abuse, and which even as now alleged to be practised is open to grave objection.

INDEX